Advance Praise for *Mergers, Acquisitions, and Other Restructuring Activities, Sixth Edition*

"DePamphilis has masterfully covered in one book all relevant managerial, strategic, financial, accounting, legal, and tax aspects of M&A in an easily understood roadmap for any M&A transaction, large or small. With totally up-to-date material, he provides the crucial information that is necessary in today's rapidly changing M&A world."

—**Lloyd Levitin,** Professor of Clinical Finance and Business Economics, University of Southern California

"After teaching M&A for ten years, I was relieved when last semester I finally switched to DePamphilis' text. His single book replaced numerous other sources that I had to use before. His academic rigor is combined with his deep personal experience as a deal maker, and thus the textbook is highly valuable to both newcomers and those who have been involved in transactions for many years."

—**Viktoria Dalko,** Professor of Global Finance, Harvard University Extension School

"*Mergers, Acquisitions, and Other Restructuring Activities, Sixth Edition,* delivers an essential understanding of corporate restructuring processes by combining insights from many case studies with academic rigor. The book points out how M&A can create value as well as the ways it can lead to value destruction. In addition to state-of-the-art valuation techniques, it explains the regulatory corporate governance framework for both the United States and Europe. It's an excellent text, and I highly recommend it."

—**Luc Renneboog,** Professor of Corporate Finance, CentRE, Tilburg University

"Great textbook that in a simple and straightforward manner combines the latest insights from academia with contemporary industry practices. It fits perfect in a class of MBA students or executives. I will be sure to use it the next time I teach M&A."

—**Karin Thorburn,** DnB Nor Professor of Finance, Norwegian School of Economics and Business Administration

"*Mergers, Acquisitions, and Other Restructuring Activities* is quite simply an outstanding text. Don DePamphilis delivers a comprehensive guide to the M&A process from start to finish. . . . In sum, *Mergers, Acquisitions, and Other Restructuring Activities* is a comprehensive, up-to-date, outstanding text."

—**Scott C. Linn,** R.W. Moore Chair in Finance and Economic Development, University of Oklahoma

MERGERS, ACQUISITIONS, AND OTHER RESTRUCTURING ACTIVITIES

SIXTH EDITION

Praise for *Mergers, Acquisitions, and Other Restructuring Activities, Fifth Edition*

"This is a truly comprehensive text and does a wonderful job at supplying the underlying motives and theory as well as the critical 'in practice' elements that many books lack. It spans all types of M&A and restructuring transactions and covers all the relevant knowledge, from academic research to the practical legal, accounting, and regulatory details. The book is up to date and teaches the state-of-the-art techniques used today. The book contains numerous cases and spreadsheet support that enable the reader to put into practice everything that is covered. The combination of great writing and active case learning make this book the best I have seen in the M&A and restructuring arena."

—**Matthew T. Billett,** Associate Professor of Finance, Henry B. Tippie Research Fellow, University of Iowa

"I am happy to recommend the fifth edition of *Mergers, Acquisitions, and Other Restructuring Activities.* Having used prior editions of Don DePamphilis' text, I can affirm that the newest edition builds on a firm foundation of coverage, real-world examples, and readability. My students have consistently responded favorably to prior editions of the book. In the newest edition, I was delighted to discover that Don is expanding his coverage of family-owned businesses, already a strength in his earlier editions, which were distinguished by their coverage of the valuation of privately held businesses. Additional attention is paid to restructuring, bankruptcy, and liquidation as well as risk management, which are clearly topics of interest to every business person in today's economic climate."

—**Kent Hickman,** Professor of Finance, Gonzaga University

"This fifth edition is one of the most comprehensive books on mergers and acquisitions. The text combines theories, valuation models, and real-life cases to give business students an overall insight into the M&A deal process. The up-to-date real-life examples and cases provide opportunities for readers to explore and apply theories to a wide variety of scenarios such as cross-border transactions, highly levered deals, firms in financial distress, and family-owned businesses. The chapter on restructuring under bankruptcy and liquidation, both inside and outside the protection of bankruptcy court, is timely and most useful in light of today's economic crisis. Overall, this is an excellent book on mergers, acquisitions, and corporate restructuring activities."

—**Tao-Hsien Dolly King,** Rush S. Dickson Professor of Finance, Associate Professor, Department of Finance, The Belk College of Business, University of North Carolina at Charlotte

"*Mergers, Acquisitions, and Other Restructuring Activities* is an interesting and comprehensive look at the most important aspects of M&A and corporate restructuring — from strategic and regulatory considerations and M&A deal processes, through several chapters on M&A valuation and deal structuring, to other types of restructuring activities. It not only provides a roadmap for M&A and other corporate restructuring transactions but also highlights key things to watch for. The book is clearly written with extensive but easy-to-follow case examples and empirical findings and cases to illustrate the points in the text. It is a book by an expert for M&A instructors and students as well as practitioners."

—**Qiao Lui,** Faculty of Business and Economics, The University of Hong Kong

"I am delighted with Don DePamphilis' *Mergers, Acquisitions, and Other Restructuring Activities, Fifth Edition.* It is a clear, comprehensive, and thorough discussion of the issues involving all restructuring activities. The use of mini-cases throughout each chapter both highlights and clarifies key elements of the decision-making process. The end-of-chapter discussion questions ideally complemented the problem set questions to challenge readers' understanding of the covered concepts. I am impressed with the current reflection of market conditions throughout the text and the extent of the changes to provide greater understanding for students. I expect to find that students will also be impressed with the clarity and structure of the text when I introduce the newest edition to my course. I recommend the fifth edition to any professor covering mergers, acquisitions, bankruptcies, or other restructuring topics which can be used with specific chapters to cover limited topics, or as a text with a complete course on restructurings."

—**John F. Manley,** Professor of Finance, Hagan School of Business, Iona College

"Mergers and Acquisitions continue to be among the preferred competitive options available to companies seeking to grow and prosper in the rapidly changing global business scenario. In this new updated and revised fifth edition of his path-breaking book, M&A expert Dr. DePamphilis illustrates how mergers, acquisitions, and other major forms of restructuring can help a company grow and prosper in the highly complex and competitive corporate takeover marketplace. Interspersed with highly relevant and up-to-date M&A case studies covering a broad range of industries are the multifarious aspects of corporate restructuring in an integrated manner adopting a lucid style. While academic research studies on the subject have been incorporated in a coherent manner at appropriate places in the book, every effort has been made by the author to deal with the intricacies of the subject by offering comprehensive coverage of the latest methods and techniques adopted in managing M&A transactions in general and in dealing with business valuations of both public and private companies in particular.

The book provides practical ways of dealing with M&As even in an economic downturn, with an exclusive chapter on corporate restructuring under bankruptcy and liquidation. With the greatly enlarged and up-to-date material on varied aspects of the subject, the book provides a plethora of real-world examples that will go a long way in making the subject easy, stimulating, and interesting to academicians and practitioners alike."

—**Donepudi Prasad,** ICFAI Business School, Hyderabad, India

"Professor DePamphilis has made significant, important, and very timely updates in this fifth edition of his text. He incorporates contemporary events such as the credit crunch and the latest accounting rules in the West plus M&A issues in emerging markets which includes family businesses. He also readdresses corporate governance, a topic that will become increasingly important in business schools the world over in M&A. This text has become, and will increasingly become, the definitive, comprehensive, and thorough reference on the subject."

—**Jeffrey V. Ramsbottom,** Visiting Professor, China Europe International Business School, Shanghai

"I think the fifth edition of *Mergers, Acquisitions, and Other Restructuring Activities* does a comprehensive job of covering the M&A field. As in the previous edition, the book is divided into five parts. These are logical and easy to follow, with a nice blend of theory, empirical research findings, and practical issues. I especially like two chapters—that on bankruptcy and liquidation is extremely relevant in today's economic conditions, and that on private equity and hedge funds is interesting because M&A activities by these players are not well-documented in the literature. Overall, I believe that MBA students will find the book useful both as a textbook in class and as a reference book for later use."

—**Raghavendra Rau,** Purdue University and Barclays Global Investors

"This book is truly outstanding among textbooks on takeovers, valuation, and corporate restructuring for several reasons: the DePamphilis book not only gives a very up-to-date overview of the recent research findings on takeovers around the world but also offers nearly 100 business case studies. The book treats all the valuation techniques in depth and also offers much institutional detail on M&A and LBO transactions. Not just takeover successes are analyzed but also how financially distressed companies should be restructured. In short, the ideal textbook for any M&A graduate course."

—**Luc Renneboog,** Professor of Corporate Finance, Tilburg University, The Netherlands

"The fifth edition of *Mergers, Acquisitions, and Other Restructuring Activities* by Professor Donald DePamphilis is an excellent book. Among its many strengths, I can easily identify three that stand out. First, it is up to date, covering recent knowledge published in most of academic journals. Second, it offers comprehensive coverage of the subject matter, including chapters on the U.S. institutional, legal, and accounting environment; on technical aspects; valuation techniques; and strategic issues. Third, it is practical by including Excel spreadsheet models and a large number of real cases. These three aspects, along with the large number of end-of-chapter discussion and review questions, problems, and exercises, make this book one of the best choices for the subject."

—**Nickolaos G. Travlos,** The Kitty Kyriacopoulos Chair in Finance and Dean,
ALBA Graduate Business School, Greece

"It is difficult to imagine that his fourth edition could be improved upon, but Dr. DePamphilis has done just that. His latest edition is clearer and better organized, and contains a wealth of vitally important new material for these challenging times. I especially recommend the new chapter on liquidation for members of boards of directors who face extreme circumstances. This is a remarkably useful book for readers at any level—students, instructors, and company executives, as well as board members. Bravo Don!"

—**Wesley B. Truitt,** Adjunct Professor, School of Public Policy, Pepperdine University

"The book is an excellent source for both academicians and practitioners. In addition to detailed cases, it provides tools contributing to value creation in M&A. A must book for an M&A course."

—**Vahap Uysal,** Assistant Professor of Finance, Price College of Business, University of Oklahoma

"An impressively detailed overview of all aspects of mergers and acquisitions. Numerous recent case studies and examples convince the reader that the material is very relevant in today's business environment."

—**Theo Vermaelen,** Professor of Finance, INSEAD

MERGERS, ACQUISITIONS, AND OTHER RESTRUCTURING ACTIVITIES

AN INTEGRATED APPROACH TO PROCESS, TOOLS, CASES, AND SOLUTIONS

———

SIXTH EDITION

DONALD M. DEPAMPHILIS, PH.D.
College of Business Administration
Loyola Marymount University
Los Angeles, California

AMSTERDAM • BOSTON • HEIDELBERG • LONDON
NEW YORK • OXFORD • PARIS • SAN DIEGO
SAN FRANCISCO • SINGAPORE • SYDNEY • TOKYO
Academic Press is an imprint of Elsevier

ELSEVIER

Academic Press is an imprint of Elsevier
525 B Street, Suite 1800, San Diego CA 92101, USA
225 Wyman Street, Waltham, MA 02451, USA
The Boulevard, Langford Lane, Kidlington, Oxford, OX5 1GB, UK

Notices
Knowledge and best practice in this field are constantly changing. As new research and experience broaden our understanding, changes in research methods, professional practices, or medical treatment may become necessary.

Practitioners and researchers must always rely on their own experience and knowledge in evaluating and using any information, methods, compounds, or experiments described herein. In using such information or methods they should be mindful of their own safety and the safety of others, including parties for whom they have a professional responsibility.

To the fullest extent of the law, neither the Publisher nor the authors, contributors, or editors assume any liability for any injury and/or damage to persons or property as a matter of products liability, negligence or otherwise, or from any use or operation of any methods, products, instructions, or ideas contained in the material herein.

Library of Congress Cataloging-in-Publication Data
DePamphilis, Donald M.
  Mergers, acquisitions, and other restructuring activities : an integrated approach
to process, tools, cases, and solutions / Donald M. DePamphilis. – 6th ed.
    p. cm.
  Includes bibliographical references and index.
  ISBN 978-0-12-385485-8 (alk. paper)
1. Organizational change—United States—Management. 2. Consolidation and merger
of corporations—United States—Management. 3. Corporate reorganizations—United
States—Management. I. Title.
    HD58.8.D467 2012
    658.1′6–dc23   2011022347

British Library Cataloguing-in-Publication Data
A catalogue record for this book is available from the British Library.

For information on all Academic Press publications,
visit our website at *www.elsevierdirect.com*

Printed in the United States
11 12 13 14 15   10 9 8 7 6 5 4 3 2 1

I extend my heartfelt gratitude to my wife, Cheryl, and my daughter, Cara, without whose patience and understanding this book could not have been completed, and to my brother, Mel, without whose encouragement this book would never have been undertaken.

Contents

Contents of the Companion Site   xvii
List of Business Case Studies   xix
Preface   xxiii
Acknowledgments   xxviii
About the Author   xxix

Part I

THE MERGERS AND ACQUISITIONS ENVIRONMENT

1. Introduction to Mergers and Acquisitions

Inside M&A: Dell Moves into Information
    Technology Services   3
Chapter Overview   4
Mergers and Acquisitions as Change Agents   4
Why Mergers and Acquisitions Happen   5
Merger and Acquisition Waves   13
Why It Is Important to Anticipate Merger Waves   19
Alternative Forms of Corporate Restructuring   19
Friendly versus Hostile Takeovers   22
The Role of Holding Companies in Mergers and
    Acquisitions   24
The Role of Employee Stock Ownership Plans in
    M&As   24
Business Alliances as Alternatives to Mergers and
    Acquisitions   25
Participants in the Mergers and Acquisitions
    Process   26
Alternative Investors and Lenders   29
Activist Investors and M&A Arbitrageurs   32
Do M&As Pay Off for Shareholders, Bondholders,
    and Society?   35
Why Some M&As Fail to Meet Expectations   44
Long-Term Performance   44
Some Things to Remember   45
Discussion Questions   45
Chapter Business Cases   47
    Case Study 1.1   Xerox Buys ACS to Satisfy
        Shifting Customer Requirements   47
    Case Study 1.2   Assessing Procter & Gamble's
        Acquisition of Gillette   49

2. Regulatory Considerations

Inside M&A: The Limitations of Regulation and
    the Lehman Brothers Meltdown   51
Chapter Overview   52
Federal Securities Laws   54
    Case Study 2.1   A Federal Judge Reprimands Hedge
        Funds in Their Effort to Control CSX   57
Antitrust Laws   61
    Case Study 2.2   Justice Department Requires
        Verizon Wireless to Sell Assets before
        Approving Alltel Merger   65
Dodd-Frank Wall Street Reform and Consumer
    Protection Act   69
    Case Study 2.3   Google Thwarted in Proposed
        Advertising Deal with Chief Rival Yahoo!   70
State Regulations Affecting Mergers and
    Acquisitions   75
National Security-Related Restrictions on Direct
    Foreign Investment in the United States   76
The U.S. Foreign Corrupt Practices Act   77
Fair Disclosure (Regulation FD)   77
Regulated Industries   78
Environmental Laws   80
Labor and Benefit Laws   80
Cross-Border Transactions   81
    Case Study 2.4   BHP Billiton and Rio Tinto
        Blocked by Regulators in an International Iron
        Ore Joint Venture   82
Some Things to Remember   83
Discussion Questions   83
Chapter Business Cases   84
    Case Study 2.5   Global Financial Exchanges Pose
        Regulatory Challenges   84
    Case Study 2.6   The Legacy of GE's Aborted
        Attempt to Merge with Honeywell   86

3. The Corporate Takeover Market:
Common Takeover Tactics, Antitakeover
Defenses, and Corporate Governance

Inside M&A: Kraft Sweetens Its Offer to Overcome
    Cadbury's Resistance   91
Chapter Overview   92
Alternative Models of Corporate Governance   94
Factors That Affect Corporate Governance   94
Alternative Takeover Tactics in the Corporate
    Takeover Market   99
What Makes the Aggressive Approach Successful?   105
Other Tactical Considerations   106
Developing a Bidding or Takeover Strategy   107
Alternative Takeover Defenses in the Corporate
    Takeover Market   108
The Impact of Takeover Defenses on Shareholder
    and Bondholder Value   121
Some Things to Remember   124
Discussion Questions   125
Chapter Business Cases   126
    Case Study 3.1   Mittal Acquires Arcelor—A
        Battle of Global Titans in the European
        Corporate Takeover Market   126
    Case Study 3.2   Verizon Acquires MCI—
        The Anatomy of Alternative Bidding
        Strategies   128

Part II

THE MERGERS AND
ACQUISITIONS PROCESS:
PHASES 1 THROUGH 10

4. Planning: Developing Business
and Acquisition Plans: Phases 1 and 2 of the
Acquisition Process

Inside M&A: Nokia's Gamble to Dominate the
    Smartphone Market Falters   135
Chapter Overview   136
A Planning-Based Approach to M&As   137
Phase 1: Building the Business Plan   139
    Case Study 4.1   CenturyTel Buys Qwest
        Communications to Cut Costs and Buy Time
        as the Landline Market Shrinks   145

Case Study 4.2   HP Redirects Its Mobile Device
    Business Strategy with the Acquisition of
    Palm   152
The Business Plan as a Communication
    Document   154
Phase 2: Building the Merger–Acquisition
    Implementation Plan   156
Some Things to Remember   162
Discussion Questions   162
Chapter Business Cases   163
    Case Study 4.3   Adobe's Acquisition of
        Omniture: Field of Dreams Marketing?   163
    Case Study 4.4   BofA Acquires Countrywide
        Financial Corporation   165
    Appendix: Common Sources of Economic,
        Industry, and Market Data   167

5. Implementation: Search through
Closing: Phases 3 through 10

Inside M&A: Bank of America Acquires Merrill
    Lynch   169
Chapter Overview   170
Phase 3: The Search Process   170
Phase 4: The Screening Process   173
Phase 5: First Contact   174
Phase 6: Negotiation   178
Phase 7: Developing the Integration Plan   186
Phase 8: Closing   188
Phase 9: Implementing Postclosing Integration   191
Phase 10: Conducting a Postclosing Evaluation   193
Some Things to Remember   194
Discussion Questions   194
Chapter Business Cases   196
    Case Study 5.1   Oracle's Efforts to Consolidate
        the Software Industry   196
    Case Study 5.2   Exxon Mobil Buys XTO Energy
        in a Bet on Natural Gas   198
    Appendix A: Thoughts on Negotiating
        Dynamics   200
    Appendix B: Legal Due Diligence Preliminary
        Information Request   202

6. Integration: Mergers, Acquisitions,
and Business Alliances

Inside M&A: General Electric's Water Business Fails
    to Meet Expectations   203

Chapter Overview　204
The Role of Integration in Successful M&As　204
Viewing Integration as a Process　206
　　Case Study 6.1　HP Acquires Compaq—
　　The Importance of Preplanning
　　Integration　208
　　Case Study 6.2　Integrating Supply Chains: Coty
　　Cosmetics Integrates Unilever Cosmetics
　　International　217
　　Case Study 6.3　Culture Clash Exacerbates Efforts
　　of the Tribune Corporation to Integrate the
　　Times Mirror Corporation　222
　　Case Study 6.4　Panasonic Moves to Consolidate
　　Past Acquisitions　224
Integrating Business Alliances　225
Some Things to Remember　227
Discussion Questions　227
Chapter Business Cases　228
　　Case Study 6.5　The Challenges of Integrating
　　Steel Giants Arcelor and Mittal　228
　　Case Study 6.6　Alcatel Merges with
　　Lucent, Highlighting Cross-Cultural
　　Issues　230

Part III

MERGER AND ACQUISITION VALUATION AND MODELING

7. A Primer on Merger and Acquisition Cash-Flow Valuation

Inside M&A: The Importance of Distinguishing
　between Operating and Nonoperating Assets　235
Chapter Overview　235
Required Returns　236
Analyzing Risk　242
Calculating Free Cash Flows　247
Applying Income or Discounted-Cash-Flow
　Methods　250
Valuing Firms Subject to Multiple Growth
　Periods　256
Valuing Firms under Special Situations　258
Using the Enterprise Method to Estimate Equity
　Value　259
Valuing Nonoperating Assets　266
Putting It All Together　270
Some Things to Remember　274

Discussion Questions　274
　Practice Problems and Answers　275
Chapter Business Cases　279
　　Case Study 7.1　Hewlett-Packard Outbids Dell
　　Computer to Acquire 3PAR　279
　　Case Study 7.2　Creating a Global Luxury Hotel
　　Chain　281

8. Applying Relative, Asset-Oriented, and Real-Option Valuation Methods to Mergers and Acquisitions

Inside M&A: A Real-Options Perspective on
　Microsoft's Dealings with Yahoo!　283
Chapter Overview　285
Applying Relative-Valuation (Market-Based)
　Methods　286
Applying Asset-Oriented Methods　297
The Replacement Cost Method　300
Valuing the Firm Using the Weighted-Average
　Method　300
Analyzing Mergers and Acquisitions in Terms of
　Real Options　302
Determining When to Use the Different Approaches
　to Valuation　314
Which Valuation Methods Are Actually Used in
　Practice　315
Some Things to Remember　316
Discussion Questions　316
　Practice Problems and Answers　317
Chapter Business Cases　320
　　Case Study 8.1　Google Buys YouTube:
　　Valuing a Firm in the Absence of Cash
　　Flows　320
　　Case Study 8.2　Merrill Lynch and BlackRock
　　Agree to Swap Assets　322

9. Applying Financial Modeling Techniques: To Value, Structure, and Negotiate Mergers and Acquisitions

Inside M&A: HP Buys EDS—The Role of Financial
　Models in Decision Making　325
Chapter Overview　326
Limitations of Financial Data　327
The Model-Building Process　329
Using Financial Models in Support of M&A
　Negotiations　349

Alternative Applications of M&A Financial
Models 353
Some Things to Remember 354
Discussion Questions 355
Practice Problems and Answers 356
Chapter Business Cases 357
Case Study 9.1 Cleveland Cliffs Fails to
Complete Takeover of Alpha Natural
Resources in a Commodity Play 357
Case Study 9.2 Mars Buys Wrigley in One Sweet
Deal 360
Appendix A: Utilizing the M&A Model on the
Companion Site to this Book 361
Appendix B: M&A Model Balance Sheet Adjustment
Mechanism 363

10. Analysis and Valuation of Privately Held Companies

Inside M&A: Cashing Out of a Privately Held
Enterprise 365
Chapter Overview 366
Demographics of Privately Held Businesses 367
Governance Issues in Privately Held and Family-
Owned Firms 368
Challenges of Valuing Privately Held
Companies 369
Process for Valuing Privately Held Businesses 371
Step 1: Adjusting Financial Statements 371
Step 2: Applying Valuation Methodologies to
Privately Held Companies 377
Step 3: Developing Discount (Capitalization)
Rates 380
Step 4: Applying Control Premiums, Liquidity,
and Minority Discounts 383
Reverse Mergers 395
Using Leveraged Employee Stock Ownership Plans
to Buy Private Companies 397
Empirical Studies of Shareholder Returns 398
Some Things to Remember 399
Discussion Questions 400
Practice Problems and Answers 400
Chapter Business Cases 401
Case Study 10.1 Panda Ethanol Goes Public in a
Shell Corporation 401
Case Study 10.2 Determining Liquidity
Discounts—The Taylor Devices and Tayco
Development Merger 403

Part IV

DEAL-STRUCTURING AND FINANCING STRATEGIES

11. Structuring the Deal: Payment and Legal Considerations

Inside M&A: Pfizer Acquires Wyeth Labs Despite
Tight Credit Markets 409
Chapter Overview 410
The Deal-Structuring Process 411
Form of Acquisition Vehicle and Postclosing
Organization 415
Legal Form of the Selling Entity 419
Form of Payment or Total Consideration 419
Managing Risk and Closing the Gap
on Price 421
Using Collar Arrangements to Preserve Shareholder
Value 427
Case Study 11.1 Flextronics Acquires
International DisplayWorks Using Fixed
Value and Fixed Share Exchange
Collars 430
Form of Acquisition 431
Case Study 11.2 Buyer Consortium Wins Control
of ABN Amro 437
Some Things to Remember 442
Discussion Questions 443
Chapter Business Cases 444
Case Study 11.3 Boston Scientific Overcomes
Johnson & Johnson to Acquire Guidant—A
Lesson in Bidding Strategy 444
Case Study 11.4 Swiss Pharmaceutical Giant
Novartis Takes Control of Alcon 446

12. Structuring the Deal: Tax and Accounting Considerations

Inside M&A: Continued Consolidation in the
Generic Pharmaceuticals Industry 449
Chapter Overview 449
General Tax Considerations and Issues 450
Taxable Transactions 450
Case Study 12.1 Cablevision Uses Tax Benefits
to Help Justify the Price Paid for Bresnan
Communications 455
Tax-Free Transactions 456

Other Tax Considerations Affecting Corporate Restructuring   463

Financial Reporting of Business Combinations   466

Impact of Purchase Accounting on Financial Statements   469

International Accounting Standards   474

Recapitalization Accounting   474

Some Things to Remember   474

Discussion Questions   475

   Practice Problems and Answers   476

Chapter Business Cases   477

   Case Study 12.2   Teva Pharmaceuticals Buys Barr Pharmaceuticals to Create a Global Powerhouse   477

   Case Study 12.3   Merck and Schering-Plough Merger: When Form Overrides Substance   480

13. Financing Transactions: Private Equity, Hedge Funds, and Leveraged Buyout Structures and Valuation

Inside M&A: Kinder Morgan Buyout Raises Ethical Questions   485

Chapter Overview   486

Characterizing Leveraged Buyouts   487

How Do LBOs Create Value?   493

When Do Firms Go Private?   495

Financing Transactions   495

Common Forms of Leveraged Buyout Deal Structures   500

Prebuyout and Postbuyout Shareholder Returns   504

Using DCF Methods to Value Leveraged Buyouts   509

LBO Valuation and Structuring Model Basics   518

Some Things to Remember   526

Discussion Questions   526

   Practice Problems and Answers   527

Chapter Business Cases   529

   Case Study 13.1   TXU Goes Private in the Largest Private Equity Transaction in History—A Retrospective Look   529

   Case Study 13.2   "Grave Dancer" Takes Tribune Corporation Private in an Ill-Fated Transaction   532

Part V

ALTERNATIVE BUSINESS AND RESTRUCTURING STRATEGIES

14. Joint Ventures, Partnerships, Strategic Alliances, and Licensing

Inside M&A: Microsoft Partners with Yahoo!—An Alternative to Takeover?   539

Chapter Overview   540

Motivations for Business Alliances   540

Critical Success Factors for Business Alliances   545

Alternative Legal Forms of Business Alliances   547

Strategic and Operational Plans   554

Resolving Business Alliance Deal-Structuring Issues   555

   Case Study 14.1   Determining Ownership Distribution in a Joint Venture   559

Empirical Findings   565

Some Things to Remember   567

Discussion Questions   567

Chapter Business Cases   568

   Case Study 14.2   Estimating the Real Cost of Comcast's Investment in NBC Universal   568

   Case Study 14.3   British Petroleum and Russia's Rosneft Unsuccessful Attempt to Swap Shares   572

15. Alternative Exit and Restructuring Strategies: Divestitures, Spin-Offs, Carve-Outs, Split-Offs, and Tracking Stocks

Inside M&A: Bristol-Myers Squibb Splits off the Rest of Mead Johnson   575

Chapter Overview   576

Commonly Stated Motives for Exiting Businesses   577

   Case Study 15.1   British Petroleum Sells Oil and Gas Assets to Apache Corporation   579

Divestitures   581

Spin-Offs   587

   Case Study 15.2   Motorola Bows to Activist Pressure   588

Case Study 15.3   Anatomy of a Spin-Off   590
Equity Carve-Outs   591
Split-Offs and Split-Ups   593
Case Study 15.4   Anatomy of a Split-Off   593
Tracking, Targeted, and Letter Stocks   595
Voluntary Liquidations (Bust-Ups)   596
Comparing Alternative Exit and Restructuring
Strategies   597
Choosing among Divestiture, Carve-Out, and
Spin-Off Restructuring Strategies   597
Determinants of Returns to Shareholders Resulting
from Restructuring Strategies   599
Some Things to Remember   609
Discussion Questions   609
Chapter Business Cases   610
Case Study 15.5   Kraft Foods Undertakes
Split-Off of Post Cereals in Merger-Related
Transaction   610
Case Study 15.6   Sara Lee Attempts to Create
Value through Restructuring   613

16. Alternative Exit and Restructuring
Strategies: Reorganization and
Liquidation

Inside M&A: Calpine Emerges from the Protection
of Bankruptcy Court   617
Chapter Overview   618
Business Failure   618
Voluntary Settlements with Creditors Outside of
Bankruptcy   619
Reorganization and Liquidation in Bankruptcy   622
Case Study 16.1   Lehman Brothers Files for
Chapter 11 in the Biggest Bankruptcy
in U.S. History   625
Analyzing Strategic Options for Failing Firms   633
Failing Firms and Systemic Risk   635
Predicting Corporate Default and Bankruptcy   637
Valuing Distressed Businesses   640
Empirical Studies of Financial Distress   644
Some Things to Remember   646
Discussion Questions   646
Chapter Business Cases   648
Case Study 16.2   The General Motors'
Bankruptcy—The Largest Government-
Sponsored Bailout in U.S. History   648
Case Study 16.3   Delta Airlines Rises from the
Ashes   652

17. Cross-Border Mergers and Acquisitions:
Analysis and Valuation

Inside M&A: InBev Buys an American Icon
for $52 Billion   655
Chapter Overview   656
Distinguishing between Developed and
Emerging Economies   656
Globally Integrated versus Segmented
Capital Markets   657
Motives for International Expansion   659
Case Study 17.1   Ford Sells Volvo to Geely in
China's Biggest Overseas Auto Deal   660
Common International Market Entry
Strategies   662
Structuring Cross-Border Transactions   665
Financing Cross-Border Transactions   667
Planning and Implementing Cross-Border
Transactions in Emerging Countries   669
Valuing Cross-Border Transactions   670
Empirical Studies of Financial Returns to
International Diversification   683
Some Things to Remember   686
Discussion Questions   686
Chapter Business Cases   688
Case Study 17.2   Overcoming Political Risk
in Cross-Border Transactions: China's
CNOOC Invests in Chesapeake Energy   688
Case Study 17.3   Wal-Mart's International
Strategy Illustrates the Challenges
and the Potential of Global Expansion   690

References   693
Glossary   715
Index   725

Contents of the Companion Site

Acquirer Due Diligence Question List

Acquisition Process: The Gee Whiz Media Integrative Case Study

Example of Applying Experience Curves to M&A

Example of Supernormal Growth Model

Example of Market Attractiveness Matrix (Updated)

Examples of Merger and Acquisition Agreements of Purchase and Sale

Excel-Based Mergers and Acquisitions Valuation and Structuring Model

Excel-Based Leveraged Buyout Valuation and Structuring Model

Excel-Based Decision Tree M&A Valuation Model

Excel-Based Model to Estimate Firm Borrowing Capacity

Excel-Based Offer Price Simulation Model (Updated)

Excel-Based Spreadsheet: How to Adjust Target Firm's Financial Statements (Updated)

Excel-Based Spreadsheet: How to Value Distressed Businesses (New)

Excel-Based Spreadsheet: Determining Home Depot's Equity Value Using the Enterprise Method (New)

Guidelines for Organizing ESOPs

Interactive Learning Library (Updated)

MCI/Verizon 2005 Merger Agreement

Primer on Cash-Flow Forecasting (Updated)

Primer on Applying and Interpreting Financial Ratios

Student Chapter PowerPoint Presentations (Updated)

Student Study Guide, Practice Questions, and Answers (Updated)

List of Business Case Studies

Chapter 1: Introduction to Mergers and Acquisitions 3

Inside M&A: Dell Moves into Information Technology Services 3
 *Strategic realignment**
1.1. Xerox Buys ACS to Satisfy Shifting Customer Requirements 47
 *Related diversification**
1.2. Assessing Proctor & Gamble's Acquisition of Gillette 49
 *Horizontal merger**

Chapter 2: Regulatory Considerations 51

Inside M&A: The Limitations of Regulation—The Lehman Brothers Meltdown 51
 *Regulatory failure**
2.1. A Federal Judge Reprimands Hedge Funds in Their Effort to Control CSX 57
 *Enforcing securities laws**
2.2. Justice Department Requires Verizon Wireless to Sell Assets before Approving Alltel Merger 65
 *Consent decrees**
2.3. Google Thwarted in Proposed Advertising Deal with Chief Rival Yahoo! 70
 *Business alliances**
2.4. BHP Billiton and Rio Tinto Blocked by Regulators in an International Iron Ore Joint Venture 82
 *International antitrust**

2.5. Global Financial Exchanges Pose Regulatory Challenges 84
 *Regulating global markets***
2.6. The Legacy of GE's Aborted Attempt to Merge with Honeywell 86
 *EU antitrust***

Chapter 3: The Corporate Takeover Market: Common Takeover Tactics, Antitakeover Defenses, and Corporate Governance 91

Inside M&A: Kraft Sweetens Its Offer to Overcome Cadbury's Resistance 91
 *Hostile takeover**
3.1. Mittal Acquires Arcelor—A Battle of Global Titans in the European Corporate Takeover Market 126
 Hostile cross-border takeover
3.2. Verizon Acquires MCI—The Anatomy of Alternative Bidding Strategies 128
 Bidding strategy

Chapter 4: Planning: Developing Business and Acquisition Plans: Phases 1 and 2 of the Acquisition Process 135

Inside M&A: Nokia's Gamble to Dominate the Smartphone Market Falters 135
 *Strategy implementation**
4.1. CenturyTel Buys Qwest Communications to Cut Costs and Buy Time as the Landline Market Shrinks 145
 *Defensive acquisition**

* A single asterisk indicates that the case study is new since the fifth edition of this book.
** A double asterisk indicates that the case study has been updated since the fifth edition.

4.2. HP Redirects Its Mobile Device
Business Strategy with the Acquisition
of Palm   152
  *Strategic realignment**
4.3. Adobe's Acquisition of Omniture: Field
of Dreams Marketing?   163
  *Industry consolidation**
4.4. BofA Acquires Countrywide Financial
Corporation   165
  *Opportunistic acquisition***

**Chapter 5: Implementation:
Search through Closing:
Phases 3 through 10   169**

Inside M&A: Bank of America Acquires
Merrill Lynch   169
  *Vision drives strategy**
5.1. Oracle's Efforts to Consolidate the
Software Industry   196
  *Strategy realignment**
5.2. Exxon Mobil Buys XTO Energy
in a Bet on Natural Gas   198
  *Related diversification**

**Chapter 6: Integration: Mergers,
Acquisitions, and Business
Alliances   203**

Inside M&A: General Electric's Water
Business Fails to Meet Expectations   203
  Culture clash
6.1. HP Acquires Compaq—The Importance
of Preplanning Integration   208
  Plan before executing
6.2. Integrating Supply Chains: Coty
Cosmetics Integrates Unilever Cosmetics
International   217
  IT integration challenges
6.3. Culture Clash Exacerbates Efforts
of the Tribune Corporation to Integrate
the Times Mirror Corporation   222
  *Incompatible cultures***

6.4. Panasonic Moves to Consolidate
Past Acquisitions   224
  *Minority investors**
6.5. The Challenges of Integrating
Steel Giants Arcelor and
Mittal   228
  *Integration implementation***
6.6. Alcatel Merges with Lucent,
Highlighting Cross-Cultural
Issues   230
  International culture clash

**Chapter 7: A Primer on Merger
and Acquisition Cash-Flow
Valuation   235**

Inside M&A: The Importance of
Distinguishing between Operating
and Nonoperating Assets   235
  Value of nonoperating assets
7.1. Hewlett-Packard Outbids Dell
Computer to Acquire 3PAR   279
  *Betting on new technology**
7.2. Creating a Global Luxury Hotel
Chain   281
  *Importance of understanding valuation
  assumptions*

**Chapter 8: Applying Relative, Asset-
Oriented, and Real-Option Valuation
Methods to Mergers and
Acquisitions   283**

Inside M&A: A Real-Options' Perspective
on Microsoft's Dealings with Yahoo!   283
  *Defining real options***
8.1. Google Buys YouTube: Valuing a
Firm in the Absence of Cash
Flows   320
  *Valuing startups***
8.2. Merrill Lynch and BlackRock Agree
to Swap Assets   322
  Determining ownership percentages

Chapter 9: Applying Financial Modeling Techniques: To Value, Structure, and Negotiate Mergers and Acquisitions   325

Inside M&A: HP Buys EDS—The Role of Financial Models in Decision Making   325
The power of models
9.1. Cleveland Cliffs Fails to Complete Takeover of Alpha Natural Resources in a Commodity Play   357
Applying simulation models
9.2 Mars Buys Wrigley in One Sweet Deal   360
*Analyzing synergy***

Chapter 10: Analysis and Valuation of Privately Held Companies   365

Inside M&A: Cashing out of a Privately Held Enterprise   365
Developing options
10.1. Panda Ethanol Goes Public in a Shell Corporation   401
Alternatives to IPO
10.2. Determining Liquidity Discounts—The Taylor Devices and Tayco Development Merger   403
*Estimating and applying discounts***

Chapter 11: Structuring the Deal: Payment and Legal Considerations   409

Inside M&A: Pfizer Acquires Wyeth Labs Despite Tight Credit Markets   409
*Financing transactions**
11.1. Flextronics Acquires DisplayWorks Using Fixed Value and Fixed Share Exchange Collars   430
*Preserving value**

11.2. Buyer Consortium Wins Control of ABN Amro   437
*Preselling assets***
11.3. Boston Scientific Overcomes Johnson & Johnson to Acquire Guidant—A Lesson in Bidding Strategy   444
*Auction process***
11.4. Swiss Pharmaceutical Giant Novartis to Take Control of Alcon   446
*Staged transactions**

Chapter 12: Structuring the Deal: Tax and Accounting Considerations   449

Inside M&A: Continued Consolidation in the Generic Pharmaceuticals Industry   449
*Addressing shareholder needs***
12.1. Cablevision Uses Tax Benefits to Help Justify the Price Paid for Bresnan Communications   455
*338 election**
12.2. Teva Pharmaceuticals Buys Barr Pharmaceuticals to Create a Global Powerhouse   477
*Tax-advantaged sale**
12.3. Merck and Schering-Plough Merger—When Form Overrides Substance   480
*Two-stage, tax-advantaged deal**

Chapter 13: Financing Transactions: Private Equity, Hedge Funds, and Leveraged Buyout Structures and Valuation   485

Inside M&A: Kinder Morgan Buyout Raises Ethical Questions   485
*Potential conflicts of interest***
13.1. TXU Goes Private in the Largest Private Equity Transaction in History—A Retrospective Look   529
*Private equity deal**

13.2. "Grave Dancer" Takes Tribune Corporation Private in an Ill-Fated Transaction   532
  Two-stage, tax-advantaged deal**

Chapter 14: Joint Ventures, Partnerships, Strategic Alliances, and Licensing   539

Inside M&A: Microsoft Partners with Yahoo!—An Alternative to Takeover?   539
  M&A alternative*
14.1. Determining Ownership Distribution in a Joint Venture   559
  Minority investment**
14.2. Estimating the Real Cost of Comcast's Investment in NBC Universal   568
  Joint venture*
14.3. British Petroleum and Russia's Rosneft Unsuccessful Attempt to Swap Shares   572
  International joint venture*

Chapter 15: Alternative Exit and Restructuring Strategies: Divestitures, Spin-Offs, Carve-Outs, Split-Ups, Split-Offs, and Tracking Stocks   575

Inside M&A: Bristol-Myers Squibb Splits off the Rest of Mead Johnson   575
  Split-offs of noncore businesses*
15.1. British Petroleum Sells Oil and Gas Assets to Apache Corporation   579
  Asset sale*
15.2 Motorola Bows to Activist Pressure   588
  Breakup*
15.3. Anatomy of a Spin-Off   590
  Spin-offs structure**
15.4. Anatomy of a Split-Off   593
  Split-off structure*
15.5. Kraft Foods Undertakes Split-Off of Post Cereals in Merger-Related Transaction   610
  Split-off related merger**

15.6. Sara Lee Attempts to Create Value through Restructuring   613
  Breakup strategy*

Chapter 16: Alternative Exit and Restructuring Strategies: Reorganization and Liquidation   617

Inside M&A: Calpine Energy Emerges from the Protection of Bankruptcy Court   617
  Chapter 11 Reorganization
16.1. Lehman Brothers Files for Chapter 11 in the Biggest Bankruptcy in U.S. History   625
  Liquidation of a financial services firm**
16.2. The General Motors Bankruptcy— The Largest Government-Sponsored Bailout in U.S. History   648
  363 reorganization*
16.3. Delta Airlines Rises from the Ashes   652
  Using Chapter 11 to renegotiate contracts

Chapter 17: Cross-Border Mergers and Acquisitions: Analysis and Valuation   655

Inside M&A: InBev Buys an American Icon for $52 Billion   655
  Cross-border auction**
17.1. Ford Sells Volvo to Geely in China's Biggest Overseas Auto Deal   660
  Geographic diversification*
17.2. Overcoming Political Risk in Cross-Border Transactions: China's CNOOC Invests in Chesapeake Energy   688
  Political risk in cross-border M&A risk*
17.3. Wal-Mart's International Strategy Illustrates the Challenges and the Potential of Global Expansion   690
  International expansion**

Preface

To the Reader

Mergers, acquisitions, business alliances, and corporate restructuring activities are increasingly commonplace in both developed and emerging countries. Given the frequency with which such activities occur, it is critical for businesspeople and officials at all levels of government to have a basic understanding of why and how such activities take place. The objective of *Mergers, Acquisitions, and Other Restructuring Activities* is to bring clarity to what can be an exciting, complex, and sometimes frustrating subject. It is intended to help the reader think of the activities involved in mergers, acquisitions, business alliances, and corporate restructuring in an integrated way.

While all of the chapters in the book contain new content and have been revised and updated, 14 of them have undergone pervasive changes. Many of the finer details in each chapter have been moved to footnotes, resulting in a more streamlined, shorter, and less complex text. The chapters contain the latest academic research, with increased focus on recent empirical findings. Additional numerical examples have been included in more chapters to illustrate the application of important concepts.

About one-fourth of the book is devoted to business valuation and financial modeling. Chapters 7 and 8 are totally focused on commonly used alternative valuation methods. Chapter 9 addresses important modeling issues not covered in prior editions.

Chapters 10, 13, 16, and 17 deal with specialized valuation applications, including valuation of private firms, leveraged buyouts, distressed companies, and cross-border transactions. These chapters describe in detail the context in which these specialized situations occur.

Chapter 1 now includes examples that illustrate the important function that economies of scale and scope often play in mergers and acquisitions. Additional details on the roles of key participants in the M&A process are also provided.

Chapter 2 has been revised extensively to reflect the implications of the far-reaching Dodd-Frank Wall Street Reform and Consumer Protection Act of 2010 (Dodd-Frank) for governance; for the environment in which mergers, acquisitions, and other corporate restructuring activities occur; and for participants in the M&A and restructuring process. The chapter also contains recent U.S. Supreme Court rulings affecting the Sarbanes-Oxley Act, the impact of Regulation FD on announcement date financial returns, and the 2010 issuance by the U.S. Department of Justice and the Federal Trade Commission of updated guidelines for approving horizontal mergers.

The implications of the "say on pay" and "clawback" provisions of the Dodd-Frank Act are explored in Chapter 3, as well as changes in Securities and Exchange Commission regulations that have made it easier for shareholders to place their candidates for the board of directors on corporate ballots.

Chapter 5 contains a more in-depth discussion of the negotiation process and how to develop effective negotiating strategies. Chapter 7 provides a more detailed discussion of the impact of risk on financial returns, the treatment of taxes in valuation, and the calculation of the market value of a firm's debt under different scenarios, as well as alternative valuation methods and how to adjust enterprise cash flow to estimate a firm's equity value per share. Chapter 8 now contains a discussion of studies documenting the valuation methods that are most commonly used in practice.

Chapter 9 includes a more rigorous discussion and illustration of how M&A Excel-based simulation models can be useful tools in the negotiation process. It also offers streamlined examples of estimating synergy and other aspects of the model-building process. The academic studies summarized in Chapter 10 that illustrate when and how to apply control premiums, liquidity, and minority discounts as part of the valuation process have been updated. The section in Chapter 11 on using collar arrangements to manage risk has been expanded, with more examples describing how to construct those based on fixed share exchange ratios and fixed value arrangements.

Chapter 12 has been updated to include a discussion of the implications of recent changes to accounting rules that apply to business combinations, additional examples, and the status of the pending convergence of GAAP with international accounting standards.

The discussion of tax structures and strategies also has been updated and streamlined. Chapter 13 has a more detailed discussion (including illustrations) of how LBOs create value and how such transactions are financed. Chapter 14 illustrates how joint ventures often are valued and how the distribution of ownership is determined. Chapter 15 includes a more detailed discussion of the divestiture process and how selling firms choose the appropriate

selling process, as well as a discussion of those factors that have an impact on purchase price premiums

Finally, Chapter 16 discusses a methodology for valuing firms that are experiencing financial distress and the Orderly Liquidation Authority created under the Dodd-Frank Act. All of the chapters reflect the latest academic research.

Three-fourths of the 72 case studies are new or have been updated from the previous edition, with most of the transactions discussed having taken place within the last four years. Eleven case studies involve cross-border or foreign transactions, four involve hostile takeovers, four deal with highly leveraged transactions, four involve private or family-owned businesses, eight address various aspects of deal structuring, and five involve firms experiencing financial distress. All of the case studies include discussion questions, with answers for all end-of-chapter and many "in-chapter" case study questions available in the Online Instructor's Manual. Finally, the case studies involve transactions in a dozen different industries.

This sixth edition contains nearly 300 end-of-chapter discussion and review questions, problems, and exercises that give readers the opportunity to test their knowledge of the material. Many of the exercises will enable students to find their own solutions based on different sets of assumptions, using Excel-based spreadsheet models that are available on the book's companion site. Solutions to all questions, problems, and exercises are available on the expanded Online Instructor's Manual. The online manual now contains more than 1,600 true/false, multiple-choice, and short essay questions, as well as numerical problems

In addition to Excel-based customizable M&A and LBO valuation and structuring software, PowerPoint presentations, and due diligence materials, the companion website provides access to an interactive learning library. The learning library enables readers to test their knowledge by having their answers to specific questions scored immediately.

The site also contains a Student Study Guide and models for estimating a firm's borrowing capacity and for adjusting a firm's financial statements, as well as numerous illustrations of concepts discussed.

Mergers, Acquisitions, and Other Restructuring Activities is intended for students in mergers and acquisitions, corporate restructuring, business strategy, management, and entrepreneurship courses. It works well at both the undergraduate and the graduate level. The text also should interest financial analysts, chief financial officers, operating managers, investment bankers, and portfolio managers. Others who may have an interest include bank lending officers, venture capitalists, government regulators, human resource managers, entrepreneurs, and board members.

From the classroom to the boardroom, this text offers something for anyone with an interest in mergers and acquisitions, business alliances, and other forms of corporate restructuring.

To the Instructor

This text is an attempt to provide organization to a topic that is inherently complex because of the diversity of applicable subject matter and the breadth of disciplines that must be involved to complete most transactions. Consequently, the discussion of M&A is not easily divisible into highly focused chapters. Efforts to compartmentalize the topic often result in the reader not understanding how seemingly independent topics are integrated. Understanding M&A involves an understanding of a full range of concepts, including management, finance, economics, business law, financial and tax accounting, organizational dynamics, and the role of leadership.

With this in mind, *Mergers and Acquisitions* provides a new organizational paradigm for discussing the complex and dynamically changing world of M&A. It is organized according to the context in which events normally occur during mergers and acquisitions and so is divided into five parts: environment, process, valuation and modeling, deal structuring and financing, and alternative business and restructuring strategies. Topics that are highly integrated are discussed within these five groupings. (See Figure P.1 for the organizational layout of the book.)

Mergers, Acquisitions, and Other Restructuring Activities equips the instructor with the information needed to communicate effectively with students who have different levels of preparation. The generous use of examples and the contemporary business cases makes the text suitable for distance-learning and self-study programs, as well as large, lecture-focused courses.

The extensive use of the end-of-chapter discussion questions, problems, and exercises (with answers available in the Online Instructor's Manual) offers the opportunity to test students' progress in mastering the material. Prerequisites for this text include familiarity with basic accounting, finance, economics, and management concepts.

Online Instructor's Manual

The Online Instructor's Manual contains PowerPoint presentations for each chapter (completely consistent with those found on the companion website), suggested learning objectives, recommended ways to teach the materials, detailed syllabi for both undergraduate- and graduate-level classes, examples of excellent papers submitted by the

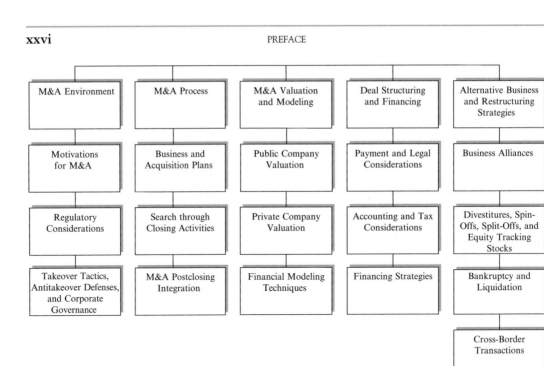

FIGURE P.1   Course layout for the use of *Mergers, Acquisitions, and Other Restructuring Activities.*

author's students, and an exhaustive test bank. It contains more than 1,600 test questions and answers (including true/false, multiple choice, short essay, case studies, and computational problems) and solutions to end-of-chapter discussion questions and case study questions.

The online manual also contains, in a file folder entitled "Preface to the Online Instructor's Manual and Table of Contents," suggestions on how to teach the course to both undergraduate and graduate classes.

Please e-mail the publisher, within North America, at *textbooks@elsevier.com* and *emea. textbook@elsevier.com* (outside North America) for access to the online manual. Include your contact information (name, department, college, address, e-mail, and phone number), along with course information, including course name and number, annual enrollment, book title, author, and ISBN.

All requests are subject to approval by the company's representatives. For instructors who have already adopted this book, please go to *textbooks.elsevier.com* (Elsevier's instructors' website) and click on the button in the upper left corner entitled "Instructors' Manual." There you will find detailed instructions on how to gain access to the online manual.

Student Study Guide

The Student Study Guide on the companion website includes chapter summaries that highlight key learning objectives for each chapter, as well as true/false, multiple-choice, and numerical questions and answers to enhance the student's learning experience.

Practical, Timely, and Diverse Examples and Current Business Cases

Each chapter begins with a vignette that is intended to illustrate a key point or points described in more detail as the chapter unfolds. Hundreds of examples, business cases, tables, and figures illustrate the application of key concepts. Many exhibits and diagrams summarize otherwise diffuse information and the results of numerous empirical studies substantiating key points made in each chapter.

Each chapter concludes with a series of 15 discussion questions and two integrative end-of-chapter case studies intended to stimulate critical thinking and test the reader's understanding of the material. Six chapters include a series of practice problems and exercises to facilitate learning the chapter's content.

Comprehensive Yet Flexible Organization

Although the text is sequential, each chapter was developed as a self-contained unit to enable adaptation to various teaching strategies and students with diverse backgrounds. The flexibility of the book's organization also makes the material suitable for courses of various lengths, from one quarter to two full semesters. The amount of time required depends on the student's level of sophistication and the instructor's desired focus.

Undergraduates have consistently demonstrated the ability to master 8 or 9 chapters during a typical semester, whereas graduate-level students are able to cover effectively 12 to 14 chapters of the book during the same period.

Acknowledgments

I would like to express my sincere appreciation for the many helpful suggestions received from a number of anonymous reviewers and the many resources of Academic Press/Butterworth-Heinemann/Elsevier. Specifically, I would like to thank Alan Cherry, Ross Bengel, Patricia Douglas, Jeff Gale, Jim Healy, Charles Higgins, Michael Lovelady, John Mellen, Jon Saxon, David Offenberg, Chris Manning, and Maria Quijada for their constructive comments.

I would also like to thank Scott Bentley, Executive Editor at Elsevier/Academic Press/Butterworth-Heinemann, for his ongoing support and guidance, as well as Editorial Project Manager Kathleen Paoni and Production Project Manager Marilyn Rash.

About the Author

Dr. DePamphilis has managed more than 30 transactions through closing, including acquisitions, divestitures, joint ventures, minority investments, licensing, and supply agreements in a variety of industries. These industries include financial services, software, metals manufacturing, business consulting, healthcare, automotive, communications, textiles, and real estate. He earned a B.A. in economics from the University of Pittsburgh and an M.A. and a Ph.D. in economics from Harvard University.

Currently clinical professor of Finance at Loyola Marymount University in Los Angeles, Dr. DePamphilis teaches mergers and acquisitions, corporate restructuring, deal making, finance, micro- and macroeconomics, and corporate governance to undergraduate, MBA, and executive MBA students. He has served as chair of the Student Investment Fund at Loyola Marymount College of Business, and he is a recipient of the University's Executive MBA Leadership Achievement Award.

Dr. DePamphilis has lectured on M&A and corporate restructuring, finance, and economics at the University of California, at Irvine, Chapman University, and Concordia University. As a visiting professor, he taught mergers and acquisitions at the Antai School of Management, Shanghai Jiao Tong University, in Shanghai.

Dr. DePamphilis's more than 25 years of experience in various industries, include positions as vice president of Electronic Commerce for Experian Corporation, vice president of Business Development at TRW

Information Systems and Services, senior vice president of Planning and Marketing at PUH Health Systems, director of Corporate Business Planning at TRW, and chief economist for National Steel Corporation. He also served as director of Banking and Insurance Economics for Chase Econometric Associates and as an economic analyst for United California Bank. While at United California, he developed a complex, interactive econometric forecasting model of the U.S. economy. He is a graduate of the TRW and National Steel Corporation Executive Management programs.

Dr. DePamphilis has authored numerous articles and books on M&A, business planning and development, marketing, and economics in peer-reviewed academic journals as well as business and trade publications. His books include the extremely popular *Mergers, Acquisitions, and Other Restructuring Activities*, now in this sixth edition; *Mergers and Acquisitions Basics: All You Need to Know;* and *Merger and Acquisition Basics: Negotiation and Deal Structuring*. This book has been translated into Chinese and Russian and is used in universities worldwide.

Dr. DePamphilis has also spoken to numerous industry and trade associations and customer groups and to Los Angeles community and business groups.

Frequently, Dr. DePamphilis serves as a consultant in litigation involving product and personal liability, patent infringement, and business valuation, including expert analysis and depositions in cases primarily related to mergers and acquisitions. He also offers target selection, negotiation support, and business valuation services.

Please forward any comments and/or suggestions you may have about this book to the author at ddepamph@lmu.edu.

PART I

THE MERGERS AND ACQUISITIONS ENVIRONMENT

"As you know we've made a lot of acquisitions lately, and the last one we made seems to have resulted in us buying ourselves."

Courtesy of www.CartoonStock.com

Part I discusses the context in which mergers, acquisitions, and corporate restructuring occur, including factors often beyond the control of the participants in the M&A process. Chapter 1 provides an overview of mergers and acquisitions by discussing basic vocabulary, the most common reasons why M&As happen, how such transactions occur in a series of somewhat predictable waves, and participants in the M&A process, from investment bankers to lenders to regulatory authorities.

The chapter also addresses whether M&As benefit shareholders, bondholders, and society, with conclusions based on recent empirical studies. The labyrinth of regulations that impact the M&A process is addressed in Chapter 2, including U.S. federal and state securities and antitrust laws, as well as environmental, labor, and benefit laws that add to the increasing complexity of such transactions. The implications of cross-border transactions, which offer an entirely new set of regulatory challenges, also are explored. Viewed in the context of a market in which control transfers from sellers to buyers, Chapter 3 addresses common takeover tactics employed as part of an overall bidding strategy, the motivation behind such tactics, and the defenses used by target firms to deter or delay such tactics. Bidding strategies are discussed for both friendly and unwanted or hostile business takeovers. In hostile transactions, the corporate takeover is viewed as a means of disciplining underperforming management, improving corporate governance practices, and reallocating assets to those who can use them more effectively.

The reader is encouraged to read about transactions currently in the news and to identify the takeover tactics and defenses employed by the parties to the transactions. One's understanding of the material can be enriched by attempting to discern the intentions of both the acquiring and target firms' boards and management and thinking about what you might have done differently to achieve similar goals.

1

Introduction to Mergers and Acquisitions

If you give a man a fish, you feed him for a day. If you teach a man to fish, you feed him for a lifetime. —**Lao Tze**

INSIDE M&A: DELL MOVES INTO INFORMATION TECHNOLOGY SERVICES

Dell Computer's growing dependence on the sale of personal computers and peripherals left it vulnerable to economic downturns. Profits had dropped more than 22% since the start of the global recession in early 2008 as business spending on information technology was cut sharply. Dell dropped from number 1 to number 3 in terms of market share, as measured by personal computer unit sales, behind lower-cost rivals Hewlett-Packard and Acer. Major competitors such as IBM and Hewlett-Packard were less vulnerable to economic downturns because they derived a larger percentage of their sales from delivering services.

Historically, Dell has grown "organically" by reinvesting in its own operations and through partnerships targeting specific products or market segments. However, in recent years, Dell attempted to "supercharge" its lagging growth through targeted acquisitions of new technologies. Since 2007, Dell has made ten comparatively small acquisitions (eight in the United States), purchased stakes in four firms, and divested two companies. The largest previous acquisition for Dell was the purchase of EqualLogic for $1.4 billion in 2007.

The recession underscored what Dell had known for some time. The firm had long considered diversifying its revenue base from the more cyclical PC and peripherals business into the more stable and less commodity-like computer services business. In 2007, Dell was in discussions about a merger with Perot Systems, a leading provider of information technology (IT) services, but an agreement could not be reached.

Dell's global commercial customer base spans large corporations, government agencies, healthcare providers, educational institutions, and small and medium firms. The firm's current capabilities include expertise in infrastructure consulting and software services, providing network-based services, and data storage hardware; nevertheless, it was still largely a manufacturer of PCs and peripheral products.

In contrast, Perot Systems offers applications development, systems integration, and strategic consulting services through its operations in the United States and ten other countries. In addition, it provides a variety of business process outsourcing services, including claims processing and call center operations. Perot's primary markets are healthcare, government, and other commercial segments. About one-half of Perot's revenue comes from the healthcare market, which is expected to benefit from the $30 billion the U.S. government has committed to spending on information technology (IT) upgrades over the next five years.

In 2008, Hewlett-Packard (HP) paid $13.9 billion for computer services behemoth EDS in an attempt to become a "total IT solutions" provider for its customers. This event, coupled with a very attractive offer price, revived merger discussions with Perot Systems. On September 21, 2009, Dell announced that an agreement had been reached to acquire Perot Systems in an all-cash offer for $30 a share in a deal valued at $3.9 billion. The tender offer (i.e., takeover bid) for all of Perot Systems' outstanding shares of Class A common stock was initiated in early November and completed on November 19, 2009, with Dell receiving more than 90% of Perot's outstanding shares.

CHAPTER OVERVIEW

In this chapter, you will gain an understanding of the underlying dynamics of mergers and acquisitions (M&As) in the context of an increasingly interconnected world. The chapter begins with a discussion of why M&As act as change agents in the context of corporate restructuring. Although other aspects of corporate restructuring are discussed elsewhere in the chapter, the focus here is on M&As, why they happen, and why they tend to cluster in waves. You will also be introduced to a variety of legal structures and strategies that are employed to restructure corporations. Moreover, the role of the various participants in the M&A process is explained. Using the results of the latest empirical studies, the chapter addresses questions of whether mergers pay off for the target and acquiring company shareholders and bondholders, as well as for society. Finally, the most commonly cited reasons for why some M&As fail to meet expectations are discussed.

Throughout this book, a firm that attempts to acquire or merge with another company is called an *acquiring company*, *acquirer*, or *bidder*. The *target company* or *target* is the firm being solicited by the acquiring company. *Takeovers* or *buyouts* are generic terms for a change in the controlling ownership interest of a corporation. A review of this chapter (including practice questions and answers) is available in the file folder entitled Student Study Guide on the companion site for this book (*www.elsevierdirect.com/companions/9780123854858*). The site also contains a Learning Interactions Library that gives students the opportunity to test their knowledge of this chapter in a "real-time" environment.

MERGERS AND ACQUISITIONS AS CHANGE AGENTS

Businesses come and go in a continuing churn, perhaps best illustrated by the ever-changing composition of the so-called "Fortune 500"—the 500 largest U.S. corporations. Only 70 of the firms on the original 1955 list of 500 are on today's list, and some 2,000 firms have appeared on it at one time or another. Most have dropped off as a result of merger, acquisition, bankruptcy, downsizing, or some other form of corporate restructuring. Consider a few examples: Chrysler, Bethlehem Steel, Scott Paper, Zenith, Rubbermaid, and Warner Lambert.

The popular media tends to use the term *corporate restructuring* to describe actions taken to expand or contract a firm's basic operations or fundamentally change its asset or financial structure. Corporate restructuring runs the gamut from reorganizing business units to takeovers and joint ventures to divestitures and spin-offs and equity carve-outs. Consequently, virtually all of the material covered in this book can be viewed as part of the corporate restructuring process. While the focus in this chapter is on corporate restructuring involving mergers and acquisitions, non-M&A corporate restructuring is discussed in more detail elsewhere in this book.

WHY MERGERS AND ACQUISITIONS HAPPEN

The reasons M&As occur are numerous, and the importance of factors giving rise to M&A activity varies over time. Table 1.1 lists some of the more prominent theories about why M&As happen. Each theory is discussed in greater detail in the remainder of this section.

Synergy

Synergy is the rather simplistic notion that the combination of two businesses creates greater shareholder value than if they are operated separately. The two basic types of synergy are operating and financial.

Operating Synergy

Operating synergy consists of both economies of scale and economies of scope, which can be important determinants of shareholder wealth creation.[1] Gains in efficiency can come from either factor and from improved managerial practices.

Economies of scale refer to the spreading of fixed costs over increasing production levels. Scale is defined by such fixed costs as depreciation of equipment and amortization of capitalized software, normal maintenance spending, and obligations such as interest expense, lease payments, long-term union, customer, and vendor contracts, and taxes. These costs are *fixed* in that they cannot be altered in the short run. By contrast, variable costs are those that change with output levels. Consequently, for a given scale or amount of fixed expenses, the dollar value of fixed expenses per unit of output and per dollar of revenue decreases as output and sales increase.

To illustrate the potential profit improvement from economies of scale, consider the merger of Firm B into Firm A. Firm A is assumed to have a plant producing at only one-half of its capacity, enabling Firm A to shut down Firm B's plant that is producing the same product and move the production to its own underutilized facility. Consequently, Firm A's profit margin improves from 6.25% before the merger to 14.58% after the merger (Table 1.2).

Economies of scope refer to using a specific set of skills or an asset currently employed in producing a specific product or service to produce related products or services, which are

[1] Houston, James, and Ryngaert, 2001; DeLong, 2003

TABLE 1.1   Common Theories of What Causes Mergers and Acquisitions

Theory	Motivation
OPERATING SYNERGY	
• Economies of Scale • Economies of Scope	Improve operating efficiency through economies of scale or scope by acquiring a customer, supplier, or competitor
FINANCIAL SYNERGY	*LOWER COST OF CAPITAL*
Diversification • New Products/Current Markets • New Products/New Markets • Current Products/New Markets	Position the firm in higher-growth products or markets
Strategic Realignment • Technological Change • Regulatory and Political Change	Acquire capabilities to adapt more rapidly to environmental changes than could be achieved if the capabilities were developed internally
Hubris (Managerial Pride)	Acquirers believe their valuation of the target is more accurate than the market's, causing them to overpay by overestimating synergy
Buying Undervalued Assets (q-Ratio)	Acquire assets more cheaply when the equity of existing companies is less than the cost of buying or building the assets
Mismanagement (Agency Problems)	Replace managers not acting in the best interests of the owners
Managerialism (agency problem)	Increase the size of a company to increase the power and pay of the managers
Tax Considerations	Obtain unused net operating losses and tax credits, asset write-ups, and substitute capital gains for ordinary income
Market Power	Increase market share to improve ability to set prices above competitive levels
Misvaluation	Investor overvaluation of acquirer's stock encourages M&As

found most often when it is cheaper to combine multiple product lines in one firm than to produce them in separate firms. For example, Procter & Gamble, the consumer products giant, uses its highly regarded consumer marketing skills to sell a full range of personal care as well as pharmaceutical products. Honda knows how to enhance internal combustion engines, so in addition to cars, the firm develops motorcycles, lawn mowers, and snowblowers. Citigroup uses the same computer center to process loan applications, deposits, trust services, and mutual fund accounts for its banks' customers.

Assume Firm A merges with Firm B and combines the data processing facilities such that a single center supports both firms' manufacturing operations. By expanding the scope of a single data processing center to support all of the manufacturing facilities of the combined firms, significant cost savings can be realized in terms of lower labor, telecommunications, leased space, and overhead costs (Table 1.3).

TABLE 1.2   Economies of Scale

Period 1: Firm A (Premerger)	Period 2: Firm A (Postmerger)
ASSUMPTIONS	*ASSUMPTIONS*
• Price = $4 per unit of output sold • Variable costs = $2.75 per unit of output • Fixed costs = $1,000,000 • Firm A is producing 1,000,000 units of output per year • Firm A is producing at 50% of plant capacity	• Firm A acquires Firm B, which is producing 500,000 units of the same product per year • Firm A closes Firm B's plant and transfers production to Firm A's plant • Price = $4 per unit of output sold • Variable costs = $2.75 per unit of output • Fixed costs = $1,000,000

Profit = price × quantity − variable costs − fixed costs
     = $4 × 1,000,000 − $2.75 × 1,000,000 −
     $1,000,000 = $250,000
	Profit = price × quantity − variable costs − fixed costs
	     = $4 × 1,500,000 − $2.75 × 1,500,000 − $1,000,000
	     = $6,000,000 − $4,125,000 − $1,000,000 = $875,000

Profit margin (%)[a] = 250,000/4,000,000 = 6.25% Fixed costs per unit = $1,000,000/$1,000,000 = $1.00	Profit margin (%)[b] = 875,000/6,000,000 = 14.58% Fixed cost per unit = $1,000,000/1,500,000 = $0.67

[a] *Margin per $ of revenue = $4.00 − $2.75 − $1.00 = $.25*
[b] *Margin per $ of revenue = $4.00 − $2.75 − $.67 = $.58*

TABLE 1.3   Economies of Scope

Premerger	Postmerger

• Firm A's data processing center supports five manufacturing facilities
 	
• Firm B's data processing center supports three manufacturing facilities
	• Firm A's and Firm B's data processing centers are combined into a single operation to support all eight manufacturing facilities
	
	• By combining the centers, Firm A is able to achieve the following annual pretax savings:
	  ○ Direct labor costs = $840,000
	  ○ Telecommunications expenses = $275,000
	  ○ Leased space expenses = $675,000
	  ○ General and administrative expenses = $230,000

Financial Synergy

Financial synergy refers to the impact of mergers and acquisitions on the cost of capital of the acquiring firm, or the newly formed firm, resulting from the merger or acquisition. The cost of capital is the minimum return required by investors and lenders to induce them to buy a firm's stock or to lend to the firm. In theory, the cost of capital could be reduced if the merged firms have cash flows that do not move up and down in tandem (i.e., so-called coinsurance), realize financial economies of scale from lower securities issuance and transactions costs, or result in a better matching of investment opportunities with internally generated funds.

Combining a firm that has excess cash flows with one whose internally generated cash flow is insufficient to fund its investment opportunities may result in a lower cost of borrowing. A firm in a mature industry that is experiencing slowing growth may produce cash flows well in excess of available investment opportunities. Another firm in a high-growth industry may not have enough cash to realize its investment opportunities. Reflecting their different growth rates and risk levels, the firm in the mature industry may have a lower cost of capital than the one in the high-growth industry, and combining the two firms could lower their average cost of capital.

Diversification

Buying firms outside of a company's current primary lines of business is called *diversification*, and is typically justified in one of two ways. Diversification may create financial synergy that reduces the cost of capital, or it may allow a firm to shift its core product lines or markets into ones that have higher growth prospects, even ones that are unrelated to the firm's current products or markets. The product–market matrix shown in Table 1.4 identifies a firm's primary diversification options.

A firm that is facing slower growth in its current markets may be able to accelerate growth through related diversification by selling its current products in new markets that are somewhat unfamiliar and, therefore, more risky. Such was the case when pharmaceutical giant Johnson & Johnson announced its ultimately unsuccessful takeover attempt of Guidant Corporation in late 2004. J&J was seeking an entry point for its medical devices business in the fast-growing market for implant devices, in which it did not then participate. A firm may attempt to achieve higher growth rates by developing or acquiring new products with which it is relatively unfamiliar and then selling them in familiar and less risky current markets.

Retailer J. C. Penney's $3.3 billion acquisition of the Eckerd Drugstore chain (a drug retailer) in 1997 or Johnson & Johnson's $16 billion acquisition of Pfizer's consumer healthcare products line in 2006 are two examples of related diversification. In each instance, the firm assumed additional risk, but less so than with unrelated diversification if it had developed new products for sale in new markets.

There is considerable evidence that investors do not benefit from unrelated diversification. Firms that operate in a number of largely unrelated industries, such as General Electric,

TABLE 1.4   The Product–Market Matrix

Markets Products	Current	New
Current	Lower Growth/Lower Risk	Higher Growth/Higher Risk (Related Diversification)
New	Higher Growth/Higher Risk (Related Diversification)	Highest Growth/Highest Risk (Unrelated Diversification)

are called *conglomerates*. The share prices of conglomerates often trade at a discount—as much as 10 to 15%[2]—compared to shares of focused firms or to their value were they broken up. This discount is called the *conglomerate discount* or *diversification discount*. Investors often perceive companies that are diversified in unrelated areas as riskier because management has difficulty understanding these companies and often fails to provide full funding for the most attractive investment opportunities.[3] Moreover, outside investors may have a difficult time understanding how to value the various parts of highly diversified businesses.[4] Researchers differ on whether the conglomerate discount is overstated.[5]

Other researchers find evidence that the most successful mergers in developed countries are those that focus on deals that promote the acquirer's core business, largely reflecting their familiarity with such businesses and their ability to optimize investment decisions.[6] Related acquisitions may even be more likely to generate higher financial returns than unrelated acquisitions.[7] This should not be surprising, since related firms are more likely to be able to realize cost savings due to overlapping functions and product lines than are unrelated firms.

In contrast to the conglomerate discount often found in developed economies, diversified firms in developing countries, where access to capital markets is limited, may sell at a premium to more focused firms.[8] Under these circumstances, corporate diversification may enable more efficient investment, since diversified firms may use cash generated by mature subsidiaries to fund those with higher growth potential.

Strategic Realignment

The strategic realignment theory suggests that firms use M&As to make rapid adjustments to changes in their external environments. Although change can come from many different sources, this theory considers primarily changes in the regulatory environment and technological innovation—two factors that, over the past 30 years, have been major forces in creating new opportunities for growth or threatening to make obsolete firms' primary lines of business.

[2] Berger and Ofek, 1995; Lins and Servaes, 1999

[3] Morck, Shleifer, and Vishny, 1990

[4] Best and Hodges, 2004

[5] Some researchers argue that diversifying firms are often poor performers before they become conglomerates (Campa and Simi, 2002; Hyland, 2001), while others conclude that the conglomerate discount is a result of how the sample studied is constructed (Villalonga, 2004; Graham, Lemmon, and Wolf, 2002). Several suggest that the conglomerate discount is reduced when firms either divest or spin off businesses in an effort to achieve greater focus on the core business portfolio (Shin and Stulz, 1998; Dittmar and Shivdasani, 2003.

[6] Harding and Rovit, 2004; Megginson et al., 2003

[7] Singh and Montgomery, 2008

[8] Fauver, Houston, and Narrango, 2003

Regulatory Change

Those industries that have been subject to significant deregulation in recent years—financial services, healthcare, utilities, media, telecommunications, defense—have been at the center of M&A activity,[9] because deregulation breaks down artificial barriers and stimulates competition. During the first half of the 1990s, for instance, the U.S. Department of Defense actively encouraged consolidation of the nation's major defense contractors to improve their overall operating efficiency. In some states, utilities that are required to sell power to competitors that can resell the power in the utility's own marketplace often respond with M&As to achieve greater operating efficiency.

Since the Telecommunications Reform Act of 1996, local and long-distance companies have been encouraged to compete in one another's markets, and cable companies are offering both Internet access and local telephone service. Following the Financial Services Modernization Act of 1999, commercial banks were allowed to move beyond their historical role of accepting deposits and granting loans by merging with securities firms and insurance companies. However, the Dodd-Frank Wall Street Reform and Consumer Protection Act of 2010 (see Chapter 2) reversed this trend, particularly for large commercial banks.

Technological Change

Technological advances create new products and industries. The development of the airplane created the passenger airline, avionics, and satellite industries. The emergence of satellite delivery of cable networks to regional and local stations ignited explosive growth in the cable industry. Today, with the expansion of broadband technology, we are witnessing the convergence of voice, data, and video technologies on the Internet The emergence of digital camera technology reduced dramatically the demand for analog cameras and film and sent household names such as Kodak and Polaroid scrambling to adapt.

Hubris and the "Winner's Curse"

Acquirers may tend to overpay for targets, having been overoptimistic when evaluating synergies. Competition among bidders also is likely to result in the winner overpaying because of hubris, even if significant synergies are present.[10] Studies show that CEOs who were previously successful in making acquisitions and those who appear to be overconfident, as measured by their overinvestment in their own firm's stocks, have a tendency to make value-destroying acquisitions.[11]

In an auction environment with bidders, the range of bids for a target company is likely to be quite wide because senior managers tend to be very competitive and sometimes self-important. Their desire not to lose can drive the purchase price of an acquisition well in excess of its actual economic value (i.e., cash-generating capability). The winner pays more than the company is worth and may ultimately feel remorse at having done so—hence what has come to be called the "winner's curse."

[9] Mitchell and Mulherin, 1996; Mulherin and Boone, 2000

[10] Roll, 1986

[11] Billet and Qian, 2008; Malmendier and Tate, 2008

Buying Undervalued Assets: The q-Ratio

The q-ratio is the ratio of the market value of the acquiring firm's stock to the replacement cost of its assets. Firms interested in expansion can choose to invest in new plant and equipment or obtain the assets by acquiring a company with a market value less than what it would cost to replace the assets (i.e., a market-to-book or q-ratio that is less than 1). This theory is very useful in explaining M&A activity when stock prices drop well below the book value (or historical cost) of many firms. When gasoline refiner Valero Energy Corp. acquired Premcor Inc. in 2005, the $8 billion transaction created the largest refiner in North America. It would have cost an estimated 40% more for Valero to build a new refinery with equivalent capacity.[12]

Mismanagement

Agency problems arise when there is a difference between the interests of current managers and the firm's shareholders. This happens when management owns a small fraction of the outstanding shares of the firm. These managers, who serve as agents of the shareholder, may be more inclined to focus on their own job security and lavish lifestyles than on maximizing shareholder value. When the shares of a company are widely held, the cost of such mismanagement is spread across a large number of shareholders, each of whom bears only a small portion. This allows for toleration of the mismanagement over long periods. Mergers often take place to correct situations where there is a separation between what managers and owners (shareholders) want. Low stock prices put pressure on managers to take actions to raise the share price or become the target of acquirers, who perceive the stock to be undervalued[13] and who are usually intent on removing the underperforming management of the target firm. Agency problems also contribute to management-initiated buyouts, particularly when managers and shareholders disagree over how excess cash flow should be used.[14]

Managerialism

The managerialism motive for acquisitions asserts that managers make acquisitions for selfish reasons, be it to add to their prestige, to build their spheres of influence, to augment their compensation, or for self-preservation.[15] But ascribing acquisition to the managerialism motive ignores the pressure that managers of larger firms are under to sustain earnings growth to support their firms' share price. As the market value of a firm increases, senior managers are compelled to make ever larger investment bets to sustain increases in shareholder value. Small acquisitions simply do not have sufficient impact on earnings growth to justify the effort required to complete them. Consequently, even though the resulting acquisitions may destroy value, the motive for making them may be more to support shareholder interests than to preserve management autonomy.

[12] Zellner, May 9, 2005

[13] Fama and Jensen, 1983

[14] Mehran and Peristiani, 2006

[15] Masulis, Wang, and Xie, 2007

Tax Considerations

Tax benefits, such as loss carryforwards and investment tax credits, can be used to offset the taxable income of firms that combine through M&As. Acquirers of firms with accumulated losses may use them to offset future profits generated by the combined firms. Unused tax credits held by target firms may also be used to lower future tax liabilities. Additional tax shelters (i.e., tax savings) are created due to the purchase method of accounting, which requires the book value of the acquired assets to be revalued to their current market value for purposes of recording the acquisition on the books of the acquiring firm. The resulting depreciation of these generally higher asset values reduces the amount of future taxable income generated by the combined companies, as depreciation expense is deducted from revenue in calculating a firm's taxable income.

The taxable nature of the transaction often plays a more important role in determining whether a merger takes place than any tax benefits that accrue to the acquiring company. The seller may view the tax-free status of the transaction as a prerequisite for the deal to take place. A properly structured transaction can allow the target shareholders to defer any capital gain resulting from the transaction until they actually sell the acquirer's stock received in exchange for their shares. If the transaction is not tax-free, the seller typically will want a higher purchase price to compensate for the tax liability resulting from the transaction.[16] These issues are discussed in more detail in Chapter 12.

Market Power

The market power theory suggests that firms merge to improve their monopoly power to set product prices at levels not sustainable in a more competitive market There is very little empirical support for this theory. Many recent studies conclude that increased merger activity is much more likely to contribute to improved operating efficiency of the combined firms than to increased market power (see the section of this chapter entitled "Do M&As Pay off for Society?").

Misvaluation

In the absence of full information, investors may periodically over- or undervalue a firm. Acquirers may profit by buying undervalued targets for cash at a price below their actual value or by using equity (even if the target is overvalued), as long as the target is less overvalued than the bidding firm's stock.[17] Overvalued shares enable the acquirer to purchase a target firm in a share-for-share exchange by issuing fewer shares, which reduces the probability of diluting the ownership position of current acquirer shareholders in the newly combined company. That's important because dilution represents a significant cost to the current shareholders of the acquiring firm; their shares represent claims on the firm's earnings, cash flows, assets, and liabilities.

---

[16] Ayers, Lefanowicz, and Robinson, 2003

[17] Dong et al., 2006; Ang and Cheng, 2006

Whenever a firm increases its shares outstanding, it reduces the proportionate ownership position of current shareholders. Overvalued shares tend to reduce this cost. Consider an acquirer who offers the target firm shareholders $10 for each share they own. If the acquirer's current share price is $10, the acquirer would have to issue one new share for each target share outstanding. If the acquirer's share price is valued at $20, only 0.5 new shares would have to be issued, and so forth. Consequently, the initial dilution of the current acquirer's shareholders' ownership position in the new firm is less the higher the acquirer's share price compared to the price offered for each share of target stock outstanding. There is evidence that the effects of misevaluation tend to be short-lived, since the initial overvaluation of an acquirer's share price is reversed in one to three years as investors' enthusiasm about potential synergies wanes.[18]

MERGER AND ACQUISITION WAVES

While there is little question that the future of M&A activity will continue to evolve, reflecting new global competition and the changing regulatory climate, it will continue to be possible to draw parallels with the past. These insights should help us to understand when to make acquisitions and how to structure and finance future M&As.

Why M&A Waves Occur

M&A activity in the United States has tended to cluster in six multiyear waves since the late 1890s. There are two competing explanations for this phenomenon. One argues that merger waves occur when firms in industries react to "shocks" in their operating environments,[19] such as from deregulation; the emergence of new technologies, distribution channels, or substitute products; or a sustained rise in commodity prices. The size and length of the M&A wave depends to a large part on how many industries are affected by these shocks, as well as the extent of the impact. Some shocks, such as the emergence of the Internet, are pervasive in their impact; others are more specific, such as deregulation of utilities or rapidly escalating commodity prices. In response to shocks, firms within the industry often acquire either all or parts of other firms.

The second argument is based on the misvaluation idea discussed previously and suggests that managers use overvalued stock to buy the assets of lower-valued firms. For M&As to cluster in waves, goes the argument, valuations of many firms (measured by their price-to-earnings or market-to-book ratios compared to other firms) must increase at the same time. Managers whose stocks are believed to be overvalued move concurrently to acquire companies whose stock prices are lesser valued[20] and, reflecting the influence of over-valuation, the method of payment would normally be stock.[21]

---

[18] Petmezas, 2009

[19] Martynova and Renneboog, 2008a; Brealey and Myers, 2003; Mitchell and Mulherin, 1996

[20] Rhodes-Kropf and Viswanathan, 2004; Shleifer and Vishny, 2003

[21] Numerous studies confirm that long-term fluctuations in market valuations and the number of takeovers are positively correlated. See Dong et al., 2006, and Ang and Cheng, 2006. However, whether high valuations contribute to greater takeover activity or whether increased M&A activity boosts market valuations is less clear.

Evidence suggests that the "shock" argument is a stronger one, especially if it is modified to include the effects of the availability of capital in causing and sustaining merger waves. Shocks alone, without sufficient liquidity to finance the transactions, will not initiate a wave of merger activity. Moreover, readily available, low-cost capital may cause a surge in M&A activity even if industry shocks are absent,[22] and this was particularly important in the most recent M&A boom.

The First Wave (1897–1904): Horizontal Consolidation

M&A activity was spurred by a drive for efficiency, lax enforcement of the Sherman Anti-Trust Act, westward migration, and technological change. Mergers during this period were largely horizontal and resulted in increased concentration in primary metals, transportation, and mining. In 1901, J.P. Morgan created America's first billion-dollar corporation, U.S. Steel, which was formed by the combination of 785 separate companies, the largest of which was Carnegie Steel. Other giants formed during this era included Standard Oil, Eastman Kodak, American Tobacco, and General Electric. Fraudulent financing and the 1904 stock market crash ended the boom.

The Second Wave (1916–1929): Increasing Concentration

Activity during this period was a result of the entry of the United States into World War I and the postwar economic boom. Mergers also tended to be horizontal and further increased industry concentration; for example, Samuel Insull built an empire of utilities with operations in 39 states. The stock market crash of 1929, along with passage of the Clayton Act that further defined monopolistic practices, brought this era to a close.

The Third Wave (1965–1969): The Conglomerate Era

A rising stock market and the longest period of uninterrupted growth in U.S. history up to that time resulted in record price-to-earnings (P/E) ratios. Companies given high P/E ratios by investors learned how to grow earnings per share (EPS) through acquisition rather than through reinvestment. Companies with high P/E ratios would often acquire firms with lower P/E ratios and increase the EPS of the combined companies, which in turn boosted the share price of the combined companies—as long as the P/E applied to the stock price of the combined companies did not fall below the P/E of the acquiring company before the transaction. To maintain this pyramiding effect, though, target companies had to have earnings growth rates that were sufficiently attractive to convince investors to apply the higher multiple of the acquiring company to the combined companies. In time, the number of high-growth, relatively low P/E companies declined as conglomerates bid their P/Es up. The higher prices paid for the targets, coupled with the increasing leverage of the conglomerates, caused the "pyramids" to collapse.

The Fourth Wave (1981–1989): The Retrenchment Era

The 1980s, a decade that saw the rise of the corporate raider, were characterized by the breakup of many major conglomerates and a proliferation of the hostile takeover and the leveraged buyout (LBO) as raider's primary acquisition strategies. A leveraged buyout or highly leveraged transaction involves the purchase of a company financed primarily by debt. While LBOs commonly involve privately owned firms, the term often is applied to a firm that

---

[22] Harford, 2005

buys back its stock using primarily borrowed funds to convert from a publicly owned to a privately owned company (see Chapter 13).

LBOs and takeovers of U.S. companies by foreign acquirers became more common. Conglomerates began to divest unrelated acquisitions made in the 1960s and early 1970s; in fact, of the acquisitions made outside of the acquirer's main line of business between 1970 and 1982, some 60% had been sold by 1989.[23]

For the first time, takeovers of U.S. companies by foreign firms exceeded in number and dollars the acquisitions by U.S. firms of companies in Europe, Canada, and the Pacific Rim (excluding Japan). Foreign purchasers were motivated by the size of the market, limited restrictions on takeovers, the sophistication of U.S. technology, and the weakness of the dollar against major foreign currencies. Foreign companies also tended to pay substantial premiums for U.S. companies, since the strength of their currencies lowered the effective cost of acquisitions. Moreover, favorable accounting practices allowed foreign buyers to write off goodwill in the year in which it occurred, unlike U.S. firms that at that time had to charge goodwill expense against earnings for many years.[24]

Toward the end of the 1980s, the level of merger activity tapered off in line with a slowing economy and widely publicized LBO bankruptcies. Moreover, the junk bond market dried up as a major source of financing with the demise of Drexel Burnham, the leading underwriter and "market-maker" for high-yield securities.

The Fifth Wave (1992–2000): The Age of the Strategic Mega-Merger

While M&A activity did diminish during the 1990 recession, the number of transactions and the dollar volume rebounded sharply beginning in 1992. The longest economic expansion and stock market boom in U.S. history, uninterrupted by recession, was powered by a combination of the information technology revolution, continued deregulation, reductions in trade barriers, and the global trend toward privatization. Both the dollar volume and the number of transactions continued to set records through the end of the 1990s before contracting sharply when the Internet bubble burst, a recession hit the United States in 2001, and global growth weakened.

The Sixth Wave (2003–2007): The Rebirth of Leverage

U.S. financial markets, especially from 2005 through 2007, were characterized by an explosion of highly leveraged buyouts and private equity investments (i.e., takeovers financed by limited partnerships) and the proliferation of complex securities collateralized by pools of debt and loan obligations of varying levels of risk. Much of the financing of these transactions, as well as mortgage-backed security issues, has taken the form of syndicated debt (i.e., debt purchased by underwriters for resale to the investing public).

---

[23] Wasserstein, 1998

[24] Goodwill represents the excess of the purchase price paid by the acquirer for the net assets acquired (i.e., assets purchased revalued to their current market values less acquired liabilities). Prior to December 15, 2001, the value of goodwill on the acquirer's balance sheet had to be written off (i.e., amortized) over as long as 40 years. This is no longer required, but it must be checked for impairment in the wake of any significant event that may reduce the value of the goodwill to less than what is shown on the acquirer's balance sheet. Whenever this occurs, the value of the goodwill must be revised downward to reflect these events, with the amount of the downward revision charged against the firm's current earnings.

The syndication process disperses such debt among many different investors. The issuers of the debt discharge much of the responsibility for the loans to others. Under such circumstances, lenders have an incentive to increase the volume of lending to generate fee income by reducing their underwriting standards to accept riskier loans.[25] Once sold to others, loan originators are likely to reduce monitoring of such loans.[26] These practices, coupled with exceedingly low interest rates made possible by a world awash in liquidity and highly accommodative monetary policies, contributed to excessive lending and encouraged acquirers to overpay significantly for target firms.

Declining home prices and a few highly publicized defaults in 2007 triggered concerns among lenders that the market value of their assets was actually well below the value listed on their balance sheets. Subsequent write-downs in the value of these assets reduced bank capital. Regulators require banks to maintain certain capital-to-asset ratios. To restore these ratios to a level comfortably above regulatory requirements, lenders restricted new lending. Bank lending continued to lag, despite efforts by the Federal Reserve to increase sharply the amount of liquidity in the banking system. Thus, the repackaging and sale of debt in many different forms contributed to instability in the financial markets in 2008. Limited credit availability not only affected the ability of private equity and hedge funds to finance new or refinance existing transactions, but also limited the ability of other businesses to fund their normal operations. Compounded by rapidly escalating oil prices in 2007 and during the first half of 2008, these conditions contributed to the global economic slowdown in 2008 and 2009 and the concomitant slump in M&A transactions, particularly those that were highly leveraged.

Table 1.5 provides the historical data underlying the trends in both global and U.S. merger and acquisition activity in recent years. M&A activity worldwide reached a historical peak in 2000 in terms of both the number and the dollar value of transactions, following surging economic growth and the Internet bubble of the late 1990s. During 2000, the dollar value of transactions in the United States accounted for nearly one-half of the global total. The ensuing 2001 recession, escalating concerns about terrorism, and the subsequent decline in the world's stock markets caused both the number and the dollar value of global and U.S. transactions to decline through 2002.

By then, though, conditions were in place for a resurgence in M&A activity, and by 2007 the dollar value and number of announced global M&A transactions outside of the United States reached new highs. However, global merger activity dropped precipitously in 2008 and again in 2009, reflecting a lack of credit, plunging equity markets, and the worldwide financial crisis.[27] The drop-off in 2009 would have been greater had it not been for government-backed acquisitions accounting for 8.5% of the value of global deal volume. Global M&A activity in 2010 showed an improvement from 2009 to about $2.7 trillion, reflecting low interest rates, increasing corporate cash balances, rising equity markets, and continued growth in emerging markets.

---

[25] Brunnermeier, 2009.

[26] Under the Dodd-Frank legislation of 2010, mortgage loan originators are required to retain ownership in at least 5% of loans that are securitized and sold by the originator.

[27] According to Dealogic, 1,307 previously announced deals valued at $911 billion were cancelled in 2008, underscoring the malaise affecting the global M&A market. Deals sponsored by private equity firms and hedge funds hit a five-year low worldwide, falling 71% in 2008 from the prior year to $88 billion.

TABLE 1.5   Trends in Announced Mergers and Acquisitions[a]

Year	Global M&As		U.S. M&As		U.S. Share of Global M&As	
	Number	$ Value (billions)	Number	$ Value (billions)	Number (%)	$ Value (%)
1995	22,027	980	3,510	356	15.9	36.3
1996	23,166	1,146	5,848	495	25.2	43.2
1997	22.642	1,676	7,800	657	34.5	39.2
1998	27,256	2,581	7,809	1,192	28.7	46.2
1999	31,701	3,439	9,278	1,426	29.3	41.5
2000	37.204	3,497	9,566	1,706	25.7	48.8
2001	28,828	1,745	8,290	759	28.8	43.5
2002	26.270	1,207	7,303	441	27.7	36.5
2003	27,753	1,333	8,131	559	29.3	41.9
2004	31,467	1,979	9,783	812	31.1	41.0
2005	33,574	2,775	10,644	1,045	31.7	37.7
2006	38,602	3,794	10,977	1,563	28.4	41.2
2007	43,817	4,169	11,296	1,571	25.8	37.7
2008	39,597	2,936	8,614	851	21.8	29.0
2009	32,081	2,144	6,940	697	21.6	32.5
2010	35,228	2,705	8,126	852	23.1	31.5

[a] *All valuations include the value of debt assumed by the acquirer.*
Source: *Compiled from information available from Thompson Reuters, Dealogic, and Bloomberg.*

Similarities and Differences among Merger Waves

While patterns of takeover activity and their profitability vary significantly across M&A waves, there are common elements. Mergers have tended to occur during periods of sustained high rates of economic growth, low or declining interest rates, and a rising stock market. Historically, each merger wave has differed in terms of a specific development, such as the emergence of a new technology; industry focus, such as rail, oil, or financial services; degree of regulation; and type of transaction, such as horizontal, vertical, conglomerate, strategic, or financial (discussed in more detail later in this chapter). Table 1.6 compares the six historical U.S. merger waves. Merger waves are also present in cross-border or international M&As. Merger waves in Europe seem to follow those in the United States, with a short lag.[28]

[28] Brakman, Garretsen, and Van Marrewijk, 2005

TABLE 1.6   U.S. Historical Merger Waves

Time Period	Driving Force(s)	Type of M&A Activity	Key Impact	Key Transactions	Factors Contributing to End of Wave
1897–1904	Drive for efficiency Lax antitrust law enforcement Westward migration Technological change	Horizontal consolidation	Increasing concentration: Primary metals Transportation Mining	U.S. Steel Standard Oil Eastman Kodak American Tobacco General Electric	Fraudulent financing 1904 stock market crash
1916–1929	Entry into World War I Post–World War I boom	Largely horizontal consolidation	Increased industry concentration	Samuel Insull builds utility empire in 39 states called Middle West Utilities	1929 stock market crash Clayton Antitrust Act
1965–1969	Rising stock market Sustained economic boom	Growth of conglomerates	Financial engineering leading to conglomeration	LTV ITT Litton Industries Gulf and Western Northwest Industries	Escalating purchase prices Excessive leverage
1981–1989	Rising stock market Economic boom Underperformance of conglomerates Relative weakness of U.S. dollar Favorable regulatory environment Favorable foreign accounting practices	Retrenchment era Rise of hostile takeovers Corporate raiders Proliferation of financial buyers using highly leveraged transactions Increased takeover of U.S. firms by foreign buyers	Breakup of conglomerates Increased use of junk (unrated) bonds to finance transactions	RJR Nabisco MBO Beecham Group (U.K.) buys SmithKline Campeau of Canada buys Federated Stores	Widely publicized bankruptcies 1990 recession
1992–2000 *(1999)*	Economic recovery Booming stock market Internet revolution Lower trade barriers Globalization	Age of strategic mega-merger	Record levels of transactions in terms of numbers and prices	AOL acquires Time Warner Vodafone AirTouch acquires Mannesmann Exxon buys Mobil	Slumping economy and stock market in 2001–2002 Escalating terrorism

TABLE 1.6 Cont'd

Time Period	Driving Force(s)	Type of M&A Activity	Key Impact	Key Transactions	Factors Contributing to End of Wave
2003–2007 2008	Low interest rates Rising stock market Booming global economy Globalization High commodity prices	Age of cross-border transactions, horizontal megamergers, and growing influence of private equity investors	Increasing synchronicity among world's economies	Mittal acquires Arcelor P&G buys Gillette Verizon acquires MCI Blackstone buys Equity Office Properties	Loss of confidence in global capital markets Economic slowdown in industrial nations

WHY IT IS IMPORTANT TO ANTICIPATE MERGER WAVES

Not surprisingly, evidence shows that the stock market rewards firms that see and act on promising opportunities early and punishes those that merely imitate. Those pursuing these opportunities early on pay lower prices for target firms than do the followers. One review of 3,194 public companies that acquired other firms between 1984 and 2004 found that the deals completed during the first 15% of a consolidation wave have share prices that outperform significantly the overall stock market, as well as those deals that follow much later in the cycle, when the purchase price of target firms tends to escalate.[29] Consequently, those that are late in pursuing acquisition targets are more likely to overpay.

ALTERNATIVE FORMS OF CORPORATE RESTRUCTURING

Corporate restructuring activities are often broken into two specific categories. Operational restructuring may entail changes in the composition of a firm's asset structure by acquiring new businesses or by the outright or partial sale or spin-off of companies or product lines. Operational restructuring could also include downsizing by closing unprofitable or nonstrategic facilities. Financial restructuring describes actions by a firm to change its total debt and equity structure, such as share repurchases or adding debt either to lower the

---

[29] McNamara et al. (2008) define a merger consolidation wave as a cycle in which the peak year had a greater than 100% increase from the first year of the wave, followed by a decline in acquisition activity of greater than 50% from the peak year. For some of the 12 industries studied, consolidation waves were as long as six years. There is also evidence that acquisitions early in the M&A cycle produce financial returns over 50% and, on average, create 14.5% more value for acquirer shareholders. See Gell et al., 2008.

corporation's overall cost of capital or as part of an antitakeover defense. The focus in this book is on business combinations and breakups rather than on operational downsizing and financial restructuring.

When firms combine, the resulting transaction can be known by many names: mergers, consolidations, acquisitions, or takeovers. Whether a deal is called a merger or an acquisition often depends on how management wishes to present the transaction to its own employees, its customers, and the investing public. Regardless of how such transactions are characterized, mergers are viewed mainly as friendly in that both the acquiring and target firms want the transaction to happen, while acquisitions may be friendly or hostile. These considerations are discussed in more detail following.

Mergers and Consolidations

Mergers can be described from a legal perspective and from an economic perspective. This distinction is relevant to discussions concerning deal structuring, regulatory issues, and strategic planning.

A Legal Perspective

Legal structures may take many forms, depending on the nature of a transaction. A merger is a combination of two or more firms, often comparable in size, in which all but one ceases to exist legally; the combined organization continues under the original name of the surviving firm. In a typical merger, shareholders of the target firm—after voting to approve the merger—exchange their shares for those of the acquiring firm. Those not voting in favor (minority shareholders) are required to accept the merger and exchange their shares for acquirer shares or cash. When target shareholders accept cash for their stock, they will no longer have any continuing interest in the combined firms. Such mergers often are referred to as cash-out mergers.

A *statutory merger* is one in which the acquiring or surviving company automatically assumes the assets and liabilities of the target in accordance with the statutes of the state in which the combined companies will be incorporated. A *subsidiary merger* involves the target becoming a subsidiary of the parent. To the public, the target firm may be operated under its brand name, but it will be owned and controlled by the acquirer. Most states require a majority of the shareholders to approve a merger; some require two-thirds. Some states also allow shareholders to dissent from such transactions and to have a court appraise the value of their shares and to force the acquirer to pay a price determined by the court.

Although the terms *mergers* and *consolidations* often are used interchangeably, a *statutory consolidation*—which involves two or more companies joining to form a new company—is technically not a merger. All legal entities that are consolidated are dissolved during the formation of the new company, which usually has a new name, and shareholders in the firms being consolidated typically exchange their shares for shares in the new company. In a merger, either the acquirer or the target survives. The combination of Daimler-Benz and Chrysler to form DaimlerChrysler is an example of a consolidation. The new corporate entity created as a result of consolidation, or the surviving entity following a merger, usually assumes ownership of the assets and liabilities of the consolidated or merged organizations.

An Economic Perspective

Business combinations may also be defined depending on whether the merging firms are in the same or different industries and on their positions in the corporate value chain.[30] These definitions are particularly important for antitrust analysis.

A *horizontal merger* occurs between two firms within the same industry. Procter & Gamble and Gillette (2006) in household products, Oracle and PeopleSoft in business application software (2004), oil giants Exxon and Mobil (1999), SBC Communications and Ameritech (1998) in telecommunications, and NationsBank and BankAmerica (1998) in commercial banking are all examples. *Conglomerate mergers* are those in which the acquiring company purchases firms in largely unrelated industries, such as the mid-1980s acquisition by U.S. Steel of Marathon Oil to form USX.

Vertical mergers involve firms that participate at different stages of the production or value chain (Figure 1.1). A simple value chain in the basic steel industry may distinguish between raw materials, such as coal or iron ore; steel making, such as "hot metal" and rolling operations; and metals distribution. Similarly, a value chain in the oil and gas industry would separate exploration activities from production, refining, and marketing. An Internet value chain might distinguish between infrastructure providers such as Cisco, content providers such as Dow Jones, and portals such as Google.

In a vertical merger, companies that do not own operations in each major segment of the value chain "backward integrate" by acquiring a supplier or "forward integrate" by acquiring a distributor. When paper manufacturer Boise Cascade acquired Office Max, an office products distributor, in 2003, the $1.1 billion transaction represented forward integration. America Online's purchase of media and content provider Time Warner in 2000 is an example of backward integration.[31] More recently, PepsiCo backward integrated through a $7.8 billion purchase of its two largest bottlers in 2010 in order to realize $400 million in annual cost efficiencies.

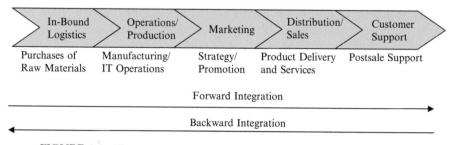

FIGURE 1.1   The corporate value chain. Note: *IT refers to information technology.*

---

[30] Porter, 1985

[31] According to Gugler et al. (2003), horizontal, conglomerate, and vertical mergers accounted for 42%, 54%, and 4% of the 45,000 transactions analyzed between 1981 and 1998, respectively.

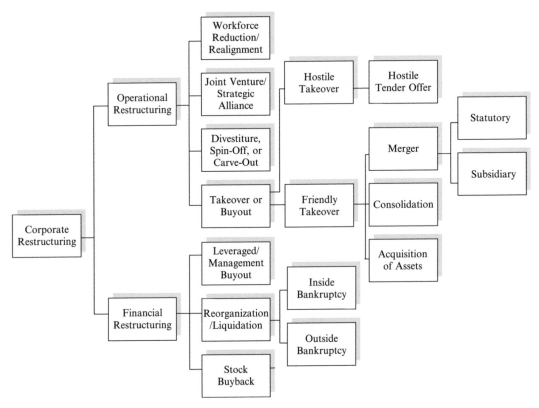

FIGURE 1.2   The corporate restructuring process.

Acquisitions, Divestitures, Spin-Offs, Carve-Outs, and Buyouts

Generally speaking, an acquisition occurs when one company takes a controlling owner-ship interest in another firm, a legal subsidiary of another firm, or selected assets of another firm, such as a manufacturing facility. An acquisition may involve the purchase of another firm's assets or stock, with the acquired firm continuing to exist as a legally owned subsidiary. In contrast, a divestiture is the sale of all or substantially all of a company or product line to another party for cash or securities. A spin-off is a transaction in which a parent creates a new legal subsidiary and distributes shares in the subsidiary to its current shareholders as a stock dividend. An equity carve-out is a transaction in which the parent firm issues a portion of its stock or that of a subsidiary to the public (see Chapter 15). Figure 1.2 provides a summary of the various forms of corporate restructuring.

Alternative Takeover strategies

FRIENDLY VERSUS HOSTILE TAKEOVERS

The term *takeover* is widely used when one firm assumes control of another. In a friendly takeover of control, the target's board and management are receptive to the idea and recom-mend shareholder approval. To gain control, the acquiring company usually must offer a premium to the current stock price. The excess of the offer price over the target's premerger share price is called a purchase premium, or acquisition premium,[32] and reflects the perceived value of obtaining a controlling interest (i.e., the ability to direct the activities of the firm) in the target, the value of expected synergies (e.g., cost savings) resulting from combining the two firms, and any overpayment for the target firm. Overpayment is the amount an acquirer pays for a target firm in excess of the present value of future cash flows, including synergy. The size of the premium can fluctuate widely from one year to the next. During the 30-year period ending in 2010, U.S. purchase price premiums averaged 43%, reaching a high of 63% in 2003 and a low of 31% in 2007.[33]

Analysts often attempt to identify the amount of premium paid for a controlling interest (i.e., *control premium*) and the amount of incremental value created that the acquirer is willing to share with the target's shareholders. An example of a pure control premium is a conglomerate willing to pay a price significantly above the prevailing market price for a target firm to gain a controlling interest, even though potential operating synergies are limited. In this instance, the acquirer often believes it will recover the value of the control premium by making better management decisions for the target firm. It is important to emphasize that what is often called a control premium in the popular press is actually a purchase or acquisition premium that includes both a premium for synergy and a premium for control.

A formal proposal to buy shares in another firm, usually for cash or securities, or both, is called a *tender offer*. While tender offers are used in a number of circumstances, they most often result from friendly negotiations (i.e., negotiated tender offers) between the boards of the acquirer and the target firm. Those that are unwanted by the target's board are referred to as *hostile tender offers*. *Self-tender offers* are used when a firm seeks to repurchase its stock.

An *unfriendly takeover*, or *hostile takeover*, occurs when the initial approach was unsolicited, the target was not seeking a merger, the approach was contested by the target's management, and control changed hands (i.e., usually requiring the purchase of more than half of the target's voting common stock). The acquirer may attempt to circumvent management by offering to buy shares directly from the target's shareholders (i.e., a hostile tender offer) and by buying shares in a public stock exchange (i.e., an *open market purchase*).

Friendly takeovers are often consummated at a lower purchase price than hostile transactions. A hostile takeover attempt may attract new bidders who might not otherwise have been interested in the target—called putting the target *in play*. In the ensuing auction, the final purchase price may be bid up to a point well above the initial offer price. Acquirers prefer friendly takeovers because the postmerger integration process is usually more expeditious when both parties are cooperating fully. For these reasons, most transactions tend to be friendly.

---

[32] U.S. merger premiums averaged about 38% between 1973 and 1998 (Andrade, Mitchell, and Stafford, 2001). Rossi and Volpin (2004) document an average premium of 44% during the 1990s for U.S. mergers. The authors also find premiums in 49 countries ranging from 10% for Brazil and Switzerland to 120% for Israel and Indonesia. The wide range of estimates may reflect the value attached to the special privileges associated with control in various countries.

[33] *Mergerstat Review*, 2010

THE ROLE OF HOLDING COMPANIES IN MERGERS AND ACQUISITIONS

A holding company is a legal entity having a controlling interest in one or more companies. The primary function of a holding company is to own stock in other corporations. In general, the parent firm has no wholly owned operating units. The segments owned by the holding company are separate legal entities, which in practice are controlled by the holding company. The key advantage of the holding company structure is the leverage achieved by gaining effective control of other companies' assets at a lower overall cost than if the firm were to acquire 100% of the target's outstanding shares.

Effective control sometimes can be achieved by owning as little as 30% of the voting stock of another company when the firm's bylaws require approval of major decisions by a majority of votes cast rather than a majority of the voting shares outstanding. This is particularly true when the target company's ownership is highly fragmented, with few shareholders owning large blocks of stock. Effective control generally is achieved by acquiring less than 100% but usually more than 50% of another firm's equity. One firm is said to have effective control when control has been achieved by buying voting stock; it is not likely to be temporary, there are no legal restrictions on control (such as from a bankruptcy court), and there are no powerful minority shareholders.

The holding company structure can create significant management challenges. Because it can gain effective control with less than 100% ownership, the holding company is left with minority shareholders, who may not always agree with the strategic direction of the company. Consequently, implementing holding company strategies may become very contentious. Furthermore, in highly diversified holding companies, managers also may have difficulty making optimal investment decisions because of their limited understanding of the different competitive dynamics of each business. The holding company structure also can create significant tax problems for its shareholders. Subsidiaries of holding companies pay taxes on their operating profits. The holding company then pays taxes on dividends it receives from its subsidiaries. Finally, holding company shareholders pay taxes on dividends they receive from the holding company. This is equivalent to triple taxation of the subsidiary's operating earnings.

(ESOPS)

THE ROLE OF EMPLOYEE STOCK OWNERSHIP PLANS IN M&AS

An *employee stock ownership plan* (ESOP) is a trust fund that invests in the securities of the firm sponsoring the plan. Designed to attract and retain employees, ESOPs are defined contribution employee benefit pension plans that invest at least 50% of the plan's assets in the common shares of the firm sponsoring them. The plans may receive the employer's stock or cash, which is used to buy the sponsoring employer's stock. The sponsoring corporation can make tax-deductible contributions of cash, stock, or other assets to the trust. The plan's trustee holds title to the assets for the benefit of the employees. The trustee is charged with investing the trust assets productively, and the trustee often can sell, mortgage, or lease the assets.

Stock acquired by the ESOP is allocated to accounts for individual employees based on some formula and vested over time. ESOP participants must be allowed to vote their allocated shares at least on major issues, such as selling the company. However, there is no requirement that they be allowed to vote on other issues such as choosing the board of directors. Cash contributions made by the sponsoring firm to pay both interest and principal payments on bank loans to ESOPs are tax deductible by the firm. Dividends paid on stock contributed to ESOPs also are deductible if they are used to repay ESOP debt. The sponsoring firm could use tax credits equal to 0.5% of payroll if contributions in that amount were made to the ESOP. Finally, lenders must pay taxes on only one-half of the interest received on loans made to ESOPs owning more than 50% of the sponsoring firm's stock.

ESOPs may be used to restructure firms. If a subsidiary cannot be sold at what the parent firm believes to be a reasonable price, and liquidating the subsidiary would be disruptive to customers, the parent may divest the subsidiary to employees through a shell corporation. A *shell corporation* is one that is incorporated but has no significant assets. The shell sets up the ESOP, which borrows the money to buy the subsidiary; the parent guarantees the loan. The shell operates the subsidiary, whereas the ESOP holds the stock. As income is generated from the subsidiary, tax-deductible contributions are made by the shell to the ESOP to service the debt. As the loan is repaid, the shares are allocated to employees, who eventually own the firm. ESOPs also may be used by employees in leveraged or management buyouts to purchase the shares of owners of privately held firms. This is particularly common when the owners have most of their net worth tied up in their firms. The mechanism is similar to owner-initiated sales to employees.

ESOPs also provide an effective antitakeover defense. A firm concerned about the potential for a hostile takeover creates an ESOP. The ESOP borrows with the aid of the sponsoring firm's guarantee and uses the loan proceeds to buy stock issued by the sponsoring firm. While the loan is outstanding, the ESOP's trustees retain voting rights on the stock. Once the loan is repaid, it is generally assumed that employees will tend to vote against bidders who they believe are jeopardizing their jobs.

BUSINESS ALLIANCES AS ALTERNATIVES TO MERGERS AND ACQUISITIONS

In addition to mergers and acquisitions, businesses also may combine through joint ventures (JVs), strategic alliances, minority investments, franchises, and licenses. The term *business alliance* is used to refer to all forms of business combinations other than mergers and acquisitions. See Chapter 14 for more details.

Joint ventures are cooperative business relationships formed by two or more separate parties to achieve common strategic objectives. While the JV is often an independent legal entity such as a corporation or partnership, it may take any organizational form deemed appropriate by the parties involved. Each JV partner continues to exist as a separate entity; JV corporations have their own management reporting to a board of directors. A *strategic alliance* generally falls short of creating a separate legal entity and may be an agreement to sell each firm's products to the other's customers or to codevelop a technology, product, or process. The terms of such an agreement may be legally binding or largely informal. *Minority investments* require little commitment of management time and may be highly liquid if the investment is in a publicly traded company. A company may choose to assist small or start-up companies in the development of products or technologies it finds useful, often receiving representation on the board in exchange for the investment. Such investments may also be opportunistic in that passive investors take a long-term position in a firm believed to have significant appreciation potential. For example, Warren Buffett's Berkshire Hathaway firm invested $5 billion in Goldman Sachs in 2008 by acquiring convertible preferred stock that pays a 10% dividend.

Licenses, which require no initial capital, provide a convenient way for companies to extend their brands to new products and new markets. They simply license their brand names to others. A company may also gain access to a proprietary technology through the licensing process. A *franchise* is a specialized form of license agreement that grants a privilege to a dealer from a manufacturer or franchise service organization to sell the franchiser's products or services in a given area. Under a franchise agreement, the franchiser may offer the franchisee consultation, promotional assistance, financing, and other benefits in exchange for a share of the franchise's revenue. Franchises represent a low-cost way for the franchiser to expand. The success of franchising, though, has been largely limited to industries such as fast-food services and retailing, in which a successful business model can be easily replicated.

The major attraction of these alternatives to outright acquisition is the opportunity for each partner to gain access to the other's skills, products, and markets at a lower overall cost in terms of management time and money. Major disadvantages include limited control, the need to share profits, and the potential loss of trade secrets and skills to competitors.

PARTICIPANTS IN THE MERGERS AND ACQUISITIONS PROCESS

The first category of key players includes the firms and individuals that provide specialized services during mergers and acquisitions. These include investment banks, lawyers, accountants, proxy solicitors, and public relations personnel.

Investment Banks

Amid the turmoil of the 2008 credit crisis, the traditional model of the mega-independent investment bank as a highly leveraged, largely unregulated, innovative securities underwriter and M&A advisor floundered. Lehman Brothers was liquidated, and Bear Stearns and Merrill Lynch were acquired by commercial banks JPMorgan Chase and Bank of America, respectively. In an effort to attract retail deposits and to borrow from the U.S. Federal Reserve System (the "Fed"), Goldman Sachs and Morgan Stanley converted to commercial bank holding companies.

Despite these developments, traditional investment banking activities will continue to be in demand. These include providing strategic and tactical advice and acquisition opportunities; screening potential buyers and sellers; making initial contact with a seller or buyer; and providing negotiation support, valuation, and deal-structuring guidance. Along with these traditional investment banking functions, the large "universal banks" (e.g., Bank of America/Merrill Lynch) will maintain substantial broker-dealer operations, serving wholesale and retail clients in brokerage and advisory capacities to assist with the complexity and often huge financing requirements of mega-transactions.

With fees averaging more than $300,000, investment bankers derive significant income from writing so-called *fairness opinion letters*—written and signed third-party assertions that certify the appropriateness of the price of a proposed deal involving a tender offer, merger, asset sale, or leveraged buyout. Such letters discuss the price and terms of the deal in the context of comparable transactions and are obtained by about 80% of target firms and more than one-third of acquirers. A typical fairness opinion provides a range of "fair" prices, with the presumption that the actual deal price should fall within that range. Although such opinions are intended to inform investors, they often are developed as legal protection for members of the boards of directors against possible shareholder challenges of their decisions.[34] Researchers have found that fairness opinion letters reduce significantly the risk of lawsuits associated with M&A transactions and reduce the size of the premium paid for targets if they result in acquirers performing more rigorous due diligence and deal negotiation.[35]

The largest investment banks are unlikely to consider any transaction valued at less than $100 million. In selecting an investment bank as a transaction advisor, the average magnitude of the abnormal returns on the announcement dates for those deals for which they serve as advisor is far more important than the investment bank's size or market share.[36] In other words, results count. Smaller, more focused boutique advisors may be able to generate substantially higher returns for their clients than the mega-investment banks because of proprietary industry knowledge and relationships.

The large investment banks are more likely to be able to assist in funding large transactions because of their current relationships with institutional lenders and broker distribution networks. After registering with the Securities and Exchange Commission (SEC), such securities may be offered to the investing public as an *initial public offering* (IPO), at a price agreed on by the issuer and the investment banking group. Security issues may avoid the public markets and be *privately placed* with institutional investors, such as pension funds and insurance companies.[37]

Investment banks charge an advisory fee that generally varies with the size of the transaction. Often contingent on completion of the deal, the fee may run about 1 to 2% of the value of the transaction; in some cases, the fee may exceed this amount if the advisors achieve certain goals. Fairness opinion fees often amount to about one-fourth of the total advisory fee paid on a transaction,[38] and typically they are paid regardless of whether the deal is consummated.

[34] Problems associated with fairness opinions include the potential conflicts of interest with investment banks that generate large fees. In many cases, the investment bank that brings the deal to a potential acquirer is the same one that writes the fairness opinion. Moreover, these letters are often out of date by the time shareholders vote on the deal, they do not address whether the firm could have gotten a better deal, and the overly broad range of values given in such letters reduces their relevance. Courts agree that because the opinions are written for boards of directors, investment bankers have no obligation to the shareholders (Henry, 2003).

[35] Kisgen et al., 2009

[36] Bao and Edmans, 2008

[37] Unlike public offerings, private placements do not have to be registered with the SEC if the securities are purchased for investment rather than for resale.

[38] Sweeney, 1999

Lawyers

Lawyers play a pervasive role in most M&A transactions.[39] They are intimately involved in structuring the deal, evaluating risk, negotiating many of the tax and financial terms and conditions (based on input received from accountants; see following), arranging financing, and coordinating the timing and sequence of events to complete the transaction. Specific tasks include drafting the agreement of purchase and sale and other transaction-related documentation, providing opinion of counsel letters to the lender, and defining due diligence activities.

For complicated transactions, legal teams can consist of more than a dozen attorneys, each bringing specialized expertise in a given aspect of the law such as M&As, corporate, tax, employee benefits, real estate, antitrust, securities, environmental, and intellectual property. In a hostile transaction, the team may grow to include litigation experts. In relatively small private transactions, lawyers play an active role in preacquisition planning, including estate planning for individuals or for family-owned firms, tax planning, and working with management and other company advisors to help better position a client for a sale.

Accountants

Accountants[40] provide advice on financial structuring, perform financial due diligence, and help create the most appropriate tax structure of a deal. A transaction can be structured in many ways, each structure having different tax implications for the parties involved. Because there is often a conflict in the tax advantages associated with the sales agreement from the buyer's and seller's perspectives, the accountant must understand both points of view and find a mechanism whereby both parties benefit. Income tax, capital gains, sales tax, and sometimes gift and estate taxes are all at play in negotiating a merger or acquisition.

In addition to tax considerations, accountants prepare financial statements and perform audits. Many agreements require that the books and records of the acquired entity be prepared in accordance with Generally Accepted Accounting Principles (GAAP), so the accountant must be intimately familiar with those principles to ensure that they have been applied appropriately. In performing due diligence, accountants also perform the role of auditors by reviewing the target's financial statements and operations through onsite visits and interviews with managers.

The roles of the lawyer and accountant may blur, depending on the size and complexity of the transaction. Sophisticated law firms with experience in mergers and acquisitions usually have the capacity to assist with the tax analysis. Furthermore, lawyers are often required to review financial statements for compliance with prevailing securities' laws.

---

[39] Leading M&A law firms in terms of their share of the dollar value of transactions include, at the time of this writing, Wachtell Lipton Rosen & Katz; Simpson Thatcher & Bartlett; Skadden Arps Slate Meagher & Flom; Sullivan & Cromwell; and Davis Polk & Wardwell.

[40] As of this writing, the accounting industry is dominated by the group of firms called the "big four": Ernst & Young, PricewaterhouseCoopers, KPMG, and Deloitte & Touche. Large regional firms (e.g., Grant Thornton and BDO Seidman) likely have some national and possibly some international clients, but they are largely tied to specific regional accounts. Local accounting firms operate in a number of cities and tend to focus on small businesses and individuals.

Proxy Solicitors

Proxy contests (discussed in detail in Chapter 3) are attempts to change the management control or policies of a company by gaining the right to cast votes on behalf of other shareholders. In contests for the control of the board of directors of a target company, it can be difficult to compile mailing lists of stockholders' addresses. The acquiring firm or dissident shareholders hire a proxy solicitor[41] to obtain these addresses. The target's management may also hire proxy solicitors to design strategies for educating shareholders and communicating why they should follow the board's recommendations.

Public Relations Firms

It is vital to communicate a consistent position during a takeover attempt. Inconsistent messages reduce the credibility of the parties involved. From the viewpoint of the acquiring company in a hostile takeover attempt, the message to the shareholders must be that the plans for the company will increase shareholder value more than the plans of incumbent management. Often, the target company's management will hire a private investigator[42] to develop detailed financial data on the company and do background checks on key personnel, later using that information in the public relations campaign in an effort to discredit publicly the management of the acquiring firm.

ALTERNATIVE INVESTORS AND LENDERS

Institutional investors and lenders are organizations that pool large sums of money to invest in or lend to companies, and they are an important financing source for mergers and acquisitions.

Commercial Banks

Traditionally, the model of a commercial bank is one that accepts checking, savings, and money market accounts and lends these funds to borrowers. This model has evolved into one in which banks sell many of the loans they originate to other players in the financial system for whom buying, selling, and collecting on loans is their primary business. Commercial banks also derive an increasing share of their profits from fees charged for various types of services offered to depositors and fees charged for underwriting and other investment banking services. However, the so-called Dodd-Frank legislation passed in 2010 and discussed in detail in Chapter 2 created new restrictions on these activities.

---

[41] Georgeson & Company and D. F. King & Company are two major proxy solicitor firms.

[42] There are many private investigators, but Kroll Associates is by far the largest such firm that frequently investigates target management.

Insurance Companies

An insurance company offers to mitigate risk for its customers in exchange for an insurance premium. The main source of profit for insurance companies is the sale of insurance products, but they also make money by investing premium income that is not being paid out to customers to cover losses.

Pension Funds

Employers establish pension funds to generate income over the long term to provide pensions for employees when they retire. Typically, pension funds are managed by a financial advisory service for the company and its employees, although some larger corporations operate their pension funds in-house. Pension funds control large amounts of capital and are the largest institutional investors in many countries.

Mutual Funds

Mutual funds are pools of money professionally managed for the benefit of investors. They may focus on stocks, bonds, cash, or a combination of these asset classes. A mutual fund's portfolio is structured and maintained to match the investment objectives stated in its prospectus. Mutual funds can influence corporate policies by exercising the voting rights associated with their stockholdings.

Hedge and Private Equity Funds

Private equity funds and hedge funds usually are limited partnerships (for U.S. investors) or offshore investment corporations (for non-U.S. or tax-exempt investors) in which the general partner has made a substantial personal investment.[43] This structure allows the general partner to achieve extensive control over the funds he or she manages. Other characteristics of partnerships that make them attractive include favorable tax benefits, a finite life, and investor liability limited to the amount of their investment. Institutional investors such as pension funds, endowments, insurance companies, and private banks, as well as high net worth individuals, typically invest in these types of funds. Once a partnership has reached its target size, the partnership closes to further investment, whether from new or from existing investors.

Hedge funds and private equity funds are distinguished by their investment strategies, lockup periods (i.e., the length of time investors are required to commit funds), and the liquidity of their portfolios. Hedge fund investment strategies include trading a variety of financial instruments—debt, equity, options, futures, and foreign currencies—as well as higher-risk strategies such as corporate restructurings (e.g., LBOs) and credit derivatives (e.g., credit default swaps, which involve insuring the borrower against potential issuer default). Hedge fund investors typically find it easier to withdraw their money than those who invest in private equity funds because they are subject to much shorter lockup periods. Because hedge funds need to maintain liquidity to satisfy investor withdrawals, they focus on investments

---

[43] For an exhaustive discussion of hedge fund investing, see Stefanini (2006).

that can be converted to cash relatively easily, such as comparatively small investments in companies. Another way hedge funds maintain sufficient liquidity to satisfy investor withdrawals is to sell their investments after six to 18 months, with lockup periods for partners ranging from one to three years.

In contrast, private equity fund managers often make highly illiquid investments in nonpublicly listed securities of private companies. Investments often are made during the first two or three years of the fund and are maintained for five to seven years—during which time there are few new investments. Such funds invest in IPOs, LBOs, and corporate restructurings, and they attempt to control risk by becoming more actively involved in managing the firm in which they have invested. Private equity fund partnerships usually last about ten years, after which cash or shares in companies in the portfolio are distributed.

In the past, one could generalize by saying that hedge funds are traders, while private equity funds are more likely to be long-term investors. This distinction has blurred in recent years as hedge funds have taken more active roles in acquiring entire companies.[44] The blurring of the differences between hedge and private equity funds reflects increased competition occurring due to the growth in the number of funds and the huge infusion of capital that occurred between 2005 and mid-2007, making it more difficult for fund managers to generate superior returns.

Like mutual funds, hedge and private equity funds receive a management fee from participating investors, averaging about 2% of the assets under management. Hedge fund managers also receive "carried interest" of 20% of any profits realized from the sale of portfolio companies before any monies are distributed to investors. Furthermore, hedge funds and private equity investors typically receive fees from their portfolio companies for completing transactions, arranging financing, performing due diligence, and monitoring business performance while the company is in the fund's portfolio.[45]

With the passage of the Dodd-Frank Wall Street Reform and Consumer Protection Act of 2010, hedge funds and private equity advisors are required to register with the SEC as investment advisers and provide information about their trades and portfolios needed to assess

---

[44] For example, the hedge fund Highfields Capital Management, which owned 7% of Circuit City, made a bid to buy the entire company in 2005. That same year, hedge fund manager Edward Lampert, after buying a large stake in Kmart, engineered an $11 billion takeover of Sears. The Blackstone Group (a private equity firm) and Lio Capital (a hedge fund) banded together to purchase the European beverage division of Cadbury Schweppes in early 2006. Blackstone also acted like a hedge fund that same year with its purchase of a 4.5% stake in Deutsche Telekom. According to Dealogic, hedge funds accounted for at least 50 leveraged buyouts in 2006.

[45] Kaplan and Schoar (2005) found little evidence that private equity funds on average outperform the overall stock market once their fees are taken into account. In contrast, hedge funds have tended to outperform the overall market by one to two percentage points, even after fees are considered, although the difference varies with the time period selected (*The Deal*, 2006). Moreover, hedge fund returns appeared to be less risky than the overall market, as measured by the standard deviation of their returns. These data may be problematic, since hedge fund financial returns are self-reported and not subject to public audit. Furthermore, such returns could be upward biased due to the failure to report poorly performing funds. Metrick and Yasuda (2007) found that for a sample of 238 LBO funds from 1992 to 2006, the average private equity fund collected about $10.35 in management fees for every $100 under management compared with $5.41 for every $100 under management that came from carried interest. Consequently, about two-thirds of fund income comes from fees.

potential risk to the financial system (so-called systemic risk). The data will be shared with the systemic risk regulator as mandated by the Act.

Sovereign Wealth Funds

Sovereign wealth funds are government-backed or -sponsored investment funds whose primary function is to invest accumulated reserves of foreign currencies and earn a profit. Countries that had accumulated huge quantities of U.S. dollars would, through such funds, reinvest the money in U.S. Treasury securities. Recently, these funds have begun to grow and are increasingly taking equity positions in foreign firms, making high-profile investments in public companies. However, the disarray in the global capital markets in 2008 and 2009, and the resulting slide in the value of their investments, has caused many such funds to retrench by investing more in government securities than in individual firms.

Venture Capital Firms

Venture capitalists (VCs) are a significant source of funds for financing both start-ups and acquisitions, and they are sometimes willing to lend when the more traditional sources, such as banks, insurance companies, and pension funds, are unwilling because of perceived risk. Representing private equity capital, typically from institutional investors and individuals with high net worth, VC firms identify and screen opportunities, transact and close deals, monitor performance, and provide advice, adding value by providing managerial and technical expertise in addition to their capital contributions. VC firms typically provide capital to early-stage, high-potential growth companies with the expectation of generating a return through an eventual IPO or sale to a strategic investor. Investments generally are made in cash in exchange for shares in a company, and VCs usually demand a large equity position in the firm in exchange for paying a relatively low per-share price.[46]

Angel Investors

Angel investors are wealthy individuals who often band together in "investment clubs" or loose networks. Their objective is to generate deal flow, pool money, and share expertise. Some angel groups imitate professional investment funds, some affiliate with universities, while others engage in for-profit philanthropy.

ACTIVIST INVESTORS AND M&A ARBITRAGEURS

Institutional activism has become an important factor in mergers and acquisitions. Institutions often play the role of activist investors to affect the policies of companies in which they invest and especially to discipline corporate management. M&A arbitrageurs sometimes support activist investors in their efforts to change a firm's board, management, or policies.

---

[46] General partners of venture capital firms receive a 2 to 3% fee and 15 to 25% of any capital gains from initial public offerings and mergers. The remaining 75 to 85% of capital gains, plus a return of principal, goes back to investors in the VC fund (Bygrave and Timmons, 1992). Only 2 to 4% of the firms contacting VC firms actually receive funding (Vachon, 1993).

Mutual Funds and Pension Funds

Institutional ownership of public firms increased substantially over the past few decades.[47] While regulations restrict the ability of institutions to discipline corporate management, institutional investors with huge portfolios can be very effective in demanding governance changes.[48] In the 1980s, pension funds, mutual funds, and insurance firms were often passive investors; however, they became more forceful in the 1990s, and there is further evidence that institutions are taking increasingly aggressive stands against management. These organizations are challenging management on hot-button issues such as antitakeover defenses, lavish severance benefits for CEOs, and employee stock option accounting. Voting against management, though, can be problematic, since some mutual funds manage retirement plans and, increasingly, provide a host of outsourcing services—from payroll to health benefits—for their business clients. Mutual funds may own stock, on behalf of individual or institutional clients, in these same firms.[49]

Pressure from institutional activists may account for the general decline in the number of executives serving as both board chairman and CEO of companies.[50] Sometimes, CEOs choose to negotiate with activists rather than face a showdown at an annual shareholders meeting. Activists are also finding that they may avoid the expense of a full-blown proxy fight simply by threatening to vote in certain ways on supporting a chief executive officer or a management proposal. This may mean a "no" vote, although in some instances the only options are to vote in the affirmative or abstain. Abstaining is a way to indicate dissatisfaction with a CEO or a firm's policy without jeopardizing future underwriting or the M&A business for the institution.[51] It should be noted, though, that institutional investor activism by mutual funds and pension funds has often failed to achieve significant benefits for shareholders.[52]

---

[47] The percent of equity held by institutions was 49.1% in 2001, compared to 31% in 1970 (*Federal Reserve Bulletin*, December 2003, p. 33).

[48] The Investment Company Act of 1940 restricts the ability of institutions to discipline corporate management. For example, mutual funds, to achieve diversification, are limited in the amount they can invest in any one firm's outstanding stock. State regulations often restrict the share of a life insurance or property casualty company's assets that can be invested in stock to as little as 2%.

[49] A study of the 24 largest mutual funds in the United States indicated that in 2004 American Funds, T. Rowe Price, and Vanguard voted against management and for key shareholder proposals 70%, 61%, and 51% of the time, respectively—sharply higher than in 2003. However, industry leader Fidelity voted against management only 33% of the time (Farzad, October 16, 2006; Davis and Kim, 2007).

[50] Goyal and Park, 2002. The number of executives serving in both positions in their companies declined from about 91% during the 1980s to 58% during the 1990s (Kini, Kracaw, and Mian, 2004).

[51] In an unprecedented expression of no confidence in early 2003, 43% of the votes cast were opposed to Michael Eisner continuing as chairman and CEO of Disney. Even though Eisner won a majority of the votes, the Disney board voted to strip him of his role as chairman. Later that year, Eisner announced that he would retire when his contract expired in 2006.

[52] Karpoff, 2001; Romano, 2001; Gillan and Starks, 2007

Hedge Funds and Private Equity Firms

In recent years, hedge funds and private equity investors have increasingly played the role of activist investors—and with much greater success than other institutional investors. Activist hedge funds are successful (or partially so) about two-thirds of the time in their efforts to change a firm's strategic, operational, or financial strategies. They seldom seek control (with ownership stakes averaging about 9%) and are most often nonconfrontational. Research shows that there is an approximate 7% abnormal financial return to shareholders around the announcement that the hedge fund is initiating some form of action.[53]

The relative success of hedge funds as activists can be attributed to the fact that their managers, who manage large pools of relatively unregulated capital, are highly motivated by the prospect of financial gain. Because hedge funds are not subject to the same regulations governing mutual funds and pension funds, they can hold highly concentrated positions in small numbers of firms. Moreover, hedge funds are not limited by the same conflicts of interest that afflict mutual funds and pension funds, because they have few financial ties to the management of the firms whose shares they own and, unlike mutual funds, do not have other business such as clients services at risk.

Hedge funds as activist investors tend to have the greatest impact on financial returns to shareholders when they prod management to put a company up for sale. However, their impact rapidly dissipates if the sale of the company is unsuccessful.[54] Firms once targeted by activists are more likely to be acquired.

M&A Arbitrageurs (Arbs)

When a bid is made for a target company, the target company's stock price often trades at a small discount to the actual bid—reflecting the risk that the offer may not be accepted. Merger arbitrage refers to an investment strategy that attempts to profit from this spread. Arbitrageurs (arbs) buy the stock and make a profit on the difference between the bid price and the current stock price if the deal is consummated. Hedge fund managers often play the role of arbs.

Arbs may accumulate a substantial percentage of the stock held outside of institutions so they can be in a position to influence the outcome of the takeover attempt. For example, if other offers for the target firm appear, arbs promote their positions directly to managers and institutional investors with phone calls and through leaks to the financial press. Their intent is to sell their shares to the highest bidder. Acquirers involved in a hostile takeover attempt often encourage hedge funds to buy as much target stock as possible, with the objective of gaining control of the target later by buying the stock from the hedge funds.

Studies show that the price of a target company's stock often starts to rise in advance of the announcement of a takeover attempt, the result of arb activity (and, possibly, insider

---

[53] Brav et al. (2006) argue that activist hedge funds occupy a middle ground between internal monitoring by large shareholders and external monitoring by corporate raiders. Clifford (2007) and Klein and Zur (2009) also found that hedge fund activism can generate significant abnormal financial returns to shareholders.

[54] Greenwood and Schor (2007) found that under such circumstances, there is little change in the firm's share price during the 18 months following the sale of the company, even if the firm follows the activist's recommendations and buys back shares or adds new directors.

trading).[55] If one firm in an industry is acquired, it is commonplace for the share prices of other firms in the same industry to increase because those firms are viewed as potential takeover targets.

Arbs also provide market liquidity—the ease with which a security can be bought or sold without affecting its current market price—during transactions. In a cash-financed merger, the merger arbitrageur seeking to buy the target firm's shares provides liquidity to the target's shareholders who want to sell on the announcement day or shortly thereafter. Arbitrageurs may actually reduce liquidity for the acquirer's stock in a stock-for-stock merger because they immediately "short" the acquirer shares (i.e., sell borrowed shares—paying interest to the share owner based on the value of the shares when borrowed—hoping to buy them back at a lower price). The downward pressure that widespread arb short-selling puts on the acquirer's share price at the time the transaction is announced makes it difficult for others to sell without incurring a loss from the premerger announcement price. Merger arbitrage short-selling may account for about one-half of the downward pressure on acquirer share prices around the announcement of a stock-financed merger.[56] Merger arbitrage also has the potential to be highly profitable.[57]

The implications of M&A for shareholders, Bondholders & society.

DO M&AS PAY OFF FOR SHAREHOLDERS, BONDHOLDERS, AND SOCIETY?

The answer to whether mergers and acquisitions pay off seems to depend on who is paid and over what period. On average, total shareholder gains around the announcement date of an acquisition or merger are significantly positive; however, most of the gain accrues to target firm shareholders. Moreover, in the three to five years after a takeover, many acquirer firms either underperform compared with their industry peers or destroy shareholder value. It is less clear whether this subpar performance and value destruction are due to the acquisition or to other factors.

Researchers use a wide variety of approaches to measure the impact of takeovers on shareholder value.[58] What follows is a discussion of the results of the two most common types of analysis of pre- and postmerger returns: The "event study" that examines abnormal stock returns to the shareholders of both bidders and targets around the announcement of an offer (the "event") and includes both successful (i.e., completed transactions) and unsuccessful takeovers; and the use of accounting measures to gauge the postmerger impact on shareholder value.

[55] Ascioglu, McInish, and Wood, 2002

[56] Mitchell, Pulvino, and Stafford, 2004

[57] A number of studies find that such arbitrage generates financial returns ranging from 4.5% to more than 100% in excess of what would be considered normal in a highly competitive market (Jindra and Walkling, 1999; Mitchell and Pulvino, 2001).

[58] In an analysis of 88 empirical studies between 1970 and 2006, Zola and Meier (2008) identify 12 different approaches to measuring the impact of takeovers on shareholder value. Of these studies, 41% use the event study method to analyze premerger returns, and 28% utilize long-term accounting measures to analyze postmerger returns.

Premerger Returns to Shareholders

Positive abnormal returns represent gains for shareholders, which can be explained by such factors as improved efficiency, pricing power, or tax benefits. They are abnormal in the sense that they exceed what an investor normally expects to earn for accepting a certain level of risk. For example, if an investor can reasonably expect to earn a 10% return on a stock but actually earns 25% due to a takeover, the abnormal or excess return to the shareholder is 15%. Abnormal returns are calculated by subtracting the actual return from a benchmark indicating investors' required returns, which often are approximated by the capital asset pricing model or the return on the S&P 500 stock index. Abnormal returns are forward looking in that share prices usually represent the present value of expected future cash flows. Therefore, the large announcement returns may reflect anticipated future synergies resulting from the combination of the target and acquiring firms. Table 1.7 provides some empirical evidence of abnormal returns to bidders and targets around announcement dates.

High Returns for Target Shareholders in Successful and Unsuccessful Bids

While averaging 30% between 1962 and 2001, abnormal returns for tender offers have risen steadily over time,[59] reflecting the frequent bidder strategy of offering a substantial premium to preempt other potential bidders and the potential for revising the initial offer because of competing bids. Other contributing factors include the increasing sophistication of takeover defenses, as well as federal and state laws requiring bidders to notify target shareholders of their intentions before completing the transaction. Moreover, the abnormal gains tend to be higher for shareholders of target firms, whose financial performance is expected to deteriorate over the long term.[60] This may suggest that the bidding firms see the highest potential for gain among those target firms whose management is viewed as incompetent. Returns from hostile tender offers typically exceed those from friendly mergers, which are characterized by less contentious negotiated settlements between the boards and management of the bidder and the target firm. Moreover, friendly takeovers often do not receive competing bids.

Unsuccessful takeovers may also result in significant announcement date returns for target company shareholders, but much of the gain dissipates if another bidder does not appear. The immediate gain in target share prices disappears within a year if the takeover attempt fails.[61] To realize abnormal returns, target firm shareholders must sell their shares shortly after the announcement of a failed takeover attempt.

Returns to Acquirer Shareholders May Not Be So Disappointing

In the aggregate, abnormal returns are modest to slightly negative for successful takeovers, whether through tender offers or mergers. Bidder returns generally have declined slightly over time as the premiums paid for targets have increased. Even if the abnormal returns are zero or slightly negative, these returns are consistent with returns in competitive markets in which financial returns are proportional to the risk assumed by the average competitor in

[59] Bhagat et al., 2005

[60] Ghosh and Lee, 2000

[61] Akhigbe, Borde, and Whyte, 2000; Bradley, Desai, and Kim, 1988; Sullivan, Jensen, and Hudson, 1994

TABLE 1.7   Empirical Evidence on Abnormal Returns to Bidders and Targets around Announcement Dates[a]

Total Gains from Takeovers[b]	Target Shareholders	Bidder Shareholders
1. Takeovers increase on average the combined market value of the merged firms, with target shareholders earning large positive returns and bidding firm shareholders on average showing little or no abnormal return. 2. Largest gains are realized at the beginning of a takeover wave. 3. Takeovers with the largest losses come during the second half of a takeover wave.	1. For the two-week period around the announcement date, returns range from 14% to 44%. 2. Average returns vary by time period: • 1960s: 18% to 19% • 1980s: 32% to 35% • 1990s: 32% to 45% 3. Average returns vary by type of bid: • Hostile bids: 32% • Friendly bids: 22% 4. Returns are higher for all-cash bids than for all-equity offers. 5. Target share prices often react as much as six weeks prior to an announcement, reflecting speculation or insider trading.	1. For the two-week period around the announcement date, average returns are close to zero when the target is a public firm; some studies show small positive gains and others small losses. 2. Returns can be 1.5% to .6% when the target is a private firm (or a subsidiary of a public firm) due to improved performance from increased monitoring by the acquiring firm, the frequent absence of multiple bidders, and the liquidity discount resulting from difficulty in valuing such firms. 3. In the U.S., all-equity financed takeovers of public firms frequently exhibit negative abnormal returns and underperform all-cash bids. 4. In Europe, all-equity financed M&As are frequently associated with positive returns (often exceeding all-cash bids), reflecting the greater concentration of ownership and the tendency of holders of large blocks of stock to more closely monitor management.

[a] Results are based on 65 studies of successful nonfinancial (friendly and hostile) M&As in the U.S., U.K., and Continental Europe. Studies include horizontal, vertical, and conglomerate mergers, as well as tender offers. The studies also include related and unrelated takeovers: all-stock, all-cash, and mixed forms of payment involving both public and private firms.

[b] Includes the sum of returns to target and acquirer shareholders.

Source: Adapted from Martynova and Renneboog (2008).

the industry. For unsuccessful takeovers, bidder shareholders have experienced negative returns in the 5 to 8% range,[62] perhaps reflecting investors' reassessment of the acquirer's business plan more than concerns about the acquisition.[63]

Bidders with low leverage show a tendency to pay high purchase premiums.[64] Not surprisingly, such bidders are in a position to pay higher prices than are more leveraged bidders. However, this tendency may also result in such bidders overpaying for target firms.

[62] Bradley, Desai, and Kim, 1988

[63] Grinblatt and Titman, 2002

[64] Morellec and Zhdanov, 2008; Uysal, 2006

Focusing on aggregate returns to acquirer shareholders can be highly misleading. The results can be distorted by a relatively few large transactions.[65] Whether abnormal returns to acquirers are positive or negative varies with the characteristics of the acquirer, the target, and the deal (discussed in more detail following). Furthermore, while event studies treat acquisitions as a single event, gains from a specific acquisition often depend on subsequent acquisitions undertaken to implement a firm's business strategy,[66] and because of potential synergies among the acquired firms, the success or failure of these acquisitions should be evaluated in the context of the entire strategy and not as standalone transactions. Finally, there is evidence that the initial stock market reaction to the announcement of an acquisition often is biased or incomplete.[67]

Postmerger Returns to Shareholders

The objective of examining postmerger accounting or other performance measures such as cash flow and operating profit, usually during the three- to five-year period following closing, is to assess how performance changed. The evidence, however, is conflicting about the long-term impact of M&A activity. Where some studies find a better than average chance that M&As create shareholder value, others find that as many as 50 to 80% have underperformed their industry peers or failed to earn their cost of capital.[68] What may seem

[65] Moeller et al., 2005. Acquirer returns around transaction dates were in the aggregate positive during the 1990s (around 1.5%), particularly during the 1990–1997 period. However, losses incurred by a relatively few mega-transactions between 1998 and 2001 offset much of the gains during the earlier period.

[66] Barkema and Schijven, 2008. For example, in an effort to become the nation's largest consumer lender, Bank of America spent more than $100 billion to acquire credit card company MBNA in 2005, mortgage lender Countrywide in 2007, and the investment firm Merrill Lynch in 2008.

[67] Harrison et al., 2005. Event studies assume that markets are highly efficient, and that share prices reflect all of the public and private information available with respect to the transaction. In practice, much of the information provided by the seller to the buyer is confidential and therefore largely unavailable to the public. Furthermore, the investing public often is unaware of the target's specific business plan at the time of the announcement, making a comparison of whether to continue to hold or to sell the target's stock difficult. Zola and Meier (2008) note that short-term event studies results do not correlate with any of the other measures of M&A performance because the "blip" in the financial returns of the buyer and seller on or about the announcement date often reflects the "collective bet" by investors on the probable success or failure of the merger. Such bets are often wrong, providing evidence contrary to the often presumed efficiency of the financial markets.

[68] In a review of 26 studies of postmerger performance during the three to five years after the merger, Martynova and Renneboog (2008a) found that 14 showed a decline in operating returns, 7 provided positive (but statistically insignificant) changes in profitability, and 5 showed a positive and statistically significant increase in profitability. The diversity of conclusions about postmerger returns may be the result of sample and time selections, methodology employed in the studies, or factors unrelated to the merger, such as a slowing economy (Barber and Lyon, 1997; Fama, 1998; Lyon, Barber, and Tsai, 1999). Using a sample of 1,300 transactions from 1993 to 2002, Dutta and Jog (2009) did not find evidence of any systematic long-term deterioration in acquirer financial performance and attribute findings of such deterioration to the choice of benchmarks, differing methodologies, and statistical techniques.

like a hubris-driven inability of CEOs and boards to learn from the past (since the number and size of transactions continue to increase over time) looks more like the result of methodological issues and the failure to distinguish among alternative situations in which M&As occur, leading to an understatement of potential returns to acquirers.[69]

Acquirer Returns Vary by Characteristics of Acquirer, Target, and Deal

There is strong evidence that abnormal returns to acquirer shareholders are largely situational, varying according to the size of the acquirer, the type and size of the target (i.e., publicly traded or private), and the form of payment (i.e., cash or stock) (Table 1.8).

Smaller Acquirers Tend to Realize Higher Returns

The size of the acquirer and the financial returns realized on mergers and acquisitions are inversely related, with relatively smaller acquirers, on average, realizing larger abnormal returns than larger acquirers. Why does this happen? It seems to be a function of management overconfidence and the empire-building tendencies of large firms. For the 20-year period ending in 2001, researchers found that large firms destroyed shareholder wealth, while small firms created wealth.[70]

Acquirer Returns

Returns Are Often Positive for Private or Subsidiary Targets

U.S. acquirers of private firms or subsidiaries of publicly traded firms often realize positive excess returns of 1.5 to 2.6%.[71] Acquirers are inclined to pay less for nonpublicly traded companies due to the difficulty of buying private firms or subsidiaries of public companies. In both cases, shares are not publicly traded, and access to information is limited. Moreover, there may be fewer bidders for nonpublicly traded companies. Consequently, these targets may be acquired at a discount from their actual economic value (i.e., cash-generation potential). As a consequence of this discount, bidder shareholders are able to realize a larger share of the anticipated synergies resulting from combining the acquirer and target firms.

---

[69] Presumably, the longer the postmerger period analyzed, the greater the likelihood that other factors, wholly unrelated to the merger, will affect financial returns. Moreover, these longer-term studies are not able to compare how well the acquirer would have done without the acquisition.

[70] Moeller et al., 2004. Small firms are defined as the smallest 25% of firms listed on the New York Stock Exchange each year during that 20-year period. Forty-six percent of a sample of 12,023 transactions involved acquisitions of private firms, 32% involved acquisitions of subsidiaries, and the remaining 22% involved acquisitions of public firms. Regardless of how they were financed (i.e., stock or cash) or whether they were public or private targets, acquisitions made by smaller firms had announcement returns 1.55% higher than a comparable acquisition made by a larger firm.

[71] Moeller et al., 2005; Fuller et al., 2002; Ang and Kohers, 2001. Similar results were found in an exhaustive study of U.K. acquirers (Draper and Paudyal, 2006) making bids for private firms or subsidiaries of public firms, where the positive abnormal returns were attributed to the relative illiquidity of such businesses.

TABLE 1.8   Acquirer Returns Differ by Characteristics of the Acquirer, Target, and Deal

Characteristic	Empirical Support
TYPE OF TARGET	
Acquirer returns are often positive when the targets are privately owned (or are subsidiaries of public companies) and slightly negative when the targets are publicly traded (i.e., so-called "listing effect") regardless of the country.	Faccio et al. (2006) Draper and Paudyal (2006) Moeller et al. (2005) Fuller et al. (2002)
FORM OF PAYMENT	
• Acquirer returns on equity-financed acquisitions of public firms often *less than* cash-financed deals in the United States.	Schleifer and Vishny (2003) Megginson et al. (2003) Heron and Lie (2002) Linn and Switzer (2001)
• Acquirer returns on equity-financed acquisitions of public or private firms frequently *more than* all-cash-financed deals in the European Union countries.	Martynova and Renneboog (2008a)
• Acquirer returns on equity-financed acquisitions of private firms often exceed significantly cash deals, particularly when the target is difficult to value.	Chang (1998) Officer et al. (2009)
ACQUIRER/TARGET SIZE	
• Smaller acquirers may realize higher returns than larger acquirers.	Moeller et al. (2004) Moeller et al. (2005) Gorton et al. (2009)[a]
• Relatively small deals may generate higher acquirer returns than larger ones.	Hackbarth et al. (2008) Frick and Torres (2002)
• Acquirer returns may be higher when the size of the acquisition is large relative to the buyer and small relative to the seller.	Gell et al. (2008)

[a] *Size is measured not in absolute but in relative terms compared to other firms within an industry.*

Relatively Small Deals May Generate Higher Returns

Average target size appears to play an important role in determining financial returns to acquirer shareholders.[72] High-tech firms often acquire small, but related, target firms to fill gaps in their product offerings. Consequently, the contribution of these acquisitions should not be viewed individually but in terms of their impact on the implementation of the acquirer's overall business strategy. Larger deals tend to be more risky for acquirers[73] and, as a percentage of the acquiring firms' equity, experience consistently lower postmerger performance, possibly reflecting the challenges of integrating large target firms and realizing projected synergies on a timely basis.

Under certain circumstances, though, larger deals may offer significant positive abnormal rates of returns. For instance, acquirer's returns from buying product lines

---

[72] For the 10-year period ending in 2000, high-tech companies, averaging 39% annual total return to shareholders, acquired targets with an average size of less than $400 million, about 1% of the market value of the acquiring firms (Frick and Torres, 2002).

[73] Hackbarth and Morellec, 2008

and subsidiaries of other companies tend to be higher when the size of the asset is large relative to the buyer and small relative to the seller.[74] The implication is that parent firms interested in funding new opportunities are more likely to divest relatively small businesses that are not germane to their core business strategy at relatively low prices to raise capital quickly. Buyers are able to acquire sizeable businesses at favorable prices, increasing the likelihood that they will be able to earn their cost of capital.

Cash Deals Often Exceed Equity-Financed Deals

Managers tend to issue stock when they believe it is overvalued. Over time, investors learn to treat such decisions as signals that the stock is overvalued and sell their shares when the new equity issue is announced, causing the firm's share price to decline. There is considerable evidence that bidding firms that use cash to purchase the target firm exhibit better long-term performance than do those using stock, since investors anticipate that stock-financed mergers underperform precisely because investors treat stock financing as a signal that shares are overvalued.[75] However, equity financed transactions in the European Union often display higher acquirer returns due to the existence of large block shareholders, whose active monitoring tends to improve the acquired firm's performance. Such shareholders are less common in the United States.

Using stock to acquire a firm often results in announcement period gains to bidder shareholders that dissipate within three to five years, even when the acquisition was successful.[76] These findings imply that shareholders, selling around the announcement dates, may realize the largest gains from either tender offers or mergers.

Some argue that equity overvaluation occurs when a firm's management cannot expect to make investments that will sustain the current share price except by chance.[77] Management will be enticed to pursue larger, more risky investments (such as unrelated acquisitions) in a vain attempt to support the overvalued share price. These actions destroy shareholder value, since the firm is unable to earn its cost of capital, and the longer-term performance of the combined firms suffers because the stock price declines to its industry average performance.

Abnormal returns to acquirers are negatively related to equity offers but not to cash offers. However, there appears to be no difference in abnormal returns for cash offers for public firms, equity offers for public firms, and equity offers for private firms when such firms exhibit similar business-specific risk (e.g., institutional ownership, growth rates, leverage, etc.).[78]

[74] Gell et al., 2008

[75] Schleifer and Vishny, 2003; Megginson et al., 2003; Heron and Lie, 2002; Linn and Switzer, 2001

[76] Deogun and Lipin, 2000; Black et al., 2000; Agrawal and Jaffe, 1999; Rau and Vermaelen, 1998

[77] Jensen, 2005

[78] Moeller et al., 2007

While still underperforming cash deals, successful acquirers that use stock as the form of payment significantly outperform unsuccessful attempts by a wide margin.[79] It seems that the successful stock-financed acquirers' relatively better performance results from their ability to use their overvalued stock to buy the target firm's assets fairly inexpensively.[80]

Acquirer Experience May Not Improve Performance

Experience is a necessary but not sufficient condition for successful acquisitions. It contributes to improved financial returns, it appears, only if it is applied to targets in the same or similar industries or in the same or similar geographic or cultural regions.[81] Abnormal returns to serial acquirers (i.e., firms that make numerous and frequent acquisitions) have tended to decline from one transaction to the next.[82] This is typically attributed to the CEO of the serial acquirer becoming overconfident with each successive acquisition. The CEO then tends to overestimate the value of synergies and the ease with which they can be realized. Now subject to hubris, the CEO tends to overpay for acquisitions.[83]

Bidder Returns Are Good Predictors of Completed Transactions

There is evidence that the magnitude of abnormal returns to acquirers around the announcement date is a good predictor either of whether the initial offer price will be renegotiated or that the deal will be cancelled.[84] The acquirer's management will react to a significant negative decline in their stock immediately following a merger announcement as investors display their displeasure with the deal. Cancellation is much less likely if an agreement of purchase and sale was signed before the announcement, since reneging on a signed agreement can result in expensive litigation.

[79] Savor and Lu, 2009. Over the first year, the mean abnormal financial return for acquirers using stock is a negative 7%, reaching a negative cumulative 13% at the end of three years. However, acquirers using stock who fail in their takeover attempts do even worse, experiencing negative returns of 21% and 32% after one year and three years, respectively, following their aborted takeover attempts.

[80] Studies of European firms indicate that postmerger returns to bidders using stock often are higher than those using cash. These results may reflect the greater concentration of ownership in European firms than in the United States and the tendency of large shareholders to more closely monitor the actions of management (Martynova and Renneboog, 2008).

[81] This is the conclusion from Barkema and Schijven (2008), an extensive survey of the literature on how firms learn from past acquisitions.

[82] Fuller et al., 2002; Billett and Qian, 2005; Conn et al., 2005; Ismail, 2005

[83] These findings are in sharp contrast with the findings that acquirers have great potential to learn from their mistakes, suggesting that serial acquirers are more likely to earn returns in excess of their cost of capital (Harding and Rovit, 2004). Atkas et al. (2007) propose an alternative explanation for the role of hubris in the decline in abnormal acquirer returns for serial acquirers. If acquirers are learning from prior acquisitions, they should improve their selection of, and ability to integrate, target firms. Therefore, the risk of each successive acquisition should decline. If risk associated with the successive acquisitions declines faster than the abnormal return, risk-adjusted acquirer returns can rise. If so, CEOs of highly acquisitive firms should be willing to bid more aggressively for targets as the perceived risk associated with such targets declines. As such, abnormal returns are simply declining in line with the level of perceived risk for experienced acquirers.

[84] Luo (2005), based on a sample of 1,576 transactions between 1995 and 2001.

Bondholder Payoffs

Mergers and acquisitions have relatively little impact on abnormal returns either to the acquirer or to the target bondholders, except in special situations. The limited impact on bondholder wealth is due to the relationship between leverage and operating performance.[85] How M&As affect bondholder wealth reflects, in part, the extent to which an increase in leverage that raises the potential for default is offset by the discipline that increasing leverage imposes on management to improve operating performance.[86] Other things being equal, increasing leverage will lower current bondholder wealth, while improving operating performance will improve bondholder wealth.

However, bondholders, in certain circumstances, may benefit from M&As. For example, bondholders of target firms whose debt is below investment grade tend to experience positive abnormal returns if the acquirer has a higher credit rating. In addition, when loan covenant agreements for firms that are subject to takeovers include poison puts that allow bondholders to sell their bonds back to the company at a predetermined price, bondholders experience positive abnormal returns when a change of control takes place.[87]

Payoffs for Society

While mergers and acquisitions have continued to increase in number and average size, since 1970, M&A activity has not increased industry concentration in terms of the share of output or value produced by the largest firms in an industry.[88] Further, most empirical studies show that M&A activity results in improved operating efficiencies and lower product prices than would have been the case without the merger. Gains in aggregate shareholder value are attributed more to the improved operating efficiency of the combined firms than to increased market or pricing power.[89] In fact, corporate transactions seem to result in an overall improvement in efficiency by transferring assets from those who are not using them effectively to those who can.[90]

[85] Renneboog and Szilagyi, 2007

[86] The empirical evidence is ambiguous. A study by Billett, King, and Mauer (2004) shows slightly negative abnormal returns to acquirer bondholders regardless of the acquirer's bond rating; the researchers used a sample of 831 U.S. transactions between 1979 and 1998. However, they also find that target firm holders of below-investment-grade bonds earn average excess returns of 4.3% or higher around the merger announcement date, when the target firm's credit rating is less than the acquirer's and when the merger is expected to decrease the target's risk or leverage. Maquierira, Megginson, and Nail (1998) show positive excess returns to acquirer bondholders of 1.9%, and .5% for target bondholders, but only for nonconglomerate transactions; their sample includes 253 U.S. transactions from 1963 to 1996. Another study, using a sample of 225 European transactions between 1995 and 2004, finds small positive returns to acquirer bondholders of .56% around the announcement date of the transaction (Renneboog and Szilagyi, 2006).

[87] Billet, Jiang, and Lee, 2010

[88] Carlton and Perloff, 1999

[89] Shahrur, 2005; Ghosh, 2004; Song and Walking, 2000; Akhigbe, Borde, and Whyte, 2000

[90] See Maksimovic and Phillips (2001), an exhaustive study of 10,079 transactions between 1974 and 1992.

WHY SOME M&AS FAIL TO MEET EXPECTATIONS

The notion that most M&As fail in some substantive manner is not supported by the evidence. In fact, the failure of an M&A to meet expectations depends to a great extent on how you define failure. The failure rate is low if failure is defined as the eventual sale or liquidation of the business, but it is higher if failure is defined as the inability to meet or exceed financial objectives. Managers are often very satisfied with their acquisitions if they are able achieve strategic objectives, so the failure rate is also low if failure is defined as not achieving strategic, nonfinancial objectives.[91]

No single factor seems likely to be the cause of M&As failing to meet expectations. There are, however, three explanations that are most commonly used to explain failure: overpaying (often due to overestimating synergies), the slow pace of postmerger integration, and a flawed strategy.[92] Overpaying for a target firm increases the hurdles an acquirer must overcome to earn its cost of capital, since there is little or no margin of error in achieving anticipated synergies on a timely basis.[93]

Consequently, the postmerger share price for such firms should underperform broader industry averages as future growth slows to more normal levels. By substantially overpaying for an acquisition, acquirers are condemned to having to improve profitability dramatically to earn the financial returns required by investors on a higher net asset base (including the fair market value of the target's net assets). Failure to achieve integration in a timely manner often results in customer attrition, loss of key employees, and the failure to realize anticipated synergies (see Chapter 6). Finally, under any circumstances, success will be elusive if the strategy justifying the acquisition is severely flawed.

LONG-TERM PERFORMANCE

There is little compelling evidence that growth strategies undertaken as an alternative to M&As fare any better. Such alternatives include solo ventures, in which firms reinvest excess cash flows, and business alliances, including joint ventures, licensing, franchising, and minority investments. Failure rates among alternative strategies tend to be remarkably similar to those documented for M&As.[94]

[91] Brouthers, 1998

[92] Articles indicating the importance of overpaying and/or overestimating synergy as a cause of M&As failing to meet expectations include Cao (2008), Harper and Schneider (2004), Christofferson, McNish, and Sias (2004), Henry (2002), Bekier, Bogardus, and Oldham (2001), Chapman et al. (1998), Agrawal, Jaffee, and Mandelker (1999), Rau and Vermaelen (1998), Sirower (1997), Mercer Management Consulting (1998), Hillyer and Smolowitz (1996), and Bradley, Desai, and Kim (1988). Articles referencing the slow pace of integration include Adolph (2006), Carey and Ogden (2004), Coopers & Lybrand (1996), and Mitchell (1998). Articles discussing the role of poor strategy include Mercer Management Consulting (1998) and Bogler (1996).

[93] In an exhaustive study of 22 different papers examining long-run postmerger returns, Agrawal and Jaffe (1999) separated financial performance following mergers and hostile tender offers. Reviewing a number of arguments purporting to explain postmerger performance, they deemed most convincing the argument that acquirers tend to overpay for so-called high-growth glamour companies based on their past performance.

[94] AC Nielsen (2002) estimates the failure rate for new product introductions at well over 70%. Failure rates for alliances of all types exceed 60% (Ellis, 1996; Klein, 2004).

SOME THINGS TO REMEMBER

M&As represent only one of several ways of executing business plans. There are alternatives, from the various forms of business alliances to a solo venture. Which method is chosen depends on management's desire for control, willingness to accept risk, and the range of opportunities present at a particular moment in time.

Although M&As clearly pay off for target company shareholders around announcement dates, shareholder wealth creation in the three to five years following closing is problematic. Abnormal returns to acquirers of private (unlisted) firms or subsidiaries of public firms frequently show larger returns than M&As involving publicly listed firms. U.S. acquirers using cash rather than equity often show larger returns compared to those using equity, although these results are reversed for European acquirers. Also, abnormal returns tend to be larger when acquirers are relatively small and the target is relatively large compared to the acquirer but represents a small portion of the selling firm. Finally, acquirer returns tend to be larger when the transaction occurs early in a merger wave.

The most common reasons for a merger to fail to satisfy expectations are the overestimation of synergies and subsequent overpayment, the slow pace of postmerger integration, and the lack of a coherent business strategy. Empirical studies also suggest that M&As tend to pay off for society due to the improved operating efficiency of the combined firms. The success rate for M&As is very similar to alternative growth strategies that may be undertaken.

DISCUSSION QUESTIONS

1.1 Discuss why mergers and acquisitions occur.

1.2 What are the advantages and disadvantages of holding companies in making M&As?

1.3 How might a leveraged ESOP be used as an alternative to a divestiture, to take a company private, or as a defense against an unwanted takeover?

1.4 What is the role of the investment banker in the M&A process?

1.5 Describe how arbitrage typically takes place in a takeover of a publicly traded company.

1.6 Why is potential synergy often overestimated by acquirers in evaluating a target company?

1.7 What are the major differences between the merger waves of the 1980s and 1990s?

1.8 In your judgment, what are the motivations for two M&As currently in the news?

1.9 What are the arguments for and against corporate diversification through acquisition? Which do you support and why?

1.10 What are the primary differences between operating and financial synergy? Give examples to illustrate your statements.

1.11 At a time when natural gas and oil prices were at record levels, oil and natural gas producer Andarko Petroleum announced the acquisition of two competitors, Kerr-McGee Corp. and Western Gas Resources, for $16.4 billion and $4.7 billion in cash, respectively. These purchase prices represented a substantial 40% premium for Kerr-McGee and a 49% premium for Western Gas. The acquired assets strongly complement Andarko's existing operations, providing the scale and focus necessary to cut overlapping expenses and concentrate resources in adjacent properties. What do you believe were the primary forces driving

Andarko's acquisition? How will greater scale and focus help Andarko cut costs? Be specific. What are the key assumptions implicit in your answer to the first question?

1.12 Mattel, a major U.S. toy manufacturer, virtually gave away The Learning Company (TLC), a maker of software for toys, to rid itself of a disastrous acquisition that actually had cost the firm hundreds of millions of dollars. Mattel, which had paid $3.5 billion for TLC, sold the unit to an affiliate of Gores Technology Group for rights to a share of future profits. Was this related or unrelated diversification for Mattel? Explain your answer. How might your answer to the first question have influenced the outcome?

1.13 AOL acquired Time Warner in a deal valued at $160 billion. Time Warner is the world's largest media and entertainment company, whose major business segments include cable networks, magazine publishing, book publishing, direct marketing, recorded music and music publishing, and film and TV production and broadcasting. AOL viewed itself as the world leader in providing interactive services, Web brands, Internet technologies, and electronic commerce services. Would you classify this business combination as a vertical, horizontal, or conglomerate transaction? Explain your answer.

1.14 Pfizer, a leading pharmaceutical company, acquired drug maker Pharmacia for $60 billion. The purchase price represented a 34% premium to Pharmacia's preannouncement price. Pfizer was betting that size is what mattered in the new millennium. As the market leader, Pfizer was finding it increasingly difficult to sustain the double-digit earnings growth demanded by investors. Such growth meant the firm needed to grow revenue by $3 billion to $5 billion annually while maintaining or improving profit margins. This became more difficult due to the skyrocketing costs of developing and commercializing new drugs. Expiring patents on a number of so-called blockbuster drugs intensified pressure to bring new drugs to market. In your judgment, what were Pfizer's primary motivations for acquiring Pharmacia? Categorize these in terms of the primary motivations for mergers and acquisitions discussed in this chapter.

1.15 Dow Chemical, a leading chemical manufacturer, acquired Rohm and Haas Company for $15.3 billion. While Dow has competed profitably in the plastics business for years, this business has proven to have thin margins and to be highly cyclical. By acquiring Rohm and Haas, Dow would be able to offer less cyclical and higher-margin products such as paints, coatings, and electronic materials. Would you consider this related or unrelated diversification? Explain your answer. Would you consider this a cost-effective way for the Dow shareholders to achieve better diversification of their investment portfolios?

Answers to these Chapter Discussion Questions are available in the Online Instructor's Manual for instructors using this book.

CHAPTER BUSINESS CASES

CASE STUDY 1.1
Xerox Buys ACS to Satisfy Shifting Customer Requirements

In anticipation of a shift from hardware and software spending to technical services by its corporate customers, IBM announced an aggressive move away from its traditional hardware business and into services in the mid-1990s. Having sold its commodity personal computer business to Chinese manufacturer Lenovo in mid-2005, IBM became widely recognized as a largely "hardware neutral" systems integration, technical services, and outsourcing company.

Because information technology (IT) services have tended to be less cyclical than hardware and software sales, the move into services by IBM enabled the firm to tap a steady stream of revenue at a time when customers were keeping computers and peripheral equipment longer to save money. The 2008–2009 recession exacerbated this trend as corporations spent a smaller percentage of their IT budgets on hardware and software.

These developments were not lost on other IT companies. Hewlett-Packard (HP) bought tech services company EDS in 2008 for $13.9 billion. On September 21, 2009, Dell announced its intention to purchase another information technology services company, Perot Systems, for $3.9 billion. One week later, Xerox, traditionally an office equipment manufacturer, announced a cash and stock bid for Affiliated Computer Systems (ACS) totaling $6.4 billion.

Each firm was moving to position itself as a total solution provider for its customers, achieving differentiation from its competitors by offering a broader range of both hardware and business services. While each firm focused on a somewhat different set of markets, all three shared an increasing focus on the government and healthcare segments.

However, by retaining a large proprietary hardware business, each firm faced challenges in convincing customers that they could provide objectively enterprise-wide solutions that reflected the best option for their customers.

Previous Xerox efforts to move beyond selling printers, copiers, and supplies and into services achieved limited success due largely to poor management execution. While some progress in shifting away from the firm's dependence on printers and copier sales was evident, the pace was far too slow. Xerox was looking for a way to accelerate transitioning from a product-driven company to one whose revenues were more dependent on the delivery of business services.

With annual sales of about $6.5 billion, ACS handles paper-based tasks such as billing and claims processing for governments and private companies. With about one-fourth of ACS's revenue derived from the healthcare and government sectors through long-term contracts, the acquisition gives Xerox a greater penetration into markets that should benefit from the 2009 government stimulus spending and 2010 healthcare legislation. More than two-thirds of ACS's revenue comes from the operation of client back office operations such as accounting, human resources, claims management, and other business management outsourcing services, with the rest coming from providing technology consulting services. ACS would also triple Xerox's service revenues to $10 billion.

Xerox hopes to increases its overall revenue by bundling its document management services with ACS's client back office operations. Only 20% of the two firms' customers overlap. This allows for significant cross-

CASE STUDY 1.1   (cont'd)

selling of each firm's products and services to the other firm's customers. Xerox is also betting that it can apply its globally recognized brand and worldwide sales presence to expand ACS internationally.

A perceived lack of synergies between the two firms, Xerox's rising debt levels, and the firm's struggling printer business fueled concerns about the long-term viability of the merger, sending Xerox's share price tumbling by almost 10% on the news of the transaction. With about $1 billion in cash at closing in early 2010, Xerox needed to borrow about $3 billion. Standard & Poor's downgraded Xerox's credit rating to triple-B-minus, one notch above junk.

Integration is Xerox's major challenge. The two firms' revenue mixes are very different, as are their customer bases, with government customers often requiring substantially greater effort to close sales than Xerox's traditional commercial customers. Xerox intends to operate ACS as a standalone business, which will postpone the integration of its operations consisting of 54,000 employees with ACS's 74,000. If Xerox intends to realize significant incremental revenues by selling ACS services to current Xerox customers, some degree of integration of the sales and marketing organizations would seem to be necessary.

It is hardly a foregone conclusion that customers will buy Affiliated Computer Systems services simply because ACS sales representatives gain access to current Xerox customers. Presumably, additional incentives are needed, such as some packaging of Xerox hardware with ACS's IT services. However, this may require significant price discounting at a time when printer and copier profit margins already are under substantial pressure.

Customers are likely to continue, at least in the near term, to view Xerox, Dell, and HP more as product than as service companies. The sale of services will require significant spending to rebrand these companies so that they will be increasingly viewed as service vendors. The continued dependence of all three firms on the sale of hardware may retard their ability to sell packages of hardware and IT services to customers. With hardware prices under continued pressure, customers may be more inclined to continue to buy hardware and IT services from separate vendors to pit one vendor against another. Moreover, with all three firms targeting the healthcare and government markets, pressure on profit margins could increase for all three firms. The success of IBM's services strategy could suggest that pure information technology service companies are likely to perform better in the long run than those that continue to have a significant presence in both production and sale of hardware as well as IT services.

Discussion Questions

1. Discuss the advantages and disadvantages of Xerox's intention to operate ACS as a standalone business. As an investment banker supporting Xerox, would you have argued in support of integrating ACS immediately, at a later date, or of keeping the two businesses separate indefinitely? Explain your answer.

2. How are Xerox and ACS similar, and how are they different? In what way will their similarities and differences help or hurt the long-term success of the merger?

3. Based on your answers to questions 1 and 2, do you believe that investors reacted correctly or incorrectly to the announcement of the transaction?

Answers to these questions are found in the Online Instructor's Manual available to instructors using this book.

CASE STUDY 1.2
Assessing Procter & Gamble's Acquisition of Gillette

The potential seemed almost limitless, as the Procter & Gamble (P&G) company announced that it had completed its purchase of Gillette Company (Gillette) in late 2005. P&G's chairman and CEO, A.G. Lafley, predicted that the acquisition of Gillette would add one percentage point to the firm's annual revenue growth rate, while Gillette's chairman and CEO, Jim Kilts, opined that the successful integration of the two best companies in consumer products would be studied in business schools for years to come.

Five years after closing, things have not turned out as expected. While cost savings targets were achieved, operating margins faltered due to lagging sales. Gillette's businesses, such as its pricey razors, have been buffeted by the 2008–2009 recession and have been a drag on P&G's top line rather than a boost. Moreover, most of Gillette's top managers have left. P&G's stock price at the end of 2010 stood about 12% above its level on the acquisition announcement date, less than one-fourth the appreciation of the share prices of such competitors as Unilever and Colgate-Palmolive during the same period.

On January 28, 2005, P&G enthusiastically announced that it had reached an agreement to buy Gillette in a share-for-share exchange valued at $55.6 billion. This represented an 18% premium over Gillette's preannouncement share price. P&G also announced a stock buyback of $18 billion to $22 billion, funded largely by issuing new debt. The combined companies would retain the P&G name and have annual 2005 revenue of more than $60 billion. Half of the new firm's product portfolio would consist of personal care, healthcare, and beauty products, with the remainder consisting of razors and blades and batteries. The deal was expected to dilute

P&G's 2006 earnings by about 15 cents per share. To gain regulatory approval, the two firms would have to divest overlapping operations, such as deodorants and oral care.

P&G had long been viewed as a premier marketing and product innovator. Consequently, P&G assumed that its R&D and marketing skills in developing and promoting women's personal care products could be used to enhance and promote Gillette's women's razors. Gillette was best known for its ability to sell an inexpensive product (e.g., razors) and hook customers into a lifetime of refills (e.g., razor blades). Although Gillette was the number 1 and number 2 supplier in the lucrative toothbrush and men's deodorant markets, respectively, it has been much less successful in improving the profitability of its Duracell battery brand. Despite its number 1 market share position, Duracell had been beset by intense price competition from Energizer and Rayovac which generally sell for less.

Suppliers such as P&G and Gillette had been under considerable pressure from the continuing consolidation in the retail industry due to the ongoing growth of Wal-Mart and industry mergers at that time, such as Sears and Kmart. About 17% of P&G's $51 billion in 2005 revenues and 13% of Gillette's $9 billion annual revenue came from sales to Wal-Mart. Moreover, the sales of both Gillette and P&G to Wal-Mart had grown much faster than sales to other retailers. The new company, P&G believed, would have more negotiating leverage with retailers for shelf space and in determining selling prices, as well as with its own suppliers, such as advertisers and media companies. The broad geographic presence of P&G was expected to facilitate the marketing of such products as

CASE STUDY 1.2   *(cont'd)*

razors and batteries in huge developing markets, such as China and India. Cumulative cost cutting was expected to reach $16 billion, including layoffs of about 4% of the new company's workforce of 140,000. Such cost reductions were to be realized by integrating Gillette's deodorant products into P&G's structure as quickly as possible. Other Gillette product lines, such as the razor and battery businesses, were to remain intact.

P&G's corporate culture was often described as conservative, with a "promote-from-within" philosophy. While Gillette's CEO was to become vice chairman of the new company, the role of other senior Gillette managers was less clear in view of the perception that P&G is laden with highly talented top management. To obtain regulatory approval, Gillette agreed to divest its Rembrandt toothpaste and its Right Guard deodorant businesses, while P&G agreed to divest its Crest toothbrush business.

The Gillette acquisition illustrates the difficulty in evaluating the success or failure of mergers and acquisitions for acquiring company shareholders. Assessing the true impact of the Gillette acquisition remains elusive, even after five years. Though the acquisition represented a substantial expansion of P&G's product offering and geographic presence, the ability to isolate the specific impact of a single event (i.e., an acquisition) becomes clouded by the introduction of other major and often uncontrollable events (e.g., the 2008–2009 recession) and their lingering effects. While revenue and margin improvement have been below expectations, Gillette has bolstered P&G's competitive position in the fast-growing

Brazilian and Indian markets, thereby boosting the firm's longer-term growth potential, and has strengthened its operations in Europe and the United States. Thus, in this ever-changing world, it will become increasingly difficult with each passing year to identify the portion of revenue growth and margin improvement attributable to the Gillette acquisition and that due to other factors.

Discussion Questions

1. Is this deal a merger or a consolidation from a legal standpoint? Explain your answer.
2. Is this a horizontal or vertical merger? What is the significance of this distinction from a regulatory perspective? Explain your answer.
3. What are the motives for the deal? Discuss the logic underlying each motive you identify.
4. Immediately following the announcement, P&G's share price dropped by 2% and Gillette's share price rose by 13%. Explain why this may have happened.
5. P&G announced that it would be buying back $18 billion to $22 billion of its stock over the 18 months following the closing of the transaction. Much of the cash required to repurchase these shares required significant new borrowing by the new company. Explain what P&G is trying to achieve in buying back its own stock. Explain how the incremental borrowing may help or hurt P&G in the long run.

Answers to these questions are found in the Online Instructor's Manual available to instructors using this book.

Regulatory Considerations

Character is doing the right thing when no one is looking. —**J. C. Watts**

INSIDE M&A: THE LIMITATIONS OF REGULATION AND THE LEHMAN BROTHERS MELTDOWN

Even though regulations are needed to promote appropriate business practices, they may also produce a false sense of security. Regulatory agencies often are coopted by those they are supposed to be regulating due to an inherent conflict of interest. The objectivity of regulators can be skewed by the prospect of future employment in the firms they are responsible for policing. No matter how extensive, regulations are likely to fail to achieve their intended purpose in the absence of effective regulators.

Consider the 2008 credit crisis that shook Wall Street to its core. On September 15, 2008, Lehman Brothers Holdings announced that it had filed for bankruptcy. Lehman's board of directors decided to opt for court protection after attempts to find a buyer for the entire firm collapsed. With assets of $639 billion and liabilities of $613 billion, Lehman is the largest bankruptcy in history in terms of assets. The next biggest bankruptcies were WorldCom and Enron, with $126 billion and $81 billion in assets, respectively.

In the months leading up to Lehman's demise, there were widespread suspicions that the book value of the firm's assets far exceeded their true market value and that a revaluation of these assets was needed. However, little was known about Lehman's aggressive use of repurchase agreements or repos. Repos are widely used short-term financing contracts in which one party agrees to sell securities to another party (a so-called counterparty), with the obligation to buy them back, often the next day. Because the transactions are so short-term in nature, the securities serving as collateral continue to be shown on the borrower's balance sheet. The cash received as a result of the repo would increase the borrower's cash balances and be offset by a liability reflecting the obligation to repay the loan. Consequently, the borrower's balance sheet would not change as a result of the short-term loan.

In early 2010, a report compiled by bank examiners indicated how Lehman manipulated its financial statements, with government regulators, the investing public, credit rating agencies, and Lehman's board of directors being totally unaware of the accounting tricks. Lehman departed from common accounting practices by booking these repos as sales of securities rather than as short-term loans. By treating the repos as a sale of securities (rather than a loan),

51

the securities serving as collateral for the repo were removed from the books, and the proceeds generated by the repo were booked as if they had been used to pay off an equivalent amount of liabilities. The resulting reduction in liabilities gave the appearance that the firm was less leveraged than it actually was despite the firm's continuing obligation to buy back the securities. Since the repos were undertaken just prior to the end of a calendar quarter, their financial statements looked better than they actually were.[1]

The firm's outside auditing firm, Ernst & Young, was aware of the moves but continued to pronounce the firm's financial statements to be in accordance with generally accepted accounting principles. The Securities and Exchange Commission (SEC), the recipient of the firm's annual and quarterly financial statements, failed to catch the ruse. In the weeks before the firm's demise, the Federal Reserve had embedded its own experts within the firm and they too failed to uncover Lehman's accounting chicanery. Passed in 2002, Sarbanes-Oxley, which had been billed as legislation that would prevent any recurrence of Enron-style accounting tricks, also failed to prevent Lehman from "cooking its books." As required by the Sarbanes-Oxley Act, Richard S. Fuld, Lehman's chief executive at the time, certified the accuracy of the firm's financial statements submitted to the SEC.

When all else failed, market forces uncovered the charade. It was the much maligned "short-seller" who uncovered Lehman's scam. Although not understanding the extent to which the firm's financial statements were inaccurate, speculators borrowed Lehman stock and sold it in anticipation of buying it back at a lower price and returning it to its original owners. In doing so, they effectively forced the long-insolvent firm into bankruptcy. Without short-sellers forcing the issue, it is unclear how long Lehman could have continued the sham.

CHAPTER OVERVIEW

This chapter focuses on the key elements of selected federal and state regulations and their implications for M&As. Considerable time is devoted to discussing the prenotification and disclosure requirements of current legislation and how decisions are made within the key securities law and antitrust enforcement agencies. Furthermore, the implications of the Dodd-Frank bill passed in 2010 are discussed in detail. This chapter provides only an overview of the labyrinth of environmental, labor, benefit, and foreign (for cross-border transactions) laws that affect M&As. Table 2.1 provides a summary of applicable legislation.

A review of this chapter is available (including practice questions) in the file folder entitled Student Study Guide on the companion site to this book (*www.elsevierdirect.com/companions/9780123854858*). The companion site also contains a Learning Interactions Library, enabling students to test their knowledge of this chapter in a "real-time" environment.

---

[1] Lehman temporarily moved as much as $50 billion of assets off its books in the months leading up to its financial collapse in September 2008. The firm used a version of a repo called repo 105 in which the firm paid $105 or more for each $100 they received if the counterparty agreed to hold onto the securities for several weeks. Because the counterparty agreed to hold the securities for a matter of weeks rather than the customary day or two, Lehman booked the transaction as a sale. It was viewed as a sale because Lehman did not own the securities for an extended period. While such transactions may be valid if done for sound business practices, the intent in this instance was to engage in massive deception.

TABLE 2.1   Laws Affecting Mergers and Acquisitions

Law	Intent
FEDERAL SECURITIES LAWS	
Securities Act (1933)	Prevents the public offering of securities without a registration statement; defines minimum data requirements and noncompliance penalties
Securities Exchange Act (1934)	Established the Securities and Exchange Commission (SEC) to regulate securities trading. Empowers SEC to revoke registration of a security if issuer is in violation of any provision of the 1934 act
Section 13	Defines content and frequency of, as well as events triggering, SEC filings
Section 14	Defines disclosure requirements for proxy solicitation
Section 16(a)	Defines what insider trading is and who is an insider
Section 16(b)	Defines investor rights with respect to insider trading
Williams Act (1968)	Regulates tender offers
Section 13D	Defines disclosure requirements
Sarbanes-Oxley Act (2002)	Initiates extensive reform of regulations governing financial disclosure, governance, auditing standards, analyst reports, and insider trading
FEDERAL ANTITRUST LAWS	
Sherman Act (1890)	Made "restraint of trade" illegal. Establishes criminal penalties for behaviors that unreasonably limit competition
Section 1	Makes mergers creating monopolies or "unreasonable" market control illegal
Section 2	Applies to firms already dominant in their served markets to prevent them from "unfairly" restraining trade
Clayton Act (1914)	Outlawed certain practices not prohibited by the Sherman Act, such as price discrimination, exclusive contracts, and tie-in contracts, and created civil penalties for illegally restraining trade. Also established law governing mergers
Celler-Kefauver Act of 1950	Amended Clayton Act to cover asset as well as stock purchases
Federal Trade Commission Act (1914)	Established a federal antitrust enforcement agency; made it illegal to engage in deceptive business practices
Hart-Scott-Rodino Antitrust Improvement Act (1976)	Requires a waiting period before a transaction can be completed and sets regulatory data submission requirements
Title I	Defines what must be filed
Title II	Defines who must file and when
Title III	Enables state attorneys general to file triple damage suits on behalf of injured parties
OTHER LEGISLATION AFFECTING M&AS	
Dodd-Frank Wall Street Reform and Consumer Protection Act (2010)	Reforms executive compensation; introduces new hedge/private equity fund registration requirements; provides oversight for credit rating agencies; increases Federal Reserve and SEC regulatory authority; gives government authority to liquidate systemically risky firms; and enables government regulation of consumer financial products

Continued

I. THE MERGERS AND ACQUISITIONS ENVIRONMENT

TABLE 2.1　Laws Affecting Mergers and Acquisitions—Cont'd

Law	Intent
State Antitakeover Laws	Define conditions under which a change in corporate ownership can take place; may differ by state
State Antitrust Laws	Similar to federal antitrust laws; states may sue to block mergers, even if the mergers are not challenged by federal regulators
Exon-Florio Amendment to the Defense Protection Act of 1950	Establishes authority of the Committee on Foreign Investment in the United States (CFIUS) to review the impact of foreign direct investment (including M&As) on national security
U.S. Foreign Corrupt Practices Act	Prohibits payments to foreign government officials in exchange for obtaining new business or retaining existing contracts
Regulation FD (Fair Disclosure)	All material disclosures of nonpublic information made by publicly traded corporations must be disclosed to the general public
Industry Specific Regulations	Banking, communications, railroads, defense, insurance, and public utilities
Environmental Laws (federal and state)	Define disclosure requirements
Labor and Benefit Laws (federal and state)	Define disclosure requirements
Applicable Foreign Laws	Cross-border transactions subject to jurisdictions of countries in which the bidder and target firms have operations

FEDERAL SECURITIES LAWS

Whenever either the acquiring or the target company is publicly traded, the two are subject to the substantial reporting requirements of the current federal securities laws. Passed in the early 1930s, these laws were a direct result of the loss of confidence in the securities markets following the crash of the stock market in 1929.[2]

Securities Act of 1933

Originally administered by the FTC, this legislation requires that all securities offered to the public must be registered with the government. Registration requires, but does not guarantee, that the facts represented in the registration statement and prospectus are accurate. Also, the law makes providing inaccurate or misleading statements in the sale of securities to the public punishable with a fine, imprisonment, or both. The registration process requires

[2] See the Securities and Exchange Commission website (*www.sec.gov*) and Coffee, Seligman, and Sale (2008) for a comprehensive discussion of federal securities laws.

a description of the company's properties and business, a description of the securities, information about management, and financial statements certified by public accountants.

Securities Exchange Act of 1934

The Securities Exchange Act extends disclosure requirements stipulated under the Securities Act of 1933 covering new issues to include securities already trading on the national exchanges. The Act also established the Securities and Exchange Commission, the purpose of which is to protect investors from illegal financial practices or fraud by requiring full and accurate financial disclosure by firms offering stocks, bonds, and other securities to the public. In 1964, coverage was expanded to include securities traded on the Over-the-Counter (OTC) market. The act also covers proxy solicitations (i.e., mailings to shareholders requesting their vote on a particular issue) by a company or shareholders. For a more detailed discussion of proxy solicitations, see Chapter 3.

The 2010 Dodd-Frank Wall Street Reform and Consumer Protections Act, discussed in more detail later in this chapter, strengthened the SEC's enforcement powers by allowing the commission to impose financial penalties against any person, rather than just regulated entities. Furthermore, it expands federal court jurisdiction by allowing the SEC to bring enforcement actions against persons, even when the violations take place outside of the United States.

Reporting Requirements

Companies that are required to file annual and other periodic reports with the SEC are those with assets of more than $10 million and whose securities are held by more than 500 shareholders. Even if both parties are privately owned, an M&A transaction is subject to federal securities laws if a portion of the purchase price is going to be financed by an initial public offering of stock or a public offering of debt by the acquiring firm.

Section 13: Periodic Reports

Form 10K, or the annual report, summarizes and documents the firm's financial activities during the preceding year. The four key financial statements that must be included are the income statement, the balance sheet, the statement of retained earnings, and the statement of cash flows. Form 10K also includes a relatively detailed description of the business, the markets served, major events and their impact on the business, key competitors, and competitive market conditions. Form 10Q is a highly succinct quarterly update of such information.

If an acquisition or divestiture is deemed significant, Form 8K must be submitted to the SEC within 15 days of the event. Form 8K describes the assets acquired or disposed, the type and amount of consideration (i.e., payment) given or received, and the identity of the person (or persons) for whom the assets were acquired. In an acquisition, Form 8K also must identify who is providing the funds used to finance the purchase and the financial statements of the acquired business. Acquisitions and divestitures are usually deemed significant if the equity interest in the acquired assets or the amount paid or received exceeds 10% of the total book value of the assets of the registrant and its subsidiaries.

Section 14: Proxy Solicitations

Where proxy contests for control of corporate management are involved, the act requires the names and interests of all participants in the proxy contest. Proxy materials must be filed in advance of their distribution to ensure that they are in compliance with disclosure requirements. If the transaction involves shareholder approval of either the acquirer or the target firm, any materials distributed to shareholders must conform to the SEC's rules for proxy materials.

Insider Trading Regulations

Insider trading involves individuals who buy or sell securities based on knowledge that is not available to the general public. Historically, insider trading has been covered under the Securities and Exchange Act of 1934. Section 16(a) of the act defines "insiders" as corporate officers, directors, and any person owning 10% or more of any class of securities of a company. The Sarbanes-Oxley Act (SOA) of 2002 amended Section 16(a) of the 1934 act by requiring that insiders disclose any changes in ownership within two business days of the transaction, with the SEC posting the filing on the Internet within one business day after the filing is received.

The SEC is responsible for investigating insider trading. Regulation 10b-5, issued by the SEC, prohibits the commission of fraud in relation to securities transactions. In addition, Regulation 14e-3 prohibits trading securities in connection with a tender offer based on information that is not available to the general public. Individuals found guilty of engaging in insider trading may be subject to substantial penalties and forfeiture of any profits.[3]

The Williams Act: Regulation of Tender Offers

Passed in 1968, the Williams Act consists of a series of amendments to the Securities Act of 1934. The Williams Act was intended to protect target firm shareholders from lightning-fast takeovers in which they would not have enough information or time to assess adequately the value of an acquirer's offer. This protection was achieved by requiring more disclosure by the bidding company, establishing a minimum period during which a tender offer must remain open, and authorizing targets to sue bidding firms.

The disclosure requirements of the Williams Act apply to anyone, including the target, asking shareholders to accept or reject a takeover bid. The major sections of the Williams Act as they affect M&As are in Sections 13(D) and 14(D). The Williams Act requirements apply to all types of tender offers, including those negotiated with the target firm (i.e., negotiated or friendly tender offers), those undertaken by a firm to repurchase its own stock (i.e., self-tender offers), and those that are unwanted by the target firm (i.e., hostile tender offers).[4]

---

[3] According to the Insider Trading Sanctions Act of 1984, those convicted of engaging in insider trading are required to give back their illegal profits. They also are required to pay a penalty three times the magnitude of such profits. A 1988 U.S. Supreme Court ruling gives investors the right to claim damages from a firm that falsely denied it was involved in negotiations that subsequently resulted in a merger.

[4] The Williams Act is vague as to what constitutes a tender offer so as not to construe any purchase by one firm of another in the open market as a tender offer. The courts have ruled that a tender offer generally is characterized by a bidder announcing publicly its desire to purchase a substantial block of another firm's stock with the intention of ultimately gaining control or if a substantial portion of another firm's shares are acquired in the open market or through a privately negotiated block purchase of the firm's shares.

Sections 13(D) and 13(G): Ownership Disclosure Requirements

Section 13(D) of the Williams Act is intended to regulate "substantial share" or large acquisitions and serves to provide an early warning for a target company's shareholders and management of a pending bid. Any person or firm acquiring 5% or more of the stock of a public corporation must file a Schedule 13(D) with the SEC within 10 days of reaching that percentage threshold.

The permitted reporting delay allows for potential abuse of the disclosure requirement. In late 2010, activist hedge fund investor William Ackman and real estate company Vornado Realty Trust surprised Wall Street when they disclosed that they had acquired nearly 27% of mega-retailer J.C. Penney's outstanding shares. Once the investors exceeded the 5% reporting threshold, they rapidly accumulated tens of millions of shares during the ensuing ten-day period, driving J.C. Penney's share price up to 45%.

The information required by Schedule 13(D) includes the identity of the acquirer, his or her occupation and associations, sources of financing, and the purpose of the acquisition. If the purpose of buying the stock is to take control of the target firm, the acquirer must reveal its business plan for the target firm. The plans could include the breakup of the firm, suspending dividends, a recapitalization of the firm, or the intention to merge it with another firm. Otherwise, the purchaser of the stock could indicate that the accumulation was for investment purposes only.

Under Section 13(G), any stock accumulated by related parties, such as affiliates, brokers, or investment bankers working on behalf of the person or firm, are counted toward the 5% threshold. This is intended to prevent an acquirer from avoiding filing by accumulating more than 5% of the target's stock through a series of related parties. Institutional investors, such as registered brokers and dealers, banks, and insurance companies, can file a Schedule 13(G)—a shortened version of Schedule 13(D)—if the securities were acquired in the normal course of business. Case Study 2.1 illustrates how derivatives may have been used to circumvent SEC disclosure requirements.

CASE STUDY 2.1
A Federal Judge Reprimands Hedge Funds in Their Effort to Control CSX

Investors who are seeking to influence a firm's decision making often try to accumulate voting shares. Such investors may attempt to acquire shares without attracting the attention of other investors, who could bid up the price of the shares and make it increasingly expensive to accumulate the stock. To avoid alerting other investors, certain derivative contracts called "cash settled equity swaps" allegedly have been used to gain access indirectly to a firm's voting shares without having to satisfy 13(D) prenotification requirements.

Using an investment bank as a counterparty, a hedge fund could enter into a contract obligating the investment bank to give dividends paid on and any appreciation of the stock of a target firm to the hedge fund in exchange for an interest payment made by the hedge fund. The amount of the interest paid is usually based on the London Interbank Offer Rate (LIBOR)

CASE STUDY 2.1   *(cont'd)*

plus a markup reflecting the perceived risk of the underlying stock. The investment bank usually hedges or defrays risk associated with its obligation to the hedge fund by buying stock in the target firm. In some equity swaps, the hedge fund has the right to purchase the underlying shares from the counterparty.

Upon taking possession of the shares, the hedge fund discloses ownership of the shares. Since the hedge fund does not actually own the shares prior to taking possession, it does not have the right to vote the shares and technically does not have to disclose ownership under Section 13(D). However, to gain significant influence, the hedge fund can choose to take possession of these shares immediately prior to a board election or a proxy contest. To avoid the appearance of collusion, many investment banks have refused to deliver shares under these circumstances or to vote in proxy contests.

In an effort to surprise a firm's board, several hedge funds may act together by each buying up to 4.9% of the voting shares of a target firm, without signing any agreement to act in concert. Each fund could also enter into an equity swap for up to 4.9% of the target firm's shares. The funds together could effectively gain control of a combined 19.6% of the firm's stock (i.e., each fund would own 4.9% of the target firm's shares and have the right to acquire via an equity swap another 4.9%). The hedge funds could subsequently vote their shares in the same way with neither fund disclosing their ownership stakes until immediately before an election.

The Children's Investment Fund (TCI), a large European hedge fund, acquired 4.1% of the voting shares of CSX, the third largest U.S. railroad, in 2007. In April 2008, TCI submitted its own candidates for the CSX board of directors' election to be held in June of that year. CSX accused TCI and another hedge fund, 3G Capital Partners, of violating disclosure laws by coordinating their accumulation of CSX shares through cash-financed equity swap agreements. The two hedge funds owned outright a combined 8.1% of CSX stock and had access to an additional 11.5% of CSX shares through cash-settled equity swaps.

In June 2008, the SEC ruled in favor of the hedge funds, arguing that cash-settled equity swaps do not convey voting rights to the swap party over shares acquired by its counterparty to hedge their equity swaps. Shortly after the SEC's ruling, a federal judge concluded that the two hedge funds had deliberately avoided the intent of the disclosure laws. However, the federal ruling came after the board election and could not reverse the results in which TCI was able to elect a number of directors to the CSX board. Nevertheless, the ruling by the federal court established a strong precedent limiting future efforts to use equity swaps as a means of circumventing federal disclosure requirements.

Discussion Questions

1. Do you agree or disagree with the federal court's ruling? Defend your position.
2. What criteria might have been used to prove collusion between TCI and 3G in the absence of signed agreements to coordinate their efforts to accumulate CSX voting shares?

Section 14(D): Rules Governing the Tender Offer Process

Although Section 14(D) of the Williams Act relates to public tender offers only, it applies to acquisitions of any size. The 5% notification threshold also applies.

Obligations of the acquirer. An acquiring firm must disclose its intentions, business plans, and any agreements between the acquirer and the target firm in a Schedule 14(D)-1. This schedule is called a *tender offer statement*. The commencement date of the tender offer is defined as the date on which the tender offer is published, advertised, or submitted to the target. Schedule 14(D)-1 must contain the identity of the target company and the type of securities involved; the identity of the person, partnership, syndicate, or corporation that is filing; and any past contracts between the bidder and the target company. The schedule also must include the source of the funds used to finance the tender offer, its purpose, and any other information material to the transaction.

Obligations of the target firm. The management of the target company cannot advise its shareholders how to respond to a tender offer until it has filed a Schedule 14(D)-9 with the SEC within ten days after the tender offer's commencement date. This schedule is called a *tender offer solicitation/recommendation statement*. Target management may only tell its shareholders to defer responding to the tender offer until it has completed its consideration of the offer.

Shareholder rights: 14(D)-4 through 14(D)-7. The tender offer must be left open for a minimum of 20 trading days. The acquiring firm must accept all shares that are tendered during this period. The firm making the tender offer may get an extension of the 20-day period if it believes that there is a better chance of getting the shares it needs. The firm must purchase the shares tendered at the offer price, at least on a pro rata basis, unless the firm does not receive the total number of shares it requested under the tender offer. The tender offer also may be contingent on attaining the approval of the Department of Justice (DoJ) and the Federal Trade Commission (FTC). Shareholders have the right to withdraw shares that they may have tendered previously as long as the tender offer remains open. The law also requires that when a new bid for the target is made from another party, the target firm's shareholders must have an additional ten days to consider the bid.

The "best price" rule: 14(D)-10. The "best price" rule requires that all shareholders be paid the same price in a tender offer. Consequently, if a bidder increases what it is offering to pay for the remaining target firm shares, it must pay the higher price to those who have already tendered their shares. As a result of SEC rule changes on October 18, 2006, the best price rule was clarified to underscore that compensation for services that might be paid to shareholders should not be included as part of the price paid for their shares. The rule changes also protect special compensation arrangements that are approved by independent members of a firm's board and specifically exclude compensation in the form of severance and other employee benefits. The rule changes make it clear that the best price rule applies only to the consideration (i.e., cash, securities, or both) offered and paid for securities tendered by shareholders.

Acquirers routinely initiate two-tiered tender offers, in which target shareholders receive a higher price if they tender their shares in the first tier (round) than do those submitting their shares in the second tier. The best price rule in these situations simply means that all shareholders tendering their shares in the first tier must be paid the price offered for those shares in the first tier, and those tendering shares in the second tier are paid the price offered for second-tier shares.

The Sarbanes-Oxley Act of 2002

The Sarbanes-Oxley Act was signed in the wake of the egregious scandals at such corporate giants as Enron, MCI WorldCom, ImClone, Qwest, Adelphia, and Tyco. The act has implications ranging from financial disclosure to auditing practices to corporate governance. Section 302 of the act requires quarterly certification of financial statements and disclosure controls and procedures for CEOs and CFOs. Section 404 requires most public companies to certify annually that their internal control system is operating successfully. The legislation, in concert with new listing requirements at public stock exchanges, requires a greater number of directors on the board who do not work for the company (i.e., so-called independent directors). In addition, the act requires board audit committees to have at least one financial expert, while the full committee must review financial statements every quarter after the CEO and chief financial officer certify them.

The SOA offers the potential for a reduction in investor risk of losses due to fraud and theft.[5] The act also provides for an increase in reliable financial reporting, transparency or visibility in a firm's financial statements, and greater accountability. However, the egregious practices of some financial services firms (e.g., AIG, Bear Stearns, and Lehman Brothers) in recent years cast doubt on how effective the SOA has been in achieving its transparency and accountability objectives.

The costs associated with implementing SOA have been substantial. As noted in a number of studies (see Chapter 13), there is growing evidence that the monitoring costs imposed by Sarbanes-Oxley have been a factor in many small firms going private since the introduction of the legislation. However, shareholders of large firms that are required to overhaul their existing governance systems under Sarbanes-Oxley may in some cases benefit significantly.[6] In an effort to reduce some of the negative effects of Sarbanes-Oxley, the SEC allowed foreign firms to avoid having to comply with the reporting requirements of the Act. As of June 15, 2007, foreign firms whose shares traded on U.S. exchanges constituted less than 5% of the global trading volume of such shares during the previous 12 months are no longer subject to the Sarbanes-Oxley Act. This regulatory change affects about 360 of the 1,200 foreign firms listed on U.S. stock exchanges.[7]

New York Stock Exchange listing requirements far exceed the auditor independence requirements of the Sarbanes-Oxley Act. Companies must have board audit committees consisting of at least three independent directors and a written charter describing their responsibilities in detail. Moreover, the majority of all board members must be independent, and nonmanagement directors must meet periodically without management. Board compensation and nominating committees must consist of independent directors. Shareholders must be able to vote on all stock option plans.

The SOA also created a quasi-public oversight agency, the Public Company Accounting Oversight Board (PCAOB). The PCAOB is charged with registering auditors, defining specific

---

[5] Coates (2007)

[6] Chaochharia and Grinstein (2007) conclude that large firms that are the least compliant with the rules around the announcement dates of certain rule implementations are more likely to display significantly positive abnormal financial returns. In contrast, small firms that are less compliant earn negative abnormal returns.

[7] Grant, 2007

processes and procedures for compliance audits, quality control, and enforcing compliance with specific SOA mandates.

ANTITRUST LAWS

Federal antitrust laws exist to prevent individual corporations from assuming so much market power that they can limit their output and raise prices without concern for any significant competitor reaction. The DoJ and the FTC have the primary responsibility for enforcing federal antitrust laws. The FTC was established in the Federal Trade Commission Act of 1914 with the specific purpose of enforcing antitrust laws such as the Sherman, Clayton, and Federal Trade Commission Acts.[8]

Generally speaking, national laws do not affect firms outside their domestic political boundaries. There are two important exceptions: antitrust laws and laws applying to the bribery of foreign government officials.[9] Outside the United States, antitrust regulation laws are described as competitiveness laws, and are intended to minimize or eliminate anticompetitive behavior. As illustrated in Case Study 2.6, the European Union antitrust regulators were able to thwart the attempted takeover of Honeywell by General Electric—two U.S. corporations with operations in the European Union. Remarkably, this occurred following the approval of the proposed takeover by U.S. antitrust authorities. The other exception, the Foreign Corrupt Practices Act, is discussed later in this chapter.

The Sherman Act

Passed in 1890, the Sherman Act makes illegal all contracts, combinations, and conspiracies that "unreasonably" restrain trade. Examples include agreements to fix prices, rig bids, allocate customers among competitors, or monopolize any part of interstate commerce. Section I of the Sherman Act prohibits new business combinations that result in monopolies or in a significant concentration of pricing power in a single firm. Section II applies to firms that already are dominant in their targeted markets. The act applies to all transactions and businesses involved in interstate commerce or, if the activities are local, all transactions and business "affecting" interstate commerce. Most states have comparable statutes prohibiting monopolistic conduct, price-fixing agreements, and other acts in restraint of trade having strictly local impact.

The Clayton Act

Passed in 1914 to strengthen the Sherman Act, the Clayton Act was created to outlaw certain practices not prohibited by the Sherman Act and so help government stop a monopoly before it developed. Section 5 of the act made price discrimination between customers illegal,

---

[8] For excellent discussions of antitrust law, see the DoJ (*www.usdoj.gov*) and FTC (*www.ftc.gov*) websites and the American Bar Association (2006).

[9] Truitt, 2006

unless it could be justified by cost savings associated with bulk purchases. Tying of contracts—in which a firm refuses to sell certain important products to a customer unless the customer agrees to buy other products from the firm—also was prohibited. Section 7 prohibits one company from buying the stock of another company if their combination results in reduced competition within the industry. Interlocking directorates also were made illegal when the directors were on the boards of competing firms.

Unlike the Sherman Act, which contains criminal penalties, the Clayton Act is a civil statute. The Clayton Act allows private parties that were injured by the antitrust violation to sue in federal court for three times their actual damages. State attorneys general also may bring civil suits. If the plaintiff wins, the costs must be borne by the party that violated the prevailing antitrust law, in addition to the criminal penalties imposed under the Sherman Act.

Acquirers soon learned how to circumvent the original statutes of the Clayton Act of 1914, which applied to the purchase of stock. They simply would acquire the assets, rather than the stock, of a target firm. In the Celler-Kefauver Act of 1950, the Clayton Act was amended to give the FTC the power to prohibit assets as well as stock purchases.

The Federal Trade Commission Act of 1914

This act created the FTC, consisting of five full-time commissioners appointed by the president for a seven-year term. The commissioners are supported by a staff of economists, lawyers, and accountants to assist in the enforcement of antitrust laws.

The Hart-Scott-Rodino Antitrust Improvements Act of 1976

Acquisitions involving companies of a certain size cannot be completed until certain information is supplied to the federal government and a specified waiting period has elapsed. The premerger notification allows the FTC and the DoJ sufficient time to challenge acquisitions believed to be anticompetitive before they are completed. Once the merger has taken place, it is often difficult to break it up. Table 2.2 provides a summary of prenotification filing requirements.

Title I: What Must Be Filed?

Title I of the Act gives the DoJ the power to request internal corporate records if it suspects potential antitrust violations. The information requirements include background information on the "ultimate parent entity" of the acquiring and target parents, a description of the transaction, and all background studies relating to the transaction. The ultimate parent entity is the corporation at the top of the chain of ownership if the actual buyer is a subsidiary.

Title II: Who Must File and When?

Title II addresses the conditions under which filings must take place. As of January 28, 2010, to comply with the size of transaction test, transactions in which the buyer purchases voting securities or assets valued in excess of $63.4 million must be reported under the HSR Act. However, according to the size of person test, transactions valued at less than

TABLE 2.2 Regulatory Prenotification Filing Requirements

	Williams Act	Hart-Scott-Rodino Act
Required filing	1. Schedule 13(D) within 10 days of acquiring 5% stock ownership in another firm 2. Ownership includes stock held by affiliates or agents of the bidder 3. Schedule 14(D)-1 for tender offers 4. Disclosure required even if 5% accumulation not followed by a tender offer	HSR filing is necessary when[a]: 1. Size of transaction test: The buyer purchases assets or securities >$63.4 million or 2. Size of person test[b]: Buyer or seller has annual sales or assets ≥$126.9 million and other party has sales or assets ≥$12.7 million Thresholds in (1) and (2) are adjusted annually by the increase in gross domestic product.
File with whom	Schedule 13(D) 1. 6 copies to SEC 2. 1 copy via registered mail to target's executive office 3. 1 copy via registered mail to each public exchange on which target stock traded Schedule 14(D)-1 1. 10 copies to SEC 2. 1 copy hand-delivered to target's executive offices 3. 1 copy hand-delivered to other bidders 4. 1 copy mailed to each public exchange on which target stock traded (each exchange also must be phoned)	1. Premerger Notification Office of the Federal Trade Commission 2. Director of Operations of the DoJ Antitrust Division
Time period	1. Tender offers must stay open a minimum of 20 business days 2. Begins on date of publication, advertisement, or submission of materials to target 3. Unless the tender offer has been closed, shareholders may withdraw tendered shares up to 60 days after the initial offer	1. Review/waiting period: 30 days 2. Target must file within 15 days of bidder's filing 3. Period begins for all cash offers when bidder files; for cash/stock bids, period begins when both bidder and target have filed 4. Regulators can request 20-day extension

[a] Note that these are the thresholds as of January 28, 2010.
[b] The "size of person" test measures the size of the "ultimate parent entity" of the buyer and seller. The ultimate parent entity is the entity that controls the buyer and seller and is not itself controlled by anyone else. Transactions valued at more than $252.7 million are reportable even if the size of person test is not met.

$63.4 million may still require filing if the acquirer or the target firm has annual net sales or total assets of at least $126.9 million and the other party has annual net sales or total assets of at least $12.7 million. These thresholds are adjusted upward by the annual rate of increase in gross domestic product.

Bidding firms must execute an HSR filing at the same time they make an offer to a target firm. The target firm also is required to file within 15 days following the bidder's filing. Filings consist of information on the operations of the two companies and their financial statements. The waiting period begins when both the acquirer and the target have filed. Either the FTC or the DoJ may request a 20-day extension of the waiting period for transactions involving securities and 10 days for cash tender offers. If the acquiring firm believes that there is little likelihood of anticompetitive effects, it can request early termination. In practice, only about one-fifth of total transactions annually require HSR filings; of these only about 4% are challenged by the regulators.[10]

If the regulatory authorities suspect anticompetitive effects, they will file a lawsuit to obtain a court injunction to prevent completion of the proposed transaction. Although it is rare for either the bidder or the target to contest the lawsuit, because of the expense involved, and even rarer for the government to lose, it does happen.[11] If fully litigated, a government lawsuit can result in substantial legal expenses as well as a significant cost in management time. Even if the FTC's lawsuit is overturned, the benefits of the merger often have disappeared by the time the lawsuit has been decided. Potential customers and suppliers are less likely to sign lengthy contracts with the target firm during the period of trial. New investment in the target is likely to be limited, and employees and communities where the target's operations are located would be subject to uncertainty. For these reasons, both regulators and acquirers often seek to avoid litigation.

How Does HSR Affect State Antitrust Regulators?

Title III expands the powers of state attorneys general to initiate triple-damage suits on behalf of individuals in their states injured by violations of the antitrust laws. This additional authority gives states the incentive to file such suits to increase state revenues.

Procedural Rules

When the DoJ files an antitrust suit, it is adjudicated in the federal court system. When the FTC initiates the action, it is heard before an administrative law judge at the FTC. The results of the hearing are subject to review by the commissioners of the FTC. Criminal actions are reserved for the DoJ, which may seek fines or imprisonment for violators. Individuals and companies also may file antitrust lawsuits. The FTC reviews complaints that have been recommended by its staff and approved by the commission. The commission as a whole then votes whether to accept or reject the hearing examiner's findings. The decision of the commission can then be appealed in the federal circuit courts. Under current guidelines, the FTC is committed to making a final decision on a complaint within 13 months.

As an alternative to litigation, a company may seek to negotiate a voluntary settlement of its differences with the FTC. Such settlements usually are negotiated during the review process and are called *consent decrees*. The FTC then files a complaint in the federal court along with the proposed consent decree. The federal court judge routinely approves the consent decree.

---

[10] In 2007, there were 2,201 HSR filings with the FTC (about one-fifth of total transactions) compared to 1,768 in 2006 (Barnett, 2008). Of these, about 4% typically are challenged and about 2% require second requests for information (Lindell, 2006). This represents a continuation of a longer-term trend. About 97% of the 37,701 M&A deals filed with the FTC between 1991 and 2004 were approved without further scrutiny (*Business Week*, 2008).

[11] Regulators filed a suit on February 27, 2004, to block Oracle's $26 per share hostile bid for PeopleSoft on antitrust grounds. On September 9, 2004, a U.S. District Court judge denied a request by U.S. antitrust authorities that he issue an injunction against the deal, arguing that the government failed to prove that large businesses can turn to only three suppliers (i.e., Oracle, PeopleSoft, and SAP) for business applications software.

The Consent Decree

A typical *consent decree* requires the merging parties to divest overlapping businesses or restrict anticompetitive practices. If a potential acquisition is likely to be challenged by the regulatory authorities, an acquirer may seek to negotiate a consent decree in advance of consummating the deal. In the absence of a consent decree, a buyer often requires that an agreement of purchase and sale include a provision that allows the acquirer to back out of the transaction if it is challenged by the FTC or the DoJ on antitrust grounds. There is evidence that consent decrees to limit potential increases in business pricing power following a merger have proven successful by creating viable competitors.[12] Case Study 2.2 illustrates how regulators may use consent decrees to maintain competitive markets.

CASE STUDY 2.2
Justice Department Requires Verizon Wireless to Sell Assets before Approving Alltel Merger

In late 2008, Verizon Wireless, a joint venture between Verizon Communications and Vodafone Group, agreed to sell certain assets to obtain Justice Department approval of their $28 billion deal with Alltel Corporation. The merger created the nation's largest wireless carrier. Under the terms of the deal, Verizon Wireless planned to buy Alltel for $5.9 billion and assume $22.2 billion in debt. The combined firms would have about 78 million subscribers nationwide.

The consent decree was required following a lawsuit initiated by the Justice Department and seven states to block the merger. Fearing the merger would limit competition, drive up consumer prices, and potentially reduce the quality of service, the settlement would require Verizon Wireless to divest assets in 100 markets in 22 states.

The proposed merger had raised concerns about what the impact would be on competition in the mainly rural, inland markets that Alltel served. Consumer advocates had argued that Verizon would not have the same incentive as Alltel to strike roaming agreements with other regional and small wireless carriers that would rely on it to provide service in areas where they lacked operations. By requiring the sale of assets, the Department of Justice hoped to ensure continued competition in the affected markets.

Discussion Questions
1. Do you believe requiring consent decrees that oblige the acquiring firm to dispose of certain target company assets is an abuse of government power? Why or why not?
2. What alternative actions could the government take to limit market power resulting from a business combination?

[12] In a report evaluating the results of 35 divestiture orders entered between 1990 and 1994, the FTC concluded that the use of consent decrees to limit market power resulting from a business combination has proven to be successful by creating viable competitors (Federal Trade Commission, 1999b). The study found that the divestiture is likely to be more successful if it is made to a firm in a related business rather than a new entrant into the business.

Antitrust Merger Guidelines for Horizontal Mergers

Understanding an industry begins with understanding its market structure. *Market structure* may be defined in terms of the number of firms in an industry; their concentration, cost, demand, and technological conditions; and ease of entry and exit. Intended to clarify the provisions of the Sherman and Clayton Acts, the DoJ issued largely quantitative guidelines in 1968 indicating the types of M&As the government would oppose. The guidelines were presented in terms of specific market share percentages and concentration ratios.

Concentration ratios were defined in terms of the market shares of the industry's top four or eight firms. Because of their rigidity, the guidelines have been revised to reflect the role of both quantitative and qualitative data. Qualitative data include factors such as the enhanced efficiency that might result from a combination of firms, the financial viability of potential merger candidates, and the ability of U.S. firms to compete globally.

In 1992, both the FTC and the DoJ announced a new set of guidelines indicating that they would challenge mergers creating or enhancing market power, even if there are measurable efficiency benefits. *Market power* is defined as a situation in which the combined firms will be able to profitably maintain prices above competitive levels for a significant period. M&As that do not increase market power are acceptable. The 1992 guidelines were revised in 1997 to reflect the regulatory authorities' willingness to recognize that improvements in efficiency over the long term could more than offset the effects of increases in market power. Consequently, a combination of firms that enhances market power would be acceptable to the regulatory authorities if it could be shown that the increase in efficiency resulting from the combination more than offsets the increase in market power. Numerous recent empirical studies support this conclusion (see Chapter 1).

In general, horizontal mergers—those between current or potential competitors—are most likely to be challenged by regulators. Vertical mergers—those involving customer-supplier relationships—are considered much less likely to result in anticompetitive effects, unless they deprive other market participants of access to an important resource.

On August 19, 2010, the 1992 guidelines were updated to further clarify how the antitrust authorities determine what constitutes anticompetitive business combinations. In general, regulators consider targeted customers and the potential for price discrimination, market definition, market share and concentration, so-called unilateral effects, coordinated effects, ease of entry, realized efficiencies, potential for business failure, and partial acquisitions. These are considered next.

Targeted Customers and the Potential for Price Discrimination

Price discrimination occurs when sellers can improve profits by raising prices to some targeted customers but not to others. For such discrimination to exist, there must be evidence that certain customers are charged higher prices even though the cost of doing business with them is no higher than selling to other customers who are charged lower prices. Furthermore, customers charged higher prices must have few alternative sources of supply.

Market Definition

Markets are defined by regulators solely in terms of the customers' ability and willingness to substitute one product for another in response to a price increase. Markets are defined by applying a hypothetical monopolist test to identify a set of products that are reasonably substitutable for the products sold by one of the merging firms. The market may be geographically defined with scope limited by such factors as transportation costs, tariff and nontariff barriers, exchange rate volatility, and so on.

Market Share and Concentration

Regulators, which are subject to data availability, calculate market shares for all firms currently producing products in the relevant market. The number of firms in the market and their respective market shares determine market concentration. Such ratios measure how much of the total output of an industry is produced by the n largest firms in the industry. The shortcomings of this approach include the frequent inability to define accurately what constitutes an industry, the failure to reflect ease of entry or exit, foreign competition, regional competition, and the distribution of firm size.

In an effort to account for the distribution of firm size in an industry, the FTC measures concentration using the *Herfindahl-Hirschman Index* (HHI), which is calculated by summing the squares of the market shares for each firm competing in the market. For example, a market consisting of five firms with market shares of 30, 25, 20, 15, and 10%, respectively, would have an HHI of 2,250 ($30^2 + 25^2 + 20^2 + 15^2 + 10^2$). Note that an industry consisting of five competitors with market shares of 70, 10, 5, 5, and 5%, respectively, will have a much higher HHI score of 5,075, because the process of squaring the market shares gives the greatest weight to the firm with the largest market shares.

The HHI ranges from 10,000 for an almost pure monopoly to approximately 0 in the case of a highly competitive market. The index gives more weight to the market shares of larger firms to reflect their relatively greater pricing power. The FTC developed a scoring system, shown in Figure 2.1, that is used as one factor in determining whether the FTC will challenge a proposed merger or acquisition.

Unilateral Effects

Competition within a market may be lessened significantly merely by the elimination of a firm through a merger or acquisition. For example, a merger between two firms selling differentiated products may reduce competition by enabling the merged firms to profit by unilaterally raising the price of one or both products above the premerger level. Furthermore, a merger between two competing sellers prevents buyers from negotiating lower prices by

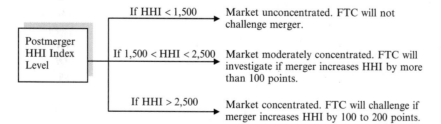

FIGURE 2.1   FTC actions at various market share concentration levels. HHI, Herfindahl-Hirschman Index. Source: *FTC Merger Guidelines (www.ftc.gov).*

playing one seller against the other. Finally, in markets involving undifferentiated products, a firm having merged with a large competitor may restrict output in order to raise prices.

Coordinated Effects

After a merger that diminishes competition, a firm may be better able to coordinate its output and pricing decisions with the remaining firms in the industry. Such actions could include a simple understanding of what a firm would or would not do under certain circumstances. For example, if the firm with dominant market share were to reduce output, others might follow suit with the implied intent of raising product prices.

Ease of Entry

The ease of entry into the market by new competitors is considered a very important factor in determining if a proposed business combination is anticompetitive. Ease of entry is defined as entry that would be timely, likely to occur, and sufficient to counter the competitive effects of a combination of firms that temporarily increases market concentration. Barriers to entry—such as proprietary technology or knowledge, patents, government regulations, exclusive ownership of natural resources, or huge investment requirements—can limit the number of new competitors and the pace at which they enter a market.

Efficiencies

Increases in efficiency that result from a merger or acquisition can enhance the combined firms' ability to compete and thus result in lower prices, improved quality, better service, or innovation. However, efficiencies are difficult to measure and verify because they will be realized only after the merger has taken place. An example of verifiable efficiency improvements would be a reduction in the average fixed cost of production due to economies of scale.

Alternative to Imminent Failure

Regulators also take into account the likelihood that a firm will fail if it is not allowed to merge with another firm. The regulators must weigh the potential cost of the failing firm, such as a loss of jobs, against any potential increase in market power that might result from the merger of the two firms. In 2008, U.S. antitrust regulators approved the merger of XM Radio and Sirius Radio, the U.S. satellite radio industry's only competitors, virtually creating a monopoly in that industry.[13]

Partial Acquisitions

Regulators may also review acquisitions of minority positions involving competing firms if it is determined that the partial acquisition results in the effective control of the target firm. For example, a partial acquisition can lessen competition by giving the acquirer the ability to influence the competitive conduct of the target firm in that the acquirer may have the right to appoint members of the board of directors. Furthermore, the minority investment also

---

[13] The authorities recognized that neither firm would be financially viable if compelled to remain independent. The firms also argued successfully that other forms of media, such as conventional radio, represented viable competition, since they were free and XM and Sirius offered paid subscription services.

may blunt competition if the acquirer gains access to non–publicly available competitive information.

Antitrust Guidelines for Vertical Mergers

The guidelines described for horizontal mergers also apply to vertical mergers between customers and suppliers. Vertical mergers may become a concern if an acquisition by a supplier of a customer prevents the supplier's competitors from having access to the customer. Alternatively, the acquisition by a customer of a supplier can become a concern if it prevents the customer's competitors from having access to the supplier.

Antitrust Guidelines for Collaborative Efforts

In 2000, the FTC and DoJ jointly issued new guidelines intended to explain how the agencies analyze antitrust issues with respect to collaborative efforts. *Collaborative effort* is the term used by the regulatory agencies to describe a range of horizontal agreements among competitors, such as joint ventures, strategic alliances, and other competitor agreements. Note that competitors include both actual and potential ones.

Regulators evaluate the impact on market share and the potential increase in market power resulting from a proposed collaborative effort. The agencies may be willing to overlook any temporary increase in market power if the participants can demonstrate that future increases in efficiency and innovation will result in lower overall selling prices or increased product quality in the long term. In general, the agencies are less likely to find a collaborative effort to be anticompetitive if (1) the participants have continued to compete through separate, independent operations or through participation in other collaborative efforts; (2) the financial interest in the effort by each participant is relatively small; (3) each participant's ability to control the effort is limited; (4) effective safeguards prevent information sharing; and (5) the duration of the collaborative effort is short.

The regulatory agencies have established two "safety zones" that provide collaborating firms with a degree of certainty that the agencies will not challenge them. First, the market shares of the collaborative effort and the participants collectively account for no more than 20% of the served market. Second, for R&D activities, there must be at least three or more independently controlled research efforts in addition to those of the collaborative effort.

Market share considerations overwhelmed other factors when the Justice Department threatened to file suit if Google and Yahoo! proceeded to implement an advertising alliance in late 2008 (see Case Study 2.3).

DODD-FRANK WALL STREET REFORM AND CONSUMER PROTECTION ACT

Comprehensive in scope, the Dodd-Frank Act (the Act) substantially changed federal regulation of financial services firms, as well as some nonfinancial public companies. Generally speaking, the Act's objectives include restoring public confidence in the financial system and preventing future financial crises that threaten the viability of financial markets. The Act's

CASE STUDY 2.3
Google Thwarted in Proposed Advertising Deal with Chief Rival Yahoo!

A proposal that gave Yahoo! an alternative to selling itself to Microsoft was killed in the face of opposition by U.S. government antitrust regulators. The deal called for Google to place ads alongside some of Yahoo!'s search results. Google and Yahoo! would share in the revenues generated by this arrangement. The deal was supposed to bring Yahoo! $250 million to $450 million in incremental cash flow in the first full year of the agreement. The deal was especially important to Yahoo!, due to the continued erosion in the firm's profitability and share of the online search market.

The Justice Department argued that the alliance would have limited competition for online advertising, resulting in higher fees charged to online advertisers. The regulatory agency further alleged that the arrangement would make Yahoo! more reliant on Google's already superior search capability and reduce Yahoo!'s efforts to invest in its own online search business. The regulators feared this would limit innovation in the online search industry.

On November 6, 2008, Google and Yahoo! announced the cessation of efforts to implement an advertising alliance. Google expressed concern that continuing the effort would result in a protracted legal battle and risked damaging lucrative relationships with their advertising partners.

The Justice Department's threat to block the proposal is a sign that Google can expect increased scrutiny in the future. High-tech markets often lend themselves to becoming "natural monopolies" in markets in which special factors foster market dominance by a single firm. Examples include Intel's domination of the microchip business, as economies of scale create huge barriers to entry for new competitors; Microsoft's preeminent market share in PC operating systems and related application software, due to its large installed customer base; and Google's dominance of Internet search, resulting from its demonstrably superior online search capability.

Discussion Questions

1. In what way might the DoJ actions result in increased concentration in the online search business in the future?
2. What are the arguments for and against regulators permitting "natural monopolies"?

provisions range from giving shareholders a say on executive compensation to greater transparency in the derivatives markets to new powers granted to the Federal Deposit Insurance Corporation (FDIC) to liquidate financial firms whose failure would threaten the U.S. financial system (i.e., systemic risk).

While the implications of the legislation are far reaching, the focus in this book is on those aspects of the Act directly impacting corporate governance; the environment in which mergers, acquisitions, and other restructuring activities take place; and participants in the corporate restructuring process. The provisions of the Act that have the greatest impact on the subject matter addressed in this book are summarized in Table 2.3 according to the categories governance and executive compensation, systemic regulation and emergency

TABLE 2.3   Selected Dodd-Frank Act Provisions

Provision	Requirements
GOVERNANCE AND EXECUTIVE COMPENSATION[a]	
Say-on-Pay	In a nonbinding vote on the board, shareholders may vote on executive compensation packages every two or three years.
Say on Golden Parachutes	Proxy statements seeking shareholder approval of acquisitions, mergers, or sale of substantially all of the company's assets must disclose any agreements with executive officers of the target or acquiring firm with regard to present, deferred, or contingent compensation.
Institutional Investor Disclosure	Institutional managers (e.g., mutual funds, pension funds) must disclose their say on pay and on golden parachutes' voting records annually.
Clawbacks	Public companies are required to develop and disclose mechanisms for recovering incentive-based compensation paid during the three years prior to earnings restatements.
Proxy Access	SEC has authority to require U.S. public firms to include shareholder nominees submitted in proxy materials.
Broker Discretionary Voting	Public stock exchanges are required to prohibit brokers from voting shares without direction from owners in the election of directors, executive compensation, or any other significant matter as determined by the SEC.
Compensation Committee Independence	SEC to define rules requiring stock exchanges to prohibit listing any issuer that does not comply with independence requirements governing compensation committee members and consultants.
SYSTEMIC REGULATION AND EMERGENCY POWERS	
Financial Stability Oversight Council	To mitigate systemic risk, the Council, which consists of ten voting members and is chaired by the Secretary of the Treasury, monitors U.S. financial markets to identify domestic or foreign banks and some nonbank firms whose default or bankruptcy would risk the financial stability of the United States.
New Federal Reserve (Fed) Bank and Nonbank Holding Company Supervision Requirements	Bank and nonbank holding companies with consolidated assets exceeding $50 billion must • Submit plans for their rapid and orderly dissolution in the event of failure (i.e., living wills) • Provide periodic reports about the nature of their credit exposure • Limit their credit exposure to any unaffiliated company to 25% of its capital • Conduct semiannual "stress tests" to determine capital adequacy • Provide advance notice of intent to purchase voting shares in financial services firms
Limitations on Leverage	For bank holding companies whose consolidated assets exceed $50 billion, the Fed may require the firm to maintain a debt-to-equity ratio of no more than 15-to-1.
Limits on Size	The size of any single bank or nonbank cannot exceed 10% of deposits nationwide. The limitation does not apply to mergers involving troubled banks.
Capital Requirements	Bank capital requirements are to be left to the regulatory agencies and should reflect the perceived risk of bank or nonbank institutions.

Continued

TABLE 2.3　Selected Dodd-Frank Act Provisions—Cont'd

Provision	Requirements
Savings and Loan Regulations	Fed gains supervisory authority over all savings and loan holding companies and their subsidiaries.
Federal Deposit Insurance Corporation (FDIC)	The FDIC may guarantee obligations of solvent insured depository institutions if the Fed and the Systemic Risk Council determine that a liquidity event has occurred in the financial markets (i.e., investors cannot sell assets without incurring an unusual and significant loss).
Orderly Liquidation Authority	The FDIC may seize and liquidate a financial services firm whose failure threatens the financial stability of the United States to ensure the speedy disposition of the firm's assets and to ensure that losses are borne by shareholders and bondholders, while losses of public funds are limited.[b]

CAPITAL MARKETS

Provision	Requirements
Office of Credit Ratings	Proposes rules for internal controls, independence, transparency, and penalties for poor performance, making it easier for investors to sue for "unrealistic" ratings. Office to conduct annual audits of rating agencies.
Securitization	Issuers of asset-backed securities must retain an interest of at least 5% of any security sold to third parties.
Hedge and Private Equity Fund Registration	Advisers to private equity and hedge funds with $100 million or more in assets under management must register with the SEC as investment advisers; those with less than $100 million will be subject to state registration. Registered advisors to provide reports and be subject to periodic examinations.
Clearing and Trading of Over-the-Counter (OTC) Derivatives	Commodity Futures Trading Commission (CFTC) and SEC to mandate central clearing of certain OTC derivatives on a central exchange and the real-time public reporting of volume and pricing data, as well as the parties to the transaction.

FINANCIAL INSTITUTIONS

Provision	Requirements
Volcker Rule	Prohibits insured depository institutions and their holding companies from buying and selling securities with their own money (so-called proprietary trading) or sponsoring or investing in hedge funds or private equity funds. Underwriting and market-making activities are exempt. Proprietary trading may occur outside the United States as long as the bank does not own or control the entity in which it is investing. Sponsoring private funds is defined as serving as a general partner or in some way gaining control of such funds. Banks may sponsor such funds if they provide trust or investment advisory services and if the bank's name is not used in marketing the fund.
Consumer Financial Protection Bureau	Creates an agency to write rules governing all financial institutions offering consumer financial products, including banks, mortgage lenders, and credit card companies, as well as pay day lenders. The authority will apply to banks and credit unions with assets over $10 billion and all mortgage-related businesses. While institutions with less than $10 billion will have to comply, they will be supervised by their current regulators.
Federal Insurance Office	Monitors all aspects of the insurance industry (other than health insurance and long-term care), coordinates international insurance matters, consults with states regarding insurance issues of national importance, and recommends insurers that should be treated as systemically important.

[a] *See Chapter 3 for more details.*
[b] *See Chapter 16 for more details.*

powers, capital markets (i.e., the ways businesses are financed), and financial institutions. These provisions are discussed in more detail in the chapters in which they are most applicable.

The full impact of the bill is not likely to be known for years, since many of the rules needed to implement the new regulatory powers have yet to be written by the regulators. However, certain things seem likely. The regulatory costs associated with operating large financial firms will escalate sharply, potentially impacting both the cost and availability of credit. With the growth of such firms likely to slow, large banks are more likely to be valued as regulated utilities rather than as growth stocks.

On the plus side, large banks may warrant higher valuation multiples if investors view them as less risky. Smaller community banks and credit unions (i.e., those with less than $10 billion in total assets) are less affected by the act, since they will avoid many of its provisions such as new capital requirements and FDIC assessments to help pay for the new legislation. While these smaller institutions will have to comply with the new consumer protection bureau's regulations, enforcement will remain with their current federal and state regulators, enabling these institutions to "shop" for the most favorable regulator.

Conglomerates with significant investments in financial institutions may choose to exit such businesses as compliance costs and the potential for slower earnings growth diminishes their attractiveness. Also, the Volcker rule, which restricts the ability of banks to invest alongside their borrowers, will limit banks as lenders and investors in LBOs, a common practice during the LBO boom that ended in 2007. The elimination of broker discretionary voting in such matters as executive compensation and board elections removes votes that senior management and directors often counted on in past proxy solicitations.

Increasing the ease with which credit rating agencies can be sued in addition to increasing bank capital requirements could limit the availability of credit and boost the cost of borrowing. The new law exposes the rating agencies to liability as experts if they allow ratings to be included in public documents for bond sales such as registration statements filed with the SEC. While this liability could be mitigated by no longer requiring such ratings in prospectuses, investors will still demand some means of evaluating credit risk or higher financial returns to compensate for the uncertainty associated with some investments.

Does the Dodd-Frank Act End Government Bailouts?

Not likely. Intended to provide an efficient method of liquidating firms deemed "too big to fail," the Orderly Liquidation Authority (OLA) in some ways enhances the government's ability to deal with such firms. The OLA establishes a payments priority that differs somewhat from Chapter 7 of the U.S. Bankruptcy Code. The new priority is intended to ensure that the brunt of losses in liquidation is borne by shareholders and creditors, not the taxpayer. If the government cannot recoup all taxpayer funds provided to the firm to fund the liquidation, it may enact a special assessment on other financial institutions regulated by the Federal Reserve.

Since it is similar to the current FDIC model for taking over and dismantling failing banks, the OLA is likely to perpetuate regulation through deal making. The FDIC commonly has liquidated failing banks by merging the bank with another financially healthy bank or has sold the assets to other investors, often with federal guarantees to pay for future losses on the acquired assets.[14] Such guarantees are equivalent to an infusion of taxpayer funds into the failing firm (i.e., a bailout). Moreover, by selling failing institutions to larger banks, which is usually the case, the OLA is making more banks larger and more interconnected and potentially "too big to fail." Finally, the OLA applies only to firms whose operations are entirely domestic, since there is currently no cross-border mechanism for resolving bank failures with operations in multiple countries. Consequently, none of the existing large multinational financial firms will be affected by the OLA.

As the receiver of the failing company, the OLA also allows for the FDIC to provide financial assistance to the firm to fund the receivership in exchange for a senior claim on the firm's assets. While the Act forbids the use of taxpayer monies to prevent the liquidation of any financial company, the government has demonstrated a willingness in times of crisis to stretch the law, as was done with the Toxic Asset Recovery Program (TARP) in 2008. Consequently, such funds may be used to sustain rather than wind down the firm. See Chapter 16 for more details on the OLA.

Finally, if the Fed and the Financial Stability Oversight Council concur, the FDIC can guarantee the liabilities of any solvent financial institution if they perceive a danger to the stability of the financial system. This authority gives these agencies wide latitude, since the criteria for implementing guarantees are highly subjective. The mere exercising of the OLA to dismantle an insolvent bank could negatively impact other banks as investors became concerned about the solvency of other financial institutions. This contagion could be used to justify government guarantees of the liabilities of these institutions.

Does the Dodd-Frank Act Address Systemic Risk Adequately?

Yes and no. It is doubtful that the Act discourages sufficiently individual firms from putting the system at risk. Since a failing firm posing systemic risk imposes costs on the financial markets well in excess of the costs it incurs, additional disincentives for assuming excessive risk need to exist—for example, paying in advance in proportion to the firm's contribution of risk to the system. The Act does not do this and threatens to make the situation worse by requiring other large financial firms to pay for the costs of liquidating the failing firms through a special FDIC assessment at a time when firms subject to the assessment are also likely to be experiencing financial duress.

The Act also fails to address huge systemically important segments of the financial markets. These include the implicit government guarantees of debt issued by the Federal National Mortgage Association (Fannie Mae) and Federal Home Loan Mortgage Corporation (Freddie Mac), which own more than one-half of all U.S. residential mortgages, including a large percentage of subprime mortgages. Other systemically important markets not covered by the Act include the sale and repurchase agreements (repo) market, whose failure was at the center of the Lehman bankruptcy and the potential for runs on money market funds, which, following the Lehman bankruptcy, helped bring financial markets to a standstill.

[14] For example, in 2008, the FDIC agreed to pay for any losses incurred by JPMorgan Chase of up to $30 billion to induce the bank to buy the failing investment bank Bear Stearns.

STATE REGULATIONS AFFECTING MERGERS AND ACQUISITIONS

Numerous regulations affecting takeovers exist at the state level. The regulations often differ from one state to another, making compliance with all applicable regulations a challenge. State regulations often are a result of special interests that appeal to state legislators to establish a particular type of antitakeover statute to make it more difficult to complete unfriendly takeover attempts. Such appeals usually are made in the context of an attempt to save jobs in the state.

State Antitakeover Laws

With almost one-half of U.S. corporations incorporated in Delaware, Delaware corporate law has a substantial influence on publicly traded corporations. Delaware corporate law generally defers to the judgment of business managers and board directors in accordance with the "business judgment rule," except in change of control situations. In takeover situations, managers are subject to an *enhanced business judgment* test. This requires a target board to show that there are reasonable grounds to believe that a danger to corporate viability exists and that the adoption of certain defensive measures is reasonable. While Delaware law is the norm for many companies, firms incorporated in other states often are subject to corporate law that may differ significantly from Delaware law. What follows is a discussion of commonalities across states.[15]

States regulate corporate charters. *Corporate charters* define the powers of the firm and the rights and responsibilities of its shareholders, boards of directors, and managers. However, states are not allowed to pass any laws that impose restrictions on interstate commerce or that conflict in any way with federal laws regulating interstate commerce. State laws affecting M&As tend to apply only to corporations incorporated in the state or that conduct a substantial amount of their business within the state.

These laws often contain *fair price provisions*, requiring that all target shareholders of a successful tender offer receive the same price as those tendering their shares. In a specific attempt to prevent highly leveraged transactions, such as leveraged buyouts, some state laws include *business combination provisions*, which may specifically rule out the sale of the target's assets for a specific period. By precluding such actions, these provisions limit LBOs from using the proceeds of asset sales to reduce indebtedness.

Other common characteristics of state antitakeover laws include cash-out and share control provisions. *Cash-out provisions* require a bidder whose purchases of stock exceed a stipulated amount to buy the remainder of the target stock on the same terms granted those shareholders whose stock was purchased at an earlier date. By forcing the acquiring firm to purchase 100% of the stock, potential bidders lacking substantial financial resources effectively are eliminated from bidding on the target. *Share control provisions* require that a bidder obtain prior approval from stockholders holding large blocks of target stock once the bidder's purchases of stock exceed some threshold level. The latter provision can be

---

[15] For an excellent discussion of the state of antitakeover law in the various states, see Barzuza, 2009.

particularly troublesome to an acquiring company when the holders of the large blocks of stock tend to support target management.

State Antitrust Laws

As part of the Hart-Scott-Rodino Act of 1976, the states were granted increased antitrust power. State laws are often similar to federal laws. Under federal law, states have the right to sue to block mergers, even if the DoJ or FTC does not challenge them.

State Securities Laws

State blue sky laws are designed to protect individuals from investing in fraudulent security offerings. State restrictions can be more onerous than federal ones. An issuer seeking exemption from federal registration will not be exempt from all relevant registration requirements until a state-by-state exemption has been received from all of the states in which the issuer and offerees reside.

NATIONAL SECURITY-RELATED RESTRICTIONS ON DIRECT FOREIGN INVESTMENT IN THE UNITED STATES

While in existence for more than 50 years, the Committee on Foreign Investment in the United States (CFIUS) made the headlines in early 2006 when Dubai Ports Worldwide proposed to acquire control of certain U.S. port terminal operations. The subsequent political firestorm catapulted what had previously been a relatively obscure committee into the public limelight. CFIUS operates under the authority granted by Congress in the Exon-Florio amendment (Section 721 of the Defense Production Act of 1950). CFIUS includes representatives from an amalgam of government departments and agencies with diverse expertise to ensure that all national security issues are identified and considered in the review of foreign acquisitions of U.S. businesses.

The president can block the acquisition of a U.S. corporation based on recommendations made by CFIUS under certain conditions. These conditions include the existence of credible evidence that the foreign entity exercising control might take action that threatens national security and that existing laws do not adequately protect national security if the transaction is permitted.[16]

Concerns expressed by CFIUS about a proposed technology deal prevented U.S. networking company 3Com from being taken private by Bain Capital in early 2008. Under the terms of the transaction, a Chinese networking equipment company, Huaewi Technologies, would have obtained a 16.6% stake and board representation in 3Com. CFIUS became alarmed because of 3Com's sales of networking security software to the U.S. military.

---

[16] Following the public furor over the proposed Dubai Ports Worldwide deal, CFIUS was amended to cover investments involving critical infrastructure. The intention is to cover cross-border transactions involving energy, technology, shipping, and transportation. Some argue that it may also apply to large U.S. financial institutions in that they represent an important component of the U.S. monetary system.

THE U.S. FOREIGN CORRUPT PRACTICES ACT

The Foreign Corrupt Practices Act prohibits individuals, firms, and foreign subsidiaries of U.S. firms from paying anything of value to foreign government officials in exchange for obtaining new business or retaining existing contracts. Even though many nations have laws prohibiting bribery of public officials, enforcement tends to be lax. Of the 38 countries that signed the 1997 Anti-Bribery Convention of the Organization for Economic Cooperation and Development, more than one-half of the signatories have little or no enforcement mechanisms for preventing the bribery of foreign officials, according to a 2010 study by Transparency International. Three of the world's fastest-growing economies—China, India, and Russia—have not yet signed the agreement.

The U.S. law permits "facilitation payments" to foreign government officials if relatively small amounts of money are required to expedite goods through foreign custom inspections or to gain approval for exports. Such payments are considered legal according to U.S. law and the laws of countries in which such payments are considered routine.[17]

FAIR DISCLOSURE (REGULATION FD)

The U.S. Securities and Exchange Commission adopted this regulation on August 15, 2000, to address concerns about the selective release of information by publicly traded firms. The rule aims to promote full and fair disclosure. Regulation FD requires that a publicly traded firm that discloses material nonpublic information to certain parties must release that information to the general public. Such parties could include stock analysts or holders of the firm's securities who may well trade on the basis of the information.

Rather than less information about stock prices provided by managers concerned about litigation, there are indications that there has been an increase in voluntary disclosure following the adoption of the Regulation FD. In theory, an increase in the availability of such information should reduce earnings' "surprises" and lower stock price volatility. However, studies provide conflicting results, with one study reporting an increase in share price volatility and another showing no change following the implementation of Regulation FD.[18] Investors may view the reliability of such information as problematic.

Consistent with the trend toward increased voluntary disclosure of information, the fraction of U.S. acquirers disclosing synergy estimates when announcing a deal has increased from 7% in 1995 to 27% of total transactions in 2008, with much of the increase coming since the introduction of Regulation FD. A public disclosure of synergy can help the acquirer to communicate the potential value of the deal to those investors lacking the same level of information available to the firm's board and management. Deals in which synergies are disclosed tend to be larger than average (i.e., potentially more complex), are more likely to

---

[17] Truitt, 2006

[18] All studies show an increase in voluntary disclosure by firms (e.g., Heflin et al., 2003; Bailey et al., 2003; and Dutordoir et al., 2010). However, Bailey et al. (2003) report an increase in the variation of analysts' forecasts but no change in the volatility of share prices following the introduction of Regulation FD. In contrast, Heflin et al. (2003) finds no change in the variation of analysts' forecasts but a decrease in share price volatility.

involve equity whose value depends on the future earnings of the combined acquiring and target firms, and take longer to complete, which introduces additional uncertainty. Disclosing synergies expected from a deal is associated with an increase in average announcement period abnormal returns of 2.6%.[19]

REGULATED INDUSTRIES

In addition to the DoJ and the FTC, a variety of other agencies monitor activities (including M&As) in certain industries, such as commercial banking, railroads, defense, and cable TV.

Banking

According to the Bank Merger Act of 1966, any bank merger not challenged by the attorney general within 30 days of its approval by the pertinent regulatory agency cannot be challenged under the Clayton Antitrust Act. Currently, three agencies review banking mergers. Which agency has authority depends on the parties involved in the transaction. The Office of the Comptroller of the Currency has responsibility for transactions in which the acquirer is a national bank. The Federal Deposit Insurance Corporation oversees mergers where the acquiring bank or the bank resulting from combining the acquirer and target will be a federally insured, state-chartered bank that operates outside the Federal Reserve System. The third agency is the Board of Governors of the Federal Reserve System (the Fed). It has the authority to regulate mergers in which the acquirer or the resulting bank will be a state bank that is also a member of the Federal Reserve System. Although all three agencies conduct their own review, they consider reviews undertaken by the DoJ in their decision-making process.

The regulatory landscape for acquiring so-called thrift institutions changed significantly in 2010. The Dodd-Frank legislation eliminated the Office of Thrift Supervision and transferred responsibility for regulating savings and loan associations, credit unions, and savings banks (collectively referred to as thrift institutions) to other regulators. Specifically, the Fed will supervise savings and loan holding companies and their subsidiaries; the FDIC will gain supervisory authority of all state savings banks; and the Office of the Comptroller of the Currency will supervise all federal savings banks.

M&A transactions involving financial institutions resulting in substantial additional leverage or in increased industry concentration will also come under the scrutiny of the Financial Stability Oversight Council created by the Dodd-Frank Act to monitor so-called systemic risk. The Council is empowered, among other things, to limit bank holding companies with $50 billion or more in assets or a nonbank financial company that is regulated by the Federal Reserve from merging with, acquiring, or consolidating with another firm. In extreme cases, the Council may require the holding company to divest certain assets if such company is deemed to constitute a threat to the financial stability of U.S. financial markets. Under the new legislation, the size of any single bank or nonbank cannot exceed 10% of deposits nationwide. However, this constraint may be relaxed for mergers involving failing banks.

[19] Dutordoir et al., May 17, 2010.

The impetus for much of this new regulation came from the rapidity with which financial markets gave way in 2008. In one instance the regulatory authorities chose to intervene, and in another instance they did not (i.e., Lehman Brothers—see the case study at the beginning of this chapter). In an effort to minimize damage to the financial markets, the Federal Reserve moved well beyond its traditional regulatory role when it engineered a merger between commercial bank J. P. Morgan Chase and failing investment bank Bear Stearns.

Communications

The federal agency charged with oversight defers to the DoJ and the FTC for antitrust enforcement. The Federal Communications Commission (FCC) is an independent U.S. government agency directly responsible to Congress. Established by the 1934 Communications Act, the FCC is charged with regulating interstate and international communication by radio, television, wire, satellite, and cable. The FCC is responsible for the enforcement of such legislation as the Telecommunications Act of 1996. This act is intended to promote competition and reduce regulation while promoting lower prices and higher-quality services.[20]

Railroads

The Surface Transportation Board (STB), the successor to the Interstate Commerce Commission (ICC), governs mergers of railroads. Under the ICC Termination Act of 1995, the STB employs five criteria to determine if a merger should be approved. These criteria include the impact of the proposed transaction on the adequacy of public transportation, the impact on the areas currently served by the carriers involved in the proposed transaction, and the burden of the total fixed charges resulting from completing the transaction. In addition, the interest of railroad employees is considered, as well as whether the transaction would have an adverse impact on competition among rail carriers in regions affected by the merger.

Defense

During the 1990s, the defense industry in the United States underwent substantial consolidation. This is consistent with the Department of Defense's (DoD) philosophy that it is preferable to have three or four highly viable defense contractors that could more effectively compete than a dozen weaker contractors. Although defense industry mergers are technically subject to current antitrust regulations, the DoJ and FTC have assumed a secondary role to the DoD. As noted previously, efforts by a foreign entity to acquire national security–related assets must be reviewed by the Council on Foreign Investment in the United States.

Other Regulated Industries

Historically, the insurance industry was regulated largely at the state level. Acquiring an insurance company normally requires the approval of state government and is subject to substantial financial disclosure by the acquiring company. Under the Dodd-Frank Act, the

---

[20] See the Federal Communications Commission website (*www.fcc.gov*).

Federal Insurance Office was created within the U.S. Treasury to monitor all nonhealthcare-related aspects of the insurance industry. As a "systemic" regulator, its approval will be required for all acquisitions of insurance companies whose size and interlocking business relationships could have repercussions on the U.S. financial system.

The acquisition of more than 10% of a U.S. airline's shares outstanding is subject to approval by the Federal Aviation Administration. Effective March 8, 2008, the 27-nation European Union and the United States agreed to reduce substantially restrictions on cross-border flights under the Open Skies Act.

Public utilities are highly regulated at the state level. Like insurance companies, their acquisition requires state government approval. In 2006, the federal government eliminated the 1935 Public Utility Holding Company Act, which limited consolidation among electric utilities unless in geographically contiguous areas. Proponents of the repeal argue that mergers would produce economies of scale, improve financial strength, and increase investment in the nation's aging electricity transmission grid.

ENVIRONMENTAL LAWS

Failure to comply adequately with environmental laws can result in enormous potential liabilities to all parties involved in a transaction. These laws require full disclosure of the existence of hazardous materials and the extent to which they are being released into the environment. Such laws include the Clean Water Act (1974), the Toxic Substances Control Act of 1978, the Resource Conservation and Recovery Act (1976), and the Comprehensive Environmental Response, Compensation, and Liability Act (Superfund) of 1980. Additional reporting requirements were imposed in 1986 with the passage of the Emergency Planning and Community Right to Know Act (EPCRA). In addition to EPCRA, several states also passed "right-to-know" laws, such as California's Proposition 65. The importance of state reporting laws has diminished because EPCRA is implemented by the states.

LABOR AND BENEFIT LAWS

A diligent buyer also must ensure that the target is in compliance with the labyrinth of labor and benefit laws. These laws govern such areas as employment discrimination, immigration law, sexual harassment, age discrimination, drug testing, and wage and hour laws. Labor and benefit laws include the Family Medical Leave Act, the Americans with Disabilities Act, and the Worker Adjustment and Retraining Notification Act (WARN). WARN governs notification before plant closings and requirements to retrain workers.

Employee benefit plans frequently represent one of the biggest areas of liability to a buyer. The greatest potential liabilities often are found in defined pension benefit plans, postretirement medical plans, life insurance benefits, and deferred compensation plans. Such liabilities arise when the reserve shown on the seller's balance sheet does not accurately indicate the true extent of the future liability. The potential liability from improperly structured benefit plans grows with each new round of legislation, starting with the passage of the Employee Retirement Income and Security Act of 1974. With it the laws affecting employee retirement and pensions were strengthened by additional legislation, including the Multi-Employer Pension Plan Amendments Act of 1980, the Retirement Equity Act of 1984, the Single Employer Pension Plan Amendments Act of 1986, the Tax Reform Act of 1986, and the Omnibus Budget Reconciliation Acts of 1987, 1989, 1990, and 1993. Buyers and sellers also must be aware of the Unemployment Compensation Act of 1992, the Retirement Protection Act of 1994, and Statements 87, 88, and 106 of the Financial Accounting Standards Board.[21]

The Pension Protection Act of 2006 places a potentially increasing burden on acquirers of targets with underfunded pension plans. The new legislation requires employers with defined benefit plans to make sufficient contributions to meet a 100% funding target and erase funding shortfalls over seven years. Furthermore, the legislation requires employers with so-called "at-risk" plans to accelerate contributions. At-risk plans are those whose pension fund assets cover less than 70% of future pension obligations.

CROSS-BORDER TRANSACTIONS

Transactions involving firms in different countries are complicated by having to deal with multiple regulatory jurisdictions in specific countries or regions such as the European Union. The number of antitrust regulatory authorities globally has grown to over 100 from 6 in the early 1990s.[22] More antitrust agencies mean more international scrutiny, potentially conflicting philosophies among regulators, and substantially longer delays in completing all types of business combinations.

The collapse of the General Electric and Honeywell transaction in 2001 underscores how much philosophical differences in the application of antitrust regulations can jeopardize major deals (see Case Study 2.6). The GE–Honeywell deal was under attack from the day it was announced in October 2000. Rival aerospace companies, including United Technologies, Rockwell, Lufthansa, Thales, and Rolls Royce, considered it inimical to their ability to compete. U.S. antitrust regulators focus on the impact of a proposed deal on customers; in contrast, EU antitrust regulators were more concerned about maintaining a level playing field for rivals in the industry. Reflecting this disparate thinking, U.S. antitrust regulators approved the transaction rapidly, concluding that it would have a salutary impact on customers. EU regulators refused to approve the transaction without GE making major concessions, which it was unwilling to do.

While the demise of the GE–Honeywell transaction reflects the risks of not properly coordinating antitrust regulatory transactions, the 2007 combination of information companies Thomson and Reuters highlights what happens when regulatory authorities are willing to work together. The transaction required approval from antitrust regulators in U.S., European, and Canadian agencies. Designing a deal that was acceptable to each country's regulator required extensive cooperation and coordination.

Antitrust law also can restrict the formation of other types of business combinations, such as joint ventures, when the resulting entity is viewed as limiting competition. Despite the potential for huge cost savings, regulators would not approve the creation of a mammoth JV between BHP Billiton and Rio Tinto in 2010. See Case Study 2.4.

[21] Sherman, 2006

[22] *New York Times*, 2001

CASE STUDY 2.4
BHP Billiton and Rio Tinto Blocked by Regulators in an International Iron Ore Joint Venture

The revival in demand for raw materials in many emerging economies fueled interest in takeovers and joint ventures in the global mining and energy sectors in 2009 and 2010. BHP Billiton (BHP) and Rio Tinto (Rio), two global mining powerhouses, had hoped to reap huge cost savings by combining their Australian iron ore mining operations when they announced their JV in mid-2009. However, after more than a year of regulatory review, BHP and Rio announced in late 2010 that they would withdraw their plans to form an iron ore JV corporation valued at $116 billion after regulators in a number of countries indicated that they would not approve the proposal due to antitrust concerns.

BHP and Rio, headquartered in Australia, are the world's largest producers of iron ore, an input critical to the production of steel. Together, these two firms control about one-third of the global iron ore output. The estimated annual synergies from combining the mining and distribution operations of the two firms were estimated to be $10 billion. The synergies would come from combining BHP's more productive mining capacity with Rio's more efficient distribution infrastructure, enabling both firms to eliminate duplicate staff and redundant overhead and enabling BHP to transport its ore to coastal ports more cheaply.

The proposal faced intense opposition from the outset from steel producers and antitrust regulators. The greatest opposition came from China, which argued that the combination would concentrate pricing power further in the hands of the top iron ore producers. China imports about 50 million tons of iron ore monthly, largely from Australia, due to its relatively close proximity.

The European Commission, the Australian Competition and Consumer Commission, the Japan Fair Trade Commission, the Korea Fair Trade Commission, and the German Federal Cartel Office all advised the two firms that their proposal would not be approved in its current form. While some regulators indicated that they would be willing to consider the JV if certain divestitures and other "remedies" were made to alleviate concerns about excessive pricing power, others such as Germany said that they would not approve the proposal under any circumstances.

Discussion Questions

1. A "remedy" to antitrust regulators is any measure that would limit the ability of parties in a business combination to achieve what is viewed as excessive market or pricing power. What remedies do you believe could have been put in place by the regulators that might have been acceptable to both Rio and BHP? Be specific.

2. Why do you believe that the antitrust regulators were successful in this instance but so unsuccessful limiting the powers of cartels such as the Organization of Petroleum Exporting Countries (OPEC), which currently controls more than 40% of the world's oil production?

SOME THINGS TO REMEMBER

The Securities Acts of 1933 and 1934 established the SEC and require that all securities offered to the public must be registered with the government. The Williams Act consists of a series of amendments to the 1934 Securities Exchange Act intended to provide target firm shareholders with sufficient information and time to adequately assess the value of an acquirer's offer. Federal antitrust laws exist to prevent individual corporations from assuming too much market power. Numerous state regulations affect M&As, such as state antitakeover and antitrust laws.

A number of industries also are subject to regulatory approval at the federal and state levels. Considerable effort must be made to ensure that a transaction is in full compliance with applicable environmental and employee benefit laws. Finally, gaining regulatory approval in cross-border transactions can be nightmarish because of the potential for the inconsistent application of antitrust laws, as well as differing reporting requirements, fee structures, and legal jurisdictions.

DISCUSSION QUESTIONS

2.1 What were the motivations for the Federal Securities Acts of 1933 and 1934?

2.2 What was the rationale for the Williams Act?

2.3 What factors do U.S. antitrust regulators consider before challenging a transaction?

2.4 What are the obligations of the acquirer and target firms according to the Williams Act?

2.5 Discuss the pros and cons of federal antitrust laws.

2.6 Why is premerger notification (HSR filing) required by U.S. antitrust regulatory authorities?

2.7 When is a person or firm required to submit a Schedule 13(D) to the SEC? What is the purpose of such a filing?

2.8 What is the rationale behind state antitakeover legislation?

2.9 Give examples of the types of actions that may be required by the parties to a proposed merger subject to a FTC consent decree.

2.10 How might the growth of the Internet affect the application of current antitrust laws?

2.11 Having received approval from the DoJ and the FTC, Ameritech and SBC Communications received permission from the FCC to combine to form the nation's largest local telephone company. The FCC gave its approval of the $74 billion transaction, subject to conditions requiring that the companies open their markets to rivals and enter new markets to compete with established local phone companies, in an effort to reduce the cost of local phone calls and give smaller communities access to appropriate phone service. SBC had considerable difficulty in complying with its agreement with the FCC. Between December 2000 and July 2001, SBC paid the U.S. government $38.5 million for failing to provide rivals with adequate access to its network. The government noted that SBC failed repeatedly to make available its network in a timely manner, meet installation deadlines, and notify competitors when their orders were filled. Comment on the fairness and effectiveness of using the imposition of heavy fines to promote government-imposed outcomes rather than free market determined outcomes.

2.12 In an effort to gain approval of their proposed merger from the FTC, top executives from Exxon Corporation and Mobil Corporation argued that they needed to merge because of the increasingly competitive world oil market. Falling oil prices during much of the late 1990s put a squeeze on oil industry profits. Moreover, giant state-owned oil companies pose a competitive threat because of their access to huge amounts of capital. To offset these factors, Exxon and Mobil argued that they had to combine to achieve substantial cost savings. Why were the Exxon and Mobil executives emphasizing efficiencies as a justification for this merger?

2.13 How important is properly defining the market segment in which the acquirer and target companies compete in determining the potential increase in market power if the two firms are permitted to combine? Explain your answer.

2.14 Comment on whether antitrust policy can be used as an effective means of encouraging innovation. Explain your answer.

2.15 The Sarbanes-Oxley Act has been very controversial. Discuss the arguments for and against the act. Which side do you find more convincing and why?

Answers to these Chapter Discussion Questions are available in the Online Instructor's Guide for instructors using this book.

CHAPTER BUSINESS CASES

CASE STUDY 2.5
Global Financial Exchanges Pose Regulatory Challenges

The year 2010 marked a turnaround for the NYSE Group, the world's largest stock and derivatives exchange measured by market capitalization. A product of the combination of the New York Stock Exchange and Euronext NV (the European exchange operator), the NYSE Group reversed the three-year slide in both its U.S. and European market share. Albeit modest, the improvement in market share was attributable largely to the decision to increase information technology spending rather than to any significant change in the regulatory environment. The key to unlocking the full potential of the international exchange remained the willingness of countries to harmonize the international regulatory environment for trading stocks and derivatives.

Valued at $11 billion, the mid-2007 merger created the first transatlantic stock and derivatives market. Organizationally, the NYSE Group operates as a holding company, with its U.S. and European operations run largely independently. The combined firms trade stocks and derivatives through the New York Stock Exchange, on the electronic Euronext Liffe Exchange in London, and on the stock exchanges in Paris, Lisbon, Brussels, and Amsterdam.

In recent years, most of the world's major exchanges have gone public and pursued acquisitions. Before this 2007 deal, the NYSE merged with electronic trading firm Archipelago Holdings, while NASDAQ Stock Market Inc. acquired the electronic trading unit of rival Instinet. This consolidation of exchanges within countries and between countries is being driven by declining trading fees, improving trading information technology, and relaxed cross-border restrictions on capital flows and in part by increased regulation in the United States. U.S. regulation, driven by Sarbanes-Oxley, contributed to the transfer

CASE STUDY 2.5 *(cont'd)*

of new listings (IPOs) overseas. The strategy chosen by U.S. exchanges for recapturing lost business is to follow these new listings overseas.

Larger companies that operate across multiple continents also promise to attract more investors to trading in specific stocks and derivatives contracts, which could lead to less expensive, faster, and easier trading. As exchange operators become larger, they can more easily cut operating and processing costs by eliminating redundant or overlapping staff and facilities and, in theory, pass the savings along to investors. Moreover, by attracting more buyers and sellers, the gap between prices at which investors are willing to buy and sell any given stock (i.e., the bid and ask prices) should narrow. The presence of more traders means more people are bidding to buy and sell any given stock. This results in prices that more accurately reflect the true underlying value of the security because of more competition. Furthermore, the cross-border mergers also should make it easier and cheaper for individual investors to buy and sell foreign shares. Finally, corporations now can sell their shares on several continents through a single exchange.

Before these benefits can be fully realized, numerous regulatory hurdles have to be overcome. Even if exchanges merge, they must still abide by local government rules when trading in the shares of a particular company, depending on where the company is listed. Generally, companies are not eager to list on multiple exchanges worldwide because that subjects them to many countries' securities regulations and a bookkeeping nightmare.

At the local level, little has changed in how markets are regulated. European companies list their shares on exchanges owned by the NYSE Group. These exchanges still are overseen by individual national regulators, which cooperate but are technically separate. In the United States, the Securities and Exchange Commission continues to oversee the NYSE but does not have a direct say over Europe, except in that it oversees the parent company, the NYSE Group, since it is headquartered in New York.

EU member states continue to set their own rules for clearing and settlement of trades. If the NYSE and Euronext are to achieve a more unified and seamless trading system, regulators must reach agreement on a common set of rules. Achieving this goal seems to remain well in the future. Consequently, it may be years before much of the anticipated synergies are realized.

Discussion Questions

1. What key challenges face regulators resulting from the merger of financial exchanges in different countries? How do you see these challenges being resolved?
2. In what way are these regulatory issues similar to or different from those confronting the SEC and state regulators and the European Union and individual country regulators?
3. Who should or could regulate global financial markets? Explain your answer.
4. In your opinion, would the merging of financial exchanges increase or decrease international financial stability?

Answers to these case study questions are found in the Online Instructor's Manual available to instructors using this book.

CASE STUDY 2.6
The Legacy of GE's Aborted Attempt to Merge with Honeywell

Many observers anticipated significant regulatory review because of the size of the transaction and the increase in concentration it would create in the markets served by the two firms. Most believed, however, that, after making some concessions to regulatory authorities, the transaction would be approved due to its perceived benefits. Although the pundits were indeed correct in noting that it would receive close scrutiny, they were completely caught off guard by divergent approaches taken by the U.S. and EU antitrust authorities. U.S regulators ruled that the merger should be approved because of its potential benefits to customers. In marked contrast, EU regulators ruled against the transaction based on its perceived negative impact on competitors.

Honeywell's avionics and engines unit would add significant strength to GE's jet engine business. The deal would add about 10 cents to General Electric's 2001 earnings and could eventually result in $1.5 billion in annual cost savings. The purchase also would enable GE to continue its shift away from manufacturing and into services, which already constituted 70% of its revenues in 2000.[23] The best fit was clearly in the combination of the two firms' aerospace businesses. Revenues from these two businesses alone would total $22 billion, combining Honeywell's strength in jet engines and cockpit avionics with GE's substantial business in larger jet engines. As the largest supplier in the aerospace industry, GE and Honeywell could offer airplane manufacturers "one-stop shopping" for everything from engines to complex software systems by cross-selling each other's products to their biggest customers.

Honeywell had been on the block for a number of months before the deal was consummated with GE. Its merger with Allied Signal had not been going well and contributed to deteriorating earnings and a much lower stock price. Honeywell's shares had declined in price by more than 40% since its acquisition of Allied Signal. While the euphoria surrounding the deal in late 2000 lingered into the early months of 2001, rumblings from the European regulators began to create an uneasy feeling among GE's and Honeywell's management.

Mario Monti, the European competition commissioner at that time, expressed concern about possible "conglomerate effects" or the total influence a combined GE and Honeywell would wield in the aircraft industry. He was referring to GE's perceived ability to expand its influence in the aerospace industry through service initiatives. General Electric's service offerings help to differentiate it from others at a time when the prices of many industrial parts are under pressure from increased competition, including low-cost manufacturers overseas. In a world in which manufactured products are becoming increasingly commodity-like, the true winners are those able to differentiate their product offerings. GE and Honeywell's European competitors complained to the European Union regulatory commission that GE's extensive services offering would give it entrée into many more points of contact among airplane manufacturers, from communications

---

[23] *BusinessWeek*, 2000b

CASE STUDY 2.6   (cont'd)

systems to the expanded line of spare parts GE would be able to supply. This so-called range effect or portfolio power is a relatively new legal doctrine that has not been tested in transactions of this size.[24]

On May 3, 2001, the U.S. Department of Justice approved the buyout after the companies agreed to sell Honeywell's helicopter engine unit and take other steps to protect competition. The U.S. regulatory authorities believed that the combined companies could sell more products to more customers and therefore could realize improved efficiencies, although it would not hold a dominant market share in any particular market. Thus, customers would benefit from GE's greater range of products and possibly lower prices, but they still could shop elsewhere if they chose. The U.S. regulators expressed little concern that the bundling of products and services could hurt customers, since buyers can choose from among a relative handful of viable suppliers.

In order to understand the European position, it is necessary to comprehend the nature of competition in the European Union. France, Germany, and Spain spent billions subsidizing their aerospace industry over the years. The GE–Honeywell deal has been attacked by their European rivals, from Rolls-Royce and Lufthansa to French avionics manufacturer Thales. Although the European Union imported much of its antitrust law from the United States, the antitrust law doctrine evolved in fundamentally different ways. In Europe, the main goal of antitrust law is to guarantee that all companies are able to compete on an equal playing field. The implication is that the European Union is just as concerned about how a transaction affects

rivals as it is about how it affects consumers. Complaints from competitors are taken more seriously in Europe, whereas in the United States it is the impact on consumers that constitutes the litmus test. Europeans accepted the legal concept of "portfolio power," which argues that a firm may achieve an unfair advantage over its competitors by bundling goods and services. Also, in Europe, the European Commission's Merger Task Force can prevent a merger without taking a company to court.

The EU authorities continued to balk at approving the transaction without major concessions from the participants—concessions that GE believed would render the deal unattractive. On June 15, 2001, GE submitted its final offer to the EU regulators in a last-ditch attempt to breathe life into the moribund deal. GE knew that if it walked away, it could continue as it had before the deal was struck, secure in the knowledge that its current portfolio of businesses offered substantial revenue growth or profit potential. Honeywell clearly would fuel such growth, but it made sense to GE's management and shareholders only if it would be allowed to realize potential synergies between the GE and Honeywell businesses.

GE said it was willing to divest Honeywell units with annual revenues of $2.2 billion, including regional jet engines, air-turbine starters, and other aerospace products. Anything more would jeopardize the rationale for the deal. Specifically, GE was unwilling to agree not to bundle (i.e., sell a package of components and services at a single price) its products and services when selling to customers. Another stumbling block was the GE

[24] Murray, 2001

CASE STUDY 2.6 *(cont'd)*

Capital Aviation Services unit, the airplane-financing arm of GE Capital. The EU Competition Commission argued that that this unit would use its influence as one of the world's largest purchasers of airplanes to pressure airplane manufacturers into using GE products. The commission seemed to ignore that GE had only an 8% share of the global airplane leasing market and would therefore seemingly lack the market power the commission believed it could exert.

On July 4, 2001, the European Union vetoed the GE purchase of Honeywell, marking the first time a proposed merger between two U.S. companies has been blocked solely by European regulators. Having received U.S. regulatory approval, GE could ignore the EU decision and proceed with the merger as long as it would be willing to forego sales in Europe. GE decided not to appeal the decision to the EU Court of First Instance (the second highest court in the European Union), knowing that it could take years to resolve the decision, and withdrew its offer to merge with Honeywell.

On December 15, 2005, a European court upheld the European regulator's decision to block the transaction, although the ruling partly vindicated GE's position. The European Court of First Instance said regulators were in error in assuming without sufficient evidence that a combined GE–Honeywell could crush competition in several markets. However, the court demonstrated that regulators would have to provide data to support either approval or rejection of mergers by ruling on July 18, 2006, that regulators erred in approving the combination of Sony BMG in 2004. In this instance, regulators failed to provide sufficient data to document their decision. These decisions affirm that the European Union needs strong economic justification to overrule cross-border deals. GE and Honeywell, in filing the suit, said that their appeal had been made to clarify European rules with an eye toward future deals, since they had no desire to resurrect the deal.

In the wake of these court rulings and in an effort to avoid similar situations in other geographic regions, coordination among antitrust regulatory authorities in different countries has improved. For example, in mid-2010, the U.S. Federal Trade Commission reached a consent decree with scientific instrument manufacturer Agilent in approving its acquisition of Varian, in which Agilent agreed to divest certain overlapping product lines. While both firms are based in California, each has extensive foreign operations, which necessitated gaining the approval of multiple regulators. Throughout the investigation, FTC staff coordinated enforcement efforts with the staffs of regulators in the European Union, Australia, and Japan. This cooperation was under the auspices of certain bilateral cooperation agreements, the OECD Recommendation on Cooperation among its members, and the European Union Best Practices on Cooperation in Merger Investigation protocol.

Discussion Questions

1. What are the important philosophical differences between U.S. and EU antitrust regulators? Explain the logic underlying these differences. To what extent are these differences influenced by political rather than economic considerations? Explain your answer.

2. This is the first time that a foreign regulatory body prevented a deal involving only U.S. firms from going through. What are the long-term implications, if any, of this precedent?

CASE STUDY 2.6 *(cont'd)*

3. What were the major stumbling blocks between GE and the EU regulators? Why do you think these were stumbling blocks? Do you think the EU regulators were justified in their position?

4. Do you think that competitors are using antitrust to their advantage? Explain your answer.

5. Do you think the EU regulators would have taken a different position if the deal had involved a less visible firm than General Electric? Explain your answer.

Answers to these case study questions are found in the Online Instructor's Manual available to instructors using this book.

The Corporate Takeover Market
Common Takeover Tactics, Antitakeover Defenses, and Corporate Governance

Treat a person as he is, and he will remain as he is. Treat him as he could be, and he will become what he should be. —**Jimmy Johnson**

INSIDE M&A: KRAFT SWEETENS ITS OFFER TO OVERCOME CADBURY'S RESISTANCE

Despite speculation that offers from U.S.-based candy company Hershey and the Italian confectioner Ferreiro would be forthcoming, Kraft's bid on January 19, 2010, was accepted unanimously by Cadbury's board of directors. Kraft, the world's second (after Nestlé) largest food manufacturer (after Nestlé) , raised its offer over its initial September 7, 2009, bid to $19.5 billion to win over the board of the world's second largest candy and chocolate maker. Kraft also assumed responsibility for $9.5 billion of Cadbury's debt.

Kraft's initial bid evoked a raucous response from Cadbury's chairman Roger Carr, who derided the offer that valued Cadbury at $16.7 billion as showing contempt for his firm's well-known brand, and dismissed the hostile bidder as a low-growth conglomerate. Immediately following the Kraft announcement, Cadbury's share price rose by 45% (7 percentage points more than the 38% premium implicit in the Kraft offer). The share prices of other food manufacturers also rose due to speculation that they could become takeover targets.

The ensuing four-month struggle between the two firms was reminiscent of the highly publicized takeover of U.S. icon Anheuser-Busch in 2008 by Belgian brewer InBev. The Kraft-Cadbury transaction stimulated substantial opposition from senior government ministers and trade unions over the move by a huge U.S. firm to take over a British company deemed to be a national treasure. However, like InBev's takeover of Anheuser-Busch, what started as a donnybrook ended on friendly terms, with the two sides reaching final agreement in a single weekend.

Determined to become a global food and candy giant, Kraft decided to bid for Cadbury after the U.K.-based firm spun off its Schweppes beverages business in the United States in 2008. The separation of Cadbury's beverage and confectionery units resulted in Cadbury becoming the world's largest pure confectionery firm following the spinoff. Confectionery companies tend to trade at a higher value, so adding the Cadbury's chocolate and gum business could enhance Kraft's attractiveness to competitors. However, this status was soon eclipsed by Mars's acquisition of Wrigley in 2008.

A takeover of Cadbury would help Kraft, the biggest food conglomerate in North America, to compete with its larger rival, Nestle. Cadbury would strengthen Kraft's market share in Britain and would open India, where Cadbury is among the most popular chocolate brands. It would also expand Kraft's gum business and give it a global distribution network. Nestle lacked a gum business and was struggling with declining sales as recession-plagued consumers turned away from its bottled water and ice cream products. Cadbury and Kraft fared relatively well during the 2008–2009 global recession, with Cadbury's confectionery business proving resilient despite price increases in the wake of increasing sugar prices. Kraft had benefited from rising sales of convenience foods because consumers ate more meals at home during the recession.

The differences in the composition of the initial and final Kraft bids reflected a series of crosscurrents. Irene Rosenfeld, Kraft CEO, not only had to contend with vituperative comments from Cadbury's board and senior management, but also was soundly criticized by major shareholders who feared Kraft would pay too much for Cadbury. Specifically, the firm's largest shareholder, Warren Buffett's Berkshire Hathaway with a 9.4% stake, expressed concern that the amount of new stock that would have to be issued to acquire Cadbury would dilute the ownership position of existing Kraft shareholders. In an effort to placate dissident Kraft shareholders while acceding to Cadbury's demand for an increase in the offer price, Ms. Rosenfeld increased the offer by 7% by increasing the cash portion of the purchase price.

The new bid consisted of $8.17 cash and 0.1874 new Kraft shares, compared to Kraft's original offer of $4.89 cash and 0.2589 new Kraft shares for each Cadbury share outstanding. The change in the composition of the offer price meant that Kraft would issue 265 million new shares compared with its original plan to issue 370 million. The change in the terms of the deal meant that Kraft would no longer have to get shareholder approval for the new share issue, since it was able to avoid the NYSE requirement that firms issuing shares totaling more than 20% of the number of shares currently outstanding must receive shareholder approval to do so.

CHAPTER OVERVIEW

The corporate takeover has been dramatized in Hollywood as motivated by excessive greed, reviled in the press as a job destroyer, hailed as a means of dislodging incompetent management, and often heralded by shareholders as a source of windfall gains. The reality is that corporate takeovers may be a little of all of these things. This chapter discusses the effectiveness of commonly used tactics to acquire a company and evaluates the effectiveness of takeover defenses.

The market in which such takeover tactics and defenses are employed is called the *corporate takeover market* (also known as the market for corporate control), which serves two important functions in a free market economy. First, it facilitates the allocation of resources to sectors in which they can be used most efficiently. Second, it serves as a mechanism for disciplining underperforming corporate managers. By replacing such managers through hostile takeover attempts or proxy fights, the corporate takeover market can help to promote good *corporate governance*, which in turn can improve corporate financial performance.[1]

What is "corporate governance"? The common definition is fairly straightforward: The term refers broadly to the rules and processes by which a business is controlled, regulated, or operated. There is, though, no universally accepted goal for corporate governance. Traditionally, the goal has been to protect shareholder rights. More recently, this has expanded to encompass additional corporate stakeholders, including customers, employees, the government, lenders, communities, regulators, and suppliers. For our discussion here, corporate governance is about leadership and accountability, and it involves all factors internal and external to the firm that interact to protect the rights of corporate stakeholders.

Figure 3.1 illustrates the range of factors affecting corporate governance, including the corporate takeover market. A chapter review (including practice questions) is available in the file

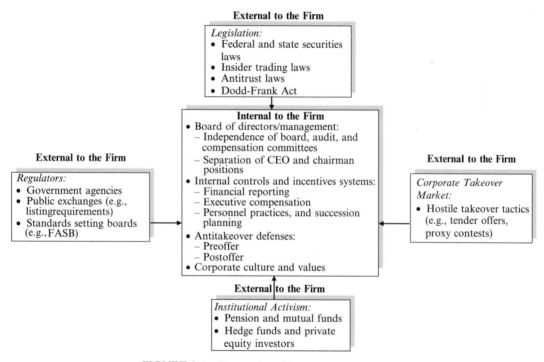

FIGURE 3.1   Factors that affect corporate governance.

[1] Carline et al. (2009) argue that mergers resulting in increased board equity ownership tend to promote improved firm performance because directors have a greater incentive to take a more proactive role in the firm. However, the relationship between board equity ownership and firm performance breaks down if the ownership becomes heavily concentrated in a few directors or if the size of the board increases significantly. Firm performance also benefits from an increase in the size of shareholdings in the hands of investors independent of the firm. Such large stockholders are likely to take a more active role in monitoring firm performance.

folder entitled Student Study Guide on the companion site to this book (*www.elsevierdirect.com/companions/9780123854858*). The companion site also contains a Learning Interactions Library, which gives students the opportunity to test their knowledge of this chapter in a "real-time" environment.

ALTERNATIVE MODELS OF CORPORATE GOVERNANCE

The ultimate goal of a successful corporate governance system should be to hold those in power accountable for their actions. Where capital markets are liquid, investors discipline bad managers by selling their shares; this is called the market model of corporate governance. Where capital markets are illiquid, bad managers are disciplined by those owning large blocks of stock in the firm or by those whose degree of control is disproportionate to their ownership position. This is called the control model of corporate governance, and it may develop through the concentration of shares having multiple voting rights (i.e., so-called supervoting shares) in the hands of a few investors. Table 3.1 provides a summary of the characteristics of these two common corporate governance models.

FACTORS THAT AFFECT CORPORATE GOVERNANCE

The following sections describe those factors internal and external to the firm, including mergers and acquisitions, that impact corporate governance. While the discussion in this chapter deals primarily with domestic considerations, how cross-border transactions impact governance is described in considerable detail in Chapter 17.

Internal Factors

Corporate governance is affected by the integrity and professionalism of the firm's board of directors, as well as by the effectiveness of the firm's internal controls and incentive systems, takeover defenses, and corporate culture and values.

The Board of Directors/Management

The board advises the firm's CEO, who runs the daily operations, and reviews the quality of recommendations the CEO receives from others in corporate management. The board also hires, fires, and sets CEO compensation. Moreover, the board is expected to oversee management, corporate strategy, and the company's financial reports to shareholders, as well as deal

TABLE 3.1   Alternative Models of Corporate Governance

Market Model Applicable When	Control Model Applicable When
Capital markets are highly liquid	Capital markets are illiquid
Equity ownership is widely dispersed	Equity ownership is heavily concentrated
Board members are largely independent	Board members are largely "insiders"
Ownership and control are separate	Ownership and control overlap
Financial disclosure is high	Financial disclosure is limited
Shareholders focus more on short-term gains	Shareholders focus more on long-term gains

with situations in which managers, as agents of the shareholder, make decisions that are not in the best interests of shareholders (i.e., the agency problem discussed in Chapter 1).

Some board members may be employees or family members (most often from the extended family of the firm's founder). Other board members may be affiliated with the firm through a banking relationship, a law firm retained by the firm, or someone who represents a customer or supplier. Such members may be subject to potential conflicts of interest that cause them to act in ways not necessarily in the shareholders' best interests. This has led some observers to argue that boards should be composed primarily of independent directors and different individuals should hold the CEO and board chairman positions.[2] The empirical evidence that firm performance is improved by more independent boards and the separation of the CEO and board positions generally supports these conclusions.[3] In the early 1990s, about 40% of boards were composed of senior corporate managers or individuals affiliated with the corporation. However, in recent years, more than 90% of boards have only one or two nonindependent directors.[4]

Today, boards average about ten members, about one-half of their average size during the 1970s. There is evidence that smaller boards tend to be more effective, since each member can wield more influence, thereby effectively reducing the power of the CEO. Smaller boards also are more likely to replace a CEO due to poor performance.[5] However, more complicated firms may benefit from larger boards capable of providing a broader range of advice to the CEO.[6]

Internal Controls and Incentive Systems

Compensation is an integral part of the incentive systems internal to firms that are used to manage the firm in the manner the board deems most appropriate. In an attempt to rectify widespread abuses, a provision in the Dodd-Frank Act of 2010 (discussed in detail in Chapter 2) includes giving shareholders of publicly traded firms the right to vote on executive compensation (i.e., the so-called "say on pay"). Under the new rules, such votes must occur at least once every three years, beginning with the first shareholder meeting after January 21, 2011. Furthermore, companies are required to hold a "frequency" vote at least once every six years in order to allow shareholders to decide how often they would like to be presented with the "say on pay" vote.

---

[2] Various researchers (Hermalin, 2006; Huson et al., 2001) have documented a number of trends regarding board composition. The proportion of independent directors has steadily increased in the United States and in other countries; outside directors rose from an average of 35% in 1989 to 61% in 1999. Second, the use of incentive compensation for outside directors has increased significantly. Some 84% of firms reporting to a Conference Board Survey used stock-based compensation for outside directors in 1997 as compared to only 6% in 1989. Unfortunately, empirical studies have not consistently demonstrated that such proposals improve shareholder wealth (Economic Report to the President, 2003, p. 90).

[3] Byrd and Hickman (1992), Yermack (1996), and Shivdansani (1993) find that firm value is positively influenced by outsider-dominated boards. However, Masulis et al. (2007) find no statistically significant association between such a board structure and acquirer returns.

[4] Gordon, 2007

[5] Yermack, 1996

[6] Coles et. al., 2008

While shareholder votes on executive pay and on golden parachutes are nonbinding on boards of directors under the new legislation, the potential for restraining the most egregious pay packages is significant based on the European experience. The United Kingdom has allowed shareholders to vote on executive pay since 2002. GlaxoSmithKline became the first firm to suffer a defeat at its annual shareholders meeting, when 50% of the votes cast were against the board's recommendation for the CEO's compensation package. Rather than ignore the vote, the board enlisted Deloitte & Touche to modify the compensation recommendations that were subsequently approved in the 2004 shareholders meeting.

Similar laws were passed throughout Europe and in Australia. In 2004, the Netherlands required companies to submit compensation to a binding vote; in 2005, Sweden and Australia both adopted requirements for nonbinding shareholder votes. Since then, Norway, Spain, Portugal, Denmark, and France have followed suit.

While shareholder interest in say on pay proposals escalated in Europe, perhaps contributing to comparatively smaller average executive pay packages in Europe than in the United States, it has been tepid in the United States. In 2008, Verizon saw its pay package, which it had voluntarily submitted for a shareholder vote, receive a 90% approval. Support for Bank of America's executive pay package topped 70%, despite the furor over the Merrill Lynch bonus debacle. In 2009, Goldman Sachs's executive compensation plan received 96% support from shareholders. About 85% of Citigroup's shareholders backed its pay proposal, despite the near financial collapse of the firm and subsequent government bailout.

The Dodd-Frank Act also requires publicly traded firms to develop mechanisms for recovering compensation based on inaccurate financial statements or if the recipient is fired due to misconduct. The act states that compensation paid during the three years prior to a corporate earnings restatement or from the date of dismissal of the employee is recoverable. Some firms have had mechanisms for recovering executive compensation even before "clawbacks" were required in the 2010 law. *Clawbacks* are ways of recovering executive compensation if it is later discovered that such compensation was paid in error. For example, most major banks put clawback mechanisms in place in 2009.

While clawback mechanisms provide a means of recovering compensation once the damage has been done, there are other ways to align managerial interests with those of shareholders. These include linking option strike prices (i.e., prices at which options can be converted into company shares) to the performance of the company's stock price relative to the stock market, ensuring that increases in the stock market do not benefit managers whose companies are underperforming. Another way to achieve this alignment is for managers to own a significant portion of the firm's outstanding stock or for the manager's ownership of the firm's stock to make up a substantial share of his or her personal wealth. On average, management in the United States tends to own about one-fifth of corporate shares outstanding.[7]

An alternative to concentrating ownership in management is for one or more shareholders who are not managers to accumulate a significant block of voting shares. Corporations having outside shareholders with large blocks of stock (so-called blockholders) may be easier to acquire, thereby increasing the risk to managers that they will be ousted for poor performance.

---

[7] The proportion of shares owned by managers of public firms in the United States grew from an average of 12.9% in 1935 to an average of 21.1% in 1998 (Economic Report to the President, 2003, p. 86).

How board members are compensated also impacts firm value. There is evidence that boards in which equity stakes in the firm are more evenly distributed among the members tend to exhibit better operating performance than firms in which ownership tends to be concentrated among a few.[8] This may reflect the tendency for a few board members owning controlling stakes to seek to entrench themselves and to extract benefits that accrue primarily to those with a controlling interest. This is discussed in more detail in Chapter 10.

Antitakeover Defenses

A firm's management and board may employ defenses to gain leverage in negotiating with a potential suitor or to solidify current management's position within the firm. There is a range of defensive actions; these are detailed later in this chapter.

Corporate Culture and Values

While internal systems and controls are important, good governance also results when the employee culture is instilled with appropriate core values and behaviors. Setting the right tone and direction comes from the board of directors and senior management and their willingness to behave in a manner consistent with what they demand from other employees. For a more detailed discussion of the role of corporate culture, see Chapter 6.

Factors External to the Firm

Federal and state legislation, the court system, regulators, institutional activists, and the corporate takeover market all play an important role in maintaining good corporate governance practices.

Legislation and the Legal System

In the United States, the Securities Acts of 1933 and 1934 form the basis for modern securities legislation; these acts created the Securities and Exchange Commission (SEC) and charged it with writing and enforcing securities regulations. The U.S. Congress has since transferred some enforcement tasks to public stock exchanges, such as the New York Stock Exchange (NYSE), which operate under SEC oversight as self-regulating organizations. The SEC itself has delegated certain responsibilities for setting and maintaining accounting standards to the Financial Accounting Standards Board.

Under the Sarbanes-Oxley Act (SOA) of 2002, the SEC is overseeing the new Public Company Accounting Oversight Board (PCAOB), whose primary task is to develop, maintain, and enforce standards that guide auditors in monitoring and certifying corporate financial reports. The aim of the Sarbanes-Oxley Act was to achieve greater corporate transparency with respect to financial statements, but the events of 2008 and 2009 in the financial and real estate markets underscore how legislated solutions often fail to achieve their intended results.

State legislation also has a significant impact on governance practices by requiring corporate charters to define the responsibilities of boards and of managers with respect to shareholders.

---

[8] Carline, Linn, and Yadav, 2009

Regulators

The SEC, the Federal Trade Commission (FTC), and the Department of Justice (DoJ) can discipline firms with inappropriate governance practices through formal and informal investigations, lawsuits, and settlements. In mid-2003, the SEC approved new listing standards that would put many lucrative, stock-based pay plans to a shareholder vote, thus giving investors in more than 6,200 companies listed on the NYSE, Nasdaq, and other major markets significant control over CEO pay packages. In January 2007, the SEC implemented additional disclosure requirements for CEO pay and perks that exceed $10,000 in value. The Dodd-Frank Act requires publicly traded or listed firms, through new rules adopted by the stock exchanges, to have fully independent compensation committees, based on new standards that consider the source of compensation for the director and whether the director is affiliated with the company.

In late 2010, the SEC voted to allow large shareholders to put their own nominees for board seats on the same ballot as those nominated by the board, allowing such shareholders to avoid the cost of promoting their own slate of candidates. To avoid a lengthy list of nominees, shareholders have to own a 3% stake in a company for at least three years to qualify. Shareholders cannot borrow stock to meet the minimum 3% level, and they will have to certify in writing that they do not intend to use the new rules to change control of the company or to gain more than 25% of the board seats.

Institutional Activists

Pension funds, hedge funds, private equity investors, and mutual funds have become increasingly influential institutions that can affect the policies of companies in which they invest. As discussed in Chapter 1, there is growing evidence that institutional activism, in combination with merger and acquisition activity, has become an important factor in disciplining underperforming managers.

The Corporate Takeover Market

Changes in corporate control can occur because of a hostile (i.e., bids contested by the target's board and management) or friendly takeover of a target firm or because of a proxy contest initiated by dissident shareholders. When a firm's internal mechanisms that govern management control are relatively weak, the corporate takeover market seems to act as a "court of last resort" to discipline inappropriate management behavior.[9] Strong internal governance mechanisms, by contrast, lessen the role of the takeover threat as a disciplinary factor. Moreover, the disciplining effect of a takeover threat on a firm's management can be reinforced when it is paired with a large shareholding by an institutional investor.[10]

Several theories have been put forth to explain why managers might resist a takeover attempt. The *management entrenchment theory* suggests that managers use a variety of takeover defenses to ensure their longevity with the firm. Hostile takeovers, or the threat of such takeovers, have historically been useful for maintaining good corporate governance by removing bad managers and installing better ones.[11] Indeed, there is evidence of frequent management

[9] Kini, Kracaw, and Mian, 2004

[10] Cremers and Nair, 2005

[11] Morck, Shleifer, and Vishny, 1988

turnover even if a takeover attempt is defeated, since takeover targets are often poor financial performers.[12] An alternative viewpoint is the *shareholder interest's theory*, which suggests that management resistance to proposed takeovers is a good bargaining strategy to increase the purchase price to the benefit of the target firm's shareholders.[13]

Proxy contests are attempts by a dissident group of shareholders to gain representation on a firm's board of directors or to change management proposals. While those that address issues other than board representation do not bind a firm's board of directors, there is evidence that boards are becoming more responsive—perhaps reflecting fallout from the Enron-type scandals in 2001 and 2002.[14] Even unsuccessful proxy contests often lead to a change in management, a restructuring of the firm, or investor expectations that the firm ultimately will be acquired. According to proxy solicitor Georgeson, Inc., the number of proxy contests in the United States rose from 25 in 2005 to a peak of 57 in 2009, before declining to 35 in 2010.

ALTERNATIVE TAKEOVER TACTICS IN THE CORPORATE TAKEOVER MARKET

As noted in Chapter 1, takeovers may be classified as friendly or hostile. The process for implementing a friendly takeover is described briefly in the next section and in considerable detail in Chapter 5. Hostile takeover tactics are described extensively in the following sections.

The Friendly Approach in the Corporate Takeover Market

In friendly takeovers, a negotiated settlement is possible without the acquirer resorting to aggressive tactics. The potential acquirer initiates an informal dialogue with the target's top management, and the acquirer and target reach an agreement on the key issues early in the process. Typically, these include the long-term business strategy of the combined firms, how they will operate in the short term, and who will be in key management positions. Often, a *standstill agreement* is negotiated in which the acquirer agrees not to make any further investments in the target's stock for a stipulated period. This compels the acquirer to pursue the acquisition on friendly terms alone, at least for the period covered by the agreement. It also permits negotiations to proceed without the threat of more aggressive tactics such as those discussed in the following sections.

The Hostile Approach in the Corporate Takeover Market

If initial efforts to take control of a target firm are rejected, an acquirer may choose to adopt a more aggressive approach. Several types of hostile takeover tactics may be used, including the bear hug, the proxy contest, and the tender offer.

---

[12] Economic Report to the President, 2003, p. 81

[13] Franks and Mayer, 1996; Schwert, 2000

[14] According to Ertimur (2008), boards implemented 41% of nonbinding shareholder proposals for majority voting in 2004, versus only 22% in 1997. A board was more likely to adopt a shareholder proposal if a competitor had adopted a similar plan.

The Bear Hug: Limiting the Target's Options

With a *bear hug*, the acquirer mails a letter that includes an acquisition proposal to the target company's CEO and board of directors. The letter arrives with no warning and demands a rapid decision. The bear hug usually involves a public announcement as well. The aim is to move the board to a negotiated settlement. Directors who vote against the proposal may be subject to lawsuits from target stockholders, especially if the offer is at a substantial premium to the target's current stock price.

Once the bid is made public, the company is effectively "put into play" (i.e., likely to attract additional bidders). Institutional investors[15] and arbitrageurs add to the pressure by lobbying the board to accept the offer. Arbitrageurs ("arbs") are likely to acquire the target's stock and to sell the bidder's stock short in an effort to profit from the anticipated rise in the target's share price and the fall in the acquirer's share price. The accumulation of stock by arbs makes purchases of blocks of stock by the bidder easier, as they often are quite willing to sell their shares.

Proxy Contests in Support of a Takeover

There are three primary forms of the *proxy contest*. In one, dissident shareholders attempt to win representation on the board of directors. In another, they seek to change a firm's bylaws or force management to take some particular action (e.g., dividend payments and share repurchases) by obtaining the right to vote on behalf of other shareholders. Finally, proxy contests may concern management proposals (e.g., an acquisition). Most commonly, dissidents initiate a proxy fight to remove management due to poor corporate performance, or they to promote a specific type of restructuring of the firm (e.g., sell or spin off a business) or the outright sale of the business, or want to force a distribution of excess cash to shareholders.[16]

Proxy fights enable dissident shareholders to replace specific board members or management with those more willing to support their positions. By replacing board members, proxy contests can be an effective means of gaining control without owning 50.1% of the voting stock, or they can be used to eliminate takeover defenses, such as poison pills, as a precursor of a tender offer, or to oust recalcitrant target firm board members. For example, in late 2010, Air Products & Chemicals, after being rejected several times by Airgas Inc., succeeded in placing three of its own nominees on the Airgas board and, in doing so, voted to remove Peter McCausland, the founder and chairman of Airgas, who had led the resistance to the Air Products' offer.

Implementing a Proxy Contest

When the bidder is also a shareholder in the target firm, the proxy process may begin with the bidder attempting to call a special stockholders' meeting. Alternatively, the bidder may present a proposal to replace the board or management at a regularly scheduled stockholders' meeting. Before the meeting, the bidder may open an aggressive public relations campaign,

---

[15] Institutional investors are organizations that pool large sums of money and invest those sums in companies. They include banks, insurance companies, retirement or pension funds, hedge funds, and mutual funds. Institutional investors now account, on average, for more than two-thirds of the shareholdings of publicly traded firms (Bogle, 2007).

[16] Faleye, 2004

with direct solicitations sent to shareholders and full-page advertisements in the press to convince shareholders to support the bidder's proposals. The target often responds with its own campaign. Once shareholders receive the proxies, they may choose to sign and send them directly to a designated collection point such as a brokerage house or bank. Shareholders may change their votes until they are counted—which often takes place under the strict supervision of inspectors to ensure accuracy. Both the target firm and the bidder generally have their own proxy solicitors present during the tabulation process.

Legal Filings in Undertaking Proxy Contests

SEC regulations cover proxy solicitations under Section 14(A) of the Securities Exchange Act of 1934. All materials distributed to shareholders must be submitted to the SEC for review at least ten days before they are distributed. The party attempting to solicit proxies from the target's shareholders must file a *proxy statement* and Schedule 14(A) with the SEC and mail it to the target's shareholders. Proxy statements may be obtained from the companies involved and on the SEC's website,[17] and they are excellent sources of information about a proposed transaction.

The Impact of Proxy Contests on Shareholder Value

Only one-fifth to one-third of all proxy fights actually result in a change in board control. Despite this low success rate, there is some empirical evidence that proxy fights result in positive abnormal returns to shareholders of the target company regardless of the outcome.[18] The reasons for these gains may include the eventual change in management at firms embroiled in proxy fights, the tendency for new management to restructure the firm, investor expectations of a future change in control due to M&A activity, and possible special cash payouts for firms with excess cash holdings. When management prevails in proxy contests, shareholder value often tends to decline, since little changes in terms of how the firm is being managed.[19]

The Hostile Tender Offer

A *hostile tender offer* is a deliberate effort to go around the target's board and management to reach the target's shareholders directly with an offer to purchase their shares. In a traditional merger, minority shareholders are said to be frozen out of their positions, since they must agree to the terms of the agreement negotiated by the board once the majority of the firm's shareholders approve the proposal. This majority approval requirement is intended to prevent minority shareholders from stopping a merger until they are paid a premium over the purchase price agreed to by the majority. Following the tender offer, the target firm becomes a partially owned subsidiary of the acquiring company.

---

[17] *www.sec.gov*

[18] In studies covering proxy battles during the 1980s through the mid-1990s, abnormal returns ranged from 6 to 19%, even if the dissident shareholders were unsuccessful in the proxy contest (Mulherin and Poulsen, 1998; Faleye, 2004).

[19] Listokin, 2009

While target boards often discourage unwanted bids initially, they are more likely to relent when a hostile tender offer is initiated.[20]Although they have become more common in recent years, hostile takeovers are relatively rare outside the United States.

Pretender Offer Tactics: Toehold Bidding Strategies

Potential bidders may purchase stock in a target before a formal bid to accumulate stock at a price lower than the eventual offer price. Such purchases are normally kept secret to avoid driving up the price and increasing the average price paid for such shares. The primary advantage to the bidder of accumulating target stock before an offer is the potential leverage achieved with the voting rights associated with the stock it has purchased. This voting power is important in a proxy contest to remove takeover defenses, win shareholder approval under state antitakeover statutes, or elect members of the target's board. In addition, the bidder can sell this stock later if the takeover attempt is unsuccessful. Toehold positions also may discourage competing bids.

Once the bidder has established a toehold ownership position in the voting stock of the target through open-market purchases, the bidder may attempt to call a special stockholders' meeting in an effort to replace the board of directors or remove takeover defenses. The conditions under which such a meeting can be called are determined by the firm's articles of incorporation governed by the laws of the state in which the firm is incorporated.[21]

While rare in friendly takeovers, toehold bidding strategies are commonplace in hostile transactions, comprising about one-half of all such takeovers. In friendly transactions, bidders are concerned about alienating a target firm's board and management with such actions; however, in potentially hostile situations, the target firm would have rejected the initial bid under any circumstances. On average, toehold positions represent about 20% of the target's outstanding shares in hostile transactions and about 11% in friendly takeovers. The frequency of toehold bidding has declined since the early 1990s in line with the widespread adoption of takeover defenses and a decline in the frequency of hostile transactions.[22]

Implementing a Tender Offer

Tender offers can be for cash, stock, debt, or some combination of the three. Unlike mergers, tender offers frequently use cash as the form of payment. Securities transactions involve a longer period to complete the takeover because new security issues must be registered with and approved by the SEC and because states have their own security registration requirements. If the tender offer involves a share-for-share exchange, it is referred to as an *exchange offer*. Whether cash or securities, the offer is made directly to target shareholders,

[20] In a study of 1,018 tender offers in the United States between 1962 and 2001, Bhagat et al. (2005) found that target boards resisted tender offers about one-fifth of the time. In a study of 49 countries, Rossi and Volpin (2004) found that only about 1% of 45,686 M&A transactions considered between 1990 and 2002 were opposed by target firm boards.

[21] A copy of a firm's articles of incorporation can usually be obtained for a nominal fee from the Office of the Secretary of State in the state in which the firm is incorporated.

[22] Betton, Eckbo, and Thorburn, 2009

is extended for a specific period, and may be unrestricted (any-or-all offer) or restricted to a certain percentage or number of the target's share.

Tender offers restricted to purchasing less than 100% of the target's outstanding shares may be oversubscribed. Because the Williams Act of 1968 requires equal treatment of all shareholders tendering shares, the bidder may either purchase all of the target stock that is tendered or purchase only a portion of the tendered stock. For example, if the bidder has extended a tender offer for 70% of the target's outstanding shares, and 90% of the target's stock actually is offered, the bidder may choose to prorate the purchase of stock by buying only 63% (i.e., 0.7×0.9) of the tendered stock from each shareholder.

If the bidder chooses to revise the tender offer, the waiting period is automatically extended. If another bid is made to the target shareholders, the waiting period must also be extended by another 10 days to provide adequate time to consider the new bid. Once initiated, tender offers for publicly traded firms are usually successful, although the success rate is lower if it is contested.[23]

Multitiered Offers

The form of the bid for the target firm can be presented to target shareholders either as a one- or as a two-tiered offer. In a *one-tiered offer*, the acquirer announces the same offer to all target shareholders, which offers the potential to purchase control of the target quickly and thus discourage other potential bidders from attempting to disrupt the transaction.

In a *two-tiered offer*, the acquirer offers to buy a certain number of shares at one price and more shares at a lower price at a later date. The form of payment in the second tier may also be less attractive, consisting of securities rather than cash. The intent of the two-tiered approach is to give target shareholders an incentive to tender their shares early in the process to receive the higher price. Furthermore, since those shareholders tendering their shares in the first tier enable the acquirer to obtain a controlling interest, their shares are worth more than those who may choose to sell in the second tier.

Once the bidding firm accumulates enough shares to gain control of the target (usually 50.1%), the bidder may initiate a so-called *back end merger* by calling a special shareholders' meeting seeking approval for a merger in which minority shareholders are required to accede to the majority vote. Alternatively, the bidder may operate the target firm as a partially owned subsidiary, later merging it into a newly created wholly owned subsidiary.

Many state statutes have been amended to require equal treatment for all tendering shareholders as part of two-tiered offers. Many states also give target shareholders *appraisal rights* that allow those not tendering shares in the first or second tier to ask the state court to determine a "fair value" for the shares. The minority shares may be subject to a "minority discount," since they are worth less to the bidder than those acquired in the process of gaining control. State statutes may also contain *fair price provisions* in which all target shareholders, including those in the second tier, receive the same price and redemption rights, enabling target shareholders in the second tier to redeem their shares at a price similar to that paid in the first tier.

---

[23] According to Mergerstat, the success rate of total attempted tender offers between 1980 and 2000 was more than 80%, with the success rate for uncontested offers more than 90% and that for contested offers (i.e., those by the target's board) slightly more than 50%.

An acquirer seeking a controlling interest in the target firm may initiate a *creeping takeover strategy*, which involves purchasing target voting stock in relatively small increments until the acquirer has gained effective control of the firm. This may occur at less than 50.1% if the target firm's ownership is widely dispersed. If about 60% of a firm's eligible shareholders vote in elections for directors, a minority owning as little as 35% can elect its own slate of directors.

Minority shareholders have demonstrated an ability to exercise significant bargaining power and obtain decent financial returns in freeze-outs or situations in which the acquirer is increasing ownership incrementally. U.S. freeze-out bids have shown approximate 15% excess returns[24]; excess financial returns approaching 12% have been found in other countries with well-developed stock markets and good governance practices.[25]

There are a number of disadvantages to owning less than 100% of the target's voting stock. These include the potential for dissident minority shareholders owning significant blocks of stock to disrupt efforts to implement important management decisions, the cost incurred in providing financial statements to both majority and minority shareholders, and current accounting and tax rules. Owning less than 50.1% means that the target cannot be consolidated for purposes of financial reporting but instead must be accounted for using the equity method. Since the equity method will include the investor's share of the target's income, it will not change consolidated income; however, the target's assets, liabilities, revenues, and expenses are not shown on the investor's financial statements. Consequently, potential increases in borrowing capacity from showing a larger asset or sales base would not be realized. Furthermore, target losses cannot be used to offset bidder gains, since consolidation for tax purposes requires owning 80.1% of the target.

In 2011, Panasonic Corporation spent $8.4 billion to buy out the remaining shares of both Sanyo Electric Company and Panasonic Electric Works Company, in which it owned a narrow majority of the outstanding shares. By converting these units into wholly owned subsidiaries, Panasonic hopes to facilitate decision making and to reduce administrative overlap as it shifts from its traditional focus on the home electronics market to renewable energy products. See Case Study 6.6 in Chapter 6 for more details.

Legal Filings in Undertaking Tender Offers

Federal securities laws impose a number of reporting, disclosure, and antifraud requirements on acquirers initiating tender offers. Once the tender offer has been made, the acquirer cannot purchase any target shares other than the number specified in the tender offer. Section 14(D) of the Williams Act requires that any individual or entity making a tender offer resulting in owning more than 5% of any class of equity must file a Schedule 14(D)-1 and all solicitation materials with the SEC.

Advantages of the Hostile Takeover

Although hostile takeovers today are more challenging than in the past, they have certain advantages over the friendly approach. One is that the friendly approach surrenders the element of surprise. Even a few days' warning gives the target's management time to take

[24] Bates et. al., 2006

[25] Croci and Petmezas, 2009

action to impede the actions of the suitor. Negotiation also raises the likelihood of a leak and a spike in the price of the target's stock as arbs seek to profit from the spread between the offer price and the target's current stock price. The speculative increase in the target's share price can add dramatically to the cost of the transaction. The bidder's initial offer generally includes a premium over the target's current share price, and because that premium usually is expressed as a percentage of the target's share price, a speculative increase in the target firm's current share price will add to the overall purchase price paid by the acquiring firm. For these reasons, a bidder may opt for a hostile approach.

WHAT MAKES THE AGGRESSIVE APPROACH SUCCESSFUL?

Successful hostile takeovers depend on the premium offered to target shareholders, the board's composition, and the composition, sentiment, and investment horizon of the target's current shareholders. Other factors include the provisions of the target's bylaws and the potential for the target to implement additional takeover defenses.

The target's board will find it more difficult to reject offers exhibiting substantial premiums to the target's current stock price. Despite the pressure of an attractive premium, the composition of the target's board also greatly influences what the board does and the timing of its decisions. A board that is dominated by independent directors, nonemployees, or nonfamily members is more likely to resist offers in an effort to induce the bidder to raise the offer price or to gain time to solicit competing bids than to protect itself and current management.[26]

Furthermore, the final outcome of a hostile takeover is heavily dependent on the composition of the target's stock ownership, how stockholders feel about management's performance, and how long they intend to hold the stock. Firms held predominately by short-term investors (i.e., less than four months) are more likely to receive a bid and exhibit a lower average premium of as much as 3% when acquired, and researchers speculate that firms held by short-term investors have a weaker bargaining position with the bidder due to the limited loyalty of short-term shareholders.[27]

To assess these factors, an acquirer compiles (to the extent possible) lists of stock ownership by category: management, officers, employees, and institutions such as pension and mutual funds. This information can be used to estimate the target's *float*—the number of shares that are outstanding, are not held by block shareholders, and are available for trading by the public. The larger the share of stock held by corporate officers, family members, and employees, the smaller the number of shares that are likely to be easily purchased by the bidder, since these types of shareholders are less likely to sell their shares.

Finally, an astute bidder will always analyze the target firm's bylaws (often easily accessible through a firm's website) for provisions potentially adding to the cost of a takeover. Such provisions could include a staggered board, the inability to remove directors without cause, or super-majority voting requirements for approval of mergers. These and other measures are detailed later in this chapter.

[26] The shareholder gain from the inception of the offer to its resolution is 62.3% for targets with an independent board, as compared with 40.9% for targets without an independent board (Shivdasani, 1993).

[27] Gaspara and Massa, 2005

OTHER TACTICAL CONSIDERATIONS

The average time between signing the initial agreement and completing or terminating an agreement is about six months, which gives both buyer and seller an incentive to hold up a deal to renegotiate the terms based on new information. Several strategies have been designed to minimize this so-called "hold-up problem."

To heighten the chance of a successful takeover, the bidder will include a variety of provisions in a *letter of intent* (LOI) designed to discourage the target firm from backing out of any preliminary agreements. The LOI is a preliminary agreement between two companies intending to merge that stipulates major areas of agreement between the parties, as well as their rights and limitations. It may contain a number of features protecting the buyer; among the most common is the *no-shop agreement*, which prohibits the target from seeking other bids or going public with information not currently readily available.

Contracts often grant the target the right to forgo the merger and pursue an alternative strategy and the acquirer to withdraw from the agreement. However, the right to break the agreement is usually not free. *Breakup or termination fees* are sums paid to the initial bidder or target if the transaction is not completed. They include legal and advisory expenses, executive management time, and the costs associated with opportunities that may have been lost to the bidder who was involved in trying to close this deal.[28]

Termination fees are used more frequently on the target side than on that of the acquirer because targets have greater incentives to break contracts and seek other bidders. Such fees give the target firm some degree of leverage with the bidder. Averaging about 3% of the purchase price and found in about two-thirds of all M&A deals, such fees tend to result in an approximately 4% higher premium paid to target firms. The higher premium represents the amount paid by the bidder for "insurance" that it will be compensated for expenses incurred if the transaction is not completed and for motivating the target to complete the deal.[29]

Breakup fees paid by the bidder to the target firm are called *reverse breakup fees*, and they have become more common in recent years as buyers, finding it increasingly difficult to finance transactions, have opted to back out of signed agreements. Pharmaceutical behemoth Pfizer's 2009 purchase agreement to buy Wyeth contained a reverse termination fee in which Pfizer could withdraw from the contract only if it received a credit rating downgrade and its lenders refused to extend loans based on the downgrade. Had this happened, Pfizer would have been legally bound to pay Wyeth a $4.5 billion payment equal to an eye-popping 6.6% of the $68 billion purchase price.

The *stock lockup*, an option granted to the bidder to buy the target firm's stock at the first bidder's initial offer, is another form of protection for the bidder. It is triggered whenever the target firm accepts a competing bid. Because the target may choose to sell to a higher bidder, the stock lockup arrangement usually ensures that the initial bidder will make a profit on its purchase of the target's stock. The initial bidder also may require that the seller agree to a

---

[28] In a sample of 1100 stock mergers between 1994 and 1999, Hotchkiss, Qian, and Song (2004) found a target termination or breakup fee included in the initial agreement in 55% of all deals, while in 21% of the deals both target and acquirer termination fees were included.

[29] Officer, 2003

crown jewels lockup, in which the initial bidder has an option to buy important strategic assets of the seller, if the seller chooses to sell to another party. Target firms may use lockup options to enhance their bargaining power in dealing with a bidding firm.[30]

DEVELOPING A BIDDING OR TAKEOVER STRATEGY

The tactics that may be used in developing a bidding strategy should be viewed as a series of decision points, with objectives and options usually well defined and understood before a takeover attempt is initiated. A poorly thought-out strategy can result in unsuccessful bidding for the target firm, which can be costly to CEOs, who may lose their jobs.[31]

Common bidding strategy objectives include winning control of the target, minimizing the control premium, minimizing transaction costs, and facilitating postacquisition integration. If minimizing the purchase price and transaction costs, while maximizing cooperation between the two parties, is considered critical, the bidder may choose the "friendly" approach, which has the advantage of generally being less costly than more aggressive tactics and minimizes the loss of key personnel, customers, and suppliers during the fight for control of the target. Friendly takeovers avoid an auction environment, which may raise the target's purchase price. Moreover, friendly acquisitions facilitate premerger integration planning and increase the likelihood that the combined businesses will be quickly integrated following closing.

If the target is unwilling to reach a negotiated settlement, the acquirer is faced with the choice of abandoning the effort or resorting to more aggressive tactics. Such tactics are likely to be less effective because of the extra time they give the target's management to put additional takeover defenses in place. In reality, the risk of loss of surprise may not be very great because of the prenotification requirements of current U.S. law.

Reading Figure 3.2 from left to right, the bidder initiates contact casually through an intermediary (sometimes called a *casual pass*) or through a more formal inquiry. If the target's management and board reject the bidder's initial offer, the bidder's options under the friendly approach are to either walk away or adopt more aggressive tactics. In the latter case, the bidder may undertake a simple bear hug, hoping that pressure from large institutional shareholders and arbs will nudge the target toward a negotiated settlement.

If the bear hug fails to convince the target's management to negotiate, the bidder may choose to buy stock in the open market in order to accumulate a toehold in the target's stock. This is most effective when ownership in the target is concentrated among relatively few shareholders. The bidder may accumulate a sufficient number of voting rights to call a special stockholders' meeting if a proxy fight is deemed necessary to change board members or dismember the target's defenses. In addition, such maneuvers may discourage competing bids.

If the target's defenses are viewed as relatively weak, the bidder may forgo a proxy contest and initiate a tender offer for the target's stock. If the target's defenses appear formidable, however, the bidder may implement a proxy contest and a tender offer concurrently. That,

---

[30] Burch, 2001

[31] In a sample of 714 acquisitions between 1990 and 1998, Lehn and Zhao (2006) found that 47% of acquiring firm CEOs were replaced within five years. Moreover, top executives are more likely to be replaced at firms that have made poor acquisitions sometime during the previous five years.

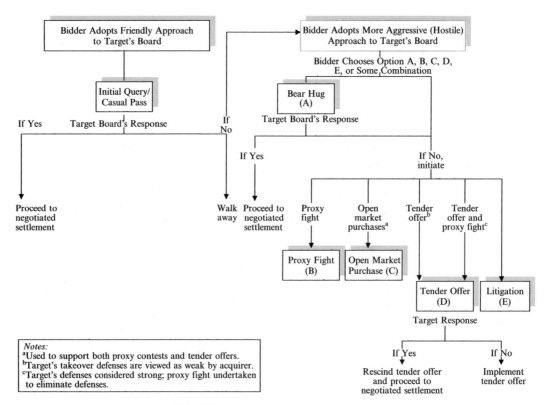

FIGURE 3.2   Alternative takeover tactics.

however, is a very expensive strategy. Tender offers are costly because they are offers to buy up to 100% of the target's outstanding stock at a significant premium. A proxy fight, while less expensive, may still be costly, reflecting extensive litigation, which is likely.

Litigation is a common tactic used to pressure the target board to relent to the bidder's proposal or remove defenses. It is most effective if the firm's defenses appear to be especially onerous. The bidder may initiate litigation that accuses the target's board of not giving the bidder's offer sufficient review, or the bidder may argue that the target's defenses are not in the best interests of the target's shareholders and serve only to entrench senior management. Table 3.2 summarizes common bidder objectives and the advantages and disadvantages of the various tactics that may be employed to achieve these objectives.

ALTERNATIVE TAKEOVER DEFENSES IN THE CORPORATE TAKEOVER MARKET

Takeover defenses are impediments to potential bidders and are designed either to slow down an unwanted offer or to force a suitor to raise the bid to get the target's board to rescind the defense. Takeover defenses can be grouped in two categories: those put in place before

TABLE 3.2   Advantages and Disadvantages of Alternative Takeover Tactics

COMMON BIDDER STRATEGY OBJECTIVES

- Gain control of the target firm
- Minimize the size of the control premium
- Minimize transactions costs
- Facilitate postacquisition integration

Tactics	Advantages	Disadvantages
Casual Pass (i.e., informal inquiry)	May learn target is receptive to offer	Gives advance warning
Bear Hug (i.e., letter to target board forcefully proposing takeover)	Raises pressure on target to negotiate a deal	Gives advance warning
Open Market Purchases (i.e., acquirer buys target shares on public markets)	• May lower cost of transaction • Creates profit if target agrees to buy back bidder's toehold position (i.e., greenmail) • May discourage other bidders	• Can result in a less than controlling interest • Limits on the amount that can be purchased without disclosure • Some shareholders could hold out for higher price • Could suffer losses if takeover attempt fails • Could alienate target management and make a friendly takeover even more difficult
Proxy Contest (i.e., effort to obtain target shareholder support to change target board)	• Less expensive than tender offer • May obviate need for tender offer	• Relatively low probability of success if target stock widely held • Adds to transactions costs
Tender Offer (i.e., direct offer to target shareholders to buy shares)	• Pressures target shareholders to sell stock • Bidder is not bound to the purchased tendered shares unless the desired number of shares is tendered	• Tends to be most expensive tactic • Disruptive to postclosing integration due to potential loss of key target management, customers, and suppliers
Litigation (i.e., lawsuits accusing target board of improper conduct)	• Puts pressure on targeted board	• Expenses

receiving an offer (preoffer) and those implemented after receipt of an offer (postoffer). Table 3.3 shows the most commonly used pre- and postoffer defenses; companies use, on average, three of these when confronted with a takeover attempt.[32] As you will learn later in this chapter, they are effective to varying degrees.

[32] Field and Karpoff, 2002

TABLE 3.3 Alternative Preoffer and Postoffer Takeover Defenses

Preoffer Defenses	Postoffer Defenses
Poison Pills[a]: Flip-Over Rights Plans Flip-In Rights Plans	*Greenmail* (bidder's investment purchased at a premium to what they paid as inducement to refrain from any further activity.)

Shark Repellents (implemented by changing bylaws or charter):
Strengthening the Board's Defenses
  Staggered or Classified Board Elections
  "For Cause" Provisions
Limiting Shareholder Actions
  Calling Special Meetings
  Consent Solicitations
  Advance Notice Provisions
  Super-Majority Rules
Other Shark Repellents
  Antigreenmail Provisions
  Fair Price Provisions
  Supervoting Stock
  Reincorporation
	Standstill Agreements (often used in conjunction with an agreement to buy bidder's investment.)

Golden Parachutes	Pac-Man Defense White Knights Employee Stock Ownership Plans Leveraged Recapitalization Share Repurchase or Buyback Plans Corporate Restructuring Litigation

[a] *While many different types of poison pills are used, only the most common forms are discussed in this text. Note also that the distinction between pre and postoffer defenses is becoming murky as poison pill plans are increasingly put in place immediately following the announcement of a bid. Pills can be adopted without a shareholder vote because they are issued as a dividend and the board has exclusive authority to issue dividends.*

Preoffer Defenses

Preoffer defenses are used to prevent a sudden, unexpected hostile bid from gaining control of the company before management has time to assess its options properly. If the preoffer defenses succeed in delaying the change in control, the target firm has time to erect additional defenses after the unsolicited offer has been received. Such defenses generally fall into three categories: poison pills, shark repellents, and golden parachutes.

Poison Pills

Often referred to as shareholder rights plans, poison pills are a new class of securities that a company issues to its current shareholders. Because pills are issued as a dividend and the board has the exclusive authority to issue dividends, a pill can often be adopted without a shareholder vote (unless the firm's bylaws limit such action). Consequently, poison pills can be adopted not only before but also after the onset of a hostile bid, which means that even a company that does not have a poison pill in place can be regarded as having a "shadow poison pill" that could be used in the event of a hostile bid.[33] Such pills could be issued as rights offerings to the firm's current shareholders, other than the bidder, which if exercised would substantially dilute the bidder's ownership position.

Poison pill securities have no value unless an investor acquires a specific percentage (sometimes as low as 10%) of the target firm's voting stock. If this threshold percentage is exceeded and the pill is a so-called *flip-in pill*, the poison pill securities are activated and typically allow existing target shareholders to purchase additional shares of the target firm's common stock at a discount from the current market price. Alternatively, if the pill is a *flip-over pill*, existing shareholders may purchase additional shares of the acquirer or surviving firm's common shares (i.e., the shares of the combined companies), also at a discount.

Triggering the flip-in pill increases the acquirer's cost of the transaction by increasing the number of target shares that need to be purchased for cash in a cash-for-share exchange or the number of new shares that must be issued by the acquirer in a share-for-share exchange. In a cash-for-share exchange, the change in the acquirer's cash outlay will depend on the number of target shareholders exercising their right to buy additional target shares. For example, if the number of target shares outstanding doubled and the price per share offered by the acquirer remained unchanged, the amount of cash required to buy all or a specific portion of the target's shares would double. In share-for-share exchange, the increased number of acquirer shares issued imposes a cost on acquirer shareholders by diluting their ownership position. News Corp. was using the flip-in poison pill when the firm announced on November 8, 2004, that it would give its shareholders the right to buy one share of the firm's stock at half price for each share they owned in the event any party sought to buy a 15% stake in the firm. Assuming all shareholders exercised their rights, this would effectively double the cost of a takeover. The pill would exclude the purchaser of the 15% stake.

Table 3.4 illustrates the dilution of the acquirer's shareholders ownership position resulting from a poison pill in a share-for-share exchange offer. Assume that the acquirer has 1 million shares currently outstanding and has agreed to acquire the 1 million shares of target stock outstanding by exchanging one share of acquirer stock for each share of target stock. To complete the transaction, the acquirer must issue 1 million shares of new stock, with the target's stock being cancelled. The total number of shares outstanding for the new company would be 2 million shares (i.e., 1 million of existing acquirer stock plus 1 million in newly issued shares). Target company and acquirer shareholders would each own one-half of the new company. However, if target company shareholders were able to buy 1 million new shares of target stock at a nominal price because of a flip-in pill, the number of shares that now must be acquired would total 2 million. The total number of shares of the new company would be 3 million, of which the target company's shareholders would own two-thirds and acquirer shareholders one-third.

Note that a flip-in or flip-over pill has the same dilutive effect on acquirer shareholders. With the flip-in pill, target shareholders purchased 1 million new shares of target stock, while

---

[33] Coates, 2000. According to *sharkrepellent.com*, almost one-fourth of first-time pill adoptions in 2007 were implemented when the firm was "in play." This compares to about 3% of all first-time pill adoptions in 2002.

TABLE 3.4   Acquirer Shareholder Dilution Due to Poison Pill

	New Company Shares Outstanding[a]		Ownership Distribution in New Company (%)	
Flip-In Pill Defenses[b]	**Without Pill**	**With Pill**	**Without Pill**	**With Pill**
Target Firm Shareholders				
Shares Currently Outstanding	1,000,000	2,000,000	50	67[c]
Total Shares Outstanding	1,000,000	2,000,000		
Acquiring Firm Shareholders				
Shares Currently Outstanding	1,000,000	1,000,000		
New Shares Issued	1,000,000	2,000,000	50	33
Total Shares Outstanding	2,000,000	3,000,000		
Flip-Over Pill Defense[d]	**Without Pill**	**With Pill**	**Without Pill**	**With Pill**
Target Firm Shareholders				
Shares Currently Outstanding	1,000,000	1,000,000	50	67
Total Shares Outstanding	1,000,000	1,000,000		
Acquiring Firm Shareholders				
Shares Currently Outstanding	1,000,000	1,000,000	50	33
New Shares Issued	1,000,000	2,000,000		
Total Shares Outstanding	2,000,000	3,000,000		

[a] *Acquirer agrees to exchange one share of acquirer stock for each share of target stock. The target shares outstanding are cancelled.*
[b] *Poison pill provisions enable each target shareholder to buy one share of target stock for each share they own at a nominal price.*
[c] *2,000,000/3,000,000*
[d] *One million new shares must be issued to target shareholders exercising their right to buy shares in the surviving or new company at a nominal price.*

for a flip-over pill they bought 1 million new shares of the acquirer or surviving firm's shares. In either case, the acquirer had to issue 1 million new shares.

Proponents of the pill defense argue that it prevents a raider from acquiring a substantial portion of the firm's stock without board permission. Since the board generally has the power to rescind the pill, bidders are compelled to negotiate with the target's board, which could result in a higher offer price. Pill defenses may be most effective when used with staggered board defenses, in which a raider would be unable to remove the pill without winning two successive elections; this increases the likelihood of remaining independent.[34] Detractors argue that pill defenses simply serve to entrench management and encourage disaffected shareholders to litigate.

Shark Repellents

Shark repellents are specific types of takeover defenses achieved by amending either a *corporate charter* or the *corporation bylaws*. The charter gives the corporation its legal existence. The corporate charter consists of the *articles of incorporation,* a document filed with a state government by the founders of a corporation, and a *certificate of incorporation,* a document received from the state once the articles have been approved. The corporation's powers thus

---

[34] According to Bebchuk et al. (2002), the likelihood of remaining independent rises from 34 to 61% with such a combination of defenses, and the probability that the first bidder will be successful drops from 34 to 14%.

derive from the laws of the state and from the provisions of the charter. Rules governing the internal management of the corporation are described in the corporation's bylaws, which are determined by the corporation's founders.

Shark repellents are put in place largely to reinforce the ability of a firm's board of directors to retain control. They predate poison pills as a defense, and their success in slowing down takeovers and making them more expensive has been mixed—which, in fact, partly explains why the poison pill and other more creative defenses were developed.

Today, shark repellents have largely become supplements to poison pill defenses. Their primary role is to make it more difficult to gain control of the board through a proxy fight at an annual or special meeting. In practice, shark repellents as described here require amendments to the firm's charter, which necessitate a shareholder vote. Although there are many variations of shark repellents, the most typical are staggered board elections, restrictions on shareholder actions, antigreenmail provisions, supervoting, and debt-based defenses. Table 3.5 summarizes the primary advantages and disadvantages of each type of shark repellent defense in three categories: those that strengthen the board's defenses, those that limit shareholder actions, and all others. Table 3.5 also includes poison pills and golden parachutes (detailed below).

Strengthening the Board's Defenses

Corporate directors are elected at annual shareholder meetings by a vote of the holders of a majority of shares, who are present and entitled to vote. However, the mechanism for electing directors differs among corporations, with voting shares being cast either through a straight vote or cumulatively. With straight voting, shareholders may cast all their votes for each

TABLE 3.5 Advantages and Disadvantages of Preoffer Takeover Defenses

Type of Defense	Advantages for Target Firm	Disadvantages for Target Firm
Poison Pills: Raising the Cost of Acquisition		
Flip-Over Pills (rights to buy stock in the acquirer, activated with 100% change in ownership)	Dilute ownership position of current acquirer shareholders Rights redeemable by buying them back from shareholders at nominal price	Ineffective in preventing acquisition of <100% of target (bidders could buy controlling interest only and buy remainder after rights expire) Subject to hostile tender contingent on target board's redemption of pill Makes issuer less attractive to white knights
Flip-In Pills (rights to buy stock in the target, activated when acquirer purchases <100% change in ownership)	Dilute target stock regardless of amount purchased by potential acquirer Discriminatory as not given to investor who activated the rights Rights redeemable at any point prior to triggering event	Not permissible in some states due to discriminatory nature No poison pill provides any protection against proxy contests

Continued

TABLE 3.5   Advantages and Disadvantages of Preoffer Takeover Defenses—Cont'd

Type of Defense	Advantages for Target Firm	Disadvantages for Target Firm
Shark Repellents: Strengthening the Board's Defenses		
Staggered or Classified Boards	Delay assumption of control by a majority shareholder	May be circumvented by increasing size of board unless prevented by charter or bylaws
Limitations on When Can Remove Directors	"For cause" provisions narrow range of reasons for removal	Can be circumvented unless supported by a super-majority requirement for repeal
Shark Repellents: Limiting Shareholder Actions		
Limitations on Calling Special Meetings	Limit ability to use special meetings to add board seats, remove, or elect new members	States may require a special meeting if a certain percentage of shareholders request a meeting.
Limiting Consent Solicitations	Limits ability of dissident shareholders to expedite a proxy contest process	May be subject to court challenge
Advance Notice Provisions	Give board time to select its own slate of candidates and to decide an appropriate response	May be subject to court challenge
Super-Majority Provisions	May be applied selectively to events such as hostile takeovers	Can be circumvented unless a super-majority of shareholders is required to change provision
Other Shark Repellents		
Antigreenmail Provision	Eliminates profit opportunity for raiders	Eliminates greenmail as a takeover defense
Fair Price Provisions	Increase the cost of a two-tiered tender offer	Raise the cost to a White Knight, unless waived by typically 95% of shareholders
Supervoting Stock *Dual class Recapitalization.*	Concentrates control by giving "friendly" shareholders more voting power than others	Difficult to implement because requires shareholder approval and only useful when voting power can be given to pro-management shareholders
Reincorporation	Takes advantage of most favorable state antitakeover statutes	Requires shareholder approval; time consuming to implement unless subsidiary established before takeover solicitation
Golden Parachutes	Embolden target management to negotiate for a higher premium and raises the cost of a takeover to the hostile bidder	Negative public perception; make termination of top management expensive; cost not tax deductible

member of the board of directors, thereby virtually ensuring that the majority shareholder(s) will elect all of the directors. For example, assume that a corporation has four directors up for election and has two shareholders, one owning 80 shares (i.e., the majority shareholder) and one owning 20 shares (i.e., the minority shareholder); with each share having one vote, the majority shareholder will always elect the director for whom it casts its votes.

In contrast, *cumulative voting* systems are designed to allow for minority participation. Cumulative voting in the election of directors means that each shareholder is entitled to as many votes as shall equal the number of shares the shareholder owns, multiplied by the number of directors to be elected. Furthermore, the shareholder may cast all of these votes for a single candidate or for any two or more candidates. With cumulative voting, all directors are elected at the same time. Using the same example, the majority shareholder will have 320 votes (80 × 4), and the minority shareholder will have 80 votes (20 × 4). If the minority shareholder casts all of her votes for herself, she is assured of a seat, since the majority shareholder cannot outvote the minority shareholder for all four board seats. That is, while there are many possible combinations, if the majority shareholder were to cast 81 votes for each of three seats, he would have only 77 votes remaining (i.e., 320 – 243) for the last seat. As the number of directors increases, it becomes easier for the minority shareholder to win a seat (or seats), since the majority shareholder's votes must be spread over more directors to block the minority shareholder. Consequently, it is generally easier to win seats as the number of directors up for election increases.

In states where cumulative voting is mandatory, companies sometimes distribute the election of directors over a number of years to make it harder for a dissident minority shareholder to gain control of the board. This makes it more difficult for the minority shareholder to elect a director when there is cumulative voting because there are fewer directors to be elected at one time. A *staggered or classified board election* involves dividing the firm's directors into a number of different classes. Only one class is up for reelection each year. For example, a 12-member board may have directors divided into four classes, with each director elected for a four-year period. In the first year, the three directors in what might be called "Class 1" are up for election; in the second year, "Class 2" directors are up for election; and so on.

This means that an insurgent stockholder, even one who holds the majority of the stock, would have to wait for three election cycles to gain control of the board. Moreover, the size of the board is limited by the firm's bylaws to preclude the insurgent stockholder from adding board seats to take control of the board. The likelihood of litigation is highest, and pressure on the board is greatest, whenever the offer price for the target is substantially above the target firm's current share price. Studies show that staggered boards can be effective in helping a target to ward off a hostile takeover attempt.[35]

Opposition to staggered boards has been growing over time. According to proxy solicitor Georgeson Inc., the average share of votes cast in favor of declassifying boards in the 187 shareholder proposals to declassify boards between 2006 and 2010 averaged 65%. FactSet Research Systems has noted that between 2000 and 2009, the number of S&P 500 companies with classified boards declined from 300 to 164.

---

[35] Bebchuk, Coates, and Subramanian, 2002 and 2003

For cause provisions specify the conditions for removing a member of the board of directors, narrowing the range of permissible reasons and limiting the flexibility of dissident shareholders in contesting board seats.

Limiting Shareholder Actions

The board can also reinforce its control by restricting the ability of shareholders to gain control of the firm by bypassing the board altogether. Limits can be set on shareholders' ability to call special meetings, engage in consent solicitations, and use super-majority rules (explained below). Firms frequently rely on the conditions under which directors can be removed (i.e., the "for cause" provision discussed earlier) and a limitation on the number of board seats as defined in the firm's bylaws or charter.

In some states, shareholders may take action—without a special shareholders' meeting—to add to the number of seats on the board, remove specific board members, or elect new members. These states allow dissident shareholders to obtain shareholder support for their proposals simply by obtaining the written consent of shareholders under what is known as *consent solicitation*, a process that still must abide by the disclosure requirements applicable to proxy contests. The process circumvents delays inherent in setting up a meeting to conduct a stockholder vote.

There is an important difference between a consent solicitation and a proxy contest. Whereas the winning vote in a proxy fight is determined as a percentage of the number of votes actually cast (unless majority voting rules are in place, which require the counting of votes withheld), the winning vote in a consent solicitation is determined as a percentage of the number of shares outstanding. A dissident shareholder may, therefore, find it easier to win by initiating a proxy contest because many shareholders simply do not vote.

Corporate bylaws may include *advance notice provisions* that require shareholder proposals and board nominations to be announced well in advance, sometimes as long as two months, of an actual vote. This buys time for the target's management. *Super-majority rules* require a higher level of approval than is standard to amend the charter or for certain types of transactions, such as a merger or acquisition. Such rules are triggered when an "interested party" acquires a specific percentage of the ownership shares (e.g., 5 to 10%). Super-majority rules may require that as many as 80% of the shareholders approve a proposed merger, or a simple majority of all shareholders except the "interested party."

Other Shark Repellents

Other shark repellent defenses include antigreenmail provisions, fair price provisions, supervoting stock, reincorporation, and golden parachutes.

Antigreenmail Provisions

During the 1980s, many raiders profited by taking an equity position in a target firm, threatening takeover, and subsequently selling their ownership position back to the target firm at a premium over what they paid for the target's shares. The practice was dubbed "greenmail"—derived from "blackmail" and "greenback." In response, many corporations adopted charter amendments called *antigreenmail provisions* that restrict the firm's ability to repurchase shares at a premium.

Fair Price Provisions

Requirements that any acquirer pay minority shareholders at least fair market price for their stock are called *fair price provisions*. The fair market price may be expressed as some historical multiple of the company's earnings or as a specific price equal to the maximum price paid when the buyer acquired shares in the company. In two-tiered tender offers, the fair price provision forces the bidder to pay target shareholders who tender their stock in the second tier the same terms offered to those tendering their stock in the first tier.

Supervoting Stock   *(98, 99)*

A firm may create more than one class of stock for many reasons, including separating the performance of individual operating subsidiaries, compensating subsidiary operating management, maintaining control with the founders, and preventing hostile takeovers. As a take-over defense, a firm may undertake a *dual class recapitalization*, the objective of which is concentrating stock with the greatest voting rights in the hands of those who are most likely to support management. One class of stock may have 10 to 100 times the voting rights of another class of stock. Such stock is called *supervoting stock*.

Supervoting stock is issued to all shareholders along with the right to exchange it for ordinary stock. Most shareholders are likely to exchange it for ordinary stock because the stock with the multiple voting rights usually has a limited resale market and pays a lower dividend than other types of voting stock the corporation issues. Typically, management retains the special stock, which effectively increases the voting control of the corporation in the hands of management. Ford Motor's class B common stock, which is not publicly traded but is held by the Ford family, has 40% of the voting power even though it represents less than 10% of the firm's total outstanding stock.

Under the voting rights policies of the SEC and major public exchanges, U.S. firms are allowed to list dual class shares. Once such shares are listed, however, firms cannot reduce the voting rights of existing shares or issue a new class of superior voting shares. Several hundred U.S. companies have issued dual class shares, including the *New York Times*, Dow Jones, the *Washington Post*, Coors, Tyson Foods, Facebook, Adelphia, Comcast, Viacom, Ford, and Google. Still, such shares are far more common in other countries.[36]

Reincorporation

In some instances, a potential target firm may change the state within which it is incorporated to one where the laws are more favorable for implementing takeover defenses. This is done by creating a subsidiary in the new state, into which the parent is merged at a later date. Several factors need to be considered in selecting a state for such *reincorporation*, including how the state's courts have ruled in lawsuits alleging breach of corporate director fiduciary

---

[36] Research by Gompers, Ishii, and Metrick (2010) suggests that firms with dual class shares often underperform in the overall stock market. This may result from efforts to entrench controlling shareholders by erecting excessive takeover defenses and policies that are not in the best interests of noncontrolling shareholders, such as excessive compensation for key managers and board members. Moreover, such firms often have excessive leverage due to an unwillingness to raise additional funds by selling shares that could dilute the controlling shareholders' power.

responsibility in takeover situations, as well as the state's laws pertaining to poison pills, staggered boards, and hostile tender offers. Reincorporation requires shareholder approval.

Golden Parachutes

Employee severance arrangements that are triggered whenever a change in control takes place are called *golden parachutes*. A change in control usually is defined as any time an investor accumulates more than a fixed percentage of the corporation's voting stock. A golden parachute typically covers only a few dozen employees, who are terminated following the change in control and to whom the company is obligated to make a lump-sum payment. They are designed to raise the bidder's cost of the acquisition, rather than to gain time for the target board. Such severance packages may serve the interests of shareholders by making senior management more willing to accept an acquisition.

The 1986 Tax Act imposed stiff penalties on these types of plans if they create payments that exceed three times the employee's average pay over the previous five years, and it treats them as income and thus not tax-deductible by the paying corporation. The employee receiving the parachute payment must pay a 20% surcharge in addition to the normal tax due on the parachute payment. More recently, the Dodd-Frank bill of 2010 gives shareholders the opportunity to express their disapproval of golden parachutes through a nonbinding vote.

Postoffer Defenses

Once an unwanted suitor has approached a firm, there are a variety of additional defenses that can be introduced. These include greenmail to dissuade the bidder from continuing the pursuit; defenses designed to make the target less attractive, such as restructuring and recapitalization strategies; and efforts to place an increasing share of the company's ownership in friendly hands by establishing employee stock ownership plans (ESOPs) or seeking white knights. Table 3.6 summarizes the advantages and disadvantages of these postoffer defenses.

Greenmail

Greenmail (introduced earlier) is the practice of paying a potential acquirer to leave you alone. It consists of a payment to buy back shares at a premium price in exchange for the acquirer's agreement not to commence a hostile takeover. In exchange for the payment, the potential acquirer is required to sign a *standstill agreement*, which typically specifies the amount of stock, if any, the investor can own, the circumstances under which the raider can sell stock currently owned, and the terms of the agreement. Courts view greenmail as discriminatory because not all shareholders are offered the opportunity to sell their stock back to the target firm at an above-market price. Nevertheless, courts in some states (e.g., Delaware) have found it to be an appropriate response if done for valid business reasons. Courts in other states (e.g., California) have favored shareholder lawsuits, contending that greenmail breaches fiduciary responsibility.[37]

[37] Wasserstein, 1998, pp. 719–720

TABLE 3.6   Advantages and Disadvantages of Postoffer Takeover Defenses

Type of Defense	Advantages for Target Firm	Disadvantages for Target Firm
Greenmail	Encourages raider to go away (usually accompanied by a standstill agreement)	Reduces risk to raider of losing money on a takeover attempt; unfairly discriminates against nonparticipating shareholders; often generates litigation; triggers unfavorable tax consequences and negative publicity
Standstill Agreement	Prevents raider from returning for a specific time period	Increases amount of greenmail paid to get raider to sign standstill; provides only temporary reprieve
White Knights	May be a preferable to the hostile bidder	Involves loss of target's independence
ESOPs	Alternative to white knight and highly effective if used in conjunction with certain states' antitakeover laws	Employee support not guaranteed; ESOP cannot overpay for stock because transaction could be disallowed by federal law
Recapitalization	Makes target less attractive to bidder and may increase target shareholder value if incumbent management motivated to improve performance	Increased leverage reduces target's borrowing capacity
Share Buyback Plans	Reduce number of target shares available for purchase by bidder, arbs, and others who may sell to bidder	*(can't self tender without SEC)* Securities laws limit ability to self-tender without SEC filing once hostile tender under way; reduction in the shares outstanding may facilitate bidder's gaining control
Corporate Restructuring	Going private may be an attractive alternative to bidder's offer for target shareholders and for incumbent management	Going private, sale of attractive assets, making defensive acquisitions, or liquidation may reduce target's shareholder value vs. bidder's offer
Litigation	May buy time for target to build defenses and increases takeover cost to the bidder	May have negative impact on target shareholder returns

White Knights

A target company seeking to avoid being taken over by a specific bidder may try to be acquired by a *white knight*: another firm that is considered a more appropriate suitor. To complete such a transaction, the white knight must be willing to acquire the target on terms more favorable than those of other bidders. Fearing that a bidding war might ensue, the white knight often demands some protection in the form of a lockup. This may involve giving the white knight options to buy stock in the target that has not yet been issued at a fixed price, or the option to acquire specific target assets at a fair price. Such lockups usually make the target less attractive to other bidders. If a bidding war does ensue, the knight may exercise the stock options and sell the shares at a profit to the acquiring company. German drug and chemical firm Bayer AG's white knight bid for Schering AG in 2006 (which was recommended by the Schering board) was designed to trump a hostile offer from a German rival, Merck KGaS—and it succeeded in repelling Merck.

Employee Stock Ownership Plans

ESOPs are trusts that hold a firm's stock as an investment for its employees' retirement program. They can be established quickly, with the company either issuing shares directly to the ESOP or having an ESOP purchase shares on the open market. The stock held by an ESOP is likely to be voted in support of management in the event of a hostile takeover attempt.

Leveraged Recapitalization

A company may recapitalize by assuming substantial amounts of new debt, which is used to either buy back stock or finance a dividend payment to shareholders. The additional debt reduces the company's borrowing capacity and leaves it in a highly leveraged position, making it less attractive to a bidder that may have wanted to use that capacity to help finance a takeover. Moreover, the payment of a dividend or a stock buyback may persuade shareholders to support the target's management in a proxy contest or hostile tender offer. The primary differences between a leveraged recapitalization and a leveraged buyout are that the firm remains a public company and that management does not take a significant equity stake in the firm. Recapitalization may require shareholder approval, depending on the company's charter and the laws of the state in which it is incorporated.[38]

Share Repurchase or Buyback Plans

Firms repurchase shares to reward shareholders, signal undervaluation, fund ESOPs, adjust capital structure, and defend against unwanted takeovers.[39] These repurchases can be executed either through a tender offer or by direct purchases of shares in public markets. When used as an antitakeover tactic, share repurchase or buyback plans aim to reduce the number of shares that could be purchased by the potential acquirer or by arbitrageurs who will sell to the highest bidder. This tactic reflects the belief that when a firm initiates a tender offer for a portion of its own shares, the shareholders who offer their shares for sale are those who are most susceptible to a tender offer by a hostile bidder. This leaves the target firm's shares concentrated in the hands of shareholders who are less likely to sell, thereby reducing float. So for a hostile tender offer to succeed in purchasing the remaining shares, the premium offered would have to be higher. The resulting higher premium might discourage some prospective bidders.

There is considerable evidence that buyback strategies are an effective deterrent.[40] The repurchase tactic, however, may be subject to the "law of unintended consequences."

---

[38] Whether the recapitalization actually weakens the target firm over the long term depends on its impact on shareholder value. Shareholders will benefit from the receipt of a dividend or from capital gains resulting from a stock repurchase. Furthermore, the increased debt service requirements of the additional debt will shelter a substantial amount of the firm's taxable income and may encourage management to be more conscientious about improving the firm's performance. Thus, the combination of these factors may result in current shareholders benefiting more from this takeover defense than from a hostile takeover of the firm.

[39] According to Billett and Xue (2007), firms frequently increase their share repurchase activities when confronted with an imminent takeover threat.

[40] Potential acquirers are less likely to pursue firms with substantial excess cash, which could be used to adopt highly aggressive share repurchase programs (Harford, 1999; Pinkowitz, 2002; Faleye, 2004).

Reducing the number of shares on the open market makes it easier for the buyer to gain control because fewer shares have to be purchased to achieve 50.1% of the target's voting shares.

Corporate Restructuring

Restructuring may involve taking the company private, selling attractive assets, undertaking a major acquisition, or even liquidating the company. "Going private" typically involves the management team's purchase of the bulk of a firm's shares. This may create a win–win situation for shareholders, who receive a premium for their stock and management, which retains control. To avoid lawsuits, the price paid for the stock must represent a substantial premium to the current market price. Alternatively, the target may make itself less attractive by divesting assets the bidder wants.

The cash proceeds of such sales could fund other defenses, such as share buybacks or payment of a special stockholder dividend. A target company also may undertake a so-called *defensive acquisition* to draw down any excess cash balances and to exhaust its current borrowing capacity. A firm may choose to liquidate the company, pay off outstanding obligations to creditors, and distribute the remaining proceeds to shareholders as a *liquidating dividend*. This makes sense only if the liquidating dividend exceeds what the shareholders would have received from the bidder.

Litigation

Takeover litigation often includes antitrust concerns, alleged violations of federal securities laws, inadequate disclosure by the bidder as required by the Williams Act, and alleged fraudulent behavior. Targets often seek a court injunction to stop the takeover attempt, at least temporarily, until the court has decided the merits of the allegations. By preventing the potential acquirer from acquiring more stock, the target firm is buying more time to erect additional defenses. While litigation is seldom successful in preventing a takeover, it may uncover additional information such as inadequate disclosure by the bidder through the ensuing discovery or fact-finding process that enables more substantive lawsuits.

THE IMPACT OF TAKEOVER DEFENSES ON SHAREHOLDER AND BONDHOLDER VALUE

Chapter 1 discussed the dramatic increase in abnormal financial returns—more than 30%, on average—since the 1960s to target shareholders around the time of a hostile tender offer announcement. Meanwhile, average abnormal returns to acquirer shareholders have deteriorated from marginally positive to slightly negative. Abnormal returns to target shareholders in friendly takeovers have remained at about 20%. What has spurred this increase in target company shareholder returns when hostile bids are at work? It could be potential improvements in efficiency, tax savings, or market power. However, if any of these were the explanation, we would be right to expect abnormal returns for mergers to show a correspondingly large increase over time—which they have not. Consequently, the explanation must lie elsewhere.

It is probably more than coincidental that the increase in abnormal returns began with the introduction of the 1967 Wallace Act prenotification period, which provides a respite for target firms to erect takeover defenses and search for other potential bidders. Takeover defenses such as poison pills, although unlikely to prevent a takeover, can add significantly to the overall purchase price. The purchase price can be boosted even further by an auction that might take place, as the initial bidder loses precious time in trying to overcome myriad defenses the target may be employing. Thus, the increasing sophistication of takeover defenses since 1980 would seem to be a highly plausible explanation—that is, at least intuitively—for the sustained increase in abnormal returns to target shareholders following the announcement of a hostile tender offer.

Unfortunately, this is a difficult intuitive argument to substantiate. Some empirical evidence seems to suggest that takeover defenses in general have virtually no statistically significant impact on shareholder returns.[41] Other evidence points to poison pills having a positive impact.[42] Studies that find a positive return seem to support the idea that incumbent management acts in the best interests of shareholders (the shareholder's interest hypothesis), while those studies that find a negative return seem to support the notion that incumbent management acts in its own interests (the management entrenchment hypothesis).

Overall, despite multiple studies, the research is largely contradictory.[43] While some studies demonstrate a correlation between firm performance and takeover defenses, it is difficult to substantiate that the correlation is a result of takeover defenses protecting incompetent management or simply reflecting the tendency of poorly managed firms to have takeover defenses.

[41] DeAngelo and Rice (1983) found no statistically significant negative results. Karpoff and Walkling (1996) found that shareholder efforts to remove takeover defenses had no significant impact on shareholder returns, suggesting that such efforts were viewed by investors as largely inconsequential. Field and Karpoff (2002), in a study of 1,019 initial public offerings between 1988 and 1992, found that takeover defenses had no impact on the takeover premiums of firms acquired after the IPO.

[42] Comment and Schwert (1995) found that poison pills would have a positive impact on shareholder returns if their addition by the target were viewed by investors as a signal that a takeover was imminent or that the firm's management would use such a defense to improve the purchase price during negotiations. The existence of poison pills often requires the bidder to raise its bid or to change the composition of its bid to an all-cash offer to put the target's board under pressure to dismantle its pill defenses. Timing also is important. For example, whenever a merger announcement coincided with the announcement of a poison pill, abnormal returns to target shareholders increased by 3 to 4%. Several studies suggest that investors react positively to the announcement of the adoption of takeover defenses if the firm's management interests are viewed as aligned with those of the shareholders, and negatively if management is viewed as seeking to entrench itself (Boyle et al., 1998; Malekzadeh et al., 1998).

[43] Comment and Schwert (1995) present a comprehensive review of previous studies, including Malatesta and Walkling (1988), Ryngaert (1988), Karpoff and Malatesta (1989), and Romano (1993). From these studies, the authors found that most takeover defensives, such as staggered boards, super-majority provisions, fair-price provisions, reincorporation, and dual capitalization resulted in a slightly negative decline in shareholder returns of about 0.5%.

Takeover Defenses May Destroy Shareholder Value

Despite the largely mixed results from earlier studies, more recent research suggests that takeover defenses may actually destroy shareholder value. For instance, the creation of a detailed "management entrenchment index" revealed that during the 1990s, firms at which management's interests are more aligned with those of the shareholders (i.e., firms employing good governance practices) had larger positive abnormal returns than firms with a high entrenchment index (i.e., those not employing good governance practices).[44] However, the close correlation between a firm's governance practices and abnormal returns disappeared in the 2000s, since investors had already bid up the prices of those firms that had implemented good governance practices in the 1990s and penalized those that had not.[45]

Another large study provides additional evidence of the destructive effect of takeover defenses, finding that managers at firms protected by takeover defenses are less subject to the disciplinary power of the market for corporate control and are more likely to engage in "empire building" acquisitions that destroy shareholder value.[46]

When firms move immediately from staggered board elections to annual elections of directors, they experience a cumulative abnormal return of 1.82%, reflecting investor expectations that the firm is more likely to be subject to a takeover. Often, such firms come under considerable pressure from activist shareholders, and the presence of a greater proportion of independent directors means that these firms are often more willing to submit to the demands of those activists.[47]

Takeover Defenses and Public Offerings

Event studies (a research approach introduced in Chapter 1) examine only how takeover defenses affect shareholder wealth after the corporation has been formed, shareholders have purchased its stock, and employees and managers have been hired. It may be the case, though, that takeover defenses create significant firm value at the very point the firm is formed. Consequently, fully evaluating the impact of takeover defenses on firm value requires giving consideration both to the potentially beneficial effects before the event of a takeover attempt and to the potentially destructive effects on firm value after the announcement. Takeover defenses may add to firm value before a takeover attempt if they help the firm

---

[44] Bebchuk et al. (2005) created a management entrenchment index in an effort to assess which of 24 provisions tracked by the Investor Responsibility Research Center (IRRC) had the greatest impact on shareholder value. The index, which is negatively correlated with firm value between 1990 and 2003, comprises staggered boards, limits to shareholder bylaw amendments, super-majority requirements for mergers, super-majority requirements for charter amendments, poison pills, and golden parachutes. No correlation between firm value and 18 other IRRC provisions during the sample period was found. The researchers note that the mere existence of correlation does not necessarily mean that these takeover defenses cause a reduction in the value of the firm. The correlation could reflect the tendency of underperforming firms that are likely to be takeover targets to adopt takeover defenses.

[45] Bebchuk, Cohen, and Wang, 2010

[46] Masulis et al., 2007

[47] Guo et al., 2008

attract, retain, and motivate effective managers and employees. Furthermore, such defenses give the new firm time to implement its business plan fully and invest in upgrading the skills of employees.[48] There is also evidence that investors may prefer the adoption of takeover defenses during the early stages of a firm's development.[49]

Takeover Defenses and Bondholders

Companies with limited takeover defenses are often vulnerable to hostile takeovers, which may hurt bondholders.[50] While the increased potential for takeover may benefit shareholder investors, existing bondholders stand to lose if the takeover results in a significant increase in leverage. This is typical of a leveraged buyout. Higher leverage can reduce the value of outstanding debt by increasing the potential for future bankruptcy.

SOME THINGS TO REMEMBER

The market in which takeover tactics and defenses are employed is called the corporate takeover market, which in a free market economy facilitates the allocation of resources and disciplines underperforming managers. By replacing such managers, the corporate takeover market can help protect stakeholder interests by promoting good corporate governance. In addition to the corporate takeover market, other factors external to the firm—such as federal and state legislation, the court system, regulators, and institutional activism—serve important roles in maintaining good corporate governance practices. Corporate governance is also affected by the integrity and professionalism of the firm's board of directors, as well as the effectiveness of the firm's internal controls and incentive systems, takeover defenses, and corporate culture.

Takeovers often are divided into friendly and hostile categories. If the friendly approach is considered inappropriate or is unsuccessful, the acquiring company may attempt to limit the options of the target's senior management by making a formal acquisition proposal, usually involving a public announcement, to the target's board of directors. Alternatively, the bidder may undertake a proxy contest, to change the composition of the target's board, or a tender offer, to go directly to shareholders.

Takeover defenses are designed to raise the overall cost of the takeover attempt and provide the target firm with more time to install additional takeover defenses. Preoffer defenses usually require shareholder approval and fall into three categories: poison pills, shark repellents, and golden parachutes. Postoffer defenses are those undertaken in response to a bid.

---

[48] Stout, 2002

[49] This is suggested by the finding of Coates (2001) that the percentage of IPO firms with staggered boards in their charters at the time of the initial public offering rose from 34% in the early 1990s to 82% in 1999.

[50] Cremers et al., 2004

DISCUSSION QUESTIONS

3.1 What are the management entrenchment and shareholder's interests hypotheses? Which seems more realistic in your judgment? Explain your answer.

3.2 What are the advantages and disadvantages of the friendly and hostile approaches to a corporate takeover? Be specific.

3.3 What are proxy contests and how are they used?

3.4 What is a tender offer? How does it differ from open market purchases of stock?

3.5 How are target shareholders affected by a hostile takeover attempt?

3.6 How are bidder shareholders affected by a hostile takeover attempt?

3.7 What are the primary advantages and disadvantages of commonly used takeover defenses?

3.8 Of the most commonly used takeover defenses, which seem to have the most favorable impact on target shareholders? Explain your answer.

3.9 How may golden parachutes for senior management help a target firm's shareholders? Are such severance packages justified in your judgment? Explain your answer.

3.10 How might recapitalization as a takeover defense help or hurt a target firm's shareholders?

3.11 Anheuser-Busch (AB) rejected InBev's all-cash offer price of $65 per share on June 30, 2008, saying it undervalued the company, despite the offer representing a 35% premium to AB's preannouncement share price. InBev refused to raise its offer, while repeating its strong preference for a friendly takeover. Speculate as to why InBev refused to raise its initial offer price. Why do you believe that InBev continued to prefer a friendly takeover? What do you think InBev should have done to raise pressure on the AB board to accept the offer?

3.12 What do you believe are the primary factors a target firm's board should consider when evaluating a bid from a potential acquirer?

3.13 If you were the CEO of a target firm, what strategy would you recommend to convince institutional shareholders to support your position in a proxy battle with the bidding firm?

3.14 Anheuser-Busch reduced its antitakeover defenses in 2006, when it removed its staggered board structure. Two years earlier, it did not renew its poison pill provision. Speculate as to why the board acquiesced in these instances. Explain how these events may have affected the firm's vulnerability to a takeover.

3.15 In response to Microsoft's efforts to acquire the firm, the Yahoo! board adopted a "change in-control" compensation plan in May 2008. The plan stated that if a Yahoo! employee's job is terminated by Yahoo! without cause (i.e., the employee is performing his or her duties appropriately) or if an employee leaves voluntarily due to a change in position or responsibilities within two years after Microsoft acquires a controlling interest in Yahoo!, the employee will receive one year's salary. Also, the plan provides for accelerated vesting of all stock options. Yahoo! notes that the adoption of the severance plan is an effort to ensure that employees are treated fairly if Microsoft wins control. Microsoft views the tactic as an effort to discourage a takeover. With whom do you agree and why?

Answers to these Chapter Discussion Questions are available in the Online Instructor's Manual for instructors using this book.

CHAPTER BUSINESS CASES

CASE STUDY 3.1
Mittal Acquires Arcelor—A Battle of Global Titans in the European Corporate Takeover Market

Ending five months of maneuvering, Arcelor agreed on June 26, 2006, to be acquired by larger rival Mittal Steel Co. for $33.8 billion in cash and stock. The takeover battle was one of the most acrimonious in recent European Union history. Hostile takeovers are now increasingly common in Europe. The battle is widely viewed as a test case as to how far a firm can go in attempting to prevent an unwanted takeover.

Arcelor was created in 2001 by melding steel companies in Spain, France, and Luxembourg. Most of its 90 plants are in Europe. In contrast, most of Mittal's plants are outside of Europe in areas with lower labor costs. Lakshmi Mittal, Mittal's CEO and a member of an important industrial family in India, started the firm and built it into a powerhouse through two decades of acquisitions in emerging nations. The company is headquartered in the Netherlands for tax reasons. Prior to the Arcelor acquisition, Mr. Mittal owned 88% of Mittal's stock.

Mittal acquired Arcelor to accelerate steel industry consolidation and thus reduce industry overcapacity. The combined firms could have more leverage in setting prices and negotiating contracts with major customers, such as auto and appliance manufacturers, and suppliers, such as iron ore and coal vendors, and they could eventually realize $1 billion annually in pretax cost savings.

After having been rebuffed by Guy Dolle, Arcelor's president, in an effort to consummate a friendly merger, Mittal launched a tender offer in January 2006 consisting of mostly stock and cash for all of Arcelor's outstanding equity. The offer constituted a 27% premium

over Arcelor's share price at that time. The reaction from Arcelor's management, European unions, and government officials was swift and furious. Guy Dolle stated flatly that the offer was "inadequate and strategically unsound." European politicians supported Mr. Dolle. Luxembourg's prime minister, Jean Claude Juncker, said a hostile bid "calls for a hostile response." Trade unions expressed concerns about potential job loss.

Dolle engaged in one of the most aggressive takeover defenses in recent corporate history. In early February, Arcelor doubled its dividend and announced plans to buy back about $8.75 billion in stock at a price well above the then current market price for Arcelor stock. These actions were taken to motivate Arcelor shareholders not to tender their shares to Mittal. Arcelor also backed a move to change the law so that Mittal would be required to pay in cash. However, the Luxembourg parliament rejected that effort.

To counter these moves, Mittal Steel said in mid-February that if it received more than one-half of the Arcelor shares submitted in the initial tender offer, it would hold a second tender offer for the remaining shares at a slightly lower price. Mittal pointed out that it could acquire the remaining shares through a merger or corporate reorganization. Such rhetoric was designed to encourage Arcelor shareholders to tender their shares during the first offer.

In late 2005, Arcelor outbid German steelmaker Metallgeschaft to buy Canadian steelmaker Dofasco for $5 billion. Mittal was proposing to sell Dofasco to raise money

CASE STUDY 3.1 *(cont'd)*

and avoid North American antitrust concerns. Following completion of the Dofasco deal in April 2006, Arcelor set up a special Dutch trust to prevent Mittal from getting access to the asset. The trust is run by a board of three Arcelor appointees. The trio has the power to determine if Dofasco can be sold during the next five years. Mittal immediately sued to test the legality of this tactic.

In a deal with Russian steel maker OAO Severstahl, Arcelor agreed to exchange its shares for Alexei Mordashov's 90% stake in Severstahl. The transaction would give Mr. Mordashov a 32% stake in Arcelor. Arcelor also scheduled an unusual vote that created very tough conditions for Arcelor shareholders to prevent the deal with Severstahl from being completed. Arcelor's board stated that the Severstahl deal could be blocked only if at least 50% of all Arcelor shareholders would vote against it. However, Arcelor knew that only about one-third of its shareholders actually attend meetings. This is a tactic permissible under Luxembourg law, where Arcelor is incorporated.

Investors holding more than 30% of the Arcelor shares signed a petition to force the company to make the deal with Severstahl subject to a traditional 50.1% or more of actual votes cast. After major shareholders pressured the Arcelor board to at least talk to Mr. Mittal, Arcelor demanded an intricate business plan from Mittal as a condition that had to be met. Despite Mittal's submission of such a plan, Arcelor still refused to talk. In late May, Mittal raised its bid by 34% and said that if the bid succeeded, Mittal would eliminate his firm's two-tiered share structure, giving the Mittal family shares ten times the voting rights of other shareholders.

A week after receiving the shareholder petition, the Arcelor board rejected Mittal's sweetened bid and repeated its support of the Severstahl deal. Shareholder anger continued, and many investors said they would reject the share buyback. Some investors opposed the buyback because it would increase Mr. Mordashov's ultimate stake in Arcelor to 38% by reducing the number of Arcelor shares outstanding. Under the laws of most European countries, any entity owning more than a third of a company is said to have effective control. Arcelor cancelled a scheduled June 21 shareholder vote on the buyback. Despite Mr. Mordashov's efforts to enhance his bid, the Arcelor board asked both Mordashov and Mittal to submit their final bids by June 25.

Arcelor agreed to Mittal's final bid, which had been increased by 14%. The new offer consisted of $15.70 in cash and 1.0833 Mittal shares for each Arcelor share. The new bid is valued at $50.54 per Arcelor share, up from Mittal's initial bid in January 2006 of $35.26. The final offer represented an unprecedented 93% premium over Arcelor's share price of $26.25 immediately before Mittal's initial bid. Lakshmi Mittal will control 43.5% of the combined firm's stock. Mr. Mordashov will receive a $175 million breakup fee due to Arcelor's failure to complete its agreement with him. Finally, Mittal agreed not to make any layoffs beyond what Arcelor already has planned.

Discussion Questions

1. Identify the takeover tactics employed by Mittal. Explain why each one was used.
2. Identify the takeover defenses employed by Arcelor. Explain why each was used.
3. Using the information in this case study, discuss the arguments for and against

CASE STUDY 3.1 *(cont'd)*

encouraging hostile corporate takeovers. Be as specific as possible.

4. Was Arcelor's board and management acting to protect their own positions (i.e., according to the management entrenchment hypothesis) or the best interests of the shareholders (i.e., the shareholder's interests hypothesis)? Explain your answer.

Answers to these questions are found in the Online Instructor's Manual available to instructors using this book.

CASE STUDY 3.2
Verizon Acquires MCI—The Anatomy of Alternative Bidding Strategies

While many parties were interested in acquiring MCI, the major players included Verizon and Qwest. U.S.-based Qwest is an integrated communications company that provides data, multimedia, and Internet-based communication services on a national and global basis. The acquisition would ease the firm's huge debt burden of $17.3 billion because the debt would be supported by the combined company with a much larger revenue base and give it access to new business customers and opportunities to cut costs.

Verizon Communications, created through the merger of Bell Atlantic and GTE in 2000, is the largest telecommunications provider in the United States. The company provides local exchange, long distance, Internet, and other services to residential, business, and government customers. In addition, the company provides wireless services to over 42 million customers in the United States through its 55%–owned JV with Vodafone Group PLC. Verizon stated that the merger would enable it to more efficiently provide a broader range of services, give the firm access to MCI's business customer base, accelerate new product development using MCI's fiber-optic network infrastructure, and create substantial cost savings.

By mid-2004, MCI had received several expressions of interest from Verizon and Qwest regarding potential strategic relationships. By July, Qwest and MCI entered into a confidentiality agreement and proceeded to perform more detailed due diligence. Ivan Seidenberg, Verizon's chairman and CEO, inquired about a potential takeover and was rebuffed by MCI's board, which was evaluating its strategic options. These included Qwest's proposal regarding a share-for-share merger, following a one-time cash dividend to MCI shareholders from MCI's cash in excess of its required operating balances. In view of Verizon's interest, MCI's board of directors directed management to advise Richard Notebaert, the chairman and CEO of Qwest, that MCI was not prepared to move forward with a potential transaction. The stage was set for what would become Qwest's laboriously long and ultimately unsuccessful pursuit of MCI, in which the firm would improve its original offer four times, only to be rejected by MCI in each instance even though the Qwest bids exceeded Verizon's.

After assessing its strategic alternatives, including the option to remain a standalone company, MCI's board of directors concluded

CASE STUDY 3.2   *(cont'd)*

that the merger with Verizon was in the best interests of the MCI stockholders. MCI's board of directors noted that Verizon's bid of $26 in cash and stock for each MCI share represented a 41.5% premium over the closing price of MCI's common stock on January 26, 2005. Furthermore, the stock portion of the offer included "price protection" in the form of a collar (i.e., the portion of the purchase price consisting of stock would be fixed within a narrow range if Verizon's share price changed between the signing and closing of the transaction).

The merger agreement also provided for the MCI board to declare a special dividend of $5.60 once the firm's shareholders approved the deal. MCI's board of directors also considered the additional value that its stockholders would realize, since the merger would be a tax-free reorganization in which MCI shareholders would be able to defer the payment of taxes until they sold their stock. Only the cash portion of the purchase price would be taxable immediately. MCI's board of directors also noted that a large number of MCI's most important business customers had indicated that they preferred a transaction between MCI and Verizon rather than a transaction between MCI and Qwest.

While it is clearly impossible to know for sure, the sequence of events reveals a great deal about Verizon's possible bidding strategy. Any bidding strategy must begin with a series of management assumptions about how to approach the target firm. It was certainly in Verizon's best interests to attempt a friendly rather than a hostile takeover of MCI, due to the challenges of integrating these two complex businesses. Verizon also employed an increasingly popular technique in which the merger agreement includes a special dividend payable by the target firm to its shareholders contingent upon their approval of the transaction. This

special dividend is an inducement to gain shareholder approval.

Given the modest 3% premium over the first Qwest bid, Verizon's initial bidding strategy appears to have been based on the low end of the purchase price range it was willing to offer MCI. Verizon was initially prepared to share relatively little of the potential synergy with MCI shareholders, believing that a bidding war for MCI would be unlikely in view of the recent spate of mergers in the telecommunications industry and the weak financial position of other competitors. SBC and Nextel were busy integrating AT&T and Sprint, respectively. Moreover, Qwest appeared to be unable to finance a substantial all-cash offer due to its current excessive debt burden, and its stock appeared to have little appreciation potential because of ongoing operating losses. Perhaps stunned by the persistence with which Qwest pursued MCI, Verizon believed that its combination of cash and stock would ultimately be more attractive to MCI investors than Qwest's primarily all-cash offer, due to the partial tax-free nature of the bid.

Throughout the bidding process, many of the hedge funds criticized MCI's board publicly for accepting the initial Verizon bid. Since its emergence from Chapter 11, hedge funds had acquired significant positions in MCI's stock, with the expectation that MCI would constitute an attractive merger candidate. In particular, Carlos Slim Helu, the Mexican telecommunications magnate and largest MCI shareholder, complained publicly about the failure of MCI's board to get full value for the firm's shares. Pressure from hedge funds and other dissident MCI shareholders triggered a shareholder lawsuit to void the February 14, 2005, signed merger agreement with Verizon.

In preparation for a possible proxy fight, Verizon entered into negotiations with Carlos Slim

CASE STUDY 3.2   (cont'd)

Helu to acquire his shares. Verizon acquired Helu's 13.7% stake in MCI in April 2005. Despite this purchase, Verizon's total stake in MCI remained below the 15% ownership level that would trigger the MCI rights plan.

About 70% (i.e., $1.4 billion) of the cash portion of Verizon's proposed purchase price consisted of a special MCI dividend payable by MCI itself when the firm's shareholders approved the merger agreement. Verizon's management argued that the deal would cost their shareholders only $7.05 billion (i.e., the $8.45 billion purchase price consisting of cash and stock, less the MCI special dividend). The $1.4 billion special dividend reduced MCI's cash in excess of what was required to meet its normal operating cash requirements.

Qwest consistently attempted to outmaneuver Verizon by establishing a significant premium between its bid and Verizon's, often as much as 25%. Qwest realized that its current level of indebtedness would preclude it from significantly increasing the cash portion of the bid. Consequently, it had to rely on the premium to attract enough investor interest, particularly among hedge funds, to pressure the MCI board to accept the higher bid. However, Qwest was unable to convince enough investors that its stock would not simply lose value once more shares were issued to consummate the stock and cash transaction.

Qwest could have initiated a tender or exchange offer directly to MCI shareholders, proposing to purchase or exchange their shares without going through the merger process. The tender process requires lengthy regulatory approval. However, if Qwest initiated a tender offer, it could trigger MCI's poison pill. Alternatively, a proxy contest might have been preferable because Qwest already had a

bid on the table, and the contest would enable Qwest to lobby MCI shareholders to vote against the Verizon bid. This strategy would have avoided triggering the poison pill.

Ultimately, Qwest was forced to capitulate simply because it did not have the financial wherewithal to increase the $9.9 billion bid. It could not borrow any more because of its excessive leverage. Additional stock would have contributed to earnings dilution and caused the firm's share price to fall.

It is unusual for a board to turn down a higher bid, especially when the competing bid is 17% higher. In accepting the Verizon bid, MCI stated that a number of its large business customers had expressed a preference for the company to be bought by Verizon rather than Qwest. MCI noted that these customer concerns posed a significant risk in being acquired by Qwest. The MCI board's acceptance of the lower Verizon bid could serve as a test case of how well MCI directors conducted their fiduciary responsibilities. The central issue is how far boards can go in rejecting a higher offer in favor of one they believe offers more long-term stability for the firm's stakeholders.

Ron Perlman, the 1980s takeover mogul, saw his higher all-cash bid rejected by the board of directors of Revlon Corporation, which accepted a lower offer from another bidder. In a subsequent lawsuit, a court overruled the decision by the Revlon board in favor of the Perlman bid. Consequently, from a governance perspective, legal precedent compels boards to accept higher bids from bona fide bidders where the value of the bid is unambiguous, as in the case of an all-cash offer. However, for transactions in which the purchase price is composed largely of acquirer stock, the value is less certain. As a

CASE STUDY 3.2 *(cont'd)*

result, the target's board may rule that the lower bidder's shares have higher appreciation potential or at least are less likely to decline than those shares of other bidders.

MCI's president and CEO Michael Capellas and other executives could collect $107 million in severance, payouts of restricted stock, and monies to compensate them for taxes owed on the payouts. In particular, Capellas stands to receive $39.2 million if his job is terminated "without cause" or if he leaves the company "for good reason."

Discussion Questions

1. Discuss how changing industry conditions have encouraged consolidation within the telecommunications industry.

2. What alternative strategies could Verizon, Qwest, and MCI have pursued? Was the decision to acquire MCI the best alternative for Verizon? Explain your answer.

3. Who are the winners and losers in the Verizon–MCI merger? Be specific.

4. What takeover tactics were employed or threatened to be employed by Verizon? By Qwest? Be specific.

5. What specific takeover defenses did MCI employ?

6. How did the actions of certain shareholders affect the bidding process? Be specific.

7. In your opinion, did the MCI board act in the best interests of their shareholders? Of all their stakeholders? Be specific.

8. Do you believe that the potential severance payments that could be paid to Capellas were excessive? Explain your answer. What are the arguments for and against such severance plans for senior executives?

9. Should the antitrust regulators approve the Verizon-MCI merger? Explain your answer.

10. Verizon's management argued that the final purchase price from the perspective of Verizon shareholders was not $8.45 billion but rather $7.05 billion. This was so, they argued, because MCI was paying the difference of $1.4 billion from their excess cash balances as a special dividend to MCI shareholders. Why is this misleading?

Answers to these discussion questions are available in the Online Instructor's Manual for instructors using this book.

THE MERGERS AND ACQUISITIONS PROCESS

Phases 1 through 10

"I need anger management. All my takeovers are hostile."

Courtesy of www.CartoonStock.com.

Part II views mergers and acquisitions not as business strategies but rather as a means of implementing business strategies. Business strategies define a firm's vision and long-term objectives and how it expects to achieve these ends. M&As simply represent one means of implementing the business strategy. The firm may choose from a range of reasonable alternative implementation strategies, including "going it alone" or partnering, or by acquiring another firm.

Chapters 4 through 6 discuss the various activities often undertaken in a merger or acquisition. These activities comprise the ten phases of an M&A process. While not all mergers and acquisitions unfold in exactly the same way, the process outlined in this section serves as a road map for executing such transactions. The process is sufficiently flexible to be applicable to alternatives to M&As such as business alliances, which are discussed in Chapter 14.

Chapter 4 focuses on how to develop a business plan or strategy and, if an acquisition is viewed as the best way of realizing the business strategy, how to develop an acquisition plan. Chapter 5 deals with identifying, making initial contact with the potential target, and developing the necessary legal documents prior to beginning due diligence and formal negotiations. While initial valuations provide a starting point, the actual purchase price is determined during the negotiation period. If agreement can be reached, planning the integration of the target firm begins between the signing of the purchase agreement and the closing. The motivation for each phase of the process is discussed in detail. Chapter 6 discusses common obstacles arising during the postclosing integration effort and how to deal successfully with such challenges.

4

Planning: Developing Business and Acquisition Plans
Phases 1 and 2 of the Acquisition Process

If you don't know where you are going, any road will get you there. —**Lewis Carroll, Alice in Wonderland**

INSIDE M&A: NOKIA'S GAMBLE TO DOMINATE THE SMARTPHONE MARKET FALTERS

The ultimate success or failure of any M&A transaction in satisfying expectations often is heavily dependent on the answer to a simple question. Was the justification for buying the target firm based on a sound business strategy? No matter how bold, innovative, or precedent-setting a bad strategy is, it is still a bad strategy.

In a bold move that is reminiscent of the rollout of Linux, Nokia, a Finnish phone handset manufacturer, announced in mid-2008 that it had reached an agreement to acquire Symbian, its supplier of smartphone operating system software.[1] Nokia also announced its intention to give away Symbian's software for free in response to Google's decision in December 2008 to offer its Android operating system at no cost to handset makers.

This switch from a model in which developers had to pay a license fee to create devices using the Symbian operating system software to a free (open source) model was designed to supercharge the introduction of innovative handheld products that relied on Symbian software. Any individual or firm can use and modify the Symbian code for any purpose for free. In doing so, Nokia is hoping that a wave of new products using Symbian software would blunt the growth of Apple's proprietary system and Google's open source Android system.

Nokia is seeking to establish an industry standard based on the Symbian software, using it as a platform for providing online services to smartphone users, such as music and photo sharing. According to Forrester Research, the market for such services is expected to reach

[1] A smartphone is a single handheld device that can take care of all of the user's handheld computing and communication needs.

$92 billion in 2012 (almost twice its size when Nokia acquired Symbian), with an increasing portion of these services delivered via smartphones.

In its *vision* for the future, Nokia seems to be positioning itself as the premier supplier of online services to the smartphone market. Its *business strategy* or *model* is to dominate the smartphone market with handsets that rely on the Symbian operating system. Nokia hopes to exploit economies of scale by spreading any fixed cost associated with online services over an expanding customer base. Such fixed expenses could include a requirement by content service providers that Nokia pay a minimum level of royalties in addition to royalties that vary with usage.

Similarly, the development cost incurred by service providers can be defrayed by selling into a growing customer base. The *implementation strategy* involved the acquisition of the leading supplier of handset operating systems and subsequently to give away the Symbian software free. The success or failure of this vision, business strategy, and implementation strategy depends on whether Symbian can do a better job of recruiting other handset makers, service providers, and consumers than Nokia's competitors.

The strategy to date seems to be unraveling. At the time of the acquisition, Symbian supplied almost 60% of the operating system software for smartphones worldwide. Market researcher Ovum estimates that the firm's global market share fell to less than 50% in 2010 and predicts the figure could decline to one-third by 2015, reflecting the growing popularity of Google's Android software.[2] Android has had excellent success in the U.S. market, leapfrogging over Apple's 24% share to capture 27% of the smartphone market, according to the NPD Group. Research-In-Motion (RIM), the maker of the Blackberry, remained the U.S. market share leader in 2010 at 33%.

CHAPTER OVERVIEW

A poorly designed or inappropriate business strategy is among the reasons most frequently given when mergers and acquisitions fail to satisfy expectations. Too often, the overarching role that planning should take in conceptualizing and implementing business combinations is ignored. Some companies view mergers and acquisitions as a business growth strategy. Here, in accord with the view of many successful acquirers,[3] M&As are not considered a business strategy but rather a means of implementing a business strategy. While firms may accelerate overall growth in the short run through acquisition, the higher growth rate often is not sustainable without a business plan—which serves as a road map for identifying additional acquisitions to fuel future growth. Moreover, the business plan facilitates the integration of the acquired firms and the realization of synergy.

This chapter focuses on the first two phases of the acquisition process—building the business and acquisition plans—and on the tools commonly used to evaluate, display, and communicate information to key constituencies both inside (e.g., board of directors and management) and outside (e.g., lenders and stockholders) of the corporation. Phases 3

---

[2] For more information, see *www.guardian.co.uk/business/2010/feb/04/symbian-smartphone-software-open-source.*

[3] Palter and Srinivasan, 2006

through 10 are discussed in Chapter 5. Subsequent chapters detail the remaining phases of the M&A process.

The planning concepts described here are largely prescriptive in nature: They recommend certain strategies based on the results generated by applying specific tools (e.g., experience curves) and answering checklists of relevant questions. Although these tools introduce some degree of rigor to strategic planning, their application should not be viewed as a completion of the planning process. Business plans must be updated frequently to account for changes in the firm's operating environment and its competitive position within that environment. Indeed, business planning is not an event but an evolving process.[4]

A review of this chapter (including practice questions) is available in the file folder entitled Student Study Guide on the companion site to this book *(www.elsevierdirect. com/companions/9780123854858).* The companion site also contains a Learning Interactions Library, which gives students the opportunity to test their knowledge of this chapter in a "real-time" environment.

A PLANNING-BASED APPROACH TO M&AS

The acquisition process envisioned here can be separated into two stages. The *planning* stage comprises developing business and acquisition plans. The *implementation* stage (discussed in Chapter 5) includes search, screening, target contact negotiation, integration planning, closing, integration, and evaluation activities.

Key Business Planning Concepts

A planning-based acquisition process is comprised of both a business plan and a merger/acquisition plan, which together drive all subsequent phases of the acquisition process. The *business plan* articulates a mission or vision for the firm and a *business strategy* for realizing that mission for all of the firm's stakeholders. *Stakeholders* are constituent groups such as customers, shareholders, employees, suppliers, lenders, regulators, and communities. The business strategy is oriented to the long term and usually cuts across organizational lines to affect many different functional areas. Typically, it is broadly defined and provides relatively little detail.

With respect to business strategy, it can be important to distinguish between the corporate level and the business level. *Corporate-level strategies* are set by the management of a diversified or multiproduct firm and generally cross business unit organizational lines. They entail decisions about financing the growth of certain businesses, operating others to generate cash, divesting some units, or pursuing diversification. *Business-level strategies* are set by the management of a specific operating unit within the corporate organizational structure and may involve that unit attempting to achieve a low-cost position in the markets it serves, differentiating its product offering, or narrowing its operational focus to a specific market niche.

The *implementation strategy* refers to the way in which the firm chooses to execute the business strategy. It is usually far more detailed than the business strategy. The *merger/acquisition plan* is a specific type of implementation strategy and describes in detail the motivation for the

---

[4] For a more detailed discussion of business planning, see Hunger and Wheeler, 2007.

acquisition and how and when it will be achieved. *Functional strategies* describe in detail how each major function within the firm (e.g., manufacturing, marketing, and human resources) will support the business strategy. *Contingency plans* are actions that are taken as an alternative to the firm's current business strategy.

The selection of which alternative action to pursue may be contingent on certain events called *trigger points* (e.g., failure to realize revenue targets or cost savings), at which point a firm faces a number of alternatives, sometimes referred to as *real options*. These include abandoning, delaying, or accelerating an investment strategy. Unlike the strategic options discussed later in this chapter, real options are decisions that can be made *after* a business strategy has been implemented.

The Merger and Acquisition Process

A merger and acquisition process can be thought of as a series of activities culminating in the transfer of ownership from the seller to the buyer. Some individuals shudder at the thought of following a structured process because they believe it may delay responding to opportunities, both anticipated and unanticipated. Anticipated opportunities are those identified as a result of the business planning process: understanding the firm's external operating environment, assessing internal resources, reviewing a range of reasonable options, and articulating a clear vision of the future of the business and a realistic strategy for achieving that vision.[5] Unanticipated opportunities may emerge as new information becomes available. Having a well-designed business plan does not delay pursuing opportunities; rather, it provides a way to evaluate the opportunity, rapidly and substantively, by determining the extent to which the opportunity supports realization of the business plan.

Figure 4.1 illustrates the ten phases of the M&A process described in this and subsequent chapters. These phases fall into two distinct sets of activities: pre- and postpurchase decision activities. Negotiation, with its four largely concurrent and interrelated activities, is the crucial phase of the acquisition process. The decision to purchase or walk away is determined as a result of continuous iteration through the four activities comprising the negotiation phase.

The phases of the M&A process are summarized as follows:

Phase 1: Business Plan—Develop a strategic plan for the entire business.
Phase 2: Acquisitions Plan—Develop the acquisition plan supporting the business plan.
Phase 3: Search—Actively search for acquisition candidates.
Phase 4: Screen—Screen and prioritize potential candidates.
Phase 5: First Contact—Initiate contact with the target.
Phase 6: Negotiation—Refine valuation, structure the deal, perform due diligence, and develop the financing plan.
Phase 7: Integration Plan—Develop a plan for integrating the acquired business.
Phase 8: Closing—Obtain the necessary approvals, resolve postclosing issues, and execute the closing.
Phase 9: Integration—Implement the postclosing integration.
Phase 10: Evaluation—Conduct the postclosing evaluation of acquisition.

[5] Hill and Jones, 2001

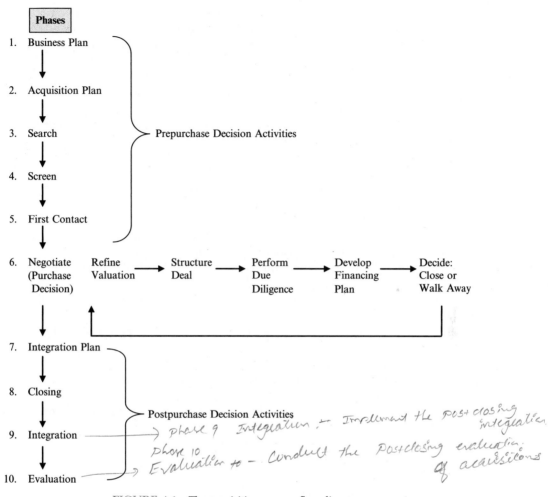

FIGURE 4.1   The acquisition process flow diagram.

PHASE 1: BUILDING THE BUSINESS PLAN

A well-designed business plan results from eight key activities, summarized below. In practice, the process of developing a business plan can be facilitated by addressing a number of detailed questions corresponding to each of these activities.[6]

The first activity is *external analysis* to determine where to compete—that is, which industry or market(s)—and how to compete—that is, how the firm can most effectively compete in its chosen market(s)). This is followed by *internal analysis*, or self-assessment of the firm's

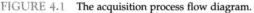

[6] Extensive checklists can be found in Porter (1985). Answering these types of questions requires gathering substantial economic, industry, and market information.

strengths and weaknesses relative to its competition. The combination of these two activities—the external and internal analyses—is often called *SWOT analysis* because it determines the strengths, weaknesses, opportunities, and threats of a business. Once this exhaustive analysis is completed, management has a clearer understanding of emerging opportunities and threats to the firm and of the firm's primary internal strengths and weaknesses. Information gleaned from the external and internal analyses drives the development of business, implementation, and functional strategies.

The third activity is to define a *mission statement* that summarizes where and how the firm has chosen to compete, based on the external analysis, as well as management's basic operating beliefs and values. Fourth, *objectives* are set, and quantitative measures of financial and nonfinancial performance are developed. Having completed these steps, the firm is ready to *select a business strategy* that is most likely to achieve the objectives in an acceptable period, subject to constraints identified in the self-assessment. The business strategy defines, in general terms, how the business intends to compete (i.e., through cost leadership, differentiation, or increased focus).

Next, an *implementation strategy* is selected that articulates the best way to implement the business strategy from among a range of reasonable options. It may be that the firm opts to act on its own, partner with others, or acquire/merge with another firm. This is followed by development of a *functional strategy* that defines the roles, responsibilities, and resource requirements of each major functional area within the firm needed to support the business strategy.

The final step is to establish *strategic controls* to monitor actual performance to plan, implement incentive systems, and take corrective actions as necessary. These controls are put in place to heighten the prospect that the mission, objectives, and strategies will be realized on schedule. They may involve establishing bonus plans and other incentive mechanisms to motivate all employees to achieve their individual objectives on or ahead of schedule. Systems are also put in place to track the firm's actual performance to plan. Significant deviations from the implementation plan may require switching to contingency plans. Let's look at each of these steps in greater detail.

External Analysis

The external analysis involves the development of an understanding of the business's customers and their needs, the market/industry competitive dynamics or factors determining profitability and cash flow, and emerging trends that affect customer needs and industry competition. This analysis begins with answering two basic questions: where to compete and how to compete. The primary output of the external analysis is the identification of important growth opportunities and competitive threats.

Determining Where to Compete

There is no more important activity in building a business plan than deciding where a firm should compete. It begins with identifying the firm's current and potential customers and their primary needs, and it is based on the process of market segmentation, which involves identifying customers with common characteristics and needs.

Whether it is made up of individual consumers or other firms, collections of customers comprise *markets*. A collection of markets is said to comprise an *industry*—for example, the automotive industry, which comprises the new and used car markets as well as the after-market for replacement parts. Markets may be further subdivided by examining cars by makes and model years. The automotive market could also be defined regionally (e.g., New England, North America, Europe) or by country. Each subdivision, whether by product or geographic area, defines a new market within the automotive industry.

Identifying a target market involves a three-step process. First, the firm establishes evaluation criteria to distinguish the attractiveness of multiple potential target markets. These criteria may include market size and growth rate, profitability, cyclicality, the price sensitivity of customers, the amount of regulation, the degree of unionization, and entry and exit barriers. The second step is to subdivide industries and the markets within these industries repeatedly and analyze the overall attractiveness of these markets in terms of the evaluation criteria. For each market, each of the criteria is given a numerical weight (some even at zero) reflecting the firm's perception of their relative importance as applied to that market. Higher numbers imply greater perceived importance. The markets are then ranked from 1 to 5 according to the evaluation criteria, with 5 indicating that the firm finds a market to be highly favorable in terms of a specific criterion. In the third step, a weighted average score is calculated for each market, and the markets are ranked according to their respective scores.

For an illustration of this process, see the document entitled "An Example of a Market-Attractiveness Matrix" on the companion site to this book.

Determining How to Compete

Determining how to compete requires a clear understanding of the factors that are critical for successfully competing in the targeted market. This outward-looking analysis applies to the primary factors governing the firm's external environment. Understanding the market/industry competitive dynamics (i.e., how profits and cash flow are determined) and knowing the areas in which the firm must excel in comparison with the competition (e.g., high-quality or low-cost products) are crucial if the firm is to compete effectively in its chosen market.

Market profiling entails collecting sufficient data to assess and characterize accurately a firm's competitive environment within its chosen markets. Using Michael Porter's well-known "Five Forces" framework (also known as the Porter or Modified Porter framework), the market or industry environment can be described in terms of competitive dynamics such as the firm's customers, suppliers, current competitors, potential competitors, and product or service substitutes.[7]

The three potential determinants of the intensity of competition in an industry include competition among existing firms, the threat of entry of new firms, and the threat of substitute products or services. While the degree of competition determines whether there is potential to earn abnormal profits (i.e., those in excess of what would be expected for the degree of assumed risk), the actual profits or cash flows are influenced by the relative bargaining power of the industry's customers and suppliers.

This framework may be modified to include other factors that determine actual industry profitability and cash flow, such as the severity of government regulation or the impact of global influences such as fluctuating exchange rates. Labor costs may also be included.

---

[7] Porter, 1985

While they represent a relatively small percentage of total expenses in many areas of manufacturing, they frequently constitute the largest expense in the nonmanufacturing sector. The analysis should also include factors such as the bargaining power of labor.

Figure 4.2 brings together these competitive dynamics. The data required to analyze industry competitive dynamics include types of products and services; market share (in terms of dollars and units); pricing metrics; selling and distribution channels and associated costs;

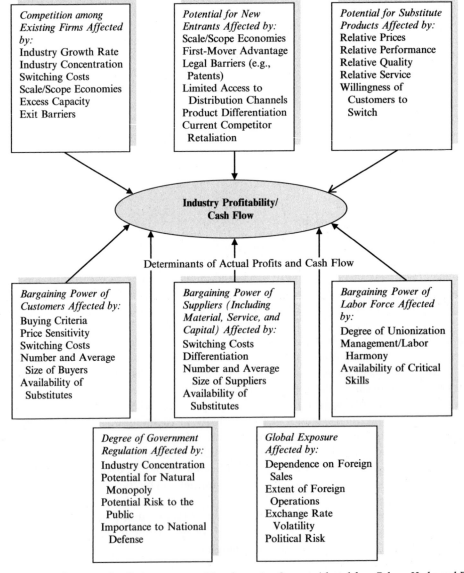

FIGURE 4.2 Defining market/industry competitive dynamics. Source: *Adapted from Palepu, Healy, and Bernard, 2004.*

type, location, and age of the production facilities; product quality metrics; customer service metrics; compensation by major labor category; research and development (R&D) expenditures; supplier performance metrics; and financial performance (in terms of growth and profitability). These data must be collected on all significant competitors in the firm's chosen markets.

Determinants of the Intensity of Industry Competition

The overall intensity of industry competition is a function of different factors in several categories. The first category includes industry growth rate, industry concentration, degree of differentiation and switching costs, scale and scope economies, excess capacity, and exit barriers, all of which affect the intensity of competition among current industry competitors. If an industry is growing rapidly, existing firms have less need to compete for market share. If an industry is highly concentrated, firms can more easily coordinate their pricing activities; in contrast, this is more difficult in a highly fragmented industry in which price competition is likely to be very intense.

If the cost of switching from one supplier to another is minimal because of low perceived differentiation, customers are likely to switch based on relatively small differences in price. In industries in which production volume is important, companies may compete aggressively for market share to realize economies of scale. Moreover, firms in industries exhibiting substantial excess capacity often reduce prices to fill unused capacity. Finally, competition may be intensified in industries in which it is difficult for firms to exit due to high exit barriers, such as large unfunded pension liabilities and single-purpose assets.

The second category is the potential for new entrants offering products and services similar to those provided by firms currently competing in the industry. Current competitors within an industry characterized by low barriers to entry have limited pricing power. Attempts to raise prices resulting in abnormally large profits will attract new competitors, thereby adding to the industry's productive capacity. In contrast, high entry barriers may give existing competitors significant pricing power. Barriers to new entrants include situations in which the large-scale operations of existing competitors give them a potential cost advantage due to economies of scale. New entrants may enter only if they are willing to invest in substantial additional new capacity. The "first-mover advantage"—that is, being an early competitor in an industry—may also create entry barriers because first-movers achieve widespread brand recognition, establish industry standards, and/or develop exclusive relationships with key suppliers and distributors. Finally, legal constraints, such as copyrights and patents, may inhibit the entry of new firms.

The third category includes the potential for substitute products and services. The selling price of one product compared to a close substitute—called the relative price—determines the threat of substitution, along with the performance of competing products, perceived quality, and the willingness of the customer to switch. Potential substitutes could come from current or potential competitors and include those that are substantially similar to existing products and those performing the same function—for example, an MP3 rather than a CD, a Kindle wireless reading device rather than a book, or even a paperless airline ticket.

Determinants of Actual Profits and Cash Flow

The bargaining powers of customers, suppliers, and the labor force are all important factors that affect profits and cash flow. Others include the degree of government regulation and global exposure. The relative bargaining power of buyers depends on their primary buying criteria (i.e., price, quality/reliability, service, convenience, or some combination), price sensitivity or elasticity, switching costs, and their number and size compared to the number and size of suppliers. For example, a customer whose primary criterion for making a purchase is product quality and reliability may be willing to pay a premium for a BMW because it is perceived to have higher relative quality. Customers are more likely to be highly price sensitive in industries characterized by largely undifferentiated products and low switching costs. Finally, buyers are likely to have considerable bargaining power when there are relatively few large buyers relative to the number of suppliers.

The relative leverage of suppliers reflects the ease with which customers can switch suppliers, perceived differentiation, their number, and how critical they are to the customer. Switching costs are highest when customers must pay penalties to exit long-term supply contracts, or when new suppliers would have to undergo an intensive learning process to meet the customers' requirements. Moreover, reliance on a single or a small number of suppliers shifts pricing power from the buyer to the seller. Examples include Intel's global dominance of the microchip market and Microsoft's worldwide supremacy in the market for personal computer operating systems.

Work stoppages create opportunities for competitors to gain market share. Customers are forced to satisfy their product and service needs elsewhere. Although the loss of customers may be temporary, it may become permanent if the customer finds that another firm's product or service is superior. Frequent work stoppages also may have long-term impacts on productivity and production costs as a result of a less-motivated labor force and increased labor turnover.

Governments may choose to regulate industries that are heavily concentrated, that are natural monopolies (e.g., electric utilities), or that provide a potential risk to the public. Regulatory compliance adds significantly to an industry's operating costs. Regulations also create barriers to both entering and exiting an industry.

Global exposure is the extent to which participation in an industry necessitates having a multinational presence. For example, the automotive industry is widely viewed as a global industry in which participation requires having assembly plants and distribution networks in major markets throughout the world. As the major auto assemblers move abroad, they need their parts suppliers to build nearby facilities to ensure "just-in-time" delivery. Global exposure introduces the firm to significant currency risk as well as political risk that could result in the confiscation of the firm's properties.

Case Study 4.1 illustrates how a second-tier U.S. telecommunications company is attempting to adapt to secular changes in the telecommunications market.

Internal Analysis

The primary output of internal analysis is to determine the firm's strengths and weaknesses. What are they compared to the competition? Can the firm's critical strengths be easily duplicated and surpassed by the competition? Can they be used to gain advantage in the firm's chosen market? Can competitors exploit the firm's key weaknesses? These questions must be answered as objectively as possible for the information to be useful in formulating a viable strategy.

Ultimately, competing successfully means doing a better job than the competitors of satisfying the needs of the firm's targeted customers. A self-assessment identifies those strengths or competencies—so-called *success factors*—necessary to compete successfully in

CASE STUDY 4.1
CenturyTel Buys Qwest Communications to Cut Costs and Buy Time as the Landline Market Shrinks

In what could best be described as a defensive acquisition, CenturyTel, the fifth largest local phone company in the United States, acquired Qwest Communications, the country's third largest, in mid-2010 in a stock swap valued at $10.6 billion. While both firms are dwarfed in size by AT&T and Verizon, these second-tier telecommunications firms will control a larger share of the shrinking landline market.

The combined firms will have about 17 million phone lines serving customers in 37 states. This compares to AT&T and Verizon with about 46 and 32 million landline customers, respectively. The deal would enable the firms to reduce expenses in the wake of the annual 10% decline in landline usage as people switch from landlines to wireless and cable connections. Expected annual cost savings total $575 million; additional revenue could come from upgrading Qwest's landlines to handle DSL Internet.

In 2010, about one-fourth of U.S. homes used only cell phones, and cable behemoth Comcast, with 7.6 million residential and business phone subscribers, ranked as the nation's fourth largest landline provider. CenturyTel has no intention of moving into the wireless and cable markets, which are maturing rapidly and are highly competitive.

While neither Qwest nor CenturyTel owns wireless networks and therefore cannot offset the decline in landline customers as AT&T and Verizon are attempting to do, the combined firms are expected to thrive in rural areas where they have extensive coverage. In such geographic areas, broadband cable Internet access and fiber-optics data transmission line coverage limited. The lack of fast cable and fiber-optics transmission makes voice over Internet protocol (VOIP)—Internet phone service offered by cable companies and independent firms such as Vonage—unavailable. Consequently, customers are forced to use landlines if they want a home phone. Furthermore, customers in these areas must use landlines to gain access to the Internet through dial-up access or through a digital subscriber line (DSL).

Discussion Questions

1. How would you describe CenturyTel's business strategy? Be specific.
2. Describe the key factors both external and internal to the firm that you believe are driving this strategy.
3. Why might the acquisition of Qwest be described as defensive?

the firm's chosen or targeted market. These may include high market share compared to the competition, product line breadth, cost-effective sales distribution channels, age and geographic location of production facilities, relative product quality, price competitiveness, R&D effectiveness, customer service effectiveness, corporate culture, and profitability.

Recall that the combination of external and internal analyses just detailed can be done as a SWOT analysis; it determines the strengths, weaknesses, opportunities, and threats of a business. Table 4.1 illustrates a hypothetical SWOT analysis—in this case for Amazon.com. It suggests that Amazon.com sees becoming an online department store as its greatest opportunity, while its greatest threat is the growing online presence of sophisticated competitors.

TABLE 4.1   Hypothetical Amazon.com SWOT Matrix

	Opportunity	Threat
	To be perceived by Internet users as the preferred online "department store" to exploit accelerating online retail sales	Wal-Mart, Best Buy, Costco, and so on, are all increasing their presence on the Internet
Strengths	• Brand recognition • Convenient online order entry system • Information technology infrastructure • Fulfillment infrastructure for selected products (e.g., books)	• Extensive experience in online marketing, advertising, and fulfillment (i.e., satisfying customer orders)
Weaknesses	• Inadequate warehousing and inventory management systems to support rapid sales growth • Limited experience in merchandising noncore retail products (e.g., pharmaceuticals, sports equipment) • Limited financial resources	• Substantially smaller retail sales volume limits ability to exploit purchase economies • Limited financial resources • Limited name recognition in selected markets (e.g., consumer electronics) • Retail management depth

The SWOT analysis then summarizes how Amazon.com might perceive its major strengths and weaknesses in the context of this opportunity and threat. This is the sort of information that allows management to set a direction in terms of where and how the firm intends to compete, which is then communicated to the firm's stakeholders in the form of a mission/vision statement and a set of quantifiable financial and nonfinancial objectives.

Defining the Mission Statement

In 2009, Apple Computer's board and management changed the way they wished to be perceived by the world by changing their company name to Apple Inc. The change was intended to be transformative, reflecting the firm's desire to change from being a computer hardware and software company to a higher-margin, faster-growing consumer electronics firm characterized by iPod and IPhone-like products. In a word, the firm was establishing a new corporate mission.

At a minimum, a corporate mission statement seeks to describe the corporation's purpose for being and where the corporation hopes to go. The mission statement should not be so general as to provide little practical direction. A good mission statement should include references to the firm's targeted markets, which should reflect the fit between the corporation's primary strengths and competencies, and its ability to satisfy customer needs better than the competition. It should define the product or service offering relatively broadly to allow for the introduction of new products that might be derived from the firm's core competencies. Distribution channels—how the firm chooses to distribute its products—should be identified, as should the customers targeted by the firm's products and services. The mission statement should state management beliefs with respect to the firm's primary stakeholders; these establish the underpinnings of how the firm intends to behave toward those stakeholders.

Setting Strategic or Long-Term Business Objectives

A business objective is what must be accomplished within a specific period. A good business objective is measurable and has a set time frame in which to be realized. Typical corporate objectives include revenue growth rates, minimum acceptable financial returns, and market share; these and several others are discussed in more detail below. A good business objective might state that the firm seeks to increase revenue from the current $1 billion to $5 billion by a given year. A poorly written objective would simply state that the firm seeks to increase revenue substantially.

Common Business Objectives

Corporations typically adopt a number of common business objectives. For instance, the firm may seek to achieve a rate of *return* that will equal or exceed the return required by its shareholders (cost of equity), lenders (cost of debt), or the combination of the two (cost of capital) by a given year. The firm may set a *size* objective, seeking to achieve some critical mass defined in terms of sales volume to realize economies of scale by a given year.

Several common objectives relate to *growth*. Accounting-related growth objectives include seeking to grow earnings per share (EPS), revenue, or assets at a specific rate of growth per year. Valuation-related growth objectives may be expressed in terms of the firm's price-to-earnings ratio, book value, cash flow, or revenue.

Diversification objectives are those where the firm desires to sell current products in new markets, new products in current markets, or new products in new markets. For example, the firm may set an objective to derive 25% of its revenue from new products by a given year. It is also common for firms to set *flexibility* objectives, aiming to possess production facilities and distribution capabilities that can be shifted rapidly to exploit new opportunities as they arise. For example, the major automotive companies have increasingly standardized parts across car and truck platforms to reduce the time required to introduce new products, giving them greater flexibility to facilitate a shift in production from one region to another. *Technology* objectives may reflect a firm's desire to possess capabilities in core or rapidly advancing technologies. Microchip and software manufacturers, as well as defense contractors, are good examples of industries in which keeping current with, and even getting ahead of, new technologies is a prerequisite for survival.

Selecting the Appropriate Corporate, Business, and Implementation Strategies

Each level of strategy serves a specific purpose. Implementation strategies, which are necessarily more detailed than corporate-level strategies, provide specific guidance for a firm's business units.

Corporate-Level Strategies

Corporate-level strategies are adopted at the corporate level and may include all or some of the business units that are either wholly or partially owned by the corporation. A *growth strategy* entails a focus on accelerating the firm's consolidated revenue, profit, and cash-flow growth. This strategy may be implemented in many different ways, as is discussed later in this chapter. A *diversification strategy* involves a decision at the corporate level to enter new businesses. These businesses may be related or completely unrelated to the corporation's existing business portfolio.

An *operational restructuring strategy*, sometimes called a turnaround or defensive strategy, usually refers to the outright or partial sale of companies or product lines, downsizing by closing unprofitable or nonstrategic facilities, obtaining protection from creditors in bankruptcy court, or liquidation. A *financial restructuring strategy* describes actions by the firm to change its total debt and equity structure. The motivation for this strategy may be better utilization of excess corporate cash balances through share-repurchase programs, reducing the firm's cost of capital by increasing leverage or increasing management's control by acquiring a company's shares through a management buyout.

Business-Level Strategies

A firm should choose its business strategy from among the range of reasonable alternatives that will enable it to achieve its stated objectives in an acceptable period, subject to resource constraints. These include limitations on the availability of management talent and funds. Business strategies fall into one of four basic categories: price or cost leadership; product differentiation; focus or niche strategies; or hybrid strategies.

Price or Cost Leadership

The price or cost leadership strategy reflects the influence of a series of tools, including the experience curve and product life cycle, introduced and popularized by the Boston Consulting Group (BCG).[8] This strategy is designed to make a firm the cost leader in its market by constructing efficient production facilities, tightly controlling overhead expenses, and eliminating marginally profitable customer accounts.

The *experience curve* postulates that as the cumulative historical volume of a firm's output increases, cost per unit of output decreases geometrically as the firm becomes more efficient in producing that product. Therefore, the firm with the largest historical output should also be the lowest-cost producer. This implies that the firm should enter markets as early as possible and reduce product prices aggressively to maximize market share. For an illustration of how to construct an experience curve, see the Word document entitled *Example of Applying Experience Curves* on the companion site to this book.

The applicability of the experience curve varies across industries. It seems to work best for largely commodity-type industries, in which scale economies can lead to substantial reductions in per unit production costs, such as PC or cell phone handset manufacturing. The strategy of continuously driving down production costs may make the most sense for the existing industry market share leader. If the leader already has a cost advantage over its competitors because of its significantly larger market share, it may be able to improve its cost advantage by pursuing market share more aggressively through price-cutting.

BCG's second major contribution is the *product life cycle*, which characterizes a product's evolution in four stages: embryonic, growth, maturity, and decline. Strong sales growth and low barriers to entry characterize the first two stages. Over time, however, entry becomes more costly as early entrants into the market accumulate market share and experience lower

---

[8] Boston Consulting Group, 1985

per unit production costs as a result of the effects of the experience curve. New entrants have substantially poorer cost positions thanks to their small market shares compared with earlier entrants, and they cannot catch up to the market leaders as overall market growth slows. During the later phases, characterized by slow market growth, falling product prices force marginal and unprofitable firms out of the market or force them to consolidate with other firms.

Management can obtain insight into the firm's probable future cash requirements and, in turn, its value by determining its position in its industry's product life cycle. During the high-growth phase, firms in the industry normally have high investment requirements associated with capacity expansion and increasing working capital needs. Operating cash flow is normally negative. During the mature and declining growth phases, investment requirements are lower, and cash flow becomes positive.

In addition to its applicability to valuing the firm, the product life cycle also can be useful in selecting the firm's business strategy. In the early stages of the product life cycle, the industry tends to be highly fragmented, with many participants having very small market shares. Often, firms in the early stages adopt a niche strategy in which they focus their marketing efforts on a relatively small and homogeneous customer group. If economies of scale are possible, the industry will begin to consolidate as firms aggressively pursue cost leadership strategies.

Product Differentiation

Differentiation encompasses a range of strategies in which the product offered is perceived by customers to be slightly different from other product offerings in the marketplace. Brand image is one way to accomplish differentiation. Another is to offer customers a range of features or functions. For example, many banks issue MasterCard or Visa credit cards, but each bank tries to differentiate its card by offering a higher credit line, a lower interest rate or annual fee, or awards programs. Apple Computer has used innovative technology to stay ahead of competitors selling MP3 players, most recently with the video capabilities of its newer iPods. Providing alternative distribution channels is another way to differentiate—for example, giving customers the ability to download products from online sites. Other firms compete on the basis of consistent product quality by providing excellent service or by offering customers outstanding convenience.

Focus or Niche Strategies

Firms adopting focus or niche strategies tend to concentrate their efforts by selling a few products or services to a single market, and they compete primarily by understanding their customers' needs better than the competition does. In this strategy, the firm seeks to carve a specific niche with respect to a certain group of customers, a narrow geographic area, or a particular use of a product. Examples include the major airlines, airplane manufacturers (e.g., Boeing), and major defense contractors (e.g., Lockheed-Martin).

Hybrid Strategies

Hybrid strategies involve some combination of the three strategies that were just discussed (Table 4.2). For example, Coca-Cola pursues both a differentiated and a highly market-focused strategy. The company derives the bulk of its revenues by focusing on the

TABLE 4.2   Hybrid Strategies

	Cost Leadership	Product Differentiation
Niche focus approach	Cisco Systems, WD-40	Coca-Cola, McDonald's
Multimarket approach	Wal-Mart, Oracle	America Online, Microsoft

worldwide soft drink market, and its main product is differentiated in that consumers perceive it to have a distinctly refreshing taste. Fast-food industry giant McDonald's pursues a similarly focused yet differentiated strategy, competing on the basis of providing fast food of a consistent quality in a clean, comfortable environment.

Implementation Strategies

Once a firm has determined the appropriate business strategy, it must turn its attention to deciding the best means of implementation. Generally, a firm has five choices: Implement the strategy based solely on internal resources (the solo venture, go it alone, or build approach); partner with others; invest; acquire; or swap assets. Each has significantly different implications. Table 4.3 compares the advantages and disadvantages of these options.

In theory, the decision to choose among alternative options should be made based on the discounting of the projected cash-flow stream to the firm resulting from each option. In practice, many other considerations are at work.

The Role of Intangible Factors

Although financial analyses are conducted to evaluate the various strategy implementation options, the ultimate choice may depend on unquantifiable factors such as the senior manager's risk profile, patience, and ego. The degree of control offered by the various alternatives is often the central issue senior management must confront as this choice is made. Although the solo venture and acquisition options offer the highest degree of control, they can be the most expensive, although for very different reasons. Typically, a build strategy will take considerably longer to realize key strategic objectives, and it may have a significantly lower current value than the alternatives—depending on the magnitude and timing of cash flows generated from the investments. Gaining control through acquisition can also be very expensive because of the substantial premium the acquirer normally has to pay to gain a controlling interest in another company.

The joint venture may be a practical alternative to either a build or an acquire strategy; it gives a firm access to skills, product distribution channels, proprietary processes, and patents at a lower initial expense than might otherwise be required. The joint venture is frequently a precursor to an acquisition because it gives both parties time to assess the compatibility of their respective corporate cultures and strategic objectives.

Asset swaps may be an attractive alternative to the other options, but in most industries they are generally very difficult to establish unless the physical characteristics and use of the assets are substantially similar. The practice is relatively common in the commercial

TABLE 4.3 Strategy Implementation

Basic Options	Advantages	Disadvantages
Solo venture or build (organic growth)	• Control	• Capital/expense[a] requirements • Speed
Partner (shared growth/shared control) • Marketing/distribution alliance • Joint venture • License • Franchise	• Limits capital and expense investment requirements • May be precursor to acquisition	• Lack of or limited control • Potential for diverging objectives • Potential for creating a competitor
Invest (e.g., minority investments in other firms)	• Limits initial capital/expense requirements	• High risk of failure • Lack of control • Time
Acquire or merge	• Speed • Control	• Capital/expense requirements • Potential earnings dilution
Swap assets	• Limits use of cash • No earnings dilution • Limits tax liability if basis in assets swapped remains unchanged	• Finding willing parties • Reaching agreement on assets to be exchanged

[a]*Expense investment refers to expenditures made on such things as application software development, database construction, research and development, training, and advertising to build brand recognition, which (unlike capital expenditures) usually are expensed in the year in which the monies are spent.*

and industrial real estate industry. Firms in the cable industry also use asset swaps to achieve strategic objectives. In recent years, cable companies have been swapping customers to allow a single company to dominate a specific geographic area and realize the full benefits of economies of scale and scope.[9]

Analyzing Assumptions

With the assumptions displayed, the reasonableness of the various options can be compared more readily. The option with the highest net present value is not necessarily the preferred strategy if the assumptions underlying the analysis strain credulity. Understanding the assumptions underlying the chosen strategy and those underlying alternative strategies forces senior management to make choices based on a discussion of the reasonableness of

[9] There are many other examples of asset swaps. In 2005, Citigroup exchanged its fund management business for Legg Mason's brokerage and capital markets businesses, with the difference in the valuation of the businesses paid in cash and stock. Similarly, Royal Dutch Shell and Russia's Gazprom reached a deal to swap major natural gas-producing properties in late 2005. In 2007, British Petroleum swapped half of its stake in its Toledo, Ohio, oil refinery for half of Husky Energy's position in the Sunrise oil sands field in Alberta, Canada.

the assumptions associated with each option. This is generally preferable to placing a dispro-portionately high level of confidence in the numerical output of computer models.

In Case Study 4.2, Hewlett-Packard opportunistically acquired struggling smartphone maker Palm in an effort to exploit the growth and profit potential of that market. The case study illustrates how a firm can react to changes in its external environment and the recognition of its competitive disadvantage in not possessing the requisite core technologies and skills. A key question is whether the acquisition of a small player with an aging proprietary technology will enable the firm to leapfrog the "800-pound gorillas" that dominate the current market.

CASE STUDY 4.2
HP Redirects Its Mobile Device Business Strategy with the Acquisition of Palm

With global PC market growth slowing, Hewlett-Packard (HP), number one in PC sales worldwide, sought to redirect its business strategy for mobile devices. Historically, the firm has relied on such partners as Microsoft to provide the operating systems for its mobile phones and tablet computer products. However, the strategy seems to have contributed to the firm's declining smartphone sales by limiting its ability to differentiate its products and by delaying new mobile product introductions.

HP has been selling a smartphone version of its iPaq handheld device since 2007, although few consumers even knew HP made such devices, since its products were aimed at business people. Sales of iPaq products fell to $172 million in 2009 from $531 million in 2007 and to less than $100 million (excluding sales of Palm products) in 2010.

With smartphone sales expected to exceed laptop sales in 2012, according to industry consultant IDC, HP felt compelled to move aggressively into the market for handheld mobile devices. The major challenge facing HP is to overcome the substantial lead that Apple, Google, and Research-In-Motion (RIM) have in the smartphone market.

To implement the new business strategy, HP acquired Palm in mid-2010 in a deal valued at $1.4 billion (including warrants and convertible preferred stock). HP acquired Palm at a time when its smartphone sales were sliding, with Palm's share of the U.S. market dropping below 5% in 2010. Palm was slow to recognize the importance of applications (apps) designed specifically for smartphones in driving sales. Palm has several hundred apps, while the numbers for Apple's iPhone and Google's Android are in the tens of thousands.

HP is hoping to leverage Palm's smartphone operating system (webOS) to become a leading competitor in the rapidly growing smartphone market, a market that had been largely pioneered by Palm. HP hopes that webOS will provides an ideal common "platform" to link the firm's mobile devices and create a unique experience for the user of multiple HP mobile devices. The intent is to create an environment where users can get a common look and feel and a common set of services irrespective of the handset they choose.

HP also acquired 452 patents and another 406 applications on file. Palm offers one key potential competitive advantage in that its operating system can run several tasks at once, just as a PC does; however, other smartphones are expected to have this capability in the near future.

By buying Palm, HP signals a "go it alone" strategy in smartphones and tablet computers

CASE STUDY 4.2   *(cont'd)*

at the expense of Microsoft. HP is also hoping that by having a proprietary system, it will be able to differentiate its mobile products in a way that Apple and Google have in introducing their proprietary operating systems and distinguishing "look and feel."

Through its sales of computer servers, software, and storage systems, HP has significant connections with telecommunications carriers like Verizon that could help promote devices based on Palm's technology. Also, because of its broad offering of PCs, printers, and other consumer electronics products, HP has leverage over electronics retailers for shelf space.

Discussion Questions

1. To what extent could the acquisition of Palm by HP be viewed as a "make versus buy decision" by HP?
2. How would you characterize the HP strategy for mobility products (cost leadership, differentiation, focus, or a hybrid) and why?

Functional Strategies

Functional strategies focus on short-term results and generally are developed by functional areas; they also tend to be very detailed and highly structured. These strategies result in a series of concrete actions for each function or business group, depending on the company's organization. It is common to see separate plans with specific goals and actions for the marketing, manufacturing, R&D, engineering, and financial and human resources functions. Functional strategies should include clearly defined objectives, actions, timetables for achieving those actions, resources required, and identifying the individual responsible for ensuring that the actions are completed on time and within budget.

Specific functional strategies might read as follows:

- Set up a product distribution network in the northeastern United States that is capable of handling a minimum of 1 million units of product annually by 12/31/20XX. (Individual responsible: Oliver Tran; estimated budget: $5 million.)
- Develop and execute an advertising campaign to support the sales effort in the northeastern United States by 10/31/20XX. (Individual responsible: Maria Gomez; estimated budget: $0.5 million.)
- Hire a logistics manager to administer the distribution network by 9/15/20XX. (Individual responsible: Patrick Petty; estimated budget: $250,000.)
- Acquire a manufacturing company with sufficient capacity to meet the projected demand for the next three years by 6/30/20XX at a purchase price not to exceed $250 million. (Individual responsible: Chang Lee.)

Perhaps an application software company is targeting the credit card industry. The following is an example of how the company's business mission, business strategy, implementation strategy, and functional strategies are related.

- *Mission*: To be recognized by our customers as the leader in providing accurate, high-speed, high-volume transactional software for processing credit card remittances by 20XX.
- *Business Strategy*: Upgrade our current software by adding the necessary features and functions to differentiate our product and service offering from our primary competitors and satisfy projected customer requirements through 20XX.
- *Implementation Strategy*: Purchase a software company at a price not to exceed $400 million that is capable of developing "state-of-the-art" remittance processing software by 12/21/20XX. (Individual responsible: Donald Stuckee.) (Note that this assumes that the firm has completed an analysis of available options, including internal development, collaborating, licensing, or acquisition.)
- *Functional Strategies to Support the Implementation Strategy*:
  - *Research and Development*: Identify and develop new applications for remittance processing software.
  - *Marketing and Sales*: Assess the impact of new product offerings on revenue generated from current and new customers.
  - *Human Resources*: Determine appropriate staffing requirements to support the combined firms.
  - *Finance*: Identify and quantify potential cost savings generated from improved productivity as a result of replacing existing software with the newly acquired software and from the elimination of duplicate personnel in our combined companies. Evaluate the impact of the acquisition on our combined companies' financial statements.
  - *Legal*: Ensure that all target company customers have valid contracts and that these contracts are transferable without penalty. Also, ensure that we will have exclusive and unlimited rights to use the remittance processing software.
  - *Tax*: Assess the tax impact of the acquisition on our cash flow.

Strategic Controls

Strategic controls include both incentive and monitoring systems. *Incentive systems* include bonus, profit sharing, or other performance-based payments made to motivate both acquirer and target company employees to work to implement the business strategy for the combined firms. Typically, these will have been agreed to during negotiation. Incentives often include *retention bonuses* for key employees of the target firm if they remain with the combined companies for a specific period following completion of the transaction.

Monitoring systems are implemented to track the actual performance of the combined firms against the business plan. They may be accounting-based and monitor financial measures such as revenue, profits, and cash flow, or they may be activity-based and monitor variables that drive financial performance. These include customer retention, average revenue per customer, employee turnover, and revenue per employee.

THE BUSINESS PLAN AS A COMMUNICATION DOCUMENT

The necessary output of the planning process is a document that communicates effectively with key decision makers and stakeholders. A good business plan should be short, focused, and well documented. There are many ways to develop such a document. Exhibit 4.1 outlines the key features that should be addressed in a good business plan—one that is so well reasoned and compelling that decision makers accept its recommendations.

The executive summary may be the most important and difficult piece of the business plan to write. It must communicate succinctly and compellingly what is being proposed, why it is being proposed, how it is to be achieved, and by when. It must also identify the major resource requirements and risks associated with the critical assumptions underlying the plan. The executive summary is often the first and only portion of the business plan that is read by a time-constrained CEO, lender, or venture capitalist. As such, it may represent the first and last chance to catch the attention of the key decision maker. Supporting documentation should be referred to in the business plan text but presented in the appendices.

EXHIBIT 4.1 TYPICAL BUSINESS UNIT-LEVEL BUSINESS PLAN FORMAT

1. **Executive summary**. In one or two pages, describe what you are proposing to do, why, how it will be accomplished, by what date, critical assumptions, risks, and major resource requirements.
2. **Industry/market definition**. Define the industry or market in which the firm competes in terms of size, growth rate, product offering, and other pertinent characteristics.
3. **External analysis**. Describe industry/market competitive dynamics in terms of the factors affecting customers, competitors, potential entrants, product or service substitutes, and suppliers, and how these factors interact to determine profitability and cash flow (e.g., Porter 5 forces model; see Figure 4.2). Discuss the major opportunities and threats that exist because of the industry's competitive dynamics. Information accumulated in this section should be used to develop the assumptions underlying revenue and cost projections in building financial statements.
4. **Internal analysis**. Describe the company's strengths and weaknesses and how they compare with the competition's. Identify which of these strengths and weaknesses are important to the firm's targeted customers, and explain why. These data can be used to develop cost and revenue assumptions underlying the businesses' projected financial statements.
5. **Business mission/vision statement**. Describe the purpose of the corporation, what it intends to achieve, and how it wishes to be perceived by its stakeholders. For example, an automotive parts manufacturer may envision itself as being perceived by the end of the decade as the leading supplier of high-quality components worldwide by its customers and as fair and honest by its employees, the communities in which it operates, and its suppliers.
6. **Quantified strategic objectives** (including completion dates). Indicate both financial (e.g., rates of return, sales, cash flow, share price) and nonfinancial goals (e.g., market share; being perceived by customers or investors as number 1 in the targeted market in terms of market share, product quality, price, innovation).
7. **Business strategy**. Identify how the mission and objectives will be achieved (e.g., become a cost leader, adopt a differentiation strategy, focus on a specific market segment, or some combination of these). Show how the chosen business strategy satisfies a key customer need or builds on a major strength possessed by the firm. For example, a firm whose targeted customers are highly price sensitive may pursue a cost leadership strategy to enable it to lower selling prices and increase market share and profitability. Alternatively, a firm with a well-established

brand name may choose to pursue a differentiation strategy by adding features to its product that are perceived by its customers as valuable.

8. **Implementation strategy**. From a range of reasonable options (i.e., solo venture or "go it alone" strategy; partner via a joint venture or less formal business alliance, license, or minority investment; or acquire–merge), indicate which option will enable the firm to best implement its chosen business strategy. Indicate why the chosen implementation strategy is superior to alternative options. For example, an acquisition strategy may be appropriate if the perceived "window of opportunity" is believed to be brief. Alternatively, a solo venture may be preferable if there are few attractive acquisition opportunities or the firm believes it has the necessary resources to develop the needed processes or technologies.

9. **Functional strategies**. Identify plans and resources required by major functional areas, including manufacturing, engineering, sales and marketing, research and development, finance, legal, and human resources.

10. **Business plan financials and valuation**. Provide projected annual income, balance sheet, and cash-flow statements for the firm, and estimate the firm's value based on the projected cash flows. State key forecast assumptions underlying the projected financials and valuation.

11. **Risk assessment**. Evaluate the potential impact on valuation by changing selected key assumptions one at a time. Briefly identify contingency plans (i.e., alternative ways of achieving the firm's mission or objectives) that will be undertaken if critical assumptions prove inaccurate. Identify specific events that will cause the firm to pursue a contingency plan. Such "trigger points" can include deviations in revenue growth of more than x percent or the failure to acquire or develop a needed technology within a specific period.

PHASE 2: BUILDING THE MERGER–ACQUISITION IMPLEMENTATION PLAN

If a firm decides to execute its strategy through an acquisition, it will need an acquisition plan. Here, the steps of the acquisition planning process are discussed, including detailed components of an acquisition plan, how to conduct an effective search process, and how to make initial contact with a potential target firm.[10]

The acquisition plan is a specific type of implementation strategy that focuses on tactical or short-term issues rather than strategic or longer-term issues. It includes management objectives, a resource assessment, a market analysis, senior management's preferences regarding management of the acquisition process, a timetable, and the name of the individual responsible for making it all happen. These and the criteria to use when searching acquisition targets are codified in the first part of the planning process; once a target has been identified, several additional steps must be taken, including contacting the target, developing a negotiation strategy, determining the initial offer price, and developing both financing and integration plans.

---

[10] Note that if the implementation of the firm's business strategy required some other business combination, such as a joint venture or business alliance, the same logic of the acquisition planning process described here would apply.

Development of the acquisition plan should be directed by the "deal owner"—typically a high-performing manager for the specific acquisition. Senior management should, very early in the process, appoint the deal owner to this full- or part-time position. It can be someone in the firm's business development unit, for example, or a member of the firm's business development team with substantial deal-making experience. Often, it is the individual who will be responsible for the operation and integration of the target, with an experienced deal maker playing a supporting role. The first steps in the acquisition planning process are undertaken prior to selecting the target firm and involve codifying the plan elements that are necessary before the search for an acquisition target can begin.

Plan Objectives

The acquisition plan's stated objectives should be completely consistent with the firm's strategic objectives. Financial and nonfinancial objectives alike should support realization of the business plan objectives. Moreover, as is true with business plan objectives, the acquisition plan objectives should be quantified and include a date when such objectives are expected to be realized.

Financial objectives in the acquisition plan could include a minimum rate of return or operating profit, revenue, and cash-flow targets to be achieved within a specified period. Minimum or required rates of return targets may be substantially higher than those specified in the business plan, which relate to the required return to shareholders or to total capital (i.e., debt plus equity). The required return for the acquisition may reflect a substantially higher level of risk as a result of the perceived variability of the amount and timing of the expected cash flows resulting from the acquisition.

Nonfinancial objectives address the motivations for making the acquisition that support the achievement of the financial returns stipulated in the business plan. They could include obtaining rights to specific products, patents, copyrights, or brand names; providing growth opportunities in the same or related markets; developing new distribution channels in the same or related markets; obtaining additional production capacity in strategically located facilities; adding R&D capabilities; and acquiring access to proprietary technologies, processes, and skills.[11] Because these objectives identify the factors that ultimately determine whether a firm will achieve its desired financial returns, they may provide substantially more guidance than financial targets. Table 4.4 illustrates how these and other acquisition plan objectives can be linked with business plan objectives.

Resource/Capability Evaluation

Early in the acquisition process, it is important to determine the maximum amount of the firm's available resources that senior management will commit to a merger or acquisition. This information is used when the firm develops target selection criteria before undertaking a search for target firms.

Financial resources that are potentially available to the acquirer include those provided by internally generated cash flow in excess of normal operating requirements, plus funds from the equity and debt markets. In cases where the target firm is known, the potential financing

[11] DePamphilis, 2001

TABLE 4.4   Examples of Linkages between Business and Acquisition Plan Objectives

Business Plan Objective	Acquisition Plan Objective
Financial: The firm will • Achieve rates of return that will equal or exceed its cost of equity or capital by 20XX • Maintain a debt/total capital ratio of x%	*Financial returns:* The target firm should have • A minimum return on assets of x% • A debt/total capital ratio $\leq y$% • Unencumbered assets of z million • Cash flow in excess of operating requirements of x million
Size: The firm will be the number 1 or 2 market share leader by 20XX • Achieve revenue of x million by 20XX	*Size:* The target firm should be at least x million in revenue
Growth: The firm will achieve through 20XX annual average • Revenue growth of x% • Earnings per share growth of y% • Operating cash-flow growth of z%	*Growth:* The target firm should • Have annual revenue, earnings, and operating cash-flow growth of at least x%, y%, and z%, respectively • Provide new products and markets • Possess excess annual production capacity of x million units
Diversification: The firm will reduce earnings variability by x%	*Diversification:* The target firm's earnings should be largely uncorrelated with the acquirer's earnings
Flexibility: The firm will achieve flexibility in manufacturing and design	*Flexibility:* The target firm should use flexible manufacturing techniques
Technology: The firm will be recognized by its customers as the industry's technology leader	*Technology:* The target firm should own important patents, copyrights, and other forms of intellectual property
Quality: The firm will be recognized by its customers as the industry's quality leader	*Quality:* The target firm's product defects must be less than x per million units manufactured
Service: The firm will be recognized by its customers as the industry's service leader	*Warranty record:* The target firm's customer claims per million units sold should be not greater than x
Cost: The firm will be recognized by its customers as the industry's low-cost provider	*Labor costs:* The target firm should be nonunion and not subject to significant government regulation
Innovation: The firm will be recognized by its customers as the industry's innovation leader	*R&D capabilities:* The target firm should have introduced new products accounting for at least x% of total revenue in the last two years

pool includes funds provided by the internal cash flow of the combined companies in excess of normal operating requirements, the capacity of the combined firms to issue equity or increase leverage, and the proceeds from selling assets not required for implementing the acquirer's business plan.

Financial theory suggests that an acquiring firm will always be able to attract sufficient funding for an acquisition if it can demonstrate that it can earn its cost of capital. In practice, senior management's risk tolerance plays an important role in determining what the acquirer believes it can afford to spend on a merger or acquisition. Consequently, risk-averse management may be inclined to commit only a small portion of the total financial resources that are potentially available to the firm.

There are three basic types of risk that confront any senior management team that is considering an acquisition, and they affect how management feels about the affordability of an acquisition opportunity. How these risks are perceived will determine how much of the potentially available resources management will be willing to commit to making an acquisition.

Operating risk addresses the ability of the buyer to manage the acquired company. Generally, it is perceived to be higher for M&As in markets unrelated to the acquirer's core business. The limited understanding of managers in the acquiring company of the competitive dynamics of the new market and the inner workings of the target firm may negatively affect the postmerger integration efforts, as well as the ongoing management of the combined companies.

Financial risk refers to the buyer's willingness and ability to leverage a transaction, as well as the willingness of shareholders to accept dilution of near-term earnings per share (EPS). To retain a specific credit rating, the acquiring company must maintain certain levels of financial ratios, such as debt-to-total capital and interest coverage (i.e., earnings before interest and taxes divided by interest expense).

A firm's incremental debt capacity can be approximated by comparing the relevant financial ratios to those of comparable firms in the same industry that are rated by the credit rating agencies. The difference represents the amount the firm, in theory, could borrow without jeopardizing its current credit rating.[12] Senior management could also gain insight into how much EPS dilution equity investors may be willing to tolerate through informal discussions with Wall Street analysts and an examination of comparable transactions financed by issuing stock.

Overpayment risk involves the dilution of EPS or a reduction in its growth rate resulting from paying significantly more than the economic value of the acquired company. The effects of overpayment on earnings dilution can last for years.[13]

[12] For example, suppose the combined acquirer and target firms' interest coverage ratio is 3 and the combined firms' debt-to-total-capital ratio is 0.25. Assume further that other firms within the same industry with comparable interest coverage ratios have debt-to-total-capital ratios of 0.5. Consequently, the combined acquirer and target firms could increase borrowing without jeopardizing their combined credit rating until their debt-to-total-capital ratio equals 0.5.

[13] To illustrate the effects of overpayment risk, assume that the acquiring company's shareholders are satisfied with the company's projected annual average increase in EPS of 20% annually for the next five years. The company announces it will be acquiring another company and that a series of "restructuring" expenses will slow EPS growth in the coming year to 10%. However, management argues that the savings resulting from combining the two companies will raise the combined companies' EPS growth rate to 30% in the second through fifth year of the forecast. The risk is that the savings cannot be realized in the time assumed by management and the slowdown in earnings will extend well beyond the first year.

Management Preferences

Senior management's preferences for conducting the acquisition process are usually expressed in terms of boundaries or limits. To ensure that the process is managed in a manner consistent with management's risk tolerance and biases, management must provide guidance to those responsible for finding and valuing the target as well as negotiating the transaction. Substantial upfront participation by management will help dramatically in the successful implementation of the acquisition process. Unfortunately, senior management frequently avoids providing significant input early in the process. This inevitably leads to miscommunication, confusion, and poor execution later. Exhibit 4.2 provides examples of the more common types of management guidance that might be found in an acquisition plan.

Timetable

The final component of a properly constructed acquisition plan is a schedule that recognizes all of the key events that must take place in the acquisition process. Each event should have beginning and ending dates and milestones along the way and should identify who is responsible for ensuring that each milestone is achieved. The timetable of events should be aggressive but realistic. It should be sufficiently aggressive to motivate all involved to work as expeditiously as possible to meet the plan's management objectives, while avoiding the overoptimism that may demotivate individuals if uncontrollable circumstances delay reaching certain milestones.

Exhibit 4.3 recaps the components of a typical acquisition planning process. The first four elements were discussed in detail in this chapter; the remaining items will be the subject of the next chapter.

EXHIBIT 4.2 EXAMPLES OF MANAGEMENT GUIDANCE PROVIDED TO ACQUISITION TEAMS

1. Determining the criteria used to evaluate prospective candidates (e.g., size, price range, current profitability, growth rate, geographic location, and cultural compatibility).
2. Specifying acceptable methods for finding candidates (e.g., soliciting board members; analyzing competitors; and contacting brokers, investment bankers, lenders, law firms, and the trade press).
3. Establishing roles and responsibilities for the acquisition team, including the use of outside consultants, and defining the team's budget.
4. Identifying acceptable sources of financing (e.g., equity issues, bank loans, unsecured bonds, seller financing, or asset sales).
5. Establishing preferences for an asset or stock purchase and form of payment (cash, stock, or debt).
6. Setting a level of tolerance for goodwill (i.e., the excess of the purchase price over the fair market value net acquired assets).
7. Indicating the degree of openness to partial rather than full ownership.
8. Specifying willingness to launch an unfriendly takeover.
9. Setting affordability limits (which can be expressed as a maximum price of after-tax earnings, earnings before interest and taxes, or cash flow multiple or maximum dollar amount).
10. Indicating any desire for related or unrelated acquisitions.

EXHIBIT 4.3 ACQUISITION PLAN FOR THE ACQUIRING FIRM

1. **Plan objectives.** Identify the specific purpose of the acquisition. This should include specific goals to be achieved (e.g., cost reduction, access to new customers, distribution channels or proprietary technology, expanded production capacity) and how the achievement of these goals will better enable the acquiring firm to implement its business strategy.
2. **Timetable.** Establish a timetable for completing the acquisition, including integration if the target firm is to be merged with the acquiring firm's operations.
3. **Resource/capability evaluation.** Evaluate the acquirer's financial and managerial capability to complete an acquisition. Identify affordability limits in terms of the maximum amount the acquirer should pay for an acquisition. Explain how this figure is determined.
4. **Management preferences.** Indicate the acquirer's preferences for a "friendly" acquisition; controlling interest; using stock, debt, cash, or some combination; and so on.
5. **Search plan**. Develop criteria for identifying target firms and explain plans for conducting the search, why the target ultimately selected was chosen, and how you will make initial contact with the target firm. See Chapter 5.
6. **Negotiation strategy.** Identify key buyer/seller issues. Recommend a deal structure that addresses the primary needs of all parties involved. Comment on the characteristics of the deal structure. Such characteristics include the proposed acquisition vehicle (i.e., the legal structure used to acquire the target firm), the postclosing organization (i.e., the legal framework used to manage the combined businesses following closing), and the form of payment (i.e., cash, stock, or some combination). Other characteristics include the form of acquisition (i.e., whether assets or stock are being acquired) and tax structure (i.e., whether it is a taxable or a nontaxable transaction). Indicate how you might "close the gap" between the seller's price expectations and the offer price. These considerations will be discussed in more detail in Chapter 5.
7. **Determination of initial offer price.** Provide projected 5-year income, balance sheet, and cash-flow statements for the acquiring and target firms individually and for the consolidated acquirer and target firms with and without the effects of synergy. (Note that the projected forecast period can be longer than 5 years if deemed appropriate.) Develop a preliminary minimum and maximum purchase price range for the target. List key forecast assumptions. Identify an initial offer price, the composition (i.e., cash, stock, debt, or some combination) of the offer price, and why you believe this price is appropriate in terms of meeting the primary needs of both target and acquirer shareholders. The appropriateness of the offer price should reflect your preliminary thinking about the deal structure. See Chapters 11 and 12 for a detailed discussion of the deal-structuring process.
8. **Financing plan.** Determine if the proposed offer price can be financed without endangering the combined firm's creditworthiness or seriously eroding near-term profitability and cash flow. For publicly traded firms, pay particular attention to the near-term impact of the acquisition on the earnings per share of the combined firms.
9. **Integration plan.** Identify integration challenges and possible solutions. See Chapter 6 for a detailed discussion of how to develop integration strategies. For financial buyers, identify an "exit strategy." Highly leveraged transactions are discussed in detail in Chapter 13.

SOME THINGS TO REMEMBER

The success of an acquisition is frequently dependent on the focus, understanding, and discipline inherent in a thorough and viable business plan that addresses four overarching questions: Where should the firm compete? How should the firm compete? How can the firm satisfy customer needs better than the competition? Why is the chosen strategy preferable to other reasonable options?

An acquisition is only one of many options available for implementing a business strategy. The decision to pursue an acquisition often rests on the desire to achieve control and a perception that the acquisition will result in achieving the desired objectives more rapidly than other options. Once a firm has decided that an acquisition is critical to realizing the strategic direction defined in the business plan, a merger/acquisition plan should be developed.

DISCUSSION QUESTIONS

4.1 Why is it important to think of an acquisition or merger in the context of a process rather than as a series of semirelated, discrete events?

4.2 How does planning facilitate the acquisition process?

4.3 What major activities should be undertaken in building a business plan?

4.4 What is market segmentation and why is it important?

4.5 What basic types of strategies do companies commonly pursue and how are they different?

4.6 What is the difference between a business plan and an acquisition plan?

4.7 What are the advantages and disadvantages of using an acquisition to implement a business strategy compared with a joint venture?

4.8 Why is it important to understand the assumptions underlying a business plan or an acquisition plan?

4.9 Why is it important to get senior management heavily involved early in the acquisition process?

4.10 In your judgment, which of the elements of the acquisition plan discussed in this chapter are the most important and why?

4.11 After having acquired the OfficeMax superstore chain in 2003, Boise Cascade announced the sale of its core paper and timber products operations in late 2004 to reduce its dependence on this highly cyclical business. Reflecting its new emphasis on distribution, the company changed its name to OfficeMax, Inc. How would you describe the OfficeMax mission and business strategy implicit in these actions?

4.12 Dell Computer is one of the best-known global technology companies. In your opinion, who are Dell's primary customers? Current and potential competitors? Suppliers? How would you assess Dell's bargaining power with respect to its customers and suppliers? What are Dell's strengths and weaknesses versus its current competitors?

4.13 In your opinion, what market need(s) was Dell Computer able to satisfy better than its competition? Be specific.

4.14 Discuss the types of analyses inside GE that may have preceded GE's 2008 announcement that it would spin off its consumer and industrial businesses to its shareholders.

4.15 Ashland Chemical, the largest U.S. chemical distributor, acquired chemical manufacturer Hercules Inc. for $3.3 billion in 2008. This move followed Dow Chemical Company's purchase of Rohm & Haas. The justification for both acquisitions was to diversify earnings and offset higher oil costs. How will this business combination offset escalating oil costs?

Answers to these Chapter Discussion Questions are available in the Online Instructor's Manual for instructors using this book.

CHAPTER BUSINESS CASES

CASE STUDY 4.3
Adobe's Acquisition of Omniture: Field of Dreams Marketing?

On September 14, 2009, Adobe announced its acquisition of Omniture for $1.8 billion in cash or $21.50 per share. Adobe CEO Shantanu Narayen announced that the firm was pushing into new business at a time when customers were scaling back on purchases of the company's design software. Omniture would give Adobe a steady source of revenue, which could mean investors would focus less on Adobe's ability to migrate its customers to product upgrades such as Adobe Creative Suite.

Adobe's business strategy was to develop a new line of software that was compatible with Microsoft applications. As the world's largest developer of design software, Adobe licenses such software as Flash, Acrobat, Photoshop, and Creative Suite to website developers. Revenues grow as a result of increased market penetration and inducing current customers to upgrade to newer versions of the design software.

In recent years, a business model has emerged in which customers can "rent" software applications for a specific time period by directly accessing the vendors' servers online or downloading the software to the customer's site. Moreover, software users have shown a tendency to buy from vendors with multiple product offerings to achieve better product compatibility.

Omniture makes software designed to track the performance of websites and online advertising campaigns. Specifically, its Web analytic software allows its customers to measure the effectiveness of Adobe's content creation software. Advertising agencies and media companies use Omniture's software to analyze how consumers use websites. It competes with Google and other smaller participants. Omniture charges customers fees based on monthly website traffic, so sales are somewhat less sensitive than Adobe's. When the economy slows, Adobe has to rely on squeezing more revenue from existing customers. Omniture benefits from the takeover by gaining access to Adobe customers in different geographic areas and more capital for future product development. With annual revenues of more than $3 billion, Adobe is almost ten times the size of Omniture.

Immediately following the announcement, Adobe's stock fell 5.6% to $33.62, after having gained about 67% since the beginning of 2009. In contrast, Omniture shares jumped 25% to $21.63, slightly above the offer price of $21.50 per share. While Omniture's share price move reflected the significant premium

CASE STUDY 4.3   *(cont'd)*

of the offer price over the firm's preannouncement share price, the extent to which investors punished Adobe reflected widespread unease with the transaction.

Investors seem to be questioning the price paid for Omniture, whether the acquisition would actually accelerate and sustain revenue growth, the impact on the future cyclicality of the combined businesses, the ability to effectively integrate the two firms, and the potential profitability of future revenue growth. Each of these factors is considered next.

Adobe paid 18 times projected 2010 earnings before interest, taxes, depreciation, and amortization, a proxy for operating cash flow. Considering that other Web acquisitions were taking place at much lower multiples, investors reasoned that Adobe had little margin for error. If all went according to the plan, the firm would earn an appropriate return on its investment. However, the likelihood of any plan being executed flawlessly is problematic.

Adobe anticipates that the acquisition will expand its addressable market and growth potential. In addition, Adobe anticipates significant cross-selling opportunities in which Omniture products can be sold to Adobe customers. With its much larger customer base, this may represent a substantial new outlet for Omniture products. The presumption is that by combining the two firms, Adobe will be able to deliver more value to its customers. Adobe plans to merge its programs that create content for websites with Omniture's technology. For designers, developers, and online marketers, Adobe believes that integrated development software will streamline the creation and delivery of relevant content and applications.

The size of the market for such software is difficult to gauge. Not all of Adobe's customers will require the additional functionality that will be offered. Google Analytic Services, offered free of charge, has put significant pressure on Omniture's earnings. However, firms with large advertising budgets are less likely to rely on the viability of free analytic services.

Adobe also is attempting to diversify into less cyclical businesses. However, both Adobe and Omniture are impacted by fluctuations in the volume of retail spending. Less retail spending implies fewer new websites and fewer upgrades of existing websites, which directly impacts Adobe's design software business. Moreover, less advertising and retail activity on electronic commerce sites negatively impacts Omniture's revenues. Omniture receives fees based on the volume of activity on a customer's site.

Integrating the Omniture measurement capabilities into Adobe software design products and cross-selling Omniture products into the Adobe customer base require excellent coordination and cooperation between Adobe and Omniture managers and employees. Achieving such cooperation often is a major undertaking, especially when the Omniture shareholders, many of whom were employees, were paid in cash. The use of Adobe stock would have given them additional impetus to achieve these synergies in order to boost the value of their shares.

Achieving cooperation may be slowed by the lack of organizational integration of Omniture into Adobe. Omniture will become a new business unit within Adobe, with Omniture's CEO, Josh James, joining Adobe as a senior vice president of the new business. James will report to Narayen. This arrangement may have been made to preserve Omniture's corporate culture.

Adobe is betting that the potential increase in revenues will grow profits for the combined firms despite Omniture's lower margins.

CASE STUDY 4.3 *(cont'd)*

Whether the acquisition will contribute to overall profit growth or not depends on which products contribute to future revenue growth. The lower margins associated with Omniture's products will slow overall profit growth if the future growth in revenue comes largely from Omniture's Web analytic products.

Discussion Questions

1. Who are Adobe's and Omniture's customers and what are their needs?
2. Which factors external to Adobe and Omniture seem to be driving the transaction? Be specific.
3. Which factors internal to Adobe and Omniture seem to be driving the transaction? Be specific.
4. How will the combined firms be able to better satisfy these needs than the competition can?
5. Do you believe the transaction can be justified based on your understanding of the strengths and weaknesses of the two firms and perceived opportunities and threats to them in the marketplace? Be specific.

Answers to these questions are found in the Online Instructor's Manual available for instructors using this book.

CASE STUDY 4.4
BofA Acquires Countrywide Financial Corporation

On July 1, 2008, Bank of America Corp. (BofA) announced that it had completed its acquisition of mortgage lender Countrywide Financial Corp. (Countrywide) for $4 billion, a 70% discount from the firm's book value at the end of 2007. Countrywide originates, purchases, and securitizes residential and commercial loans; provides loan closing services, such as appraisals and flood determinations; and performs other residential real estate–related services. This marked another major (but risky) acquisition by Bank of America's chief executive Kenneth Lewis in recent years.

BofA's long-term intent has been to become the nation's largest consumer bank while achieving double-digit earnings growth. The acquisition will help the firm realize that vision and create the second largest U.S. bank.

In 2003, BofA paid $48 billion for Fleet-Boston Financial, which gave it the most branches, customers, and checking deposits of any bank in the United States. In 2005, BofA became the largest credit card issuer when it bought MBNA for $35 billion.

The purchase of the troubled mortgage lender averted the threat of a collapse of a major financial institution because of the U.S. 2007–2008 subprime loan crisis. Regulators in the United States were quick to approve the takeover because of the potentially negative implications for U.S. capital markets of a major

CASE STUDY 4.4   *(cont'd)*

bank failure. Countrywide had lost $1.2 billion in the third quarter of 2007. Countrywide's exposure to the subprime loan market (i.e., residential loans made to borrowers with poor or nonexistent credit histories) had driven its shares down by almost 80% from year-earlier levels. The bank was widely viewed as teetering on the brink of bankruptcy as it lost access to short-term debt markets, its traditional source of borrowing.

Bank of America deployed 60 analysts to Countrywide's headquarters in Calabasas, California. After four weeks of analyzing Countrywide's legal and financial challenges and modeling how its loan portfolio was likely to perform, BofA offered an all-stock deal valued at $4 billion. The deal valued Countrywide at $7.16 per share, a 7.6 discount to its closing price the day before the announcement. BofA issued 0.18 shares of its stock for each Countrywide share. The deal could have been renegotiated if Countrywide had experienced a material change that adversely affected the business between the signing of the agreement of purchase and sale and the closing of the deal. BofA made its initial investment of $2 billion in Countrywide in August 2007, purchasing preferred shares convertible to a 16% stake in the company. By the time of the announced acquisition in early January 2008, Countrywide had a $1.3 billon paper loss on the investment.

The acquisition provided an opportunity to buy a market leader at a distressed price. The risks related to the amount of potential loan losses, the length of the U.S. housing slump, and potential lingering liabilities associated with Countrywide's questionable business practices. The purchase made BofA the nation's largest mortgage lender and servicer, consistent with the firm's business strategy, which is to help consumers meet all their financial needs. BofA has been one of the relatively few major banks to be successful in increasing revenue and profit following acquisitions by "cross-selling" its products to the acquired bank's customers. Countrywide's extensive retail distribution network enhances BofA's network of more than 6,100 banking centers throughout the United States. BofA had anticipated almost $700 million in after-tax cost savings in combining the two firms. Almost two-thirds of these savings had been realized by the end of 2010. In mid-2010, BofA agreed to pay $108 million to settle federal charges that Countrywide had incorrectly collected fees from 200,000 borrowers who had been facing foreclosure.

Discussion Questions

1. How did the acquisition of Countrywide fit BofA's business strategy? Be specific. What were the key assumptions implicit in BofA's business strategy? How did the existence of BofA's mission and business strategy help the firm move quickly in acquiring Countrywide?

2. How would you classify the BofA business strategy (cost leadership, differentiation, focus, or some combination)? Explain your answer.

3. Describe what the likely objectives of the BofA acquisition plan might have been. Be specific. What key assumptions were implicit in BofA's acquisition plan? What were some of the key risks associated with integrating Countrywide? In addition to the purchase price, how would you determine BofA's potential resource commitment in making this acquisition?

CASE STUDY 4.4 *(cont'd)*

4. What capabilities did the acquisition of FleetBoston Financial and MBNA provide BofA? How did the acquisition of Countrywide complement previous acquisitions?
5. What alternatives to outright acquisition did BofA have? Why do you believe

BofA chose to acquire Countrywide rather than to pursue an alternative strategy? Be specific.

Answers to these case discussion questions are available in the Online Instructor's Manual for instructors using this book.

APPENDIX
Common Sources of Economic, Industry, and Market Data

Economic Information
Business Cycle Development (U.S. Department of Commerce)
Current Business Reports (U.S. Department of Commerce)
Economic Indicators (U.S. Department of Commerce)
Economic Report of the President to the Congress (U.S. Government Printing Office)
Long-Term Economic Growth (U.S. Department of Commerce)
Regional statistics and forecasts from large commercial banks
Monthly Labor Review (U.S. Department of Labor)
Monthly Bulletin of Statistics (United Nations)
Overseas Business Reports (By country, published by U.S. Department of Commerce)
World Trade Annual (United Nations)
U.S. Industrial Outlook (U.S. Department of Commerce)
Survey of Current Business (U.S. Department of Commerce)
Statistical Yearbook (United Nations)

Statistical Abstract of the United States (U.S. Department of Commerce)

Industry Information
Forbes (Mid-January issues provide performance data on firms in various industries)
Business Week (Provides weekly economic and business information, and quarterly profit and sales rankings of corporations)
Fortune (April issues include listings of financial information on corporations within selected industries)
Industry Survey (Published quarterly by Standard and Poor's Corporation)
Industry Week (March–April issue provides information on 14 industry groups)
Inc. (May and December issues give information on entrepreneurial firms)

Directories of National Trade Associations
Encyclopedia of Associations
Funk and Scott's *Index of Corporations and Industries*
Thomas' *Register of American Manufacturers*
The Wall Street Journal Index

Implementation: Search through Closing
Phases 3 through 10

A man that is very good at making excuses is probably good at nothing else. —**Ben Franklin**

INSIDE M&A: BANK OF AMERICA ACQUIRES MERRILL LYNCH

Against the backdrop of the Lehman Brothers' Chapter 11 bankruptcy filing, Bank of America (BofA) CEO Kenneth Lewis announced on September 15, 2008, that the bank had reached agreement to acquire mega–retail broker and investment bank Merrill Lynch. Hammered out in a few days, investors expressed concern that BofA's swift action on the all-stock $50 billion transaction would saddle the firm with billions of dollars in problem assets by pushing BofA's share price down by 21%.

BofA saw the takeover of Merrill as an important step toward achieving its long-held vision of becoming the number 1 provider of financial services in its domestic market. The firm's business strategy was to focus its efforts on the U.S. market by expanding its product offering and geographic coverage. The firm implemented its business strategy by acquiring selected financial services companies to fill gaps in its product offering and geographic coverage. The existence of a clear and measurable vision for the future enabled BofA to make acquisitions as the opportunity arose.

Since 2001, the firm completed a series of acquisitions valued at more than $150 billion. The firm acquired FleetBoston Financial, greatly expanding its network of branches on the East Coast, and LaSalle Bank to improve its coverage in the Midwest. The acquisitions of credit card–issuing powerhouse MBNA, U.S. Trust (a major private wealth manager), and Countrywide (the nation's largest residential mortgage loan company) were made to broaden the firm's financial services offering.

The acquisition of Merrill makes BofA the country's largest provider of wealth management services to go with its current status as the nation's largest branch banking network and the largest issuer of small business, home equity, credit card, and residential mortgage loans. The deal creates the largest domestic retail brokerage and puts the bank among the top five largest global investment banks. Merrill also owns 45% of the profitable asset manager BlackRock Inc., worth an estimated $10 billion. BofA expects its retail network to help sell Merrill and BlackRock's investment products to BofA customers.

The hurried takeover encouraged by the U.S. Treasury and Federal Reserve did not allow for proper due diligence. The extent of the troubled assets on Merrill's books was largely unknown. While the losses at Merrill proved to be stunning in the short run—$15 billion alone in the fourth quarter of 2008—the acquisition by Bank of America averted the possible demise of Merrill Lynch. By the end of the first quarter of 2009, the U.S. government had injected $45 billion in loans and capital into BofA in an effort to offset some of the asset write-offs associated with the acquisition. Later that year, Lewis announced his retirement from the bank.

Mortgage loan losses and foreclosures continued to mount throughout 2010, with a disproportionately large amount of such losses attributable to the acquisition of the Countrywide mortgage loan portfolio. While BofA's vision and strategy may still prove to be sound, the rushed execution of the Merrill acquisition, coupled with problems surfacing from other acquisitions, could hobble the financial performance of BofA for years to come.

CHAPTER OVERVIEW

This chapter starts with the presumption that a firm has developed a viable business plan that requires an acquisition to realize the firm's strategic direction. Whereas Chapter 4 addressed the creation of business and acquisition plans (Phases 1 and 2), this chapter focuses on Phases 3 through 10 of the acquisition process, including search, screening, first contact, negotiation, integration planning, closing, integration implementation, and evaluation. The negotiation phase is the most complex aspect of the acquisition process, involving refining the preliminary valuation, deal structuring, due diligence, and developing a financing plan. It is in the negotiation phase that all elements of the purchase price are determined.

A review of this chapter (including the practice questions) is contained in the file folder entitled Student Study Guide on the companion site for this book (*www.elsevierdirect.com/companions/9780123854858*). The companion site also contains a comprehensive acquirer due-diligence question list, redacted agreements of purchase and sale for stock and asset purchases, and a Learning Interactions Library, which gives students the opportunity to test their knowledge of this chapter in a "real-time" environment.

PHASE 3: THE SEARCH PROCESS

The first step in searching for potential acquisition candidates is to establish a relatively small number of primary screening or selection criteria. These should include the industry and size of the transaction, which is best defined in terms of the maximum purchase price a firm is willing to pay. This can be expressed as a maximum price-to-earnings, book, cash flow, or revenue ratio, or as a maximum purchase price stated in terms of dollars. It also may be appropriate to add a geographic restriction to the selection criteria.

Consider a private acute-care hospital holding company that wants to buy a skilled nursing facility within 50 miles of its largest hospital in Allegheny County, Pennsylvania. Management believes it cannot afford to pay more than $45 million for the facility. Its primary selection criteria could include an industry (skilled nursing), location (Allegheny County), and maximum price (five times cash flow, not to exceed $45 million).

Similarly, a Texas-based manufacturer of patio furniture with manufacturing operations in the southwestern United States seeks to expand its sales in California. The company decides to seek a patio furniture manufacturer that it can purchase for no more than $100 million. Its primary selection criteria could include an industry (outdoor furniture), a location (California, Arizona, and Nevada), and a maximum purchase price (15 times after-tax earnings, not to exceed $100 million).

The next target selection step is to develop a search strategy that employs the selection criteria. This typically involves using computerized databases and directory services such as Disclosure, Dun & Bradstreet, Standard & Poor's *Corporate Register*, and Capital IQ to identify qualified candidates. Firms also may query their law, banking, and accounting firms to identify other candidates. Investment banks, brokers, and leveraged buyout firms are also fertile sources of potential candidates, although they are likely to require an advisory or finder's fee.

The Internet makes research much easier than in the past; today, analysts have much more information at their fingertips than ever before. Such services as Google Finance, Yahoo! Finance, Hoover's, and EDGAR Online enable researchers to quickly obtain data about competitors and customers. These sites provide easy access to a variety of public documents filed with the Securities and Exchange Commission. Exhibit 5.1 provides a comprehensive listing of alternative information sources.

EXHIBIT 5.1 SOURCES OF INFORMATION ON INDIVIDUAL COMPANIES

SEC Filings (Public Companies Only)

10-K: Provides detailed information on a company's annual operations, business conditions, competitors, market conditions, legal proceedings, risk factors in holding the stock, and other related information.

10-Q: Updates investors about a company's operations each quarter.

S-1: Filed when a company wants to register new stock. Can contain information about the company's operating history and business risks.

S-2: Filed when a company is completing a material transaction, such as a merger or acquisition. Provides substantial detail underlying the terms and conditions of the transaction, the events surrounding the transaction, and justification for the merger or acquisition.

8-K: Filed when a company faces a "material event," such as a merger.

Schedule 14A: A proxy statement. Gives details about the annual meeting and biographies of company officials and directors, including stock ownership and pay.

Websites

www.aol.com	*http://edgarscan.pwcglobal.com/serviets.edgarscan*
www.bizbuysell.com	*www.factset.com*
www.capitaliq.com	*http://finance.yahoo.com*
www.dialog.com	*www.freeedgar.com*
www.edgar-online.com	*www.lexisnexis.com*

www.mergernetwork.com   *www.sec.gov*
www.mergers.net   *www.worldm-anetwork.com*
www.onesource.com   www. Hooversonline. Com
                                 www. quicken. Com
                                 www. washington researchers. com.

Organizations

Value Line Investment Survey: Information on public companies
Directory of Corporate Affiliations: Corporate affiliations
Lexis/Nexis: Database of general business and legal information
Thomas Register: Organizes firms by products and services
Frost & Sullivan: Industry research
Findex.com: Financial information
Competitive Intelligence Professionals: Information about industries
Dialog Corporation: Industry databases
Wards Business Directory of U.S. and public companies
Predicasts: Provides databases through libraries
Business Periodicals Index: Business and technical article index
Dun & Bradstreet Directories: Information about private and public companies
Experian: Information about private and public companies
Nelson's Directory of Investment Research: Wall Street Research Reports
Standard & Poor's Publications: Industry surveys and corporate records
Harris Infosource: Information about manufacturing companies
Hoover's Handbook of Private Companies: Information on large private firms
Washington Researchers: Information on public and private firms, markets, and industries
The *Wall Street Journal* Transcripts: Wall Street research reports
Directory of Corporate Affiliations (published by Lexis-Nexis Group)

If confidentiality is not an issue, a firm may seek to advertise its interest in acquiring a particular type of firm in *The Wall Street Journal* or trade press. While this may generate substantial interest, it is less likely to generate high-quality prospects. Rather, it will probably result in a lot of responses from those interested in getting a free valuation of their own company or from brokers claiming that their clients fit the buyer's criteria as a ruse to convince you that you need the broker's services.[1]

Finding reliable information about privately owned firms is a major problem. Sources such as Dun & Bradstreet or Experian may only provide fragmentary data. Publicly available information may offer additional details. For example, surveys by trade associations or the U.S. Census Bureau often include industry-specific average sales per employee. A private firm's sales can be estimated by multiplying this figure by an estimate of the firm's workforce, which may be obtained by searching the firm's product literature, website, or trade show speeches, or even by counting the number of cars in the parking lot during each shift. Obtaining data on privately owned firms will be discussed in more detail in Chapter 10.

---

[1] It is important to respond in writing if you receive a solicitation from a broker or finder, particularly if you reject their services. If at a later date you acquire the firm they claim to have represented, the broker or finder may sue your firm for compensation.

Increasingly the number of companies—even midsize firms—are moving investment banking "in-house." Rather than use brokers or so-called "finders"[2] as part of their acquisition process, they are identifying potential targets, doing valuation, and performing due diligence on their own. This reflects efforts to save on investment banking fees, which can easily be more than $5 million plus expenses on a $500 million transaction.[3]

PHASE 4: THE SCREENING PROCESS

The screening process is a refinement of the initial search process. It begins by pruning the initial list of potential candidates created using the primary criteria discussed earlier. Because relatively few primary criteria are used, the initial list may be lengthy. It can be shortened using secondary selection criteria, but care should be taken to limit the number of these criteria. An excessively long list of selection criteria will severely limit the number of candidates that pass the screening process. The following selection criteria should be quantifiable whenever possible.

Market Segment: The search process involves the specification of the target industry and perhaps results in a lengthy list of acquisition candidates. The list can be shortened by identifying a target segment within the industry. For example, a steel fabricated products company may decide to diversify into the aluminum fabricated products industry. Whereas the primary search criterion might have been firms in the aluminum flat-rolled products industry, a secondary criterion could stipulate a segmenting of the market to identify only those companies that manufacture aluminum tubular products.

Product Line: The product line criterion identifies a specific product line within the target market segment. For example, the same steel fabrication company may decide to focus its search on companies manufacturing aluminum tubular products used for lawn and patio furniture.

Profitability: The profitability criterion should be defined in terms of the percentage return on sales, assets, or total investment. This allows a more accurate comparison among candidates of different sizes. A firm with after-tax earnings of $5 million on sales of $100

[2] A broker has a fiduciary responsibility to either the potential buyer or the potential seller and is not permitted to represent both parties. Compensation is paid by the client to the broker. A finder is someone who introduces both parties but represents neither party. The finder has no fiduciary responsibility to either party and is compensated by one or both parties. If you choose to use a broker or finder, make sure the fees and terms are clearly stipulated in writing. Keep a written record of all telephone conversations and meetings with the finder or broker. These may be used in court at a later date if the broker or finder sues for fees that may be in dispute.

[3] Actual fee formulas are most often based on the purchase price. The so-called Lehman formula was at one time a commonly used fee structure in which broker or finder fees would be equal to 5% of the first $1 million of the purchase price, 4% of the second, 3% of the third, 2% of the fourth, and 1% of the remainder. Today, this formula is often ignored in favor of a negotiated fee structure consisting of a basic fee (or retainer) paid regardless of whether the deal is consummated, an additional closing fee paid on closing, and an "extraordinary" fee paid under unusual circumstances that may delay the eventual closing, such as gaining antitrust approval or achieving a hostile takeover. Fees vary widely, but 1% of the total purchase price plus reimbursement of expenses is often considered reasonable.

million may be less attractive than a firm earning $3 million on sales of $50 million because the latter firm may be more efficient.

Degree of Leverage: Debt-to-equity or debt-to-total-capital ratios are used to measure the level of leverage or indebtedness. The acquiring company may not want to purchase a company whose heavy debt burden may cause the combined company's leverage ratios to jeopardize its credit rating.

Market Share: The acquiring firm may be interested only in firms that are number 1 or 2 in market share in the targeted industry, or in firms whose market share is some multiple (e.g., 2 × the next largest competitor). Firms that have substantially greater market share than their competitors often are able to achieve lower-cost positions than their competitors because of economies of scale and experience curve effects.

Cultural Compatibility: While cultural compatibility between the acquirer and the target may be more difficult to quantify than other measures, public statements about the target's vision for the future and its governance practices, as well as its reputation as a responsible corporate citizen within its industry, will provide some subjective measure. Insights can be gained by examining employee demographics, such as the approximate average age and diversity of the workforce, and how long the potential target has been in business. America Online's 2001 acquisition of Time Warner highlighted how difficult it can be to integrate a young, heterogeneous employee population with a much older, more homogeneous group. Also, as a much newer firm, AOL had a much less structured management style than was found in Time Warner's more staid environment. Finally, an acquirer needs to determine whether it can adapt to the challenges of dealing with foreign firms, such as different languages and customs.

PHASE 5: FIRST CONTACT

Using both the primary and secondary selection criteria makes it possible to bring the search to a close and begin the next part of the acquisition planning process. This begins with contacting the selected target company. For each target firm, it is necessary to develop an approach strategy in which the potential acquirer develops a profile of each firm to be contacted in order to be able to outline the reasons the target firm should consider an acquisition proposal. Such reasons could include the need for capital, a desire by the owner to "cash out," and succession planning issues (see Chapter 10).

Research efforts should extend beyond publicly available information and include interviews with customers, suppliers, ex-employees, and trade associations in an effort to better understand the strengths, weaknesses, and objectives of potential target firms. Insights into management, ownership, performance, and business plans help provide a compelling rationale for the proposed acquisition and heighten the prospect of obtaining the target firm's interest.

The approach for initiating contact with a target company depends on the size of the company, whether the target is publicly or privately held, and the acquirer's time frame for completing a transaction. The latter can be extremely important. If time permits, there is no substitute for developing a personal relationship with the sellers—especially if theirs is a privately held firm. Developing a rapport often makes it possible to acquire a company that is not thought to be for sale.

Personal relationships must be formed only at the highest levels within a privately held target firm. Founders or their heirs often have a strong paternalistic view of their businesses, whether they are large or small. Such firms often have great flexibility in negotiating a deal that "feels right," rather than simply holding out for the highest possible price. In contrast, personal relationships can only go so far in negotiating with a public company that has a fiduciary responsibility to its shareholders to get the best price. If time is a critical factor, acquirers may not have the luxury of developing close personal relationships with the seller. Under these circumstances, a more expeditious approach must be taken.

For small companies with which the buyer has no direct contacts, it may only be necessary to initiate contact through a vaguely worded letter expressing interest in a joint venture or marketing alliance. During the follow-up telephone call, be prepared to discuss a range of options with the seller.

Preparation before the first telephone contact is essential. If possible, script your comments. Get to the point quickly but indirectly. Identify yourself, your company, and its strengths. Demonstrate your understanding of the contact's business and how an informal partnership could make sense. Be able to explain the benefits of your proposal to the contact—quickly and succinctly. If the opportunity arises, propose a range of options, including an acquisition. Listen carefully to the contact's reaction. If the contact is willing to entertain the notion of an acquisition, request a face-to-face meeting.[4]

Whenever possible, use an intermediary to make contact, generally at the highest level possible in the target firm's organization. In some instances, the appropriate contact is the most senior manager, but it could be a disaffected large shareholder. Intermediaries include members of the acquirer's board of directors or the firm's outside legal counsel, accounting firm, lender, broker/finder, or investment banker. Intermediaries can be less intimidating than if you take a direct approach.

For publicly traded companies, contact also should be made through an intermediary at the highest level possible. Discretion is extremely important because of the target's concern about being "put into play"—that is, when circumstances suggest that it may be an attractive investment opportunity for other firms. Even rumors of an acquisition can have substantial, adverse consequences for the target. Current or potential customers may express concern about the uncertainty associated with a change of ownership.

Such a change could imply variation in product or service quality, reliability, and the level of service provided under product warranty or maintenance contracts. Suppliers worry about possible disruptions in their production schedules as the transition to the new owner takes place. Employees worry about possible layoffs or changes in compensation. Competitors will do what they can to fan these concerns in an effort to persuade current customers to switch and potential customers to defer buying decisions; key employees will be encouraged to defect to the competition. Shareholders may experience a dizzying ride as arbitrageurs,

---

[4] To ensure confidentiality, choose a meeting place that provides sufficient privacy. Create a written agenda for the meeting after soliciting input from all participants. The meeting should start with a review of your company and your perspective on the outlook for the industry. Encourage the potential target firm to provide information on its own operations and its outlook for the industry. Look for areas of consensus.

buying on the rumor, bid up the price of the stock, only to bail out if denial of the rumor appears credible.

Discussing Value

Neither the buyer nor the seller has any incentive to be the first to provide an estimate of value. It is difficult to back away from a number put on the table by either party should new information emerge. Getting a range may be the best that you can do. Discussing values for recent acquisitions of similar businesses is one way to get a range. Another is to agree to a formula for calculating the purchase price. For example, the purchase price may be defined in terms of a price to current year earnings multiple. This enables both of the parties to proceed to performing due diligence to reach a consensus on the actual current year's earnings for the target firm.

Preliminary Legal Documents

Typically, and early on, parties to M&A transactions negotiate a confidentiality agreement, term sheet, and letter of intent.

Confidentiality Agreement

All parties to the deal are likely to want a confidentiality agreement (also called a nondisclosure agreement), which is generally mutually binding—that is, it covers all parties to the transaction. In negotiating the confidentiality agreement, the buyer requests as much audited historical data and supplemental information as the seller is willing to provide. The prudent seller requests similar information about the buyer to assess the buyer's financial credibility. It is important for the seller to determine the buyer's credibility early in the process so as not to waste time with a potential buyer incapable of raising the financing to complete the transaction. The agreement should cover only information that is not publicly available and should have a reasonable expiration date. Note that the confidentiality agreement can be negotiated independently or as part of the term sheet or letter of intent.

Term Sheet

A term sheet outlines the primary terms with the seller and is often used as the basis for a more detailed letter of intent. It may not be necessary to involve lawyers and accountants at this stage. It is the last point before the parties to the potential transaction start incurring significant legal, accounting, and consulting expenses.

A standard term sheet is typically two to four pages long and stipulates the total consideration or purchase price (often as a range), what is being acquired (i.e., assets or stock), limitations on the use of proprietary data, a *no-shop provision* that prevents the seller from sharing the terms of the buyer's proposal with other potential buyers with the hope of instigating an auction environment, and a termination date. Many transactions skip the term sheet and go directly to negotiating a letter of intent.

Letter of Intent

Unlike the confidentiality agreement, not all parties to the transaction may want a Letter of Intent (LOI). While the LOI can be useful in identifying areas of agreement and disagreement early in the process, the rights of all parties to the transaction, and certain protective provisions, it may delay the signing of a definitive purchase agreement and may also result in some legal risk to either the buyer or the seller if the deal is not consummated. Public companies that sign a letter of intent for a transaction that is likely to have a "material" impact on the buyer or seller may need to announce the LOI publicly to comply with securities law.

The LOI formally stipulates the reason for the agreement and major terms and conditions. It also indicates the responsibilities of both parties while the agreement is in force, a reasonable expiration date, and how all fees associated with the transaction will be paid. Major terms and conditions include a brief outline of the structure of the transaction, which may entail the payment of cash or stock for certain assets and the assumption of certain target company liabilities. The letter may also specify certain conditions, such as an agreement that selected personnel of the target will not compete with the combined companies for some period should they leave. Another condition may indicate that a certain portion of the purchase price will be allocated to the noncompete agreement.[5] The LOI also may place a portion of the purchase price in escrow.

The proposed purchase price may be expressed as a specific dollar figure, as a range, or as a multiple of some measure of value, such as operating earnings or cash flow. The LOI also specifies the types of data to be exchanged and the duration and extent of the initial due diligence. The LOI usually will terminate if the buyer and the seller do not reach an agreement by a certain date. Legal, consulting, and asset transfer fees (i.e., payments made to governmental entities when ownership changes hands) may be paid for by the buyer or seller, or they may be shared.

Depending on how it is written, the LOI may or may not be legally binding. A well-written LOI usually contains language limiting the extent to which the agreement binds the two parties. Price or other provisions are generally subject to *closing conditions*, such as the buyer having full access to all of the seller's books and records; having completed due diligence; obtaining financing; and having received approval from boards of directors, stockholders, and regulatory bodies. Other standard conditions include requiring signed employment contracts for key target firm executives and the completion of all necessary M&A documents. Failure to satisfy any of these conditions will invalidate the agreement.

A well-written LOI should also describe the due diligence process in some detail. It should stipulate how the potential buyer should access the potential seller's premises, the frequency and duration of such access, and how intrusive such activities should be. The LOI should indicate how the buyer should meet and discuss the deal with the seller's employees, customers, and suppliers. Sometimes the provisions of a standard confidentiality agreement are negotiated as part of the LOI. The letter of intent becomes the governing document for the deal that the potential acquirer can show to prospective financing sources.

---

[5] Such an allocation of the purchase price is in the interests of the buyer because the amount of the allocation can be amortized over the life of the agreement. As such, it can be taken as a tax-deductible expense. However, it may constitute taxable income for the seller.

The LOI may create legal liabilities if one of the parties is later accused of not negotiating in "good faith." This is the basis for many lawsuits filed when transactions are undertaken but not completed as a result of disagreements that emerge during lengthy and often heated negotiations.

In recent years, some letters of intent have included *go-shop* provisions, which allow the seller to continue to solicit higher bids for several months. However, if the seller accepts another bid, the seller must pay a breakup fee to the bidder with whom it has a signed agreement.

PHASE 6: NEGOTIATION

The negotiation phase often is the most complex aspect of the acquisition process. It is interactive and iterative. Activities unfold concurrently. It is during this phase that the actual purchase price paid for the acquired business is determined, and often it will be quite different from the initial valuation of the target company, which was probably made before due diligence and with only limited, publicly available information.

In this section, the emphasis is on negotiation in the context of problem-solving or interest-based bargaining, in which parties look at their underlying interests rather than simply stating positions and making demands. In most successful negotiations, parties to the transaction search jointly for solutions to problems. All parties must be willing to make concessions that satisfy their own needs, as well as the highest-priority needs of the others involved in the negotiation.

The negotiation phase consists of four iterative activities that may begin at different times but tend to overlap (Figure 5.1). Due diligence starts as soon as the target is willing to allow it to begin and, if permitted, runs throughout the negotiation process. Another activity is refining the preliminary valuation based on new information uncovered as part of due diligence, enabling the buyer to better understand the value of the target. A third activity is deal structuring, which involves meeting the needs of both parties by addressing issues of risk and reward. The final activity entails a financing plan, which provides a reality check for the buyer by defining the maximum amount the buyer can reasonably expect to finance and, in turn, pay for the target company. Each of these activities is detailed next.

Refining Valuation

The starting point for negotiation is to update the preliminary target company valuation based on new information. A buyer requests and reviews at least three to five years of historical financial data. While it is highly desirable to examine data that have been audited in accordance with Generally Accepted Accounting Principals, such data may not be available for small, privately owned companies. The historical data should be *normalized*, or adjusted for nonrecurring gains, losses, or expenses. Nonrecurring gains or losses can result from the sale of land, equipment, product lines, patents, software, or copyrights. Nonrecurring expenses include severance payments, employee signing bonuses, and settlements of litigation. These adjustments allow the buyer to smooth out irregularities and better understand the dynamics of the business. Once the data have been normalized, each major expense

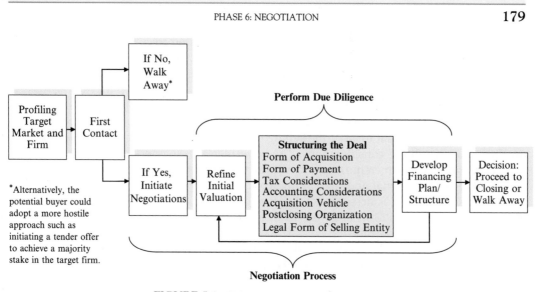

FIGURE 5.1   Viewing negotiation as a process.

category should be expressed as a percentage of revenue. By observing year-to-year changes in these ratios, sustainable trends in the data are more discernible.

Deal Structuring

In purely financial terms, deal structuring involves the allocation of cash-flow streams (with respect to amount and timing), the allocation of risk, and, therefore, the allocation of value between different parties to the transaction. However, because of the human element involved in negotiation, deal structuring must also be a process of identifying and satisfying as many of the highest-priority objectives of the parties involved in the transaction as possible, subject to their tolerance for risk. The process begins with each party determining its own initial negotiating position, potential risks, options for managing risk, levels of tolerance for risk, and conditions under which either party will "walk away" from the negotiations. (These elements of negotiation are discussed in more detail in Appendix A at the end of this chapter.)

In practice, deal structuring is about understanding potential sources of disagreement—from simple arguments over basic facts to substantially more complex issues, such as the form of payment and legal, accounting, and tax structures. It also requires understanding the potential conflicts of interest that can influence the outcome of discussions. For example, when a portion of the purchase price depends on the long-term performance of the acquired business, its management—often the former owner—may not behave in a manner that serves the acquirer's best interests.

Decisions made throughout the deal-structuring process influence various attributes of the deal, including how ownership is determined, how assets are transferred, how ownership is protected (i.e., governance), and how risk is apportioned among parties to the transaction. Other attributes include the type, number, and complexity of the documents required for closing; the types of approvals required; and the time needed to complete the transaction. These decisions also will influence how the combined companies will be managed, the amount and timing of resources committed, and the magnitude and timing of current and future tax liabilities.[6]

Given its complexity, the deal-structuring process should be viewed as comprising a number of interdependent components. At a minimum, these include the acquisition vehicle, postclosing organization, legal form of the selling entity, form of payment, form of acquisition, and tax and accounting considerations. The *acquisition vehicle* refers to the legal structure (e.g., corporation or partnership) used to acquire the target company. The *postclosing organization* is the organizational and legal framework (e.g., corporation or partnership) used to manage the combined businesses following the completion of the transaction. The *legal form of the selling entity* refers to whether the seller is a C or Subchapter S Corporation, a limited liability company, or a partnership.

The *form of payment* may consist of cash, common stock, debt, or some combination. Some portion of the payment may be deferred or be dependent on the future performance of the acquired entity. The *form of acquisition* reflects what is being acquired (e.g., stock or assets) and how ownership will be transferred. As a general rule, a transaction is taxable if the remuneration paid to the target company's shareholders is primarily something other than the acquirer's stock, and it is nontaxable (i.e., tax deferred) if what they receive is largely acquirer stock.

Finally, *accounting considerations* refer to the potential impact of financial reporting requirements on the earnings volatility of business combinations, due to the need to periodically revalue acquired assets to their fair market value as new information becomes available. Fair market value is what a willing buyer and seller, having access to the same information, would pay for an asset.[7]

Conducting Due Diligence

Due diligence is an exhaustive review of records and facilities and typically continues throughout the negotiation phase. Although some degree of protection is achieved through a well-written contract, legal documents should never be viewed as a substitute for conducting formal due diligence. Table 5.1 lists convenient online sources of information that are helpful in conducting due diligence. A detailed preliminary acquirer due diligence question list is provided on the companion site to this book. While due diligence is most often associated with buyers, both sellers and lenders will also conduct due diligence.[8]

The acquirer typically attempts to protect itself through due diligence, extensive representations and warranties (i.e., claims and promises made by the seller), or some combination of the two. In some instances, buyers and sellers may agree to an abbreviated due diligence period on the theory that the buyer can be protected in a well-written purchase agreement in

---

[6] McCarthy, 1998

[7] For a more detailed discussion of how to structure M&A transactions, see *M&A Negotiations and Deal Structuring—All You Need to Know* by Donald M. DePamphilis (2010b).

[8] For a detailed discussion of the due diligence process and best practices, see Selim (2003).

TABLE 5.1 Convenient Information Sources for Conducting Due Diligence

Web Address	Content
Securities and Exchange Commission	**Financial Information/Security Law Violations**
– *www.sec.gov* – *http://www.sec.gov/litigation.shtml*	– Public filings for almost 10 years available through the EDGAR database – Enforcement actions
U.S. Patent Office	**Intellectual Property Rights Information**
– *www.uspto.gov* – *www.uspto.gov/patft/index.html*	– Search patent database – Database if you have patent number
Federal Communications Commission	**Regulates Various Commercial Practices**
– *www.fcc.gov* – *http://www.fcc.gov/searchtools.html*	– General information – Access to database of individuals sanctioned for illegal marketing practices
U.S. and States Attorneys General Offices	**Information on Criminal Activities**
– *http://www.naag.org/ag/full_ag_table.php*	– Listing of states attorneys general
National Association of Securities Dealers	**Regulates Securities Industry**
– *www.nasdr.com* – *http://www.nasdr.com*	– Information on investment bankers – Database
Better Business Bureau (BBB)	**Compiles Consumer Complaints**
– *http://search.bbb.org/search.html*	– Database
Paid Services	**Information On**
– U.S. Search (*www.ussearch.com*) – KnowX (*www.knowx.com*)	– Criminal Violations – Liens/bankruptcies – Credit history – Litigation

which the seller is required to make certain representations and warrant that they are true. These could include the seller's acknowledgment that it owns all assets listed in the agreement "free and clear" of any liens, with a mechanism for compensating the buyer for any material loss (defined in the contract) should the representation be breached (i.e., found not to be true). Relying on reps and warranties as a substitute for a thorough due diligence is rarely a good idea.

An expensive and exhausting process, due diligence is, by its nature, highly intrusive, and it places considerable demands on managers' time and attention. Frequently, the buyer wants as much time as necessary to complete due diligence, while the seller will want to limit the length and scope as much as possible.

Due diligence rarely works to the advantage of the seller because a long and detailed due diligence is likely to uncover items the buyer will use as a reason to lower the purchase price. Consequently, sellers may seek to terminate due diligence before the buyer feels it is appropriate.[9] If the target firm succeeds in reducing the amount of information disclosed to the target firm, it can expect to be required to make more representations and warranties as to the accuracy of its claims and promises in the purchase and sale agreement.[10]

The Components of Due Diligence

Three primary reviews comprise due diligence; they are of equal importance and often occur concurrently. The *strategic and operational review* conducted by senior operations and marketing management asks questions that focus on the seller's management team, operations, and sales and marketing strategies. The *financial review* directed by financial and accounting personnel focuses on the accuracy, timeliness, and completeness of the seller's financial statements.

A *legal review*, which is conducted by the buyer's legal counsel, deals with corporate records, financial matters, management and employee issues, tangible and intangible assets of the seller, and material contracts and obligations of the seller, such as litigation and claims. A rigorous due diligence requires the creation of comprehensive checklists. The interview process provides invaluable sources of information. By asking the same questions of a number of key managers, the acquirer is able to validate the accuracy of its conclusions.

Buyer Due Diligence

Buyers use due diligence to validate assumptions underlying valuation. The primary objectives of buyer's due diligence are to identify and confirm sources of value or synergy and mitigate real or potential liability by looking for fatal flaws that reduce value. Table 5.2 categorizes potential sources of value from synergy that may be uncovered or confirmed during due diligence and the impact these may have on operating performance.

Seller Due Diligence

Although the bulk of due diligence is performed by the buyer on the seller, the prudent seller should also perform due diligence on the buyer and on its own personnel and operations. By investigating the buyer, the seller can determine whether the buyer has the financial wherewithal to finance the purchase. As part of its internal due diligence, a seller often requires its managers to sign affidavits attesting (to the "best of their knowledge") to the truthfulness of what is being represented in the contract that pertains to their areas of responsibility. In doing so, the seller hopes to mitigate liability stemming from inaccuracies in the seller's representations and warranties made in the definitive agreement of purchase and sale.

[9] One way sellers try to limit due diligence is to sequester the acquirer's team in a data room. Typically, this is a conference room filled with file cabinets and boxes of documents requested by the buyer's due diligence team. Formal presentations by the seller's key managers are given in the often cramped conditions of the data room. In other instances, the potential buyer may have limited access to information on a password-protected website, also called a virtual data room.

[10] A buyer is well advised to rely more on an on-site review of facilities and records and personnel interviews than on a seller's contract obligations. Should a seller declare bankruptcy, disappear, or move assets to offshore accounts, receiving remuneration for breach of contract may be impossible.

TABLE 5.2   Identifying Potential Sources of Value

Potential Source of Value	Examples	Potential Impact
Operating Synergy		

• Eliminating functional overlap
• Productivity improvement
• Purchasing discounts
• Working capital management
• Facilities management
  – Economies of scale
  – Economies of scope
• Organizational realignment
	• Reduce duplicate overhead positions
	• Increased output per employee
	• Volume discounts on material purchases
	• Reduced days in receivables due to improved collection of accounts receivable
	• Fewer days in inventory due to improved inventory turns
	• Increased production in underutilized facilities
	• Data centers, R&D functions, call centers, and so on, support multiple product lines/operations
	• Reduce the number of layers of management
		• Improved margins
		• Same
		• Same
		• Improved return on total assets
		• Same
		• Improved return on total assets
		• Same
		• Improved communication
		• Reduced bureaucratic inertia

Financial Synergy		
• Increased borrowing capacity • Increased leverage	• Target has little debt and many unencumbered assets • Access to lower–cost source of funds	• Increased access to financing • Lower cost of capital
Marketing/Product Synergy		
• Access to new distribution channels • Cross-selling opportunities • Research and development • Product development	• Increased sales opportunities • Selling acquirer products to target customers and vice versa • Cross-fertilization of ideas • Increased advertising budget	• Increased revenue • Same • More innovation • Improved market share
Control		
• Opportunity identification • More proactive management style	• Acquirer sees opportunities not seen by target's management • More decisive decision making	• New growth opportunities • Improved financial returns

Lender Due Diligence

If the acquirer is borrowing to buy a target firm, the lender(s) will want to perform their own due diligence independent of the buyer's effort. Multiple lender due diligences, often performed concurrently, can be quite burdensome to the target firm's management and employees, and the seller should agree to these disruptive activities only if confident that the transaction will be consummated within a reasonable period.

Developing the Financing Plan

The last of the four negotiation phase activities is to develop the balance sheet, income, and cash-flow statements for the combined firms. Unlike the financial projections of cash flow made to value the target, these statements should include the expected cost of financing the transaction. Developing the financing plan is a key input in determining the purchase price because it places a limitation on the amount the buyer can offer the seller. The financing plan is appended to the acquirer's business and acquisition plans and is used to obtain financing for the transaction. No matter the size of the transaction, lenders and investors will want to see a coherent analysis of why the proposed transaction is a good investment opportunity. How transactions are financed is discussed in more detail in Chapter 13.

Defining the Purchase Price

The three commonly used definitions of purchase price are total consideration, total purchase price/enterprise value, and net purchase price. Each serves a different purpose.

Total Consideration

In the purchase agreement, the *total consideration* consists of cash (C), stock (S), new debt issues (D), or some combination of all three. It is a term commonly used in legal documents to reflect the different types of remuneration received by target company shareholders. Note that the remuneration can include both financial and nonfinancial assets, such as real estate. Nonfinancial compensation sometimes is referred to as *payment in kind*. The debt counted in the total consideration is what the target company shareholders receive as payment for their stock, along with any cash or acquiring company stock.

Each component of the total consideration may be viewed in present value terms; therefore, the total consideration is itself expressed in present value terms (PV_{TC}). The present value of cash is its face value. The stock component of the total consideration is the present value (PV_S) of future dividends or net cash flows or the acquiring firm's stock price per share times the number of shares to be exchanged for each outstanding share of the seller's stock. New debt issued by the acquiring company as part of the compensation paid to shareholders can be expressed as the present value (PV_{ND}) of the cumulative interest payments plus principal discounted at some appropriate market rate of interest (see Chapter 7).

Total Purchase Price/Enterprise Value

The *total purchase price* (PV_{TPP}) or *enterprise value* of the target firm consists of the total consideration (PV_{TC}) plus the market value of the target firm's debt (PV_{AD}) assumed by the acquiring company. The enterprise value is sometimes expressed as the total purchase price plus net debt. *Net debt* includes the market value of debt assumed by the acquirer less cash and marketable securities on the books of the target firm.

The enterprise value of the firm often is quoted in the media as the purchase price because it is most visible to those who are not familiar with the details. It is important to analysts and shareholders alike, because it approximates the total investment made by the acquiring firm.

It is an approximation because it does not necessarily measure liabilities the acquirer is assuming that are not visible on the target firm's balance sheet. Nor does it reflect the potential for recovering a portion of the total consideration paid to target company shareholders by selling undervalued or redundant assets.

Net Purchase Price

The *net purchase price* (PV_{NPP}) is the total purchase price plus other assumed liabilities (PV_{OAL})[11] less the proceeds from the sale of discretionary or redundant target assets (PV_{DA})[12] that are on or off the balance sheet. PV_{OAL} are those assumed liabilities not fully reflected on the target firm's balance sheet or in the estimation of the economic value of the target firm.

The net purchase price is the most comprehensive measure of the actual price paid for the target firm. It includes all known cash obligations assumed by the acquirer as well as any portion of the purchase price that is recovered through the sale of assets. The various definitions of price can be summarized as follows:

Total consideration $= PV_{TC} = C + PV_S + PV_{ND}$

Total purchase price or enterprise value $= PV_{TPP} = PV_{TC} + PV_{AD}$

Net purchase price $= PV_{NPP} = PV_{TPP} + PV_{OAL} - PV_{DA} = (C + PV_S + PV_{ND} + PV_{AD}) + PV_{OAL} - PV_{DA}$

Although the total consideration is most important to the target company's shareholders as a measure of what they receive in exchange for their stock, the acquirer's shareholders often focus on the total purchase price/enterprise value as the actual amount paid for the target firm. However, the total purchase price tends to ignore other adjustments that should be made to determine actual or pending "out-of-pocket" cash spent by the acquirer. The net purchase price reflects adjustments to the total purchase price and is a much better indicator of

[11] If all the target firm's balance sheet reserves reflected accurately all known future obligations and there were no significant potential off-balance sheet liabilities, there would be no need to adjust the purchase price for assumed liabilities other than for short- and long-term debt assumed by the acquiring company. Earnings would accurately reflect the expected impact of known liabilities. Operating cash flows, which reflect both earnings and changes in balance sheet items, would also accurately reflect future liabilities. In practice, reserves are often inadequate to satisfy pending claims. This is particularly true if the selling company attempts to improve current earnings performance by understating reserves. Common examples include underfunded or underreserved employee pension and healthcare obligations and uncollectable receivables, as well as underaccrued vacation and holidays, bonuses, and deferred compensation, such as employee stock options. To the extent that such factors represent a future use of cash, the present value of their future impact, to the extent possible, should be estimated.

[12] Discretionary assets are undervalued or redundant assets that can be used by the buyer to recover some portion of the purchase price. Such assets include land valued at its historical cost on the balance sheet or equipment whose resale value exceeds its fully depreciated value. Other examples include cash balances in excess of normal working capital needs and product lines or operating units considered nonstrategic by the buyer. The sale of discretionary assets is not considered in the calculation of the economic value of the target firm because economic value is determined by future operating cash flows before consideration is given to how the transaction will be financed.

whether the acquirer overpaid for the target firm. The application of the various definitions of the purchase price is addressed in more detail in Chapter 9.

PHASE 7: DEVELOPING THE INTEGRATION PLAN

Part of the premerger integration planning process involves the preclosing due diligence activity. One of the responsibilities of the due diligence team is to identify ways in which assets, processes, and other resources can be combined to realize cost savings, productivity improvements, or other perceived synergies. This information is also essential for refining the valuation process by enabling planners to understand better the necessary sequencing of events and the resulting pace at which the expected synergies may be realized.

Contract-Related Issues

Integration planning also involves addressing human resource, as well as customer and supplier issues that overlap the change of ownership. These are *transitional* issues to resolve as part of the purchase agreement, and it is critical that the seller's responsibilities be negotiated before closing to make the actual transition as smooth as possible. Also, a cooperative effort is most likely made prior to closing. For example, the agreement may stipulate how target company employees will be paid and how their benefit claims will be processed.[13]

A prudent buyer will want to include assurances in the purchase agreement to limit its postclosing risk. Most seller representations and warranties made to the buyer refer to the past and present condition of the seller's business. They pertain to items such as the ownership of securities; real and intellectual property; current levels of receivables, inventory, and debt; and pending lawsuits, worker disability, customer warranty claims; and an assurance that the target's accounting practices are in accordance with Generally Accepted Accounting Principles.

---

[13] Systems must be in place to ensure that employees of the acquired company continue to be paid without disruption. If the number of employees is small, this may be accommodated easily by loading the acquirer's payroll computer system with the necessary salary and personal information before closing or by having a third-party payroll processor perform these services. For larger operations or where employees are dispersed geographically, the target's employees may continue to be paid for a specific period using the target's existing payroll system. As for benefits, employee healthcare or disability claims tend to escalate just before a transaction closes, and studies show that employees, whether they leave or stay with the new firm, file more disability claims for longer periods after downsizing (*The Wall Street Journal*, November 21, 1996). The sharp increase in such expenses can pose an unexpected financial burden for the acquirer if the responsibility for paying such claims has not been addressed in the merger agreement. For example, the agreement may read that all claims incurred within a specific number of days before closing but not submitted by employees for processing until after closing will be reimbursed by the seller after the closing. Alternatively, such claims may be paid from an escrow account containing a portion of the purchase price set aside to cover these types of expenses.

Although "reps and warranties" apply primarily to the past and current state of the seller's business, they do have ramifications for the future. For example, if a seller claims there are no lawsuits pending and a lawsuit is filed shortly after closing, the buyer may seek to recover damages from the seller.

The buyer also may insist that certain conditions be satisfied before closing can take place. Common conditions include employment contracts, agreements not to compete, financing, and regulatory and shareholder approval. Finally, the buyer will want to make the final closing contingent on receiving approval from the appropriate regulatory agencies and shareholders of both companies before any money changes hands.

Earning Trust

Decisions made before closing affect postclosing integration activity.[14] Successfully integrating firms requires getting employees in both firms to work toward achieving common objectives. This comes about through building credibility and trust, not through superficial slogans, pep talks, and empty promises. Trust comes from cooperation, keeping commitments, and experiencing success.

Choosing the Integration Manager and Other Critical Decisions

The buyer should designate an integration manager who possesses excellent interpersonal and project management skills. During the integration phase, interpersonal skills are frequently more important than professional and technical skills. The buyer must also determine what is critical to continuing the acquired company's success during the first 12 to 24 months after the closing. Critical activities include identifying key managers, vendors, and customers, and determining what is needed to retain them as valued assets.

Preclosing integration planning activities should also determine the operating norms or standards required for continued operation of the businesses: executive compensation, labor contracts, billing procedures, product delivery times, and quality metrics. Finally, there must be a communication plan for all stakeholders that can be implemented immediately following closing.[15] Chapter 6 describes in detail the way in which the integration plan is implemented.

---

[14] Benefits packages, employment contracts, and retention bonuses to keep key employees typically are negotiated before the closing. Contractual covenants and conditions also affect integration. Earnouts, which are payments made to the seller based on the acquired business achieving certain profit or revenue targets, and deferred purchase price payments, which involve placing some portion of the purchase price in escrow until certain contractual conditions have been realized, can limit the buyer's ability to integrate the target effectively into the acquirer's operations.

[15] Porter and Wood, 1998

PHASE 8: CLOSING

In the closing phase of the acquisition process, you obtain all necessary shareholder, regulatory, and third-party consents (e.g., customer and vendor contracts) and also complete the definitive purchase agreement. Like all other phases, this activity benefits from significant planning at the outset if it is to go smoothly, but this is often impractical because so many activities tend to converge on the closing date.

Assigning Customer and Vendor Contracts

In a purchase of assets, many customer and vendor contracts cannot be assigned to the buyer without receiving written approval from the other parties. While this may be largely a formality, both vendors and customers may view it as an opportunity to attempt to negotiate more favorable terms. Licenses must be approved by the licensor, which can be a major impediment to a timely closing if not properly planned. For example, a major software vendor demanded a substantial increase in royalty payments before agreeing to transfer the software license to the buyer. The vendor knew that the software was critical for the ongoing operation of the target company's data center. From the buyer's perspective, the exorbitant increase in the fee had an adverse impact on the economics of the transaction and nearly caused the deal to collapse.

Gaining the Necessary Approvals

The buyer's legal counsel is responsible for ensuring that the transaction is in full compliance with securities, antitrust, and state corporation laws. Significant planning before closing is again crucial to minimizing roadblocks that a target company may place before the buyer. Great care must be exercised to ensure that all filings required by law have been made with the Federal Trade Commission and the Department of Justice. Finally, many transactions require approval by the acquirer and target company shareholders.

Completing the Acquisition/Merger Agreement

The acquisition/merger agreement is the cornerstone of the closing documents. It indicates all of the rights and obligations of the parties both before and after the closing. This agreement also may be referred to as the purchase agreement or, more formally, as the definitive agreement of purchase and sale; its length depends on the complexity of the transaction.

Deal Provisions

In an asset or stock purchase, this section of the agreement defines the consideration or form of payment and how it will be paid and the specific assets or shares to be acquired. In a merger, this section of the agreement defines the number (or fraction) of acquirer shares to be exchanged for each target share.

Price

The purchase price or total consideration may be fixed at the time of closing, subject to future adjustment, or it may be contingent on future performance. In asset transactions, it is common to exclude cash on the target's balance sheet from the transaction; the price paid for noncurrent assets, such as plant and intangible assets, will be fixed, but the price for current assets will depend on their levels at closing following an audit.

Allocation of Price

The buyer typically has an incentive to allocate as much of the purchase price as possible to depreciable assets, such as fixed assets, customer lists, and noncompete agreements, which will enable the buyer to depreciate or amortize these upwardly revised assets and reduce future taxable income. However, such an allocation may constitute taxable income to the seller. Both parties should agree on how the purchase price should be allocated to the various assets acquired in an asset transaction before closing. This eliminates the chance that the parties involved will take conflicting positions for tax reporting purposes.

Payment Mechanism

Payment may be made at closing by wire transfer or cashier's check, or the buyer may defer the payment of a portion of the purchase price by issuing a promissory note to the seller. The buyer may agree to put the unpaid portion of the purchase price in escrow or through a holdback allowance, thereby facilitating the settlement of claims that might be made in the future.[16]

Assumption of Liabilities

The seller retains those liabilities not assumed by the buyer. In instances such as environmental liabilities, unpaid taxes, and inadequately funded pension obligations, the courts may go after the buyer and seller. In contrast, the buyer assumes all known and unknown liabilities in a merger or purchase of shares.

Representations and Warranties

The reps and warranties should provide for full disclosure of all information that is germane to the transaction, typically covering the areas of greatest concern to both parties. Areas commonly covered include financial statements, corporate organization and good standing, capitalization, absence of undisclosed liabilities, current litigation, contracts, title to assets, taxes and tax returns, no violation of laws or regulations, employee benefit plans, labor issues, and insurance coverage.

Covenants

Covenants are agreements by the parties about actions they agree to take or refrain from taking between signing the definitive agreement and the closing. For example, the seller may be required to continue conducting business in the usual and customary manner. The seller

---

[16] The escrow account involves the buyer putting a portion of the purchase price in an account held by a third party, while the holdback allowance generally does not.

often will be required to seek approval for all expenditures that may be considered out of the ordinary, such as one-time dividend payments or sizeable increases in management compensation.

Closing Conditions

The satisfaction of negotiated conditions determines whether a party to the agreement must go forward and consummate the deal. These conditions could include the continued accuracy of the seller's reps and warranties and the extent to which the seller is living up to its obligations under the covenants. Other examples include obtaining all necessary legal opinions, the execution of other agreements (e.g., promissory notes), and the absence of any "material adverse change" in the condition of the target company.

The effects of material adverse change clauses (MACs) in agreements of purchase and sale became very visible during the disruption in the financial markets in 2008. Many firms that had signed M&A contracts looked for a way out. The most common challenge in negotiating such clauses is defining what constitutes materiality—for example, is it a 20% reduction in earnings or sales? Because of the inherent ambiguity, the contract language is usually vague, and it is this very ambiguity that has enabled so many acquirers to withdraw from contracts. Lenders, too, use these clauses to withdraw financing (see the following).

Indemnification

In effect, indemnification is the reimbursement of the other party for a loss incurred following closing for which they were not responsible. The definitive agreement requires the seller to indemnify or absolve the buyer of liability in the event of misrepresentations or breaches of warranties or covenants. Similarly, the buyer usually agrees to indemnify the seller. Both parties generally want to limit the period during which the indemnity clauses remain in force.[17]

Other Closing Documents

In addition to resolving the issues just outlined, closing may be complicated by the number and complexity of other documents required to complete the transaction. In addition to the agreement of purchase and sale, the more important documents often include patents, licenses, royalty agreements, trade names, and trademarks; labor and employment agreements; leases; mortgages, loan agreements, and lines of credit; stock and bond commitments and details; supplier and customer contracts; distributor and sales representative agreements; stock option and employee incentive programs; and health and other benefit plans (which must be in place at closing to eliminate lapsed coverage).

Closing documents may also include complete descriptions of all foreign patents, facilities, and investments; insurance policies, coverage, and claims pending; intermediary fee arrangements; litigation pending for and against each party; environmental compliance issues resolved or on track to be resolved; seller's corporate minutes of the board of directors

---

[17] At least one full year of operation and a full audit are necessary to identify claims. Some claims (e.g., environmental) extend beyond the survival period of the indemnity clause. Usually, neither party can submit claims to the other until some minimum threshold, expressed in terms of the number or dollar size of claims, has been exceeded.

and any other significant committee information; and articles of incorporation, bylaws, stock certificates, and corporate seals.[18]

Financing Contingencies

Most well-written agreements of purchase and sale contain a financing contingency. The buyer is not subject to the terms of the contract if the buyer cannot obtain adequate funding to complete the transaction. Breakup fees can be particularly useful to ensure that the buyer will attempt as aggressively as possible to obtain financing. In some instances, the seller may require the buyer to put a nonrefundable deposit in escrow to be forfeited if the buyer is unable to obtain financing to complete the transaction.

Lenders, too, exercise financial contingencies, invoking material adverse change clauses to back out of lending commitments. For example, concerned that they would have to discount such loans when they were resold, Morgan Stanley and UBS balked at commitments to fund the purchase of Reddy Ice Holdings and Genesco in late 2007. Similarly, that same year Lehman and J.P. Morgan were part of a group of banks that helped force Home Depot to take $1.8 billion less for its construction supply business.[19]

PHASE 9: IMPLEMENTING POSTCLOSING INTEGRATION

The postclosing integration activity is widely viewed as among the most important phases of the acquisition process. Postclosing integration is discussed in considerable detail in Chapter 6. What follows is a discussion of those activities required immediately following closing. Such activities generally fall into five categories, which are discussed in the next sections.

Communication Plans

Implementing an effective communication plan immediately after the closing is crucial for retaining employees of the acquired firm and maintaining or boosting morale and productivity. The plan should address employee, customer, and vendor concerns. The message always should be honest and consistent. Employees need to understand how their compensation, including benefits, might change under the new ownership. Employees may find a loss of specific benefits palatable if they are perceived as offset by improvements in other benefits or working conditions. Customers want reassurance that there will be no deterioration in product or service quality or delivery time during the transition from old to new ownership.

---

[18] Sherman, 2006

[19] Although only the tenth largest transaction of 2007 in terms of price, the Home Depot deal became one of the most important by midyear as among the first of the large, highly leveraged transactions to be renegotiated following the collapse of the subprime mortgage market in late summer.

Vendors also are very interested in understanding how the change in ownership will affect their sales to the new firm.

Whenever possible, communication is best done on a face-to-face basis. Senior officers of the acquiring company can be sent to address employee groups (on site, if possible). Senior officers also should contact key customers (preferably in person or at least by telephone) to provide the needed reassurances. Meeting reasonable requests for information from employees, customers, and vendors immediately following closing with complete candor will contribute greatly to the sense of trust among stakeholders that is necessary for the ultimate success of the acquisition.

Employee Retention

Retaining middle-level managers should be a top priority during this phase of the acquisition process. Frequently, senior managers of the target company that the buyer chooses to retain are asked to sign employment agreements as a condition of closing. Without these signed agreements, the buyer would not have completed the transaction. Although senior managers provide overall direction for the firm, middle-level managers execute the day-to-day operations. Plans should be in place to minimize the loss of such people. Bonuses, stock options, and enhanced sales commission schedules are commonly put in place to keep such managers.

Satisfying Cash-Flow Requirements

Invariably, operating cash-flow requirements are higher than expected. Conversations with middle-level managers following closing often reveal areas in which maintenance expenditures have been deferred. Receivables previously thought to be collectable may have to be written off. Production may be disrupted as employees of the acquired firm find it difficult to adapt to new practices introduced by the acquiring company's management or if inventory levels are inadequate to maintain desired customer delivery times. Finally, more customers than had been anticipated may be lost to competitors that use the change in ownership as an opportunity to woo them away with various types of incentives.

Employing Best Practices

An important motivation for takeovers is to realize specific operating synergies, which result in improved operating efficiency, product quality, customer service, and on-time delivery. The parties in a transaction are likely to excel in different areas. An excellent way for the combined companies to take advantage of their individual strengths is to use the "best practices" of both. However, in some areas, neither company may be employing what its customers believe to be the best practices in the industry. In these circumstances, management should look beyond its own operations to accept the practices of other companies in the same or other industries.

Cultural Issues

Corporate cultures reflect the set of beliefs and behaviors of the management and employees of a corporation. Some corporations are very paternalistic, and others are very "bottom-line" oriented. Some empower employees, whereas others believe in highly centralized control. Some promote problem solving within a team environment; others encourage individual performance. Inevitably, different corporate cultures impede postacquisition integration efforts. The key to success is taking the time to explain to all of the new firm's employees what behaviors are expected and why and to tell managers that they should "walk the talk."

PHASE 10: CONDUCTING A POSTCLOSING EVALUATION

The primary reasons for conducting a postclosing evaluation of all of the acquisitions are to determine whether the acquisition is meeting expectations, to determine corrective actions if necessary, and to identify what was done well and what should be done better during future acquisitions.

Do Not Change Performance Benchmarks

Once the acquisition appears to be operating normally, evaluate the actual performance against that projected in the acquisition plan. Success should be defined in terms of actual to planned performance. Too often, management simply ignores the performance targets in the acquisition plan and accepts less than plan performance to justify the acquisition. This may be appropriate if circumstances beyond the firm's control cause a change in the operating environment. Examples include a recession, which slows the growth in revenue, or changing regulations, which preclude the introduction of a new product.

Ask the Difficult Questions

The types of questions asked should vary, depending on the time elapsed since the closing. After six months, what has the buyer learned about the business? Were the original valuation assumptions reasonable? If not, what did the buyer not understand about the target company and why? What did the buyer do well? What should have been done differently? What can be done to ensure that the same mistakes are not made in future acquisitions? After 12 months, is the business meeting expectations? If not, what can be done to put the business back on track? Is the cost of fixing the business offset by expected returns? Are the right people in place to manage the business for the long term? After 24 months, does the acquired business still appear attractive? If not, should it be divested? If yes, when and to whom?

Learn from Mistakes

It always pays to take the time to identify lessons learned from each transaction. This is often a neglected exercise and results in firms repeating the same mistakes. This occurs even in the most highly acquisitive firms because those involved in the acquisition process may change from one acquisition to another. Lessons learned in an acquisition completed by the management of one of the firm's product lines may not be readily communicated to those about to undertake acquisitions in other parts of the company. Highly acquisitive companies can benefit greatly by dedicating certain legal, human resource, marketing, financial, and business development resources to support acquisitions made throughout the company.

SOME THINGS TO REMEMBER

The acquisition process consists of 10 identifiable phases. During the first phase, the business plan defines the overall direction of the business. If an acquisition is believed necessary to implement the firm's business strategy, an acquisition plan, developed during the second phase, defines the key objectives, available resources, and management preferences for completing an acquisition. The next phase consists of the search for appropriate acquisition candidates. To initiate this phase, selection criteria need to be developed. The screening phase is a refinement of the search phase and entails applying more criteria to reduce the list of candidates that surfaced during the search process.

How the potential acquirer initiates first contact depends on the urgency of completing a transaction, the size of the target, and the availability of intermediaries with highly placed contacts within the target firm. The negotiation phase consists of refining valuation, structuring the deal, conducting due diligence, and developing a financing plan. Integration planning is a highly important aspect of the acquisition process that must be done before closing. The closing phase includes wading through the logistical quagmire of getting all the necessary third-party consents and regulatory and shareholder approvals. The postclosing integration phase entails communicating effectively with all stakeholders, retaining key employees, and identifying and resolving immediate cash-flow needs. The postclosing evaluation phase is the most commonly overlooked phase because many firms stop short of formally questioning how effective they were in managing the acquisition process.

DISCUSSION QUESTIONS

5.1 What resources are commonly used to conduct a search for potential acquisition targets?

5.2 Identify at least three criteria that might be used to select a manufacturing firm as a potential acquisition candidate. A financial services firm? A high-technology firm?

5.3 Identify alternative ways to make "first contact" with a potential acquisition target. Why is confidentiality important? Under what circumstances might a potential acquirer make its intentions public?

5.4 What are the advantages and disadvantages of a letter of intent?

5.5 How do the various activities undertaken concurrently as part of the negotiation phase affect the determination of the purchase price?

5.6 What are the differences between total consideration, total purchase price/enterprise value, and net purchase price? How are these different concepts used?

5.7 What is the purpose of the buyer and seller in performing due diligence?

5.8 What is the purpose of a financing plan? In what sense is it a "reality check"?

5.9 Why is preclosing integration planning important?

5.10 What key activities make up a typical closing?

5.11 In a rush to complete its purchase of health software producer HBO, McKesson did not perform adequate due diligence but rather relied on representations and warranties in the agreement of sale and purchase. Within six months following closing, McKesson announced that it would have to reduce revenue by $327 million and net income by $191.5 million for the preceding three fiscal years to correct for accounting irregularities. The company's stock fell by 48%. If HBO's financial statements had been declared to be in accordance with GAAP, would McKesson have been justified in believing that HBO's revenue and profit figures were 100% accurate? Explain your answer.

5.12 Find a transaction currently in the news. Speculate as to what criteria the buyer may have employed to identify the target company as an attractive takeover candidate. Be specific.

5.13 In mid-2008, Fresenius, a German manufacturer of dialysis equipment, acquired APP Pharmaceuticals for $4.6 billion. The deal includes an earn-out, under which Fresenius will pay as much as $970 million if APP reaches certain future financial targets. What is the purpose of the earn-out? How does it affect the buyer and seller?

5.14 Material adverse change clauses (MACs) are a means for the parties to the contract to determine who will bear the risk of adverse events that occur between the signing of an agreement and the closing. MACs are frequently not stated in dollar terms. How might MACs affect the negotiating strategies of the parties to the agreement during the period between signing and closing?

5.15 Despite disturbing discoveries during due diligence, Mattel acquired The Learning Company (TLC), a leading developer of software for toys, in a stock-for-stock transaction valued at $3.5 billion. Mattel had determined that TLC's receivables were overstated, a $50 million licensing deal had been prematurely put on the balance sheet, and TLC's brands were becoming outdated.

TLC also had substantially exaggerated the amount of money put into research and development for new software products. Nevertheless, driven by the appeal of rapidly becoming a big player in the children's software market, Mattel closed on the transaction even though aware that TLC's cash flows were overstated. After restructuring charges associated with the acquisition, Mattel's consolidated net loss was $82.4 million on sales of $5.5 billion. Mattel's stock fell by more than 35% to end the year at about $14 per share. What could Mattel have done to better protect its interests?

Answers to these Chapter Discussion Questions are available in the Online Instructor's Manual for instructors using this book.

CHAPTER BUSINESS CASES

CASE STUDY 5.1
Oracle's Efforts to Consolidate the Software Industry

Oracle's completion of its $7.4 billion takeover of Sun Microsystems on January 28, 2010, illustrated how in somewhat more than five years the firm has been able to dramatically realign its focus. Once viewed as the premier provider of proprietary database and middleware services (accounting for about three-fourths of the firm's revenue), Oracle is now seen as a leader in enterprise resource planning, customer relationship management, and supply chain management software applications. The purpose of this case study is to show how industry-wide trends, coupled with increasing recognition within Oracle of its own limitations, compelled the firm to radically restructure its operations.

In the past, the corporate computing market was characterized by IBM selling customers systems that included most of the hardware and software in a single package. Later, minicomputer manufacturers pursued a similar strategy in which they would build all of the crucial pieces of a large system, including its chips, main software, and networking technology. The traditional model was upended by the rise of more powerful and standardized computers based on readily available chips from Intel and an innovative software market. Customers could choose the technology they preferred (i.e., "best of breed") and assemble those products in their own data centers. Prices of hardware and software declined under intensifying competitive pressure as more and more software firms entered the fray.

Although the enterprise software market grew rapidly in the 1990s, by the early 2000s, market growth showed signs of slowing.

This market consists primarily of large Fortune 500 firms with multiple operations across many countries. Such computing environments tend to be highly complex and require multiple software applications that must work together on multiple hardware systems.

In recent years, users of information technology have sought ways to reduce the complexity of getting disparate software applications to work together. Although some buyers still prefer to purchase the "best of breed" software, many are moving to purchase suites of applications that are compatible. However, while customers seeking to simplify their IT operations are better able to choose from a wider array of products from firms such as Oracle and SAP, they are finding that they are increasingly locked into a single vendor.

Oracle, an industry leader, sought to bring about what its CEO Larry Ellison believed was needed industry consolidation. Oracle's big move into enterprise applications came with its 2004 $10.3 billion purchase of PeopleSoft. From there, Oracle proceeded to acquire 55 firms, with more than one-half focused on strengthening the firm's software applications business. Revenues have almost doubled since then to $23 billion in 2009, and they have continued to grow through the 2008–2009 recession. Oracle's intensifying focus on business applications software largely reflected the slowing growth of its database product line, which accounts for more than three-fourths of the company's sales.

Oracle, like most of the successful software firms, generates substantial and sustainable cash flow as a result of the way in which

CASE STUDY 5.1 *(cont'd)*

business software is sold. Customers buy licenses to obtain the right to utilize a vendor's software and periodically renew the license in order to receive upgrades. Healthy cash flow minimized the need for Oracle to borrow. Consequently, it was able to sustain its acquisitions by borrowing and paying cash for companies rather than to issue stock and avoid diluting existing shareholders.

Oracle has experience in streamlining other firms' supply chains and in reducing costs. For most software firms, the largest single cost is the cost of sales. Consequently, in acquiring other software firms, Oracle attempted to add other firms' revenue streams while reducing costs by pruning unprofitable products and redundant overhead during the integration of the acquired firms.

For example, since acquiring Sun, Oracle has rationalized and consolidated Sun's manufacturing operations and substantially reduced the number of products the firm offers. Fewer products will mean less administrative and support overhead. Furthermore, Oracle has introduced a "build to order" mentality rather than a "build to inventory" marketing approach. With a focus on "build to order," hardware is manufactured only when orders are received rather than for inventory in anticipation of future orders. By aligning production with actual orders, Oracle is able to reduce substantially the cost of carrying inventory; however, it does run the risk of lost sales from customers who need their orders satisfied immediately. Oracle has also pared down the number of suppliers in order to realize savings from volume purchase discounts. While lowering its cost position in this manner, Oracle has sought to distinguish itself from its competitors by being known as

a full-service provider of integrated software solutions.

Prior to the Sun acquisition, Oracle's primary competitor in the enterprise software market was SAP. However, the acquisition of Sun's vast hardware business pits Oracle for the first time against Hewlett-Packard, IBM, Dell Computer, and Cisco Systems, all of which have made acquisitions of software services companies in recent years, moving well beyond their traditional specialties in computers or networking equipment. In 2009, Cisco Systems diversified from its networking roots and began selling computer servers, a move that brought them into competition with HP, Dell, and IBM. Traditionally, Cisco had teamed with hardware vendors HP, Dell, and IBM. HP countered Cisco by investing more in its existing networking products and acquiring 3Com, also a networking company for $2.7 billion in November 2009. HP also bought EDS in 2008 for $13.8 billion in an effort to sell more equipment and services to customers often served by IBM. The individual firm seems to be pursuing a "me too" strategy in which they can claim to their customers that they and they alone have all the capabilities to be an end-to-end service provider. Which firm is most successful in the long run may well be the one that successfully integrates its acquisitions the best.

Investors' concern about Oracle's strategy is that the frequent acquisitions make it difficult to measure how well the company is growing. With many of the acquisitions falling in the $5 million to $100 million range, relatively few of Oracle's acquisitions have been viewed as material for financial reporting purposes. Consequently, Oracle is not

CASE STUDY 5.1   *(cont'd)*

obligated to provide pro forma financial data about these acquisitions, and investors have found it difficult to ascertain the extent to which Oracle has grown organically (i.e., grown the revenue resulting from prior acquisitions) versus simply by acquiring new revenue streams. Ironically, in the short run, Oracle's acquisition binge has resulted in increased complexity as each new acquisition means more products must be integrated.

Discussion Questions

1. How would you characterize the Oracle business strategy (i.e., cost leadership, differentiation, niche, or a combination of all three)? Explain your answer.

2. Conduct an external and internal analysis of Oracle. Briefly describe those factors that influenced the development of Oracle's business strategy. Be specific.

3. In what way do you think the Oracle strategy was targeting key competitors? Be specific.

4. What other benefits for Oracle and for the remaining competitors such as SAP do you see from further industry consolidation? Be specific.

Answers to these questions are found in the Online Instructor's Manual available for instructors using this book.

CASE STUDY 5.2
Exxon Mobil Buys XTO Energy in a Bet on Natural Gas

Exxon Mobil Corporation has stated publicly that it is committed to being the world's premier petroleum and petrochemical company and that the firm's primary focus in the coming decades will likely remain on its core businesses of oil and gas exploration and production, refining, and chemicals. According to the firm, there appears to be "a pretty bright future" for drilling in previously untapped shales—such as the natural gas–rich Barnett Shale of North Texas and the Haynesville Shale in northwest Louisiana and East Texas—as a result of technological advances in horizontal drilling and hydraulic fracturing. No single energy source available currently solves the dual challenge of meeting growing energy needs while reducing CO_2 emissions. The firm seeks a set of solutions ranging from producing hydrocarbons more effectively to using them more efficiently to improving existing alternatives and developing policies that encourage long-term planning and investments.[20]

Traditionally, energy companies have extracted natural gas by drilling vertical wells into pockets of methane that are often trapped above oil deposits. With this newer technology in use for the last 20 years, energy companies now drill horizontal wells and fracture them with high-pressure water, a practice known as "fracking." That technique has enabled energy firms to release natural gas trapped in the vast shale oil fields in the United States, as well as to recover gas and

[20] Rex Tillerson, ExxonMobil CEO, 2009 ExxonMobil Annual Report.

CASE STUDY 5.2 (cont'd)

oil from fields previously thought to have been depleted. The natural gas and oil recovered in this manner are often referred to as "unconventional energy resources."

In an effort to bolster its position in the development of unconventional natural gas and oil, Exxon announced on December 14, 2009, that it had reached an agreement to buy XTO Energy in an all-stock deal valued at $31 billion. The deal also included Exxon's assumption of $10 billion in XTO's current debt. Exxon agreed to issue 0.7098 of a share of common stock for each share of XTO common stock. This represented a 25% premium to XTO shareholders at the time of the announcement. XTO shares jumped 15% to $47.86, while Exxon's fell by 4.3% to $69.69. The deal values XTO's natural gas reserves at $2.96 per thousand cubic feet of proven reserves, in line with recent deals. This price is about one-half of the NYMEX natural gas futures price at that time.

Known as a wildcat or an independent energy producer, the 23-year-old XTO competed aggressively with other independent drillers in the natural gas business, which had boomed with the onset of horizontal drilling and well fracturing to extract energy from older oil fields. However, independent energy producers like XTO typically lack the financial resources required to unlock unconventional gas reserves, unlike the large multinational energy firms like Exxon.

The geographic overlap between the proven reserves of the two firms was significant, with both Exxon and XTO having a presence in the states of Colorado, Louisiana, Texas, North Dakota, Pennsylvania, New York, Ohio, and Arkansas. The two firms' combined proven reserves are the equivalent of 45 trillion cubic feet of gas and include shale gas, coal bed methane, and shale oil. These reserves also complement Exxon's U.S. and international holdings.

Exxon is the global leader in oil and gas extraction and the largest publicly traded firm in terms of market value. Given its size, it is difficult to achieve rapid future earnings growth organically through reinvestment of free cash flow. Consequently, mega-firms such as Exxon often turn to large acquisitions to offer their shareholders significant future earnings growth.

Given the long lead time required to add to proven reserves and the huge capital requirements to do so, energy companies by necessity must have exceedingly long-term planning and investment horizons. Acquiring XTO is a bet on the future of natural gas. Moreover, XTO has substantial technical expertise in recovering unconventional natural gas resources, which complement Exxon's global resource base, advanced R&D, proven operational capabilities, global scale, and financial capacity.

In the five-year period ending in 2008, the U.S. Energy Information Administration estimates, the U.S. total proven natural gas reserves increased by 30% to 245 trillion cubic feet, or the equivalent of 41 billion barrels of oil. Unconventional natural gas is projected by the EIA to meet most of the nation's domestic natural gas demand by 2030, representing a substantial change in the overall energy consumption pattern in the United States. At current consumption rates, the nation can count on natural gas for nearly a century. In addition to its abundance, natural gas is the cleanest burning of the fossil fuels.

A sizeable purchase price premium, the opportunity to share in any upside appreciation in

CASE STUDY 5.2 *(cont'd)*

Exxon's share price, and the tax-free nature* of the transaction convinced XTO shareholders to approve the deal. Exxon's commitment to manage XTO on a stand-alone basis as a wholly-owned subsidiary in which a number of former XTO managers would be retained garnered senior management support.

Discussion Questions

1. What was the total purchase price/ enterprise value of the transaction?
2. Why did Exxon Mobil's shares decline and XTO Energy's shares rise substantially immediately following the announcement of the takeover?
3. What do you think Exxon Mobil believes are its core skills? Based on your answer to this question, would you characterize this

transaction as a related or unrelated acquisition? Explain your answer.
4. Identify what you believe are the key environmental trends that encouraged Exxon Mobil to acquire XTO Energy.
5. How would you describe Exxon Mobil's long-term objectives, business strategy, and implementation strategy? What alternative implementation strategies could Exxon have pursued? Why do you believe it chose an acquisition strategy? What are the key risks involved in Exxon Mobil's takeover of XTO Energy?

Answers to these case study discussion questions are found in the Online Instructor's Manual available to instructors using this book.

* When target firm shareholders receive primarily acquirer shares for their shares, the transaction is deemed to be tax free in that no taxes are due until the acquirer shares are sold. See Chapter 12 for more details on tax-free transactions.

APPENDIX A
Thoughts on Negotiating Dynamics

Negotiating is essentially a process in which two or more parties that represent different interests attempt to achieve a consensus on a particular issue. It is useful to start a negotiation by determining any areas of disagreement, which can be done by having all of the parties review the facts pertaining to the deal at the beginning. Generally, parties reach agreement on most facts relatively easily.

From there, it is easy to identify areas in dispute. Good negotiators make concessions on issues that are not considered deal breakers—anything to which a party cannot agree without making the deal unacceptable—but only if they receive something in return. If deal breakers occur, they must be the highest priority in a negotiation and must be resolved if a negotiated settlement is to be reached.

APPENDIX A (cont'd)

The easiest areas of disagreement should be resolved first. By the time only a few remain, all of the parties to the negotiation have invested a great deal of money, time, and emotional commitment in the process and will be looking forward to resolving any remaining issues quickly.

Sound planning is the key to successful negotiation. Prior to negotiating, each party should determine its own goals (i.e., highest-priority needs) and prioritize those goals. Is money the major issue, or is it more about gaining control? Each party should also make an effort to identify the other party's goals and priorities based on public statements and actions, as well as information uncovered during due diligence. With clearly identified goals, each party can develop strategies for achieving those goals. Each party needs to recognize that allowances must be made so other parties can achieve—or at least *believe* they have achieved—their primary goals.

All moves in a negotiation should be supported by the most objective rationale possible; a well-reasoned and well-structured proposal is difficult to counter. The first move of any negotiation can set the tone for the entire process.

A reasonable offer is more likely to appeal to the other side and is more likely to elicit a reasonable counteroffer. Skilled negotiators often employ a series of techniques to reach consensus. For example, negotiators may try to determine the minimum outcome that the other party will accept and then to adjust its demands accordingly, without giving up its highest-priority objectives.

Traditional negotiating has been referred to as the "win–lose" approach, based on the assumption that one's gain is necessarily another's loss. This is true when only one issue is at stake. For example, if a seller accepts a lower cash purchase price, and if cash is a high-priority concern to the buyer and the seller, the buyer gains at the seller's expense.

"Win–win" negotiations, in contrast, presume there are outcomes in which both parties to a negotiation gain; these are negotiations that involve multiple related issues. In a win–win negotiation, one party can concede what it believes to be a relatively low-priority item in exchange for the other party's acceptance of something else that is highly important.

When it comes to issues of money, it can be important to reach agreement first on a formula or a framework for determining what both parties believe is a fair value. This may require intense discussion. A formula might be that the purchase price will be some multiple of earnings or cash flow; a framework might consist of a series of steps, such as the extent of due diligence, to be allowed before a purchase price is proposed. The formula or framework can help avoid the thorny issue of how much to offer at the outset and enables negotiators to proceed to the data collection or due diligence stage (DePamphilis, 2010a).

APPENDIX B

Legal Due Diligence Preliminary Information Request

The due diligence question list, found in the file folder entitled "Acquirer Due Diligence Question List" on the companion site to this book, applies mainly to transactions involving large public companies. For smaller, privately owned target firms, the list may be substantially more focused. Normally, the length and complexity of a "due diligence question list" submitted by the acquiring firm to the target firm's management team is determined through negotiation. The management of the target firm normally would view a lengthy list as both intrusive and costly to complete. Consequently, the target firm's management often will try to narrow both the number and breadth of the questions included in the initial request for information. The request for such a list often is included as part of the letter of intent signed by the acquirer and target firms. Note that all references to the company in the due diligence question list refer to the target.

CHAPTER

6

Pos closing Integlalion

Integration
Mergers, Acquisitions, and Business Alliances

Success breeds a disregard for the possibility of failure. —**Hyman P. Minsky**

INSIDE M&A: GENERAL ELECTRIC'S WATER BUSINESS FAILS TO MEET EXPECTATIONS

When Jeffrey Immelt, General Electric's CEO, assumed his position in September 2001, he identified water as one of five industries that would fuel future growth for the firm. Since 2001, GE has invested more than $4 billion in acquiring four companies to grow its water treatment business. In an unusual strategy for GE, the firm's intention was to build a business from scratch through acquisition to enter the $400 billion global water treatment business. In doing so, GE would be competing against a number of global competitors. GE had historically entered many new markets by growing a small portion of a larger existing business unit through a series of relatively small but highly complementary acquisitions.

GE's experience in integrating these so-called "bolt-on" acquisitions emboldened the firm to pursue this more aggressive strategy. However, the challenge proved to be more daunting than originally assumed. The largest of the units, which sells chemicals, faced aggressive price competition in what has become a commodity business. Furthermore, expectations of huge contracts to build water treatment plants were slower to materialize than expected.

Amid the unit's failure to spur revenue growth, GE has been struggling to meld thousands of employees from competing corporate cultures into its own highly disciplined culture with its focus on excellent financial performance. As the cornerstone to accelerating revenue growth, GE attempted to restructure radically the diverse sales forces of the four acquired companies. The new sales and marketing structure divided the combined sales forces into teams that are geographically focused. Within each region, one sales team is responsible for pursuing new business opportunities. More than 1,500 engineers have been retrained to sell the unit's entire portfolio, from chemicals to equipment that removes salt and debris from water.

Another group is focused on servicing customers in "vertical markets," or industries such as dairy products, electronics, and healthcare. However, the task of retraining even highly educated engineers to do substantially different things has required much more time and expense than anticipated. For example, in an effort to rapidly redirect the business, GE retrained a group of 2,000 engineers who had previously sold chemicals to sell sophisticated equipment. The latter sales effort required a much different set of skills than what the engineers had been originally trained to do.

Reflecting these problems, in mid-2006, Immelt admitted that the water business unit's operating profit was well below forecast and replaced George Oliver, the executive he had put in charge of the water business in 2002. "We probably moved quicker than we should have in some areas," Immelt conceded, adding that "training has taken longer than expected."[1]

CHAPTER OVERVIEW

After a transaction closes, integration is on the agenda. The category into which the acquirer falls will influence considerably the extent of integration and the pace at which it takes place. *Financial* buyers—those who buy a business for eventual resale—tend not to integrate the acquired business into another entity. Rather than manage the business, they are inclined to monitor the effectiveness of current management and intervene only if there is a significant and sustained deviation between actual and projected performance. In contrast, *strategic* buyers want to make a profit by managing the acquired business for an extended period, either as a separate subsidiary in a holding company or by merging it into another business.

For our purposes here, assume that integration is the goal of the acquirer immediately after the transaction closes. The integration phase is an important contributor to the ultimate success of the merger or acquisition, and ineffective integration is commonly given as one of the primary reasons that M&As sometimes fail to meet expectations. A practical process makes for effective integration. The critical success factors include careful premerger planning, candid and continuous communication, adopting the right pace for combining the businesses, appointing an integration manager and team with clearly defined goals and lines of authority, and making the difficult decisions early in the process. The chapter concludes with a discussion of how to overcome some of the unique obstacles encountered in integrating business alliances. A chapter review (consisting of practice questions and answers) is available in the file folder entitled Student Study Guide on the companion site to this book (*www.elsevierdirect. com/companions/9780123854858*). The companion site also contains a Learning Interactions Library, which gives students the opportunity to test their knowledge of this chapter in a "real-time" environment.

THE ROLE OF INTEGRATION IN SUCCESSFUL M&AS

Rapid integration is more likely to result in a merger that achieves the acquirer's expectations.[2] For our purposes, the term *rapid* is defined as relative to the pace of normal operations for a firm. Andersen Consulting studied 100 global acquisitions, each valued at more than $500 million, and concluded that most postmerger activities are completed within six

[1] Kranhold, 2006

[2] Coopers & Lybrand, 1996; Marks, 1996

months to one year and that integration done quickly generates the financial returns expected by shareholders and minimizes employee turnover and customer attrition.[3]

Realizing Projected Financial Returns

A simple example demonstrates the importance of rapid integration to realizing projected financial returns. Suppose a firm's current market value of $100 million accurately reflects the firm's future cash flows discounted at its cost of capital (i.e., the financial return the firm must earn or exceed to satisfy the expectations of its shareholders and lenders). Assume an acquirer is willing to pay a $25 million premium for this firm over its current share price, believing it can recover the premium by realizing cost savings resulting from integrating the two firms. The amount of cash the acquirer will have to generate to recover the premium will increase the longer it takes to integrate the target company. If the cost of capital is 10% and integration is completed by the end of the first year, the acquirer will have to earn $27.5 million by the end of the first year to recover the premium plus its cost of capital ($25 + ($25 × 0.10)). If integration is not completed until the end of the second year, the acquirer will have to earn an incremental cash flow of $30.25 million ($27.5 + ($27.5 × 0.10)), and so on.

The Impact of Employee Turnover

Although there is little evidence that firms necessarily experience an actual reduction in their total workforce following an acquisition, there is evidence of increased turnover among management and key employees after a corporate takeover.[4] Some loss of managers is intentional as part of an effort to eliminate redundancies and overlapping positions, but other managers quit during the integration turmoil. In many acquisitions, talent and management skills represent the primary value of the target company to the acquirer—especially in high-technology and service companies, for which assets are largely the embodied knowledge of their employees[5]—and it is difficult to measure whether employees who leave represent a significant "brain drain" or loss of key managers. If it does, though, this loss degrades the value of the target company, making the recovery of any premium paid to target shareholders difficult for the buyer.

The cost also may be high simply because the target firm's top, experienced managers are removed as part of the integration process and replaced with new managers—who tend to have a high failure rate in general. When a firm selects an insider (i.e., a person already in the employ of the merged firms) to replace a top manager (e.g., a CEO), the failure rate of the successor (i.e., the successor is no longer with the firm 18 months later) is 34%. When the board selects an outside successor (i.e., a person selected who is not in the employ of the merged firms) to replace the departing senior manager, the 18-month failure rate is 55%. Therefore, more than half of the time, an outside successor will not succeed, with an insider succeeding about two-thirds of the time.[6]

[3] Andersen Consulting, 1999

[4] Shivdasani, 1993; Walsh and Ellwood, 1991

[5] Lord and Ranft, 2000

[6] Dalton, 2006

The cost of employee turnover does not stop with the loss of key employees. The loss of any significant number of employees can be very costly. Current employees have already been recruited and trained; lose them, and you will incur new recruitment and training costs to replace them with equally qualified employees. Moreover, the loss of employees is likely to reduce the morale and productivity of those who remain.

Acquisition-Related Customer Attrition

During normal operations, a business can expect a certain level of churn in its customer list. Depending on the industry, normal churn as a result of competitive conditions can be anywhere from 20 to 40%. A newly merged company will experience a loss of another 5 to 10% of its existing customers as a direct result of a merger,[7] reflecting uncertainty about on-time delivery and product quality and more aggressive postmerger pricing by competitors. Moreover, many companies lose revenue momentum as they concentrate on realizing expected cost synergies. The loss of customers may continue well after closing.[8]

Rapid Integration Does Not Mean Doing Everything at the Same Pace

Rapid integration may result in more immediate realization of synergies, but it also contributes to employee and customer attrition. Therefore, intelligent integration involves managing these tradeoffs by quickly identifying and implementing projects that offer the most immediate payoff and deferring those whose disruption would result in the greatest revenue loss. Acquirers often will postpone integrating data processing and customer service call centers until much later in the integration process if such activities are seen as pivotal to maintaining on-time delivery and high-quality customer service.

VIEWING INTEGRATION AS A PROCESS

Integrating an acquired business into the acquirer's operations involves six major activities that fall loosely into the sequence premerger planning, resolving communication issues, defining the new organization, developing staffing plans, integrating functions and departments, and building a new corporate culture. Some of the activities are continuous and, in some respects, unending. In practice, for instance, communicating with all of the major stakeholder groups and developing a new corporate culture are largely continuous activities, running through the integration period and beyond. Table 6.1 outlines the sequence.

[7] Down, 1995

[8] A McKinsey study of 160 acquisitions by 157 publicly traded firms in 11 different industries in 1995 and 1996 found that, on average, these firms grew four percentage points less than their peers during the three years following closing. Moreover, 42% of the sample actually lost ground. Only 12% of the sample showed revenue growth significantly ahead of their peers (Bekier, Bogardus, and Oldham, 2001).

TABLE 6.1   Viewing Merger Integration as a Process

Integration Planning	Developing Communication Plans	Creating a New Organization	Developing Staffing Plans	Functional Integration	Building a New Corporate Culture
Premerger Planning: • Refine valuation • Resolve transition issues • Negotiate contractual assurances	Stakeholders: • Employees • Customers • Suppliers • Investors • Lenders • Communities (including regulators)	Learn from the past	Determine personnel requirements for the new organization	Revalidate due diligence data	Identify cultural issues through corporate profiling
		Business needs drive organizational structure	Determine resource availability	Conduct performance benchmarking	Integrate through shared: • Goals • Standards • Services • Space
		Establish staffing plans and timetables		Integrate functions: • Operations • Information technology • Finance • Sales • Marketing • Purchasing • R&D • Human resources	
		Develop compensation strategy			
		Create needed information systems			

Premerger Integration Planning

Even though some argue that integration planning should begin as soon as the merger is announced,[9] assumptions made before the closing based on information accumulated during due diligence must be reexamined once the transaction is consummated to ensure their validity. The premerger integration planning process enables the acquiring company to refine its original

[9] Carey and Ogden, 2004

estimate of the value of the target and deal with transition issues in the context of the merger agreement. Furthermore, it gives the buyer an opportunity to insert into the agreement the appropriate representations (claims) and warranties (guarantees), as well as conditions of closing that facilitate the postmerger integration process. Finally, the planning process creates a postmerger integration organization to expedite the integration process after the closing.

To minimize potential confusion, it is critical to get the integration manager involved in the process as early as possible—ideally, as soon as the target has been identified, or at least well before the evaluation and negotiation process begins.[10] Doing so makes it more likely that the strategic rationale for the deal remains well understood by those involved in conducting due diligence and postmerger integration. The 2002 acquisition of Compaq Computer by Hewlett-Packard offers some interesting insights into the benefits of preclosing planning (see Case Study 6.1).

CASE STUDY 6.1
HP Acquires Compaq—The Importance of Preplanning Integration

The proposed marriage between Hewlett-Packard (HP) and Compaq Computer got off to a rocky start when the sons of the founders came out against the transaction. The resulting long, drawn-out proxy battle threatened to divert management's attention from planning for the postclosing integration effort. The complexity of the pending integration effort appeared daunting. The two companies would need to meld employees in 160 countries and assimilate a large array of products ranging from personal computers to consulting services. When the transaction closed on May 7, 2002, critics predicted that the combined businesses, like so many tech mergers over the years, would become stalled in a mess of technical and personal entanglements.

Instead, HP's then CEO Carly Fiorina methodically began to plan for integration prior to the deal closing. She formed an elite team that studied past tech mergers, mapped out the merger's most important tasks, and checked regularly whether key projects were on schedule. A month before the deal was even announced on September 4, 2001, Carly Fiorina and Compaq CEO Michael Capellas each

tapped a top manager to tackle the integration effort. The integration managers immediately moved to form a 30-person integration team. The team learned, for example, that during Compaq's merger with Digital some server computers slated for elimination were never eliminated. In contrast, HP executives quickly decided what to jettison. Every week they pored over progress charts to review how each product exit was proceeding. By early 2003, Hewlett-Packard had eliminated 33 product lines it had inherited from the two companies, thereby reducing the remaining number to 27. Another 6 were phased out in 2004.

After reviewing other recent transactions, the team recommended offering retention bonuses to employees the firms wanted to keep, as Citigroup had done when combining with Travelers. The team also recommended that moves be taken to create a unified culture to avoid the kind of divisions that plagued AOL Time Warner. HP executives learned to move quickly, making tough decisions early with respect to departments, products, and executives. By studying the 1984 merger between Chevron and Gulf Oil, in which it

[10] Uhlaner and West, 2008

CASE STUDY 6.1 *(cont'd)*

took months to name new managers, integration was delayed and employee morale suffered. In contrast, after Chevron merged with Texaco in 2001, new managers were appointed in days, contributing to a smooth merger.

Disputes between HP and former Compaq staff sometimes emerged over issues such as the different approaches to compensating sales people. These issues were resolved by setting up a panel of up to six sales managers enlisted from both firms to referee the disagreements. Hewlett-Packard also created a team to deal with combining the corporate cultures and hired consultants to document the differences. A series of workshops involving employees from both organizations was established to find ways to bridge actual or perceived differences. Teams of sales personnel from both firms were set up to standardize ways to market to common customers. Schedules were set up to ensure that agreed-upon tactics were actually implemented in a timely manner. The integration managers met with Fiorina weekly.

The results of this intense preplanning effort were evident by the end of the first year

following closing. HP eliminated duplicate product lines and closed dozens of facilities. The firm cut 12,000 jobs, 2,000 more than had been planned at that point in time, from its combined 150,000 employees. HP achieved $3 billion in savings from layoffs, office closures, and consolidating its supply chain. Its original target was for savings of $2.4 billion after the first 18 months.

Despite realizing greater than anticipated cost savings, operating margins by 2004 in the PC business fell far short of expectations. This shortfall was due largely to declining selling prices and a slower than predicted recovery in PC unit sales. The failure to achieve the level of profitability forecast at this time of the acquisition contributed to the termination of Fiorina in early 2005.

Discussion Questions

1. Explain how premerger planning aided in the integration of HP and Compaq.
2. What did HP learn by studying other mergers? Give examples.
3. Cite key cultural differences between the two organizations. How were they resolved?

Putting the Postmerger Integration Organization in Place before Closing

A postmerger integration organization with clearly defined goals and responsibilities should be in place before the closing. For friendly mergers, the organization—including supporting work teams—should consist of individuals from both the acquiring and target companies with a vested interest in the newly formed company. During a hostile takeover, of course, it can be problematic to assemble such a team, given the lack of trust that may exist between the parties to the transaction. The acquiring company will likely find it difficult to access needed information and involve the target company's management in the planning process before the transaction closes.

If the plan is to integrate the target firm into one of the acquirer's business units, it is critical to place responsibility for integration in that business unit. Personnel from the business unit should be well represented on the due diligence team to ensure that they understand how best to integrate the target to realize synergies expeditiously.

The Postmerger Integration Organization: Composition and Responsibilities

The postmerger integration organization should consist of a management integration team (MIT) and integration work teams focused on implementing a specific portion of the integration plan. Senior managers from the two merged organizations serve on the MIT, which is charged with implementing synergies identified during the preclosing due diligence. Involving senior managers from both firms captures the best talent from both organizations and also sends a comforting signal to all employees that decision makers who understand their particular situations are on board.

The MIT's emphasis during the integration period should be on activities that create the greatest value for shareholders. Exhibit 6.1 summarizes the key tasks the MIT must perform to realize anticipated synergies.

In addition to driving the integration effort, the MIT ensures that the managers not involved in the endeavor remain focused on running the business. Dedicated integration work teams perform the detailed integration work. These work teams should also include employees from both the acquiring and target companies. Other team members might include outside advisors, such as investment bankers, accountants, attorneys, and consultants.

The MIT allocates dedicated resources to the integration effort and clarifies non-team-membership roles and enables day-to-day operations to continue at premerger levels. The MIT should be careful to give the work teams not only the responsibility to do certain tasks but also the authority and resources to get the job done. To be effective, the work teams must have access to timely, accurate information and should receive candid, timely feedback. The teams need to be kept informed of the broader perspective of the overall integration effort to avoid becoming too narrowly focused.

EXHIBIT 6.1 **KEY MANAGEMENT INTEGRATION TEAM RESPONSIBILITIES**

1. Build a master schedule of what should be done by whom and by what date.
2. Determine the required economic performance for the combined entity.
3. Establish work teams to determine how each function and business unit will be combined (e.g., structure, job design, and staffing levels).
4. Focus the organization on meeting ongoing business commitments and operational performance targets during the integration process.
5. Create an early warning system consisting of performance indicators to ensure that both integration activities and business performance stay on plan.
6. Monitor and expedite key decisions.
7. Establish a rigorous communication campaign to aggressively support the integration plan. Address both internal (e.g., employees) and external (e.g., customers, suppliers, and regulatory authorities) constituencies.

Developing Communication Plans for Key Stakeholders

Before publicly announcing an acquisition, the acquirer should prepare a communication plan targeted at major stakeholder groups, developed jointly by the MIT and the public relations (PR) department or outside PR consultant.

Employees: Addressing the "Me" Issues Immediately

Employees are interested in any information pertaining to the merger and how it will affect them. They want to know how changes affect the overall strategy, business operations, job security, working conditions, and total compensation. Thus, consistent and candid communication is of paramount importance.

Target firm employees typically represent a substantial portion of the acquired company's value, particularly for technology and service-related businesses with few tangible assets. The CEO should lead the effort to communicate to employees at all levels through on-site meetings or via teleconferencing. Communication with employees should be as frequent as possible; it is better to report that there is no change than to remain silent. Direct communication to all employees at both firms is critical. Deteriorating job performance and absences from work are clear signs of workforce anxiety.

Many companies find it useful to create a single information source that is accessible to all employees, be it an individual whose job is to answer questions or a menu-driven automated phone system programmed to respond to commonly asked questions. The best way to communicate in a crisis, however, is through regularly scheduled employee meetings.

All external communication in the form of press releases should be coordinated with the PR department to ensure that the same information is released concurrently to all employees. Internal e-mail systems, voice mail, or intranets may be used to facilitate employee communications. In addition, personal letters, question-and-answer sessions, newsletters, or videotapes are highly effective ways to deliver messages.

Customers: Undercommitting and Overdelivering

Attrition can be minimized if the newly merged firm commits to customers that it will maintain or improve product quality, on-time delivery, and customer service. Commitments should be realistic in terms of what needs to be accomplished during the integration phase. The firm must communicate to customers realistic benefits associated with the merger. From the customer's perspective, the merger can increase the range of products or services offered or provide lower selling prices as a result of economies of scale and new applications of technology.

Suppliers: Developing Long-Term Vendor Relationships

Although substantial cost savings are possible by "managing" suppliers, the new company should seek long-term relationships rather than simply ways to reduce costs. Aggressive negotiation may win high-quality products and services at lower prices in the short run, but that may be transitory if the new company is a large customer of the supplier and if the supplier's margins are squeezed continually. The supplier's product or service quality will suffer, and the supplier eventually may exit the business. (See the next section for suggestions of how to manage suppliers effectively following an acquisition.)

Investors: Maintaining Shareholder Loyalty

The new firm must be able to present to investors a compelling vision of the future. Target shareholders will become shareholders in the newly formed company. Loyal shareholders tend to provide a more stable ownership base and may contribute to lower share price volatility. All firms attract particular types of investors—some with a preference for high dividends and others for capital gains—and they may clash over their preferences, as America Online's acquisition of Time Warner in January 2000 illustrates. The combined market value of the two firms lost 11% in the four days following the announcement, as investors fretted over what had been created and there was a selling frenzy that likely involved investors who bought Time Warner for its stable growth and America Online for its meteoric growth rate of 70% per year.

Communities: Building Strong, Credible Relationships

Good working relations with surrounding communities are simply good public relations. Companies should communicate plans to build or keep plants, stores, or office buildings in a community as soon as they can be confident that these actions will be implemented. Such steps often translate into new jobs and increased taxes for the community.

Creating a New Organization

Despite being a time-consuming process that involves appointing dozens of managers—including heads of key functions, groups, and even divisions—creating a new top management team must be given first priority. The role of each senior manager must be clearly defined to achieve effective collaboration.

Establishing a Structure

Building new reporting structures for combining companies requires knowledge of the target company's prior organization, some sense as to the effectiveness of this organization in the decision-making process, and the future business needs of the newly combined companies. Previous organization charts provide insights into how individuals from both target and acquiring companies will interact within the new company because they reveal the experiences and future expectations of individuals with regard to reporting relationships. The next step is to move from the past into the future by creating a structure that focuses on meeting the business needs of the combined companies.

There are three basic types of structures. In a *functional organization*, which tends to be the most centralized and is becoming less common, people are assigned to specific groups or departments such as accounting, engineering, marketing, sales, distribution, customer service, manufacturing, or maintenance. In a *product or service organization*, functional specialists are grouped by product line or service offering, and each has its own accounting, human resources, sales, marketing, customer service, and product development staffs.

These types of organizations tend to be somewhat decentralized, and the individuals in them often have multiple reporting relationships, such as a finance manager reporting to a product line manager and the firm's CFO. *Divisional organizations* continue to be the dominant form of organizational structure, in which groups of products are combined into independent divisions or "strategic business units." Such organizations have their own management teams and tend to be highly decentralized.

The popularity of decentralized versus centralized management structures varies with the state of the economy. During recessions, when top management is under great pressure to cut costs, companies may tend to move toward centralized management structures, only to decentralize when the economy recovers. Highly decentralized authority can retard the pace of integration because there is no single authority to resolve issues or determine policies.

A centralized structure may make postmerger integration much easier. Senior management can dictate policies governing all aspects of the combined companies, centralize all types of functions that provide support to operating units, and resolve issues among the operating units. Still, centralized control can be highly detrimental and can destroy value if policies imposed by the central headquarters are inappropriate for the operating units—such as policies that impose too many rigid controls, focus on the wrong issues, hire or promote the wrong managers, or establish the wrong performance measures. Moreover, centralized companies often have multiple layers of management and centralized functions providing services to the operating units. The parent companies pass on the costs of centralized management and support services to the operating units, and these costs often outweigh the benefits.[11]

The right structure may be an evolving one. The substantial benefits of a well-managed, rapid integration of two businesses suggest a centralized management structure initially with relatively few layers of management. In general, flatter organizations are common among large companies. The distance between the CEO and division heads, measured in terms of intermediate positions, has decreased substantially, while the span of a CEO's authority has widened.[12] This does not mean that all integration activities should be driven from the top, with no input from middle managers and supervisors of both companies. It does mean taking decisive and timely action based on the best information available. Once integration is viewed as relatively complete, the new company should move to a more decentralized structure in view of the well-documented costs of centralized corporate organizations.

Developing Staffing Plans

Staffing plans should be formulated as early as possible in the integration process. In friendly acquisitions, the process should begin before closing. The early development of such plans provides an opportunity to include key personnel from both firms in the integration effort. Other benefits include the increased likelihood of retaining employees with key skills and talents, maintaining corporate continuity, and team building. Figure 6.1 describes the logical sequencing of staffing plans and the major issues addressed in each segment.

[11] Campbell, Sadler, and Koch, 1997

[12] Wulf and Rajan (2003) report a 25% decrease in intermediate positions between 1986 and 1999, with about 50% more positions reporting directly to the CEO.

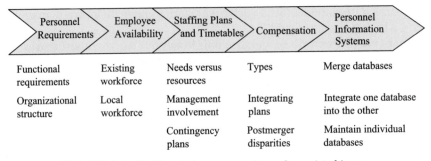

FIGURE 6.1   Staffing strategy sequencing and associated issues.

Personnel Requirements

The appropriate organizational structure is one that meets the current functional requirements of the business and is flexible enough to be expanded to satisfy future requirements. Creating such a structure should involve input from all levels of management, be consistent with the combined firm's business strategy, and reflect expected sales growth. Before establishing the organizational structure, the integration team should agree on the specific functions needed to run the combined businesses and to project each function's personnel requirements based on a description of the function's ideal structure to achieve its objectives.

Employee Availability

Employee availability refers to the number of each type of employee required by the new organization. The skills of the existing workforce should be documented and compared with the current and future requirements of the new company. The local labor pool can be a source of potential new hires for the combined firms to augment the existing workforce. Data should be collected on the educational levels, skills, and demographic composition of the local workforce, as well as prevailing wage rates by skill category.

Staffing Plans and Timetables

A detailed staffing plan can be developed once the preceding steps are completed. Gaps in the firm's workforce that need to be filled by outside recruitment can be readily identified. The effort to recruit externally should be tempered by its potentially adverse impact on current employee morale. Filling needed jobs should be prioritized and phased in over time in recognition of the time required to fill certain types of positions and the impact of major hiring programs on local wage rates in communities with a limited availability of labor.

Compensation

Merging compensation plans must be done in compliance with prevailing regulations and with a high degree of sensitivity. Total compensation consists of base pay, bonuses or incentive plans, benefits, and special contractual agreements. Bonuses may take the form of a lump sum of cash or stock paid to an employee for meeting or exceeding targets. Special contractual agreements may consist of noncompete agreements, in which key employees, in exchange for an agreed-on amount of compensation, sign agreements not to compete against the newly formed company if they should leave. Special agreements also may take the form of golden parachutes (i.e., lucrative severance packages) for senior management. Finally, retention bonuses often are given to employees if they agree to stay with the new company for a specific period.[13]

Personnel Information Systems

The acquiring company may choose to merge all personnel data into a new database, merge one corporate database into another, or maintain the separate personnel databases of each business. A single database enables authorized users to access employee data more readily, plan more efficiently for future staffing requirements, and conduct workforce analyses. Maintenance expenses associated with a single database also may be lower. The decision to keep personnel databases separate may reflect plans to divest the unit in the future.

Functional Integration

So far, you have learned about the steps involved in *planning* the integration process. Now let's look at functional integration—the actual *execution* of the plans.

First, the management integration team needs to determine the extent to which the two companies' operations and support staffs can be centralized or decentralized. The main areas of focus should be information technology (IT), manufacturing operations, sales, marketing, finance, purchasing, R&D, and the requirements to staff these functions. However, before any actual integration takes place, it is crucial to revalidate data collected during due diligence and benchmark all operations by comparing them to industry standards.

Revalidating Due Diligence Data

Data collected during due diligence should be revalidated immediately after closing. The pressure exerted by both buyer and seller to complete the transaction often results in a haphazard preclosing due diligence review. For example, to compress the time devoted to due diligence, sellers often allow buyers access only to senior managers. Middle-level managers, supervisory personnel, and equipment operators may be excluded from the interview process. For similar reasons, site visits by the buyer often are limited to those with the largest number of employees, and so risks and opportunities that might exist at other sites are ignored or remain undiscovered.

The buyer's legal and financial reviews typically are conducted only on the largest customer and supplier contracts, promissory notes, and operating and capital leases. Receivables are evaluated, and physical inventory is counted using sampling techniques. The effort to determine whether intellectual property has been properly protected, with key trademarks or service marks registered and copyrights and patents filed, is often spotty.

---

[13] Following its acquisition of Merrill Lynch in 2008, Bank of America offered Merrill's top financial advisers retention bonuses to minimize potential attrition—believing that the loss of the highest producers among Merrill's 17,000 brokers would seriously erode the value of the firm.

Benchmarking Performance

Benchmarking important functions such as the acquirer and target manufacturing and IT operations and processes is a useful starting point for determining how to integrate these activities. Standard benchmarks include the International Organization of Standards' (ISO) 9000 Quality Systems—Model for Quality Assurance in Design, Development, Production, Installation, and Servicing. Other benchmarks that can be used include the U.S. Food and Drug Administration's Good Manufacturing Practices and the Department of Commerce's Malcolm Baldrige Award.[14]

Integrating Manufacturing Operations

The data revalidation process for integrating and rationalizing facilities and operations requires in-depth discussions with key target company personnel and on-site visits to all facilities. The objective should be to reevaluate overall capacity, the potential for future cost reductions, the age and condition of facilities, the adequacy of maintenance budgets, and compliance with environmental laws and safety laws. The integration should consider carefully whether target facilities that duplicate manufacturing capabilities are potentially more efficient than those of the buyer. As part of the benchmarking process, the operations of both the acquirer and the target company should be compared with industry standards to properly evaluate their efficiency.

Process effectiveness is an accurate indicator of overall operational efficiency.[15] Four processes should be examined. The first two are *production planning* and *materials ordering*. Production planning is often inaccurate, particularly when the operations require long-term sales forecasts. The production planning and materials ordering functions need to coordinate activities because the quantity and composition of the materials ordered depend on the accuracy of sales projections. Inaccurate projections result in shortages or costly excess inventory accumulation.

The third process to examine, *order entry*, may offer significant opportunities for cost savings. Companies that produce in anticipation of sales often carry large finished goods inventories. For this reason, companies such as personal computer manufacturers are building inventory according to orders received to minimize working capital requirements. A key indicator of the effectiveness of *quality control*, the last of the processes to examine, is the percentage of products that have to be reworked due to their failure to meet quality standards. Companies whose "first-run yield" (i.e., the percentage of finished products that do not have to be reworked due to quality problems) is in the 70 to 80% range may have serious quality problems.

Plant consolidation begins with adopting a set of common systems and standards for all manufacturing activities. Such standards include cycle time between production runs, cost per unit of output, first-run yield, and scrap rates. Links between the different facilities are then created by sharing information management and processing systems, inventory control, supplier relationships, and transportation links. Vertical integration can be achieved by focusing on different stages of production. Different facilities specialize in the production of selected components, which are then shipped to other facilities to assemble the finished product. Finally, a company may close certain facilities whenever there is excess capacity.

[14] Sanderson and Uzumeri (1997, p. 135) provide a comprehensive list of standards-setting organizations.

[15] Porter and Wood, 1998

Integrating Information Technology

IT spending constitutes an ever-increasing share of most business budgets—and about 80% of software projects fail to meet their performance expectations or deadlines.[16] Nearly one-half are scrapped before completion, and about one-half cost two to three times their original budgets and take three times as long as expected to complete.[17]

Managers seem to focus too much on technology and not enough on the people and processes that will use that technology. If the buyer intends to operate the target company independently, the information systems of the two companies may be kept separate as long as communications links between them can be established. If the buyer intends to integrate the target, though, the process can be daunting. Nearly 70% of buyers choose to combine their information systems immediately after closing, and almost 90% of acquirers eventually combine these operations.[18] Case Study 6.2 describes how Dutch fragrance maker Coty successfully overcame many of the challenges of integrating its supply chain with that of Unilever Cosmetics International.

CASE STUDY 6.2
Integrating Supply Chains: Coty Cosmetics Integrates Unilever Cosmetics International

In mid-August of 2005, Coty, one of the world's largest cosmetics and fragrance manufacturers, acquired Unilever Cosmetics International (UCI), a subsidiary of the Unilever global conglomerate, for $800 million. Coty viewed the transaction as one in which it could become a larger player in the prestigious fragrance market of expensive perfumes. Coty believed it could reap economies of scale from having just one sales force, marketing group, and the like, selling and managing the two sets of products. It hoped to retain the best people from both organizations. However, Coty's management understood that if the deal were not done quickly enough, it might not realize the potential cost savings and would risk losing key personnel.

By mid-December, Coty's information technology (IT) team had just completed moving the UCI employees from Unilever's infrastructure to Coty's. This involved such tedious work as switching employees from Microsoft's Outlook to Lotus Notes. Coty's IT team was faced with the challenge of combining and standardizing the two firms' supply chains, including order entry, purchasing, processing, financial, warehouse, and shipping systems.

At the end of 2006, Coty's management announced that it anticipated that the two firms would be fully integrated by June 30, 2006. From an IT perspective, the challenges were daunting. The new company's supply chain spanned ten countries and employed four different enterprise resource planning (ERP) systems that had three warehouse systems running five major distribution facilities on two continents. ERP is an information system

---

[16] *Financial Times*, 1996

[17] *The Wall Street Journal*, November 18, 1996

[18] Cossey, 1991

CASE STUDY 6.2 *(cont'd)*

or process that integrates all of the production and related applications across an entire corporation.

On January 11–12, 2006, 25 process or function "owners," including the heads of finance, customer service, distribution, and IT, met to create the integration plan for the firm's disparate supply chains. In addition to the multiple distribution centers and ERP systems, operations in each country had unique processes that had to be included in the integration planning effort.

For example, Italy was already using the SAP system on which Coty would eventually standardize. The largest customers there placed orders at the individual store level and expected products to be delivered to these stores. In contrast, the United Kingdom used a legacy (i.e., a highly customized, nonstandard) enterprise resource planning system, and Coty's largest customer in the United Kingdom, the Boots pharmacy chain, placed orders electronically and had them delivered to central warehouses.

Coty's IT team, facing a very demanding schedule, knew it could not accomplish all that needed to be done in the time frame required. Therefore, it started with any system that directly affected the customer, such as sending an order to the warehouse, shipment notification, and billing. The decision to focus on "customer-facing" systems came at the expense of internal systems, such as daily management reports tracking sales and inventory levels. These systems were to be completed after the June 30, 2006, deadline imposed by senior management.

To minimize confusion, Coty created small project teams that consisted of project managers, IT directors, and external consultants. Smaller teams did not require costly overhead, like dedicated office space, and eliminated chains of command that might have prevented senior IT management from receiving timely, candid feedback on actual progress against the integration plan. The use of such teams is credited with allowing Coty's IT department to combine sales and marketing forces as planned at the beginning of the 2007 fiscal year in July 2006.

While much of the "customer-facing" work was done, many tasks remained. The IT department now had to go back and work out the details it had neglected during the previous integration effort, such as those daily reports its senior managers wanted and the real-time monitoring of transactions. By setting priorities early in the process and employing small, project-focused teams, Coty was able to successfully integrate the complex supply chains of the firms in a timely manner.

Discussion Questions

1. Do you agree with Coty management's decision to focus on integrating "customer-facing" systems first? Explain your answer.
2. How might this emphasis on integrating "customer-facing" systems have affected the new firm's ability to realize anticipated synergies? Be specific.
3. Discuss the advantages and the disadvantages of using small project teams. Be specific.

Integrating Finance

Some target companies will be operated as stand-alone operations, while others will be completely merged with the acquirer's existing business. Many international acquisitions involve companies in areas that are geographically remote from the parent company and operate largely independently from the parent. This requires a great deal of effort to ensure that the buyer can monitor financial results from a distance, even if the parent has its representative permanently on site. The acquirer should also establish a budgeting process and signature approval levels to control spending.

Integrating Sales

Whether the sales forces of the two firms are wholly integrated or operated independently depends on their relative size, the nature of their products and markets, and their geographic location. A relatively small sales force may be readily combined with the larger sales force if they sell sufficiently similar products and serve sufficiently similar markets. The sales forces may be kept separate if the products they sell require in-depth understanding of the customers' needs and a detailed knowledge of the product.

It is quite common for firms that sell highly complex products such as robotics or enterprise software to employ a particularly well-trained and very sophisticated sales force that must employ the "consultative selling" approach; this may require keeping the sales forces of merged firms separate. Sales forces in globally dispersed businesses often are kept separate to reflect the uniqueness of their markets. However, support activities such as sales training or technical support often are centralized.

Significant cost savings may be achieved by integrating sales forces, which eliminates duplicate sales representatives and related support expenses, such as travel and entertainment expenses, training, and management. A single sales force may also minimize potential confusion by allowing customers to deal with a single sales representative when purchasing multiple products and services.

Integrating Marketing

Enabling the customer to see a consistent image in advertising and promotional campaigns may be the greatest challenge facing the integration of the marketing function. Steps to ensure consistency, however, should not confuse the customer by radically changing a product's image or how it is sold. The location and degree of integration of the marketing function depend on the global nature of the business, the diversity or uniqueness of product lines, and the pace of change in the marketplace.

A business that has operations worldwide may be inclined to decentralize its marketing department to the local countries in order to increase awareness of the local laws and cultural patterns. Companies with a large number of product lines that can be grouped into logical categories, or that require extensive product knowledge, may decide to disperse the marketing function to the various operating units to keep marketing personnel as close to their customers as possible.

Integrating Purchasing

Managing the merged firm's purchasing function aggressively and efficiently can reduce the total cost of goods and services purchased by merged companies by 10 to 15%.[19] The opportunity to reap such substantial savings from suppliers comes immediately after the closing of the transaction. A merger creates uncertainty among both companies' suppliers, particularly if they might have to compete against each other for business with the combined firms. Many will offer cost savings and new partnership arrangements, given the merged organization's greater bargaining power to renegotiate contracts. The new company may choose to realize savings by reducing the number of suppliers. As part of the premerger due diligence, both the acquirer and the acquired company should identify a short list of their most critical suppliers, with a focus on those accounting for the largest share of purchased materials expenses.

Integrating Research and Development

Often, the buyer and seller R&D organizations are working on duplicate projects or projects not germane to the buyer's long-term strategy. The integration team must define future areas of R&D collaboration and set priorities for future R&D research (subject to senior management approval).

Barriers to R&D integration abound. Some projects require considerably more time (measured in years) to produce results than others. Another obstacle is that some personnel stand to lose in terms of titles, prestige, and power if they collaborate. Finally, the acquirer's and the target's R&D financial return expectations may differ. The acquirer may wish to give R&D a higher or lower priority in the combined operation of the two companies.

A starting point for integrating R&D is to have researchers from both companies share their work with each other and colocate. Work teams also can follow a balanced scorecard approach for obtaining funding for their projects, scoring R&D projects according to their impact on key stakeholders, such as shareholders and customers. Those projects receiving the highest scores are fully funded.

Integrating Human Resources

Traditionally, human resources departments have been highly centralized and have been responsible for conducting opinion surveys, assessing managerial effectiveness, developing hiring and staffing plans, and providing training. HR departments are often instrumental in conducting strategic reviews of the strengths and weaknesses of potential target companies, integrating the acquirer's and target's management teams, recommending and implementing pay and benefit plans, and disseminating information about acquisitions. In recent years, as highly centralized HR functions have been found to be very expensive and nonresponsive, the trend has been to move the HR function to the operating unit, where hiring and training may be done more effectively. Most of the traditional human resources

---

[19] In an analysis of 50 M&As, Chapman et al. (1998) found that companies were able to recover at least half of the premium paid for the target company by moving aggressively to manage their purchasing activities. For these firms, purchased goods and services, including office furniture, raw materials, and outside contractors, constituted up to 75% of their total spending.

activities are conducted at the operating units, with the exception of the administration of benefit plans, management of human resources' information systems, and (in some cases) organizational development.[20]

Building a New Corporate Culture

Corporate culture is a common set of values, traditions, and beliefs that influence management and employee behavior within a firm. Large, diverse businesses have an overarching culture and a series of subcultures that reflect local conditions. When two companies with different cultures merge, the newly formed company often will take on a new culture that is quite different from either the acquirer's or the target's culture. Cultural differences can instill creativity in the new company or create a contentious environment.

Tangible symbols of culture include statements hung on walls containing the firm's mission and principles, as well as status associated with the executive office floor and designated parking spaces. Intangible forms include the behavioral norms communicated through implicit messages about how people are expected to act. Since they represent the extent to which employees and managers actually "walk the talk," these messages are often far more influential in forming and sustaining corporate culture than the tangible trappings of corporate culture.[21]

Trust in the corporation is undermined immediately after a merger, in part by the ambiguity of the new organization's identity. Employee acceptance of a common culture can build identification with and trust in the corporation. As ambiguity abates and acceptance of a common culture grows, trust can be restored, especially among those who closely identified with their previous organization.[22]

Identifying Cultural Issues through Cultural Profiling

The first step in building a new corporate culture is to develop a cultural profile of both acquirer and acquired companies through employee surveys and interviews and by observing management styles and practices. The information is then used to show the similarities and the differences between the two cultures, as well as their comparative strengths and weaknesses.

The relative size and maturity of the acquirer and target firms can have major implications for cultural integration. Start-up companies typically are highly unstructured and informal in terms of dress and decision making. Compensation may be largely stock options and other forms of deferred income. Benefits, beyond those required by state and federal law, and "perks" such as company cars are largely nonexistent. Company policies frequently do not

---

[20] Porter and Wood, 1998

[21] Kennedy and Moore (2003) argue that the most important source of communication of cultural biases in an organization is the individual behavior of others, especially those with the power to reward appropriate and to punish inappropriate behavior.

[22] Maguire and Phillips, 2008

exist, are not in writing, or are drawn up only as needed. Internal controls covering employee expense accounts are often minimal. In contrast, larger, mature companies are often more highly structured, with well-defined internal controls, compensation structures, benefits packages, and employment policies all in place because the firms have grown too large and complex to function in an orderly manner without them. Employees usually have clearly defined job descriptions and career paths.

Once senior management reviews the information in the cultural profile, it must decide which characteristics of both cultures to emphasize. The most realistic expectation is that employees in the new company can be encouraged to adopt a shared vision, a set of core values, and behaviors deemed important by senior management. Anything more is probably wishful thinking: A company's culture evolves over a long period, but getting to the point where employees wholly embrace management's desired culture may take years at best or may never be achieved.

Case Study 6.3 illustrates how the Tribune Corporation's inattention to the profound cultural differences between itself and the Times Mirror Corporation may have contributed to the failure of this merger to meet expectations.

CASE STUDY 6.3
Culture Clash Exacerbates Efforts of the Tribune Corporation to Integrate the Times Mirror Corporation

The Chicago-based Tribune Corporation owned 11 newspapers, including such flagship publications as the *Chicago Tribune*, the *Los Angeles Times*, and *Newsday*, as well as 25 television stations. Attempting to offset the long-term decline in newspaper readership and advertising revenue, Tribune acquired Times Mirror (owner of the *Los Angeles Times* newspaper) for $8 billion in 2000. The merger combined two firms that historically had been intensely competitive and had dramatically different corporate cultures. The *Tribune* was famous for its emphasis on local coverage, with even its international stories having a connection to Chicago. In contrast, the *L.A. Times* had always maintained a strong overseas and Washington, D.C., presence, with local coverage often ceded to local suburban newspapers. To some Tribune executives, the *L.A.*

Times was arrogant and overstaffed. To *L.A. Times* executives, *Tribune* executives seemed too focused on the "bottom line" to be considered good newspaper people.[23]

The overarching strategy for the new company was to sell packages of newspaper and local TV advertising in the big urban markets. It soon became apparent that the strategy would be unsuccessful. Consequently, Tribune's management turned to aggressive cost cutting to improve profitability. The *Tribune* wanted to encourage centralization and cooperation among its newspapers to cut overlapping coverage and redundant jobs.

Coverage of the same stories by different newspapers owned by Tribune added substantially to costs. After months of planning, Tribune moved five bureaus belonging to Times Mirror papers (including the *L.A. Times*) to the same location as its four other

[23] Ellison, 2006

CASE STUDY 6.3 *(cont'd)*

bureaus in Washington, D.C. *L.A. Times'* staffers objected strenuously to the move, saying that their stories needed to be tailored to individual markets and they did not want to share reporters with local newspapers. As a result of the consolidation, Tribune's newspapers shared as much as 40% of the content from Washington, D.C., among the papers in 2006, compared to as little as 8% in 2000. Such changes allowed for significant staffing reductions.

In trying to achieve cost savings, the firm ran aground in a culture war. Historically, Times Mirror, unlike Tribune, had operated its newspapers more as a loose confederation of separate newspapers. Moreover, Tribune wanted more local focus, while the *L.A. Times* wanted to retain its national and international presence. The controversy came to a head when the *L.A. Times'* editor was forced out in late 2006.

Many newspaper stocks, including Tribune's, had lost more than half of their value between 2004 and 2006. The long-term decline in readership within Tribune appears to have

been exacerbated by the internal culture clash. As a result, the Chandler Trusts, Tribune's largest shareholder, put pressure on the firm to boost shareholder value. In September, the Tribune announced that it wanted to sell the entire newspaper; however, by November, after receiving bids that were a fraction of what had been paid to acquire the newspaper, it was willing to sell parts of the firm. The Tribune was taken private by legendary investor Sam Zell in 2007 and later went into bankruptcy in 2009, a victim of the recession and its bone-crushing debt load. See Case Study 13.4 for more details.

Discussion Questions

1. Why do you believe the Tribune Corporation thought it could overcome the substantial cultural differences between itself and the Times Mirror Corporation? Be specific.
2. What would you have done differently following closing to overcome the cultural challenges faced by Tribune? Be specific.

Overcoming Cultural Differences

Sharing common goals, standards, services, and space can be a highly effective and practical way to integrate disparate cultures.[24] Common goals drive different units to cooperate. For example, at the functional level, setting exact timetables and processes for new product development can drive different operating units to collaborate as project teams strive to introduce the product by the target date. At the corporate level, incentive plans spanning many years can focus all operating units to pursue the same goals. Although it is helpful in the integration process to have shared or common goals, individuals must still have specific goals to minimize the tendency of some to underperform while benefiting from the collective performance of others.

[24] Malekzadeh and Nahavandi, 1990

Shared standards or practices enable one unit or function to adopt the "best practices" found in another. Standards include operating procedures, technological specifications, ethical values, internal controls, employee performance measures, and comparable reward systems throughout the combined companies.

Some functional services can be centralized and shared by multiple departments or operating units. Commonly centralized services include accounting, legal, public relations, internal audit, and information technology. The most common way to share services is to use a common staff. Alternatively, a firm can create a support services unit and allow operating units to purchase services from it or to buy similar services outside the company.

Mixing offices or even locating acquired company employees in space adjacent to the parent's offices is a highly desirable way to improve communication and idea sharing. Common laboratories, computer rooms, libraries, and lunchrooms also facilitate communication and cooperation.[25]

When Time Is Critical

Although every effort should be made to merge corporate cultures by achieving consensus around certain core beliefs and behaviors, the need for nimble decision making may require a more expeditious approach. Japanese corporations have long had a reputation for taking the time to build consensus before implementing corporate strategies. Historically, this approach has served them well. However, in the increasingly fast pace of the global marketplace, this is a luxury they may not be able to afford. Case Study 6.4 illustrates a growing trend among Japanese conglomerates to buy out minority shareholders in their majority-owned subsidiaries in order to gain full control.

CASE STUDY 6.4
Panasonic Moves to Consolidate Past Acquisitions

Increased competition in the manufacture of rechargeable batteries and other renewable energy products threatened to thwart Panasonic Corporation's move to achieve a dominant global position in renewable energy products. The South Korean rivals Samsung Electronics Company and LG Electronics Inc. were increasing investment to overtake Panasonic in this marketplace. These firms have already been successful in surpassing Panasonic's leadership position in flat-panel televisions.

Despite having a majority ownership in several subsidiaries, Sanyo Electric Company,

---

[25] The challenges are enormous in companies with disparate cultures. In early 2006, Jeffrey Bewkes, the president of Time Warner, stopped requiring corporate units to cooperate. It was a complete turnabout from the philosophy espoused following the firm's 2001 merger with AOL. Then, executives promised to create a well-oiled vertically integrated profit generator. Books and magazines and other forms of content would feed the television, movie, and Internet operations. The 2006 change encouraged managers to cooperate only if they could not make more money on the outside. Other media companies such as Viacom and Liberty Media have broken themselves up because their efforts to achieve corporate-wide synergies with disparate media businesses proved unsuccessful.

CASE STUDY 6.4 *(cont'd)*

and Panasonic Electric Works Company that are critical to its long-term success in the manufacture and sale of renewable energy products, Panasonic has been frustrated by the slow pace of decision making and strategy implementation. In particular, Sanyo Electric has been reluctant to surrender decision making to Panasonic. Despite appeals by Panasonic president Fumio Ohtsubo for collaboration, Panasonic and Sanyo have continued to compete for customers. Sanyo Electric maintains a brand that is distinctly different from the Panasonic brand, thereby creating confusion among customers.

Sanyo Electric, the global market share leader in rechargeable lithium ion batteries, also has a growing presence in solar panels. Panasonic Electric Works makes lighting equipment, sensors, and other key components for making homes and offices more energy efficient.

To gain greater decision-making power, Panasonic acquired the remaining publicly traded shares in both Sanyo Electric and Panasonic Electric Works in March 2011 and plans to merge these two operations into the parent. Plans call for combining certain overseas sales operations and production facilities of Sanyo Electric and Panasonic Electric

Works, as well as using Panasonic factories to make Sanyo products.

The firm expects to fully consolidate the two businesses by early 2012. The challenge to Panasonic is gaining full control without alienating key employees who may be inclined to leave and destroying those attributes of the Sanyo culture that are needed to expand Panasonic's global position in renewable energy products.

This problem is not unique to Panasonic. Many Japanese companies consist of large interlocking networks of majority-owned subsidiaries that are proving less nimble than firms with more centralized authority. After four straight years of operating losses, Hitachi Ltd. spent 256 billion yen ($2.97 billion) to buy out minority shareholders in five of its majority-owned subsidiaries in order to achieve more centralized control.

Discussion Questions

1. Describe the advantages and disadvantages of owning less than 100% of another company.
2. When does it make sense to buy a minority interest, a majority interest, or 100% of the publicly traded shares of another company?

INTEGRATING BUSINESS ALLIANCES

Business alliances, particularly those created to consolidate resources such as manufacturing facilities or sales forces, also must pay close attention to integration activities. Unlike M&As, alliances usually involve shared control. Successful implementation requires maintaining a good working relationship between venture partners. When partners cannot maintain a good working relationship, the alliance is destined to fail. The breakdown in the working relationship is often a result of an inadequate integration.[26]

[26] Lynch, 1993, pp. 189–205.

Integrating Mechanisms

Robert Porter Lynch suggests six integration mechanisms to apply to business alliances: leadership, teamwork and role clarification, control by coordination, policies and values, consensus decision making, and resource commitments.

Leadership

Although the terms *leadership* and *management* often are used interchangeably, there are critical differences. A leader sets direction and makes things happen, whereas a manager follows through and ensures that things continue to happen. Leadership involves vision, drive, enthusiasm, and selling skills; management involves communication, planning, delegating, coordinating, problem solving, making choices, and clarifying lines of responsibility. Successful alliances require the proper mix of both sets of skills. The leader must provide direction, values, and behaviors to create a culture that focuses on the alliance's strategic objectives as its top priority. Managers foster teamwork and promote stability in the shared control environment of the business alliance.

Teamwork and Role Clarification

Teamwork is the underpinning that makes alliances work. Teamwork comes from trust, fairness, and discipline. Teams reach across functional lines and often consist of diverse experts or lower-level managers with critical problem-solving skills. The team provides functional managers with broader, flexible staffing to augment their own specialized staff. Teams tend to create better coordination and communication at lower levels of the alliance, as well as between partners in the venture. Because teams represent individuals with varied backgrounds and possibly conflicting agendas, they may foster rather than resolve conflict.

Coordination

In contrast to an acquisition, no one company is in charge. Alliances do not lend themselves to control through mandate; rather, control in the alliance is best exerted through coordination. The best alliance managers are those who coordinate activities through effective communication. When problems arise, the manager's role is to manage the decision-making process, not necessarily to make the decision.

Policies and Values

Alliance employees need to understand how decisions are made, what has high priority, who will be held accountable, and how rewards will be determined. When people know where they stand and what to expect, they are better able to deal with ambiguity and uncertainty. This level of clarity can be communicated through a distinct set of policies and procedures that are well understood by joint venture or partnership employees.

Consensus Decision Making

Consensus decision making does not mean that decisions are based on unanimity; rather, decisions are based on the premise that all participants have had an opportunity to express their opinions and they are willing to accept the final decision. Like any other business, operating decisions must be made within a reasonable time frame. The formal decision-making structure varies with the type of legal structure. Joint ventures often have a board of directors and a management committee that meet quarterly and monthly, respectively. Projects normally are governed by steering committees. Many alliances are started to take advantage of complementary skills or resources available from alliance participants. The alliance can achieve its strategic objective only if all parties to the alliance provide the resources they agreed to commit.

SOME THINGS TO REMEMBER

Successfully integrated M&As are those that demonstrate leadership by candidly and continuously communicating a clear vision, a set of values, and clear priorities to all employees. Successful integration efforts are those that are well planned, that appoint an integration manager and a team with clearly defined lines of authority, and that make the tough decisions early in the process, be they about organizational structure, reporting relationships, spans of control, personnel selection, roles and responsibilities, or workforce reduction. The focus must be on those issues with the greatest near-term impact.

Because alliances involve shared control, the integration process requires good working relationships with other participants. Successful integration also requires leadership that is capable of defining a clear sense of direction and well-defined priorities and managers who accomplish their objectives as much by coordinating activities through effective communication as by unilateral decision making. Finally, the successful integration of business alliances, as well as mergers and acquisitions, demands that the necessary resources, in terms of the best people, the appropriate skills, and sufficient capital, be committed to the process.

DISCUSSION QUESTIONS

6.1 Why is the integration phase of the acquisition process considered so important?

6.2 Why should acquired companies be integrated quickly?

6.3 Why might the time required to integrate acquisitions vary by industry?

6.4 What are the costs of employee turnover?

6.5 Why is candid and continuous communication so important during the integration phase?

6.6 What messages might be communicated to the various audiences or stakeholders of the new company?

6.7 Cite examples of difficult decisions that should be made early in the integration process.

6.8 Cite the contract-related "transition issues" that should be resolved before closing.

6.9 How does the process for integrating business alliances differ from that of integrating an acquisition?

6.10 How are the processes for integrating business alliances and M&As similar?

6.11 When Daimler Benz acquired Chrysler Corporation, it announced that it could take six to eight years to fully integrate the combined firm's global manufacturing operations and certain functions such as purchasing. Why do you believe it might take that long?

6.12 In your judgment, are acquirers more likely to under- or overestimate anticipated cost savings? Explain your answer.

6.13 Cite examples of expenses you believe are commonly incurred in integrating target companies. Be specific.

6.14 A common justification for mergers of competitors are the potential cross-selling opportunities they provide. Comment on the challenges that might be involved in making such a marketing strategy work.

6.15 Billed as a merger of equals, Citibank and Travelers resorted to a co-CEO arrangement when they merged in 1998. Why do you think they adopted this arrangement? What are the advantages and disadvantages of such an arrangement?

Answers to these Chapter Discussion Questions are available in the Online Instructor's Manual for instructors using this book.

CHAPTER BUSINESS CASES

CASE STUDY 6.5
The Challenges of Integrating Steel Giants Arcelor and Mittal

The merger of Arcelor and Mittal into ArcelorMittal in June 2006 resulted in the creation of the world's largest steel company.[27] With 2007 revenues of $105 billion and its steel production accounting for about 10% of global output, the behemoth has 320,000 employees in 60 countries, and it is a global leader in all its target markets. Arcelor was a product of three European steel companies (Arbed, Aceralia, and Usinor). Similarly, Mittal resulted from a series of international acquisitions. The two firms' downstream (raw material) and upstream (distribution) operations proved to be highly complementary, with Mittal owning much of its iron ore and coal reserves and Arcelor having extensive distribution and service center operations. Like most mergers, ArcelorMittal faced the challenge of integrating management teams; sales, marketing, and product functions; production facilities; and purchasing operations. Unlike many mergers involving direct competitors, a relatively small portion of the cost savings would come from eliminating duplicate functions and operations.

ArcelorMittal's top management set three driving objectives before undertaking the post-merger integration effort: Achieve rapid integration, manage daily operations effectively, and accelerate revenue and profit growth. The third objective was viewed as the primary motivation for the merger. The goal was to combine what were viewed as entities having highly complementary assets and skills. This goal was quite different from the way Mittal had grown historically, which was a result of acquisitions of turnaround targets focused on cost and productivity improvements.

The formal phase of the integration effort was to be completed in six months. Consequently, it was crucial to agree on the role of the management integration team (MIT); the key aspects of the integration process, such as how decisions would be made; and

---

[27] This case relies on information provided in an interview with Jerome Ganboulan (formerly of Arcelor) and William A. Scotting (formerly of Mittal), the two executives charged with directing the postmerger integration effort; it is adapted from De Mdedt and Van Hoey (2008).

CASE STUDY 6.5 (cont'd)

team members' roles and responsibilities. Activities were undertaken in parallel rather than sequentially. Teams consisted of employees from the two firms. People leading task forces came from the business units.

The teams were then asked to propose a draft organization to the MIT, including the profiles of the people who were to become senior managers. Once the senior managers were selected, they were to build their own teams to identify the synergies and create action plans for realizing the synergies. Teams were formed before the organization was announced, and implementation of certain actions began before detailed plans had been fully developed. Progress to plan was monitored on a weekly basis, enabling the MIT to identify obstacles facing the 25 decentralized task forces and, when necessary, to resolve issues.

Considerable effort was spent on getting line managers involved in the planning process and selling the merger to their respective operating teams. Initial communication efforts included the launch of a top-management "road show." The new company also established a website and introduced Web TV. Senior executives conducted two- to three-minute interviews on various topics, giving everyone with access to a personal computer the ability to watch the interviews onscreen.

Owing to the employee duress resulting from the merger, uncertainty was high, as employees with both firms wondered how the merger would affect them. To address employee concerns, managers were given a well-structured message about the significance of the merger and the direction of the new company. Furthermore, the new brand, Arcelor-Mittal, was launched in a meeting attended

by 500 of the firm's top managers during the spring of 2007.

External communication was conducted in several ways. Immediately following the closing, senior managers traveled to all the major cities and sites of operations, talking to local management and employees at these sites. Typically, media interviews were also conducted around these visits, providing an opportunity to convey the ArcelorMittal message to the communities through the press. In March 2007, the new firm held a media day in Brussels. Journalists were invited to the different businesses to review the progress themselves.

Within the first three months following the closing, customers were informed about the advantages of the merger for them, such as enhanced R&D capabilities and wider global coverage. The sales forces of the two organizations were charged with the task of creating a single "face" to the market.

ArcelorMittal's management viewed the merger as an opportunity to conduct interviews and surveys with employees to gain an understanding of their views about the two companies. Employees were asked about the combined firm's strengths and weaknesses and how the new firm should present itself to its various stakeholder groups. This process resulted in a complete rebranding of the combined firms.

ArcelorMittal management set a target for annual cost savings of $1.6 billion, based on experience with earlier acquisitions. The role of the task forces was first to validate this number from the bottom up and then tell the MIT how the synergies would be achieved. As the merger progressed, it was necessary to get the business units to assume ownership of the process in order to formulate the initiatives, timetables, and key

CASE STUDY 6.5   *(cont'd)*

performance indicators that could be used to track performance against objectives.

In some cases, the synergy potential was larger than anticipated while it was smaller in other situations. The expectation was that synergy could be realized by mid-2009. The integration objectives were included in the 2007 annual budget plan. As of the end of 2008, the combined firms had realized their goal of an annualized cost savings of $1.6 billion, six months earlier than originally expected.

The integration was deemed complete when the new organization, the brand, the "one face to the customer" requirement, and the synergies were finalized. This occurred within eight months of the closing. However, integration would continue for some time to achieve cultural integration. Cultural differences within the two firms were significant. In effect, neither company was homogeneous from a cultural perspective. ArcelorMittal management viewed this diversity as an advantage in that it provided an opportunity to learn new ideas.

Discussion Questions

1. Why is it important to establish both top-down (i.e., provided by top management) and bottom-up (provided by operating units) estimates of synergy?

2. How did ArcelorMittal attempt to bridge cultural differences during the integration? Be specific.

3. Why are communication plans so important? What methods did Arcelor-Mittal employ to achieve these objectives? Be specific.

4. Comment on ArcelorMittal management's belief that the cultural diversity within the combined firms was an advantage. Be specific.

5. The formal phase of the postmerger integration period was to be completed within six months. Why do you believe that ArcelorMittal's management was eager to integrate the two businesses rapidly? Be specific. What integration activities were to extend beyond the proposed six-month integration period?

Answers to these questions are found in the Online Instructor's Manual for instructors using this book.

CASE STUDY 6.6
Alcatel Merges with Lucent, Highlighting Cross-Cultural Issues

Alcatel SA and Lucent Technologies signed a merger pact on April 3, 2006, to form a Paris-based telecommunications equipment giant. The combined firms would be led by Lucent's chief executive officer Patricia Russo. Her charge would be to meld two cultures during a period of dynamic industry change. Lucent and Alcatel were considered natural merger partners because they had overlapping

product lines and different strengths. More than two-thirds of Alcatel's business came from Europe, Latin America, the Middle East, and Africa. The French firm was particularly strong in equipment that enabled regular telephone lines to carry high-speed Internet and digital television traffic. Nearly two-thirds of Lucent's business was in the United States. The new company was expected to eliminate

CASE STUDY 6.6 (cont'd)

10% of its workforce of 88,000 and save $1.7 billion annually within three years by eliminating overlapping functions.

While billed as a merger of equals, Alcatel of France, the larger of the two, would take the lead in shaping the future of the new firm, whose shares would be listed in Paris, not in the United States. The board would have six members from the current Alcatel board and six from the current Lucent board, as well as two independent directors that had to be European nationals. Alcatel CEO Serge Tehuruk would serve as the chairman of the board. Much of Russo's senior management team, including the chief operating officer, the chief financial officer, the head of the key emerging markets unit, and the director of human resources, would come from Alcatel. To allay U.S. national security concerns, the new company would form an independent U.S. subsidiary to administer American government contracts. This subsidiary would be managed separately by a board composed of three U.S. citizens acceptable to the U.S. government.

International combinations involving U.S. companies have had a spotty history in the telecommunications industry. For example, British Telecommunications PLC and AT&T Corp. saw their joint venture, Concert, formed in the late 1990s, collapse after only a few years. Even outside the telecom industry, transatlantic mergers have been fraught with problems. For example, Daimler Benz's 1998 deal with Chrysler, which was also billed as a merger of equals, was heavily weighted toward the German company from the outset.

In integrating Lucent and Alcatel, Russo faced a number of practical obstacles, including who would work out of Alcatel's Paris headquarters. Russo, who became Lucent's chief executive in 2000 and does not speak French, had to navigate the challenges of doing business in France. The French government has a big influence on French companies and remains a large shareholder in the telecom and defense sectors. Russo's first big fight would be dealing with the job cuts that were anticipated in the merger plan. French unions tend to be strong, and employees enjoy more legal protections than elsewhere.

Hundreds of thousands took to the streets in mid-2006 to protest a new law that would make it easier for firms to hire and fire younger workers. Russo has extensive experience with big layoffs. At Lucent, she helped orchestrate spin-offs, layoffs, and buyouts involving nearly four-fifths of the firm's workforce.

Making choices about cuts in a combined company would likely be even more difficult, with Russo facing a level of resistance in France unheard of in the United States, where it is generally accepted that most workers are subject to layoffs and dismissals. Alcatel has been able to make many of its job cuts in recent years outside France, thereby avoiding the greater difficulty of shedding French workers. Lucent workers feared that they would be dismissed first simply because it was easier than dismissing their French counterparts.

After the 2006 merger, the company posted six quarterly losses and took more than $4.5 billion in write-offs, while its stock plummeted more than 60%. An economic slowdown and tight credit limited spending by phone companies. Moreover, the market was getting more competitive, with China's Huawei aggressively pricing its products. However, other telecommunications equipment manufacturers that face the same conditions have not

CASE STUDY 6.6   *(cont'd)*

fared nearly as badly as Alcatel-Lucent. Melding two fundamentally different cultures (Alcatel's entrepreneurial and Lucent's centrally controlled) has proven daunting. Customers who were uncertain about the new firm's products migrated to competitors, forcing Alcatel-Lucent to slash prices even more. Despite the aggressive job cuts, a substantial portion of the projected $3.1 billion in savings from the layoffs were lost to discounts the company made to customers in an effort to rebuild market share.

Frustrated by the lack of progress in turning around the business, the Alcatel-Lucent board announced in July 2008 that Patricia Russo, the American chief executive, and Serge Tchuruk, the French chairman, would leave the company by the end of the year. The board also announced that, as part of the shake-up, the board's size would be reduced, with Henry Schacht, a former chief executive at Lucent, stepping down. Perhaps hamstrung by its dual personality, the French-American company seemed poised to take on a new personality of its own by jettisoning the previous leadership.

Discussion Questions

1. Explain the logic behind combining the two companies. Be specific.
2. What major challenges were the management of the combined companies likely to face? How would you recommend resolving these issues?
3. Most corporate mergers are beset by differences in corporate cultures. How do cross-border transactions compound these differences?
4. Why do you think mergers, both domestic and cross-border, are often communicated by the acquirer and target firms' management as mergers of equals?
5. In what way would you characterize this transaction as a merger of equals? In what ways should it not be considered a merger of equals?

Answers to these questions are found in the Online Instructor's Manual for instructors using this book.

MERGER AND ACQUISITION VALUATION AND MODELING

"Make them a four billion dollar takeover offer, but don't cause a fuss."

Courtesy of www.CartoonResource.com

Part III covers alternative valuation methods and basic financial modeling techniques, as well as how such models may be applied in the merger and acquisition process. All valuation methods are subject to significant limitations, and a valuation approach reflecting a variety of the alternative methodologies is likely to provide a more accurate estimate of firm value than any single approach.

Chapter 7 provides a primer on how to construct valuation cash flows and the discount rates necessary to convert projected cash flows to a present value. Alternatives to discounted-cash-flow (DCF) methods are discussed in Chapter 8, including relative-valuation, asset-oriented, and replacement-cost techniques. Implicit in the DCF approach to valuation is that management has no flexibility once an investment decision has been made. In practice, management may decide to accelerate, delay, or abandon investments as new information becomes available. The significance of this decision-making flexibility may be reflected in the value of the target firm by adjusting discounted cash flows for the value of so-called real options.

Chapter 9 discusses how to build financial models, which can be used to answer several sets of questions. The first set pertains to valuation. How much is the target company worth without the effects of synergy? What is the value of expected synergy? What is the maximum price the acquiring company should pay for the target? The second set of questions pertains to financing. Can the proposed purchase price be financed? What combination of potential sources of funds—both internally generated and external sources—provides the lowest cost of funds for the acquirer, subject to known constraints (e.g., existing loan covenants)? The final set of questions pertains to deal structuring. What is the impact on the acquirer's financial performance if the deal is structured as a taxable rather than a nontaxable transaction? What is the impact on financial performance and valuation if the acquirer is willing to assume certain target company liabilities? (Deal structuring considerations are discussed in detail in Chapters 11 and 12.) Finally, Chapter 10 addresses the unique challenges of valuing privately held firms and how to adjust purchase prices for liquidity and minority discounts, as well as for the value of control.

7

A Primer on Merger and Acquisition Cash-Flow Valuation

The greater danger for most of us is not that our aim is too high and we might miss it, but that it is too low and we reach it. —**Michelangelo**

pg. 218-219

INSIDE M&A: THE IMPORTANCE OF DISTINGUISHING BETWEEN OPERATING AND NONOPERATING ASSETS

In 2006, Verizon Communications and MCI Inc. executives completed a deal in which MCI shareholders received $6.7 billion for 100% of MCI stock. Verizon's management argued that the deal cost their shareholders only $5.3 billion in Verizon stock, with MCI having agreed to pay its shareholders a special dividend of $1.4 billion contingent on their approval of the transaction. The $1.4 billion special dividend reduced MCI's cash in excess of what was required to meet its normal operating cash requirements.

To understand the actual purchase price, it is necessary to distinguish between operating and nonoperating assets. Without the special dividend, the $1.4 billion in cash would have transferred automatically to Verizon as a result of the purchase of MCI's stock. Verizon would have had to increase its purchase price by an equivalent amount to reflect the face value of this nonoperating cash asset. Consequently, the purchase price would have been $6.7 billion. With the special dividend, the excess cash transferred to Verizon was reduced by $1.4 billion, and the purchase price was $5.3 billion.

In fact, the alleged price reduction was no price reduction at all. It simply reflected Verizon's shareholders' receiving $1.4 billion less in net acquired assets. Moreover, since the $1.4 billion represents excess cash that would have been reinvested in MCI or paid out to shareholders anyway, the MCI shareholders were simply getting the cash earlier than they may have otherwise.

CHAPTER OVERVIEW

The five basic methods of valuation are income or discounted cash flow (DCF), market based, asset oriented, replacement cost, and the contingent claims or real-options approach. This chapter provides an overview of the basics of valuing mergers and acquisitions (M&A)

using discounted-cash-flow methods. The remaining valuation methods are discussed in Chapter 8.

In addition to these methods, investment bankers often use the leveraged buyout method (LBO) of valuation to assess whether a particular target firm may be of interest to private equity investors (i.e., so-called financial sponsors) as an acquisition opportunity. As is true of DCF methods, the LBO approach requires the projection of cash flows to identify an internal rate of return (IRR) for a private equity investor. The IRR is the discount rate that equates the projected cash flows and terminal value or expected value of the target firm when sold with the initial equity investment. The LBO method is discussed in detail in Chapter 13. The special challenges of valuing private firms, distressed companies, and cross-border transactions are addressed in detail in Chapters 10, 16, and 17, respectively.

This chapter begins with a brief review of rudimentary finance concepts, including measuring risk and return, the capital asset pricing model, and the effects of operating and financial leverage on risk and return. The cash-flow definitions, free cash flow to equity (equity value) or to the firm (enterprise value), discussed in this chapter are used in valuation problems in subsequent chapters. The chapter concludes with an illustration of the commonly used enterprise method to value a firm's operating and nonoperating assets and liabilities to determine equity value.[1]

A review of this chapter (including additional practice problems with solutions) is available in the file folder entitled "Student Study Guide" in the companion site to this book (*www. elsevierdirect.com/companions/9780123854858*). The companion site also contains a Learning Interactions Library, which gives students the opportunity to test their knowledge of this chapter in a "real-time" environment, and a discussion of how to project cash flows in a file entitled "Primer on Cash Flow Forecasting."

REQUIRED RETURNS

Investors require a minimum rate of return on an investment to compensate them for the level of perceived risk associated with that investment. The required rate of return must be at least equal to what the investor can receive on alternative investments exhibiting a comparable level of perceived risk.[2]

Cost of Equity and the Capital Asset Pricing Model

The cost of equity (k_e) is the rate of return required to induce investors to purchase a firm's equity. The cost of equity also can be viewed as an *opportunity cost*, because it represents the rate of return investors could earn by investing in equities of comparable risk. The cost of equity can be estimated using the capital asset pricing model (CAPM), which measures the relationship between expected risk and expected return. It postulates that investors require higher rates of return for accepting higher levels of risk. Specifically, the CAPM

---

[1] For more exhaustive analyses of valuation, see Copeland, Koller, and Murrin (2005).

[2] For an excellent discussion of the basic concepts of finance, see Gitman (2008).

states that the expected return on an asset or security is equal to a risk-free rate of return plus a risk premium.

A *risk-free rate of return* is one for which the expected return is certain. It is the reward paid to an investor for postponing current consumption spending without taking any risk. It represents the time value of money. For a return to be considered risk free over some future period, it must be free of default risk, and there must be no uncertainty about the reinvestment rate (i.e., the rate of return that can be earned at the end of the investor's holding period). Despite widespread agreement on the use of U.S. Treasury securities as assets that are free of default risk, there is some controversy over whether a short- or long-term Treasury rate should be used in applying the CAPM.

Whether you should use a short- or long-term rate depends on how long the investor intends to hold the investment. Consequently, the investor who anticipates holding an investment for five or ten years needs to use either a five- or ten-year Treasury bond rate. A three-month Treasury bill rate is not free of risk for a five- or ten-year period, since interest and principal received at maturity must be reinvested at three-month intervals, resulting in considerable reinvestment risk. In this book, a ten-year Treasury bond rate is used to represent the risk-free rate of return. This would be most appropriate for a strategic acquirer interested in valuing a target firm with the intent of operating the firm over an extended time period.

Estimating Market Risk Premiums

The *market risk* or *equity premium* refers to the additional rate of return in excess of the risk-free rate that investors require to purchase a firm's equity. While the risk premium represents the perceived risk of the stock and should therefore be forward looking, obtaining precise estimates of future market returns often is exceedingly difficult. The objectivity of Wall Street analysts' projections is problematic, and efforts to develop sophisticated models show results that vary widely. Consequently, analysts often look to historical data, despite results that vary based on the time periods selected and whether returns are calculated as arithmetic or geometric averages. CAPM relates the cost of equity (k_e) to the risk-free rate of return and market risk premium as follows:

$$\text{CAPM}: k_e = R_f + \beta(R_m - R_f) \tag{7.1}$$

where

R_f = risk-free rate of return
β = beta (See the section of this chapter entitled "Analyzing Risk.")
R_m = expected rate of return on equities
$R_m - R_f$ = 5.5% (i.e., the difference between the return on a diversified portfolio of stocks and the risk-free rate)

The 5.5% equity risk premium used in this book is consistent with long-term arithmetic and geometric averages calculated elsewhere.[3] Despite its intuitive appeal, the CAPM has

---

[3] Based on survey results of 510 finance and economics professors, Welch (2001) estimates an equity premium over a 30-year horizon of 5.5%. Using data provided by Dimson, March, and Staunton (2003), the equity risk premium relative to bonds during the period from 1900 to 2002 was 5.75% in the United States and 4.9% for a 16-country average.

limitations. Betas tend to vary over time and are quite sensitive to the time period and methodology employed in their estimation.[4] Some analysts argue that the "risk premium" should be changed to reflect fluctuations in the stock market. However, history shows that such fluctuations are relatively short term in nature. Consequently, the risk premium should reflect more long-term considerations, such as the expected holding period of the investor or acquiring company. Therefore, for the strategic or long-term investor or acquirer, the risk premium should approximate the 5.5% premium long-term historical average.[5]

Since CAPM measures a stock's risk only relative to the overall market and ignores returns on assets other than stocks, some analysts have begun using *multifactor models*. Such models adjust the CAPM by adding other risk factors that determine asset returns, such as firm size, bond default premiums, bond term structure (i.e., the difference between short- and long-term interest rates on securities that differ only by maturity), and inflation.

Studies show that, of these factors, firm size appears to be among the most important.[6] The size factor serves as a proxy for factors such as smaller firms being subject to higher default risk and generally being less liquid than large capitalization firms.[7] Table 7.1 provides

TABLE 7.1   Estimates of the Size Premium

Market Value (000,000)	Percentage Points Added to CAPM Estimate
>$18,600	0.0
$7,400 to $18,600	0.6
$2,700 to $7,400	1.0
$1,100 to $2,700	1.5
$450 to $1,100	2.3
$200 to $450	2.7
$100 to $200	5.8
<$100 million	9.2

Source: *Adapted from estimates provided by Ibbotson's* Stocks, Bills, Bonds, and Inflation Valuation Edition 2010 Yearbook.

[4] For a detailed discussion of these issues, see Fama and French (1992, 1993, 2006). Other studies show that the market risk premium is unstable—lower during periods of prosperity and higher during periods of economic slowdowns (Claus and Thomas, 2001; Easton et al., 2001).

[5] In a survey of 200 companies, Escherich (1998) found that most firms estimate the cost of equity using CAPM and use an equity risk premium of between 5 and 7%. In a survey of 1,500 finance professors, Fernandez (2011) found that the average equity risk premium used in 2010 was 6% in the United States and 5.3% in Europe. Fernanadez also found in a survey of 2,400 analysts and companies that analysts in the United States and Europe used 5.1% and 5%, respectively, while companies used 5.3% in the United States and 5.7% in Europe. Similar results were found in a survey of 150 finance textbooks in which the five-year moving average ending in 2009 was 5.7%.

[6] Bernard, Healy, and Palepu, 2000

[7] Berk, 1995

estimates of the amount of the adjustment to the cost of equity to correct for firm size, as measured by market value, based on actual data since 1926. The analyst should use this data as a guideline only. Specific firm business risk is largely unobservable. Consequently, in applying a firm size premium, analysts should use their judgment in selecting a proper size premium. This magnitude of the firm size premium should be tempered by such factors as a comparison of the firm's key financial ratios (e.g., liquidity and leverage) with comparable firms and after interviewing management. The selection of the proper magnitude is addressed in more detail in Chapter 10.

Equation (7.1) can be rewritten to reflect an adjustment for firm size as follows:

$$\text{CAPM: } k_e = R_f + \beta(R_m - R_f) + FSP \quad \longrightarrow \text{Multifactor Model} \quad (7.2)$$

where

FSP = firm size premium

Assume that a firm has a market value of less than $100 million and a β of 1.75. Also assume that the risk-free rates of return and equity premium are 5% and 5.5%, respectively. The firm's cost of equity using the CAPM method adjusted for firm size can be estimated as follows:

$$k_e = 0.05 + 1.75(0.055) + 0.092 = 0.238 \times 100 = 23.8\% \text{ (see Table 7.1)}$$

Pretax Cost of Debt

The cost of debt represents the cost of borrowing each additional dollar of debt. It reflects the current level of interest rates and the level of default risk as perceived by investors. Interest paid on debt is tax deductible by the firm; in bankruptcy, bondholders are paid before shareholders as the firm's assets are liquidated. Default risk, the likelihood the firm will fail to repay interest and principal on a timely basis, can be measured by the firm's credit rating. Default rates vary from an average of 0.52% for AAA-rated firms over a 15-year period to 54.38% for those rated CCC by Standard & Poor's Corporation.[8]

Interest paid by the firm on its current debt can be used as an estimate of the current cost of debt if the financial condition of the firm and the prevailing level of interest rates have not changed since the firm last borrowed. However, when conditions have changed, the analyst must estimate the cost of debt reflecting current market interest rates and default risk.

In estimating the current cost of debt, analysts commonly use the yield to maturity (YTM)[9] of the company's long-term, option-free bonds.[10] This requires knowing the price of the se-

---

[8] Burrus and McNamee, 2002

[9] Yield to maturity is the internal rate of return on a bond held to maturity, assuming scheduled payment of principal and interest, that takes into account the capital gain or loss on a discount bond or capital loss on a premium bond.

[10] To calculate the yield to maturity using a Hewlett-Packard 12C calculator, enter the quoted price (as a percent of par), using PV; enter the annual coupon rate (as a percentage), using PMT; key in the settlement (purchase) date; and press ENTER. Key in the maturity (redemption) date. Press f and YTM.

Note: Using day-month-year format, key in 1 or 2 digits of the day and press decimal point. Key in 2 digits of the month and 4 digits of the year.

TABLE 7.2   Weighted-Average Yield to Maturity of Microsoft's Long-Term Debt

Coupon Rate (%)	Maturity	Book Value (face value in $ millions)	Percentage of Total Debt	Price (% of par)	Yield to Maturity (%)
0.88	9/27/2013	1,250	0.25	99.44	1.09
2.95	6/1/2014	2,000	0.40	104.27	1.63
4.20	6/1/2019	1,000	0.20	105.00	3.50
5.20	6/1/2039	750	0.15	100.92	5.14
		5,000	1.00		2.40

curity and its coupon and face value.[11] In general, the cost of debt is estimated by calculating the yield to maturity (YTM) on each of the firm's outstanding bond issues. We then compute a weighted average YTM, with the estimated YTM for each issue weighted by its percentage of total debt outstanding. In Table 7.2, Microsoft's weighted average YTM on the bulk of its long-term debt on January 24, 2011, was 2.4%. The source for the YTM for each debt issue was found in the Financial Industry Regulatory Authority's (FINRA) Trace database *www.finra.org/marketdata*.[12] The book or face value of the debt comes from Microsoft's 2009 10K. Microsoft is rated AAA by Standard & Poor's Corporation.

YTM represents the most reliable estimate of a firm's cost of debt as long as the firm's debt is investment grade. Investment grade bonds are those whose credit quality is considered to be among the most secure by independent bond rating agencies. A rating of BBB or higher by Standard & Poor's and Baa or higher by Moody's Investors Service is considered to be investment grade.

For investment grade bonds, the difference between the expected rate of return and the promised rate of return is small. The promised rate of return assumes that the interest and principal are paid on time. The yield to maturity is affected by the cost of debt, the probability of default, and the expected recovery rate on the debt if the firm defaults, and it is a good proxy for actual future returns on investment grade debt, since the potential for default or bankruptcy is relatively low.

Noninvestment grade debt is rated less than BBB by Standard & Poor's and Baa by Moody's, and it represents debt with a default risk that is significant due to the firm's high leverage, deteriorating cash flows, or both. The difference between the expected rate of return and the promised rate can be substantial. Ideally, the expected yield to maturity would be calculated based on the current market price of the noninvestment grade bond, the probability of default, and the potential recovery rate following default.[13] However, such data are

[11] YTM is distorted by corporate bonds, which also have conversion or callable features, since their value will affect the bond's value.

[12] FINRA is the largest independent regulator for all securities firms in the Unites States. See *http://cxa.marketwatch.com/finra/MarketData/CompanyInfo/default.aspx*.

[13] Titman and Martin (2011), pp. 144–147.

frequently unavailable. A practical alternative is to use the YTM for a number of similarly rated bonds of other firms. Such bonds include a so-called *default premium*, which reflects the compensation that lenders require over the risk-free rate to buy noninvestment grade debt. This methodology assumes that the risk characteristics of the proxy firms approximate those of the firm being analyzed.

To illustrate this process, on January 24, 2011, HCA Healthcare Inc.'s 9% fixed rate noncallable bond that would reach maturity on December 15, 2015 (rated CCC by Standard & Poor's and Caa1 by Moody's) had a YTM of 7.41% on that date, according to FINRA's TRACE database. With five-year U.S. Treasury bonds offering a yield to maturity of 1.94%, the implied default risk premium was 5.47% (i.e., 7.41 minus 1.94). This same process could then be repeated for a number of similarly rated bonds in order to calculate an average YTM.

For nonrated firms, the analyst may estimate the current pretax cost of debt for a specific firm by comparing debt-to-equity ratios, interest coverage ratios, and operating margins with those of similar rated firms. The analyst would then use the interest rates paid by these comparably rated firms as the pretax cost of debt for the firm being analyzed. Much of this information can be found in local libraries in such publications as Moody's *Company Data;* Standard & Poor's *Descriptions, the Outlook, and Bond Guide;* and Value Line's *Investment Survey.* In the United States, the FINRA TRACE database also is an excellent source of interest rate information.

Cost of Preferred Stock

Preferred stock exhibits some of the characteristics of long-term debt in that its dividend is generally constant and preferred stockholders are paid before common shareholders in the event the firm is liquidated. Unlike interest payments on debt, preferred dividends are not tax deductible. Because preferred stock is riskier than debt but less risky than common stock in bankruptcy, the cost to the company to issue preferred stock should be less than the cost of equity but greater than the cost of debt. Viewing preferred dividends as paid in perpetuity, the cost of preferred stock (k_{pr}) can be calculated as dividends per share of preferred stock (d_{pr}) divided by the market value of the preferred stock (PR) (see the section of this chapter entitled "Zero-Growth Valuation Model"). Consequently, if a firm pays a $2 dividend on its preferred stock whose current market value is $50, the firm's cost of preferred stock is 4% (i.e., $2 ÷ $50). The cost of preferred stock can be generalized as follows:

$$k_{pr} = \frac{d_{pr}}{PR} \tag{7.3}$$

Cost of Capital

The weighted-average cost of capital (WACC) is the broadest measure of the firm's cost of funds and represents the return that a firm must earn to induce investors to buy its common stock, preferred stock, and bonds. The WACC is calculated using a weighted average of the firm's cost of equity (k_e), cost of preferred stock (k_{pr}), and pretax cost of debt (i):

$$\text{WACC} = k_e \times \frac{E}{(D+E+PR)} + i \times (1-t) \times \frac{D}{(D+E+PR)} + k_{pr} \times \frac{PR}{(D+E+PR)} \tag{7.4}$$

where

E = the market value of common equity

D = the market value of debt

PR = the market value of preferred stock

t = the firm's marginal tax rate

A portion of interest paid on borrowed funds is recoverable by the firm because of the tax deductibility of interest. For every dollar of taxable income, the tax owed is equal to $1 multiplied by t. Since each dollar of interest expense reduces taxable income by an equivalent amount, the actual cost of borrowing is reduced by $(1 - t)$. Therefore, the after-tax cost of borrowed funds to the firm is estimated by multiplying the pretax interest rate, i, by $(1 - t)$.

Note that the weights, $[E/(D + E + PR)]$, $[D/(D + E + PR)]$, and $[PR/(D + E + PR)]$, associated with the cost of equity, preferred stock, and debt, respectively, reflect the firm's target capital structure or capitalization. These are targets in that they represent the capital structure the firm hopes to achieve and sustain in the future. The actual market value of equity, preferred stock, and debt as a percentage of total capital (i.e., $D + E + PF$) may differ from the target. Market values rather than book values are used because the WACC measures the cost of issuing debt, preferred stock, and equity securities. Such securities are issued at market and not book value. The use of the target capital structure avoids the circular reasoning associated with using the current market value of equity to construct the weighted average cost of capital, which is subsequently used to estimate the firm's current market value.

Non-interest-bearing liabilities, such as accounts payable, are excluded from the estimation of the cost of capital for the firm to simplify the calculation of WACC.[14] Estimates of industry betas, cost of equity, and WACC are provided by firms such as Ibbotson Associates, Value Line, Standard & Poor's, and Bloomberg. Such estimates provide a "reality check," since they serve as a benchmark against which the analyst's estimate of a firm's WACC can be compared.

ANALYZING RISK /Risk Assessment

Risk is the degree of uncertainty associated with the outcome of an investment. It takes into consideration the probability of a loss as well as a gain on an investment. Risk consists of a *diversifiable risk* (also called *nonsystematic risk*) component, such as strikes, defaulting on debt repayments, and lawsuits, that are specific to a firm, and a *nondiversifiable risk* (also called *systematic risk*) component, such as inflation and war, that affects all firms. *Beta* (β) is a measure of nondiversifiable risk or the extent to which a firm's (or asset's) return changes because of a change in the market's return.

An *equity beta* is a measure of the risk of a stock's financial returns compared with the risk of the financial returns to the general stock market, which in turn is affected by the overall

[14] Although such liabilities have an associated cost of capital, it is assumed to have been included in the price paid for the products and services whose purchase generated the accounts payable. Consequently, the cost of capital associated with these types of liabilities affects cash flow through its inclusion in operating expenses (e.g., the price paid for raw materials).

economy. When $\beta = 1$, the stock is as risky as the general market. When $\beta < 1$, the stock is less risky, whereas when $\beta > 1$, the stock is more risky than the overall stock market. Investors are compensated only for risk that cannot be eliminated through diversification (i.e., systematic or nondiversifiable risk).

The value of β may be estimated by applying linear regression analysis to explain the relationship between the dependent variable, stock returns (R_j), and the independent variable, market returns (R_m). The intercept or constant term (also referred to as *alpha*) of the regression equation provides a measure of R_j's performance compared with the general market during the regression period. In Wall Street parlance, alpha is the premium (or discount) an investment earns above (below) some performance benchmark, such as the S&P 500 index.

The following equations express R_j as defined by the linear regression model and R_j as defined by the CAPM:

$$R_j = \alpha + \beta R_m \text{(regression equation formulation)}$$
$$R_j = R_f + \beta(R_m - R_f)$$
$$= R_f + \beta R_m - \beta R_f$$
$$= R_f(1 - \beta) + \beta R_m \text{(CAPM formulation)}$$

If α is greater than $R_f(1 - \beta)$, this particular stock's rate of return, R_j, performed better than would have been expected using the CAPM during the same time period. The cumulative daily difference between α (i.e., actual returns) and $R_f(1 - \beta)$ (i.e., expected returns) is a measure of "abnormal" or "excess return" for a specified number of days around the announcement of a transaction (see Exhibit 7.1).

In practice, betas are frequently estimated using the most recent three to five years of data. Consequently, betas are sensitive to the time period selected. The relationship between the

EXHIBIT 7.1 ESTIMATING β FOR PUBLICLY TRADED COMPANIES

Calculate the return to the jth company's shareholders as capital gains (or losses) plus dividends paid during the period adjusted for stock splits that take place in the current period. This adjusted return should then be regressed against a similarly defined return for a broadly defined market index.

$$\frac{SP \times (P_{jt} - P_{jt-1}) + SP \times \text{Dividends}}{P_{jt-1}} = \alpha + \beta \frac{(S\&P500_t - S\&P500_{t-1}) + \text{Dividends}}{S\&P500_{t-1}}$$

Notes:

1. SP is equal to 2 for a two-for-one stock split, 1.5 for a three-for-two split, and 1.33 for a four-for-three split, and so on. If we do not adjust for stock splits that may take place in the current period, the stock price will drop, resulting in a negative return.

2. Betas for public companies can be obtained from estimation services such as Value Line, Standard & Poor's, Ibbotson, and Bloomberg. Betas for private companies can be obtained by substituting a beta for comparable publicly traded companies (see Chapter 10).

overall market and a specific firm's equity beta may change significantly if a large sector of stocks that make up the overall index increase or decrease substantially.[15] Estimates of public company equity betas may be obtained by going to *finance.yahoo.com*, *finance.google.com*, and *reuters.com*.

Alternatively, a firm's beta may be calculated based on the betas of a sample of similar firms—that is, firms facing similar business risk (usually in the same industry) and those with similar capital structures. We unlever the betas of the firms in the sample to eliminate the effects of their current capital structures on their betas. Finally, we average the unlevered betas and relever them to reflect the capital structure of the firm whose beta we are trying to estimate. This process is described in detail in the next section.

Effects of Financial and Operating Leverage on Beta

The volatility of a firm's financial returns is affected by the cyclicality of the industry in which it competes, its cost structure, and its capital structure. The following discussion introduces the concepts of unlevered and levered betas as ways to measure the effects of a firm's cost and capital structures on its beta and, in turn, the firm's financial returns.

In the absence of debt, the equity β is called an *unlevered* β, denoted β_u. The unlevered beta of a firm is determined by the type of industry in which the firm operates (e.g., cyclical or noncyclical) and its *operating leverage* (i.e., the firm's ratio of fixed expenses to total cost of sales). Operating leverage magnifies the volatility of a firm's earnings and financial returns.[16] Table 7.3 illustrates the effects of operating leverage on financial returns.

The three cases reflect the same level of fixed expenses but varying levels of revenue and the resulting impact on after-tax earnings and financial returns. The Case 1 illustration assumes that the firm's total cost of sales is 80% of revenue and that fixed expenses comprise 60% of the total cost of sales. Note the volatility of the firm's return on equity resulting from fluctuations of 25% in the firm's revenue in Cases 2 and 3.

If a firm borrows, the unlevered equity beta must be adjusted to reflect the additional risk associated with *financial leverage* (i.e., the firm's ratio of debt to equity). The resulting beta is called a *leveraged* or *levered* β, denoted β_l. Table 7.4 illustrates the effects of financial leverage on financial returns. The three cases reflect varying levels of debt but the same earnings before interest and taxes. Note how increasing leverage magnifies financial returns to equity.

---

[15] While over longer periods of time the impact on beta is problematic, it may be quite substantial over relatively short time periods. For example, the telecommunications, media, and technology sectors of the S&P 500 rose dramatically in the late 1990s and fell precipitously after 2000. Other sectors were relatively unaffected by the wild fluctuations in the overall market, resulting in a reduction in their betas. To illustrate, the equity beta for electric utilities fell to 0.1 in 2001 from 0.6 in 1998, falsely suggesting that the sector's risk and, in turn, cost of equity had declined.

[16] Recall that operating profits equal total revenue less fixed and variable costs. If revenue, fixed, and variable costs are $100, $50, and $25 million, respectively, the firm's operating profits are $25 million. If revenue doubles to $200 million, the firm's profit increases fourfold to $100 million (i.e., $200 – $50 – $50).

TABLE 7.3   How Operating Leverage Affects Financial Returns[a]

	Case 1	Case 2: Revenue Increases by 25%	Case 3: Revenue Decreases by 25%
Revenue	100	125	75
Fixed	48	48	48
Variable[b]	32	40	24
Total Cost of Sales	80	88	72
Earnings Before Taxes	20	37	3
Tax Liability @ 40%	8	14.8	1.2
After-Tax Earnings	12	22.2	1.8
Firm Equity	100	100	100
Return on Equity (%)	12	22.2	1.8

[a] All figures are in millions of dollars unless otherwise noted.
[b] In Case 1, variable costs represent 32% of revenue. Assuming this ratio is maintained, variable costs in Cases 2 and 3 are estimated by multiplying total revenue by 0.32.

TABLE 7.4   How Financial Leverage Affects Financial Returns[a]

	Case 1: No Debt	Case 2: 25% Debt to Total Capital	Case 3: 50% Debt to Total Capital
Equity	100	75	50
Debt	0	25	50
Total Capital	100	100	100
Earnings before Interest and Taxes	20	20	20
Interest @ 10%	0	2.5	5
Income before Taxes	20	17.5	15
Less Income Taxes @ 40%	8	7.0	6
After-Tax Earnings	12	10.5	9
After-Tax Returns on Equity (%)	12	14	18

[a] All figures are in millions of dollars unless otherwise noted.

If a firm's stockholders bear all the risk from operating and financial leverage and interest paid on debt is tax deductible, levered and unlevered betas can be calculated as follows for a firm whose debt-to-equity ratio is denoted by D/E:

$$\beta_1 = \beta_u[1 + (1-t)(D/E)] \quad \text{and} \tag{7.5}$$

$$\beta_u = \beta_1/[1 + (1-t)(D/E)] \tag{7.6}$$

III. MERGER AND ACQUISITION CASH FLOW VALUATION

Shareholders view risk as the potential for a firm not to earn sufficient future cash flow to satisfy their minimum required financial returns. Equation (7.5) implies that increases in a firm's leverage denoted by (D/E) will, other things unchanged, increase this risk as measured by the firm's levered beta because the firm's interest payments represent fixed expenses that must be paid before any payments can be made to shareholders. However, this increased risk is offset somewhat by the tax deductibility of interest, which reduces shareholder risk by increasing after-tax cash flow available for shareholders. The reduction in the firm's tax liability due to the tax deductibility of interest is often referred to as a *tax shield*. Therefore, the levered beta will, unless offset by other factors, increase with an increase in leverage and decrease with an increase in tax rates.

In summary, β_u is determined by the characteristics of the industry in which the firm competes and its degree of operating leverage. The value of β_l is determined by the same factors and the degree of the firm's financial leverage. Estimating a firm's beta by regressing the percent change in its share price plus dividends against the percent change in a broadly defined index plus dividends over some historical period, as illustrated in Exhibit 7.1, assumes the historical relationship will hold in the future. However, this often is not the case.

An alternative to using historical information is to estimate beta using a sample of similar firms and applying Eqs. (7.5) and (7.6). This involves a three-step procedure (Table 7.5). In step 1, select a sample of firms with similar cyclicality and operating leverage (i.e., firms usually in the same industry). Step 2 requires calculating the average unleveraged beta for firms in the sample to eliminate the effects of their current capital structures on their betas. Finally, in step 3, we relever the average unleveraged beta using the debt-to-equity ratio and the marginal tax rate of the firm whose beta we are trying to estimate (i.e., the target firm).

TABLE 7.5　Estimating Abbot Labs' Equity Beta Using Similar Firms

| Firm | Step 1: Select sample of firms having similar cyclicality and operating leverage | | Step 2: Compute average of firms' unleveraged betas | Step 3: Relever average unleveraged beta using target's debt/equity ratio |
	Levered Equity Beta[a]	Debt/ Equity[a]	Unlevered Equity Beta[b]	Abbot Labs' Relevered Equity Beta[c]
Abbot Labs	0.2900	0.2662	0.2501	NA
Johnson & Johnson	0.6000	0.0762	0.5738	NA
Merck	0.6600	0.3204	0.5536	NA
Pfizer	0.6800	0.3044	0.5750	NA
			Average = 0.4881	0.4209

[a] Yahoo! Finance (1/29/2011). Beta estimates are based on the historical relationship between the firm's share price and a broadly defined stock index.
[b] $\beta_u = \beta_l / [1 + (1 - t)(D/E)]$, where β_u and β_l are unlevered and levered betas; marginal tax rate is 0.4.
　Abbot Labs $(\beta_u) = 0.2900 / [1 + (1 - 0.4)0.2662)] = 0.2501$
　Johnson & Johnson $(\beta_u) = 0.6000 / [1 + (1 - 0.4)0.0762)] = 0.5738$
　Merck $(\beta_u) = 0.6600 / [1 + (1 - 0.4)0.3204)] = 0.5536$
　Pfizer $(\beta_u) = 0.6800 / [1 + (1 - 0.4)0.3044)] = 0.5750$
[c] $\beta_l = \beta_u [1 + (1 - t)(D/E)]$ using the target firm's (Abbot Labs') debt/equity ratio and marginal tax rate.
　Abbot Labs' relevered beta $= 0.4881[1 + (1 - 0.4)0.2662)] = 0.4209$

Using Eqs. (7.5) and (7.6), the effects of different amounts of leverage on the cost of equity also can be analyzed.[17] The process is as follows:

1. Determine a firm's current equity β^* and $(D/E)^*$;
2. Estimate the unleveraged beta to eliminate the effects of the firm's current capital structure:

$$\beta_u = \beta^*/[1 + (1 - t)(D/E)^*];$$

3. Estimate the firm's leveraged beta: $\beta_1 = \beta_u [1 + (1 - t)(D/E)^{**}]$; and
4. Estimate the firm's cost of equity for the new leveraged beta

where β^* and $(D/E)^*$ represent the firm's current equity beta and the market value of the firm's debt-to-equity ratio before additional borrowing takes place; $(D/E)^{**}$ is the firm's debt-to-equity ratio after additional borrowing occurs; and t is the firm's marginal tax rate.

In an acquisition, an acquirer may anticipate increasing significantly the target firm's current debt level after the closing. To determine the impact on the target's beta of the increased leverage, the target's levered beta, which reflects its preacquisition leverage, must be converted to an unlevered beta, reflecting the target firm's operating leverage and the cyclicality of the industry in which the firm competes. To measure the increasing risk associated with new borrowing, the resulting unlevered beta is then used to estimate the levered beta for the target firm (see Exhibit 7.2).

EXHIBIT 7.2 ESTIMATING THE IMPACT OF CHANGING DEBT LEVELS ON THE COST OF EQUITY

Assume that a target's current or preacquisition debt-to-equity ratio is 25%, current levered beta is 1.05, and marginal tax rate is 0.4. After the acquisition, the debt-to-equity ratio is expected to rise to 75%. What is the target's postacquisition levered beta?

Answer: Using Eqs. (7.5) and (7.6):

$$\beta_u = \beta_1^*/[1 + (1 - t)(D/E)^*] = 1.05/[1 + (1 - 0.4)(0.25)] = 0.91$$
$$\beta_1 = \beta_u[1 + (1 - t)(D/E)^{**}] = 0.91[1 + (1 - 0.4)(0.75)] = 1.32$$

where $(D/E)^*$ and $(D/E)^{**}$ are the target's pre- and postacquisition debt-to-equity ratios and β_1^* is the target's preacquisition equity beta.

CALCULATING FREE CASH FLOWS

Two common definitions of cash flow used for valuation purposes are free cash flow to the firm (FCFF), or enterprise cash flow, and cash flow to equity investors (FCFE), or equity cash flow. These cash flows (often referred to as valuation cash flows) require adjusting GAAP-based cash flows provided in companies' financial statements. How valuation cash flows are constructed is discussed next.

[17] The reestimation of a firm's beta to reflect a change in leverage requires that we first deleverage the firm to remove the effects of the firm's current level of debt on its beta and then releverage the firm using its new level of debt to estimate the new levered beta.

Free Cash Flow to the Firm (Enterprise Cash Flow)

Free cash flow to the firm represents cash available to satisfy all investors holding claims against the firm's resources. These claim holders include common stockholders, lenders, and preferred stockholders. This definition assumes implicitly that a firm can always get financing if it can generate sufficient future cash flows to meet or exceed minimum returns required by investors and lenders. Consequently, enterprise cash flow is calculated before the sources of financing are determined and, as such, is not affected by the firm's financial structure. However, in practice, the financial structure may affect the firm's cost of capital and, therefore, its value due to the potential for bankruptcy (see Chapter 16 for a more detailed discussion of financial distress).

FCFF can be calculated by adjusting operating earnings before interest and taxes (EBIT) as follows:

$$
\begin{aligned}
\text{FCFF} = \ &\text{EBIT}(1 - \text{Tax Rate}) + \text{Depreciation and Amortization} \\
&- \text{Gross Capital Expenditures} - \Delta\text{Net Working Capital}
\end{aligned}
\tag{7.7}
$$

Under this definition, only cash flow from operating and investment activities, but not financing activities, is included. The tax rate refers to the firm's marginal tax rate. Net working capital is defined as current operating assets less cash balances in excess of the amount required to meet normal operating requirements less current operating liabilities. In some instances, firms may have negative working capital. While this is possible for a certain time period, it is unlikely to be sustained; consequently, it is preferable to set net working capital to zero in this instance.

Assets lose value or wear out over time. There is a cash outflow when the asset is acquired initially; however, because assets can continue to generate revenue over many years, GAAP accounting requires that the initial cost of the asset be spread over the expected useful life of the asset to better align costs with the revenue generated in each year. Since such depreciation and amortization expenses do not constitute an actual cash outlay, they are added back to operating income in the calculation of cash flow.

Selecting the Right Tax Rate

The calculation of after-tax operating income requires multiplying EBIT by either a firm's marginal tax rate (i.e., the rate paid on each additional dollar of earnings) or effective tax rate (i.e., taxes due divided by taxable income). The effective tax rate is calculated from actual taxes paid, based on accounting statements prepared for tax-reporting purposes. The marginal tax rate in the United States is usually 40%—35% for federal taxes for firms earning more than $10 million and 5% for most state and local taxes—and it is typically used to calculate after-tax income from new investment projects.

The effective rate is usually less than the marginal tax rate and varies among firms due to the use of tax credits to reduce actual taxes paid or accelerated depreciation to defer the payment of taxes. While favorable tax rules may temporarily reduce the effective tax rate, it is unlikely to be permanently reduced. Once tax credits have been used and the ability to further defer taxes has been exhausted, the effective rate can exceed the marginal rate at some point in the future.

Because favorable tax treatment cannot be extended indefinitely, the marginal tax rate should be used if taxable income is going to be multiplied by the same tax rate during each future period. However, an effective tax rate lower than the marginal rate may be used in the early years of cash-flow projections and eventually increased to the firm's marginal tax rate if the analyst has reason to believe that the current favorable tax treatment is likely to continue into the foreseeable future. However, whatever the analyst chooses to do with respect to the selection of a tax rate, it is critical to use the marginal rate in calculating after-tax operating income in perpetuity. Otherwise, the implicit assumption is that taxes can be deferred indefinitely.

Dealing with Operating Leases

For many firms, their future operating lease commitments are substantial. Leased assets qualifying as operating leases do not require a firm to record an asset or a liability on the balance sheet; instead, the lease charge is recorded as an expense on the firm's income statement, and future lease commitments are recorded in footnotes to the firm's financial statements.

As noted later in this chapter, future lease commitments should be discounted to the present at the firm's pretax cost of debt (i), since leasing equipment represents an alternative to borrowing to buy a piece of equipment, and its present value (PV_{OL}) should be included in the firm's total debt outstanding. Once operating leases are converted to debt, operating lease expense (OLE_{EXP}) must be added to EBIT because it is a financial expense and EBIT represents operating income before such expenses. Lease payments include both an interest expense component to reflect the cost of borrowing and a depreciation component to reflect the anticipated decline in the value of the leased asset.

An estimate of depreciation expense associated with the leased asset (DEP_{OL}) then must be deducted from EBIT, as is depreciation expense associated with other fixed assets owned by the firm, to calculate an "adjusted" EBIT ($EBIT_{ADJ}$). DEP_{OL} may be estimated by dividing the firm's gross plant and equipment by its annual depreciation expense. Studies show that the median asset life for leased equipment is 10.9 years.[18] The $EBIT_{ADJ}$ then is used to calculate free cash flow to the firm. EBIT may be adjusted as follows:

$$EBIT_{ADJ} = EBIT + OLE_{EXP} - DEP_{OL} \qquad (7.8)$$

For example, if EBIT, OLE_{EXP}, PV_{OL}, and the estimated useful life of the leased equipment are $15 million, $2 million, $30 million, and ten years, respectively, $EBIT_{ADJ}$ equals $14 million (i.e., $15 + $2 − ($30/10)).

Free Cash Flow to Equity Investors (Equity Cash Flow)

Free cash flow to equity investors is the cash flow remaining for returning cash through dividends or share repurchases to current common equity investors or for reinvesting in the firm after the firm satisfies all obligations.[19] These obligations include debt payments,

[18] Lim, Mann, and Mihov, 2004

[19] Damodaran, 2002

capital expenditures, changes in net working capital, and preferred dividend payments. FCFE can be defined as follows:

FCFE = Net Income + Depreciation and Amortization − Gross Capital Expenditures
− ΔNet Working Capital + New Debt and Equity Issues − Principal
Repayments − Preferred Dividends

$$(7.9)$$

Exhibit 7.3 summarizes the key elements of enterprise cash flow, Eq. (7.6), and equity cash flow, Eq. (7.9). Note that equity cash flow reflects operating, investment, and financing activities, whereas enterprise cash flow excludes cash flow from financing activities.

EXHIBIT 7.3 DEFINING VALUATION CASH FLOWS: EQUITY AND ENTERPRISE CASH FLOWS

Free Cash Flow to Common Equity Investors (Equity Cash Flow: FCFE)
FCFE = {Net Income + Depreciation and Amortization − ΔWorking Capital}[a]
− Gross Capital Expenditures[b] + {New Preferred Equity Issues − Preferred Dividends
+ New Debt Issues − Principal Repayments}[c]

⟹ Cash flow (after taxes, debt repayments and new debt issues, preferred dividends, preferred equity issues, and all reinvestment requirements) available for paying dividends and/or repurchasing common equity.

Free Cash Flow to the Firm (Enterprise Cash Flow: FCFF)
FCFF = {Earnings Before Interest & Taxes (1 − Tax Rate) + Depreciation and Amortization
− Δ Working Capital}[a] − Gross Capital Expenditures[b]

⟹ Cash flow (after taxes and reinvestment requirements) available to repay lenders and/or pay common and preferred dividends and repurchase equity.

[a]Cash from operating activities.
[b]Cash from investing activities.
[c]Cash from financing activities.

APPLYING INCOME OR DISCOUNTED-CASH-FLOW METHODS

The firm's ability to generate future cash flows often is referred to as its economic value. DCF methods provide estimates of the economic value of a company at a moment in time, which do not need to be adjusted if the intent is to acquire a small portion of it. However, if the intention is to obtain a controlling interest in the firm, a control premium must be added to the firm's estimated economic value to determine the purchase price. A controlling interest generally is considered more valuable to an investor than is a minority interest because the investor has the right to approve important decisions affecting the business. Minority investment positions often are subject to discounts because of their lack of control. Control premiums and minority discounts are discussed in detail in Chapter 10.

Enterprise Discounted-Cash-Flow Model (Enterprise or FCFF Method)

The enterprise valuation method, or FCFF, approach discounts the after-tax free cash flow available to the firm from operations at the weighted-average cost of capital to obtain the estimated enterprise value. The firm's *enterprise value* (often referred to as *firm value*) reflects the market value of the entire business. It represents the sum of investor claims on the firm's cash flows from all those holding securities. These include those holding long-term debt, preferred stock, common shareholders, and minority shareholders.

Enterprise value is commonly calculated as the market value of the firm's common equity plus long-term debt, preferred stock, and minority interest less cash and cash equivalents.[20] It is commonly assumed that cash and cash equivalents are available to meet such obligations.[21]

The firm's estimated common equity value then is determined by subtracting the market value of the firm's debt and other investor claims on cash flow, such as preferred stock, from the enterprise value. The estimate of equity derived in this manner equals the value of equity determined by discounting the cash flow available to the firm's shareholders at the cost of equity, if assumptions about cash flow and discount rates are consistent. The enterprise method is used when the analyst has limited information about the firm's debt repayment schedules or interest expense.

Equity Discounted-Cash-Flow Model (Equity or FCFE Method)

The equity valuation, or FCFE approach, discounts the after-tax cash flows available to the firm's shareholders at the cost of equity. This approach is more direct than the enterprise method when the objective is to value the firm's equity, and may be appropriate for financial services firms in which the cost of capital for various operations within the firm may be very difficult to estimate.[22] By focusing on FCFE, the analyst needs to estimate only the financial services firm's cost of equity. The enterprise or FCFF method and the equity or FCFE method are illustrated in the following sections of this chapter using three cash-flow growth scenarios: zero-growth, constant-growth, and variable-growth rates.

---

[20] Other long-term liabilities such as the firm's pension and healthcare obligations may be ignored if they are fully funded. However, the unfunded portion of such liabilities should be added to enterprise value, while any recoverable surplus should be deducted.

[21] The total amount of cash and cash equivalents would only be available to meet investor claims if the firm were being liquidated. Otherwise, some portion of such cash would be required to meet continuing operations of the company.

[22] For example, a retail commercial banking operation typically finances its operations using interest-free checking accounts. Determining the actual cost of acquiring such accounts is often quite arbitrary.

The Zero-Growth Valuation Model

This model assumes that free cash flow is constant in perpetuity. The value of the firm at time zero (P_0) is the discounted or capitalized value of its annual cash flow. In this instance (see Exhibit 7.4), the discount rate and the capitalization rate are the same (see Chapter 10 for further discussion of the difference between discount and capitalization rates).[23] The subscript FCFF or FCFE refers to the definition of cash flow used in the valuation.

$$P_{0,FCFF} = FCFF_0/WACC \qquad (7.10)$$

where $FCFF_0$ is free cash flow to the firm at time 0 and WACC is the cost of capital.

$$P_{0,FCFF} = FCFF_0/k_e \qquad (7.11)$$

where $FCFE_0$ is free cash flow to common equity at time 0 and k_e is the cost of equity.

While simplistic, the zero-growth method has the advantage of being easily understood by all parties involved in a negotiation. Moreover, there is little evidence that more complex methods provide consistently better valuation estimates, due to their greater requirement for more inputs and assumptions. This method is often used to value commercial real estate transactions and small privately owned businesses.

EXHIBIT 7.4 THE ZERO-GROWTH VALUATION MODEL

1. What is the enterprise value of a firm whose annual $FCFF_0$ of $1 million is expected to remain constant in perpetuity and whose cost of capital is 12% (see Eq. (7.10))?

$$P_{0,FCFF} = \$1/0.12 = \$8.3 \text{ million}$$

2. Calculate the weighted-average cost of capital (see Eq. (7.4)) and the enterprise value of a firm whose capital structure consists only of common equity and debt. The firm desires to limit its debt to 30% of total capital.[a] The firm's marginal tax rate is 0.4 and its beta is 1.5. The corporate bond rate is 8% and the ten-year U.S. Treasury bond rate is 5%. The expected annual return on stocks is 10%. Annual FCFF is expected to remain at $4 million indefinitely.

$$k_e = 0.05 + 1.5(0.10 - 0.05) = 0.125 = 12.5\%$$
$$WACC = 0.125 \times 0.7 + 0.08 \times (1 - 0.4) \times 0.3 = 0.088 + 0.014 = 0.102 = 10.2\%$$
$$P_{0,FCFF} = \$4/0.102 = \$39.2 \text{ million}$$

[a]If you only know a firm's debt-to-equity ratio (D/E), it is possible to calculate the firm's debt-to-total capital ratio ($D/D + E$) by dividing (D/E) by ($1 + D/E$), since $D/(D + E) = (D/E)/(1 + D/E) = [(D/E)/(D + E)/E] = (D/E) \times (E/D + E) = D/(D + E)$.

---

[23] The present value of a constant payment in perpetuity is a diminishing series because it represents the sum of the PVs for each future period. Each PV is smaller than the preceding one; therefore, the perpetuity is a diminishing series that converges to 1 divided by the discount rate.

The Constant-Growth Valuation Model

The constant-growth model is applicable for firms in mature markets, characterized by a moderate and somewhat predictable rate of growth. Examples of such industries include beverages, cosmetics, personal care products, prepared foods, and cleaning products. To project growth rates, extrapolate the industry's growth rate over the past five to ten years. The constant-growth model assumes that cash flow grows at a constant rate, g, which is less than the required return, k_e. The assumption that k_e is greater than g is a necessary mathematical condition for deriving the model. In this model, next year's cash flow to the firm ($FCFF_1$), or the first year of the forecast period, is expected to grow at the constant rate of growth, g. Therefore, $FCFF_1 = FCFF_0 (1 + g)$:

$$P_{0,FCFF} = FCFF_1/(WACC - g) \qquad (7.12)$$

$$P_{0,FCFE} = FCFE_1/(k_e - g), \text{where } FCFE_1 = FCFE_0(1 + g) \qquad (7.13)$$

where $FCFE_1 = FCFE_0 (1 + g)$.[24]

This simple valuation model also provides a means of estimating the risk premium component of the cost of equity as an alternative to relying on historical information, as is done in the capital asset pricing model. This model was developed originally to estimate the value of stocks in the current period (P_0) using the level of expected dividends (d_1) in the next period. This formulation provides an estimate of the present value of dividends growing at a constant rate forever. Assuming the stock market values stocks correctly and we know P_0, d_1, and g, we can estimate k_e. Therefore,

$$P_0 = d_1/(k_e - g) \text{ and } k_e = (d_1/P_0) + g \qquad (7.14)$$

For example, if d_1 is $1, g is 10%, and $P_0 = 10, k_e is 20%. See Exhibit 7.5 for an illustration of how to apply the constant-growth model.

EXHIBIT 7.5 THE CONSTANT-GROWTH MODEL

1. Determine the enterprise value of a firm whose projected free cash flow to the firm (enterprise cash flow) next year is $1 million, WACC is 12%, and expected annual cash-flow growth rate is 6% (see Eq. (7.12)).

$$P_{0,FCFF} = \$1/(0.12 - 0.06) = \$16.7 \text{ million}$$

2. Estimate the equity value of a firm whose cost of equity is 15% and whose free cash flow to equity holders (equity cash flow) in the prior year is projected to grow 20% this year and then at a constant 10% annual rate thereafter. The prior year's free cash flow to equity holders is $2 million (see Eq. (7.13)).

$$P_{0,FCFE} = [(\$2.0 \times 1.2)(1.1)]/(0.15 - 0.10) = \$52.8 \text{ million}$$

---

[24] Note that the zero growth model is a special case of the constant-growth model for which g equals 0.

The Variable-Growth (Supernormal or Nonconstant) Valuation Model

Many firms experience periods of high growth followed by a period of slower, more stable growth. Examples of such industries include cellular phones, personal computers, and cable TV. Firms within such industries routinely experience double-digit growth rates for periods of five to ten years because of low penetration of these markets in the early years of the product's life cycle. As the market becomes saturated, growth inevitably slows to a rate more in line with the overall growth of the economy or the general population. The PV of such firms is equal to the sum of the PV of the discounted cash flows during the high-growth period plus the discounted value of the cash flows generated during the stable growth period. The discounted value of the cash flows generated during the stable growth period is often called the *terminal, sustainable, horizon,* or *continuing growth value*.

The terminal value may be estimated using the constant-growth model. Free cash flow during the first year beyond the nth or final year of the forecast period, $FCFF_{n+1}$, is divided by the difference between the assumed cost of capital and the expected cash-flow growth rate beyond the nth-year forecast period. The terminal value is the value in the nth year of all future cash flows beyond the nth year. Consequently, to convert the terminal value to its value in the current year, it is necessary to discount the terminal value by applying the discount rate used to convert the nth-year value to a present value.

The use of the constant-growth model provides consistency in estimating the value of the firm created beyond the end of the forecast period. It enables the application of discounted-cash-flow methodology in estimating value during both variable and stable growth periods. However, the selection of the earnings growth rate and cost of capital must be done very carefully. Small changes in assumptions can result in dramatic swings in the terminal value and, therefore, in the valuation of the firm.

Table 7.6 illustrates the sensitivity of a terminal value of $1 million to different spreads between the cost of capital and the stable growth rate. Note that, using the constant-growth model formula, the terminal value declines dramatically as the spread between the cost of

TABLE 7.6 Impact of Changes in Assumptions on Terminal Value

Difference between Cost of Capital and Cash-Flow Growth Rate	Terminal Value ($ millions)
3%	33.3[a]
4%	25.0
5%	20.0
6%	16.7
7%	14.3

[a] $1.0/0.03

capital and expected stable growth for cash flow increases by 1 percentage point. Note also that terminal values can be estimated in numerous other ways.[25]

Using the definition of free cash flow to the firm, $P_{0,FCFF}$ can be estimated using the variable-growth model as follows:

$$P_{0,FCFF} = \sum_{t=1}^{n} \frac{FCFF_0 \times (1 + g_t)^t}{(1 + WACC)^t} + \frac{P_n}{(1 + WACC)^n} \qquad (7.15)$$

where

$$P_n = \frac{FCFF_n \times (1 + g_m)}{(WACC_m - g_m)}$$

$FCFF_0 = FCFF$ in year 0
$WACC$ = weighted-average cost of capital through year n
$WACC_m$ = cost of capital assumed beyond year n (*Note:* $WACC > WACC_m$)
P_n = value of the firm at the end of year n (terminal value)
g_t = growth rate through year n
g_m = stabilized or long-term growth rate beyond year n (*Note:* $g_t > g_m$)

Similarly, the value of the firm to equity investors can be estimated using Eq. (7.15). However, projected free cash flows to equity (FCFE) are discounted using the firm's cost of equity.

The cost of capital is assumed to differ between the high-growth and the stable-growth period when applying the variable-growth model. High-growth rates usually are associated with increased levels of uncertainty. In applying discounted-cash-flow methodology, the discount rate reflects risk. Consequently, the discount rate during the high-growth (i.e., less predictable) period or periods should generally be higher than during the stable-growth period. For example, a high-growth firm may have a beta significantly above 1. However, when the growth rate becomes stable, it is reasonable to assume that the beta should approximate 1. A reasonable approximation of the discount rate to be used during the stable-growth period is the industry average cost of equity or weighted average cost of capital.

Equation (7.15) can be modified to use the growing-annuity model[26] to approximate growth during the high-constant-growth period and the constant-growth model for the terminal period. This formulation requires fewer computations if the number of annual cash-flow projections is large. As such, $P_{0,FCFF}$ also can be estimated as shown in the following equation.

[25] The price-to-earnings, price-to-cash-flow, or price-to-book techniques value the target as if it were sold at the end of a specific number of years. At the end of the forecast period, the terminal year's earnings, cash flow, or book value is projected and multiplied by a P/E, cash-flow, or book-value multiple believed to be appropriate for that year. The terminal value also may be estimated by assuming the firm's cash flow or earnings in the last year of the forecast period will continue in perpetuity. This is equivalent to the zero-growth valuation model discussed previously.

[26] Ross et al. (2009), pp. 238–240.

$$P_{0,FCFF} = \frac{FCFF_0(1+g)}{(WACC-g)} \times \{1 - [(1+g)/(1+WACC)]^n\} + \frac{P_n}{(1+WACC)^n} \qquad (7.16)$$

See Exhibit 7.6 for an illustration of when and how to apply the variable-growth model.

EXHIBIT 7.6 THE VARIABLE-GROWTH VALUATION MODEL

Estimate the enterprise value of a firm (P_0) whose free cash flow is projected to grow at a compound annual average rate of 35% for the next five years. Growth then is expected to slow to a more normal 5% annual growth rate. The current year's cash flow to the firm is $4 million. The firm's weighted-average cost of capital during the high-growth period is 18% and 12% beyond the fifth year, as growth stabilizes. The firm's cash in excess of normal operating balances is assumed to be zero. Therefore, using Eq. (7.15), the present value of cash flows during the high-growth forecast period is as follows:

$$PV_{t-5} = \frac{\$4.00 \times 1.35}{1.18} + \frac{\$4.00 \times 1.35^2}{1.18^2} + \frac{\$4.00 \times 1.35^3}{1.18^3}$$

$$+ \frac{\$4.00 \times 1.35^4}{1.18^4} + \frac{\$4.00 \times 1.35^5}{1.18^5}$$

$$= \$5.40/1.18 + \$7.29/1.18^2 + \$9.84/1.18^3 + \$13.29/1.18^4 + \$17.93/1.18^5$$

$$= \$4.58 + \$5.24 + \$5.99 + \$6.85 + \$7.84 = \$30.50$$

Calculation of the terminal value is as follows:

$$PV_5 = \frac{[(\$4.00 \times 1.35^5 \times 1.05]/(0.12 - 0.05)}{1.18^5}$$

$$= \frac{\$18.83/0.07}{2.29} = \$117.60$$

$$P_{0,FCFF} = PV_{t-5} + PV_5 = \$30.50 + \$117.60 = \$148.10$$

Alternatively, using the growing annuity model to value the high-growth period and the constant-growth model to value the terminal period (see Eq. (7.16)), the present value of free cash flow to the firm could be estimated as follows:

$$PV_{0,FCFF} = \frac{\$4.00 \times 1.35}{(0.18 - 0.35)} \times \{1 - [(1.35/1.18)]^5\} + \frac{[(\$4.00 \times 1.35^5 \times 1.05]/(0.12 - 0.05)}{1.18^5}$$

$$= \$30.50 + \$117.60$$

$$= \$148.10$$

VALUING FIRMS SUBJECT TO MULTIPLE GROWTH PERIODS

Some companies display initial periods of what could be described as hypergrowth, followed by an extended period of rapid growth, before stabilizing at a more normal and sustainable growth rate. Initial public offerings and start-up companies may follow this model.

This pattern reflects growth over their initially small revenue base, the introduction of a new product, or the sale of an existing product to a new or underserved customer group. Calculating the discounted cash flows is computationally more difficult for firms expected to grow for multiple periods, each of whose growth rates differ, before assuming a more normal long-term growth rate. Because each period's growth rate differs, the cost of capital in each period differs. Consequently, each year's cash flows must be discounted by the "cumulative cost of capital" from prior years. A more detailed discussion of this method is provided on the companion site to this book in the file folder entitled "Example of Supernormal Growth Model."

Determining Growth Rates

Projected growth rates for sales, profit, cash flow, or other financial variables can be readily calculated based on the historical experience of the firm or of the industry. See the document entitled "Primer on Cash-Flow Forecasting" on the companion site to this text for a discussion of how to apply regression analysis to projecting a firm's cash flow.

The Duration of the High-Growth Period

Intuition suggests that the length of the high-growth period should be longer when the current growth rate of a firm's cash flow is much higher than the stable growth rate. This is particularly true when the high-growth firm has a relatively small market share and there is little reason to believe that its growth rate will slow in the foreseeable future. For example, if the industry is expected to grow at 5% annually and the target firm, which has only a negligible market share, is growing at three times that rate, it may be appropriate to assume a high-growth period of five to ten years.

Moreover, if the terminal value constitutes a substantial percentage (e.g., three-fourths) of the total PV, the annual forecast period should be extended beyond the customary five years to at least ten years. The extension of the time period reduces the impact of the terminal value in determining the market value of the firm. Historical evidence shows that sales and profitability tend to revert to normal levels within five to ten years.[27] This suggests that the conventional use of a five- to ten-year annual forecast before calculating a terminal value makes sense.[28]

[27] Between 1979 and 1998, sales growth for the average U.S. firm reverted to an average of 7 to 9% within five years. Firms with initial growth rates in excess of 50% experience a decline to about 6% growth within three years; those with the lowest initial growth rate tend to increase to about 8% by year 5. See Palepu, Healy, and Bernard (2004), pp. 10-2 and 10-3.

[28] More sophisticated forecasts of growth rates involve an analysis of the firm's customer base. Annual revenue projections are made for each customer or product and summed to provide an estimate of aggregate revenue. A product or service's life cycle (see Chapter 4) is a useful tool for making such projections. In some industries, a product's life cycle may be a matter of months (e.g., software) or years (e.g., an automobile). This information is readily available by examining the launch dates of new products and services in an industry in publications provided by the industry's trade associations. By determining where the firm's products are in their life cycle, the analyst can project annual unit volume by product.

The Stable or Sustainable Growth Rate

The stable growth rate generally is going to be less than or equal to the overall growth rate of the industry in which the firm competes or the general economy. Stable growth rates in excess of these levels implicitly assume that the firm's cash flow eventually will exceed that of its industry or the general economy. Similarly, for multinational firms, the stable growth rate should not exceed the projected growth rate for the world economy or a particular region of the world.

Determining the Appropriate Discount Rate

The appropriate discount rate is generally the target's cost of capital if the acquirer is merging with a higher-risk business, resulting in an increase in the cost of capital of the combined firms. However, either the acquirer's or the target's cost of capital may be used if the two firms are equally risky and based in the same country.

VALUING FIRMS UNDER SPECIAL SITUATIONS

A firm's cash flows may be affected by temporary, long-term, or cyclical factors. Each scenario requires a different solution. How each scenario can be addressed is discussed next.

Firms with Temporary Problems

When cash flow is temporarily depressed as a result of strikes, litigation, warranty claims, employee severance, or other one-time events, it is generally safe to assume that cash flow will recover in the near term. One solution is to base projections on cash flow prior to the one-time event. Alternatively, actual cash flow could be adjusted for the one-time event by adding back the pretax reduction in operating profits of the one-time event and recalculating after-tax profits. If the cost of the one-time event is not displayed on the firm's financial statements, it is necessary to compare each expense item as a percentage of sales in the current year with the prior year. Any expense items that look abnormally high should be "normalized" by applying an average ratio from prior years to the current year's sales. Alternatively, the analyst could use the prior year's operating margin to estimate the current year's operating income.

Firms with Longer-Term Problems

Deteriorating cash flow may be symptomatic of a longer-term deterioration in the firm's competitive position due to poor strategic decisions having been made by management. Under such circumstances, the analyst must decide whether the firm is likely to recover and how long it would take to restore the firm's former competitive position. The answer to such questions requires the identification of the cause of the firm's competitive problems. Firms with competitive problems often are less profitable than key competitors or the average firm in the industry.

Therefore, the firm's recovery can be included in the forecast of cash flows by allowing its operating profit margin to increase gradually to the industry average or the level of the industry's most competitive firm. The speed of the adjustment depends on the firm's problems. For example, replacing outmoded equipment or back-office processing systems may be done more quickly than workforce reductions when the labor force is unionized or if the firm's products are obsolete.

Cyclical Firms

The projected cash flows of firms in highly cyclical industries can be distorted, depending on where the firm is in its business cycle. The most straightforward solution is to project cash flows based on an average historical growth rate during a prior full business cycle for the firm. Alternatively, if the recovery from a recession is expected to be sluggish, the analyst may extend the forecast period to as much as ten years and allow the currently depressed level of cash flow to gradually grow to its more normal historical level.

USING THE ENTERPRISE METHOD TO ESTIMATE EQUITY VALUE

A firm's common equity value often is determined by first estimating its enterprise value, adding the value of nonoperating assets, and then deducting the value of debt and other nonequity claims on future cash flows. What follows is a discussion of how to value nonequity claims and nonoperating assets. If these factors already are included in the projections of future cash flows, they should not be deducted from the firm's enterprise value. This approach is especially useful when a firm's capital structure (i.e., debt–to–total capital ratio) is expected to remain stable.

Valuing Nonequity Claims

Nonequity claims commonly include long-term debt, operating leases, deferred taxes, unfunded pension liabilities, preferred stock, employee options, and minority interests. How to value these items is discussed next.

Determining the Market Value of Long-Term Debt

The current value of a firm's debt generally is independent of its enterprise value for stable or financially healthy companies. This is not true for financially distressed or unstable firms and for hybrid securities such as convertible debt and convertible preferred stock.

Financially Stable Firms

In some instances, the analyst may not know the exact principal repayment schedule for the target firm's debt. To determine the market value of debt, treat the book value of all of the firm's debt as a conventional coupon bond, in which interest is paid annually or semiannually and the principal is repaid at maturity. The coupon is the interest on all of the firm's debt, and the principal at maturity is a weighted average of the maturity of all of the debt outstanding.

The weighted-average principal at maturity is the sum of the amount of debt outstanding for each maturity date multiplied by its share of total debt outstanding. The estimated current market value of the debt then is calculated as the sum of the annuity value of the interest expense per period plus the present value of the principal (see Exhibit 7.7).[29]

Note that the book value of debt may be used unless interest rates have changed significantly since the debt was incurred or the likelihood of default is high. In these situations, value each bond issued by the firm separately by discounting cash flows at yields to maturity for comparably rated debt with similar maturities issued by similar firms. Book value also may be used for floating rate debt, since its market value is unaffected by fluctuations in interest rates.

In the United States, the current market value of a company's debt can be determined using the FINRA TRACE database. For example, the Home Depot Inc.'s 5.40% fixed coupon bond maturing on March 1, 2016, was priced at $112.25 on September 5, 2010, or 1.1225 times par value. Multiply this number by the amount of debt outstanding, which is $3,040,000, to determine its market value of $3,412,400 on that date.

Financially Distressed Firms

Valuing debt for distressed or troubled firms is more challenging than for healthier companies. The value of the debt reflects the riskiness of the firm and fluctuates with the cash flows of the firm and will usually be a fraction of its book value. Because the debt takes on the riskiness of equity, debt and equity are not independent, and the calculation of a firm's equity value cannot be calculated by simply subtracting the market value of the firm's debt from the firm's enterprise value.

One method is to utilize scenarios as described in Chapter 8 (see Exhibit 8.11) in which the firm's enterprise value is estimated using two scenarios: one in which the firm is able to return to financial health and one in which the firm's position deteriorates. For each scenario, calculate the firm's enterprise value and deduct the book value of the firm's debt and other non-equity claims. Each scenario is weighted by the probability the analyst attaches to each scenario, such that the resulting equity value estimate represents a probability weighted average of the scenarios.

Hybrid Securities (Convertible Bonds and Preferred Stock)

Convertible bonds and stock represent conventional debt and preferred stock plus a conversion feature or call option to convert the bonds or stock to shares of common equity at a stipulated price per share. Since the value of the debt reflects the value of common equity, it is not independent of the firm's enterprise value and therefore cannot be deducted from the firm's enterprise value to estimate equity value. One approach to valuing such debt and preferred stock is to assume that all of it will be converted into equity when a target firm is acquired. This makes the most sense when the offer price for the target exceeds the price per share at which the debt can be converted. See Exhibit 9.8 in Chapter 9 for an illustration of this method.

---

[29] The only debt that must be valued is the debt outstanding on the valuation date. Future borrowing is irrelevant if we assume that cash inflows generated from investments financed with future borrowings are sufficient to satisfy interest and principal payments associated with these borrowings.

EXHIBIT 7.7 ESTIMATING THE MARKET VALUE OF A FIRM'S DEBT AND CAPITALIZED OPERATING LEASES

According to its 10K report, Gromax, Inc. has two debt issues outstanding, with a total book value of $220 million. Annual interest expense on the two issues totals $20 million. The first issue, whose current book value is $120 million, matures at the end of five years; the second issue, whose book value is $100 million, matures in ten years. The weighted average maturity of the two issues is 7.27 years (i.e., $5 \times (120/220) + 10 \times (100/220)$). The current cost of debt maturing in seven to ten years is 8.5%.

The firm's 10K also shows that the firm has annual operating lease expenses of $2.1, $2.2, $2.3, and $5 million in the fourth year and beyond (the 10K indicated the firm's cumulative value in the fourth year and beyond to be $5 million). (For our purposes, we may assume that the $5 million is paid in the fourth year.) What is the total market value of the firm's total long-term debt, including conventional debt and operating leases?

Int (Annuity value Int) + Principal Amt

$$PV_D(\text{Long-Term Debt})^a = \$20 \times \frac{[(1 - (1/(1.085)^{7.27})]}{.085} + \frac{\$220}{(1.085)^{7.27}}$$

Install $X \left(1 - \dfrac{1}{Int}\right)^{n} \Big/ Int$

$$= \$105.27 + \$121.55$$

$$= \$226.82$$

$$PV_{OL}(\text{Operating Leases}) = \frac{\$2.1}{(1.085)} + \frac{\$2.2}{(1.085)^2} + \frac{\$2.3}{(1.085)^3} + \frac{\$5.0}{(1.085)^4}$$

$$= \$1.94 + \$1.87 + \$1.80 + \$3.61$$

$$= \$9.22$$

$$PV_{TD}(\text{Total Debt}) = \$226.82 + \$9.22 = \$236.04$$

[a]The present value of debt is calculated using the PV of an annuity formula for 7.27 years and an 8.5% interest rate plus the PV of the principal repayment at the end of 7.27 years. Alternatively, rather than using the actual formulas, a present value interest factor annuity table and a present value interest factor table could have been used to calculate the PV of debt.

Determining the Market Value of Operating Leases

Both capital and operating leases also should be counted as outstanding debt of the firm. When a lease is classified as a capital lease, the present value of the lease expenses is treated as debt. Interest is imputed on this amount that corresponds to debt of comparable risk and maturity. This imputed interest is shown on the income statement. Although operating lease expenses are treated as operating expenses on the income statement, they are not counted as part of debt on the balance sheet for financial reporting purposes. For valuation purposes, operating leases should be included in debt because failure to meet lease payments results in the loss of the leased asset, which contributes to the generation of operating cash flows.

Future operating lease expenses are shown in financial statement footnotes. These future expenses should be discounted at an interest rate comparable to current bank lending rates for unsecured assets. The discount rate may be approximated using the firm's current pretax cost of debt, reflecting the market rate of interest that lessors would charge the firm. If future operating lease expenses are not available, the analyst can approximate the principal amount of the operating leases by discounting the current year's operating lease payment as a perpetuity using the firm's cost of debt (see Exhibit 7.7).

Determining the Cash Impact of Deferred Taxes

Deferred tax assets and liabilities arise when the tax treatment of an item is temporarily different from its financial accounting treatment. Deferred taxes can arise from many sources, such as uncollectible accounts receivable, warranties, options expensing, pensions, leases, net operating losses, depreciable assets, inventories, installment receivables, and intangible drilling and development costs. Deferred taxes have a current and a future or noncurrent impact on cash flow. The current impact is reflected by adding the change in deferred tax liabilities and subtracting the change in deferred tax assets in the calculation of working capital. The noncurrent impact of deferred assets generally is shown in other long-term assets and deferred tax liabilities in other long-term liabilities on the firm's balance sheet.

For example, GAAP may allow the current deduction of a $20,000 product warranty expense, reducing taxable income for reporting the firm's financial performance in the current accounting period to its shareholders. However, the tax authorities may allow only an $8,000 current tax deduction—that is, the amount actually paid by the firm during the current period to satisfy claims. The remaining $12,000 represents a balance sheet reserve set up by the firm in anticipation of future claims. Consequently, there will be a temporary difference if the tax authorities allow for the remaining $12,000 to be deducted in subsequent years. Assuming the firm's marginal tax rate is 40%, the firm would show a tax savings of $8,000 (i.e., $20,000 × 0.4) for financial reporting purposes; for tax purposes, however, tax savings would only be $3,200 (i.e., $8,000 × 0.4). Therefore, actual taxes paid during the current period are $4,800 (i.e., $8,000 – $3,200) higher than they would have been had the IRS allowed the deduction of the entire expense.

A *deferred tax asset* is a future tax benefit in that deductions not allowed in the current period may be realized in some future period. In the preceding example, the $12,000 is deductible when an equivalent amount of warranty claims are paid, resulting in future tax savings of $4,800 (i.e., 0.4 × $12,000).[30] In this instance, the deferred tax asset would equal $4,800. A *deferred tax liability* represents the increase in taxes payable in future years as a result of taxable temporary differences existing at the end of the current year. The excess of accelerated depreciation taken for tax purposes over straight-line depreciation often used for financial reporting results in a reduction in the firm's current tax liability but an increase in future tax liabilities when the rate of the firm's spending on plant and equipment slows. The amount of the deferred tax liability would equal the excess of accelerated over straight-line depreciation times the firm's marginal tax rate.

For valuation purposes, noncurrent deferred taxes may be valued separately, with deferred tax assets added to and deferred tax liabilities subtracted from the present value of the firm's operating cash flows in the estimation of the firm's equity value. Alternatively, the PV of net deferred tax liabilities (i.e., deferred tax assets less deferred tax liabilities) may be deducted from the firm's enterprise value in calculating equity value. The use of

[30] GAAP requires a firm to reduce the amount of a deferred tax asset by an offsetting valuation allowance if, based on available information, it is more likely than not that that some portion of or the entire deferred asset will not be realized.

net deferred tax liabilities is appropriate, since deferred tax liabilities generally are larger than deferred tax assets for most firms in the absence of significant NOLs.[31]

The impact of timing differences can be incorporated into present value estimates by including the impact of the factors affecting a firm's effective tax rate in projections of the individual components of cash flow.[32] Alternatively, the analyst could make assumptions about how the firm's effective tax rate will change and value current and future deferred tax liabilities separately from the calculation of the present value of the projected cash flows. As such, the impact on free cash flow of a change in deferred taxes can be approximated by the difference between a firm's marginal and effective tax rate multiplied by the firm's operating income before interest and taxes. The author recommends calculating the impact of deferred taxes separately, since they can arise from many sources.

The greatest challenge with deferred taxes is determining when they are likely to come due. The choice of tax rate in estimating future after-tax operating income has different implications under alternative scenarios. The first scenario assumes after-tax operating income is calculated using the firm's current effective tax rate indefinitely, implicitly assuming that the firm's deferred tax liabilities will never have to be repaid. In the second scenario, the analyst estimates after-tax operating income using the firm's marginal rate indefinitely, which implies that the firm cannot defer taxes beyond the current period. In the final scenario, the analyst assumes the effective tax rate is applicable for a specific number of years (e.g., five years) before reverting to the firm's marginal tax rate.

The use of the effective tax rate for five years increases the deferred tax liability to the firm during that period as long as the effective rate is below the marginal rate. The deferred tax liability at the end of the fifth year can be estimated by adding to the current cumulated deferred tax liability the incremental liability for each of the next five years. This incremental liability is the sum of projected EBIT times the difference between the marginal and effective tax rates. Assuming tax payments on the deferred tax liability at the end of the fifth year will be spread equally over the following ten years, the present value of the tax payments during that ten-year period is then estimated and discounted back to the current period (see Exhibit 7.8).

If you take the benefit in advance → Deferred Tax Liab.

---

[31] In some instances, differences between the tax liability for financial reporting and for tax purposes are permanent. Examples include nondeductible goodwill and the 50% limitation on the deductibility of meals and entertainment expenses for tax purposes. The tax treatment of goodwill depends on the expenditures that created the goodwill. If an acquisition is structured as a stock purchase (unless the parties agree to a 338 election), no amortization of goodwill is permitted under current accounting practices. If the purchase is structured as an asset purchase, goodwill is amortized over 15 years using straight-line depreciation. For financial reporting to shareholders, goodwill is not normally amortized unless the assets are viewed as impaired. When goodwill is tax deductible and is being amortized on the firm's tax return, it creates a deferred tax liability once the amortization period is up (see Chapter 12 for more details on the tax treatment of goodwill and other intangibles).

[32] Copeland et al., 2005

EXHIBIT 7.8 ESTIMATING COMMON EQUITY VALUE BY DEDUCTING THE MARKET VALUE OF DEBT, PREFERRED STOCK, AND DEFERRED TAXES FROM THE ENTERPRISE VALUE

Operating income, depreciation, working capital, and capital spending are expected to grow 10% annually during the next five years and 5% thereafter. The book value of the firm's debt is $300 million, with annual interest expense of $25 million and term to maturity of four years. The debt is a conventional "interest only" note with a repayment of principal at maturity. The firm's annual preferred dividend expense is $20 million. The prevailing market yield on preferred stock issued by similar firms is 11%. The firm does not have any operating leases, and pension and healthcare obligations are fully funded. The firm's current cost of debt is 10%. The firm's weighted-average cost of capital is 12%. Because it is already approximating the industry average, it is expected to remain at that level beyond the fifth year. Because of tax deferrals, the firm's current effective tax rate of 25% is expected to remain at that level for the next five years. The firm's current net deferred tax liability is $300 million. The projected net deferred tax liability at the end of the fifth year is expected to be paid off in ten equal amounts during the following decade. The firm's marginal tax rate is 40% and will be applied to the calculation of the terminal value. What is the value of the firm to common equity investors?

Financial Data (in $ million)

	Current Year	Year 1	Year 2	Year 3	Year 4	Year 5
EBIT	$200	$220	$242	$266.2	$292.8	$322.1
EBIT $(1-t)$	$150	$165	$181.5	$199.7	$219.6	$241.6
Depreciation (straight line)	$8	$8.8	$9.7	$10.7	$11.7	$12.9
ΔNet Working Capital	$30	$33	$36.3	$39.9	$43.9	$48.3
Gross Capital Spending	$40	$44	$48.4	$53.2	$58.6	$64.4
Free Cash Flow to the Firm	$88	$96.8	$106.5	$117.3	$128.8	$141.8

$$P_{0,\text{FCFF}}{}^a = \frac{\$88.0(1.10)}{(0.12-0.10)} \times \left\{1 - [1.10/1.12]^5\right\} + \frac{\$93.5^b \times (1.05)/(0.12-0.05)}{(1.12)^5}$$

$$= \$416.98 + \$795.81$$

$$= \$1,212.80$$

$$PV_D(\text{Debt})^c = \$25 \times \frac{[1 - (1/(1.10)^4)]}{0.10} + \frac{\$300}{1.10^4}$$

$$= \$25(3.17) + \$300(0.683)$$

$$= \$79.25 + \$204.90$$

$$= \$284.15$$

$$PV_{\text{PFD}}(\text{Preferred Stock})^d = \$20/0.11 = \$181.82$$

$$\text{Deferred Tax Liability by end of Year 5} = \$300 + (\$220 + \$242 + \$266.2 + \$292.8$$
$$+\$322.1)(0.40 - 0.25)$$

$$= \$501.47$$

$$PV_{DEF}(\text{Deferred Taxes}) = (\$501.47/10) \times \frac{[(1 - (1/(1.12)^{10})]/(1.12)^5}{0.12}$$

$$= (\$50.15 \times 5.65)/1.76$$

$$= \$160.99$$

$$P_{0,FCFE} = \$1,212.80 - \$284.15 - \$181.82 - \$160.99 = \$585.84$$

Notes:
[a]See Eq. (7.16).
[b]The terminal value reflects the recalculation of the fifth year after-tax operating income using the marginal tax rate of 40% and applying the constant-growth model. Fifth-year free cash flow equals $322.1(1 - 0.4) + \$12.9 - \$48.3 - \$64.4 = \$93.5$.
[c]The present value of debt is calculated using the PV of an annuity for four years and a 10% interest rate plus the PV of the principal repayment at the end of four years. The firm's current cost of debt of 10% is higher than the implied interest rate of 8% ($25/$300) on the loan currently on the firm's books. This suggests that the market rate of interest has increased since the firm borrowed the $300 million "interest only" note.
[d]The market value of preferred stock (PV_{PFD}) is equal to the preferred dividend divided by the cost of preferred stock.

Determining the Cash Impact of Unfunded Pension Liabilities

Publicly traded firms are required to identify the present value of their unfunded pension obligations. If not shown as a separate line item on the firm's balance sheet, they typically are shown in the company's notes to the balance sheet. If the unfunded liability is not shown explicitly in the footnote, the footnote should indicate where it has been included.

Determining the Cash Impact of Employee Options

Firms commonly offer key employees incentive compensation in the form of options to buy stock. Holders of such options have the right, but not the obligation, to buy a firm's common stock at a stipulated price (i.e., exercise price). Since such options may be exercised over a number of years, the firm's share price could eventually exceed the exercise price, making such options valuable. Exercising these options impacts cash flows as firms attempt to repurchase shares to mitigate the dilution in earnings per share and the wealth transfer from current shareholders to option holders who buy newly issued shares at a discount to the prevailing share price at the time options are exercised. Consequently, the present value of these future cash outlays to repurchase stock should be deducted from the firm's enterprise value.[33] Accounting rules require firms to report the present value of all stock options outstanding based on estimates provided by option pricing models (see Chapter 8) in the footnotes to financial statements.

---

[33] The effects of this cash outflow may be more than offset by the additional shareholder value created by the incentive of option holders to work more efficiently and to innovate more to increase the value of their options. Note also that because such options represent employee compensation, they are tax deductible for firms.

Determining the Cash Impact of Other Provisions and Contingent Liabilities

Provisions (i.e., reserves set up for anticipated charges) for future layoffs due to restructuring usually are recorded on the balance sheet in undiscounted form, since they usually represent cash outlays to be made in the near term. Such provisions should be deducted from enterprise value because they are equivalent to debt.

Contingent liabilities, whose future cash outlays depend on the occurrence of certain events, are not shown on the balance sheet but rather in footnotes. Examples include pending litigation and loan guarantees. Since such expenses are tax deductible, estimate the present value of future after-tax cash outlays discounted at the firm's cost of debt and deduct from the firm's enterprise value.

Determining the Market Value of Minority Interests

When a firm owns less than 100% of another business, it is shown on the firm's consolidated balance sheet. That portion of the business not owned by the firm is shown as a minority interest. Note that for valuation purposes the minority interest has a claim on the assets of the majority-owned subsidiary and not on the parent firm's assets. If the less than wholly-owned subsidiary is publicly traded, value the minority interest by multiplying the minority's ownership share by the market value of the subsidiary. If the subsidiary is not publicly traded and you as an investor in the subsidiary have access to its financials, value the subsidiary by discounting the subsidiary's cash flows at the cost of capital appropriate for the industry in which it competes. Alternatively, value the subsidiary using multiples of earnings or cash flow available for comparable publicly traded firms (see Chapter 8).

VALUING NONOPERATING ASSETS

Other assets not directly used in operating the firm also may contribute to the value of the firm, including such nonoperating assets as cash in excess of normal operating requirements, investments in other firms, and unused or underutilized assets. The value of such assets should be added to the value of the discounted cash flows from operating assets to determine the total value of the firm.

Cash and Marketable Securities

Cash and short-term marketable securities, held in excess of the target firm's minimum operating cash balance, represent value that should be added to the present value of net operating assets to determine the value of the firm. If a firm has cash balances in excess of those required to satisfy operating requirements at the beginning of the forecast period, the valuation approach outlined in this chapter, which focuses on cash flow generated from net operating assets, assumes implicitly that it is treated as a one-time cash payout to the target firm's shareholders. Otherwise, the excess cash should be added to the present value of the firm's operating cash flows. On an ongoing basis, projected excess cash flows are assumed implicitly to be paid out to shareholders either as dividends or share repurchases.

Note that the estimate of the firm's minimum cash balance should be used in calculating net working capital in determining free cash flow from operations.

What constitutes the minimum cash balance depends on the firm's *cash conversion cycle*. This cycle reflects the firm's tendency to build inventory, sell products on credit, and later collect accounts receivable. The delay between the investment of cash in the production of goods and the eventual receipt of cash in this process reflects the amount of cash tied up in working capital. The length of time cash is committed to working capital can be estimated as the sum of the firm's inventory conversion period plus the receivables collection period less the payables deferral period.

The inventory conversion period is the average length of time in days required to produce and sell finished goods. The receivables collection period is the average length of time in days required to collect receivables. The payables deferral period is the average length of time in days between the purchase of and payment for materials and labor. To finance this investment in working capital, a firm must maintain a minimum cash balance equal to the average number of days its cash is tied up in working capital times the average dollar value of sales per day. The inventory conversion and receivables collection periods are calculated by dividing the dollar value of inventory and receivables by average sales per day. The payments deferral period is estimated by dividing the dollar value of payables by the firm's average cost of sales per day. See Exhibit 7.9 for an illustration of how to estimate minimum and excess cash balances.

EXHIBIT 7.9 ESTIMATING MINIMUM AND EXCESS CASH BALANCES

Prototype Incorporated's current inventory, accounts receivable, and accounts payable are valued at $14 million, $6.5 million, and $6 million, respectively. Projected sales and cost of sales for the coming year total $100 million and $75 million, respectively. Moreover, the value of the firm's current cash and short-term marketable securities is $21,433,000. What minimum cash balance should the firm maintain? What is the firm's current excess cash balance?

$$\frac{\$14,000,000}{\$100,000,000/365} + \frac{\$6,500,000}{\$100,000,000/365} - \frac{\$6,000,000}{75,000,000/365} =$$

$$51.1 \text{days} \quad + \quad 23.7 \text{days} \quad - \quad 29.2 \text{days} \quad = 45.6 \text{ days}$$

Minimum Cash Balance $= 45.6$ days $\times \$100,000,000/365 = \$12,493,151$

Excess Cash Balance $= \$21,433,000 - \$12,493,151 = \$8,939,849$

While excess cash balances should be added to the present value of operating assets, any cash deficiency should be subtracted from the value of operating assets to determine the value of the firm. This reduction in the value reflects the need for the acquirer to invest additional working capital to make up any deficiency.

The method illustrated in Exhibit 7.9 may not work for firms that manage working capital aggressively, so receivables and inventory are very low relative to payables. An alternative is to compare the firm's cash and marketable securities as a percent of revenue with the industry average. If the firm's cash balance exceeds the industry average, the firm has excess cash balances, assuming there are no excess cash balances for the average firm in the industry. For example, if the industry average cash holdings as a percent of annual revenue is 5% and the target firm has 8%, the target holds excess cash equal to 3% of its annual revenue.

Investments in Other Firms

Many target firms have investments in other firms. These investments generally have value and need to be included in any valuation of the target's nonoperating assets. Such investments, for financial reporting purposes, may be classified as minority passive investments, minority active investments, or majority investments. These investments need to be valued individually and added to the present value of the firm's operating assets to determine the total value of the firm. Table 7.7 describes their accounting treatment and valuation methodology.

Unutilized and Undervalued Assets

Real estate on the books of the target firm at historical cost may have an actual market value substantially in excess of the value stated on the balance sheet. In other cases, a firm may have more assets on hand to satisfy future obligations than it currently might need (e.g., an over-funded pension fund). Examples of intangible assets include patents, copyrights, licenses,

TABLE 7.7   Investments in Other Firms

Percent Ownership of Firm	Accounting Treatment	Valuation Methodology
Minority, Passive Investments (Investment <20% of other firm)	• Assets held to maturity are carried at book value with interest or dividends shown on income statement • Investments available for sale are carried at market value, with unrealized gains/losses included as equity and not as income • Trading investments are shown at market value with unrealized gains/losses shown on the income statement[a]	• For investments recorded on investing firm's balance sheet at book value: 1. Value firm in which investment held 2. Multiply the firm's value by the proportionate share held by the investing firm to determine the investment's market value 3. Add the investment's market value to the value of the investing firm's nonoperating assets • For investments recorded at market value, add to the investing firm's nonoperating assets
Minority, Active Investments—Equity Method (Investment is between 20% and 50% of the other firm's value)	• Initial acquisition value is adjusted for proportional share of subsequent profits/losses • Market value estimated on liquidation and gain/loss reported on income statement	• Valuation Steps: 1. Value the firms in which the investments are held 2. Multiply each firm's resulting market value by the investing firm's proportionate ownership share 3. Add the resulting estimated value to the investing firm's nonoperating assets

TABLE 7.7 Cont'd

Percent Ownership of Firm	Accounting Treatment	Valuation Methodology
Majority Investments (Investment >50% of other firm's value)	• Requires consolidation of both firms' balance sheets[b] • Shares held by other investors are shown as a noncontrolling or minority interest in the shareholders' equity account of the consolidated firms' balance sheet	• If the parent owns 100% of the subsidiary, value the two on a consolidated basis[c] • If the parent owns less than 100%, value the parent and subsidiary on a consolidated basis and subtract the market value of minority interest[d]

[a] *Financial services firms may have to revalue their assets more frequently to reflect changes in their market value. Under so-called "mark to market" requirements, banks could be required to revalue their assets daily.*

[b] *A firm may be required to consolidate both firms' balance sheets even if it owns less than 50% if its ownership position gives it effective control of the other firm.*

[c] *If the subsidiary is in a different industry from the parent, a weighted-average cost of capital reflecting the different costs of capital for the two businesses should be used to discount cash flows generated by the consolidated businesses.*

[d] *If a subsidiary is valued at $500 million and the parent owns 75% of the subsidiary, the value of the subsidiary to the parent is $375 million (i.e., $500 million − 0.25 × $500 million to reflect the value owned by minority shareholders).*

and trade names. Intangible assets may represent significant sources of value on a target firm's balance sheet. However, they tend to be difficult to value. There is evidence that the value of intangible spending, such as R&D expenditures, is indeed factored into a firm's current share price.[34] Despite this evidence, it is doubtful that the value of intellectual property rights, such as patents, which a firm may hold but not currently use, is reflected fully in the firm's current share price. In the absence of a predictable cash-flow stream, their value may be estimated using the Black–Scholes model (see Chapter 8) or the cost of developing comparable inventions or technologies.

Patents

How patents are valued depends on whether they have current applications, are linked to existing products or services, or can be grouped and treated as a single patent portfolio. Many firms have patents for which no current application within the firm has yet been identified. However, the patent may have value to an external party. Before closing, the buyer and seller may negotiate a value for a patent that has not yet been licensed to a third party based on the cash flows that can reasonably be expected to be generated over its future life. In cases where the patent has been licensed to third parties, the valuation is based on the expected future royalties to be received from licensing the patent over its remaining life.

When a patent is linked to a specific product, it is normally valued based on the "cost avoidance" method. This method uses after-tax market-based royalty rates paid on comparable patents multiplied by the projected future stream of revenue from the products whose production depends on the patent discounted to its present value at the cost of capital.

Products and services often depend on a number of patents. This makes it exceedingly difficult to determine the amount of the cash flow generated by the sale of the products or

[34] Chan, Lakonishok, and Sougiannis, 1999

services to be allocated to each patent. In this case, the patents are grouped together as a single portfolio and valued as a group using a single royalty rate applied to a declining percentage of the company's future revenue. The declining percentage of revenue reflects the likely diminishing value of the patents with the passage of time. This cash-flow stream is then discounted to its present value.

Trademarks and Service Marks

A trademark is the right to use a name associated with a company, product, or concept. A service mark is the right to use an image associated with a company, product, or concept. Trademarks and service marks have recognition value. Examples include Bayer Aspirin and Kellogg's Corn Flakes. Name recognition reflects the firm's longevity, cumulative advertising expenditures, the overall effectiveness of its marketing programs, and the consistency of perceived product quality. The cost avoidance approach,[35] the PV of projected license fees,[36] or the use of recent transactions can be helpful in estimating a trademark's value.

Overfunded Pension Plans

Defined benefit pension plans require firms to accumulate financial assets to enable them to satisfy estimated future employee pension payments. During periods of rising stock markets, such as during the 1990s, firms with defined benefit pension plans routinely accumulated assets in excess of the amount required to meet expected obligations. As owners of the firm, shareholders have the legal right to these excess assets. In practice, if such funds are liquidated and paid out to shareholders, the firm has to pay taxes on the pretax value of these excess assets. Therefore, the after-tax value of such funds may be added to the present value of projected operating cash flows.

PUTTING IT ALL TOGETHER

Table 7.8 shows how Home Depot's equity value is estimated by first determining the firm's total operating value, adding the value of nonoperating assets to derive enterprise value, and subtracting the value of all nonequity claims to calculate equity value. Home Depot is the largest home improvement materials retailer in the United States.

---

[35] The underlying assumption in applying the cost-avoidance approach to the valuation of trademarks and service marks is that cumulative advertising and promotion campaigns build brand recognition. The initial outlays for promotional campaigns are the largest and tend to decline as a percentage of sales over time as the brand becomes more recognizable. Consequently, the valuation of a trademark associated with a specific product or business involves multiplying projected revenues by a declining percentage to reflect the reduced level of spending, as a percentage of sales, required to maintain brand recognition. These projected expenditures then are adjusted for taxes (because marketing expenses are tax deductible) and discounted to the present at the acquiring firm's cost of capital.

[36] Companies may license the right to use a trademark or service mark. The acquiring company may apply the license rate required to obtain the rights to comparable trademarks and service marks to a percentage of the cash flows that reasonably can be expected to be generated by selling the products or services under the licensed trademark or service mark. The resulting cash flows then are discounted to the present using the acquirer's cost of capital. Alternatively, a value may be determined by examining recent outright purchases of comparable trademarks or, in the case of the Internet, Web addresses or domain names.

TABLE 7.8 Determining Home Depot's Equity Value Using the Enterprise Method

| | History | | Projections | | | | | | | | | |
Assumptions	2008	2009	2010	2011	2012	2013	2014	2015	2016	2017	2018	2019
Net Sales Growth Rate %	-0.078	-0.072	-0.040	0.010	0.020	0.040	0.050	0.050	0.040	0.040	0.035	0.030
Operating Profit Margin %	0.061	0.073	0.070	0.065	0.068	0.070	0.072	0.075	0.075	0.078	0.080	0.080
Depreciation Expenditure % of Sales	0.026	0.025	0.025	0.025	0.025	0.025	0.025	0.025	0.025	0.025	0.025	0.025
Effective Tax Rate %	0.356	0.342	0.340	0.340	0.340	0.340	0.340	0.340	0.340	0.340	0.340	0.340
Marginal Tax Rate %			0.400	0.400	0.400	0.400	0.400	0.400	0.400	0.400	0.400	0.400
Working Capital % of Sales	0.048	0.057	0.060	0.060	0.060	0.060	0.060	0.060	0.060	0.060	0.060	0.060
Gross P&E % of Sales	0.049	0.026	0.035	0.035	0.035	0.035	0.035	0.035	0.035	0.035	0.035	0.035
WACC (2010–2019) %[a]			0.073									
WACC Terminal Period %			0.070									
Terminal Period Growth Rate %			0.030									
Valuation ($ million)												
Net Sales	71,288	66,176	63,529	64,164	65,448	68,065	71,469	75,042	78,044	81,166	84,006	86,527
Operating Income (EBIT)	4,359	4,803	4,447	4,171	4,450	4,765	5,146	5,628	5,853	6,331	6,721	6,922
Plus: Operating Lease Expense			802	717	640	584	535	535	535	535	535	535
Less: Operating Lease Depreciation[b]			258	258	258	258	258	258	258	258	258	258
Equals: Adjusted EBIT			4,991	4,630	4,832	5,091	5,423	5,905	6,130	6,608	6,998	7,199
Adjusted EBIT(1 – t)			3,294	3,056	3,189	3,360	3,579	3,897	4,046	4,361	4,618	4,751
Plus: Depreciation & Amortization	1,785	1,707	1,906	1,925	1,963	2,042	2,144	2,251	2,341	2,435	2,520	2,596
Minus: Δ Net Working Capital[c]		1,328	275	38	77	157	204	214	180	187	170	151
Minus: Gross P&E Expenditure	1,847	966	2,224	2,246	2,291	2,382	2,501	2,626	2,732	2,841	2,940	3,028
Equals: Enterprise Cash Flow[d]			2,702	2,697	2,785	2,862	3,017	3,308	3,476	3,768	4,028	4,168

Continued

TABLE 7.8 Determining Home Depot's Equity Value Using the Enterprise Method—Cont'd

Assumptions	History		Projections								
	2008	2009	2010	2011	2012	2013	2014	2015	2016	2017	2018	2019
PV (2010–2019)			22,048									
Terminal Value			47,638									
Total Operating Value			69,686									
Plus:												
Excess Cash[e]			0									
Other Long-Term Assets[f]			256									
Equals: Enterprise Value			69,942									
Less:												
Market Value of Debt[g]			9,469									
Capitalized Operating Leases			6,450									
PV Net Noncurrent DTLs[h]			1,102									
Stock Options			158									
Equals: Equity Value			52,763									
Number of Shares (Millions)			1,683									
Equity Value Per Share			$31.35									

Explanatory Notes

[a]WACC calculation:

$k_e = 0.0265 + 1.10 (0.055) = 8.43\%$, where 2.65% is the ten-year Treasury bond rate on September 5, 2010, and 1.21 is the firm's beta provided by Yahoo! Finance/Capital IQ.

$I = 6.85\%$, pretax cost of debt estimated as the yield to maturity on BBB+ rated debt per Yahoo! Finance on 9/5/2010. Weights for debt and equity of 31% and 69%, respectively, are based on firm's current debt-to-capital ratio held constant throughout the forecast period.

$WACC = 8.70 \times 0.69 + 6.85 (1 - 0.4) \times 0.31 = 7.28$

WACC for terminal period equal to average for comparable retail companies per Yahoo! Finance.

[b]Operating Leases:

Capitalized value of operating leases = PV of lease expense provided in financial statement footnotes discounted at firm's cost of debt. Operating lease equipment estimated useful life = 25 years; estimated annual operating lease depreciation expense = $6.450/25 = $258.

[c]Working Capital $3,537 $3,812 $3,850 $3,927 $4,084 $4,288 $4,503 $4,683 $4,870 $5,040 $5,192.

[d]Terminal period enterprise cash flow recalculated using 40% marginal tax rate.

[e]Excess cash is zero, since minimum balances estimated using Exhibit 7.9 method exceed actual year-end 2009 cash balances.

[f]Excludes goodwill but includes $33 million in notes receivable.

ᵍMarket Value of Home Depot Debt:

Coupon	Maturity Date	Face Value (000)		Percent of Par Value (9/5/10)	Market Value
5.20%	March 2011	$1,000,000	×	1.02630	$1,026,300
6.19%	March 2012	$40,000	×	1.03366	$41,346
6.74%	May 2013	$14,285	×	1.03650	$14,806
5.25%	December 2013	$1,258,000	×	1.02630	$1,291,085
5.88%	December 2036	$2,960,000	×	1.10650	$3,275,240
5.40%	March 2016	$3,040,000	×	1.12250	$3,412,400

Capitalized Leases (payments vary from 2010 through 2056) | | | | | $408,000

Total Long-Term Debt | | | | | $9,469,177

ʰ PV of Net Noncurrent DTLs (Net Deferred Tax Assets – Deferred Tax Liabilities) Calculation:

Future Value as of 2019 = $3,570 Adds current net deferred tax liability to the sum of the projected EBIT times the difference between marginal and effective tax rates.

Present Value = $1,102 2019 net deferred tax liability paid off in equal amounts during following decade.

The exhibit is divided into three panels. The top panel displays the primary assumptions underlying the valuation. The second panel shows how the total operating value of the firm is determined. The bottom panel—"Explanatory Notes"—provides details on how various line items in the exhibit were calculated. Cash flow is projected for ten years, reflecting the anticipated slow recovery of the firm's free cash flow from the 2008–2009 recession. The actual formula used to construct the Excel-based model underlying this exhibit is provided in an Excel file entitled "Determining Home Depot's Equity Value Using the Enterprise Method" on the companion site to this book.

SOME THINGS TO REMEMBER

Value is created for shareholders when firms invest capital that generates future cash flows at financial returns exceeding their cost of capital. Therefore, firms earning financial returns in excess of their cost of capital should focus on growth, while those earning less than their cost of capital should concentrate on improving their returns.

Discounted-cash-flow methods such as the zero-, constant-, and variable-growth methods are widely used to estimate the value of the firm. GAAP-based cash flows must be adjusted to create valuation cash flows for this purpose. Such cash flows include FCFF or enterprise cash flow, cash available for investors and lenders, which reflects cash from operating and investing activities. Alternatively, FCFE, free cash flow to equity investors or equity cash flow, includes cash from operating, investing, and financing activities. The present value of enterprise cash flows often is referred to as the enterprise value of the firm. Valuation estimates based on equity cash flows are called the equity value. A common technique for estimating equity value is to deduct the market value of the target firm's debt and other nonequity claims from its enterprise value.

DISCUSSION QUESTIONS

7.1. What is the significance of the weighted-average cost of capital? How is it calculated? Do the weights reflect the firm's actual or target debt–to–total capital ratio? Explain your answer.

7.2. What does a firm's β measure? What is the difference between an unlevered and levered β? Why is this distinction significant?

7.3. Under what circumstances is it important to adjust the capital asset pricing model for firm size? Why?

7.4. What are the primary differences between FCFE and FCFF?

7.5. Explain the conditions under which it makes the most sense to use the zero-growth and constant-growth DCF models. Be specific.

7.6. Which DCF valuation methods require the estimation of a terminal value? Why?

7.7. Do small changes in the assumptions pertaining to the estimation of the terminal value have a significant impact on the calculation of the total value of the target firm? If so, why?

7.8. How would you estimate the equity value of a firm if you knew its enterprise value and the present value of all nonoperating assets, nonoperating liabilities, and long-term debt?

7.9. Why is it important to distinguish between operating and nonoperating assets and liabilities when valuing a firm? Be specific.

7.10. Explain how you would value a patent under the following situations: a patent with no current application, a patent linked to an existing product, and a patent portfolio.

Answers to these Chapter Discussion Questions are available in the Online Instructor's Manual for instructors using this book.

Practice Problems and Answers

7.11. ABC Incorporated shares are currently trading for $32 per share. The firm has 1.13 billion shares outstanding. In addition, the market value of the firm's outstanding debt is $2 billion. The ten-year Treasury bond rate is 6.25%. ABC has an outstanding credit record and earned a AAA rating from the major credit rating agencies. The current interest rate on AAA corporate bonds is 6.45%. The historical risk premium over the risk-free rate of return is 5.5 percentage points. The firm's beta is estimated to be 1.1, and its marginal tax rate, including federal, state, and local taxes, is 40%.

a. What is the cost of equity?

b. What is the after-tax cost of debt?

c. What is the weighted average cost of capital?

Answers:

a. 12.3%

b. 3.9%

c. 11.9%

7.12 HiFlyer Corporation does not currently have any debt. Its tax rate is 0.4 and its unlevered beta is estimated by examining comparable companies to be 2.0. The ten-year bond rate is 6.25%, and the historical risk premium over the risk-free rate is 5.5%. Next year, HiFlyer expects to borrow up to 75% of its equity value to fund future growth.

a. Calculate the firm's current cost of equity.

b. Estimate the firm's cost of equity after the firm increases its leverage to 75% of equity.

Answers:

a. 17.25%

b. 22.2%

[handwritten annotations in right margin:] D/E 75% eq / equity / So Debt = 75 / Equity = 100.

[handwritten annotations:] $(6.25 + 2 \times 5.5)$ $\beta_{Lev} = 2\left(1 + 0.6 \times \frac{75}{100} \frac{D}{E}\right) = 6.25 + 2.9 \times 5.5$

7.13. Abbreviated financial statements are given for Fletcher Corporation in Table 7.9. Year-end working capital in 2009 was $160 million, and the firm's marginal tax rate was 40% in both 2010 and 2011. Estimate the following for 2010 and 2011:

a. Free cash flow to equity

b. Free cash flow to the firm

Answers:

a. $16.4 million in 2010 and −$26.8 million in 2011

b. $44.4 million in 2010 and $1.2 million in 2011

7.14. In 2011, No Growth Incorporated had operating income before interest and taxes of $220 million. The firm was expected to generate this level of operating income indefinitely. The firm had depreciation expense of $10 million that year. Capital spending totaled $20 million during 2011. At the end of 2010 and 2011, working capital totaled $70 million and $80 million, respectively. The firm's combined marginal state, local, and federal tax rate was 40%, and its outstanding debt had a market value of $1.2 billion. The ten-year Treasury bond rate is 5%, and

TABLE 7.9   Abbreviated Financial Statements for Fletcher Corporation ($ million)

	2010	2011
Revenues	$600	$690
Operating expenses	520	600
Depreciation	16	18
Earnings before interest and taxes	64	72
Less interest expense	5	5
Less taxes	23.6	26.8
Equals: net income	35.4	40.2
Addendum		
Year-end working capital	150	200
Principal repayment	25	25
Capital expenditures	20	10

the borrowing rate for companies exhibiting levels of creditworthiness similar to No Growth is 7%. The historical risk premium for stocks over the risk-free rate of return is 5.5%. No Growth's beta was estimated to be 1.0. The firm had 2.5 million common shares outstanding at the end of 2011. No Growth's target debt–to–total capital ratio is 30%.

a. Estimate free cash flow to the firm in 2011.
b. Estimate the firm's weighted average cost of capital.
c. Estimate the enterprise value of the firm at the end of 2011, assuming that it will generate the value of free cash flow estimated in (a) indefinitely.
d. Estimate the value of the equity of the firm at the end of 2011.
e. Estimate the value per share at the end of 2011.

Answers:
a. $112 million $\quad 220x(1-0.4)+10-10-20 \qquad (5+\frac{10.5}{1x5.5}, \frac{4.2}{7x06})$
 $\qquad\qquad\qquad 10.5 \times 0.7 + 4.2 \times 0.3$
b. 8.61%
c. $1,300.8 million $112/8.61\%$
d. $100.8 million $FCFF - Mkt$ sale of $Debt = 1300.8 - 1200 = 100.8$
e. $40.33 $(100.8/2.5)$ value of $Eq/\#$ of shs o/s.

7.15. Carlisle Enterprises, a specialty pharmaceutical manufacturer, has been losing market share for three years because several key patents have expired. Free cash flow to the firm is expected to decline rapidly as more competitive generic drugs enter the market. Projected cash flows for the next 5 years are $8.5 million, $7 million, $5 million, $2 million, and $0.5 million. Cash flow after the fifth year is expected to be negligible. The firm's board has decided to sell the firm to a larger pharmaceutical company that is interested in using Carlisle's product offering to fill gaps in its own product line until it can develop similar drugs. Carlisle's WACC is 15%. What purchase price must Carlisle obtain to earn its cost of capital? *Answer:* $17.4 million

7.16. Ergo Unlimited's current year's free cash flow to equity is $10 million. It is projected to grow at 20% per year for the next five years. It is expected to grow at a more modest 5% beyond the fifth year. The firm estimates that its cost of equity will be 12% during the next five years and then will drop to 10% beyond the fifth year as the business matures. Estimate the firm's current market value.

Answer: $358.3 million

7.17. In the year in which it intends to go public, a firm has revenues of $20 million and net income after taxes of $2 million. The firm has no debt, and revenue is expected to grow at 20% annually for the next five years and 5% annually thereafter. Net profit margins are expected to remain constant throughout. Annual capital expenditures equal depreciation, and the change in working capital requirements is minimal. The average beta of a publicly traded company in this industry is 1.50 and the average debt-to-equity ratio is 20%. The firm is managed conservatively and will not borrow through the foreseeable future. The Treasury bond rate is 6%, and the marginal tax rate is 40%. The normal spread between the return on stocks and the risk-free rate of return is believed to be 5.5%. Reflecting the slower growth rate in the sixth year and beyond, the discount rate is expected to decline to the industry average cost of capital of 10.4%. Estimate the value of the firm's equity.

Answer: $63.41 million

7.18. The information in Table 7.10 is available for two different common stocks: Company A and Company B.

a. Estimate the cost of equity for each firm.

b. Assume that the companies' growth rates will continue at the same rate indefinitely. Estimate the per share value of each company's common stock.

Answers:

a. Company A = 15.45%; Company B = 12.2%

b. Company A = $13.42; Company B = $61.00

7.19. You have been asked to estimate the beta of a high-technology firm that has three divisions with the characteristics shown in Table 7.11.

a. What is the beta of the equity of the firm?

b. If the risk-free return is 5% and the spread between the return on all stocks is 5.5%, estimate the cost of equity for the software division.

c. What is the cost of equity for the entire firm?

TABLE 7.10 Common Stocks in Problem 7.18

	Company A	Company B
Free cash flow per-share at the end of year 1	$1.00	$5.00
Growth rate in cash flow per share	8%	4%
Beta	1.3	0.8
Risk-free return	7%	7%
Expected return on all stocks	13.5%	13.5%

III. MERGER AND ACQUISITION CASH FLOW VALUATION

TABLE 7.11   High-Technology Company in Problem 7.19

Division	Beta	Market Value ($ million)
Personal computers	1.60	100
Software	2.00	150
Computer mainframes	1.20	250

d. Free cash flow to equity investors in the current year (FCFE) for the entire firm is $7.4 million and for the software division is $3.1 million. If the total firm and the software division are expected to grow at the same 8% rate into the foreseeable future, estimate the market value of the firm and of the software division.

Answers:

a. 1.52

b. 16%

c. 13.4%

d. PV (total firm) = $147.96; PV (software division) = $41.88

7.20 Financial Corporation wants to acquire Great Western Inc. Financial has estimated the enterprise value of Great Western at $104 million. The market value of Great Western's long-term debt is $15 million, and cash balances in excess of the firm's normal working capital requirements are $3 million. Financial estimates the present value of certain licenses that Great Western is not currently using to be $4 million. Great Western is the defendant in several outstanding lawsuits. Financial Corporation's legal department estimates the potential future cost of this litigation to be $3 million, with an estimated present value of $2.5 million. Great Western has 2 million common shares outstanding. What is the adjusted equity value of Great Western per common share?

Answer: $46.75/share

Answers to these Practice Problems are available in the Online Instructor's Manual for instructors using this book.

CHAPTER BUSINESS CASES

CASE STUDY 7.1
Hewlett-Packard Outbids Dell Computer to Acquire 3PAR

On September 2, 2010, a little more than two weeks after Dell's initial bid for 3PAR, Dell Computer withdrew from a bidding war with Hewlett-Packard when HP announced that it had raised its previous offer by 10% to $33 a share. Dell's last bid had been for $32 per share, which had trumped HP's previous bid the day before of $30 per share. The final HP bid valued 3PAR at $2.1 billion versus Dell's original offer of $1.1 billion.

3Par was sought after due to the growing acceptance of its storage product technology in the emerging "cloud computing" market. 3PAR's storage products enable firms to store and manage their data more efficiently at geographically remote data centers accessible through the Internet. While 3Par has been a consistent money loser, its revenues had been growing at more than 50% annually since it went public in 2007. The deal valued 3Par at 12.5 times 2009 sales in an industry that has rarely spent more than 5 times sales to acquire companies. HP's motivation for its rich bid seems to have been a bet on a fast-growing technology that could help energize the firm's growth. While impressive at $115 billion in annual revenues and $7.7 billion in net income in 2009, the firm's revenue and earnings has slowed due to the 2008–2009 global recession and the maturing personal computer market.

Table 7.12 provides selected financial data on 3PAR and a set of valuation assumptions. Note that HP's marginal tax rate is used rather than 3PAR's much lower effective tax rate to reflect potential tax savings to HP from 3PAR's cumulative operating losses. Given HP's $10 billion plus pretax profit, HP is expected to fully utilize 3PAR's deferred tax assets in the current tax year. The continued 3PAR high sales growth rate reflects the HP expectation that its extensive global sales force can expand the sale of 3PAR products.

To support further development of the 3PAR products, the valuation assumptions reflect an increase in plant and equipment spending in excess of depreciation and amortization through 2015; however, beyond 2015, capital spending is expected to grow at the same rate as depreciation as the business moves from a growth to a maintenance mode. 3PAR's operating margin is expected to show a slow recovery, reflecting the impact of escalating marketing expenses and the cost of training the HP sales force in the promotion of the 3PAR technology.

Discussion Questions

1. Estimate 3PAR's equity value per share based on the assumptions and selected 3PAR data provided in Table 7.12.
2. Why is it appropriate to utilize at least a ten-year annual time horizon before estimating a terminal value in valuing firm's such as 3PAR?
3. What portion of the purchase price can be financed by 3PAR's nonoperating assets?
4. Does the deal still make sense to HP if the terminal period growth rate is 3% rather than 5%? Explain your answer.

Answers to these questions are found in the Online Instructor's Manual available to instructors using this book.

TABLE 7.12 3PAR Valuation Assumptions and Selected Historical Data

Assumptions	History		Projections								
	2009	2010	2011	2012	2013	2014	2015	2016	2017	2018	2019
Sales Growth Rate %	0.508	0.450	0.400	0.400	0.400	0.350	0.300	0.250	0.200	0.100	0.100
Operating Margin % of Sales	-0.020	-0.010	-0.010	0.020	0.040	0.080	0.100	0.120	0.150	0.150	0.150
Depreciation Expense % of Sales	0.036	0.034	0.060	0.060	0.060	0.060	0.060	0.070	0.070	0.070	0.060
Marginal Tax Rate %		0.400	0.400	0.400	0.400	0.400	0.400	0.400	0.400	0.400	0.400
Working Capital % of Sales	0.104	0.114	0.100	0.100	0.100	0.100	0.100	0.100	0.100	0.100	0.100
Gross P&E % of Sales	0.087	0.050	0.080	0.080	0.080	0.080	0.080	0.070	0.070	0.060	0.060
WACC (2010–2019) %		0.093									
WACC (Terminal Period) %		0.085									
Terminal Period Growth Rate %		0.050									
Working Capital ($ Million)	112.8	126.4									
Total Cash ($ Million)	103.7	111.2									
Minimum Cash (5% of Sales)	8.4	12.65									
W Cap Excluding Excess Cash	17.5	27.85									
Selected Financial Data ($ Million)											
Sales	168										
Depreciation Expense & Amortization	6.1										
Gross Plant & Equipment	14.6										
Excess Cash	98.55										
Deferred Tax Assets	73.1										
PV of Operating Leases	22.0										
Number of Shares Outstanding	61.8										

CASE STUDY 7.2
Creating a Global Luxury Hotel Chain

Fairmont Hotels & Resorts Inc. announced on January 30, 2006, that it had agreed to be acquired by Kingdom Hotels and Colony Capital in an all-cash transaction valued at $45 per share. The transaction is valued at $3.9 billion, including assumed debt. The purchase price represents a 28% premium over Fairmont's closing price on November 4, 2005, the last day of trading when Kingdom and Colony expressed interest in Fairmont. The combination of Fairmont and Kingdom will create a luxury global hotel chain with 120 hotels in 24 countries. Discounted cash-flow analyses, including estimated synergies and terminal value, value the firm at $43.10 per share. The net asset value of Fairmont's real estate is believed to be $46.70 per share.

Discussion Questions

1. Is it reasonable to assume that the acquirer could actually be getting the operation for "free," since the value of the real estate per share is worth more than the purchase price per share? Explain your answer.
2. Assume the acquirer divests all of Fairmont's hotels and real estate properties but continues to manage the hotels and properties under long-term management contracts. How would you estimate the net present value of the acquisition of Fairmont to the acquirer? Explain your answer.

Answers to these questions are found in the Online Instructor's Manual available to instructors using this book.

CHAPTER

8

Applying Relative, Asset-Oriented, and Real-Option Valuation Methods to Mergers and Acquisitions

Most people are about as happy as they make up their minds to be. —**Abraham Lincoln**

INSIDE M&A: A REAL-OPTIONS PERSPECTIVE ON MICROSOFT'S DEALINGS WITH YAHOO!

In a bold move to transform two relatively weak online search businesses into a competitor capable of challenging market leader Google, Microsoft proposed to buy Yahoo! for $44.6 billion on February 2, 2008. At $31 per share in cash and stock, the offer represented a 62% premium over Yahoo!'s prior day closing price. Despite boosting its bid to $33 per share to offset a decline in the value of Microsoft's share price following the initial offer, Microsoft was rebuffed by Yahoo!'s board and management. In early May of 2008, Microsoft withdrew its bid to buy the entire firm and substituted an offer to acquire the search business only. Incensed at Yahoo!'s refusal to accept the Microsoft bid, activist shareholder Carl Icahn initiated an unsuccessful proxy fight to replace the Yahoo! board. Throughout this entire melodrama, critics continued to ask how Microsoft could justify an offer valued at $44.6 billion when the market prior to the announcement had valued Yahoo! at only $27.5 billion.

Microsoft could have continued to slug it out with Yahoo! and Google as it had been for the last five years, but this would have given Google more time to consolidate its leadership position. Despite having spent billions of dollars on Microsoft's online service (Microsoft Network, or MSN) in recent years, the business remains a money loser (with losses exceeding one-half billion dollars in 2007). Furthermore, MSN accounted for only 5% of the firm's total revenue at that time.

Microsoft argued that its share of the online Internet search (i.e., ads appearing with search results) and display (i.e., website banner ads) advertising markets would be dramatically increased by combining Yahoo! with MSN. Yahoo! also is the leading consumer e-mail service. Anticipated cost savings from combining the two businesses were expected to reach $1 billion annually. Longer term, Microsoft expected to bundle search and advertising capabilities into the Windows operating system to increase the usage of the combined firms' online services by offering compatible new products and enhanced search capabilities.

The two firms have very different cultures. The iconic Silicon Valley–based Yahoo! often is characterized as a company with a freewheeling, fun-loving culture, potentially incompatible with Microsoft's more structured and disciplined environment. Melding or eliminating overlapping businesses represents a potentially mind-numbing effort given the diversity and complexity of the numerous sites available. To achieve the projected cost savings, Microsoft would have to choose which of the businesses and technologies would survive. Moreover, the software driving all of these sites and services is largely incompatible.

As an independent, or stand-alone, business, the market valued Yahoo! at approximately $17 billion less than Microsoft's valuation. Microsoft was valuing Yahoo! based on its intrinsic stand-alone value plus perceived synergy resulting from combining Yahoo! and MSN. Standard discounted-cash-flow analysis assumes implicitly that once Microsoft makes an investment decision, it cannot change its mind. In reality, once an investment decision is made, management often has a number of opportunities to make future decisions based on the outcome of things that are currently uncertain. These opportunities, or real options, include the decision to expand (i.e., accelerate investment at a later date), delay the initial investment, or abandon an investment. With respect to Microsoft's effort to acquire Yahoo!, the major uncertainties dealt with the actual timing of an acquisition and whether the two businesses could be integrated successfully. For Microsoft's attempted takeover of Yahoo!, such options included the following:

Base case. Buy 100% of Yahoo! immediately.

Option to expand. If Yahoo! accepts the bid, accelerate investment in new products and services contingent on the successful integration of Yahoo! and MSN.

Option to delay. (1) Temporarily walk away, keeping open the possibility of returning for 100% of Yahoo! if circumstances change; (2) offer to buy only the search business with the intent of purchasing the remainder of Yahoo! at a later date; or (3) enter into a search partnership, with an option to buy at a later date.

Option to abandon. If Yahoo! accepts the bid, spin off or divest combined Yahoo!/MSN if integration is unsuccessful.

The decision tree in Figure 8.1 illustrates the range of real options (albeit an incomplete list) available to the Microsoft board at the time of its offer. Each branch of the tree represents a specific option. The decision tree framework is helpful in depicting the significant flexibility that senior management often has in changing an existing investment decision at some point in the future.

With neither party making headway against Google, Microsoft again approached Yahoo! in mid-2009, which resulted in an announcement in early 2010 of an Internet search agreement between the two firms. Yahoo! transferred control of its Internet search technology to Microsoft in an attempt to boost its sagging profits. Microsoft is relying on a ten-year arrangement with Yahoo! to help counter the dominance of Google in the Internet search market. Both firms hope to be able to attract more advertising dollars paid by firms willing to pay for links on the firms' sites. (See Chapter 14's *Inside M&A* case study for more details about this partnership.)

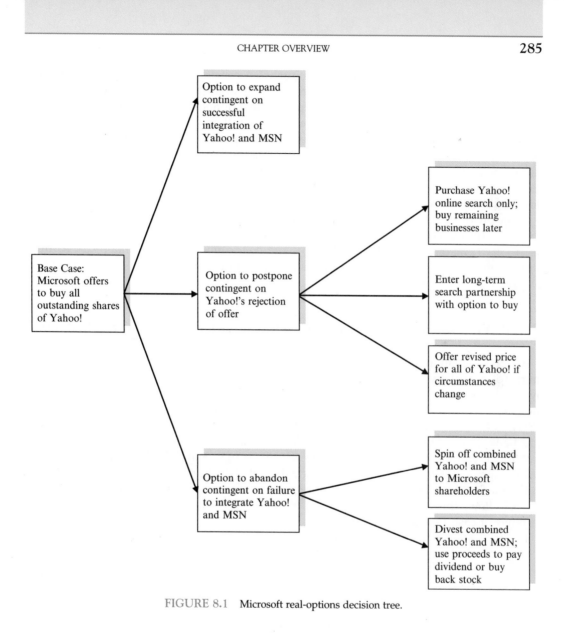

FIGURE 8.1   Microsoft real-options decision tree.

CHAPTER OVERVIEW

Chapter 7 discussed in detail how DCF analysis is applied to M&A valuation. This chapter addresses alternative methods of valuation. These methods include relative-valuation (i.e., market-based) methods, asset-oriented methods, real-options analysis (i.e., contingent claims), and replacement cost. Relative-valuation methods include comparable company, comparable transactions, comparable industry techniques, and value-driver-based valuation. Asset-oriented methods include tangible book value and liquidation- or breakup-valuation techniques.

The chapter discusses in detail how to look at M&A valuation in the context of real options. This involves identifying preclosing and postclosing strategic and tactical alternatives and associated risks available to M&A participants. Real-options valuation is illustrated both in the context of a decision tree framework and as call and put options, when the assets underlying the option exhibit the characteristics of financial options. A weighted-average valuation approach, which attempts to incorporate the analyst's relative confidence in the various valuation methods, also is discussed. The chapter concludes with a summary of the strengths and weaknesses of alternative valuation methods (including discounted cash flow) and when it is appropriate to apply each methodology.

A review of this chapter (including additional practice problems with solutions) is available in the file folder entitled "Student Study Guide" on the companion site to this book (*www. elsevierdirect.com/companions/9780123854858*). The companion site also contains a Learning Interactions Library, which gives students the opportunity to test their knowledge of this chapter in a "real-time" environment.

APPLYING RELATIVE-VALUATION (MARKET-BASED) METHODS

Relative valuation involves valuing assets based on how similar assets are valued in the marketplace. Relative-valuation methods assume a firm's market value can be approximated by a value indicator for comparable companies, comparable transactions, or comparable industry averages. Value indicators could include the firm's earnings, operating cash flow, EBITDA (i.e., earnings before interest and taxes, depreciation, and amortization), sales, and book value. This approach often is described as market based, since it reflects the amounts investors are willing to pay for each dollar of earnings, cash flow, sales, or book value at a moment in time. As such, it reflects theoretically the collective wisdom of investors in the marketplace. Because of the requirement for positive current or near-term earnings or cash flow, this approach is meaningful only for companies with a positive, stable earnings or cash-flow stream.

If comparable companies are available, the market value of a target firm T (MV_T) can be estimated by solving the following equation:

$$MV_T = (MV_C/VI_C) \times VI_T \qquad (8.1)$$

where

MV_C = market value of the comparable company C
VI_C = value indicator for the comparable company C
VI_T = value indicator for firm T
(MV_C/VI_C) = market value multiple for the comparable company

For example, if the P/E ratio for the comparable firm is equal to 10 (MV_C/VI_C) and the after-tax earnings of the target firm are $2 million ($VI_T$), the market value of the target firm at that moment in time is $20 million ($MV_T$). Relative-value methods are used widely for three reasons. First, such methods are relatively simple to calculate and require far fewer assumptions than discounted-cash-flow techniques. Second, relative valuation is easier to explain than are DCF methods. Finally, the use of market-based techniques is more likely to reflect current market demand and supply conditions. The relationship expressed in Eq. (8.1) can be used to estimate the value of the target firm in all of the relative-valuation and asset-oriented methods discussed in this chapter.

The analyst must be careful to follow certain guidelines in applying relative-valuation methods. First, when using multiples (i.e., MV_C/VI_C), it is critical to ensure that the multiple is defined in the same way for all comparable firms. For example, in using a price-to-earnings ratio, earnings may be defined as trailing (i.e., prior), current, or projected. Whichever way earnings are defined, the definition must be applied consistently to all firms in the sample. Also, the numerator and the denominator of the multiple must be defined in the same way. If the numerator in the price-to-earnings ratio is defined as price per share, the denominator also must be calculated as earnings per share. Second, the analyst must examine the distribution of the multiples of the firms being compared and eliminate outliers. Outliers are those whose values are substantially different from others in the sample. Failure to do so can distort the average or median of the sample.[1]

The Comparable Companies Method

Applying the comparable companies approach requires that the analyst identify companies that are substantially similar to the target firm. Generally speaking, a comparable firm is one whose profitability, potential growth rate in earnings or cash flows, and perceived risk are similar to those of the firm to be valued. By defining comparable companies broadly, it is possible to utilize firms in other industries. As such, a computer hardware manufacturer can be compared to a telecommunications firm as long as they are comparable in terms of profitability, growth, and risk. Consequently, if the firm to be valued has a 15% return on equity (i.e., profitability),[2] expected earnings or cash-flow growth rates of 10% annually (i.e., growth), and a beta of 1.3 or debt to equity ratio of 1 (i.e., risk), the analyst must find a firm with similar characteristics in either the same industry or another industry. In practice, analysts often look for comparable firms in the same industry and that are similar in terms of such things as markets served, product offering, degree of leverage, and size.[3]

To determine if the firms you have selected are truly comparable, estimate the correlation between the operating income or revenue of the firm to be valued and the comparable firms. If the correlation is positive and high, the firms are comparable. Similarly, if the firm has multiple product lines, collect comparable firms for each product line and estimate the degree of correlation.

Even when companies appear to be substantially similar, there are likely to be significant differences in these data at any one moment in time. These differences may result from investor overreaction to one-time events. For example, the announcement of a pending acquisition

[1] For a more detailed discussion of these issues, see Stowe et al. (2007).

[2] Rather than using a financial return to measure profitability, the actual dollar value of profits could be used to identify firms that are also comparable in size.

[3] As noted in Chapter 7, smaller firms, other things being equal, are more prone to default than larger firms, which generally have a larger asset base and a larger and more diversified revenue stream than smaller firms. Consequently, the analyst should take care not to compare firms that are substantially different in size unless convinced that the firms are truly comparable in terms of profitability, growth, and risk.

may boost the share prices of competitors as investors anticipate takeover bids for these firms. The impact of such events abates with the passage of time. Consequently, comparisons made at different times can provide distinctly different results. By taking an average of multiples over six months or one year, these differences may be minimized. Note that valuations derived using the comparable companies method do not include a purchase price premium.

Table 8.1 illustrates how to apply the comparable companies method to value Spanish oil company Repsol YPF. Repsol is a geographically diversified integrated oil and gas firm engaged in all aspects of the petroleum business, including exploration, development, and production of crude oil and natural gas; petroleum refining; petrochemical production; and marketing of petroleum products. Repsol has economic and political risks and growth characteristics similar to other globally diversified integrated oil and gas companies. The estimated value of Repsol based on the comparable companies method is $51.81 billion versus its actual June 25, 2008, market capitalization of $49.83 billion.

The analyst needs to be mindful of changes in fundamentals that can affect multiples. These fundamentals include a firm's ability to generate and grow earnings and cash flow through reinvestment in its operations, as well as the risk associated with the firm's earnings and cash flows. Since multiples are affected by each of these variables, changes in the variables affect them. Firms with lower earnings and cash-flow generation potential, lower growth prospects, and higher risk should trade at multiples less than firms with higher earnings and cash-flow

TABLE 8.1   Valuing Repsol YPF Using Comparable Integrated Oil Companies

	Target Valuation Based on Following Multiples (MV_C/VI_C)				
	Trailing P/E[a]	Forward P/E[b]	Price/Sales	Price/Book	Average
Comparable Company	Col. 1	Col. 2	Col. 3	Col. 4	Cols. 1–4
Exxon Mobil Corp. (XOM)	11.25	8.73	1.17	3.71	
British Petroleum (BP)	9.18	7.68	0.69	2.17	
Chevron Corp. (CVX)	10.79	8.05	0.91	2.54	
Royal Dutch Shell (RDS-B)	7.36	8.35	0.61	1.86	
ConocoPhillips (COP)	11.92	6.89	0.77	1.59	
Total SA (TOT)	8.75	8.73	0.80	2.53	
Eni SpA (E)	3.17	7.91	0.36	0.81	
PetroChina Co. (PTR)	11.96	10.75	1.75	2.10	
Average Multiple (MV_C/VI_C) Times	9.30	8.39	0.88	2.16	
Repsol YPF Projections (VI_T)[c]	$4.38	$3.27	$92.66	$26.49	
Equals Estimated Market Value of Target[c]	$40.72	$27.42	$81.77	$57.32	$51.81

[a] Trailing 52-week averages.
[b] Projected 52-week averages.
[c] Billions of dollars.

TABLE 8.2   Factors Influencing Valuation Multiples

Multiple	Factor
Price-to-Earnings Ratio	Earnings Growth Rate (positive)
	Payout Ratio (negative)[a]
Price-to-Book Ratio	Return on Equity (positive)
	Payout Ratio (negative)
	Earnings Growth Rate (positive)
Price-to-Revenue Ratio	Net Profit Margin (positive)
	Payout Ratio (negative)
	Earnings Growth Rate (positive)
Enterprise Value Multiples	Cash-Flow Growth Rate (positive)

[a] *Payout ratios refer to dividends as a percent of earnings available for common equity. One minus the payout ratio equals the rate at which a firm is retaining earnings for reinvestment. Therefore, increasing payout ratios indicate a lower firm reinvestment rate.*

generation capability, higher growth prospects, and less risk. Consequently, the analyst needs to understand why one firm's multiple is less than a comparable firm's before concluding that it is under- or overvalued. For example, a firm with a P/E of 10 may not be more expensive than a comparable firm with a P/E of 8 if the former's growth prospects, profitability, and rate at which profits are reinvested in the firm are higher than the latter firm's.

Table 8.2 summarizes the relationships between various multiples and their underlying determinants. The word *positive* or *negative* in parentheses next to the factors influencing the multiples indicates the direction of causality. For example, assuming nothing else is changing, price-to-earnings ratios should increase as expected earnings increase and decrease as dividend payout ratios rise, reflecting a lower rate of reinvestment of earnings in the firm.

Recent Comparable Transactions Method

The comparable transactions approach is conceptually similar to the comparable companies approach. This valuation technique also is referred to as the *precedent transactions method*. The multiples used to estimate the value of the target are based on purchase prices of comparable companies that recently were acquired. Price-to-earnings, sales, cash-flow, EBITDA, and book-value ratios are calculated using the purchase price for the recent comparable transaction. Earnings, sales, cash-flow, EBITDA, and book value for the target subsequently are multiplied by these ratios to obtain an estimate of the market value of the target company. The estimated value of the target firm obtained using recent comparable transactions already reflects a purchase price premium, unlike the comparable companies approach to valuation. The obvious limitation to the comparable transactions method is the difficulty in finding truly comparable, recent transactions. Note that comparable recent transactions can be found in other industries as long as they are similar to the target firm in terms of profitability, expected earnings, and cash flow; growth; and perceived risk. Table 8.1 could be used to illustrate how the recent transaction valuation method may be applied simply by replacing the data in the column headed "Comparable Company" with data for "Recent Comparable Transactions."

Same or Comparable Industry Method

Using this approach, the target company's net income, revenue, cash-flow, EBITDA, and book value are multiplied by the ratio of the market value of shareholders' equity to net income, revenue, cash-flow, EBITDA, and book value for the average company in the target firm's industry or a comparable industry (see Exhibit 8.1). Such information can be obtained from Standard & Poor's, Value Line, Moody's, Dun & Bradstreet, and Wall Street analysts. The primary advantage of this technique is the ease of use. Disadvantages include the presumption that industry multiples are actually comparable. The use of the industry average may overlook the fact that companies, even in the same industry, can have drastically different expected growth rates, returns on invested capital, and debt-to-total capital ratios.

Valuations Based on Projections May Be Superior to Those Using Historical Data

An analyst using industry or comparable company multiples needs to decide whether or not to use multiples based on current or projected earnings or cash flows or some other measure of value. While projections based on Wall Street analysts' forecasts may not be unbiased, empirical evidence suggests that forecasts of earnings and other value indicators are better predictors of a firm's value than value indicators based on historical data.[4]

Earnings Show Better Short-Run Correlation with Stock Returns Than Cash Flow

Considerable attention has been paid to whether cash flow, earnings, or dividends are better predictors of a firm's value.[5] Studies suggest that cash flows and earnings are highly positively correlated with stock returns over long periods, such as five-year intervals. However, for shorter time periods, earnings show a stronger correlation with stock

---

[4] Moonchul and Ritter, 1999; Liu, Nissim, and Thomas, 2002

[5] In valuation, differences in earnings, cash flows, and dividends are often attributable to timing differences (i.e., differences between when a cash outlay is recorded and when it is actually incurred). For example, when a firm buys a piece of equipment, it generally pays for the equipment in the period in which it is received. However, for financial reporting purposes, the purchase price of the equipment is amortized over its estimated useful life. Proponents of using earnings as a measure of value rather than cash flow argue that earnings reflect value changes regardless of when they occur. For example, a firm's contractual obligation to provide future health care or pension benefits when an employee retires is reflected in current compensation and reduces earnings by an expense equal to the present value of that deferred compensation. In contrast, current cash flows are unaffected by this obligation. The bottom line is that, over the life of the firm, the present values of future earnings, cash flows, and dividends will be equal if based on internally consistent assumptions. See Lui et al. (2002).

EXHIBIT 8.1 VALUING A TARGET COMPANY USING THE SAME OR COMPARABLE INDUSTRIES METHOD

As of June 25, 2008, Repsol YPF, a Spanish integrated oil and gas producer, had projected earnings per share for the coming year of $3.27 (see Table 8.1). The industry average price-to-earnings ratio at that time for integrated oil and gas companies was 12.4. Estimate the firm's price per share (see Eq. (8.1)).

$$MV_T = (MV_{IND}/VI_{IND}) \times VI_T$$
$$= 12.4 \times \$3.27$$
$$= \$40.54/\text{share}(6/25/08 \text{ acutal price} = \$39.18) \tag{8.1}$$

where

MV_T = market value per share of the target company

MV_{IND}/VI_{IND} = market value per share of the average firm in the industry divided by a value indicator for that average firm in the industry (e.g., industry average price-to-earnings ratio)

VI_T = value indicator for the target firm (e.g., projected earnings per share)

---

returns than cash flows.[6] As a practical matter, cash flow is more often used for valuation than earnings or dividends simply because firms often do not pay dividends or generate profits for a significant period.

Enterprise Value to EBITDA Method

In recent years, analysts have increasingly used the relationship between enterprise value to earnings before interest and taxes, depreciation, and amortization to value firms. Note that enterprise value can be defined in terms of either the asset or the liability side of the balance sheet. Recall that in Chapter 7 enterprise value was discussed from the perspective of the asset or "left-hand" side of the balance sheet as the present value of free cash flow to the firm (i.e., cash flows generated from operating assets and liabilities available for lenders and common and preferred shareholders). Thus defined, enterprise value was adjusted for the value of nonoperating assets and liabilities to estimate the value of common equity. In this chapter, enterprise value is viewed from the perspective of the liability or "right-hand" side of the balance sheet.

[6] Cheng, Liu, and Schaefer, 1996; Dechow, 1994; Sloan, 1996. For a sample of 25,843 firms in ten countries from 1987 to 2004, Liu, Nissim, and Thomas (2007) argue that forecasted earnings may be better predictors of firm value than projected cash flows. The authors found that industry multiples based on forecasted earnings are superior predictors of actual equity values of firms traded on public stock exchanges than industry multiples based forecasted cash flow. Forecasted earnings also were found to be superior as a measure of value than dividend-based valuations. Kaplan and Ruback (1995) and Kim and Ritter (1999) argue that the choice of which multiple or method (relative valuation or DCF) to use is ambiguous. Furthermore, for a sample of 51 highly leveraged transactions between 1983 and 1989, Kaplan and Ruback question whether one forecasting method is superior to another by noting that both the DCF and the relative multiple methods exhibit similar levels of valuation accuracy.

The enterprise value to EBITDA multiple relates the total market value of the firm from the perspective of the liability side of the balance sheet (i.e., long-term debt plus preferred and common equity), excluding cash, to EBITDA. In practice, other long-term liabilities often are ignored and cash is assumed to be equal to cash and short-term marketable securities on the balance sheet. Ignoring other long-term liabilities such as the firm's pension and healthcare obligations only makes sense if they are fully funded.

In constructing the enterprise value, the market value of the firm's common equity value (MV_{FCFE}) is added to the market value of the firm's long-term debt (MV_D) and the market value of preferred stock (MV_{PF}). Cash and short-term marketable securities are deducted from the enterprise value of the firm, since interest income from such cash is not counted in the calculation of EBITDA. Consequently, the inclusion of cash would overstate the enterprise value to EBITDA multiple. The enterprise value (EV) to EBITDA method is commonly expressed as follows:

$$EV/EBITDA = [MV_{FCFE} + MV_{PF} + (MV_D - Cash)]/EBITDA \qquad (8.2)$$

where (MV_D – Cash) is often referred to as net debt.

The enterprise value to EBITDA method is useful because more firms are likely to have negative earnings rather than negative earnings before interest and taxes, depreciation, and amortization. Consequently, relative-valuation methods are more often applicable when EBITDA is used as the value indicator. Furthermore, net or operating income can be significantly affected by the way the firm chooses to calculate depreciation (e.g., straight line versus accelerated). Such problems do not arise if the analyst uses a value indicator such as EBITDA that is estimated before deducting depreciation and amortization expense. Finally, the multiple can be compared more readily among firms exhibiting different levels of leverage than for other measures of earnings, since the numerator represents the total value of the firm irrespective of its distribution between debt and equity, and the denominator measures earnings before interest.

A major shortcoming of EBITDA as a value indicator is that it provides a good estimate of the firm's assets already in place but ignores the impact of new investment on future cash flows. This is not a problem as long as the firm is not growing and, as such, will not be experiencing changes in working capital and increased maintenance investment. Despite this shortcoming, EBITDA is more often used than a multiple based on free cash flow to the firm (FCFF), since FCFF is frequently negative due to changes in working capital and the fact that capital spending often exceeds internally generated funds. For these reasons, EBITDA multiples are most often used for mature businesses for which most of the value comes from the firm's existing assets. See Exhibit 8.2 for an illustration of how to apply this method.

EXHIBIT 8.2 VALUING A TARGET FIRM USING THE ENTERPRISE VALUE TO EBITDA METHOD

Repsol and Eni are geographically diversified integrated oil and gas companies. As of December 31, 2006, the market value of Repsol's common equity was $40.36 billion, and Eni's was $54.30 billion. Neither firm had preferred stock outstanding. Repsol's and Eni's outstanding debt consists primarily of interest-only notes with a balloon payment at maturity. The average maturity date for Repsol's debt is 12 years; for Eni's, it is 10 years. Market rates of interest for firms like Repsol and Eni at that time for debt maturing within 10 to 12 years were 7.5% and 7%, respectively. Repsol's and Eni's current income, balance sheet, and cash-flow statements as of December 31, 2006, are shown in the following table.

Financial Statements

	Repsol YPF	Eni SpA
	($ billion)	
Income Statement (12/31/06)		
Revenue	72.70	114.70
Cost of Sales	48.60	75.90
Other Expenses	16.10	11.20
Earnings before Interest and Taxes	8.00	27.60
Interest Expense	0.70	0.30
Earnings before Taxes	7.30	27.30
Taxes	3.10	14.10
Net Income	4.20	13.20
Balance Sheet (12/31/06)		
Cash	3.80	6.20
Other Current Assets	14.60	29.80
Long-Term Assets	42.70	77.20
Total Assets	61.10	113.20
Current Liabilities	13.30	28.30
Long-Term Debt	14.60	8.80
Other Long-Term Liabilities	8.80	26.40
Total Liabilities	36.70	63.50
Shareholders' Equity	24.40	49.70
Equity + Total Liabilities	61.10	113.20
Cash Flow (12/31/06)		
Net Income	4.20	13.20
Depreciation	4.10	8.10
Change in Working Capital	−0.40	1.10
Investments	−6.90	−9.30
Financing	−1.20	−9.40
Change in Cash Balances	−0.20	3.70

Source: *EDGAR Online*
Which firm has the higher enterprise value to EBITDA ratio? (Hint: Use Eq. (8.2).)
Answer: *Repsol.*

Market Value of Existing Debt

$$PV_D \text{(PV of Repsol Long-Term Debt)}^a = \$0.7 \times \frac{\left[\left(1 - (1/(1.075)^{12})\right)\right]}{0.075} + \frac{\$14.6}{(1.075)^{12}}$$

Given in income statement → Int Exp

$$= \$0.7 \times 7.74 + \$6.13 = \$11.55 \text{ billion}$$

$$PV_D \text{(PV of Eni Long-Term Debt)}^b = \$0.3 \times \frac{\left[(1 - (1/(1.070)^{10}))\right]}{0.07} + \frac{\$8.8}{(1.07)^{10}}$$

$$= \$0.3 \times 7.02 + \$4.47 = \$6.58 \text{ billion}$$

Enterprise to EBITDA Ratio

(Market value of equity + Market Value of Debt – Cash) / (EBIT + Depreciation):[c]

Repsol : ($40.36 + $11.55 – $3.8)/($8.0 + $4.1) = 3.98
Eni :   ($54.30 + $6.58 – $6.2)/($27.60 + $8.1) = 1.53

[a] The present value of debt is calculated using the PV of an annuity formula for 12 years and a 7.5% interest rate plus the PV of the principal repayment of $14.6 billion at the end of 12 years. Alternatively, rather than using the actual formulas, a present value interest factor annuity table and a present value interest factor table could have been used to calculate the PV of debt. Note that only annual interest expense of $0.7 million is used in the calculation of the PV of the annuity payment because the debt is treated as a balloon note.
[b] The present value of debt is calculated using the PV of an annuity formula for 10 years and a 7% interest rate plus the PV of the principal repayment of $8.8 billion at the end of 10 years.
[c] Note that a firm's financial statements frequently include depreciation expense in the cost of sales. Therefore, EBITDA may be calculated by adding EBIT from the income statement and depreciation expense shown on the cash-flow statement.

Adjusting Relative-Valuation Methods for Firm Growth Rates

Assume that Firm A and Firm B are direct competitors and have price-to-earnings ratios of 20 and 15, respectively. Which is the cheaper firm? It is not possible to answer this question without knowing how fast the earnings of the two firms are growing. The higher P/E ratio for Firm A may be justified if its earnings are expected to grow significantly faster than Firm B's future earnings.

For this reason, relative-valuation methods may be adjusted for differences in growth rates among firms. The most common adjustment is the PEG ratio, commonly calculated by dividing the firm's price-to-earnings ratio by the expected growth rate in earnings. This relative-valuation method is simple to compute and provides a convenient mechanism for comparing firms with different growth rates. The comparison of a firm's P/E ratio to its projected earnings is helpful in identifying stocks of firms that are under- or overvalued. Conceptually, firms with P/E ratios less than their projected growth rates may be considered undervalued, while those with P/E ratios greater than their projected growth rates may be viewed as overvalued. It is critical for the analyst to remember that growth rates by themselves do not increase multiples, such as a firm's price-to-earnings ratio, unless coupled with improving financial returns. Investors are willing to pay more for each dollar of future earnings only if they expect to earn a higher future rate of return. They may be willing to pay considerably more for a stock whose PEG ratio is greater than 1 if they believe the increase in earnings will result in future financial returns that significantly exceed the firm's cost of equity.

The PEG ratio can be helpful in evaluating the potential market values of a number of different firms in the same industry in selecting which may be the most attractive acquisition target. While the PEG ratio uses P/E ratios, other value indicators may be used. This method may be generalized as follows

$$\frac{(MV_T/VI_T)}{VI_{TGR}} = A \quad \text{and}$$

$$MV_T = A \times VI_{TGR} \times VI_T$$

(8.3)

where

A = PEG ratio—that is, market price–to–value indicator ratio (MV_T/VI_T) relative to the growth rate of the value indicator (VI_{TGR}), which could include the growth in net income, cash flow, EBITDA, revenue, and the like.

VI_{TGR} = projected growth rate of the value indicator. Because this method uses an equity multiple (e.g., price per share/net income per share), consistency suggests that the growth rate in the value indicator should be expressed on a per-share basis. Therefore, if the value indicator is net income per share, the growth in the value indicator should be the growth rate for net income per share and not net income.

Equation (8.3) gives an estimate of the implied market value per share for a target firm based on its PEG ratio. As such, PEG ratios are useful for comparing firms whose expected future growth rates are positive and different to determine which is likely to have the higher firm value. For firms whose projected growth rates are 0 or negative, this method implies zero firm value for firms that are not growing and a negative value for those whose projected growth rates are negative. The practical implication for such firms is that those that are not growing are not likely to increase in market value, while those exhibiting negative growth are apt to experience declining firm values. Exhibit 8.3 illustrates how to apply the PEG ratio.

EXHIBIT 8.3 APPLYING THE PEG RATIO

An analyst is asked to determine whether Basic Energy Service (BES) or Composite Production Services (CPS) is more attractive as an acquisition target. Both firms provide engineering, construction, and specialty services to the oil, gas, refinery, and petrochemical industries.

BES and CPS have projected annual earnings per share growth rates of 15% and 9%, respectively. BES's and CPS's current earnings per share are $2.05 and $3.15, respectively. The current share prices as of June 25, 2008, for BES are $31.48 and for CPX are $26.00. The industry average price-to-earnings ratio and growth rate are 12.4 and 11%, respectively. Based on this information, which firm is a more attractive takeover target as of the point in time the firms are being compared? (*Hint:* Use Eq. (8.3).) The PEG ratio focuses on P/E ratios and earnings growth rates. What other factors if known might change your answer to the previous question?

Industry average PEG ratio: $12.4/0.11 = 112.73^{a}$

BES: Implied share price $= 112.73 \times 0.15 \times \$2.05 = \$34.66$

CPX: Implied share price $= 112.73 \times 0.09 \times \$3.15 = \$31.96$

Answer: The difference between the implied and actual share prices for BES and CPX is \$3.18 (i.e., \$34.66 − \$31.48) and \$5.96 (\$31.96 − \$26.00), respectively. CPX is more undervalued than BES at this moment in time. However, BES could be a more attractive acquisition target than CPX if it can generate increasing future financial returns and if its projected earnings stream is viewed as less risky. Therefore, BES could exhibit greater potential and less uncertain future profitability than CPX.

[a] Solving $MVT = A \times VITGR \times VIT$ using an individual firm's PEG ratio provides the firm's current or share price in period T, since this formula is an identity. An industry average PEG ratio may be used to provide an estimate of the firm's intrinsic value. This implicitly assumes that the target firm and the average firm in the industry exhibit the same relationship between price-to-earnings ratios and earnings growth rates.

Data Source: *Yahoo! Finance.*

Value-Driver-Based Valuation

In the absence of earnings, other factors that drive the creation of value for a firm may be used for valuation purposes. Such factors commonly are used to value start-up companies and initial public offerings, which often have little or no earnings performance records. Measures of profitability and cash flow are simply manifestations of value indicators. These indicators are dependent on factors both external and internal to the firm. Value drivers exist for each major function within the firm, including sales, marketing, and distribution; customer service; operations and manufacturing; and purchasing.

There are both micro value drivers and macro value drivers. *Micro value drivers* are those that directly influence specific functions within the firm. Micro value drivers for sales, marketing, and distribution could include product quality measures, such as part defects per 100,000 units sold, on-time delivery, the number of multiyear subscribers, and the ratio of product price to some measure of perceived quality. Customer service drivers could include average waiting time on the telephone, the number of billing errors as a percent of total invoices, and the time required to correct such errors. Operational value drivers include the average collection period, inventory turnover, and the number of units produced per manufacturing employee hour. Purchasing value drivers include average payment period, on-time vendor delivery, and the quality of purchased materials and services. *Macro value drivers* are more encompassing than micro value drivers in that they affect all aspects of the firm. Examples of macro value drivers include market share, overall customer satisfaction measured by survey results, total asset turns (i.e., sales to total assets), revenue per employee, and "same store sales" in retailing.

Using value drivers to value businesses is straightforward. First, the analyst needs to determine the key determinants of value (i.e., the value drivers for the target firm). Second, the market value for comparable companies is divided by the value driver selected for the target to calculate the dollars of market value per unit of value driver. Third, this figure is multiplied by the same indicator or value driver for the target company. For example, assume that the primary macro value driver or determinant of a firm's market value in a particular industry is market share. How investors value market share can be estimated by dividing the market leader's market value by its market share. If the market leader has a market value and market share of $300 million and 30%, respectively, the market is valuing each percentage point of market share at $10 million (i.e., $300 million ÷ 30). If the target company in the same industry has a 20% market share, an estimate of the market value of the target company is $200 million (20 points of market share times $10 million).

Similarly, the market value of comparable companies could be divided by other known value drivers. Examples include the number of visitors or page views per month for an Internet content provider, the number of subscribers to a magazine, cost per hotel room for a hotel chain, and the number of households with TVs in a specific geographic area for a cable TV company. Using this method, AT&T's acquisitions of the cable companies TCI and Media One in the late 1990s would appear to have been a "bargain." AT&T spent an average of $5,000 per household (the price paid for each company divided by the number of customer households acquired) in purchasing these companies' customers. In contrast, Deutsche Telekom and Mannesmann spent $6,000 and $7,000 per customer, respectively, in buying mobile phone companies One 2 One and Orange PLC.[7]

The major advantage of this approach is its simplicity. Its major disadvantage is the implied assumption that a single value driver or factor is representative of the total value of the business. The bankruptcy of many dotcom firms between 2000 and 2002 illustrates how this valuation technique can be misused. Many of these firms had never shown any earnings, yet they exhibited huge market valuations. Investors often justified these valuations by using page views and subscribers of supposedly comparable firms to value any firm associated with the Internet. These proved to be poor indicators of the firm's ability to generate future earnings or cash flow.

APPLYING ASSET-ORIENTED METHODS

What follows is a discussion of valuation based on applying tangible book value, liquidation value, and breakup value.

Tangible Book Value or Equity per Share Method

Book value is a much-maligned value indicator because book asset values rarely reflect actual market values (see Exhibit 8.4). They may over- or understate market value. For example, the value of land frequently is understated on the balance sheet, whereas inventory often is overstated if it is old or obsolete. The applicability of this approach varies by industry. Although book values generally do not mirror actual market values for manufacturing companies, they may be more accurate for distribution companies, whose assets are largely composed of inventory exhibiting high inventory turnover rates. Examples of such companies include pharmaceutical distributor Bergen Brunswick and personal computer distributor Ingram Micro. Book value is also widely used for valuing financial services companies, where tangible book value is primarily cash or liquid assets. Tangible book value is book value less goodwill.

[7] *Business Week*, 2000a

EXHIBIT 8.4 VALUING COMPANIES USING BOOK VALUE

Ingram Micro Inc. and its subsidiaries distribute information technology products worldwide. The firm's market price per share on August 21, 2008, was $19.30. Ingram's projected five-year average annual net income growth rate is 9.5%, and its beta is 0.89. The firm's shareholders' equity is $3.4 billion and goodwill is $0.7 billion. Ingram has 172 million (0.172 billion) shares outstanding. The following firms represent Ingram's primary competitors.

	Market Value/Tangible Book Value	Beta	Projected Five-Year Net Income Growth Rate (%)
Tech Data	0.91	0.90	11.6
Synnex Corporation	0.70	0.40	6.9
Avnet	1.01	1.09	12.1
Arrow	0.93	0.97	13.2

Ingram's tangible book value per share $(VI_T) = (\$3.4 - \$0.7)/0.172 = \$15.70$

Based on risk as measured by the firm's beta and the five-year projected earnings growth rate, Synnex is believed to exhibit significantly different risk and growth characteristics from Ingram and is excluded from the calculation of the industry average market value to tangible book value ratio. Therefore, the appropriate industry average ratio $(MV_{IND}/VI_{IND}) = 0.95$—that is, $(0.91 + 1.01 + 0.93)/3$.

Ingram's implied value per share $= MV_T = (MV_{IND}/VI_{IND}) \times VI_T = 0.95 \times \$15.70 = \$14.92$

Based on the implied value per share, Ingram was overvalued on August 21, 2008, when its share price was $19.30.

Data Source: *Yahoo! Finance.*

Liquidation or Breakup Value

The terms *liquidation* and *breakup value* often are used interchangeably. However, there are subtle distinctions. Liquidation or breakup value is the projected price of the firm's assets sold separately less its liabilities and expenses incurred in liquidating or breaking up the firm. Liquidation may be involuntary, as a result of bankruptcy, or voluntary, if a firm is viewed by its owners as worth more in liquidation than as a going concern. The *going concern value* of a company may be defined as the firm's value in excess of the sum of the value of its parts. Breakup and liquidation strategies are explored further in Chapters 15 and 16.

During the late 1970s and throughout most of the 1980s, highly diversified companies routinely were valued by investors in terms of their value if broken up and sold as discrete operations, as well as their going concern value as a consolidated operation. Companies lacking real synergy among their operating units or sitting on highly appreciated assets often were viewed as more valuable when broken up or liquidated. In early 2007, the Blackstone

Group, a major private equity investor who acquired Equity Office Properties Trust (EOP) for $36 billion, moved aggressively to break up the business after having arranged the sale prior to closing of many of the properties held by the real estate investment trust.

Analysts may estimate the liquidation value of a target company to determine the minimum value of the company in the worst-case scenario of business failure and eventual liquidation. It is particularly appropriate for financially distressed firms. Analysts often make a simplifying assumption that the assets can be sold in an orderly fashion, which is defined as a reasonable amount of time to solicit bids from qualified buyers. *Orderly fashion* often is defined as 9 to 12 months. Under these circumstances, high-quality receivables typically can be sold for 80% to 90% of their book value. Inventories might realize 80 to 90% of their book value, depending on the condition and the degree of obsolescence. The value of inventory may also vary, depending on whether it consists of finished, intermediate, or raw materials. More rapid liquidation might reduce the value of inventories to 60 to 65% of their book value. The liquidation value of equipment varies widely depending on age and condition.

Inventories need to be reviewed in terms of obsolescence, receivables in terms of the ease with which they may be collected, equipment in terms of age and effectiveness, and real estate in terms of current market value. Equipment such as lathes and computers with a zero book value may have a significant economic value (i.e., useful life). Land can be a hidden source of value because it frequently is undervalued on GAAP balance sheets. Prepaid assets, such as insurance premiums, sometimes can be liquidated with a portion of the premium recovered. The liquidation value is reduced dramatically if the assets have to be liquidated in "fire sale" conditions, under which assets are sold to the first rather than the highest bidder (see Exhibit 8.5).

Exhibit 8.6 illustrates a hypothetical estimation of the breakup value of a firm consisting of multiple operating units. The implicit assumption is that the interdependencies among the four operating units are limited such that they can be sold separately without a significant degradation of the value of any individual unit.

EXHIBIT 8.5 CALCULATING LIQUIDATION VALUE

Titanic Corporation has declared bankruptcy, and the firm's creditors have asked the trustee to estimate its liquidation value assuming orderly sale conditions. Note that this example does not take into account legal fees, taxes, management fees, and contractually required employee severance expenses. In certain cases, these expenses can comprise a substantial percentage of the proceeds from liquidation.

Balance Sheet Item	Book Value ($ million)	Orderly Sale Value ($ million)
Cash	100	100
Receivables	500	450
Inventory	800	720
Equipment (after depreciation)	200	60
Land	200	300
Total Assets	1,800	1,630
Total Liabilities	1,600	1,600
Shareholders' Equity	200	30

EXHIBIT 8.6 CALCULATING BREAKUP VALUE

Sea Bass Inc. consists of four operating units. The value of operating synergies among the units is believed to be minimal. All but $10 million in debt can be allocated to each of the four units. Such debt is associated with financing the needs of the corporate overhead structure. Legal, consulting, and investment banking fees, as well as severance expenses associated with terminating corporate overhead personnel, amount to $10 million. What is the breakup value of Sea Bass Inc.?

Operating Unit	Estimated After-Tax Equity Value ($ million)
Unit 1	100
Unit 2	125
Unit 3	50
Unit 4	75
Total Equity Value	350
Less any unallocated liabilities held at the corporate level, corporate overhead expense, and costs associated with the breakup	20
Total Breakup Value	330

THE REPLACEMENT COST METHOD

The replacement cost approach estimates what it would cost to replace the target firm's assets at current market prices using professional appraisers less the present value of the firm's liabilities. The difference provides an estimate of the market value of equity. This approach does not take into account the going concern value of the company, which reflects how effectively the assets are being used in combination (i.e., synergies) to generate profits and cash flow. Valuing the assets separately in terms of what it would cost to replace them may seriously understate the firm's true going concern value. This approach may also be inappropriate if the firm has a significant amount of intangible assets on its books due to the difficulty in valuing such assets.

VALUING THE FIRM USING THE WEIGHTED-AVERAGE METHOD

Predicting future cash flows and determining the appropriate discount rate are often very difficult. Consequently, relative-valuation multiples often are used in lieu of DCF valuation. However, no multiple is universally accepted as the best measure of a firm's value. Consequently, the weighted-average method of valuation represents a compromise position.[8] This approach involves calculating the expected value (EXPV) or weighted average of a range of potential outcomes.

[8] Kaplan and Ruback (1995) and Liu et al. (2002) provide empirical support for using multiple methods of valuation to estimate the economic value of an asset.

Note that the weights, which must sum to one, reflect the analyst's relative confidence in the various methodologies employed to value a business. Assuming that an analyst is equally confident in the accuracy of both methods, the expected value of a target firm valued at $12 million using discounted cash flow and $15 million using the comparable companies method can be written as follows:

$$\text{EXPV} = 0.5 \times \$12 + 0.5 \times \$15 = \$13.5 \text{ million}$$

Neither valuation method in this example includes a purchase price premium. Consequently, a premium will have to be added to the expected-value estimate to obtain a reasonable purchase estimate for the target firm.

Adjusting Valuation Estimates for Purchase Price Premiums

As explained in Chapter 1, the purchase premium reflects both the perceived value of obtaining a controlling interest in the target and the value of expected synergies (e.g., cost savings) resulting from combining the two firms. When using the weighted-average or expected-value valuation method, it is important to remember that unless adjusted to reflect a premium, the individual valuation methods discussed in Chapter 7 and in this chapter will not reflect the amount over market value that must be paid to gain a controlling interest in the target firm.

The exception is the recent transactions method, which already reflects a purchase price premium. The premium generally will be determined as a result of the negotiation process and should reflect premiums paid on recent acquisitions of similar firms and the percentage of synergy provided by the target firm. If the investor is interested in purchasing less than 100% of the voting shares of the target, it is necessary to adjust the purchase price for control premiums or minority discounts. How these adjustments are made is explained in detail in Chapter 10.[9]

Exhibit 8.7 illustrates a practical way of calculating the expected value of the target firm, including a purchase premium, using estimates provided by multiple valuation methods. In the example, the purchase price premium associated with the estimate provided by the recent comparable transactions method is applied to estimates provided by the other valuation methodologies.

---

[9] Adjustments to estimated market values should be made with care. For example, the analyst should be careful not to mechanically add an acquisition premium to the target firm's estimated value based on the comparable companies method if there is evidence that the market values of "comparable firms" already reflect the effects of acquisition activity elsewhere in the industry. For example, rival firms' share prices will rise in response to the announced acquisition of a competitor, regardless of whether the proposed acquisition is ultimately successful or unsuccessful (Song and Walking, 2000). Akhigbe, Borde, and Whyte (2000) find that the increase in rivals' share prices may be even greater if the acquisition attempt is unsuccessful because investors believe that the bidder will attempt to acquire other firms in the same industry. There is evidence that the effects of merger activity in one country are also built into merger premiums in other countries in regions that are becoming more integrated, such as the European Union (Bley and Medura, 2003).

EXHIBIT 8.7 WEIGHTED-AVERAGE VALUATION OF ALTERNATIVE METHODOLOGIES

An analyst has estimated the value of a company using multiple valuation methodologies. The discounted-cash-flow value is $220 million, the comparable transactions value is $234 million, the P/E-based value is $224 million, and the firm's breakup value is $200 million. The analyst has greater confidence in certain methodologies than others. The purchase price paid for the recent comparable transaction represented a 20% premium over the value of the firm at the time of the takeover announcement. Estimate the weighted-average value of the firm using all valuation methodologies and the weights or relative importance the analyst assigns to each methodology.

Estimated Value ($ million) Col. 1	Estimated Value Including 20% Premium ($ million) Col. 2	Relative Weight (as determined by analyst) Col. 3	Weighted Average ($ million) Col. 2 × Col. 3
220	264.0	0.30	79.2
234	234.0[a]	0.40	93.6
224	268.8	0.20	53.8
200	240.0	0.10	24.0
		1.00	250.6

[a] Note that the comparable recent transactions estimate already contains a 20% purchase price premium.

ANALYZING MERGERS AND ACQUISITIONS IN TERMS OF REAL OPTIONS

An *option* is the exclusive right, but not the obligation, to buy, sell, or use property for a specific period of time in exchange for a predetermined amount of money. Options traded on financial exchanges, such as puts and calls, are called *financial options*. Options that involve real assets, such as licenses, copyrights, trademarks, and patents, are called *real options*. Other examples of real options include the right to buy land, commercial property, and equipment. Such assets can be valued as call options if their current value exceeds the difference between the asset's current value and some predetermined level. For example, if a business has an option to lease office space at a predetermined price, the value of that option increases as lease rates for this type of office space increase. The asset can be valued as a put option if its value increases as the value of the underlying asset falls below a predetermined level. For example, if a business has an option to sell a commercial office building at a predetermined price, the value of that option increases as the value of the office building declines. In either instance, the option holder can choose to exercise (or not exercise) the option now or at some time in the future.

The term *real options* refers to management's ability to adopt and later revise corporate investment decisions. It should not be confused with a firm's *strategic options*, such as adopting a cost leadership, differentiation, or a focused business strategy (see Chapter 4). Since management's ability to adopt and subsequently change investment decisions can greatly alter the value of a project, it should be considered in capital budgeting methodology. If we view a merger or acquisition as a single project, real options should be considered as an integral part of M&A valuation.

Traditional DCF techniques fail to account for management's ability to react to new information and make decisions that affect the outcome of a project. However, real options can be costly to obtain (e.g., the right to extend a lease or purchase property), complex to value, and dependent on highly problematic assumptions. They should not be considered unless they are clearly identifiable, management has the time and resources to exploit them, and they would add significantly to the value of the underlying investment decision.[10]

Identifying Real Options Embedded in M&A Decisions

Investment decisions, including M&As, often contain certain "embedded options," such as the ability to accelerate growth by adding to the initial investment (i.e., expand), delay the timing of the initial investment (i.e., delay), or walk away from the project (i.e., abandon). The case study at the beginning of this chapter illustrates the real options available to Microsoft in its attempt to take over Yahoo!. If Yahoo! were to accept Microsoft's early 2008 bid, Microsoft could choose to accelerate investment contingent on the successful integration of Yahoo! and MSN (i.e., option to expand) or spin off or divest the combined MSN/Yahoo! business if the integration effort were unsuccessful (option to abandon). Absent a negotiated agreement with Yahoo!, Microsoft could walk away, keeping open the possibility of returning to acquire or partner with Yahoo! at a later date if the Yahoo! board became more receptive (option to delay). Ultimately, Microsoft entered into a search partnership with Yahoo! in 2009.

In late 2008, Swiss mining company Xstrata PLC executed what could be characterized as an option to delay when it dropped its $10 billion bid for platinum producer Lonmin PLC because of its inability to get financing due to turmoil in the credit markets. However, Xstrata signaled that it would resume efforts to acquire Lonmin at a later date by buying 24.9% of the firm's depressed shares in the open market. Already owning 10.7% of the target's shares, the additional purchase gave Xstrata a 35.6% stake in Lonmin at a low average cost, effectively blocking potential competing bids. Drug company Eli Lilly's purchase of ImClone Systems for $6.5 billion in late 2008 at a sizeable 51% premium may have reflected an embedded option to expand. A significant portion of ImClone's future value seems to depend on the commercial success of future drugs derived from the firm's colon cancer–fighting drug Erbitux.

Frequently, the existence of the real option increases the value of the expected NPV of an investment. For example, the NPV of an acquisition of a manufacturer may have a lower value than if the NPV is adjusted for a decision made at a later date to expand capacity. If the additional capacity is fully utilized, the resulting higher level of future cash flows may increase the acquisition's NPV. In this instance, the value of the real option to expand is the difference between the NPV with and without expansion. An option to abandon an investment (i.e., divest or liquidate) often increases the NPV because of its effect on reducing risk.

[10] For an intuitive discussion of real options, see Boer (2002); for a more rigorous discussion of applying real options, see Damodaran (2002, pp. 772–815).

By exiting the business, the acquirer may be able to recover a portion of its original investment and truncate projected negative cash flows associated with the acquisition. Similarly, an acquirer may be able to increase the expected NPV by delaying the decision to acquire 100% of the target firm until the acquirer can be more certain about projected cash flows.

Preclosing Options and Associated Risks

Expand, delay, and abandon options exist in the period prior to closing an acquisition. An example of an option to delay closing occurs when a potential acquirer chooses to purchase a "toehold" position in the target firm to obtain leverage by acquiring voting shares in the target. The suitor is required to prenotify the target firm and publicly file its intentions with the SEC if its share of the target firm's outstanding stock reaches 5%. At this point the acquirer may choose to delay adding to its position or choose to move aggressively through a tender offer to achieve a controlling interest in the target firm. The latter option is an example of an option to expand its toehold position. An opportunity cost is associated with each choice. If the suitor fails to expand its position, additional bidders who are made aware of its intentions may bid up the target firm's share price to a level considered prohibitive by the initial potential acquirer. If the acquirer moves aggressively, it may lose the potential for reaching agreement with the target firm's board and management on friendly terms. The costs associated with a hostile takeover attempt include a potentially higher purchase price and the possible loss of key employees, customers, and suppliers during a more contentious integration of the target into the acquiring firm.

Other examples of delay options include an acquiring firm choosing to delay a merger until certain issues confronting the target are resolved, such as outstanding litigation or receiving regulatory approval (e.g., FDA approval for a new drug). The suitor may simply choose not to bid at that time and run the risk of losing the target firm to another acquirer or to negotiate an exclusive call option to buy the target at a predetermined price within a specified time period.

Normally, a breakup or termination fee is paid by the seller to the buyer if the seller decides to sell to another bidder following the signing of agreement of purchase and sale with the initial bidder. In a reverse termination fee arrangement, the bidder pays the seller a fee to withdraw from the transaction, often due to financial failure (i.e., the inability to obtain financing). The reverse fee could be viewed as a real option held by the buyer to abandon the deal. In mid-2008, Excel Technologies' shares traded at a 7.5% discount to a tender offer that was scheduled to close in 30 days. The size of the discount reflected investor concern that the buyer, GSI Group, would exercise its $9 million reverse termination fee to withdraw from the contract, since its stock had fallen by 35% since the deal's announcement, reflecting investor displeasure with the proposed takeover.

Postclosing Options and Associated Risks

Following closing, the acquirer also has the opportunity to expand, delay, or abandon new investment in the target firm. Acquiring firms generally have some degree of control over the timing of their investment decisions. For example, the acquiring firm's management may choose to make the level of investment in the target firm following closing contingent on the performance of actual cash flows compared to projected cash flows. If actual performance exceeds expectations, the acquirer may choose to accelerate its level of investment. In contrast, if performance is disappointing, the acquirer may opt to delay investment or even abandon the target firm either through divestiture or liquidation.

Valuing Real Options for Mergers and Acquisitions

Three ways to value real options are discussed in this book. The first is to use discounted cash flow, relative valuation, or asset-oriented methods and ignore alternative real options by assuming that their value is essentially zero. This suggests implicitly that management will not change the decision to invest once it has been made. The second is to value the real options in the context of a decision tree analysis. A decision tree is an expanded timeline that branches into alternative paths whenever an event can have multiple outcomes.[11] The points at which the tree branches are called *nodes*. The decision tree is most useful whenever the investment decision is subject to a relatively small number of probable outcomes and the investment decision can be made in clearly defined stages. The third method involves the valuation of the real option as a put or call, assuming that the underlying asset has the characteristics of financial options. Valuing real options in this manner is often referred to as *contingent claim valuation*. A *contingent claim* is a claim that pays off only if certain events occur.

Several methods are employed for valuing financial options. The standard method for valuing a financial option is the Black-Scholes model, which is typically applied to "European options." Such options can be exercised only at the expiration date of the option (i.e., a single, predefined date). This is an example of a "closed-form" model, in which the underlying assumptions do not vary over time. A more flexible, albeit often more complex, valuation method is a lattice-based option valuation technique, such as the binomial valuation model.[12] While the binomial options model offers greater flexibility in terms of allowing assumptions to vary over time, the Black-Scholes offers greater simplicity. For this reason, the real options expressed as call or put options are valued in this book using the Black-Scholes method.[13]

Valuing Real Options Using a Decision Tree Framework

Table 8.3 illustrates how the presence of real options may affect the NPV associated with an acquisition in which management has identified two cash-flow scenarios (i.e., those associated with a successful acquisition and those with an unsuccessful one). Each pair of cash-flow scenarios is associated with what are believed to be the range of reasonable options associated with acquiring the target firm. These include the option to immediately proceed with, delay,

[11] See Lasher (2005), pp. 428–433.

[12] Such models are sometimes used to value so-called American options, which may be exercised at any time before the expiration date. The binomial option-pricing model is based on the notion that the value of the underlying asset in any time period can change in one of two directions (i.e., either up or down), thereby creating a lattice of alternative asset pricing points. Because the lattice model, unlike the Black-Scholes model, values the asset (e.g., stock price) underlying the option at various points in time, such important economic assumptions as risk and the risk-free rate of return can be assumed to vary over time. While the binomial model allows for changing key assumptions over time, it often requires a large number of inputs, in terms of expected future prices at each node or pricing point.

[13] For a recent discussion of alternative real-option valuation methods, see Hitchner (2006).

TABLE 8.3   The Impact of Real Options on Valuing Mergers and Acquisitions

	Year 0	Year 1	Year 2	Year 3	Year 4	Year 5	Year 6	Year 7	Year 8	Year 9
First Branch: Option for Immediate Investment/Acquisition										
Enterprise Cash Flows		*Projected Target Firm Cash Flows*								
Successful Case	−300	30	35	40	45	50	55	60	65	
Unsuccessful Case	−300	−5	−5	−5	−5	−5	−5	−5	−5	
Weighted Cash Flows										
Successful Case (60%)	0	18	21	24	27	30	33	36	39	
Unsuccessful Case (40%)	0	−2	−2	−2	−2	−2	−2	−2	−2	
Expected Enterprise Cash Flow	−300	16	19	22	25	28	31	34	37	
Expected NPV Yr 1–8 @ 15%									**−166**	
Expected Terminal Value @ 13%; sustainable growth rate = 5%									159	
Expected Total NPV									**−7**	
Second Branch: Option to Abandon (Divest or Liquidate)										
Enterprise Cash Flows		*Projected Target Firm Cash Flows*								
Successful Case	−300	30	35	40	45	50	55	60	65	
Unsuccessful Case	−300	−5	−5	−5	−5	−5	−5	−5	−5	
Weighted Cash Flows										
Successful Case (60%)	0	18	21	24	27	30	33	36	39	
Unsuccessful Case (40%)	0	−2	−2	150	0	0	0	0	0	
Expected Enterprise Cash Flow	−300	16	19	174	27	30	33	36	39	
Expected NPV Yr 1–6 @15%									**−75**	
Expected Terminal Value @ 13%; sustainable growth rate = 5%									167	
Expected Total NPV									92	
Third Branch: Option to Delay Investment/Acquisition										
Enterprise Cash Flows		*Projected Target Firm Cash Flows*								
Successful Case	0	−300	35	40	45	50	55	60	65	70
Unsuccessful Case	0	−300	0	0	0	0	0	0	0	0
Weighted Cash Flows										
Successful Case (60%)	0	0	21	24	27	30	33	36	39	42
Unsuccessful Case (40%)	0	0	0	0	0	0	0	0	0	0
Expected Enterprise Cash Flow	0	−300	21	24	27	30	33	36	39	42
Expected NPV @ 15%									**−146**	
Expected Terminal Value @ 13%; sustainable growth rate = 5%									180	
Expected Total NPV									34	

Note: The NPV for the delay option is discounted at the end of year 1, while the other options are discounted from year 0 (i.e., the present).

or abandon the acquisition. Each outcome is shown as a "branch" on a tree. Each branch shows the cash flows and probabilities associated with each cash-flow scenario displayed as a timeline. The probability of realizing the "successful" cash-flow projections is assumed to be 60%; the "unsuccessful" one, 40%. The expected enterprise cash flow of the target firm is the sum of the projected cash flows of both the "successful" and "unsuccessful" scenarios multiplied by the estimated probability associated with each scenario. The target firm is assumed to have been acquired for $300 million, and the NPV is estimated using a 15% discount rate. The terminal value is calculated using the constant-growth method with an assumed terminal-period growth rate of 5%. With an NPV of –$7 million, the immediate investment option suggests that the acquisition should not be undertaken. However, the analyst should evaluate alternative options to determine if they represent attractive investment strategies.

By recognizing that the target firm could be sold or liquidated, the expected NPV based on projected enterprise cash flows is $92 million, suggesting that the acquisition should be undertaken. This assumes that the target firm is sold or liquidated at the end of the third year following its acquisition for $152 million. Note that the cash flow in year 3 is $150 million, reflecting the difference between $152 million and the –$2 million in operating cash flow during the third year. The expected NPV with the option to delay is estimated at $34 million. Note that the investment is to be made after a one-year delay only if the potential acquirer feels confident that competitive market conditions will support the projected "successful" scenario cash flows. Consequently, the "unsuccessful" scenario's cash flows are zero.

Figure 8.2 summarizes the results provided in Table 8.3 in a decision tree framework. Of the three options analyzed, valuing the target including the value of the cash flows associated

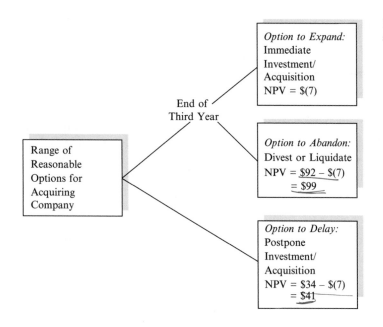

FIGURE 8.2 Real-options decision tree. Note: *See Table 8.3 for data.*

with the option to abandon would appear to be the most attractive investment strategy based on net present value (NPV). The values of the abandon and delay options are estimated as the difference between each of their NPVs and the NPV for the "immediate investment or acquisition" case.

Valuing Real Options Using the Black-Scholes Model

Options to assets whose cash flows have large variances and a long time before they expire are typically more valuable than those with smaller variances and less time remaining. The greater variance and time to expiration increase the chance that the factors affecting cash flows will change a project from one with a negative NPV to one with a positive NPV. If we know the values of five variables, we can use the Black-Scholes model to establish a theoretical price for an option. The limitations of the Black-Scholes model are the difficulty in estimating key assumptions (particularly risk), its assumptions that interest rates and risk are constant, that it can be exercised only on the expiration date, and that taxes and transaction costs are minimal. The basic Black-Scholes formula[14] for valuing a call option is given as follows:

$$C = SN(d_1) - Ee^{-Rt}N(d_2) \qquad (8.4)$$

where

$C = $ theoretical call option value

$$d_1 = \frac{\ln(S/E) + \left[R + (1/2)\sigma^2\right]t}{\sigma\sqrt{t}}$$

$d_2 = d_1 - \sigma\sqrt{t}$
$S = $ stock price or underlying asset price
$E = $ exercise or strike price
$R = $ risk-free interest rate corresponding to the life of the option
$\sigma^2 = $ variance (a measure of risk) of the stock's or underlying asset's return
$t = $ time to expiration of the option
$N(d_1)$ and $N(d_2) = $ cumulative normal probability values of d_1 and d_2

The term Ee^{-Rt} is the present value of the exercise price when continuous discounting is used. The terms $N(d_1)$ and $N(d_2)$, which involve the cumulative probability function, are the terms that take risk into account. $N(d_1)$ and $N(d_2)$ measure the probability that the value of the call option will pay off and the probability that the option will be exercised, respectively. These two values are Z-scores from the normal probability function, and they can be found in cumulative normal distribution function tables for the standard normal random variable in many statistics.

The variance (i.e., risk) to be used in the Black-Scholes model can be estimated in number of ways. First, risk could be estimated as the variance in the stock prices of similar firms or the assets whose cash flows enable the valuation of the option. For example, the average variance

[14] Modified versions of the Black–Scholes model are discussed in Arzac (2006).

in the share prices of U.S. oil services companies could be used as the variance in the valuation of a real option associated with the potential purchase of an oil services firm.[15] Second, the variance of cash flows from similar prior investments can be used. For example, drugs often require more than ten years and a cumulative expenditure of more than $1 billion before they become commercially viable. A pharmaceutical company may use the variance associated with the cash flows of previously developed comparable drugs in valuing an option to invest in a new drug. A third method is to use the standard deviation (i.e., the square root of the variance) calculated by using commonly available software to conduct Monte Carlo simulation analyses.[16]

Assuming that the necessary inputs (e.g., risk) can be estimated, a real option can be valued as a put or call option. The NPV of an investment can be adjusted for the value of the real option as follows:

$$\text{Total NPV} = \text{Present Value} - \text{Investment} + \text{Option Value} \tag{8.5}$$

OPTION TO EXPAND

To value a firm with an option to expand, the analyst must define the potential value of the option. For example, suppose a firm has an opportunity to enter a new market. The analyst must project cash flows that accrue to the firm if it enters the market. The cost of entering the market becomes the option's exercise price and the present value of the expected cash flows resulting from entering the market becomes the value of the firm or underlying asset. The present value is likely to be less than the initial entry costs, or the firm would already have entered the market. The variance of the firm's value can be estimated by using the variances of the market values of publicly traded firms that currently participate in that market. The option's life is the length of time during which the firm expects to achieve a competitive advantage by entering the market now. Exhibit 8.8 illustrates how to value an option to expand.

---

[15] In another example, assume a potential acquirer of an oil company recognizes that, in buying the target, it would have a call option (real option to expand) to develop the firm's oil reserves at a later date. The acquirer could choose to value the target firm as a stand-alone entity and the option to develop the firm's reserves at some time in the future separately. Assuming the volume of reserves is known with certainty, the variance in world oil prices may be used as a proxy for the risk associated with an option to develop the reserves. If there is uncertainty with respect to the volume of reserves and the price of oil, the uncertainties can be combined by recognizing that the value of the reserves represents the price of oil times the quantity of reserves and estimating the variance of the dollar value of the reserves.

[16] For each simulation, a range of outcomes is generated based on the predefined probability distributions provided by the analyst for the inputs (e.g., sales growth, inflation) driving the cash flows. The analyst selects one outcome from each simulation and calculates the present values of the cash flows based on the selected outcomes. The average of the range of present values calculated from running repeated simulations is the expected value of the project. By squaring the standard deviation associated with the range of present values, a variance can be calculated to be used in valuing the real option.

EXHIBIT 8.8 VALUING AN OPTION TO EXPAND USING THE BLACK-SCHOLES MODEL

AJAX Inc. is negotiating to acquire Comet Inc. to broaden its product offering. Based on its projections of Comet's cash flows as a stand-alone business, AJAX cannot justify paying more than $150 million for Comet. However, Comet is insisting on a price of $160 million. Following additional due diligence, AJAX believes that by applying its technology, Comet's product growth rate could be accelerated significantly. By buying Comet, AJAX is buying an option to expand in a market in which it is not participating currently by retooling Comet's manufacturing operations. The cost of retooling to fully utilize AJAX's technology requires an initial investment of $100 million. The present value of the expected cash flows from making this investment today is $80 million. Consequently, based on this information, paying the higher purchase price cannot be justified by making the investment in retooling now.

However, if Comet (employing AJAX's new technology) could be first to market with the new product offering, it could achieve a dominant market share. While the new product would be expensive to produce in small quantities, the cost of production is expected to fall as larger volumes are sold, making Comet the low-cost manufacturer. Moreover, because of patent protection, AJAX believes that it is unlikely that competitors will be able to develop a superior technology for at least ten years. An analysis of similar investments in the past suggests that the variance of the projected cash flows is 20%. The option is expected to expire in ten years, reflecting the time remaining on AJAX's patent. The current ten-year Treasury bond rate (corresponding to the expected term of the option) is 6%. Is the value of the option to expand, expressed as a call option, sufficient to justify paying Comet's asking price of $160 million (see Eq. (8.4))?

Solution

Value of the asset (PV of cash flows from retooling Comet's operations)	= $80 million
Exercise price (PV of the cost of retooling Comet's operations)	= $100 million
Variance of the cash flows	= 0.20
Time to expiration	= 10 years
Risk-free interest rate	= .06

$$d_1 = \frac{\ln(\$80/\$100) + [0.06 + (1/2)0.2]10}{\sqrt{0.2}\sqrt{10}} = \frac{-0.2231 + 1.600}{0.4472 \times 3.1623} = \frac{1.3769}{1.4142} = 0.9736$$

$$d_2 = 0.9736 - 1.4142 = -0.4406$$

$$C = \$80(0.8340) - \$100(2.7183)^{-.06 \times 10}(0.3300) = \$66.72 - \$18.11 = \$48.61 \text{ (value of the call option)}$$

The net present value of the investment in retooling Comet's operations including the value of the call option is $28.61 million (i.e., $80 − $100 + $48.61). Including the value of the option, AJAX could pay Comet up to $178.61 million (i.e., $150 million + $28.61 million). Therefore, it does make sense for AJAX to exercise its option to retool Comet's operations, and AJAX can justify paying Comet its $160 million asking price.

Note: Z-values for d_1 and d_2 were obtained from a Cumulative Standardized Normal Distribution N(d) table in Levine, Berenson, and Stephan (1999), pp. E6–E7.

OPTION TO DELAY

The underlying asset is the project to which the firm has exclusive rights. The current value is the present value of expected cash flows from undertaking the project now. The variance of cash flows from similar past projects or acquisitions can be used to estimate the variance for the project under consideration. A firm exercises an option to delay when it decides to postpone investing in a project. The option's exercise price is the cost of making the initial investment.

The option to delay expires whenever the exclusive rights to the project end. Since the option eventually expires, excess profits associated with having the option disappear as other competitors emerge to exploit the opportunity. This opportunity cost associated with delaying implementation of an investment is similar to an adjustment made to the Black-Scholes model for stocks that pay dividends. The payment of a dividend is equivalent to reducing the value of the stock, since such funds are not reinvested in the firm to support future growth. Consequently, for a project whose expected cash flows are spread evenly throughout the option period, each year the project is delayed, the firm will lose one year of profits that it could have earned. Therefore, the annual cost of delay is $1/n$, where n is the time period for which the option is valid. If cash flows are not spread evenly, the cost of delay may be estimated as the projected cash flow for the next period as a percent of the current present value (see Exhibit 8.9). Equation (8.4) may be modified to reflect these considerations.

$$C = SN(d_1)e^{-DYt} - Ee^{-Rt}N(d_2) \qquad (8.6)$$

where

$$d_1 = \frac{\ln(S/E) + \left[R + (1/2)\sigma^2\right]t}{\sigma\sqrt{t}}$$

$$d_2 = d_1 - \sigma\sqrt{t}$$

DY = dividend yield or opportunity cost

EXHIBIT 8.9 VALUING AN OPTION TO DELAY USING THE BLACK-SCHOLES MODEL

Aztec Corp. has an opportunity to acquire Pharmaceuticals Unlimited, which has a new cancer-fighting drug recently approved by the Food and Drug Administration. While current market studies indicate that the new drug's market acceptance will be slow due to competing drugs, it is believed that the drug will have meteoric growth potential in the long term as new applications are identified. The R&D and commercialization costs associated with exploiting new applications are expected to require an upfront investment of $60 million. However, Aztec can delay making this investment until it is more confident of the new drug's actual growth potential.

It is believed that Pharmaceuticals Unlimited's research and development efforts give it a five-year time period before competitors will have similar drugs on the market to exploit these new applications. However, if the higher growth for the new drug and its related applications do not materialize, Aztec estimates that the NPV for Pharmaceuticals Unlimited will be $(30). That is, if the new cancer-fighting drug does not realize its potential, it makes no sense for Aztec to acquire Pharmaceuticals Unlimited. Cash flows from previous drug introductions have exhibited a variance equal to 50% of the present value of the cash flows. Simulating alternative growth scenarios for this new drug provides an expected value of $40 million. The five-year Treasury bond rate (corresponding to the expected term of the option) is 6%. Despite the negative NPV associated with the acquisition, does the existence of the option to delay, valued as a call option, justify Aztec acquiring Pharmaceuticals Unlimited (see Eq. (8.6))?

Solution

Value of the asset (PV of projected cash flows for the new drug)	= $40 million
Exercise price (investment required to fully develop the new drug)	= $60 million
Variance of the cash flows	= 0.5
Time to expiration (t)	= 5 years
Risk-free interest rate	= 0.06
Dividend yield or opportunity cost (cost of delay = 1/5)	= 0.2

$$d_1 = \frac{\ln(\$40/\$60) + [0.06 - 0.2 + (1/2)0.5]5}{\sqrt{0.5}\sqrt{5}} = \frac{-0.4055 + 0.5500}{0.7071 \times 2.2361} = \frac{0.1445}{1.5811} = 0.0914$$

$d_2 = 0.0914 - 1.5811 = -1.4897$

$C = \$40(0.5359)2.7183^{-0.2\times5} - \$60(0.0681)(2.7183)^{-0.06\times5}$

$\quad = \$40 \times (0.5359) \times 0.3679 - \$60 \times (0.0681) \times 0.7408$

$\quad = \$7.89 - \$3.03 = \$4.86$ million (value of the call option)

The modest $4.86 million value of the call option is insufficient to offset the negative NPV of $30 million associated with the acquisition. Consequently, Aztec should not acquire Pharmaceuticals Unlimited.

Note: Z-values for d_1 and d_2 were obtained from a Cumulative Standardized Normal Distribution N(d) table in Levine, Berenson, and Stephan (1999), pp. E6–E7.

OPTION TO ABANDON

For a project with a remaining life of n years, the value of continuing the project should be compared to its value in liquidation or sale (i.e., abandonment). The project should be continued if its value exceeds the liquidation value or sale value. Otherwise, the project should be abandoned. The option to abandon is equivalent to a put option (i.e., the right to sell an asset for a predetermined price at or before a stipulated time). The Black-Scholes formula for valuing a call option can be rewritten to value a put option (P) as follows (see Eq. (8.4)):

$$P = S\{1 - N(d_2)\}e^{-Rt} - E\{1 - N(d_1)\}e^{-DYt} \tag{8.7}$$

where

P = theoretical put option value

$$d_1 = \frac{\ln(S/E) + \left[R + DY(1/2)\sigma^2\right]t}{\sigma\sqrt{t}}$$

$$d_2 = d_1 - \sigma\sqrt{t}$$

Exhibit 8.10 illustrates how the abandonment or put option can be applied.

EXHIBIT 8.10 VALUING AN OPTION TO ABANDON USING THE BLACK-SCHOLES MODEL

BETA Inc. has agreed to acquire a 30% ownership stake in Bernard Mining for $225 million to help finance the development of new mining operations. The mines are expected to have an economically useful life of 35 years. BETA estimates that the present value of its share of the cash flows would be $210 million, resulting in a negative NPV of $15 million (i.e., $210 million – $225 million). To induce BETA to make the investment, Bernard Mining has given BETA a put option enabling it to sell its share (i.e., abandon its investment) to Bernard at any point during the next five years for $175 million. The put option limits the downside risk to BETA.

In evaluating the terms of the deal, BETA needs to value the put option, whose present value will vary depending on when it is exercised. BETA estimates the average variance in the present values of future cash flows to be 20%, based on the variance of the share prices of publicly traded similar mining companies. Since the value of the mines will diminish over time as the reserves are depleted, the present value of the investment will diminish over time because there will be fewer years of cash flows remaining. The dividend yield or opportunity cost is estimated to be 1/number of years of profitable reserves remaining. The risk-free rate of return is 4%. Is the value of the put option sufficient to justify making the investment despite the negative net present value of the investment without the inclusion of the option value (see Eq. (8.7))?

Solution

Present or expected value of BETA's 30% share of Bernard   = $210 million
Exercise price of put option   = $175 million
Time to expiration of put option   = 5
Variance   = 20%
Dividend yield (1/35)   = 0.029

$$d_1 = \frac{\ln(\$210/\$175) + (0.04 - 0.029 + (1/2)0.2)5}{\sqrt{0.2} \times \sqrt{5}} = \frac{0.1823 + 0.5550}{0.4472 \times 2.2361} = \frac{0.7373}{1.0} = 0.7373$$

$$d_2 = 0.7373 - 1.000 = -0.2627$$

$$p = \$210 \times (1 - 0.6026) \times 2.7183^{-0.04\times5} - \$175 \times (1 - 0.7673) \times 2.7183^{-0.029\times5}$$
$$= \$210 \times 0.3974 \times 0.8187 - \$175 \times 0.2327 \times 0.8650 = \$33.10$$

The value of the put option represents the additional value created by reducing risk associated with the investment. This additional value justifies the investment, as the sum of the NPV of $(15) million and the put option of $33.10 million gives a total NPV of $18.10 million.

Note: Z-scores for d_1 and d_2 were obtained from a cumulative Standardized Normal Distribution N(d) table in Levine, Berenson, and Stephan (1999), pp. E6–E7.

DETERMINING WHEN TO USE THE DIFFERENT APPROACHES TO VALUATION

Table 8.4 summarizes the circumstances under which it would be most appropriate to use each valuation methodology. These methodologies include the discounted-cash-flow (DCF) approach discussed in detail in Chapter 7, as well as the relative, asset-oriented, replacement-cost, and contingent-claims methods (i.e., real options) discussed in this chapter. If the intention is to obtain a controlling interest in the firm, a control premium must be added to the estimated economic value of the firm to determine the purchase price. The exception is the comparable recent transactions method, which already contains a premium.

TABLE 8.4   When to Use Various Valuation Methodologies

Methodology	Use Each Methodology When:
Discounted Cash Flow	• The firm is publicly traded or private with identifiable cash flows • A start-up has some history to facilitate cash-flow forecasts • An analyst has a long-term time horizon • An analyst has confidence in forecasting the firm's cash flows • Current or near-term earnings or cash flows are negative but are expected to turn positive in the future • A firm's competitive advantage is expected to be sustainable • The magnitude and timing of cash flows vary significantly
Comparable Companies	• There are many firms exhibiting similar growth, return, and risk characteristics • An analyst has a short-term time horizon • Prior, current, or near-term earnings or cash flows are positive • An analyst has confidence that the markets are, on average, right • Sufficient information to predict cash flows is lacking • Firms are cyclical. For P/E ratios, use normalized earnings (i.e., earnings averaged throughout the business cycle) • Growth rate differences among firms are large. Use the PEG ratio.
Comparable Transactions	• Recent transactions of similar firms exist • An analyst has a short-term time horizon • An analyst has confidence the markets are, on average, right • Sufficient information to predict cash flows is lacking
Same or Comparable Industry	• Firms within the same industry or comparable industry are substantially similar in terms of profitability, growth, and risk • An analyst has confidence the markets are, on average, right • Sufficient information to predict cash flows is lacking
Replacement Cost	• An analyst wants to know the current cost of replicating a firm's assets • The firm's assets are easily identifiable, tangible, and separable • The firm's earnings or cash flows are negative
Tangible Book Value	• The firms' assets are highly liquid • The firm is a financial services or product distribution business • The firm's earnings and cash flows are negative

TABLE 8.4   Cont'd

Methodology	Use Each Methodology When:
Breakup Value	• The sum of the value of the businesses or product lines comprising a firm are believed to exceed its value as a going concern
Liquidation Value	• An analyst wants to know asset values if the assets were liquidated today • Assets are separable, tangible, and marketable • Firms are bankrupt or subject to substantial financial distress • An orderly liquidation is possible
Real Options (Contingent Claims)	• Additional value can be created if management has a viable option to expand, delay, or abandon an investment • Assets not currently generating cash flows have the potential to do so • The markets have not valued the management decision-making flexibility associated with the option • Assets have characteristics most resembling financial options • The asset owner has some degree of exclusivity (e.g., a patent)

290-297

WHICH VALUATION METHODS ARE ACTUALLY USED IN PRACTICE

Practitioners tend to use price-to-earnings and cash-flow multiples in valuation more frequently than discounted-cash-flow models. The popularity of multiples reflects the combination of their relative simplicity and previously cited evidence that earnings and cash flow are highly positively correlated with stock returns over long periods such as five years or more. For shorter periods, earnings show a closer correlation with stock returns than cash flows. Cash-flow multiples are used for valuation when a firm's earnings are negative.

In a study of analysts and mutual fund managers in the United Kingdom, a researcher assessed the frequency of use of price-to-earnings ratios, dividend yields, price–to–free cash flow, sales-to-market capitalization, net asset value, and discounted cash flow. The author concluded that valuation multiples based on earnings and cash flow were the most common and DCF methods and dividend discount models were used the least.[17] A study of 26 international investment banks showed that, while P/E-based models are most commonly used in valuation, investment bankers often resort to using various methods, including DCF models and price-to-sales multiples, depending on the situation (e.g., writing fairness opinion letters).[18] A review of the *Institutional Investor All-American Analyst Reports* found market-to-book multiples were commonly used in valuing firms, while there was no evidence that DCF valuation was used.[19]

[17] Barker, 1999

[18] Demirakos et al., 2004

[19] Asquith et al., 2005

SOME THINGS TO REMEMBER

Relative-valuation and asset-oriented techniques offer a variety of alternatives to the use of discounted-cash-flow estimates. The comparable companies approach entails the multiplication of certain value indicators for the target, such as earnings, by the appropriate valuation multiple for comparable companies. Similarly, the comparable transactions method involves the multiplication of the target's earnings by the same valuation multiple for recent, similar transactions. The comparable industry approach applies industry average multiples to earnings, to cash flow, to book value, or to sales. Asset-oriented methods, such as tangible book value, are very useful for valuing financial services companies and distribution companies. Liquidation or breakup value is the projected price of the firm's assets sold separately less its liabilities and associated expenses. Since no single valuation approach ensures accuracy, analysts often choose to use a weighted average of several valuation methods to increase their level of confidence in the final estimate.

The term *real options* refers to management's ability to revise corporate investment decisions after they have been made. Since real options can be costly, complex, and dependent on questionable assumptions, they should not be considered unless they are clearly identifiable and realizable, and significantly add to the value of the underlying investment.

DISCUSSION QUESTIONS

8.1 Does the application of the comparable companies valuation method require the addition of an acquisition premium? Why or why not?

8.2 Which is generally considered more accurate: the comparable companies or recent transactions method? Explain your answer.

8.3 What key assumptions are implicit in using the comparable companies valuation method? The recent comparable transactions method?

8.4 Explain the primary differences between the income (discounted cash flow), market-based, and asset-oriented valuation methods.

8.5 Under what circumstances might it be more appropriate to use relative-valuation methods rather than the DCF approach? Be specific.

8.6 PEG ratios allow for the adjustment of relative-valuation methods for the expected growth of the firm. How might this be helpful in selecting potential acquisition targets? Be specific.

8.7 How is the liquidation value of the firm calculated? Why is the assumption of orderly liquidation important?

8.8 What are real options and how are they applied in valuing acquisitions?

8.9 Give examples of pre- and postclosing real options. Be specific.

8.10 Conventional DCF analysis does not incorporate the effects of real options into the valuation of an asset. How might an analyst incorporate the potential impact of real options into conventional DCF valuation methods?

Answers to these Chapter Discussion Questions are available in the Online Instructor's Manual for instructors using this book.

Practice Problems and Answers

8.11 BigCo's chief financial officer is trying to determine a fair value for PrivCo, a nonpublicly traded firm that BigCo is considering acquiring. Several of PrivCo's competitors, Ion International and Zenon, are publicly traded. Ion and Zenon have P/E ratios of 20 and 15, respectively. Moreover, Ion and Zenon's shares trade at a multiple of earnings before interest, taxes, depreciation, and amortization (EBITDA) of 10 and 8, respectively. BigCo estimates that next year, PrivCo will achieve net income and EBITDA of $4 million and $8 million, respectively. To gain a controlling interest in the firm, BigCo expects to have to pay at least a 30% premium to the firm's market value. What should BigCo expect to pay for PrivCo?

a. Based on P/E ratios?

b. Based on EBITDA?

Answers:

a. $91 million

b. $93.6 million

8.12 LAFCO Industries believes that its two primary product lines, automotive and commercial aircraft valves, are becoming obsolete rapidly. Its free cash flow is diminishing quickly as it loses market share to new firms entering its industry. LAFCO has $200 million in debt outstanding. Senior management expects the automotive and commercial aircraft valve product lines to generate $25 million and $15 million, respectively, in earnings before interest, taxes, depreciation, and amortization next year. The operating liabilities associated with these two product lines are minimal. Senior management also believes that it will not be able to upgrade these product lines because of declining cash flow and excessive current leverage. A competitor to its automotive valve business last year sold for 10 times EBITDA. Moreover, a company similar to its commercial aircraft valve product line sold last month for 12 times EBITDA. Estimate LAFCO's breakup value before taxes. 250 + 180 - 200

Answer: $230 million

8.13 Siebel Incorporated, a nonpublicly traded company, has 2009 after-tax earnings of $20 million, which are expected to grow at 5% annually into the foreseeable future. The firm is debt free, capital spending equals the firm's rate of depreciation, and the annual change in working capital is expected to be minimal. The firm's beta is estimated to be 2.0, the ten-year Treasury bond is 5%, and the historical risk premium of stocks over the risk-free rate is 5.5%. Publicly traded Rand Technology, a direct competitor of Siebel's, was sold recently at a purchase price of 11 times its 2009 after-tax earnings, which included a 20% premium over its current market price. Aware of the premium paid for the purchase of Rand, Siebel's equity owners would like to determine what it might be worth if they were to attempt to sell the firm in the near future. They choose to value the firm using the discounted-cash-flow and comparable recent transactions methods. They believe that either method provides an equally valid estimate of the firm's value.

a. What is the value of Siebel using the DCF method?

b. What is the value using the comparable recent transactions method?

c. What will be the value of the firm if we combine the results of both methods?

Answers:

a. $228.9 million

b. $220 million

c. $224.5 million

TABLE 8.5   Titanic Corporation Balance Sheet

Balance Sheet Item	Book Value of Assets	Liquidation Value
Cash	$10	10
Accounts receivable	$20 70	14
Inventory	$15 40	6
Net fixed assets excluding land	$8 25	2
Land	$6 120 7.2	−2·9
Total assets	$59 −2·9	
Total liabilities	$35 −35	
Shareholders' equity	$24 1·3.	

8.14 Titanic Corporation reached an agreement with its creditors to voluntarily liquidate its assets and use the proceeds to pay off as much of its liabilities as possible. The firm anticipates that it will be able to sell off its assets in an orderly fashion, realizing as much as 70% of the book value of its receivables, 40% of its inventory, and 25% of its net fixed assets (excluding land). However, the firm believes that the land on which it is located can be sold for 120% of book value. The firm has legal and professional expenses associated with the liquidation process of $2.9 million. The firm has only common stock outstanding. Using Table 8.5, estimate the amount of cash that will remain for the firm's common shareholders once all assets have been liquidated.

Answer: $1.3 million

8.15 Best's Foods is seeking to acquire the Heinz Baking Company, whose shareholders' equity and goodwill are $41 million and $7 million, respectively. A comparable bakery was recently acquired for $400 million, 30% more than its tangible book value (TBV). What was the tangible book value of the recently acquired bakery? How much should Best's Foods expect to have to pay for the Heinz Baking Company? Show your work.

Answer: The TBV of the recently acquired bakery = $307.7 million, and the likely purchase price of Heinz = $44.2 million.

8.16 Delhi Automotive Inc. is the leading supplier of specialty fasteners for passenger cars in the U.S. market, with an estimated 25% share of this $5 billion market. Delhi's rapid growth in recent years has been fueled by high levels of reinvestment in the firm. While this has resulted in the firm having "state-of-the-art" plants, it also has resulted in the firm showing limited profitability and positive cash flow. Delhi is privately owned and has announced that it is going to undertake an initial public offering in the near future. Investors know that economies of scale are important in this high-fixed-cost industry and understand that market share is an important determinant of future profitability. Thornton Auto Inc., a publicly traded firm and the leader in this market, has an estimated market share of 38% and an $800 million market value. How should investors value the Delhi IPO? Show your work.

Answer: $526.3 million

8.17 Photon Inc. is considering acquiring one of its competitors. Photon's management wants to buy a firm it believes is most undervalued. The firm's three major competitors, AJAX, BABO, and COMET, have current market values of $375 million, $310 million, and $265 million, respectively. AJAX's FCFE is expected to grow at 10% annually, while BABO's and COMET's FCFEs are projected to grow by 12 and 14% per year, respectively. AJAX, BABO, and COMET's current-year FCFEs are $24, $22, and $17 million, respectively. The industry average price-to-FCFE ratio and growth rate are 10 and 8%, respectively. Estimate the market value of each of the three potential acquisition targets based on the information provided. Which firm is the most undervalued? Which firm is most overvalued? Show your work. Answer: AJAX is most overvalued and COMET is most undervalued.

8.18 Acquirer Incorporated's management believes that the most reliable way to value a potential target firm is by averaging multiple valuation methods, since all methods have their short-comings. Consequently, Acquirer's chief financial officer estimates that the value of Target Inc. could range, before an acquisition premium is added, from a high of $650 million using discounted-cash-flow analysis to a low of $500 million using the comparable companies relative-valuation method. A valuation based on a recent comparable transaction is $672 million. The CFO anticipates that Target Inc.'s management and shareholders would be willing to sell for a 20% acquisition premium, based on the premium paid for the recent comparable transaction. The CEO asks the CFO to provide a single estimate of the value of Target Inc. based on the three estimates. In calculating a weighted average of the three estimates, she gives a value of 0.5 to the recent transactions method, 0.3 to the DCF estimate, and 0.2 to the comparable companies estimate. What is the weighted-average estimate she gives to the CEO? Show your work.
Answer: $690 million

8.19 An investor group has the opportunity to purchase a firm whose primary asset is ownership of the exclusive rights to develop a parcel of undeveloped land sometime during the next five years. Without considering the value of the option to develop the property, the investor group believes the net present value of the firm is $(10) million. However, to convert the property to commercial use (i.e., exercise the option), the investors have to invest $60 million immediately in infrastructure improvements. The primary uncertainty associated with the property is how rapidly the surrounding area will grow. Based on their experience with similar properties, the investors estimate that the variance of the projected cash flows is 5% of NPV, which is $55 million. Assume the risk-free rate of return is 4%. What is the value of the call option the investor group would obtain by buying the firm? Is it sufficient to justify the acquisition of the firm? Show your work.
Answer: The value of the option is $13.47 million. The investor group should buy the firm, since the value of the option more than offsets the $(10) million NPV of the firm if the call option were not exercised.

8.20 Acquirer Company's management believes that there is a 60% chance that Target Company's free cash flow will grow at 20% per year during the next five years from this year's level of $5 million. Sustainable growth beyond the fifth year is estimated at 4% per year. However, management also believes that there is a 40% chance that cash flow will grow at half that annual rate during the next five years, and then at a 4% rate thereafter. The discount rate is estimated to be 15% during the high-growth period and 12% during the sustainable-growth period. What is the expected value of Target Company?
Answer: $94.93 million

Answers to these Practice Problems are available in the Online Instructor's Manual for instructors using this book.

CHAPTER BUSINESS CASES

CASE STUDY 8.1
Google Buys YouTube: Valuing a Firm in the Absence of Cash Flows

YouTube ranks as one of the most heavily utilized sites on the Internet, with 1 billion views per day, 20 hours of new video uploaded every minute, and 300 million users worldwide. Despite the explosion in usage, Google continues to struggle to "monetize" the traffic on the site five years after having acquired the video sharing business. 2010 marked the first time the business turned marginally profitable.[20] Whether the transaction is viewed as successful depends on whether it is evaluated on a stand-alone basis or as part of a larger strategy designed to steer additional traffic to Google sites and promote the brand.

This case study illustrates how a value driver approach to valuation could have been used by Google to estimate the potential value of YouTube by collecting publicly available data for a comparable business. Note the importance of clearly identifying key assumptions underlying the valuation. The credibility of the valuation ultimately depends on the credibility of the assumptions.

Google acquired YouTube in late 2006 for $1.65 billion in stock. At that time, the business had been in existence only for 14 months, consisted of 65 employees, and had no significant revenues. However, what it lacked in size it made up in global recognition and a rapidly escalating number of site visitors. Under pressure to continue to fuel its own meteoric 77% annual revenue growth rate, Google moved aggressively to acquire YouTube in an attempt to assume center stage in the rapidly growing online video market. With no debt, $9 billion in cash, and a net profit margin of about 25%, Google was in remarkable financial health for a firm growing so rapidly. The acquisition was by far the most expensive by Google in its relatively short eight-year history. In 2005, Google spent $130.5 million in acquiring 15 small firms. Google seemed to be placing a big bet that YouTube would become a huge marketing hub as its increasing number of viewers attracted advertisers interested in moving from television to the Internet.

Started in February 2005 in the garage of one of the founders, YouTube displayed in 2006 more than 100 million videos daily and had an estimated 72 million visitors from around the world each month, of which 34 million were unique.[21] As part of Google, YouTube retained its name and current headquarters in San Bruno, California. In addition to receiving funding from Google, YouTube was able to tap into Google's substantial technological and advertising expertise.

To determine if Google is likely to earn its cost of equity on its investment in YouTube, we have to establish a base-year free-cash-flow estimate for YouTube. This may be done by examining the performance of a similar but more mature website, such as about.com. Acquired by *The New York Times* in February 2005 for

---

[20] Briel, 2010

[21] Unique visitors are those whose IP addresses are counted only once no matter how many times they visit a website during a given period.

CASE STUDY 8.1 *(cont'd)*

$410 million, about.com is a website offering consumer information and advice and is believed to be one of the biggest and most profitable websites on the Internet, with estimated 2006 revenues of almost $100 million. With a monthly average number of unique visitors worldwide of 42.6 million, about.com's revenue per unique visitor was estimated to be about $0.15, based on monthly revenues of $6.4 million.[22]

Assuming that these numbers could be duplicated by YouTube within the first full year of ownership by Google, YouTube could potentially achieve monthly revenue of $5.1 million (i.e., $0.15 per unique visitor × 34 million unique YouTube visitors) by the end of the year. Assuming net profit margins comparable to Google's 25%, YouTube could generate about $1.28 million in after-tax profits on those sales. If that monthly level of sales and profits could be sustained for the full year, YouTube could achieve annual sales in the second year of $61.2 million (i.e., $5.1 × 12) and profit of $15.4 million ($1.28 × 12). Assuming optimistically that capital spending and depreciation grow at the same rate and that the annual change in working capital is minimal, YouTube's free cash flow would equal after-tax profits.

Recall that a firm earns its cost of equity on an investment whenever the net present value of the investment is zero. Assuming a risk-free rate of return of 5.5%, a beta of 0.82 (per Yahoo! Finance), and an equity premium of 5.5%, Google's cost of equity would be 10%. For Google to earn its cost of equity on its investment in YouTube, YouTube would have to generate future cash flows whose present

value would be at least $1.65 billion (i.e., equal to its purchase price). To achieve this result, YouTube's free cash flow to equity would have to grow at a compound annual average growth rate of 225% for the next 15 years, and then 5% per year thereafter. Note that the present value of the cash flows during the initial 15-year period would be $605 million and the present value of the terminal period cash flows would be $1,005 million. Using a higher revenue per unique visitor assumption would result in a slower required annual growth rate in cash flows to earn the 10% cost of equity. However, a higher discount rate might be appropriate to reflect YouTube's higher investment risk. Using a higher discount rate would require revenue growth to be even faster to achieve an NPV equal to zero.

Google could easily have paid cash, assuming that the YouTube owners would prefer cash to Google stock. Perhaps Google saw its stock as overvalued and decided to use it now to minimize the number of new shares that it would have had to issue to acquire YouTube, or perhaps YouTube shareholders simply viewed Google stock as more attractive than cash.

With YouTube having achieved marginal profitability in 2010, it would appear that the valuation assumptions implicit in Google's initial valuation of YouTube may, indeed, have been highly optimistic. While YouTube continues to be wildly successful in terms of the number of site visits, with unique monthly visits having increased almost sixfold from their 2006 level, it appears to be disappointing at this juncture in terms of profitability and cash flow. The traffic continues to grow as a result of integration with social networks such

---

[22] Aboutmediakit, September 17, 2006, *http://beanadvertiser.about.com/archive/news091606.html*.

CASE STUDY 8.1   *(cont'd)*

as Facebook and initiatives such as the ability to send clips to friends as well as to rate and comment on videos. Moreover, YouTube is showing some progress in improving profitability by continuing to expand its index of professionally produced premium content. Nevertheless, on a stand-alone basis, it is problematic that YouTube will earn Google's cost of equity. However, as part of a broader Google strategy involving multiple acquisitions to attract additional traffic to Google and to promote the brand, the purchase may indeed make sense.

Discussion Questions

1. What alternative valuation methods could Google have used to justify the purchase price it paid for YouTube? Discuss the advantages and disadvantages of each.
2. The purchase price paid for YouTube represented more than 1% of Google's

then market value. If you were a Google shareholder at that time, how might you have evaluated the wisdom of the acquisition?

3. To what extent might the use of stock by Google have influenced the amount it was willing to pay for YouTube? How might the use of "overvalued" shares impact future appreciation of the stock?
4. What is the appropriate cost of equity for discounting future cash flows? Should it be Google's or YouTube's? Explain your answer.
5. What are the critical valuation assumptions implicit in the valuation method discussed in this case study? Be specific.

Answers to these questions are provided in the Online Instructor's Guide accompanying this manual.

CASE STUDY 8.2
Merrill Lynch and BlackRock Agree to Swap Assets

During the 1990s, many financial services companies began offering mutual funds to their current customers who were pouring money into the then booming stock market. Hoping to become financial supermarkets offering an array of financial services to their customers, these firms offered mutual funds under their own brand name. The proliferation of mutual funds made it more difficult to be noticed by potential customers and required the firms to boost substantially advertising expenditures at a time when increased competition was reducing mutual fund management fees. In addition, potential customers were concerned that brokers

would promote their own firm's mutual funds to boost profits.

This trend reversed in recent years, as banks, brokerage houses, and insurance companies were exiting the mutual fund management business. Merrill Lynch agreed on February 15, 2006, to swap its mutual funds business for an approximate 49% stake in money-manager BlackRock Inc. The mutual fund or retail accounts represented a new customer group for BlackRock, founded in 1987, which had previously managed primarily institutional accounts.

At $453 billion in 2005, BlackRock's assets under management had grown four times

CASE STUDY 8.2 *(cont'd)*

faster than Merrill's $544 billion mutual fund assets. During 2005, BlackRock's net income increased to $270 million, or 63% over the prior year, as compared to Merrill's 27% growth in net income in its mutual fund business to $397 million. BlackRock and Merrill stock traded at 30 and 19 times estimated 2006 earnings, respectively.

Merrill assets and net income represented 55% and 60% of the combined BlackRock and Merrill assets and net income, respectively. Under the terms of the transaction, BlackRock would issue 65 million new common shares to Merrill. Based on BlackRock's February 14, 2005, closing price, the deal is valued at $9.8 billion. The common stock gave Merrill 49% of the outstanding BlackRock voting stock. PNC Financial and employees and public shareholders owned 34% and 17%, respectively. Merrill's ability to influence board decisions is limited, since it has only 2 of 17 seats on the BlackRock board of directors.

Certain "significant matters" require a 70% vote of all board members and 100% of the nine independent members, which include the two Merrill representatives. Merrill (along with PNC) must also vote its shares as recommended by the BlackRock board.

Discussion Questions

1. Merrill owns less than half of the combined firms, although it contributed more than one-half of the combined firms' assets and net income. Discuss how you might use DCF and relative-valuation methods to determine Merrill's proportionate ownership in the combined firms.

2. Why do you believe Merrill was willing to limit its influence in the combined firms?

3. What method of accounting would Merrill use to show its investment in BlackRock?

Answers to these questions are found in the Online Instructor's Manual for instructors using this manual.

Applying Financial Modeling Techniques

To Value, Structure, and Negotiate Mergers and Acquisitions

There are two kinds of forecasters: the ones who don't know and the ones who don't know they don't know. —**John Kenneth Galbraith**

299 – 300.

INSIDE M&A: HP BUYS EDS—THE ROLE OF FINANCIAL MODELS IN DECISION MAKING

Personal computer printer behemoth Hewlett-Packard (HP), had just announced its agreement to buy Electronic Data Systems (EDS) on May 9, 2008, for $13.9 billion (including assumed debt of $700 million) in an all-cash deal. The purchase price represented a 33% premium for EDS, a systems integration, consulting, and services firm. Expressing their dismay, investors drove HP's share price down by 11% in a single day following the announcement.

In a meeting arranged to respond to questions about the deal, HP's chief executive Mark Hurd found himself barraged by concerns about how the firm intended to recover the sizeable premium it had paid for EDS. The CEO had been a Wall Street darling since he had assumed his position three years earlier. Under his direction, the firm's profits rose sharply as it successfully cut costs while growing revenue and integrating several acquisitions. Asked how HP expected to generate substantial synergies by combining two very different organizations, Mr. Hurd indicated that the firm and its advisors had done "double-digit thousands of hours" in due diligence and financial modeling and that they were satisfied that the cost synergies were there. In an effort to demonstrate how conservative they had been, the CEO indicated that potential revenue synergies had not even been included in their financial models. However, he was convinced that there were significant upside revenue opportunities.[1]

[1] Richtel, 2008

CHAPTER OVERVIEW

Financial modeling refers to the application of spreadsheet software to define simple arithmetic relationships among variables within the firm's income, balance sheet, and cash-flow statements and to define the interrelationships among the various financial statements. The primary objective in applying financial modeling techniques is to create a computer-based model, which facilitates the acquirer's understanding of the effect that changes in certain operating variables have on the firm's overall performance and valuation. Once in place, these models can be used to simulate alternative plausible valuation scenarios to determine which one enables the acquirer to achieve its financial objectives without violating identifiable constraints. Financial objectives could include earnings per share (EPS) for publicly traded firms, return on total capital for privately held firms, or internal rates of return for leveraged buyout firms. Typical constraints include Wall Street analysts' expectations for the firm's EPS, the acquirer's leverage compared with other firms in the same industry, and loan covenants limiting how the firm uses its available cash flow. Another important constraint is the risk tolerance of the acquiring company's management, which could be measured by the acquirer's target debt-to-equity ratio.

Financial models can be used to answer several sets of questions. The first set pertains to valuation. How much is the target company worth without the effects of synergy? What is the value of expected synergy? What is the maximum price the acquiring company should pay for the target? The second set of questions pertains to financing. Can the proposed purchase price be financed? What combination of potential sources of funds, both internally generated and external sources, provides the lowest cost of funds for the acquirer, subject to known constraints (e.g., existing loan covenants)? The final set of questions pertains to deal structuring. What is the impact on the acquirer's financial performance if the deal is structured as a taxable rather than a nontaxable transaction? What is the impact on financial performance and valuation if the acquirer is willing to assume certain target company liabilities? Deal-structuring considerations are discussed in detail in Chapters 11 and 12.

The purpose of this chapter is to illustrate a process for building a financial model in the context of a merger or acquisition. The process allows the analyst to determine the minimum and maximum prices for a target firm and the initial offer price. The author also provides a simulation model for assessing the impact of various offer prices on postmerger EPS and discusses how this capability can be used in the negotiating process. Finally, the flexibility of these modeling techniques is illustrated by showing how they may be applied to special situations, such as when the acquirer or target is part of a parent firm or when the objective is to value, structure, and negotiate a joint venture or business alliance. The Microsoft Excel spreadsheets and formulas for the models described in this chapter are available in the file folder entitled "Mergers and Acquisitions Valuation and Structuring Model" on the companion site to this book (*www.elsevierdirect.com/companions/9780123854858*).

A review of this chapter (including practice questions and answers) is available in the file folder entitled "Student Study Guide" on the companion site to this book. The companion site also contains a Learning Interactions Library, which gives students the opportunity to test their knowledge of this chapter in a "real-time" environment, as well as a document discussing how to interpret the financial ratios commonly generated by financial models. See Appendix A for more details on how to use the companion site M&A model,[2] and see Appendix B for a discussion of common methods of "balancing" financial models.

LIMITATIONS OF FINANCIAL DATA

The output of models is only as good as the accuracy and timeliness of the numbers used to create them and the quality of the assumptions used in making projections. Consequently, analysts must understand on what basis numbers are collected and reported. Consistency and adherence to uniform standards become exceedingly important.

Generally Accepted Accounting Principles and International Standards

U.S. public companies prepare their financial statements in accordance with *generally accepted accounting principles* (GAAP). GAAP financial statements are those prepared in agreement with guidelines established by the Financial Accounting Standards Board (FASB). GAAP is a rules-based system, giving explicit instructions for every situation that the FASB has anticipated. In contrast, *international accounting standards* (IAS) are a principles-based system, with more generalized standards to follow. All European Union publicly traded companies had to adopt the IAS system in 2007; according to the International Accounting Standards Board (IASB), more than 150 countries are expected to have adopted IAS by the end of 2011. GAAP and IAS currently exhibit significant differences. However, these differences could narrow in the coming years. The United States is considering whether to utilize international accounting standards for financial reporting purposes for all publicly traded firms.

When and the extent to which GAAP and IAS systems converge are open questions. While it may be possible to establish consistent accounting standards across countries, it is unclear if adherence to such standards can be enforced without a global regulatory authority. It is unclear that individual countries would readily submit to such an authority. Without effective enforcement, firms may largely ignore certain standards without fear of significant consequences. While multinational auditing firms may move to harmonize accounting practices, there are clear limits to their ability and willingness to do so. Multinational auditing firms usually consist of a series of legally independent, country-based partnerships. Consequently, cultural differences may create variation in the way accounting standards are applied.

In the absence of strict enforcement of consistent standards, do the benefits of converging accounting systems outweigh the cost of implementing a new system? By some estimates, the cost of converting to international accounting standards for S&P 500 companies could range from $40 to $60 billion over three years. While theoretically increased consistency and transparency could lower the cost of capital, the lack of a serious enforcement mechanism may limit the extent to which this occurs.[3]

[2] For more advanced discussions on financial modeling, see Mun (2006).

[3] Reilly, David, "Convergence Flaws," Presentation to the American Accounting Association, Tampa, Florida, January 29, 2011.

Few would argue that GAAP ensures that all transactions are accurately recorded. Nonetheless, the scrupulous application of GAAP does ensure consistency in comparing one firm's financial performance to another's. It is customary for purchase agreements in U.S. transactions to require that a target company represent that its financial books are kept in accordance with GAAP. Consequently, the acquiring company at least understands how the financial numbers were assembled. During due diligence, the acquirer can look for discrepancies between the target's reported numbers and GAAP practices. Such discrepancies could indicate potential problems.

Pro Forma Accounting

Pro forma financial statements present financial statements in a way that purports to more accurately describe a firm's current or projected performance. Because there are no accepted standards for pro forma accounting, pro forma statements may deviate substantially from standard GAAP statements. Pro forma statements frequently are used to show what an acquirer's and target's combined financial performance would look like if they were merged.

Although public companies still are required to file their financial statements with the Securities and Exchange Commission in accordance with GAAP, companies often argue that pro forma statements provide investors with a more realistic view of a company's core performance than GAAP reporting. Although pro forma statements provide useful insight into how a proposed combination of businesses might look, such liberal accounting techniques easily can be abused to hide a company's poor performance. Exhibit 9.1 suggests some ways in which an analyst can tell if a firm is engaging in inappropriate accounting practices.[4]

EXHIBIT 9.1 ACCOUNTING DISCREPANCY RED FLAGS

1. The source of the revenue is questionable. Beware of revenue generated by selling to an affiliated party, by selling something to a customer in exchange for something other than cash, or the receipt of investment income or cash received from a lender.
2. Income is inflated by nonrecurring gains. Gains on the sale of assets may be inflated by an artificially low book value of the assets sold.
3. Deferred revenue shows an unusually large increase. Deferred revenue increases as a firm collects money from customers in advance of delivering its products. It is reduced as the products are delivered. A jump in this balance sheet item could mean the firm is having trouble delivering its products.
4. Reserves for bad debt are declining as a percentage of revenue. This implies that the firm may be boosting revenue by not reserving enough to cover probable losses from customer accounts that cannot be collected.
5. Growth in accounts receivable exceeds substantially the increase in revenue or inventory. This may mean that a firm is having difficulty in selling its products (i.e., inventories are accumulating) or that it is having difficulty collecting what it is owed.
6. The growth in net income is significantly different from the growth in cash from operations. Because it is more difficult to "manage" cash flow than net income (which is subject to

---

[4] For a more detailed discussion of these issues, see Sherman and Young (2001).

distortion due to improper revenue recognition), this could indicate that net income is being deliberately misstated. Potential distortion may be particularly evident if the analyst adjusts end-of-period cash balances by deducting cash received from financing activities and adding back cash used for investment purposes. Consequently, changes in the adjusted cash balances should reflect changes in reported net income.

7. An increasing gap between a firm's income reported on its financial statements and its tax income. While it is legitimate for a firm to follow different accounting practices for financial reporting and tax purposes, the relationship between book and tax accounting is likely to remain constant over time, unless there are changes in tax rules or accounting standards.

8. Unexpected large asset write-offs. This may reflect management inertia in incorporating changing business circumstances into its accounting estimates.

9. Extensive use of related party transactions. Such transactions may not be subject to the same discipline and high standards of integrity as unrelated party transactions.

10. Changes in auditing firms that are not well justified. The firm may be seeking a firm that will accept its aggressive accounting positions.

THE MODEL-BUILDING PROCESS

The logic underlying the Excel-based M&A model found on the companion site follows the process discussed in this chapter. This process involves four discrete steps (Table 9.1). First, value the acquiring and target firms as stand-alone businesses. A *stand-alone business* is one whose financial statements reflect all the costs of running the business and all the revenues generated by the business. Second, value the consolidated acquirer (PV_A) and target (PV_T) firms, including the effects of synergy. The appropriate discount rate for the combined firms is generally the target's cost of capital; if the two firms have similar risk profiles and are based in the same country, either firm's cost of capital could be used. It is particularly important to use the target's cost of capital if the acquirer is merging with a higher-risk business, resulting in an increase in the acquirer's cost of capital.

Third, determine the initial offer price for the target firm. Fourth, determine the acquirer's ability to finance the purchase using an appropriate financial structure. The appropriate financial structure (debt–to–equity ratio) is that which satisfies certain predetermined criteria and which can be determined from a range of scenarios created by making small changes in selected value drivers. Value drivers are factors, such as product volume, selling price, and cost of sales, that have a significant impact on the value of the firm whenever they are altered (see Chapter 7).

Step 1. Value Acquirer and Target Firms as Stand-Alone Businesses

A merger or acquisition makes sense to the acquirer's shareholders only if the combined value of the target and acquiring firms exceeds the sum of their stand-alone (i.e., independent or separate) values. Consequently, in the first step of the model-building process outlined in Table 9.1, it is necessary to determine each firm's stand-alone value. This requires understanding the basis of competition within an industry.

TABLE 9.1   The Mergers and Acquisitions Model-Building Process

Step 1: Value Acquirer and Target as Stand-Alone Firms	Step 2: Value Acquirer and Target Firms, Including Synergy	Step 3: Determine Initial Offer Price for Target Firm Transaction	Step 4: Determine Combined Firms' Ability to Finance
1. Understand specific firm and industry competitive dynamics (see Chapter 4: Figure 4.2)	1. Estimate a. Sources and destroyers of value and b. Implementation costs incurred to realize synergy	1. Estimate minimum and maximum purchase price range	1. Estimate impact of alternative financing structures
2. Normalize 3–5 years of historical financial data (i.e., add or subtract nonrecurring losses/expenses or gains to smooth data)	2. Consolidate the acquirer and target stand-alone values, including the effects of synergy	2. Determine amount of synergy acquirer is willing to share with target shareholders	2. Select financing structure that a. Meets acquirer's required financial returns b. Meets target's primary needs c. Does not raise cost of debt or violate loan covenants d. Minimizes EPS dilution and short-term reduction in financial returns
3. Project normalized cash flow based on expected market growth and intensity of industry competition; calculate stand-alone values of acquirer and target firms	3. Estimate value of net synergy (i.e., consolidated firms, including synergy less stand-alone values of acquirer and target)	3. Determine appropriate composition of offer price (i.e., cash, stock, or some combination)	

Note: Key assumptions made for each step should be clearly stated.

Understand Specific Firm and Industry Competitive Dynamics

The accuracy of any valuation depends heavily on understanding the historical competitive dynamics of the industry, the historical performance of the company within the industry, and the reliability of the data used in the valuation. Competitive dynamics simply refer to the factors within the industry that determine industry profitability and cash flow. A careful examination of historical information can provide insights into key relationships among various operating variables. Examples of relevant historical relationships include seasonal or cyclical movements in the data, the relationship between fixed and variable expenses, and the impact on revenue of changes in product prices and unit sales. If these relationships can reasonably be expected to continue through the forecast period, they can be used to project valuation cash flows.

If the factors affecting sales, profit, and cash flow historically are expected to exert about the same degree of influence in the future, it is reasonable to forecast a firm's financial statements by extrapolating historical growth rates in key variables such as revenue. However, if the dynamics underlying sales growth are expected to change due to such factors as the introduction of new products, total revenue growth may accelerate from its historical trend. In contrast, the emergence of additional competitors may limit revenue growth by eroding the firm's market share and selling prices. Answers to the questions posed in Figure 9.1 provide helpful insights into how financial performance can be projected. (See Chapter 4 and Exhibit 4.2 for a more detailed discussion of the Porter Five Forces Model.)

Normalize Historical Data

To ensure that these historical relationships can be accurately defined, it is necessary to *normalize* the data by cleansing it of nonrecurring changes and questionable accounting practices. For example, cash flow may be adjusted by adding back unusually large increases in reserves or deducting large decreases in reserves from free cash flow to the firm. Similar adjustments can be made for significant nonrecurring gains or losses on the sale of assets or nonrecurring expenses, such as those associated with the settlement of a lawsuit or warranty claim. Monthly revenue may be aggregated into quarterly or even annual data to minimize period-to-period distortions in earnings or cash flow resulting from inappropriate accounting practices. While public companies are required to provide financial data for only the current and two prior years, it is highly desirable to use data spanning at least one business cycle (i.e., about five to seven years).

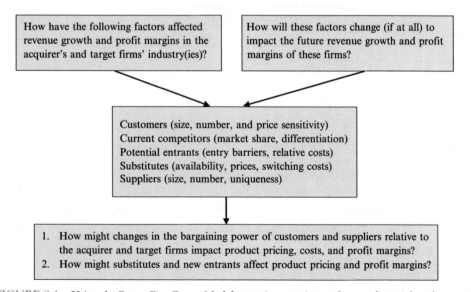

FIGURE 9.1   Using the Porter Five Forces Model to project acquirer and target financial performance.

Common-size financial statements are among the most frequently used tools to uncover data irregularities. These statements may be constructed by calculating the percentage each line item of the income statement, balance sheet, and cash-flow statement is of annual sales for each quarter or year for which historical data are available. Common-size financial statements are useful for comparing businesses of different sizes in the same industry at a specific moment in time. Such analyses are called *cross-sectional comparisons*. By expressing the target's line-item data as a percentage of sales, it is possible to compare the target company with other companies' line-item data expressed in terms of sales to highlight significant differences. For example, a cross-sectional comparison may indicate that the ratio of capital spending to sales for the target firm is much less than for other firms in the industry.

This discrepancy may simply reflect "catch-up" spending under way at the target's competitors, or it may suggest a more troubling development in which the target is deferring necessary plant and equipment spending. To determine which is true, it is necessary to calculate common-size financial statements for the target firm and its primary competitors over a number of consecutive periods. This type of analysis is called a *multiperiod comparison*. Comparing companies in this manner helps confirm whether the target simply has completed a large portion of capital spending that others in the industry are undertaking currently or is woefully behind in making necessary expenditures.[5]

Financial ratio analysis is the calculation of performance ratios from data in a company's financial statements to identify the firm's financial strengths and weaknesses. Such analysis helps in identifying potential problem areas that may require further examination during due diligence. Because ratios adjust for firm size, they enable the analyst to compare a firm's ratios with industry averages. A file entitled "A Primer on Applying and Interpreting Financial Ratios" on the companion site lists commonly used formulas for financial ratios, how they are expressed, and how they should be interpreted. These ratios should be compared with industry averages to discover if the company is out of line with others in the industry. A successful competitor's performance ratios may be used if industry average data[6] are not available.

---

[5] Even if it is not possible to collect sufficient data to undertake cross-sectional and multiperiod comparisons of both the target firm and its direct competitors, constructing common-size statements for the target firm only provides useful insights. Abnormally large increases or decreases in these ratios from one period to the next highlight the need for further examination to explain why these fluctuations occurred. If it is determined that they are one-time events, these fluctuations may be eliminated by averaging the data immediately preceding and following the period in which these anomalies occurred. The anomalous data then are replaced by the data created through this averaging process. Alternatively, anomalous data can be completely excluded from the analysis. In general, nonrecurring events affecting more than 10 percent of the net income or cash flow for a specific period should be discarded from the data to allow for a clearer picture of trends and relationships in the firm's historical financial data.

[6] Industry average data commonly is found in such publications as *The Almanac of Business and Industrial Financial Ratios* (Prentice Hall), *Annual Statement Studies* (Robert Morris Associates), *Dun's Review* (Dun and Bradstreet), *Industry Norms and Key Business Ratios* (Dun and Bradstreet), and *Value Line Investment Survey for Company and Industry Ratios* (Value Line).

Project Normalized Cash Flow

Normalized cash flows should be projected for at least five years, and possibly more, until they turn positive or the growth rate slows to what is believed to be a sustainable pace. Projections should reflect the best available information about product demand growth, future pricing, technological changes, new competitors, new product and service offerings from current competitors, potential supply disruptions, raw material and labor cost increases, and possible new product or service substitutes. Projections also should include the revenue and costs associated with known new product introductions and capital expenditures, as well as additional expenses, required to maintain or expand operations by the acquiring and target firms during the forecast period.

A simple model to project cash flow involves the projection of revenue and the various components of cash flow as a percent of projected revenue. For example, cost of sales, depreciation, gross capital spending, and the change in working capital are projected as a percent of projected revenue. What percentage is applied to projected revenue for these components of free cash flow to the firm may be determined by calculating their historical ratio to revenue. In this simple model, revenue drives cash-flow growth. Therefore, special attention must be given to projecting revenue by forecasting unit growth and selling prices, the product of which provides estimated revenue. As suggested in Chapters 4 and 7, the product life cycle concept may be used to project unit growth and prices. Common projection methods include *trend extrapolation* and *scenario analysis*.[7] See this chapter's Appendix B for a discussion of how to force the balance sheet of such models to balance (i.e., total assets equal total liabilities plus shareholders' equity).

To illustrate this process, consider the income, balance sheet, and cash-flow statements for Alanco Technologies Inc., a provider of wireless systems for tracking the movement of freight and people. In 2010, Alanco acquired StarTrak Systems, a provider of global positioning satellite tracking and wireless subscription data services to the transportation industry. Alanco believed that the acquisition would help it develop new markets for its products and services for wireless tracking and management of people and assets. With StarTrak less than 10% of the size of Alanco, Alanco believed that most of the synergy would come from cross-selling its products and services to StarTrak's customers rather than from cost savings.

Alanco's management understood that a successful acquisition would be one that would create more shareholder value at an acceptable level of risk than if the firm retained its current "go it alone" strategy. Consequently, Alanco valued its own business on a stand-alone basis (Table 9.2), StarTrak's business as a stand-alone unit (financials not shown), estimated potential synergy (Table 9.3), and combined firms including the effects of potential synergy (Table 9.4). The difference between the combined valuation with synergy and the sum of the two businesses valued as stand-alone operations provided an estimate of the potential incremental value that could be created from the acquisition of StarTrak.

---

[7] Revenue projections are commonly based on trend extrapolation, which entails extending present trends into the future using historical growth rates or multiple regression techniques. Another common forecasting method is to use scenario analysis. Cash flows under multiple scenarios are projected, with each differing in terms of key variables (e.g., growth in gross domestic product, industry sales growth, fluctuations in exchange rates) or issues (e.g., competitive new product introductions, new technologies, and new regulations).

TABLE 9.2   Step 1: Acquirer (Alanco) 5-Year Forecast and Stand-Alone Valuation

Forecast Assumptions		2011	2012	2013	2014	2015
Net Sales Growth Rate (%)		4.0	4.0	4.0	4.0	4.0
Cost of Sales (Variable)/Sales (%)		52.5	51.5	51.0	50.5	50.5
Depreciation & Amortization/Gross Fixed Assets (%)		8.3	8.3	8.3	8.3	8.3
Selling Expenses/Sales (%)		14.5	14.5	14.5	14.5	14.5
General & Administrative Expenses/Sales		19.0	18.5	18.0	17.2	16.4
Interest on Cash and Marketable Securities		5.0	5.0	5.0	5.0	5.0
Interest on New Debt (%)		8.3	8.3	8.3	8.3	8.3
Effective Tax Rate		18.0	22.0	25.0	30.0	37.0
Other Current Operations Assets/Sales (%)		35.0	35.0	35.0	35.0	35.0
Other Assets/Sales (%)		35.0	30.0	25.0	20.0	20.0
Gross Fixed Assets/Sales (%)		25.0	25.0	25.0	25.0	25.0
Minimum Cash Balance/Sales (%)		4.5	4.5	4.5	4.5	4.5
Current Liabilities/Sales (%)		30.0	30.0	28.0	26.0	25.0
Common Shares Outstanding*		426	426	426	426	426
Cost of Capital: 2011–2015 (%)	11.81					
Cost of Capital: Terminal Period (%)	10.31					
Sustainable Cash-Flow Growth Rate (%)	4.00					
Market Value of Long-Term Debt*	$1,171					

	Historical Financials				Projected Financials				
*Income Statement**	2007	2008	2009	2010	2011	2012	2013	2014	2015
Net Sales	4,779	4,698	4,596	4,670	4,857	5,051	5,253	5,463	5,682
Less: Variable Cost of Sales	2,315	2,286	2,333	2,415	2,449	2,496	2,570	2,646	2,751
– Depreciation	100	103	81	75	101	105	109	113	118
Total Cost of Sales	**2,415**	**2,389**	**2,414**	**2,490**	**2,550**	**2,601**	**2,679**	**2,759**	**2,869**
Gross Profit	2,364	2,310	2,182	2,180	2,307	2,450	2,574	2,704	2,812
Less: Sales Expense	761	786	685	681	704	732	762	792	824
– General and Administrative Expenses	780	863	868	908	923	934	946	940	942
– Amortization of Intangibles	32	41	52	52	52	52	52	52	52
– Other Expense (Income), Net	1	5	(5)	(19)	(16)	(16)	(16)	(16)	(16)
Total Sales and General and Administrative Expenses	**1,574**	**1,695**	**1,599**	**1,622**	**1,663**	**1,703**	**1,743**	**1,768**	**1,792**
Operating Income (EBIT)	790	615	583	558	644	747	831	936	1,021

TABLE 9.2   Cont'd

Income Statement*	Historical Financials				Projected Financials				
	2007	2008	2009	2010	2011	2012	2013	2014	2015
Plus: Interest Income					23	40	47	74	96
Less: Interest Expense	90	111	132	153	127	128	121	96	96
Net Profits before Taxes	700	504	451	405	540	659	757	915	1,021
Less: Taxes	201	131	62	55	97	145	189	274	376
Net Profits after Taxes	500	373	390	350	443	514	567	640	643
Balance Sheet[†]	2007	2008	2009	2010	2011	2012	2013	2014	2015
Cash	695	213	247	232	219	227	236	246	255
Other Operating Assets	1,767	1,845	1,605	1,519	1,700	1,768	1,839	1,912	1,989
Total Current Assets	**2,462**	**2,058**	**1,852**	**1,752**	**1,918**	**1,995**	**2,075**	**2,158**	**2,244**
Investments					245	582	711	1,235	1,674
Gross Fixed Assets	939	1,159	1,147	1,121	1,214	1,263	1,313	1,366	1,420
Less: Accumulated Depreciation & Amortization	337	422	422	473	574	679	788	901	1,019
Net Fixed Assets	602	737	725	648	640	584	526	465	402
Other Assets	852	1,819	2,097	1,914	1,914	1,913	1,913	1,913	1,913
Total Assets	3,915	4,613	4,674	4,313	4,718	5,075	5,224	5,771	6,233
Current Liabilities	1,173	1,317	1,565	1,502	1,457	1,515	1,471	1,420	1,420
Long-Term Debt	664	984	983	1,242	1,242	1,021	640	589	400
Other Liabilities	144	141	163	166	172	179	186	194	201
Total Liabilities	1,962	2,442	2,711	2,910	2,872	2,715	2,297	2,203	2,022
Common Stock	728	2,041	1,923	1,836	1,836	1,836	1,836	1,836	1,836
Retained Earnings	1,205	130	40	(433)	10	524	1,091	1,731	2,375
Shareholders' Equity	1,933	2,171	1,963	1,403	1,846	2,360	2,927	3,668	4,211
Total Liabilities & Shareholders' Equity	**3,915**	**4,613**	**4,674**	**4,314**	**4,718**	**5,075**	**6,224**	**5,771**	**6,233**
Shares Outstanding*	291.6	390.8	421.6	426	426	426	426	426	4.26
Earnings Per Share ($)	1.71	0.95	0.92	0.82	1.04	1.21	1.33	1.50	1.51
Long-Term Debt/Equity (%)	37	48	53	93	70	46	24	18	9.5
Addendum: Working Capital*	1,288	741	287	249	461	480	604	78	624

Continued

TABLE 9.2 Step 1: Acquirer (Alanco) 5-Year Forecast and Stand-Alone Valuation—Cont'd

Income Statement*	Historical Financials				Projected Financials				
	2007	2008	2009	2010	2011	2012	2013	2014	2015
Cash-Flow Statement									
EBIT $(1 - t)$	584	455	503	482	528	583	623	655	643
Plus: Depreciation and Amortization	132	144	133	127	153	157	161	165	170
Less: Gross Capital Expenditures	201	221	(12)	(26)	93	49	51	53	55
Less: Change in Working Capital	(200)	(548)	(454)	(37)	212	18	124	133	88
– Free Cash Flow	695	926	1,102	672	375	67	609	635	672
PV: 2011–2015	$2,100								
PV: Terminal Value	$6,342								
Total PV (Market Value of the Firm)	$8,442								
Less: Market Value of Long-Term Debt	$1,171								
Plus: Excess Cash (Investments)	$245								
Equity Value	**$7,517**								
Equity Value per Share	**$17.64**								

* In millions of dollars.
† As of December 31, 2010

TABLE 9.3 Step 2: Synergy Estimation[a]

	2011*	2012	2013	2014	2015
Incremental Sales Synergy – Sales of Alanco services to StarTrak customers		100	150	200	250
Cost of Sales Synergy – Elimination of 3rd-party manufacturing and service contracts by bringing outside manufacturing in-house	4	11	14	14	14
Selling Expense Synergy – Shutdown of Houston sales office (elimination of 20 sales employees by the end of 2011 at $100,000 per employee, including benefits)	2	3	3	3	3
General and Administrative Expense Synergy – Elimination of 38 finance and accounting personnel in Los Angeles headquarters by the end of 2011 at $80,000 per employee, including benefits	2	3	3	3	3
Implementation/Integration Expenses					
– Severance	0.7				
– Lease buyouts	0.1				
– Retention bonuses	0.2				
Total	1.0				

[a] Note that incremental sales and cost savings are realized gradually due to the time required to implement such plans.
* In millions of dollars

TABLE 9.4 Step 2: Consolidated Alanco and StarTrak 5-Year Forecast and Valuation

Forecast Assumptions					2011	2012	2013	2014	2015
Cost of Sales Synergy					4	11	14	14	14
Selling Expenses Synergy					2	3	3	3	3
G&A Expenses Synergy					2	3	3	3	3
Incremental Sales Synergy						100	0.150	200	250
Integration Expenses					(1)				
Cost of Capital: 2011–2015 (%)	11.81								
Cost of Capital: Terminal Period (%)	10.31								
Sustainable Cash-Flow Growth Rate (%)	4.0								
Market Value of Long-Term Debt*	$1,172								

Income Statement*	2007	2008	2009	2010	2011	2012	2013	2014	2015
Net Sales of Combined Firms	4,821	4,764	4,779	4,922	5,147	5,285	5,470	5,659	5,848
Incremental Sales Due to Synergy						100	150	200	250
Total Sales	**4,821**	**4,784**	**4,779**	**4,922**	**5,147**	**5,385**	**5,620**	**5,859**	**6,098**
Less: Variable Costs of Sales	2,339	2,335	2,436	2,556	2,620	2,692	2,784	2,877	2,994
Depreciation & Amortization	101	106	86	84	104	109	113	118	123
Cost of Sales Synergy					(4)	(11)	(14)	(14)	(14)
Total Cost of Sales	2,440	2,441	2,521	2,640	2,721	2,790	2,884	2,981	3,103
Gross Profit	2,380	2,343	2,258	2,282	2,426	2,595	2,736	2,879	2,995
Less: Sales Expense	767	799	712	719	748	782	817	852	886
Sales Expense Synergy					(2)	(3)	(3)	(3)	(3)
General & Administrative Expenses	785	874	891	951	965	983	997	996	990
General & Administrative Expenses Synergy					(2)	(3)	(3)	(3)	(3)
Total Sales, G&A Expenses	**1,552**	**1,673**	**1,603**	**1,670**	**1,709**	**1,759**	**1,808**	**1,842**	**1,870**
Integration Expense					1				
Amortization of Intangibles	32	41	52	52	52	52	52	52	52
Other Expense (Income), Net	2	6	(9)	(34)	(32)	(32)	(32)	(32)	(32)
Total Cost of Sales and G&A Expense	**1,586**	**1,720**	**1,646**	**1,688**	**1,731**	**1,779**	**1,828**	**1,861**	**1,890**
Operating Profits (EBIT)	794	623	612	594	696	816	909	1,018	1,105
Plus: Interest Income			2	4	29	48	58	87	113
Less: Interest Expense	91	111	132	153	127	129	122	96	96

Continued

TABLE 9.4   Step 2: Consolidated Alanco and StarTrak 5-Year Forecast and Valuation—Cont'd

Income Statement*	2007	2008	2009	2010	2011	2012	2013	2014	2015
Net Profits before Taxes	704	512	482	445	597	736	845	1,009	1,122
Less: Taxes	201	133	70	67	112	163	10	297	402
Net Profits after Taxes	502	379	411	378	485	573	635	712	719
Balance Sheet	**2007**	**2008**	**2009**	**2010**	**2011**	**2012**	**2013**	**2014**	**2015**
Cash	698	225	344	275	236	247	258	270	281
Other Operating Assets	1,779	1,861	1,665	1,605	1,787	1,868	1,949	2,031	2,113
Total Current Assets	2,477	2,086	2,009	1,880	2,023	2,115	2,207	2.301	2,394
Investments					347	742	940	1,539	2,056
Gross Fixed Assets	942	1,165	1,164	1,150	1,249	1,303	1,357	1,413	1,470
Less: Accumulated Depreciation & Amortization	338	424	427	484	588	697	810	926	1,051
Net Fixed Assets	604	741	737	667	661	606	547	485	419
Other Assets	877	1,844	2,161	2,015	2,010	2,005	1,999	1,994	1,989
Total Assets	3,958	4,672	4,907	4,562	5,040	5,468	5,693	6,319	6,861
Current Liabilities	1,185	1,332	1,610	1,544	1,530	1,599	1,563	1,520	1,524
Long-Term Debt	670	989	983	1,243	1,244	1,022	641	589	400
Other Liabilities	144	141	164	167	174	181	188	196	204
Total Liabilities	1,999	2,463	2,757	2,954	2,947	2,802	2,392	2,305	2,128
Common Stock	750	2,068	2,078	1,980	1,980	1,980	1,980	1,980	1,980
Retained Earnings	1,210	141	72	(372)	113	687	1,322	2,034	2,752
Shareholders' Equity	1,960	2,209	2,150	1,608	2,093	2,666	3,302	4,014	4,733
Total Liabilities & Shareholders' Equity	3,959	4,672	4,907	4,562	5,040	5,468	5,693	6,319	6,861
Addendum: Working Capital	1,292	754	400	336	493	517	644	781	870
Shares Outstanding*	299	399	435	445	445	445	445	445	445
Cash-Flow Statement	**2007**	**2008**	**2009**	**2010**	**2011**	**2012**	**2013**	**2014**	**2015**
EBIT$(1-t)$	567	462	523	505	565	636	683	718	708
Plus: Depreciation and Amortization	133	147	138	136	156	161	165	170	175
Less: Gross Capital Expenditures	204	223	(2)	(13)	99	54	55	56	57
Less: Change in Working Capital	(204)	(537)	(355)	(64)	157	23	128	137	88
PV: 2011–2015	$2,336								

TABLE 9.4   Cont'd

Cash-Flow Statement	2007	2008	2009	2010	2011	2012	2013	2014	2015
PV: Terminal Value	$6,964								
Total PV (Market Value of the Firm)	$9,300								
Less: Market Value of Long-Term Debt	$1,171								
Plus: Excess Cash Investment✗*	$347								
Equity Value	$8,475								

In millions of dollars.

Note that the layout in Table 9.2 is identical to those worksheets provided for the M&A Valuation and Structuring Model on the companion site. The assumptions provided in the top panel drive the forecast of the various line items for the income, balance sheet, and cash-flow statements. The historical financial data provides recent trends. As is typical of discounted cash-flow valuations, the terminal value comprises about three-fourths of the total present value (i.e., $6,342 million/$8,442 million) of Alanco's projected operating cash flows. Nonoperating assets such as the $245 million in excess cash balances are added to the total present value of the firm's operating cash flows.

Step 2. Value Acquirer and Target Firms, Including Synergy

Synergy generally is considered as those factors or sources of value that add to the economic value (i.e., ability to generate future cash flows) of the combined firms. However, factors that destroy value also should be considered in the estimation of the economic value of the combined firms. *Net synergy* (NS) is the difference between estimated sources of value and destroyers of value. The common approach to estimating the present value of net synergy is to subtract the sum of the present values of the acquirer and target firms on a stand-alone basis from the present value of the consolidated acquirer and target firms, including the estimated effects of synergy.[8] This approach has the advantage of enabling the analyst to create an interactive model to simulate alternative scenarios including different financing and deal-structuring assumptions.

Sources of Value

Look for quantifiable sources of value while conducting due diligence. The most common include the potential for cost savings resulting from shared overhead, duplicate facilities, and overlapping distribution channels. Synergy related to cost savings that are generally more easily identified seems to have a much better chance of being realized than synergy due to other sources.[9]

---

[8] Alternatively, the present value of net synergy can be estimated by calculating the present value of the difference between the cash flows from sources and destroyers of value.

[9] Christofferson, McNish, and Sias, 2004

Potential sources of value also include assets not recorded on the balance sheet at fair value and off-balance-sheet items. Common examples include land, "obsolete" inventory and equipment, patents, licenses, and copyrights. Underutilized borrowing capacity also can make an acquisition target more attractive. The addition of the acquired company's assets, low level of indebtedness, and strong cash flow from operations could enable the buyer to increase substantially the borrowing levels of the combined companies.[10]

Other sources of value could include access to intellectual property (i.e., patents, trade names, and rights to royalty streams), new technologies and processes, and new customer groups. Gaining access to new customers is often given as a justification for mergers and acquisitions. Kmart Holding Corp's acquisition of Sears, Roebuck and Co. in 2004 was in part motivated by the opportunity to sell merchandise with strong brand equity, which had been sold exclusively at Kmart (e.g., Joe Boxer) to a whole new clientele in Sears stores.

Income tax loss carryforwards and carrybacks, as well as tax credits, also may represent an important source of value for an acquirer seeking to reduce its tax liability. Loss carryforwards and carrybacks represent a firm's losses that may be used to reduce future taxable income or recover some portion of previous taxes paid by the firm. See Chapter 12 for a more detailed discussion of tax-related issues.

Destroyers of Value

Factors that can destroy value include poor product quality, wage and benefit levels above comparable industry levels, low productivity, and high employee turnover. A lack of customer contracts or badly written contracts often result in customer disputes about terms and conditions and what amounts actually are owed. Verbal agreements made with customers by the seller's sales representatives also may become obligations for the buyer. These are particularly onerous, because commissioned sales forces frequently make agreements that are not profitable for their employer.

Environmental issues, product liabilities, unresolved lawsuits, and other pending liabilities are also major potential destroyers of value for the buyer. These often serve as ticking time bombs, because the actual liability may not be apparent for years following the acquisition. Moreover, the magnitude of the liability actually may force a company into bankruptcy.[11]

---

[10] The incremental borrowing capacity can be approximated by comparing the combined firms' current debt-to-total capital ratio with the industry average. For example, assume Firm A's acquisition of Firm B results in a reduction in the combined firms' debt-to-total capital ratio to 0.25 (e.g., debt represents $250 million of the new firm's total capital of $1 billion). If the same ratio for the industry is 0.5, the new firm may be able to increase its borrowing by $250 million to raise its debt-to-total capital ratio to the industry average. Such incremental borrowing often is used to finance a portion of the purchase price paid for the target firm. See Chapter 13 for a more rigorous discussion of how to estimate incremental borrowing capacity.

[11] In the 1980s, a major producer of asbestos, Johns Manville Corporation, was forced into bankruptcy because of the discovery that certain types of asbestos, which had been used for decades for insulating buildings, could be toxic. When China's Lenovo Group acquired IBM's PC business in 2005, it disclosed that high warranty costs attributable to a single problem component contributed significantly to the IBM PC business net losses in 2002 and 2003 of $171 million and $258 million, respectively.

Implementation Costs

In calculating net synergy, it is important to include the costs associated with recruiting and training, realizing cost savings, achieving productivity improvements, and exploiting revenue opportunities. No matter how much care is taken to minimize employee attrition following closing, some employees will be lost. Often these are the most skilled. Once a merger or acquisition is announced, target company employees start to circulate their resumes. The best employees start to receive job solicitations from competitors or executive search firms. Consequently, the costs associated with replacing employees who leave following closing can escalate sharply. The firm will incur recruitment costs as well as the cost of training the new hires. Moreover, the new hires are not likely to reach the productivity levels of those they are replacing for some time.

Cost savings are likely to be greatest when firms with similar operations are consolidated and redundant, or overlapping positions are eliminated. Many analysts take great pains to estimate savings in terms of wages, salaries, benefits, and associated overhead, such as support staff and travel expenses, without accurately accounting for severance expenses associated with layoffs.[12]

Realizing productivity improvements frequently requires additional spending in new structures and equipment, retraining employees that remain with the combined companies, or redesigning work flow. Similarly, exploiting revenue-raising opportunities may require training the sales force of the combined firms in selling each firm's products or services and additional advertising expenditures to inform current or potential customers of what has taken place. See Table 9.4 for estimated sources of synergy resulting from the combination of Alanco and StarTrak, which presents the consolidated financial statements (including the effects of anticipated synergy) for the two firms. The impact of anticipated synergy is illustrated on the income statement in terms of incremental revenue, as well as savings from cost of sales and selling and general and administrative expense reductions. Note how synergy-related revenue is added to total revenue and synergy-related reductions in cost of sales, selling expenses, and general and administrative expenses are deducted from their respective line items on the income statement.

Step 3. Determine the Magnitude and Composition of the Offer Price for the Target Firm

In practice, many factors affect the amount and form of payment of the initial offer price. Which are most important depends largely on the circumstances surrounding the transaction. In some cases, these factors can be quantified (e.g., synergy), while others are largely subjective (e.g., the degree of acquirer shareholder and management risk aversion). The amount of the initial offer price may also reflect a premium for control. While the actual value of control is difficult to quantify, a bidder may be willing to pay more to gain control if it is believed that

---

[12] How a company treats its employees during layoffs has a significant impact on the morale of those who remain. Furthermore, if it is widely perceived that if a firm treats laid-off employees fairly, it will be able to recruit new employees more easily in the future. Consequently, severance packages should be as equitable as possible.

this would provide for better decision making and the implementation of a more effective strategy. The value of control and how it may be estimated is discussed in more detail in Chapter 10.

Table 9.5 identifies many of the factors that affect the magnitude and composition of the offer price. The remainder of this section of this chapter addresses how some of these factors can be incorporated into the model-building process.

Estimating the Minimum and Maximum Offer Price Range (Stock and Asset Purchases)

For transactions in which there is potential synergy between the acquirer and the target firms, the initial offer price for the target firm lies between the minimum and maximum offer prices. In a purchase of stock transaction, the minimum offer price may be defined as the target's stand-alone or present value (PV_T) or its current market value (MV_T) (i.e., the target's current stock price times its shares outstanding). The maximum price is the sum of the minimum price plus the present value of net synergy (PV_{NS}).[13] The initial offer price (PV_{IOP}) is the sum of both the minimum

TABLE 9.5   Determinants of Magnitude and Composition of Initial Offer Price

Factors Affecting	Magnitude	Composition
Acquirer's Perspective	• Estimated net synergy • Perceived contribution of target to net synergy • Willingness to share net synergy with target shareholders • Relative attractiveness of alternative investment opportunities • Number of potential bidders • Effectiveness of target's defenses • Public disclosure requirements (may result in preemptive bid) • Degree of management's risk aversion • Perceived value of control	• Current borrowing capacity • After-tax cost of debt versus cost of equity • Size and duration of potential EPS dilution (impacts attractiveness of share exchange) • Size of transaction (may make borrowing impractical) • Desire for risk sharing (may result in contingent or deferred payments) • Extent to which acquirer shares are overvalued (makes an all-equity transaction more attractive)
Target's Perspective	• Number of potential bidders • Perceived contribution of target to net synergy • Perception of bidder as friendly or hostile • Effectiveness of defenses • Size of potential tax liability (may require an increase in the purchase price) • Stand-alone valuation • Availability of recent comparable transactions • Relative attractiveness of alternative investment opportunities	• Perceived attractiveness of acquirer stock • Shareholder preference for cash versus stock • Size of potential tax liability (may make share exchange most attractive option) • Perceived upside potential of target (may result in contingent payout)

purchase price and some percentage between 0 and 1 of the PV of net synergy (see Exhibit 9.2).

The percentage of net synergy (i.e., α) that is to be shared with the target firm's share-holders may be determined by considering premiums paid on recent similar transactions, the portion of net synergy that is provided by the target, and the target firm's negotiating leverage. In addition, acquirers might make so-called preemptive bids, which represent proposals so attractive that the target firm's board would have considerable difficulty in explaining to shareholders their reasons for rejecting the offer. The acquirer's hope is that such bids will discourage other potential bidders. Finally, an acquirer may be very re-luctant to share more than a small fraction of the anticipated net synergy with target share-holders, recognizing that actually realizing the synergy on a timely basis is highly problematic.

The stand-alone value is applicable for privately held firms. In an efficient market in which both buyer and seller have access to the same information, the stand-alone value would be the price the rational seller expects to receive. In practice, markets for small, privately owned businesses are often inefficient. Either the buyer or seller may not have access to all relevant information about the economic value of the target, perhaps due to the absence of recent comparable transactions. Consequently, the buyer may attempt to purchase the target firm at a discount from what it believes is the actual economic or fair market value.

In an asset purchase, the target's net assets (i.e., total assets less total liabilities) have to be adjusted to reflect the fair market value of the target assets and liabilities that are retained by the target. Consequently, the target's adjusted net assets represent assets included in the transaction less liabilities assumed by the buyer and equal the PV of the cash flows generated by the target's adjusted net assets. Therefore, the minimum purchase price would be the liquidation value of the target's adjusted net assets; the maximum purchase price would equal the minimum price plus 100% of net synergy, and the initial offer price would equal the PV of adjusted net assets plus some portion of net synergy.

EXHIBIT 9.2 DETERMINING THE OFFER PRICE (PV_{OP})— PURCHASE OF STOCK

a. $PV_{MIN} = PV_T$ or MV_T, whichever is greater. MV_T is the target firm's current share price times the number of shares outstanding

b. $PV_{MAX} = PV_{MIN} + PV_{NS}$, where $PV_{NS} = PV$ (sources of value) − PV (destroyers of value)

c. $PV_{OP} = PV_{MIN} + \alpha\, PV_{NS}$, where $0 \le \alpha \le 1$

d. Offer price range for the target firm $= (PV_T$ or $MV_T) < PV_{OP} < (PV_T$ or $MV_T) + PV_{NS}$

---

[13] Note that the maximum price may be overstated if the current market value of the target firm reflects investor expectations of an impending takeover. As such, the current market value may already reflect some portion of future synergies. Consequently, simply adding the present value of net synergy to the current market value of the target firm can result in double-counting some portion of future synergy.

Determining the Distribution of Synergy between the Acquirer and the Target

In determining the initial offer price, the acquiring company must decide how much of the anticipated synergy it is willing to share with the target firm's shareholders. This is often determined by the portion of anticipated synergy contributed by the target firm. For example, if following due diligence, it is determined that the target would contribute 30% of the synergy resulting from combining the acquirer and target firms, the acquirer may choose to share up to 30% of the estimated net synergy with the target firm's shareholders. The actual amount of synergy shared with the target firm shareholders will reflect the relative bargaining power of the acquirer and target firms and recent comparable firm transaction prices.

It is logical that the offer price should fall between the minimum and maximum prices for three reasons. First, it is unlikely that the target company can be purchased at the minimum price, because the acquiring company normally has to pay a premium over the current market value to induce target shareholders to transfer control to another firm. In an asset purchase, the rational seller would not sell at a price below the liquidation value of the net assets being acquired, since this represents what the seller could obtain by liquidating rather than selling the assets and using a portion of the proceeds to pay off liabilities that would have been assumed by the buyer. Second, at the maximum end of the range, the acquiring company would be ceding all of the net synergy value created by the combination of the two companies to the target company's shareholders. Third, it is prudent to pay significantly less than the maximum price, because the amount of synergy actually realized often tends to be less than the amount anticipated.

Determining the Appropriate Composition of the Offer Price

The purchase price offered to the target company could consist of the acquirer's stock, debt, cash, or some combination of all three. The actual composition of the purchase price depends on what is acceptable to the target and acquiring companies and what the financial structure of the combined companies can support. Consequently, the acquirer needs to determine the appropriate financing or capital structure of the combined companies, including debt, common equity, and preferred equity. In this chapter, the initial offer price is the market value or economic value (i.e., present value of the target firm defined as a stand-alone business) plus some portion of projected net synergy. In Chapter 5, the offer or purchase price was defined in a different context, as total consideration, total purchase price or enterprise value, and net purchase price. These definitions were provided with the implicit assumption that the acquiring company had determined the economic value of the firm on a stand-alone basis and the value of net synergy. Economic value is determined before any consideration is given to how the transaction will be financed.

SHARE-EXCHANGE RATIOS

For public companies, the exchange of the acquirer's shares for the target's shares requires the calculation of the appropriate exchange ratio. The share-exchange ratio (SER) can be negotiated as a fixed number of shares of the acquirer's stock to be exchanged for each share of the target's stock. Alternatively, SER can be defined in terms of the dollar value of the negotiated offer price per share of target stock (P_{OP}) to the dollar value of the acquirer's share price (P_A). The SER is calculated by the following equation:

$$SER = P_{OP}/P_A$$

The SER, defined in this manner, can be less than, equal to, or greater than 1, depending on the value of the acquirer's shares relative to the offer price on the date set during the negotiation for valuing the transaction. For example, in a share-for-share exchange in which the offer price per target share and acquirer's share prices are $25.50 and $37.25, respectively, the target firm's shareholders would receive 0.6846 shares (i.e., $25.50 ÷ $37.25) of acquirer stock for each share of target stock they tender. Furthermore, if the number of acquirer and target shares outstanding is 10 million and 2 million, respectively, the acquirer would have to issue 1,369,200 new shares (i.e., .6846 × 2,000,000) to purchase all of the target shares. Since the target shares are canceled, the total number of shares outstanding for the combined firms is 11,369,200 (i.e., 10,000,000 + 1,369,200). The shareholders of the acquiring company would own 88% (i.e., 10,000,000 ÷ 11,369,200) of the combined firms and the target shareholders the remaining 12%.

FULLY DILUTED SHARES OUTSTANDING

When the target firm has outstanding management stock options and convertible securities, it is necessary to adjust the offer price to reflect the extent to which options and convertible securities will be exchanged for new common shares. If the acquirer is intent on buying all the target's outstanding shares, these new shares also have to be purchased. Convertible securities commonly include preferred stock and debentures. Information on the number of options outstanding and their associated exercise prices, as well as convertible securities, generally are available in the footnotes to the financial statements of the target firm.[14] With respect to convertible securities, it is reasonable to assume that such securities will be converted to common equity if the conversion price is less than the offer price for each common share. Such securities are said to be "in the money." Table 9.6 illustrates the calculation of the target firm's fully diluted shares outstanding and the impact on the equity value of the target firm.

Table 9.7 summarizes the steps involved in determining the offer price. Please pay special attention to the addendum to this exhibit because it contains formulas for estimating each row of the section entitled "Model Output."

Step 4. Determine the Combined Firms' Ability to Finance the Transaction

The consolidated target and acquiring firms' financial statements, adjusted to reflect the net effects of synergy, are run through a series of scenarios to determine the impact on such variables as earnings, leverage, covenants, and borrowing costs. For example, each scenario could represent different amounts of leverage as measured by the firm's debt-to-equity ratio.

[14] Note that "out-of-the-money" options (i.e., those whose exercise or conversion price exceeds the firm's current shares price) often are exercisable if the firm faces a change of control.

TABLE 9.6 Calculating the Target's Fully Diluted Shares Outstanding and Equity Value (Using If-Converted Method)

Assumptions about Target		Comment
Basic Shares Outstanding	2,000,000 shares	
In-the-Money Options[a]	150,000 shares	Exercise price = $15/share
Convertible Securities		
Convertible Debt (Face value = $1,000; convertible into 50 shares of common stock)	$10,000,000	Implied conversion price = $20 (i.e., $1,000/50)
Preferred Stock (Par value = $20; convertible into one share of common at $24 per share)	$5,000,000	Preferred shares outstanding = $5,000,000/$20 = 250,000
Offer Price per Share	$30	Purchase price offered for each target share outstanding

$$\text{Total Shares Outstanding}^b = 2,000,000 + 150,000 + (\$10,000,000/\$1,000) \times 50 + 250,000$$
$$= 2,000,000 + 150,000 + 500,000 + 250,000$$
$$= 2,900,000$$

$$\text{Target Equity Value}^c = 2,900,000 \times \$30 - 150,000 \times \$15$$
$$= \$87,000,000 - \$2,250,000$$
$$= \$84,750,000$$

[a] *An option whose exercise price is below the market value of the firm's share price.*
[b] *Total shares outstanding = Issued shares + Shares from "in-the-money" options and convertible securities.*
[c] *Purchase price adjusted for new acquirer shares issued for convertible shares or debt less cash received from "in-the-money" option holders.*

TABLE 9.7 Step 3: Offer Price Determination

Deal Terms and Conditions	
Cash Portion of Offer Price	0
Equity Portion of Offer Price	100%
% of Synergy Shared with Target	30%
Specific Firm Data	
Acquirer Share Price	$16.03
Target Share Price	$14.25
Target Shares Outstanding	
Basic Shares Outstanding	18.1
"In-the-Money" Options Converted to Common	0.2
Convertible Preferred Converted to Common	0.8
Total Target Shares Outstanding*	19.1
Acquirer Shares Outstanding*	426

TABLE 9.7   Cont'd

| Model Output | Stand-Alone Value | | Consolidated Acquirer + Target | | Value of Synergy |
	Acquirer	Target	Without Synergy (1)	With Synergy (2)	PV_{NS} (1)–(2)
Discounted Cash-Flow Valuations*	$7,517	$591	$8,107	$8,475	$368
Minimum Offer Price (PV_{MIN})*	$272				
Maximum Offer Price (PV_{MAX})*	$640				
Offer Price Per Share ($)	$20.02				
Purchase Price Premium per Share (%)	41%				
Cash Per Share ($)	0				
New Shares Issued by Acquirer*	23.867				
Total Shares Outstanding for the Combined Firms*	450				
Ownership Distribution in New Firm					
Acquirer Shareholders	95%				
Target Shareholders	5%				

*In millions of dollars.
Addendum:

Discounted-cash-flow valuations provided by Steps 1 and 2 of the M&A model.

Minimum offer price = target share price × total target shares outstanding = $14.25 × 19.1 = $272.18.

Maximum offer price = minimum price + net synergy = $272 + $368 = $640.

Offer price per share = (minimum offer price + 0.3 × net synergy) / total target shares outstanding = ($272 + 0.3 × $368) / 19.1 = $20.02.

Purchase price premium = (Offer price per share / target share price) − 1 = ($20.02 / $14.25) − 1 = 40.5%.

New shares issued by acquirer = share exchange ratio × total target shares outstanding = ($20.02 / $16.03) × 19.1 = 23.9 million.

Total shares outstanding of combined firms = Acquirer shares outstanding + New shares issued by acquirer = 426 + 23.9 = 450 million.

Ownership distribution:

Acquirer shareholders = acquirer shares outstanding/total shares outstanding for the combined firms = 426/450
     = 0.947 × 100 = 94.7%.

Target shareholders = 1 − 0.947 = 0.053 × 100 = 5.3%.

In theory, the optimal capital or financing structure is the one that maximizes the firm's share price. When borrowed funds are reinvested at a return above the firm's cost of capital, firm value is increased. Also, higher interest expense will result in increased tax savings due to the tax deductibility of interest. However, higher debt levels relative to equity increase the risk of default and the firm's cost of equity by raising its levered beta, which works to lower the firm's share price. Since many factors affect share price, it is difficult to determine the exact capital structure that maximizes the firm's share price.

In practice, financial managers attempt to forecast how changes in debt will affect those ratios that have an impact on a firm's creditworthiness. Such factors include the interest-coverage ratio, debt-to-equity ratio, times-interest-earned ratio, current ratio, and the like. They subsequently discuss their projected pro forma financial statements with lenders and bond rating agencies, which may make adjustments to the firm's projected financial statements. The lenders and rating agencies then compare the firm's credit ratios with those of other firms in the same industry to assess the likelihood that the borrower will be able to repay the borrowed funds (with interest) on schedule. Ultimately, interaction among the borrower, lenders, and rating agencies is what determines the amount and composition of combined firms' capital structure.

For purposes of model building, the appropriate financing structure can be estimated by selecting that structure which satisfies certain predetermined selection criteria. These selection criteria should be determined as part of the process of developing the acquisition plan (see Chapter 4). For a public company, the appropriate capital structure could be that scenario whose debt-to-equity ratio results in the highest net present value for cash flows generated by the combined businesses, the least near-term EPS dilution, no violation of loan covenants, and no significant increase in borrowing costs. Excluding EPS considerations, private companies could determine the appropriate capital structure in the same manner.

Table 9.8 displays the consolidated financial statements for Alanco and StarTrak, including the effects of synergy and financing. The addendum provides selected loan covenants and the

TABLE 9.8   Combined Firms' Financing Capacity

	Projected Financials				
Income Statement*	2011	2012	2013	2014	2015
Net Sales	5,147	5,385	5,620	5,859	6,098
Less: Cost of Sales	2,721	2,790	2,884	2,981	3,103
Gross Profit	2,426	2,595	2,736	2,879	2,995
Less: Sales, General & Administrative Expenses	1,730	1,779	1,828	1,861	1,890
Integration Expenses	(1)				
Operating Profits (EBIT)	696	816	909	1,018	1,105
Plus: Interest Income	29	48	58	87	113
Less: Interest Expense	127	129	122	96	96
Net Profits before Taxes	597	736	845	1,009	1,122
Less: Taxes	112	163	210	297	402
Net Profits after Taxes	485	573	635	712	719
Balance Sheet (December 31)					
Cash and Marketable Securities	582	989	1,198	1,809	2,340
Other Current Assets	1,787	1,868	1,949	2,301	2,113
Total Current Assets	2,369	2,857	3,147	3,840	4,453
Gross Fixed Assets	1,249	1,303	1,357	1,413	1,470

TABLE 9.8 Cont'd

Income Statement*	Projected Financials				
	2011	2012	2013	2014	2015
Less: Accumulated Depreciation	588	697	810	928	1,051
Net Fixed Assets	661	606	547	485	419
Other Assets	2,010	2,005	1,999	1,994	1,989
Total Assets	5,040	5,468	5,693	6,319	6,861
Current Liabilities	1,530	1,599	1,563	1,520	1,524
Long-Term Debt	1,244	1,022	641	589	400
Other Liabilities	174	181	188	196	204
Common Stock	1,980	1,980	1,980	1,980	1,980
Retained Earnings	113	687	1,322	2,034	2,753
Shareholders' Equity	2,093	2,666	3,302	4,014	4,733
Total Liabilities + Shareholders' Equity	5,040	5,468	5,693	6,319	6,861
Key Performance Indicators					
Long-Term Debt/Equity	59%	38%	19%	15%	8%
Interest Coverage Ratio (EBIT/Interest Expense)	5.48	6.33	7.45	10.60	11.57
Current Ratio (Current Assets/Current Liabilities)	1.55	1.79	2.01	2.53	2.92
Earnings Per Share (Note: Total shares = 450,000,000)	1.08	1.27	1.41	1.58	1.60

*In millions of dollars.
Addendum:
  Selected Loan Covenants.
  Long-Term Debt / Equity ≤ 0.75.
  Interest Coverage Ratio (EBIT/Interest Expense) ≥ 2.5.
  Current Ratio (Current Assets / Current Liabilities) ≥ 1.25.

projected performance of the combined firms with respect to these covenants and in terms of earnings per share. The pro formas suggest that the acquisition can be financed without any deterioration in earnings per share, violation of existing loan covenants, deterioration in liquidity, or increase in interest expense. *pg. 324. – 342.*

USING FINANCIAL MODELS IN SUPPORT OF M&A NEGOTIATIONS

The acquirer's initial offer generally is at the lowest point in the range between the minimum and maximum prices consistent with the acquirer's perception of what constitutes an acceptable price to the target firm. If the target's financial performance is remarkable, the target firm will command a high premium and the final purchase price will be close to the maximum price. Moreover, the acquirer may make a bid close to the maximum price to preempt other potential acquirers from having sufficient time to submit competing offers. However, in practice, hubris on the part of the acquirer's management or an auction environment may push the final negotiated purchase price to or even above the maximum economic value of the firm. Under any circumstance, increasing the offer price involves trade-offs.

The value of the offer price simulation model is that it enables the acquirer to see trade-offs between changes in the offer price and postacquisition EPS. EPS is widely used by acquirers whose shares are publicly traded as a measure of the acceptability of an acquisition. Even a short-term reduction in EPS may dissuade some CEOs from pursuing a target firm.[15]

The acquiring firm may vary the offer price by changing the amount of net synergy shared with the target firm's shareholders. Increases in the offer price affect the postacquisition EPS for a given set of assumptions about the deal's terms and conditions and firm-specific data. Terms and conditions include the cash and stock portion of the purchase price. Firm-specific data include the preacquisition share prices, the number of common shares outstanding for the acquirer and target firms, and the present value of anticipated net synergy, as well as the postacquisition projected net income available for common equity of the combined firms. Note that alternative performance measures, such as cash flow per share, can be used in place of EPS.

Table 9.9 illustrates alternative scenarios for postacquisition earnings per share generated by varying the amount of synergy shared with the target firm's shareholders based on a 75% equity/25% cash offer price. The composition reflects what the acquirer believes will best meet both the target's and its own objectives. The table shows the trade-off between increasing the offer price for a given postacquisition projection of net income and EPS. The relatively small reduction in EPS in each year as the offer price increases reflects the relatively small number of new shares the acquirer has to issue to acquire the target's shares. The data in the table reflects the resulting minimum, maximum, and initial offer price, assuming that the acquirer is willing to give up 30% of projected synergy. At that level of synergy sharing, the equity of the new firm will be 95% owned by the acquirer's current shareholders, with the remainder owned by the target firm's shareholders.

See Case Study 9.1 for an application of the offer price simulation model to Cleveland Cliffs' 2008 takeover attempt of Alpha Natural Resources Corporation. Readers are encouraged to examine the formulas underlying the Excel-Based Offer-Price Simulation Model on the companion site and to apply the model to an actual or potential transaction of their choosing. Note that the offer price simulation model in Table 9.9 is embedded in Step 3 of the worksheets entitled "Excel-Based Merger and Acquisition Valuation and Structuring Model" on the companion site.

---

[15] As noted in Chapter 8, studies suggest that cash flows and earnings are highly positively correlated with stock returns over long periods such as five-year intervals. However, for shorter time periods, earnings show a stronger correlation with stock returns than cash flows.

TABLE 9.9 Offer Price Simulation Model

Deal Terms and Conditions

Cash Portion of Offer Price (%)	0.25
Equity Portion of Offer Price (%)	0.75
Percent of Anticipated Synergy Shared with Target %	0.3

Specific Firm Data

Acquirer Share Price ($/Share)	16.03
Target Share Price ($/Share)	14.25
Target Shares Outstanding*	19.10
Acquirer Shares Outstanding, Preclosing*	426.00
PV of Anticipated Net Synergy*	368.00

Alternative Scenarios Based on Different Amounts of Synergy Shared with Target

		% Shared Synergy	Offer Price*	Offer Price per Share	Postacquisition Total Shares	Postacquisition EPS				
						2008	2009	2010	2011	2012
Calculated Data		**0.1**	**309**	**16.18**	**445**	**1.09**	**1.29**	**1.43**	**1.60**	**1.61**
Minimum Offer Price*	272	0.2	346	18.10	448	1.08	1.28	1.42	1.59	1.61
Maximum Offer Price*	640	0.3	383	20.03	450	1.08	1.27	1.41	1.58	1.60
Initial Offer Price*	383	0.4	419	21.96	452	1.07	1.27	1.40	1.57	1.59
Initial Offer Price per Share ($)	20.03	0.5	456	23.88	454	1.07	1.26	1.40	1.57	1.58
Purchase Price Premium per Share (%)	0.41	0.6	493	25.81	457	1.06	1.25	1.39	1.56	1.57
Composition of Purchase Price per Target Share		0.7	530	27.74	459	1.06	1.25	1.38	1.55	1.57
Acquirer Equity per Target Share	15.02	0.8	567	29.66	461	1.05	1.24	1.38	1.54	1.56

Continued

TABLE 9.9 Offer Price Simulation Model—Cont'd

		% Shared Synergy	Offer Price*	Offer Price per Share	Postacquisition Total Shares	Postacquisition EPS				
						2008	2009	2010	2011	2012
Cash per Target Share ($)	5.01	0.9	603	31.59	464	1.05	1.24	1.37	1.54	1.55
Share Exchange Ratio	1.25	1.0	640	33.52	466	1.04	1.23	1.36	1.53	1.54
New Shares Issued by Acquirer	23.87									
Acquirer Shares Outstanding, Postclosing (Millions)	449.87									

Ownership Distribution in New Firm

Acquirer Shareholders (%)	0.95
Target Shareholders (%)	0.05

Consolidated Acquirer and Target Net Income

	2008	2009	2010	2011	2012
Postacquisition Consolidated Net Income*	485	573	635	712	719

Note: This model is available on the companion site in an Excel worksheet entitled "Offer Price Simulation Model."
* In millions of dollars.

ALTERNATIVE APPLICATIONS OF M&A FINANCIAL MODELS

The modeling process outlined in this chapter can also be applied when the acquirer or the target is part of a larger organization or to value the assets contributed to a joint venture or business alliance.

When the Acquirer or the Target Is Part of a Larger Legal Entity

The acquirer or the target may be a wholly-owned subsidiary, an operating division, a business segment, or product line of a parent corporation. When this is the case, it should be treated as a stand-alone business (i.e., one whose financial statements reflect all the costs of running the business and all the revenues generated by the business). This is the methodology suggested for Step 1 in the modeling process outlined in this chapter (refer to Exhibit 9.1).

Wholly-owned subsidiaries differ from operating divisions, business segments, and product lines in that they are units whose stock is entirely owned by the parent firm. Operating divisions, business segments, or product lines may or may not have detailed income, balance sheet, and cash-flow statements for financial reporting purposes. The parent's management may simply collect data sufficient for tracking the unit's performance. For example, such operations may be viewed as "cost centers," responsible for controlling their own costs. Consequently, detailed costs may be reported, with little detail for assets and liabilities associated with the operation. This is especially true for product lines, which often share resources (e.g., manufacturing plants, shipping facilities, accounting and human resource departments) with other product lines and businesses. The solution is to allocate a portion of the cost associated with each resource shared by the business to the business' income statement and estimate the percentage of each asset and liability associated with the business to create a balance sheet.

As an operating unit within a larger company, administrative costs such as legal, tax, audit, benefits, and treasury may be heavily subsidized or even provided without charge to the subsidiary. Alternatively, these services may be charged to the subsidiary as part of an allocation equal to a specific percentage of the subsidiary's sales or cost of sales. If these expenses are accounted for as part of an allocation methodology, they may substantially overstate the actual cost of purchasing these services from outside parties. Such allocations are often ways for the parent to account for expenses incurred at the level of the corporate headquarters but have little to do with the actual operation of the subsidiary. Such activities may include the expense associated with maintaining the corporation's headquarters building and airplanes.

If the cost of administrative support services is provided for free or heavily subsidized by the parent, the subsidiary's reported profits should be reduced by the actual cost of providing these services. If the cost of such services is measured using some largely arbitrary allocation methodology, the subsidiary's reported profits may be increased by the difference between the allocated expense and the actual cost of providing the services.

When the target is an operating unit of another firm, it is common for its reported revenue to reflect sales to other operating units of the parent firm. Unless the parent firm contractually commits as part of the divestiture process to continue to buy from the divested operation, such revenue may evaporate as the parent firm satisfies its requirements from other suppliers. Moreover, intercompany revenue may be overstated because the prices paid for the target's output reflect artificially high internal transfer prices (i.e., the price products are sold by one business to another in the same corporation) rather than market prices. The parent firm may not be willing to continue to pay the inflated transfer prices following the divestiture.

If the unit, whose financials have been adjusted, is viewed by the parent firm as the acquirer, use its financials (not the parent's) as the acquirer in the computer model. Then proceed with Steps 1 through 4 of the model-building process described earlier in this chapter. You may wish to eliminate the earnings per share lines in the model. Similar adjustments are made for targets that are part of larger organizations.

Joint Ventures and Business Alliances

For alliances and joint ventures, the process is very much the same. The businesses or assets contributed by the partners to a joint venture (JV) should be valued on a stand-alone basis. For consistency with the model presented in this chapter, one of the partners may be viewed as the acquirer and the other as the target. Their financials are adjusted so that they are viewed on a stand-alone basis. Steps 1 and 2 enable the determination of the combined value of the JV and Step 4 incorporates the financing requirements for the combined operations. Step 3 is superfluous, as actual ownership of the partnership or JV depends on the agreed-on (by the partners) relative value of the assets or businesses contributed by each partner and the extent to which these assets and businesses contribute to creating synergy.

SOME THINGS TO REMEMBER

Financial modeling in the context of M&As facilitates the process of valuation, deal structuring, and selecting the appropriate financial structure. The methodology developed in this chapter also may be applied to operating subsidiaries and product lines of larger organizations as well as joint ventures and partnerships. The process outlined in this chapter entails a four-step procedure.

1. Value the acquirer and target firms as stand-alone businesses. All costs and revenues associated with each business should be included in the valuation. Multiple valuation methods should be used and the results averaged to increase confidence in the accuracy of the estimated value.
2. Value the combined financial statements of the acquirer and target companies including the effects of anticipated synergy. Ensure that all costs likely to be incurred in realizing synergy are included in the calculation of net synergy.

3. Determine the initial offer price for the target firm. For stock purchases, define the minimum and maximum offer price range where the potential for synergy exists as follows:

$$(PV_T \text{ or } MV_T) < P_{OP} < (PV_T \text{ or } MV_T + PV_{NS})$$

where PV_T and MV_T are the economic value of the target as a stand-alone company and the market value of the target, respectively. PV_{NS} is the present value of net synergy, and P_{OP} is the initial offer price for the target. For asset purchases, the minimum price is the liquidation value of acquired net assets (i.e., acquired assets – acquired/assumed liabilities).

4. Determine the combined companies' ability to finance the transaction. The appropriate capital structure of the combined businesses is that which enables the acquirer to meet or exceed its required financial returns, satisfies the seller's price expectations, does not significantly raise borrowing costs, and does not violate significant financial constraints (e.g., loan covenants and prevailing industry average debt service ratios).

DISCUSSION QUESTIONS

9.1 Why are financial modeling techniques used in analyzing M&As?

9.2 Give examples of the limitations of financial data used in the valuation process.

9.3 Why is it important to analyze historical data on the target company as part of the valuation process?

9.4 Explain the process of normalizing historical data and why it should be done before the valuation process is undertaken.

9.5 What are common-size financial statements, and how are they used to analyze a target firm?

9.6 Why should a target company be valued as a stand-alone business? Give examples of the types of adjustments that might have to be made if the target is part of a larger company.

9.7 Define the minimum and maximum purchase price range for a target company.

9.8 What are the differences between the final negotiated price, total consideration, total purchase price, and net purchase price?

9.9 Can the offer price ever exceed the maximum purchase price? If yes, why? If no, why not?

9.10 Why is it important to clearly state assumptions underlying a valuation?

9.11 Assume two firms have little geographic overlap in terms of sales and facilities. If they were to merge, how might this affect the potential for synergy?

9.12 Dow Chemical, a leading manufacturer of chemicals, announced in 2008 that it had an agreement to acquire competitor Rhom and Haas. Dow expected to broaden its current product offering by offering the higher-margin Rohm and Haas products. What would you identify as possible synergies between these two businesses? In what ways could the combination of these two firms erode combined cash flows?

9.13 Dow Chemical's acquisition of Rhom and Haas included a 74% premium over the firm's preannouncement share price. What is the probable process Dow employed in determining the stunning magnitude of this premium?

9.14 For most transactions, the full impact of net synergy will not be realized for many months. Why? What factors could account for the delay?

9.15 How does the presence of management options and convertible securities affect the calculation of the offer price for the target firm?

Answers to these Chapter Discussion Questions are available in the Online Instructor's Manual for instructors using this book.

Practice Problems and Answers

9.16 Acquiring Company is considering the acquisition of Target Company in a share-for-share transaction in which Target Company would receive $50.00 for each share of its common stock. Acquiring Company does not expect any change in its P/E multiple after the merger.

	Acquiring Co.	Target Co.
Earnings available for common stock	$150,000	$30,000
Number of shares of common stock outstanding	60,000	20,000
Market price per share	$60.00	$40.00

Using the preceding information about these two firms and showing your work, calculate the following:

a. Purchase price premium. (*Answer: 25%*)

b. Share-exchange ratio. (*Answer: 0.8333*)

c. New shares issued by Acquiring Company. (*Answer: 16,666*)

d. Total shares outstanding of the combined companies. (*Answer: 76,666*)

e. Postmerger EPS of the combined companies. (*Answer: $2.35*)

f. Premerger EPS of Acquiring Company. (*Answer: $2.50*)

g. Postmerger share price. (*Answer: $56.40, compared with $60.00 premerger*)

9.17 Acquiring Company is considering buying Target Company. Target Company is a small biotechnology firm that develops products licensed to the major pharmaceutical firms. Development costs are expected to generate negative cash flows during the first two years of the forecast period of $(10) million and $(5) million, respectively. Licensing fees are expected to generate positive cash flows during years 3 through 5 of the forecast period of $5 million, $10 million, and $15 million, respectively. Because of the emergence of competitive products, cash flow is expected to grow at a modest 5% annually after the fifth year. The discount rate for the first five years is estimated to be 20% and then to drop to the industry average rate of 10% beyond the fifth year. Also, the present value of the estimated net synergy by combining Acquiring and Target companies is $30 million. Calculate the minimum and maximum purchase prices for Target Company. Show your work.

Answer: Minimum price: $128.5 million; maximum price: $158.5 million.

9.18 Using the Excel-Based Offer Price Simulation Model (see Table 9.9) on the companion site, what would the initial offer price be if the amount of synergy shared with the target firm's shareholders was 50%? What is the offer price and what would the ownership distribution be if the percentage of synergy shared increased to 80% and the composition of the purchase price were all acquirer stock?

Answers to these Practice Problems are available in the Online Instructor's Manual for instructors using this book.

CHAPTER BUSINESS CASES

CASE STUDY 9.1
Cleveland Cliffs Fails to Complete Takeover of Alpha Natural Resources in a Commodity Play

In an effort to exploit the long-term upward trend in commodity prices, Cleveland Cliffs, an iron ore mining company, failed in its attempt to acquire Alpha Natural Resources, a metallurgical coal mining firm, in late 2008 for a combination of cash and stock. In a joint press release on November 19, 2008, the firms announced that their merger agreement had been terminated due to adverse "macroeconomic conditions" at that time. Nevertheless, the transaction illustrates how a simple simulation model can be used to investigate the impact of alternative offer prices on postacquisition earnings per share.

When first announced in mid-2008, the deal was valued at about $10 billion. Alpha shareholders would receive total consideration of $131.42 per share, an approximate 46% premium over the firm's preannouncement share price. The new firm was to be renamed Cliffs Natural Resources and would have become one of the largest U.S. diversified mining and natural resources firms. The additional scale of operations, purchasing economies, and elimination of redundant overhead were expected to generate about $290 million in cost savings annually. The cash and equity portions of the offer price were 17.4% and 82.6%, respectively. See Table 9.10. The present value of anticipated synergy discounted in perpetuity at Cliff's estimated cost of capital of 11% was about $2.65 billion. Posttransaction net income

projections were derived from Wall Street estimates.

Discussion Questions

1. Purchase price premiums contain a synergy premium and a control premium. The control premium represents the amount an acquirer is willing to pay for the right to direct the operations of the target firm. Assume that Cliffs would not have been justified in paying a control premium for acquiring Alpha. Consequently, the Cliffs's offer price should have reflected only a premium for synergy. According to Table 9.10, did Cliffs overpay for Alpha? Explain your answer.

2. Based on the information in Table 9.10 and the initial offer price of $10 billion, did this transaction implicitly include a control premium? How much? In what way could the implied control premium have simply reflected Cliffs potentially overpaying for the business? Explain your answer.

3. The difference in postacquisition EPS between an offer price in which Cliffs shared 100% of synergy and one in which it would share only 10% of synergy is about 22% (i.e., $3.72 ÷ $3.04 in 2008). To what do you attribute this substantial difference?

Answers to these questions are found in the Online Instructor's Manual Available to instructors using this book.

TABLE 9.10 Cleveland-Cliffs' Attempted Acquisition of Alpha Natural Resources: Offer Price Simulation Model

Deal Terms and Conditions

Cash Portion of Offer Price (%)	0.174
Equity Portion of Offer Price (%)	0.826
Percent of Anticipated Synergy Shared with Target %	1.00

Specific Firm Data

Acquirer Share Price ($/Share)	102.50
Target Share Price ($/Share)	90.27
Target Shares Outstanding*	64.40
Acquirer Shares Outstanding, Preclosing*	44.60
PV of Anticipated Net Synergy* @11% WACC)	2,650

Alternative Scenarios Based on Different Amounts of Synergy Shared with Target

		%Shared Synergy	Offer Price*	Offer Price per Share	Postacquisition Total Shares	Postacquisition EPS				
						2008	2009	2010	2011	2012
Calculated Data		0.1	6078	94.38	104	3.72	4.09	4.42	4.73	4.96
Minimum Offer Price*	5,813	0.2	6343	98.50	106	3.63	3.99	4.31	4.61	4.84
Maximum Offer Price*	8,463	0.3	6608	102.61	109	3.55	3.90	4.21	4.50	4.72
Initial Offer Price*	8,463	0.4	6873	106.73	112	3.47	3.81	4.11	4.40	4.61
Initial Offer Price per Share*	131.42	0.5	7138	110.84	114	3.39	3.72	4.02	4.30	4.51

Purchase Price Premium per Share (%)	0.46	0.6		7403	114.96	117	3.31	3.64	3.93	4.20	4.41
Composition of Purchase Price per Target Share		0.7	7668	119.07	119	3.24	3.56	3.84	4.11	4.31
Acquirer Equity per Target Share	108.55	0.8	7933	123.19	122	3.17	3.48	3.76	4.02	4.22
Cash Per Target Share ($)	22.87	0.9	8198	127.30	125	3.11	3.41	3.68	3.94	4.13
Share Exchange Ratio	1.28	1.0	8463	131.42	127	3.04	3.34	3.61	3.86	4.05
New Shares Issued by Acquirer	82.57									
Acquirer Shares Outstanding, Postclosing (Millions)	127.17									

Ownership Distribution in New Firm

Acquirer Shareholders (%)	0.35
Target Shareholders (%)	0.65

Consolidated Acquirer and Target Net Income

	2009	2010	2011	2012	2013
Post-Acquisition Consolidated Net Income*	387	425	459	491	515

* In millions of dollars.

CASE STUDY 9.2
Mars Buys Wrigley in One Sweet Deal

Under considerable profit pressure from escalating commodity prices and eroding market share, Wrigley Corporation, a U.S. based leader in gum and confectionery products, faced increasing competition from Cadbury Schweppes in the U.S. gum market. Wrigley had been losing market share to Cadbury since 2006. Mars Corporation, a privately owned candy company with annual global sales of $22 billion, sensed an opportunity to achieve sales, marketing, and distribution synergies by acquiring Wrigley Corporation.

On April 28, 2008, Mars announced that it had reached an agreement to merge with Wrigley Corporation for $23 billion in cash. Under the terms of the agreement, which were unanimously approved by the boards of the two firms, shareholders of Wrigley would receive $80 in cash for each share of common stock outstanding, a 28% premium to Wrigley's closing share price of $62.45 on the announcement date. The merged firms in 2008 would have a 14.4% share of the global confectionary market, annual revenue of $27 billion, and 64,000 employees worldwide. The merger of the two firms that were family controlled represents a strategic blow to competitor Cadbury Schweppes's efforts to continue as the market leader in the global confectionary market with its gum and chocolate business. Prior to the announcement, Cadbury had a 10% worldwide market share.

As of the September 28, 2008 closing date, Wrigley became a separate stand-alone subsidiary of Mars, with $5.4 billion in sales. The deal is expected to help Wrigley augment its sales, marketing, and distribution capabilities. To provide more focus to Mars's brands in an effort to stimulate growth, Mars would in time transfer its global nonchocolate confectionery sugar brands to Wrigley. Bill Wrigley Jr., who controls 37% of the firm's outstanding shares, remained the executive chairman of Wrigley. The Wrigley management team also remained in place after the closing.

The combined companies would have substantial brand recognition and product diversity in six growth categories: chocolate, not chocolate confectionary, gum, food, drinks, and pet care products. While there is little product overlap between the two firms, there is considerable geographic overlap. Mars is located in 100 countries, while Wrigley relies heavily on independent distributors in its growing international distribution network. Furthermore, the two firms have extensive sales forces, often covering the same set of customers.

While mergers among competitors are not unusual, the deal's highly leveraged financial structure is atypical of transactions of this type. Almost 90% of the purchase price would be financed through borrowed funds, with the remainder financed largely by a third-party equity investor. Mars's upfront costs would consist of paying for closing costs from its cash balances in excess of its operating needs. The debt financing for the transaction would consist of $11 billion and $5.5 billion provided by J.P. Morgan Chase and Goldman Sachs, respectively. An additional $4.4 billion in subordinated debt would come from Warren Buffet's investment company, Berkshire Hathaway, a nontraditional source of high-yield financing. Historically, such financing would have been provided by investment banks or hedge funds and subsequently repackaged into securities and sold to long-term investors, such as pension funds, insurance companies, and foreign investors. However, the meltdown in the global credit markets in 2008 forced investment banks and hedge funds to withdraw from the

CASE STUDY 9.2 *(cont'd)*

high-yield market in an effort to strengthen their balance sheets. Berkshire Hathaway completed the financing of the purchase price by providing $2.1 billion in equity financing for a 9.1% ownership stake in Wrigley.

Discussion Questions

1. Why was market share in the confectionery business an important factor in Mars' decision to acquire Wrigley?
2. It what way did the acquisition of Wrigley represent a strategic blow to Cadbury?
3. How might the additional product and geographic diversity achieved by combining Mars and Wrigley benefit the combined firms?
4. Speculate as to the potential sources of synergy associated with the deal. Based on this speculation, what additional information would you want to know in order to determine the potential value of this synergy?
5. Given the terms of the agreement, Wrigley shareholders would own what percent of the combined companies? Explain your answer.

Answers to these questions are found in the Online Instructor's Manual Available to instructors using this book.

APPENDIX A

Utilizing the M&A Model on the Companion Site to This Book

The spreadsheet model on the companion site follows the four-step model-building process discussed in this chapter. Each worksheet is identified by a self-explanatory title and an acronym or "short name" used in developing the worksheet linkages. Appendices A and B at the end of the Excel spreadsheets include the projected timeline, milestones, and individual(s) responsible for each activity required to complete the transaction. See Table 9.11 for a brief description of the purpose of each worksheet.

Each worksheet follows the same layout: the assumptions listed in the top panel, historical data in the lower left panel, and forecast period data in the lower right panel. In place of existing historical data, fill in the data for the firm you wish to analyze in cells not containing formulas. Do not delete existing formulas in the sections marked "historical period" or

"forecast period" unless you wish to customize the model. To replace existing data in the forecast period panel, change the forecast assumptions at the top of the spreadsheet.

A number of the worksheets use Excel's "iteration" calculation option. This option may have to be turned on for the worksheets to operate correctly, particularly due to the inherent circularity in these models. For example, the change in cash and investments affects interest income, which in turn, affects net income and the change in cash and investments. If the program gives you a "circular reference" warning, please go to Tools, Options, and Calculation and turn on the iteration feature. One hundred iterations usually are enough to solve any "circular reference," but the number may vary with different versions of Excel.

APPENDIX A   (cont'd)

Individual simulations may be made most efficiently by making relatively small incremental changes to a few key assumptions underlying the model. Key variables include sales growth rates, the cost of sales as a percent of sales, cash-flow growth rates during the terminal period, and the discount rate applied during the annual forecast period and the terminal period. Changes should be made to only one variable at a time.

TABLE 9.11   Model Structure

Step	Worksheet Title	Objective (Tab Short Name)
1	Determine Acquirer and Target Stand-Alone Valuation	Identify assumptions and estimate preacquisition value of stand-alone strategies
1	Acquirer 5-Year Forecast and Stand-Alone Valuation	Provides stand-alone valuation (BP_App_B1)
1	Acquirer Historical Data and Financial Ratios	Provides consistency check between projected and historical data (BP_App_B2)
1	Acquirer Debt Repayment Schedules	Estimate firm's preacquisition debt (BP_App_B3)
1	Acquirer Cost of Equity and Capital Calculation	Displays assumptions (BP_App_B4)
1	Target 5-Year Forecast and Stand-Alone Valuation	See above (AP_App_B1)
1	Target Historical Data and Financial Ratios	See above (AP_App_B2)
1	Target Debt Repayment Schedules	See above (AP_App_B3)
1	Target Cost of Equity and Capital Calculation	See above (AP_App_B4)
2	Value Combined Acquirer and Target Including Synergy	Identify assumptions and estimate postacquisition value
2	Combined Firm's 5-Year Forecast and Valuation	Provides valuation (AP_App_C)
2	Synergy Estimation	Displays assumptions underlying estimates (AP_App_D)
3	Determine Initial Offer Price for Target Firm	Estimate negotiating price range
3	Offer Price Determination	Estimate minimum and maximum offer prices (AP_App_E)
3	Alternative Valuation Summaries	Displays alternative valuation methodologies employed (AP_App_F)
4	Determine Combined Firm's Ability to Finance Transaction	Reality check (AP_App_G)
	Appendix A: Acquisition Timeline	Provides key activities schedule (AP_App_A1)
	Appendix B: Summary Milestones and Responsible Individuals	Benchmarks performance to timeline (AP_App_A2)

APPENDIX B

M&A Model Balance Sheet Adjustment Mechanism

Projecting each line item of the balance sheet as a percent of sales does not ensure that the projected balance sheet will balance. Financial analysts commonly "plug" into financial models an adjustment equal to the difference between assets and liabilities plus shareholders' equity. While this may make sense for one-year budget forecasting, it becomes very cumbersome in multiyear projections. Moreover, it becomes very time consuming to run multiple scenarios based on different sets of assumptions. By forcing the model to automatically balance, these problems can be eliminated. While practical, this automatic adjustment mechanism rests on the simplistic notion that a firm will borrow if cash flow is negative and add to cash balances if cash flow is positive. This assumption ignores other options available to the firm, such as using excess cash flow to reduce

outstanding debt, repurchase stock, or pay dividends.

The balance-sheet adjustment methodology illustrated in Table 9.12 requires that the analyst separate the current assets into operating and nonoperating assets. Operating assets include minimum operating cash balances and other operating assets (e.g., receivables, inventories, and assets such as prepaid items). Current nonoperating assets are investments (i.e., cash generated in excess of minimum operating balances invested in short-term marketable securities). The firm issues new debt whenever cash outflows exceed cash inflows. Investments increase whenever cash outflows are less than cash inflows. For example, if net fixed assets (NFA) were the only balance sheet item that grew from one period to the next, new debt issued (ND) would increase by an amount equal to

TABLE 9.12   Model Balance Sheet Adjustment Mechanism

Assets	Liabilities
Current Operating Assets	Current Liabilities (CL)
Cash Needed for Operations (C)	
Other Current Assets (OCA)	Other Liabilities (OL)
Total Current Operating Assets (TCOA)	
Short-Term (Nonoperating)	Long-Term Debt (LTD)
Investments (I)	Existing Debt (ED)
	New Debt (ND)
Net Fixed Assets (NFA)	
Other Assets (OA)	
Total Assets (TA)	Total Liabilities (TL)
	Shareholders' Equity (SE)

Cash Outflows Exceed Cash Inflows:
- If $(TA - I) > (TL - ND) + SE$, *the firm must borrow.*

Cash Outflows Are Less Than Cash Inflows:
- If $(TA - I) < (TL - ND) + SE$, *the firm's nonoperating investments increase.*

Cash Outflows Equal Cash Inflows:
- If $(TA - I) = (TL - ND) + SE$, *there is no change in borrowing or nonoperating investments.*

APPENDIX B　(cont'd)

the increase in net fixed assets. In contrast, if current liabilities were the only balance sheet entry to rise from one period to the next, nonoperating investments (I) would increase by an amount equal to the increase in current liabilities. In either example, the balance sheet will automatically balance.

The Microsoft Excel formulae that underlie the model's adjustment mechanism correspond to conditional or "if, then" instructions. If in a given year, the firm is borrowing (i.e., new debt is positive), the investment row in the model's Step 1 worksheet is zero for that year. The amount of new debt would equal the difference between total assets less short-term nonoperating investments and total liabilities less new debt plus shareholders' equity. If in a given year, the firm is not borrowing (i.e., new debt is zero), the investment row in the model's Step 1 worksheet is positive. The amount of short-term nonoperating investment would be equal to the difference between total liabilities less new debt plus shareholders' equity and total assets less short-term nonoperating investment. The same logic applies to the balancing mechanism for the Step 2 and Step 4 worksheets.

10

Analysis and Valuation of Privately Held Companies

Maier's Law: If the facts do not conform to the theory, they must be disposed of.

Pg. 343-346

INSIDE M&A: CASHING OUT OF A PRIVATELY HELD ENTERPRISE

When he had reached his early sixties, Anthony Carnevale starting reducing the amount of time he spent managing Sentinel Benefits Group Inc., a firm he had founded. He planned to retire from the benefits and money management consulting firm in which he was a 26% owner. Mr. Carnevale, his two sons, and two nonfamily partners had built the firm to a company of more than 160 employees with $2.5 billion under management.

Selling the family business was not what the family expected to happen when Mr. Carnevale retired. He believed that his sons and partners were quite capable of continuing to manage the firm after he left. However, like many small businesses, Sentinel found itself with a succession of planning challenges. If the sons and the company's two other nonfamily partners bought out Mr. Carnevale, the firm would have little cash left over for future growth. The firm was unable to get a loan, given the lack of assets for collateral and the somewhat unpredictable cash flow of the business. Even if a loan could have been obtained, the firm would have been burdened with interest and principal repayment for years to come.

Over the years, Mr. Carnevale had rejected buyout proposals from competitors as inadequate. However, he contacted a former suitor, Focus Financial Partners LLC (a partnership that buys small money management firms and lets them operate largely independently). After several months of negotiation, Focus acquired 100% of Sentinel. Each of the five partners—Mr. Carnevale, his two sons, and two nonfamily partners—received an undisclosed amount of cash and Focus stock. A four-person Sentinel management team is now paid based on the company's revenue and growth.

The major challenges prior to the sale dealt with the many meetings held to resolve issues such as compensation, treatment of employees, how the firm would be managed subsequent to the sale, how client pricing would be determined, and who would make decisions about staff changes. Once the deal was complete, the Carnivales found it difficult to tell employees, particularly those who had been with the firm for years. Since most employees were not directly affected, only one left as a direct result of the sale.[1]

CHAPTER OVERVIEW

A *privately owned corporation* is a firm whose securities are not registered with state or federal authorities. Consequently, they are prohibited from being traded in the public securities markets. The lack of such markets makes valuing private businesses particularly challenging. Nevertheless, the need to value such businesses may arise for a variety of reasons. Investors and small business owners may need a valuation as part of a merger or acquisition, for settling an estate, or because employees wish to exercise their stock options. Employee stock ownership plans (ESOPs) also may require periodic valuations. In other instances, shareholder disputes, court cases, divorce, or the payment of gift or estate taxes may necessitate a valuation of the business.

Other significant differences between publicly traded and privately owned companies include the availability and reliability of data, which for public companies tend to be much greater than for small private firms. Moreover, in large publicly traded corporations and large privately owned companies, managers are often well versed in contemporary management practices, accounting, and financial valuation techniques. This is frequently not the case for small privately owned businesses. Finally, managers in large public companies are less likely to have the same level of emotional attachment to the business frequently found in family-owned businesses.

This chapter discusses how the analyst deals with these problems. Issues concerning making initial contact and negotiating with the owners of privately owned businesses were addressed in Chapter 5. Consequently, this chapter focuses on the challenges of valuing private firms. Following a brief discussion of such businesses, this chapter discusses in detail the hazards of dealing with both limited and often unreliable data associated with private firms. The chapter then focuses on how to properly adjust questionable data, as well as how to select the appropriate valuation methodology and discount or capitalization rate. Considerable time is spent discussing how to apply control premiums, minority discounts, and liquidity discounts in valuing businesses. This chapter also includes a discussion of how corporate shells, created through reverse mergers, and leveraged ESOPs are used to acquire privately owned companies and how PIPE financing may be used to fund their ongoing operations.

A review of this chapter (including practice questions) is available in the file folder entitled "Student Study Guide" on the companion site to this book (*www.elsevierdirect.com/companions/ 9780123854858*). The companion site also contains a Learning Interactions Library, which gives students the opportunity to test their knowledge of this chapter in a "real-time" environment.

---

[1] Adapted from Simona Covel, "Firm Sells Itself to Let Patriarch Cash Out," *Wall Street Journal,* November 1, 2007, p. B8

DEMOGRAPHICS OF PRIVATELY HELD BUSINESSES

More than 99% of all businesses in the United States are small. They contribute about 75% of net new jobs added to the U.S. economy annually. Furthermore, such businesses employ about one-half of the U.S. nongovernment-related workforce and account for about 41% of nongovernment sales.[2]

Privately owned businesses are often referred to as *closely held*, since they are usually characterized by a small group of shareholders controlling the operating and managerial policies of the firm. Most closely held firms are family-owned businesses. All closely held firms are not small, since families control the operating policies at many large, publicly traded companies. In many of these firms, family influence is exercised by family members holding senior management positions, seats on the board of directors, and through holding supervoting stock (i.e., stock with multiple voting rights). The last factor enables control, even though the family's shareholdings often are less than 50%. Examples of large, publicly traded family businesses include Wal-Mart, Ford Motor, American International Group, Motorola, Loew's, and Bechtel Group. Each of these firms has annual revenues of more than $18 billion.

Key Characteristics

The number of firms in the United States in 2009 (the last year for which detailed data are available) totaled 32.7 million, with about 8.2 million, or one-fourth, having payrolls. The total number of firms and the number of firms with payrolls have grown at compound annual average growth rates of 2.8% and 1.6%, respectively, between 1990 and 2009. Of the firms without a payroll, most are self-employed persons operating unincorporated businesses, and they may or may not be the owner's primary source of income. Of the total number of firms in 2009, about 19%, 9%, and 72% were corporations, partnerships, and single proprietorships, respectively. These percentages have been relatively constant since the early 1990s. The M&A market for employer firms tends to be concentrated among firms with 99 or fewer employees, which account for about 98% of all firms with employees.[3]

Family-Owned Firms

Family-owned businesses account for about 89% of all businesses in the United States.[4] In such businesses, the family has effective control over the strategic direction of the business. Moreover, the business contributes significantly to the family's income, wealth, and identity. While confronted with the same business challenges as all firms, family-owned firms are beset by more severe internal issues than publicly traded firms. These issues include management succession, lack of corporate governance, informal management structure, less-skilled lower-level management, and a preference for ownership over growth.

[2] See U.S. Small Business Administration.

[3] U.S. Census Bureau

[4] Astrachan and Shanker, 2003

Firms that are family owned but not managed by family members are often well managed, since family shareholders with large equity stakes carefully monitor those who are charged with managing the business.[5] However, management by one of the founders' children typically adversely affects firm value.[6] This may result from the limited pool of family members available for taking control of the business.

Succession is one of the most difficult challenges to resolve, with family-owned firms viewing succession as the transfer of ownership more than as a transfer of management. Problems arise from inadequate preparation of the younger generation of family members and the limited pool of potential successors who might not even have the talent or the interest to take over. Mid-level management expertise often resides among nonfamily members, who often leave due to perceived inequity in pay scales with family members and limited promotion opportunities. While some firms display an ability to overcome the challenges of succession, others look to sell the business.

GOVERNANCE ISSUES IN PRIVATELY HELD AND FAMILY-OWNED FIRMS

The approach taken to promote good governance in the Sarbanes-Oxley Act (SOX) of 2002 (see Chapter 2) and under the market model of corporate governance (see Chapter 3) is to identify and apply "best practices." The focus on "best practices" has led to the development of generalized laundry lists, rather than specific actions leading to measurable results.[7] Moreover, what works for publicly traded companies may not be readily applicable to privately held or family-owed firms.

The market model relies on a large dispersed class of investors in which ownership and corporate control are largely separate. Moreover, the market model overlooks the fact that family-owned firms often have different interests, time horizons, and strategies from investors in publicly owned firms. In many countries, family-owned firms have been successful because of their shared interests and because investors place a higher value on the long-term health of the business rather than on short-term performance.[8] Consequently, the control model of corporate governance discussed in Chapter 3 may be more applicable where ownership tends to be concentrated and the right to control the business is not fully separate from ownership.

There is some empirical evidence that the control model (or some variation) is more applicable to family-owned firms than the market model.[9] Director independence appears to be less important for family-owned firms, since outside directors often can be swayed by various forms of compensation. A board consisting of owners focused on the long-term growth of the business for future generations of the family may be far more committed to the firm than

---

[5] Bennedsen et al., 2006; Perez-Gonzalez, 2006; Villalonga and Amit, 2006

[6] Claessens et al., 2002; Morck and Yeung, 2000

[7] Robinson, 2002b

[8] Habershon and Williams, 1999; de Visscher, Aronoff, and Ward, 1995

[9] Astrachan and Shanker, 2003

outsiders. While the owners are ultimately responsible for strategic direction, the board must ensure that the strategy formulated by management is consistent with the owners' desires.

Nevertheless, other studies find that private businesses are adopting many of the Sarbanes-Oxley procedures as part of their own internal governance practices. A 2004 survey conducted by Foley and Lardner found that more than 40% of the private firms surveyed voluntarily adopted the following SOX provisions: (1) executive certification of financial statements, (2) whistleblower initiatives, (3) board approval of nonaudit services provided by external auditors, and (4) adoption of corporate governance policy guidelines.[10]

CHALLENGES OF VALUING PRIVATELY HELD COMPANIES

The anonymity of many privately held firms, the potential for manipulation of information, problems specific to small firms, and the tendency of owners of private firms to manage in a way to minimize tax liabilities create a number of significant valuation issues. The challenges of valuation are compounded by the emotional attachments private business owners often have to their businesses. These issues are addressed in the next sections of this chapter.

Lack of Externally Generated Information

There is generally a lack of analyses of private firms generated by sources outside of the company. Private firms provide little incentive for outside analysts to cover them because of the absence of a public market for their securities. Consequently, there are few forecasts of their performance other than those provided by the firm's management. Press coverage is usually quite limited, and what is available is often based on information provided by the firm's management. Even highly regarded companies (e.g., Dun & Bradstreet) purporting to offer demographic and financial information on small privately held firms use largely superficial and infrequent telephone interviews with the management of such firms as their primary source of such information.

Lack of Internal Controls and Inadequate Reporting Systems

Private companies are generally not subject to the same level of rigorous controls and reporting systems as public firms. Public companies are required to prepare audited financial statements for their annual reports.[11] The SEC enforces the accuracy of these statements under the authority provided by the Securities and Exchange Act of 1934.

Although reporting systems in small firms are generally poor or nonexistent, the lack of formal controls, such as systems to monitor how money is spent and an approval process to ensure that funds are spent appropriately, invites fraud and misuse of company resources. Documentation is another formidable problem. Intellectual property is a substantial portion

[10] The audit consists of a professional examination and verification of a company's accounting documents and supporting data for the purpose of rendering an opinion as to their fairness, consistency, and conformity with generally accepted accounting principles.

[11] Foley and Lardner, 2007

of the value of many private firms. Examples of such property include system software, chemical formulas, and recipes. Often only one or two individuals within the firm know how to reproduce these valuable intangible assets. The lack of documentation can destroy a firm if such an individual leaves or dies. Moreover, customer lists and the terms and conditions associated with key customer relationships also may be largely undocumented, creating the basis for customer disputes when a change in ownership occurs.

Firm-Specific Problems

Private firms may lack product, industry, and geographic diversification. There may be insufficient management talent to allow the firm to develop new products for its current markets or expand into new markets. The company may be highly sensitive to fluctuations in demand because of significant fixed expenses. Its small size may limit its influence with regulators and unions. The company's size also may limit its ability to gain access to efficient distribution channels and leverage with suppliers and customers. Finally, the company may have an excellent product but very little brand recognition.

Common Forms of Manipulating Reported Income

Revenue and operating expenses are most commonly misstated. How this may occur is explained next.

Misstating Revenue

Revenue may be over- or understated, depending on the owner's objectives. If the intent is tax minimization, businesses operating on a cash basis may opt to report less revenue because of the difficulty outside parties have in tracking transactions. Private business owners intending to sell a business may be inclined to inflate revenue if the firm is to be sold. Common examples include manufacturers, which rely on others to distribute their products. These manufacturers can inflate revenue in the current accounting period by booking as revenue products shipped to resellers without adequately adjusting for probable returns. Membership or subscription businesses, such as health clubs and magazine publishers, may inflate revenue by booking the full value of multiyear contracts in the current period rather than prorating the payment received at the beginning of the contract period over the life of the contract.[12]

Manipulation of Operating Expenses

Owners of private businesses attempting to minimize taxes may overstate their contribution to the firm by giving themselves or family members unusually high salaries, bonuses, and benefits. The most common distortion of costs comes in the form of higher than normal salary and benefits provided to family members and key employees. Other examples of cost

---

[12] Such booking activity results in a significant boost to current profitability because not all the costs associated with multiyear contracts, such as customer service, are incurred in the period in which the full amount of revenue is booked.

manipulation include extraordinary expenses that are really other forms of compensation for the owner, his or her family, and key employees, which may include the rent on the owner's summer home or hunting lodge and salaries for the pilot and captain for the owner's airplane and yacht. Current or potential customers sometimes are allowed to use these assets. Owners frequently argue that these expenses are necessary to maintain customer relationships or close large contracts and are therefore legitimate business expenses. One way to determine if these are appropriate business expenses is to ascertain how often these assets are used for the purpose for which the owner claims they were intended. Other areas commonly abused include travel and entertainment, personal insurance, and excessive payments to vendors supplying services to the firm. Due diligence frequently uncovers situations in which the owner or a family member is either an investor in or an owner of the vendor supplying the products or services.

Alternatively, if the business owner's objective is to maximize the selling price of the business, salaries, benefits, and other operating costs may be understated significantly. An examination of the historical trend in the firm's reported profitability may reveal that the firm's profits are being manipulated. For example, a sudden improvement in operating profits in the year in which the business is being offered for sale may suggest that expenses had been overstated, revenues understated, or both during the historical period.

PROCESS FOR VALUING PRIVATELY HELD BUSINESSES

To address the challenges presented by privately owned firms, an analyst should adopt a four-step procedure. Step 1 requires adjustment of the target firm's financial data to reflect true profitability and cash flow in the current period. Determining what the business is actually capable of doing in terms of operating profit and cash flow in the current period is critical to the valuation, since all projections are biased if the estimate of current performance is skewed. Step 2 entails determining the appropriate valuation methodology. Step 3 requires the determination of the appropriate discount rate. Finally, the fourth step involves adjusting the estimated value of the private firm for a control premium (if appropriate), a liquidity discount, and a minority discount (if an investor takes a less than controlling ownership position in a firm).

STEP 1: ADJUSTING FINANCIAL STATEMENTS

The purpose of adjusting the income statement is to provide an accurate estimate of the current year's net or pretax income, earnings before interest and taxes (EBIT), or earnings before interest, taxes, depreciation, and amortization (EBITDA). The various measures of income should reflect accurately all costs actually incurred in generating the level of revenue, adjusted for doubtful accounts the firm booked in the current period. They also should reflect other expenditures (e.g., training and advertising) that must be incurred in the current period to sustain the anticipated growth in revenue.

The importance of establishing accurate current or base-year data is evident when we consider how businesses—particularly small, closely held businesses—are often valued. If the current year's profit data are incorrect, future projections of the dollar value would be inaccurate, even if the projected growth rate is accurate. Furthermore, valuations based on relative valuation methods such as price–to–current year earnings ratios would be biased to the extent estimates of the target's current income are inaccurate.

Earnings before interest and taxes, depreciation, and amortization has become an increasingly popular measure of value for privately held firms. The use of this measure facilitates the comparison of firms because it eliminates the potential distortion in earnings performance due to differences in depreciation methods and financial leverage among firms. Furthermore, this indicator is often more readily applicable in relative-valuation methods than other measures of profitability, since firms are more likely to display positive EBITDA than EBIT or net income figures. Despite its convenience, the analyst needs to be mindful that EBITDA is only one component of cash flow and ignores the impact on cash flow of changes in net working capital, investing, and financing activities. See Chapter 8 for a more detailed discussion of the use of EBITDA in relative valuation methods.

Making Informed Adjustments

While finding reliable current information on privately held firms is generally challenging, some information is available, albeit often fragmentary and inconsistent. The first step for the analyst is to search the Internet for references to the target firm. This search should unearth a number of sources of information on the target firm. Table 10.1 provides a partial list of websites containing information on private firms.

TABLE 10.1   Sources of Information on Private Firms

Source/Web Address	Content
RESEARCH FIRMS	
Washington Researchers: www.washingtonresearchers.com Fuld & Company: www.fuld.com	Provide listing of sources such as local government officials, local chambers of commerce, state government regulatory bodies, credit reporting agencies, and local citizen groups
DATABASES	
Dun & Bradstreet: smallbusiness.dnb.com	Information on firms' payments histories and limited financial data
Hoover: www.hoovers.com	Data on 40,000 international and domestic firms, IPOs, not-for-profits, trade associations, and small businesses; limited data on 18 million other companies
Integra: www.integrainfo.com	Provides industry benchmarking data
Standard & Poor's NetAdvantage: www.netadvantage.standardandpoors.com	Financial data and management and directors' bibliographies on 125,000 firms
InfoUSA: www.infousa.com	Industry benchmarking and company-specific data
Forbes: www.forbes.com/list	Provides list of top privately held firms annually
Inc: www.inc.com/inc500	Provides list of 500 of fastest-growing firms annually

Owners' and Officers' Salaries

Before drawing any conclusions, the analyst should determine the actual work performed by all key employees and the compensation received for performing a similar job in the same industry. Comparative salary information can be obtained by employing the services of a compensation consultant who is familiar with the industry or simply by scanning "employee wanted" advertisements in the industry trade press and magazines and the "help wanted" pages of the local newspaper.

Benefits

Depending on the industry, benefits can range from 14 to 50% of an employee's base salary. Certain employee benefits, such as Social Security and Medicare taxes, are mandated by law and, therefore, an uncontrollable cost of doing business. Other types of benefits may be more controllable. These include items such as pension contributions and life insurance coverage, which are calculated as a percentage of base salary. Consequently, efforts by the buyer to trim salaries that appear to be excessive also reduce these types of benefits. Efforts to reduce such benefits may contribute to higher overall operating costs in the short run. Operating costs may increase as a result of higher employee turnover and the need to retrain replacements, as well as the potential negative impact on the productivity of those that remain.

Travel and Entertainment

Travel and entertainment (T&E) expenditures tend to be one of the first cost categories cut when a potential buyer attempts to value a target company. What may look excessive to one who is relatively unfamiliar with the industry may in fact be necessary for retaining current customers and acquiring new customers. Establishing, building, and maintaining relationships is particularly important for personal and business services companies, such as consulting and law firms. Account management may require consultative selling at the customer's site. A complex product like software may require on-site training. Indiscriminant reduction in the T&E budget could lead to a loss of customers following a change in ownership.

Auto Expenses and Personal Life Insurance

Ask if such expenses represent a key component of the overall compensation required to attract and retain key employees. This can be determined by comparing total compensation paid to employees of the target firm with compensation packages offered to employees in similar positions in the same industry in the same region. A similar review should be undertaken with respect to the composition of benefits packages. Depending on the demographics and special needs of the target firm's workforce, an acquirer may choose to alter the composition of the benefits package by substituting other types of benefits for those eliminated or reduced.

Family Members

Similar questions need to be asked about family members on the payroll. Frequently, they perform real services and tend to be highly motivated because of their close affinity with the business. If the business has been in existence for many years, the loss of key family members who built relationships with customers over the years may result in a subsequent loss of key accounts. Moreover, family members may be those who possess proprietary knowledge necessary for the ongoing operation of the business.

Rent or Lease Payments in Excess of Fair Market Value

Check who owns the buildings housing the business or the equipment used by the business. This is a frequent method used to transfer company funds to the business owner, who also owns the bulding, in excess of his or her stated salary and benefits. However, rents may not be too high if the building is a "special-purpose" structure retrofitted to serve the specific needs of the tenant.

Professional Services Fees

Professional services could include legal, accounting, personnel, and actuarial services. This area is frequently subject to abuse. Once again, check for any nonbusiness relationship between the business owner and the firm providing the service. Always consider any special circumstances that may justify unusually high fees. An industry that is subject to continuing regulation and review may incur what appear to be abnormally high legal and accounting expenses.

Depreciation Expense

Accelerated depreciation methodologies may make sense for tax purposes, but they may seriously understate current earnings. For financial reporting purposes, it may be appropriate to convert depreciation schedules from accelerated to straight-line depreciation if this results in a better matching of when expenses actually are incurred and revenue actually is received.

Reserves

Current reserves may be inadequate to reflect future events. An increase in reserves lowers taxable income, whereas a decrease in reserves raises taxable income. Collection problems may be uncovered following an analysis of accounts receivable. It may be necessary to add to reserves for doubtful accounts. Similarly, the target firm may not have adequate reserves for future obligations to employees under existing pension and healthcare plans. Reserves also may have to be increased to reflect known environmental and litigation exposures.

Accounting for Inventory

During periods of inflation, businesses frequently use the last-in, first-out (LIFO) method to account for inventories. This approach results in an increase in the cost of sales that reflects the most recent and presumably highest-cost inventory; therefore, it reduces gross profit and taxable income. During periods of inflation, the use of LIFO also tends to lower the value of inventory on the balance sheet because the items in inventory are valued at the lower cost of production associated with earlier time periods. In contrast, the use of first-in, first-out (FIFO) accounting for inventory assumes that inventory is sold in the chronological order in which it was purchased. During periods of inflation, the FIFO method produces a higher ending inventory, a lower cost of goods sold, and higher gross profit. Although it may make sense for tax purposes to use LIFO, the buyer's objective for valuation purposes should be to obtain as realistic an estimate of actual earnings as possible in the current period. FIFO accounting appears to be most logical for products that are perishable or subject to rapid obsolescence and, therefore, are most likely to be sold in chronological order. In an environment in which inflation is expected to remain high for an extended time period, LIFO accounting may make more sense.

Areas That Are Commonly Understated

Projected increases in sales normally require more aggressive marketing efforts, more effective customer service support, and better employee training. Nonetheless, it is common to see the ratio of annual advertising and training expenses to annual sales decline during the period of highest projected growth in forecasts developed by either the seller or the buyer. The seller has an incentive to minimize such expenses during the forecast period to provide the most sanguine outlook possible. The buyer simply may be overly optimistic about how much more effectively the business can be managed as a result of a change in ownership; the buyer may also be excessively optimistic in an effort to induce lenders to finance the transaction. Other areas that are commonly understated in projections but that can never really be escaped include the expense associated with environmental cleanup, employee safety, and pending litigation.

Areas That Are Commonly Overlooked

In many cases, the value of the business is more in its intangible assets than in its tangible assets. The best examples include the high valuations placed on many Internet-related and biotechnology companies. The target's intangible assets may include customer lists, patents, licenses, distributorship agreements, leases, regulatory approvals (e.g., U.S. Food and Drug Administration approval of a new drug), noncompete agreements, and employment contracts. Note that for these items to represent sources of incremental value, they must represent sources of revenue or cost reduction not already reflected in the target's cash flows.

Explaining Adjustments to Financial Statements

Table 10.2 illustrates how historical and projected financial statements received from the target as part of the due diligence process could be restated to reflect what the buyer believes to be a more accurate characterization of revenue and costs. Adjusting the historical financials provides insight into what the firm could have done had it been managed differently. Similarly, adjusting the projected financials enables the analyst to use what he or she considers more realistic assumptions. Note that the cost of sales is divided into direct and indirect expenses.

Direct cost of sales relates to costs incurred directly in the production process. Indirect costs are those incurred as a result of the various functions (e.g., senior management, human resources, sales, accounting) supporting the production process. The actual historical costs are displayed above the "explanation of adjustments" line. Some adjustments represent "add backs" to profit while others reduce profit. The adjusted EBITDA numbers at the bottom of the table represent what the buyer believes to be the most realistic estimate of the profitability of the business. Finally, by displaying the data historically, the buyer can see trends that may be useful in projecting the firm's profitability.

TABLE 10.2   Adjusting the Target Firm's Financial Statements[a]

	Year 1	Year 2	Year 3	Year 4	Year 5
Revenue ($ thousands)	8000.0	8400.0	8820.0	9261.0	9724.1
Less: Direct Cost of Sales (COS), excluding depreciation & amortization	5440.0	5712.0	5997.6	6297.5	6612.4
Equals: Gross Profit	2560.0	2688.0	2822.4	2963.5	3111.7
Less: Indirect Cost of Sales					
Salaries & Benefits	1200.0	1260.0	1323.0	1389.2	1458.6
Rent	320.0	336.0	352.8	370.4	389.0
Insurance	160.0	168.0	176.4	185.2	194.5
Advertising	80.0	84.0	88.2	92.6	97.2
Travel & Entertainment	240.0	252.0	264.6	277.8	291.7
Director Fees	50.0	50.0	50.0	50.0	50.0
Training	10.0	10.0	10.0	10.0	10.0
All Other Indirect Expenses	240.0	252.0	264.6	277.8	291.7
Equals: EBITDA	260.0	276.0	292.8	310.4	329.0

Explanation of Adjustments	Add Backs/(Deductions)				
LIFO Direct COS is higher than FIFO cost; adjustment converts to FIFO costs	200.0	210.0	220.5	231.5	243.1
Eliminate part-time family members' salaries and benefits	150.0	157.5	165.4	173.6	182.3
Eliminate owner's salary, benefits, and director fees	125.0	131.3	137.8	144.7	151.9
Increase targeted advertising to sustain regional brand recognition	(50.0)	(52.5)	(55.1)	(57.9)	(60.8)
Increase T&E expense to support out-of-state customer accounts	(75.0)	(78.8)	(82.7)	(86.8)	(91.2)
Reduce office space (rent) by closing regional sales offices	120.0	126.0	132.3	138.9	145.9
Increase training budget	(25.0)	(26.3)	(27.6)	(28.9)	(30.4)
Adjusted EBITDA	705.0	743.3	783.4	825.6	869.9

[a]The reader may simulate alternative assumptions by accessing a file entitled Excel Spreadsheet for Adjusting Target Firm Financials available on the companion site.

In this illustration, the buyer believes that because of the nature of the business, inventories are more accurately valued on a FIFO rather than a LIFO basis. This change in inventory cost accounting results in a sizeable boost to the firm's profitability. Furthermore, due diligence revealed that the firm was overstaffed and it could be operated adequately by eliminating the full-time position held by the former owner (including fees received as a member of the firm's board of directors) and a number of part-time positions held by the owner's family members.

Although some cost items are reduced, others are increased. For example, office space is reduced, thereby lowering rental expense as a result of the elimination of out-of-state sales offices. However, the sales- and marketing-related portion of the travel and entertainment budget is increased to accommodate the increased travel necessary to service out-of-state customer accounts due to the closure of the regional offices. Furthermore, it is likely that advertising expenses will have to be increased to promote the firm's products in those regions. The new buyer also believes the firm's historical training budget to be inadequate to sustain the growth of the business and more than doubles spending in this category. The reader may simulate alternative assumptions by accessing the file entitled "Excel-Based Spreadsheet of How to Adjust Target Firm's Financial Statements" on the companion site.

STEP 2: APPLYING VALUATION METHODOLOGIES TO PRIVATELY HELD COMPANIES

The methodologies employed to value privately held firms are very similar to those discussed elsewhere in this book. However, they are often subject to adjustments not commonly applied to publicly traded firms.

Defining Value

The most common generic definition of "value" used by valuation professionals is fair market value. Hypothetically, *fair market value* is the cash or cash-equivalent price that a willing buyer would propose and a willing seller would accept for a business if both parties had access to all relevant information. Furthermore, fair market value assumes that neither the seller nor the buyer is under any obligation to buy or sell.

It is easier to obtain the fair market value for a public company because of the existence of public markets in which stock in the company is actively traded. The concept may be applied to privately held firms if similar publicly traded companies exist. However, because finding substantially similar companies is difficult, valuation professionals have developed a related concept called fair value. *Fair value* is applied when no strong market exists for a business, or it is not possible to identify the value of substantially similar firms. Fair value is, by necessity, more subjective because it represents the dollar value of a business based on an appraisal of its tangible and intangible assets.[13]

---

[13] Unfortunately, the standard for fair value is ambiguous, since it is interpreted differently in the context of state statutes and financial reporting purposes. In most states, fair value is the statutory standard of value applicable in cases of dissenting stockholders' appraisal rights. Following a merger or corporate dissolution, shareholders in these states have the right to have their shares appraised and receive fair value in cash. In states adopting the Uniform Business Corporation Act, fair value refers to the value of the shares immediately before the corporate decision to which the shareholder objects, excluding any appreciation or depreciation in anticipation of the corporate decision. Fair value tends to be interpreted by judicial precedents or prior court rulings in each state. In contrast, according to the Financial Accounting Standards Board Statement 157 effective November 15, 2007, fair value is the price determined in an orderly transaction between market participants (Pratt and Niculita, 2008).

Selecting the Appropriate Valuation Methodology

As noted in Chapters 7 and 8, appraisers, brokers, and investment bankers generally classify valuation methodologies into four distinct approaches: income (discounted cash flow), relative or market based, replacement cost, and asset oriented.

The Income or Discounted-Cash-Flow Approach

The validity of this method depends heavily on the particular definition of income or cash flow, the timing of cash flows, and the selection of an appropriate discount or capitalization rate. The terms *discount rate* and *capitalization rate* often are used interchangeably. Whenever the growth rate of a firm's cash flows is projected to vary over time, *discount rate* generally refers to the factor used to convert the projected cash flows to present values. In contrast, if the cash flows of the firm are not expected to grow or are expected to grow at a constant rate indefinitely, the discount rate used by practitioners often is referred to as the *capitalization rate.*

The conversion of a future income stream into a present value also is referred to as the *capitalization process.* It often applies when future income or cash flows are not expected to grow or are expected to grow at a constant rate. When no growth in future income or cash flows is expected, the capitalization rate is defined as the perpetuity growth model. When future cash flow or income is expected to grow at a constant rate, the capitalization rate commonly is defined as the difference between the discount rate and the expected growth rate (i.e., the constant growth model). Present values calculated in this manner are sometimes referred to as *capitalized values.*

Capitalization rates are commonly converted to multiples by dividing 1 by the discount rate or the discount rate less the anticipated constant growth rate in cash flows. These *capitalization multiples* can be multiplied by the current period's cash flow (i.e., if applying the perpetuity model) or the subsequent period's anticipated cash flow (i.e., if applying the constant-growth model) to estimate the market value of a firm. For example, if the discount rate is assumed to be 8% and the current level of a firm's cash flow is $1.5 million, which is expected to remain at that level in perpetuity, the implied valuation is $18.75 million—that is, $(1/0.08) \times \$1.5$ million. Alternatively, if the current level of cash flow is expected to grow at 4% annually in perpetuity, the implied valuation is $39 million—that is, $[(1.04)/(0.08 - 0.04)] \times \$1.5$ million. The capitalization multiples in the perpetuity and constant-growth cases are $1/0.08$ and $1.04/(0.08 - 0.04)$, respectively.

Several alternative definitions of income or cash flow can be used in either the discounting or capitalization process. These include free cash flow to equity holders or the firm; earnings before interest and taxes; earnings before interest, taxes, and depreciation; earnings before taxes (EBT); and earnings after taxes (EAT or NI).

Capitalization multiples and capitalization rates often are used in valuing small businesses because of their inherent simplicity. Many small business owners lack sophistication in financial matters. Consequently, a valuation concept, which is easy to calculate, understand, and communicate to the parties involved, may significantly facilitate completion of the transaction. Finally, there is little empirical evidence that more complex valuation methods necessarily result in more accurate valuation estimates.

The Relative-Value or Market-Based Approach

This approach is used widely in valuing private firms by business brokers or appraisers to establish a purchase price. The Internal Revenue Service and the U.S. tax courts have encouraged the use of market-based valuation techniques. Therefore, in valuing private companies, it is always important to keep in mind what factors the IRS thinks are relevant to the process, because the IRS may contest any sale requiring the payment of estate, capital gains, or unearned income taxes. The IRS's positions on specific tax issues can be determined by reviewing revenue rulings. A *revenue ruling* is an official interpretation by the IRS of the Internal Revenue Code, related statutes, tax treaties, and regulations.

Revenue Ruling 59-60 describes the general factors that the IRS and tax courts consider relevant in valuing private businesses. These factors include general economic conditions, the specific conditions in the industry, the type of business, historical trends in the industry, the firm's performance, and the firm's book value. In addition, the IRS and tax courts consider the ability of the company to generate earnings and pay dividends, the amount of intangibles such as goodwill, recent sales of stock, and the stock prices of companies engaged in the "same or similar" line of business.

The Replacement-Cost Approach

This approach states that the assets of a business are worth what it costs to replace them and is most applicable to businesses that have substantial amounts of tangible assets for which the actual cost to replace them can be determined easily. This method is often not useful in valuing a business whose assets are primarily intangible. Moreover, the replacement-cost approach ignores the value created in excess of the cost of replacing each asset by operating the assets as a going concern. For example, an assembly line may consist of a number of different machines, each performing a specific task in the production of certain products. The value of the total production coming off the assembly line over the useful lives of the individual machines is likely to far exceed the sum of the costs to replace each machine. Consequently, the business should be valued as a going concern rather than as the sum of the costs to replace its individual assets.[14]

The Asset-Oriented Approach

Like the replacement-cost approach, the accuracy of asset-oriented approaches depends on the overall proficiency of the appraiser hired to establish value and the availability of adequate information. Book value is an accounting concept and generally is not considered a good measure of market value because book values usually reflect historical rather than current market values. However, as noted in Chapter 8, tangible book value (i.e., book value less intangible assets) may be a good proxy for the current market value for both financial services and product distribution companies. Breakup value is an estimate of what the value of a

---

[14] The replacement-cost approach sometimes is used to value intangible assets by examining the amount of historical investment associated with the asset. For example, the cumulative historical advertising spending targeted at developing a particular product brand or image may be a reasonable proxy for the intangible value of the brand name or image. However, because consumer tastes tend to change over time, applying historical experience to the future may be highly misleading.

business would be if each of its primary assets were sold independently. This approach may not be practical if there are few public markets for the firm's assets. Liquidation value is a reflection of the firm under duress. A firm in liquidation normally must sell its assets within a specific time period. Consequently, the cash value of the assets realized is likely to be much less than their actual replacement value or value if the firm were to continue as a viable operation. Liquidation value is a reasonable proxy for the minimum value of the firm. For a listing of when to use the various valuation methodologies, see Table 8.4 in Chapter 8.

STEP 3: DEVELOPING DISCOUNT (CAPITALIZATION) RATES

While the discount or capitalization rate can be derived using a variety of methods, the focus in this chapter is on the weighted-average cost of capital or the cost of equity. The capital asset pricing model (CAPM) provides an estimate of the acquiring firm's cost of equity, which may be used as the discount or capitalization rate when the firm is debt-free.

Estimating a Private Firm's Beta and Cost of Equity

Like public firms, private firms are subject to nondiversifiable risk, such as changes in interest rates, inflation, war, and terrorism. However, to estimate the firm's beta, it is necessary to have sufficient historical data. Private firms and divisions of companies are not publicly traded and, therefore, have no past stock price information. The common solution is to estimate the firm's beta based on comparable publicly listed firms.

Assuming that the private firm is leveraged, the process commonly employed for constructing the private firm's leveraged beta is to assume that it can be estimated based on the unlevered beta for comparable firms adjusted for the private firm's target debt-to-equity ratio. The process involves the following steps. First, calculate the average beta for publicly traded comparable firms. If the comparable firms are leveraged, the resulting average is a leveraged beta for the comparable firms. Second, estimate the average debt-to-equity ratio in terms of the market values of the comparable firms. Third, estimate the average unlevered beta for the comparable firms based on information determined in the first two steps. Fourth, compute the levered beta for the private firm based on the firm's target debt–to–equity ratio set by management and the unlevered beta for comparable firms determined in the third step. Alternatively, the industry average leveraged beta could be used by assuming the private firm's current debt-to-equity ratio will eventually match the industry average.

Once estimated using the CAPM, the cost of equity may have to be adjusted to reflect risk specific to the target when it is applied to valuing a private company. The CAPM may understate significantly the specific business risk associated with acquiring the target firm. Recall from Chapter 7 that risk premiums for public companies often are determined by examining the historical premiums earned by stocks over some measure of risk-free returns, such as ten-year Treasury bonds. This same logic may be applied to calculating specific business risk premiums for small private firms. The specific business risk premium can be measured by the difference between the junk bond and risk-free rate or the return on comparable small stocks and the risk-free rate. Note that comparable small companies are more likely to be found on the NASDAQ, OTC, or regional stock exchanges than on the New York Stock Exchange.

Other adjustments for the risks associated with firm size are given by Ibbotson Associates in Table 7.1 in Chapter 7.

For example, consider an acquiring firm attempting to value a small, privately owned software company. If the risk-free return is 6%, the historical return on all stocks minus the risk-free return is 5.5%, the firm's financial returns are highly correlated with the overall stock market (i.e., the firm's β is approximately 1), and the historical return on OTC software stocks minus the risk-free return is 9%, the cost of equity (k_e) can be calculated as follows:[15]

$$k_e = \text{Risk} - \text{Free Return} + \beta \times \text{Market Risk or Equity Premium} + \text{Specific Business Risk Premium}$$
$$= 6\% + 1.0 \times 5.5\% + 9\% = 20.5\%$$

Estimating the Cost of Private Firm Debt

Private firms seldom can access public debt markets and are therefore usually not rated by the credit rating agencies. Most debt is bank debt, and the interest expense on loans on the firm's books that are more than a year old may not reflect what it actually would cost the firm to borrow currently. The common solution is to assume that private firms can borrow at the same rate as comparable publicly listed firms or estimate an appropriate bond rating for the company based on financial ratios and use the interest rate that public firms with similar ratings would pay.

For example, an analyst can easily identify publicly traded company bond ratings by going to any of the various Internet bond screening services (e.g., *finance.yahoo.com/bonds*) and searching for bonds using various credit ratings. Royal Caribbean Cruise Lines LTD had a BBB rating and a 2.7 interest coverage ratio (i.e., EBIT/interest expense) in 2009 and would have to pay 7.0 to 7.5% for bonds maturing in seven to ten years. Consequently, firms with similar interest coverage ratios could have similar credit ratings. If the private firm to be valued had a similar interest coverage ratio and wanted to borrow for a similar time period, it is likely that it would have had to pay a comparable rate of interest. Other sources of information about the interest rates that firms of a certain credit rating pay often are available in major financial newspapers such as the *Wall Street Journal, Investors' Business Daily*, and *Barron's*. Unlike the estimation of the cost of equity for small privately held firms, it is unnecessary to adjust the cost of debt for specific business risk, since such risk should already be reflected in the interest rate charged to firms of similar risk.

Estimating the Cost of Capital

In the presence of debt, the cost of capital method should be used to estimate the discount or capitalization rate. This method involves the calculation of a weighted average of the cost of equity and the after-tax cost of debt. The weights should reflect market values rather than book values. Private firms represent a greater challenge than public firms in that the market value of their equity and debt is not readily available in public markets. Calculating the cost of capital requires the use of the market rather than the book value of debt-to-total capital ratios. Private firms provide such ratios only in book terms. A common solution is to use what the firm's

---

[15] Note that the rationale for this adjustment for specific business risk is similar to that discussed in Chapter 7 in adjusting the CAPM for firm size (i.e., small firms generally are less liquid and subject to higher default risk than larger firms).

management has set as its target debt-to-equity ratio in determining the weights to be used or assume that the private firms will eventually adopt the industry average debt-to-equity ratio.

Note the importance of keeping assumptions used for the management's target debt-to-equity ratio (D/E) in computing the firm's cost of equity consistent with the weights used in calculating the weighted-average cost of capital. For example, the firm's target D/E should be consistent with the debt–to–total capital and equity–to–total capital weights used in the weighted-average cost of capital. This consistency can be achieved simply by dividing the target D/E (or the industry D/E if that is what is used) by $(1 + D/E)$ to estimate the implied debt–to–total capital ratio. Subtracting this ratio from 1 provides the implied equity–to–total capital ratio.

When the growth period for the firm's cash flow is expected to vary, the cost of capital estimated for the high-growth period can be expected to decline when the firm begins to grow at a more sustainable rate. This rate often is the industry average rate of growth. At that point, the firm presumably begins to take on the risk and growth characteristics of the typical firm in the industry. Thus, the discount rate may be assumed to be the industry average cost of capital during the sustainable- or terminal-growth period. Exhibit 10.1 illustrates how to calculate a private firm's beta, cost of equity, and cost of capital.

EXHIBIT 10.1 VALUING PRIVATE FIRMS

Acuity Lighting, a regional manufacturer and distributor of custom lighting fixtures, has revenues of $10 million and an EBIT of $2 million in the current year (i.e., year 0). The book value of the firm's debt is $5 million. The firm's debt matures at the end of five years and has annual interest expense of $400,000. The firm's marginal tax rate is 40%, the same as the industry average. Capital spending equals depreciation in year 0, and both are expected to grow at the same rate. As a result of excellent working capital management, the future change in working capital is expected to be essentially zero. The firm's revenue is expected to grow 15% annually for the next five years and 5% per year thereafter. The firm's current operating profit margin is expected to remain constant throughout the forecast period. As a result of the deceleration of its growth rate to a more sustainable rate, Acuity Lighting is expected to assume the risk and growth characteristics of the average firm in the industry during the terminal growth period. Consequently, its discount rate during this period is expected to decline to the industry average cost of capital of 11%.

The industry average beta and debt-to-equity ratio are 2 and 0.4, respectively. The ten-year U.S. Treasury bond rate is 4.5%, and the historical equity premium on all stocks is 5.5%. The specific business risk premium as measured by the difference between the junk bond and risk-free rate or the return on comparable small stocks and the risk-free rate is estimated to be 9%.

Acuity Lighting's interest coverage ratio is 2.89, which is equivalent to a BBB rating by the major credit rating agencies. BBB-rated firms are currently paying a pretax cost of debt of 7.5%. Acuity Lighting's management has established the firm's target debt-to-equity ratio at 0.5 based on the firm's profitability and growth characteristics. Estimate the equity value of the firm.

Calculate Acuity's cost of equity and weighted average cost of capital:

1. Unlevered beta for publicly traded firms in the same industry $= 2/(1 + 0.6 \times 0.4) = 1.61$, where 2 is the industry's average levered beta, 0.6 is $(1 - \text{tax rate})$, and 0.4 is the average debt-to-equity ratio for firms in this industry.
2. Acuity's levered beta $= 1.61 \times (1 + 0.6 \times 0.5) = 2.09$, where 0.5 is the target debt-to-equity ratio established by Acuity's management.

3. Acuity's cost of equity $= 4.5 + 2.09 \times 5.5 + 9 = 25$, where 4.5 is the risk-free rate and 9 is the firm size or firm specific business risk premium.
4. Acuity's after-tax cost of debt $= 7.5 \times (1 - 0.4) = 4.5$, where 7.5 is the pretax cost of debt.
5. Acuity's WACC $= (25 \times 0.67) + (4.5 \times 0.33) = 18.24$, where the firm's debt–to–total capital ratio (D/TC) is determined by dividing Acuity's debt-to-equity target (D/E) by $1 + D/E$. Therefore,

$$D/TC = 0.5/(1 + 0.5) = 0.33 \text{ and equity to total capital is } 1 - 0.33 \text{ or } 0.67.$$

Value Acuity using the FCFF DCF model using the data provided in Table 10.3.

$$\text{Present Value of FCFF} = \frac{\$1,380,000}{1.1824} + \frac{\$1,587,000}{1.1824^2} + \frac{\$1,825,050}{1.1824^3} + \frac{\$2,098,807}{1.1824^4} + \frac{\$2,413,628}{1.1824^5}$$

$$= \$1,167,118 + \$1,135,136 + \$1,104,032 + \$1,073,779 + \$1,044,355$$
$$= \$5,524,420$$

$$\text{PV of Terminal value} = [\$2,534,310/(0.11 - 0.05)]/1.1824^5 = \$18,276,220$$

$$\text{Total Present Value} = \$5,524,420 + \$18,276,220 = \$23,800,640$$

$$\text{Market value of Acuity's Debt} = \$400,000 \times \frac{[(1 - (1/(1.075)^5)]}{075} + \frac{\$5,000,000}{(1.075)^5}$$

$$= \$1,618,354 + \$3,482,793$$
$$= \$5,101,147$$

$$\text{Value of Equity} = \$23,800,640 - \$5,101,147 = \$18,699,493$$

TABLE 10.3   FCFF Model

Year	1	2	3	4	5	6
EBIT[a]	$2,300,000	$2,645,000	$3,041,750	$3,498,012	$4,022,714	$4,223,850
EBIT (1 – Tax Rate)[b]	$1,380,000	$1,587,000	$1,825,050	$2,098,807	$2,413,628	$2,534,310

[a]EBIT grows at 15% annually for the first five years and at 5% thereafter.
[b]Capital spending equals depreciation in year 0, and both are expected to grow at the same rate. Moreover, the change in working capital is zero. Therefore, free cash flow equals after-tax EBIT.

STEP 4: APPLYING CONTROL PREMIUMS, LIQUIDITY, AND MINORITY DISCOUNTS

In Exhibit 9.2 in Chapter 9, the maximum purchase price of a target firm (PV_{MAX}) is defined as its current market or stand-alone value (i.e., the minimum price or PV_{MIN}) plus the value of anticipated net synergies (i.e., PV_{NS}):

$$PV_{MAX} = PV_{MIN} + PV_{NS} \tag{10.1}$$

This is a reasonable representation of the maximum offer price for firms whose shares are traded in liquid markets and where no single shareholder (i.e., block shareholder) can direct the activities of the business. Examples of such firms could include Microsoft, IBM, and General Electric. However, when markets are illiquid and there are block shareholders with the ability to influence strategic decisions made by the firm, the maximum offer price for the firm needs to be adjusted for liquidity risk and the value of control. These concepts are explained next.

Liquidity Discounts

Liquidity is the ease with which investors can sell their stock without a serious loss in the value of their investment. An investor in a private company may find it difficult to quickly sell his or her shares because of limited interest in the company. As such, the investor may find it necessary to sell at a significant discount from what was paid for the shares. Liquidity or marketability risk may be expressed as a *liquidity* or *marketability discount*. This discount equals the reduction in the offer price for the target firm by an amount equal to the potential loss of value when sold due to the lack of liquidity in the market.

Empirical Studies of the Liquidity Discount

Liquidity discounts have been estimated using a variety of methodologies. The most popular involves so-called restricted stocks. Other studies have involved analyzing conditions prior to initial public offerings (IPOs), the cost of IPOs, option pricing models, and the value of subsidiaries of parent firms.

RESTRICTED STOCK (LETTER STOCK) STUDIES

Issued by public companies, such shares are identical to the firm's equities that are freely traded except for the restriction that they not be sold for a specific period of time.[16] The restriction on trading results in a lack of marketability of the security. Registration (with the SEC) exemptions on restricted stocks are granted under Rule 144A of Section 4(2) of the 1933 Securities Act. Restricted stock may be sold in limited amounts through private placements to investors, usually at a significant discount. However, it cannot be sold to the public, except under provisions of the SEC's Rule 144.

Prior to 1990, a holder of restricted stock had to register the securities with the SEC or qualify for exemption under Rule 144 to sell stock in the public markets. This made trading letter stock a time-consuming, costly process, as buyers had to perform appropriate due diligence. In 1990, the SEC adopted Rule 144A, allowing institutional investors to trade unregistered securities among themselves without filing registration statements. This change created a limited market for letter stocks and reduced discounts. In 1997, this rule was again amended to reduce the holding period for letter stocks before they could be sold from two years to one.

Empirical studies of restricted equities examine the difference in the price at which the restricted shares trade versus the price at which the same unrestricted equities trade in the public markets on the same date. Table 10.4 provides the results of 17 restricted stock studies. A comprehensive study undertaken by the SEC in 1971 examined restricted stock for 398 publicly traded companies and found that the median discount involving the restricted stock sales was about 26%.[17] Size effects appeared to be important, with firms

---

[16] "Letter" stock gets its name from the practice of requiring investors to provide an "investment letter" stipulating that the purchase is for investment and not for resale.

[17] *Institutional Investor*, 1971

TABLE 10.4   Empirical Studies of Liquidity Discounts

Study	Time Period (Sample Size)	Median Discount (%)
Restricted Stock Studies		
Institutional Investor Study Report	1966–1969 (398)	25.8
Gelman (1972)	1968–1970 (89)	33.0
Trout (1977)	1968–1972 (NA)	33.5
Morony (1973)	1969–1972 (146)	35.6
Maher (1976)	1969–1973 (NA)	35.4
Standard Research Consultants (1983)	1978–1982 (NA)	45.0
Wruck (1989)	1979–1985 (99)	13.5
Hertzel and Smith (1993)	1980–1987 (106)	20.1
Oliver and Meyers (2000)	1980–1996 (53)	27.0
Willamette Management Associates Inc. (Pratt and Niculita, 2008)	1981–1984 (NA)	31.2
Silber (1991)	1981–1988 (69)	33.8
Management Planning, Inc. (Pratt and Niculita, 2008)	1980–1995 (NA)	28.9
Hall and Polacek (1994)	1979–1992 (NA)	23.0
Johnson (1999)	1991–1995 (72)	20.0
Aschwald (2000)	1996–1997 (23)	21.0
Aschwald (2000)	1997–1998 (15)	13.0
Finnerty (2002)	1991–1997 (101)	20.1
Pre-IPO Studies		
Willamette Management Associates Inc. (Pratt and Niculita, 2008)	1981–1984 (NA)	45.0
Emory (2001)	1981–2000 (631)	45.9
IPO COST STUDIES		
Loughran and Ritter (2002)[a]	1990–2000 (NA)	22.0
OPTION STUDIES		
Longstaff (1995)	NA	25–35
Parent Subsidiaries Studies		
Officer (2007)	1997–2004 (122)	15–30

NA = Not available.
[a]*Measures maximum discount.*

having the highest sales volumes exhibiting the lowest discounts and the smallest firms having the largest discounts. An analysis completed on a smaller sample of 146 publicly traded firms found that restricted shares traded at a discount of 33%.[18] Other studies estimated the discount to be in the 33 to 35% range.[19] The size of liquidity discounts tends to decrease for firms with larger revenues and profitability and for smaller block sales of stock.[20] The magnitude of these estimates from the pre-1990 studies is problematic in view of the types of investors in unregistered equities. These include insurance companies and pension funds, which have long-term investment horizons and well-diversified portfolios. Such investors are unlikely to be deterred by a one- or two-year restriction on selling their investments.

Certain factors that have been found to be reliable indicators of liquidity discounts include the following: revenues, earnings, market price per share, price stability, and earnings stability.[21] Firms that were the most profitable showed 11% discounts,[22] while firms with the highest sales volumes showed discounts of 13%.[23] Firms showing the greatest earnings stability had a median discount of 16.4%.

More recent studies of restricted stock sales since 1990 indicate a median discount of about 20%.[24] Moreover, following the holding period change under Rule 144 from two years to one after 1997, the median discount declined to 13%.[25]

PRE-IPO STUDIES

An alternative to estimating liquidity discounts is to compare the value of a firm's stock sold before an IPO, usually through private placements, with the actual IPO offering price. Firms undertaking IPOs are required to disclose all transactions in their stocks for a period of three years before the IPO. Because the liquidity available is substantially less before the IPO, this difference is believed to be an estimate of the liquidity discount. Ten separate studies of 631 firms between 1980 and 2000 found a median discount of 45.9% between the pre-IPO transaction prices and the actual post-IPO prices.[26] The magnitude of the estimate remained relatively unchanged in each study. Such studies are subject to selection bias because only initial public offerings that were completed are evaluated. IPOs that were withdrawn because of unattractive market conditions may have received valuations more in line with pre-IPO private placements and therefore exhibited smaller discounts.

[18] Gelman, 1972

[19] Maher, 1976; Trout, 1977

[20] Silber, 1991

[21] The Management Planning Study cited in Mercer (1997) reported a median 28.9% discount.

[22] Hall and Polacek, 1994

[23] Johnson, 1999

[24] Johnson, 1999; Aschwald, 2000; Finnerty, 2002; Loughran and Ritter, 2002

[25] Aschwald, 2000

[26] Emory, 2001

IPO COST STUDIES

The total cost of an IPO includes both direct costs of flotation and indirect under-pricing costs. The direct costs entail management fees, underwriting fees, and selling concession (i.e., difference between gross and net proceeds of the issue) as a percentage of the amount of the issue. Indirect costs are measured by the frequent under-pricing of the securities by underwriters interested in selling the entire issue quickly. Direct costs run about 7% and indirect costs about 15%, implying that firms seeking to achieve liquidity incur an average cost of 22%.[27]

OPTION PRICING STUDIES

Such studies suggest that uncertainty and time are important determinants of liquidity discounts. With respect to uncertainty, the greater the volatility of the shares, the greater the magnitude of the discount. The longer the length of time the shareholder is restricted from selling the shares, the greater the discount. If a shareholder holds restricted stock and purchases a put option to sell the stock at the market price, the investor has effectively secured access to liquidity. The liquidity discount is the cost of the put option with an exercise price equal to the share price at the date of issue as a percent of the exercise price.[28] Maximum liquidity discounts were found to be in the 2 to 35% range for two-year holding periods and 15 to 25% for one-year holding periods.[29]

STUDIES OF PARENT SUBSIDIARIES

Sales of subsidiaries of other firms and privately owned firms often sell at discounts of 15% to 30% below acquisition multiples for comparable publicly traded firms. This discount may reflect the price paid by such firms for the liquidity provided by the acquiring firm. Discounts tend to be greater when debt is relatively expensive to obtain and when the parent's stock returns tend to underperform the market in the 12 months prior to the sale. This is consistent with the findings of several restricted stock studies, which identify profitability as a reliable indicator of the size of a firm's liquidity discount.[30]

In summary, empirical studies of liquidity discounts demonstrate that they exist, but there is substantial disagreement over their magnitude. Most empirical studies conducted prior to 1992 indicated that liquidity discounts ranged from 33 to 50% when compared to publicly traded securities of the same company.[31] More recent studies indicate that such securities trade at more modest discounts, ranging from 13 to 35%.[32] This range excludes the results of the pre-IPO studies that, for reasons discussed previously, are believed to be outliers. Four recent studies show a clustering of the discount around 20%. The decline in the liquidity

[27] Chaplinsky and Ramchand, 2000; Loughran and Ritter, 2002

[28] Alli and Thompson, 1991

[29] Longstaff, 1995

[30] Officer, 2007

[31] Gelman, 1972; Moroney, 1973; Maher, 1976; Silber, 1991

[32] Hertzel and Smith, 1993; Hall and Polacek, 1994; Longstaff, 1995; Oliver and Meyers, 2000; Aschwald, 2000; Koeplin, Sarin, and Shapiro, 2000; Finnerty, 2002; Officer, 2007

discount since 1990 reflects a reduction in the required holding period for Rule 144 security issues and improved overall market liquidity during the periods covered by these studies. The latter is due to enhanced business governance practices, lower transaction costs, and greater accessibility to information via the Internet and other sources about private firms and the industries in which they compete. Note that the 2008–2009 capital market meltdowns are likely an aberration and, as such, should not affect the magnitude of the liquidity discount in the long term.

Purchase Price Premiums, Control Premiums, and Minority Discounts

For many transactions, the purchase price premium, which represents the amount a buyer pays the seller in excess of the seller's current share price, includes both a premium for anticipated synergy and a premium for control. The value of control is distinctly different from the value of synergy. The value of synergy represents revenue increases and cost savings that result from combining two firms, usually in the same line of business. In contrast, the value of control provides the right to direct the activities of the target firm on an ongoing basis.

While control is often assumed to require a greater than 50% ownership stake, effective control can be achieved at less than 50% ownership if other shareholders own relatively smaller stakes and do not band together to offset the votes cast by the largest shareholder. Consequently, an investor may be willing to pay a significant premium to purchase a less than 50% stake if they believe that effective control over key decisions can be achieved.

Control can include the ability to select management, determine compensation, set policy and change the course of the business, acquire and liquidate assets, award contracts, make acquisitions, sell or recapitalize the company, and register the company's stock for a public offering. Control also involves the ability to declare and pay dividends, change the articles of incorporation or bylaws, or block any of the aforementioned actions. Owners of controlling blocks of voting stock may use this influence to extract special privileges or benefits not available to other shareholders, such as directing the firm to sell to companies owned by the controlling shareholder at a discount to the market price and to buy from suppliers owned by the controlling shareholder at premium prices. Furthermore, controlling shareholders may agree to pay unusually high salaries to selected senior managers, who may be family members. For these reasons, the more control a block investor has, the less influence a minority investor has and the less valuable is that person's stock. Therefore, a *control premium* is the amount an investor is willing to pay to direct the activities of the firm. Conversely, a *minority discount* is the reduction in the value of the investment because the minority owners have little control over the firm's operations.

Purchase price premiums may reflect only control premiums, when a buyer acquires a target firm and manages it as a largely independent operating subsidiary. The *pure control premium* is the value the acquirer believes can be created by replacing incompetent management, changing the strategic direction of the firm, gaining a foothold in a market not currently served, or achieving unrelated diversification.[33]

[33] Another example of a pure control premium is that paid for a firm going private through a leveraged buyout, in that the target firm generally is merged into a shell corporation with no synergy being created and managed for cash after having been recapitalized. While the firm's management team may remain intact, the board of directors usually consists of representatives of the financial sponsor (i.e., equity or block investor).

Empirical Studies of the Pure Control Premium

While many empirical studies estimate the magnitude of the liquidity risk discount, the empirical evidence available to measure the control premium is limited. As is true of the liquidity discount, empirical studies confirm the existence of a pure control premium. However, considerable disagreement continues over their size. Empirical studies to date focus on block transaction premiums, dual-class ownership, and M&A transactions.

EVIDENCE FROM BLOCK TRANSACTION PREMIUMS

An estimate of the magnitude of the pure control premium can be obtained by examining the difference between prices paid for privately negotiated sales of blocks of voting stock (defined as greater than 10,000 shares) constituting more than 5% of a firm's equity with the posttransaction share price. In an analysis of 63 block trades between 1980 and 1982, the median premium paid for these private blocks of voting stock compared to the publicly traded price was found to be about 20%.[34]

In a more recent study involving a cross-country comparison of 412 block transactions in 39 countries from 1990 to 2000, the median control was about 14%. However, estimates of the control premium ranged from –4 to 65%.[35] Negative results occur whenever the price paid for the block is less than the market price. This could occur whenever a firm is facing bankruptcy, management is widely viewed as incompetent, or the firm's products are obsolete. For example, Morgan Stanley's offer price for 40% of financially insolvent Bear Stearns voting shares in 2008 at $10 per share was $2 less than the market price on the day of the announcement.

In this same cross-country comparison, countries such as the United States, the United Kingdom, and the Netherlands exhibited median premiums of 2% compared to premiums in Brazil and the Czech Republic of 65 and 58%, respectively. The value of control appears to be less in countries with better accounting standards, better legal protection for minority shareholders, more competitive markets, an independent press, and high tax compliance.[36]

In a study of 27 control transactions in Italy between 1993 and 2003, block transaction (tender) premiums equaled about 12 to 14%, depending on the size of the block of shares to be acquired.[37] A 2008 study of block transaction premiums in China estimated median control premiums in China of 18.5%.[38] The wide variation in results across countries may reflect the small samples used in evaluating transactions in each country as well as significantly different circumstances in each country.

EVIDENCE FROM DUAL-CLASS OWNERSHIP

Dual-class ownership structures involve classes of stock that differ in voting rights. Those shares having more voting rights than other shares typically trade at much higher prices, with control premiums for most countries falling within a range of 10 to 20% of the firm's current

[34] Barclay and Holderness, 1989

[35] Dyck and Zingales, 2004

[36] Dyck and Zingales, 2004

[37] Massari, Monge, and Zanetti, 2006

[38] Weifeng, Zhaoguo, and Shasa, 2008

share price. However, the dispersion of control premiums is substantial, with the United States, Sweden, and the United Kingdom displaying premiums of 5.4, 6.5, and 12.8%, respectively, compared to Israel and Italy at 45.5 and 82%, respectively.[39] In an 18-country study in 1997, the estimated median control premium was 13%. However, the results varied widely across countries, with the United States and Sweden at 2% and Italy and Mexico at 29.4% and 36.4%, respectively. Two-thirds of the cross-country variance could be explained by a nation's legal environment, law enforcement, investor protection, and corporate charter provisions that tend to concentrate power (e.g., supermajority voting).[40]

EVIDENCE FROM MERGERS AND ACQUISITION TRANSACTIONS

The premium paid to target company shareholders in part reflects what must be paid to get the firm's shareholders to relinquish control. In a study examining 9,566 transactions between 1990 and 2000 in the United States, Japan, Germany, France, Italy, the United Kingdom, and Canada, two samples were analyzed: one in which buyers acquired a minority position and one where buyers acquired a controlling position. The study found that a controlling position commanded a premium 20 to 30% higher than the price paid for minority positions in U.S. transactions. Similar premiums were found in other market-oriented nations, such as the United Kingdom and Canada. However, premiums were much smaller in those nations (i.e., Japan, Germany, France, and Italy) in which banks routinely make equity investments in publicly traded firms.[41]

In summary, country comparison studies indicate a huge variation in median control premiums from as little as 2 to 5% in countries where corporate ownership often is widely dispersed and investor protections are relatively effective (e.g., United States and United Kingdom) to as much as 60 to 65% in countries where ownership tends to be concentrated and governance practices are relatively poor (e.g., Brazil and the Czech Republic). Median estimates across countries are 10 to 12%.

The Relationship between Liquidity Discounts and Control Premiums

Market liquidity and the value of control tend to move in opposite directions—that is, whenever it is easy for shareholders to sell their shares, the benefits of control diminish. Why? Because shareholders who are dissatisfied with the decisions made by controlling shareholders may choose to sell their shares, thereby reducing the value of the controlling shareholder's interest. Conversely, when it is difficult for shareholders to sell without incurring significant losses (i.e., the market is illiquid), investors place a greater value on control. Minority shareholders have no way to easily dispose of their investment, since they cannot force the sale of the firm and the controlling shareholder has little incentive to acquire their shares, except at a steep discount. The controlling shareholder can continue to make decisions that may not be in the best interests of the minority shareholders with minimal consequences. Therefore, the sizes of control premiums and liquidity discounts tend to be positively

[39] Zingales, 1995

[40] Nenova, 2003

[41] Hanouna, Sarin, and Shapiro, 2001

correlated, since the value of control increases as market liquidity decreases (i.e., liquidity discounts increase).

Equation (10.1) can be rewritten to reflect the interdependent relationship between the control premium (CP) and the liquidity discount (LD) as follows:

$$PV_{MAX} = (PV_{MIN} + PV_{NS})(1 + CP\%)(1 - LD\%) \text{ and}$$
$$PV_{MAX} = (PV_{MIN} + PV_{NS})(1 - LD\% + CP\% - LD\% \times CP\%) \tag{10.2}$$

where

CP% = control premium expressed as a percentage of the maximum purchase price
LD% = liquidity discount expressed as a percentage of the maximum purchase price

The multiplicative form of Eq. (10.2) results in a term (i.e., $LD\% \times CP\%$) that serves as an estimate of the interaction between the control premium and the liquidity discount.[42] Note that while CP% can be positive if it is a premium or negative if it is a minority discount, the value of LD% always is negative.

Estimating Liquidity Discounts, Control Premiums, and Minority Discounts

Given the wide variability of estimates, it should be evident that premiums and discounts must be applied to the value of the target firm with great care. The implication is that there is no such thing as a standard liquidity discount or control premium. In general, the size of the discount or premium should reflect factors specific to the firm.

Factors Affecting the Liquidity Discount

The median discount for empirical studies since 1992 is about 20%, with about 90% of the individual studies' estimated median discounts falling within a range of 13 to 35%. Table 10.5 suggests a subjective methodology for adjusting a private firm for liquidity risk, in which the analyst starts with the median liquidity discount of 20% and adjusts for factors specific to the firm to be valued. Such factors include firm size, liquid assets as a percent of total assets, financial returns, and cash-flow growth and leverage compared to the industry. While this is not intended to be an exhaustive list, these factors were selected based on the findings of empirical studies of restricted stocks.

The logic underlying the adjustments to the median liquidity discount in Table 10.5 is explained next. The liquidity discount should be smaller for more highly liquid firms, since liquid assets generally can be converted quickly to cash with minimal loss of value. Furthermore, firms whose financial returns exceed significantly the industry average have an easier time attracting investors and should be subject to a smaller liquidity discount than firms that are underperforming the industry. Likewise, firms with relatively low leverage and high cash-flow growth should be subject to a smaller liquidity discount than more leveraged firms with slower cash-flow growth because they have a lower breakeven point and are less likely to default or become insolvent.

---

[42] If control premiums and minority discounts and control premiums and liquidity discounts are positively correlated, minority discounts and liquidity discounts must be positively correlated.

TABLE 10.5   Estimating the Size of the Liquidity Discount

Factor	Guideline	Adjust 20% Median Discount as Follows
Firm size	• Large • Small	• Reduce discount • Increase discount
Liquid assets as % of total assets	• >50% • <50%	• Reduce discount • Increase discount
Financial returns	• 2 × industry median[a] • ½ × industry median	• Reduce discount • Increase discount
Cash-flow growth rate	• 2 × industry median • ½ × industry median	• Reduce discount • Increase discount
Leverage	• ½ × industry median • 2 × industry median	• Reduce discount • Increase discount
Estimated firm-specific liquidity discount		???

[a]*Industry median financial information often is available from industry trade associations, conference presentations, Wall Street analysts' reports, Yahoo! Finance, Barron's, Investors Business Daily, The Wall Street Journal, and similar publications and websites.*

Factors Affecting the Control Premium

Factors affecting the size of the control premium include the perceived competence of the target's current management, the extent to which operating expenses are discretionary, the value of nonoperating assets, and the perceived net present value of currently unexploited business opportunities. The value in replacing incompetent management is difficult to quantify, since it reflects the potential for better future decision making. The value of nonoperating assets and discretionary expenses are quantified by estimating the after-tax sale value of redundant assets and the pretax profit improvement from eliminating noncritical operating activities or individual positions. While relatively easy to measure, such actions may be impossible to implement without having control of the business.[43]

If the target business is to be run by the acquirer as it is currently, no control premium should be added to the purchase price. However, if the acquirer intends to take actions that are possible only if the acquirer owns enough of the voting stock to achieve control, the purchase price should include a control premium large enough to obtain a controlling interest. Table 10.6 provides a subjective methodology for adjusting a control premium to be applied to a specific business. Note that the 10% premium used in the table is for illustrative purposes only and is intended to provide a starting point. The actual premium selected should reflect the analyst's perception of what is appropriate given the country's legal system and propensity to enforce laws and the extent to which firm ownership tends to be concentrated or widely dispersed.

The percentages applied to the discretionary expenses' share of total expenses, nonoperating assets as a percent of total assets, and the NPV of alternative strategies are intended to

---

[43] This is true because such decisions could involve eliminating the positions of members of the family owning the business or selling an asset owned by the business but used primarily by the family owning the business.

TABLE 10.6   Estimating the Size of the Control Premium to Reflect the Value of Changing the Target's Business Strategy and Operating Practices

Factor	Guideline	Adjust 10% Median Control Premium as Follows[a]
Target management	• Retain • Replace	• No change in premium • Increase premium
Discretionary expenses	• Cut if potential savings >5% of total expenses • Do not cut if potential savings <5% of total expenses	• Increase premium • No change in premium
Nonoperating assets	• Sell if potential after-tax gain >10% of purchase price[b] • Defer decision if potential after-tax gain <10% of purchase price	• Increase premium • No change in premium
Alternative business opportunities	• Pursue if NPV >20% of target's stand-alone value • Do not pursue if NPV <20% of target's stand-alone value	• Increase premium • No change in premium
Estimated firm-specific control premium		???

[a]The 10% premium represents the median estimate from the Nenova (2003) and Dyck and Zingales (2004) studies for countries perceived to have relatively stronger investor protection and law enforcement.
[b]The purchase price refers to the price paid for the controlling interest in the target.

reflect risks inherent in cutting costs, selling assets, and pursuing alternative investment opportunities. These risks include a decline in morale and productivity following layoffs, the management time involved in selling assets and the possible disruption of the business, and the potential for overestimating the NPV of alternative investments. In other words, the perceived benefits of these decisions should be large enough to offset the associated risks. Additional adjustments not shown in Table 10.6 may be necessary to reflect state statutes affecting the rights of controlling and minority shareholders.[44]

As a practical matter, business appraisers frequently rely on the *Control Premium Study*, published annually by FactSet Mergerstat. Another source is Duff and Phelps. The use of these data is problematic, however, since the control premium estimates provided by these firms include the estimated value of synergy as well as the amount paid to gain control.[45]

---

[44] In more than one-half of the states, major corporate actions, such as a merger, sale, liquidation, or recapitalization of a firm, may be approved by a simple majority vote of the firm's shareholders. In contrast, other states require at least a two-thirds majority to approve such decisions. In these states, a minority of slightly more than one-third can block such actions. Furthermore, a majority of the states have dissolution statutes that make it possible for minority shareholders to force dissolution of a corporation if they can show there is a deadlock in their negotiations with the controlling shareholders or that their rights are being violated. If the suit is successful and the controlling shareholders do not want to dissolve the firm, the solution is to pay the minority shareholders fair value for their shares.

[45] Damodaran (2002) suggests that the way to estimate a control premium is to view it as equal to the difference between the present value of a firm if it were being operated optimally and its present value the way it is currently being managed. This approach presumes that the analyst is able to determine accurately the value-optimizing strategy for the target firm.

Factors Affecting the Minority Discount

Minority discounts reflect the loss of influence due to the power of a controlling block investor. Intuitively, the magnitude of the discount should relate to the size of the control premium. The larger the control premium, the greater the perceived value of being able to direct the activities of the business and the value of special privileges that come at the expense of the minority investor. Reflecting the relationship between control premium and minority discounts, FactSet Mergerstat estimates minority discounts by using the following formula:

$$\text{Implied Median Minority Discount} = 1 - [1/(1 + \text{median premium paid})] \qquad (10.3)$$

Equation (10.3) implies that an investor would pay a higher price for control of a company and a lesser amount for a minority stake (i.e., larger control premiums are associated with larger minority discounts). While Eq. (10.3) is routinely used by practitioners to estimate minority discounts, there is little empirical support for this largely intuitive relationship.

Exhibit 10.2 illustrates what an investor should be willing to pay for a controlling interest and for a minority interest. Note that the example assumes that 50.1% ownership is required for a controlling interest. In practice, control may be achieved with less than a majority ownership position if there are numerous other minority investors or the investor is buying supervoting shares. The reader should note how the 20% median liquidity discount rate (based on recent empirical studies) is adjusted for the specific risk and return characteristics of the target firm. Furthermore, note that the control premium is equal to what the acquirer believes is the minimum increase in value created by achieving a controlling interest. Also, observe how the direct relationship between control premiums and minority discounts is used to estimate the size of the minority discount. Finally, see how median estimates of liquidity discounts and control premiums can serve as guidelines in valuation analyses.

EXHIBIT 10.2 INCORPORATING LIQUIDITY RISK, CONTROL PREMIUMS, AND MINORITY DISCOUNTS IN VALUING A PRIVATE BUSINESS

Lighting Group Incorporated, a holding company, wants to acquire a controlling interest in Acuity Lighting, whose estimated stand-alone equity value equals $18,699,493 (see Exhibit 10.1). LGI believes that the present value of synergies due to cost savings is $2,250,000 ($PV_{SYN}$) due to the potential for bulk purchase discounts and cost savings related to eliminating duplicate overhead and combining warehousing operations. LGI believes that the value of Acuity, including synergy, can be increased by at least 10% by applying professional management methods (and implicitly by making better management decisions). To achieve these efficiencies, LGI must gain control of Acuity. LGI is willing to pay a control premium of as much as 10%. The minority discount is derived from Eq. (10.3). The factors used to adjust the 20% median liquidity discount are taken from Table 10.5. The magnitudes of the adjustments are the opinion of the analyst. LGI's analysts have used Yahoo! Finance to obtain the industry data in Table 10.7 for the home furniture and fixtures industry.

What is the maximum purchase price LGI should pay for a 50.1% controlling interest in the business? For a minority 20% interest in the business?

To adjust for presumed liquidity risk of the target firm due to lack of a liquid market, LGI discounts the amount it is willing to offer to purchase 50.1% of the firm's equity by 16%.

TABLE 10.7 Industry Data

Factor	Acuity Lighting	Home Furniture and Fixtures Industry	Adjustments to 20% Median Liquidity Discount
Median liquidity discount[a]	NA	NA	20.0%
Firm size	Small	NA	+2.0
Liquid assets as % of total assets	>50%	NA	–2.0
Return on equity	19.7%	9.7%	–2.0
Cash-flow growth rate	15%	12.6%	0.0
Leverage (debt to equity)	0.27[b]	1.02	–2.0
Estimated liquidity discount for Acuity Lighting			16.0%

[a]Median estimate of the liquidity discount of empirical studies (excluding pre-IPO studies) since 1992.
[b]From Exhibit 10.1. $5,101,147/$18,699,493 = 0.27.
NA = Not available or not applicable.

Using Eq. (10.2):

$$PV_{MAX} = (PV_{MIN} + PV_{NS})(1 - LD\%)(1 + CP\%)$$
$$= [(\$18,699,493 + \$2,250,000)(1 - 0.16)(1 + 0.10)] \times 0.501$$
$$= \$20,949,493 \times 0.924 \times 0.501$$
$$= \$9,698,023 \text{ (maximum purchase price for 50.1\%)}$$

If LGI were to acquire only a 20% stake in Acuity, it is unlikely that there would be any synergy because LGL would lack the authority to implement potential cost saving measures without the approval of the controlling shareholders. Because it is a minority investment, there is no control premium, but a minority discount for lack of control should be estimated. The minority discount is estimated using Eq. (10.3)—that is, $1 - (1/(1 + 0.10)) = 9.1$.

$$PV_{MAX} = [\$18,699,493 \times (1 - 0.16)(1 - 0.091)] \times 0.2$$
$$= \$2,855,637 \text{ (maximum purchase price for 20\%)}$$

REVERSE MERGERS

Many small businesses fail each year. In a number of cases, all that remains is a business with no significant assets or operations. Such companies are referred to as _shell corporations._ Shell corporations can be used as part of a deliberate business strategy in which a corporate legal structure is formed in anticipation of future financing, a merger, joint venture, spin-off, or some other infusion of operating assets. This may be accomplished in a transaction called a _reverse merger_, in which the acquirer (a private firm) merges with a publicly traded target (often a corporate shell) in a statutory merger in which the public firm survives. See Chapter 11 for more on reverse mergers.

The Value of Corporate Shells

Merging with an existing corporate shell of a publicly traded company may be a reasonable alternative for a firm wanting to go public that is unable to provide the two years of audited financial statements required by the SEC or is unwilling to incur the costs of going public. Thus, merging with a shell corporation may represent an effective alternative to an IPO for a small firm.

After the private company acquires a majority of the public shell corporation's stock and completes the reverse merger, it appoints new management and elects a new board of directors. The owners of the private firm receive most of the shares of the shell corporation (i.e., more than 50%) and control the shell's board of directors. The new firm must have a minimum of 300 shareholders to be listed on the NASDAQ Small Cap Market.

Shell corporations usually are of two types. The first is a failed public company whose shareholders want to sell what remains to recover some of their losses. The second type is a shell that has been created for the sole purpose of being sold as a shell in a reverse merger. The latter type typically carries less risk of having unknown liabilities.

Are Reverse Mergers Cheaper Than IPOs? *Yes*

As noted previously, direct and indirect costs of an IPO can be as much as 22% of gross proceeds, or about $1.1 million for a $5 million IPO. Reverse mergers typically cost between $50,000 and $100,000, about one-quarter of the expense of an IPO, and can be completed in about 60 days, or one-third of the time to complete a typical IPO.[46]

Despite these advantages, reverse takeovers may take as long as IPOs and are sometimes more complex. The acquiring company must still perform due diligence on the target and communicate information on the shell corporation to the exchange on which its stock will be traded and prepare a prospectus. It can often take months to settle outstanding claims against the shell corporation. Public exchanges often require the same level of information for companies going through reverse mergers as those undertaking IPOs. The principal concern is that the shell company may contain unseen liabilities, such as unpaid bills or pending litigation, which in some instances can make the reverse merger far more costly than an IPO.

Empirical studies show mixed results. One study completed in 2002 found that 32.6% of the sample of 121 reverse mergers between 1990 and 2000 were delisted from their exchanges within three years. The authors argue that reverse mergers may represent a means by which a private firm can achieve listing on a public stock exchange when it may not be fully able to satisfy the initial listing requirements if it were to undertake an IPO.[47] However, this claim is disputed in a larger and more recent study involving a sample of 286 reverse mergers and 2,860 IPOs between 1990 and 2002. The study found that private firms using the reverse merger technique to go public rather than the IPO method tend to be smaller, younger, and exhibit poorer financial performance than those that choose to go public using an IPO. Of those private firms listed on public exchanges either through a reverse merger or an IPO, 42% using reverse mergers are delisted within three years versus 27% of firms using IPOs. However, the study found that only 1.4% of their sample of reverse mergers were unable to satisfy the initial listing requirements of

---

[46] Sweeney, 2005

[47] Arellano-Ostoa and Brusco, 2002

public exchanges. See Case Study 10.1 for an example of a company taken public via a reverse merger.[48]

Financing Reverse Mergers

Private investment in public equities (PIPEs) is a commonly used method of financing reverse mergers. In a PIPE offering, a firm with publicly traded shares sells, usually at a discount, newly issued but unregistered securities, typically stock or debt convertible into stock, directly to investors in a private transaction. Hedge funds are common buyers of such issues. The issuing firm is required to file a shelf registration statement on Form S-3 with the SEC as quickly as possible (usually between 10 and 45 days after issuance) and to use its "best efforts" to complete registration within 30 days after filing.

PIPEs often are used in conjunction with a reverse merger to provide companies with not just an alternative way to go public but also financing once they are listed on the public exchange. For example, assume a private company is merged into a publicly traded firm through a reverse merger. As the surviving entity, the public company raises funds through a privately placed equity issue (i.e., PIPE financing). The private firm is now a publicly traded company with the funds to finance future working capital requirements and capital investments.[49]

USING LEVERAGED EMPLOYEE STOCK OWNERSHIP PLANS TO BUY PRIVATE COMPANIES

An ESOP is a means whereby a corporation can make tax-deductible contributions of cash or stock into a trust comprising up to 25% of its annual pre-tax payroll. The ESOP's assets are allocated to employees and are not taxed until withdrawn by employees. ESOPs generally must invest at least 50% of their assets in employer-chosen stock. Three types of ESOPs are recognized by the 1974 Employee Retirement Income Security Act: leveraged, where the ESOP borrows to purchase qualified employer securities; leverageable, where the ESOP is authorized but not required to borrow; and nonleveraged, where the ESOP may not borrow funds. As noted in Chapter 1, ESOPs offer substantial tax advantages to sponsoring firms, lenders, and participating employees.

Employees frequently use leveraged ESOPs to buy out owners of private companies who have most of their net worth in the firm. ESOPs are particularly popular for this purpose during periods of economic slowdowns when business owners wishing to sell their businesses have fewer options. ESOP valuations done by professional appraisers are often much lower than purchase prices that could be obtained in a more conventional acquisition or merger.

---

[48] Cyree and Walker, 2008

[49] To issuers, PIPEs offer the advantage of being able to be completed more quickly, cheaply, and confidentially than a public stock offering, which requires registration up front and a more elaborate investor "road show" to sell the securities to public investors. To investors, PIPEs provide an opportunity to identify stocks that overoptimistic public investors have overvalued. Such shares can be purchased as a private placement at a discount to compensate investors for the stock's underperformance following the issue. Once registered, such shares can be resold in the public markets, often before the extent of the overvaluation is recognized by public investors. As private placements, PIPEs are most suitable for raising small amounts of financing, typically in the $5 to $10 million range. Firms seeking hundreds of millions of dollars are more likely to be successful in going directly to the public financial markets in a public stock offering.

For firms having established ESOPs, the business owner sells at least 30% of their stock to the ESOP, which pays for the stock with borrowed funds. The owner may invest the proceeds and defer taxes if the investment is made within 12 months of the sale of the stock to the ESOP, the ESOP owns at least 30% of the firm, and neither the owner nor his or her family participates in the ESOP. The firm makes tax-deductible contributions to the ESOP in an amount sufficient to repay interest and principal. Shares held by the ESOP are distributed to employees as the loan is repaid. As the outstanding loan balance is reduced, the shares are allocated to employees, who eventually own the firm.[50]

EMPIRICAL STUDIES OF SHAREHOLDER RETURNS

As noted in Chapter 1, target shareholders of both public and private firms routinely experience abnormal positive returns when a bid is announced for the firm. In contrast, acquirer shareholders often experience abnormal negative returns on the announcement date, particularly when using stock to purchase publicly traded firms. However, substantial empirical evidence shows that public acquirers using their stock to buy privately held firms experience significant abnormal positive returns around the transaction announcement date. Other studies suggest that acquirers of private firms often experience abnormal positive returns regardless of the form of payment. These studies are discussed next.

A study of the returns to public company shareholders when they acquire privately held firms found an average positive 2.6% abnormal return for shareholders of bidding firms for stock offers but not cash transactions.[51] The finding of positive abnormal returns earned by buyers using stock to acquire private companies is in sharp contrast with the negative abnormal returns earned by U.S. bidders using stock to acquire publicly traded companies.

Ownership of privately held companies tends to be highly concentrated, so an exchange of stock tends to create a few very large block stockholders. Close monitoring of management and the acquired firm's performance may contribute to abnormal positive returns experienced by companies bidding for private firms. These findings are consistent with studies conducted in Canada, the United Kingdom, and Western Europe.[52]

---

[50] Only C and Sub-Chapter S corporations generating pretax incomes of at least $100,000 annually are eligible to form ESOPs.

[51] Chang, 1998

[52] Draper and Padyal (2006), in an exhaustive study of 8,756 firms from 1981 to 2001, also found that acquirers of private firms in the United Kingdom paying with stock achieved the largest positive abnormal returns due to increased monitoring of the target firm's performance. These findings are consistent with the positive abnormal announcement returns of more than 2% for acquirers of private firms in Canadian and European studies, where ownership is often more highly concentrated than the highly dispersed ownership of publicly traded firms in the United States (Ben-Amar and Andre, 2006; Bigelli and Mengoli, 2004; Boehmer, 2000; Dumontier and Pecherot, 2001). This conclusion is consistent with studies of returns to companies that issue stock and convertible debt in private placements (Fields and Mais, 1991; Hertzel and Smith, 1993; Wruck, 1989). It generally is argued that, in private placements, large shareholders are effective monitors of managerial performance, thereby enhancing the prospects of the acquired firm (Demsetz and Lehn, 1996). Wruck and Wu (2009) argue that relationships such as board representation developed between investors and issuers contribute to improved firm performance due to increased monitoring of performance and improved corporate governance. Such relationships may be a result of the private placement of securities.

Firms acquiring private firms often earn excess returns regardless of the form of payment.[53] Acquirers can also earn excess returns of as much as 2.1% when buying private firms or 2.6% for subsidiaries of public companies.[54] The abnormal returns may reflect the tendency of acquirers to pay less for nonpublicly traded companies, due to the relative difficulty in buying private firms or subsidiaries of public companies. In both cases, shares are not publicly traded and access to information is limited. Moreover, there may be fewer bidders for nonpublicly traded companies. Consequently, these targets may be acquired at a discount from their actual economic value. As a consequence of this discount, bidder shareholders are able to realize a larger share of the anticipated synergies.

Other factors that may contribute to these positive abnormal returns for acquirers of private companies include the introduction of more professional management into the privately held firms and tax considerations. Public companies may introduce more professional management systems into the target firms, thereby enhancing the target's value. The acquirer's use of stock rather than cash may also induce the seller to accept a lower price since it allows sellers to defer taxes on any gains until they decide to sell their shares.[55]

SOME THINGS TO REMEMBER

Valuing private companies is more challenging than valuing public companies, due to the absence of published share price data and the unique problems they face due to their size. Owners considering the sale of their firms may overstate revenue and understate cost; however, during the normal course of business, private firms are more likely to overstate costs and understate revenues to minimize tax liabilities. As such, it is crucial to restate the firm's financial statements to determine the current period's true profitability.

When markets are illiquid and block shareholders exert substantial control over the firm's operations, the maximum offer price for the target must be adjusted for liquidity risk and the value of control. Given the wide variability of estimates, it should be evident that premiums and discounts must be applied to the value of the target firm with great care. In general, the size of the premium or discount should reflect factors specific to the firm. The median liquidity discount from empirical studies since 1992 is about 20%. While varying widely, recent studies indicate that median pure control premiums across countries are about 12 to 14%. However, such premiums in the United States fall in the 2 to 5% range. Increasing control premiums are associated with increasing minority discounts. The author suggests that factors specific to each circumstance need to be analyzed and used to adjust these medians to the realities of the situation.

In contrast to studies involving acquisitions of U.S. public firms, buyers of private firms in the United States and abroad often realize significant abnormal positive returns, particularly in share-for-share transactions. This result reflects the concentration of ownership in private firms and the resulting aggressive monitoring of management, a tendency of buyers to acquire private firms at a discount from their economic value, and tax considerations.

---

[53] Ang and Kohers, 2001

[54] Fuller, Netter, and Stegemoller, 2002

[55] Poulsen and Stegemoller, 2002

DISCUSSION QUESTIONS

10.1 Why is it more difficult to value privately held companies than publicly traded firms?

10.2 What factors should be considered in adjusting target company data?

10.3 What is the capitalization rate, and how does it relate to the discount rate?

10.4 What are the common ways of estimating the capitalization rate?

10.5 What is the liquidity discount, and what are common ways of estimating this discount?

10.6 Give examples of private company costs that might be understated, and explain why.

10.7 How can an analyst determine if the target firm's costs and revenues are understated or overstated?

10.8 What is the difference between the concepts of fair market value and fair value?

10.9 What is the importance of IRS Revenue Ruling 59-60?

10.10 Why might shell corporations have value?

10.11 Why might succession planning be more challenging for a family firm?

10.12 How are governance issues between public and private firms the same and how are they different?

10.13 What are some of the reasons a family-owned or privately owned business may want to go public? What are some of the reasons that discourage such firms from going public?

10.14 Why are family-owned firms often attractive to private equity investors?

10.15 Rank from the highest to lowest the liquidity discount you would apply if you, as a business appraiser, had been asked to value the following businesses: (a) a local, profitable hardware store; (b) a money-losing laundry; (c) a large privately owned firm with significant excess cash balances and other liquid short-term investments; and (d) a pool-cleaning service whose primary tangible assets consist of a two-year-old truck and miscellaneous equipment. Explain your ranking.

Answers to these Discussion Questions are available in the Online Instructor's Manual for instructors using this book.

Practice Problems and Answers

10.16 It usually is appropriate to adjust the financials received from the target firm to reflect any changes that you, as the new owner, would make to create an adjusted EBITDA. Using the Excel-Based Spreadsheet on How to Adjust Target Firm's Financial Statements on the companion site, make at least three adjustments to the target's hypothetical financials to determine the impact on the adjusted EBITDA. (*Note:* The adjustments should be made in the section on the spreadsheet entitled "Adjustments to Target Firm's Financials.") Explain your rationale for each adjustment.

10.17 Based on its growth prospects, a private investor values a local bakery at $750,000. She believes that cost savings having a present value of $50,000 can be achieved by changing staffing levels and store hours. Based on recent empirical studies, she believes the appropriate liquidity discount is 20%. A recent transaction in the same city required the buyer to pay a 5% premium to the average price for similar businesses to gain a controlling interest in a bakery. What is the most she should be willing to pay for a 50.1% stake in the bakery?

Answer: $336,672 $\left(750\,000 + 50\,000\right)\left(1 - 0.2\right)\left(1 + 0.05\right)$

10.18 You have been asked by an investor to value a local restaurant. In the most recent year, the restaurant earned pretax operating income of $300,000. Income has grown an average of 4% annually during the last five years, and it is expected to continue growing at that rate into the foreseeable future. By introducing modern management methods, you believe the pretax operating-income growth rate can be increased to 6% beyond the second year and sustained at that rate through the foreseeable future. The investor is willing to pay a 10% premium to reflect the value of control. The beta and debt-to-equity ratio for publicly traded firms in the restaurant industry are 2 and 1.5, respectively. The business's target debt-to-equity ratio is 1, and its pretax cost of borrowing, based on its recent borrowing activities, is 7%. The business-specific risk for firms of this size is estimated to be 6%. The investor concludes that the specific risk of this business is less than other firms in this industry due to its sustained profit growth, low leverage, and high return on assets compared to similar restaurants in this geographic area. Moreover, per capita income in this region is expected to grow more rapidly than elsewhere in the country, adding to the growth prospects of the restaurant business. At an estimated 15%, the liquidity risk premium is believed to be relatively low due to the excellent reputation of the restaurant. Since the current chef and the staff are expected to remain if the business is sold, the quality of the restaurant is expected to be maintained. The ten-year Treasury bond rate is 5%, the equity risk premium is 5.5%, and the federal, state, and local tax rate is 40%. The annual change in working capital is $20,000, and capital spending for maintenance exceeded depreciation in the prior year by $15,000. Both working capital and the excess of capital spending over depreciation are projected to grow at the same rate as operating income. What is the business worth?

Answer: $2,110,007 2226448

Answers to these practice exercises and problems are available in the Online Instructor's Manual for instructors using this book.

CHAPTER BUSINESS CASES

CASE STUDY 10.1
Panda Ethanol Goes Public in a Shell Corporation

In early 2007, Panda Ethanol, owner of ethanol plants in west Texas, decided to explore the possibility of taking its ethanol production business public to take advantage of the high valuations placed on ethanol-related companies in the public market at that time. The firm was confronted with the choice of taking the company public through an initial public offering or by combining with a publicly traded shell corporation through a reverse merger.

After enlisting the services of a local investment banker, Grove Street Investors, Panda chose to "go public" through a reverse merger. This process entailed finding a shell corporation with relatively few shareholders who were interested in selling their stock. The investment banker identified Cirracor

CASE STUDY 10.1 *(cont'd)*

Inc. as a potential merger partner. Cirracor was formed on October 12, 2001, to provide website development services and was traded on the over-the-counter bulletin board market (i.e., a market for very low-priced stocks). The website business was not profitable, and the company had only ten shareholders. As of June 30, 2006, Cirracor listed $4,856 in assets and a negative shareholders' equity of $(259,976). Given the poor financial condition of Cirracor, the firm's shareholders were interested in either selling their shares for cash or owning even a relatively small portion of a financially viable company to recover their initial investments in Cirracor. Acting on behalf of Panda, Grove Street formed a limited liability company, called Grove Panda, and purchased 2.73 million Cirracor common shares, or 78% of the company, for about $475,000.

The merger proposal provided for one share of Cirracor common stock to be exchanged for each share of Panda Ethanol common outstanding stock and for Cirracor shareholders to own 4% of the newly issued and outstanding common stock of the surviving company. Panda Ethanol shareholders would own the remaining 96%. At the end of 2005, Panda had 13.8 million shares outstanding. On June 7, 2007, the merger agreement was amended in order to permit Panda

Ethanol to issue 15 million new shares through a private placement to raise $90 million. This brought the total Panda shares outstanding to 28.8 million. Cirracor common shares outstanding at that time totaled 3.5 million. However, to achieve the agreed-on ownership distribution, the number of Cirracor shares outstanding had to be reduced. This would be accomplished by initiating an approximate three-for-one reverse stock split immediately prior to the completion of the reverse merger (i.e., each Cirracor common share would be converted into 0.340885 shares of Cirracor common stock). As a consequence of the merger, the previous shareholders of Panda Ethanol were issued 28.8 million new shares of Cirracor common stock. The combined firm now has 30 million shares outstanding, with the Cirracor shareholders owning 1.2 million shares. Table 10.8 illustrates the effect of the reverse stock split.

A special Cirracor shareholders' meeting was required by Nevada law (i.e., the state in which Cirracor was incorporated) in view of the substantial number of new shares that were to be issued as a result of the merger. The proxy statement filed with the SEC and distributed to Cirracor shareholders indicated that Grove Panda, a 78% owner of Cirracor common stock, had already indicated that it would vote its shares

TABLE 10.8   Effects of Reverse Stock Split

	Shares Outstanding*	Ownership Distribution (%)	Shares Outstanding*	Ownership Distribution (%)
	Before Reverse Split		*After Reverse Split*	
Panda Ethanol	28.8	89.2	28.8	96
Cirracor Inc.	3.5	10.8	1.2	4

In millions of dollars.

CASE STUDY 10.1 *(cont'd)*

for the merger and the reverse stock split. Since Cirracor's articles of incorporation required only a simple majority to approve such matters, it was evident to all that approval was imminent.

On November 7, 2007, Panda completed its merger with Cirracor Inc. As a result of the merger, all shares of Panda Ethanol common stock (other than Panda Ethanol shareholders who had executed their dissenters' rights under Delaware law) would cease to have any rights as a shareholder except the right to receive one share of Cirracor common stock per share of Panda Ethanol common. Panda Ethanol shareholders choosing to exercise their right to dissent would receive a cash payment for the fair value of their stock on the day immediately before closing. Cirracor shareholders had similar dissenting rights under Nevada law. While Cirracor is the surviving corporation, Panda is viewed for accounting purposes as the acquirer. Accordingly, the financial statements shown for the surviving corporation are those of Panda Ethanol.

Discussion Questions

1. Who were Panda Ethanol, Grove Street Investors, Grove Panda, and Cirracor? What were their roles in the case study? Be specific.
2. Discuss the pros and the cons of a reverse merger versus that of an initial public offering for taking a company public. Be specific.
3. Why did Panda Ethanol undertake a private equity placement totaling $90 million shortly before implementing the reverse merger?
4. Why did Panda not directly approach Cirracor with an offer? How were the Panda Grove investment holdings used to influence the outcome of the proposed merger?

Answers to this case are provided in the Online Instructor's Manual available for instructors using this book.

CASE STUDY 10.2
Determining Liquidity Discounts—The Taylor Devices and Tayco Development Merger

This discussion[56] is a highly summarized version of how a business valuation firm evaluated the liquidity risk associated with Taylor Devices' unregistered common stock, registered common shares, and a minority investment in a business that it was planning to sell following its merger with Tayco Development. The estimated liquidity discounts were used in a joint proxy statement submitted to the SEC by the two firms to justify the value of the offer the boards of Taylor Devices and Tayco Development had negotiated.

Taylor Devices and Tayco Development agreed to merge in early 2008. Tayco would be merged into Taylor, with Taylor as the surviving entity. The merger would enable

---

[56] *Source:* SEC Form S4 filing of a joint proxy statement for Taylor Devices and Tayco Development, dated January 15, 2008.

CASE STUDY 10.2   (cont'd)

Tayco's patents and intellectual property to be fully integrated into Taylor's manufacturing operations, since intellectual property rights transfer with the Tayco stock. Each share of Tayco common would be converted into one share of Taylor common stock, according to the terms of the deal. Taylor's common stock is traded on the Nasdaq Small Cap Market under the symbol TAYD, and on January 8, 2009 (the last trading day before the date of the filing of the joint proxy statement with the SEC), the stock closed at $6.29 per share. Tayco common stock is traded over the counter on "Pink Sheets" (i.e., an informal trading network) under the trading symbol TYCO.PK, and it closed on January 8, 2009, at $5.11 per share.

A business appraisal firm was hired to value Taylor's unregistered (with the SEC) shares. The appraisal firm treated the shares as if they were restricted shares because there was no established market for trading in these shares. The appraiser reasoned that the risk of Taylor's unregistered shares is greater than for letter stocks, which have a stipulated period during which the shares cannot be sold, because the Taylor shares lacked a date indicating when they could be sold. Using this line of reasoning, the appraisal firm estimated a liquidity discount of 20%, which it believed approximated the potential loss that holders of these shares might incur in attempting to sell their shares.

The block of registered Taylor common stock differs from the unregistered shares in that they are not subject to Rule 144. Based on the trading volume of Taylor common stock over the preceding 12 months, the appraiser believed that it would likely take less than one year to convert the block of registered stock into cash and the appraisal firm

estimated the discount at 13%, consistent with the Aschwald (2000) studies.

The appraisal firm also was asked to estimate the liquidity discount for the sale of Taylor's minority investment in a real estate development business. Due to the increase in liquidity of restricted stocks since 1990, the business appraiser argued that restricted stock studies conducted before that date may provide a better proxy for liquidity discounts for this type of investment. Interests in closely held firms are more like letter stock transactions occurring before the changes in SEC Rule 144 beginning in 1990 when the holding period was reduced from three to two years and later to one after 1997. Such firms have little ability to raise capital in public markets due to their small size, and they face high transaction costs.

Based on the SEC and other prior 1990 studies, the liquidity discount for this investment was expected to be between 30 and 35%. Pre-IPO studies could push it higher to a range of 40 to 45%. Consequently, the appraisal firm argued that the discount for most minority interest investments tended to fall in the range of 25 to 45%. Because the real estate development business is smaller than nearly all of the firms in the restricted stocks studies, the liquidity discount is believed by the appraisal firm to be at the higher end of the range.

Discussion Questions

1. Describe how the various historical restricted stock studies were used by the appraiser to estimate the liquidity discount.
2. What other factors could the appraiser have used to estimate the liquidity discount on the unregistered stock?

CASE STUDY 10.2 *(cont'd)*

3. In view of your answer to question 2, how might these factors have changed the appraiser's conclusions? Be specific.

4. Based on the 13% liquidity discount that was estimated by the business appraiser, what was the actual purchase price premium paid to Tayco shareholders for each of their common shares?

Answers to these questions are available on the Online Instructor's Manual for instructors using this book.

DEAL-STRUCTURING AND FINANCING STRATEGIES

"Everything seems to be in order with the legal papers for our merger."

Courtesy of www.CartoonResource.com.

Part IV describes how consensus is reached during the bargaining process by satisfying the primary demands of the parties involved in the transaction subject to acceptable levels of risk. The chapters in this section discuss the implications of various aspects of deal structuring and how they impact how deals are done.

Chapter 11 outlines the major facets of the deal-structuring process, including the acquisition vehicle and postclosing organization, form of acquisition, form of payment, and legal form of selling entity and how changes in one area of the deal often impact significantly other parts of the agreement. Specific ways to bridge major differences on price also are discussed.

Chapter 12 addresses tax considerations, including alternative forms of taxable and nontaxable structures, and how they impact reaching agreement. This chapter also discusses such accounting issues as how business combinations are recorded for financial reporting purposes and the impact of purchase accounting on financial statements and reported earnings.

Chapter 13 focuses on how transactions are financed, with particular emphasis on financing, structuring, and valuing highly leveraged transactions and the role of private equity and hedge funds in this process. More specifically, this chapter describes how companies are taken private, how leveraged buyouts (LBOs) create value, how to estimate financing capacity, and how to develop exit strategies. Factors contributing to successful LBOs, the implications of poorly constructed deals, and LBO modeling methods also are discussed.

Structuring the Deal
Payment and Legal Considerations

If you can't convince them, confuse them. —**Harry S. Truman**

pg - 366,384

INSIDE M&A: PFIZER ACQUIRES WYETH LABS DESPITE TIGHT CREDIT MARKETS

Pfizer and Wyeth began joint operations on October 22, 2009, when Wyeth shares stopped trading and each Wyeth share was converted to $33 in cash and 0.985 of a Pfizer share. Valued at $68 billion, the cash and stock deal was first announced in late January of 2009. The purchase price represented a 12.6% premium over Wyeth's closing share price the day before the announcement and a 29% premium over the same day the prior month. Investors from both firms celebrated as Wyeth's shares rose 12.6% and Pfizer's 1.4% on the news. The announcement seemed to offer the potential for profit growth, despite storm clouds on the horizon.

As is true of other large pharmaceutical companies, Pfizer expects to experience serious erosion in revenue due to expiring patent protection on a number of its major drugs. Pfizer faces the expiration of patent rights in 2011 to the cholesterol-lowering drug Lipitor, which accounted for 25% of the firm's 2008 $52 billion in revenue. Pfizer also faces 14 other patent expirations through 2014 on drugs that, in combination with Lipitor, contribute more than one-half of the firm's total revenue. Pfizer is not alone in suffering from patent expirations. Merck, Bristol-Myers Squibb, and Eli Lilly are all facing significant revenue reduction due to patent expirations during the next five years as competition from generic drugs undercuts their pricing. Wyeth will also be losing its patent protection on its top-selling drug, the antidepressant Effexor XR.

Pfizer's strategy appears to have been to acquire Wyeth at a time when transaction prices were depressed because of the recession and tight credit markets. Pfizer anticipates saving more than $4 billion annually by combining the two businesses, with the savings being phased in over three years. Pfizer also hopes to offset revenue erosion due to patent expirations by diversifying into vaccines and arthritis treatments.

By the end of 2008, Pfizer already had a $22.5 billion commitment letter in order to obtain temporary or "bridge" financing and $26 billion in cash and marketable securities. Pfizer also announced plans to cut its quarterly dividend in half to $0.16 per share to help finance the transaction. However, there were still questions about the firm's ability to complete the transaction in view of the turmoil in the credit markets.

Many transactions that were announced during 2008 were never closed because buyers were unable to arrange financing and would later claim that the purchase agreement had been breached due to material adverse changes in the business climate and would renege on contracts. Usually, such contracts contained so-called reverse termination fees, in which the buyer would agree to pay a fee to the seller if they were unwilling to close the deal. This is called a reverse termination or breakup fee because traditionally breakup fees are paid by a seller that chooses to break a contract with a buyer in order to accept a more attractive offer from another suitor.

Negotiations, which had begun in earnest in late 2008, became increasingly contentious, not so much because of differences over price or strategy but rather under what circumstances Pfizer could back out of the deal. Under the terms of the final agreement, Pfizer would have been liable to pay Wyeth $4.5 billion if its credit rating dropped prior to closing and it could not finance the transaction. At about 6.6% of the purchase price, the termination fee was about twice the normal breakup fee for a transaction of this type.

What made this deal unique was that the failure to obtain financing as a pretext for exit could be claimed only under very limited circumstances. Specifically, Pfizer could renege only if its lenders refused to finance the transaction because of a credit downgrade of Pfizer. If lenders refused to finance primarily for this reason, Wyeth could either demand that Pfizer attempt to find alternative financing or terminate the agreement. If Wyeth had terminated the agreement, Pfizer would have been obligated to pay the termination fee.

CHAPTER OVERVIEW

Once management has determined that an acquisition is the best way to implement the firm's business strategy, a target has been selected, the target's fit with the strategy is well understood, and the preliminary financial analysis is satisfactory, it is time to consider how to properly structure the transaction. A *deal structure* is an agreement between two parties (the acquirer and target firms) defining the rights and obligations of the parties involved. The way in which this agreement is reached is called the deal-structuring process. In this chapter, the deal-structuring process is described in terms of seven interdependent components. These include the acquisition vehicle, the postclosing organization, the form of payment, the legal form of the selling entity, the form of acquisition, and accounting and tax considerations.

This chapter briefly addresses the form of the acquisition vehicle, postclosing organization, and the legal form of the selling entity because these are discussed in some detail elsewhere in this book. The chapter also discusses the interrelatedness of payment, legal, and tax forms by illustrating how decisions that are made in one area affect other aspects of the overall deal structure. The focus in this chapter is on the form of payment, form of acquisition, and alternative forms of legal structures in which ownership is conveyed. The implications of alternative tax structures for the deal-structuring process, how transactions are recorded for financial reporting purposes, and how they might affect the deal-structuring process are discussed in detail in Chapter 12.

A review of this chapter (including practice questions and answers) is available in the file folder entitled "Student Study Guide" on the companion site to this book (*www.elsevierdirect.com/companions/9780123854858*). The companion site also contains a Learning Interactions Library, which gives students the opportunity to test their knowledge of this chapter in a "real-time" environment.

THE DEAL-STRUCTURING PROCESS

The *deal-structuring process* is fundamentally about satisfying as many of the primary objectives (or needs) of the parties involved and determining how risk will be shared. Common examples of high-priority buyer objectives include paying a "reasonable" purchase price, using stock in lieu of cash (if the acquirer's stock is believed to be overvalued), and having the seller finance a portion of the purchase price by carrying a seller's note. Buyers may also want to put a portion of the purchase price in an escrow account, defer a portion of the price, or make a certain percentage of the purchase price contingent on realizing some future event to minimize risk. Common closing conditions desired by buyers include obtaining employee retention and noncompete agreements.

Sellers, who also are publicly traded companies, commonly are driven to maximize purchase price. However, their desire to maximize price may be tempered by other considerations, such as the perceived ease of doing the deal, a desire to obtain a tax-free transaction, or a desire to obtain employment contracts or consulting arrangements for key employees. Private or family-owned firms may be less motivated by price than by other factors, such as protecting the firm's future reputation and current employees, as well as obtaining rights to license patents or utilize other valuable assets. A buyer may determine the highest-priority needs of the seller by determining the average age of the primary owners, their basis in the stock of the firm, the extent to which the firm is paternalistic toward its employees, whether it is family owned, and if there are issues around who will succeed the current owner.

Risk sharing refers to the extent to which the acquirer assumes all, some, or none of the liabilities, disclosed or otherwise, of the target. The appropriate deal structure is that which satisfies, subject to an acceptable level of risk, as many of the primary objectives of the parties involved as necessary to reach overall agreement. The process may be highly complex in large transactions involving multiple parties, approvals, forms of payment, and sources of financing. Decisions made in one area inevitably affect other areas of the overall deal structure. Containing risk associated with a complex deal is analogous to catching a water balloon. Squeezing one end of the balloon simply forces the contents to shift elsewhere.

Key Components of the Deal-Structuring Process

Figure 11.1 summarizes the deal-structuring process. The process begins with addressing a set of key questions shown on the left-hand side of the exhibit. Answers to these questions help define initial negotiating positions, potential risks, options for managing risk, levels of tolerance for risk, and conditions under which the buyer or seller will "walk away" from the negotiations.

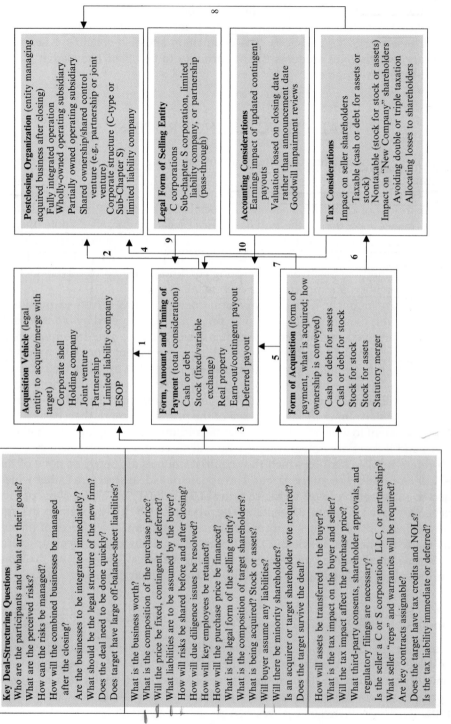

Key Deal-Structuring Questions
Who are the participants and what are their goals?
What are the perceived risks?
How can the risks be managed?
How will the combined businesses be managed after the closing?
Are the businesses to be integrated immediately?
What should be the legal structure of the new firm?
Does the deal need to be done quickly?
Does target have large off-balance-sheet liabilities?

What is the business worth?
What is the composition of the purchase price?
Will the price be fixed, contingent, or deferred?
What liabilities are to be assumed by the buyer?
How will risks be shared before and after closing?
How will due diligence issues be resolved?
How will key employees be retained?
How will the purchase price be financed?
What is the legal form of the selling entity?
What is the composition of target shareholders?
What is being acquired? Stock or assets?
Will buyer assume any liabilities?
Will there be minority shareholders?
Is an acquirer or target shareholder vote required?
Does the target survive the deal?

How will assets be transferred to the buyer?
What is the tax impact on the buyer and seller?
Will the tax impact affect the purchase price?
What third-party consents, shareholder approvals, and regulatory filings are necessary?
Is the seller a C or S corporation, LLC, or partnership?
What seller "reps" and warranties will be required?
Are key contracts assignable?
Does the target have tax credits and NOLs?
Is the tax liability immediate or deferred?

Acquisition Vehicle (legal entity to acquire/merge with target)
Corporate shell
Holding company
Joint venture
Partnership
Limited liability company
ESOP

Form, Amount, and Timing of Payment (total consideration)
Cash or debt
Stock (fixed/variable exchange)
Real property
Earn-out/contingent payout
Deferred payout

Form of Acquisition (form of payment, what is acquired; how ownership is conveyed)
Cash or debt for assets
Cash or debt for stock
Stock for stock
Stock for assets
Statutory merger

Postclosing Organization (entity managing acquired business after closing)
Fully integrated operation
Wholly-owned operating subsidiary
Partially owned operating subsidiary
Shared ownership/shared control venture (e.g., partnership or joint venture)
Corporate structure (C-type or Sub-Chapter S)
limited liability company

Legal Form of Selling Entity
C corporations
Sub-chapter S corporation, limited liability company, or partnership (pass-through)

Accounting Considerations
Earnings impact of updated contingent payouts
Valuation based on closing date rather than announcement date
Goodwill impairment reviews

Tax Considerations
Impact on seller shareholders
Taxable (cash or debt for assets or stock)
Nontaxable (stock for stock or assets)
Impact on "New Company" shareholders
Avoiding double or triple taxation
Allocating losses to shareholders

FIGURE 11.1 Mergers and acquisitions deal-structuring process.

The *acquisition vehicle* refers to the legal structure created to acquire the target company. The *postclosing organization*, or structure, is the organizational and legal framework used to manage the combined businesses following the consummation of the transaction. Commonly used structures for both acquisition vehicle and postclosing organization include the corporate, division, holding company, joint venture (JV), partnership, limited liability company (LLC), and employee stock ownership plan (ESOP) structures. Although the two structures are often the same before and after completion of the transaction, the postclosing organization may differ from the acquisition vehicle, depending on the acquirer's strategic objectives for the combined firms.

The *form of payment*, or total consideration, may consist of cash, common stock, debt, or a combination of all three types. The payment may be fixed at a moment in time, contingent on the future performance of the acquired unit, or payable over time. The form of payment influences the selection of the appropriate form of acquisition and postclosing organization. The *form of acquisition* reflects what is being acquired (stock or assets). *Accounting considerations* refer to the potential impact of financial reporting requirements on the earnings volatility of business combinations due to the need to periodically revalue acquired assets to their fair market value as new information becomes available.

Tax considerations entail tax structures and strategies that determine whether a transaction is taxable or nontaxable to the seller's shareholders and influence the choice of postclosing organization, which affects the potential for double taxation and the allocation of losses to owners. The form of acquisition also defines how the ownership of assets will be conveyed from the seller to the buyer, either by rule of law, as in a merger, or through transfer and assignment, as in a purchase of assets. The *legal form of the selling entity* (i.e., whether it is a C or S chapter corporation, LLC, or partnership) also has tax implications. These considerations are explored in greater detail later in this chapter.

Common Linkages

For simplicity, many of the linkages or interactions that reflect how decisions made in one area affect other aspects of the deal are not shown in Figure 11.1. Common linkages or interactions among various components of the deal structure are illustrated through examples, described next.

Payment's Form Influences Acquisition Vehicle and Postclosing Organization Choice (Figure 11.1, Arrows 1 and 2)

If the buyer and seller agree on a price, the buyer may offer a purchase price that is contingent on the future performance of the target. The buyer may choose to acquire and operate the acquired company as a wholly-owned subsidiary within a holding company during the term of the "earn-out." This facilitates monitoring the operation's performance during the earn-out period and minimizes the potential for post-earn-out litigation initiated by earn-out participants.

Form of Acquisition Effects (Figure 11.1, Arrows 3–6)

Choice of acquisition vehicle and postclosing organization. If the form of acquisition is a statutory merger, all known and unknown or contingent liabilities are transferred to the buyer. Under these circumstances, the buyer may choose to change the type of acquisition vehicle to one better able to protect the buyer from the liabilities of the target, such as a holding company arrangement. Acquisition vehicles and postclosing organizations that facilitate a sharing of potential risk or the purchase price include JV or partnership arrangements.

Form, timing, and amount of payment. The assumption of all seller liabilities through a merger also may induce the buyer to change the form of payment by deferring some portion of the purchase price to decrease the present value of the cost of the transaction. The buyer also may attempt to negotiate a lower overall purchase price.

Tax considerations. The transaction may be tax free to the seller if the acquirer uses its stock to acquire substantially all of the seller's assets or stock in a stock-for-stock or stock-for-assets purchase. See Chapter 12 for a discussion of M&A-related tax issues.

Tax Considerations Effects (Figure 11.1, Arrows 7 and 8)

Amount, timing, and composition of the purchase price. If the transaction is taxable to the target's shareholders, it is likely that the purchase price will be increased to compensate the target's shareholders for their tax liability. The increase in the purchase price may affect the form of payment. The acquirer may maintain the present value of the total cost of the acquisition by deferring some portion of the purchase price by altering the terms to include more debt or installment payments.

Selection of the postclosing organization. The decision as to what constitutes the appropriate organizational structure of the combined businesses is affected by these tax-related factors: the desire to minimize taxes and pass through losses to the owners. The S corporation, LLC, and the partnership eliminate double-taxation problems. Moreover, current operating losses, loss carryforwards or carrybacks, or tax credits generated by the combined businesses can be passed through to the owners if the postclosing organization is a partnership or a LLC.

Legal Form of Selling Entity Affects the Form of Payment (Figure 11.1, Arrow 9)

Because of the potential for deferring shareholder tax liabilities, target firms that qualify as C corporations often prefer to exchange their stock or assets for acquirer shares. In contrast, owners of S corporations, LLCs, and partnerships are largely indifferent as to whether the transaction is taxable or nontaxable because 100% of the proceeds of the sale are taxed at the shareholder's ordinary tax rate.

Accounting Considerations Affect the Form, Amount, and Timing of Payment (Figure 11.1, Arrow 10)

Earn-outs and other forms of contingent considerations are recorded at fair value on the acquisition date under recent changes in financial reporting guidelines (i.e., SFAS 141R and SFAS 157) effective December 15, 2009, and subsequently adjusted to fair value as new information becomes available. Such changes can increase or decrease reported earnings. Since earn-outs must be recorded at fair value on the acquisition date and subsequently adjusted, the potential for increased earnings volatility may make performance-related pay-outs less attractive as a form of payment. Furthermore, the use of equity securities to pay for

TABLE 11.1 Summary of Common Linkages within the Deal-Structuring Process

Component of Deal-Structuring Process	Influences choice of
Form, Amount, and Timing of Payment	Acquisition vehicle
	Postclosing organization
	Accounting considerations
	Tax structure (taxable or nontaxable)
Form of Acquisition	Acquisition vehicle
	Postclosing organization
	Form, amount, and timing of payment
	Tax structure (taxable or nontaxable)
Tax Considerations	Form, amount, and timing of payment
	Postclosing organization
Legal Form of Selling Entity	Tax structure (taxable or nontaxable)

target firms may be less attractive due to recent changes in financial reporting requirements.[1] Finally, the requirement to review periodically the book or carrying value of such assets as goodwill for impairment (e.g., fair market value is less than book value) may discourage acquirers from overpaying for a target firm due to the potential for future asset write-downs. These financial reporting requirements are discussed in more detail in Chapter 12. Table 11.1 provides a summary of these common linkages.

FORM OF ACQUISITION VEHICLE AND POSTCLOSING ORGANIZATION

Present in all transactions, the *acquisition vehicle* is the legal or business structure employed to acquire a target firm, and the *postclosing organization* is that used to operate the new company following closing. There are various options, as the following examples illustrate, and making the right choices for both is integral to the negotiation process.[2]

On July 9, 2000, in a share-for-share exchange valued at $41 billion, the boards of JDSU (a fiber-optic components manufacturer) and SDL (a pump laser producer) unanimously approved an agreement to merge SDL with a newly formed entity: K2 Acquisition, Inc., a

[1] The value of the transaction is not known until the closing, since the value of the transaction is measured at the close of the deal rather than at the announcement date. If the length of time between announcement and closing is substantial due to the need to obtain regulatory approval, the value of the deal may change significantly.

[2] References to business structures throughout the chapter refer to such arrangements as joint ventures and strategic business alliances (which may or may not involve legal entities). For example, the joint venture routinely is used to describe a collaboration among partners. The JV can be a corporation, partnership, or some other form of legal entity, or the JV can be an informal, non–legally binding agreement involving multiple parties collaborating in an effort to achieve specific business objectives.

wholly-owned subsidiary of JDS Uniphase created as a shell corporation to be the acquisition vehicle to complete the merger. K2 Acquisition Inc. was merged into SDL, with SDL as the surviving entity. The postclosing organization consisted of SDL as a wholly-owned subsidiary of JDS Uniphase.

In another deal, Rupert Murdoch's News Corp.—a holding company (the acquisition vehicle)—acquired a controlling interest in Hughes Electronics Corporation (a subsidiary of General Motors Corporation and owner of DirecTV) on April 10, 2003. News Corp. subsequently transferred its stake in Hughes to its Fox Entertainment Group subsidiary (the postclosing organization), in which it owned an 81% interest at the time, to strengthen Fox's competitive position while retaining control over DirecTV.

More recently, the Tribune Corporation announced on April 2, 2007, that the firm's publicly traded shares would be acquired in a multistage transaction valued at $8.2 billion. The acquisition vehicle was an employee stock ownership plan (ESOP), and the postclosing organization was a Subchapter S corporation. Converting the Tribune into a Subchapter S corporation eliminated the firm's current annual tax liability of $348 million. Such entities pay no corporate income tax but must pay all profit directly to shareholders, who then pay taxes on these distributions. Since the ESOP is the sole shareholder, the restructured Tribune would be largely tax exempt, since ESOPs are not taxed.

Finally, in a cross-border transaction, the biggest banking deal on record was announced on October 9, 2007, resulting in the dismemberment of one of Europe's largest and oldest financial services firms: ABN Amro (ABN), which was at the time the largest bank in the Netherlands. The acquisition vehicle was a buyer partnership comprising The Royal Bank of Scotland, Spain's Banco Santander, and Belgium's Fortis Bank, which won control of ABN in a buyout valued at $101 billion. The acquisition partners agreed in advance who would retain which ABN assets, and these were merged into the respective buyers' corporate subsidiaries (the postclosing organizations).

Choosing the Appropriate Form of Acquisition Vehicle

The decision about which legal entity to use as an acquisition vehicle requires consideration of a host of practical, financial, legal, and tax issues, which could include the cost and formality of organization, ease of transferability of ownership interests, continuity of existence, management, control, ease of financing, method of distribution of profits, extent of personal liability, and taxation. Each form of legal entity has markedly different risk, financing, tax, and control implications for the acquirer. The various forms of potential acquisition vehicles and their specific advantages and disadvantages are discussed in considerable detail in Chapter 14. The selection of the appropriate entity can help to mitigate risk associated with the target firm, maximize financing flexibility, and minimize the net cost of the acquisition to the acquiring firm.

The corporate structure or some variation is the most commonly used acquisition vehicle. This legal form tends to offer most of the features acquirers desire, including limited liability, financing flexibility, continuity of ownership, and deal flexibility (e.g., option to engage in a tax-free deal). Moreover, the corporate structure enables the acquirer to retain control over the implementation of the business plan and the acquisition process, something that may not be possible under partnership arrangements. When using a corporate structure as the acquisition vehicle, the target company typically is integrated into an existing operating division or product line within the corporation.

The corporate structure may also be appropriate for those situations where there is a desire to share the risk of acquiring the target or because the partner has skills and attributes viewed as valuable in operating the target after closing. Used as an acquisition vehicle, the JV corporation or partnership offers a lower level of risk than a direct acquisition of the target firm by one of the JV corporate owners or individual partners. By acquiring the target firm through the JV, the corporate investor limits the potential liability to the extent of its investment in the joint venture. The joint venture arrangement also enables the inclusion of partners with a particular skill, proprietary knowledge, intellectual property, manufacturing facility, or distribution channel that offers potential synergy with the target firm.

There are many common motivations for using other legal forms. For small, privately owned firms, an employee stock ownership plan structure may be a convenient vehicle for transferring the owner's interest in the business to the employees, while offering significant tax advantages. Non-U.S. buyers intending to make additional acquisitions may prefer a holding company structure. The advantages of this structure over a corporate merger for both foreign and domestic firms are the ability to control other companies by owning only a small portion of the company's voting stock and to gain this control without getting shareholder approval.

If the form of acquisition is a statutory merger, all known and unknown or contingent liabilities are transferred to the buyer. Under these circumstances, the buyer may choose to change the type of acquisition vehicle to one that offers better protection from the target's liabilities, such as a holding company arrangement. By merging the target firm into a subsidiary of the holding company, the acquirer may better insulate itself from the target's liabilities. Again, this risk could be shared under a joint venture or partnership arrangement.

If the buyer and seller cannot agree on a price, the buyer may offer a purchase price that is contingent on the future performance of the target. The buyer may choose to acquire and to operate the acquired company as a wholly-owned subsidiary within a holding company during the term of the earn-out (i.e., deferred payment to target owners upon achievement of certain goals). The holding company framework facilitates monitoring the target's performance during the earn-out period and minimizes the potential for post-earn-out litigation initiated by earn-out participants.

Choosing the Appropriate Postclosing Organization

The postclosing organization refers to the legal or organizational framework used to operate the acquired firm following closing, so it can be the same as that chosen for the acquisition vehicle: corporate, general partnership, limited partnership, and the limited liability company. Common organizational business structures include divisional and holding company arrangements. The choice will depend on the objectives of the acquirer.

A division generally is not a separate legal entity but rather an organizational unit, while a holding company can take on many alternative legal forms. An operating division is distinguishable from a legal subsidiary in that it typically will not have its own stock or board of directors that meets on a regular basis. However, divisions as organizational units may have managers with some of the titles normally associated with separate legal entities, such as a president or chief operating officer. Because a division is not a separate legal entity, its liabilities are the responsibility of the parent firm.

The acquiring firm may have a variety of objectives for operating the target firm after closing, including facilitating postclosing integration, minimizing risk to owners from the target's known and unknown liabilities, minimizing taxes, passing through losses to shelter the owners' tax liabilities, preserving unique target attributes, maintaining target independence during the duration of an earn-out, and preserving the tax-free status of the deal. If the acquirer is interested in integrating the target business immediately following closing, the corporate or divisional structure may be most desirable because it may make it possible for the acquirer to gain the greatest control. In other structures, such as JVs and partnerships, the dispersed ownership may render decision making slower or more contentious, since it is more likely to depend on close cooperation and consensus building that may slow efforts at rapid integration of the acquired company.

In contrast, a holding company structure in which the acquired company is managed as a wholly- or partially owned subsidiary may be preferable when the target has significant known or unknown liabilities, an earn-out is involved, the target is a foreign firm, or the acquirer is a financial investor. By maintaining the target as a subsidiary, the parent firm may be able to isolate significant liabilities within the subsidiary. Moreover, if need be, the subsidiary could be placed under the protection of the U.S. Bankruptcy Court without jeopardizing the existence of the parent.

In an earn-out agreement, the acquired firm must be operated largely independently from other operations of the acquiring firm to minimize the potential for lawsuits. If the acquired firm fails to achieve the goals required to receive the earn-out payment, the acquirer may be sued for allegedly taking actions that prevented the acquired firm from reaching the necessary goals. When the target is a foreign firm, it is often appropriate to operate it separately from the rest of the acquirer's operations because of the potential disruption from significant cultural differences. Finally, a financial buyer may use a holding company structure because they have no interest in operating the target firm for any length of time.

A partnership or JV structure may be appropriate if the risk associated with the target firm is believed to be high. Consequently, partners or JV owners can limit their financial exposure to the amount they have invested. The acquired firm may benefit from being owned by a partnership or JV because of the expertise that the different partners or owners might provide.

A partnership or LLC may be most appropriate for eliminating double taxation and passing through current operating losses, tax credits, and loss carryforwards and carrybacks to owners.[3] Cerberus Capital Management's conversion of its purchase of General Motors Acceptance Corporation (GMAC) from General Motors in 2006 from a C corporation to a limited liability company at closing reflected its desire to eliminate double taxation of income while continuing to limit shareholder liability. Similarly, when investor Sam Zell masterminded a

---

[3] It is important to maintain the existence of the target firm to preserve the tax-free status of the transaction. Preserving the tax-free status of a deal results from satisfying conditions such as maintaining continuity of ownership, which requires previous target firm shareholders to receive a significant percentage of the purchase price in acquirer stock, and continuity of business enterprise, which requires that the acquirer retains a significant share of the target's assets after closing. These concepts are detailed in Chapter 12.

leveraged buyout of media company Tribune Corporation in 2007, an ESOP was used as the *Frank* acquisition vehicle and a Subchapter-S corporation as the postclosing organization. The change in legal structure enabled the firm to save an estimated $348 million in taxes, because S corporation profits are not taxed if distributed to shareholders—which in this case included the tax-exempt ESOP as the primary shareholder.

LEGAL FORM OF THE SELLING ENTITY

Whether the seller will care about the form of the transaction (i.e., whether stock or assets are sold) may depend on whether the seller is an S, a limited liability company, partnership, or a C corporation. As noted previously, C corporations are subject to double taxation, whereas owners of S corporations, partnerships, and LLCs are not (see Exhibit 11.1).

EXHIBIT 11.1 HOW THE SELLER'S LEGAL FORM AFFECTS THE FORM OF PAYMENT

Assume that a business owner starting with an initial investment of $100,000 sells her business for $1 million. Different legal structures have different tax impacts:

1. After-tax proceeds of a stock sale are ($1,000,000 – $100,000) × (1 – 0.15) = $765,000. The S corporation shareholder or limited liability company member holding shares for more than one year pays a maximum capital gains tax equal to 15% of the gain on the sale.[a]
2. After-tax proceeds from an asset sale are ($1,000,000 – $100,000) × (1 – 0.4) × (1 – 0.15) = $900,000 × 0.51 = $459,000. A C corporation typically pays tax equal to 40% (i.e., 35% federal and 5% state and local), and the shareholder pays a maximum capital gains tax equal to 15%, resulting in double taxation of the gain on sale.

Implications
1. C corporation shareholders generally prefer acquirer stock for their stock or assets to avoid double taxation.
2. S corporation and LLC owners often are indifferent to an asset sale or stock sale because 100% of the corporation's income passes through the corporation untaxed to the owners, who are subject to their own personal tax rates. The S corporation shareholders or LLC members still may prefer a share-for-share exchange if they are interested in deferring their tax liability or are attracted by the long-term growth potential of the acquirer's stock.

[a]This is the current capital gains tax rate as of the time of this writing.

FORM OF PAYMENT OR TOTAL CONSIDERATION

The form of payment refers to the composition of the purchase price for a target firm and can be structured in many different ways. This section discusses alternative structures that can be used as payment in negotiating with a target firm's board and management and how these various forms of payment can be used to bridge differences between the seller's asking price and the price the acquirer is willing to pay.

Cash

Cash is the simplest and most commonly used means of payment for acquiring shares or assets. Although cash payments generally result in an immediate tax liability for the target company's shareholders, there is no ambiguity about the value of the transaction as long as no portion of the payment is deferred. Whether cash is used as the predominant form of payment depends on a variety of factors, including the acquirer's current leverage, potential near-term earnings per share dilution, the seller's preference for cash or acquirer stock, and the extent to which the acquirer wishes to maintain control.

A bidder may choose to use cash rather than issue voting shares if the voting control of its dominant shareholder is threatened as a result of the issuance of voting stock to acquire the target firm.[4] Issuing new voting shares would dilute the amount of control held by the dominant shareholder. The preference for using cash appears to be much higher in Western European countries, where ownership tends to be more heavily concentrated in publicly traded firms, than in the United States. In Europe, 63% of publicly traded firms have a single shareholder who directly or indirectly controls 20% or more of the voting shares; the U.S. figure is 28%.[5]

Noncash

The use of common equity may involve certain tax advantages for the parties involved—especially shareholders of the selling company. However, using shares is much more complicated than cash because it requires compliance with the prevailing security laws and may result in long-term earnings per share dilution. Using convertible preferred stock or debt can be attractive to both buyers and sellers. These securities offer holders the right (but not the obligation) to convert to common stock at a predetermined "conversion" price. Convertible preferred stock provides some downside protection to sellers in the form of continuing dividends, while providing upside potential if the acquirer's common stock price increases above the conversion point. Acquirers often find convertible debt attractive because of the tax deductibility of interest payments.

The major disadvantage in using securities of any type is that the seller may find them unattractive because of the perceived high risk of default associated with the issuer. When offered common equity, shareholders of the selling company may feel that the growth prospects of the acquirer's stock may be limited or that the historical volatility of the stock makes it unacceptably risky. Debt or equity securities may also be illiquid because of the small size of the resale market for such securities.

Acquirer stock may be a particularly useful form of payment when valuing the target firm is difficult, such as when the target firm has hard to value intangible assets, new product entries whose outcome is uncertain, or large research and development outlays. In accepting acquirer stock, a seller may have less incentive to negotiate an overvalued purchase price if it wishes to participate in any appreciation of the stock it receives. However, a seller could

---

[4] Faccio and Marsulis, 2005

[5] Faccio and Lang, 2002

attempt to negotiate the highest price possible for its business and immediately sell its stock following closing.[6]

Other forms of noncash payment include real property, rights to intellectual property, royalties, earn-outs, and contingent payments. These are discussed later in this chapter.

Cash and Stock in Combination

The bidding strategy of offering target firm shareholders multiple payment options increases the likelihood that more target firm shareholders will participate in a tender offer. It is a bidding strategy common in "auction" environments or when the bidder is unable to borrow the amount necessary to support an all-cash offer or unwilling to absorb the potential earnings per share dilution in an all-stock offer. The multiple-option bidding strategy does, however, introduce a certain level of uncertainty in determining the amount of cash the acquirer ultimately will have to pay out to target firm shareholders, since the number of shareholders choosing the all-cash or cash-and-stock option is not known prior to completion of the tender offer.

Acquirers resolve this issue by including a *proration clause* in tender offers and merger agreements that allows them to fix—at the time the tender offer is initiated—the total amount of cash they will ultimately have to pay out. For example, assume that the total cost of an acquisition is $100 million, the acquirer wishes to limit the amount of cash paid to target firm shareholders to one-half of that amount, and the acquirer offers the target firm's shareholders a choice of stock or cash. If the number of target shareholders choosing cash exceeds $50 million, the proration clause enables the acquirer to pay all target firm shareholders tendering their shares one-half of the purchase price in cash and the remainder in stock.

MANAGING RISK AND CLOSING THE GAP ON PRICE

During the negotiation phase, the buyer and seller maneuver to share the perceived risk and apportion the potential returns. In doing so, substantial differences arise between what the buyer is willing to pay and what the seller believes their business is worth. Postclosing balance sheet adjustments and escrow accounts, earn-outs and other contingent payments, contingent value rights, staging investment, rights to intellectual property, licensing fees, and consulting agreements are all typically used to consummate the deal when the buyer and seller cannot reach agreement on price.

Postclosing Price Adjustments

Postclosing adjustment price mechanisms include escrow or holdback accounts and adjustments to the target's balance sheet. Both mechanisms, most often used in cash rather than stock-for-stock purchases (particularly when the number of target shareholders is large), rely on an audit of the target firm to determine its "true" value and generally are applicable

---

[6] In a sample of 735 acquisitions of privately held firms between 1995 and 2004, Officer et al. (2007) found that acquirer stock was used as the form of payment about 80% of the time. The unusually high (for acquirers) 3.8% abnormal return earned by acquirers in this sample around the announcement suggests that sellers willing to accept acquirer stock were more likely to see significant synergies in merging with the acquiring firm.

only when what is being acquired is clearly identifiable, such as in a purchase of tangible assets. The buyer and seller typically share the cost of the audit.

With *escrow accounts*, the buyer retains a portion of the purchase price until completion of a postclosing audit of the target's financial statements. Escrow accounts may also be used to cover and claims that continue beyond a closing. For instance, Google's share-for-share purchase of YouTube involved a holdback of a portion of the purchase price because of the potential for copyright infringement litigation. When Berkshire Hathaway and Leucadia National agreed to buy Capmark Financial Group's mortgage servicing business in 2010 for $490 million, the buyers held back $40 million to cover potential indemnity claims.

Balance sheet adjustments are used most often in purchases of assets when there is a lengthy time between the agreement on price and the actual closing date. This may result from the need to obtain regulatory or shareholder approvals or from ongoing due diligence. During this period, balance sheet items may change significantly—particularly those related to working capital—so the purchase price is adjusted up or down. Balance sheet adjustments can be employed broadly to guarantee the value of the target firm's shareholder equity or, more narrowly, to guarantee the value of working capital.

With a shareholder equity guarantee, both parties agree to an estimated equity value as of the closing date. Target equity value is often calculated by taking the book value of equity on the balance sheet of the target firm at a given point and then increasing (or decreasing) it by the amount of net profit earned (or lost) between that date and closing. The purchase price is then increased or decreased to reflect any change in the book value of equity. A guarantee of this sort protects the buyer from risks such as any distribution of company profits by the seller after the signing date or unusually large salary payments or severance benefits between the contract signing and closing dates. While attractive to the buyer, the equity guarantee can be unattractive to the seller because of the difficulty in forecasting revenue during the period between signing and closing at the signing date. Consequently, sellers often will demand a higher purchase price to compensate them for this increase in risk.

Both parties may more easily reach an agreement with a working capital guarantee, which ensures against fluctuations in the company's current operating assets. It is critical, though, to define clearly what constitutes working capital and equity in the agreement of purchase and sale, since—similar to equity—what constitutes working capital may be ambiguous.

As Table 11.2 indicates, the buyer—to protect the buyer or seller—reduces the total purchase price by an amount equal to the decrease in net working capital or shareholders' equity of the target and increases the purchase price by any increase in these measures during this period.

TABLE 11.2   Balance Sheet Adjustments ($ million)

	Purchase Price		Purchase Price Reduction	Purchase Price Increase
	At Time of Negotiation	*At Closing*	*Purchase Price Reduction*	*Purchase Price Increase*
If Working Capital Equals	110	100	10	
If Working Capital Equals	110	125		15

Earn-Outs and Other Contingent Payments

Earn-outs and warrants frequently are used whenever the buyer and seller cannot agree on the probable performance of the seller's business over some future period or when the parties involved wish to participate in the upside potential of the business. Earn-out agreements may also be used to retain and motivate key target firm managers. An *earn-out agreement* is a financial contract whereby a portion of the purchase price of a company is to be paid in the future, contingent on realizing the future earnings level or some other performance measure agreed upon earlier. The terms of the earn-out are stipulated in the agreement of purchase and sale. A subscription warrant, or simply *warrant*, is a type of security—often issued with a bond or preferred stock—that entitles the holder to purchase an amount of common stock at a stipulated price. The exercise price is usually higher than the price at the time the warrant is issued. Warrants may be converted over a period of many months to many years.

The earn-out typically requires that the acquired business be operated as a wholly-owned subsidiary of the acquiring company under the management of the former owners or key executives. Both the buyer and the seller are well advised to keep the calculation of such goals and resulting payments as simple as possible because the difficulty of measuring actual performance against the goals often creates disputes.

Earn-outs may take many forms. Some are payable only if a certain performance threshold is achieved; others depend on average performance over several periods; and still others may involve periodic payments, depending on the achievement of interim performance measures rather than a single, lump-sum payment at the end of the earn-out period. The value of the earn-out is often capped. In some cases, the seller may have the option to repurchase the company at some predetermined percentage of the original purchase price if the buyer is unable to pay the earn-out at maturity.

Exhibit 11.2 illustrates how an earn-out formula could be constructed reflecting these considerations. The purchase price has two components. At closing, the seller receives a lump-sum payment of $100 million. The seller and the buyer agree to a baseline projection for a three-year period and that the seller will receive a fixed multiple of the average annual performance of the acquired business in excess of the baseline projection. Thus, the earn-out provides an incentive for the seller to operate the business as effectively as possible. Normally, the baseline projection is what the buyer used to value the seller's business. Shareholder value for the buyer is created whenever the acquired business' actual performance exceeds the baseline projection and the multiple applied by investors at the end of the three-year period exceeds the multiple used to calculate the earn-out payment. This assumes that the baseline projection accurately values the business and that the buyer does not overpay. By multiplying the anticipated multiple that investors will pay for operating cash flow at the end of the three-year period by projected cash flow, it is possible to estimate the potential increase in shareholder value.

Earn-outs tend to shift risk from the acquirer to the seller in that a higher price is paid only when the seller has met or exceeded certain performance criteria. Earn-outs may also create some perverse results during implementation. Management motivation may be lost if the acquired firm does not perform well enough to achieve any payout under the earn-out formula or if the acquired firm exceeds the performance targets substantially, effectively guaranteeing the maximum payout under the plan.

EXHIBIT 11.2 HYPOTHETICAL EARN-OUT AS PART OF THE PURCHASE PRICE

Purchase Price

1. Lump-sum payment at closing: The seller receives $100 million.
2. Earn-out payment: The seller receives four times the excess of the actual average annual net operating cash flow over the baseline projection after three years, not to exceed $35 million.

Base Year

First Full Year of Ownership	Year 1	Year 2	Year 3
Baseline Projection (Net Cash Flow)	$10	$12	$15
Actual Performance (Net Cash Flow)	$15	$20	$25

Earn-out at the end of three years[a]:

$$\frac{(\$15 - \$10) + (\$20 - \$12) + (\$25 - \$15)}{3} \times 4 = \$30.67$$

Potential increase in shareholder value[b]:

$$\left\{ \frac{(\$15 - \$10) + (\$20 - \$12) + (\$25 - \$15)}{3} \times 10 \right\} - \$30.67 = \$46$$

[a]The cash-flow multiple of 4 applied to the earn-out is a result of negotiation before closing.
[b]The cash-flow multiple of 10 applied to the potential increase in shareholder value for the buyer is the multiple the buyer anticipates that investors would apply to a three-year average of actual operating cash flow at the end of the three-year period.

Moreover, the management of the acquired firm may have an incentive to take actions not in the best interests of the acquirer. For example, management may cut back on advertising and training expenses to improve the operation's current cash-flow performance or make only those investments that improve short-term profits, while ignoring those that may generate immediate losses but favorably affect profits in the long term. As the end of the earn-out period approaches, managers may postpone investments to maximize their own bonuses under the earn-out plan.

Earn-outs may also be based on share of equity ownership when the business is sold. For example, assume an entrepreneur believes the business is worth $20 million without additional investment, and the private equity investor estimates the business to be worth only $15 million without additional investment. The entrepreneur who wants $5 million in equity investment perceives the market value, including the equity infusion, to be $25 million (i.e., $20 million stand-alone plus $5 million in equity). The implied ownership distribution is 80/20, with the entrepreneur receiving 80% (i.e., $20/$25) and the equity investor receiving 20% (i.e., $5/$25).

However, the equity investor sees the value of the business, including the equity investment, to be only $20 million (i.e., $15 million stand-alone plus $5 million equity investment).

The implied ownership is 75/25, with the entrepreneur receiving only 75% ownership (i.e., $15/$20) and the equity investor 25% ownership (i.e., $5/$20). The ownership gap of 5 percentage points can be closed by the entrepreneur and equity investor agreeing to the 80/20 distribution if certain cash-flow or profit targets can be reached prior to exiting the business sufficient to justify the $25 million net present value (see Exhibit 11.3).

EXHIBIT 11.3 **EARN-OUTS BASED ON OWNERSHIP DISTRIBUTION**

Distribution of ownership equity if average annual free cash flow is less than $5 million in years 3 to 5[a]:

Entrepreneur	75%
Private Investor	25%
Total	**100%**

Distribution of ownership equity if average annual free cash flow is greater than $5 million in years 3 to 5:

Entrepreneur	80%
Private Investor	20%
Total	**100%**

[a]A three-year average cash-flow figure is used to measure performance to ensure that the actual performance is sustainable as opposed to an aberration.

To avoid various pitfalls associated with earn-outs, also known as contingent payouts, it may be appropriate to establish more than one target. For example, it may be appropriate to include a revenue, income, and investment target, although this adds to the earn-out's complexity. Earn-outs are included in about 3% of total transactions. Earn-outs are more commonly used when the targets are small, private firms or subsidiaries of larger firms, rather than for large, publicly traded firms. Such contracts are more easily written and enforced when there are relatively few shareholders.[7] Earn-outs tend to be most common in high-tech and service industries, when the acquirer and target firms are in different industries, when the target firm has a significant number of assets not recorded on the balance sheet, when buyer access to information is limited, and when little integration will be attempted.

Earn-outs on average account for 45% of the total purchase price paid for private firms and 33% for subsidiary acquisitions, and target firm shareholders tend to realize about 62% of the potential earn-out amount. In transactions involving earn-outs, acquirers earn abnormal returns of 5.39% around the announcement date, in contrast to transactions not involving contingent payments in which abnormal returns to acquirers tend to be zero or negative. Positive abnormal returns to acquiring company shareholders may be a result of investor perception that with an earn-out the buyer is less likely to overpay and more likely to retain key target firm talent.[8]

[7] Srikant, Frankel, and Wolfson, 2001

[8] Kohers and Ang, 2000

New IRS rules may make earn-outs less attractive than in the past. Under revisions that took effect on January 1, 2009, earn-outs and other contingent payments must be revalued as new information becomes available that could introduce greater volatility into a firm's earnings.[9]

Contingent Value Rights

In M&A transactions, *contingent value rights* (CVRs) are commitments by the issuing company (i.e., the acquirer) to pay additional cash or securities to the holder of the CVR (i.e., the seller) if the share price of the issuing company falls below a specified level at some future date. CVRs provide a guarantee of future value of one of various forms of payment made to the seller—such as cash, stock, or debt—as of a given time. While relatively rare, CVRs are sometimes granted when the buyer and seller are far apart on the purchase price or when the target firm wants protection for any remaining minority shareholders fearful of being treated unfairly by the buyer.[10]

Whereas earn-outs represent call options for the target representing claims on future upside performance and are employed when there is substantial disagreement between the buyer and seller on price, CVRs are put options limiting downside loss on the form of payment received by sellers. CVRs may be traded on public exchanges.

The following examples illustrate the use of CVRs. In Tembec Inc.'s acquisition of Crestbrook Forest Products Ltd., each Crestbrook shareholder received a contingent value right, enabling the shareholder to receive a one-time payment on March 31, 2000, the size of which (up to a maximum of $1.50 per share) depended on the amount that the average price of wood pulp for 1999 exceeded $549 per ton. In 2008, French utility EDF overcame resistance from certain British Energy shareholders by offering a combination of cash and a CVR that enabled investors to share in future profits whenever electrical output and energy prices rose.

---

[9] Revisions to accounting standards (Statement of Financial Accounting Standards 141R) that apply to business combinations went into effect on January 1, 2009. The fair value of earn-outs and other contingent payouts must be estimated and recorded on the acquisition closing date. Changes in fair value resulting from changes in the likelihood or amount of the contingent payout must be recorded as charges to the income statement at that time. Under earlier accounting standards, contingent payments were charged against income only when they were actually paid.

[10] Chatterjee and Yan (2008) argue that CVRs are issued most often when the acquiring firm issues stock to the target firm's shareholders that it believes are undervalued—in what is often called information asymmetry, where one party has access to more information than others. The CVR represents a declaration by the acquirer that its current share price represents a floor and that it is confident it will rise in the future. Firms offering CVRs in their acquisitions tend to believe their shares are more undervalued than those acquirers using cash or stock without CVRs as a form of payment. The authors found that most CVRs are issued in conjunction with either common or preferred stock. Acquirers offering CVRs experience announcement period abnormal returns of 5.3%. Targets receiving CVRs earn abnormal announcement period returns of 18.4%. The size of the abnormal announcement period return is greater than that of firms not offering CVRs. The authors argue that investors view acquirers who offer CVRs as having knowledge of the postmerger performance of the acquired business not available to the broader market. Hence, the issuance of the CVR expresses buyer confidence in the future success of the transaction.

The amount of future payouts to shareholders would depend on the amount of the increase in profits. In 2011, French pharmaceutical giant Sanofi-Aventis clinched a deal to acquire U.S.-based Genzyme Corporation by offering a CVR to bridge the wide gap in the two firms' expectations for a newly introduced Genzyme drug, Lemitrada. Genzyme forecasted peak annual sales of $3.5 billion versus Sanofi's estimate of only $700 million. By some estimates, the value of the contingent value rights could be worth as much as $12 to $15 per share paid out over as long as eight years to Genzyme shareholders, depending on the eventual annual revenues produced by the drug.

Distributed or Staged Payouts

The purchase price payments can be contingent on the target satisfying an agreed-on milestone, such as achieving a profit or cash-flow target, successfully launching a new product, obtaining regulatory or patent approval, and so on. Distributing the payout over time manages risk to the acquirer by reducing some of the uncertainty about future cash flows. An acquirer could also avoid having to finance the entire cash purchase price in a large transaction at one time.

Rights, Royalties, and Fees

The rights to intellectual property, royalties from licenses, and fee-based consulting or employment agreements are other forms of payment that can be used to close the gap between what the buyer is willing to offer and what the seller expects. The right to use a proprietary process or technology for free or at a rate below that prevailing in the market may interest former owners considering business opportunities in which it would be useful. Note that such an arrangement, if priced at below market rates or free to the seller, would represent taxable income to the seller. Obviously, such arrangements should be coupled with reasonable agreements not to compete in the same industry as their former firm. Table 11.3 summarizes the advantages and disadvantages of these various forms of payment.

USING COLLAR ARRANGEMENTS TO PRESERVE SHAREHOLDER VALUE

Unlike what happens with all-cash deals, significant fluctuations in the acquirer's share price can threaten to change the terms of the deal or even to derail it altogether. Parties may need to renegotiate price as they approach closing. A solution is for the acquirer and target firms to agree on a range or collar within which the stock price can change. By setting floors and caps on the stock portion of an acquisition's price, a collar gives both sides some assurance that the deal will retain its value despite share price fluctuations. Whereas fixed share exchange ratios are most common, some transactions do allow the share exchange ratio to fluctuate within limits to compensate for the uncertain value of the deal. These limits often

TABLE 11.3   Evaluating Alternative Forms of Payment

Form of Payment	Advantages	Disadvantages
Cash (including highly marketable securities)	*Buyer:* Simplicity. *Seller:* Ensures payment if acquirer's creditworthiness questionable.	*Buyer:* Must rely solely on protections afforded in contract to recover claims. *Seller:* Creates immediate tax liability.
Stock – Common – Preferred – Convertible Preferred	*Buyer:* High P/E relative to seller's P/E may increase value of combined businesses. *Seller:* Defers taxes and provides potential price increase. Retains interest in the business.	*Buyer:* Adds complexity; potential EPS dilution. *Seller:* Potential decrease in purchase price if the value of equity received declines. May delay closing because of SEC registration requirements.
Debt – Secured – Unsecured – Convertible	*Buyer:* Interest expense tax deductible. *Seller:* Defers tax liability on principal.	*Buyer:* Adds complexity and increases leverage. *Seller:* Risk of default.
Performance-Related Earn-Outs	*Buyer:* Shifts some portion of risk to seller. *Seller:* Potential for higher purchase price.	*Buyer:* May limit integration of businesses. *Seller:* Increases uncertainty of sales price.
Purchase Price Adjustments	*Buyer:* Protection from eroding values of working capital before closing. *Seller:* Protection from increasing values of working capital before closing.	*Buyer:* Audit expense. *Seller:* Audit expense. (Note that buyers and sellers often split the audit expense.)
Real Property – Real Estate – Plant and Equipment – Business or Product Line	*Buyer:* Minimizes use of cash. *Seller:* May minimize tax liability.	*Buyer:* Opportunity cost. *Seller:* Real property may be illiquid.
Rights to Intellectual Property – License – Franchise	*Buyer:* Minimizes cash use. *Seller:* Gains access to valuable rights and spreads taxable income over time.	*Buyer:* Potential for setting up new competitor. *Seller:* Illiquid; income taxed at ordinary rates.
Royalties from – Licenses – Franchises	*Buyer:* Minimizes cash use. *Seller:* Spreads taxable income over time.	*Buyer:* Opportunity cost. *Seller:* Income taxed at ordinary rates.
Fee-Based – Consulting Contract – Employment Agreement	*Buyer:* Uses seller's expertise and removes seller as potential competitor for a limited time. *Seller:* Augments purchase price and allows seller to stay with the business.	*Buyer:* May involve demotivated employees. *Seller:* Limits ability to compete in same line of business. Income taxed at ordinary rates.
Contingent Value Rights	*Buyer:* Minimizes upfront payment. *Seller:* Provides for minimum payout guarantee.	*Buyer:* Commits buyer to minimum payout. *Seller:* Buyer may ask for purchase price reduction
Staged or Distributed Payouts	*Buyer:* Reduces amount of upfront investment. *Seller:* Reduces buyer angst about certain future events.	*Buyer:* May result in underfunding of needed investments. *Seller:* Lower present value of purchase price.

are referred to as the "collar" around the purchase price; such arrangements have become more common in recent years, with about 20% of stock mergers employing some form of collar.

A *fixed share exchange agreement* fixes the share exchange ratio (i.e., the number of acquirer shares exchanged for each target share) between the signing of the agreement of purchase and sale and closing. However, the value of the buyer's share price is allowed to fluctuate due to changes in the value of the acquirer's share price. While the buyer will know exactly how many shares will have to be issued to consummate the transaction, both the acquirer and the target will be subject to significant uncertainty about the final purchase price. The acquirer may find that the transaction will be much more expensive than anticipated if the value of its shares rises; in contrast, the seller may be greatly disappointed if the acquirer's share price declines. Fixed share exchange ratios are more common in share-for-share exchanges because they involve both firms' share prices and allow both parties to share in the risk or benefit of fluctuating share prices.

A *fixed value (offer price) agreement* fixes the value of the offer price per share by allowing the share exchange ratio to change. For example, an increase in the value of the acquirer's share price (ASP) would result in the issuance of fewer acquirer shares to keep the value of the deal unchanged, while a decrease would require that new shares be issued.

Buyers often argue that a collar arrangement to the seller is like buying insurance because it tends to reduce the seller's uncertainty about the purchase price at closing. In these cases, such buyers expect sellers to accept a lower purchase price as payment of a "premium" for such insurance.

Offer prices based on collar arrangements can be constructed as follows:

$$\text{Offer Price per Share} = \text{Share Exchange Ratio (SER)} \times \text{Acquirer's Share Price}$$
$$= \left\{ \frac{\text{Offer Price per Share}}{\text{Acquirer's Share Price}} \right\} \times \text{Acquirer's Share Price}$$

$$\text{Collar Range: } SER_L \times ASP_L(\text{lower limit}) \leq \text{Offer Price per Share} \leq SER_U \times ASP_U(\text{upper limit})$$

where $ASP_U > ASP_L$ and $SER_U < SER_L$; subscripts L and U refer to lower and upper limits.

Case Study 11.1 illustrates the use of both fixed value and fixed share exchange ratio collar agreements. Within the first collar (fixed value), the purchase price is fixed by allowing the share exchange ratio to vary, giving the seller some degree of certainty inside a narrow range within which the acquirer share price can fluctuate; the second collar (fixed share exchange) allows the acquirer's share price to vary within a stipulated range resulting in both the buyer and seller sharing the risk. Finally, if the acquirer's share price rises above a certain level, the purchase price is capped; if it falls below a predetermined price, the seller can walk away.

If the acquirer's share price has historically been highly volatile, the target may demand a collar to preserve the agreed-on share price. Similarly, the acquirer may demand a collar if the target's share price has shown great variation in the past in order to minimize the potential for overpaying if the target's share price declines significantly relative to the acquirer's share price.

CASE STUDY 11.1
Flextronics Acquires International DisplayWorks Using Fixed Value and Fixed Share Exchange Collars

Flextronics, a manufacturer of camera modules, TV tuners, and Wi-Fi module assemblies, acquired International DisplayWorks (IDW), a designer and manufacturer of LCDs and other components for handheld and industrial products, in a share-for-share deal valued at approximately $300 million in late 2009. The share exchange ratio used at closing was calculated using the Flextronics average daily closing share price for the 20 trading days ending on the fifth trading day immediately preceding the closing.[1] Transaction terms included the following three collars:

1. *Fixed Value Agreement:* The offer price was calculated using an exchange ratio floating inside a 10% collar above and below a Flextronics share price of $11.73 and a fixed purchase price of $6.55 per share for each share of IDW common stock. The range in which the exchange ratio floats can be expressed as follows:[2]

$$[\$655/\$10.55] \times \$10.55 \leq [\$6.55/\$11.73] \times \$11.73 \leq [\$6.55/\$12.90] \times \$12.90$$

$$0.6209 \times \$10.55 \leq 0.5584 \times \$11.73 \leq 0.5078 \times \$12.90$$

0.6209 shares of Flextronics' stock issued for each IDW share (i.e., $6.55/$10.55) if Flextronics' stock price declines by as much as 10%

0.5078 shares of Flextronics' stock issued for each IDW share (i.e., $6.55/$12.90) if Flextronics' stock price increases by as much as 10%

2. *Fixed Share Exchange Agreement:* The offer price was calculated using a fixed exchange ratio inside a collar 11% and 15% above and below $11.73, resulting in a floating purchase price if the average Flextronics' stock price increases or decreases between 11% and 15% from $11.73 per share.

3. IDW has the right to terminate the agreement if Flextronics's share price falls by more than 15% below $11.73. If Flextronics' share price increases by more than 15% above $11.73, the exchange ratio floats based on a fixed purchase price of $6.85 per share.[3] See Figure 11.2 for an illustration of the collar ranges and Case Study Table 11.4 on 432 for the calculation of the effects of 1% changes in Flextronics' share price on the offer price.

[1]Calculating the acquirer share price as a 20-day average ending five days prior to closing reduces the chance of using an aberrant price per share and provides time to include the final terms in the purchase agreement.
[2]The share exchange ratio varies within a range of plus or minus 10% of the Flextronics' $11.73 share price.
[3]IDW is protected against a potential "free fall" in the Flextronics' share price, while the purchase price paid by Flextronics is capped at $6.85.

The boards of directors of both the acquirer and target have a fiduciary responsibility to demand that merger terms be renegotiated if the value of the offer made by the bidder changes materially relative to the value of the target's stock or if there has been any other material change in the target's operations. Merger contracts routinely contain "material adverse effects clauses" that provide a basis for buyers to withdraw from or renegotiate the contract.

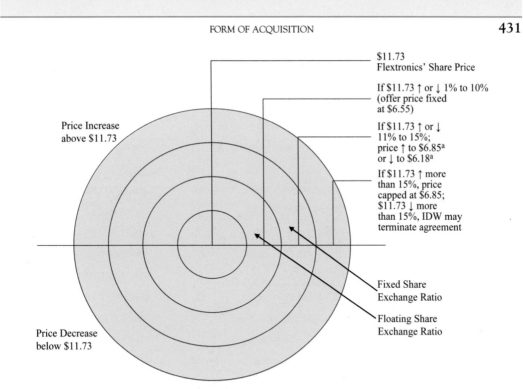

FIGURE 11.2 Multiple price collars around the share price of Flextronics' stock.
↑ *indicates increase;* ↓ *indicates decrease.*
[a]See Table 11.4 for the calculation of upper ($6.85) and lower ($6.18) bounds of offer price.

The existence of collars reduces the likelihood of having to renegotiate the terms of a merger agreement due to unanticipated changes in share prices.[11]

FORM OF ACQUISITION

Acquirers may purchase the stock or assets of a target firm; what is being acquired and the mechanism for transferring ownership of assets or stock and associated liabilities from the target to the acquirer is called the *form of acquisition*. Each form affects the negotiation and deal structuring process differently, and each has a number of advantages and disadvantages depending on the point of view—whether buyer or seller.[12] The most commonly used methods are discussed next.

An *asset purchase* involves the sale of all or a portion of the assets of the target to the buyer or its subsidiary in exchange for buyer stock, cash, debt, or some combination. The buyer may

[11] From an evaluation of 1,127 stock mergers between 1991 and 1999, approximately one-fifth of which had collar arrangements, Officer (2004) concluded that collars are more likely to be used the greater the volatility of the acquirer share price compared to that of the target share price. He further concluded that the use of collars reduces substantially the likelihood that merger terms will have to be renegotiated—a costly proposition in terms of management time and legal and investment banking advice.

[12] For more information on this topic, see DePamphilis (2010b), Chapter 11.

TABLE 11.4   Flextronics–IDW Fixed Value and Fixed Share Exchange Agreements for Case Study 11.1

	% Change[a]	Offer Price ($6.55/$11.73) × $11.73 = $6.55	% Change[a]	Offer Price ($6.55/$11.73) × $11.73 = $6.55
Floating SER	1	($6.55/$11.85) × $11.85 = $6.55	(1)	($6.55/$11.61) × $11.61 = $6.55
	2	($6.55/$11.96) × $11.96 = $6.55	(2)	($6.55/$11.50) × $11.50 = $6.55
	3	($6.55/$12.08) × $12.08 = $6.55	(3)	($6.55/$11.38) × $11.38 = $6.55
	4	($6.55/$12.20) × $12.20 = $6.55	(4)	($6.55/$11.26) × $11.26 = $6.55
	5	($6.55/$12.32) × $12.32 = $6.55	(5)	($6.55/$11.14) × $11.14 = $6.55
	6	($6.55/$12.43) × $12.43 = $6.55	(6)	($6.55/$11.03) × $11.03 = $6.55
	7	($6.55/$12.55) × $12.55 = $6.55	(7)	($6.55/$10.91) × $10.91 = $6.55
	8	($6.55/$12.67) × $12.67 = $6.55	(8)	($6.55/$10.79) × $10.79 = $6.55
	9	($6.55/$12.79) × $12.79 = $6.55	(9)	($6.55/$10.67) × $10.67 = $6.55
	10	($6.55/$12.90) × $12.90 = $6.55	(10)	($6.55/$10.56) × $10.56 = $6.55
Fixed SER	11	($6.55/$12.90) × $13.02 = $6.61	(11)	($6.55/$10.56) × $10.44 = $6.48
	12	($6.55/$12.90) × $13.14 = $6.67	(12)	($6.55/$10.56) × $10.32 = $6.40
	13	($6.55/$12.90) × $13.25 = $6.73	(13)	($6.55/$10.56) × $10.21 = $6.33
	14	($6.55/$12.90) × $13.37 = $6.79	(14)	($6.55/$10.56) × $10.09 = $6.26
	15	($6.55/$12.90) × $13.49 = $6.85	(15)	($6.55/$10.56) × $9.97 = $6.18
	>15	SER floats based on fixed $6.85 offer	>(15)	IDW may terminate agreement

[a]Percent change in Flextronics' share price. All changes in the offer price based on percent change from $11.73.

assume all, some, or none of the target's liabilities. The purchase price is paid directly to the target firm. A *stock purchase* involves the sale of the outstanding stock of the target to the buyer or its subsidiary by the target's shareholders. Unlike in an asset purchase, the purchase price in a stock purchase is paid to the target firm's shareholders. This is the biggest difference between the two methods, and has significant tax implications for the seller's shareholders (see Chapter 12).

A *statutory merger* involves the combination of the target with the buyer or a subsidiary formed to complete the merger. The corporation surviving the merger can be the buyer, the target, or the buyer's subsidiary. The assets and liabilities of the corporation that ceases to exist are merged into the surviving firm as a "matter of law" governed by the statutes of the state in which the combined businesses will be incorporated. State statutes typically address the percentage of total voting stock required for approval of the transaction, who is entitled to vote, how the votes are counted, and the rights of dissenting voters. In a statutory merger, dissenting or minority shareholders are required to sell their shares, although some state statutes grant them the right to be paid the appraised value of their shares. *Stock-for-stock* or *stock-for-assets* transactions represent alternatives to a merger. Table 11.5 highlights the primary advantages and disadvantages of these alternative forms of acquisition.

TABLE 11.5 Advantages and Disadvantages of Alternative Forms of Acquisition

Alternative Forms	Advantages	Disadvantages
Cash Purchase of Assets	*Buyer:* • Allows targeted purchase of assets • Asset write-up • May renegotiate union and benefits agreements in absence of successor clause[a] in labor agreement • May avoid need for shareholder approval • No minority shareholders *Seller:* • Maintains corporate existence and ownership of assets not acquired • Retains NOLs and tax credits	*Buyer:* • Lose NOLs[b] and tax credits • Lose rights to intellectual property • May require consents to assignment of contracts • Exposed to liabilities transferring with assets (e.g., warranty claims) • Subject to taxes on any gains resulting in asset write-up • Subject to lengthy documentation of assets in contract *Seller:* • Potential double-taxation if shell liquidated • Subject to state transfer taxes • Necessity of disposing of unwanted residual assets • Requires shareholder approval if substantially all of the firm's assets sold
Cash Purchase of Stock	*Buyer:* • Assets/liabilities transfer automatically • May avoid need to get consents to assignment for contracts • Less documentation • NOLs and tax credits pass to buyer • No state transfer taxes • May insulate from target liabilities if kept as subsidiary • No shareholder approval if funded by cash or debt • Enables circumvention of target's board in hostile tender offer *Seller:* • Liabilities generally pass to buyer • May receive favorable tax treatment if acquirer stock received in payment	*Buyer:* • Responsible for known and unknown liabilities • No asset write-up unless 338 election adopted by buyer and seller[c] • Union and employee benefit agreements do not terminate • Potential for minority shareholders[d] *Seller:* • Loss of NOLs and tax credits • Favorable tax treatment lost if buyer and seller adopt 338 election[c]
Statutory Merger	*Buyer:* • Flexible form of payment (stock, cash, or debt) • Assets and liabilities transfer automatically, without lengthy documentation • No state transfer taxes • No minority shareholders as shareholders required to tender shares (minority freeze-out) • May avoid shareholder approval	*Buyer:* • May have to pay dissenting shareholders' appraised value of stock • May be time consuming because of need for target shareholder and board approvals, which may delay closing

Continued

IV. DEAL-STRUCTURING AND FINANCING STRATEGIES

TABLE 11.5   Advantages and Disadvantages of Alternative Forms of Acquisition—Cont'd

Alternative Forms	Advantages	Disadvantages
Statutory Merger (cont'd)	*Seller:* • Favorable tax treatment if purchase price primarily in acquirer stock • Allows for continuing interest in combined companies • Flexible form of payment	*Seller:* • May be time consuming • Target firm often does not survive • May not qualify for favorable tax status
Stock-for-Stock Transaction	*Buyer:* • May operate target company as a subsidiary • See purchase of stock on previous page *Seller:* See purchase of stock on previous page	*Buyer:* • May postpone realization of synergies • See purchase of stock on previous page *Seller:* See purchase of stock earlier in this table
Stock-for-Assets Transaction	*Buyer:* • See purchase of assets on previous page *Seller:* See purchase of assets on previous page	*Buyer:* • May dilute buyer's ownership position • See purchase of assets on previous page *Seller:* See purchase of assets on previous page
Staged Transactions	• Provides greater strategic flexibility	• May postpone realization of synergies

[a] If the employer and union negotiated a "successor clause" into their collective bargaining agreement covering the workforce in the target firm, the terms of the agreement may still apply to the workforce of the new business.

[b] Net operating loss carryforwards or carrybacks.

[c] In Section 338 of the U.S. tax code, the acquirer in a purchase of 80% or more of the stock of the target may elect to treat the acquisition as if it were an acquisition of the target's assets. The seller must agree with the election.

[d] Minority shareholders in a subsidiary may be eliminated by a so-called "back-end" merger following the initial purchase of target stock. As a result of the merger, minority shareholders are required to abide by the majority vote of all shareholders and sell their shares to the acquirer. If the acquirer owns more than 90% of the target's shares, it may be able to use a short-form merger, which does not require any shareholder vote.

Purchase of Assets

In an asset purchase, a buyer acquires all rights a seller has to an asset for cash, stock, or some combination. Many state statutes require shareholder approval of a sale of "substantially all" of the target's assets. An asset purchase may be the most practical way to complete the transaction when the acquirer is interested only in a product line or division of the parent firm with multiple product lines or divisions that are not organized as separate legal subsidiaries. The seller retains ownership of the shares of stock of the business. The buyer must either create a new entity or use another existing business unit as the acquisition vehicle for the transaction. Only assets and liabilities specifically identified in the agreement of purchase and sale are transferred to the buyer.

In a *cash-for-assets* acquisition, the acquirer pays cash for the seller's assets and may choose to accept some or all of the seller's liabilities.[13] The seller shareholders must approve

[13] In cases where the buyer purchases most of the assets of a target firm, courts have ruled that the buyer is also responsible for the target's liabilities.

the transaction whenever the seller's board votes to sell all or "substantially all" of the firm's assets. For example, when Valero Oil and Gas purchased substantially all of the assets of bankrupt ethanol manufacturer VeraSun for $280 million in early 2009—five refineries and one under construction—it required VeraSun shareholder approval. Even though the purchase was fewer than half of VeraSun's total number of refineries, it represented about three-quarters of the firm's assets.[14]

When substantially all of the selling firm's assets are acquired, the selling firm's shares are extinguished if shareholders approve the liquidation of the firm. After paying for any liabilities that are not assumed by the buyer, the assets remaining with the seller and the cash received from the acquiring firm are transferred to the seller's shareholders in a liquidating distribution.

In a *stock-for-assets* transaction, once approved by the seller's board and shareholders, the seller's shareholders receive buyer stock in exchange for the seller's assets and assumed liabilities. In a second stage, the seller dissolves the corporation following shareholder ratification of such a move, leaving its shareholders with buyer stock. Consequently, the shareholders of the two firms have effectively pooled their ownership interests in the buyer's corporation, which holds the combined assets and liabilities of both firms.

Advantages and Disadvantages from the Buyer's Perspective

The *advantages* from the buyer's perspective include being selective as to which assets of the target to purchase. The buyer is generally not responsible for the seller's liabilities unless specifically assumed under the contract. However, the buyer can be held responsible for certain liabilities such as environmental claims, property taxes, and, in some states, substantial pension liabilities and product liability claims. To protect against such risks, buyers usually insist on *indemnification* that holds the seller responsible for payment of damages resulting from such claims. Of course, this is of value only as long as the seller remains solvent. Indemnification is explained in more detail later in this chapter.[15]

Another advantage is that asset purchases also enable buyers to revalue acquired assets to market value on the closing date under the purchase method of accounting (a form of financial reporting of business combinations detailed in the next chapter) This increase, or *step-up*, in the tax basis of the acquired assets to fair market value provides for higher depreciation and amortization expense deductions for tax purposes. Buyers are generally free of any undisclosed or contingent liabilities. Absent successor clauses in the contract, the asset purchase results in the termination of union agreements if less than 50% of the workforce in the

[14] Selling "substantially all" assets does not necessarily mean that most of the firm's assets have been sold; rather, it could refer to a relatively small percentage of the firm's total assets that are critical to the ongoing operation of the business. Hence, the firm may be forced to liquidate if a sale of assets does not leave the firm with "significant continuing business activity"—that is, at least 25% of total pretransaction operating assets and 25% of pretransaction income or revenue. Unless required by the firm's bylaws, the buyer's shareholders do not vote to approve the transaction.

[15] Note that in most agreements of purchase and sale, buyers and sellers agree to indemnify each other from claims for which they are directly responsible. Liability under such arrangements usually is subject to specific dollar limits and is in force only for a specific period.

new firm is unionized, thereby providing an opportunity to renegotiate agreements viewed as too restrictive. Benefits plans may be maintained or terminated at the acquirer's discretion. Buyers, though, may be reluctant to terminate contracts and benefits plans because of the potential undermining of employee productivity.

Even with all these advantages, there are still several *disadvantages* to a purchase of assets from the buyer's perspective. The buyer loses the seller's net operating losses and tax credits. Rights to assets such as licenses, franchises, and patents cannot be transferred to buyers. Such rights are viewed as belonging to the owners of the business: the target shareholders. These rights can be difficult to transfer because of the need to obtain consent from the U.S. Patent Office or other agency issuing the rights. The buyer must seek the consent of customers and vendors to transfer existing contracts to the buyer. The transaction often is more complex and costly, because acquired assets must be listed in appendices to the definitive agreement, the sale of and titles to each asset transferred must be recorded, and state title *transfer taxes* must be paid. Moreover, a lender's consent may be required if the assets to be sold are being used as collateral for loans.

The acquisition by Cadbury Schweppes plc (a confectionery and beverage company head-quartered in London, England) of Adams Inc. from Pfizer in 2003 illustrates the potential complexity of an asset purchase. Cadbury bought 100% of Adams' assets for $4.2 billion. Many Adams employees had positions with both the parent and the operating unit, and the parent supplied numerous support services to its subsidiary. Adams also operated in 40 countries, representing 40 different legal jurisdictions—quite typical in the purchase of a unit of a larger company, but no less complicated.

Advantages and Disadvantages from the Seller's Perspective

Among the *advantages*, sellers are able to maintain their corporate existence and thus ownership of tangible assets not acquired by the buyer and of intangible assets such as licenses, franchises, and patents. The seller retains the right to use the corporate identity in subsequent marketing programs unless ceded to the buyer as part of the transaction. The seller also retains the right to use all tax credits and accumulated net operating losses, which can be used to shelter future income from taxes. Such tax considerations remain with the holders of the target firm's stock.

The *disadvantages* for the seller include several issues related to taxes. Taxes also may be a problem because the seller may be subject to double taxation. If the tax basis in the assets or stock is low, the seller may experience a sizable gain on the sale. In addition, if the corporation subsequently is liquidated, the seller may be responsible for the recapture of taxes deferred as a result of the use of accelerated rather than straight-line depreciation. If the number of assets transferred is large, the amount of state transfer taxes may become onerous. Whether the seller or the buyer actually pays the transfer taxes or they are shared is negotiable. If substantially all of the target's assets are to be sold, approval must be obtained from the target's shareholders.

In late 2007, the largest banking deal in history was consummated through a purchase of the assets of one of Europe's largest financial services firms (see Case Study 11.2). The deal was made possible by a buyer group banding together to buy the firm after reaching agreement as to which of the target's assets would be owned by the each member of the consortium.

CASE STUDY 11.2
Buyer Consortium Wins Control of ABN Amro

The biggest banking deal on record was announced on October 9, 2007, resulting in the dismemberment of one of Europe's largest and oldest financial services firms, ABN Amro (ABN). A buyer consortium consisting of The Royal Bank of Scotland (RBS), Spain's Banco Santander (Santander), and Belgium's Fortis Bank (Fortis) won control of ABN, the largest bank in the Netherlands, in a buyout valued at $101 billion.

European banks had been under pressure to grow through acquisitions and compete with larger American rivals to avoid becoming takeover targets themselves. ABN had been viewed for years as a target because of its relatively low share price. However, rival banks were deterred by its diverse mixture of businesses, which was unattractive to any single buyer. Under pressure from shareholders, ABN announced that it had agreed, on April 23, 2007, to be acquired by Barclay's Bank of London for $85 billion in stock. The RBS-led group countered with a $99 billion bid consisting mostly of cash. In response, Barclay's upped its bid by 6% with the help of state-backed investors from China and Singapore. ABN's management favored the Barclay bid because Barclay had pledged to keep ABN Amro intact and its headquarters in the Netherlands. However, a declining stock market soon made the Barclay's mostly stock offer unattractive.

While the size of the transaction was noteworthy, the deal is especially remarkable in that the consortium had agreed prior to the purchase to split up ABN among the three participants. The mechanism used for acquiring the bank represented an unusual means of completing big transactions in the amidst of the subprime-mortgage-induced turmoil in the global credit markets at the time. The members of the consortium were able to select the ABN assets they found most attractive. The consortium agreed in advance of the acquisition that Santander would receive ABN's Brazilian and Italian units; Fortis would obtain the Dutch bank's consumer lending business, asset management, and private banking operations, and RBS would own the Asian and investment banking units. Merrill Lynch served as the sole investment advisor for the group's participants. Caught up in the global capital market meltdown, Fortis was forced to sell the ABN Amro assets it had acquired to its Dutch competitor ING in October 2008.

Discussion Questions

1. In your judgment, what are likely to be some of the major challenges in assembling a buyer consortium to acquire and subsequently dismember a target firm such as ABN Amro? In what ways do you think the use of a single investment advisor might have addressed some of these issues?

2. The ABN Amro transaction was completed at a time when the availability of credit was limited due to the subprime-mortgage-loan problem in the United States. How might the use of a group rather than a single buyer have facilitated the purchase of ABN Amro?

3. The same outcome could have been achieved if a single buyer had reached agreement with other banks to acquire selected pieces of ABN before completing the transaction. The pieces could then have been sold at the closing. Why might the use of the consortium been a superior alternative?

Answers to these questions are given in the Online Instructors' Guide for instructors using this textbook.

Purchase of Stock

Stock purchases often are viewed as the purchase of all of a target firm's outstanding stock. In effect, the buyer replaces the seller as owner, the business continues to operate without interruption, and the seller has no ongoing interest in, or obligation with respect to, the assets, liabilities, or operations of the business.

In *cash-for-stock* or *stock-for-stock* transactions, the buyer purchases the seller's stock directly from the seller's shareholders. If the target is a private firm, the purchase is completed by a stock purchase agreement signed by the acquirer and the target's shareholders, if they are few in number. For a public company, the acquiring firm making a tender offer to the target firm's shareholders would consummate the purchase. A tender offer is employed because public company shareholders are likely to be too numerous to deal with individually. The tender offer would be considered friendly or hostile depending on whether it was supported by the board and management of the target firm.

This is in marked contrast to a statutory merger, in which the boards of directors of the firms involved must first ratify the proposal before submitting it to their shareholders for approval. Consequently, a purchase of stock is the approach most often taken in hostile take-overs. If the buyer is unable to convince all of the seller's shareholders to tender their shares, then a minority of seller shareholders remains outstanding. The target firm would then be viewed not as a wholly-owned but rather as a partially owned subsidiary of the buyer or acquiring company. No seller shareholder approval is required in such transactions as the seller's shareholders are expressing approval by tendering their shares.

Advantages and Disadvantages from the Buyer's Perspective

When it comes to the purchase of stock, there are a number of *advantages* for the buyer. All assets are transferred with the target's stock, resulting in less need for documentation to complete the transaction. State asset transfer taxes may be avoided with a purchase of shares and net operating losses and tax credits pass to the buyer. The right of the buyer to use the target's name, licenses, franchises, patents, and permits also is preserved. Furthermore, the purchase of the seller's stock provides for the continuity of contracts and corporate identity, which obviates the need to renegotiate contracts and enables the acquirer to employ the brand recognition that may be associated with the name of the target firm. However, the consent of some customers and vendors may be required before a contract is transferred; this may apply as well to some permits.

While the acquirer's board normally approves any major acquisition, approval by shareholders is not required if the purchase is financed primarily with cash or debt. If stock that has not yet been authorized is used, shareholder approval is likely to be required. Neither the target's board nor shareholders need to approve a sale of stock; however, shareholders may simply refuse to sell their stock.

Among the *disadvantages*, the buyer is liable for all unknown, undisclosed, or contingent liabilities. The seller's tax basis is carried over to the buyer at historical cost;[16] consequently, there is no step-up in the cost basis of assets, and no tax shelter is created. Dissenting

---

[16] This is true unless the seller consents to take a 338 tax code election, which can create a tax liability for the seller. Consequently, such elections are used infrequently.

shareholders in many states have the right to have their shares appraised, with the option of being paid the appraised value of their shares or of remaining minority shareholders. The purchase of stock does not terminate existing union agreements or employee benefits plans.

The existence of minority shareholders creates significant administrative costs and practical concerns. The parent incurs significant additional expenses to submit annual reports, hold annual shareholder meetings, and conduct a formal board election process. Furthermore, implementing strategic business moves may be inhibited. See Case Studies 6.5 and 11.4 for an illustration of the challenges posed by minority investors.

Advantages and Disadvantages from the Seller's Perspective

Sellers generally prefer a stock purchase rather than an asset purchase because of its *advantages*. First, it allows them to step away from the business and be completely free of future obligations. The seller is able to defer paying taxes if the form of payment is primarily buyer stock. All obligations, disclosed or otherwise, transfer to the buyer.[17] Finally, the seller is not left with the problem of disposing of assets that the seller does not wish to retain but that were not purchased by the acquiring company.

There are, though, *disadvantages* for the seller. For instance, the seller cannot pick and choose the assets to be retained. Furthermore, the seller loses all net operating losses, tax credits, potential tax savings, and rights to intellectual property.

Mergers

When a *merger* is used to consummate the transaction, the legal structure may take one of many forms. In a merger, two or more firms combine, and all but one legally cease to exist. The combined organization continues under the original name of the surviving firm. Shareholders of the target firm exchange their shares for those of the acquiring firm after a shareholder vote approving the merger, with minority shareholders required to exchange their shares for acquirer shares.

Statutory and Subsidiary Mergers

In a *statutory merger*, the acquiring company assumes the assets and liabilities of the target in accordance with the statutes of the state in which the combined companies will be incorporated. A *subsidiary merger* involves the target becoming a subsidiary of the parent. To the public, the target firm may be operated under its brand name, but will be owned and controlled by the acquirer.

Most mergers are structured as subsidiary mergers in which the acquiring firm creates a new corporate subsidiary that merges with the target. By using a reverse triangular merger in which the target survives, the acquirer may be able to avoid seeking approval from its shareholders. While merger statutes require approval by shareholders of both the target and

---

[17] This advantage for the seller usually is attenuated by the buyer's insistence that it be indemnified from damages resulting from any undisclosed liability. However, as previously noted, indemnification clauses in contracts generally are in force for only a limited time.

acquiring firms, the parent of the acquisition subsidiary is the shareholder. Just as in a stock purchase, an assignment of contracts is generally not necessary because the target survives. In contrast, an assignment is required in a forward triangular merger because the target is merged into the subsidiary with the subsidiary surviving.

Statutory Consolidations

Although the terms *merger* and *consolidation* often are used interchangeably, this is not always accurate. Technically, a *statutory consolidation*, which involves two or more companies joining to form a new company, is not a merger. All legal entities that are consolidated are dissolved as the new company is formed, usually with a new name, whereas in a merger either the acquirer or the target survives. The new corporate entity created as a result of consolidation, or the surviving entity following a merger, usually assumes ownership of the assets and liabilities of the merged or consolidated organizations. Stockholders in merged companies typically exchange their shares for shares in the new company. The 1999 combination of Daimler-Benz and Chrysler to form DaimlerChrysler is an example of a consolidation.

Mergers of Equals

A *merger of equals* is a merger structure usually applied whenever the participants are comparable in size, competitive position, profitability, and market capitalization—which can make it unclear whether one party is ceding control to the other and which party provides the greatest synergy. Consequently, target firm shareholders rarely receive any significant premium for their shares. It is common for the new firm to be managed by the former CEOs of the merged firms as coequals and for the new firm's board to have equal representation from the boards of the merged firms.[18] In such transactions, it is relatively uncommon for the ownership split to be equally divided.[19] The 1998 formation of Citigroup from Citibank and Travelers is an example of a merger of equals.

Tender Offers

Tender offers refer to solicitations to buy stock. When a firm extends an offer to its own shareholders to buy back stock, it is called a *self-tender offer*. A *hostile tender offer* is a takeover tactic in which the acquirer bypasses the target's board and management and goes directly to the target's shareholders with an offer to purchase their shares. Unlike a merger, the tender offer specifically allows for minority shareholders to approve or deny the merger.

An alternative to a traditional merger, which accomplishes the same objective, is the *two-step acquisition*. In the first step, the acquirer buys, through a stock purchase, the majority of the target's outstanding stock from its shareholders in a tender offer and then follows up in a second step with a *squeeze-out merger* or *back-end merger* approved by the acquirer as the majority shareholder. Minority shareholders are required to take the acquisition into consideration

[18] Research by Wulf (2004) suggests that the CEOs of target firms often negotiate to retain a significant degree of control in the merged firm for both their board and management in exchange for a lower premium for their shareholders.

[19] According to Mallea (2008), only 14% have a 50/50 split.

in the back-end merger. Usually, minority shareholders are offered a lower price for their shares in the form of cash or debt. Two-step acquisitions sometimes are used to make it more difficult for another firm to make a bid because the merger can be completed quickly.

In March 2009, Merck Pharmaceuticals—seeking to close the deal quickly—acquired much smaller rival Schering-Plough through a two-step merger. Merck wanted to prevent a potential bidding war with Johnson & Johnson and the loss of profits from a joint venture Schering had with Johnson & Johnson. Merck was merged into Schering subsequent to closing. By positioning Schering as the acquirer, Merck wanted to avoid triggering a change of control provision in a longstanding drug distribution agreement between Johnson & Johnson and Schering, under which J&J would be able to cancel the agreement and take full ownership of the drugs (see Case Study 12.2).

In contrast, the Swiss pharmaceutical giant Roche reached agreement on March 12, 2009, to acquire the remaining 44% of Genentech it did not already own, but it was unable to employ the back-end merger approach. Roche was bound by an affiliation agreement between the two firms that governed prior joint business relationships. It required, in the event of a merger with Genentech, that Roche receive a favorable vote from the majority of the remaining Genentech shares it did not already own or offer the remaining Genentech shareholders a price equal to or greater than the average of fair values of such shares as determined by two investment banks appointed by the Genentech board of directors.

Share Loldus Approvals   *43 - 4²¹*

Board Approvals

Unlike purchases of target stock, mergers require approval of the acquirer's board and the target's board of directors and the subsequent submission of the proposal to the shareholders of both firms. Unless otherwise required by a firm's bylaws, a simple majority of all the outstanding voting shares must ratify the proposal. The merger agreement must then be filed with the appropriate authorities of the state in which the merger is to be consummated.

There are three exceptions under which no vote is required by the acquirer's (i.e., the surviving firm's) shareholders. The first, the so-called *small-scale merger exception*, involves a transaction not considered material. The acquiring firm's shareholder cannot vote unless their ownership in the acquiring firm is diluted by more than one-sixth or 16.67% (i.e., the acquirer owns at least 83.33% of the firm's voting shares following closing). This effectively limits the acquirer to issuing no more than 20% of its total shares outstanding.[20] The second is when a subsidiary is being merged into the parent and the parent owns a substantial majority (over 90% in some states) of the subsidiary's stock before the transaction. This is referred to as a *short-form merger* or the *parent-submerger exception*. The third exception involves use of a *triangular merger*, in which the acquirer establishes a merger subsidiary in which it is the sole shareholder; the only approval required is that of the board of directors of the subsidiary, which may be essentially the same as that of the parent or acquiring company. However, acquirer shareholders may still be required by the firm's bylaws to vote to authorize creation of new shares of stock offered in the transaction.

[20] For example, if the acquirer has 80 million shares outstanding and issues 16 million new shares (i.e., 0.2 × 80), its current shareholders are not diluted by more than one-sixth (i.e., 16/(16 + 80) equals one-sixth or 16.67%). More than 16 million new shares would violate the small-scale merger exception.

Staged Transactions

An acquiring firm may choose to complete a takeover of another firm in stages spread over an extended period of time. Staged transactions may be used to structure an earn-out, enable the target to complete the development of a technology or process, or await regulatory approval of a license or patent.

Special Applications of Basic Structures

The structures discussed previously are sufficiently flexible to accommodate a variety of different transaction types.

Leveraged Buyouts

In a *leveraged buyout* (LBO), a financial sponsor or equity investor, usually a limited partnership, creates a shell corporation funded by equity provided by the sponsor. In stage one, the shell corporation raises debt by borrowing from banks and selling debt to institutional investors. In the second stage, the shell corporation buys 50.1% of the target's stock, squeezing out minority shareholders with a back-end merger in which the remaining shareholders receive debt or preferred stock.

Single Firm Recapitalization

Firms sometimes recapitalize in order to squeeze out minority shareholders. A firm with minority shareholders creates a wholly-owned shell corporation and merges itself into the shell through a statutory merger. All stock in the original firm is canceled, with the majority shareholders in the original firm receiving stock in the surviving firm and minority shareholders receiving cash or debt.

SOME THINGS TO REMEMBER

The deal structuring process addresses satisfying as many of the primary objectives of the parties involved and determines how risk will be shared. The process begins with addressing a set of key questions, whose answers help define initial negotiating positions, potential risks, options for managing risk, levels of tolerance for risk, and conditions under which the buyer or seller will "walk away" from the negotiations.

As part of the deal structuring process, the acquisition vehicle refers to the legal structure used to purchase the target. The postclosing organization is the legal or organizational framework used to manage the combined businesses following the consummation of the transaction and may differ from the acquisition vehicle, depending on the acquirer's strategic objectives for the combined firms. The form of payment or total consideration may consist of cash, common stock, debt, or some combination. The form of acquisition refers to what is being acquired (stock or assets) and the mechanism for conveying ownership. The form of acquisition affects the form of payment, tax considerations, and the choice of acquisition vehicle and postclosing organization. Tax considerations also are affected by the legal structure of the selling entity. Finally, accounting considerations may affect the form, amount, and timing of payment.

DISCUSSION QUESTIONS

11.1 Describe the deal structuring process. Be specific.

11.2 Provide two examples of how decisions made in one area of the deal structuring process are likely to affect other areas.

11.3 For what reasons may acquirers choose a particular form of acquisition vehicle?

11.4 Describe techniques used to "close the gap" when buyers and sellers cannot agree on a price.

11.5 Why do bidders sometimes offer target firm shareholders multiple payment options (e.g., cash and stock)?

11.6 What are the advantages and disadvantages of a purchase of assets from the perspective of the buyer and seller?

11.7 What are the advantages and disadvantages of a purchase of stock from the perspective of the buyer and seller?

11.8 What are the advantages and disadvantages of a statutory merger?

11.9 What are the reasons some acquirers choose to undertake a staged or multistep takeover?

11.10 What forms of acquisition represent common alternatives to a merger? Under what circumstances might these alternative structures be employed?

11.11 Comment on the following statement: *A premium offered by a bidder over a target's share price is not necessarily a fair price; a fair price is not necessarily an adequate price.*

11.12 In early 2008, a year marked by turmoil in the global credit markets, Mars Corporation was able to negotiate a reverse breakup fee structure in its acquisition of Wrigley Corporation. This structure allowed Mars to walk away from the transaction at any time by paying a $1 billion fee to Wrigley. Speculate as to the motivation behind Mars and Wrigley negotiating such a fee structure.

11.13 Despite disturbing discoveries during due diligence, Mattel acquired The Learning Company, a leading developer of software for toys, in a stock-for-stock transaction valued at $3.5 billion. Mattel had determined that TLC's receivables were overstated because product returns from distributors were not deducted from receivables and its allowance for bad debt was inadequate. Also, a $50 million licensing deal also had been prematurely put on the balance sheet. Nevertheless, driven by the appeal of rapidly becoming a big player in the children's software market, Mattel closed on the transaction, aware that TLC's cash flows were overstated. Despite being aware of extensive problems, Mattel proceeded to acquire The Learning Company. Why? What could Mattel have done to better protect its interests? Be specific.

11.14 Describe the conditions under which an earn-out may be most appropriate.

11.15 In late 2008, Deutsche Bank announced that it would buy the commercial banking assets (including a number of branches) of the Netherlands' ABN Amro for $1.13 billion. What liabilities, if any, would Deutsche Bank have to (or want to) assume? Explain your answer.

Answers to these Chapter Discussion Questions are found in the Online Instructor's Manual for instructors using this book.

CHAPTER BUSINESS CASES

CASE STUDY 11.3
Boston Scientific Overcomes Johnson & Johnson to Acquire Guidant—A Lesson in Bidding Strategy

Johnson & Johnson, the behemoth American pharmaceutical company, announced an agreement in December 2004 to acquire Guidant for $76 per share for a combination of cash and stock. Guidant is a leading manufacturer of implantable heart defibrillators and other products used in angioplasty procedures. The defibrillator market has been growing at 20% annually, and J&J desired to reenergize its slowing growth rate by diversifying into this rapidly growing market. Soon after the agreement was signed, Guidant's defibrillators became embroiled in a regulatory scandal over failure to inform doctors about rare malfunctions. Guidant suffered a serious erosion of market share when it recalled five models of its defibrillators.

The subsequent erosion in the market value of Guidant prompted J&J to renegotiate the deal under a material adverse change clause common in most M&A agreements. J&J was able to get Guidant to accept a lower price of $63 per share in mid-November. However, this new agreement was not without risk.

The renegotiated agreement gave Boston Scientific an opportunity to intervene with a more attractive informal offer on December 5, 2005, of $72 per share. The offer price consisted of 50% stock and 50% cash. Boston Scientific, a leading supplier of heart stents, saw the proposed acquisition as a vital step in the company's strategy of diversifying into the high-growth implantable defibrillator market.

Despite the more favorable offer, Guidant's board decided to reject Boston Scientific's offer in favor of an upwardly revised offer of $71 per share made by J&J on January 11, 2005. The board continued to support J&J's lower bid, despite the furor it caused among big Guidant shareholders. With a market capitalization nine times the size of Boston Scientific, the Guidant board continued to be enamored with J&J's size and industry position relative to Boston Scientific.

Boston Scientific realized that it would be able to acquire Guidant only if it made an offer that Guidant could not refuse without risking major shareholder lawsuits. Boston Scientific reasoned that if J&J hoped to match an improved bid, it would have to be at least $77, slightly higher than the $76 J&J had initially offered Guidant in December 2004. With its greater borrowing capacity, Boston Scientific knew that J&J also had the option of converting its combination stock and cash bid to an all-cash offer. Such an offer could be made a few dollars lower than Boston Scientific's bid, since Guidant investors might view such an offer more favorably than one consisting of both stock and cash, whose value could fluctuate between the signing of the agreement and the actual closing. This was indeed a possibility, since the J&J offer did not include a collar arrangement.

Boston Scientific decided to boost the new bid to $80 per share, which it believed would deter any further bidding from J&J. J&J had been saying publicly that Guidant was already "fully valued." Boston Scientific reasoned that J&J had created a public relations nightmare for itself. If J&J raised its bid, it would upset J&J shareholders and make it look like an undisciplined buyer. J&J refused to up its offer, saying

CASE STUDY 11.3   *(cont'd)*

TABLE 11.6   Boston Scientific and Johnson & Johnson Bidding Chronology

Date	Comments
December 15, 2004	J&J reaches agreement to buy Guidant for $25.4 billion in stock and cash.
November 15, 2005	Value of J&J deal is revised downward to $21.5 billion.
December 5, 2005	Boston Scientific offers $25 billion.
January 11, 2006	Guidant accepts a J&J counteroffer valued at $23.2 billion.
January 17, 2006	Boston Scientific submits a new bid valued at $27 billion.
January 25, 2006	Guidant accepts Boston Scientific's bid when J&J fails to raise its offer.

that such an action would not be in the best interests of its shareholders. Table 11.6 summarizes the key events timeline.

A side deal with Abbott Labs made the lofty Boston Scientific offer possible. The firm entered into an agreement with Abbott Laboratories in which Boston Scientific would divest Guidant's stent business while retaining the rights to Guidant's stent technology. In return, Boston Scientific received $6.4 billion in cash on the closing date, consisting of $4.1 billion for the divested assets, a loan of $900 million, and Abbott's purchase of $1.4 billion of Boston Scientific stock. The additional cash helped fund the purchase price. This deal also helped Boston Scientific gain regulatory approval by enabling Abbott Labs to become a competitor in the stent business. Merrill Lynch and Bank of America each would lend $7 billion to fund a portion of the purchase price and provide the combined firms with additional working capital.

To complete the transaction, Boston Scientific paid $27 billion, consisting of cash and stock, to Guidant shareholders and another $800 million as a breakup fee to J&J. In addition, the firm is burdened with $14.9 billion in new debt. Within days of Boston Scientific's

winning bid, the firm received a warning from the U.S. Food and Drug Administration to delay the introduction of new products until the firm's safety procedures improved.

Between December 2004, the date of Guidant's original agreement with J&J, and January 25, 2006, the date of its agreement with Boston Scientific, Guidant's stock rose by 16%, reflecting the bidding process. During the same period, J&J's stock dropped by a modest 3%, while Boston Scientific's shares plummeted by 32%.

As a result of product recalls and safety warnings on more than 50,000 of Guidant's cardiac devices, the firm's sales and profits plummeted. Between the announcement date of its purchase of Guidant in December 2005 and year-end 2006, Boston Scientific lost more than $18 billion in shareholder value. In acquiring Guidant, Boston Scientific increased its total shares outstanding by more than 80% and assumed responsibility for $6.5 billion in debt, with no proportionate increase in earnings. In early 2010, major senior management changes occurred at Boston Scientific and it spun off several business units in an effort to improve profitability. Ongoing defibrillator recalls could shave the firm's revenue by

CASE STUDY 11.3   *(cont'd)*

$0.5 billion during the next two years.[21] In 2010, continuing product-related problems forced the firm to write off $1.8 billion in impaired goodwill associated with the Guidant acquisition. At less than $8 per share throughout most of 2010, Boston Scientific's share price is about one-fifth of its peak of $35.55 on December 5, 2005, the day the firm announced its bid for Guidant.

Discussion Questions

1. What were the key differences between the two firms' bidding strategies? Be specific.

2. What might J&J have done differently to avoid igniting a bidding war?
3. What evidence is given that J&J may not have seen Boston Scientific as a serious bidder?
4. Explain how differing assumptions about market growth, potential synergies, and the size of the potential liability related to product recalls affected the bidding.

Answers to these questions are provided in the Online Instructor's Manual for instructors using this book.

CASE STUDY 11.4
Swiss Pharmaceutical Giant Novartis Takes Control of Alcon

In December 2010, Swiss pharmaceutical company Novartis AG completed its drawn-out effort to acquire the remaining 23% of U.S.-listed eye care group Alcon Incorporated (Alcon) that it did not already own for $12.9 billion. This brought the total purchase price for 100% of Alcon to $52.2 billion. Novartis had been trying to purchase Alcon's remaining publicly traded shares since January 2010, but its original offer of 2.8 Novartis shares, valued at $153 per Alcon share met stiff resistance from Alcon's independent board of directors, which had repeatedly dismissed the Novartis bid as "grossly inadequate."

Novartis finally relented, agreeing to pay $168 per share, the average price it had paid for the Alcon shares it already owned, and

to guarantee that price by paying cash equal to the difference between $168 and the value of 2.8 Novartis shares immediately prior to closing. If the value of Novartis shares were to appreciate before closing such that the value of 2.8 shares exceeded $168, the number of Novartis shares would be reduced accordingly. By acquiring all outstanding Alcon shares, Novartis avoided any interference by minority shareholders in making major business decisions, achieved certain operating synergies, and eliminated the expense associated with having public shareholders.

In 2008, a year in which global financial markets were in turmoil due to the worst global recession since the 1930s, Novartis acquired only a minority position in global food giant Nestlé's wholly-owned subsidiary

---

[21] *Source:* The Street.com, Boston Scientific's Cash Crunch, April 1, 2010.

CASE STUDY 11.4   *(cont'd)*

Alcon for cash. Nestlé had acquired 100% of Alcon in 1978 and retained that position until 2002, when it undertook an initial public offering of 23% of its shares. In April 2008, Novartis acquired 25% of Alcon for $143 per share from Nestlé. As part of this transaction, Novartis and Nestlé received a call and a put option, respectively, which could be exercised at $181 per Alcon share from January 2010 to July 2011.

On January 4, 2010, Novartis exercised its call option to buy Nestlé's remaining 52% ownership stake in Alcon that it did not already own. By doing so, Novartis increased its total ownership position in Alcon to about 77%. The total price paid by Novartis for this position amounted to $39.3 billion ($11.2 billion in 2008 plus $28.1 billion in 2010). On the same day, Novartis also offered to acquire the remaining publicly held shares that it did not already own in a share exchange valued at $153 per share in which 2.8 shares of its stock would be exchanged for each Alcon share.

While the Nestlé deal seemed likely to receive regulatory approval, the offer to the minority shareholders was assailed immediately as too low. At $153 per share, the offer was well below the Alcon closing price on January 4, 2010, of $164.35. The Alcon publicly traded share price may have been elevated by investors anticipating a higher bid. Novartis argued that without this speculation the publicly traded Alcon share price would have been $137, and the $153 per share price Novartis offered the minority shareholders would have represented an approximate 12% premium to that price. The minority shareholders, who included several large hedge funds, argued that they were entitled

to $181 per share, the amount paid to Nestlé. Alcon's publicly traded shares dropped nearly 5% to $156.97 on the news of the Novartis takeover. Novartis' shares also lost 3%, falling to $52.81.

On August 9, 2010, Novartis received approval from European Union regulators to buy the stake in Alcon, making it easier for it to take full control of Alcon. The acquisition's approval was conditioned on Novartis divesting several ophthalmology and pharmaceutical products sold in the EU's consumer vision care market. The transaction had also received approval from the Canadian and Australian antitrust regulators pending certain divestitures by Novartis in their countries. The last required regulatory approval was received on October 1, 2010, when the U.S. Federal Trade Commission approved the deal.

With the buyout of Nestlé's stake in Alcon completed, Novartis was now faced with acquiring the remaining 23% of the outstanding shares of Alcon stock held by the public. Under Swiss takeover law, Novartis needed a majority of Alcon board members and two-thirds of shareholders to approve the terms for the merger to take effect and for Alcon shares to automatically convert into Novartis shares. Once it owned 77% of Alcon's stock, Novartis only needed to place five of its own nominated directors on the Alcon board to replace the five directors previously named by Nestlé to the board.

However, Alcon's independent directors set up an independent director committee (IDC), arguing that the price offered to the minority shareholders was too low and that the new directors, having been nominated by Novartis,

CASE STUDY 11.4 (cont'd)

should abstain from voting on the Novartis takeover because of their conflict of interest. The IDC preferred a negotiated merger to a "cram down" or forced merger in which the minority shares automatically convert to Novartis shares at the 2.8 share exchange offer.

Provisions in the Swiss takeover code require a mandatory offer whenever a bidder purchases more than 33.3% of another firm's stock. In a mandatory offer, Novartis would also be subject to the Swiss code's minimum bid rule, which would require Novartis to pay $181 per share in cash to Alcon's minority shareholders, the same bid offered to Nestlé. By replacing the Nestlé-appointed directors with their own slate of candidates and owning more than two-thirds of the Alcon shares, Novartis argued that they were not subject to mandatory bid requirements.

Novartis was betting on the continued appreciation of its shares, valued in Swiss francs, due to an ongoing appreciation of the Swiss currency and its improving operating performance, to eventually win over holders of the publicly traded Alcon shares. However, by late 2010, Novartis' patience appears to have worn thin. While not always the case, the resistance of the independent directors paid off for those investors holding publicly traded shares.

Discussion Questions

1. Speculate as to why Novartis acquired only a 25% ownership stake in Alcon in 2008.
2. Why was the price ($181 per share) at which Novartis exercised its call option in 2010 to increase its stake in Alcon to 77% so much higher than what it paid ($143 per share) for an approximate 25% stake in Alcon in early 2008?
3. Alcon and Novartis shares dropped by 5% and 3%, respectively, immediately following the announcement that Novartis would exercise its option to buy Nestlé's majority holdings of Alcon shares. Explain why this may have happened.
4. How do Swiss takeover laws compare to comparable U.S. laws? Which do you find more appropriate and why?
5. Discuss how Novartis may have arrived at the estimate of $137 per share as the intrinsic value of Alcon shares. What are the key underlying assumptions? Do you believe the minority shareholders should receive the same price as Nestlé? Explain your answer.

Answers to these case study discussion questions are available in the Online Instructor's Manual for instructors using this book.

12

Structuring the Deal
Tax and Accounting Considerations

In matters of style, swim with the current. In matters of principle, stand like a rock. —**Thomas** ✱
Jefferson

INSIDE M&A: CONTINUED CONSOLIDATION IN THE GENERIC PHARMACEUTICALS INDUSTRY

Teva Pharmaceutical Industries, a manufacturer and distributor of generic drugs, completed its takeover of Ivax Corp for $7.4 billion in early 2006 to become the world's largest manufacturer of generic drugs. For Teva, based in Israel, and Ivax, headquartered in Miami, the merger eliminated a large competitor and created a distribution chain that spans 50 countries.

To broaden the appeal of the proposed merger, Teva offered Ivax shareholders the option to receive for each of their shares either 0.8471 of American depository receipts (ADRs) representing Teva shares or $26 in cash. ADRs represent the receipt given to U.S. investors for the shares of a foreign-based corporation held in the vault of a U.S. bank. Ivax shareholders wanting immediate liquidity chose to exchange their shares for cash, while those wanting to participate in future appreciation of Teva stock exchanged their shares for Teva shares.

Following the merger, each previously outstanding share of Ivax common stock was canceled. Each canceled share represented the right to receive either of these two previously mentioned payment options. The merger agreement also provided for the acquisition of Ivax by Teva through a merger of Merger Sub, a newly formed and wholly-owned subsidiary of Teva, into Ivax. As the surviving corporation, Ivax would be a wholly-owned subsidiary of Teva. The merger involving the exchange of Teva ADRs for Ivax shares was considered as tax-free under U.S. law.

CHAPTER OVERVIEW

While Chapter 11 discussed in detail the first five components of the process, this chapter focuses on the implications of tax and accounting considerations for the deal structuring process. Taxes are an important consideration in almost any transaction, but they seldom are the

TABLE 12.1   Alternative Taxable and Nontaxable Structures

Taxable Transactions: Immediately Taxable to Target Shareholders	Nontaxable Transactions: Tax Deferred to Target Shareholders

1. Purchase of assets with cash
2. Purchase of stock with cash
3. Statutory cash mergers and consolidations
   a. Direct merger (stock-for-assets)
   b. Forward triangular merger (stock-for-assets)
   c. Reverse triangular merger (stock-for-stock)
	1. Type "A" reorganization (stock-for-assets)
	   a. Statutory stock merger or consolidation
	   b. Forward triangular merger
	   c. Reverse triangular merger
	2. Type "B" reorganization (stock-for-stock)
	3. Type "C" reorganization (stock-for-assets)
	4. Type "D" divisive merger

primary motivation for an acquisition. The fundamental economics of the transaction should always be the deciding factor, and any tax benefits simply reinforce a purchase decision.

Furthermore, recent changes in accounting standards requiring more immediate recognition of changes in the value of acquired assets could have the effect of making acquirers more disciplined in what they are willing to pay for other firms. By substantially overpaying for acquisitions, acquirers condemn themselves to having to improve profitability dramatically to earn the financial returns required by investors. If they have significantly overestimated potential synergy, they will be unable to realize these returns.

A review of this chapter (including practice questions and answers) is available in the file folder entitled "Student Study Guide" on the companion site to this book (*www.elsevierdirect.com/companions/9780123854858*). The companion site also contains a Learning Interactions Library, which gives students the opportunity to test their knowledge of this chapter in a "real-time" environment.[1]

GENERAL TAX CONSIDERATIONS AND ISSUES

The requirement to pay taxes creates a daunting array of choices for the parties to the transaction. Table 12.1 summarizes the most commonly used taxable and tax-free structures, including both statutory mergers (two-party transactions) and triangular mergers (three-party transactions). The implications of these alternative structures are explored in detail in the following sections.

TAXABLE TRANSACTIONS

A transaction generally will be considered taxable to the target firm's shareholders if it involves the purchase of the target's stock or assets for substantially all cash, notes, or some other nonequity consideration. Using the term *cash* or *boot* to represent all forms of payment other than equity, taxable transactions may take the form of a cash purchase of target assets, a

---

[1] See Stickney, Brown, and Wahlen (2007) for an excellent discussion of financial reporting and statements analysis. See Carrington (2007) for an in-depth discussion of tax accounting for mergers and acquisitions.

cash purchase of target stock, or a statutory cash merger or consolidation, which commonly includes direct cash mergers and triangular forward and reverse cash mergers.

Taxable Mergers

In a direct cash merger, the acquirer and target boards reach a negotiated settlement, and both firms receive approval from their respective shareholders. The target is then merged into the acquirer or the acquirer into the target, with only one surviving. In a consolidation, the acquirer and the target are merged into a third legal entity, with that entity surviving. Assets and liabilities on and off the balance sheet automatically transfer to the surviving firm in a direct statutory merger or consolidation.

In an effort to protect themselves from target liabilities, acquirers often employ so-called triangular mergers. In a triangular cash merger, the target firm may be merged into an acquirer's operating or shell acquisition subsidiary, with the subsidiary surviving (called a forward triangular cash merger), or the acquirer's subsidiary is merged into the target firm, with the target surviving (called a reverse triangular cash merger). Direct cash mergers and forward triangular mergers (Figure 12.1) are treated as a taxable purchase of assets with cash and reverse triangular mergers (Figure 12.2) as a taxable purchase of stock with cash. The tax consequences of these transactions are discussed in the following sections.

Taxable Purchase of Target Assets with Cash

If a transaction involves a cash purchase of target assets, which may involve none, some, or all of the target's liabilities, the target company's tax cost or basis in the acquired assets is increased or "stepped up" to its fair market value (FMV), which is equal to the purchase price (including any assumed liabilities) paid by the acquirer. The additional depreciation in future years reduces the present value of the tax liability of the combined companies. The target firm realizes an immediate gain or loss on assets sold equal to the difference

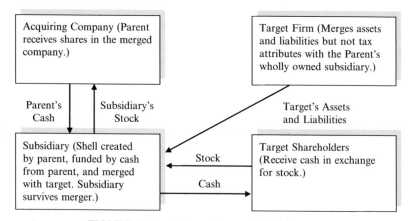

FIGURE 12.1   A forward triangular cash merger.

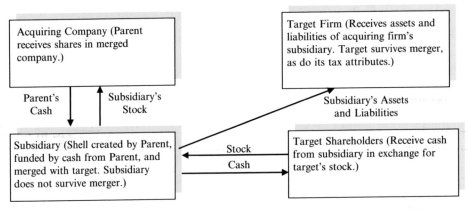

FIGURE 12.2   A reverse triangular cash merger.

between the FMV of the asset and the asset's adjusted tax basis (i.e., book value less accumulated depreciation).

The IRS views transactions resulting in the liquidation of the target firm as actual sales rather than reorganizations in which the target shareholders have an ongoing interest in the combined firms. Consequently, the target's tax attributes, such as net operating loss carryforwards and carrybacks, capital loss carryovers, and excess credit carryovers, may not be used by the acquirer following closing because they cease to exist along with the target. However, they may be used to offset any gain realized by the target resulting from the sale of its assets.

The target's shareholders could be taxed twice—once when the firm pays taxes on any gains and again when the proceeds from the sale are paid to the shareholders either as a dividend or distribution following liquidation of the corporation. A liquidation of the target firm may occur if a buyer acquires enough of the assets of the target to cause it to cease operations. To compensate the target company shareholders for any tax liability they may incur, the buyer usually will have to increase the purchase price.[2]

There is little empirical evidence that the tax shelter resulting from the ability of the acquiring firm to increase the value of acquired assets to their FMV is a highly important motivating factor for a takeover.[3] However, taxable transactions have become somewhat more attractive to acquiring firms since 1993, when a change in legislation allowed acquirers to amortize certain intangible assets for tax purposes.[4]

---

[2] Ayers, Lefanowicz, and Robinson, 2003

[3] Auerbach and Reishus, 1988

[4] Assets must qualify under Section 197 of the Internal Revenue Service Code. Such assets include goodwill, going concern value, books and records, customer lists, licenses, permits, franchises, and trademarks. A "197" intangible must be amortized over 15 years for tax purposes. Moreover, the current tax code allows operating losses (including those resulting from the write-down of impaired goodwill) to be used to recover taxes paid in the preceding two years and to reduce future tax liabilities up to 20 years.

Taxable Purchase of Target Stock with Cash

Taxable transactions often involve the purchase of the target's voting stock, with the acquirer initiating a tender offer for the target's outstanding shares, because the purchase of assets automatically triggers a tax on any gain on the sale and another tax on any payment of the after-tax proceeds to shareholders. In contrast, taxable stock purchases avoid double taxation because the transaction takes place between the acquirer and the target firm's shareholders. Target shareholders may realize a gain or loss on the sale of their stock.

The target firm does not revalue its assets and liabilities for tax purposes to reflect the amount that the acquirer paid for the shares of common stock. Rather, the values of the target's assets and liabilities before the acquisition (i.e., tax basis) are consolidated with the acquirer's financial statements following the acquisition; that is, the historical tax basis of the assets continues, and no step-up or increase in the basis of the assets occurs. The buyer loses the additional tax savings that would result from acquiring assets and writing them up to fair market value. Consequently, the buyer may want to reduce what it is willing to pay to the seller. Furthermore, since from the IRS' viewpoint the target firm continues to exist, the target's tax attributes carry over to the acquirer following the transaction, but their use may be limited by Sections 382 and 383 of the Internal Revenue Service Code (see the section of this chapter entitled "Treatment of Target Tax Attributes in M&A Deals" for more details). Table 12.2 summarizes the key characteristics of the various forms of taxable transactions.

Section 338 Election

Section 338 elections are made in connection with a taxable stock sale and apply to C corporations. The acquirer and target firms can jointly elect Section 338 of the Internal Revenue Code and thereby record assets and liabilities at their fair market value for tax purposes. This allows a purchaser of 80% or more of the voting stock and market value of the target to treat the acquisition of stock as if it were an acquisition of assets for tax purposes. The target's tax basis in the net acquired assets are increased to their fair market value and carryover to the buyer when the transaction is completed (i.e., the tax basis to the buyer is the same as for the target). Benefits to the acquirer include the avoidance of having to transfer assets and obtain consents to assignment of all contracts (as would be required in a direct purchase of assets), while still benefiting from the write-up of assets. Asset transfer, sales, and use taxes may also be avoided. Since the tax basis in the target's net acquired assets is increased to reflect the purchase price paid, the acquiring firm must pay the taxes on any gain on the sale.[5] Of course, for legal purposes, the sale of the target stock under a 338 election as an asset sale still is treated as a purchase of stock by the buyer. Consequently, the buyer remains responsible for the target's known and unknown liabilities

Section 338 elections are relatively rare because the additional tax liability triggered by the transaction often exceeds the present value of the tax savings from the step-up in the tax basis

---

[5] For Section 338(h)(10) elections that apply to acquisitions of corporate subsidiaries or S corporations, the seller bears any incremental tax cost from the stock sale, which is treated as an asset sale for tax purposes, and the selling firm's shareholders may demand a higher purchase price to compensate them for the increased tax liability.

TABLE 12.2 Key Characteristics of Alternative Taxable (to Target Shareholders) Transaction Structures

Transaction Structure	Form of Payment	Acquirer Retains Tax Attributes of Target	Target Survives?	Parent Exposure to Target Liabilities	Shareholder Vote Required? Acquirer	Shareholder Vote Required? Target	Minority Freeze Out?	Automatic Transfer of Contracts?[b]
Cash Purchase of Stock	Mostly cash, debt, or other nonequity payment	Yes, assuming no asset step-up due to 338 election[a]	Yes	High	No[d]	No, but shareholders may not sell shares	No	Yes
Cash Purchase of Assets	Mostly cash, debt, other nonequity payment	No, but can step up assets	Perhaps[c]	Low, except for assumed liabilities	No[d]	Yes, if sale of assets is substantial	No minority created	No
Statutory Cash Merger or Consolidation	Mostly cash, debt, or other nonequity payment	Yes, but no step up in assets	No, if target merged into acquirer	High, if target merged into acquirer	Yes	Yes	Yes[e]	Yes
Forward Triangular Cash Merger (IRS views as asset purchase)	Mostly cash, debt, or other nonequity payment	No, but can step up assets	No	Low—limited by subsidiary relationship	No[d]	Yes	Yes	No
Reverse Triangular Cash Merger (IRS views as stock purchase)	Mostly cash, debt, or other nonequity payment	Yes	Yes	Low—limited by subsidiary	No[d]	Yes	Yes	Yes

[a] An acquirer may treat a stock purchase as an asset purchase if it and the target agree to invoke a Section 338 election. Such an election would allow a step-up in net acquired assets and result in the loss of the target's tax attributes.

[b] Contracts, leases, licenses, and rights to intellectual property automatically transfer unless contracts stipulate consent to assignment required.

[c] The target may choose to liquidate if the sale of assets is substantial and to distribute the proceeds to its shareholders or to continue as a shell.

[d] May be required by public stock exchanges or by legal counsel if deemed material to the acquiring firm or if the parent needs to authorize new stock to pay for the acquisition and requires shareholder approval.

[e] Target shareholders must accept terms due to merger, although in some states dissident shareholders have appraisal rights for their shares.

of the net acquired assets. Generally, a 338 election is most advantageous when the target has substantial net operating losses (NOLs) or tax credit carryovers that the acquirer can use to offset any taxable gain triggered by the transaction. As explained in more detail in the section discussing the tax treatment of target firm tax attributes, these NOLs, capital loss, and tax credit carryforwards are only available for use in reducing the immediate tax liability and do not survive the acquisition if the target firm is liquidated.

In buying Bresnan Communications, Cablevision Systems used the combination of a share repurchase of its stock and tax benefits associated with the acquisition to gain support from its shareholders for the acquisition (see Case Study 12.1).

CASE STUDY 12.1
Cablevision Uses Tax Benefits to Help Justify the Price Paid for Bresnan Communications

During mid-2010, Cablevision Systems announced that it had reached an agreement to buy privately owned Bresnan Communications for $1.37 billion in a cash for stock deal. CVS's motivation for the deal reflected the board's belief that the firm's shares were undervalued and their desire to expand coverage into the western United States.

CVS is the most profitable cable operator in the industry in terms of operating profit margins, due primarily to the firm's heavily concentrated customer base in the New York City area. Critics immediately expressed concern that the acquisition would provide few immediate cost savings and relied almost totally on increasing the amount of revenue generated by Bresnan's existing customers.

CVS saw an opportunity to gain market share from satellite TV operators providing services in BC's primary geographic market. Bresnan, the nation's 13th largest cable operator, serves Colorado, Montana, Wyoming, and Utah. CVS believes it can sell bundles of services, including Internet and phone services, to current Bresnan customers. Bresnan's primary competition comes from DirecTV and DISH Network, which cannot offer phone and Internet access services.

To gain shareholder support, Cablevision Systems announced a $500 million share repurchase to placate shareholders seeking a return of cash. The deal was financed by a $1 billion nonrecourse loan and $370 million in cash from Cablevision. CVS points out that the firm's direct investment in BC will be more than offset by tax benefits resulting from the structure of the deal in which both Cablevision and Bresnan agreed to treat the purchase of Bresnan's stock as an asset purchase for tax reporting purposes (i.e., a 338 election). Consequently, CVS will be able to write up the net acquired Bresnan assets to their fair market value and use the resulting additional depreciation to generate significant future tax savings. Such future tax savings are estimated by CVS to have a net present value of approximately $400 million

Discussion Questions:
1. How is the 338 election likely to impact Cablevision System's earnings per share immediately following closing? Why?
2. As an analyst, how would you determine the impact of the anticipated tax benefits on the value of the firm?
3. What is the primary risk to realizing the full value of the anticipated tax benefits?

TAX-FREE TRANSACTIONS

As a general rule, a transaction is tax-free if the form of payment is primarily the acquirer's stock. Transactions may be partially taxable if the target shareholders receive some nonequity consideration, such as cash or debt, in addition to the acquirer's stock. This nonequity consideration, or *boot*, generally is taxable as ordinary income.

Acquirers and targets planning to enter into a tax-free transaction will frequently seek to get an *advance ruling* from the IRS to determine its tax-free status, which is formal and binding. However, the certainty of the formal letter may diminish if any of the key assumptions underlying the transaction change prior to closing. Moreover, the process of requesting and receiving a letter may take five or six months. Alternatively, acquirers may rely on the opinion of legal counsel.

If the transaction is tax-free, the acquiring company is able to transfer or carry over the target's tax basis to its own financial statements. There is no increase or step-up in assets to fair market value. A tax-free reorganization envisions the acquisition of all or substantially all of a target company's assets or shares, making tax-free structures unsuitable for the acquisition of a division within a corporation.

Qualifying a Transaction for Tax-Free Treatment

According to the Internal Revenue Code Section 368, for a transaction to qualify as tax-free, it must provide for continuity of ownership interest, continuity of business enterprise, a valid business purpose, and satisfy the *step-transaction doctrine*. Tax-free transactions require substantial continuing involvement of the target company's shareholders. To demonstrate *continuity of ownership interests*, target shareholders must continue to own a substantial part of the value of the combined target and acquiring firms. To demonstrate *continuity of business enterprise*, the acquiring corporation must either continue the acquired firm's "historic business enterprise" or use a significant portion of the target's "historic business assets" in a business.[6] This continued involvement is intended to demonstrate a long-term commitment on the part of the acquiring company to the target. To meet the continuity of business enterprise requirement, an acquirer must buy "substantially all" of the assets of the target firm. Furthermore, the transaction must demonstrate a valid business purpose, such as maximizing the profits of the acquiring corporation, rather than only be for tax avoidance. Finally, under the step-transaction doctrine, the deal cannot be part of a larger plan that would have constituted a taxable transaction.

Nontaxable or tax-free transactions usually involve mergers, with the acquirer's stock exchanged for the target's stock or assets. Nontaxable transactions also are called *tax-free reorganizations*. The continuity of ownership interests and business enterprise requirements

---

[6] The IRS is vague about exactly how it is determined that these criteria are being met. The acquirer must purchase the assets that are key to continuing the operation of the target's business, but such assets may not necessarily represent a majority of the target's total assets. However, acquirers often purchase at least 80% of the target's assets to ensure that they are in compliance with IRS guidelines.

serve to prevent transactions that more closely resemble a sale from qualifying as a tax-free reorganization.[7]

Alternative Tax-Free Reorganizations

Section 368 of the Internal Revenue Code covers eight principal forms of tax-free reorganizations. Of these, the most common include type "A" Reorganizations (statutory merger or consolidation, forward triangular mergers, and reverse triangular mergers), type "B" reorganizations (stock-for-stock acquisitions), and type "C" reorganizations (stock-for-assets acquisitions). Type "D" reorganizations may be applied to acquisitions or restructuring. An acquisitive type D reorganization requires that the acquiring firm receive at least 80% of the stock in the target firm in exchange for the acquirer's voting stock. Divisive type D reorganizations are used in spin-offs, split-offs, and split-ups, which are discussed in detail in Chapter 15.

Nontaxable "A" reorganizations involve one corporation acquiring the assets of another in exchange for acquirer stock, cash, and other consideration. A type "B" reorganizations involve one corporation acquiring the stock of another in exchange *solely* for acquirer voting stock. C reorganizations involve one corporation acquiring "substantially all" of the assets of another in exchange for acquirer voting stock. Finally, divisive "D" reorganizations involve a corporation transferring all or some of its assets to a subsidiary it controls in exchange for subsidiary stock or securities. The remaining tax-free reorganizations contained in Section 368 are less common and are not discussed in this book.

A *type A statutory merger or consolidation* does not limit the type of consideration involved in the transaction: Target company shareholders may receive cash, voting or nonvoting common or preferred stock, notes, or real property. Nor must target shareholders all be treated equally: Some may receive all stock, others all cash, and others a combination of the two. The acquirer may choose not to purchase all of the target's assets; the deal could be structured so as to permit the target to exclude certain assets from the transaction. Unlike a direct statutory merger in which all known and unknown target assets and liabilities transfer to the buyer by law, a subsidiary merger often results in the buyer acquiring only a majority interest in the target and then carrying the target as a subsidiary of the parent. The target may later be merged into the parent in a back-end merger (discussed in Chapter 11). To ensure that the target does not resemble an actual sale (thereby making the transaction taxable), at least 50% of the purchase price must be acquiring company stock to satisfy the IRS continuity of ownership interests requirement, although in some instances the figure may be as low as 40%.

Type A reorganizations are used widely because of their great flexibility. Because there is no requirement to utilize voting stock, acquiring firms enjoy more options. By issuing nonvoting stock, the acquiring corporation may acquire control of the target without diluting control of the combined or newly created company. Additional flexibility results from the buyer being able to acquire less than 100% of the target's net assets. Finally, there is no maximum

---

[7] An acquirer could merge with another firm in a tax-free transaction and immediately following closing sell the assets acquired in the tax-free transaction. The acquirer's basis in the assets would reflect their fair market value (i.e., the purchase price paid for the assets), and if the assets were resold, there would not be any taxable gain on the sale. Therefore, no taxes would have been paid on either transaction.

amount of cash that may be used in the purchase price, and the limitations articulated by both the IRS and the courts allow significantly more cash than type B and C reorganizations. In fact, this flexibility with respect to cash may be the most important consideration because it enables the acquirer to better satisfy the disparate requirements of the target's shareholders. Some will want cash, and some will want stock.

With a *type A forward triangular stock merger*, the parent funds the shell corporation by buying stock issued by the shell with its own stock (Figure 12.3). All of the target's stock is acquired by the subsidiary with the parent's stock, the target's stock is canceled, the acquirer subsidiary survives, and the target's assets and liabilities are merged into the subsidiary in a statutory merger. The parent's stock may be voting or nonvoting, and the acquirer must purchase "substantially all" of the target's assets and liabilities (defined as at least 70% and 90% of the FMV of the target's gross and net assets, respectively), unless the acquiring subsidiary is considered a "disregarded unit."[8]

Asset sales by the target firm just prior to the transaction may threaten the tax-free status of the deal if it is viewed as a violation of the step doctrine. Moreover, tax-free deals such as spin-offs are disallowed within two years before or after the merger.[9] At least 50% of the purchase price must consist of acquirer stock, with the remainder consisting of boot tailored to meet the needs of the target's shareholders. The parent indirectly owns all of the target's assets and liabilities because it owns the subsidiary's entire voting stock.

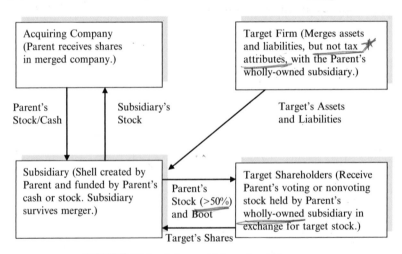

FIGURE 12.3   A forward triangular stock merger.

[8] In 2006, the IRS announced new rules establishing that the "substantially all" requirement may not apply if a so-called "disregarded unit," such as a limited liability company, is used as the acquiring subsidiary and the target firm (structured as a C corporation) ceases to exist. As such, no limitations would be placed on the amount of target net assets that would have to be acquired in order to qualify as a tax-free reorganization.

[9] The IRS imposes these limitations to preclude sellers from engaging in restructuring activities that make them more attractive to potential acquirers that might be willing to consummate a tax-free deal if the target firm were smaller.

The advantages of the forward triangular merger may include the avoidance of approval by the parent firm's shareholders. However, public exchanges on which the parent firm's stock trades still may require parent shareholder approval if the amount of the parent stock used to acquire the target exceeds some predetermined percentage of parent voting shares outstanding. Other advantages include the possible insulation of the parent from the target's liabilities, which remain in the subsidiary, and the avoidance of asset recording fees and transfer taxes, because the target's assets go directly to the parent's wholly-owned subsidiary.

With a *type A reverse triangular stock merger*, the acquirer forms a new shell subsidiary, which is merged into the target in a statutory merger (Figure 12.4). The target is the surviving entity and must hold "substantially all" of the assets and liabilities of both the target and shell subsidiary.[10] The target firm's shares are canceled, and the target shareholders receive the acquirer's or parent's shares. The parent corporation, which owned all of the subsidiary stock, now owns all of the new target stock and, indirectly, all of the target's assets and liabilities. Moreover, at least 80% of the total consideration paid to the target must be in the form of the acquirer's voting stock. This stock may be common or preferred equity. The reverse triangular merger is functionally equivalent to a type B reorganization.

The reverse merger may eliminate the need for parent company shareholder approval. Because the target firm remains in existence, the target can retain any nonassignable franchise, lease, or other valuable contract rights. This often is considered the most important advantage of the reverse triangular merger. Also, the target's liabilities are isolated in a subsidiary of the acquirer. By avoiding the dissolution of the target firm, the acquirer avoids the possible acceleration of loans outstanding. Insurance, banking, and public utility regulators may require the target to remain in existence to be granted regulatory approval.

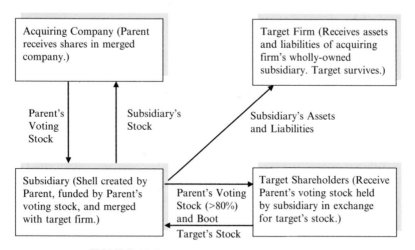

FIGURE 12.4   A reverse triangular stock merger.

[10] Note that unlike in a forward triangular merger, the "substantially all" requirement cannot be circumvented by merging a LLC created by a parent corporation with a target C corporation and exchanging parent stock for target stock.

In a *type B stock-for-stock reorganization*, the acquirer must use its voting common stock to purchase at least 80% of all of the target's outstanding voting and nonvoting stock-outs. Any cash or debt will disqualify the transaction as a type B reorganization. However, cash may be used to purchase fractional shares. Type B reorganizations are used as an alternative to a merger or consolidation. The target's stock does not have to be purchased all at once and allows for a "creeping merger" because the target's stock may be purchased over 12 months or less as part of a formal acquisition plan. Type B reorganizations may be appropriate if the acquiring company wishes to conserve cash or its borrowing capacity. Since shares are being acquired directly from shareholders, there is no need for a target shareholder vote. Finally, contracts, licenses, and so forth, transfer with the stock, thereby obviating the need to receive consent to assignment, unless specified in the contract.

The *type C stock-for-assets reorganization* is used when it is essential for the acquirer not to assume any undisclosed liabilities. It requires that at least 70% and 90% of the FMV of the target's gross and net assets, respectively, be acquired solely in exchange for acquirer voting stock. Consideration paid in cash or nonequity securities cannot exceed 20% of the fair market value of the target's assets. Any liabilities assumed by the acquirer must be deducted from the 20%, thereby reducing the amount of boot that can be used. Since assumed liabilities frequently exceed 20% of the FMV of the acquired assets, the form of payment, as a practical matter, generally is 100% stock. As part of the reorganization plan, the target subsequent to closing dissolves and distributes the acquirer's stock to the target's shareholders for the now-canceled target stock.

The requirement to use only voting stock is a major deterrent to the use of type C reorganization. While a purchase of assets will allow the acquirer to step up the basis of the acquired assets, asset purchases will result potentially in taxable gains. If the target is liquidated to enable the firm to pay the sale proceeds to its shareholders, target shareholders will then have to pay taxes on these payouts. Table 12.3 summarizes the key characteristics of alternative tax-free deal structures.

Expanding the Role of Mergers in Tax-Free Reorganizations

In late 2006, the IRS finalized regulations[11] defining the term *statutory merger* or *consolidation* for purposes of using tax-free reorganizations. Under these regulations, only the continuity of interests and continuity of business enterprise tests, and not the more restrictive "substantially all" requirement, must be satisfied. It is now possible for a merger of a corporation into a single-member (i.e., parent) limited liability company established by the parent corporation in a triangular merger to qualify as a two-party type A merger, with no limit on the amount of target net assets the buyer may acquire.[12]

For years, the IRS had contended that a foreign corporation could not participate in a type A tax-free reorganization because the term *statutory merger* referred only to a merger

[11] Under U.S. Treasury Regulation Section 1.368-2. The new rules apply to transactions taking place on or after January 22, 2006.

[12] However, the target firm must be a C corporation that ceases to exist after the transaction is completed. Because three parties are involved in the forward triangular merger, the target firm can be operated as a subsidiary, thereby insulating the parent from its liabilities.

TABLE 12.3   Key Characteristics of Alternative Tax-Free (to Target Shareholders) Transaction Structures[a]

Transaction Structure (type of reorganization)	Form of Payment	Limitation[b]	Acquirer Retains Target Tax Attributes?	Target Survives?	Parent Exposure to Target Liabilities[c]	Shareholder Vote Required? Acquirer	Target	Minority Freeze Out?	Automatic Transfer of Contracts?[d]
Statutory Merger or Consolidation (type A reorganization)	At least 50% parent voting or nonvoting stock	Assets and liabilities pass automatically to buyer	Yes, but no asset step-up	No	High	Yes	Yes	Yes	No, since target is liquidated
Forward Triangular Stock Merger (type A reorganization)	At least 50% parent voting or nonvoting stock	Must purchase at least 70% and 90% of FMV of gross and net assets unless LLC acquiring sub	Yes, but no asset step-up	No	Low, limited by subsidiary	No[f,g]	Yes	Yes	No, since target is liquidated
Reverse Triangular Stock Merger (type A reorganization)	At least 80% parent voting stock (common/preferred)	Must purchase at least 80% of voting and of nonvoting shares	Yes, but no asset step-up	Yes	Low, limited by subsidiary	No[f,g]	Yes	Yes	Yes, target retains nonassignable contracts, etc.
Purchase of Stock—without a Merger (type B reorganization)	100% parent voting stock (common/preferred)	Must purchase at least 80% of voting and of nonvoting shares	Yes, but no asset step-up	Yes	Low, limited by subsidiary	No[f]	No, as shares bought directly from shareholders	No	Yes
Purchase of Assets (type C reorganization)	100% voting stock[h]	Must purchase at least 70% and 90% of FMV of gross and net assets	Yes, but no asset step-up	No	Low,[e] except for assumed liabilities	No[f]	Yes, if sale of assets substantial	No minority created	No

[a] Target shareholders are taxed at ordinary rates on any "boot" received (i.e., anything other than acquiring company stock).

[b] Asset sales or spin-offs two years prior (may reflect effort to reduce size of purchase) or subsequent to (violates continuity requirement) closing may invalidate tax-free status. Forward triangular mergers do not require any limitations on purchase of target net assets if a so-called "disregarded unit" such as an LLC is used as the acquiring entity and the target is a C corporation that ceases to exist as a result of the transaction.

[c] Contracts, leases, licenses, and rights to intellectual property automatically transfer with the stock unless contracts stipulate consent to assignment required. Moreover, target retains any nonassignable franchise, lease, or other contract rights as long as the target is the surviving entity as in a reverse triangular merger.

[d] Acquirer may be insulated from a target's liabilities as long as it is held in a subsidiary, except for liabilities such as unpaid taxes, unfunded pension obligations, and environmental liabilities.

[e] The parent is responsible for those liabilities conveying with the assets, such as warranty claims.

[f] May be required by public stock exchanges or by legal counsel if deemed material to the acquiring firm or if the parent needs to authorize new stock.

[g] Mergers are generally ill-suited for hostile transactions because they require approval of both the target's board and its shareholders.

[h] While cash may be used to pay for up to 20% of the FMV of net assets, it must be offset by assumed liabilities, making the purchase price usually 100% stock.

completed under the laws of the United States, an individual state, or the District of Columbia. The new regulations make its easier to qualify foreign acquisitions as type A tax-free reorganizations.[13] Therefore, if a U.S. firm buys a foreign firm having U.S. shareholders, the transaction can be structured so that the purchase is free of U.S. taxes to the U.S. shareholders.

Treatment of Target Tax Attributes in M&A Deals

Tax attributes, such as net operating loss carryforwards and carrybacks, capital loss carryovers, excess credit carryovers, tax basis in company assets, and tax basis in subsidiary companies, can represent considerable value to acquiring firms. In taxable transactions, the acquirer may benefit from additional depreciation expense generated by increasing the value of net acquired assets to FMV, but not benefit from the target's other tax attributes. In nontaxable transactions, acquirers may benefit from the target's tax attributes other than those resulting from increasing the value of net acquired assets to FMV. Consequently, the target's tax attributes generally will not survive the deal if the acquirer has already stepped up net acquired assets to their fair market value. From the IRS' viewpoint, this prevents the acquirer from realizing "excessive" tax benefits from the transaction—that is, the future tax savings from writing up the net acquired assets plus savings from NOLs, and so on.

In contrast, the target's tax attributes do carry over to the acquirer in tax-free reorganizations, since the tax basis of the net acquired assets is transferred to the acquirer without having been revalued to their fair market value. The tax authorities view a tax-free transaction as a reorganization in which target shareholders retain a significant ownership position in the combined firms rather than as an actual sale of the target firm. In summary, the target's tax attributes survive in nontaxable transactions and taxable purchases of stock (except for stock acquisitions with a 338 election) but not in taxable purchases of assets.

When tax attributes do survive and carry over to the acquirer, their use is limited by Sections 382 (net operating losses) and 383 (tax credit and capital loss carryforwards). When tax attributes do not survive, they may still be used to offset any immediate gain on the sale of target assets.

Tax-Free Transactions Arising from 1031 "Like-Kind" Exchanges

The prospect of being able to defer taxable gains indefinitely is often associated with 1031 exchanges of real estate property. The potential benefits are significant, with capital gains taxes (as of this writing) of 15% at the federal level and between 10% and 15% at the state level. Furthermore, depreciation recapture taxes (i.e., taxes applied to the difference between accelerated and straight-line depreciation) also may be postponed, with applicable federal income tax rates as high as 35% and some state income tax rates approaching 10%.

By postponing the tax payments, investors have more money to reinvest in new properties. For example, assume a property was purchased ten years ago for $5 million and it is now worth $15 million. If the property were sold with no subsequent purchase of a substantially similar property within the required period, the federal capital gains tax bill would be $1.5 million (i.e., ($15 – $5) × 0.15). This ignores the potential for state taxes or depreciation

---

[13] With the advent of the new regulations, the merger of a foreign corporation into another foreign corporation (or the creation of a new corporation in a consolidation) in accordance with the host country's laws will qualify as a type A reorganization. As such, the exchange will be tax free for any U.S. shareholders in the target firm receiving acquirer shares or shares in the new company formed as a result of the consolidation.

recapture taxes that could be owed if the owner took deductions for depreciation. However, by entering into a 1031 exchange, the owner could use the entire $15 million from the sale of the property as a down payment on a more expensive property. If the investor acquires a property of a lesser value, taxes are owed on the difference. With tax rates likely to rise in the next few years, the value of tax-free exchanges will increase.

News Corp. employed a tax-free 1031 exchange in reaching an agreement in early 2007 to buy Liberty Media's 19%—or $11 billion—stake in the media giant in exchange for News Corp.'s 38.6% stake in satellite TV firm DirecTV Group, $550 million in cash, and three sports TV channels. While the two investments were approximately equal in value, Liberty's management believed that DirecTV's stock was inflated by speculation about the impending deal. The cash and media assets were added to ensure that Liberty Media was exchanging its stake in News Corp. for "like-kind" assets of an equivalent or higher value to qualify as a tax-free exchange. By structuring the deal in this manner, the transaction was viewed as an asset swap rather than a sale of assets, and Liberty Media stood to save billions of dollars in taxes that would have been owed due to its low basis in its investment in News Corp. Had the assets been divested, the two companies would have had to pay an estimated $4.5 billion in taxes due to likely gains on the sale of these assets.[14]

OTHER TAX CONSIDERATIONS AFFECTING CORPORATE RESTRUCTURING

Many parts of the tax code affect corporate restructuring activities. These include treatment of net operating losses, corporate capital gains taxes, the alternative corporate minimum tax, the treatment of greenmail for tax purposes, and Morris Trust transactions. These are discussed next.

Net Operating Losses

Net operating losses (NOLs) are created when firms generate negative taxable income or losses. NOLs can be carried back 2 years to recover past tax payments and forward 20 years to reduce future taxable income. Losses remaining after 20 years are no longer usable. When the acquired net assets are stepped up for tax purposes, the target's NOLs may be used immediately by the acquirer to offset the gain on an asset sale. For deals not resulting in an asset write-up or step-up for tax reporting purposes, the target's NOLs may be used by the acquirer in future years subject to the limitation specified in Section 382 of the IRC code.[15] An increase

---

[14] Angwin and Drucker, 2006

[15] Section 382 of the IRS code was created to prevent acquisitions of companies with substantial NOLs solely to reduce the acquirer's taxable income, without having a valid business purpose other than tax avoidance. Section 382 imposes an *annual* limit on the use of the target firm's NOLs that do survive the transaction and transfer to the acquirer equal to the minimum of the market value of the target's stock multiplied by the long-term tax-exempt interest rate, taxable income of the combined company, or the amount of unused NOLs remaining. For example, suppose that the target firm has $100 million in NOLs expiring in ten years, an acquirer buys all of the target's stock for $500 million, and the long-term tax-exempt interest rate is 5%. The *annual* limitation on the use of NOLs is $100 million × 0.05 or $5 million. Consequently, the combined firm can utilize only $5 million annually for ten years or $50 million of the target's $100 million of NOLs.

in the ownership of certain shareholders in a corporation by more than 50 percentage points over a three-year period would generally trigger the limitation.

Despite annual limits to carryforwards and carrybacks, NOLs may represent a potentially significant source of value to acquirers that should be considered during the process of valuing an acquisition target. For instance, Lucent Technologies had accumulated numerous losses after the Internet bubble burst in 2000. By acquiring Lucent in 2006, Alcatel obtained $3.5 billion in NOLs that could be used to shelter future income for many years.[16] The use of NOLs must be monitored carefully to realize the full value that could potentially result from deferring income taxes. Because the acquirer can never be certain that future income will be sufficient to realize fully the value of the NOLs before they expire, loss carryforwards alone rarely justify an acquisition.[17] Table 12.4 illustrates how an analyst might value NOLs on the books of a target corporation. Acquiring Company is contemplating buying Target Company, which has a tax loss carryforward of $8 million. Acquiring Company has a 40% tax rate. Assume the tax-loss carryforward is within the limits of the Tax Reform Act of 1986 and that the firm's cost of capital is 15%.

Corporate Capital Gains Taxes

Since both short- and long-term corporate capital gains are taxed as ordinary income and are subject to a maximum federal corporate tax rate of 34%, acquirers often adopt alternative legal structures with more favorable tax attributes for making acquisitions. These include master limited partnerships, Subchapter S corporations, and limited liability companies, in which participants are taxed at their personal tax rates for the profits distributed to them directly.

Alternative Corporate Minimum Tax

Under certain circumstances in which corporate taxes have been significantly reduced, corporations may be subject to an alternative minimum tax with a flat rate of 20%. The introduction of the alternative minimum tax has proven to reduce significantly returns to investors in leveraged buyouts, which—by intent—are highly leveraged and have little (if any) taxable income because of their high annual interest expense.

Greenmail Payments

Greenmail refers to payments made to "corporate raiders" to buy back positions they had taken in target companies (see Chapter 3 for more details). Greenmail has been made more expensive by changes in the tax code that sharply reduced the amount of such payments that can be deducted from before-tax profits.

[16] Drucker and Silver, 2006

[17] Studies show that it is easy to overstate the value of loss carryforwards because of their potential to expire before they can be fully used. Empirical analyses indicate that the actual tax savings realized from loss carryforwards tend to be about one-half of their expected value (Auerbach and Poterba, 1987).

TABLE 12.4   Valuing Net Operating Losses

Years Remaining in Loss Carryforward	Amount ($000)	Years after Acquisition	Earnings before Tax ($000)
1	2,000	1	1,800
2	2,000	2	2,000
3	800	3	1,000
4	1,200	4	1,000
5	800	5	2,000
Total	6,800	Total	7,800

Calculate Acquiring Company's tax payments without the acquisition

Years	Tax Benefit
1	720
2	800
3	400
4	400
5	800

Calculate Acquiring Company's tax payment for each year with the proposed acquisition

Years	Earnings before Taxes ($000)	Tax Loss ($000)	Amount Carried Forward ($000)	Use of Tax Loss[a] ($000)	Taxable Income ($000)	Tax Payment ($000)
1	1,800	2,000		1,800	0	0
2	2,000	2,000	200	2,000	0	0
3	1,000	800	0	1,000	0	0
4	1,000	1,200	200	1,000	0	0
5	2,000	800	0	1,000[b]	1,000	400

What is the most the Acquiring Company should pay for the Target Company if its only value is its tax loss?

Answer: The Acquiring Company should not pay more than the present value of the net tax benefit: $720,000; $800,000; $400,000; $400,000; and $400,000. The present value of the cumulative tax benefits discounted at a 15% cost of capital is $1,921,580.

[a] *Tax benefits are equal to earnings before tax times the 40% marginal tax rate of the Acquiring Company. Therefore, the tax benefit in year 1 is $1,800,000 × 0.4 = $720,000.*
[b] *The net tax benefit in the fifth year is equal to the $800,000 tax benefit less the $400,000 in tax payments required in the fifth year.*

Morris Trust Transactions

Tax code rules for Morris Trust transactions restrict how certain types of corporate deals can be structured to avoid taxes.[18] Assume that Firm A sells an operating unit to Firm B and makes a profit on the transaction on which it would owe taxes. To avoid paying those taxes, Firm A spins off the operating unit as a dividend to its shareholders. The operating unit, still owned by Firm A's shareholders, is subsequently merged with Firm B, and shareholders in Firm A thus become shareholders in Firm B. By spinning off the operating unit, Firm A avoids paying corporate taxes on taxable gains, and Firm A's shareholders defer paying personal taxes on any gains until they sell their stock in Firm B.

To make such transactions less attractive, the tax code was amended in 1997 to require that taxes be paid unless no cash changes hands and Firm A's shareholders end up as majority owners in Firm B. The practical effect of this requirement is that merger partners such as Firm B in these types of transactions must be significantly smaller than Firm A, which reduces significantly the number of potential deal candidates.

The change in the law has had a material impact on the way M&A business is conducted. For example, in 2005, Alltel announced it was getting rid of its local telephone business. Although Alltel had been in talks with phone companies, their size made the prospects of a tax-free transaction more complicated. In the end, Alltel sold the business to a far smaller firm, Valor Communications Group Inc., to meet the tax code requirements.

FINANCIAL REPORTING OF BUSINESS COMBINATIONS

Since 2001, a company maintaining its financial statements under International Financial Reporting Standards (IFRS) or Generally Accepted Accounting Principles (GAAP) needs to account for its business combinations using the purchase method (also called the acquisition method).[19] According to the *purchase method of accounting*, the purchase price or acquisition cost is determined and then, using a cost allocation approach, assigned first to tangible and then to intangible net assets and recorded on the books of the acquiring company. Net assets refer to acquired assets less assumed liabilities. Any excess of the purchase price over the fair value of the acquired net assets is recorded as goodwill. Goodwill is an asset representing future economic benefits arising from acquired assets that were not identified individually.

Revised accounting rules (SFAS 141R) have changed the standards covering business combinations to require the acquiring entity to recognize, separately from goodwill, identifiable assets and assumed liabilities at their acquisition date (closing date) fair values and to account for future changes in fair value. The intent was to achieve greater conformity with international accounting standards as applied to business combinations. SFAS 141R applies to transactions with acquisition dates on or after December 15, 2008.

Another recent accounting standard change (SFAS 157) introduces a new definition of fair value, which could have a significant impact on the way mergers and acquisition are done.

[18] Morris Trust transactions were named after a 1966 court case between the U.S. Internal Revenue Service and the Morris Trust.

[19] See IFRS 3 and SFAS (Statements of Financial Accounting Standards) 141, respectively.

Previously, the definition of "fair value" was ambiguous, and it often was used inconsistently. The effective date for SFAS 157 for financial assets and liabilities on financial statements was November 15, 2007, and for nonfinancial assets and liabilities November 15, 2008.

SFAS 141R: The Revised Standards

The revised standards in SFAS 141R require an acquirer to recognize the assets acquired, the liabilities assumed, and any noncontrolling interest in the target to be measured at their fair value as of the acquisition/closing date. Previous guidance had resulted in failure to recognize items on the date of the acquisition, such as acquisition-related expenses. The acquisition date generally corresponds to the closing date rather than the announcement or signing date, as was true under earlier guidelines.

Recognizing Acquired Net Assets and Goodwill at Fair Value

To increase the ability to compare different transactions, SFAS 141R requires recognizing 100% of the assets acquired and liabilities assumed, even if less than 100% of the target's ownership interests are acquired by the buyer. In other words, this results in the recognition of the target's business in its entirety regardless of whether 51%, 100%, or any amount in between of the target is acquired. Consequently, the portion of the target that was not acquired (i.e., the noncontrolling or minority interest) is also recognized, causing the buyer to account for the goodwill attributable to it as well as to the noncontrolling interest. Minority interest is reported in the consolidated balance sheet within the equity account, separately from the parent's equity. Moreover, the revenues, expenses, gains, losses, net income or loss, and other income associated with the noncontrolling interest should be reported on the consolidated income statement.

For example, if Firm A buys 50.1% of Firm B, reflecting its effective control, Firm A must add 100% of Firm B's acquired assets and assumed liabilities to its assets and liabilities and record the value of the 49.9% noncontrolling or minority interest in shareholders' equity. This treats the noncontrolling interest as simply another form of equity and recognizes that Firm A is responsible for managing all of the acquired assets and assumed liabilities. Previously, noncontrolling interests were recorded as a liability on the consolidated balance sheet, reflecting their claim on the consolidated firm's assets.

Similarly, 100% of Firm B's earnings are included in Firm A's income statement and added to the retained earnings of the consolidated firms. Firm B will be operated within Firm A as a majority-owned subsidiary with Firm A's investment in Firm B shown at cost, according to the equity method of accounting. The value of this investment will increase with Firm B's net income and decrease with dividends paid to Firm A.

Recognizing and Measuring Net Acquired Assets in Step or Stage Transactions

The revised standards require an acquirer in a business combination undertaken in stages (i.e., a step or stage transaction) to recognize the acquired net assets as well as the noncontrolling interest in the target firm at the full amounts of their fair values. Net acquired assets at each step must be revalued to the current fair market value. The acquirer is obligated to disclose gains or losses that arise due to the reestimation of the formerly noncontrolling interests on the income statement.

Recognizing Contingent Considerations

Contingencies are uncertainties—such as potential legal, environmental, and warranty claims about which the future may not be fully known at the time a transaction is consummated— that may result in future assets or liabilities. Under the new standards, the acquirer must report an asset or liability arising from a contingency to be recognized at its acquisition date fair value absent new information about the possible outcome. However, as new information becomes available, the acquirer must revalue the asset or liability to its current fair value reflecting the new information and record the impact of changes in the fair values of these assets or liabilities on earnings. This is likely to encourage more rigorously defined limits on liability in acquisitions, with indemnification clauses that cover specific issues rather than general indemnification clauses.

Contingent consideration or payments are an important component of many transactions and include the transfer of additional equity or cash to the previous owners of the target firm (e.g., earn-outs). Payment of contingent consideration depends on the acquired business achieving certain prespecified performance benchmarks over some period. SFAS 141R treats contingent consideration as part of the total consideration paid (i.e., purchase price) for the acquired business, which is measured at the acquisition date fair value. The revised standard also requires the reporting entity to reestimate the fair value of the contingent consideration at each reporting date until the amount of the payout (if any) is determined, with changes in fair value during the period reported as a gain or loss on the income statement. The potential for increased earnings volatility due to changes in the value of contingent liabilities may reduce the attractiveness of earnouts as a form of consideration.

In-Process Research and Development Assets

Under the new standards, the acquirer must recognize separately from goodwill the acquisition date fair values of R&D assets acquired in the business combination. Such assets will remain on the books with an indefinite life until the project's outcome is known. If the specific project is deemed a success, the firm will begin to amortize the asset over the estimated useful life of the technology; if the research project is abandoned, the R&D asset will be considered impaired and expensed.

Expensing Deal Costs

Under the new standard, transaction-related costs such as legal, accounting, and investment banking fees are recorded as an expense on the closing date and charged against current earnings. As such, firms may need to explain the nature of the costs incurred in closing a deal and the impact of such costs on the earnings of the combined firms. Financing costs, such as expenses incurred as a result of new debt and equity issues, will continue to be capitalized and amortized over time.

SFAS 157: The New Fair Value Framework

The purpose of SFAS 157 is to establish a single definition of fair value and a consistent framework for measuring fair value under GAAP to increase comparability in fair value estimates. The new definition of "fair value" under SFAS 157 is the price that would be received to sell an asset or paid to transfer a liability in an orderly transaction (i.e., not a forced liquidation or distress sale) between market participants on the date the asset or liability is to be estimated.[20]

IMPACT OF PURCHASE ACCOUNTING ON FINANCIAL STATEMENTS

A long-term asset is impaired if its fair value falls below its book or carrying value. Impairment could occur due to loss of customers, loss of contracts, loss of key personnel, obsolescence of technology, litigation, patent expiration, failure to achieve anticipated cost savings, overall market slowdown, and so on. In a case of asset impairment, the firm is required to report a loss equal to the difference between the asset's fair value and its carrying value. The write-down of assets associated with an acquisition constitutes a public admission by the firm's management of having overpaid for the acquired assets.

In an effort to minimize goodwill, auditors often require that factors underlying goodwill be tied to specific intangible assets for which fair value can be estimated, such as customer lists and brand names. These intangible assets must be capitalized and shown on the balance sheet. Consequently, if the anticipated cash flows associated with an intangible asset, such as a customer list, have not materialized, the carrying value of the customer list must be written down to reflect its current value.

Balance Sheet Considerations

For financial reporting purposes, the purchase price (PP) paid (including the fair value of any noncontrolling interest in the target at the acquisition date) for the target company consists of the fair market value of total identifiable acquired tangible and intangible assets (FMV_{TA}) less total assumed liabilities (FMV_{TL}) plus goodwill (FMV_{GW}). The difference between FMV_{TA} and FMV_{TL} is called *net asset value*.

These relationships can be summarized as follows:

$$\text{Purchase price(total consideration): } PP = FMV_{TA} - FMV_{TL} + FMV_{GW} \tag{12.1}$$

$$\text{Calculation of goodwill: } FMV_{GW} = PP - FMV_{TA} + FMV_{TL}$$
$$= PP - (FMV_{TA} - FMV_{TL}) \tag{12.2}$$

---

[20] This new definition introduces the notion that fair value is an "exit" price a market participant would pay the seller for a company, asset, or investment. An asset's "entry" price will always be the price paid, but the asset's exit price can fluctuate dramatically, reflecting changing market, industry, or regulatory conditions.

From Eq. (12.2), it should be noted that as net asset value increases, FMV_{GW} decreases. Also note that the calculation of goodwill can result either in a positive (i.e., PP > net asset value) or negative (i.e., PP < net asset value). Negative goodwill arises if the acquired assets are purchased at a discount to their FMV and is referred under SFAS 141R as a "bargain purchase."[21]

Table 12.5 provides a simple example of how the purchase method of accounting can be applied in business combinations. Assume Acquirer buys 100% of Target's equity for $1 billion in cash on December 31, 2011. Columns 1 and 2 present the preacquisition book values of the two firms' balance sheets. Column 3 reflects the restatement of the book value of the Target's balance sheet in column 2 to fair market value. As the sum of columns 1 and 3, column 4 presents the Acquirer's balance sheet, which includes the Acquirer's book value of the preacquisition balance sheet plus the fair market value of the Target's balance sheet.

Furthermore, as shown in column 3, total assets are less than shareholders' equity plus total liabilities by $100 million, reflecting the unallocated portion of the purchase price or goodwill. This $100 million is shown in column 4 as goodwill on the postacquisition Acquirer

TABLE 12.5   Example of Purchase Method of Accounting

	Acquirer Preacquisition Book Value* Column 1	Target Preacquisition Book Value* Column 2	Target Fair Market Value* Column 3	Acquirer Postacquisition Value* Column 4
Current Assets	12,000	1,200	1,200	13,200
Long-Term Assets	7,000	1,000	1,400	8,400
Goodwill				100[c]
Total Assets	19,000	2,200	2,600	21,700
Current Liabilities	10,000	1,000	1,000	11,000
Long-Term Debt	3,000	600	700	3,700
Common Equity	2,000	300	1,000[a]	3,000
Retained Earnings	4,000	300		4,000
Equity + Liabilities	19,000	2,200	2,700[b]	21,700

*In millions of dollars

[a]The fair market value of the target's equity is equal to the purchase price. Note that the value of the target's retained earnings is implicitly included in the purchase price paid for the target's equity.

[b]The difference of $100 million between the fair market value of the target's equity plus liabilities less total assets represents the unallocated portion of the purchase price.

[c]Goodwill = Purchase Price − Fair Market Value of Net Acquired Assets = $1,000 − ($2,600 − $1,000 − $700)

[21] A "bargain" purchase is a business combination in which the total acquisition date fair value of the acquired net assets exceeds the fair value of the purchase price plus the fair value of any noncontrolling interest in the target. Such a purchase may arise due to forced liquidation or distressed sales. SFAS 141R requires the acquirer to recognize that excess on the consolidated income statement as a gain attributable to the acquirer.

balance sheet to equate total assets with equity plus total liabilities. Note that the difference between the Acquirer's preacquisition and postacquisition equity is equal to the $1 billion purchase price.

Exhibit 12.1 illustrates the calculation of goodwill in a transaction in which the acquirer purchases less than 100% of the target's outstanding shares but is still required to account for all of the target's net acquired assets, including 100% of goodwill. Exhibit 12.2 lists valuation guidelines for each major balance sheet category.

EXHIBIT 12.1 ESTIMATING GOODWILL

On January 1, 2009, the closing date, Acquirer Inc. purchased 80% of Target Inc.'s 1 million shares outstanding at $50 per share for a total value of $40 million (i.e., $0.8 \times 1,000,000$ shares outstanding $\times$ $50/share). On that date, the fair value of the net assets acquired from Target was estimated to be $42 million. Acquirer paid a 20% control premium, which was already included in the $50 per share purchase price. The implied minority discount of the minority shares is 16.7% (i.e., $1 - (1 / 1 + 0.2)$).[a] What is the value of the goodwill shown on Acquirer's consolidated balance sheet? What portion of that goodwill is attributable to the minority interest retained by Target's shareholders? What is the fair value of the 20% minority interest measured on the basis of fair value per share?

Goodwill shown on Acquirer's balance sheet: From Eq. (12.2), goodwill can be estimated as follows:

$$FMV_{GW} = PP - (FMV_{TA} - FMV_{TL}) = \$50,000,000 - \$42,000,000 = \$8,000,000$$

where $50,000,000 = $50/share \times 1,000,000$ shares outstanding.
Goodwill attributable to the minority interest: Note that 20% of the total shares outstanding equals 200,000 shares with a market value of $10 million ($50/share $\times$ 200,000). Therefore, the amount of goodwill attributable to the minority interest is calculated as follows:

Fair Value of Minority Interest:	$10,000,000
Less 20% fair value of net acquired assets (0.2 × $42,000,000):	$ 8,400,000
Equal: Goodwill attributable to minority interest:	$ 1,600,000

Fair value of the minority interest per share: Since the fair value of Acquirer's interest in Target and Target's retained interest are proportional to their respective ownership interest, the value of the ownership distribution of the majority and minority owners is as follows:

Acquirer Interest (0.8 × 1,000,000 × $50/share):	$40,000,000
Target Minority Interest (0.2 × 1,000,000 × $50/share):	$10,000,000
Total Market Value:	$50,000,000

The fair market value per share of the minority interest is $41.65 (i.e., ($10,000,000/200,000) $\times$ (1 – 0.167)). The minority share value is less than the share price of the controlling shareholders (i.e., $50/share) because it must be discounted for the relative lack of influence of minority shareholders on the firm's decision-making process.

[a]See Chapter 10 for a discussion of how to calculate control premiums and minority discounts.

EXHIBIT 12.2 GUIDELINES FOR VALUING ACQUIRED ASSETS AND LIABILITIES

1. Cash and accounts receivable, reduced for bad debt and returns, are valued at their values on the books of the target on the acquisition/closing date.
2. Marketable securities are valued at their realizable value after any transaction costs.
3. Inventories are broken down into finished goods and raw materials. Finished goods are valued at their liquidation value; raw material inventories are valued at their current replacement cost. Last-in, first-out inventory reserves maintained by the target before the acquisition are eliminated.
4. Property, plant, and equipment are valued at fair market value on the acquisition/closing date.
5. Accounts payable and accrued expenses are valued at the levels stated on the target's books on the acquisition/closing date.
6. Notes payable and long-term debt are valued at the net present value of the future cash payments discounted at the current market rate of interest for similar securities.
7. Pension fund obligations are booked at the excess or deficiency of the present value of the projected benefit obligations over the present value of pension fund assets. This may result in an asset or liability being recorded by the consolidated firms.
8. All other liabilities are recorded at their net present value of future cash payments.
9. Intangible assets are booked at their appraised values on the acquisition/closing date.
10. Goodwill is the difference between the purchase price less the fair market value of the target's net asset value. Positive goodwill is recorded as an asset, whereas negative goodwill (i.e., a bargain purchase) is shown as a gain on the acquirer's consolidated income statement.

Firms capitalize (i.e., value and display as assets on the balance sheet) the costs of acquiring identifiable intangible assets. The value of such assets can be ascertained from similar transactions made elsewhere. The acquirer must consider the future benefits of the intangible asset to be at least equal to the price paid. Specifically, identifiable assets must have a finite life. Intangible assets are listed as identifiable if the asset can be separated from the firm and sold, leased, licensed, or rented—such as patents and customer lists. Intangible assets also are viewed as identifiable if they are contractually or legally binding. An example is the purchase of a firm that has a leased manufacturing facility whose cost is less than the current cost of a comparable lease. The difference would be listed as an intangible asset on the consolidated balance sheet of the acquiring firm.[22]

---

[22] Many assets, such as intangibles, are not specifically identified on the firm's balance sheet. In the United States, companies expense the cost of investing in intangibles in the year in which the investment is made; the rationale is the difficulty in determining whether a particular expenditure results in a future benefit (i.e., an asset, not an expense). For example, the value of the Coca-Cola brand name clearly has value extending over many years, but there is no estimate of this value on the firm's balance sheet.

TABLE 12.6   Balance Sheet Impacts of Purchase Accounting

Target Inc. December 31, 2010, Purchase Price (Total Consideration)		**$500,000,000**
Fair Values of Target Inc.'s Net Assets on December 31, 2010		
Current Assets	$ 40,000,000	
Plant and Equipment	200,000,000	
Customer List	180,000,000	
Copyrights	120,000,000	
Current Liabilities	(35,000,000)	
Long-Term Debt	(100,000,000)	
Value Assigned to Identifiable Net Assets		$405,000,000
Value Assigned to Goodwill		$95,000,000
Carrying Value as of December 31, 2010		$500,000,000
Fair Values of Target Inc.'s Net Assets on December 31, 2011		$400,000,000[a]
Current Assets	$ 30,000,000	
Plant and Equipment	175,000,000	
Customer List	100,000,000	
Copyrights	120,000,000	
Current Liabilities	(25,000,000)	
Long-Term Debt	(90,000,000)	
Fair Value of Identifiable Net Assets		$310,000,000
Value of Goodwill		$90,000,000
Carrying Value after Impairment on December 31, 2011		$400,000,000
Impairment Loss (Difference between December 31, 2011, and December 31, 2010, carrying values)		$100,000,000

[a]Note that the December 31, 2011, carrying value is estimated based on the discounted value of projected cash flows of the reporting unit and therefore represents the fair market value of the unit on that date. The fair value is composed of the sum of fair value of identifiable net assets plus goodwill.

Table 12.6 illustrates the balance sheet impacts of purchase accounting on the acquirer's balance sheet and the effects of impairment subsequent to closing. Assume that Acquirer Inc. purchases Target Inc. on December 31, 2010 (the acquisition/closing date) for $500 million. Identifiable acquired assets and assumed liabilities are shown at their fair value on the acquisition date. The excess of the purchase price over the fair value of net acquired assets is shown as goodwill. The fair value of the "reporting unit" (i.e., Target Inc.) is determined annually to ensure that its fair value exceeds its carrying (book) value. As of December 31, 2011, it is determined that the fair value of Target Inc. has fallen below its carrying value due largely to the loss of a number of key customers.

Income Statement and Cash Flow Considerations

For reporting purposes, an upward valuation of tangible and intangible assets, other than goodwill, raises depreciation and amortization expenses, which lowers operating and net income. For tax purposes, goodwill created after July 1993 may be amortized up to 15 years and is tax deductible. Goodwill booked before July 1993 is not tax deductible. Cash flow benefits from the tax deductibility of additional depreciation and amortization expenses that are written off over the useful lives of the assets. If the purchase price paid is less than the target's net asset value, the acquirer records a one-time gain equal to the difference on its income statement. If the carrying value of the net asset value subsequently falls below its fair market value, the acquirer records a one-time loss equal to the difference.

INTERNATIONAL ACCOUNTING STANDARDS

Ideally, financial reporting would be the same across the globe, but at this writing it is not yet the case, although the bodies responsible for setting standards have pledged to work diligently to achieve that objective. The overarching objective of the International Accounting Standards Board (IASB), one of those bodies, is the convergence of accounting standards worldwide and the establishment of global standards, sometimes referred to as "global GAAP." The IASB issues International Financial Reporting Standards (IFRS), and since 2005, firms across the European Union have had to conform to IFRS directives. Concerns in the United States about moving to international standards from GAAP include higher taxes if the conversion results in increases in reported earnings, increased implementation costs, and increased litigation, because the IFRS is principles-based and allows more latitude in using professional judgment.

RECAPITALIZATION ACCOUNTING

An acquisition resulting in a change in control (i.e., a change in majority voting power) must use purchase accounting for recording the net assets of the acquired business on the acquirer's financial statements. However, under certain circumstances that arise with a leveraged buyout, control may change without changing the basis of the acquired assets and liabilities. In an LBO, some of the target's shareholders will continue to own stock in the postacquisition firm. If the target's shareholders continue to own more than 20% of the firm, the acquired net assets do not have to be restated to fair market value, avoiding any negative impact on earnings resulting from higher depreciation of assets. Consequently, when the firm is sold at a later date, its financial returns are likely to be more attractive under recapitalization than purchase accounting.

SOME THINGS TO REMEMBER

Taxes are an important but rarely an overarching consideration in most M&A transactions. The deciding factor in any transaction should be whether it makes good business sense. A transaction generally is considered taxable to the seller if the buyer uses mostly cash, notes, or some nonequity consideration to purchase the target's stock or assets. Conversely, the transaction is generally considered tax free if mostly acquirer stock is used to purchase the stock or assets of the target firm. Tax considerations and strategies are likely to have an important impact on how a deal is structured by affecting the amount, timing, and composition of the price offered to a target firm and how the combined firms are organized following closing.

For financial reporting purposes, all M&As (except those qualifying for recapitalization accounting) must be recorded using the purchase method of accounting. The excess of the purchase price, including the fair value of any noncontrolling (i.e., minority) interest in the target on the acquisition date, over the fair market value of acquired net assets is treated as goodwill on the combined firm's balance sheet. If the fair market value of the target's net assets later falls below its carrying value, the acquirer must record a loss equal to the difference. This threat may introduce additional discipline for acquirers when negotiating with target company boards and management, since such an event would be a public admission that management had overpaid for past acquisitions. Furthermore, recent changes in accounting standards requiring business combinations to be valued on the acquisition date may make equity-financed transactions less attractive due to the potential for significant changes in value between signing and closing. However, this concern may be mitigated somewhat by the use of collar arrangements. The requirement to value contingent liabilities at closing and update them over time could contribute to earnings instability and make earn-outs a less attractive form of payment.

DISCUSSION QUESTIONS

12.1 When does the IRS consider a transaction to be nontaxable to the target firm's shareholders? What is the justification for the IRS' position?

12.2 What are the advantages and disadvantages of a tax-free transaction for the buyer?

12.3 Under what circumstances can the assets of the acquired firm be increased to fair market value when the transaction is deemed a taxable purchase of stock?

12.4 When does it make sense for a buyer to use a type A tax-free reorganization?

12.5 When does it make sense for a buyer to use a type B tax-free reorganization?

12.6 What are net operating loss carryforwards and carrybacks? Why might they add value to an acquisition?

12.7 Explain how tax considerations affect the deal structuring process.

12.8 How does the purchase method of accounting affect the income statements, balance sheets, and cash-flow statements of the combined companies?

12.9 What is goodwill and how is it created?

12.10 Under what circumstances might an asset become impaired? How might this event affect the way in which acquirers bid for target firms?

12.11 Why do boards of directors of both acquiring and target companies often obtain so-called fairness opinions from outside investment advisors or accounting firms? What valuation methodologies might be employed in constructing these opinions? Should stockholders have confidence in such opinions? Why or why not?

12.12 Archer Daniel Midland (ADM) wants to acquire AgriCorp to augment its ethanol. manufacturing capability. AgriCorp wants the transaction to be tax-free for its shareholders. ADM wants to preserve AgriCorp's significant investment tax credits and tax loss carryforwards so that they transfer in the transaction. Also, ADM plans on selling certain unwanted AgriCorp assets to help finance the transaction. How would you structure the deal so that both parties' objectives could be achieved?

12.13 Tangible assets are often increased to fair market value following a transaction and depreciated faster than their economic lives. What is the potential impact on post-transaction EPS, cash flow, and the balance sheet?

12.14 Discuss how the form of acquisition (i.e., asset purchase or stock deal) could affect the net present value or internal rate of return of the deal calculated postclosing.

12.15 What are some of the important tax-related issues the boards of the acquirer and target companies may need to address prior to entering negotiations? How might the resolution of these issues affect the form of payment and form of acquisition?

Answers to these Chapter Discussion Questions are found in the Online Instructor's Manual for instructors using this book.

Practice Problems and Answers

12.16 Target Company has incurred $5 million in losses during the past three years. Acquiring Company anticipates pretax earnings of $3 million in each of the next three years. What is the difference between the taxes that Acquiring Company would have paid before the merger as compared to actual taxes paid after the merger, assuming a marginal tax rate of 40%? Show your work.

Answer: $2 million.

12.17 Acquiring Company buys Target Company for $5 million in cash. As an analyst, you are given the premerger balance sheets for the two companies (Table 12.7). Assuming plant and equipment are revalued upward by $500,000, what will be the combined companies' shareholders' equity plus total liabilities? What is the difference between Acquiring Company's shareholders' equity and the shareholders' equity of the combined companies? Show your work

Answer: The combined companies' shareholders' equity plus total liabilities is $7.1 million, and the change between the combined companies' and Acquiring Company's shareholders' equity is $5 million. Note that the change in the acquirer's equity equals the purchase price.

Answers to these problems can be found in the Online Instructor's Manual available to instructors using this book.

TABLE 12.7 Premerger Balance Sheets for Companies ($ million)

	Acquiring Company	Target Company
Current Assets	600,000	800,000
Plant and Equipment	1,200,000	1,500,000
Total Assets	1,800,000	2,300,000
Long-Term Debt	500,000	300,000
Shareholders' Equity	1,300,000	2,000,000
Shareholders' Equity + Total Liabilities	1,800,000	2.300,000

CHAPTER BUSINESS CASES

CASE STUDY 12.2
Teva Pharmaceuticals Buys Barr Pharmaceuticals to Create a Global Powerhouse

On December 23, 2008, Teva Pharmaceuticals Ltd. completed its acquisition of U.S.-based Barr Pharmaceuticals Inc. The merged businesses created a firm with a significant presence in 60 countries worldwide and about $14 billion in annual sales. Teva Pharmaceutical Industries Ltd. is headquartered in Israel and is among the top 20 pharmaceutical companies in the world. It also is the world's leading generic pharmaceutical company. The firm develops, manufactures, and markets generic and human pharmaceutical ingredients called biologics, as well as animal health pharmaceutical products. Over 80% of Teva's revenue is generated in North America and Europe.

Barr is a U.S.-headquartered global specialty pharmaceutical company that operates in more than 30 countries. Barr's operations are based primarily in North America and Europe, with its key markets being the United States, Croatia, Germany, Poland, and Russia. With annual sales of about $2.5 billion, Barr is engaged primarily in the development, manufacturing, and marketing of generic and proprietary pharmaceuticals and is one of the world's leading generic drug companies. In addition, Barr also is involved actively in the development of generic biologic products, an area that Barr believes provides significant prospects for long-term earnings and profitability.

Based on the average closing price of Teva American Depository Shares (ADSs) on NASDAQ on July 16, 2008, the last trading day in the United States before the merger's announcement, the total purchase price was approximately $7.4 billion, consisting of a combination of Teva shares and cash. Each ADS represents one ordinary share of Teva deposited with a custodian bank.[23] As a result of the transaction, Barr shareholders owned approximately 7.3% of Teva after the merger.

The merger agreement provided that each share of Barr common stock issued and outstanding immediately prior to the effective time of the merger was to be converted into the right to receive 0.6272 ordinary shares of Teva, which trade in the United States as American Depository Shares, and $39.90 in cash. The 0.6272 represents the share exchange ratio stipulated in the merger agreement.

The value of the portion of the merger consideration comprising Teva ADSs could have changed between signing and closing. The share exchange ratio was a fixed ratio agreed to by the parties to the negotiation. The market value of the Teva ADSs that Barr shareholders received in the merger could have increased or decreased as the trading price of Teva's ADSs increased or decreased and, therefore, it could have been different on the closing date than what it was on the

---

[23] ADSs may be issued in uncertificated form or certified as an American Depositary Receipt, or ADR. ADRs provide evidence that a specified number of ADSs have been deposited by Teva commensurate with the number of new ADSs issued to Barr shareholders.

CASE STUDY 12.2   *(cont'd)*

signing date. In fact, the differences between signing and closing were minimal.

By most measures, the offer price for Barr shares constituted an attractive premium over the value of Barr shares prior to the merger announcement. Based on the closing price of a Teva ADS on the NASDAQ Stock Exchange on July 16, 2008, the consideration for each outstanding share of Barr common stock for Barr shareholders represented a premium of approximately 42% over the closing price of Barr common stock on July 16, 2008, the last trading day in the United States before the merger announcement.

Since the merger qualified as a tax-free reorganization under U.S. federal income tax laws, a U.S. holder of Barr common stock generally did not recognize any gain or loss under U.S. federal income tax laws on the exchange of Barr common stock for Teva ADSs. A U.S. holder generally would recognize a gain on cash received in exchange for the holder's Barr common stock.

Teva was motivated to acquire Barr because of its desire to achieve increased economies of scale and scope, as well as greater geographic coverage with significant growth potential in emerging markets. Barr's U.S. generic drug offering is highly complementary with Teva's and extends Teva's product offering and product development pipeline into new and attractive product categories, such as a substantial women's healthcare business. The merger also is a response to the ongoing global trend of consolidation among the purchasers of pharmaceutical products as governments are increasingly becoming the primary purchaser of generic drugs.

Under the merger agreement, a wholly-owned Teva corporate subsidiary, the Boron Acquisition Corp. (i.e., the acquisition vehicle)

merged with Barr, with Barr surviving the merger as a wholly-owned subsidiary of Teva. Immediately following the closing of the merger, Barr was merged into a newly formed limited liability company (i.e., postclosing organization), also wholly owned by Teva, which is the surviving company in the second step of the merger. As such, Barr became a wholly-owned subsidiary of Teva and ceased to be traded on the New York Stock Exchange.

The merger agreement contained standard preclosing covenants, in which Barr agreed to conduct its business only in their ordinary course of business (i.e., as it has historically in a manner consistent with common practices) and not to alter any supplier, customer, or employee agreements or declare any dividends or buy back any outstanding stock. Barr also agreed not to engage in one or more transactions or investments or assume any debt exceeding $25 million. The firm also promised not to change any accounting practices in any material way or in a manner inconsistent with generally accepted accounting principles. Barr also committed not to solicit alternative bids from any other possible investors between the signing of the merger agreement and the closing.

Teva agreed that from the period immediately following closing and ending on the first anniversary of closing that it would require Barr or its subsidiaries to maintain each Barr compensation and benefit plan in existence prior to closing. All annual base salary and wage rates of each Barr employee would be maintained at no less than the levels in effect before closing. Bonus plans also would be maintained at levels no less favorable than those in existence before the closing of the merger.

CASE STUDY 12.2 *(cont'd)*

The key closing conditions that applied to both Teva and Barr included satisfaction of required regulatory and shareholder approvals, compliance with all prevailing laws, and that no representations and warranties were found to have been breached. Moreover, both parties had to provide a certificate signed by the chief executive officer and the chief financial officer that their firms had performed in all material respects all obligations required to be performed in accordance with the merger agreement prior to the closing date and that neither business had suffered any material damage between the signing and closing.

The merger agreement had to be approved by a majority of the outstanding voting shares of Barr common stock. Shareholders failing to vote or abstaining were counted as votes against the merger agreement. Shareholders were entitled to vote on the merger agreement if they held Barr common stock at the close of business on the record date, which was October 10, 2008. Since the shares issued by Teva in exchange for Barr's stock had already been authorized and did not exceed 20% of Teva's shares outstanding (i.e., the threshold on some public stock exchanges at which firms are required to obtain shareholder approval), the merger was not subject to a vote of Teva's shareholders.

Teva and Barr each filed notification of the proposed transaction with the U.S. Federal Trade Commission and the Antitrust Division of the U.S. Department of Justice in order to comply with the Hart-Scott-Rodino Antitrust Improvements Act of 1976. Each party subsequently received a request for additional information (commonly referred to as a "second request") from the U.S. FTC in connection with the pending acquisition. The effect of the second request was to extend the HSR waiting period until 30 days after the parties had substantially complied with the request, unless that period was terminated sooner by the FTC. Teva and Barr received FTC and Justice Department approval once potential antitrust concerns had been dispelled. Given the global nature of the merger, the two firms also had to file with the European Union Antitrust Commission as well as with other countries' regulatory authorities.

Discussion Questions

1. Why do you believe that Teva chose to acquire the outstanding stock of Barr rather than selected assets? Explain your answer.
2. Mergers of businesses with operations in many countries must seek approval from a number of regulatory agencies. How might this affect the time between the signing of the agreement and the actual closing? How might the ability to realize synergy following the merger of the two businesses be affected by actions required by the regulatory authorities before granting their approval? Be specific.
3. What is the importance of the preclosing covenants signed by both Teva and Barr?
4. What is the importance of the closing conditions in the merger agreement? What could happen if any of the closing conditions are breached (i.e., violated)?
5. Speculate as to why Teva offered Barr shareholders a combination of Teva stock and cash for each Barr share outstanding and why Barr was willing to accept a fixed share exchange ratio rather than some type of collar arrangement.

CASE STUDY 12.3
Merck and Schering-Plough Merger: When Form Overrides Substance

If it walks like a duck and quacks like a duck, is it really a duck? That is a question Johnson & Johnson might ask about a 2009 transaction involving pharmaceutical companies Merck and Schering-Plough. On August 7, 2009, shareholders of Merck and Company ("Merck") and Schering-Plough Corp. (Schering-Plough) voted overwhelmingly to approve a $41.1 billon merger of the two firms. With annual revenues of $42.4 billion, the new Merck will be second in size only to global pharmaceutical powerhouse Pfizer Inc.

At closing on November 3, 2009, Schering-Plough shareholders received $10.50 and 0.5767 of a share of the common stock of the combined company for each share of Schering-Plough stock they held, and Merck shareholders received one share of common stock of the combined company for each share of Merck that they held. Merck shareholders voted to approve the merger agreement, and Schering-Plough shareholders voted to approve both the merger agreement and the issuance of shares of common stock in the combined firms. Immediately after the merger, the former shareholders of Merck and Schering-Plough owned approximately 68% and 32%, respectively, of the shares of the combined companies.

The motivation for the merger reflects the potential for $3.5 billion in pretax annual cost savings, with Merck reducing its workforce by about 15% through facility consolidations, a highly complementary product offering, and the substantial number of new drugs under development at Schering-Plough. Furthermore, the deal increases Merck's international presence, since 70% of Schering-Plough's revenues come from abroad. The combined firms both focus on biologics (i.e., drugs derived

from living organisms). The new firm has a product offering that is much more diversified than either firm had separately.

The deal structure involved a reverse merger, which allowed for a tax-free exchange of shares and for Schering-Plough to argue that it was the acquirer in this transaction. The importance of the latter point is explained in the following section.

To implement the transaction, Schering-Plough created two merger subsidiaries—that is, Merger Subs 1 and 2—and moved $10 billion in cash provided by Merck and 1.5 billion new shares (i.e., so-called "New Merck" shares approved by Schering-Plough shareholders) in the combined Schering-Plough and Merck companies into the subsidiaries. Merger Sub 1 was merged into Schering-Plough, with Schering-Plough becoming the surviving firm. Merger Sub 2 was combined with Merck, with Merck surviving as a wholly-owned subsidiary of Schering-Plough. The end result is the appearance that Schering-Plough (renamed Merck) acquired Merck through its wholly-owned subsidiary (Merger Sub 2). In reality, Merck acquired Schering-Plough.

Former shareholders of Schering-Plough and Merck become shareholders in the new Merck. The "New Merck" is simply Schering-Plough renamed Merck. This structure allows Schering-Plough to argue that no change in control occurred and that a termination clause in a partnership agreement with Johnson & Johnson should not be triggered. Under the agreement, J&J has the exclusive right to sell a rheumatoid arthritis drug it had developed called Remicade, and Schering-Plough has the exclusive right to sell the drug outside of the United States, reflecting its stronger

CASE STUDY 12.3 *(cont'd)*

international distribution channel. If the change of control clause were triggered, rights to distribute the drug outside the United States would revert back to J&J. Remicade represented $2.1 billion or about 20% of Schering-Plough's 2008 revenues and about 70% of the firm's international revenues.

Consequently, retaining these revenues following the merger was important to both Merck and Schering-Plough.

The multistep process for implementing this transaction is illustrated in the following steps and figures. From a legal perspective, all these actions occur concurrently.

Step 1: Schering-Plough renamed Merck (denoted in the figures as "New Merck"):

a. Schering-Plough creates two wholly-owned merger subs.

b. Schering-Plough transfers cash provided by Merck and newly issued "New Merck" stock into Merger Sub 1 and only "New Merck" stock into Merger Sub 2.

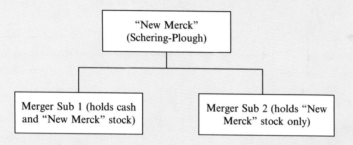

Step 2: Schering-Plough Merger:

a. Merger Sub 1 merges into Schering-Plough in a reverse merger, with Schering-Plough surviving.

b. To compensate shareholders, Schering-Plough shareholders exchange their shares for cash and stock in "New Merck."

c. Former Schering-Plough shareholders now hold stock in "New Merck."

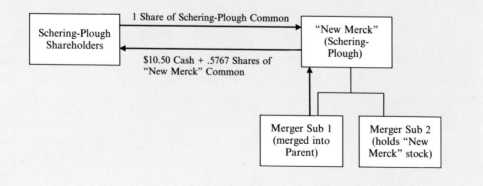

CASE STUDY 12.3   *(cont'd)*

Step 3: Merck Merger:
a. Merger Sub 2 merges into Merck, with Merck surviving.
b. To compensate shareholders, Merck shareholders exchange their shares for shares in "New Merck."
c. Former shareholders in Merck now hold shares in "New Merck" (i.e., a renamed Schering-Plough).
d. Merger Sub 2, a subsidiary of "New Merck," now owns Merck.

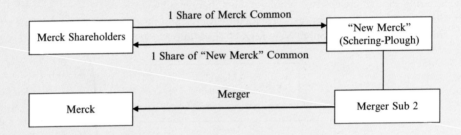

This figure shows the combined company as a result of Steps 1 through 3.

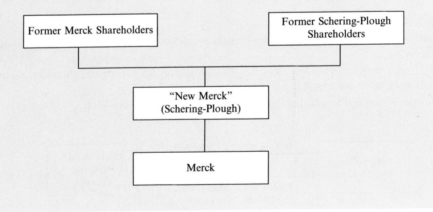

CASE STUDY 12.3 *(cont'd)*

Concluding Comments

In reality, Merck was the acquirer. Merck provided the money to purchase Schering-Plough, and Richard Clark, Merck's chairman and CEO, will run the newly combined firm when Fred Hassan, Schering-Plough's CEO, steps down. The new firm has been renamed Merck to reflect its broader brand recognition. Three-fourths of the new firm's board consists of former Merck directors, with the remainder coming from Schering-Plough's board. These factors would give Merck effective control of the combined Merck and Schering-Plough operations. Finally, former Merck shareholders own almost 70% of the outstanding shares of the combined companies.

J&J initiated legal action in August 2009, arguing that the transaction was a conventional merger and, as such, triggered the change of control provision in its partnership agreement it had with Schering-Plough. Schering-Plough argued that the reverse merger bypasses the change of control clause in the agreement, and that, consequently, J&J could not terminate the joint venture. In the past, courts in the United States have tended to focus on the form rather than the spirit of a transaction. The implications of the form of a transaction are usually relatively explicit, while determining what was actually intended (i.e., the spirit) in a deal is often more subjective.

In late 2010, an arbitration panel consisting of former federal judges indicated that a final ruling would be forthcoming in 2011. Potential outcomes could include J&J receiving rights to Remicade with damages to be paid by Merck; a finding that the merger did not constitute a change in control, which would keep the distribution agreement in force; or a ruling allowing Merck to continue to sell Remicade overseas but providing for more royalties to J&J.

Discussion Questions

1. Do you agree with the argument that the courts should focus on the form or structure of an agreement and not try to interpret the actual intent of the parties to the transaction? Explain your answer.
2. How might allowing the form of a transaction to override the actual spirit or intent of the deal impact the cost of doing business for the parties involved in the drug distribution agreement? Be specific.
3. How did the use of a reverse merger facilitate the transaction?

Answers to these questions are provided in the Online Instructor's Manual for instructors using this book.

C H A P T E R

13

Financing Transactions
Private Equity, Hedge Funds, and Leveraged Buyout Structures and Valuation

A billion dollars isn't what it used to be. —**Nelson Bunker Hunt**

INSIDE M&A: KINDER MORGAN BUYOUT RAISES ETHICAL QUESTIONS

In the largest management buyout in U.S. history at that time, Kinder Morgan Inc.'s management proposed to take the oil and gas pipeline firm private in 2006 in a transaction that valued the firm's outstanding equity at $13.5 billion. Under the proposal, chief executive Richard Kinder and other senior executives would contribute shares valued at $2.8 billion to the newly private company. An additional $4.5 billion would come from private equity investors, including Goldman Sachs Capital Partners, American International Group Inc., and the Carlyle Group. Including assumed debt, the transaction was valued at about $22 billion. The transaction also was notable for the governance and ethical issues it raised. Reflecting the struggles within the corporation, the deal did not close until mid-2007.

The top management of Kinder Morgan Inc. waited more than two months before informing the firm's board of its desire to take the company private. It is customary for boards governing firms whose managements are interested in buying out public shareholders to create a committee within the board consisting of independent board members to solicit other bids. While the Kinder Morgan board did eventually create such a committee, the board's lack of awareness of the pending management proposal gave management an important lead over potential bidders in structuring a proposal. By being involved early on in the process, a board has more time to negotiate terms more favorable to shareholders. The transaction also raised questions about the potential conflicts of interest in cases where investment bankers who were hired to advise management and the board on the "fairness" of the offer price also were potential investors in the buyout.

Kinder Morgan's management hired Goldman Sachs in February 2006 to explore "strategic" options for the firm to enhance shareholder value. The leveraged buyout option was proposed by Goldman Sachs on March 7, followed by their proposal to become the primary investor in the LBO on April 5. The management buyout group hired a number of law firms and other investment banks as advisors and discussed the proposed buyout with credit-rating firms to assess how much debt the firm could support without experiencing a downgrade in its credit rating.

On May 13, 2006, the full board was finally made aware of the proposal. The board immediately demanded that a standstill agreement that had been signed by Richard Kinder, CEO and leader of the buyout group, be terminated. The agreement did not permit the firm to talk to any alternative bidders for a period of 90 days. While investment banks and buyout groups often propose such an agreement to ensure that they can perform adequate due diligence, this extended period is not necessarily in the interests of the firm's shareholders because it puts alternative suitors coming in later at a distinct disadvantage. Later bidders simply lack sufficient time to make an adequate assessment of the true value of the target and structure their own proposals. In this way, the standstill agreement could discourage alternative bids for the business.

A special committee of the board was set up to negotiate with the management buyout group, and it was ultimately able to secure a $107.50 per share price for the firm, significantly higher than the initial offer. The discussions were rumored to have been very contentious due to the board's annoyance with the delay in informing them.[1] Reflecting the strong financial performance of the firm and an improving equity market, Kinder Morgan raised $2.4 billion in early 2011 in the largest private equity–backed IPO in history. The majority of the IPO proceeds were paid out to the firm's private equity investors as a dividend.

CHAPTER OVERVIEW

This chapter discusses how transactions are financed, with an emphasis on the financing, structuring, and valuation of highly leveraged transactions. In a *leveraged buyout* (LBO), borrowed funds are used to pay for most of the purchase price, with the remainder provided by a financial sponsor, such as a private equity investor group or hedge fund. LBOs can be of an entire company or divisions of a company. LBO targets can be private or public firms. Typically, the tangible assets of the firm to be acquired are used as collateral for the loans. The most highly liquid assets often are used as collateral for obtaining bank financing. Such assets commonly include receivables and inventory.

The firm's fixed assets commonly are used to secure a portion of long-term senior financing. Subordinated debt, either unrated or low-rated debt, is used to raise the balance of the purchase price. This debt often is referred to as *junk bond financing*. When a public company is subject to an LBO, it is said to be *going private* in a public-to-private transaction because the equity of the firm has been purchased by a small group of investors and is no longer publicly traded. Buyers of the firm targeted to become a leveraged buyout often consist of managers from the firm that is being acquired. The LBO that is initiated by the target firm's incumbent management is called a *management buyout* (MBO).

[1] Berman and Sender, 2006

This chapter begins with a discussion of the changing face of LBOs. Subsequent sections discuss how such transactions often are financed, alternative LBO structures, the risks associated with poorly constructed deals, how to take a company private, how to develop viable exit strategies, and how to estimate a firm's financing capacity. The terms *buyout firm* and *financial sponsor* are used interchangeably, as they are in the literature on the subject, throughout the chapter to include the variety of investor groups, such as private equity investors and hedge funds, that commonly engage in LBO transactions. Empirical studies of pre- and postbuyout returns to shareholders also are reviewed. The chapter concludes with a discussion of how to analyze and value highly leveraged transactions and to construct LBO models.

A detailed Microsoft Excel-Based Leveraged Buyout Valuation and Structuring Model is available on this book's companion site (*www.elsevierdirect.com/companions/ 9780123854858*). The site also contains a review of this chapter (including practice questions and answers) in the file folder entitled "Student Study Guide" and a Learning Interactions Library, which gives students the opportunity to test their knowledge of this chapter in a "real-time" environment.

CHARACTERIZING LEVERAGED BUYOUTS

An LBO investor is frequently called a *financial buyer* or *financial sponsor*. Such investors are inclined to use a large amount of debt to finance as much of the target's purchase price as possible. Leverage makes the potential returns to equity much more attractive than in unleveraged transactions (Table 13.1).

TABLE 13.1   Impact of Leverage on Return to Shareholders[a]

	All-Cash Purchase	50% Cash/50% Debt	20% Cash/80% Debt
Purchase Price	$100	$100	$100
Equity (Cash Investment)	100	50	20
Borrowings	0	50	80
Earnings before Interest, Taxes, Depreciation, and Amortization	20	20	20
Interest @ 10%	0	5	8
Depreciation and Amortization	2	2	2
Income before Taxes	18	13	10
Less Income Taxes @ 40%	7.2	5.2	4
Net Income	$10.8	$7.8	$6
After-Tax Return on Equity	10.8%	15.6%	30%

[a]*Unless otherwise noted, all numbers are in millions of dollars.*

Historically, empirical studies of LBOs have been subject to small samples due to limited data availability, survival bias,[2] and a focus on the conversion of public to private firms. Recent studies based on larger samples make some of the conclusions of earlier studies problematic.[3] These more recent studies are discussed in the following sections.

The Changing Nature of LBOs since 1970

In an exhaustive study of 21,397 private equity transactions that could be identified between 1970 and 2007, Stromberg (2008) confirmed that private equity investments accelerated sharply in recent years from their longer-term trend, peaking in 2006 and 2007. In 2007, more than 14,000 LBOs operated globally as compared to about 5,000 in the year 2000 and only 2,000 in the mid-1990s. The major insights provided by this study are discussed next.

The Private Equity Market Is a Global Phenomenon

While private equity investors have been more active in the United States for a longer time period, the number of non-U.S. private equity transactions has grown to be larger than that of the United States. The ability to conduct public-to-private LBO transactions in different countries is influenced by the ability to squeeze out minority shareholders. The United States, United Kingdom, and Ireland tend to be at the less-restrictive end of the spectrum, while Italy, Denmark, Finland, and Spain tend to be far more restrictive.[4] Although remaining relatively flat throughout the 1990s in both the United States and Western Europe following the recession early in the decade, LBO growth exploded between 2001 and 2007, particularly outside the United States.

Pure Management Buyouts Rare

Only one in five LBOs deals between 1970 and 2007 involved pure management buyouts, in which individual investors (typically the target firm's management) acquired the firm in a leveraged transaction. The majority were undertaken by a traditional private equity financial sponsor providing most of the equity financing.

LBO Transactions Widespread

While private equity transactions take place in a wide variety of industries, including chemicals, machinery, and retailing, buyout activity has shifted increasingly to the high-growth, "high-tech" market segments. The shift in the type of target may reflect a change in the composition of U.S. industry or simply a shortage of targets deemed appropriate by private equity investors in the more traditional industries.

---

[2] Failed firms were excluded from the performance studies because they no longer existed.

[3] The data for the large sample studies come from Standard & Poor's Capital IQ and the U.S. Census Bureau databases. The studies compare a sample of LBO target firms with a "control sample." Selected for comparative purposes, firms in control samples are known to be similar to the private equity transaction sample in all respects except for not having undergone an LBO.

[4] Wright et al., 2008

Sales to Strategic Buyers Represent Primary Exit Strategy

LBO financial sponsors and management are able to realize their expected financial returns on exiting or "cashing out" of the business. Constituting about 13% of total transactions since the 1970s, initial public offerings (i.e., IPOs) declined in importance as an exit strategy. At 39% of all exits, the most common ways of exiting buyouts is through a sale to a strategic buyer; the second most common method, at 24%, is a sale to another buyout firm in so-called secondary buyouts.

Selling to a strategic buyer usually results in the best price because the buyer may be able to generate significant synergies by combining the firm with its existing business. If the original buyout firm's investment fund is coming to an end, the firm may be able to sell the LBO to another buyout firm that is looking for new investment opportunities. This option is best used when the LBO's management is still enthusiastic about growing the firm rather than cashing out. Consequently, the LBO may be attractive to another buyout firm.

An IPO is often less attractive due to the massive amount of public disclosure required, the substantial commitment of management time, the difficulty in timing the market, and the potential for incorrectly valuing the IPO. The original investors also can cash out while management remains in charge of the business through a leveraged recapitalization: borrowing additional funds to repurchase stock from other shareholders. This strategy may be employed once the firm has paid down its original debt level.

LBOs Not Prone to "Quick Flips"

"Quick flips," those LBOs exited in less than two years after the initial investment, accounted for only 8% of the total deals and have declined in recent years. LBOs tend to remain in place for long periods, with almost 40% continuing to operate 10 years after the initial LBO announcement. Smaller firms tend to stay in the LBO ownership form longer than larger firms. The median firm remains under LBO ownership for nine years. These findings are in stark contrast to earlier studies of public-to-private transactions, which found the median LBO target remained private for 6.8 years.[5]

Most LBOs Involve Acquisitions of Private Firms

While receiving most of the research in prior studies, public-to-private transactions accounted for 6.7% of all transactions between 1970 and 2007, although they did make up about 28% of the dollar value of such transactions, since public companies tend to be larger than private firms. Acquisitions of private firms constituted 47% of all transactions between 1970 and 2007. During the same period, buyouts of divisions of companies accounted for 31% of the transactions and 31% of the total value of transactions.

The Effects of LBOs on Innovation

It has long been recognized that economic growth is influenced significantly by the rate of innovation, which is in turn affected by the level of R&D spending.[6] Although early studies found a correlation between more debt and lower R&D spending,[7] more recent studies

[5] Kaplan, 1991

[6] Jaffe and Trajtenberg, 2002

[7] Hall, 1992; Himmelberg and Petersen, 1994

demonstrate that increased leverage tends to reduce R&D only for the smallest firms.[8] Studies show that LBOs increase R&D spending on an absolute basis and relative to their peers[9] and that private equity-financed LBOs may tend to improve the rate of innovation.[10]

The Effects of LBOs on Employment Growth

In an international study of 5,000 LBOs between 1980 and 2005 (the largest such study to date), Davis and colleagues (2008) found that companies owned by buyout firms maintained employment levels on par with competitors in the first year after the buyout. However, their employment levels dropped relative to a control (i.e., comparison) sample consisting of non-LBO firms in the second and third years following the buyout. By the end of five years, cumulative job growth was in the aggregate about 2 percentage points less than firms in the control sample. In manufacturing, employment levels at firms subject to buyout were very similar to those at competitor firms; in retailing, services, and financial services, employment tended to be significantly lower. Job creation as a result of investment in new ventures (i.e., greenfield operations) tends to be higher at firms experiencing buyouts than at competitor firms.

The authors note that their findings are consistent with the notion that private equity groups act as catalysts to shrink the inefficient segments of underperforming firms. Furthermore, greenfield operations undertaken by firms having undergone buyouts accelerate the expansion of such firms in new, potentially more productive directions. The job creation rate in these new ventures tends to be substantially higher than those in current businesses, creating the potential for higher long-term employment gains than at firms not having undergone buyouts.

Hedge Funds as Investors of Last Resort

Since 1995, hedge funds have participated in more than one-half of the private placements of equity securities (i.e., equity issues outside of public markets) in the United States. Contributing more than one-fourth of the total capital raised, hedge funds have consistently been the largest single investor group in these types of transactions.[11]

Firms using private placements tend to be small, young, and poorly performing. Because it is often difficult to get reliable information, these firms have difficulty obtaining financing.[12] These

---

[8] Hao and Jaffe, 1993

[9] Lichtenberg and Siegel, 1990

[10] Lerner, Sorensen, and Stromberg (2011) examined the impact of private equity investment on the rate of innovation for a sample of 495 firms with at least one successful patent application filed from three years prior to five years following a private equity investment. The authors found that the rate of innovation, as measured by the quantity and generality of patents, does not change following private equity investments. However, such firms tend to concentrate their innovation efforts in areas in which the firm has historically focused. In fact, the patents of private equity–backed firms applied for in the years following the investment by the private equity firm are more frequently cited, suggesting some improvement in the rate of innovation.

[11] Brophy et al., 2009

[12] Wu, 2004

transactions often are referred to as private investments in public equity (PIPES).[13] Because of difficulty in raising financing, firms issuing private placements of equities often have little leverage in negotiating with investors. Consequently, many of the private placements grant investors "repricing rights," which protect investors from a decline in the price of their holdings by requiring firms to issue more shares whenever the price of the privately placed shares decreases.

Hedge funds are often willing to purchase PIPES because of the way in which they insulate their portfolios from price declines. Hedge funds can purchase PIPE securities that cannot be sold in public markets until they are registered with the SEC at discounts from the issuing firms and simultaneously sell short the securities of the issuing firms that are already trading on public markets. Although firms obtaining funding from hedge funds perform relatively poorly, hedge funds investing in PIPE securities perform relatively well, because they buy such securities at substantial discounts (affording some protection from price declines), protect their investment through repricing rights and short-selling, and sell their investments after a relatively short period. By being able to protect their investments in this manner, hedge funds are able to serve "as investors of last resort" for firms having difficulty borrowing.

Competition in the LBO Market

To finance the increased average size of targets taken private in 2006, buyout firms started to bid for target firms as groups of investors. The tendency of buyout firms to invest as a group is often referred to as *clubbing*. The HCA, SunGard, and Kinder Morgan transactions all involved at least four private equity investor funds. While mitigating risk, banding together to buy large LBO targets also made buyout firms vulnerable to accusations of colluding in an effort to limit the prices offered for target firms. The empirical evidence concerning whether club deals actually benefit target firm shareholders by enabling the payment of higher purchase prices is mixed.[14]

Factors in Successful LBOs

While many factors contribute to the success of LBOs, studies suggest that target selection, not overpaying, and improving operating performance are among the most important.

Target Selection

Traditionally, firms that represent good candidates for an LBO are those that have substantial unused borrowing capacity, tangible assets, predictable positive operating cash flow, and assets that are not critical to the continuing operation of the business.[15] Competent and highly

---

[13] See Chapter 10 for a more detailed discussion of PIPE transactions.

[14] Meuleman and Wright (2007) and Guo et al. (2008) found some evidence that "clubbing" is associated with higher target transaction prices. However, Officer, Ozbas, and Sensoy (2008) argue that club deals are likely to be detrimental to public company shareholders by undermining the auction process that might result from having multiple suitors. In analyzing 325 public-to-private LBO transactions between 1998 and 2007, the U.S. General Accountability Office (2008) could find no correlation between club deals and prices paid for target firms.

[15] Carow and Roden, 1998

motivated management is always crucial to the eventual success of the LBO. Finally, firms in certain types of industries or that are part of larger firms often represent attractive opportunities.

Unused Borrowing Capacity and Redundant Assets

Factors enhancing borrowing capacity include cash balances on the books of the target company in excess of working capital requirements, a low debt–to–total capital ratio (as compared with the industry average), and a demonstrated ability to generate consistent earnings and cash-flow growth. Firms with undervalued assets may use such assets as collateral for loans from asset-based lenders. Undervalued assets also provide a significant tax shelter because they may be revalued and depreciated or amortized over their allowable tax lives. In addition, operating assets, such as subsidiaries that are not germane to the target's core business and that can be sold quickly for cash, can be divested to accelerate the payoff of either the highest cost debt or the debt with the most restrictive covenants.

Management Competence and Motivation

Even though management competence is a necessary condition for success, it does not ensure that the firm's performance will meet investor expectations. Management must be highly motivated by the prospect of abnormally large returns in a relatively short time. Consequently, management of the firm to be taken private is normally given an opportunity to own a significant portion of the equity of the firm.

Attractive Industries

Typical targets are in mature industries, such as manufacturing, retailing, textiles, food processing, apparel, and soft drinks. Such industries usually are characterized by large tangible book values, modest growth prospects, relatively stable cash flow, and limited research and development, new product, or technology requirements. Such industries are generally not dependent on technologies and production processes that are subject to rapid change. Empirical studies have shown that industries that have high free cash flows and limited growth opportunities are good candidates for LBOs.[16]

Large Company Operating Divisions

The best candidates for management buyouts often are underperforming divisions of larger companies, in which the division is no longer considered critical to the parent firm's overarching strategy. Frequently, such divisions are saddled with excessive administrative overhead, often required by the parent, and expenses are allocated to the division by the parent for services, such as legal, auditing, and treasury functions, that could be purchased less expensively from sources outside the parent firm.

Firms without Change of Control Covenants

Such covenants in bond indentures are clauses either limiting the amount of debt a firm can add or requiring the company to buy back outstanding debt, sometimes at a premium, whenever a change of control occurs. Firms with bonds lacking such covenants are twice as likely to be the target of an LBO.[17]

[16] Opler and Titman, 1993; Phan, 1995

[17] Billett, Jiang, and Lie, 2010

Not Overpaying

Overpaying for LBOs can be disastrous. Failure to meet debt service obligations in a timely fashion often requires that the LBO firm renegotiate the terms of the loan agreements with the lenders. If the parties to the transaction cannot reach a compromise, the firm may be forced to file for bankruptcy, often wiping out the initial investors. Highly leveraged firms also are subject to aggressive tactics from major competitors, who understand that taking on large amounts of debt raises the breakeven point for the firm. If the amount borrowed is made even more excessive as a result of having paid more than the economic value of the target firm, competitors may opt to gain market share by cutting product prices. The ability of the LBO firm to match such price cuts is limited because of the need to meet required interest and principal repayments.

Improving Operating Performance

Tactics employed to improve performance include negotiating employee wage and benefit concessions in exchange for a profit-sharing or stock ownership plan and outsourcing services once provided by the parent. Other options include moving the corporate headquarters to a less-expensive location, pruning unprofitable customer accounts, and eliminating such perks as corporate aircraft. As board members, buyout specialists, such as LBO funds, tend to take a much more active role in monitoring management performance.

HOW DO LBOS CREATE VALUE?

LBOs create value by reducing debt, improving operating performance, and properly timing the sale of the business. LBOs often do not pay taxes for five to seven years or longer following the buyout due to the tax deductibility of interest and the additional depreciation resulting from the write-up of net acquired assets to fair market value. The firm's profits are likely to be shielded from taxes until a substantial portion of the outstanding debt is repaid and the assets depreciated. LBO investors (i.e., the sponsor group) utilize cumulative free cash flow to increase firm value by repaying debt and improving operating performance.

Debt Reduction

When debt is repaid, the equity value of the firm increases in direct proportion to the reduction in outstanding debt—equity increases by $1 for each $1 of debt repaid—assuming the financial sponsor can sell the firm for at least what it paid for the company. Debt reduction also contributes to cash flow by eliminating future interest and principal payments.

Operating Margin Improvement

By reinvesting cumulative free cash flow, the firm's operating margins can increase by improving efficiency, introducing new products, and making strategic acquisitions. The subsequent increase in margins will augment operating cash flow, which in turn raises the firm's equity value, if the level of risk is unchanged.

Timing the Sale of the Firm

The amount of the increase in firm value depends to a significant extent on the valuation that multiple investors place on each dollar of earnings, cash flow, or EBITDA when the firm is sold. LBO investors create value by timing the sale of the firm to coincide with the firm's

TABLE 13.2   LBOs Create Value by Reducing Debt, Improving Margins, and Increasing Exit Multiples

	Case 1: Debt Reduction	Case 2: Debt Reduction + Margin Improvement	Case 3: Debt Reduction + Margin Improvement + Higher Exit Multiples
LBO Formation Year			
Total Debt	$400,000,000	$400,000,000	$400,000,000
Equity	100,000,000	100,000,000	100,000,000
Transaction Value	$500,000,000	$500,000,000	$500,000,000
Exit Year (Year 7) Assumptions			
Cumulative Cash Available for Debt Repayment[a]	$150,000,000	$185,000,000	$185,000,000
Net Debt[b]	$250,000,000	$215,000,000	$215,000,000
EBITDA	$100,000,000	$130,000,000	$130,000,000
EBITDA Multiple	7.0×	7.0×	8.0×
Transaction Value[c]	$700,000,000	$910,000,000	$1,040,000,000
Equity Value[d]	$450,000,000	$695,000,000	$825,000,000
Internal Rate of Return	24%	31.9%	35.2%
Cash on Cash Return[e]	4.5×	6.95×	8.25×

[a]*Cumulative cash available for debt repayment and EBITDA increase between Case 1 and Case 2 due to improving margins and lower interest and principal repayments reflecting the reduction in net debt.*
[b]*Net Debt = Total Debt − Cumulative Cash Available for Debt Repayment = $400 million − $185 million = $215 million.*
[c]*Transaction value = EBITDA in the 7th Year × EBITDA multiple in the 7th Year.*
[d]*Equity Value = Transaction Value in the 7th Year − Net Debt.*
[e]*The equity value when the firm is sold divided by the initial equity contribution. The IRR represents a more accurate financial return because it accounts for the time value of money.*

leverage declining to the industry-average leverage and with favorable industry conditions.[18] This typically occurs when the firm takes on the risk characteristics of the average firm in the industry and when the industry in which the business competes is most attractive to investors, a point at which valuation multiples are likely to be the highest.[19]

Table 13.2 provides a numerical example of how LBOs create value by "paying down" debt, by improving the firm's operating margins, and by increasing the market multiple applied to the firm's EBITDA in the year in which the firm is sold. Each case assumes that the sponsor group pays $500 million for the target firm and finances the transaction by borrowing $400 million and contributing $100 million in equity. The sponsor group is assumed to exit the LBO at the end of seven years. In Case 1, all cumulative free cash

[18] Guo et al. (2011) find that operating performance, tax benefits, and market multiples applied when the investor group exits the business each contribute about one-fourth of the financial returns to buyout investors.

[19] The annual ROE of the firm will decline, as the impact of leverage declines, to the industry average ROE, which usually occurs when the firm's debt–to–total capital ratio approximates the industry average ratio. At this point, the financial sponsor is unable to earn excess returns by continuing to operate the business. Table 13.1 illustrates this point. ROE is highest when leverage is highest and lowest when leverage is zero, subject to the caveat that ROE could decline due to escalating borrowing costs if debt were to be viewed by lenders as excessive.

flow is used to reduce outstanding debt. Case 2 assumes the same exit multiple as Case 1 but that cumulative free cash flow is higher due to margin improvement and lower interest and principal repayments as a result of debt reduction. Case 3 assumes the same cumulative free cash flow available for debt repayment and EBITDA as in Case 2 but a higher exit multiple.

WHEN DO FIRMS GO PRIVATE?

Firms are inclined to go private if the board and management believe that the firm's current share price is undervalued, the need for liquidity is low, the cost of governance is high, and the potential loss of control is high. While access to liquid public capital markets enables a firm to lower its cost of capital, participating in public markets creates the potential for significant disagreements between the board and management on one hand and shareholders on the other.[20] The Sarbanes-Oxley Act of 2002 may also have contributed to the cost of governance, causing some firms (particularly smaller firms) to go private to avoid such costs.[21]

FINANCING TRANSACTIONS

This section discusses how transactions are financed and addresses the complex capital structures of highly leveraged transactions, such as leveraged buyouts, and ways of selecting the appropriate capital structure. In addition to an acquirer using excess cash on hand, financing options range from borrowing to issuing equity to seller financing. These are discussed next.

Financing Options: Borrowing

An acquirer or financial sponsor may tap into an array of alternative sources of borrowing, including asset- and cash-flow–based lending, long-term financing, and leveraged bank loans.

Asset-Based or Secured Lending

Under asset-based lending, the borrower pledges certain assets as collateral. These loans are often short-term (i.e., less than one year in maturity) and secured by assets that can be liquidated easily, such as accounts receivable and inventory. Borrowers often seek *revolving*

---

[20] Boot, Gopalan, and Thakor, 2008

[21] There is evidence that the Sarbanes-Oxley Act of 2002 contributed to the cost of governance for firms as a result of the onerous reporting requirements of the bill. This has been a particular burden to smaller firms. Some studies estimate that the cost of being a public firm was more than $4 million in 2004, almost twice the cost incurred in the prior year (Engel, Hayes, and Xang, 2004; Hartman, 2005; Kamar, Karaca-Mandic, and Talley, 2006). Leuz, Triantis, and Wang (2008) document a spike in delistings of public firms attributable to the passage of the Sarbanes-Oxley Act of 2002.

lines of credit that they draw upon on a daily basis to run their business. Under a revolving credit arrangement, the bank agrees to make loans up to a maximum for a specified period, usually a year or more. As the borrower repays a portion of the loan, an amount equal to the repayment can be borrowed again under the terms of the agreement. In addition to interest on the notes, the bank charges a fee for the commitment to hold the funds available. For a fee, the borrower may choose to convert the revolving credit line into a term loan. A *term loan* usually has a maturity of two to ten years and typically is secured by the asset that is being financed, such as new capital equipment.[22]

Loan documents define the rights and the obligations of the parties to the loan. The *loan agreement* stipulates the terms and conditions under which the lender will loan the firm funds; the *security agreement* specifies which of the borrower's assets will be pledged to secure the loan; and the *promissory note* commits the borrower to repay the loan, even if the assets, when liquidated, do not fully cover the unpaid balance.[23] If the borrower defaults on the loan, the lender can seize and sell the collateral to recover the value of the loan.[24] Loan agreements often have *cross-default provisions* that allow a lender to collect its loan immediately if the borrower is in default on a loan to another lender.

These documents contain certain security provisions and protective positive and negative covenants limiting what the borrower may do as long as the loan is outstanding. Typical *security provisions* include the assignment of payments due under a specific contract to the lender, an assignment of a portion of the receivables or inventories, and a pledge of marketable securities held by the borrower. An *affirmative protective covenant* in a loan agreement specifies the actions the borrower agrees to take during the term of the loan.

Typically, these include furnishing periodic financial statements to the lender, carrying sufficient insurance to cover insurable business risks, maintaining a minimum amount of net working capital, and retaining key management personnel acceptable to the lending institution. *Negative covenants* restrict the actions of the borrower. They include limiting the amount of dividends that can be paid; the level of salaries and bonuses that may be given to the borrower's employees; the total amount of indebtedness that can be assumed

---

[22] Acquiring firms often prefer to borrow funds on an unsecured basis because the added administrative costs involved in pledging assets as security significantly raise the total cost of borrowing. Secured borrowing can be onerous because the security agreements can severely limit a company's future borrowing, ability to pay dividends, make investments, and manage working capital aggressively.

[23] The security agreement is filed at a state regulatory office in the state where the collateral is located. Future lenders can check with this office to see which assets a firm has pledged and which are free to be used as future collateral. The filing of this security agreement legally establishes the lender's security interest in the collateral.

[24] The process of determining which of a firm's assets are free from liens is made easier today by commercial credit reporting repositories such as Dun & Bradstreet, Experian, Equifax, and Transunion.

by the borrower; investments in plant and equipment and acquisitions; and the sale of certain assets.

Cash-Flow or Unsecured Lenders

Cash-flow lenders view the borrower's future cash-flow generation capability as the primary means of recovering a loan and the borrower's assets as a secondary source of funds in the event of default by the borrower. In the mid-1980s, LBOs' capital structures assumed increasing amounts of unsecured debt. To compensate for additional risk, the unsecured lenders would receive both a higher interest rate and warrants that were convertible into equity at some future date.

Unsecured debt that lies between senior debt and the equity layers is often referred to as *mezzanine financing*. It includes senior subordinated debt, subordinated debt, bridge financing, and LBO partnership financing. It frequently consists of high-yield junk bonds, which may also include zero coupon deferred interest debentures (i.e., bonds whose interest is not paid until maturity) used to increase the postacquisition cash flow of the acquired entity. Unsecured financing often consists of several layers of debt, each subordinate in liquidation to the next most senior issue. Those with the lowest level of security typically offer the highest yields to compensate for their higher level of risk in the event of default. *Bridge financing* consists of unsecured loans, often provided by investment banks or hedge funds, to supply short-term financing pending the placement of subordinated debt (i.e., long-term or "permanent" financing). The usual expectation is that bridge financing will be replaced six to nine months after the closing date of the LBO transaction.

On March 17, 2009, Pfizer Pharmaceuticals announced that it had successfully sold $13.5 billion in senior, unsecured long-term debt in maturities of 3, 6, 10, and 20 years to replace short-term bridge financing that had been issued to complete its acquisition of Wyeth Pharmaceuticals. Accounting for about one-third of the $68 billion purchase price, the bridge financing, consisting of $22.5 billion, had to be repaid by December 31, 2009. The five banks that originally had provided the bridge loans had syndicated (sold) portions of the loans to a total of 29 other banks such that no single bank financed more than $1.5 billion of the total $22.5 billion.

Types of Long-Term Financing

The attractiveness of long-term debt is its relatively low after-tax cost and the potential for leverage to improve earnings per share and returns on equity. However, too much debt can increase the risk of default on loan repayments and bankruptcy.

Long-term debt issues are classified by whether they are *senior* or *junior* in liquidation. Senior debt has a higher-priority claim to a firm's earnings and assets than junior debt. Unsecured debt also may be classified according to whether it is subordinated to other types of debt. In general, subordinated debentures are junior to other types of debt, including bank loans, and even may be junior to all of a firm's other debt. *Debentures* are unsecured, backed only by the overall creditworthiness of the borrower.

Convertible bonds are types of debt that are convertible, at some predetermined ratio (i.e., a specific number of shares per bond), into shares of stock of the issuing company. Such debt often is referred to as a hybrid security because it has both debt and equity characteristics. It normally has a relatively low coupon rate. The bond buyer is compensated primarily by the ability to convert the bond to common stock at a substantial discount from the stock's market value. Issuers of such debt benefit by having to make a lower cash interest payment. However, current shareholders will experience earnings or ownership dilution when the bondholders convert their bonds into new shares.

The extent to which a debt issue is junior to other debt depends on the restrictions placed on the company in an agreement called an *indenture*, which is a contract between the firm that issues the long-term debt securities and the lenders. The indenture details the nature of the issue, specifies the way in which the principal must be repaid, and specifies affirmative and negative covenants applicable to the long-term debt issue. Typical covenants include maintaining a minimum interest coverage ratio, minimum level of working capital, maximum amount of dividends that the firm can pay, and restrictions on equipment leasing and issuing additional debt.

Debt issues often are rated by various *credit rating agencies* according to their relative degree of risk.[25] The agencies consider various factors, such as a firm's earnings stability, interest coverage ratios, the amount of debt in the firm's capital structure, the degree of subordination of the issue being rated, and the firm's past performance, in meeting its debt service requirements.[26]

Junk Bonds

Junk bonds are high-yield bonds that credit-rating agencies have deemed either to be below investment grade or to have no rating.[27] When originally issued, junk bonds frequently yield more than 4 percentage points above the yields on U.S. Treasury debt of comparable maturity.

[25] Prospectuses promoting bond sales have typically included ratings from the various agencies as a measure of risk provided by a third party. Prior to the Dodd-Frank Act of 2010 (see Chapter 2), institutional investors, including banks, insurers, and money market funds, were permitted to rely solely on credit ratings when making investment decisions. The Dodd-Frank Act now seeks to compel such investors to conduct an independent investigation into the factors influencing the risk associated with a security to diminish their reliance on credit rating agencies. The Act intends to achieve this objective by expunging from existing federal securities regulations the requirement that ratings from credit rating agencies be included in bond prospectuses. The Act also makes it easier to sue the rating agencies for credit ratings that turn out to be too optimistic, thereby discouraging the agencies from allowing the use of their ratings in bond prospectuses.

[26] Rating agencies include Moody's Investors Services and Standard & Poor's Corporation. Each has its own scale for identifying the risk of an issue. For Moody's, the ratings are Aaa (the lowest risk category), Aa, A, Baa, Ba, B, Caa, Ca, and C (the highest risk). For S&P, AAA denotes the lowest risk category, and risk rises progressively through ratings AA, A, BBB, BB, B, CCC, CC, C, and D.

[27] Moody's usually rates noninvestment-grade bonds Ba or lower; for S&P, it is BB or lower.

Junk bond financing exploded in the early 1980s but dried up by the end of the decade.[28] Three-fourths of the proceeds of junk bonds issued between 1980 and 1986 were used to finance the capital requirements of high-growth corporations; the remainder was used to finance takeovers.[29]

Leveraged Bank Loans

Leveraged loans are defined as unrated or noninvestment-grade bank loans whose interest rates are equal to or greater than the London Interbank Rate (LIBOR) plus 150 basis points (1.5 percentage points). Leveraged loans include second mortgages, which typically have a floating rate and give lenders a lower level of security than first mortgages. Some analysts include other forms of debt instruments in this market, such as mezzanine or senior unsecured debt, discussed earlier in this chapter, and *payment-in-kind notes*, for which interest is paid in the form of more debt.

In the United States, the volume of such loans substantially exceeds the volume of junk bond issues. This represents a revival in bank loan financing as an alternative to financing transactions with junk bonds after junk bond issues dried up in the late 1980s; at the time, bank loans were more expensive. Leveraged loans are often less costly than junk bonds for borrowers because they have higher seniority in a firm's capital structure than high-yield bonds.

Globally, the syndicated loan market, including leveraged loans, senior unsecured debt, and payment-in-kind notes, is growing more rapidly than public markets for debt and equity. Syndicated loans are those typically issued through a consortium of institutions, including hedge funds, pension funds, and insurance companies to individual borrowers.

Financing Options: Common and Preferred Equity

There are many varieties of common stock, and some pay dividends and provide voting rights. Other common shares (often called super-voting shares) have multiple voting rights. In addition to voting rights, common shareholders sometimes receive rights offerings that allow them to maintain their proportional ownership in the company in the event that the company issues another stock offering. Common shareholders with rights may, but are not obligated to, acquire as many shares of the new stock as needed to maintain their proportional ownership in the company.

Although preferred stockholders receive dividends rather than interest payments, their shares often are considered a fixed income security. Dividends on preferred stock are generally

---

[28] Rapid growth of the junk bond market coincided with a growing deterioration during the 1980s in their quality, as measured by interest coverage ratios (i.e., earnings before interest and taxes/interest expense), debt/net tangible book value, and cash flow as a percentage of debt (Wigmore, 1994). Cumulative default rates for junk bonds issued in the late 1970s reached as high as 34T by 1986 (Asquith, Mullins, and Wolff, 1989), but firms that emerged from bankruptcy managed to recover some portion of the face value of the junk bond. Altman and Kishore (1996) found that recovery rates for senior secured debt averaged about 58% of the original principal and that the actual realized spread between junk bonds and ten-year U.S. Treasury securities was actually about 4 percentage points between 1978 and 1994, rather than more than 4 percentage points when they were issued originally. This source of LBO financing dried up in the late 1980s after a series of defaults of overleveraged firms, coupled with alleged insider trading and fraud at companies such as Drexel Burnham, the primary market maker for junk bonds at that time.

[29] Yago and Bonds, 1991

constant over time, like interest payments on debt, but the firm is generally not obligated to pay them at a specific time.[30] In liquidation, bondholders are paid first, then preferred stockholders, and common stockholders are paid last. To conserve cash, LBOs frequently issue *paid in kind (PIK) preferred stock*, where dividends are paid in the form of more preferred stock.

Seller Financing

Seller financing is a highly important source of financing and one way to "close the gap" between what a seller wants and a buyer is willing to pay on the purchase price. It involves the seller deferring the receipt of a portion of the purchase price until some future date—in effect, providing a loan to the buyer. A buyer may be willing to pay the seller's asking price if a portion is deferred because the buyer recognizes that the loan will reduce the purchase price in present value terms. The advantages to the buyer include a lower overall risk of the transaction because of the need to provide less capital at the time of closing and the shifting of operational risk to the seller if the buyer ultimately defaults on the loan to the seller.[31] Table 13.3 summarizes the alternative forms of financing.

COMMON FORMS OF LEVERAGED BUYOUT DEAL STRUCTURES

Due to the epidemic of bankruptcies of cash-flow–based LBOs in the late 1980s, the most common form of LBO today is the asset-based LBO. This type of LBO can be accomplished in two ways: the sale of assets by the target to the acquiring company, with the seller using the cash received to pay off outstanding liabilities, or a merger of the target into the acquiring company (direct merger) or a wholly-owned subsidiary of the acquiring company (subsidiary merger). For small companies, a reverse stock split may be used to take the firm private. An important objective of "going private" transactions is to reduce the number of shareholders to below 300 to enable the public firm to delist from many public stock exchanges.

In a *direct merger*, the company to be taken private merges with a company controlled by the financial sponsor. If the LBO is structured as a direct merger, in which the seller receives cash for stock, the lender will make the loan to the buyer once the security agreements are in place and the target's stock has been pledged against the loan. The target then is merged into the acquiring company, which is the surviving corporation. Payment of the loan proceeds usually is made directly to the seller in accordance with a "letter of direction" drafted by the buyer.

In a *subsidiary merger*, the company controlled by the financial sponsor creates a new subsidiary that merges with the target. The subsidiary then makes a tender offer for the outstanding public shares. This may be done to avoid any negative impact that the new company

---

[30] Unpaid dividends may accumulate for eventual payment by the issuer if the preferred stock is a special cumulative issue.

[31] Many businesses do not want to use seller financing, since it requires that they accept the risk that the note will not be repaid. Such financing is necessary, though, when bank financing is not an option. The drying up of bank lending in 2008 and 2009 due to the slumping economy and crisis of confidence in the credit markets resulted in increased reliance on seller financing to complete the sale of small- to intermediate-size businesses.

TABLE 13.3 Alternative Financing by Type of Security and Lending Source

Type of Security		Debt	
	Backed by	Lenders Loan up to	Lending Source
Secured Debt			
Short-Term (<1 Year) Debt	Liens generally on receivables and inventories	50–80%, depending on quality	Banks and finance companies
Intermediate-Term (1–10 Years) Debt	Liens on land and equipment	80% of appraised value of equipment and 50% of real estate	Life insurance companies, private equity investors, pension and hedge funds
Unsecured or Mezzanine Debt (Subordinated and Junior Subordinated Debt, including Seller Financing) – First Layer – Second Layer – Etc. Bridge Financing Payment-in-Kind	Cash-generating capabilities of the borrower	Face value of securities	Life insurance companies, pension funds, private equity, and hedge funds
Equity			
Preferred Stock— Payment-in-Kind	Cash-generating capabilities of the borrower		Life insurance companies, pension funds, hedge funds, private equity, and angel investors
Common Stock	Cash-generating capabilities of the borrower		Life insurance, pension, private equity, hedge, and venture capital funds; angel investors

might have on existing customer or creditor relationships. If some portion of the parent's assets are to be used as collateral to support the ability of its operating subsidiary to fund the transaction, both the parent and the subsidiary may be viewed as having a security interest (i.e., an implied guarantee) in the debt. As such, they may be held jointly and severally liable for the debt. To avoid this situation, the parent may make a capital contribution to the subsidiary rather than provide collateral or a loan guarantee.

A *reverse stock split* enables a corporation to reduce the number of shares outstanding. The total number of shares will have the same market value immediately after the reverse split as before, but each share will be worth more. Reverse splits may be used to take a firm private where a firm is short of cash. Therefore, the majority shareholders retain their stock after the split, while the minority shareholders receive a cash payment.

On January 9, 2008, MagStar Technologies, a Minnesota-based manufacturer of conveyor systems, announced a 1 for 2,000 reverse split of the firm's common stock, intending to take it private. Under the terms of the split, each 2,000 shares of the firm's common stock would be converted into 1 share of common stock, and holders of fewer than 2,000 shares of common stock on the record date would receive cash of $0.425 per presplit share. The anticipated split would reduce the number of shareholders to less than 300, the minimum required to list on many public exchanges. The company immediately stopped filing reports with the SEC. Under Minnesota law, the board of directors of a company may amend the firm's articles of incorporation to conduct the reverse split without shareholder approval.

Legal Pitfalls of Improperly Structured LBOs

Fraudulent conveyance laws are applicable whenever a company goes into bankruptcy following events such as a highly leveraged transaction. Under the law, the new company created by the LBO must be strong enough financially to meet its obligations to current and future creditors. If the new company is found by the court to have been inadequately capitalized, the lender could be stripped of its secured position in the company's assets, or its claims on the assets could be made subordinate to those of the general or unsecured creditors. Consequently, lenders, sellers, directors, or their agents, including auditors and investment bankers, may be required to compensate the general creditors. Fraudulent conveyance laws are intended to preclude shareholders, secured creditors, and others from benefiting at the expense of unsecured creditors. While fraudulent conveyance cases ordinarily do not get very far in court, the extreme leverage of many transactions during 2006 and 2007 has spawned increasing allegations of fraud.[32]

Leveraged Buyout Capital Structures

LBOs tend to have complicated capital structures consisting of bank debt, high-yield debt, mezzanine debt, and private equity provided primarily by the LBO sponsor (Figure 13.1). As secured debt, the bank debt generally is the most senior in the capital structure in the event of liquidation. Usually maturing within five to seven years, interest rates on such loans often vary at a fixed spread or difference over the London interbank offering rate. Bank loans usually must be paid off before other types of debt. Bank credit facilities consist of revolving credit and term loans.[33] A revolving credit facility is used to satisfy daily liquidity requirements, secured by the firm's most liquid assets such as receivables and inventory. Term loans are usually secured by the firm's longer-lived assets and are granted in tranches or slices, denoted as A, B, C, and D, with A the most senior and D the lowest of all bank financing. While bank debt in the A tranche usually must be amortized or paid off before other forms of debt can be paid, the remaining tranches generally involve little or no amortization. While lenders in the A tranche often sell such loans to other commercial banks, loans in the B, C, and D tranches often are sold to hedge funds and mutual funds. In recent years, bank debt would make up about 40% of the total capital structure.

---

[32] In late 2009, a group of junior creditors led by Centerbridge Partners charged that Chicago billionaire Sam Zell's $8.2 billion transaction to take the Tribune Company public in 2007 left the firm insolvent from the start. If provable, the court might invalidate more than $10 billon in claims held by senior lenders who financed the deal, forcing them to write off the entire amount.

[33] Credit or loan facilities may represent a single loan or a collection of loans to a borrower. Such facilities vary in terms of what is being financed, the type of collateral, terms, and duration.

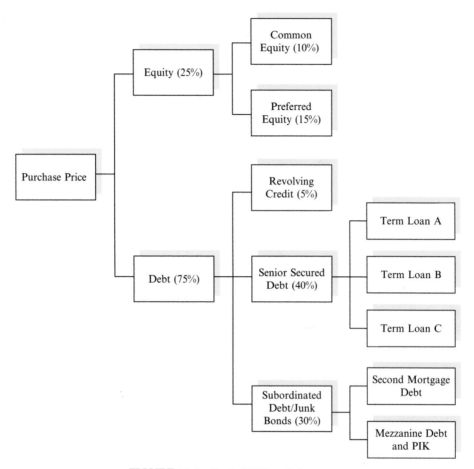

FIGURE 13.1   Typical LBO capital structure.

The next layer of LBO capital structure consists of unsecured subordinated debt, also referred to as *junk bonds*. Interest is fixed and represents a constant percentage or spread over the U.S. Treasury bond rate. The amount of the spread depends on the credit quality of the debt. Often callable at a premium, this debt usually has a seven- to ten-year maturity range, with the debt often paid off in a single payment. Such loans often are referred to as *bullet loans*.

As an alternative to high-yield publicly traded junk bonds, second mortgage or lien loans became popular between 2003 and mid-2007. Often called mezzanine debt, such loans are privately placed with hedge funds and collateralized loan obligation (CLO) investors. They are secured by the firm's assets but are subordinated to the bank debt in liquidation. By pooling large numbers of first and second mortgage loans (so-called noninvestment-grade or leveraged loans) and subdividing the pool into tranches, CLO investors sell the tranches to institutional investors such as pension funds and insurance companies. This type of debt is often issued with warrants to buy equity in the firm. The final layer of the capital structure consists of equity contributed by the financial sponsor (usually a single or a number of private equity or hedge funds) and management. The equity component consists of both preferred and common shares.

PREBUYOUT AND POSTBUYOUT SHAREHOLDER RETURNS

The following sections summarize the key factors affecting financial returns to shareholders before and after a leveraged buyout transaction.

Prebuyout Returns to Target Shareholders

The studies that are cited in Table 13.4 show that the premium paid by LBOs and MBOs to target company shareholders often exceeds 40% in nondivisional buyouts. These empirical studies also include so-called *reverse LBOs* (RLBOs)—public companies taken private and later taken public through an IPO. The latter IPO is called a *secondary public offering*.

Divisional buyouts represent opportunities for improved operating efficiency, since the division is removed from the bureaucracy of the parent. Although this may be a source of gain for the acquirer, it does not seem to be true for the shareholders of the parent firm divesting the division. The parent firm's shareholders receive only minuscule returns. The size of these returns may reflect the division's small share of the parent corporation's total market value. The fact that parent shareholders experience any gain at all may suggest that the parent's resources are redeployed to higher return investments.

TABLE 13.4 Empirical Studies[a] of Returns to Shareholders (Prebuyout Returns)

Nondivisional Buyouts	Premium Paid to Target Shareholders
DeAngelo, DeAngelo, and Rice (1984) (Sample size = 72 U.S. MBOs)	56% (1973–1983)[b] 76% (when there are 3 or more bids)
Lowenstein (1985) (Sample size = 28 U.S. MBOs)	48% (1979–1984)
Lehn and Poulsen (1988) (Sample size = 92 U.S. LBOs)	41% (1980–1984)
Kaplan (1989) (Sample size = 76 U.S. LBOs)	42% (1980–1986)
Renneboog, Simons, and Wright (2007) (Sample size = 97 U.K. LBOs)	40% (1997–2003)
Divisional Buyouts	**Return to Parent Corporation Shareholders**
Hite and Vetsuypens (1989) (Sample size = 151 MBOs)	0.55% (1983–1987)
Muscarella and Vetsuypens (1990) (Sample size = 45 MBOs)	1.98% (1983–1988)

[a]*MBO, management buyout; LBO, leveraged buyout.*
[b]*The years in parentheses represent the time period in which the study took place.*

Factors Determining Prebuyout Target Shareholder Returns

Table 13.5 summarizes a portion of the extensive empirical research that attempts to identify the factors that explain the sizable gains in share price accruing to prebuyout target shareholders. Although a number of factors are at work, the sizeable returns to these shareholders seem to reflect buyout firms' anticipated improvements in operating performance (i.e., cost reduction, productivity improvement, and revenue enhancement) due to management incentives, as well as large tax benefits. The anticipated improved operating performance is consistent with arguments that large abnormal returns to LBO target shareholders reflect investor undervaluation of the target prior to the announcement of an LBO.[34]

Anticipated Improvement in Operating Performance and Tax Benefits

The most often cited sources of these returns are from tax benefits and expected post-LBO improvements in operating performance as a result of management incentives and the discipline imposed on management to repay debt. Because tax benefits are highly predictable, their value is largely reflected in premiums offered to shareholders of firms subject to LBOs.[35]

Wealth Transfer Effects

The evidence supporting wealth transfer effects is mixed. The exception may be for very large LBOs, such as RJR Nabisco, where largely anecdotal evidence suggests that a significant transfer of wealth may have taken place between the firm's pre-LBO debt holders and shareholders.

Superior Knowledge

There is little evidence to support the notion that LBO investors have knowledge of a business that is superior to the firm's public shareholders. Such knowledge, the theory suggests, would enable LBO investors to pay such high premiums because they understand better how to achieve cost savings and productivity improvements.

More Efficient Decision Making

There is also little empirical evidence to support the notion that decision making is more efficient. Nonetheless, the intuitive appeal of the simplified decision-making process of a private company is compelling when contrasted with a public company with multiple constituents directly or indirectly affecting decision making, including the board of directors with outside directors, public shareholders, public company regulatory agencies, and Wall Street analysts.

---

[34] Renneboog et al., 2007; Weir, Laing, and Wright, 2005

[35] Jensen (1986) argues that debt imposes a discipline that forces managers to stay focused on maximizing operating cash flows. Tax benefits are largely predictable and built into the premium offered for the public shares of the target firm as a result of the negotiation process (Kaplan, 1989b; Newbould, Chatfield, and Anderson, 1992). Successful MBOs are associated with improved operating performance, including increased efficiency and more aggressive marketing plans, while firms undertaking MBOs that were not completed showed no subsequent improvement in operating performance (Ofek, 1994).

TABLE 13.5   Factors Contributing to Pre-LBO Buyout Returns to Target Shareholders

Factor	Theory	Evidence[a]
MANAGEMENT INCENTIVES		
Equity Ownership Kaplan (1991) (sample size = 76 MBOs)	Management will improve performance when their ownership stake increases.	Management ownership increased for MBOs between 1980 and 1986 from 8.3% before the buyout to 29% after the buyout.
Incentive (Profit Sharing) Plans Muscarella and Vetsuypens (1990) (sample size = 72 reverse LBOs)	Stock option and share appreciation plans motivate management to take cost-cutting actions that might otherwise have been unacceptable.	96% of LBOs had at least one and 75% had two incentive plans in place during the 1983–1988 period. The change in shareholder gain is positively correlated with the fraction of shares owned by LBO's officers.
Improved Operating Performance Holthausen and Larker (1996) (sample size = 90 reverse LBOs)	Equity ownership and incentive plans motivate management to initiate aggressive cost-reduction plans and to change marketing strategies.	For the 1983–1988 period, sales were up by 9.4% in real terms, and operating profits were up by 45.4% between the LBO announcement date and the secondary initial public offering. Firm performance also was highly correlated with the amount of ownership by officers and directors.
Kaplan (1989b)		Operating income in LBO firms increased more than in other firms in the same industry during 2 years following the LBO.
TAX SHELTER BENEFITS		
Kaplan (1989a)	An LBO can be tax-free for as long as 5–7 years.	Median value of tax shelter contributed 30% of the premium.
Lehn and Poulsen (1988)		Premium paid to pre-LBO shareholders positively correlated with pre-LBO tax liability/equity.
UNDERVALUATION		
Renneboog, Simons, and Wright (2007); Weir, Laing, and Wright (2005)	Investors undervalue the target firm prior to LBO.	Both studies report large abnormal returns in recent LBO wave consistent with those recorded in the 1980s.
WEALTH TRANSFER EFFECTS		
Lehn and Poulsen (1988)	Premiums represent a transfer of wealth from bondholders to common stockholders.	Found no evidence that bondholders and preferred stockholders lose value when an LBO is announced.
Travlos and Cornett (1993)		Found small losses associated with the LBO announcement.
Billet, King, and Mauer (2004) (sample size = 3073 LBOs)		Found no evidence of wealth transfer between bondholders and stockholders.

TABLE 13.5   Cont'd

	INVESTOR GROUP HAS BETTER INFORMATION THAN PUBLIC SHAREHOLDERS ON MBO TARGET	
Kaplan (1988) and Smith (1990)	Investor group believes target worth more than shareholders believe it is.	Found no evidence to support this theory.
	IMPROVED EFFICIENCY IN DECISION MAKING	
Travlos and Cornett (1993)	Private firms are less bureaucratic and do not incur reporting and servicing costs associated with public shareholders.	Shareholder-related expenses are not an important factor; difficult to substantiate more efficient decision making.

^{a}MBO, managed buyout; LBO, leveraged buyout.

Postbuyout Returns to LBO Shareholders

Table 13.6 summarizes a cross-section of the studies of returns to shareholders following a leveraged buyout. A number of empirical studies suggest that investors in LBOs earned abnormal profits on their initial investments. Overall, studies suggest specifically that public to private LBOs (particularly MBOs) improve a firm's operating profits and cash flow, irrespective of methodology, benchmarks, and time period. However, there is evidence that more recent public to private LBOs may have a more modest impact on operating performance than those of the 1980s.[36]

Factors Determining Postbuyout Returns

Postbuyout empirical studies imply that the effect of increased operating efficiency following a leveraged buyout is not fully reflected in the pre-LBO premium. These studies may be subject to selection or survivor bias in that only LBOs that are successful in significantly improving their operating performance are able to undertake a secondary public offering. In many instances, the abnormal returns earned by postbuyout shareholders were the result of the LBO being acquired by another firm within the three years immediately following the LBO announcement.[37]

In a larger sample and within a longer time period than in earlier studies, reverse LBOs showed a much larger three-year cumulative return (except for those "flipped" within one year of acquisition) than earlier studies.[38] Researchers suggest that new owners choosing to retain their investment longer have more time to put the proper controls and reporting–

[36] Cumming et al. (2007) in a summary of much of the literature on post-LBO performance conclude that LBOs and especially MBOs enhance firm operating performance. However, Guo et al. (2011) find that the improvement in operating performance following public to private LBOs has been more modest during the 1990–2006 period than during the 1980s. Weir et al (2007) find similar results over roughly the same period.

[37] Mian and Rosenfeld, 1993

[38] Cao and Lerner, 2006

TABLE 13.6   Postbuyout Returns to LBO Shareholders[a]

Empirical Study	Impact on Postbuyout Performance
Muscarella and Vetsuypens (1990) (Sample Size = 45 MBOs 1983–1987)	Of 41 firms going public, median annual return was 36.6% in 3 years following buyout.
Kaplan (1991) (Sample size = 21 MBOs 1979–1986)	Median annualized return was 26% higher than the gain on the S&P 500 during the 3-year postbuyout period.
Mian and Rosenfeld (1993) (Sample Size = 85 reverse LBOs 1983–1989)	Of the 33 LBOs that were acquired by another firm during the 3 years following the LBO, cumulative abnormal returns exceeded 21%. Of those not acquired, cumulative abnormal returns were zero.
Holthausen and Larker (1996) (Sample Size = 90 reverse LBOs 1983–1988)	Firms outperformed their industries over the 4 years following the secondary IPO.
Groh and Gottschaig (2006) (Sample size = 152 LBOs 1981–2004)	Risk-adjusted performance of U.S. LBOs significantly superior to S&P 500 stock index
Renneboog, Simons, and Wright (2006) (Sample size = 97 LBOs 1997–2004)	Share prices higher in aftermath of LBO
Guo et al. (2011) (Sample size = 192 LBOs 1990–2006)	Median postbuyout 3-year cumulative returns of 40.9%. Gains tend to be larger for firms that are more leveraged and when the CEO has been replaced at the time of the buyout. However, median operating performance is more modest than improvements recorded during 1980s.
Cao and Lerner (2009) (Sample Size = 496 reverse LBOs 1980–2002)	Reverse LBOs outperform other IPOs and the overall stock market, exhibiting a cumulative 3-year return of 43.8%. In contrast, "quick flips" (i.e., buyout firm sells its investment within a year of acquisition) underperformed the S&P 500 by a cumulative 5 percentage points during the following 3-year period.

[a]MBO, managed buyout; LBO, leveraged buyout.

monitoring systems in place for firms to survive the rigor of being a public company. In contrast, unless those systems are in place when acquired, firms resold within a year simply lack the time to adequately prepare for participating in public markets. Other factors contributing to postbuyout returns include professional management, tighter monitoring by owners, and often the reputations of the private equity firm investor groups.[39]

[39] Katz (2008) reports that private equity–sponsored firms display superior long-term share price performance after they go public, reflecting professional ownership, tighter monitoring, and often the reputations of the private equity firm owners. Gurung and Lerner (2008) find that private equity groups have a greater capacity to squeeze more productivity out of companies they buy during times of financial stress than other types of acquirers. The authors attribute this success to the willingness of private equity sponsors to make the difficult choices of restructuring and shutting down poorly performing operations in times of economic downturns. The authors also find that private equity–owned firms are strong at adopting "lean manufacturing" practices.

USING DCF METHODS TO VALUE LEVERAGED BUYOUTS

An LBO can be evaluated from the perspective of common equity investors only or all those who supply funds, including common and preferred investors and lenders. Conventional capital budgeting procedures may be used to evaluate the LBO. The transaction makes sense from the viewpoint of all investors if the present value (PV) of the cash flows to the firm (PV_{FCFF}) or enterprise value, discounted at the weighted-average cost of capital, equals or exceeds the total investment consisting of debt, common equity, and preferred equity ($I_{D + E + PFD}$) required to buy the outstanding shares of the target company:

$$PV_{FCFF} - I_{D + E + PFD} \geq 0 \tag{13.1}$$

Equation (13.1) implies that the target firm can earn its cost of capital and return sufficient cash flow to all investors and lenders, enabling them to meet or exceed their required returns.

However, it is possible for a leveraged buyout to make sense to common equity investors but not to other investors, such as pre-LBO debt holders and preferred stockholders. Once the LBO has been consummated, the firm's perceived ability to meet its obligations to current debt and preferred stockholders often deteriorates because the firm takes on a substantial amount of new debt. The firm's pre-LBO debt and preferred stock may be revalued in the open market by investors to reflect this higher perceived risk, resulting in a significant reduction in the market value of both debt and preferred equity owned by pre-LBO investors. Although there is little empirical evidence to show that this is typical of LBOs, this revaluation may characterize large LBOs, such as RJR Nabisco in 1989, HCA in 2006, and TXU Corp. in 2007.

What follows is a discussion of two methods for valuing leveraged buyouts. The cost of capital method attempts to adjust future cash flows for changes in the cost of capital as the firm reduces its outstanding debt. The second method, adjusted present value, sums the value of the firm without debt plus the value of future tax savings resulting from the tax deductibility of interest.

Valuing LBOs: The Cost of Capital Method

As long as the debt-to-equity ratio is expected to be constant, applying conventional capital budgeting techniques that discount future cash flows with a constant weighted-average cost of capital (CC) is appropriate. However, the extremely high leverage associated with leveraged buyouts significantly increases the riskiness of the cash flows available to equity investors as a result of the increase in fixed interest and principal repayments that must be made to lenders. Consequently, the cost of equity should be adjusted for the increased leverage of the firm. However, since the debt is to be paid off over time, the cost of equity decreases over time. Therefore, in valuing a leveraged buyout, the analyst must project free cash flows. Instead of discounting the cash flows at a constant discount rate, however, the discount rate must decline with the firm's declining debt-to-equity ratio. A five-step methodology for adjusting the discount rate to reflect a firm's declining leverage is discussed next.

Project Annual Cash Flows (Step 1)

Step 1 involves projecting free cash flow to equity (FCFE)—that is, the cash flow available for common equity investors, annually until the LBO has achieved its target debt-to-equity (D/E) ratio. The target D/E ratio often is the industry average ratio or a ratio that would appear to be acceptable to strategic buyers or investors in secondary IPOs.

Project Debt-to-Equity Ratios (Step 2)

The decline in debt-to-equity ratios depends on known debt repayment schedules and the projected growth in the market value of shareholders' equity. The market value of common equity can be assumed to grow in line with the projected growth in net income.

Calculate Terminal Value (Step 3)

Calculate the terminal value of equity (TVE) and of the firm in year t:

$$TVE = FCFE_{t+1}/(k_e - g) \tag{13.2}$$

k_e, and g represent the cost of equity and the cash-flow growth rate that can be sustained during the stable-growth or terminal period. TVE represents the present value of equity of the dollar proceeds available to the firm at time t, generated by selling equity to the public, to a strategic buyer, or to another LBO firm.

Adjust Discount Rate to Reflect Changing Risk (Step 4)

The high leverage associated with a leveraged buyout increases the risk of the cash flows available for equity investors. As the LBO's extremely high debt level is reduced, the cost of equity needs to be adjusted to reflect the decline in risk, as measured by the firm's levered beta (β_{FL}). This adjustment may be estimated starting with the firm's levered beta in period 1 (β_{FL1}) as follows:

$$\beta_{FL1} = \beta_{IUL1} (1 + (D/E)_{F1} (1 - t_F)) \tag{13.3}$$

β_{IUL1} is the industry unlevered β in period 1; $(D/E)_{F1}$ and t_F are the firm's debt-to-equity ratio and marginal tax rate, respectively, and $\beta_{IUL1} = \beta_{IL1}/[1 + (D/E)_{I1}(1 - t_I)]$, where β_{IL1}, $(D/E)_{I1}$, and t_I are the industry's levered β, debt-to-equity ratio, and tax rate, respectively. The firm's β in each successive period should be recalculated using the firm's projected debt-to-equity ratio for that period. The firm's cost of equity (k_e) must be recalculated each period using that period's estimated β determined by Eq. (13.3).

Because the firm's cost of equity changes over time, the firm's cumulative cost of equity is used to discount projected cash flows.[40] This reflects the fact that each period's cash flows generate a different rate of return. The cumulative cost of equity is represented as follows:

$$PV_1 = FCFE_1/(1 + k_{e1})$$
$$PV_2 = FCFE_2/[(1 + k_{e1})(1 + k_{e\,2})]$$

$$\cdot$$
$$\cdot \tag{13.4}$$
$$\cdot$$

$$PV_n = FCFE_n/[(1 + k_{e1})(1 + k_{e2}) \ldots (1 + k_{e\,n-1})(1 + k_{en})]$$

---

[40] Recall that the future value of $1 (FV$1) in two years invested at a 5% return in the first year and 8% in the second year is $1 × [(1 + 0.05)(1 + 0.08)] = $1.13; the present value of $1 received in two years earning the same rates of return (PV$1) is /[(1 + 0.05)(1 + 0.08)] = $0.88.

Determine If Deal Makes Sense (Step 5)

Making sense of the deal requires calculating the PV of FCFE discounted by the cumulative cost of equity generalized by Eq. (13.4) in Step 4, including the terminal value estimated by Eq. (13.2) in Step 3. Compare this result to the value of the equity invested in the firm, including transaction-related fees. The deal makes sense to common equity investors if the PV of FCFE exceeds the value of the equity investment in the deal. The deal makes sense to lenders and noncommon equity investors if the PV of FCFF exceeds the total cost of the deal (see Eq. (13.1)). Table 13.7 shows how to calculate the value of an LBO using the cost of capital method.

Valuing LBOs: Adjusted Present Value Method

Some analysts suggest that the problem of a variable discount rate can be avoided by separating the value of a firm's operations into two components: the firm's value as if it were debt-free and the value of interest tax savings. The total value of the firm is the present value of the firm's free cash flows to equity investors plus the present value of future tax savings discounted at the firm's unlevered cost of equity. The unlevered cost of equity is often viewed as the appropriate discount rate rather than the cost of debt or a risk-free rate because tax savings are subject to risk, since the firm may default on its debt or be unable to utilize the tax savings due to continuing operating losses.[41]

TABLE 13.7   Present Value of Equity Cash Flow Using the Cost of Capital Method

Assumptions	2003	2004	2005	2006	2007	2008	2009	2010
Market Value of 12% PIK Preferred Equity ($ million)	22	24.6	27.6	30.9	34.6	38.8	43.4	48.6
Market Value of Common Equity ($ million)	3	2.3	3.3	4.0	5.0	5.4	5.7	6.0
Equity[a] ($ million)	25	27.0	30.9	34.9	39.6	44.2	49.1	54.6
Debt ($ million)	47	39.5	31.5	23.8	19.2	14.3	8.8	2.7
Comparable Firm								
Price/Earnings Ratio	6							
Levered Beta (β)	2.4							
Debt/Equity Ratio	0.3							
Unlevered Beta[b]	2.0							
Marginal Tax Rate	0.4							

Continued

[41] Brigham and Ehrhardt (2005), p. 597

TABLE 13.7 Present Value of Equity Cash Flow Using the Cost of Capital Method—Cont'd

Assumptions	2003	2004	2005	2006	2007	2008	2009	2010
10-Year Treasury Bond Rate	0.05							
Risk Premium on Stocks (%)	0.055							
Terminal Period Growth Rate (%)	0.045							
Terminal Period Cost of Equity (%)	0.10							

Year	Debt/ Equity	Leveraged Beta[c]	Cost of Equity	Cumulative Discount Factor[d]	Adjusted Equity Cash Flow[e]	PV of Adjusted Equity Cash Flow[f]
2004	1.5	3.8	0.260	$1/(1.26) = 0.7937$	0.3	0.3
2005	1.0	3.3	0.230	$1/[(1.26)(1.23)] = 0.6452$	0.2	0.1
2006	0.7	2.9	0.208	$1/[(1.26)(1.23)(1.208)] = 0.5341$	1.8	1.0
2007	0.5	2.6	0.194	$1/[(1.26)(1.23)(1.208)(1.194)] = 0.4474$	7.4	3.3
2008	0.3	2.4	0.184	$1/[(1.26)(1.23)(1.208)(1.194)(1.184)] = 0.3778$	7.7	2.9
2009	0.2	2.3	0.174	$1/[(1.26)(1.23)(1.208)(1.194)(1.184)(1.174)] = 0.3218$	8.1	2.6
2010	0.0	2.1	0.165	$1/[(1.26)(1.23)(1.208)(1.194)(1.184)(1.174)(1.165)] = 0.2762$	8.5	2.4
PV (2004–2010)						12.5
Terminal Value						44.7
Total PV						57.2

[a]Market value of common equity is assumed to grow by the rate of growth in income available to common stock (i.e., 2004: (0.77)%; 2005: 43.4%; 2006: 21.2%; 2007: 25%; 2008: 8%; 2009: 5.6%; and 2010: 5.3%. PIK preferred equity is assumed to equal its book value and to grow at its 12% dividend rate, and debt outstanding reflects its known principal repayment schedule.
[b]Comparable firm unlevered $\beta_u = \beta_l/(1 + (D/E)(1 - t))$.
[c]Firm's leveraged beta $\beta_l = \beta_u(1 + (D/E)(1 - t))$.
[d]Because of the changing D/E ratio, the discount factor is expressed in multiplicative form to reflect the differing cash-flow streams generated by investments made at each level of the D/E ratio.
[e]Adjusted equity cash flows come from Table 13.12.
[f]PV of adjusted equity cash flow equals the cumulative discount factor times the adjusted equity cash flow.

The justification for the adjusted present value (APV) method reflects the theoretical notion that firm value should not be affected by the way in which it is financed.[42] However, recent studies suggest that for LBOs, the availability and cost of financing does indeed impact financing and investment decisions.[43]

In the presence of taxes, firms are often less leveraged than they should be, given the potentially large tax benefits associated with debt. Firms can increase market value by increasing leverage to the point at which the additional contribution of the tax shield to the firm's market value begins to decline.[44] However, management's decision to increase leverage affects and is affected by the firm's credit rating. Consequently, the tax benefits of higher leverage may be partially or entirely offset by the higher probability of default associated with an increase in leverage.[45]

For the APV method to be applicable in highly leveraged transactions, the analyst needs to introduce the costs of financial distress (i.e., a firm's inability to pay interest and principal on its debt on a timely basis). The direct cost of financial distress includes the costs associated with reorganization in bankruptcy and ultimately liquidation (see Chapter 16). Such costs include legal and accounting fees. However, financial distress can have a material cost even on firms that are able to avoid bankruptcy or liquidation. These indirect costs include the loss of customers, employee turnover, less favorable terms from suppliers, higher borrowing costs, lost opportunities, management distraction costs, higher operating expenses, and reduced overall competitiveness.

Consequently, in applying the APV method, the present value of a highly leveraged transaction (PV_{HL}) would reflect the present value of the firm without leverage (PV_{UL}) plus the present value of tax savings (i.e., interest expense, i, times the firm's marginal tax rate, t, or tax shield PV_{ti} resulting from leverage) less the present value of expected financial distress PV_{FD}).

$$PV_{HL} = PV_{UL} + PV_{ti} - PV_{FD} \qquad (13.5)$$

where $PV_{FD} = \mu FD$.

FD is the expected cost of financial distress, and μ is the probability of financial distress. Unfortunately, FD and μ cannot be easily or reliably estimated and are often ignored by analysts using the APV method. Failure to include an estimate of the cost and probability of

---

[42] Brealey and Myers, 1996. This concept assumes investors have access to perfect information, the firm is not growing and no new borrowing is required, and there are no taxes and transaction costs and implicitly that the firm is free of default risk. Under these assumptions, the decision to invest is affected by the earning power and risk associated with the firm's assets and not by the way the investment is financed.

[43] Axelson et al. (2009) argue that the capital structure in buyouts requires a different explanation than in public firms, where investment decisions are believed to be made independently of the way in which they are financed. With respect to LBOs, the availability of financing appears to impact the decision to invest in LBOs, unlike public firms. This paper is consistent with the widely held view among buyout practitioners that the size and frequency of LBOs are driven by the availability and cost of financing.

[44] Graham, 2000

[45] Molina (2006) and Almeida and Philippon (2007) show that the risk-adjusted costs of distress can be so large as to totally offset the tax benefits derived from debt. This is particularly true during periods of economic downturns.

financial distress is likely to result in an overestimate of the value of the firm using the APV method. Despite these concerns, many analysts continue to apply the APV method because of its relative simplicity, as illustrated in the following five-step process.

Project Annual Cash Flows and Interest Tax Savings (Step 1)

For the period during which the debt–to–total capital ratio is changing, the analyst should project free cash flows to equity and the interest-related tax savings. During the firm's terminal period, the debt–to–total capital structure is assumed to be stable and the free cash flows are projected to grow at a constant rate.

Value Target Excluding Tax Savings (Step 2)

Estimate the unlevered cost of equity (COE) for discounting cash flows during the period in which the capital structure is changing and the weighted-average cost of capital (WACC) for discounting during the terminal period. The WACC is estimated using the COE and after-tax cost of debt and the proportions of debt and equity that make up the firm's capital structure in the final year of the period during which the capital structure is changing.

Estimate Present Value of Tax Savings (Step 3)

Project the annual tax savings resulting from the tax deductibility of interest. Discount projected tax savings at the firm's unlevered cost of equity, since it reflects a higher level of risk than either the WACC or after-tax cost of debt. Tax savings are subject to risk comparable to the firm's cash flows in that a highly leveraged firm may default and the tax savings go unused.

Calculate Total Value of Firm (Step 4)

To determine the total value of the firm, add the present value of the firm's cash flows to equity, interest tax savings, and terminal value discounted at the firm's unlevered cost of equity and subtract the present value of the expected cost of financial distress (see Eq. (13.5)). Note that the terminal value is calculated using WACC but that it is discounted to the present using the unlevered COE. This is done because it represents the present value of cash flows in the final year of the period in which the firm's capital structure is changing and beyond.

Determine Whether Deal Makes Sense (Step 5)

This requires that the present value of Eq. (13.5) less the value of equity invested in the transaction (i.e., NPV) be greater than or equal to 0. The magnitude of the cost of financial distress can range from 10 to 25% of a firm's predistressed market value.[46] The probability of financial distress

---

[46] Andrade and Kaplan, 1998. Branch (2002) concludes that the impact of bankruptcy on a firm's predistressed value falls within a range of 12 to 20%. More recently, Korteweg (2010) estimates that the impact falls within a range of 15 to 30% of predistressed firm value.

can be estimated by analyzing bond ratings[47] and the cumulative probabilities of default for bonds in different ratings classes over five- and ten-year periods (see Table 13.8).[48]

TABLE 13.8 Bond Rating and Probability of Default

Rating	Cumulative Probability of Distress (%)	
	5 Years	10 Years
AAA	0.04	0.07
AA	0.44	0.51
A+	0.47	0.57
A	0.20	0.66
A−	3.00	5.00
BBB	6.44	7.54
BB	11.90	19.63
B+	19.20	28.25
B	27.50	36.80
B-	31.10	42.12
CCC	46.26	59.02
CC	54.15	66.60
C+	65.15	75.16
C	72.15	81.03
C−	80.00	87.16

Source: Altman, 2007.

[47] While the failure of the credit rating agencies to anticipate the extreme financial distress in the credit markets experienced in 2008 and 2009 casts doubt on the use of credit ratings to assess financial distress, the lack of better alternatives supports their use for this purpose. Credit research departments of the major credit rating agencies use extensive models to assess the likelihood of default and bankruptcy. As discussed in Chapter 16, the probability of default is reflected in credit ratings and the maturity of the debt issue and is displayed in the credit spreads associated with the various bond issues. In general, higher-rated firms tend to issue debt with smaller credit spreads and default less than those with lower credit ratings. Furthermore, the size of credit spreads tends to increase with the maturity date of the bond, as does the frequency of default.

[48] Altman and Kishore, 2001; Altman, 2007. Cumulative probability is the likelihood that a random variable will be less than or equal to each value that the random variable can assume. Intuitively, cumulative probability estimates reflect the likelihood of a particular outcome based on previous outcomes or events. Cumulative probabilities are used when reductions in cash flows due to financial distress in earlier years impact cash flows in subsequent years as the firm may be forced to underinvest in subsequent years. Assume that the probability of a firm experiencing financial distress in year 1 is 20%. If the firm ceases to exist at the end of the first year due to financial distress, there will not be any cash flows in year 2. If we assume that the likelihood of distress in year 2 is again 20%, the likelihood of the firm producing cash flows in the third year is now only 64% (i.e., $(1 - 0.2)(1 - 0.2)$).

Table 13.9 illustrates the APV method. Assuming that the firm has a B credit rating, the present value of the expected cost of bankruptcy is $5.62 million and is calculated as the cumulative probability of default over ten years for a B-rated company (i.e., 0.3680 per Table 13.8) times the expected cost of bankruptcy (i.e., 0.25 × $61.07 million).[49] Note that the estimate provided by the APV method is $61.07 million before the adjustment for financial distress. This is 6.8% (i.e., ($61.07/$57.2) − 1) more than the estimate provided using the

TABLE 13.9   Present Value of Equity Cash Flows Using the APV Method

Assumptions	2004	2005	2006	2007	2008	2009	2010
Marginal Tax Rate (t)	0.4						
Comparable Company Unlevered Beta	2						
10-Year Treasury Bond Rate	0.05						
Firm's Credit Rating	B						
Expected Cost of Bankruptcy as % of Firm Market Value (per Andrade and Kaplan, 1998, and Korteweg, 2010)	0.2500						
Cumulative Probability of Default for a B-Rated Firm over 10 Years (see Table 13.8)	0.3680						
Risk Premium on Stocks	0.0550						
Terminal Period Growth Rate	0.0450						
2004–2010 Unlevered Cost of Equity[a]	0.1700						
Terminal Period WACC[b]	0.1200						
Adjusted Equity Cash Flow[c]	0.3	0.2	1.8	7.4	7.7	8.1	8.5
Plus: Tax Shield[d]	1.8	1.6	1.3	1.0	0.8	0.6	0.4
Plus: Terminal Value[e]							123.8
Equals: Total Cash Flow	2.2	1.8	3.2	8.4	8.5	8.7	132.7
PV of 2004–2010 Cash Flows							$61.07
Less: PV Expected Cost of Bankruptcy[f]							5.62
PV of Cash Flows Adjusted for Expected Cost of Bankruptcy							$55.45

[a]Cost of Equity (k_e) = 0.06 + 2.0(0.055).
[b]WACC = k_e × W1 + Pref × W2 + i × (1 − 0.t) × W3, where k_e = unlevered cost of equity; Pref = yield on preferred stock; i = interest rate on outstanding debt; W1 = common equity's share of total terminal year capital; W2 = preferred stock's share of total terminal year capital; W3 = debt's share of total terminal year capital; and t = marginal tax rate.
[c]Adjusted equity cash flows come from Table 13.12.
[d]Tax shield is the product of total interest expense times the marginal tax rate.
[e]The terminal value is calculated using the constant-growth method estimated based on total 2010 cash flow, terminal period WACC, and terminal period sustainable period cash flow growth rate.
[f]Equals 0.3680 (i.e., cumulative probability of default over ten years for a B-rated company) × (0.25 × $61.07) (i.e., expected cost of bankruptcy).

[49] Per Andrade and Kaplan, 1998.

CC method, shown in Table 13.7. After adjusting for financial distress, the estimate declines to $55.45 million versus $57.2 million, estimated using the cost of capital method, a difference of approximately 3%.

Comparing Cost of Capital and Adjusted Present Value Methods

Although the proposition that the value of the firm should be independent of the way in which it is financed may make sense for a firm whose debt-to-capital ratio is relatively stable and similar to the industry's, it is highly problematic when it is applied to highly leveraged transactions. Without adjusting for the cost of financial distress, the APV method implies that the value of the firm could be increased by continuously taking on more debt. Therefore, the primary drawback to the APV method is the implication that the firm should optimally use 100% debt financing to take maximum advantage of the tax shield created by the tax deductibility of interest.[50]

The primary advantage of the APV method is its relative computational simplicity. Although somewhat more complex, the cost of capital method attempts to adjust for the changing level of risk over time, as the LBO reduces its leverage over time. Thus, the CC method takes into account what is actually happening in practice.[51] Table 13.10 summarizes the process steps as well as the strengths and weaknesses of the cost of capital and adjusted present value methods.

TABLE 13.10 Comparative LBO Valuation Methodologies

Process Steps	Cost of Capital Method	Adjusted Present Value Method
Step 1	Project annual cash flows, including all financing considerations and tax savings, until anticipate exiting the business	Project annual cash flows to equity investors and interest tax savings
Step 2	Project annual debt-to-equity ratios	Value target, including terminal value but without tax savings
Step 3	Calculate terminal value	Estimate PV of tax savings
Step 4	Adjust discount rate to reflect declining cost of equity as debt is repaid	Add PV of firm without debt, including terminal period and PV of tax savings
Step 5	Determine if NPV of projected cash flows ≥ 0	Determine if NPV of projected cash flows ≥ 0
Advantages	• Adjusts discount rate to reflect diminishing risk	• Simplicity
Disadvantages	• Calculations more tedious than alternative methods	• Ignores effects of leverage on discount rate as debt repaid • To incorporate effects of leverage, requires estimation of cost of and probability of financial distress for highly leveraged firms • Unclear whether true discount rate is cost of debt, unlevered k_e, or somewhere between the two

---

[50] Booth, 2002

[51] For an excellent discussion of alternative valuation methods for highly leveraged firms, see Ruback (2002).

LBO VALUATION AND STRUCTURING MODEL BASICS

An LBO analysis is applied when there is the potential for a financial buyer or sponsor to acquire a business. Investment bankers frequently employ such analyses in addition to discounted cash flow and relative valuation methods in valuing businesses they are attempting to sell. The objective is to provide financial buyers with a leveraged buyout opportunity that offers a financial return in excess of their desired rate of return, while allowing the target firm to retain sufficient financial flexibility to meet potential future operating challenges.

The following sections discuss a simple approach to evaluating LBO opportunities and a useful template for building LBO models. The Excel-based spreadsheets underlying these sections, found on the companion site to this book, are entitled "Excel-Based LBO Valuation and Structuring Model" and "Excel-Based Model to Estimate Borrowing Capacity." The reader is encouraged to examine the formulas that support these spreadsheets.

Evaluating LBO Opportunities

LBO analyses are similar to DCF valuations in that they require projected cash flows, terminal values, present values, and discount rates. However, the DCF analysis solves for the present value of the firm, while the LBO analysis solves for the discount rate or internal rate of return (IRR). The IRR is the discount rate that equates the projected cash flows and terminal value with the initial equity investment. Because the IRR is the discount rate at which the NPV is zero, the IRR can be derived from a DCF valuation.

The IRR is the critical decision variable in an analysis of a leveraged buyout opportunity because of the central role played by leverage. Without the lift to financial returns provided by leverage, financial buyers rarely can compete with strategic buyers, who can generally justify paying more for a target firm due to potential synergy.

The LBO analysis also requires the determination of whether there is sufficient future cash flow to operate the target firm while meeting interest and principal repayments and potentially paying dividends to the private equity investors. Financial buyers often will attempt to determine the highest amount of debt possible (i.e., the borrowing capacity of the target firm) to minimize their equity investment in order to maximize the IRR, although they may sometimes sacrifice some financial return to remain invested for a longer time period.[52] Borrowing capacity is defined as the amount of debt a firm can borrow without materially increasing its cost of borrowing or violating loan covenants on existing debt, while maintaining the ability to engage in future borrowing to satisfy unexpected liquidity requirements.

---

[52] Financial sponsors may attempt to strike a balance between maximizing IRR and the total cash amount taken out of the investment on the exit date. For example, by holding an investment for five rather than three years, the sponsor may experience a lower IRR but may increase the multiple applied on the exit date by waiting for more favorable market conditions. The motivation for this behavior may reflect investor desire to remain invested longer to minimize the cost of redeploying the funds.

While analysts differ on the measure of cash flow to use in evaluating LBO opportunities, EBITDA is commonly used despite its significant shortcomings.[53] The following equations illustrate the linkages between the target firm's purchase price and the firm's borrowing capacity and the financial sponsor's equity contribution.

$$PP_{TF} = (EV/EBITDA) \times EBITDA_{TF} \tag{13.6}$$

$$(D_{TF} + E_{TF})/EBITDA_{TF} = PP_{TF}/EBITDA_{TF} \tag{13.7}$$

where

D_{TF} = net debt (i.e., total debt less cash and marketable securities held by the target firm)
E_{TF} = financial sponsor's equity contribution to the target firm's purchase price
PP_{TF} = estimated purchase price of the target firm
$EBITDA_{TF}$ = target firm earnings before interest, taxes, depreciation, and amortization
$EV/EBITDA$ = appropriate recent LBO transaction enterprise value to EBITDA multiple

Equation (13.6) shows how the dollar value of the purchase price can be determined by multiplying an appropriate enterprise value multiple by the target firm's EBITDA. If the estimated purchase price for the target firm is six times EBITDA, the implied unlevered financial return for an all equity deal would be 16.7% annually (i.e., equity investors would be willing to pay $6 for each dollar of sustainable cash flow).[54]

Equation (13.7) equates the target firm's enterprise value (i.e., the sum of net debt and equity) to EBITDA multiple with the firm's purchase price to EBITDA multiple and illustrates how the purchase price may be financed from debt or equity contributed by the financial sponsor. For a given purchase price, level of net debt, and EBITDA, it is possible to estimate the financial sponsor's initial equity contribution by solving this equation for E_{TF}.

---

[53] Some analysts use EBITDA as a proxy for cash flow. By not deducting interest, taxes, depreciation, and amortization, EBITDA supporters argue that it represents a convenient proxy for the cash available to meet the cost (i.e., interest, depreciation, and amortization) of long-term assets. In essence, EBITDA provides a simple way of determining how long the firm can continue to service its debt without additional financing.

Furthermore, EBITDA is not affected by the method the firm employs in depreciating its assets. Critics of the use of EBITDA as a measure of cash flow argue that it can be dangerously misleading because it ignores changes in working capital. It implicitly assumes that capital expenditures needed to maintain the business are equal to depreciation. However, from the dotcom debacle in 2000, we know that a firm could have an attractive EBITDA–to–interest expense ratio but still have insufficient cash to finance interest expense, working capital, and needed capital outlays that exceed the long-term growth trend. Such critics argue that free cash flow to the firm (i.e., enterprise cash flow) is a better measure of how much cash a company is generating, since it includes changes in working capital and capital expenditures.

[54] The implied unlevered return for an enterprise value multiple of 6 (which equals the purchase price paid to EBITDA for the target firm ratio) is calculated as the reciprocal of the purchase price paid for the target firm–to–EBITDA ratio—that is, EBITDATF / PPTF = 1/6 = 16.7%. Note that these returns are based on EBITDA. Actual unlevered after-tax returns to financial investors would be lower, reflecting the deduction of taxes, depreciation, and amortization expense. Leveraged returns would also be reduced by the deduction of interest expense.

What follows is a simple three-step process employed to assess the attractiveness of a firm as a potential LBO target. Step 1 involves estimating the maximum borrowing capacity of the firm. Step 2 entails determining the purchase price necessary to buy out the target firm's shareholders and estimating the initial equity contribution to be made by the financial sponsor. Step 3 entails calculating the IRR on the financial sponsor's initial equity investment. The deal would make sense to the financial sponsor if the resulting IRR were equal to or greater than their target IRR.

Step 1: Determine a Firm's Borrowing Capacity

An LBO analysis usually starts with the determination of cash available for financing a target firm's future debt obligations and the sources of such debt. This requires the projection of cash flow from operations. Any projected cash flow in excess of the need to meet the firm's normal operating requirements may be used to satisfy future principal and interest repayments. Once available future cash flow has been determined, the total debt that can be supported by the firm's projected cash flows may be estimated and confirmed in discussions with potential lenders. When the maximum amount of debt is determined, the financial sponsor can identify the sources of such debt, which include senior bank loans, subordinated debt, high-yield debt, and mezzanine financing.

Table 13.11 illustrates a simple model to estimate a firm's borrowing capacity. The estimate of borrowing capacity is expressed as a multiple of EBITDA. The model is divided into three panels: assumptions, estimating cash available for debt reduction, and estimating borrowing capacity. Year 0 represents the year immediately prior to the closing date (i.e., the beginning of year 1). The beginning debt figures are shown as of December 31 in year 0.

Assume that, based on similar transactions, the analyst believes that a buyout firm will be able to borrow about 5.5 times EBITDA of $200 million (i.e., about $1.1 billion), and the buyout firm has a target debt mix consisting of 75% senior and 25% subordinated debt. Further assume that investors in the buyout firm wish to exit the business within eight years once the senior debt has been repaid. To accomplish this objective, the investors intend to use 100% of cash available for debt reduction to pay off senior debt, and the subordinated debt is payable as a balloon note beyond year 8.

Using a trial-and-error method, insert a starting value for senior debt of $800 million in year 0. This $800 million starting number is in line with the firm's assumed target debt mix (i.e., 0.75 × total potential borrowing of $1.1 billion is approximately equal to $800 million). The amount of senior debt outstanding at the end of the eighth year is $75.7 million. If we now try $700 million in senior debt in year 0, the amount of senior debt outstanding at the end of the eighth year is $(63.3). Using the midpoint between $700 and $800 million, we insert $750 million for senior debt in year 0, resulting in $6.2 million in remaining debt at the end of the eighth year. Additional fine-tuning results in a zero balance at the end of year 8 if we use a starting value of $745.6 million for senior debt. Consequently, the firm's maximum total debt (i.e., borrowing capacity) based on the assumptions underlying Table 13.11 is estimated at $1,045.6 million.

TABLE 13.11 Determining Borrowing Capacity

Assumptions	Year 0	Year 1	Year 2	Year 3	Year 4	Year 5	Year 6	Year 7	Year 8
Sales Growth %	0	1.05	1.05	1.05	1.05	1.05	1.05	1.05	1.05
COS as % of Sales	0.5	0.5	0.5	0.5	0.5	0.5	0.5	0.5	0.5
Sales, General and Admin. Expense as % of Sales	0.1	0.1	0.1	0.1	0.1	0.1	0.1	0.1	0.1
Depreciation as % of Sales	0.03	0.03	0.03	0.03	0.03	0.03	0.03	0.03	0.03
Amortization as % of Sales	0.01	0.01	0.01	0.01	0.01	0.01	0.01	0.01	0.01
Interest on Cash and Marketable Securities %	0.03	0.03	0.03	0.03	0.03	0.03	0.03	0.03	0.03
Interest on Senior Debt %	0.07	0.07	0.07	0.07	0.07	0.07	0.07	0.07	0.07
Interest on Subordinated Debt %	0.09	0.09	0.09	0.09	0.09	0.09	0.09	0.09	0.09
Tax rate	0.4	0.4	0.4	0.4	0.4	0.4	0.4	0.4	0.4
Cash & Marketable Securities as % Sales	0.01	0.01	0.01	0.01	0.01	0.01	0.01	0.01	0.01
Change in Working Capital as % of Sales	0.02	0.02	0.02	0.02	0.02	0.02	0.02	0.02	0.02
Capital Expenditures as % of Sales	0.03	0.03	0.03	0.03	0.03	0.03	0.03	0.03	0.03
Cash Available for Debt Reduction ($ million)									
Sales	500.0	525.0	551.3	578.8	607.8	638.1	670.0	703.6	738.7
Less: Cost of Sales	250.0	262.5	275.6	289.4	303.9	319.1	335.0	351.8	369.4
Less: Sales General Administrative Expense	50.0	52.5	55.1	57.9	60.8	63.8	67.0	70.4	73.9
Equals: EBITDA	200.0	210.0	220.5	231.5	243.1	255.3	268.0	281.4	295.5
Less: Depreciation	15.0	15.8	16.5	17.4	18.2	19.1	20.1	21.1	22.2
Less: Amortization	5.0	5.3	5.5	5.8	6.1	6.4	6.7	7.0	7.4
Plus: Interest Income	0.2	0.2	0.2	0.2	0.2	0.2	0.2	0.2	0.2
Less: Interest Expense									
Senior Debt		52.2	47.9	43.1	37.7	31.7	24.9	17.4	9.1
Subordinated Debt		27.0	27.0	27.0	27.0	27.0	27.0	27.0	27.0
Total Interest Expense		*79.2*	*74.9*	*70.1*	*64.7*	*58.7*	*51.9*	*44.4*	*36.1*
Equals: Income Before Tax		110.0	123.7	138.4	154.3	171.3	189.5	209.1	230.0
Less: Taxes Paid		44.0	49.5	55.4	61.7	68.5	75.8	83.6	92.0
Equals: Net Income After Tax		66.0	74.2	83.1	92.6	102.8	113.7	125.4	138.0

Continued

TABLE 13.11　Determining Borrowing Capacity—Cont'd

Assumptions	Year 0	Year 1	Year 2	Year 3	Year 4	Year 5	Year 6	Year 7	Year 8
Plus: Depreciation and Amortization Expense		21.0	22.1	23.2	24.3	25.5	26.8	28.1	29.5
Less Change in Working Capital		10.5	11.0	11.6	12.2	12.8	13.4	14.1	14.8
Less Capital Expenditures		15.8	16.5	17.4	18.2	19.1	20.1	21.1	22.2
Equals: Cash Available for Debt Reduction		60.7	68.7	77.3	86.5	96.4	107.0	118.4	130.6
Borrowing Capacity									
Cash Balance	5.0	5.3	5.5	5.8	6.1	6.4	6.7	7.0	7.4
Senior Debt Outstanding at Year End[a]	745.6	684.8	616.1	538.9	452.4	356.0	249.0	130.6	0.0
Subordinated Debt Outstanding at Year End[b]	300.0	300.0	300.0	300.0	300.0	300.0	300.0	300.0	300.0
Total Debt	*1045.6*	*984.8*	*916.1*	*838.9*	*752.4*	*656.0*	*549.0*	*430.6*	*300.0*
Net Debt to EBITDA Ratio	5.20	4.66	4.13	3.60	3.07	2.55	2.02	1.51	0.99
Interest Coverage (EBITDA/ Net Interest Expense	0.00	2.66	2.95	3.31	3.77	4.37	5.18	6.36	8.23

[a]Assumes 100% of cash available for debt reduction is used to pay off senior debt.
[b]Subordinated debt payable as a balloon note in year 10.

Step 2: Estimate the Financial Sponsor's Initial Equity Contribution

Equation (13.6) provides an estimate of the target firm's purchase price. The preliminary valuation or purchase price estimate for the target firm is often based on an average multiple of enterprise value to EBITDA for recent comparable transactions times the target firm's EBITDA. A higher multiple might be used if potential bidders for the target firm include strategic buyers, who may justify a higher premium due to perceived synergy. The multiples are often based on a 12- to 24-month trailing average EBITDA and projections for 12 to 24 months into the future. In practice, valuations are usually based on the historical multiples, which may be adjusted up or down depending on their perceived riskiness to the target firm's future cash flows.

Assume the financial sponsor believes that the appropriate enterprise to EBITDA multiple to be applied to the target firm's EBITDA based on a review of recent comparable LBO transactions is 7. From Eq. (13.6), the purchase price for the target firm (PP_{TF}) can be estimated as 7 × $210 (Year 1 EBITDA in Table 13.12 or $1,470 million.

Using this purchase price estimate and the target firm's maximum borrowing capacity of $1,045.6 million determined in Step 1 and multiplying both sides by $EBITDA_{TF}$, we can solve Eq. (13.7) to estimate the financial sponsor's initial equity contribution at $424.4 million (i.e., $1,470 − $1,045.6).

Step 3: Analyze Financial Returns

The most important calculation to the financial sponsor is the IRR. The calculation considers the initial investment in the firm and additional capital contributions as cash outflows and any dividend payments as cash inflows plus the exit or residual value of the business when sold. The financial multiple applied to the equity value on the exit date is usually the same as used by the financial sponsor when determining the target firm's preliminary valuation. The equity value of the firm is the sale value on the exit date less the value of debt repaid and any fees incurred in selling the business.

Due to their high sensitivity to the multiple applied to exit year cash flows and the number of years the investment is to be held, financial returns are usually displayed as a range reflecting different assumptions about exit multiples. If the calculated IRR is less than the target IRR, the financial sponsor can substitute lower purchase prices into Eq. (13.7), as described in Step 2, resulting in lower initial capital contributions, and recalculate the IRR until it exceeds the target IRR or walk away from considering the target firm as an LBO candidate.

Standard LBO Formats Used in Building LBO Models

Once the financial sponsor concludes that it is an attractive LBO candidate, the target firm's balance sheet is restated to reflect the new debt and equity structure of the business. The firm's financial statements are again projected to reflect the firm's new financial structure.

Table 13.12 summarizes the key elements of the analysis. The *Sources and Uses of Funds* section in the table shows how the transaction is to be financed. Representing total funds required, the Uses section shows where the cash will go and includes payments to the target firm's owners, including cash, any equity retained by the seller, any seller's notes, and any excess cash retained by the sellers. The Uses section also contains the refinancing of any existing debt on the balance sheet of the target firm and any transaction fees. The Sources section describes various sources of financing including new debt, any existing cash that is being used to finance the transaction, and the common and preferred equity being contributed by the financial sponsor. The equity contribution represents the difference between uses and all other sources of financing. The *Pro Forma Capital Structure* segment provides the percent distribution of the firm's capital structure among the various types of debt and equity. The *Equity Ownership* section illustrates the distribution of ownership between the financial sponsor and management. The *Internal Rates of Return* section provides the projected financial returns in both percentages and dollar amounts for three potential exit years (i.e., 2014, 2015, and 2016), as well as the multiple applied to the exit year's cash flow. The final segment, entitled *Financial Projections and Analysis*, provides summarized income, cash-flow, and balance sheet data. The table displays five years of historical data from 2001 to 2005 and five years of projected data from 2006 to 2010.

Supporting income, cash-flow, and balance sheet statements can be found on the companion site in a file folder entitled "LBO Structuring and Valuation Model." The pro forma Excel-based balance sheet reflects changes to the existing balance sheet of the target firm altered to reflect the new capital structure of the firm. The new balance sheet also reflects the goodwill resulting from the excess of the purchase price over the fair market value of the net acquired assets and any interest expense that can be capitalized under current accounting rules.

TABLE 13.12 Leveraged Buyout Model Output Summary

	Sources (Cash Inflows) and Uses (Cash Outflows) of Funds				Pro Forma Capital Structure		
Sources of Funds	Amount	Interest Rate (%)	Uses of Funds	Amount	Form of Debt and Equity	Market Value	% of Total Capital
Cash from Balance Sheet	$0.0	0.0	Cash to Owners	$70.0	Revolving Loan	$12.0	16.7
New Revolving Loan	$12.0	9.0	Seller's Equity	$0.0	Senior Debt	$20.0	27.8
New Senior Debt	$20.0	9.0	Seller's Note	$0.0	Subordinated Debt	$15.0	20.8
New Subordinated Debt	$15.0	12.0	Excess Cash	$0.0	Total Debt	$47.0	65.3
New Preferred Stock (PIK)	$22.0	12.0	Paid to Owners	$70.0	Preferred Equity	$22.0	30.6
New Common Stock	$3.0	0.0	Debt Repayment	$0.0	Common Equity	$3.0	4.2
			Buyer Expenses	$2.0	Total Equity	$25.0	34.7
Total Sources	$72.0		Total Uses	$72.0	Total Capital	$72.0	

Equity Investment	Ownership Distribution ($)			% Distribution		Fully Diluted Ownership Distribution				
	Common	Preferred	Total	Common	Preferred	Common	Warrants	Preoption Ownership	Performance Options	Fully Diluted Ownership
Equity Investor	1.5	22.0	23.5	50.0	100.0	50.0%	0.0%	50.0%	0.0%	50.0%
Management	1.5	0.0	1.5	50.0	0.0	50.0%	0.0%	50.0%	0.0%	50.0%
Total Equity Investment	$3.0	$22.0	$25.0	100.0	100.0	100.0%	0.0%	100.0%	0.0%	100.0%

Internal Rates of Return	Total Investor Return (%)			Equity Investor Investment Gain ($)			Management Investment Gain ($)		
	2014	2015	2016	2014	2015	2016	2014	2015	2016
Multiple of Adjusted Equity Cash Flow									
8 × Terminal Yr. CF	0.42	0.35	0.33	$66.6	$78.9	$96.0	$4.3	$5.0	$6.1
9 × Terminal Yr. CF	0.46	0.39	0.35	$73.8	$86.6	$104.5	$4.7	$5.5	$6.7
10 × Terminal Yr. CF	0.51	0.42	0.37	$81.0	$94.2	$113.0	$5.2	$6.0	$7.2

Financial Projections and Analysis	2001	2002	2003	2004	2005	2006	2007	2008	2009	2010
Net Sales	$177.6	$183.5	$190.4	$197.1	$205.0	$214.2	$223.8	$233.9	$244.4	$255.4
Annual Growth Rate	4.2%	3.3%	3.8%	3.5%	4.0%	4.5%	4.5%	4.5%	4.5%	4.5%
EBIT as Percentage of Net Revenue	5.5%	1.3%	5.1%	8.5%	9.5%	10.2%	11.2%	11.4%	11.4%	11.4%
Adjusted Enterprise Cash Flow[a]	$4.2	$0.2	$0.1	$9.5	$9.6	$10.8	$13.0	$13.4	$14.2	$14.9
Adjusted Equity Cash Flow[b]	$4.2	$0.2	$0.1	$0.3	$0.2	$1.8	$7.4	$7.7	$8.1	$8.5
Total Debt Outstanding	0	0	$47.0	$39.5	$31.5	$23.8	$19.2	$14.3	$8.8	$2.7
Total Debt/Adjusted Enterprise Cash Flow	0.0	0.0	NA	4.1	3.3	2.2	1.5	1.1	0.6	0.2
EBIT/Interest Expense	0	0	0	3.6	4.9	6.6	10.1	13.3	18.6	30.9
PV of Adjusted Equity Cash Flow at 26%	$57.2									
PV of 2004–2010 Adj. Equity CF/Terminal Value	28.1%									

[a] EBIT$(1 − t)$ + Depreciation and Amortization − Gross Capital Spending − Change in Working Capital − Change in Investments Available for Sale.
[b] Net Income + Depreciation and Amortization − Gross Capital Spending − Change in Working Capital − Principal Repayments − Change in Investments Available for Sale (i.e., Increases in such investments are a negative cash-flow entry but represent cash in excess of normal operating needs).

The balance sheet projections are based on the pro forma balance sheet, with the debt outstanding and interest expense reflecting the repayment schedules associated with each type of debt. The model also reflects a projected sale value on the assumed exit date. The internal rates of return represent the average annual compounded rate at which the financial sponsor's equity investment grows, assuming that there are no dividend payments or additional equity contributions.

SOME THINGS TO REMEMBER

A successful LBO is a result of knowing what to buy, not overpaying, and being able to substantially improve operating performance. Good candidates are those that have substantial tangible assets, unused borrowing capacity, predictable positive operating cash flow, and assets that are not critical to the continuing operation of the business. Successful LBOs rely heavily on management incentives to improve operating performance and the discipline imposed by the demands of satisfying interest and principal repayments.

DISCUSSION QUESTIONS

13.1 What potential conflicts arise between management and shareholders in an MBO? How can these conflicts be minimized?

13.2 In what ways have private equity and hedge funds exhibited increasing similarities in recent years?

13.3 What are the primary ways in which an LBO is financed?

13.4 How do loan and security covenants affect the way in which an LBO is managed? Note the differences between positive and negative covenants.

13.5 What are the primary factors that explain the magnitude of the premium paid to pre-LBO shareholders?

13.6 What are the primary uses of junk bond financing?

13.7 Describe common strategies LBO firms use to exit their investment. Discuss the circumstances under which some methods of "cashing out" are preferred to others.

13.8 Describe some of the legal problems that can arise from an improperly structured LBO.

13.9 Is it possible for an LBO to make sense to equity investors but not to other investors in the deal? If so, why? If not, why not?

13.10 How does the risk of an LBO change over time? How can the impact of changing risk be incorporated into the valuation of the LBO?

13.11 In an effort to take the firm private, Cox Enterprises announced on August 3, 2004, a proposal to buy the remaining 38% of Cox Communications' shares that it did not already own. Cox Enterprises stated that the increasingly competitive cable industry environment makes investment in the cable industry best done through a private company structure. Why would the firm believe that increasing future levels of investment would be best done as a private company?

13.12 Following Cox Enterprises' announcement on August 3, 2004, of its intent to buy the remaining 38% of Cox Communications' shares that it did not already own, the Cox Communications board of directors formed a special committee of independent directors to consider the proposal. Why?

13.13 Qwest Communications agreed to sell its slow but steadily growing yellow pages business, QwestDex, to a consortium led by the Carlyle Group and Welsh, Carson, Anderson, and Stowe for $7.1 billion in late 2002. Why do you believe the private equity groups found the yellow pages business attractive? Explain the following statement: "A business with high growth potential may not be a good candidate for an LBO."

13.14 Describe the potential benefits and costs of LBOs to stakeholders, including shareholders, employers, lenders, customers, and communities, in which the firm undergoing the buyout may have operations. Do you believe that on average LBOs provide a net benefit or a cost to society? Explain your answer.

13.15 Sony's long-term vision has been to create synergy between its consumer electronics products business and its music, movies, and games. On September 14, 2004, a consortium consisting of Sony Corporation of America, Providence Equity Partners, Texas Pacific Group, and DLJ Merchant Banking Partners agreed to acquire MGM for $4.8 billion. In what way do you believe that Sony's objectives might differ from those of the private equity investors making up the remainder of the consortium? How might such differences affect the management of MGM? Identify possible short-term and long-term effects.

Answers to these Chapter Discussion Questions are available in the Online Instructor's Manual for instructors using this book.

Practice Problems and Answers

13.16 Assume that, based on similar transactions, an analyst believes that a buyout firm will be able to borrow about 5.5 times first-year EBITDA of $200 million (i.e., about $1.1 billion) and that the buyout firm has a target senior to subordinated debt split of 75% to 25%. Further assume that investors in the buyout firm wish to exit the business within eight years after having repaid all of the senior debt. To accomplish this objective, the investors intend to use 100% of cash available for debt reduction to pay off senior debt; the subordinated debt will be is payable as a balloon note beyond year 8. Using the scenario in the template "Excel-Based Model to Estimate Firm Borrowing Capacity" on the companion site as the base case, answer the following questions:

    a. Will the buyout firm be able to exit its investment by the eighth year if sales grow at 3% rather than the 5% assumed in the base case and still satisfy the assumptions in the base case scenario? After rerunning the model using the lower sales growth rate, what does this tell you about the model's sensitivity to relatively small changes in assumptions?

    b. How does this slower sales growth scenario affect the amount the buyout firm could borrow initially if the investors still want to exit the business by the eighth year after paying off 100% of the senior debt and maintain the same senior to subordinated debt split?

13.17 By some estimates, as many as one-fourth of the LBOs between 1987 and 1990 (the first mega-LBO boom) went bankrupt. The data in Table 13.13 illustrate the extent of the leverage associated with the largest completed LBOs of 2006 and 2007 (the most recent mega-LBO

TABLE 13.13   Top Ten Completed Buyouts of 2006 and 2007 Ranked by Deal Enterprise Value

Target	Bidder(s)	Enterprise Value (EV)	Net Debt	Equity	Value of Equity	Interest Coverage[a]
		($ billion)	% of EV	% of EV	($ billion)	Ratio
TXU	KKR, TPG, Goldman Sachs	43.8	89.5	?	?	1.0
Equity Office Properties	Blackstone	38.9	Sold	NA	NA	Sold
HCA	Bain, KKR, Merrill Lynch	32.7	82.4	?	?	1.6
Alltel	TPG, Goldman Sachs	27.9	Sold	NA	NA	Sold
First Data	KKR	27.7	79.2	?	?	1.0
Harrah's Entertainment	TPG, Apollo	27.4	83.7	?	?	0.8
Hilton Hotels	Blackstone	25.8	75.9	?	?	1.1
Alliance Boots	KKR	20.8	83.5	?	?	1.1
Freescale Semiconductor	Blackstone, Permira, Carlyle, TPG	17.6	49.6	?	?	1.6
Intelsat	BC Partners	16.4	88.9	?	?	1.0
Average		27.9	81	?	?	1.0

[a]EBITDA less capital expenditures divided by estimated interest expense.
Source: The Economist, July 2008, p. 85.

boom). Equity Office Properties and Alltel have been sold. Use the data given in Table 13.13 to calculate the equity contribution made by the buyout firms as a percent of enterprise value and the dollar value of their equity contribution. What other factors would you want to know in evaluating the likelihood that these LBOs will end up in bankruptcy?

Answers to these problems are available in the Online Instructor's Manual for instructors using this book.

CHAPTER BUSINESS CASES

CASE STUDY 13.1
*TXU Goes Private in the Largest Private Equity Transaction
in History—A Retrospective Look*

Valued at $48 billion, the 2007 buyout of TXU, a Dallas-based energy giant, is the largest private equity deal in history. To complete the deal, an investor group moved aggressively to get approval from major stakeholders, including shareholders, consumers, legislators, regulators, environmentalists, and lenders. The buyout was a bet that the price of natural gas would continue to climb, benefiting the firm's natural gas revenues. However, the price of gas plummeted along with the U.S. economy, eroding TXU's cash flow. Since the transaction closed in October 2007, investors who bought $40 billion of TXU's bonds and loans have experienced large losses. Most of the bonds were trading between 70 and 80 cents on the dollar during most of 2010. The other $8 billion used to finance the deal came from private equity investors, banks, and large institutional investors. While the firm met its debt service obligations in 2010, it faces a $20 billion debt repayment coming due in 2014.

Wall Street banks were competing in 2007 to make loans to buyout firms on easier terms, with the banks also investing their own funds as a part of the deal. The allure to the banks was the prospect of dividing up as much as $1.1 billion in fees for originating the loans, repackaging such loans into pools called collateralized loan obligations, and reselling them to long-term investors such as pension funds and insurance companies. In doing so, the loans would be removed from the banks' balance sheets, eliminating potential losses that could arise if the deal soured at a later date. Furthermore, the deal appeared to be attractive as an investment opportunity as some banks put up $500 million of their own cash for a stake in TXU.

Under the terms of the February 2, 2007, merger agreement, ownership was transferred through a forward triangular cash merger–that is, a subsidiary merger. The financial sponsor group, which consisted of Kohlberg Kravis Roberts & Co., Texas Pacific Group, and Goldman Sachs, created a shell corporation referred to as Merger Sub Parent and its wholly-owned subsidiary Merger Sub. TXU was merged into Merger Sub, with Merger Sub surviving. Each outstanding share of TXU common stock was converted into the right to receive $69.25 in cash. Total cash required for the purchase was provided by the financial sponsor group and lenders (Creditor Group) to the Merger Sub (Figure 13.2). Regulatory authorities required that the debt associated with the transaction be held at the Merger Sub Parent holding company level so as not to further leverage the utility.

Subsequent to closing, the new company was reorganized into independently operated businesses under a new holding company, controlled by the Sponsor Group, called Texas Holdings (TH). Merger Sub (which owns TXU) was renamed Energy Future Holdings (EFH). TH's direct subsidiaries are EFH and Oncor (an energy distribution business formerly held by TXU). EFH's primary direct subsidiary is Texas Competitive Electric Holdings, which holds TXU's public utility operating assets and liabilities. All TXU non-Sponsor Group-related debt incurred to finance the transaction

CASE STUDY 13.1   *(cont'd)*

is held by EFH, while any debt incurred by the Sponsor Group is shown on the TH balance sheet (Figure 13.3).

Loan covenants limit EFH's and its subsidiaries' ability to incur additional indebtedness or issue preferred stock; pay dividends on, repurchase, or make distributions of capital stock or make other restricted payments; make investments; sell or transfer assets; consolidate, merge, sell, or dispose of all or substantially all its assets; and repay, repurchase, or modify debt. A breach of any of these covenants could result in an event of default. Table 13.14 illustrates selected covenants in which certain ratios must be maintained either above or below stipulated thresholds. Note that EFH was in violation of certain covenants when actual December 31, 2009, ratios are compared with required threshold levels.

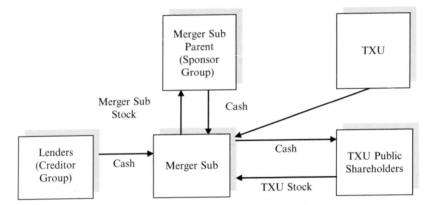

FIGURE 13.2   Forward triangular cash merger.

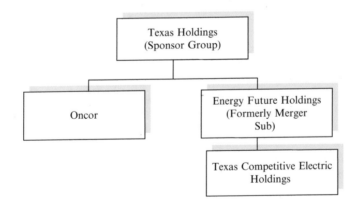

FIGURE 13.3   Postmerger organization.

CASE STUDY 13.1 *(cont'd)*

TABLE 13.14   EFH Holdings Debt Covenants

	December 31, 2009	Threshold Level as of December 31, 2009
Maintenance Covenant		
TCEH Secured Facilities:		
– Secured debt to adjusted EBITDA Ratio	4.76 to 1.00	Must not exceed 7.25 to 1.00
Debt Incurrence Covenants		
EFH Corp Senior Notes		
– EFH Corp fixed charge coverage ratio	1.2 to 1.0	At least 2.0 to 1.0
– TCEH fixed charge coverage ratio	1.5 to 1.0	At least 2.0 to 1.0
EFH Corp 9.75% Notes		
– EFH Corp fixed charge coverage ratio	1.2 to 1.0	At least 2.0 to 1.0
– TCEH fixed charge coverage ratio	1.5 to 1.0	At least 2.0 to 1.0
TCEH Senior Notes		
– TCEH fixed charge coverage ratio	1.5 to 1.0	At least 2.0 to 1.0
TCEH Senior Secured Facilities		
– TCEH fixed charge coverage ratio	1.5 to 1.0	At least 2.0 to 1.0
Restricted Payments/Limitations on Investments Covenants		
EFH Corp Senior Notes		
– General restrictions		
– EFH Corp fixed charge coverage ratio	1.4 to 1.0	At least 2.0 to 1.0
– General restrictions		
– EFH fixed charge coverage ratio	1.2 to 1.0	At least 2.0 to 1.0
– EFH Corp leverage ratio	9.4 to 1.0	≤7.0 to 1.0
EFH Corp 9.75% Notes		
– General restrictions		
– EFH Corp fixed charge coverage ratio	1.4 to 1.0	At least 2.0 to 1.0
– General restrictions		
– EFH Corp fixed charge coverage ratio	1.2 to 1.0	At least 2.0 to 1.0
– EFH Corp leverage ratio	9.4 to 1.0	≤7.0 to 1.0
TCEH Senior Notes		
– TCEH fixed charge coverage ratio	1.5 to 1.0	At least 2.0 to 1.0

CASE STUDY 13.1   (cont'd)

Discussion Questions:
1. How does the postclosing holding company structure protect the interests of the financial sponsor group, creditors, and the utility's customers, employees, and other stakeholder groups?
2. What was the purpose of the preclosing covenants and closing conditions as described in the merger agreement?
3. Loan covenants exist to protect the lender. How might such covenants inhibit EFH from meeting its 2014 $20 billion obligations?
4. As CEO of EFH, what would you recommend to the board of directors as an appropriate strategy for paying the $20 billion in debt that is maturing in 2014?

5. In the fourth quarter of 2008 and first quarter of 2009, EFC Holdings recorded goodwill impairment charges of about $8 billion. The substantial write-down of the net acquired suggests that the purchase price paid for TXU was too high. How might this impact KKR, TPG, and Goldman's abilities to earn financial returns expected by their investors on the TXU acquisition? How might this write-down impact EFH's ability to meet the $20 billion debt maturing in 2014?

Answers to this case study is provided in the Online Instructors Manual for instructors using this book.

CASE STUDY 13.2
"Grave Dancer" Takes Tribune Corporation Private in an Ill-Fated Transaction

At the closing in late December 2007, well-known real estate investor Sam Zell described the takeover of the Tribune Company as "the transaction from hell." His comments were prescient in that what had appeared to be a cleverly crafted, albeit highly leveraged, deal from a tax standpoint was unable to withstand the credit malaise of 2008. The end came swiftly when the 161-year-old Tribune filed for bankruptcy on December 8, 2008.

On April 2, 2007, the Tribune Corporation announced that the firm's publicly traded shares would be acquired in a multistage transaction valued at $8.2 billion. Tribune owned at that time 9 newspapers, 23 television stations, a 25% stake in Comcast's Sports-Net Chicago, and the Chicago Cubs baseball team. Publishing accounts for 75% of the firm's total $5.5 billion annual revenue, with the remainder coming from broadcasting and entertainment. Advertising and circulation revenue had fallen by 9% at the firm's three largest newspapers (*Los Angeles Times*, *Chicago Tribune*, and *Newsday* in New York) between 2004 and 2006. Despite aggressive efforts to cut costs, Tribune's stock had fallen more than 30% since 2005.

The transaction was implemented in two stages. Sam Zell acquired a controlling 51% interest in the first stage followed by a back-end merger in the second stage in which the remaining outstanding Tribune shares were acquired. In the first stage, Tribune initiated a cash tender offer for 126 million shares (51% of total shares) for $34 per share, totaling $4.2 billion. The tender was financed using

CASE STUDY 13.2   *(cont'd)*

$250 million of the $315 million provided by Sam Zell in the form of subordinated debt, plus additional borrowing to cover the balance. Stage 2 was triggered when the deal received regulatory approval. During this stage, an employee stock ownership plan (ESOP) bought the rest of the shares at $34 a share (totaling about $4 billion), with Zell providing the remaining $65 million of his pledge. Most of the ESOP's 121 million shares purchased were financed by debt guaranteed by the firm on behalf of the ESOP. At that point, the ESOP held all of the remaining stock outstanding, valued at about $4 billion. In exchange for his commitment of funds, Mr. Zell received a 15-year warrant to acquire 40% of the common stock (newly issued) at a price set at $500 million.

Following closing in December 2007, all company contributions to employee pension plans were funneled into the ESOP in the form of Tribune stock. Over time, the ESOP would hold all the stock. Furthermore, Tribune was converted from a C corporation to a Subchapter S corporation, allowing the firm to avoid corporate income taxes. However, it would have to pay taxes on gains resulting from the sale of assets held less than ten years after the conversion from a C to an S corporation (Figure 13.4).

The purchase of Tribune's stock was financed almost entirely with debt, with Zell's equity contribution amounting to less than 4% of the purchase price. The transaction resulted in Tribune being burdened with $13 billion in debt (including the approximate $5 billion currently owed by Tribune). At this level, the firm's debt was ten times EBITDA, more than two and a half times that of the average media company. Annual interest and principal repayments reached $800 million (almost three times their preacquisition level), about 62% of the firm's previous EBITDA cash flow of $1.3 billion. Even though the

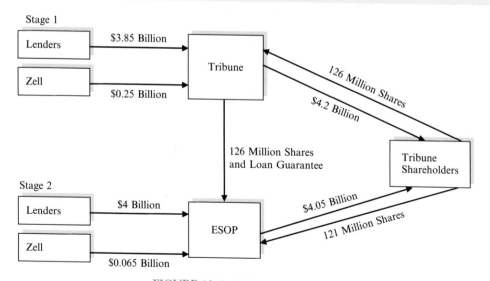

FIGURE 13.4   Tribune deal structure.

CASE STUDY 13.2 *(cont'd)*

ESOP owned the company, it was not be liable for the debt guaranteed by Tribune.

The conversion of Tribune into a Subchapter S corporation eliminated the firm's current annual tax liability of $348 million. Such entities pay no corporate income tax but must pay all profit directly to shareholders, who then pay taxes on these distributions. Since the ESOP was the sole shareholder, Tribune was expected to be largely tax exempt, since ESOPs are not taxed.

In an effort to reduce the firm's debt burden, the Tribune Company announced in early 2008 the formation of a partnership in which Cablevision Systems Corporation would own 97% of *Newsday* for $650 million, with Tribune owning the remaining 3%. However, Tribune was unable to sell the Chicago Cubs (which had been expected to fetch as much as $1 billion) and the minority interest in SportsNet Chicago to help reduce the debt amid the 2008 credit crisis. The worsening of the recession, accelerated by the decline in newspaper and TV advertising revenue, as well as newspaper circulation, thereby eroded the firm's ability to meet its debt obligations.

By filing for Chapter 11 bankruptcy protection, the Tribune Company sought a reprieve from its creditors while it attempted to restructure its business. Although the extent of the losses to employees, creditors, and other stakeholders is difficult to determine, some things are clear. Any pension funds set aside prior to the closing would remain with the employees, but it is likely that equity contributions made to the ESOP on behalf of the employees since the closing would be lost. The employees would become general creditors of Tribune. As a holder of subordinated debt, Mr. Zell had priority over the employees if the firm was liquidated and the proceeds distributed to the creditors.

Those benefiting from the deal included Tribune's public shareholders, including the Chandler family, which owned 12% of Tribune as a result of its prior sale of Times Mirror to Tribune, and Dennis FitzSimons, the firm's former CEO, who received $17.7 million in severance and $23.8 million for his holdings of Tribune shares. Citigroup and Merrill Lynch received $35.8 million and $37 million, respectively, in advisory fees. Morgan Stanley received $7.5 million for writing a fairness opinion letter. Finally, Valuation Research Corporation received $1 million for providing a solvency opinion indicating that Tribune could satisfy its loan covenants.

What appeared to be one of the most complex deals of 2007, which was designed to reap huge tax advantages, soon became a victim of the downward-spiraling economy, the credit crunch, and its own leverage. A lawsuit filed in late 2008 on behalf of Tribune employees contended that the transaction was flawed from the outset and intended to benefit Sam Zell and his advisors and Tribune's board. Even if the employees win, they will simply have to stand in line with other Tribune creditors awaiting the resolution of the bankruptcy court proceedings.

Discussion Questions

1. What are the acquisition vehicle, postclosing organization, form of payment, form of acquisition, and tax strategy described in this case study?
2. Describe the firm's strategy to finance the transaction.
3. Is this transaction best characterized as a merger, an acquisition, a leveraged buyout, or a spin-off? Explain your answer.

CASE STUDY 13.2 *(cont'd)*

4. Is this transaction taxable or nontaxable to Tribune's public shareholders? To its post-transaction shareholders? Explain your answer.
5. Comment on the fairness of this transaction to the various stakeholders involved. How would you apportion the responsibility for the eventual bankruptcy of Tribune among Sam Zell and his advisors, Tribune's board, and the largely unforeseen collapse of the credit markets in late 2008?

Answers to these case study discussion questions are available in the Online Instructor's Manual for instructors using this book.

PART V

ALTERNATIVE BUSINESS AND RESTRUCTURING STRATEGIES

"Don't think of it as a divorce. Think of it as a spinoff."

Courtesy of www.Cartoonstock.com.

The preceding sections of this book dealt primarily with mergers and acquisitions as a means of fueling corporate growth within a specific country. Part V addresses alternative strategic options for growth, including cross-border M&A transactions and business alliances. This section also discusses what can be done if corporations believe that more value can be created by exiting certain businesses or product lines or by reorganizing or liquidating either outside of or under the protection of the bankruptcy court.

Chapter 14 outlines the common motives for entering business alliances, ranging from minority investments to joint ventures as alternatives to mergers and acquisitions, as well as the critical success factors for establishing alliances, alternative legal forms, and ways of resolving common deal-structuring issues. Common exit strategies or restructuring strategies, discussed in Chapters 15 and 16, describe how corporations choose from among a range of restructuring options, including divestitures, spin-offs, split-ups, equity carve-outs, and split-offs to improve shareholder value.

Chapter 16 focuses on failing firms that may attempt to preserve shareholder value by negotiating voluntarily with creditors to restructure their outstanding debt outside of bankruptcy court; alternatively, such firms may choose or be compelled to seek the protection of the court system. This chapter also describes methodologies for predicting corporate default or bankruptcy and also how to value failing businesses. Finally, Chapter 17 outlines common motives for international expansion and describes widely used international market entry strategies. Ways to value, structure, and finance cross-border transactions also are discussed in detail in Chapter 17.

Joint Ventures, Partnerships, Strategic Alliances, and Licensing

Humility is not thinking less of you. It is thinking less about you. —**Rick Warren**

INSIDE M&A: MICROSOFT PARTNERS WITH YAHOO! —AN ALTERNATIVE TO TAKEOVER?

Business alliances sometimes represent a less expensive alternative to mergers and acquisitions. This notion may have motivated Microsoft when the firm first approached Yahoo! about a potential partnership in November 2006 and again in mid-2007. Frustrated with their inability to partner with Yahoo!, Microsoft initiated a hostile takeover bid in 2008 valued at almost $48 billion or $33 per share, only to be spurned by Yahoo!. Following the withdrawal of Microsoft's offer, Yahoo!'s share price fell into the low to mid-teens and remained in that range throughout 2010.

Reflecting the slumping share price and a failed effort to create a search partnership with Google, Yahoo!'s cofounder, Jerry Yang, was replaced by Carol Bartz in early 2009. The U.S. Justice Department had threatened to sue to block the proposed partnership between Yahoo! and Google on antitrust grounds.

Microsoft again approached Yahoo! with a partnering proposal in mid-2009, which resulted in an announcement on February 18, 2010, of an Internet search agreement between the two firms. As a result of the agreement, Yahoo! transferred control of its Internet search technology to Microsoft. Microsoft is relying on a ten-year arrangement with Yahoo! to help counter the dominance of Google in the Internet search market. By gaining access to each other's Internet users, both firms hope to be able to attract more advertising dollars from companies willing to pay for links on Microsoft's and Yahoo!'s websites. With Microsoft's search technology believed to be superior to Yahoo!'s, searches requested through Yahoo!'s site will be implemented using Microsoft's search software.

Regulatory agencies in both the United States and the European Union had no trouble approving the proposal because the combined Yahoo! and Microsoft Internet search market share is dwarfed by Google's. Google is estimated to have about two-thirds of the search market, followed by Yahoo! at 7% and Microsoft with about 3%.

Yahoo! could profit handsomely from the deal, since it will retain 88% of the revenue from search ads on its website during the first five years of the ten-year contract. Microsoft will pay most of the costs of implementing the partnership by giving Yahoo! $150 million to defray its expenses. Microsoft also agreed to absorb about 400 of Yahoo!'s nearly 14,000 employees. Ironically, Microsoft may get much of what it wanted (namely Yahoo!'s user base) at a fraction of the cost it would have paid to acquire the entire company.

CHAPTER OVERVIEW

For many years, joint ventures (JVs) and alliances have been commonplace in high-technology industries; many segments of manufacturing; the oil exploration, mining, and chemical industries; media and entertainment; financial services; pharmaceutical and bio-technology firms; and real estate. They have taken the form of licensing, distribution, co-marketing, research and development agreements, and equity investments. What all of these arrangements have in common is that they generally involve sharing the risk, reward, and control among all participants.

The term *business alliance* is used throughout this chapter to describe the various forms of cooperative relationships common in business today, including joint ventures, partnerships, strategic alliances, equity partnerships, licensing agreements, and franchise alliances. The primary theme of this chapter is that well-constructed business alliances often represent viable alternatives to mergers and acquisitions, and they always should be considered one of the many options for achieving strategic business objectives. The principal differences in the various types of business alliances were discussed in some detail in Chapter 1 and are therefore only summarized in Table 14.1. This chapter discusses the wide variety of motives for business alliances and the factors common to most successful ones. Also addressed are the advantages and disadvantages of alternative legal structures, important deal-structuring issues, and empirical studies that purport to measure the contribution of business alliances to creating shareholder wealth.

A review of this chapter (including practice questions and answers) is available in the file folder entitled "Student Study Guide" on the companion site to this book (*www.elsevierdirect.com/companions/9780123854858*). The companion site also contains a Learning Interactions Library, which gives students the opportunity to test their knowledge of this chapter in a "real-time" environment.

MOTIVATIONS FOR BUSINESS ALLIANCES

Money alone rarely provides the basis for a successful long-term business alliance. A partner often can obtain funding from a variety of sources but may be able to obtain access to a set of skills or nonfinancial resources only from a specific source. The motivation for an alliance can include risk sharing, gaining access to new markets, globalization, cost reduction, a desire to acquire (or exit) a business, or the favorable regulatory treatment often received compared with M&As.

TABLE 14.1   Key Differences among Business Alliances

Type	Key Characteristics
Joint Ventures	• Independent legal entity involving two or more parties • May be organized as a corporation, partnership, or other legal/business organization selected by the parties • Ownership, responsibilities, risks, and rewards allocated to parties • Each party retains corporate identity and autonomy • Created by parties contributing assets for a specific purpose and for a limited duration
Strategic Alliances (e.g., technology transfer, R&D sharing, and cross-marketing)	• Do not involve the formation of separate legal entities • May be precursor to JV, partnership, or acquisition • Generally not passive but involve cross-training, coordinated product development, and long-term contracts based on performance metrics, such as product quality, rather than price
Equity Partnerships	• Have all the characteristics of an alliance • Involve making minority investment in other party (e.g., 5% to 10%) • Minority investor may have an option to buy a larger stake in other party
Licensing – Product – Process – Merchandise and Trademark	• Patent, trademark, or copyright licensed in exchange for a royalty or fee • Generally no sharing of risk or reward • Generally stipulates what is being sold, how and where it can be used, and for how long • Payments usually consist of an initial fee and royalties based on a percentage of future license sales
Franchising Alliances	• Network of alliances in which partners linked by licensing agreements (e.g., fast-food chains, hardware stores) • Often grant exclusive rights to sell or distribute goods or services in specific geographic areas or markets • Licensees may be required to purchase goods and services from other firms in the alliance
Network Alliances	• Interconnecting alliances among companies crossing international and industrial boundaries • May involve companies collaborating in one market while competing in others (e.g., computers, airlines, cellular telephones) • Most often formed to access skills from different but increasingly interconnected industries
Exclusive Agreements	• Usually involve rights for manufacturing or marketing specific products or services • Each party benefits from the specific skills or assets the other party brings to the relationship

Risk Sharing

Risk is the potential for losing, or at least not gaining, value. Risk often is perceived to be greater the more money, management time, or other resources a company has committed to an endeavor and the less certain the outcome. To mitigate perceived risk, companies often enter into alliances to gain access to know-how and scarce resources or to reduce the amount of resources they would have to commit if they were to do it on their own. For example, in late 2004, General Motors and DaimlerChrysler, the world's largest and fifth largest auto manufacturers, respectively, agreed to jointly develop hybrid gasoline–electric engines for cars and light trucks. Neither corporation felt comfortable in assuming the full cost and risk associated with developing this new automotive technology. Moreover, each company would be willing to contribute the results of its own internal R&D efforts to the joint development of a technology to be shared by the two companies.[1]

Sharing Proprietary Knowledge

Developing new technologies can be extremely expensive. Given the pace at which technology changes, the risk is high that a competitor will be able to develop a superior technology before a firm can bring its own new technology to market. Consequently, high-technology companies with expertise in a specific technology segment often combine their efforts with another company or companies with complementary know-how to reduce the risk of failing to develop the "right" technology. Evidence shows that such alliances often do result in knowledge sharing between alliance partners.

Examples of technology JVs include the well-known Microsoft and Intel partnership in which the two cooperate to enhance the "Wintel" world, which combines Windows operating systems with Intel microchips. More recently, Chinese battery maker BYD Ltd. and German automaker Daimler AG, a leader in electric car technology, announced a 50/50 joint venture in mid-2010, headquartered in China, targeted at the Chinese electric car market.

Sharing Management Skills and Resources

Firms often lack the management skills and resources to solve complex tasks and projects. These deficiencies can be remedied by aligning with other firms that possess the requisite skills and proprietary knowledge. Building contractors and real estate developers have collaborated for years by pooling their resources to construct, market, and manage large, complex commercial projects. The contribution of Dow Chemical management personnel to a JV with Cordis, a small pacemaker manufacturer, enabled the JV to keep pace with accelerating production.

Reflecting the bureaucratic inertia often found in mega-corporations, large pharmaceutical firms actively seek partnerships with smaller, more nimble and innovative firms as a way of revitalizing their new drug pipelines. Such relationships are also commonplace among biotechnology firms. Small biotechnology firms are in fact likely to fund their R&D through JVs with large corporations, with the larger partner receiving the controlling interest.[2]

---

[1] Gomes-Casseres et al. 2006

[2] Lerner, Shane, and Tsai, 2003

In mid-2006, Nokia, a Finnish firm specializing in wireless communications, and Siemens, a German company with a strong position in fixed-line telecommunications, agreed to pool their networking equipment divisions in a joint venture to develop integrated network products. In early 2009, Walt Disney Studios announced that it had entered a long-term distribution agreement with DreamWorks Studios to utilize its marketing skills to distribute six DreamWorks' films annually.

In 2009, Italy's Fiat acquired a 35% stake in U.S. car maker Chrysler in exchange for sharing products and platforms for small cars with Chrysler. The deal was designed to help Fiat boost its sales volumes to compete in the global auto market and to enable Chrysler to enter more foreign markets, gain access to fuel-efficient technology, and expand its small-car offering.

Sharing Substantial Capital Outlays

As the U.S. cellular phone market became saturated, wireless carriers fought tenaciously to increase market share in a maturing market. Increased price competition and the exorbitant costs of creating and supporting national networks contributed to consolidation in the industry. Regional and foreign carriers were encouraged to join forces to achieve the scale necessary to support these burdensome costs. Vodafone and Verizon Communications joined forces in 1999 to form Verizon Wireless. SBC and Bell Atlantic formed the Cingular Wireless partnership, which acquired AT&T Wireless in early 2004.

Securing Sources of Supply

The chemical industry is highly vulnerable to swings in costs of energy and other raw materials. Chemical companies such as Dow, Hercules, and Olin have used JVs to build new plants throughout the world. When shortages of raw materials threaten future production, these firms commonly form JVs to secure future sources of supply. Similarly, CNOOC, the large Chinese oil concern, has been busily trying to invest in oil and natural gas assets in highly diverse geographic areas to obtain reliable sources of supply. CNOOC's efforts have ranged from outright acquisition (e.g., the attempted takeover of Unocal in the United States) to long-term contracts (e.g., Canadian tar sands) to joint ventures in various locations in Africa (e.g., Sudan and Kenya).

Cost Reduction

In the 1980s and 1990s, retailers and financial services, firms outsourced back-office activities, such as information and application processing, to IBM, EDS, and the like. Others outsourced payroll processing and the management of benefits to such firms as ADP. More recently, firms entered so-called logistics alliances. These alliances cover both transportation and warehousing services and utilize a single provider for them.[3]

Companies also may choose to combine their manufacturing operations in a single facility with the capacity to meet the production requirements of all parties involved. By building a large facility, the firms jointly can benefit from economies of scale. This type of arrangement is commonplace within the newspaper industry in major cities in which several newspapers are engaged in "head-to-head" competition. Similar cost benefits may be realized if one party

---

[3] Schmid, 2001

closes its production facility and satisfies its production requirements by buying at preferred prices from another party with substantial unused capacity. Other examples of competitors combining operating units to achieve economies of scale include Sony and Ericsson combining their mobile-handset units to compete with Nokia and Motorola in the late 1990s, as well as Hitachi and Mitsubishi forming an $8 billion-a-year semiconductor joint venture in 2000. In 2005, Canon and Toshiba created a new manufacturing operation to satisfy their requirements for SED displays for TVs by investing a combined $1.8 billion in a JV.

Gaining Access to New Markets

Accessing new customers is often a highly expensive proposition involving substantial initial marketing costs, such as advertising, promotion, warehousing, and distribution expenses. The cost may be prohibitive unless alternative distribution channels providing access to the targeted markets can be found. For example, in late 2006, eBay granted Google the exclusive right to display text advertisements on eBay's auction websites outside the United States, with eBay sharing in the revenue generated by the advertisements. Earlier that same year, Yahoo! signed a similar agreement with eBay for sites within the United States. Both Google and Yahoo! were able to expand their advertising reach without having to make substantial additional investments.

A company may enter into an alliance to sell its products through another firm's direct sales force, telemarketing operation, retail outlets, or Internet site. The alliance may involve the payment of a percentage of revenue generated in this manner to the firm whose distribution channel is being used. Alternatively, firms may enter into a "cross-marketing" relationship, in which they agree to sell the other firm's products through their own distribution channels. The profitability of these additional sales can be significant because neither firm has to add to its overhead expense or to its investment in building or expanding its distribution channels.

Globalization

The dizzying pace of international competition increased the demand for alliances and JVs to enable companies to enter markets in which they lack production or distribution channels or in which laws prohibit 100% foreign ownership of a business. Moreover, a major foreign competitor might turn out to be an excellent partner in fighting domestic competition. Alternatively, a domestic competitor could become a partner in combating a foreign competitor.

The automotive industry uses alliances to provide additional production capacity, distribution outlets, technology development, and parts supply. Many companies, such as General Motors and Ford, take minority equity positions in other companies within the industry to gain access to foreign markets. By aligning with Lenovo Group as a strategic partner in 2007, IBM has an opportunity to enlarge dramatically its market share in China. More recently, Nissan and Daimler announced in 2010 the formation of a partnership in which the firms would share the cost of developing engines and small-car technologies with projected savings totaling $5.3 billion. As part of the arrangement, each firm will buy a 3.1% stake in the other.

A Prelude to Acquisition or Exit

Rather than acquire a company, a firm may choose to make a minority investment in another company. In exchange for the investment, the investing firm may receive board representation, preferred access to specific proprietary technology, and an option to purchase a controlling interest in the company. The investing firm is able to assess the quality of management, cultural compatibility, and the viability of the other firm's technology without having to acquire a controlling interest in the firm.

Alternatively, a parent intending to exit a subsidiary may do so by contributing the unit to a joint venture and negotiating as part of the deal a put or call option with the other JV partners. A call option gives the partners the right to purchase the unit, and the put option gives the parent the right to sell the unit to the other partners. The price and a time period during which the options may be exercised are determined during the formation of the JV. For example, GE negotiated a put option with Comcast in 2010 when GE announced that it would be contributing its NBC Universal subsidiary to a JV corporation in which Comcast and GE would own 51% and 49% stakes, respectively (see Case Study 14.2 for more details).

Favorable Regulatory Treatment

As noted in Chapter 2, the Department of Justice has looked on JVs far more favorably than mergers or acquisitions. Mergers result in a reduction in the number of firms; JVs increase the number of firms because the parents continue to operate while another firm is created. Project-oriented JVs often are viewed favorably by regulators. Regulatory authorities tend to encourage collaborative research, particularly when the research is shared among all the parties to the JV.

CRITICAL SUCCESS FACTORS FOR BUSINESS ALLIANCES

Research suggests that the success of a JV or alliance depends on a specific set of identifiable factors.[4] These factors most often include synergy; cooperation; clarity of purpose, roles, and responsibilities; accountability; a "win–win" situation; compatible time frames and financial expectations for the partners; and support from top management.

Synergy

Successful alliances are characterized by partners that have attributes that either complement existing strengths or offset significant weaknesses. Examples include economies of scale and scope, access to new products, distribution channels, and proprietary know-how. As with any merger or acquisition, the perceived synergy should be measurable to the extent possible. Interestingly, successful alliances are often those in which the partners contribute a skill or resource in addition to or other than money. Such alliances often make good economic sense and, as such, are able to get financing.

[4] Kantor, 2002; Child and Faulkner, 1998; Lynch, 1990, 1993

Cooperation

All parties involved must be willing to cooperate at all times. A lack of cooperation contributes to poor communication and reduces the likelihood that the objectives of the joint venture or alliance will be realized. Not surprisingly, companies with similar philosophies, goals, rewards, operating practices, and ethics are more likely to cooperate over the long run.

Clarity of Purpose, Roles, and Responsibilities

The purpose of the business alliance must be evident to all involved. A purpose that is widely understood drives timetables, division of responsibility, commitments to milestones, and measurable results. Internal conflict and lethargic decision making inevitably result from poorly defined roles and responsibilities of those participating in the alliance.

Accountability

Successful alliances hold managers accountable for their actions. Once roles and responsibilities have been clearly defined and communicated, measurable goals to be achieved in identifiable time frames should be established for all of the managers. Such goals should be directly tied to the key objectives for the alliance. Incentives should be in place to reward good performance with respect to goals, and those who fail to perform adequately should be held accountable.

Win–Win Situation

All parties to an alliance must believe they are benefiting from the activity for it to be successful. Johnson & Johnson's alliance with Merck & Company in the marketing of Pepcid AC is a classic win–win situation. Merck contributed its prescription drug Pepcid AC to the alliance so that J&J could market it as an over-the-counter drug. With Merck as the developer of the upset stomach remedy and J&J as the marketer, the product became the market share leader in this drug category. In contrast, the attempt by DaimlerChrysler, Ford, and GM to form an online auction network for parts, named Covisint, in early 2000 failed in part because of the partners' concern that they would lose competitive information.

Compatible Time Frames and Financial Expectations

The length of time an alliance agreement remains in force depends on the partners' objectives, the availability of resources needed to achieve these objectives, and the accuracy of the assumptions on which the alliance's business plans are based. Incompatible time frames are a recipe for disaster. The management of a small Internet business may want to "cash out" within the next 18 to 24 months, whereas a larger firm may wish to gain market share over a number of years.

Support from the Top

Top management of the parents of a business alliance must involve themselves aggressively and publicly. Such support should be unambiguous and consistent. Tepid support or, worse, indifference filters down to lower-level managers and proves to be highly demotivating. Middle-level managers tend to focus their time and effort on those activities that tend to maximize their compensation and likelihood of promotion. These activities may divert time and attention from the business alliance.

ALTERNATIVE LEGAL FORMS OF BUSINESS ALLIANCES

As is true of M&As, determining the legal form of a business alliance should follow the creation of a coherent business strategy. The choice of legal structure should be made only when the parties to the business alliance are comfortable with the venture's objectives, potential synergy, and preliminary financial analysis of projected returns and risk. Business alliances may assume a variety of legal structures, including corporate, partnership, franchise, equity partnership, or written contract.[5] The five basic legal structures are discussed in detail in this section. Each has its own implications with respect to taxation, control by the owners, ability to trade ownership positions, limitations on liability, duration, and ease of raising capital (Table 14.2).

Corporate Structures

A corporation is a legal entity created under state law in the United States with an unending life and limited financial liability for its owners. Corporate legal structures include a generalized corporate form (also called a C-type corporation) and the Subchapter S (S-type) corporation. The S-type corporation contains certain tax advantages intended to facilitate the formation of small businesses, which are perceived to be major contributors to job growth.[6]

C-Type Corporations

A JV corporation normally involves a stand-alone business. The corporation's income is taxed at the prevailing corporate tax rates. Corporations other than S-type corporations are subject to "double" taxation. Taxes are paid by the corporation when profits are earned and again by the shareholders when the corporation issues dividends. Moreover, setting up a corporate legal structure may be more time consuming and costly than other legal forms because of legal expenses incurred in drafting a corporate charter and bylaws. Although the

[5] Technically, a "handshake" agreement is also an option. However, given the inordinate risk associated with the lack of a written agreement, those seeking to create a business alliance are encouraged to avoid this type of arrangement. However, in some cultures, this type of informal agreement may be the most appropriate. Efforts to insist on a detailed written agreement or contractual relationship may be viewed as offensive.

[6] Truitt, 2006

TABLE 14.2 Alternative Legal Forms Applicable to Business Alliances

Legal Form	Advantages	Disadvantages
Corporate Structures		
C Corporation	Continuity of ownership Limited liability Provides operational autonomy Provides for flexible financing	Double taxation Inability to pass losses on to shareholders Relatively high setup costs including charter and bylaws
Subchapter S	Facilitates tax-free merger Avoids double taxation Limited liability	Maximum of 100 shareholders Excludes corporate shareholders Must distribute all earnings Allows only one class of stock Lacks continuity of C corporation Difficult to raise large sums of money
Limited Liability Company (LLC)	Limited liability Owners can be managers without losing limited liability Avoids double taxation Allows an unlimited number of members (i.e., owners) Allows corporate shareholders Can own more than 80% of another company Allows flexibility in allocating investment, profits, losses, and operational responsibilities among members Life set by owners Can sell shares to "members" without SEC registration Allows foreign corporations as investors	Owners also must be active participants in the firm Lacks continuity of a corporate structure State laws governing LLC formation differ, making it difficult for LLCs doing business in multiple states Member shares often illiquid because consent of members required to transfer ownership
Partnership Structures		
General Partnership	Avoids double taxation Allows flexibility in allocating investment, profits, losses, and operational responsibilities	Partners have unlimited liability Lacks continuity of corporate structure Partnership interests illiquid Partners jointly and severally liable
Limited Liability Partnership	Life set by general partner Limits partner liability (except for general partner) Avoids double taxation State laws are consistent (covered under the Uniform Limited Partnership Act)	Each partner has authority to bind the partnership to contracts Partnership interests illiquid Partnership dissolved if a partner leaves Private partnerships limited to 35 partners
Franchise Alliance	Allows repeated application of a successful business model Minimizes start-up expenses Facilitates communication of common brand and marketing strategy	Success depends on quality of franchise sponsor support Royalty payments (3–7% of revenue)

TABLE 14.2 Cont'd

Legal Form	Advantages	Disadvantages
Equity Partnership	Facilitates close working relationship Potential prelude to merger May preempt competition	Limited tactical and strategic control
Written Contract	Easy start-up Potential prelude to merger	Limited control Lacks close coordination Potential for limited commitment

corporate legal structure has adverse tax consequences and may be more costly to establish, it does offer a number of important advantages over other legal forms. The four primary characteristics of a C-type corporate structure include managerial autonomy, continuity of ownership or life, ease of transferring ownership and raising money, and limited liability. These characteristics are discussed next.

Managerial autonomy most often is used when the JV is large or complex enough to require a separate or centralized professional management organization. The corporate structure works best when the JV requires some operational autonomy to be effective. The parent companies would continue to set strategy, but the JV's management would manage the day-to-day operations.

Unlike other legal forms, the corporate structure has an indefinite life, since it does not have to be dissolved as a result of the death of the owners or if one of the owners wishes to liquidate its ownership position. A corporate legal structure may be warranted if the JV's goals are long term and the parties choose to contribute cash directly to the JV. In return for the cash contribution, the JV partners receive stock in the new company. If the initial strategic reasons for the JV change and the JV no longer benefits one of the partners, the stock in the JV can be sold. Alternatively, the partner–shareholder can withdraw from active participation in the JV corporation but remain a passive shareholder in anticipation of potential future appreciation of the stock. In addition, the corporate structure facilitates a tax-free merger, in which the stock of the acquiring firm can be exchanged for the stock or assets of another firm. In practice, the transferability of ownership interests is strictly limited by the stipulations of a shareholder agreement created when the corporation is formed.

Under a corporate structure ownership can be easily transferred, which facilitates raising money. A corporate structure also may be justified if the JV is expected to have substantial future financing requirements. A corporate structure provides a broader array of financing options than other legal forms, including the ability to sell shares and the issuance of corporate debentures and mortgage bonds. The ability to sell new shares enables the corporation to raise funds to expand while still retaining control if less than 50.1% of the corporation's shares are sold.

Under the corporate structure, the parent's liability is limited to the extent of its investment in the corporation. Consequently, an individual stockholder cannot be held responsible for the debts of the corporation or of other shareholders. However, a corporation's owner can be held personally liable if he or she directly injures someone or personally guarantees a bank loan or a business debt on which the corporation defaults. Other exceptions to personal liability include the failure to deposit taxes withheld from employees' wages or the commission of intentional fraud that causes harm to the corporation or to someone else. Finally, an owner may be liable if he or she treats the corporation as an extension of his or her personal affairs by failing to adequately capitalize the corporation, hold regular directors and shareholders meetings, or keeps business records and transactions separate from the other owners.

Subchapter S Corporations

Effective December 31, 2004, a firm having 100 or fewer shareholders may qualify as an S-type corporation and elect to be taxed as if it were a partnership and thus avoid double taxation. The maximum number of shareholders was increased from 76 to 100 under the 2004 American Jobs Creation Act. This act allows the members of a single family to be considered as a single shareholder. For example, a husband and wife (and their estates) would be treated as a single shareholder. Members of a family are individuals with a common ancestor, lineal descendants of the common ancestor, and the spouses of such lineal descendants or common ancestor. Moreover, an ESOP maintained by an S corporation is not in violation of the maximum number of shareholders' requirement because the S corporation contributes stock to the ESOP.

The major disadvantages to an S-type corporation are the exclusion of any corporate shareholders, the requirement to issue only one class of stock, the necessity of distributing all earnings to the shareholders each year, and that no more than 25% of the corporation's gross income may be derived from passive income. To be treated as an S-type corporation, all shareholders must simply sign and file IRS Form 2553.

C corporations may convert to Subchapter S corporations to eliminate double taxation on dividends. Asset sales within ten years of the conversion from a C to an S corporation are subject to taxes on capital gains at the prevailing corporate income tax rate. However, after ten years, such gains are tax-free to the S corporation but are taxable when distributed to shareholders at their personal tax rates. In 2007, turnaround specialist Sam Zell, after taking the Tribune Corporation private, converted the firm to an S corporation to take advantage of the favorable tax treatment (see Case Study 13.2). Sales of assets acquired by an S corporation, or after a ten-year period following conversion from one form of legal entity to an S corporation, are taxed at the capital gains tax rate, which is generally more favorable than the corporate income tax rate. The ten-year "built-in-gains" period is designed by the IRS to discourage C corporations from converting to Subchapter S corporations to take advantage of the more favorable capital gains tax rates on gains realized by selling corporate assets. Gains on the sale of assets by C corporations are taxed at the prevailing corporate tax rate rather than a more favorable capital gains tax rate.

As discussed next, the limited liability company offers its owners the significant advantage of greater flexibility in allocating profits and losses and is not subject to the many restrictions of the S corporation. Consequently, the overall popularity of the S corporation has declined.

Limited Liability Company

Like a corporation, the LLC limits the liability of its owners (called *members*) to the extent of their investment. Like a limited partnership, the LLC passes through all of the profits and losses of the entity to its owners without itself being taxed. To obtain this favorable tax status, the IRS generally requires that the LLC adopt an organization agreement that eliminates the characteristics of a C corporation: management autonomy, continuity of ownership or life, and free transferability of shares. Management autonomy is limited by expressly placing decisions about major issues pertaining to the management of the LLC (e.g., mergers or asset sales) in the hands of all its members. LLC organization agreements require that they be dissolved in case of the death, retirement, or resignation of any member, thereby eliminating continuity of ownership or life. Free transferability is limited by making a transfer of ownership subject to the approval of all members.

Unlike S-type corporations, LLCs can own more than 80% of another corporation and have an unlimited number of members. Also, corporations as well as non-U.S. residents can own LLC shares. Equity capital is obtained through offerings to owners or members. Capital is sometimes referred to as *interests* rather than *shares*, since the latter denotes something that may be freely traded. The LLC can sell shares or interests to members without completing the costly and time-consuming process of registering them with SEC, which is required for corporations that sell their securities to the public. However, LLC shares are not traded on public exchanges. This arrangement works well for corporate JVs or projects developed through a subsidiary or affiliate. The parent corporation can separate a JV's risk from its other businesses while getting favorable tax treatment and greater flexibility in the allocation of revenues and losses among owners. Finally, LLCs can incorporate before an initial public offering tax-free. This is necessary because they must register such issues with the SEC. The life of the LLC is determined by the owners and is generally set for a fixed number of years in contrast to the typical unlimited life for a corporation.

The LLC's management structure may be determined in whatever manner the members desire. Members may manage the LLC directly or provide for the election of a manager, officer, or board to conduct the LLC's activities. Members hold final authority in the LLC, having the right to approve extraordinary actions such as mergers or asset sales.

The LLC's drawbacks are evident if one owner decides to leave. All other owners must formally agree to continue the firm. Also, all the LLC's owners must take active roles in managing the firm. LLC interests are often illiquid, since transfer of ownership is subject to the approval of other members. LLCs must be set for a limited time, typically 30 years. Each state has different laws about LLC formation and governance, so an LLC that does business in several states might not meet the requirements in every state. LLCs are formed when two or more "persons" (i.e., individuals, LLPs, corporations, etc.) agree to file articles of organization with the secretary of state's office. The most common types of firms to form LLCs are family-owned businesses, professional services firms such as lawyers, and companies with foreign investors.

Partnership Structures

Frequently used as an alternative to a corporation, partnership structures include general partnerships and limited partnerships. While the owners of a partnership are not legally required to have a partnership agreement, it usually makes sense to have one. The partnership agreement spells out how business decisions are to be made and how profits and losses will be shared.

General Partnerships

Under the general partnership legal structure, investment, profits, losses, and operational responsibilities are allocated to the partners. The arrangement has no effect on the autonomy of the partners. Because profits and losses are allocated to the partners, the partnership is not subject to tax. The partnership structure also offers substantial flexibility in how the profits and losses are allocated to the partners. Typically, a corporate partner forms a special-purpose subsidiary to hold its interest. This not only limits liability but also may facilitate disposition of the JV interest in the future. The partnership structure is preferable to the other options when the business alliance is expected to have a short (three to five years) duration and if high levels of commitment and management interaction are necessary for short time periods.

The primary disadvantage of the general partnership is that all the partners have unlimited liability and may have to cover the debts of less financially sound partners. Each partner is said to be jointly and severally liable for the partnership's debts. For example, if one of the partners negotiates a contract resulting in a substantial loss, each partner must pay for a portion of the loss, based on a previously determined agreement on the distribution of profits and losses. Because each partner has unlimited liability for all the debts of the firm, creditors of the partnership may claim assets from one or more of the partners if the remaining partners are unable to cover their share of the loss. Another disadvantage includes the ability of any partner to bind the entire business to a contract or other business deal. Consequently, if one partner purchases inventory at a price that the partnership cannot afford, the partnership is still obligated to pay.

Partnerships also lack continuity in that they must be dissolved if a partner dies or withdraws, unless a new partnership agreement can be drafted. To avoid this possibility, a partnership agreement should include a buy–sell condition or right of first refusal allowing the partners to buy out a departing partner's interest so the business can continue. Finally, partnership interests may also be difficult to sell because of the lack of a public market, thus making it difficult to liquidate the partnership or to transfer partnership interests.

Forming a partnership generally requires applying for a local business license or tax registration certificate. If the business name does not contain all of the partners' last names, the partnership must register a fictitious or assumed business name in the county in which it is established. The body of law governing partnerships is the Uniform Partnership Act (UPA).

Limited Partnerships

A limited liability partnership is one in which one or more of the partners can be designated as having limited liability as long as at least one partner has unlimited liability. Those who are responsible for the day-to-day operations of the partnership's activities, whose individual acts are binding on the other partners, and who are personally liable for the partnership's total liabilities are called *general partners*. Those who contribute only money and are not involved in management decisions are called *limited partners*. Usually limited partners receive income, capital gains, and tax benefits, whereas the general partner collects fees and a percentage of the capital gain and income.

Typical limited partnerships are in real estate, oil and gas, and equipment leasing, but they also are used to finance movies, R&D, and other projects. Public limited partnerships are sold through brokerage firms, financial planners, and other registered securities representatives.

Public partnerships may have an unlimited number of investors, and their partnership plans must be filed with the SEC. Private limited partnerships are constructed with fewer than 35 limited partners, who each invest more than $20,000. Their plans do not have to be filed with the SEC.

The sources of equity capital for limited partnerships are the funds supplied by the general and limited partners. The total amount of equity funds needed by the limited partnerships is typically committed when the partnership is formed. Therefore, ventures that are expected to grow are not usually set up as limited partnerships. LLPs are very popular for accountants, physicians, attorneys, and consultants. With the exception of Louisiana, every state has adopted either the Uniform Limited Partnership Act or the Revised Uniform Limited Partnership Act.

Franchise Alliance

Franchises typically involve a franchisee making an initial investment to purchase a license, plus additional capital investment for real estate, machinery, and working capital. For this initial investment, the franchisor provides training, site-selection assistance, and discounts resulting from bulk purchasing. Royalty payments for the license typically run 3% to 7% of annual franchisee revenue. Franchise success rates exceed 80% over a five-year period as compared with some types of start-ups, which have success rates of less than 10% after five years.[7] The franchise alliance is preferred when a given business format can be replicated many times. Moreover, franchise alliances are also appropriate when there needs to be a common, recognizable identity presented to customers of each of the alliance partners and close operational coordination is required. In addition, a franchise alliance may be desirable when a common marketing program needs to be coordinated and implemented by a single partner.[8]

The franchisor and franchisee operate as separate entities, usually as corporations or LLCs. The four basic types of franchises are distributor (auto dealerships), processing (bottling plants), chain (restaurants), and area franchises (a geographic region is licensed to a new franchisee to subfranchise to others). Franchisors are required to comply with the Federal Trade Commission's Franchise Rule, which requires franchisors to make presale disclosures nationwide to prospective franchisees. Registration of franchises falls under state law modeled on the Uniform Franchise Offering Circular, which requires franchisors to make specific presale disclosures to prospective franchisees, including their financial statements for the preceding three years, as well as the terms and conditions of the franchise agreement, territory restrictions, and the like.

Equity Partnership

An equity partnership involves a company's purchase of stock (resulting in a less than controlling interest) in another company or a two-way exchange of stock by the two companies. It often is referred to as a *partnership* because of the equity ownership exchanged. Equity partnerships commonly are used in purchaser–supplier relationships, technology development,

[7] Lynch, 1990

[8] Multistate franchises must be careful to be in full compliance with the franchise laws of the states in which they have franchisees.

marketing alliances, and in situations in which a larger firm makes an investment in a smaller firm to ensure its continued financial viability. In exchange for an equity investment, a firm normally receives a seat on the board of directors and possibly an option to buy a controlling interest in the company. The equity partnership may be preferred when there is a need to have a long-term or close strategic relationship, to preempt a competitor from making an alliance or acquisition, or as a prelude to an acquisition or merger.

In early 2011, British Petroleum and Russian oil and gas exploration and development giant Rosneft exchanged shares prior to forming a JV to develop oil and gas properties in the Arctic Sea. The purpose of the share exchange may have been to ensure that both parties would remain motivated to work together, since a successful JV may significantly increase the market value of both firms. As noted in Case Study 14.3, the viability of this JV may be in jeopardy unless pending lawsuits are resolved.

Written Contract

The written contract is the simplest form of legal structure. This form is used most often with strategic alliances because it maintains an "arms-length" or independent relationship between the parties to the contract. The contract normally stipulates such things as how the revenue is divided, the responsibilities of each party, the duration of the alliance, and confidentiality requirements. No separate business entity is established for legal or tax purposes. The written contract most often is used when the business alliance is expected to last less than three years, frequent close coordination is not required, capital investments are made independently by each party to the agreement, and the parties have had little previous contact.

STRATEGIC AND OPERATIONAL PLANS

Planning should precede deal-structuring activities. Before any deal-structuring issues are addressed, the prospective parties must agree on the basic strategic direction and purpose of the alliance as defined in the alliance's strategic plan, as well as the financial and nonfinancial goals established in the operation's plan.

The strategic plan identifies the primary purpose or mission of the business alliance; communicates specific quantifiable targets, such as financial returns or market share and milestones; and analyzes the business alliance's strengths and weaknesses, and opportunities and threats relative to the competition. The purpose of a business alliance could take various forms, as diverse as R&D, cross-selling the partners' products, or jointly developing an oil field. The roles and responsibilities of each partner in conducting the day-to-day operations of the business alliance are stipulated in an operations plan. Teams representing all parties to the alliance should be involved from the outset of the discussions in developing both a strategic and an operations plan for the venture. The operations plan (i.e., annual budget) should reflect the specific needs of the proposed business alliance. The operations plan should be written by those responsible for implementing the plan. The operations plan is typically a one-year plan that outlines for managers what is to be accomplished, when it is to be accomplished, and what resources are required.

RESOLVING BUSINESS ALLIANCE
DEAL-STRUCTURING ISSUES

The purpose of deal structuring in a business alliance is to allocate risks, rewards, resource requirements, and responsibilities fairly among participants. Table 14.3 summarizes the key issues and related questions that need to be addressed as part of the

TABLE 14.3   Business Alliance Deal-Structuring Issues

Issue	Key Questions
Scope	Which products are included and which are excluded? Who receives rights to distribute, manufacture, acquire, or license technology or purchase future products or technology?
Duration	How long is the alliance expected to exist?
Legal Form	What is the appropriate legal structure—stand-alone entity or contractual?
Governance	How are the interests of the parent firms to be protected? Who is responsible for specific accomplishments?
Control	How are strategic decisions to be addressed? How are day-to-day operational decisions to be handled?
Resource Contributions and Ownership Determination	Who contributes what and in what form? Cash? Assets? Guarantees/loans? Technology including patents, trademarks, copyrights, and proprietary knowledge? How are contributions to be valued? How is ownership determined?
Financing Ongoing Capital Requirements	What happens if additional cash is needed?
Distribution	How are profits and losses allocated? How are dividends determined?
Performance Criteria	How is performance to the plan measured and monitored?
Dispute Resolution	How are disagreements resolved?
Revision	How will the agreement be modified?
Termination	What are the guidelines for termination? Who owns the assets on termination? What are the rights of the parties to continue the alliance activities after termination?
Transfer of Interests	How are ownership interests to be transferred? What are the restrictions on the transfer of interests? How will new alliance participants be handled? Will there be rights of first refusal, drag-along, tag-along, or put provisions?
Tax	Who receives tax benefits?
Management/Organization	How is the alliance to be managed?
Confidential Information	How is confidential information handled? How are employees and customers of the parent firms protected?
Regulatory Restrictions and Notifications	Which licenses are required? Which regulations need to be satisfied? Which agencies need to be notified?

business alliance deal-structuring process. This section discusses how these issues most often are resolved.[9]

Scope

A basic question in setting up a business alliance involves which products specifically are included and excluded from the business alliance. This question deals with defining the scope of the business alliance. Scope outlines how broadly the alliance will be applied in pursuing its purpose. For example, an alliance whose purpose is to commercialize products developed by the partners could be broadly or narrowly defined in specifying what products or services are to be offered, to whom, in what geographic areas, and for what time period. Failure to define scope adequately can lead to situations in which the alliance may be competing with the products or services offered by the parent firms. With respect to both current and future products, the alliance agreement should identify who receives the rights to market or distribute products, manufacture products, acquire or license technology, or purchase products from the venture.

In certain types of alliances, intellectual property may play a very important role. It is common for a share in the intangible benefits of the alliance, such as rights to new developments of intellectual property, to be more important to an alliance participant than its share of the alliance's profits. What started out as a symbiotic marketing relationship between two pharmaceutical powerhouses, Johnson & Johnson and Amgen, deteriorated into a highly contentious feud. The failure to properly define which parties would have the right to sell certain drugs for certain applications and future drugs that may have been developed as a result of the alliance laid the groundwork for a lengthy legal battle between these two corporations.

Duration

The participants need to agree on how long the business alliance is to remain in force. Participant expectations must be compatible. The expected longevity of the alliance is also an important determinant in the choice of a legal form. For example, the corporate structure more readily provides for a continuous life than a partnership structure because of its greater ease of transferring ownership interests. There is conflicting evidence on how long most business alliances actually last.[10] The critical point is that most business alliances have a finite life, corresponding to the time required to achieve their original strategic objectives.

---

[9] For an excellent discussion of deal structuring in this context, see Ebin (1998), Freeman and Stephens (1994), and Fusaro (1995).

[10] Mercer Management Consulting, in ongoing research, concludes that most JVs last only about three years (Lajoux, 1998), whereas Booz-Allen and Hamilton (1993) reported an average life span of seven years.

TABLE 14.4 Key Factors Affecting Choice of Legal Entity

Determining Factors: Businesses with	Should Select
High liability risks	C corporation, LLP, or LLC
Large capital/financing requirements	C corporation
Desire continuity of existence	C corporation
Desire for managerial autonomy	C corporation
Desire for growth through M&A	C corporation
Owners who are also active participants	LLC
Foreign corporate investors	LLC
Desire to allocate investments, profits, losses, and operating responsibilities among owners	LLC and LLP
High pretax profits	LLC and LLP
Project focus/expected limited existence	LLP
Owners who want to remain inactive	LLP and C corporation
Large marketing expenses	Franchise
Strategies that are easily replicated	Franchise
Close coordination among participants not required	Written "arms-length" agreement
Low risk/low capital requirements	Sole proprietorship or partnership

Legal Form

Businesses that are growth oriented or intend to eventually go public through an IPO generally become a C corporation due to its financing flexibility, unlimited life, continuity of ownership, and ability to combine on a tax-free basis with other firms. With certain exceptions concerning frequency, firms may convert from one legal structure to a C corporation before going public. The nature of the business greatly influences the legal form that is chosen (Table 14.4).

Governance

In the context of a business alliance, *governance* may be defined broadly as an oversight function providing for efficient, informed communication between two or more parent companies. The primary responsibilities of this oversight function are to protect the interests of the corporate parents, approve changes to strategy and annual operating plans, allocate resources needed to make the alliance succeed, and arbitrate conflicts among lower levels of management. Historically, governance of business alliances has followed either a quasi-corporate or quasi-project approach. For example, the oil industry traditionally has managed alliances by establishing a board of directors to provide oversight of managers and protect the interests of nonoperating owners.

In contrast, in the pharmaceutical and the automotive industries, where nonequity alliances are common, firms treat governance the same as project management by creating a steering committee that allows all participants to comment on issues confronting the alliance. For highly complex alliances, governance may have to be implemented through multiple boards of directors, steering committees, operating committees, alliance managers, and project committees.

Resource Contributions and Ownership Determination

As part of the negotiation process, the participants must agree on a fair value for all tangible and intangible assets contributed to the business alliance. The valuation of partner contributions is important in that it often provides the basis for determining ownership shares in the business alliance. The shares of the corporation or the interests in the partnership are distributed among the owners in accordance with the value contributed by each participant. The partner with the largest risk, the largest contributor of cash, or the person who contributes critical tangible or intangible assets generally is given the greatest equity share in a JV.

It is relatively easy to value tangible or "hard" contributions such as cash, promissory cash commitments, contingent commitments, stock of existing corporations, and assets and liabilities associated with an ongoing business in terms of actual dollars or their present values. A party that contributes "hard" assets, such as a production facility, may want the contribution valued in terms of the value of increased production rather than its replacement cost or lease value. The contribution of a fully operational, modern facility to a venture interested in being first to market with a particular product may provide far greater value than if the venture attempted to build a new facility because of the delay inherent in making the facility fully operational.

In contrast, intangible or "soft" or "in-kind" contributions such as skills, knowledge, services, patents, licenses, brand names, and technology are often much more difficult to value. Partners providing such services may be compensated by having the business alliance pay a market-based royalty or fee for such services. If the royalties or fees paid by the alliance are below standard market prices for comparable services, the difference between the market price and what the alliance actually is paying may become taxable income to the alliance.

Alternatively, contributors of intellectual property may be compensated by receiving rights to future patents or technologies developed by the alliance. Participants in the business alliance that contribute brand identities, which facilitate the alliance's entry into a particular market, may require assurances that they can purchase a certain amount of the product or service, at a guaranteed price, for a specific time period. See Case Study 14.1 for an illustration of how the distribution of ownership between General Electric and Vivendi Universal Entertainment may have been determined in the formation of NBC Universal.

CASE STUDY 14.1
Determining Ownership Distribution in a Joint Venture

In 2003, Vivendi Universal Entertainment contributed film and television assets valued at $14 billion to create NBC Universal, a joint venture with TV network NBC, which was wholly owned by General Electric at that time. NBC Universal was valued at $42 billion at closing. NBC Universal's EBITDA was estimated to be $3 billion, of which GE contributed two-thirds and VUE accounted for the remaining one-third. EBITDA multiples for recent transactions involving TV media firms averaged 14 times EBITDA at that time. GE provided VUE an option to buy $4 billion in GE stock, assumed $1.6 billion in VUE debt, and paid the remainder of the $14 billion purchase price in the form of NBC Universal stock. At closing, VUE converted the option to buy GE stock into $4 billion in cash. GE owned 80% of NBC Universal and VUE owned 20%. How might this ownership distribution have been determined?

Solution

Step 1: Estimate the total value of the joint venture.

$3 billion $\times$ 14 = $42 billion

Step 2: Estimate the value of assets contributed by each partner.

Reflecting the relative contribution of each partner to EBITDA ($\frac{2}{3}$ from GE; $\frac{1}{3}$ from VUE), GE's contributed assets were valued at $28 billion (i.e., $\frac{2}{3}$ of $42 billion) and VUE's at $14 billion (i.e., $\frac{1}{3}$ of $42 billion).

Step 3: Determine the form of payment.

$4.0 billion (GE stock)
$1.6 billion (assumed Vivendi debt)
$8.4 billion (value of VUE's equity
    position in NBC Universal
    = $14 – $4.0 – $1.6)
$14.0 billion (purchase price paid by GE to Vivendi for VUE assets)

Step 4: Determine ownership distribution.

At closing, Vivendi chose to receive a cash infusion of $5.6 billion (i.e., $4 billion in cash in lieu of GE stock + $1.6 billion in assumed VUE debt). Thus,

VUE's ownership of NBC Universal
= ($14 billion – $5.6 billion)/$42 billion
= $8.4 billion/$42 billion
= 0.2

GE's ownership of NBC Universal
= 1 – 0.2 = 0.8

Financing Ongoing Capital Requirements

The business alliance may finance future capital requirements that cannot be financed out of operating cash flow by calling on the participants to make a capital contribution, issuing additional equity or partnership interests, or borrowing. Cingular's 2004 purchase of AT&T Wireless in an all-cash offer totaling $41 billion (the largest all-cash purchase on record) resulted in SBC and Bell Atlantic (co-owners of the Cingular JV) contributing 60% and 40% of the purchase price, respectively, to the joint venture to fund the acquisition. Their percentage equity contributions reflected their ownership shares of the joint venture.

If it is decided that the alliance should be able to borrow, the participants must agree on an appropriate financial structure for the enterprise. *Financial structure* refers to the amount of equity that will be contributed to the business alliance and how much debt it will carry. Alliances established through a written contract obviate the need for such a financing decision because each party to the contract finances its own financial commitments to the alliance. Because of their more predictable cash flows, project-based JVs, particularly those that create a separate corporation, sometimes sell equity directly to the public or though a private placement.

Owner or Partner Financing

The equity owners or partners may agree to make contributions of capital in addition to their initial investments in the enterprise. The contributions usually are made in direct proportion to their equity or partnership interests. If one party chooses not to make a capital contribution, the ownership interests of all the parties are adjusted to reflect the changes in their cumulative capital contributions. This adjustment results in an increase in the ownership interests of those making the contribution and a reduction in the interests of those not making contributions.

Equity and Debt Financing

JVs formed as a corporation may issue different classes of either common or preferred stock. JVs established as partnerships raise capital through the issuance of limited partnership units to investors, with the sponsoring firms becoming general partners. An LLC structure may be necessary when one of the owners is a foreign investor. When a larger company aligns with a smaller company, it may make a small equity investment in the smaller firm to ensure it remains solvent or to benefit from potential equity appreciation. Such investments often include an option to purchase the remainder of the shares, or at least a controlling interest, at a predetermined price if the smaller firm or the JV satisfies certain financial targets. Non-project-related alliances or alliances without financial track records often find it very difficult to borrow. Banks and insurance companies generally require loan guarantees from the participating owners. Such guarantees give lenders recourse to the participating owners in the event the alliance fails to repay its debt.

Control

Control is distinguishable from ownership by the use of agreements among investors or voting rights or by issuing different classes of shares. The most successful JVs are those in which one party is responsible for most routine management decisions, with the other parties participating in decision making only when the issue is fundamental to the business alliance. The business alliance agreement must define what issues are to be considered fundamental to the alliance and address how they are to be resolved, either by majority votes or by veto rights given to one or more of the parties. The owner who is responsible for the results of the alliance will want operational control. Operational control should be placed with the owner best able to manage the JV.

The owner who has the largest equity share but not operational control is likely to insist on being involved in the operation of the business alliance by having a seat on the board of directors or steering committee. The owner also may insist on having veto rights over such issues as changes in the alliance's purpose and scope, overall strategy, capital expenditures over a certain amount of money, key management promotions, salary increases applying to the general employee population, the amount and timing of dividend payments, buyout conditions, and acquisitions or divestitures.

Distribution Issues

Distribution issues relate to dividend policies and how profits and losses are allocated among the owners. The dividend policy determines the cash return each partner should receive. How the cash flows of the venture will be divided generally depends on the initial equity contribution of each partner, ongoing equity contributions, and noncash contributions in the form of technical and managerial resources. Allocation of profits and losses normally follows directly from the allocation of shares or partnership interests. When the profits flow from intellectual property rights contributed by one of the parties, royalties may be used to compensate the party contributing the property rights. When profits are attributable to distribution or marketing efforts of a partner, fees and commission can be used to compensate the partners. Similarly, rental payments can be used to allocate profits attributable to specific equipment or facilities contributed by a partner.

Performance Criteria

The lack of adequate performance measurement criteria can result in significant disputes among the partners and eventually contribute to the termination of the venture. Performance criteria should be both measurable and simple enough to be understood and used by the partners and managers at all levels and spelled out clearly in the business alliance agreement. Nonfinancial performance measures should be linked to financial return drivers. For example, factors such as market share, consistent product quality, and customer service may be critical to success in the marketplace. In licensing arrangements, the licensor should require that the licensee provide a forecast of unit sales and the value contributed by the license in such sales to provide a basis for auditing the licensee royalty payments. The balanced scorecard technique may be applied to measuring alliance performance by having the partners agree on a small number (i.e., five to ten) of relevant indicators. The indicators should include financial and nonfinancial, short- and long-term, and internal and customer-focused measures.[11]

Dispute Resolution

How disputes are resolved is affected by the choice of law provision, the definition of what constitutes an impasse, and the arbitration clause provided in the alliance agreement. The *choice of law provision* in the agreement indicates which state's or country's laws have

---

[11] Examples of performance indicators include return on investment, operating cash flow, profit margins, asset turnover, market share, on-time delivery, and customer satisfaction survey results. Managers will ignore performance indicators if their compensation is not linked to their actual performance against these measures. The top alliance managers should be evaluated against the full list of balanced scorecard performance measures. The performance of lower-level managers should be evaluated only against those measures over which they have some degree of control.

jurisdiction in settling disputes. This provision should be drafted with an understanding of the likely outcome of litigation in any of the participants' home countries or states and the attitude of these countries' or states' courts in enforcing choice of law provisions in the JV agreements.[12] The *deadlock or impasse clause* defines what events trigger dispute-resolution procedures. Care should be taken not to define the events triggering dispute-resolution procedures so narrowly that minor disagreements are subject to the dispute mechanism. Finally, an *arbitration clause* addresses major disagreements by defining the type of dispute subject to arbitration and how the arbitrator will be selected.

Revision

Changing circumstances and partner objectives may prompt a need to revise the objectives of the business alliance. If one of the parties to the agreement wishes to withdraw, the participants should have agreed in advance how the withdrawing party's ownership interest would be divided among the remaining parties. Moreover, a product or technology may be developed that was not foreseen when the alliance first was conceived. The alliance agreement should indicate that the rights to manufacture and distribute the product or technology might be purchased by a specific alliance participant. If agreement cannot be reached on revising the original agreement, it may be necessary to terminate the enterprise.

Termination

A business alliance may be terminated as a result of the completion of a project, successful operations resulting in merger of the partners, diverging strategic objectives of the partners, and failure of the alliance to achieve stated objectives. Termination provisions in the alliance agreement should include buyout clauses enabling one party to purchase another's ownership interests, prices of the buyout, and how assets and liabilities are to be divided if the venture fails or the partners elect to dissolve the operation. In some instances, a JV may convert to a simple licensing arrangement. Consequently, the partner may disengage from the JV without losing all benefits by purchasing rights to the product or technology.

Transfer of Interests

JV and alliance agreements often limit how and to whom parties to the agreements can transfer their interests. This is justified by noting that each party entered the agreement with the understanding of who its partners would be. In agreements that permit transfers under certain conditions, the partners or the JV itself may have *right of first refusal* (i.e., the party wishing to leave the JV first must offer its interests to other participants in the JV). Parties

[12] In international JVs, the choice of common law or civil law countries for settling disputes can have profoundly different outcomes. Common law countries, found typically in North America and Western Europe, rely on case law (i.e., resolutions of prior disputes) for guidance in resolving current disputes. In contrast, civil law countries, located primarily in Asia, do not rely on case law but allow magistrates to apply their interpretation of existing statutes to resolve current disputes. Consequently, the outcome of certain types of disputes may be less predictable in civil rather than common law countries.

to the agreement may have the right to "put" or sell their interests to the venture, and the venture may have a call option or right to purchase such interests. There also may be tag-along and drag-along provisions, which have the effect of a third-party purchaser acquiring not only the interest of the JV party whose interest it seeks to acquire but also the interests of other parties as well. A *drag-along* provision *requires* a party not otherwise interested in selling its ownership interest to the third party to do so. A *tag-along* provision gives a party to the alliance, who was not originally targeted by the third party, the *option* to join the targeted party in conveying its interest to the third party.

Buyout clauses in alliances that give one party an option to sell its share of the partnership to the other at a fixed price can backfire. Examples abound. AOL Time Warner had to pay a German media firm $6.75 billion for its half of AOL Europe, four times its estimated value at the time. The best alliance agreements avoid clauses such as fixed or minimum buyout prices, short payment periods, and strict payment options, such as cash only, to avoid giving sub-stantial leverage to one party over the other. In early 2005, General Motors and Fiat agreed to dissolve their five-year partnership after GM agreed to pay Fiat $2 billion in cash to avoid having to exercise a put option to buy the financially weak Fiat Auto.

Taxes

As is true for a merger, the primary tax concerns of the JV partners are to avoid the recog-nition of taxable gains on the formation of the venture and minimize taxes on the distribution of its earnings. In addition to the double taxation of dividends discussed earlier, the corporate structure may have other adverse tax consequences. If the partner owns less than 80% of the alliance, its share of the alliance's results cannot be included in its consolidated income tax return. This has two effects. First, when earnings are distributed, they are subject to an inter-corporate dividend tax, which can be 7% if the partner's ownership interest in the venture is 20% or more. Second, losses of the business alliance cannot be used to offset other income earned by the participant. For tax purposes, the preferred alternative to a corporate legal structure is to use a pass-through legal structure, such as a limited liability company or partnership.

A partnership can be structured in such a way that some partners receive a larger share of the profits, whereas others receive a larger share of the losses. This flexibility in tax planning is an important factor stimulating the use of partnerships and LLCs. These entities can allocate to each JV partner a portion of a particular class of revenue, income, gain, loss, or expense.[13]

Services provided to the JV, such as accounting, auditing, legal, human resource, and trea-sury services, are not viewed by the IRS as being "at risk" if the JV fails. The JV should pay prevailing market fees for such services. Services provided to the JV in return for equity may be seen as taxable to the JV by the IRS if such services are not truly "at risk."

---

[13] These special allocations can be made in the documents governing the creation of the partnership or LLC. Thus, partners or LLC members need not share the results of the venture on a pro rata basis. When one of the partners contributes technology, patent rights, or other property to the JV, the contribution may be structured so that the partner receives equity in exchange for the contribution. Otherwise, it will be viewed by the IRS as an attempt to avoid making cash contributions and treated as taxable income to the JV.

Management and Organizational Issues

Before a business alliance agreement is signed, the partners must decide what type of organizational structure provides the most effective management and leadership.

Steering or Joint Management Committee

Control of business alliances most often is accomplished through a steering committee. The steering committee is the ultimate authority for ensuring that the venture stays focused on the strategic objectives agreed to by the partners. To maintain good communication, co-ordination, and teamwork, the committee should meet at least monthly. The committee should provide operations managers with sufficient autonomy so they can take responsibility for their actions and be rewarded for their initiative.

Methods of Dividing Ownership and Control

A common method of control is the *majority–minority* framework, which relies on identifying a clearly dominant partner, usually the one having at least a 50.1% ownership stake. In this scenario, the equity, control, and distribution of rewards reflect the majority–minority relationship. This type of structure promotes the ability to make rapid corrections, defines who is in charge, and is most appropriate for high-risk ventures, where quick decisions often are required. The major disadvantage of this approach is that the minority partner may feel powerless and become passive or alienated.

Another method of control is the *equal division of power* framework, which usually means that equity is split equally. This assumes that the initial contribution, distribution, decision making, and control are split equally. This approach helps keep the partners actively engaged in the management of the venture. It is best suited for partners sharing a strong common vision for the venture and possessing similar corporate cultures. However, the approach can lead to deadlocks and the eventual dissolution of the alliance.

Under the *majority rules* framework, the equity distribution may involve three partners. Two of the partners have large equal shares, whereas the third partner may have less than 10%. The minority partner is used to break deadlocks. This approach enables the primary partners to remain engaged in the enterprise without stalemating the decision-making process.

In the *multiple party* framework, no partner has control; instead, control resides with the management of the venture. Consequently, decision making can be nimble and made by those who best understand the issues. This framework is well suited for international ventures, where a country's laws may prohibit a foreign firm from having a controlling interest in a domestic firm. In this instance, it is commonplace for a domestic company to own the majority of the equity but for the operational control of the venture to reside with the foreign partner. In addition to a proportional split of the dividends paid, the foreign company may receive additional payments in the form of management fees and bonuses.[14]

---

[14] Armstrong and Hagel, 1997

Regulatory Restrictions and Notifications

From an antitrust perspective, the Department of Justice historically looked on business alliances far more favorably than mergers or acquisitions. Nonetheless, JVs may be subject to Hart-Scott-Rodino filing requirements because the parties to the JV are viewed as acquirers and the JV itself is viewed as a target. For JVs between competitors to be acceptable to regulators, competitors should be able to do something together that they could not do alone. In general, competitors can be relatively confident that a partnership will be acceptable to regulators if, in combination, they control no more than 20% of the market. Project-oriented ventures are looked at most favorably. Collaborative research is encouraged, particularly when the research is shared among all the parties to the alliance. Alliances among competitors are likely to spark a review by regulators because they have the potential to result in price fixing and dividing up the market.

EMPIRICAL FINDINGS

Reflecting their flexibility and relatively low capital requirements, business alliances are becoming increasingly popular ways to implement business strategies. Under the right conditions, alliances can generate significant abnormal financial returns.

Abnormal Returns

Empirical evidence shows that JVs and strategic alliances create value for their participants (Table 14.5). Abnormal returns average about 1.5% around the announcement date of the formation of a business alliance. Partners in horizontal JVs (i.e., those involving partners in the same industry) tend to share equally in wealth creation. However, for vertical JVs, suppliers

TABLE 14.5   Abnormal Returns to Alliance Participants around Announcement Dates

Empirical Study	Abnormal (Excess) Return
McConnell and Nantell (1985): 136 JVs 1972–1979	2.15%
Woolridge and Snow (1990): 767 JVs 1972–1987	2.45%
Koh and Venkatraman (1991): 239 technology firms in JVs 1972–1986	0.87%
Chan, Kensinger, Keown, and Martin (1997): 345 strategic alliances 1983–1992	0.64% for both horizontal and nonhorizontal alliances 3.54% for horizontal alliances involving technical knowledge transfer
Das, Sen, and Sengupta (1998): 119 strategic alliances 1987–1991	1% (for technology transfer alliances)
Johnson and Houston (2000): 191 JVs 1991–1995	1.67%
Kale, Dyer, and Singh (2002): 1,572 strategic alliances 1988–1997	1.35% (for firms with significant alliance experience); otherwise 0.18%

experience a greater portion of the wealth created.[15] Moreover, the increase in wealth is often much greater for horizontal alliances involving the transfer of technical knowledge than for non-technical alliances.[16] Firms with greater alliance experience enjoy a greater likelihood of success and greater wealth creation than those with little experience.[17] Finally, strategic alliances most often represent the final form of cooperation between partners and do not often represent a prelude to a more formal arrangement, such as a joint venture corporation or a merger. However, investors in those firms participating in the alliance tend to react more favorably around the announcement date of the alliance if they believe the partners will eventually merge.[18]

Strategic alliances can have a salutary effect on the share prices of their suppliers and customers and a negative impact on the share prices of competitors. For alliances created to share technologies or develop new technical capabilities, suppliers benefit from increased sales to the alliance and customers benefit from using the enhanced technology developed by the alliance in their products. Competitors' share prices decline due to lost sales and earnings to the alliance.[19]

The Growing Role of Business Alliances

The average large company now has more than 30 alliances.[20] Although the average number of merger transactions per year exceeds the number of new alliances, alliance formation is accelerating.[21] The acceleration in alliance formation in part reflects a loosening of antitrust regulatory policies with respect to business alliances.

Despite rapid growth, studies show that most companies have yet to develop the skill to implement alliances successfully, with as many as 60% of all business alliances failing to meet expectations.[22] These studies make no allowance for different levels of experience in forming and managing alliances among the firms in their samples. Cumulative experience seems to be an important factor in increasing the likelihood that an alliance will meet expectations, with reported financial returns from alliances increasing with the number of businesses alliances implemented.[23]

[15] Johnson and Houston, 2000

[16] Chan, Kensinger, Keown, and Martin, 1997; Das, Sen, and Sengupta, 1998

[17] Kale, Dyer, and Singh, 2002

[18] Marciukaityte, Roskelley, and Wang, 2009

[19] Chang, 2008

[20] Kalmbach and Roussel, 1999

[21] Robinson, 2002a

[22] Kalmbach and Roussel (1999) indicate that 61% of the alliances are viewed as either disappointments or outright failures. This figure substantiates earlier findings by Robert Spekman of the Darden Graduate School of Business Administration that 60% of all ventures fail to meet expectations (Ellis, 1996). Klein (2004) reports that 55% of alliances fall apart within three years of their formation.

[23] According to a Booz-Allen survey of 700 alliances (Booz-Allen and Hamilton, 1993), financial returns on investment are directly related to a company's experience in forming and managing business alliances. Companies with one or two alliances in place tended to earn a 10% average return on investment as compared with 15% for those with three to five, 17% for those with six to eight, and 20% for those with nine or more.

SOME THINGS TO REMEMBER

Business alliances may represent attractive alternatives to M&As. The motivations for business alliances can include risk sharing, gaining access to new markets, accelerating new product introduction, technology sharing, globalization, a desire to acquire (or exit) a business, and the perception that they are often more acceptable to regulators than acquisitions or mergers. Furthermore, business alliances may assume a variety of legal structures: corporate, LLCs, partnership, franchise, equity partnership, or written contract. Key deal-structuring issues in forming alliances include the alliance's scope, duration, legal form, governance, and control mechanism. The valuation of resource contributions ultimately determines ownership interests. Alliance agreements also must be flexible enough to be revised when necessary and contain mechanisms for breaking deadlocks, transferring ownership interests, and dealing with the potential for termination.

Empirical studies suggest that alliances formed by partners in the same industry are more likely to create value than those that are not. Partners in such horizontal alliances are more likely to share equally in the benefits than parties to vertical alliances between a customer and a supplier. In such arrangements, studies suggest that suppliers tend to experience a disproportionate amount of the benefit. Finally, the greatest value creation seems to occur for horizontal alliances that result in a technology or knowledge transfer among the parties to the alliance. Nonetheless, the success rate of business alliances in terms of meeting participants' expectations does not seem to be materially different from that of M&As.

DISCUSSION QUESTIONS

14.1 Under what circumstances does a business alliance represent an attractive alternative to a merger or acquisition?

14.2 Compare and contrast a corporate and partnership legal structure.

14.3 What are the primary motives for creating a business alliance? How do they differ from the motives for a merger or acquisition?

14.4 What factors are critical to the success of a business alliance?

14.5 Why is a handshake agreement a potentially dangerous form of business alliance? Are there any circumstances under which such an agreement may be appropriate?

14.6 What is a limited liability company? What are its advantages and disadvantages?

14.7 Why is defining the scope of a business alliance important?

14.8 Discuss ways of valuing tangible and intangible contributions to a JV.

14.9 What are the advantages and disadvantages of the various organizational structures that could be used to manage a business alliance?

14.10 What are the common reasons for the termination of a business alliance?

14.11 Google invested $1 billion for a 5% stake in Time Warner's America Online unit as part of a partnership that expands the firm's existing search engine deal to include collaboration on advertising, instant messaging, and video. Under the deal, Google would have the usual customary rights afforded a minority investor. What rights or terms do you believe Google would have negotiated in this transaction? What rights do you believe Time Warner might want?

14.12 Conoco Phillips announced the purchase of 7.6% of the stock of Lukoil (a largely government-owned Russian oil and gas company) for $2.36 billion during a government auction of Lukoil's stock. Conoco would have one seat on Lukoil's board. As a minority investor, how could Conoco protect its interests?

14.13 Johnson & Johnson sued Amgen over their 14-year alliance to sell a blood-enhancing treatment called erythropoietin. The relationship had begun in the mid-1980s with J&J helping commercialize Amgen's blood-enhancing treatment, but the partners ended up squabbling over sales rights and a spin-off drug. The companies could not agree on future products for the JV. Amgen won the right in arbitration to sell a chemically similar medicine that can be taken weekly rather than daily. Arbitrators ruled that the new formulation was different enough to fall outside the licensing pact between Amgen and J&J. What could these companies have done before forming the alliance to have mitigated the problems that arose after the alliance was formed? Why do you believe they may have avoided addressing these issues at the outset?

14.14 General Motors, the world's largest auto manufacturer, agreed to purchase 20% of Japan's Fuji Heavy Industries, Ltd., the manufacturer of Subaru vehicles, for $1.4 billion. Why do you believe that initially General Motors may have wanted to limit its investment to 20%?

14.15 Through its alliance with Best Buy, Microsoft is selling its products—including Microsoft Network (MSN) Internet access services and hand-held devices such as digital telephones, hand-held organizers, and WebTV that connect to the Web—through kiosks in Best Buy's 354 stores nationwide. In exchange, Microsoft has invested $200 million in Best Buy. What do you believe were the motivations for this strategic alliance?

Answers to these Chapter Discussion Questions are available in the Online Instructor's Manual for instructors using this book.

CHAPTER BUSINESS CASES

CASE STUDY 14.2
Estimating the Real Cost of Comcast's Investment in NBC Universal

Following months of intense review, regulators approved the creation of a media giant consisting of Comcast Corporation and General Electric's NBC Universal on January 17, 2011. GE and Comcast had announced a deal on December 2, 2009, to form a joint venture consisting of NBCU and selected Comcast assets. The transaction is noteworthy for its potential impact on the entertainment industry, its complexity, and as an exit strategy for GE

from the media and entertainment business. The transaction also illustrates the payment of a significant control premium by Comcast.

Comcast is primarily a cable company and provider of programming content, with 23.8 million cable customers, 15.7 million high-speed Internet customers, and 7.4 million voice customers. Comcast hopes to be able to diversify its holdings as it faces encroaching threats from online video and more

CASE STUDY 14.2 *(cont'd)*

aggressive competition from satellite and phone companies that offer subscription TV services by adding more content to its video-on-demand offerings. Furthermore, by having an interest in NBCU's digital properties such as Hulu.com, Comcast is hoping to capitalize on any shift of its cable customers to viewing their favorite TV programs online. Comcast also will have more control over the videos that users watch on the web. By having a controlling interest in NBC Universal, Comcast could offer popular films on movies-on-demand channels ahead of or on the same day as a DVD release.

Comcast's strategy is to achieve vertical integration by owning the content it distributes through its cable operations. Previous attempts to do this, such as AOL's acquisition of Time Warner in 2001, have ended in failure largely because the cultures of the two firms did not mesh. Some media companies have successfully merged—for example, Time Warner's merger with Turner Broadcasting. Having learned from AOL's headlong rush to achieve synergy, Comcast is taking an approach that will allow the NBC Universal JV to operate largely independently of the parents.

General Electric is a diversified infrastructure, finance, and media firm whose products include aircraft engines and power generation to financial services, medical imaging, and television programming. The GE decision to sell reflects the deteriorating state of the broadcast television industry and a desire to exit a business that never quite fit well with its industrial side. NBC has been moored in fourth place among the major broadcast networks, and the economics of the broadcast television industry have deteriorated in recent years amid declining overall ratings

and a decline in advertising. In contrast, cable channels have continued to thrive because they rely on a steady stream of subscriber fees from cable companies such as Comcast. Moreover, while NBCU was profitable in 2009, it is expected to go into the red in the coming years. The Comcast deal helps GE to reduce its debt as it tries to shore up its big finance arm, which got hit in the 2008 financial crisis, and to focus more on its manufacturing and infrastructure operations.

The joint venture will be 51% owned by Comcast and 49% owned by GE, with Comcast managing the JV. GE will contribute to the joint venture NBCU businesses valued at \$30 billion, including cable networks, movies, television programming, and theme parks.

Comcast will contribute its cable channels, ten regional sports networks, and digital media properties, such as its equity interest in Hulu.com (jointly owned by NBC, News Corporation, and Walt Disney Company), valued collectively at \$7.25 billion. Comcast will also pay GE up to \$6.5 billion in cash subject to a balance sheet adjustment between signing and closing. In addition, NBCU will borrow \$9.1 billion from lenders and distribute the cash to GE, bringing the total cash received by GE for selling a 51% stake in NBCU to \$15.6 billion. By having NBCU borrow the \$9.1 billion, Comcast and GE may be able to protect themselves from NBCU's creditors if the firm eventually goes into bankruptcy because such loans are backed by NBCU's assets and cash flow.

GE will acquire Vivendi's 20% interest in NBCU for \$5.8 billion. The Vivendi agreement values NBCU at \$29 billion (\$5.8 ÷ 0.2), reflecting a slight minority discount for the Vivendi stake. GE expects to realize

CASE STUDY 14.2   *(cont'd)*

$8 billion in cash from the receipt of $6.5 billion from Comcast and loan proceeds of $9.1 billion at closing after paying Vivendi for its 20% stake in NBCU, NBCU's preclosing debt, and associated transaction fees.

GE has put options allowing it to sell one-half of its interest after three and a half years and its remaining interest at the end of the seventh year following closing. The JV is obligated to buy out GE only if its debt levels do not exceed two and three-quarters times EBITDA as a result of the purchase of the GE interest and if the JV is able to maintain investment-grade credit ratings.

Comcast has a call option to buy GE's interest at specific intervals at a 20% premium to the public market value of its stock

Table 14.6 shows how the two parties valued the JV. While it has been widely reported that Comcast paid $13.75 billion for a stake in NBC Universal, the real cost to Comcast was much greater. The actual price could have been almost $23 billion.

As the controlling shareholder, Comcast must show the debt accumulated by the JV on its consolidated balance sheet. As such, this additional debt may have the effect of reducing

TABLE 14.6   NBC Universal Joint Venture Valuation and Purchase Price Determination ($ billion)

NBC Universal Joint Venture Valuation ($ billion)[a]	**$37.25**
Comcast Purchase Price for 51% of NBC Universal JV	
– Cash from Comcast paid to GE	$6.50
– Cash proceeds paid to GE from NBCU borrowings[b]	9.10
– Contributed assets (Comcast network)	7.25
Total	**$22.85**
GE Purchase Price for 49% of NBC Universal JV	
– Contributed assets (NBCU)	$30.00
– Cash from Comcast paid to GE	(6.50)
– Cash proceeds paid to GE from NBCU borrowings	(9.10)
Total	**$14.40**
Implied Control/Purchase Premium Paid by Comcast[c]	20.3%
Implied Minority/Liquidity Discount to GE's Purchase Price[d]	(21.1)%

[a] *Equals the sum of NBCU ($30 billion) plus the fair market value of contributed Comcast properties ($7.25 billion) and assumes no incremental value due to synergy.*

[b] *The $9.1 billion borrowed by NBCU will be carried on the consolidated books of Comcast, since it has the controlling interest in the joint venture. Since it reduces Comcast's borrowing capacity by that amount, it represents a portion of the purchase price. In practice, the additional $9.1 billion in debt from the JV on Comcast's consolidated balance sheet may not reduce the firm's borrowing capacity by an equivalent amount if lenders view the JV's cash-flow potential sufficient to more than offset the debt service requirements of the debt. Nonetheless, the additional debt will reduce Comcast's overall borrowing capacity. As such, some portion of the debt should be included in the purchase price Comcast paid for a 51% stake in the JV, making the actual purchase price much closer to $23 billion than the widely reported $13.75 billion.*

[c] *The control premium represents the excess of the purchase price paid over the fair market value of the net acquired assets and is calculated as follows: {[$22.85/(0.51 × $37.25)] – 1} × 100 = {[$22.85/$19.00] – 1} × 100 = 20.28%.*

[d] *The minority/liquidity discount represents the excess of the fair market value of the net acquired assets over the purchase price and is calculated as follows: {[$14.40/(0.49 × $37.25)] – 1} × 100 = (21.1)%.*

CASE STUDY 14.2 *(cont'd)*

Comcast's borrowing capacity dollar for dollar. Since the deal required NBCU to borrow $9.1 billion and then transfer the proceeds to GE, this debt should be included in the calculation of the purchase price paid by Comcast. Including the debt raises the purchase price to $22.85 billion. In practice, the reduction in Comcast's borrowing capacity is likely to be less because lenders will take into consideration the firm's substantial cash-generating ability.

As a result of its 51% interest, Comcast will own $19 billion in net assets of the JV (i.e., 0.51 × $37.25 billion). The excess of the $22.85 billion over the $19 billion in net assets constitutes an approximate 20% premium paid by Comcast for control and anticipated strategic and operating synergies. The premium may be excessive, since there were no other firms that expressed serious interest in buying NBC Universal.

GE's purchase price for 49% of the joint venture is $14.4 billion. This figure represents the fair market value of NBCU less the cash proceeds received from Comcast and from NBCU and includes a combined 21% minority and liquidity discount, reflecting its lack of control and inability to "cash out" of its ownership interest until the put exercise dates. Both the estimated control premium and the minority/liquidity discount are likely to be overstated because no estimate of synergy was included in the calculation of the NBCU valuation due to a lack of information.

To gain approval, the U.S. Federal Communications Commission and the Department of Justice required Comcast and NBCU to relinquish their voting rights and board representation to Hulu, although they could continue to

remain part owners. Furthermore, Comcast would have to ensure what the FCC called "reasonable access" to its programming for its competitors. Comcast also may not discriminate against programming that competes with its own offerings.

Critics suggest there is little overlap between Comcast and NBCU's businesses to provide significant cost savings. Moreover, big media deals have a poor track record, as illustrated by the AOL Time Warner debacle. Comcast is placing a big bet that it will be able to successfully combine content and distribution.

Discussion Questions

1. Speculate as to why GE may have found it difficult to manage NBC Universal. Be specific.

2. In theory, GE is responsible for 49% of NBC Universal's debt because it owns 49% of the joint venture. Do you believe that Comcast should be responsible for only 51% of the debt rather than the entire $9.1 billion? Explain your answer.

3. Speculate as to the potential circumstances in which either Comcast or GE would be likely to exercise their call or put options. Which party do you believe is likely to exercise its options first and why?

4. What are the likely challenges Comcast and GE will have in integrating the various businesses that make up the joint venture? Be specific.

Answers to these case study questions are found in the Online Instructor's Manual for instructors using this book.

CASE STUDY 14.3
British Petroleum and Russia's Rosneft
Unsuccessful Attempt to Swap Shares

Extending its already close ties with Russia, British Petroleum PLC announced an agreement to exchange shares with Russia's largest oil company, OAO Rosneft, on January 14, 2011. Rosneft is 75% owned by the Russian government. BP and Rosneft also announced the formation of a JV to develop three massive offshore exploration blocks that Rosneft owns in northern Russia. The two firms said they will jointly explore three areas in the South Kara Sea in the Russian Arctic, spending between $1.4 and $2 billion on seismic tests and drilling wells in the initial exploration phase. The JV will be two-thirds owned by Rosneft, with the remainder owned by BP.

Reflecting Europe's escalating dependence on Russia for an increasing share of its energy resources, particularly for clean-burning natural gas, the agreement is backed by Britain's prime minister, David Cameron, and Russia's prime minister, Vladimir Putin. Russia holds one-fifth of the world's proven reserves of natural gas, and, by some estimates, the South Kara Sea contains some of the largest reserves of oil and gas in the world.

The deal comes in the wake of BP's sale of assets to raise funds to cover the costs of the Gulf of Mexico oil spill in mid-2010. Such costs are expected to eventually total $40 billion. Rosneft, which had announced in late 2010 that it was seeking a partner for exploiting its Arctic leases, indicated that BP's experience in dealing with such problems gives it an edge over other potential partners. Rosneft also regards BP's deep-water drilling technology and experience as cutting edge. BP's expertise received another vote of confidence when Australia granted BP licenses to initiate extensive drilling activity off its coast several days after the Rosneft announcement.

The share exchange gives Rosneft a 5% interest in British Petroleum's voting shares, making it BP's single largest shareholder. In return, BP receives a 9.5% ownership stake in Rosneft. Each stake is valued at about $7.8 billion. Both firms agreed to hold each other's equity for at least two years before selling any stock. BP's shares currently pay a dividend about twice that of Rosneft's. BP and Rosneft have stated publicly that they believe investors have significantly undervalued their firms. The Russian government has a particularly strong interest in seeing the value of its holdings appreciate, since it announced plans to privatize a number of largely state-owned enterprises, including Rosneft, in 2014 in order to raise funds.

At the time of the announcement, BP's market capitalization was about $154 billion. With almost 90% of its shares owned by the Russian government and Sherbank, Russia's biggest retail savings bank, the firm's stock trading in public markets tends to be limited and not reflective of Rosneft's true value. However, the terms of the share exchange imply a market capitalization for Rosneft of about $81 billion.

The transaction represents the first time there has been a cross-shareholding between major international oil firms and a major government-owned national oil company. Unlike more conventional oil and gas JVs, the Rosneft JV will not own the oil leases but merely the right to develop them. This structure is similar to Russian oil company Gazprom's agreement with France's Total SA and Norway's Statoil for the development of the Shtokman gas field in early 2008.

CASE STUDY 14.3 *(cont'd)*

Rosneft became Russia's leading extraction and refining company after purchasing assets of the former privately owned oil giant Yukos at state-sponsored auctions, in which the global community decried what appeared to be the Russian government expropriation of the privately owned assets. In 2006, Rosneft conducted one of the largest IPOs in history by issuing nearly 15% of its shares on the Russian Trading System and the London Stock Exchange. With the shares priced at $7.55 each, the offering raised about $10.7 billion. Most of the proceeds went to the Russian government. BP began its relationship with Rosneft by buying $1 billion in shares in the firm's initial public offering, equivalent to 1.3%. Thus, the recent agreement brings BP's ownership interest in Rosneft to 10.8%.

Previous attempts to invest in Russia and to create partnerships between Russian state oil companies and Western oil firms have failed due to outright expropriation by the Russian government or heavy-handed tactics employed by certain Russian billionaires (so-called oligarchs) with close ties to the Russian government. For example, Russian officials forced Shell Oil to sell control of its Sakhalin II oil and gas development to state-owned Gazprom. BP and Gazprom signed a global joint venture in 2007 in which each was to contribute assets valued at $1.5 billion, but it was later dissolved due to disagreements between BP and large Russian investors. TNK-BP, BP's 50%-owned JV with a group of Russian billionaire business people, has also had a troubled history. The JV that contributes a quarter of BP's global production and nearly a fifth of its reserves was rocked by a shareholder dispute in 2008 that cost BP some of its control. BP chief executive Bob Dudley had served as chief executive of that JV for five years until he was expelled by BP's Russian partners during the disagreement.

On news of the agreement, BP's partners in the TNK-BP JV stated that BP had not notified them adequately and that the Rosneft deal violated their "right of first refusal" as stated in the JV agreement. The partners were successful in getting a court injunction in the United Kingdom to block the implementation of the JV in February 2011. TNK-BP at the time of this writing is considering a legal claim against BP for damages of up to $10 billion for allegedly reneging on its commitment to use TNK-BP as its main vehicle for investment in Russia. These developments raise serious questions about the longer-term viability of the BP-Rosneft JV.

Discussion Questions

1. Speculate as to the purpose of the share swap between BP and Rosneft.
2. What is the purpose of the two-year lockup period during which neither partner can sell its stock? How might the lockup period impact the value of each firm's holdings?
3. Would you expect the share exchange to be dilutive to BP shareholders in the short run? In the long run? Explain your answer.
4. Why would you expect the publicly traded Rosneft shares not to reflect the true value of the firm?
5. How would you estimate the market capitalization for Rosneft based on the terms of the share exchange? Show your work.
6. How can BP best protect its interests in the JV with Rosneft in the highly uncertain political and economic environment of Russia?

Answers to these case study questions are provided in the Online Instructor's Manual for instructors using this book.

CHAPTER

15 16-

Alternative Exit and Restructuring Strategies
Divestitures, Spin-Offs, Carve-Outs, Split-Ups, Split-Offs, and Tracking Stocks

Experience is the name everyone gives to their mistakes. —*Oscar Wilde*

INSIDE M&A: BRISTOL-MYERS SQUIBB SPLITS OFF THE REST OF MEAD JOHNSON

Facing the loss of patent protection for its blockbuster drug Plavix, a blood thinner, in 2012, Bristol-Myers Squibb Company decided to split off its 83% ownership stake in Mead Johnson Nutrition Company in late 2009 through an offer to its shareholders to exchange their Bristol-Myers shares for Mead Johnson shares. The decision was part of a longer-term restructuring strategy that included the sale of assets to raise money for acquisitions of biotechnology drug companies and the elimination of jobs to reduce annual operating expenses by $2.5 billion by the end of 2012.

Bristol-Myers anticipated a significant decline in operating profit following the loss of patent protection as increased competition from lower-priced generics would force sizeable reductions in the price of Plavix. Furthermore, Bristol-Myers considered Mead Johnson, a baby formula manufacturer, as a noncore business that was pursuing a focus on biotechnology drugs. Bristol-Myers shareholders greeted the announcement positively, with the firm's shares showing the largest one-day increase in eight months.

In the exchange offer, Bristol-Myers shareholders were able to exchange some, none, or all of their shares of Bristol-Myers common stock for shares of Mead Johnson common stock at a discount. The discount was intended to provide an incentive for Bristol-Myers shareholders to tender their shares. Also, the rapid appreciation of the Mead Johnson shares in the months leading up to the announced split-off suggested that these shares could have attractive long-term appreciation potential.

While the transaction did not provide any cash directly to the firm, it did indirectly augment Bristol-Myer's operating cash flow by $214 million annually. This represented the difference between the $350 million that Bristol-Myers paid in dividends to Mead Johnson shareholders and the $136 million it received in dividends from Mead Johnson each year. By reducing the number of Bristol-Myers shares outstanding, the transaction also improved Bristol-Myers' earnings per share by 4% in 2011. Finally, by splitting-off a noncore business, Bristol-Myers was increasing its attractiveness to investors interested in a "pure play" in biotechnology pharmaceuticals.

The exchange was tax free to Bristol-Myers shareholders participating in the exchange offer, who also stood to gain if the now independent Mead Johnson Corporation were acquired at a later date. The newly independent Mead Johnson had a poison pill in place to discourage any takeover within six months to a year following the split-off. The tax-free status of the transaction could have been disallowed by the IRS if the transaction were viewed as a "disguised sale" intended to allow Bristol-Myers to avoid paying taxes on gains incurred if it had chosen to sell Mead Johnson.

CHAPTER OVERVIEW

Many corporations, particularly large, highly diversified organizations, are constantly reviewing ways in which they can enhance shareholder value by changing the composition of their assets, liabilities, equity, and operations. These activities generally are referred to as restructuring strategies. Restructuring may embody both growth and exit strategies. Growth strategies have been discussed elsewhere in this book. The focus in this chapter is on those strategic options allowing the firm to maximize shareholder value by redeploying assets through downsizing or refocusing the parent company.

As such, this chapter discusses the myriad motives for exiting businesses, the various restructuring strategies for doing so, and why firms select one strategy over other options. In this context, equity carve-outs, spin-offs, divestitures, and split-offs are discussed separately rather than as a specialized form of a carve-out.[1] The chapter concludes with a discussion of what empirical studies say are the primary determinants of financial returns to shareholders resulting from undertaking the various restructuring strategies.

Voluntary and involuntary restructuring and reorganization (both inside and outside the protection of bankruptcy court) also represent exit strategies for firms and are discussed in detail in Chapter 16. A review of this chapter (including practice questions with answers) is available in the file folder entitled "Student Study Guide" on the companion site to this book (*www.elsevierdirect.com/companions/9780123854858*). The companion site also contains a Learning Interactions Library, which gives students the opportunity to test their knowledge of this chapter in a "real-time" environment.

---

[1] In some accounting texts, divestitures (referred to as sell-offs), spin-offs, and split-offs are all viewed as different forms of equity carve-outs and discussed in terms of how they affect the parent firm's shareholders' equity for financial reporting purposes.

COMMONLY STATED MOTIVES FOR EXITING BUSINESSES

Theories abound as to why corporations choose to exit certain businesses, including increasing corporate focus, a desire to exit underperforming businesses, a lack of fit, regulatory concerns, and tax considerations. Other motives include a need to raise funds, reduce risk, discard unwanted businesses from prior acquisitions, avoid conflicts with customers, and increase financial transparency (i.e., the ease with which investors can understand a firm's true financial performance).

Increasing Corporate Focus

Managing highly diverse and complex portfolios of businesses is both time consuming and distracting and may result in funding those businesses with relatively unattractive investment opportunities with cash flows generated by units offering more favorable opportunities. This is particularly true when the businesses are in largely unrelated industries and senior managers lack sufficient understanding of such businesses to make appropriate investment decisions. Consequently, firms often choose to simplify their business portfolio by focusing on those units with the highest growth potential and by exiting those businesses that are not germane to the firm's core business strategy.

In 2005, Agilent announced that it had reached an agreement to sell its semiconductor unit and its stake in a lighting technology company for $3.6 billion to emphasize its core measurement products business. Similarly, Sara Lee announced in early 2006 that it would divest or spin off businesses accounting for as much as 40% of its current revenue to concentrate its resources on its food and beverage business (see Case Study 15.6 for more details). In 2010, Fiat announced that it would spin off its trucking operations to focus on its core car operations and to enable investors to more easily value the firm.

Underperforming Businesses

Parent firms often exit businesses that consistently fail to meet or exceed the parent's hurdle rate requirements. In 2004, IBM announced the sale of its ailing PC business to China's Lenovo Group. In May 2007, General Electric announced the sale of its plastics operations for $11.6 billion to Saudi Basic Industries Corporation as part of the firm's strategy to sell lower-return businesses and move into faster-growing and potentially higher-return businesses such as healthcare and water processing. In late 2007, Daimler announced it was divesting its Chrysler operations to private equity investor firm Cerberus in exchange for Cerberus's willingness to pay off $18 billion in future retirement and healthcare liabilities. Daimler had acquired Chrysler in 1998 for $36 billion.

Regulatory Concerns

A firm with substantial market share purchasing a direct competitor may create concerns about violations of antitrust laws. Regulatory agencies still may approve the merger if the acquiring firm is willing to divest certain operations that, in combination with similar units in the acquiring company, are deemed to be anticompetitive. As a result of an antitrust suit filed by the Department of Justice, the government and AT&T reached an agreement effective January 1, 1984, to break up AT&T's 22 operating companies into 7 regional Bell operating companies (RBOCs). The RBOCs became responsible for local telephone service, and AT&T kept responsibility for long-distance service and certain telecommunications equipment manufacturing operations. In another instance, the Justice Department required AlliedSignal and Honeywell to divest overlapping businesses before approving their merger in 1999.

Lack of Fit

Perceived synergies associated with certain businesses may be insufficient to offset the overhead expenses that come with their being part of the parent company. This may have been a factor in AT&T's choice to break up its business in the mid-1990s into three entities, each with its own stock traded on the public exchanges. In late 1999, a failed attempt to redirect the business into more lucrative telecommunications industry segments, such as broadband and wireless, caused AT&T to again undertake a strategy to spin off or divest some portions of the firm.

Companies may divest units after they have had time to learn more about the business. Raytheon sold its D.C. Heath textbook publishing company to Houghton Mifflin Company in 1995. Although largely operated as a stand-alone, D.C. Heath did not fit with the other three larger core Raytheon businesses, which included defense electronics, engineering, and avionics. Similarly, TRW's decision to sell its commercial and consumer information services businesses in 1997 came after years of trying to find a significant fit with its space and defense businesses.

Tax Considerations

Restructuring actions may provide tax benefits that cannot be realized without a restructuring of the business. Marriott Corporation contributed its hotel real estate operations to a Real Estate Investment Trust (REIT) in 1989 through a spin-off. Because REITs do not pay taxes on income that is distributed to shareholders, Marriott was able to enhance shareholder value by eliminating the double taxation of income, once by the parent and again when paid as dividends.

Raising Funds or Worth More to Others

Parent firms may choose to fund new initiatives or reduce leverage through the sale or partial sale of units no longer considered strategic or that underperform corporate expectations. Sales may also result from a financially failing firm's need to raise capital. Examples include Andarko's announcement in late 2006 of the sale of its Canadian gas properties to Canadian Natural Resources for $4.1 billion to help finance its purchase of two smaller competitors earlier in the year and Chrysler's sale of its highly profitable tank division to avoid bankruptcy in the early 1980s. Similarly, Navistar, formerly International Harvester, sold its profitable Solar Turbines operation to Caterpillar Tractor to reduce its indebtedness.

Others may view a firm's operating units as much more valuable than the parent itself and be willing to pay a "premium" price for such businesses. In early 2010, GE completed its sale of its fire alarm and security systems unit at a substantial profit to United Technologies for $1.82 billion to eliminate what it considered a noncore business. In contrast, United Technologies desired to increase its focus in the security business and had acquired a series of home security firms. In late 2010, British Petroleum completed a sale of "mature" oil and gas properties to Apache Corporation for $7 billion in order to finance a portion of the costs associated with the Gulf of Mexico oil well "blowout" (see Case Study 15.1).

CASE STUDY 15.1
British Petroleum Sells Oil and Gas Assets to Apache Corporation

In the months that followed the oil spill in the Gulf of Mexico, British Petroleum agreed to create a $20 billion fund to help cover the damages and cleanup costs associated with the spill. The firm had agreed to contribute $5 billion to the fund before the end of 2010. To help meet this obligation and to help finance the more than $4 billion already spent on the spill, the firm announced on July 20, 2010, that it had reached an agreement to sell Apache Corporation its oil and gas fields in Texas and southeast New Mexico worth $3.1 billion; gas fields in Western Canada for $3.25 billion; and oil and gas properties in Egypt for $650 million. All of these properties had been in production for years, and their output rates were declining.

Apache is a Houston-based independent oil and gas exploration firm with a reputation for being able to extract additional oil and gas from older properties. Also, Apache had operations near each of the BP properties, enabling them to take control of the acquired assets with existing personnel.

In what appears to have been a premature move, Apache agreed to acquire Mariner Energy's and Devon Energy's offshore assets in the Gulf of Mexico for a total of $3.75 billion just days before the BP oil rig explosion in the Gulf. The acquisitions made Apache a major player in the Gulf just weeks before the United States banned temporarily deepwater drilling exploration in federal waters.

The announcement of the sale of these properties came as a surprise because BP had been rumored to be attempting to sell its stake in the oil fields of Prudhoe Bay, Alaska. The sale had been expected to fetch as much as $10 billion. The sale failed to materialize because of lingering concerns that BP might at some point seek bankruptcy protection and because the firm's creditors could seek to reverse an out-of-court asset sale as a fraudulent conveyance of assets. Fraudulent conveyance refers to the illegal transfer of assets to another party in order to defer, hinder, or defraud creditors. Under U.S. bankruptcy laws, courts might order that any asset sold by a company in distress, such as BP, must be encumbered with some of the liabilities of the seller if it can be shown that the distressed firm undertook the sale with the full knowledge that it would be filing for bankruptcy protection at a later date.

Ideally, buyers would like to purchase assets "free and clear" of the environmental liabilities associated with the Gulf oil spill. Consequently, a buyer of BP assets would have to incorporate such risks in determining the purchase price for such assets. In some

CASE STUDY 15.1   (cont'd)

instances, buyers will buy assets only after the seller has gone through the bankruptcy process in order to limit fraudulent conveyance risks.

Discussion Questions

1. In what sense were the BP properties strategically more valuable to Apache than to British Petroleum?

2. How could Apache have protected itself from risks that they might be required at some point in the future to be liable for some portion of the BP Gulf–related liabilities? What are some of the ways Apache could have estimated the potential costs of such liabilities? Be specific.

Risk Reduction

A firm may reduce its perceived risk associated with a particular unit by selling a portion of the business to the public. For example, major tobacco companies have been under pressure for years to divest or spin off their food businesses because of the litigation risk associated with their tobacco subsidiaries. RJR Nabisco bowed to such pressure in 1998 with the spin-off of Nabisco Foods. For similar reasons, Altria spun off its Kraft food operations in 2007. Parent firms may attempt to dump debt or other liabilities by assigning them to a subsidiary and later exiting those businesses. In early 2002, Citigroup sold 21% of its Travelers Property Casualty unit in a $3.9 billion initial public offering (IPO), announcing that the remainder would be sold off later. The parent's motivation for this exit strategy could have been to distance itself from the potential costs of asbestos-related claims by Travelers' policyholders. Similarly, Goodrich passed on its asbestos liabilities to EnPro Industries, its diversified industrial products subsidiary, which it spun off in mid-2002.

Discarding Unwanted Businesses from Prior Acquisitions

Acquirers often find themselves with certain assets and operations of the acquired company that do not fit their primary strategy. These redundant assets may be divested to raise funds to help pay for the acquisition and enable management to focus on integrating the remaining businesses into the parent without the distraction of having to manage nonstrategic assets. In 2002, Northrop Grumman Corporation announced that it would acquire TRW. Northrop stated that it would retain TRW's space and defense businesses and divest its automotive operations, which were not germane to Northrop's core defense business. Nestlé acquired Adams, Pfizer's chewing gum and confectionery business, in early 2003 for $4.6 billion. Pfizer viewed Adams as a noncore business it had acquired as part of its $84 billion acquisition of Warner-Lambert in 2000.

Avoiding Conflicts with Customers

For years, many of the regional Bell operating companies (i.e., RBOCs) that AT&T spun off in 1984 had been interested in competing in the long-distance market, which would put them in direct competition with their former parent. Similarly, AT&T sought to penetrate the regional telephone markets by gaining access to millions of households by acquiring cable TV companies. In preparation for the implementation of these plans, AT&T announced in 1995 that it would divide the company into three publicly traded global companies. The primary reason for the breakup was to avoid conflicts between AT&T's former equipment manufacturer and its main customers, the RBOCs.

Increasing Transparency

Firms may be opaque to investors due to their diverse business and product offerings. General Electric is an example of such a corporation, operating dozens of separate businesses in many countries. Even with access to financial and competitive information on each business, it is challenging for any analyst or investor to value properly such a diversified firm. By reducing the complexity of its operations and making information more readily available, a firm may increase the likelihood that investors will value the corporation accurately.

DIVESTITURES

A *divestiture* is the sale of a portion of a firm's assets to an outside party, generally resulting in a cash infusion to the parent. Such assets may include a product line, subsidiary, or division. Between 1970 and 2009, divestitures averaged about one-third of total M&A transactions.[2] The number of divestitures as a percentage of M&A volume surged in the early to mid-1970s (reaching a peak of 54% in 1975), in the early 1990s (reaching a high of 42% in 1992), in the early 2000s (hitting 40% in 2002), and again between 2008 and 2010 (topping out at 50% in 2010). These peak activity levels followed the merger and acquisition boom periods of the late 1960s, the 1980s, the second half of the 1990s, and from 2003 to 2007.

Motives for Divestitures

Divestitures often represent a way of raising cash. A firm may choose to sell an undervalued or underperforming operation that it determines to be nonstrategic or unrelated to the core business and use the proceeds of the sale to fund investments in potentially higher-return opportunities, including paying off debt. Alternatively, the firm may choose to divest the undervalued business and return the cash to shareholders through either a liquidating dividend[3] or share repurchase. Moreover, an operating unit may simply be worth more if sold

---

[2] *FactSet Mergerstat Review*

[3] A liquidating dividend is a payment made to shareholders exceeding the firm's net income. It is a "liquidating" dividend because the firm must sell assets to make the payment.

than if retained by the parent. Some firms try to identify operating units that are worth more if sold by periodically conducting business portfolio reviews.

Corporate Portfolio Reviews

The parent conducts a financial analysis to determine if the business is worth more to shareholders if it is sold and the proceeds either returned to the shareholders or reinvested in opportunities offering higher returns. Weighing the future of certain current businesses with other perceived opportunities, General Electric announced in late 2006 that it was selling its silicone and quartz business for $3.4 billion to private equity firm Apollo Management. GE's portfolio of companies has been undergoing change since the current CEO, Jeffrey Immelt, took control in September 2001. Since then, GE has completed transactions valued at more than $110 billion in buying and selling various operating units.

To Sell or Not to Sell

An analysis undertaken to determine if a business should be sold involves a multistep process. These steps include determining the after-tax cash flows generated by the unit, an appropriate discount rate reflecting the risk of the business, the after-tax market value of the business, and the after-tax value of the business to the parent. The decision to sell or retain the business depends on a comparison of the after-tax value of the business to the parent with the after-tax proceeds from the sale of the business. These steps are outlined next.

Step 1: Calculating After-Tax Cash Flows

To decide if a business is worth more to the shareholder if sold, the parent must first estimate the after-tax cash flows of the business viewed on a stand-alone basis. This requires adjusting the cash flows for intercompany sales and the cost of services (e.g., legal, treasury, and audit) provided by the parent. *Intercompany sales* refer to operating unit revenue generated by selling products or services to another unit owned by the same parent. Intercompany sales should be restated to ensure they are valued at market prices.[4] Moreover, services provided by the parent to the business may be subsidized (i.e., provided at below actual cost) or at a markup over actual cost. To reflect these factors, operating profits should be reduced by the amount of any subsidies and increased by any markup over what the business would have to pay if it purchased comparable services from sources outside of the parent firm.

---

[4] For example, in a vertically integrated business, such as a steel manufacturer that obtains both iron ore and coal from its operating subsidiaries, the majority of the revenue generated by the iron ore and coal operations often comes from sales to the parent company's steelmaking operations. The parent may value this revenue for financial reporting purposes using product transfer prices, which may reflect current market prices or some formula, such as a predetermined markup over the cost of production. If the transfer prices do not reflect actual market prices, intercompany revenue may be artificially high or low, depending on whether the transfer prices are higher or lower than actual market prices. Intercompany revenues associated with the operating unit should be restated to reflect actual market prices.

Step 2: Estimating the Discount Rate

Once the after-tax stand-alone cash flows have been determined, a discount rate should be estimated that reflects the risk characteristics of the industry in which the business competes. The cost of capital of other firms in the same industry (or firms in other industries exhibiting similar profitability, growth, and risk characteristics) is often a good proxy for the discount rate of the business being analyzed.

Step 3: Estimating the After-Tax Market Value of the Business

The discount rate then is used to estimate the present or market value of the projected after-tax cash flows of the business as if it were a stand-alone business. The valuation is based on the cash flows determined in Step 1.

Step 4: Estimating the Value of the Business to the Parent

The after-tax equity value (EV) of the business as part of the parent is estimated by subtracting the market value of the business's liabilities (L) from its after-tax market value (MV) as a stand-alone operation. This relationship can be expressed as follows:

$$EV = MV - L$$

EV is a measure of the after-tax market value of the shareholder equity of the business, where the shareholder is the parent firm.

Step 5: Deciding to Sell

The decision to sell or retain the business is made by comparing the EV with the after-tax sale value (SV) of the business. Assuming other considerations do not outweigh any after-tax gain on the sale of the business, the decision to sell or retain can be summarized as follows:

$$\text{If } SV > EV, \text{divest.}$$
$$\text{If } SV < EV, \text{retain.}$$

Although the sale value may exceed the equity value of the business, the parent may choose to retain the business for strategic reasons. For example, the parent may believe that the business's products (e.g., ties) may facilitate the sale of other products the firm offers (e.g., custom shirts). The firm may lose money on the sale of ties but make enough money on the sale of custom shirts to earn a profit on the combined sales of the two products. In another instance, one subsidiary of a diversified parent may provide highly complex components critical to the assembly of finished products produced by other subsidiaries of the parent firm. The parent may incur a loss on the components to ensure the continued high quality of its highly profitable finished products.

Timing of the Sale

Obviously, the best time to sell a business is when the owner does not need to sell or the demand for the business to be divested is greatest. The decision to sell also should reflect the broader financial environment. Selling when business confidence is high, stock prices are rising, and interest rates are low is likely to fetch a higher price for the unit. If the business to be sold is highly cyclical, the sale should be timed to coincide with the firm's peak year earnings. Businesses also can be timed to sell when they are considered most popular.[5]

The Selling Process

The selling process may be reactive or proactive (Figure 15.1). *Reactive sales* occur when the parent is unexpectedly approached by a buyer, either for the entire firm or for a portion of the firm, such as a product line or subsidiary. If the bid is sufficiently attractive, the parent firm may choose to reach a negotiated settlement with the bidder without investigating other options. This may occur if the parent is concerned about potential degradation of its business, or that of a subsidiary, if its interest in selling becomes public knowledge.

In contrast, *proactive sales* may be characterized as public or private solicitations. In a *public sale or auction*, a firm announces publicly that it is putting itself, a subsidiary, or a product line up for sale. In this instance, potential buyers contact the seller. This is a way to identify easily interested parties; unfortunately, this approach can also attract unqualified bidders (i.e., those lacking the resources necessary to complete the deal) or those seeking to obtain proprietary information through the due diligence process. In a *private or controlled sale*, the parent firm may hire an investment banker or undertake on its own to identify potential buyers to be contacted. Once a preferred potential buyer has been identified or list of what are believed to be qualified buyers has been compiled, contact is made.[6]

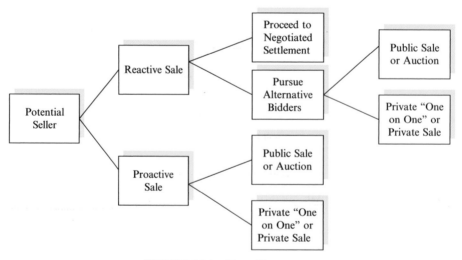

FIGURE 15.1   The selling process.

[5] In 1980, the oil exploration business was booming; by 1983, it was in the doldrums. It recovered by the mid-1990s. What's hot today can fizzle tomorrow. A similar story could be told about many of the high-flying Internet-related companies of the late 1990s.

[6] See the discussion of the screening and contacting process in Chapter 5 for more details.

In either a public or private sale, interested parties are asked to sign confidentiality agreements before they are given access to proprietary information. The challenge for the selling firm is to manage efficiently this information, which can grow into thousands of pages of documents and spreadsheets, and to provide easy and secure access to all interested parties. Increasingly, such information is offered online through so-called *virtual data rooms* (VDR).[7]

In a private sale, bidders may be asked to sign a standstill agreement requiring them not to make an unsolicited bid. Parties willing to sign these agreements are then asked to submit preliminary, nonbinding "indications of interest" (i.e., a single number or a bid within a range). Those parties submitting preliminary bids are then ranked by the selling company in terms of the size of the bid, form of payment, the ability of the bidder to finance the transaction, form of acquisition, and ease of doing the deal. The last factor involves an assessment of the difficulty in obtaining regulatory approval, if required, and the integrity of the bidder. A small number of those submitting preliminary bids are then asked to submit a best and final offer. Such offers must be legally binding on the bidder. At this point, the seller may choose to initiate an auction among the most attractive bids or go directly into negotiating a purchase agreement with a single party.

Choosing the Right Selling Process

Firms may choose to negotiate with a single firm, to control the number of potential bidders, or to engage in a public auction (Table 15.1). Large firms often choose to sell themselves, major product lines, or subsidiaries through "one on one" negotiations with a single bidder

TABLE 15.1   Choosing the Right Selling Process

Selling Process	Advantages/Disadvantages
One on One Negotiations (single bidder)	Enables seller to select buyer with greatest synergy
	Minimizes disruptive due diligence
	Limits potential for loss of proprietary information to competitors
	May exclude potentially attractive bidders
Public Auction (no limit on number of bidders)	Most appropriate for small, private, or hard to value firms
	May discourage bidders concerned about undisciplined bidding by uninformed bidders
	Potentially disruptive due to multiple due diligences
Controlled Auction (limited number of bidders)	Enables seller to select a number of potential buyers with greatest synergy
	Sparks competition without disruptive effects of public auctions
	May exclude potentially attractive bidders

[7] The VDR is intended to replace the traditional paper-based data room and the challenges of keeping such information current and secure. Because the VDR is searchable electronically, potential bidders have easier and more rapid access to the specific information they are seeking. Since multiple parties can access the information simultaneously from anywhere in the world unaware of the presence of others, the VDR provides for more efficient and thorough due diligence. VDRs also allow for online questions and answers. The major limitations of the VDR are the expense and technical expertise required and the inability to meet the management of the unit to be sold in person.

deemed to have the greatest synergy with the selling firm. Such firms' sellers are concerned about the potential deleterious effects of making the sale public and the disruptive effects of allowing many firms to perform due diligence. This approach also may be adopted to limit the potential for losing bidders who may also be competitors from obtaining proprietary information as a result of due diligence. An auction among a number of bidders may be undertaken to elicit the highest offer when selling smaller, more difficult to value firms. The private or controlled sale among a small number of carefully selected bidders may spark competition to boost the selling price while minimizing the deleterious effects of public auctions. Paradoxically, public auctions may actually discourage some firms from bidding due to the potential for overly aggressive bidding by relatively uninformed bidders to boost the bid price to excessive levels.

Approximately one-half of corporate M&A transactions involve "one on one" negotiations. The remaining transactions include deals in which the sellers contacted an average of 10 potential bidders, with some contacting as many as 150. The number of bidders actually signing confidentiality agreements averages 4, with some deals involving as many as 60. About one-third of the time, sellers receive more than one legally binding bid, and about 12% of sellers receive additional bids once a formal merger agreement has been announced. The average length of time from the start of the solicitation process to completion is about a year, with about 90% of deals involving a breakup fee averaging about 3% of the value of the deal.[8]

The mere fact that most transactions involve relatively few bidders does not suggest that the bidding process is not competitive.[9] In most cases, simply the threat of rival bids is sufficient to increase bids even in "one on one" negotiations. Such latent competition tends to influence bid prices the most when market liquidity is greatest such that potential bidders have relatively inexpensive access to funds through borrowing or new equity issues.

Ultimately, the premium a target firm receives over its current share price is influenced by a variety of factors. Table 15.2 provides a summary of those factors that have been found to be significant determinants of the magnitude of purchase price premiums.

Tax and Accounting Considerations for Divestitures

The divesting firm is required to recognize a gain or loss for financial reporting purposes equal to the difference between the fair value of the consideration received for the divested operation and its book value. However, if the transaction is an exchange of similar assets or an equivalent interest in similar productive assets, the company should not recognize a gain or loss other than a loss resulting from the impairment of value.[10] For tax purposes, the gain or loss is the difference between the proceeds and the parent's tax (i.e., cost) basis in the stock or assets. Capital gains are taxed at the same rate as other business income.

[8] Boone and Mulherin, 2009

[9] Aktas et al., 2010

[10] If the divested division or subsidiary is a discontinued segment, the parent firm must estimate the gain or loss from the divestiture on the date that management approves a formal plan to dispose of the division or subsidiary.

TABLE 15.2 Factors Affecting Purchase Price Premiums

Factor	Explanation
Net Synergy Potential	Purchase premiums are likely to increase the greater the magnitude of perceived net synergy (see Chapter 9). Net synergy often is the greatest in highly related firms (Betton et al., 2009). Moreover, premiums are likely to be larger if most of the synergy is provided by the target.
Desire for Control	Buyers may pay more to gain control of firms exhibiting weak financial performance because of potential gains from making better business decisions (see Chapter 10).
Growth Potential	Targets displaying greater growth potential relative to competitors generally command higher premiums (Betton et al., 2008).
Information Asymmetry (i.e., one bidder has more information than other bidders)	Informed bidders are likely to pay lower premiums because less informed bidders fear overpaying and either withdraw from or do not participate in the bidding process (Dionne et al., 2010).
Target Size	Buyers pay more for smaller targets due to the anticipated ease of integration (Moeller, 2005).
Target's Eagerness to Sell	Targets with a strong desire to sell typically receive lower premiums due to their relatively weak negotiating positions (Aktas et al., 2010).
Run-up in Preannouncement Target Share Price	Share price run-up causes bidders unsure of having adequate information to revalue their bids upward (Betton et al., 2009).
Type of Purchase	Hostile transactions tend to command higher premiums than friendly transactions (Moeller, 2005).
Hubris	Excessive confidence may lead bidders to overpay (Hayward et al., 1997).
Type of Payment	Cash purchases usually require an increased premium to compensate target shareholders for the immediate tax liability they incur (Hayward et al., 1997). Conversely, target shareholders receiving acquirer stock often receive lower premiums because of the deferred tax liability in such situations.
Leverage	Highly leveraged buyers are disciplined by their lenders not to overpay; relatively unleveraged buyers often are prone to pay excessive premiums.[a]

[a] Gondhaleker et al. (2004) argue that highly leveraged buyers are monitored closely by their lenders and are less likely to overpay. Morellec and Zhdanov (2008) find that relatively unleveraged buyers often pay more for target firms.

SPIN-OFFS

A *spin-off* is a transaction in which a parent creates a new legal subsidiary and distributes shares it owns in the subsidiary to its current shareholders as a stock dividend. Such distributions are made in direct proportion to the shareholders' current holdings of the parent's stock. Consequently, the proportional ownership of shares in the new legal subsidiary is the same as the stockholders' proportional ownership of shares in the parent firm. The new entity has its own management and operates independently from the parent company.

Unlike the divestiture or equity carve-out (explained later in this chapter), the spin-off does not result in an infusion of cash to the parent company. Some of the more notable spin-offs include the spin-off of Medco by Merck, Allstate by Sears, Payless by May Department Stores, Dean Witter/Discover by Sears, CBS by Westinghouse, and Pizza Hut, KFC, and Taco Bell by PepsiCo. In early 2011, Motorola Inc. completed its ongoing restructuring effort by spinning off Motorola Mobility to its shareholders and renaming the remaining business Motorola Solutions (see Case Study 15.2).

CASE STUDY 15.2
Motorola Bows to Activist Pressure

Under pressure from a proxy battle with activist investor Carl Icahn (who owned a 6.4% stake in the firm), Motorola felt compelled to make a dramatic move before its May 2008 shareholders' meeting. Icahn had submitted a slate of four directors to replace those that were up for reelection and demanded that the wireless handset and network manufacturer take actions to improve profitability. Shares of Motorola, which had a market value of $22 billion, had fallen more than 60% since October 2006, making the firm's board vulnerable in the proxy contest.

Signaling its willingness to take dramatic action, Motorola announced on March 26, 2008, its intention to create two independent, publicly traded companies. The two new companies would consist of the firm's former Mobile Devices operation (including its Home Devices businesses consisting of modems and set-top boxes) and its Enterprise Mobility Solutions & Wireless Networks business. In addition to the planned spin-off, Motorola agreed to nominate two people supported by Carl Icahn to the firm's board.

Originally scheduled for 2009, the breakup was postponed due to the upheaval in the financial markets that year. The breakup would result in a tax-free distribution to Motorola's shareholders, with shareholders receiving shares of the two independent and publicly traded firms.

Mobile Devices designs, manufactures, and sells mobile handsets globally, and it has lost more than $5 billion during the last three years. The Enterprise Mobility Solutions & Wireless Networks business manufactures, designs, and services public safety radios, handheld scanners and telecommunications network gear for businesses and government agencies, and generates nearly all of Motorola's current cash flow. This business also makes network equipment for wireless carriers such as Spring Nextel and Verizon Wireless.

By dividing the company in this manner, Motorola would separate its loss-generating Mobility Devices division from its other businesses. Although it is the third largest handset manufacturer globally, its handset business had been losing market share to Nokia and Samsung Electronics for years. Following the breakup, the Mobility Devices unit will be renamed Motorola Mobility, and the Enterprise Mobility Solutions & Networks operation will be called Motorola Solutions.

Motorola's board is seeking to ensure the financial viability of Motorola Mobility by eliminating its outstanding debt and through a cash infusion. To do so, Motorola intends to buy back nearly all of its outstanding $3.9

CASE STUDY 15.2 *(cont'd)*

billion debt and to transfer as much as its $4 billion in cash to Motorola Mobility.

Furthermore, Motorola Solutions would assume responsibility for the pension obligations of Motorola Mobility. If Motorola Mobility were to be forced into bankruptcy shortly after the breakup, Motorola Solutions may be held legally responsible for some of the business's liabilities. The court would have to prove that Motorola had conveyed the Mobility Devices unit (renamed Motorola Mobility following the breakup) to its shareholders, fraudulently knowing that the unit's financial viability was problematic.

Once free of debt and other obligations and when it is flush with cash, Motorola Mobility would be in a better position to make acquisitions and to develop new phones. It would also be more attractive as a takeover target. A stand-alone firm is unencumbered by intercompany relationships, including such things as administrative support or parts and services supplied by other areas of Motorola. Moreover, all of the liabilities and assets associated with the handset business already would have been identified, making it easier for a potential partner to value the business.

In mid-2010, Motorola Inc. announced that it had reached an agreement with Nokia Siemens Networks, a Finnish–German joint venture, had reached an agreement with Motorola Inc. to buy its wireless networks operations, formerly part of Motorola's Enterprise Mobility Solutions and Wireless Network Devices business. On January 4, 2011, Motorola Inc. spun off the common shares of Motorola Mobility it held as a tax-free dividend to its shareholders and renamed the firm Motorola Solutions. Each shareholder of record as of December 21, 2010, would receive one share of Motorola Mobility common for every eight shares of Motorola Inc. common stock they held. Table 15.3 shows the timeline of Motorola's restructuring effort.

Discussion Questions

1. In your judgment, did Motorola's breakup make sense? Explain your answer.
2. What other restructuring alternatives could Motorola have pursued to increase shareholder value? Why do you believe it pursued this breakup strategy rather than some other option?

TABLE 15.3 Motorola Restructuring Timeline

Motorola (Beginning 2010)	Motorola (Mid-2010)	Motorola (Beginning 2011)
Mobility Devices	Mobility Devices	Motorola Mobility spin-off
Enterprise Mobility Solutions & Wireless Networks	Enterprise Mobility Solutions*	Motorola Inc. renamed Motorola Solutions

Wireless Networks sold to Nokia-Siemens.

Motives for Spin-Offs

In addition to the motives for exiting businesses discussed earlier, spin-offs provide a means of rewarding shareholders with a nontaxable dividend (if properly structured). Parent firms with a low tax basis in a business may choose to spin off the unit as a tax-free distribution to shareholders rather than sell the business and incur a substantial tax liability. In addition, the unit, now independent of the parent, has its own stock to use for possible acquisitions. Finally, the managers of the business that is to be spun off have a greater incentive to improve the unit's performance if they own stock in the unit.

Tax and Accounting Considerations for Spin-Offs

If properly structured, spin-offs are generally not taxable to shareholders. According to the Internal Revenue Service Code Section 355, a spin-off must be undertaken for reasons other than tax avoidance such as to increase management focus or improve profitability. The parent must control the subsidiary to be spun off by owning at least 80% of each class of the unit's voting and nonvoting stock, and parent firm shareholders must maintain a continuity of interest in both the parent firm and the subsidiary. Finally, both the parent and the spun-off subsidiary must remain in operation during the five years following the spin-off.[11]

For financial reporting purposes, the parent firm should account for the spin-off of a subsidiary's stock to its shareholders at book value with no gain or loss recognized, other than any reduction in value due to impairment. The reason for this treatment is that the ownership interests are essentially the same before and after the spin-off. See Case Study 15.3 for a description of how a spin-off may be structured.

CASE STUDY 15.3
Anatomy of a Spin-Off

On October 18, 2006, Verizon Communications' board of directors declared a dividend to the firm's shareholders consisting of shares in a company comprising the firm's domestic print and Internet yellow pages directories publishing operations (Idearc Inc.). The dividend consisted of 1 share of Idearc stock for every 20 shares of Verizon common stock. Idearc shares were valued at $34.47 per share. On the dividend payment date, Verizon shares were valued at $36.42 per share. The 1-to-20 ratio constituted a 4.73% yield— that is, $34.47/($36.42 \times 20)$—approximately

equal to Verizon's then current cash dividend yield.

Because of the spin-off, Verizon would contribute to Idearc all its ownership interest in Idearc Information Services and other assets, liabilities, businesses, and employees currently employed in these operations. In exchange for the contribution, Idearc would issue to Verizon shares of Idearc common stock to be distributed to the Verizon shareholders. In addition, Idearc would issue senior unsecured notes to Verizon in an amount approximately equal to the $9 billion

[11] A spin-off cannot be used to avoid the payment of taxes on capital gains that might have been incurred if the parent had chosen to sell a subsidiary in which it had a low tax basis.

CASE STUDY 15.3 *(cont'd)*

in debt that Verizon incurred in financing Idearc's operations historically. Idearc would also transfer $2.5 billion in excess cash to Verizon. Verizon believed it owned such cash balances, since they were generated while Idearc was part of the parent.

Verizon announced that the spin-off company would enable the parent and Idearc to focus on their core businesses, which might facilitate expansion and growth of each firm. The spin-off would also allow each company to determine its own capital structure, enable Idearc to pursue an acquisition strategy using its own stock, and permit Idearc to enhance its equity-based compensation programs offered to its employees. Because of the spin-off, Idearc would become an independent public company. Moreover, no vote of Verizon shareholders was required to approve the spin-off, since it constituted the payment of a dividend permissible by the board of directors according to the bylaws of the firm. Finally, Verizon shareholders had no appraisal rights in connection with the spin-off.

In late 2009, Idearc entered Chapter 11 bankruptcy because it was unable to meet its outstanding debt obligations. In September 2010, a trustee for Idearc's creditors filed a lawsuit against Verizon, alleging that the firm breached its fiduciary responsibility by knowingly spinning off a business that was not financially viable. The lawsuit further contends that Verizon benefited from the spin-off at the expense of the creditors by transferring $9 billion in debt from its books to Idearc and receiving $2.5 billion in cash from Idearc.

Discussion Questions

1. How do you believe the Idearc shares were valued for purposes of the spin-off? Be specific.
2. Do you believe that it is fair for Idearc to repay a portion of the debt incurred by Verizon relating to Idearc's operations even though Verizon included Idearc's earnings in its consolidated income statement? Is the transfer of excess cash to the parent fair? Explain your answer.
3. Do you believe shareholders should have the right to approve a spin-off? Explain your answer?
4. To what extent do you believe that Verizon's activities could be viewed as fraudulent? Explain your answer.

EQUITY CARVE-OUTS

Equity carve-outs exhibit characteristics similar to spin-offs. Both result in the subsidiary's stock being traded separately from the parent's stock. They also are similar to divestitures and IPOs in that they provide cash to the parent. However, unlike the spin-off or divestiture, the parent generally retains control of the subsidiary in a carve-out transaction. Retention of at least 80% of the unit enables consolidation for tax purposes, and retention of more than 50% enables consolidation for financial reporting purposes.[12] A potentially significant

[12] Allen and McConnell (1998) found a median retention of subsidiary shares of 69 percent, while Vijh (2002) found a median ownership stake of 72 percent.

drawback to the carve-out is the creation of minority shareholders. General Motors 2006's sale of a 51% stake in its then profitable GMAC finance unit to private investor group Cerberus for $14 billion is a recent example of an equity carve-out. In this transaction, GM retained the right (i.e., a call option) to buy back GMAC during the ten-year period following the close of the transaction.

Motives for Equity Carve-Outs

As is true of a divestiture, equity carve-outs provide an opportunity to raise funds for reinvestment in the subsidiary, to pay off debt, or to pay a dividend to the parent firm. Moreover, a carve-out frequently is a prelude to a divestiture, since it provides an opportunity to value the business by selling stock in a public stock exchange. The stock created for purposes of the carve-out often is used in incentive programs for the unit's management and as an *acquisition currency* (i.e., form of payment) if the parent later decides to grow the subsidiary. The two basic forms of an equity carve-out are the initial public offering and the subsidiary equity carve-out. These are discussed in the following sections.

Initial Public Offerings

An *initial public offering* is the first offering to the public of the common stock of a formerly privately held firm. The sale of the stock provides an infusion of cash to the parent. The cash may be retained by the parent or returned to shareholders. United Parcel Service's IPO of 5 percent of its stock in 1999 is an example of an IPO.

Subsidiary Equity Carve-Outs

The *subsidiary carve-out* is a transaction in which the parent creates a wholly-owned independent legal subsidiary, with stock and a management team that are different from the parent's, and issues a portion of the subsidiary's stock to the public. Usually, only a minority share of the parent's ownership in the subsidiary is issued to the public. Although the parent retains control, the subsidiary's shareholder base may be different from that of the parent due to the public sale of equity. The cash raised may be retained in the subsidiary or transferred to the parent as a dividend, a stock repurchase, or an intercompany loan. An example of a subsidiary carve-out is the sale to the public by Phillip Morris in 2001 of 15% of its wholly-owned Kraft subsidiary. Phillip Morris' voting power over Kraft was reduced only to 97.7% because Kraft had a dual-class share structure in which only low-voting shares were issued in the public stock offering.

Equity Carve-Outs as Staged Transactions

Equity may be sold to the public in several stages. A partial sale of equity either in a wholly-owned subsidiary (a subsidiary equity carve-out) or in the consolidated business (an IPO) may be designed to raise capital and establish a market price for the stock. Later, once a market has been established for the stock, the remainder of the subsidiary's stock may be issued to the public. Alternatively, the parent may choose to spin off its remaining shares in the subsidiary to the parent's shareholders as a dividend. Few carve-outs remain under the parent's control in the long term. In a study of more than 200 carve-outs, only 8% of the firms held more than 50% of the equity of their carve-outs after five years, 31% of the parents held less than 25% of the equity, and 39% of the carve-outs had been acquired or merged with third parties.[13] Hewlett-Packard's staged spin-off of its Agilent Technologies subsidiary is an example of a staged transaction. It began with an equity carve-out of a minority position in its wholly-owned Agilent subsidiary in late 1999. The remainder of the unit's stock was sold in 2000.

SPLIT-OFFS AND SPLIT-UPS

A *split-off* is similar to a spin-off in that a firm's subsidiary becomes an independent firm and the parent firm does not generate any new cash. However, unlike a spin-off, the split-off involves an offer to exchange parent stock for stock in the parent firm's subsidiary. For example, in 2004, Viacom spun off its movie rental chain by exchanging shares in its 81%–owned Blockbuster Inc. subsidiary for Viacom common shares. Split-offs tend to be less common than spin-offs because they most often arise when a portion of the parent firm's shareholders prefer to own the shares of a subsidiary of the parent rather than the parent's shares.

A *split-up* refers to a restructuring strategy in which a single company splits into two or more separately managed firms. Through a series of split-offs, shareholders of the original or parent firm may choose to exchange their shares in the parent firm for shares in the new companies. Following the split, the original firm's shares are canceled, and it ceases to exist.

Split-offs normally are non–pro rata stock distributions, in contrast to spin-offs, which generally are pro rata or proportional distributions of shares. In a pro rata distribution, a shareholder owning 10% of the outstanding parent company stock would receive 10% of the subsidiary whose shares were distributed. A non–pro rata distribution takes the form of a tender or exchange offer in which shareholders can accept or reject the distribution. Case Study 15.4 describes how such a non–pro rata distribution took place for the Bristol-Myers Squibb split-off discussed in the Inside M&A case study at the beginning of this chapter.

CASE STUDY 15.4
Anatomy of a Split-Off

Under the Bristol-Myers Squibb exchange offer of Mead Johnson shares for shares of its common stock, announced on November 16, 2009, each BMS shareholder would receive $1.11 for each $1 of BMS stock tendered and accepted in the exchange offer. The exchange was subject to an upper limit of 0.6027 shares of MJ common stock per share of BMS common.

On December 4, 2009, BMS amended the offer by increasing the maximum share exchange ratio to 0.6313, indicating it would accept for exchange a maximum of 269,281,601 shares of its stock and that if the exchange offer were

[13] Annema, Fallon, and Goedhart, 2002

CASE STUDY 15.4 *(cont'd)*

oversubscribed, all shares tendered would be subject to proration. The proration formula was determined by dividing the maximum number of MJ shares BMS was willing to exchange by the number of BMS shares actually tendered.

The actual ratio at which shares of Bristol-Myers' common stock and shares of Mead Johnson's common stock were exchanged was determined by computing a simple three-day average of the shares of the two firms during December 8–10, 2009, subject to the 0.6313 upper limit. On December 16, 2009, Bristol-Myers announced it would exchange up to 170 million shares of Mead Johnson common stock (i.e., all that it owned) for outstanding shares of its stock at an exchange ratio of 0.6313 shares of Mead Johnson common stock for each share of Bristol-Myers common stock tendered and accepted in the exchange offer.

Assuming that the three-day average of the BMS and MJ share prices was $24.30 and $43.75, respectively. BMS shareholders whose tendered shares were accepted in the exchange offer received the higher of $26.97 (i.e., $24.30 × 1.11) or $27.62 (i.e., 0.6313 ×

$43.75). Therefore, a BMS shareholder tendering 100 shares of BMS stock would have received the share equivalent of $2,762 ($27.62 × 100) or 63.13 MJ shares at $43.75 per share (i.e., $2,762 ÷ $43.75). Fractional shares were paid in cash.

The actual number of BMS shares tendered totaled 500,547,697, resulting in a proration ratio of 53.80% (i.e., 269,281,601 ÷ 500,547,697). Each shareholder tendering BMS shares would only have 53.80% of their tendered shares accepted for the exchange.

Discussion Questions

1. Why did Bristol-Myers Squibb offer its shareholders $1.11 worth of Mead Johnson stock for each $1 of Bristol-Myers Squibb stock tendered and accepted in the exchange offer?

2. Why did Bristol-Myers Squibb prorate the number of shares tendered in the exchange offer?

Answers to these questions are provided in the Online Instructors Manual for instructors using this textbook.

Motives for Split-Offs

Divestiture may not be an option for disposing of a business in which the parent owns less than 100% of the stock because potential buyers often want to acquire all of a firm's outstanding stock. By acquiring less than 100%, a buyer inherits minority shareholders who may disagree with the new owner's future business decisions. Consequently, split-offs are best suited for disposing of a less than a 100% investment stake in a subsidiary. Moreover, the split-off reduces the pressure on the spun-off firm's share price because shareholders who exchange their stock are less likely to sell the new stock. Presumably, those shareholders willing to make the exchange believe the stock in the subsidiary has greater appreciation potential than the parent's stock. The exchange also increases the earnings per share of the parent firm by reducing the number of its shares outstanding as long as the impact of the reduction in the number of shares outstanding exceeds the loss of the subsidiary's earnings. Finally, split-offs are generally tax free to shareholders as long as they conform to the IRS requirements previously described for spin-offs.

TRACKING, TARGETED, AND LETTER STOCKS

Such stocks are separate classes of common stock of the parent corporation. The parent firm divides its operations into two or more operating units and assigns a common stock to each operation. Tracking stock is a class of common stock that links the shareholders' return to the operating performance of a particular business segment or unit. Dividends paid on the tracking stock rise or fall with the performance of the business segment. Tracking stock represents an ownership interest in the company as a whole, rather than a direct ownership interest in the targeted business segment. For voting purposes, holders of tracking stock with voting rights may vote their shares on issues related to the parent and not the subsidiary. The parent's board of directors and top management retain control of the subsidiary for which a tracking stock has been issued, since the subsidiary is still legally a part of the parent. Tracking stocks may be issued to current parent company shareholders as a dividend, used as payment for an acquisition, or, more commonly, issued in a public offering. Once the tracking stock is listed on a public exchange, the subsidiary must file separate financial statements with the Securities and Exchange Commission.

Thirty-two U.S. firms had issued 50 tracking stocks as of the end of 2009. The concept was introduced in 1984 when General Motors issued a class of stock identified as E stock, often referred to as *letter stock* at that time, to buy Electronic Data Systems (EDS). In 1985, GM issued another class of stock called H stock when it acquired Hughes Corporation. In 1991, U.S. Steel Company created a USX-Marathon stock for its oil business and a USX stock for its steel operations. The next year, USX created a third tracking stock when it sold shares of the USX-Delhi group in an IPO. Few tracking stocks have been issued in recent years, perhaps due to inherent governance issues and their poor long-term performance. Relatively recent issues include AT&T Wireless, Alcatel, and Disney in 2000, as well as Sony, Sprint PCS, and CarMax in 2001.

Motives for Tracking Stocks

The purpose in creating tracking stock is to enable the financial markets to value the different operations within a corporation based on their own performance. Such stocks represent *pure plays* to the extent that they give investors an opportunity to invest in a single operating unit of a diversified parent firm. Moreover, the operating unit files financial statements with the SEC separate from those of the parent's, even though its financial performance is included in the parent's consolidated financial statements. However, there is little empirical evidence that issuing a tracking stock for a subsidiary creates pure-play investment opportunities, since the tracking stock tends to be correlated more with the parent's other outstanding stocks than with the stocks in the industry in which the subsidiary competes.[14] Tracking or targeted stocks provide the parent company with an alternative means of raising capital for a specific operation by selling a portion of the stock to the public and an alternative "currency" for making acquisitions. In addition, stock-based incentive programs to attract and retain key managers can be implemented for each operation with its own tracking stock.

---

[14] D'Souza and Jacob, 2000

Tax and Accounting Considerations for Tracking Stocks

For financial reporting purposes, a distribution of tracking stock divides the parent firm's equity structure into separate classes of stock without a legal split-up of the firm. Tracking stocks may be issued as dividends to the parent's current shareholders. Unlike the case with spin-offs, the IRS currently does not require that the business for which the tracking stock is created be at least five years old and that the parent retain a controlling interest in the business for the stock to be exempt from capital gains taxes. Unlike a spin-off or carve-out, the parent retains complete ownership of the business. In general, a proportionate distribution by a company to its shareholders in the company's stock is tax free to shareholders.

Problems with Tracking Stocks

Conflicts among the parent's operating units often arise in determining how the parent's overhead expenses are allocated to the business units and what price one business unit is paid for selling products to other business units. Tracking stocks also can stimulate shareholder lawsuits. Although the unit for which a tracking stock has been created may be largely autonomous, the potential for conflict of interest is substantial because the parent's board and the target stock's board are the same. The parent's board approves overall operating unit and capital budgets. Decisions made in support of one operating unit may appear to be unfair to those holding a tracking stock in another unit. Thus, tracking stocks can pit classes of shareholders against one another and lead to lawsuits.[15] Tracking stocks also may not have voting rights. Further, the chances of a hostile takeover of a firm with a tracking stock are virtually zero because the firm is controlled by the parent. Hence, there is no takeover premium built into the stock price.

VOLUNTARY LIQUIDATIONS (BUST-UPS)

Chapter 16 includes a detailed discussion of involuntary bankruptcy-related liquidations. Such transactions occur when creditors and the bankruptcy court concur that they will realize more value through liquidation than by reorganizing the firm. *Voluntary liquidations* or *bust-ups* reflect the judgment that the sale of individual parts of the firm could realize greater value than the value created by a continuation of the combined corporation. This may occur when management views the firm's growth prospects as limited.[16] This option generally is pursued only after other restructuring strategies have failed to improve the firm's overall market value. Unlike spin-offs and divestitures, which may be viewed as discrete events, the liquidation process generally represents a series of individual transactions during which the firm's assets are sold.

---

[15] When GM sold part of its Hughes unit and all of EDS, holders of H shares sued the GM board of directors, complaining that they were underpaid.

[16] Erwin and McConnell, 1997

COMPARING ALTERNATIVE EXIT AND RESTRUCTURING STRATEGIES

Table 15.4 summarizes the primary characteristics of each of the restructuring strategies discussed in this chapter. Note that divestitures and carve-outs provide cash to the parent, whereas spin-offs, split-ups, and bust-ups do not. The parent remains in existence in all restructuring strategies except split-ups and voluntary liquidations. A new legal entity generally is created with each restructuring strategy, except for voluntary liquidations. With the exception of the carve-out, the parent generally loses control of the division involved in the restructuring strategy. Only spin-offs, split-ups, and split-offs are generally not taxable to shareholders, if properly structured.

CHOOSING AMONG DIVESTITURE, CARVE-OUT, AND SPIN-OFF RESTRUCTURING STRATEGIES

Parent firms that engage in divestitures often are highly diversified in largely unrelated businesses and have a desire to achieve greater focus or raise cash.[17] Parent firms that use carve-out strategies usually operate businesses in somewhat related industries exhibiting some degree of synergy and a desire to raise cash. Consequently, the parent firm may pursue a carve-out rather than a divestiture or spin-off strategy to retain perceived synergy.[18] Evidence shows that the timing of the carve-out is influenced by when management sees its subsidiary's assets as overvalued.[19] Firms engaging in spin-offs often are highly diversified but less so than those that are prone to pursue divestiture strategies and have little need to raise cash.[20] Table 15.5 identifies characteristics of parent firm operating units that are subject to certain types of restructuring activities.

The decision to exit a business is essentially a two-stage process. The first stage involves the firm deciding to exit a line of business or product line for one or more of the reasons described earlier in this chapter. The second stage entails selecting the appropriate exit strategy. Divestitures, carve-outs, and spin-offs are the most commonly used restructuring strategy when a parent corporation is considering partially or entirely exiting a business. The decision as to which of these three strategies to use is often heavily influenced by the parent firm's need for cash, the degree of synergy between the business to be divested or spun off and the parent's other operating units, and the potential selling price of the division.[21] However, these factors are not independent. Parent firms needing cash are more likely to divest or engage in an equity carve-out for operations exhibiting high selling prices relative to their synergy value. Parent firms not needing cash are more likely to spin off units exhibiting low selling prices and synergy with the parent. Parent firms with moderate cash needs are likely to

[17] Bergh, Johnson, and Dewitt, 2007

[18] Powers, 2001

[19] Powers, 2003; Chen and Guo, 2005

[20] John and Ofek, 1995; Kaplan and Weisbach, 1992

[21] Powers, 2001

TABLE 15.4   Key Characteristics of Alternative Exit/Restructuring Strategies

	Alternative Strategies						
Characteristics	Divestitures	Equity Carve-Outs/ IPOs	Spin-Offs	Split-Ups	Split-Offs	Voluntary Liquidation (Bust-Ups)	Tracking Stocks
Cash Infusion to Parent	Yes	Yes	No	No	No	No	Yes
Parent Ceases to Exist	No	No	No	Yes	No	Yes	No
New Legal Entity Created	Sometimes	Yes[a]	Yes	Yes	No	No	No
New Shares Issued	Sometimes	Yes	Yes	Yes	Yes	No	Yes
Parent Remains in Control	No	Generally	No	No	No	No	Yes
Taxable to Shareholders	Yes[c]	Yes[b]	No[c]	No[c]	No[c]	Yes	No[d]

[a] Applies to subsidiary carve-outs only.
[b] The proceeds are taxable if returned to shareholders as a dividend or tax deferred if used to repurchase the parent's stock.
[c] The transaction is generally not taxable if properly structured.
[d] Only dividend payments and shareholder gains on the sale of stock are taxable.

TABLE 15.5   Characteristics of Parent Company Operating Units That Undergo Divestiture, Carve-Out, or Spin-Off

Exit/Restructuring Strategy	Characteristics of Operating Unit Subject to Exit/Restructuring Strategy
Divestitures	• Usually unrelated to other businesses owned by parent • Operating performance generally worse than the parent's consolidated performance • Slightly underperform their peers in year before announcement date • Generally sell at a lower price than carve-outs, which is measured by market value to book assets
Carve-Outs	• Generally more profitable and faster growing than spun-off or divested businesses • Operating performance often exceeds parent's • Usually operate in industries characterized by high market to book values • Generally outperform peers in year before announcement date
Spin-Offs	• Generally faster growing and more profitable than divested businesses • Most often operate in industries related to other industries in which the parent operates • Operating performance worse than parent's • Slightly underperform peers in year before announcement date

Sources: *Ravenscroft and Scherer (1991), Cho and Cohen (1997), Hand and Skantz (1997), Kang and Shivdasani (1997), Powers (2001, 2003), Chen and Guo (2005), and Bergh (2007).*

engage in equity carve-outs when the unit's selling price is low relative to perceived synergy. Table 15.6 illustrates this two-stage procedure.

It may seem that a divestiture or carve-out generally would be preferable to a spin-off if the after-tax proceeds from the sale of all or a portion of the operating unit exceed its after-tax equity value to the firm. Unlike a spin-off, a divestiture or carve-out generates a cash infusion to the firm. However, a spin-off may create greater shareholder wealth for several reasons. First, a spin-off is tax free to the shareholders if it is properly structured. In contrast, the cash proceeds from an outright sale may be taxable to the parent to the extent a gain is realized.

Moreover, management must be able to reinvest the after-tax proceeds in a project that has a reasonable likelihood of returning the firm's cost of capital. If management chooses to return the cash proceeds to shareholders as a dividend or through a stock repurchase, the shareholders also must pay taxes on the dividend at their ordinary tax rate or on any gain realized through the share repurchase at the generally lower capital gains tax rate. Second, a spin-off enables the shareholders to decide when to sell their shares. Third, a spin-off may be less traumatic than a divestiture for an operating unit. The divestiture process can degrade value if it is lengthy. Employees leave, worker productivity generally suffers, and customers may not renew contracts until the new owner is known.

DETERMINANTS OF RETURNS TO SHAREHOLDERS RESULTING FROM RESTRUCTURING STRATEGIES

In general, restructuring strategies create shareholder value by increasing parent firm focus and by transferring businesses to those who can operate them more efficiently. These factors are reflected in the abnormal financial returns frequently associated with the announcement of corporate restructurings.

Preannouncement Abnormal Returns

Empirical studies indicate that the alternative restructuring and exit strategies discussed in this chapter generally provide positive abnormal returns to the shareholders of the company implementing the strategy. This should not be surprising, since such actions often are undertaken to correct many of the problems associated with highly diversified firms, such as having invested in underperforming businesses, having failed to link executive compensation to the performance of the operations directly under their control, and being too difficult for investors and analysts to evaluate. Alternatively, restructuring strategies involving a divisional or asset sale may create value simply because the asset is worth more to another investor. Table 15.7 provides a summary of the results of selected empirical studies of restructuring activities.

Divestitures

The empirical evidence suggests that divestitures generally create value by increasing the diversified firm's focus and reducing the conglomerate discount (see Chapter 1), transferring assets to those that can use them more effectively, resolving agency conflicts, and mitigating

TABLE 15.6 Divestitures, Carve-Outs, and Spin-Offs: Selecting the Appropriate Restructuring Strategy

Stage One Considerations (Primary Motive for Restructuring)	Stage Two Considerations Need for Cash Value of Business/Degree of Business Strategy	Appropriate Restructuring Strategy	Restructuring Strategy More Likely If Parent
	Needs Cash →		
	High Price/High Synergy	Carve-Out	Can retain synergy
	Low Price/High Synergy	Carve-Out	Can retain synergy
	High Price/Low Synergy	Divestiture	Can shield taxable gains[a]
	Low Price/Low Synergy	Divestiture	
Change Strategy/Increase Focus	Little Need for Cash →		
	HighPrice/High Synergy	Carve-Out	Can retain synergy
	Low Price/High Synergy	Carve-Out	Can retain synergy
	High Price/Low Synergy	Spin-Off	Cannot shield potential gains
	Low Price/Low Synergy	Spin-Off	Cannot shield potential gains
Underperforming Businesses →	Needs Cash →	Divestiture	Can shield taxable gains
	Little Need for Cash →	Spin-Off	Cannot shield potential gains
Regulatory Concerns →		Divestiture/Spin-Off	Carve-out not an option
Lack of Fit →	Needs Cash →	Divestiture	Can shield taxable gains
	Little Need for Cash →	Spin-Off	Cannot shield potential gains
Tax Considerations →		Spin-Off	Cannot shield potential gains
Raising Funds/Worth More to Others →		Divestiture	Can shield taxable gains
Risk Reduction →		Carve-Out	Can shield taxable gains
Moving Away from Core Business →		Divestiture/Carve-Out	Can shield taxable gains
Discarding Unwanted Businesses from Prior Acquisitions →		Divestiture	Can shield taxable gains
Avoiding Customer Conflicts →	Needs Cash →	Divestiture	Can shield taxable gains
	Little Need for Cash →	Spin-Off	Cannot shield taxable gains

[a]Parent can shield any taxable gains on the sale by offsetting such gains with losses incurred elsewhere in the consolidated firm.

TABLE 15.7   Returns to Shareholders of Firms Undertaking Restructuring Actions

Restructuring Action	Average Preannouncement Abnormal Returns
Divestitures	1.6%
Spin-Offs	3.7%
Tracking Stocks	3.0%
Equity Carve-Outs	4.5%
Voluntary Liquidations (bust-ups)	17.3%

Study	Preannouncement Abnormal Returns by Study[a]
Divestitures	
Alexander, Benson, and Kampmeyer (1984): 53, 1964–1973	0.17%
Linn and Rozeff (1984): 77, 1977–1982	1.45%
Jain (1985): 1,107, 1976–1978	0.70%
Klein (1986): 202, 1970–1979	1.12%
	When percentage of equity sold <10%: none
	>10 and <50%: 2.53%
	>50%: 8.09%
Lang, Poulsen, and Stulz (1995): 93, 1984–1989	2.0% for firms distributing proceeds to shareholders; (0.5)% for those reinvesting proceeds
Allen (2000): 48, 1982–1991	0.8%
Mulherin and Boone (2000): 139, 1990–1998	2.6%
Clubb and Stouraitis (2002): 187, 1984–1994	1.1%
Dittmar and Shivdasani (2002): 188, 1983–1994	2.6%
Bates (2005): 372, 1990–1998	1.2% for firms using proceeds to reduce debt; 0.7% for firms using proceeds to repurchase stock or pay dividends
Slovin, Sushka, and Polonchek (2005): 327, 1983–2000	1.9% for seller receiving cash
	3.2% for seller receiving equity
Spin-Offs	
Hite and Owers (1983): 56, 1963–1979	3.8%
Miles and Rosenfeld (1983): 62, 1963–1981	2.33%
Michaely and Shaw (1995): 91, master limited partnerships 1981–1989	4.5%
Loh, Bezjak, and Toms (1995): 59, 1982–1987	1.5%
J.P. Morgan (1995): 77, since beginning of 1995	5%
	6% if spin-off >10% of parent's equity
	4% if spin-off <10% of parent's equity
Vroom and van Frederikslust (1999): 210 worldwide spin-offs, 1990–1998	2.6%
Mulherin and Boone (2000): 106, 1990–1998	4.51%
Davis and Leblond (2002): 93, 1980–1999	2.92%
Veld and Veld-Merkoulova (2004): 200, 1987–2000	2.66%
Maxwell and Rao (2003): 80, 1976–1997	3.60%
McNeil and Moore (2005): 153, 1980–1996	3.5%
Harris and Glegg (2007): 58 cross-border spin-offs, 1990–2006	2.23%

Continued

TABLE 15.7   Returns to Shareholders of Firms Undertaking Restructuring Actions—Cont'd

Study	Preannouncement Abnormal Returns by Study[a]
Tracking Stocks	
Logue, Seward, and Walsh (1996): 9, 1991–1995	2.9%
D'Souza and Jacob (2000): 19, 1984-1998	3.6%
Elder and Westra (2000): 35, 1984–1999	3.1%
Haushalter and Mikkelson (2001): 31, 1994–1996	3.0%
Chemmanur and Paeglis (2000): 19, 1984–1998	3.1%
Billet and Vijh (2004): 29, 1984–1999	2.2%
Equity Carve-Outs/IPOs	
Schipper and Smith (1986): 81, 1965–1983	1.7%
Michaely and Shaw (1995): 91 limited partnerships, 1981–1989	4%
Allen and McConnell (1998): 188, 1978–1993	6.63% when proceeds used to pay off debt; zero otherwise
Vijh (1999): 628, 1981–1995	6.2%
Mulherin and Boone (2000): 125, 1990–1998	2.3%
Prezas, Tarimcilar, and Vasudevan (2000): 237, 1985–1996	5.8%
Hulburt, Miles, and Wollridge (2002): 245, 1981–1994	2.1%
Hogan and Olson (2004): 458, 1990–1998	8.8%
Wagner (2004): 71, 1984–2002	1.7%
Voluntary Liquidations	
Skantz and Marchesini (1987): 37, 1970–1978	21.4%[b]
Hite, Owers, and Rogers (1987): 49, 1966–1975	13.6%[b]
Kim and Schatzberg (1987): 73, 1963–1981	14%
Erwin and McConnell (1997): 61, 1970–1991	20%

[a] *Abnormal mean returns measured from one to three before and including announcement date of restructuring action.*
[b] *Abnormal mean returns measured during the month of the announced restructuring action.*

financial distress. Abnormal returns around the announcement date of the restructuring strategy average 1.6% for sellers. Buyers average abnormal returns of about 0.5%.[22] While both sellers and buyers gain from a divestiture, most of the gain appears to accrue on average to the seller. However, how the total gain is divided ultimately depends on the relative bargaining strength of the seller and the buyer.

INCREASING FOCUS of Divesting Firms

A substantial body of evidence indicates that reducing a firm's complexity can improve financial returns to shareholders. The difficulty in managing diverse portfolios of businesses in many industries and the difficulty in accurately valuing these portfolios contributed to the breakup of conglomerates in the 1970s and 1980s. Of the acquisitions made between 1970 and 1982 by companies in industries unrelated to the acquirer's primary industry focus, 60% were divested by 1989. Abnormal returns earned by the shareholders of a firm divesting a business

[22] Hanson and Song, 2000; John and Ofek, 1995; Sicherman and Pettway, 1992

result largely from improved management of the assets that remain after the divestiture is completed. With 75% of the divested units unrelated to the selling firm, these returns may be attributed to increased focus and the ability of management to understand fewer lines of business.[23] Divesting firms tend also to improve their investment decisions in their remaining businesses following divestitures by achieving levels of investment in core businesses comparable to their more focused peers.[24]

Firms tend to sell operations representing a relatively small portion of the parent's total operations. Such sales often are of previously acquired units with a profitability that has improved or represent businesses no longer considered critical to the parent's business strategies.[25]

Restructuring decisions, such as divestitures, and investment decisions are interdependent. A parent may divest a unit to raise cash to finance what ultimately turns out to be a successful investment decision. While the divestiture was related to the successful investment, it does not follow that the decision to divest resulted in better investment decision making. Therefore, other factors unrelated to the divestiture decision, such as the firm's competitive position in high-growth markets, often explain the success of the firm's investment decisions.[26]

TRANSFERRING ASSETS TO THOSE WHO CAN USE THEM MORE EFFICIENTLY

Divestitures result in productivity gains by redeploying assets from less productive sellers to more productive buyers, who believe they can generate a higher financial return than the seller.[27]

RESOLVING DIFFERENCES BETWEEN MANAGEMENT AND SHAREHOLDERS (AGENCY CONFLICTS)

A firm's senior managers serve as agents of the shareholders in conducting the firm's operations. Conflicts arise when management and shareholders disagree about major corporate decisions. What to do with the proceeds of the sale of assets can result in such a conflict, since they can be reinvested in the seller's remaining operations, paid to shareholders, or used to reduce the firm's outstanding debt. Abnormal returns on divestiture announcement dates

[23] Petty, Keown, Scott, and Martin, 1993; John and Ofek, 1995

[24] Dittmar and Shivdasani, 2003

[25] Maksimovic and Phillips (2001) and Kaplan and Weisback (1992) found that firms tend to sell noncore operations, while Moeller, Schlingemann, and Stulz (2004) demonstrated that divested units tend to represent a relatively small portion of the parent's operations. Kaplan and Weisback argue that firms tend to sell previously acquired units more because of the improvement in their profitability or because they no longer support the parent's strategy than because they have failed to achieve expectations.

[26] Colak and Whited, 2007

[27] Using Tobin q-ratios (i.e., the ratio of the market value of a firm to the cost of replacing the firm's assets) as a proxy for better-managed firms, Datta, Iskandar-Datta, and Raman (2003) found that announcement period returns are highest for transactions in which the buyer's q-ratio is higher than the seller's. This implies that the assets are being transferred to a better-managed firm. Maksimovic and Phillips's (2001) findings also support this conclusion.

tend to be positive when the proceeds are used to pay off debt[28] or distributed to the shareholders.[29] Such results are consistent with a lack of shareholder confidence in management's ability to invest funds intelligently.

The form of payment appears to affect excess returns. Abnormal returns to sellers are much smaller when the seller receives cash rather than buyer equity. Asset sales paid for with buyer shares generate abnormal or excess returns of about 10% for buyers and 3% for sellers on or about the announcement date of the divestiture. The higher returns for buyers may reflect information communicated to the seller not generally known by the investing public about the synergy between the divested asset and the buyer's operations and the overall future earnings potential of the buyer's business. In contrast, excess returns to sellers receiving cash average about 3% for sellers and about zero for buyers.[30]

MITIGATING FINANCIAL DISTRESS

Not surprisingly, empirical studies indicate that firms sell assets when they need cash. The period before a firm announces asset sales often is characterized by deteriorating operating performance.[31] Firms that divest assets often have lower cash balances, cash flow, and bond credit ratings than firms exhibiting similar growth, risk, and profitability characteristics.[32] Firms experiencing financial distress are more likely to utilize divestitures as part of their restructuring programs than other options because they generate cash.[33]

Spin-Offs

At 3.7%, the average abnormal return to parent firm shareholders associated with spin-off announcements is more than twice the 1.6% average return on divestitures. However, the differences in announcement date returns between spin-offs and divestitures is smaller than it appears if we note that some portion of the total gain in wealth created by divestitures is shared with the buying firm's shareholders. In contrast, the jump in the parent firm's share price following the announcement of a spin-off reflects the total gain due to the spin-off. Including the abnormal return to the buyer's shareholders of 0.5%, the total gain from a divestiture is 2.1%. Much of the remaining gap between abnormal returns to shareholders from spin-offs versus divestitures may be attributable to tax considerations. Spin-offs generally are tax-free, while any gains realized on divested assets can be subject to double taxation. With spin-offs, shareholder value is created by increasing the focus of the parent by spinning off unrelated units, providing greater transparency, and transferring wealth from bondholders to shareholders.

[28] Lang et al., 1995; Kaiser and Stouraitis, 2001

[29] Slovin et al., 2005

[30] Slovin et al., 2005

[31] Lang et al., 1995; Schlingemann et al., 2003

[32] Officer, 2007

[33] Nixon, Roenfeldt, and Sicherman, 2000; Ofek, 1993

INCREASING FOCUS

Spin-offs increasing the parent's focus show significant positive announcement date returns. However, spin-offs of subsidiaries that are in the same industry as the parent firm do not result in positive announcement date returns because they do little to enhance corporate focus.[34] Spin-offs that increase parent focus also improve operating performance more than spin-offs that do not increase focus.[35] There is also a reduction in the diversification discount when a spin-off increases corporate focus but not for those that do not.[36]

Like divestitures, spin-offs eliminate the tendency to use the cash flows of efficient businesses to finance investment in less efficient business units; firms are more likely to invest in their attractive businesses after the spin-off.[37]

ACHIEVING GREATER TRANSPARENCY (ELIMINATING INFORMATION ASYMMETRIES)

Divestitures and spin-offs that tend to reduce a firm's complexity help to improve investors' ability to evaluate the firm's operating performance. The coverage of publicly traded firms by financial analysts provides an important source of information for investors. By reducing complexity, financial analysts are better able to forecast earnings accurately.[43] Analysts tend to revise upward their earnings forecasts of the parent in response to a spin-off.[39] These findings are consistent with the observation that reduced information asymmetries tend to increase shareholder value.

WEALTH TRANSFERS

Evidence shows that spin-offs transfer wealth from bondholders to stockholders for several reasons.[40] First, spin-offs reduce the assets available for liquidation in the event of business failure. Therefore, investors may view the firm's existing debt as more risky.[41] Second, the loss of the cash flow generated by the spin-off may result in less total parent cash flow to cover interest and principal repayments on the parent's current debt.

[34] Daley, Mehrotra, and Sivakumar, 1997

[35] Desai and Jain, 1997

[36] Burch and Nanda (2001) and Seoungpil and Denis (2004) demonstrate that spin-offs reduce the magnitude of the discount for firms trading at a conglomerate discount prior to the spin-off. Such firms are also more inclined to invest in their remaining high-growth segments.

[37] Gertner, Powers, and Scharfstein, 2002

[38] Gilson et al. (2001) note a substantial increase in analyst coverage and earnings forecast accuracy in the three years following a spin-off or equity carve-out.

[39] Huson and MacKinnon, 2003

[40] Maxwell and Rao (2003), in a sample of 80 spin-offs between 1976 and 1997, note that bondholders on average suffer a negative abnormal return of 0.8% in the month of the spin-off announcement. Stockholders experience an increase of about 3.6% during the same period.

[41] Note that assets actually pledged as collateral to current debt may not be spun off without violating loan covenants.

Equity Carve-Outs

Investors view the announcement of a carve-out as the beginning of a series of restructuring activities, such as a reacquisition of the unit by the parent, a spin-off, a secondary offering, or an M&A. The sizeable announcement date abnormal returns to parent firm shareholders averaging 4.5% reflect investor-anticipated profit from these secondary events. These abnormal positive returns are realized only when the parent firm retains a controlling interest after a carve-out announcement allowing the parent to initiate these secondary actions.[42] Furthermore, these returns tend to increase with the size of the carve-out.[43] Announcement date returns are significant for both parent firm stock and bond investors when the parent of the carve-out unit indicates that the majority of the proceeds resulting from the carve-out will be used to redeem debt.[44]

Managers use their inside information about the subsidiary's growth prospects to decide how much of the subsidiary to issue to the public. They are more inclined to retain a larger percentage of the business if they feel the unit's growth prospects are favorable.[45] Carve-outs may show poorer operating performance than their peers when their parents keep less than 50% of the subsidiary's equity. Either the parent chooses not to consolidate the carved-out unit due to its expected poor performance or it intends to transfer cash from minority-owned businesses through intercompany loans or dividends.[46] Value is created by increased parent focus, providing a source of financing, and resolving differences between the parent firm's management and shareholders (i.e., agency issues).

INCREASING FOCUS

Parents and subsidiaries involved in carve-outs are frequently in different industries. Positive announcement date returns often are higher for carve-outs of unrelated subsidiaries. This is consistent with the common observation that carve-outs are undertaken for businesses that do not fit with the parent's business strategy. It is unclear if operating performance improves following equity carve-outs.[47] Evidence has shown that both parents and carved-out subsidiaries tend to improve their operating performance relative to their industry peers in the year following the carve-out.[48] However, other studies have shown that operating performance declines following a carve-out.[49]

[42] Otsubo, 2009

[43] Allen and McConnell, 1998; Vijh, 2002

[44] The carve-out proceeds boost bondholder returns as current debt is repurchased. The reduction in outstanding debt means less interest expense is incurred and more cash is available for dividend payments and share repurchases of stock held by current shareholders. See Thompson and Apilado (2009).

[45] Powers, 2003

[46] Atanasov, Boone, and Haushalter, 2005

[47] Vijh, 2002

[48] Hulbert et al., 2002

[49] Powers et al., 2003; Boone, Haushalter, and Mikkelson, 2003

PROVIDING A SOURCE OF FINANCING

Equity carve-outs can help to finance the needs of the parent or the subsidiary involved in the carve-out. Firms may use carve-outs to finance their high-growth subsidiaries.[50] Corporations tend to choose equity carve-outs and divestitures over spin-offs when market to book value and revenue growth of the carved-out unit are high to maximize the cash proceeds of the sale of equity or asset sales.[51]

RESOLVING AGENCY ISSUES

There is evidence that investor reaction to the announcement of a carve-out is determined by how the proceeds are used. Firms announcing that the proceeds will be used to repay debt or pay dividends earn a 7% abnormal return compared to minimal returns for those announcing that the proceeds will be reinvested in the firm.[52]

Tracking Stocks

Reflecting initial investor enthusiasm, a number of studies show that tracking stocks experience significant positive abnormal returns around their announcement date. Studies addressing the issue of whether the existence of publicly listed tracking shares increases the demand for other stock issued by the parent give mixed results.[53] However, there is some evidence that investors become disenchanted with tracking stocks over time. In 11 instances between 1984 and 1999, excess returns to shareholders averaged 13.9% around the date of the announcement that target stock structures would be removed.[54]

Voluntary Liquidations (Bust-Ups)

The exceptional average 17.3% abnormal returns for voluntary liquidations or bust-ups may reflect investors' concurrence with management that continued operation of the firm is likely to erode shareholder value. Busting up the firm enables shareholders to redeploy the proceeds of the liquidation to potentially more attractive alternative investments. Consistent with a perceived lack of investment options, empirical research indicates that firms that voluntarily liquidate have low market-to-book ratios, cash balances well in excess of their operating needs, and low debt-to-equity levels. Such firms also tend to have high equity ownership by senior managers who tend to gain significantly by liquidating the firm.[55] The high abnormal returns also may reflect the potential for firms announcing their intention to voluntarily liquidate to receive acquisition bids.[56]

[50] Schipper and Smith, 1986

[51] Chen and Guo, 2005

[52] Allen and McConnell (1998)

[53] Clayton and Qian (2004) found evidence that parent shares rise following the issuance of publicly listed tracking stocks. However, Elder et al. (2000) found no evidence that tracking shares lead to greater interest in the parent's and other subsidiary shares.

[54] Billet and Vijh, 2004

[55] Fleming and Moon, 1995

[56] Hite, Owers, and Rogers, 1987

Post-Carve-Out and Post-Spin-Off Returns to Shareholders

Carve-outs and spin-offs are more likely to outperform the broader stock market indices because their share prices reflect speculation that they will be acquired rather than any improvement in the operating performance of the units once they have been spun off from the parent. One-third of spin-offs are acquired within three years after the unit is spun off by the parent. Once those spin-offs that have been acquired are removed from the sample, the remaining spin-offs perform no better than their peers.[57]

Many historical studies that show superior post-spin-off returns are indeed heavily biased by the inclusion of one or two firms in the sample with excess returns that are the result of having been acquired. Spin-offs simply may create value by providing an efficient method of transferring corporate assets to the acquiring companies.[58] The probability of acquisition is higher for units that are subject to a carve-out than it is for similar firms that are in the same industry.[59]

Spin-offs involving parents and subsidiaries that are in different countries often show significant positive abnormal returns. The magnitude of the wealth gain accruing to holders of stock in the unit spun off by the parent is higher in countries where takeover activity is also high. This reflects the increased likelihood that the spun-off units will become takeover targets.[60]

In a study of 232 spin-offs and equity carve-outs during the 1990s, Booz-Allen Hamilton found that only 26% of the units outperformed the broader stock market indices during the two years following their separation from the parent.[61] Smaller spin-offs (i.e., those with a market cap of less than $200 million) tend to outperform larger ones (i.e., those with a market cap greater than $200 million).[62] This may be a result of a tendency of investors who are relatively unfamiliar with the business that is spun off by the parent to undervalue the spin-off. Carve-outs that are largely independent of the parent (i.e., in which the parent generally owned less than 50% of the spin-off's equity) tended to significantly outperform the S&P 500.[63] The evidence for the long-term performance of tracking stocks is mixed.[64]

---

[57] Cusatis, Miles, and Woolridge, 1993

[58] McConnell, Ozbilgin, and Wahal, 2001

[59] Hulbert et al., 2002

[60] Harris and Glegg, 2007

[61] Scherreik, 2002

[62] J.P. Morgan, 1999

[63] Annema et al., 2002

[64] Chemmanur and Paeglis (2000) found that the stock of parent firms tends to underperform the major stock indices, while the average tracking stock outperforms its industry stock index. However, Billett and Vijh (2004) found negative financial returns following the issue date for tracking stocks and positive, but statistically insignificant, returns for parents.

SOME THINGS TO REMEMBER

Divestitures, spin-offs, equity carve-outs, split-ups, split-offs, and voluntary bust-ups are commonly used restructuring and exit strategies to redeploy assets by returning cash or non-cash assets through a special dividend to shareholders or to use cash proceeds to pay off debt. On average, these restructuring strategies create positive abnormal financial returns for shareholders around the announcement date because they tend to correct problems facing the parent. However, the longer-term performance of spin-offs, carve-outs, and tracking stocks is problematic. The extent to which such stocks outperform their industry stock indices reflects more the likelihood that they will be acquired than improved operating performance.

DISCUSSION QUESTIONS

15.1 How do tax and regulatory considerations influence the decision to exit a business?

15.2 How would you decide when to sell a business?

15.3 What are the major differences between a spin-off and an equity carve-out?

15.4 Under what conditions is a spin-off tax free to shareholders?

15.5 Why would a firm decide to voluntarily split up?

15.6 What are the advantages and the disadvantages of tracking stocks to the investors and the firm?

15.7 What factors contribute to the high positive abnormal returns to shareholders before the announcement of a voluntary bust-up?

15.8 What factors influence a parent firm's decision to undertake a spin-off rather than a divestiture or equity carve-out?

15.9 How might the form of payment affect the abnormal return to sellers and buyers?

15.10 How might spin-offs result in a wealth transfer from bondholders to shareholders?

15.11 Explain how executing successfully a large-scale divestiture can be highly complex. This is especially true when the divested unit is integrated with the parent's functional departments and other units operated by the parent. Consider the challenges of timing, interdependencies, regulatory requirements, and customer and employee perceptions.

15.12 On April 25, 2001, in an effort to increase shareholder value, USX announced its intention to split U.S. Steel and Marathon Oil into two separately traded companies. The breakup gives holders of Marathon Oil stock an opportunity to participate in the ongoing consolidation within the global oil and gas industry. Holders of USX–U.S. Steel Group common stock (target stock) would become holders of newly formed Pittsburgh-based United States Steel Corporation. What other alternatives could USX have pursued to increase shareholder value? Why do you believe it pursued the breakup strategy rather than some of the alternatives?

15.13 Hewlett-Packard announced in early 1999 the spin-off of its Agilent Technologies unit to focus on its main business of computers and printers. HP retained a controlling interest until mid-2000, when it spun off the rest of its shares in Agilent to HP shareholders as a tax-free transaction. Discuss the reasons why HP may have chosen a staged transaction rather than an outright divestiture or spin-off of the business.

15.14 After months of trying to sell its 81% stake in Blockbuster Inc., Viacom undertook a spin-off in mid-2004. Why would Viacom choose to spin off rather than divest its Blockbuster unit? Explain your answer.

15.15 Since 2001, GE, the world's largest conglomerate, had been underperforming the S&P 500 stock index. In late 2008, the firm announced that it was considering spinning off its consumer and industrial unit. What do you believe are GE's motives for its proposed restructuring? Why do you believe it chose a spin-off rather than an alternative restructuring strategy?

Answers to these Chapter Discussion Questions can be found in the Online Instructor's Manual for instructors using this book.

CHAPTER BUSINESS CASES

CASE STUDY 15.5
Kraft Foods Undertakes Split-Off of Post Cereals in Merger-Related Transaction

In August 2008, Kraft Foods announced an exchange offer related to the split-off of its Post Cereals unit and the closing of the merger of its Post Cereals business into a wholly-owned subsidiary of Ralcorp Holdings. Kraft is a major manufacturer and distributor of foods and beverages; Post is a leading manufacturer of breakfast cereals; and Ralcorp manufactures and distributes brand-name products in grocery and mass merchandise food outlets. The objective of the transaction was to allow Kraft shareholders participating in the exchange offer for Kraft Sub stock to become shareholders in Ralcorp and Kraft to receive almost $1 billion in cash or cash equivalents on a tax-free basis.

Prior to the transaction, Kraft borrowed $300 million from outside lenders and established Kraft Sub, a shell corporation wholly owned by Kraft. Kraft subsequently transferred the Post assets and associated liabilities, along with the liability Kraft incurred in raising $300 million, to Kraft Sub in exchange for all of Kraft Sub's stock and $660 million in debt securities issued by Kraft

Sub to be paid to Kraft at the end of ten years. In effect, Post was conveyed to Kraft Sub in exchange for assuming Kraft's $300 million liability, 100% of Kraft Sub's stock, and Kraft Sub debt securities with a principal amount of $660 million. The consideration that Kraft received, consisting of the debt assumption by Kraft Sub, the debt securities from Kraft Sub, and the Kraft Sub stock, is considered tax free to Kraft, since it is viewed simply as an internal reorganization rather than a sale.* Kraft later converted to cash the securities received from Kraft Sub by selling them to a consortium of banks.

In the related split-off transaction, Kraft shareholders had the option to exchange their shares of Kraft common stock for shares of Kraft Sub, which owned the assets and liabilities of Post. If Kraft was unable to exchange all of the Kraft Sub common shares, it would distribute the remaining shares as a dividend (i.e., spin-off) on a pro rata basis to Kraft shareholders.

With the completion of the merger of Kraft Sub with Ralcorp Sub, which was a Ralcorp wholly-owned subsidiary, the common shares

CASE STUDY 15.5 *(cont'd)*

of Kraft Sub were exchanged for shares of Ralcorp stock on a one-for-one basis. Consequently, Kraft shareholders tendering their Kraft shares in the exchange offer owned 0.6606 of a share of Ralcorp stock for each Kraft share exchanged as part of the split-off.

Concurrent with the exchange offer, Kraft closed the merger of Post with Ralcorp. Kraft shareholders received Ralcorp stock valued at $1.6 billion, resulting in their owning 54% of the merged firm. By satisfying the Morris Trust tax code regulations,** the transaction was tax free to Kraft shareholders. Ralcorp Sub was later merged into Ralcorp. As such, Ralcorp assumed the liabilities of Ralcorp Sub, including the $660 million owed to Kraft.

The purchase price for the Post Cereals business equaled $2.56 billion. This price consisted of $1.6 billion in Ralcorp stock received by Kraft shareholders and $960 million in cash equivalents received by Kraft. The $960 million included the assumption of the $300 million liability by Kraft Sub and the $660 million in debt securities received from Kraft Sub.[†] The steps that were involved in the transaction are described in Exhibit 15.1.

Discussion Questions

1. The merger of Post with Ralcorp could have been achieved through a spin-off. Explain the details of how this might have happened.
2. Speculate as to why Kraft chose to split off rather than spin off Post as part its plan to merge Post with Ralcorp. Be specific.
3. Why was this transaction subject to the Morris Trust tax regulations (see Chapter 12)?
4. How is value created for the Kraft and Ralcorp shareholders in this type of transaction?

Answers to this case study are found in the Online Instructors Manual for instructors using this book.

---

[*] The intracompany transfer of certain assets and associated liabilities is considered a tax-free event if it complies with the requirements of a D reorganization under Section 355 of the U.S. Internal Revenue Code.

[**] Split-offs and spin-offs undertaken as part of a merger must be structured to satisfy Morris Trust tax code rules if they are to be tax-free. Such rules require that the shareholders of the parent undertaking the split-off or spin-off end up as majority shareholders in the merged firm.

[†] The $660 million represents the book value of the debt on the merger closing date. The more correct representation in calculating the purchase price would be to estimate its market value.

EXHIBIT 15.1 STRUCTURING THE TRANSACTION

Step 1: Kraft creates a shell subsidiary (Kraft Sub) and transfers Post assets and liabilities and $300 million in Kraft debt into the shell in exchange for Kraft Sub stock plus $660 million in Kraft Sub debt securities. Kraft also implements an exchange offer of Kraft Sub for Kraft common stock.

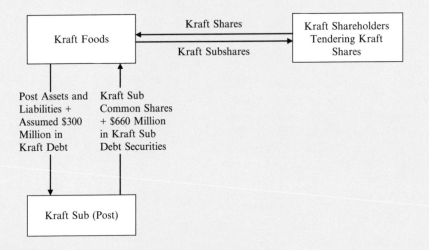

Step 2: Kraft Sub, as an independent company, is merged in a forward triangular tax-free merger with a Sub of Ralcorp (Ralcorp Sub) in which Kraft Sub shares are exchanged for Ralcorp shares, with Ralcorp Sub surviving.*

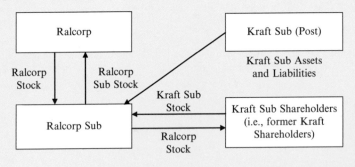

* The merger is tax free to Kraft Sub shareholders in that it results in Kraft Sub shareholders owning a significant ongoing interest in Ralcorp and Ralcorp owning the Kraft Sub assets. Consequently, both the continuity of interests and continuity of business enterprise principles are satisfied. See Chapter 12 for a more detailed discussion of these issues.

CASE STUDY 15.6
Sara Lee Attempts to Create Value through Restructuring

After spurning a series of takeover offers, Sara Lee, a global consumer goods company, announced in early 2011 its intention to split the firm into two separate publicly traded companies. The two companies would consist of the firm's North American retail and food service division and its international beverage business. The announcement comes after a long string of restructuring efforts designed to increase shareholder value. It remains to be seen if the latest effort will be any more successful than earlier efforts.

Reflecting a flawed business strategy, Sara Lee had struggled for more than a decade to create value for its shareholders by radically restructuring its portfolio of businesses. The firm's business strategy had evolved from one designed in the mid-1980s to market a broad array of consumer products, from baked goods to coffee to underwear under the highly recognizable brand name of Sara Lee, into one that was designed to refocus the firm on the faster-growing food and beverage and apparel businesses. Despite acquiring several European manufacturers of processed meats in the early 1990s, the company's profits and share price continued to founder.

In September 1997, Sara Lee embarked on a major restructuring effort designed to boost both profits, which had been growing by about 6% during the previous five years, and the company's lagging share price. The restructuring program was intended to reduce the firm's degree of vertical integration, shifting it from a manufacturing and sales orientation to one focused on marketing the top brands of the firm. Increasingly it viewed itself as more of a marketing than a manufacturing enterprise.

Sara Lee outsourced and/or sold 110 of its manufacturing and distribution facilities over the next two years. Nearly 10,000 employees, representing 7% of the workforce, were laid off. The proceeds from the sale of facilities and the cost savings from outsourcing were either reinvested in the firm's core food businesses or used to repurchase $3 billion in company stock. In 1999 and 2000, the firm acquired several brands in an effort to bolster its core coffee operations, including names such as Chock full o'Nuts, Hills Bros, and Chase & Sanborn.

Despite these restructuring efforts, the firm's stock price continued to drift lower. In an attempt to reverse its misfortunes, the firm announced an even more ambitious restructuring plan in 2000. Sara Lee would focus on three main areas: food and beverages, underwear, and household products. The restructuring efforts resulted in the shutdown of a number of meat packing plants and a number of small divestitures, resulting in a 10% reduction (about 13,000 people) in the firm's workforce.

Sara Lee also completed the largest acquisition in its history, purchasing The Earthgrains Company for $1.9 billion plus the assumption of $0.9 billion in debt. With annual revenue of $2.6 billion, Earthgrains specialized in fresh packaged bread and refrigerated dough. However, despite ongoing restructuring activities, Sara Lee continued to underperform the broader stock market indices.

In February 2005, Sara Lee executed its most ambitious plan to transform the firm into a company focused on the global food, beverage, and household and body care

CASE STUDY 15.6 *(cont'd)*

businesses. To this end, the firm announced plans to dispose of 40% of its revenues, totaling more than $8 billion, including its apparel, European packaged meats, U.S. retail coffee, and direct sales businesses.

In 2006, the firm announced that it had completed the sale of its branded apparel business in Europe, its Global Body Care and European Detergents units, and its European meat processing operations. Furthermore, the firm spun off its U.S. Branded Apparel unit into a separate publicly traded firm called HanesBrands Inc. The firm raised more than $3.7 billion in cash from the divestitures. The firm was now focused on its core businesses: food, beverages, and household and body care.

In late 2008, Sara Lee announced that it would close its kosher meat processing business and sold its retail coffee business. In 2009, the firm sold its Household and Body Care business to Unilever for $1.6 billion and its hair care business to Procter & Gamble for $0.4 billion.

In 2010, the proceeds of the divestitures carried out the prior year were used to repurchase $1.3 billion of Sara Lee's outstanding shares. The firm also announced its intention to repurchase another $3 billion of its shares during the next three years. If completed, this would amount to about one-third of its approximate $10 billion market capitalization at the end of 2010.

What remains of the firm are food brands in North America, including Hillshire Farm, Ball Park, and Jimmy Dean processed meats, and Sara Lee baked goods and Earthgrains. A food distribution unit will also remain in North America, as will its beverage and bakery operations. Sara Lee is rapidly moving to become a food, beverage, and bakery firm. As it becomes more focused, it could become a takeover target.

Has the restructuring program started in 2005 worked? To answer this question, it is necessary to determine the percentage change in Sara Lee's share price from the announcement date of the restructuring program to the end of 2010, as well as the percentage change in the share price of HanesBrands Inc., which was spun off on August 18, 2006. The Sara Lee shareholders of record received one share of HanesBrands Inc. for every eight Sara Lee shares they held.

Sara Lee's share price jumped by 6%, closing at $19.56 when the restructuring was announced on February 21, 2005. Six years later, the stock price ended 2010 at $14.90, an approximate 24% decline since the announcement of the restructuring program in early 2005. Immediately following the spin-off, HanesBrands' stock traded at $22.06 per share; at the end of 2010, the stock traded at $25.99, a 17.8% increase.

A shareholder owning 100 shares of Sara Lee when the spin-off was announced would have been entitled to 12.5 shares of HanesBrands. However, they would have actually received 12 shares plus $11.03 for fractional shares (i.e., 0.5 × $22.06).

Individual shareholders of record who had 100 Sara Lee shares on the date of the announcement of the restructuring program and held their shares until the end of 2010 would have seen their investment decline 24% from $1,956 (100 shares × $19.56 per share) to $1,486.56 by the end of 2010. However, this would have been partially offset by the appreciation of the HanesBrands shares between 2006 and 2010. Therefore, the total

CASE STUDY 15.6 *(cont'd)*

value of the hypothetical shareholders' investment would have decreased by 7.5% from $1,956 to $1,809.47 (i.e., $1,486.56 + 12 HanesBrands shares × $25.99 + $11.03). This compares to a more modest 5% loss for investors who put the same $1,956 into a Standard & Poor's 500 stock index fund during the same period.

Why did Sara Lee underperform the broader stock market indices during this period? Despite the cumulative buyback of more than $4 billion of its outstanding stock, Sara Lee's fully diluted earnings per share dropped from $0.90 per share in 2005 to $0.52 per share in 2009. Furthermore, the book value per share, a proxy for the breakup or liquidation value of the firm, dropped from $3.28 in 2005 to $2.93 in 2009, reflecting the ongoing divestiture program. While the HanesBrands spin-off did create value for the shareholder, the amount was far too modest to offset the decline in Sara Lee's market value. During the same period, total revenue grew at a tepid average annual rate of about 3% to about $13 billion in 2009.

Discussion Questions

1. In what sense is the Sara Lee business strategy in effect a breakup strategy? Be specific.
2. Would you expect investors to be better off buying Sara Lee stock or investing in a similar set of consumer product businesses in their own personal investment portfolios? Explain your answer.
3. Why did the 2005 restructuring program appear to have been unsuccessful in achieving a sustained increase in Sara Lee's earnings per share and in creating value for the Sara Lee shareholders?
4. Why is a breakup strategy conceptually simple to explain but often difficult to implement? Be specific.
5. Explain why Sara Lee may have chosen to spin off rather than to divest HanesBrands Inc. Be specific.

Answers to these questions are found in the Online Instructor's Manual available for instructors using this book.

CHAPTER

16

Alternative Exit
and Restructuring Strategies
Reorganization and Liquidation

What matters is not the size of the dog in the fight but the size of the fight in the dog.
—*Vince Lombardi*

INSIDE M&A: CALPINE EMERGES FROM THE PROTECTION OF BANKRUPTCY COURT

Following approval of its sixth Plan of Reorganization by the U.S. Bankruptcy Court for the Southern District of New York, Calpine Corporation was able to emerge from Chapter 11 bankruptcy on January 31, 2008. Burdened by excessive debt and court battles with creditors on how to use its cash, the electric utility had sought Chapter 11 protection by petitioning the bankruptcy court in December 2005. After settlements with certain stakeholders, all classes of creditors voted to approve the Plan of Reorganization, which provided for the discharge of claims through the issuance of reorganized Calpine Corporation common stock, cash, or a combination of cash and stock to its creditors.

Shortly after exiting bankruptcy, Calpine canceled all of its then outstanding common stock and authorized the issuance of 485 million shares of reorganized Calpine Corporation common stock for distribution to holders of unsecured claims. In addition, the firm issued warrants (i.e., securities) to purchase 48.5 million shares of reorganized Calpine Corporation common stock from the holders of the canceled (i.e., previously outstanding) common stock. The warrants were issued on a pro rata basis reflecting the number of shares of "old common stock" held at the time of cancellation. These warrants carried an exercise price of $23.88 per share and expired on August 25, 2008. Relisted on the New York Stock Exchange, the reorganized Calpine Corporation common stock began trading under the symbol CPN on February 7, 2008, at about $18 per share.

The firm had improved its capital structure while in bankruptcy. On entering bankruptcy, Calpine carried $17.4 billion of debt with an average interest rate of 10.3%. By retiring unsecured debt with reorganized Calpine Corporation common stock and selling certain assets,

Calpine was able to repay or refinance certain project debt, thereby reducing the prebankruptcy petition debt by approximately $7 billion. On exiting bankruptcy, Calpine negotiated approximately $7.3 billion of secured "exit facilities" (i.e., credit lines) from Goldman Sachs, Credit Suisse, Deutsche Bank, and Morgan Stanley. About $6.4 billion of these funds were used to satisfy cash payment obligations under the Plan of Reorganization. These obligations included the repayment of a portion of unsecured creditor claims and administrative claims, such as legal and consulting fees, as well as expenses incurred in connection with the "exit facilities" and immediate working capital requirements. On emerging from Chapter 11, the firm carried $10.4 billion of debt with an average interest rate of 8.1%.

CHAPTER OVERVIEW

The focus of this chapter is on bankruptcy and liquidation as alternative restructuring or exit strategies for failing firms. Bankruptcy enables a failing firm to reorganize, while protected from its creditors, or to cease operation by selling its assets to satisfy all or a portion of the firm's outstanding debt. How reorganization and liquidation take place both inside and outside the protection of the bankruptcy court are examined in detail. This chapter also discusses common strategic options for failing firms and how to value such firms, the current state of bankruptcy prediction models, and empirical studies of the performance of firms experiencing financial distress.

A review of this chapter (including practice questions with answers) is available in the file folder entitled "Student Study Guide" on the companion site to this book (*www.elsevierdirect. com/companions/9780123854858*). The companion site also contains a Learning Interactions Library, which gives students the opportunity to test their knowledge of this chapter in a "real-time" environment.

BUSINESS FAILURE

Failing firms may be subject to financial distress as measured by declining asset values, liquidity, and cash flow. The term *financial distress* does not have a strict technical or legal definition. The term applies to a firm that is unable to meet its obligations or a specific security on which the issuer has defaulted. Firms whose debt yields more than 10 percentage points above the risk-free rate often are considered financially distressed. Moody's credit rating agency defines *default* as any missed or delayed disbursement of interest or principal, bankruptcy, receivership, or an exchange diminishing the value of what is owed to bondholders. For example, the issuer might offer bondholders a new security or package of securities (such as preferred or common stock or debt with a lower coupon or par value) that are worth less than what they are owed.[1]

Technical insolvency arises when a firm is unable to pay its liabilities as they come due. *Legal insolvency* occurs when a firm's liabilities exceed the fair market value of its assets. Creditors' claims cannot be satisfied unless the firm's assets can be liquidated for more than the book value of the firm's liabilities. A federal legal proceeding designed to protect the technically or legally insolvent firm from lawsuits by its creditors until a decision can be made to shut down or to continue to operate the firm is called *bankruptcy*. A firm is not bankrupt or in

---

[1] Keenan, Shotgrin, and Sobehart, 1999

bankruptcy until it files, or its creditors file, a petition for reorganization or liquidation with the federal bankruptcy courts.

The terms *liquidity* and *solvency* often are used inappropriately. Liquidity is the ability of a business to have sufficient cash on hand (as opposed to tied up in receivables and inventory) to meet its immediate obligations without having to incur significant losses in selling assets. Insolvency means that a firm cannot pay its bills under any circumstances. A liquid business is more likely to be solvent (i.e., able to pay its bills); however, not all businesses that are liquid are solvent, and not all solvent businesses have adequate liquidity.

Receivership can be an alternative to bankruptcy in which a court- or government-appointed individual (i.e., a receiver) takes control of the assets and affairs of a business to administer them according to the court's or government's directives. The purpose of a receiver may be to serve as a custodian while disputes between officers, directors, or stockholders are settled or to liquidate the firm's assets. Under no circumstances can the firm's debt be discharged without the approval of the bankruptcy court. In most states, receivership cannot take effect unless a lawsuit is under way and the court has determined that receivership is appropriate. *Conservatorship* represents a less restrictive alternative to receivership. While the receiver is expected to terminate the rights of shareholders and managers, a conservator is expected to merely assume these rights temporarily.

For example, in July 2008, the failing IndyMac Bank was taken into administrative receivership by the Federal Deposit Insurance Corporation, and the bank's assets and secured liabilities were transferred into a "bridge bank" called *IndyMac Federal Bank* until the assets could be liquidated. Also, in September 2008, the CEO and the boards of the Federal National Mortgage Association and the Federal Home Loan Mortgage Corporation were dismissed, and the firms were put under the conservatorship of the Federal Housing Finance Agency while their asset portfolios were reduced.

A debtor firm and its creditors may choose to reach a negotiated settlement outside of bankruptcy, within the protection of the court, or through a prepackaged bankruptcy, which represents a blend of the first two options. The following sections discuss each of these options.

VOLUNTARY SETTLEMENTS WITH CREDITORS OUTSIDE OF BANKRUPTCY

An insolvent firm may reach an agreement with its creditors to restructure its obligations out of court to avoid the costs of bankruptcy proceedings. The debtor firm usually initiates the voluntary settlement process because it generally offers the best chance for the current owners to recover a portion of their investments either by continuing to operate the firm or through a planned liquidation of the firm. This process normally involves the debtor firm requesting a meeting with its creditors. At this meeting, a committee of creditors is selected to analyze the debtor firm's financial position and recommend a course of action: whether the firm continues to operate or is liquidated.

Increasingly, distressed companies are choosing to restructure outside of bankruptcy court.[2] Smaller firms are inclined to use out-of-court settlements because of the excessive

---

[2] Lovly, 2007

expenses associated with reorganizing in bankruptcy courts. Small business bankruptcy filings cost $50,000 to $100,000 in legal expenses and court filing fees. Legal and fee expenses well in excess of $100,000 are common.[3] More midsized companies moving into international markets also contribute to the growth in out-of-court restructurings. Such firms may not be able to restructure through U.S. bankruptcy courts if the ruling is not recognized overseas. Large companies often have a difficult time achieving out-of-court settlements because they usually have hundreds of creditors.

Voluntary Settlements Resulting in Continued Operation

Plans to restructure the debtor firm developed cooperatively with creditors commonly are called *workouts*. A *workout* is an arrangement outside of bankruptcy by a debtor and its creditors for payment or rescheduling of payment of the debtor's obligations. Because of the firm's weak financial position, the creditors must be willing to restructure the insolvent firm's debts to enable it to sustain its operations. *Debt restructuring* involves concessions by creditors that lower an insolvent firm's payments so that it may remain in business. Restructuring normally is accomplished in three ways: an extension, a composition, or a debt-for-equity swap.

An *extension* occurs when creditors agree to lengthen the period during which the debtor firm can repay its debt. Creditors often agree to temporarily suspend both interest and principal repayments. A *composition* is an agreement in which creditors agree to receive less than the full amount they are owed. A *debt-for-equity swap* occurs when creditors surrender a portion of their claims on the firm in exchange for an ownership position in the firm. If the reduced debt service payments enable the firm to prosper, the value of the stock in the long run may far exceed the amount of debt the creditors were willing to forgive.

Exhibit 16.1 depicts a debt restructure of a bankrupt company that would enable the firm to continue operation by converting debt to equity. Although the firm, Survivor Incorporated, has positive earnings before interest and taxes, these is not enough to meet its interest payments. When principal payments are considered, cash flow becomes negative, rendering the firm technically insolvent. As a result of the restructuring of the firm's debt, Survivor Inc. is able to continue to operate; however, the firm's lenders now have a controlling interest in the firm. Note that the same type of restructuring could take place either voluntarily outside the courts or as a result of reorganizing under the protection of the bankruptcy court. The latter scenario is discussed later in this chapter.

EXHIBIT 16.1 SURVIVOR INC. RESTRUCTURES ITS DEBT

Survivor Inc. currently has 400,000 shares of common equity outstanding at a par value of $10 per share. The current rate of interest on its debt is 8%, and the debt is amortized over 20 years. The combined federal, state, and local tax rate is 40%. The firm's cash flow and capital position are shown in Table 16.1.

[3] Buljevich, 2005

TABLE 16.1   Cash Flow and Capital Position

Income and Cash Flow		Total Capital	
Earnings before Interest and Taxes	$500,000	Debt	$10,000,000
Interest	$800,000	Equity	$4,000,000
Earnings before Taxes	$(300,000)	**Total**	**$14,000,000**
Taxes	$120,000		
Earnings after Taxes	$(180,000)	Debt/Total Capital	71.4%
Depreciation	$400,000		
Principal Repayment	$(500,000)		
Cash Flow	$(280,000)		

Assume that bondholders are willing to convert $5 million of debt to equity at the current par value of $10 per share. This necessitates that Survivor Inc. issue 500,000 new shares. These actions result in a positive cash flow, a substantial reduction in the firm's debt-to-total capital ratio, and a transfer of control to the bondholders. The former stockholders now own only 44.4% (4 million/9 million) of the company. The revised cash flow and capital position are shown in Table 16.2.

TABLE 16.2   Revised Cash Flow and Capital Position

Income and Cash Flow		Total Capital	
Earnings before Interest and Taxes	$500,000	Debt	$5,000,000
Interest	$400,000	Equity	$9,000,000
Earnings before Taxes	$100,000	**Total**	**$14,000,000**
Taxes	$40,000		
Earnings after Taxes	$60,000	Debt/Total Capital	35.7%
Depreciation	$400,000		
Principal Repayment	$(250,000)		
Cash Flow	$210,000		

Voluntary Settlement Resulting in Liquidation

If the creditors conclude that the insolvent firm's situation cannot be resolved, liquidation may be the only acceptable course of action. Liquidation can be conducted outside the court in a private liquidation or through the U.S. bankruptcy court. If the insolvent firm is willing to accept liquidation and all creditors agree, legal proceedings are not necessary. Creditors normally prefer private liquidations to avoid lengthy and costly litigation. Through a process called an *assignment*, a committee representing creditors grants the power to liquidate the firm's assets to a third party, called an *assignee* or *trustee*. The responsibility of the assignee is to sell the assets as quickly as possible while obtaining the best possible price. The assignee distributes the proceeds of the asset sales to the creditors and the firm's owners if any monies remain.

REORGANIZATION AND LIQUIDATION IN BANKRUPTCY

In the absence of a voluntary settlement out of court, the debtor firm may seek protection from its creditors by initiating bankruptcy or may be forced into bankruptcy by its creditors. When the debtor firm files the petition with the bankruptcy court, the bankruptcy is said to be *voluntary*. When creditors do the filing, the action is said to be *involuntary*. Once either a voluntary or an involuntary bankruptcy petition is filed, the debtor firm is protected from any further legal action related to its debts until the bankruptcy proceedings have been completed. The filing of a petition triggers an *automatic stay* once the court accepts the request, which provides a period that suspends all judgments, collection activities, foreclosures, and repossessions of property by the creditors on any debt or claim that arose before the filing of the bankruptcy petition.

The Evolution of U.S. Bankruptcy Laws and Practices

U.S. bankruptcy laws focus on rehabilitating and reorganizing debtors in distress. Except for Chapter 12, all the chapters of the present Bankruptcy Code are odd-numbered. Chapters 1, 3, and 5 cover matters of general application, while Chapters 7, 9, 11, 12, and 13 concern liquidation (business or nonbusiness), municipality bankruptcy, business reorganization, family farm debt adjustment, and wage-earner or personal reorganization, respectively. Chapter 15 applies to international cases.

The Bankruptcy Reform Act of 1978

The Bankruptcy Reform Act of 1978 substantially changed the bankruptcy laws by adding a strong business reorganization mechanism, referred to as Chapter 11 of the U.S. Bankruptcy Code. Chapter 11 replaced the old Chapters 10 through 12 of the U.S. Bankruptcy Code. Similarly, a more powerful personal bankruptcy, Chapter 13, replaced the old laws. In general, the Reform Act of 1978 made it easier for both businesses and individuals to file a bankruptcy and reorganize. The 1978 law also broadened the conditions under which companies could file so that a firm could declare bankruptcy without having to wait until it was virtually insolvent. The intent of making the Bankruptcy Code less rigid was to increase the likelihood that creditors and owners would reach agreement on plans to reorganize rather than liquidate insolvent firms, which offered the prospect of saving jobs, government tax revenue, and enabling creditors to recover a larger portion of their claims.

The Bankruptcy Reform Act of 1994

During the 1980s and early 1990s, the number of bankruptcy filings reached record levels. Most of the filings were for Chapter 11 reorganization. As the frequency and complexity of cases grew, concerns about the level of professional fees and the perceived loss of value of assets in a number of bankruptcy cases increased the demand for new legislation. In response, the U.S. Congress passed the Bankruptcy Reform Act of 1994, which contained provisions to expedite bankruptcy proceedings and encourage individual debtors to use Chapter 13 to reschedule their debts rather than use Chapter 7 to liquidate.

The Bankruptcy Abuse Prevention and Consumer Protection Act of 2005

On April 19, 2005, the Bankruptcy Abuse Prevention and Consumer Protection Act (BAPCPA) became law. The new legislation primarily affects consumer filings, making it more difficult for a person or estate to file for Chapter 7 bankruptcy. The BAPCPA affects business filers as well, with the heaviest influence on smaller businesses (i.e., those with less than $2 million in debt).

Prior to BAPCPA, commercial enterprises used Chapter 11 reorganization to continue operating a business and repay creditors through a court-approved plan of reorganization. The debtor had the exclusive right to file a plan of reorganization for the first 120 days after it filed the case. The court ultimately approved or disapproved the reorganization plan. If approved, the plan enabled the debtor to reduce its debts by repaying a portion of its obligations and discharging other obligations. The debtor could also terminate onerous contracts and leases, recover assets, and restructure its operations.

BAPCPA changed this process by (1) reducing the maximum length of time during which debtors have an exclusive right to submit a plan; (2) shortening the time that debtors have to accept or reject leases; and (3) limiting compensation under key employee retention programs. Prior to BAPCPA, a debtor corporation had the opportunity to request a bankruptcy judge to extend the period for submission of the plan of reorganization as long as it could justify its request. Once the judge ruled that the debtor has been given sufficient time, any creditor could submit a reorganization plan. The new law caps the exclusivity period at 18 months from the day of the bankruptcy filing. The debtor then has an additional two months to win the creditors' acceptance of the plan, thereby providing a *debtor-in-position* a maximum of 20 months before creditors can submit their reorganization plans.[4]

Before BAPCPA, Chapter 11 litigation often took several years before the reorganized firm emerged from bankruptcy. United Airlines exited from bankruptcy in February 2006 after 38 months in Chapter 11, the longest period under court protection in U.S. bankruptcy history. UAL used the time to radically restructure the company and trim $7 billion in annual

---

[4] In addition to increased privileges for creditors via the amended bankruptcy laws, lessors (i.e., owners of the leased asset) also benefit from BAPCPA amendments. "Good-cause" extensions are restricted to 90 days without written consent of the lessor. Under prior legislation, leases could be extended indefinitely as long as the debtor-in-position continued making payments due under the commercial lease. Under the new legislation, the trustee or debtor-in-possession no longer would be able to get endless extensions, even if the debtor is paying the rent according to the terms of the lease agreement. BAPCPA also limits pay for key employees. Payments to management employees cannot be more than ten times the amount paid to nonmanagement employees.

costs, including two rounds of employee pay cuts and the elimination of 25,000 jobs. The firm also transferred successfully its defined benefit pension plans to the U.S Pension Benefit Guaranty Corporation and further reduced its cost structure by shedding more than 100 planes from its fleet, cutting some U.S. flights, and expanding internationally.

Finally, Chapter 15 was added to the U.S. Bankruptcy Code by BAPCPA of 2005 to reflect the adoption of the Model Law on Cross-Border Insolvency passed by the United Nations Commission on International Trade Law (UNCITRAL) in 1997. The purpose of UNCITRAL is to provide for better coordination among legal systems for cross-border bankruptcy cases. Chapter 15 is discussed in more detail later in this chapter.

Filing for Chapter 11 Reorganization

Chapter 11 reorganization may involve a corporation, sole proprietorship, or partnership. Since a corporation is viewed as separate from its owners (i.e., the shareholders), the Chapter 11 bankruptcy of a corporation does not put the personal assets of the stockholders at risk, other than the value of their investment in the firm's stock. In contrast, sole proprietor-ships and owners are not separate; a bankruptcy case involving a sole proprietorship includes both the business and personal assets of the owner–debtor. Like a corporation, a partnership exists as a separate entity apart from its partners. In a partnership bankruptcy case, the part-ners may be sued such that their personal assets are used to pay creditors. The partners them-selves may have to file for bankruptcy.

Figure 16.1 summarizes the process for filing for reorganization under Chapter 11. The pro-cess begins by filing in a federal bankruptcy court. In the case of an involuntary petition, a hearing must be held to determine whether the firm is insolvent. If the firm is found to be insolvent, the court enters an *order for relief*, which initiates the bankruptcy proceedings. On the filing of a reorganization petition, the filing firm becomes the *debtor-in-possession* of all the assets and has a maximum of 20 months to convince creditors to accept its reorgani-zation plan, after which the creditors can submit their own proposal. In the case of fraud, creditors may request that the court appoint a trustee instead of the debtor to manage the firm during the reorganization period.

The U.S. Trustee (the bankruptcy department of the U.S. Justice Department) appoints one or more committees to represent the interests of creditors and shareholders. The purpose of these committees is to work with the debtor-in-possession to develop a reorganization plan for exiting Chapter 11. Creditors and shareholders are grouped according to the similarity of claims. In the case of creditors, the plan must be approved by holders of at least two-thirds of the dollar value of the claims, as well as a simple majority of the creditors in each group. In the case of shareholders, two-thirds of those in each group (e.g., common and preferred shareholders) must approve the plan. Following acceptance by creditors, bondholders,

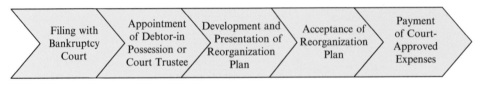

FIGURE 16.1 Procedures for reorganizing during bankruptcy.

and stockholders, the bankruptcy court also must approve the reorganization plan. Even if creditors or shareholders vote to reject the plan, the court is empowered to ignore the vote and approve the plan if it finds the plan fair to creditors and shareholders as well as feasible. Finally, the debtor-in-possession is responsible for paying the expenses approved by the court of all parties whose services contributed to the approval or disapproval of the plan.

Although intended to give firms time to restructure, whether a business is likely to be successful in Chapter 11 in part depends on the type of business and the circumstances under which it seeks the protection of the bankruptcy court. The credit crisis of 2008, which saw global banks write down more than $300 billion in assets and caused the hurried sales of Bear Stearns, Merrill Lynch, Wachovia, and Washington Mutual, also forced investment banking behemoth Lehman Brothers to seek protection from its creditors.

Case Study 16.1 illustrates the race against time to salvage as much of the firm's franchise as possible and how circumstances overcame Lehman's plans to restructure the business. Lehman Brothers had a plan in place to restructure operations, reduce the overall cost structure, and improve performance. Top executives intended to sell a majority of the firm's investment management business, which included money manager Neuberger Berman, and spin off its troubled real estate loans into a publicly traded unit. The firm also had explored the sale of its broker–dealer operations (i.e., a broker network and securities trading business). However, plans take time to implement, and, with the loss of confidence in the capital markets in general and Lehman in particular, the firm simply ran out of time and options.

CASE STUDY 16.1
Lehman Brothers Files for Chapter 11 in the Biggest Bankruptcy in U.S. History

A casualty of the 2008 credit crisis that shook Wall Street to its core, Lehman Brothers Holdings, Inc., a holding company, announced on September 15, 2008, that it had filed a petition under Chapter 11 of the U.S. Bankruptcy Code. Lehman's board of directors decided to opt for court protection after attempts to find a buyer for the entire firm collapsed. With assets of $639 billion and liabilities of $613 billion, Lehman is the largest bankruptcy in history in terms of assets. The next biggest bankruptcies were WorldCom and Enron with $126 billion and $81 billion in assets, respectively.

None of the holding company's subsidiaries was included in the filing, enabling customers of Lehman's brokerage, Neuberger Berman Holdings, to continue to use their accounts to trade. Furthermore, by excluding its units from the bankruptcy filing, the customers of its broker–dealer operations would not be subject to claims by LBHI's more than 100,000 creditors in the bankruptcy case.

Prior to the Dodd-Frank Act of 2010 (see Chapter 2) limiting such rights, counterparties could cancel contracts when a financial services firm went bankrupt. Lehman would normally hedge or protect its investments by taking opposite positions to minimize potential losses in its derivatives portfolios. Derivatives are financial instruments whose value changes in response to the value of the underlying assets over a specific period. For example, if the firm purchased a contract to buy oil at a specific price at some point in the future, it would also sell a contract at a somewhat lower price to another party (called a *counterparty*) to minimize losses if the price of oil dropped. Thus, the bankruptcy filing left Lehman's investment positions unprotected.

CASE STUDY 16.1   *(cont'd)*

On September 20, 2008, Barclays PLC, a major U.K. bank, acquired Lehman's broker–dealer operations for $250 million and paid an additional $1.5 billion for the firm's New York headquarters building and two New Jersey–based data centers. Coming just five days after Lehman filed for bankruptcy, the deal reflected the urgency to find buyers for those businesses whose value consisted primarily of their employees. Barclays did not buy any of Lehman's commercial real estate assets or private equity and hedge fund investments. However, Barclays did agree to take $47.4 billion in securities and assume $45.5 billion in trading liabilities.

On September 24, 2008, Japanese brokerage Nomura Securities acquired Lehman's Japanese and Australian operation for $250 million. Lehman's investment management group, Neuberger Berman, was sold in late December 2008 to a Neuberger management group for $922 million. Under the deal, Neuberger's management would own 51 percent of the firm, and Lehman's creditors would control the remainder. Other Lehman assets, consisting primarily of complex derivatives ranging from oil price futures to credit default swaps (i.e., debt insurance) to options on stock indices, with more than 8,000 counterparties, were expected to take years to identify, value, and liquidate. The firm also could expect to face numerous lawsuits.

The October 18, 2008, auction of $400 billion of Lehman's debt issues was valued at 8.5 cents on the dollar. Because such debt was backed by only the firm's creditworthiness, the buyers of the Lehman debt had purchased insurance from other financial institutions to mitigate the risk of a Lehman default. The existence of these credit default swap arrangements meant that the insurers were required to pay Lehman bondholders $366 billion (i.e., $0.915 \times \$400$ billion). Purchasers of this debt were betting that, following Lehman's liquidation, holders of this debt would receive more than 8.5 cents on the dollar and the insurers would be able to satisfy their obligations.

Hedge funds also were affected by the Lehman bankruptcy. Hedge funds borrowed heavily from Lehman, putting up certain assets as collateral for the loans. While legal, Lehman was using this collateral to borrow from other firms. By using its customers' collateral as its own collateral, Lehman and other firms could borrow more money, using the proceeds to make additional investments. When Lehman filed for bankruptcy, the court took control of such assets until who was entitled to the assets could be determined. Moreover, while derivative agreements were designed to terminate whenever a party declares bankruptcy and be settled outside of court, Lehman's general creditors may lay claim to any collateral whose value exceeds the value of the derivative agreements. Disentangling these claims will take years.

In early 2010, a report compiled by bank examiners described how Lehman manipulated its financial statements, leaving the investing public, the credit rating agencies, government regulators, and Lehman's board of directors totally unaware of the accounting tricks. By departing from common accounting practices, Lehman appeared to be less levered than it actually was. It was pressure from speculators, sensing that the firm was in disarray, that uncovered the scam by selling Lehman's stock short and accomplishing what the regulators and credit rating agencies could not. See the Inside M&A case study at the beginning of Chapter 2 for more details on Lehman's accounting practices.

CASE STUDY 16.1 *(cont'd)*

Discussion Questions

1. Why did Lehman choose not to seek Chapter 11 protection for its subsidiaries?

2. How does Chapter 11 bankruptcy protect Lehman's creditors? How does it potentially hurt them? Explain your answers.

3. Do you believe the U.S. bankruptcy process was appropriate in this instance? Explain your answer.

4. Do you believe the U.S. government's failure to bail out Lehman, thereby forcing the firm to file for bankruptcy, exacerbated the global credit meltdown in October 2008? Explain your answer.

U.S. automotive parts manufacturer Dana Corporation used Chapter 11 bankruptcy in 2008 to achieve substantial cost savings from employees and suppliers, price increases from customers, and concessions from its creditors. These actions enabled the firm to avoid liquidation, which may have resulted in a much larger loss of jobs and tax revenue in the communities in which the firm had operations, while enabling creditors to recover a larger portion of their claims.

Implementing Chapter 7 Liquidation

If the bankruptcy court determines that reorganization is infeasible, the failing firm may be forced to liquidate. A trustee is given the responsibility to liquidate the firm's assets, keep records, examine creditors' claims, disburse the proceeds, and submit a final report on the liquidation. The priority in which the claims are paid is stipulated in Chapter 7 of the Bankruptcy Reform Act, which must be followed by the trustee when the firm is liquidated.[5] All secured creditors are paid when the firm's assets that were pledged as collateral are liquidated. If the proceeds of the sale of these assets are inadequate to satisfy all of the secured creditors' claims, they become unsecured or general creditors for the amount that was not recovered. If the proceeds of the sale of pledged assets exceed secured creditors' claims, the excess proceeds are used to pay general creditors.

Liquidation under Chapter 7 does not mean that all employees lose their jobs. When a large firm enters Chapter 7 bankruptcy, a division of the company may be sold intact to other companies during the liquidation. For example, the sale of several Lehman Brothers operating units in 2008, while the firm was in bankruptcy, preserved the jobs of as many as 10,000 of the firm's 25,000 employees in place before the bankruptcy.

Fully secured creditors, such as bondholders or mortgage lenders, have a legally enforceable right to the collateral securing their loans or the equivalent value. A creditor is fully

---

[5] Chapter 7 distributes the liquidation proceeds according to the following priorities: (1) administrative claims (e.g., lawyers' fees, court costs, accountants' fees, trustees' fees, and other costs necessary to liquidate the firm's assets), (2) statutory claims (e.g., tax obligations, rent, consumer deposits, and unpaid wages and benefits owed before the filing up to some threshold), (3) secured creditors' claims, (4) unsecured creditors' claims, and (5) equity claims.

secured if the value of the collateral for its loan to the debtor equals or exceeds the amount of the debt. For this reason, fully secured creditors are not entitled to participate in any distribution of liquidated assets that the bankruptcy trustee might make.

Exhibit 16.2 describes how a legally bankrupt company could be liquidated. In this illustration, the bankruptcy court, owners, and creditors could not agree on an appropriate reorganization plan for DOA Inc. Consequently, the court ordered that the firm be liquidated in accordance with Chapter 7. Note that this illustration would differ from a private or voluntary out-of-court liquidation in two important respects. First, the expenses associated with conducting the liquidation would be lower because the liquidation would not involve extended legal proceedings. Second, the distribution of proceeds could reflect a priority of claims negotiated between the creditors and the owners that differs from those set forth in Chapter 7 of the Bankruptcy Reform Act.

EXHIBIT 16.2 LIQUIDATION OF DOA INC. UNDER CHAPTER 7

DOA has the balance sheet shown in Table 16.3. The only liability that is not shown on the balance sheet is the cost of the bankruptcy proceedings, which are treated as expenses and are

TABLE 16.3   DOA Balance Sheet

Assets		Liabilities	
Cash	$ 35,000	Accounts Payable	$750,000
Accounts Receivable	2,300,000	Bank Notes Payable	3,000,000
Inventories	2,100.000	Accrued Salaries	720,000
Total Current Assets	$4,435,000	Unpaid Benefits	140,000
Land	1,500,000	Unsecured Customer Deposits	300,000
Net Plant and Equipment	2,000,000	Taxes Payable	400,000
Total Fixed Assets	$ 3,500,000	Total Current Liabilities	$5,310,000
Total Assets	**$ 7,935,000**	**First Mortgage**	**2,500,000**
		Unsecured Debt	200,000
		Total Long-Term Debt	$2,700,000
		Preferred Stock	50,000
		Common Stock	100,000
		Paid in Surplus	500,000
		Retained Earnings	(725,000)
		Total Stockholders' Equity	$ (75,000)
		Total Shareholders' Equity and Total Liabilities	**$7,935,000**

not capitalized. The sale of DOA's assets generates $5.4 million in cash. The distribution of the proceeds is displayed in Table 16.4. Note that the proceeds are distributed in accordance with the priorities stipulated in the current commercial bankruptcy law and that the cost of administering the bankruptcy totals 18% (i.e., $972,000 ÷ $5,400,000) of the proceeds from liquidation.

Once all prior claims have been satisfied, the remaining proceeds are distributed to the unsecured creditors. The pro rata or proportional settlement percentage of 27.64% is calculated by dividing funds available for unsecured creditors by the amount of unsecured creditor claims (i.e., $1,368 ÷ $4,950). The shareholders receive nothing because not all unsecured creditor claims have been satisfied (Table 16.5).

TABLE 16.4   Distribution of Liquidation Proceeds

	Amount
Proceeds from Liquidation	$5,400,000
Expenses of Administering Bankruptcy	972,000
Salaries Owed Employees	720,000
Unpaid Employee Benefits	140,000
Unsecured Customer Deposits	300,000
Taxes	400,000
Funds Available for Creditors	$2,868,000
First Mortgage (From sale of fixed assets)	1,500,000
Funds Available for Unsecured Creditors	$1,368,000

TABLE 16.5   Pro Rata Distribution of Funds among Unsecured Creditors

Unsecured Creditor Claims	Amount	Settlement at 27.64%
Unpaid Balance from First Mortgage	$1,000,000	$ 276,400
Accounts Payable	750,000	207,300
Notes Payable	3,000,000	829,200
Unsecured Debt	200,000	55,280
Total	**$4,950,000**	**$1,368,000**

"Section 363 Sales" from Chapter 11

So-called 363 sales have become increasingly popular in recent years when time is critical. Section 363 bankruptcies allow a firm to enter a court-supervised sale of assets—usually an auction—as the best means of protecting the value of such assets. Unlike typical bankruptcies, firms may emerge in as little as 30 to 60 days.

The auction process starts with a prospective buyer setting the initial purchase price and terms, as well as negotiating a *topping fee* to be paid if it is not successful in buying the assets. Often referred to as a *stalking horse*, the identity of the initial bidder may be concealed. *Credit bids* occur when secured creditors propose to buy the assets. Such bidders can bid up to the amount of the debt owed before offering any cash. In 2010, creditors outbid an investor group to acquire the *Philadelphia Inquirer* for an amount equal to $318 million, about one-half of what they were owed by the newspaper.

Creditors opposing the sale have only 10 to 20 days to file written objections to the court, although the period may be shortened to as little as a few days by the bankruptcy judge. The bankruptcy judge decides how the proceeds of the auction are distributed among secured creditors.

The Chapter 11 bankruptcy proceedings of automakers General Motors and the Chrysler in 2009 are among the most visible 363 sales. Chrysler LLC was sold to a new company managed by Italian carmaker Fiat that would operate as Chrysler Group LLC and consist of the Chrysler, Jeep, Dodge, and Mopar brands. The ownership distribution of the new company emerging from Chapter 11 was United Auto Workers (55%), Fiat (20%, growing to 35% once certain milestones had been reached), the U.S. government (8%), and the Canadian government (2%). The outcome of this proceeding was particularly controversial in that the *absolute priority rule* appears to have been violated. Under this federal bankruptcy code rule, no unsecured creditor can receive an interest in a reorganized firm before secured creditors are paid in full or are provided a fair distribution. However, in this instance, the UAW received for its pension obligations—an unsecured claim—a much higher ownership stake than the value of the cash received by secured creditors.

The resolution of the GM 363 sale involved splitting the firm into two companies. The U.S. and Canadian operations only were included in the GM bankruptcy filing. "New GM" contained the "good assets," while all the other assets were retained in "Old GM." "New GM" represented a new corporation containing only the attractive assets held by the U.S. and Canadian operations and is primarily owned by the U.S. and Canadian governments, a UAW healthcare trust, and the creditors of "Old GM." Following approval of the Chapter 11 plan of reorganization, a postliquidating trust directed by a court-appointed trustee was established to dispose of "Old GM" assets, with the proceeds going to the creditors. For a more detailed discussion, see Case Study 16.2 at the end of the chapter.

Chapter 15: Dealing with Cross-Border Bankruptcy

As noted previously in this chapter, the purpose of Chapter 15 of the U.S. Bankruptcy Code is to provide mechanisms for resolving insolvency cases involving assets, lenders, and other parties in various countries. In general, a Chapter 15 case is ancillary or secondary to the primary proceeding brought in another country, which is typically the debtor's home country. As an alternative to Chapter 15, the debtor may proceed with a Chapter 7 or Chapter 11 case in the United States. As part of a Chapter 15 proceeding, the U.S. Bankruptcy Court may authorize a trustee to act in a foreign country on its behalf.

Under Chapter 15, an ancillary case is initiated by a "foreign representative" filing a petition for recognition of a "foreign proceeding." As such, Chapter 15 gives the foreign representative the right to petition the U.S. court system for resolving insolvency issues. Once processed by the U.S. court, the petition gives the court the authority to issue an order recognizing the foreign proceeding as either a "foreign main proceeding" or a "foreign nonmain proceeding." A foreign main proceeding is a proceeding in a country where the debtor's main interests are located. A foreign nonmain proceeding is a proceeding in a country where the debtor has an establishment not representing its primary holdings. If recognized as a foreign main proceeding, the court imposes an automatic stay on assets in dispute in the United States and authorizes the foreign representative to operate the debtor's business.[6]

In late 2008, judges in Canada and the United States approved key elements of an agreement enabling Hollinger Inc., a Canadian-based newspaper holding company, to emerge from the protection of bankruptcy court. Bondholders sent Hollinger into insolvency protection in Canada and Chapter 15 in the United States. A key component of the agreement with Davidson Kempner, holder of about 40 percent of the more than $100 million owed by Hollinger, involved the elimination of the supervoting control shares held by a major stockholder. The shareholder agreed to convert supervoting shares in Hollinger's largest investment (i.e., Sun-Times Media Group) for one-vote, one-share common stock. Hollinger's creditors would receive the new shares as part of an agreement to dispense with the debt they are owed.

Motivations for Filing for Bankruptcy

Although most companies that file for bankruptcy do so because of their deteriorating financial position, companies increasingly are seeking bankruptcy protection to enhance negotiating leverage, avoid litigation, and minimize exposure to potentially onerous future liabilities. In the mid-1980s, Johns Manville Corporation used bankruptcy to negotiate a reduction in huge liability awards granted in the wake of asbestos-related lawsuits. Similarly, Texaco used the threat of bankruptcy in the early 1990s as a negotiating ploy to reduce the amount of court-ordered payments to Occidental Petroleum resulting from the court's determination that Texaco had improperly intervened in a pending merger transaction. More recently, a bankruptcy judge in late 2004 approved a settlement enabling two subsidiaries of the energy giant Halliburton to emerge from bankruptcy and to limit their exposure to potential future asbestos claims by establishing a $4.2 billion trust fund to pay such claims.

In 2001, LTV sold its plants while in bankruptcy to W.L. Ross and Company, which restarted the plants in 2002 in a new company, the International Steel Group. By simply buying assets, ISI eliminated its obligation to pay pension, healthcare, or insurance liabilities,

---

[6] Chapter 15 also gives foreign creditors the right to participate in U.S. bankruptcy cases and prohibits discrimination against foreign creditors. The Chapter 15 proceeding attempts to promote collaboration between U.S and foreign courts, since the participants in the proceeding must cooperate fully.

which remained with LTV. Delphi, the ailing auto parts manufacturer, used its bankrupt status to threaten to abrogate union contracts to gain substantial wage and benefit concessions from its employees in 2007.

Effectiveness of Chapter 11 Reorganization versus Chapter 7 Liquidation

Chapter 7 liquidations appear to be as costly as Chapter 11 reorganization, in terms of legal expenses and related fees, as well as the time required to complete the proceedings. However, Chapter 11 reorganization allows creditors to recover relatively more of their claims than under liquidation. In liquidation, bankruptcy professionals, including attorneys, accountants, and trustees, often end up with the majority of the proceeds generated by selling the assets of the failing firm.[7]

Professional Fees Associated with the Bankruptcy Process

Factors explaining most of the variation in professional fees from one bankruptcy to another include company size, duration, complexity, and the number of parties involved. These factors measure not only the need for professional services but also the opportunity to bill.[8] Efforts to contain costs have prompted a greater use of auctions and other market-based techniques to privatize bankruptcy. These techniques include *prepackaged bankruptcies* with a reorganization plan in place at the time of the bankruptcy filing, acquisition of distressed debt by *vulture investors* willing to support the proposed plan of reorganization, and voluntary auction-based sales while a firm is under the protection of Chapter 11. Despite the increasing use of innovative ways of expediting the bankruptcy process, the cost of professional services remains high. While large and complex, estimated fees paid to bankruptcy advisors, such as appraisers and investment bankers, and legal fees since the Lehman Brothers liquidation began in September 2008, exceeded $800 million by the end of 2010.

Prepackaged Bankruptcies

Under a *prepackaged bankruptcy*, the debtor negotiates with creditors well in advance of filing for a Chapter 11 bankruptcy. Because there is general approval of the plan before the filing, the formal Chapter 11 reorganization that follows generally averages only a few months and results in substantially lower legal and administrative expenses.[9] More than one-fifth of major

[7] Bris, Welch, and Zhu, 2006

[8] In a study of 74 large public bankruptcies between 1998 and 2003, Lopucki and Doherty (2007) found that company size (measured by assets), case duration (measured in days), and the number of parties involved in the proceedings (measured in terms of the numbers of professional firms working) explain 87% of the case-to-case variation in professional fees. The study reviewed 74 large public company bankruptcies between 1998 and 2003. Fees and expenses increased about 9% annually during that period. The authors argue that these factors measure not only the need for professional services but also the opportunity for professionals to bill. The authors came to the same conclusion after adjusting for differences in case complexity by including such variables in their analysis as the number of employees, docket length, and the number of parties to the reorganization plan.

[9] Altman, 1993; Betker, 1995; Tashjian, Lease, and McConnell, 1996

bankruptcy cases between 2001 and 2005 were prepackaged deals.[10] Prepackaged bankrupt-cies are often a result of major creditors anticipating a potential liquidation in bankruptcy as occurring at "fire sale" prices.[11] Prepackaged bankruptcies work best when a limited number of sophisticated secured creditors are involved, enabling the negotiations to proceed rapidly.

In a true prepackaged bankruptcy, creditors approve a reorganization plan before filing for bankruptcy. The bankruptcy court then approves the plan and the company emerges from bankruptcy quickly. Minority creditors are often required by the court to accept a plan of re-organization. The confirmation of a plan of reorganization over the objections of one or more classes of creditors sometimes is referred to as a *cram down*.

Prepackaged bankruptcy provides tax benefits not found in workouts. If a firm enters into a workout in which a voluntary negotiated agreement with debtors is achieved, the firm may lose its right to claim net operating losses in its tax filing.[12] In bankruptcy, the firm may claim the right to NOLs if the court rules the firm insolvent (i.e., negative net worth). In addition, if a debtor company reaches a voluntary agreement outside of bankruptcy court whereby creditors agree to cancel a certain percentage of debt, the amount is treated as in-come for tax purposes. A similar debt restructuring in bankruptcy does not create such a tax liability.

On November 4, 2010, U.S. movie studio Metro-Goldwyn-Mayer filed a prepackaged Chapter 11 bankruptcy in New York that had the approval of nearly all of its creditors. The week before, creditors had approved a plan to forgive more than $4 billion in debt for ownership stakes in the restructured studio and to replace existing management. The bank-ruptcy was approved the following month, with the reorganized firm emerging from court protection having raised $600 million in new financing.

ANALYZING STRATEGIC OPTIONS FOR FAILING FIRMS

A failing firm's strategic options are to merge with another firm, reach an out-of-court vol-untary settlement with creditors, or file for Chapter 11 bankruptcy. Note that the prepackaged bankruptcy discussed earlier in this chapter constitutes a blend of the second and third options. The firm may voluntarily liquidate as part of an out-of-court settlement or be forced to liquidate under Chapter 7 of the Bankruptcy Code. Table 16.6 summarizes the implications of each option. The choice of which option to pursue is critically dependent on which provides the greatest present value for creditors and shareholders. To evaluate these options, the firm's management needs to estimate the going concern, selling price, and liquidation values of the firm.

---

[10] Lovly, 2007

[11] Eckbo and Thorburn, 2008

[12] This could occur if the original creditors exchange their debt for equity and the original equity holders own less than 50% of the company. As such, the Internal Revenue Service would view this as a loss of control by the original shareholders and a violation of the "continuity of interests" principle discussed in Chapter 12.

TABLE 16.6　Alternative Strategies for Failing Firms

Assumptions	Options: Failing Firm	Outcome: Failing Firm
Selling Price > Going Concern or Liquidation Value	1. Is acquired by another firm 2. Merges with another firm	1. Continues as subsidiary of acquirer 2. Merged into acquirer and ceases to exist
Going Concern Value > Sale or Liquidation Value	1. Reaches out-of-court settlement with creditors 2. Seeks bankruptcy protection under Chapter 11 3. Seeks prepackaged settlement with primary creditors before entering Chapter 11	1. Continues with debt for equity swap, extension, and composition 2. Continues in reorganization
Liquidation Value > Sale or Going Concern Value	1. Reaches out-of-court settlement with creditors 2. Liquidates under Chapter 7	1. Ceases to exist; assignee liquidates assets and distributes proceeds reflecting terms of negotiated settlement with creditors 2. Ceases to exist; trustee supervises liquidation and distributes proceeds according to statutory priorities

Merging with Another Firm

If the failing firm's management estimates that the sale price of the firm is greater than the going concern or liquidation value, management should seek to be acquired by or to merge with another firm. If there is a strategic buyer, management must convince the firm's creditors that they will be more likely to receive what they are owed and shareholders are more likely to preserve share value if the firm is acquired rather than liquidated or allowed to remain independent. In some instances, buyers are willing to acquire failing firms only if their liabilities are reduced through the bankruptcy process. Hence, it may make sense to force the firm into bankruptcy to have some portion of its liabilities discharged during the process of Chapter 11 reorganization.[13] Alternatively, the potential buyer could reach agreement in advance of bankruptcy reorganization with the primary creditors (i.e., a prepackaged bankruptcy) and employ the bankruptcy process to achieve compliance from the minority creditors.

Sales within the protection of Chapter 11 reorganization may be accomplished either by a negotiated private sale to a particular purchaser or through a public auction. The latter is often favored by the court, since the purchase price is more likely to reflect the true market value of the assets. Generally, a public auction can withstand any court challenge by creditors questioning whether the purchaser has paid fair market value for the failing firm's assets. International Steel Group's acquisition of LTV Steel's assets in 2002 and the bankrupt Bethlehem Steel in early 2003, and U.S. Steel's purchase of bankrupt National Steel shortly thereafter, are examples of such transactions. In 2005, Time Warner Inc. and Comcast Corp. reached an agreement to buy bankrupt cable operator Adelphia Communications Corporation while it

---

[13] To protect it from litigation, Washington Construction Group required Morrison Knudsen Corporation to file for bankruptcy as a closing condition in the agreement of purchase and sale in 2000.

was in Chapter 11 for nearly $18 billion. Time Warner and Comcast paid Adelphia bond-holders and other creditors in cash and warrants for stock in a new company formed by combining Time Warner's cable business and Adelphia.

Bidders tend to overpay for firms purchased out of Chapter 11, with such strategies benefiting target firm but not acquirer shareholders. In most cases, the acquirers fail to successfully restructure the target firms.[14]

Reaching an Out-of-Court Voluntary Settlement with Creditors

Alternatively, the going concern value of the firm may exceed the sale or liquidation value. Management must be able to demonstrate to creditors that a restructured or downsized firm would be able to repay its debts if creditors were willing to accept less, extend the maturity of the debt, or exchange debt for equity.

A voluntary settlement may be difficult to achieve because the debtor often needs the approval of all its creditors. Known as the *holdout problem*, smaller creditors have an incentive to attempt to hold up the agreement unless they receive special treatment. Consensus may be accomplished by paying all small creditors 100 percent of what they are owed and the larger creditors an agreed-on percentage. Other factors limiting voluntary settlements, such as a debt-for-equity swap, include a preference by some creditors for debt rather than equity and the lack of the necessary information to enable proper valuation of the equity offered to the creditors. Because of these factors, there is some evidence that firms attempting to restructure outside of Chapter 11 bankruptcy have more difficulty in reducing their indebtedness than those that negotiate with creditors while under the protection of Chapter 11.[15] If management cannot reach agreement with the firm's creditors, it may seek protection under Chapter 11.

Voluntary and Involuntary Liquidations

The failing firm's management, shareholders, and creditors may agree that the firm is worth more in liquidation than in sale or as a continuing operation. If management cannot reach agreement with its creditors on a private liquidation, the firm may seek Chapter 7 liquidation. The proceeds of a private liquidation are distributed in accordance with the agreement negotiated with creditors, while the order in which claimants are paid under Chapter 7 is set by statute.

FAILING FIRMS AND SYSTEMIC RISK

In response to the meltdown in global financial markets in 2008 and 2009, the U.S. Congress passed the Dodd-Frank Wall Street Reform and Consumer Protections Act of 2010 (Dodd-Frank). Among other things, the Act created a new government mechanism to dismantle

---

[14] In a study of 38 takeovers of distressed firms from 1981 to 1988, Clark and Ofek (1994) found that bidders tend to overpay for these types of firms. Although this strategy may benefit the failing firm's shareholders, such takeovers do not seem to benefit the acquirer's shareholders. Clark and Ofek also found that the acquiring firms often fail successfully to restructure the target firms.

[15] Gilson, 1997

financial services firms whose imminent demise would endanger the U.S. financial system and economy.

The objectives of the resolution authority are to ensure a speedy liquidation of a firm through a mechanism called the Orderly Liquidation Authority (OLA), that the losses are primarily borne by the firm's shareholders and creditors, while minimizing the loss of taxpayer funds, and to penalize current management. Because the measure applies to corporations that are subject to the U.S. Bankruptcy Code, a determination by the designated government authorities that a company poses a systemic risk would enable the Federal Deposit Insurance Corporation (FDIC) to seize the firm and liquidate it under the OLA, thereby preempting any proceedings under the Bankruptcy Code. The OLA is solely a liquidation remedy and, unlike Chapter 11 of the U.S. Bankruptcy Code, does not allow for reorganization or rehabilitation as an option.

The new authority is modeled after the FDIC's resolution authority for insured depository institutions under the Federal Deposit Insurance Act. With the FDIC assuming full control as receiver, the debtor-in-position (i.e., the current management) is removed. The ability of the FDIC to seize a bank holding company allows it to conduct coordinated proceedings for the bank and its affiliates. The OLA gives the FDIC the right to terminate all contracts, including derivative contracts. The FDIC is required to resolve claims within 180 days of receivership having taken effect. Secured creditors faced with the prospect of loss of the value of their collateral may request expedited resolution of their claims within 90 days. However, as receiver, the FDIC may merge the firm with another or transfer any asset or liability without approval, consignment, or consent of creditors or other stakeholders. Officers and directors of the firm in receivership are exposed to significant financial liability. Their incentive and other compensation earned in the three years prior to receivership may be subject to "clawback" (i.e., repayment).

The order in which claimants are paid during liquidation is similar to that defined under Chapter 7, except that the government puts itself first. The cash proceeds of assets would first be used to pay the government, then to pay wages up to $11,725 per employee, and subsequently to pay senior and unsecured creditors, senior executives, and finally shareholders. If the government cannot recoup all of the taxpayer funds provided to the firm to fund the liquidation, it may enact a special assessment on other financial institutions regulated by the Federal Reserve.

The OLA applies only to U.S. companies that are bank holding companies, nonbank financial firms supervised by the Federal Reserve Board of Governors (the Fed), companies predominantly engaged in activities that the Fed determines are financial in nature, subsidiaries of such companies (other than insured depositor institutions or insurance companies), and brokers and dealers registered with the SEC and members of the Securities Investor Protection Corporation (SIPC), a fund designed to insure clients against broker/dealer fraud. The liquidation of insured depository institutions will continue to be the responsibility of the FDIC under the agency's current mandate. While insurance companies will continue to be subject to state regulation, their holding companies and unregulated affiliates are covered by the OLA.

The OLA is initiated with a request from the secretary of the Treasury that the FDIC be appointed receiver of a failing firm whose failure would jeopardize the U.S. financial system. To take effect, the request must be approved by a two-thirds vote of each of the Federal Reserve Board and the board of the FDIC, or by the SEC (in the case of a broker or dealer) or the Federal Insurance Office (in the case of an insurance company). Firms subject to the OLA must be in default or in danger of default and they must represent systemic risk.[16] If the board of directors of the failing firm agrees, the approval of the Federal Reserve and a second regulator is not required, since only a decision by the Treasury secretary is needed. Furthermore, any decision by the firm's board to accept receivership will not subject the board to liability.

The advantages of the OLA are that it provides the government with both the authority and a clear process for winding down expeditiously failing firms that are deemed a risk to the financial system. However, the resolution process for dealing with failing systemically risky firms can itself destabilize the financial system, since the process could panic investors and lenders. Furthermore, the OLA is applicable only to firms whose operations are wholly domestic, since there is currently no cross-border mechanism for resolving banks operating in multiple countries. Consequently, large, multinational banks will be unaffected by the OLA.

PREDICTING CORPORATE DEFAULT AND BANKRUPTCY

The ability to accurately anticipate default is an important component of any lender's risk management system. While the predictive accuracy of statistical models has improved significantly over the years, the widespread defaults during the 2008 and 2009 global recession underscore the need for further research.

Alternative Models

A review of 165 bankruptcy prediction studies published from 1930 to 2006 examined how modeling trends have changed by decade. Discriminant analysis was the primary method used to develop models in the 1960s and 1970s. However, the primary modeling methods shifted by the 1980s to logit analysis and neural networks. While the number of factors used in building the models varied by decade, the average model used about ten variables. In analyzing model accuracy, multivariate discriminant analysis and neural networks seem to be the most promising, and increasing the number of variables in the model does not guarantee greater accuracy. Interestingly, two-factor models are often as accurate as models with as many as 21 factors.[17]

An international study analyzed the empirical findings and methodologies employed in 46% studies applied in ten countries from 1968 to 2003. The study documented that bankruptcy prediction models typically used financial ratios to forecast business failure, with about 60 of the studies reviewed using only financial ratios. The remaining studies used both financial ratios and other information. The financial ratios typically included measures of liquidity, solvency, leverage, profitability, asset composition, firm size, and growth rate. The other information included macroeconomic, industry-specific, location, and firm-specific variables. This study concluded that the predictive accuracy of the various types of models investigated was very similar, correctly identifying failing firms about 80% of the time for

---

[16] The determination of whether a company is in default or in danger of default requires the application of certain insolvency tests to establish the likelihood that the firm will enter Chapter 11; that anticipated losses will deplete the firm's capital; and that assets will likely be less than the firm's obligations. See the section of this chapter entitled "Predicting Corporate Default and Bankruptcy" for more on the specific tests for insolvency.

[17] Bellovary, Giacomino, and Akers, 2007

firms in the sample employed in estimating the models. However, accuracy dropped substantially for out-of-sample predictions.[18]

Documenting potential problems with bankruptcy prediction models, researchers have found that model results often vary by industry and time period. Model accuracy also tends to decline when applied to periods different from those employed to develop the models (i.e., in-sample versus out-of-sample predictions). Moreover, applying models to industries other than those used to develop the models often results in greatly diminished accuracy.[19]

In view of the extensive literature on the subject, the following subsections discuss categories of models that differ by methodology and choice of variables used to predict bankruptcy. The intent of these subsections is to provide an overview of the state of such models.[20]

Models That Differ by Methodology

Bankruptcy prediction models tend to fall into three major categories: credit scoring models, structural models, and reduced form models.

Credit Scoring Models

One of the earliest (1960s) quantitative efforts to predict bankruptcy relied on discriminant analysis to distinguish between bankrupt and nonbankrupt firms.[21] Discriminant analysis uses a combination of independent variables to assign a score (i.e., a Z score) to a particular firm. This score then is used to distinguish between bankrupt and nonbankrupt firms by using a cutoff point. The Z score model formalized the more qualitative analysis of default risk offered by credit rating agencies such as Moody's Investors Services. Five key financial ratios were used to determine a firm's Z score. The likelihood of default for firms with low Z scores is less than for firms with high Z scores. The most significant financial ratios for predicting default are earnings before income and taxes as a percent of total assets and the ratio of sales to total assets. The major shortcoming of this approach is that it is a snapshot of a firm's financial health at a moment in time, and it does not reflect changes in a company's financial ratios over time. Tests of this methodology applied to more recent samples found that the earlier models' ability to classify bankrupt companies correctly fell from 83.5 to 57.8%.[22]

To compensate for the shortcomings of the discriminant model, analysts developed models to predict the probability of a firm defaulting over some future period. The model postulated that the default rate depended not only on the firm's current financial ratios but also on such forward-looking market variables as market capitalization, abnormal financial returns, and the volatility of such financial returns. The only financial ratios with significant predictive power are earnings before interest and taxes to total liabilities and the market value of equity to total liabilities.[23]

---

[18] Aziz and Dar, 2006

[19] Grice and Dugan, 2001

[20] For a more rigorous discussion of bankruptcy prediction models, see Jones and Hensher (2008).

[21] Altman, 1968

[22] Grice and Ingram, 2001

[23] Shumway, 2001

Structural Models

While credit scoring models do not estimate the probability of default, structural models attempt to do so. Often employing probit analysis, structural models are debt-pricing models that link the probability of default to the structure of a firm's assets and liabilities. Structural models of credit risk assume that firms default when they violate a debt covenant, their cash flow falls short of required debt payments, their assets become more valuable in competitors' hands, or their shareholders decide that servicing the debt is no longer in their best interests. Structural models can be very difficult to develop for firms with complex debt structures.

Logistic (logit) or probit regression models provide a conditional probability of an observation belonging to a particular category. Logit and probit models do not require assumptions as restrictive as discriminant analysis. Supporters of this approach argue that logit regression fits the characteristics of the default prediction problem. The dependent variable is binary (default/nondefault). The logit model yields a score between 0 and 1, which gives the probability of the firm defaulting.[24]

Reduced Form Models

In contrast to structural models, reduced form models use market prices of the distressed firm's debt as the only source of information about the firm's risk profile. Such prices are a proxy for the variables used in the structural models. Although easier to estimate, such models lack a specific link between credit risk and the firm's assets and liabilities and assume that the timing of default is random in that investors with incomplete data do not know how far the firm is from default. Default is triggered by some measure of distress crossing a threshold level or default boundary.[25]

Other Modeling Methods

While statistical discriminant analysis and probit or logit methods dominate the literature, they are not the only techniques used in bankruptcy prediction. Neural networks are a type of artificial intelligence that attempts to mimic the way a human brain works. Neural networks are particularly effective when the networks have a large database of prior examples.[26] The cumulative sums (CUSUM) methods represent a class of models that account for serial correlation (i.e., interdependencies) in the data and incorporate information from more than one period.[27] The options-based approach to bankruptcy prediction builds on option-pricing theory to explain business bankruptcy, relying on such variables as firm volatility to predict default.[28]

---

[24] A partial list of structural credit risk models includes the following: Kim, Ramaswamy, and Sundaresan, 1993; Leland, 1994; Longstaff and Schwartz, 1995; and Hsu, Saa-Requejo, and Santa-Clara, 2002.

[25] See Jarrow and Turnbull (1995) for examples of reduced form models.

[26] Platt et al., 1999

[27] Kahya and Theodosiou, 1999

[28] Charitou and Trigeorgis, 2000

Models Differing in Choice of Variables Used to Predict Bankruptcy

Accounting data are sometimes used to predict credit ratings, which serve as proxies for the probability of default.[29] Some analysts argue that the probability of failure depends on the length of the time horizon considered[30] or demonstrate a correlation between default rates and loss in the event of default and the business cycle.[31] "Shocks," such as recession and credit crunches, contribute to default by negatively affecting firm assets or cash flow.[32] Other studies use net worth as a key factor that affects a firm's ability to raise financing in a liquidity crisis[33] or equity returns and debt service ratios as measures of distress.[34]

VALUING DISTRESSED BUSINESSES

The intent of this section is to discuss ways of incorporating the impact of potential financial distress, default, and ultimately bankruptcy on the value of the firm. Historical performance may prove a poor guide to determining the future financial performance of businesses experiencing declining revenue and profitability, since it is unclear when or if they will recover.

Standard DCF methods attempt to adjust for financial distress by increasing the discount rate. Since the bulk of the firm's total value will come from its terminal value, this adjustment implies that the firm will be able to generate cash flows in perpetuity despite its weakened state. Consequently, it is likely that the value of the firm will be overstated.

To adjust DCF estimates, it is necessary to estimate the likelihood and cost of financial distress. In practice, it is extremely difficult to estimate the probability of a specific outcome such as the event of bankruptcy. We need to estimate not only the probability of a specific outcome annually but also the cumulative probability of that outcome, since a firm experiencing distress in one year is likely to continue to experience distress in subsequent years. Thus, the effect of financial distress tends to accumulate because a firm may be less able to reinvest such that future cash flows are reduced below what they would have been had the firm not experienced financial distress.

While there are many ways to value distressed firms, a common approach is the adjusted present value, or APV, method (see Chapter 13). The APV method requires the estimation of the value of the firm without debt by discounting the projected cash flows by the unlevered cost of equity; calculating the present value of interest tax savings at the unlevered cost of equity, since these tax benefits are subject to the same risk as the cash flows of an unlevered firm; and estimating the probability and cost of financial distress.

Table 16.7 illustrates the inclusion of financial distress in the valuation of the McClatchy Company using the adjusted present value method. McClatchy Company is a U.S.-based

[29] Blume, Lim, and MacKinlay, 1998; Molina, 2006; Avamov et al., 2006

[30] Duffie, Saita, and Wang, 2007

[31] Altman et al., 2003

[32] Hennessy and Whited, 2007; Anderson and Corverhill, 2007

[33] White, 1989

[34] Gilson, John, and Lang, 1990; Asquith, Gerthner, and Scharfstein, 1994

TABLE 16.7 Present Value of McClatchy Company Using the Adjusted Present Value Method

Company Data	2010	2011	2012	2013	2014	2015
Price/Share on March 10, 2010	5.19					
Fully Diluted Shares Outstanding	84,470,000					
Market Value (MV) of Equity March 10, 2010	$438,399,300	$650,896,030	$854,892,890	$1,054,809,813	$1,307,204,929	$1,616,136,550
Market Value (MV) of Debt March 10, 2010[a]	$740,249,905	$666,224,915	$599,602,423	$539,642,181	$485,677,963	$437,110,166
MV of Debt/MV of Equity Ratio	1.69	1.02	0.70	0.51	0.37	0.27
Weighted Average Maturity of McClatchy Debt	9.6 years					
McClatchy Credit Rating	B–					A
General Assumptions						
Comparable Company Unlevered Beta[b]	1.1344					
10-Year Treasury Bond Rate (%)	3.65					
Cumulative Probability of Default for Firm Rated B–[c]	0.4212					
Equity Premium	0.055					
McClatchy Company Assumptions						
Price/Earnings Ratio	6.00	4.00	4.00	4.00	5.00	6.00
Target Debt/Equity Ratio for 2015	0.33					
Implied Target Debt/Total Capital Ratio for 2015[d]	0.25					
Current Cost of Debt[e]	10.65					0.08
Expected Cost of Financial Distress (% of firm value)	0.15–0.40					
Terminal Period Growth Rate	0.03					
Unlevered Cost of Equity (2011–2015)[f]	0.0989					
Terminal Period WACC[g]	0.0862					

Continued

TABLE 16.7 Present Value of McClatchy Company Using the Adjusted Present Value Method—Cont'd

Company Data	2010	2011	2012	2013	2014	2015
Revenue	$1,471,584,000	$1,398,004,800	$1,342,084,608	$1,315,242,916	$1,328,395,345	$1,354,963,252
Net Income (3.8% of revenue)	$54,090,000	$53,124,182	$50,999,215	$49,979,231	$50,479,023	$51,488,604
Depreciation (8% of revenue)	$142,889,000	$111,840,384	$107,366,769	$105,219,433	$106,271,628	$108,397,060
Change in Working Capital (3.5% of revenue)	$73,579,000	$48,930,168	$46,972,961	$46,033,502	$46,493,837	$54,198,530
Gross Capital Spending	$13,574,000	$13,980,048	$20,131,269	$26,304,858	$33,209,884	$33,874,081
Principal Repayments	$64,200,000	$74,024,991	$66,622,491	$59,960,242	$53,964,218	$48,567,796
Dividends Paid	$14,905,000	$10,905,000	$5,905,000	$5,905,000	$5,905,000	$5,905,000
Equity Cash Flow	$30,721,000	$17,124,360	$18,734,262	$16,995,061	$17,177,712	$17,340,256
Interest expense	$107,353,000	$96,617,700	$86,955,930	$78,260,337	$70,434,303	$63,390,873
Tax Shield (40% of interest expense)	$42,941,200	$38,647,080	$34,782,372	$31,304,135	$28,173,721	$25,356,349
Adjusted Present Value						
PV Equity Cash Flow at 9.89%	$2,026,598					
PV Terminal Value	$1,445,999,847					
Total PV	$1,448,026,445					
Plus: PV of Tax Shield	$3,868,418					

	at 15%	at 20%	at 25%	at 30%	at 35%	at 40%
Adjusted Present Value of Firm	$1,451,894,863					
Less: Expected Cost of Financial Distress at 15%	$217,784,229					
Expected Cost of Financial Distress at 20%		$290,378,973				
Expected Cost of Financial Distress at 25%			$362,973,716			
Expected Cost of Financial Distress at 30%				$435,568,459		
Expected Cost of Financial Distress at 35%					$508,163,202	
Expected Cost of Financial Distress at 40%						$580,757,945
Less: Market Value of Debt	$740,249,837	$740,249,837	$740,249,837	$740,249,837	$740,249,837	$740,249,837
Equals: Equity Value	$493,860,796	$421,266,053	$348,671,310	$276,076,567	$203,481,824	$130,887,081
Equals: Equity Value Per Share	$5.85	$4.99	$4.13	$3.27	$2.41	$1.55

[a] $Market\ value\ of\ debt = Interest\ expense \times \{[1 - 1/(1+i)^n]/1+i\} + Face\ value\ of\ debt/(1+i)^n$
$= \$107,353,000 \times \{[1 - 1/(1.1065)^{9.6}]/1.1065\} + 1,796,436,000/(1.1065)^{9.6} = 60,298,095 + 679,951,810 = \$740,249,905.$

[b] $Comparable\ company\ unlevered\ beta = Comparable\ company\ levered\ beta/[(1 + (1 - marginal\ tax\ rate) \times (comparable\ company\ debt/equity)]$
$= 1.924/(1 + (1 - 0.4) \times 1.16) = 1.1344$ (Based on top 10 U.S. newspapers in terms of market capitalization).

[c] See Table 13.9 in Chapter 13.

[d] $Implied\ debt\text{-}to\text{-}total\ capital\ ratio = (D/E)/(1 + D/E) = 0.33/1.33 = 0.25.$

[e] Cost of debt equals the risk-free rate of 3.65 percent plus a 7 percent default spread based on McClatchy's rating of B− from S&P.

[f] $Unleveraged\ cost\ of\ equity = 0.0365 + 1.1344\ (0.055) = 0.0989.$

[g] $Terminal\ period\ WACC = 0.25 \times (1 - 0.4) \times 0.08 + 0.75 \times 0.0989 = 0.012 + 0.0742 = 0.0862.$

newspaper publisher owning 30 daily newspapers and 43 nondailies in 29 regional markets. The company also owns local websites offering a variety of content, engages in direct marketing and direct mail operations, and has minority interests in a series of digital businesses.

The entire newspaper industry has been experiencing long-term erosion in its readership base and a subsequent decline in advertising revenue. The decline in revenues was exacerbated by the 2008–2009 recession. The model assumes that the deterioration in revenues will continue through 2013 before showing a modest improvement in 2014–2015 as the firm transforms itself from primarily a print business to a digital media business. The key assumption in calculating the terminal value is an assumed 3% growth in cash flow in perpetuity.

As of March 10, 2010, the company was viewed by the major credit rating agencies as experiencing considerable financial distress and was rated below investment grade by Standard & Poor's credit rating agency. Such firms carry a B– credit rating and have an estimated cumulative probability of default of about 42% (see Table 13.9 in Chapter 13). Table 16.7 adjusts the value of the firm for the expected cost of bankruptcy ranging from 15% to 40% of the firm's APV. The cost of bankruptcy is assumed to be included in the cost of financial distress. The value of the firm's share price varies from a high of $5.85 (at 15%) to a low of $1.55 (at 40%). The firm's price per share of $5.19 at the time of the valuation suggests that investors believed the impact of financial distress was limited. See Chapter 13 for a more detailed discussion of the probability and cost of financial distress. The Excel model underlying Table 16.7 is available on the companion site in a file folder entitled "Estimating the Cost of Financial Distress."

EMPIRICAL STUDIES OF FINANCIAL DISTRESS

Many of the quantitative studies of firms in financial distress reveal an array of sometimes surprising results.

Attractive Returns to Firms Emerging from Bankruptcy Often Temporary

When firms emerge from bankruptcy, they often cancel the old stock and issue new common stock. Empirical studies show that such firms often show very attractive financial returns to holders of the new stock immediately following the announcement that the firm is emerging from bankruptcy.[35] However, long-term performance often deteriorates, with some studies showing that 40% of the firms studied experienced operating losses in the three years after emerging from Chapter 11. Almost one-third subsequently filed for bankruptcy or had to restructure their debt. After five years, about one-quarter of all firms that reorganized were liquidated, merged, or refiled for bankruptcy.[36] The most common reason for firms having to again file for bankruptcy is excessive debt, with such firms typically having 3:1 debt-to-equity ratios.

[35] Alderson and Betker, 1996; Eberhart, Altman, and Aggarwal, 1999

[36] Hotchkiss, 1995; France, 2002

Returns to Financially Distressed Stocks Unexpectedly Low

As a class, distressed stocks offer low financial rates of return despite their high risk of business failure.[37] In theory, one would expect such risky assets to offer financial returns commensurate with risk. The low financial return for distressed stocks tends to be worse for stocks with low analyst coverage, institutional ownership, and price per share. Factors potentially contributing to these low returns could include unexpected events, valuation errors by uninformed investors, and the characteristics of distressed stocks. Unexpected events could include the economy being worse than expected. Valuation errors include investors not understanding the relationship between variables used to predict failure and the risk of failure and therefore not having fully discounted the value of stocks to offset this risk. The characteristics of failing firms are such that some investors may have an incentive to hold such stocks despite their low returns. For example, majority owners of distressed stocks can benefit by buying the firm's output or assets at bargain prices. Consequently, the benefits from having control could exceed the low returns associated with financially distressed stocks.

Low returns to financially distressed stocks also may be related to the future potential for asset recovery. If expected recovery rates are high, the distressed firm's shareholders may deliberately trigger default by missing payments if they believe they can recover a significant portion of the value of their shares through renegotiation of credit terms with lenders. Consequently, the lower perceived risk of such shares would result in commensurately lower financial returns.[38]

IPOs More Likely to Experience Bankruptcy than Established Firms

Firms that have recently undergone IPOs tend to experience a much higher incidence of financial distress and bankruptcy than more established firms.[39] These findings are consistent with other studies showing that a portfolio of IPOs performs well below the return on the S&P 500 stock index for up to five years after the firms go public.[40] Some observers attribute this underperformance to the limited amount of information available on these firms.[41]

Financially Ailing Firms Can Be Contagious

A contagion in this context describes a situation in which the financial distress of one firm often spreads to other firms. For example, a declaration of bankruptcy by one firm can negatively impact rival firms and suppliers. The extent to which this may happen depends on whether the factors contributing to financial distress are impacting all firms within an

---

[37] Campbell, Hilscher, and Szilagyi, 2008

[38] Garlappi and Yan, 2011

[39] Beneda, 2007

[40] Aggarwal and Rivoli, 1990; Ritter, 1991; and Loughran, Ritter, and Rydqvist, 1994

[41] Grinblatt and Titman, 2002

industry or relate to a specific firm. The effects of financial distress may also differ depending on the degree to which an industry is concentrated. Studies show that rival stock prices react negatively to a competitor's bankruptcy in most industries; however, rival share prices may increase whenever a competitor declares bankruptcy in highly concentrated industries. The latter reflects the likelihood that the remaining competitors in concentrated industries will gain market share, enabling them to benefit from increased economies of scale and pricing power.[42] Furthermore, firms experiencing financial distress or in Chapter 11 are likely to experience declining sales and in turn to reduce their demand for raw materials and services from suppliers. When such firms represent important customers, suppliers often experience significant declines in valuations.[43]

There also is evidence that industry bankruptcies raise the cost of borrowing and reduce the access to credit of other industry participants by reducing the value of the collateral used to secure debt financing.[44] Specifically, firms experiencing financial distress are forced to sell assets and to reduce their purchases of similar assets, putting downward pressure on the value of such assets. Consequently, firms owning similar assets whose value has fallen will be forced to borrow less, pay more for credit, or both.

SOME THINGS TO REMEMBER

Bankruptcy is a federal legal proceeding designed to protect the technically or legally insolvent firm from lawsuits by its creditors until a decision is made to liquidate or reorganize the firm. In the absence of a voluntary settlement out of court, the debtor firm may voluntarily seek protection from its creditors by initiating bankruptcy or be forced into bankruptcy by its creditors. Once a petition is filed, the debtor firm is protected from any further legal action related to its debts until the bankruptcy proceedings are completed.

DISCUSSION QUESTIONS

16.1 Why are strong creditor rights important to an efficiently operating capital market? What is the purpose of bankruptcy in promoting capital market efficiency?

16.2 Of all the possible stakeholders in the bankruptcy process, which are likely to benefit the most? Which are likely to benefit the least? Explain your answer.

16.3 What are the advantages to the lender and the debtor firm's shareholders of reaching a negotiated settlement outside of bankruptcy court? What are the primary disadvantages?

16.4 How does the Bankruptcy Abuse Prevention and Consumer Protection Act of 2005 differ from the Bankruptcy Reform Act of 1978? In what ways do you feel that it represents an improvement? In what ways could the more recent legislation discourage reorganization in Chapter 11? Be specific.

[42] Lang and Stulz, 1992

[43] Hertzel, Li, Officer, and Rodgers, 2008

[44] Benmelech and Bergman, 2011

16.5 What are prepackaged bankruptcies? In what ways do they represent streamlining of the credit recovery process?

16.6 Why would creditors make concessions to a debtor firm? Give examples of common types of concessions. Describe how these concessions affect the debtor firm.

16.7 Although most companies that file for bankruptcy do so because of their deteriorating financial position, companies increasingly are seeking bankruptcy protection to avoid litigation. Give examples of how bankruptcy can be used to avoid litigation.

16.8 What are the primary options available to a failing firm? What criteria might the firm use to select a particular option? Be specific.

16.9 Describe the probable trend in financial returns to shareholders of firms that emerge from bankruptcy. To what do you attribute these trends? Explain your answer.

16.10 Identify at least two financial or nonfinancial variables that have been shown to affect firm defaults and bankruptcies. Explain how each might affect the likelihood that the firm will default or seek Chapter 11 protection.

16.11 On June 25, 2008, JHT Holdings, Inc., a Kenosha, Wisconsin–based package delivery service company, filed for bankruptcy. The firm had annual revenues of $500 million. What would the firm have to demonstrate for its petition to be accepted by the bankruptcy court?

16.12 Dura Automotive emerged from Chapter 11 protection in mid-2008. The firm obtained exit financing consisting of a $110 million revolving credit facility, a $50 million European first-lien term loan, and an $84 million U.S. second-lien loan. The reorganization plan specified how a portion of the proceeds of these loans would be used. What do you believe might be typical stipulations in reorganization plans for using such funds? Be specific.

16.13 What are the primary factors contributing to business failure? Be specific.

16.14 In recent years, hedge funds engaged in so-called loan-to-own prebankruptcy investments, in which they acquired debt from distressed firms at a fraction of face value. Subsequently, they moved the company into Chapter 11, intent on converting the acquired debt into equity in a firm with sharply reduced liabilities. The hedge fund also provided financing to secure its interest in the business. The emergence from Chapter 11 was typically accomplished under Section 363(k) of the Bankruptcy Code, which gives debtors the right to bid on the firm in a public auction sale. During the auction, the firm's debt was valued at face rather than market value, discouraging bidders other than the hedge fund, which acquired the debt prior to bankruptcy at distressed levels. Without competitive bidding, there was little chance of generating additional cash for the general creditors. Is this an abuse of the Chapter 11 bankruptcy process? Explain your answer.

16.15 American Home Mortgage Investments filed for Chapter 11 bankruptcy in late 2008. The company indicated that it chose this course of action because it represented the best means of preserving the firm's assets. W.L. Ross and Company agreed to provide the firm $50 million in debtor-in-possession financing to meet its anticipated cash needs while in Chapter 11. Comment on the statement that bankruptcy provides the best means of asset preservation. Why would W.L. Ross and Company lend money to a firm that had just filed for bankruptcy?

Answers to these Chapter Discussion Questions are found in the Online Instructor's Manual for instructors using this book.

CHAPTER BUSINESS CASES

CASE STUDY 16.2
The General Motors' Bankruptcy—The Largest Government-Sponsored Bailout in U.S. History

Rarely has a firm fallen as far and as fast as General Motors. Founded in 1908, GM dominated the car industry through the early 1950s, with its share of the U.S. car market reaching 54% in 1954, which proved to be the firm's high-water mark. Efforts in the 1980s to cut costs by building brands on common platforms blurred their distinctiveness. Following increasing healthcare and pension benefits paid to employees, concessions made to unions in the early 1990s to pay workers even when their plants were shut down reduced the ability of the firm to adjust to changes in the cyclical car market. GM was increasingly burdened by so-called legacy costs (i.e., healthcare and pension obligations to a growing retiree population).

Over time, GM's labor costs soared compared to the firm's major competitors. To cover these costs, GM continued to make higher-margin medium- to full-size cars and trucks, which in the wake of higher gas prices could only be sold with the help of highly attractive incentive programs. Forced to support an escalating array of brands, the firm was unable to provide sufficient marketing funds for any one of its brands.

With the onset of one of the worst global recessions in the post–World War II years, auto sales worldwide collapsed by the end of 2008. All automakers' sales and cash flows plummeted. Unlike Ford, GM and Chrysler were unable to satisfy their financial obligations. The U.S. government, in an unprecedented move, agreed to lend General Motors and Chrysler $13 billion and $4 billion, respectively.

The intent was to buy time to develop an appropriate restructuring plan.

Having essentially ruled out the liquidation of GM and Chrysler, continued government financing was contingent on gaining major concessions from all of the major stakeholders such as lenders, suppliers, and labor unions. With car sales continuing to show harrowing double-digit year over year declines during the first half of 2009, the threat of bankruptcy was used to motivate the disparate parties to come to an agreement. With available cash running perilously low, Chrysler entered bankruptcy in early May; General Motors filed on June 1, with the government providing debtor-in-possession financing during their time in bankruptcy. In its bankruptcy filing for its U.S. and Canadian operations only, GM listed $82.3 billion in assets and $172.8 billion in liabilities. In less than 45 days each, both GM and Chrysler emerged from government-sponsored sale in bankruptcy court, a feat that many thought impossible.

Judge Robert E. Gerber of the U.S. Bankruptcy Court of New York approved the sale in view of the absence of alternatives considered more favorable to the government's option. GM emerged from the protection of the court on July 10, 2009, in an economic environment characterized by escalating unemployment and eroding consumer income and confidence. Even with less debt and liabilities, fewer employees, the elimination of most "legacy costs," and a reduced number of dealerships and brands, GM found itself operating in an environment in 2009 in which U.S.

CASE STUDY 16.2   *(cont'd)*

vehicle sales totaled an anemic 10.4 million units. This compared to more than 16 million in 2008. GM's 2009 market share slipped to a post–World War II low of about 19%.

While the bankruptcy option had been under consideration for several months, its attraction grew as it became increasingly apparent that time was running out for the cash-strapped firm. Having determined from the outset that liquidation of General Motors either inside or outside of the protection of bankruptcy would not be considered, the government initially considered a prepackaged bankruptcy in which agreement is obtained among major stakeholders prior to filing for bankruptcy. The presumption is that since agreement with many parties had already been obtained, developing a plan of reorganization to emerge from Chapter 11 would move more quickly. However, this option was not pursued because of the concern that the public would simply view the post–Chapter 11 GM as simply a smaller version of its former self. The government in particular was seeking to position GM as an entirely new firm capable of profitably designing and building cars that the public wanted.

Time was of the essence. The concern was that consumers would not buy GM vehicles while the firm was in bankruptcy. Consequently, a strategy was devised in which General Motors would be divided into two firms: "old GM," which would contain the firm's unwanted assets, and "new GM," which would own the most attractive assets. "New GM" would then emerge from bankruptcy in a sale to a new company owned by various stakeholder groups, including the U.S. and Canadian governments, a union trust fund, and bondholders. Only GM's U.S. and Canadian operations were included in the bankruptcy filing. Figure 16.2 illustrates the GM bankruptcy process.

Buying distressed assets can be accomplished through a Chapter 11 reorganization plan or through a postconfirmation trustee. Alternatively, a 363 sale transfers the acquired assets free and clear of any liens, claims, and encumbrances. The sale of GM's attractive assets to "new GM" was ultimately completed under Section 363 of the U.S. Bankruptcy Code. Historically, firms used this tactic to sell failing plants and redundant equipment. In recent

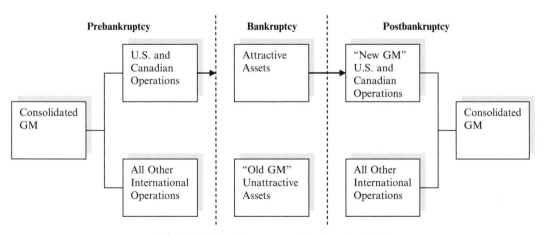

FIGURE 16.2   The process of bankruptcy at GM.

V. ALTERNATIVE BUSINESS AND RESTRUCTURING STRATEGIES

CASE STUDY 16.2   *(cont'd)*

years, so-called 363 sales have been used to completely restructure businesses, including the 363 sales of entire companies. A 363 sale requires only the approval of the bankruptcy judge, while a plan of reorganization in Chapter 11 must be approved by a substantial number of creditors and meet certain other requirements to be approved. A plan of reorganization is much more comprehensive than a 363 sale in addressing the overall financial situation of the debtor and how its exit strategy from bankruptcy will affect creditors. Once a 363 sale has been consummated and the purchase price paid, the bankruptcy court decides how the proceeds of sale are allocated among secured creditors with liens on the assets sold.

Total financing provided by the U.S. and Canadian (including the province of Ontario) governments amounted to $69.5 billion. U.S. taxpayer-provided financing totaled $60 billion, which consisted of $10 billion in loans and the remainder in equity. The government decided to contribute $50 billion in the form of equity to reduce the burden on GM of paying interest and principal on its outstanding debt. Nearly $20 billion was provided prior to the bankruptcy, $11 billion to finance the firm during the bankruptcy proceedings, and an additional $19 billion in late 2009.

In exchange for these funds, the U.S. government owns 60.8% of "new GM's common shares, while the Canadian and Ontario governments own 11.7% in exchange for their investment of $9.5 billion. The United Auto Workers' new voluntary employee beneficiary association (VEBA) received a 17.5% stake in exchange for assuming responsibility for retiree medical and pension obligations. Bondholders and other unsecured creditors received a 10% ownership position. The U.S. Treasury and the VEBA also received $2.1

billion and $6.5 billion in preferred shares, respectively.

The new firm, which employs 244,000 workers in 34 countries, intends to further reduce its head count of salaried employees to 27,200 by 2012. The firm will also have shed 21,000 union workers from the 54,000 UAW workers it employed prior to declaring bankruptcy in the United States and close 12 to 20 plants. General Motors did not include its foreign operations in Europe, Latin America, Africa, the Middle East, or Asia Pacific in the Chapter 11 filing. Annual vehicle production capacity for the firm will decline to 10 million vehicles in 2012, compared with 15 to 17 million in 1995. The firm exited bankruptcy with consolidated debt at $17 billion and $9 billion in 9% preferred stock, which is payable on a quarterly basis. GM has a new board, on which Canada and the UAW healthcare trust each have a seat.

Following bankruptcy, General Motors has four core brands—Chevrolet, Cadillac, Buick, and GMC—that are sold through 3,600 dealerships, down from its existing 5,969-dealer network. The business plan calls for an IPO whose timing will depend on the firm's return to sufficient profitability and stock market conditions.

By offloading worker healthcare liabilities to the VEBA trust and seeding it mostly with stock instead of cash, GM has eliminated the need to pay more than $4 billion annually in medical costs. Concessions made by the UAW before GM entered bankruptcy have made GM more competitive in terms of labor costs with Toyota.

Assets to be liquidated by Motors Liquidation Company (i.e., "old GM") were split into four trusts, including one financed by $536 million in existing loans from the federal government. These funds were set aside to clean up 50 million square feet of industrial

CASE STUDY 16.2 *(cont'd)*

manufacturing space at 127 locations spread across 14 states. Another $300 million was set aside for property taxes, plant security, and other shutdown expenses. A second trust will handle claims of the owners of GM's prebankruptcy debt, who are expected to get 10% of the equity in GM when the firm goes public and warrants to buy additional shares at a later date. The remaining two trusts are intended to process litigation (e.g., asbestos-related claims). The eventual sale of the remaining assets could take four years, with most of the environmental cleanup activities completed within a decade (Lattman and de la Merced, 2010).

Reflecting the overall improvement in the U.S. economy and in its operating performance, GM repaid $10 billion in loans to the U.S. government in April 2010. Seventeen months after emerging from bankruptcy, the firm completed successfully the largest IPO in history on November 17, 2010, raising $23.1 billion. The IPO was intended to raise cash for the firm and to reduce the government's ownership in the firm, reflecting the firm's concern that ongoing government ownership will hurt sales. Following completion of the IPO, government ownership of GM remained at 33%, with the government continuing to have three board representatives.

GM is likely to continue to receive government support for years to come. In an unusual move, GM was allowed to retain $45 billion in tax loss carryforwards, which will eliminate the firm's tax payments for years to come. Normally, tax losses are preserved following bankruptcy only if the equity in the reorganized company goes to creditors who have been in place for at least 18 months. Despite not meeting this criterion, the Treasury simply overlooked these regulatory requirements in allowing

these tax benefits to accrue to GM. Having repaid its outstanding debt to the government, GM continued to owe the U.S. government $36.4 billion ($50 billion less $13.6 billion received from the IPO) at the end of 2010. Assuming a corporate marginal tax rate of 35%, the government would lose another $15.75 billion in future tax payments as a result of the loss carryforward. The government also is providing $7,500 tax credits to buyers of GM's new all-electric car, the Chevrolet Volt.

Discussion Questions

1. Do you agree or disagree that the taxpayer-financed bankruptcy represented the best way to save jobs? Explain your answer.
2. Discuss the relative fairness to the various stakeholders in a bankruptcy of a more traditional Chapter 11 bankruptcy, in which a firm emerges from the protection of the bankruptcy court following the development of a plan of reorganization versus an expedited sale under Section 363 of the federal bankruptcy law. Be specific.
3. Identify what you believe to be the real benefits and costs of the government bailout of General Motors. Be specific.
4. The first round of government loans to GM occurred in December 2008. The firm did not file for bankruptcy until June 1, 2009. Discuss the advantages and disadvantages of the firm having filed for bankruptcy much earlier in 2009. Be specific.
5. What alternative restructuring strategies do you believe may have been considered for GM? Of these, do you believe that the 363 sale in bankruptcy represented the best course of action? Explain your answers.

Answers to these Case Study questions are found in the Online Instructor's Manual available for instructors using this book.

CASE STUDY 16.3
Delta Airlines Rises from the Ashes

On April 30, 2007, Delta Airlines emerged from bankruptcy leaner but still an independent carrier after a 19-month reorganization during which it successfully fought off a $10 billion hostile takeover attempt by US Airways. The challenge facing Delta's management was to convince creditors that it would become more valuable as an independent carrier than it would be as part of US Airways.

Ravaged by escalating jet fuel prices and intensified competition from low-fare, low-cost carriers, Delta had lost $6.1 billion since the September 11, 2001, terrorist attack on the World Trade Center. The final crisis occurred in early August 2005 when the bank that was processing the airline's Visa and MasterCard ticket purchases started holding back money until passengers had completed their trips as protection in case of a bankruptcy filing. The bank was concerned that it would have to refund the passengers' ticket prices if the airline curtailed flights and the bank had to be reimbursed by the airline. This move by the bank cost the airline $650 million, further straining the carrier's already limited cash reserves. Delta's creditors were becoming increasingly concerned about the airline's ability to meet its financial obligations. Running out of cash and unable to borrow to satisfy current working capital requirements, the airline felt compelled to seek the protection of the bankruptcy court in late August 2005.

Delta's decision to declare bankruptcy occurred at about the same time as a similar decision by Northwest Airlines. United Airlines and US Airways were already in bankruptcy. United had been in bankruptcy almost three years at the time Delta entered Chapter 11, and US Airways had been in bankruptcy court twice since the 9/11 terrorist attacks shook the airline industry. At the time Delta declared bankruptcy, about one-half of the domestic carrier capacity was operating under bankruptcy court oversight.

Delta underwent substantial restructuring of its operations. An important component of that restructuring effort involved turning over its underfunded pilot's pension plans to the Pension Benefit Guaranty Corporation (PBGC), a federal pension insurance agency, while winning concessions on wages and work rules from its pilots. The agreement with the pilot's union would save the airline $280 million annually, and the pilots would be paid 14% less than they were before the airline declared bankruptcy. To achieve an agreement with its pilots to transfer control of their pension plan to the PBGC, Delta agreed to give the union a $650 million interest-bearing note upon terminating and transferring the pension plans to the PBGC. The union would then use the airline's payments on the note to provide supplemental payments to members who would lose retirement benefits as a result of the PBGC limits on the amount of Delta's pension obligations it would be willing to pay. The pact covers more than 6,000 pilots.

The overhaul of Delta, the nation's third largest airline, left it a much smaller carrier than the one that sought protection of the bankruptcy court. Delta shed about one jet in six used by its mainline operations at the time of the bankruptcy filing, and it cut more than 20% of the 60,000 employees it had just prior to entering Chapter 11. Delta's domestic carrying capacity has fallen by about 10% since it petitioned for Chapter 11 reorganization, allowing it to fill about 84% of its seats on U.S. routes. This compared to only 72% when it filed for bankruptcy.

CASE STUDY 16.3 *(cont'd)*

The much higher utilization of its planes boosted revenue per mile flown by 15% since it entered bankruptcy, enabling the airline to better cover its fixed expenses. Delta also sold one of its "feeder" airlines, Atlantic Southeast Airlines, for $425 million.

Delta would have $2.5 billion in exit financing to fund operations and a cost structure of about $3 billion a year less than when it went into bankruptcy. The purpose of the exit financing facility is to repay the company's $2.1 billion debtor-in-possession credit facilities provided by GE Capital and American Express, make other payments required on exiting bankruptcy, and increase its liquidity position. With ten financial institutions providing the loans, the exit facility consisted of a $1.6 billion first-lien revolving credit line, secured by virtually all of the airline's unencumbered assets, and a $900 million second-lien term loan.

As required by the Plan of Reorganization approved by the bankruptcy court, Delta cancelled its preplan common stock on April 30, 2007. Holders of preplan common stock did not receive a distribution of any kind under the Plan of Reorganization. The company issued new shares of Delta common stock as payment of bankruptcy claims and as part of a postbankruptcy compensation program for Delta employees. Issued in May 2007, the new shares were listed on the New York Stock Exchange.

Discussion Questions

1. To what extent do you believe the factors contributing to the airline's bankruptcy were beyond the control of management? To what extent do you believe past airline mismanagement may have contributed to the bankruptcy?
2. Comment on the fairness of the bankruptcy process to shareholders, lenders, employees, communities, government, and so forth. Be specific.
3. Why would lenders be willing to lend to a firm emerging from Chapter 11? How did the lenders attempt to manage their risks? Be specific.
4. In view of the substantial loss of jobs, as well as wage and benefit reductions, do you believe that firms should be allowed to reorganize in bankruptcy? Explain your answer.
5. How does Chapter 11 potentially affect adversely competitors of those firms emerging from bankruptcy? Explain your answer.

Answers to these case study questions are found in the Online Instructor's Manual for instructors using this book.

Cross-Border Mergers and Acquisitions
Analysis and Valuation

Courage is not the absence of fear. It is doing the thing you fear the most. — **Rick Warren**

INSIDE M&A: INBEV BUYS AN AMERICAN ICON FOR $52 BILLION

For many Americans, Budweiser is synonymous with American beer, and American beer is synonymous with Anheuser-Busch. Ownership of the American icon changed hands on July 14, 2008, when beer giant Anheuser-Busch agreed to be acquired by Belgian brewer InBev for $52 billion in an all-cash deal. The combined firms would have annual revenue of about $36 billion and control about 25% of the global beer market and 40% of the U.S. market. The purchase is the largest in a wave of consolidations in the global beer industry, reflecting an attempt to offset rising commodity costs by achieving greater scale and purchasing power. While expecting to generate annual cost savings of about $1.5 billion, InBev stated publicly that the transaction is more about the two firms being complementary rather than overlapping.

The announcement marked a reversal from AB's position the previous week when it said publicly that the InBev offer undervalued the firm and subsequently sued InBev for "misleading statements" it had allegedly made about the strength of its financing. To court public support, AB publicized its history as a major benefactor in its hometown area (St. Louis, Missouri). The firm also argued that its own long-term business plan would create more shareholder value than the proposed deal. AB also investigated the possibility of acquiring the half of Grupo Modelo, the Mexican brewer of Corona beer, that it did not already own to make the transaction too expensive for InBev.

While it publicly professed to want a friendly transaction, InBev wasted no time in turning up the heat. The firm launched a campaign to remove Anheuser's board and replace it with its own slate of candidates, including a Busch family member. However, AB was under substantial pressure from major investors to agree to the deal, since the firm's stock had been lackluster during the preceding several years. In an effort to gain additional shareholder support, InBev raised its initial $65 bid to $70. To eliminate concerns over its ability to finance the deal, InBev agreed to fully document its credit sources rather than rely on the more traditional but less certain credit commitment letters.

In an effort to placate AB's board, management, and the myriad politicians who railed against the proposed transaction, InBev agreed to name the new firm Anheuser-Busch InBev and keep Budweiser as the new firm's flagship brand and St. Louis as its North American headquarters. In addition, AB would be given two seats on the board, including August A. Busch IV, AB's CEO and patriarch of the firm's founding family. InBev also announced that AB's 12 U.S. breweries would remain open.

By the end of 2010, the combined firms seemed to be progressing well, with the debt accumulated as a result of the takeover being paid off faster than planned. Earnings per share exceeded investor expectations. The sluggish growth in the U.S. market was offset by increased sales in Latin America. Challenges remain, however, since AB Inbev still must demonstrate that it can restore growth in the United States.[1]

CHAPTER OVERVIEW

There are as many motives as there are strategies for international expansion. This chapter addresses common motives for international expansion, as well as the advantages and disadvantages of a variety of international market entry strategies. However, the focus in this chapter is on M&A as a market entry or expansion mode because cross-border M&As comprise on average one-fourth of all global transactions and more than one-half of direct foreign investment annually.[2] Moreover, foreign direct investment has replaced international trade as the driving force behind global integration of product markets. Given its focus on M&As, this chapter also addresses the challenges of M&A deal structures, financing, valuation, and execution in both developed and emerging countries. Finally, the chapter summarizes empirical studies investigating the actual benefits to both target and acquiring company shareholders of international diversification.

A chapter review (including practice questions with answers) is available in the file folder entitled "Student Study Guide" on the companion site to this book (*www.elsevierdirect.com/companions/9780123854858*). The companion site also contains a Learning Interactions Library, which gives students the opportunity to test their knowledge of this chapter in a "real-time" environment.

DISTINGUISHING BETWEEN DEVELOPED AND EMERGING ECONOMIES

Throughout the chapter, the term *local country* refers to the target's country of residence, while *home country* refers to the acquirer's country of residence. *Developed countries* are those having significant and sustainable per capita economic growth, globally integrated capital markets, a well-defined legal system, transparent financial statements, currency convertibility, and a stable government. According to the World Bank, *emerging countries* have a growth

---

[1] Schultes, 2010

[2] Hopkins, 2008; Kang and Johansson, 2001; Letto-Gillies, Meschi, and Simonetti, 2001; Chen and Findlay, 2002

TABLE 17.1 Examples of Developed and Emerging Economies

Developed Economies		Emerging Economies	
Australia	Japan	Argentina	Mexico
Austria	Netherlands	Brazil	Morocco
Belgium	New Zealand	China	Pakistan
Canada	Norway	Colombia	Peru
Denmark	Portugal	Czech Republic	Philippines
Finland	Singapore	Egypt	Poland
France	Spain	Hungary	Russia
Germany	Sweden	India	South Africa
Greece	Switzerland	Indonesia	Sri Lanka
Hong Kong	United Kingdom	Israel	Taiwan
Ireland	United States	Jordan	Thailand
Italy		Korea	Turkey
		Malaysia	Venezuela

Source: Morgan Stanley Capital International (www.msci.com).

rate in per capita gross domestic product significantly below that of developed countries. Note that while many emerging countries show annual gross domestic product (GDP) growth well in excess of that of developed countries, their per capita GDP growth rate, generally considered a better measure of economic well-being, is usually much lower.

Table 17.1 provides examples of developed and emerging economies as defined by Morgan Stanley Capital International. Other organizations, such as the Organization for Economic Cooperation and Development and the United Nations, include a somewhat different mix of countries. Despite definitional differences, Brazil, Russia, India, and China make everyone's list of emerging nations. These four countries (often grouped together under the acronym BRIC) constitute about four-fifths of the total GDP of emerging countries.[3]

GLOBALLY INTEGRATED VERSUS SEGMENTED CAPITAL MARKETS

The world's economies have become more interdependent since WWII due to expanding international trade. As restrictions to foreign investment have been removed, country financial markets also have displayed similar interdependence or integration such that fluctuations in financial returns in one country's equity markets impact returns in other countries' equity markets. Between 1960 and 1990, the correlation among equity market financial returns for seven large developed countries increased, reflecting the emergence of a global capital market.[4] Furthermore, the correlation between equity market returns in emerging economies compared to global financial market returns has increased following the liberalization of their stock markets.[5]

[3] *The Economist*, 2006b

[4] Longin and Solnik, 1995

[5] Bekaert and Harvey, 2000

TABLE 17.2   Long-Term Movements in Country Financial Return Correlations between 1980 and 2003

Country Grouping	Average Correlation
All Countries	0.37
G7	0.37
Europe	0.54
Far East	0.30
U.S. versus Far East	0.27
U.S. versus Europe	0.39
U.S. versus All Other Countries	0.35

Source: Bekaert, Hodrick, and Zhang (2009).

However, in contrast to earlier studies, there does not seem to have been an increase in the upward trend in correlation among financial returns for 23 developed countries between 1980 and 2003 (Table 17.2).[6] The major exception is the correlation among equity market returns in European countries. However, the correlation appears to be highly sensitive to the time period examined. For example, the correlation between the performance of U.S. and European stocks increased from less than 30% in the 1970s to 90% for the five-year period ending in 2006.[7]

Globally integrated capital markets provide foreigners with unfettered access to local capital markets and local residents with access to foreign capital markets. Factors contributing to the integration of global capital markets include the reduction in trade barriers, removal of capital controls, the harmonization of tax laws, floating exchange rates, and the free convertibility of currencies. Improving accounting standards and corporate governance also encourage cross-border capital flows. Transaction costs associated with foreign investment portfolios have also fallen because of advances in information technology and competition. Consequently, multinational corporations can more easily raise funds in both domestic and foreign capital markets. This increase in competition among lenders and investors has resulted in a reduction in the cost of capital for such firms.

Unlike globally integrated capital markets, *segmented capital markets* exhibit different bond and equity prices in different geographic areas for identical assets in terms of risk and maturity. Arbitrage should drive the prices in different markets to be the same, since investors sell those assets that are overvalued to buy those that are undervalued. Segmentation arises when investors are unable to move capital from one market to another due to capital controls or simply because they prefer to invest in their local markets. Segmentation or local bias may arise because of investors having better information about local rather than more remote firms.[8]

[6] Bekaert, Hodrick, and Zhang, 2009

[7] Blackman, 2006

[8] Kang, 2008

Investors in segmented markets bear a higher level of risk by holding a disproportionately large share of their investments in their local market as opposed to the level of risk if they invested in a globally diversified portfolio. Reflecting this higher level of risk, investors and lenders in such markets require a higher rate of return to local market investments than if investing in a globally diversified portfolio of stocks. Therefore, the cost of capital for firms in segmented markets without easy access to global markets often is higher than the global cost of capital.

There is evidence that capital markets in some countries may be segmented to the extent that local factors are more important in determining cash flows, access to capital, and share prices of small firms than of large firms.[9] Consequently, the share price of a major French retailer like Carrefour may trade very much like the giant U.S. retailer Wal-Mart. However, the stock of a small French retail discount chain, affected more by factors in its local market segment, may trade differently from either Carrefour or Wal-Mart and exhibit a much higher cost of capital.

MOTIVES FOR INTERNATIONAL EXPANSION

The reasons firms expand internationally include the desire to achieve geographic diversification, accelerate growth, consolidate industries, utilize natural resources and lower labor costs elsewhere, and leverage intangible assets. Other motives include minimizing tax liabilities, avoiding entry barriers, fluctuating exchange rates, and following customers into foreign markets. Each of these is discussed in the following sections.

Geographic and Industrial Diversification

Firms may diversify by investing in different industries in the same country, the same industries in different countries, or different industries in different countries. Firms investing in industries or countries whose economic cycles are not highly correlated may lower the overall volatility in their consolidated earnings and cash flows. By increasing earnings and cash flow predictability, such firms may reduce their cost of capital.[10]

Accelerating Growth

Foreign markets represent an opportunity for domestic firms to grow. Large firms experiencing slower growth in their domestic markets have a greater likelihood of making foreign acquisitions, particularly in rapidly growing emerging markets.[11] U.S. firms have historically invested in potentially higher-growth foreign markets. Similarly, the United States represents a large, growing, and politically stable market. Consequently, foreign firms have increased their exports to and direct investment (including M&As) in the United States. For

[9] Eun, Huang, and Lai, 2007

[10] Numerous studies show that diversified international firms often exhibit a lower cost of capital than firms whose investments are not well diversified (Chan, Karolyi, and Stulz, 1992; Stulz 1995a, 1995b; Stulz and Wasserfallen, 1995; and Seth, Song, and Petit, 2002).

[11] Graham, Martey, and Yawson, 2008

example, facing increasingly saturated home markets, many European telecommunications companies, such as Vodafone and Spain's Telefonica, set their sights on emerging markets to fuel future expansion.[12]

Reflecting the increasing cost of bringing drugs to market and the loss of patent protection on high-revenue-generating drugs, the global healthcare industry has been undergoing consolidation during much of the last decade. As part of the ongoing trend, chemical and drug manufacturer Merck acquired Millipore, a manufacturer of products to help develop and process drugs, in 2010.

Although headquartered in the United States, Millipore does about 40% of its business in Europe. The deal enabled Merck to diversify into the higher-growth and higher-margin biologics business to help offset declining margins in its chemical business.

That same year, Spanish bank Banco Bilbao Vizcaya Argentaria (BBVA) acquired a 24.9% stake in Turkey's largest bank, Turkiye Garanti Bankasi (Garanti), giving it access to a market that is growing much faster than its own domestic market. The price paid represented a 10 percent discount to Garanti's average closing price, reflecting BBVA's less than controlling interest. Also in 2010, China's Geely Automotive acquired Ford Motor Company's Volvo subsidiary in an attempt to substantially increase its international sales (see Case Study 17.1).

CASE STUDY 17.1
Ford Sells Volvo to Geely in China's Biggest Overseas Auto Deal

Despite a domestic car market in which car sales exceeded the U.S. market for the first time in 2009, Chinese auto manufacturers moved aggressively to expand their international sales. In an effort to do so, Zhejiang Geely Holding Company, China's second largest non-government-owned car manufacturer, acquired Ford's money-losing Volvo operation in mid-2010 for $1.8 billion. The purchase price consisted of a $200 million note and $1.6 billion in cash.

Geely sees this acquisition as a way of moving from being a maker of low-priced cars affordable in the Chinese mass market to selling luxury cars and penetrating the European car market. Geely has publicly stated that it hopes to have one-half of its revenue coming from international sales by 2015. With 2,500 dealerships in more than 100 countries, acquiring Volvo is seen as a significant first step in achieving this goal.

As part of the agreement, Ford will continue to sell Volvo engines and other components and to provide engineering and technology support for an unspecified period of time. Geely intends to maintain car production in Sweden and to build another factory in China within the next several years.

Discussion Questions

1. With the world's largest and fastest-growing domestic car market, why do you believe Chinese carmakers are interested in expanding internationally?

2. What factors are likely to motivate Geely and other Chinese carmakers to ensure strict enforcement of intellectual property laws?

---

[12] The number of cell phone subscribers in Europe has been increasing at a tepid 6 to 8% pace as compared to 34% in the Middle East and 55% per annum in Africa (Bryan-Low, 2005).

Industry Consolidation

Excess capacity in many industries often drives M&A activity, as firms strive to achieve greater economies of scale and scope as well as pricing power with customers and suppliers. The highly active consolidation in recent years in the metals industries (e.g., steel, nickel, and copper) represents an excellent example of this global trend. Global consolidation has also been common in such industries as financial services, media, oil and gas, telecommunications, and pharmaceuticals.

Once industries become more concentrated, smaller competitors often are compelled to merge, thereby accelerating the pace of consolidation. In late 2006, midsize European drug maker Merck KGaA agreed to buy Swiss biotechnology company Serono SA for $11 billion, and Germany's Alana AF said it would sell its comparatively low-market-share pharmaceutical business to Danish drug manufacturer Nycomed for $5 billion. Smaller drug companies found it difficult to compete with behemoths Pfizer Inc. and GlaxoSmithKline PLC, which have much larger research budgets and sales forces. Midsize firms also are more likely to be reliant on a few drugs for the bulk of their revenue, which makes them highly vulnerable to generic copies of their drugs.

Consolidation also results from buyers seeking to exploit what are believed to be undervalued assets. In late 2010, Canadian banks Toronto-Dominion and Bank of Montreal, largely unscathed by the global financial crisis, acquired U.S. consumer lenders Chrysler Financial for $6.3 billion and Wisconsin-based Marshall & Ilsley for $4.1 billion, respectively, to increase their market share in the consumer loan market.

Utilization of Lower Raw Material and Labor Costs

Emerging markets may be particularly attractive, since they often represent low labor costs, access to inexpensive raw materials, and low levels of regulation.[13] Thus, shifting production overseas represents an opportunity to significantly reduce operating expenses and become more competitive in global markets. The salutary impact of lower labor costs often is overstated because worker productivity in emerging countries tends to be significantly lower than in more developed countries.

Leveraging Intangible Assets

Firms with significant expertise, brands, patents, copyrights, and proprietary technologies seek to grow by exploiting these advantages in emerging markets. Foreign buyers may seek to acquire firms with intellectual property so that they can employ such assets in their own domestic markets.[14] Firms with a reputation for superior products in their home markets might find that they can successfully apply this reputation in foreign markets (e.g., Coke, Pepsi, and McDonald's).[15] Firms seeking to leverage their capabilities are likely to acquire controlling

[13] Dunning, 1988

[14] Eun, Kolodny, and Scherage, 1996; Morck and Yeung, 1991

[15] Caves, 1982

interests in foreign firms.[16] However, as Wal-Mart discovered, sometimes even a widely recognized brand name is insufficient to overcome the challenges of foreign markets (see Case Study 17.3).

Minimizing Tax Liabilities

Firms in high-tax countries may shift production and reported profits by building or acquiring operations in countries with more favorable tax laws. Evidence supporting the notion that such strategies are common is mixed.[17]

Avoiding Entry Barriers

Quotas and tariffs on imports imposed by governments to protect domestic industries often encourage foreign direct investment. Foreign firms may acquire existing facilities or start new operations in the country imposing the quotas and tariffs to circumvent such measures.

Fluctuating Exchange Rates

Changes in currency values can have a significant impact on where and when foreign direct investments are made. Appreciating foreign currencies relative to the dollar reduce the overall cost of investing in the United States. The impact of exchange rates on cross-border transactions has been substantiated in a number of studies.[18]

Following Customers

Often suppliers are encouraged to invest abroad to better satisfy the immediate needs of their customers. For example, auto parts suppliers worldwide have set up operations next to large auto manufacturing companies in China. By doing so, parts suppliers were able to reduce costs and make parts available as needed by the auto companies.

COMMON INTERNATIONAL MARKET ENTRY STRATEGIES

The method of market entry chosen by a firm reflects the firm's risk tolerance, perceived risk, competitive conditions, and overall resources. Common entry strategies include greenfield or solo ventures, mergers and acquisitions, joint ventures, export, and licensing. The literature discussing the reasons why a firm chooses one strategy over another is extensive. Figure 17.1 summarizes the factors influencing the choice of entry strategy.

[16] Ferreira and Tallman, 2005

[17] Servaes and Zenner (1994) found a positive correlation between cross-border mergers and differences in tax laws. However, Manzon, Sharp, and Travlos (1994) and Dewenter (1995) found little correlation.

[18] Georgopoulos, 2008; Feliciano and Lipsey, 2002; Vasconcellos and Kish, 1998; Harris and Ravenscraft, 1991; Vasconcellos, Madura, and Kish, 1990

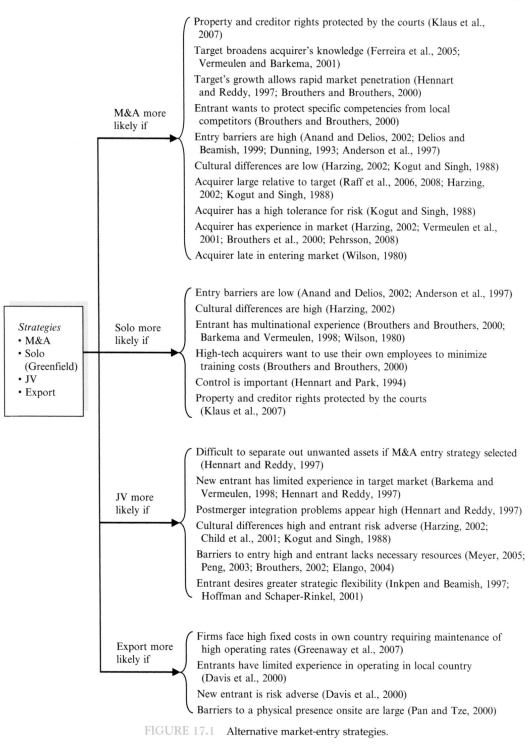

FIGURE 17.1   Alternative market-entry strategies.

V. ALTERNATIVE BUSINESS AND RESTRUCTURING STRATEGIES

M&As can provide quick access to a new market; however, they are subject to many of the same problems associated with domestic M&As. They often are very expensive, complex to negotiate, subject to myriad regulatory requirements, and sometimes beset by intractable cultural issues. The challenges of implementing cross-border transactions are compounded by substantial cultural differences and frequently by local country political and regulatory considerations.

In a greenfield or solo venture, a foreign firm starts a new business in the local country, enabling the firm to control technology, production, marketing, and product distribution. Studies show that firms with significant intangible assets (e.g., proprietary know-how) are frequently able to earn above-average returns, which can be leveraged in a greenfield or start-up venture.[19] However, the firm's total investment is at risk, and the need to hire local residents ensures that the firm is able to face the challenges associated with managing a culturally diverse employee base.

Joint ventures allow firms to share the risks and costs of international expansion, develop new capabilities, and gain access to important resources.[20] Most strategic alliances are with a local firm that understands the competitive conditions, legal and social norms, and cultural standards of the country. Local firms may be interested in alliances to gain access to the technology, brand recognition, and innovative products of the foreign firm. Despite these benefits, many alliances fail due to conflict between partners (see Chapter 14).

Alliances tend to produce higher financial returns if the partners have an equity interest.[21] In contrast to earlier studies showing increasing use of alliances and joint ventures in entering foreign markets, more recent studies show a decline in the frequency of such activity. Factors contributing to this decline include lower coordination costs between domestic and foreign operations due to easier communication; reduced transportation costs; and integration of global financial markets.

Exporting does not require the expense of establishing local operations. However, exporters must establish some means of marketing and distributing their products at the local level. The disadvantages of exporting include high transportation costs, exchange rate fluctuations, and possible tariffs placed on imports into the local country. Moreover, the exporter has limited control over the marketing and distribution of its products in the local market. Recent studies show that firms exhibiting relatively low productivity (a proxy for cash flow) are more likely to enter foreign markets by exporting than via acquisition or investing in greenfield operations.[22]

Licensing allows a firm to purchase the right to manufacture and sell another firm's products within a specific country or set of countries. The licensor is normally paid a royalty on each unit sold. The licensee takes the risks and makes the investments in facilities for manufacturing, marketing, and distribution of goods and services. Consequently, licensing is possibly the least costly form of international expansion. Therefore, licensing is an increasingly popular entry mode for smaller firms with insufficient capital and limited brand recognition.[23] Disadvantages include the lack of control over the manufacture and marketing of the

[19] Brouthers and Brouthers, 2000

[20] Zahra and Elhagrasey, 1994

[21] Pan, Li, and Tse, 1999

[22] Raff, Ryan, and Staehler, 2008

[23] Hitt and Ireland, 2000

firm's products in other countries. The risk may be high if the firm's brand or trademark is put in jeopardy. Furthermore, licensing often is the least profitable entry strategy because the profits must be shared between the licensor and licensee. Finally, the licensee may learn the technology and sell a similar competitive product after the license expires.

STRUCTURING CROSS-BORDER TRANSACTIONS

Acquisition vehicles, forms of payment and acquisition, and tax strategies are discussed in detail elsewhere in this book. This section discusses those aspects of deal structuring most pertinent to cross-border transactions.

Acquisition Vehicles

Non-U.S. firms seeking to acquire U.S. companies often use C corporations, limited liability companies, or partnerships to acquire the shares or assets of U.S. targets. C corporations are relatively easy to organize quickly, since all states permit such structures and no prior government approval is required. There is no limitation on non-U.S. persons or entities acting as shareholders in U.S. corporations, except for certain regulated industries. A limited liability company is attractive for joint ventures in which the target would be owned by two or more unrelated parties, corporations, or nonresident investors. While not traded on public stock exchanges, LLC shares can be sold freely to members. This facilitates the parent firm operating the acquired firm as a subsidiary or JV. A partnership may have advantages for investors from certain countries (e.g., Germany), where income earned from a U.S. partnership is not subject to taxation. A holding company structure enables a foreign parent to offset gains from one subsidiary with losses generated by another, serves as a platform for future acquisitions, and provides the parent with additional legal protection in the event of lawsuits.

U.S. companies acquiring businesses outside the United States encounter obstacles atypical of domestic acquisitions. These include investment and exchange control approvals, tax clearances, clearances under local competition (i.e., antitrust) laws, and unusual due diligence problems. Other problems involve the necessity of agreeing on an allocation of the purchase price among assets located in various jurisdictions and compliance with local law relating to the documentation necessary to complete the transaction. Much of what follows also applies to non-U.S. firms acquiring foreign firms.

The laws governing foreign firms have an important impact on the choice of acquisition vehicle, since the buyer must organize a local company to hold acquired shares or assets in a way that is consistent with local country law. In common-law countries (e.g., the United Kingdom, Canada, Australia, India, Pakistan, Hong Kong, Singapore, and other former British colonies), the acquisition vehicle will be a corporation-like structure. Corporations in the United Kingdom and other commonwealth countries are similar to those in the United States. In civil law countries (which include Western Europe, South America, Japan, and Korea), the acquisition will be in the form of a share company or limited liability company. *Civil law* is synonymous with *codified law, continental law,* or the *Napoleonic Code.* Practiced in some Middle Eastern Muslim countries and some countries in Southeast Asia (e.g., Indonesia and Malaysia), Islamic law is based on the Koran.

In the European Union, there is no overarching law or EU directive requiring a specific corporate form. Rather, corporate law is the responsibility of each member nation. In many civil law countries, smaller enterprises often use a limited liability company, while larger enterprises, particularly those with public shareholders, are referred to as *share companies*. The rules applicable to limited liability companies tend to be flexible and are particularly useful for wholly-owned subsidiaries. In contrast, share companies are subject to numerous restrictions and applicable securities laws. However, their shares trade freely on public exchanges.

Share companies tend to be more heavily regulated than U.S. corporations. Share companies must register with the commercial registrar in the location of their principal place of business. Bureaucratic delays from several weeks to several months between the filing of the appropriate documents and the organization of the company may occur. Most civil law countries require that there be more than one shareholder. Usually there is no limitation on foreigners acting as shareholders.

Limited liability companies outside the United States are generally subject to fewer restrictions than share companies. A limited liability company typically is required to have more than one quota holder (i.e., investor). In general, either domestic or foreign corporations or individuals may be quota holders in the LLC.[24]

Form of Payment

U.S. target shareholders most often receive cash rather than shares in cross-border transactions.[25] Shares and other securities require registration with the Securities and Exchange Commission and compliance with all local securities (including state) laws if they are resold in the United States. Acquirer shares often are less attractive to potential targets because of the absence of a liquid market for resale or because the acquirer is not widely recognized by the target firm's shareholders.

Form of Acquisition

While a foreign buyer may acquire shares or assets directly, share acquisitions are generally the simplest form of acquisition. Share acquisitions result in all assets and liabilities of the target firm, on or off the balance sheet, transferred to the acquirer by "rule of law." Asset purchases result in the transference of all or some of the assets of the target firm to the acquirer (see Chapter 11).

For acquisitions outside the United States, share acquisitions are the simplest mechanism for conveying ownership, since licenses, permits, franchises, contracts, and leases generally transfer to the buyer, without the need to get approval from licensors, permit holders, and the like, unless otherwise stipulated in the contract. The major disadvantage of a share purchase is that all the target's known and unknown liabilities transfer to the buyer. When the target is in a foreign country, full disclosure of liabilities is often limited, and some target assets transfer encumbered by tax liens or other associated liabilities.

---

[24] For an excellent discussion of alternative corporate structures in common and civil law countries, see Truitt (2006).

[25] Ceneboyan, Papaiaoannou, and Travlos, 1991

While asset sales generally make sense in acquiring a single line of business, they often are more complicated in foreign countries when the local law requires that the target firm's employees automatically become the acquirer's employees with the sale of the assets. Mergers are not legal or practical in all countries, often due to the requirement that minority shareholders must assent to the will of the majority vote.

Tax Strategies

A common strategy used by foreign companies buying U.S. firms is the *tax-free reorganization*, or merger, in which target shareholders receive mostly acquirer stock in exchange for substantially all of the target's assets or shares. The target firm merges with a U.S. subsidiary of the foreign acquirer in a statutory merger under state laws. To qualify as a U.S. corporation for tax purposes, the foreign firm must own at least 80% of the stock of the domestic subsidiary. As such, the transaction can qualify as a type A tax-free reorganization (see Chapter 12). Target company shareholders receive voting or nonvoting stock of the foreign acquirer in exchange for their stock in the target firm.

Another form of deal structure is the taxable purchase, which involves the acquisition by ~~~ of the shares or assets of another, usually in exchange for cash or debt. Such a

~~~ because the target firm's shareholders recognize a taxable gain or

riangular merger in cash is the most common form of *taxable*

merges with a U.S. subsidiary of the foreign acquirer, with

eceiving acquirer shares as well as cash, although cash is

it. This structure is useful when the foreign acquirer is will-

me target company shareholders want shares, while others

a third form of transaction used in cross-border transactions.

the U.S. target corporation and its shareholders tax-free treat-

ince of shares of the foreign acquirer. In general, a hybrid trans-

target shareholders and tax free to others. To structure hybrid

npany shareholders may exchange their common shares for a

hile the foreign acquirer or its U.S. subsidiary buys the remain-

This transaction is tax free to target company shareholders taking

to those selling their shares for cash.[26]

ING CROSS-BORDER TRANSACTIONS

sed to finance cross-border transactions. The proceeds of the debt

either to purchase the target's outstanding shares for cash or to

ares issued to target shareholders to minimize potential earnings

ancing exist in capital markets in the acquirer's home, the target's local

sion of the different tax laws in various countries, see PriceWaterhouseCoopers

country, or in some third country. Domestic capital sources available to cross-border acquirers include banks willing to provide bridge financing and lines of credit, bond markets, and equity markets.

Debt Markets

Eurobonds represent a common form of financing for cross-border transactions. Eurobonds are debt instruments expressed in terms of U.S. dollars or other currencies and sold to investors outside the country in whose currency they are denominated. A typical Eurobond transaction could be a dollar-denominated bond issued by a French firm through an underwriting group. The underwriting group could comprise the overseas affiliate of a New York commercial bank, a German commercial bank, and a consortium of London banks. Bonds issued by foreign firms and governments in local markets have existed for many years. Such bonds are issued in another country's domestic bond market, denominated in its currency, and subject to that country's regulations. Bonds of a non-U.S. issuer registered with the SEC for sale in the U.S. public bond markets are called *yankee bonds*. Similarly, a U.S. company issuing a bond in Japan would be issuing a "samurai" bond.

Equity Markets

The American depository receipt (ADR) market evolved as a means of enabling foreign firms to raise funds in the U.S. equity markets. ADRs represent the receipt for the shares of a foreign-based corporation held in a U.S. bank. Such receipts entitle the holder to all dividends and capital gains. American depositary shares (ADS) are shares issued under a deposit agreement representing the underlying common share, which trades in the issuer's market. The acronyms ADS and ADR often are used interchangeably. The Euroequity market reflects equity issues by a foreign firm tapping a larger investor base than the firm's home equity market.

If the acquirer is not well known in the target's home market, target shareholders may be able to sell the shares only at a discount in their home market. In this instance, the buyer may have to issue shares in its home market or possibly to the international equities market and use the proceeds to acquire the target for cash. Alternatively, the acquirer may issue shares in the target's market to create a resale market for target shareholders or offer target shareholders the opportunity to sell the shares in the buyer's home market through an investment banker.

Sovereign Funds

Sovereign wealth funds (SWFs) are government-backed or -sponsored investment funds whose primary function is to invest accumulated reserves of foreign currencies. For years, such funds, in countries that had accumulated huge quantities of dollars, would reinvest in U.S. Treasury securities. However, in recent years, such funds have become more sophisticated, increasingly taking equity positions in foreign firms and diversifying their currency holdings. Collectively, the sovereign funds control about $3.4 trillion in assets.[27] The biggest shift in recent years has been the funds' willingness to make high-profile investments in public companies. For the most part, the sovereign funds appear to be long-term, sophisticated investors. In addition to providing a source of capital, sovereign wealth funds, as politically connected large investors, may contribute to the value of a firm in which they invest by providing access to the SWF's home market and to government-related contracts.[28]

PLANNING AND IMPLEMENTING CROSS-BORDER TRANSACTIONS IN EMERGING COUNTRIES

Entering emerging economies poses a host of new challenges not generally encountered in developed countries, which include a range of political and economic risks.

Political and Economic Risks

It is difficult to differentiate between political and economic risks, since they are often highly interrelated. Examples of political and economic risks include excessive local government regulation, confiscatory tax policies, restrictions on cash remittances, currency inconvertibility, restrictive employment policies, outright expropriation of assets of foreign firms, civil war or local insurgencies, and corruption. Another, sometimes overlooked, challenge is the failure of the legal system in an emerging country to honor contracts.[29]

Many of these risks result in gyrating exchange rates, which heighten the level of risk associated with foreign direct investment in an emerging country. Unanticipated changes in exchange rates can influence substantially the competitiveness of goods produced in the local market for export to the global marketplace. Furthermore, changes in exchange rates alter the value of assets invested in the local country and earnings repatriated from the local operations to the parent corporation in the home country. Not surprisingly, the degree of economic and political freedom correlates positively with foreign direct investment. When they believe that their property rights are going to respected and relatively few restrictions are placed on managing investments and repatriating earnings, foreigners are more inclined to invest directly in the local country.[30]

Recent developments also highlight the importance of rising nationalism and protectionism amid the global economic slowdown in recent years. Australian mining giant BHP Billiton abandoned its effort to acquire Canadian fertilizer producer Potash Corporation in 2010. Regulatory authorities blocked the takeover amidst public furor over the potential loss

---

[27] Teslik, 2010

[28] Sojli and Tham, 2010

[29] Khanna, Palepu, and Sinha, 2005

[30] Bengoa and Sanchez-Robles (2003) and Berggren and Jordahl (2005) demonstrate a strong positive relationship between foreign direct investment and the Heritage Foundation's Freedom Index. This index contains about 50 variables divided into 10 categories, measuring various aspects of economic and political freedoms.

of control of the nation's natural resources. The reaction was somewhat unusual for Canada, a traditionally free-trade supporter.

Sources of Information for Assessing Political and Economic Risk

Information sources include consultants in the local country, joint venture partners, a local legal counsel, or appropriate government agency, such as the U.S. Department of State. Other sources of information include the major credit rating agencies such as Standard & Poor's, Moody's, and Fitch IBCA. Trade magazines, such as *Euromoney* and *Institutional Investor*, provide overall country risk ratings updated semiannually. The Economic Intelligence Unit also provides numerical risk scores for individual countries. The *International Country Risk Guide*, published by the Political Risk Services Group, offers overall numerical risk scores for individual countries, as well as separate scores for political, financial, and economic risks.

Using Insurance to Manage Risk

The decision to buy political risk insurance depends on the size of the investment and the perceived level of risk. Parties have a variety of sources from which to choose. For instance, the export credit agency in a variety of countries such as Export Import Bank (United States), SACE (Italy), Hermes (Germany), and so forth, may offer coverage for companies based within their jurisdictions. The Overseas Private Investment Corporation is available to firms based in the United States, while the World Bank's Multilateral Investment Guarantee Agency is available to all firms. These government and quasi-governmental insurers are the only substantial providers of war and political violence coverage.

Using Options and Contract Language to Manage Risk

In emerging countries, where financial statements may be haphazard and gaining access to the information necessary to adequately assess risk is limited, it may be impossible to perform an adequate due diligence. Under these circumstances, acquirers may protect themselves by including a put option in the agreement of purchase and sale. Such an option enables the buyer to require the seller to repurchase shares from the buyer at a predetermined price under certain circumstances. Alternatively, the agreement could include a clause requiring a purchase price adjustment. For example, in late 2005, the Royal Bank of Scotland purchased shares in the Bank of China. If subsequent to closing there were material restatements to the Bank of China's financial statements, the purchase price would have been adjusted in the Royal Bank's favor.

VALUING CROSS-BORDER TRANSACTIONS

The methodology for valuing cross-border transactions using discounted-cash-flow analysis is similar to that employed when both the acquiring and target firms are within the same country. The basic differences between within-country and cross-border valuation methods is that the latter involves converting cash flows from one currency to another and adjusting the discount rate for risks not generally found when the acquirer and target firms are within the same country.

Converting Foreign Target Cash Flows to Acquirer Domestic Cash Flows

Cash flows of the target firm can be expressed in its own currency including expected inflation (i.e., nominal terms), its own currency without inflation (i.e., real terms), or the acquirer's currency. Real cash-flow valuation adjusts all cash flows for inflation and uses real discount rates. Normally, M&A practitioners utilize nominal cash flows except when inflation rates are high. Under these circumstances, real cash flows are preferable. Real cash flows are determined by dividing the nominal cash flows by the country's gross domestic product deflator or some other broad measure of inflation. Future real cash flows are estimated by dividing future nominal cash flows by the current GDP deflator, increased by the expected rate of inflation. Real discount rates are determined by subtracting the expected rate of inflation from nominal discount rates. Nominal or real cash flows should give the same NPVs if the expected rate of inflation used to convert future cash flows to real terms is the same inflation rate used to estimate the real discount rate.

Inflation in the target country may affect the various components of the target firm's cash flows differently. For example, how the inventory component of working capital is affected by inflation reflects in part how sensitive certain raw materials and the like are to inflation and how such inventory is recorded (i.e., LIFO or FIFO basis). Moreover, straight-line depreciation may not adequately account for the true replacement cost of equipment in an inflationary environment. Since conversion of the various components of cash flow from local to home country currency may result in unnecessary distortions, it is advisable to project the target's cash flows in terms in its own currency, then convert the cash flows into the acquirer's currency. This requires estimating future exchange rates between the target (local) and acquirer's (home) currency.

Interest rates and expected inflation in one country versus another affect exchange rates between the two countries. The current rate at which one currency can be exchanged for another is called the *spot exchange rate*. Consequently, the translation to the acquirer's currency can be achieved by using future spot exchange rates estimated either from relative interest rates (the interest rate parity theory) in each country or from the relative rates of expected inflation (the purchasing power parity theory).[31]

When Target Firms Are in Developed (Globally Integrated) Capital Market Countries

For developed countries, such as those in Western Europe, the interest rate parity theory provides a useful framework for estimating *forward currency exchange rates* (i.e., future spot exchange rates). To illustrate this process, consider a U.S. acquirer's valuation of a firm in the European Union (EU), with projected cash flows expressed in terms of euros. The target's cash flows can be converted into dollars by using a forecast of future dollar-to-euro spot rates. The *interest rate parity theory* relates forward or future spot exchange rates to differences in

---

[31] For a detailed discussion of the interest rate parity and purchasing power parity theories, see Shapiro (2005).

interest rates between two countries adjusted by the spot rate. Therefore, dollar/euro exchange rate $(\$/€)_n$ (i.e., the future or forward exchange rate), n periods into the future, is expected to appreciate (depreciate) according to the following relationship:

$$(\$/€)_n = \{(1 + R_{\$n})^n/(1 + R_{€n})^n\} \times (\$/€)_0 \qquad (17.1)$$

Similarly, the euro-to-dollar exchange rate $(€/\$)_n$, n periods into the future, would be expected to appreciate (depreciate) according to the following relationship:

$$(€/\$)_n = \{(1 + R_{€n})^n/(1 + R_{\$n})^n\} \times (€/\$)_0 \qquad (17.2)$$

Note that $(\$/€)_0$ and $(€/\$)_0$ represent the spot rate for the dollar-to-euro and euro-to-dollar exchange rates, respectively; $R_{\$n}$ and $R_{€n}$ represent the interest rate in the United States and the European Union, respectively. Equations (17.1) and (17.2) imply that if U.S. interest rates rise relative to those in the European Union, investors will buy dollars with euros at the current spot rate and sell dollars for euros in the forward or futures market to offset the risk of exchange rate changes n periods into the future. By doing so, investors avoid the potential loss of the value of their investment expressed in terms of dollars when they wish to convert their dollar holdings back into euros. In this way, the equality in these two equations is maintained. Exhibit 17.1 illustrates how to convert a target company's nominal free cash flows to the firm (FCFF) expressed in euros (i.e., the local country or target's currency) to those expressed in dollars (i.e., home country or acquirer's currency).

EXHIBIT 17.1 **CONVERTING EURO-DENOMINATED INTO DOLLAR-DENOMINATED FREE CASH FLOWS TO THE FIRM USING THE INTEREST RATE PARITY THEORY**

	2008	2009	2010
Target's Euro-Denominated			
FCFF Cash Flows (millions)	€124.5	€130.7	€136.0
Target Country's Interest Rate (%)	4.50	4.70	5.30
U.S. Interest Rate (%)	4.25	4.35	4.55
Current Spot Rate $(\$/€) = 1.2044$			
Projected Spot Rate $(\$/€)$	1.2015	1.1964	1.1788
Target's Dollar-Denominated			
FCFF Cash Flows (millions)	$149.59	$156.37	$160.32

Note: Calculating the projected spot rate using Eq. (17.1):

$$(\$/€)_{2008} = \{(1.0425)/(1.0450)\} \times 1.2044 = 1.2015$$
$$(\$/€)_{2009} = \{(1.0435)^2/(1.0470)^2\} \times 1.2044 = 1.1964$$
$$(\$/€)_{2010} = \{(1.0455)^3/(1.0530)^3\} \times 1.2044 = 1.1788$$

When Target Firms Are in Emerging (Segmented) Capital Market Countries

Cash flows are converted as before using the interest rate parity theory or the purchasing power parity theory. The latter is used if there is insufficient information about interest rates in the emerging market. The *purchasing power parity theory* states that one currency appreciates (depreciates) with respect to another currency according to the expected relative rates of inflation between the two countries. To illustrate, the dollar/Mexican peso exchange rate, $(\$/\text{Peso})_n$, and the Mexican peso/dollar exchange rate, $(\text{Peso}/\$)_n$, n periods from now (i.e., future exchange rates), is expected to change according to the following relationships:

$$(\$/\text{Peso})_n = ((1 + P_{us})^n/(1 + P_{mex})^n) \times (\$/\text{Peso})_0 \qquad (17.3)$$

and

$$(\text{Peso}/\$)_n = ((1 + P_{mex})^n/(1 + P_{us})^n) \times (\text{Peso}/\$)_0 \qquad (17.4)$$

where P_{us} and P_{mex} are the expected inflation rates in the United States and Mexico, respectively, and $(\$/\text{Peso})_0$ and $(\text{Peso}/\$)_0$ are the dollar-to-peso and peso-to-dollar spot exchange rates, respectively. If future U.S. inflation is expected to rise faster than the Mexican inflation rate, the forward dollar-to-peso exchange rate—that is, future spot rates shown by Eq. (17.4)—would depreciate as U.S. citizens sell dollars for pesos to buy relatively cheaper Mexican products. See Exhibit 17.2 for an illustration of how this might work in practice.

EXHIBIT 17.2 **CONVERTING PESO-DENOMINATED INTO DOLLAR-DENOMINATED FREE CASH FLOWS TO THE FIRM USING THE PURCHASING POWER PARITY THEORY**

	2008	2009	2010
Target's Peso-Denominated			
FCFF Cash Flows (millions of pesos)	P1,050.5	P1,124.7	P1,202.7
Current Mexican Expected Inflation Rate = 6%			
Current U.S. Expected Inflation Rate = 4%			
Current Spot Rate ($/Peso) = 0.0877			
Projected Spot Rate ($/Peso)	0.0860	0.0844	0.0828
Target's Dollar-Denominated			
FCFF Cash Flows (millions of $)	$90.34	$94.92	$99.58

Note: Calculating the projected spot rate using Eq. (17.3):

$$(\$/\text{Peso})_{2008} = \{(1.04)/(1.06)\} \times 0.0877 = 0.0860$$
$$(\$/\text{Peso})_{2009} = \{(1.04)^2/(1.06)^2\} \times 0.0877 = 0.0844$$
$$(\$/\text{Peso})_{2010} = \{(1.04)^3/(1.06)^3\} \times 0.0877 = 0.0828$$

Selecting the Correct Marginal Tax Rate

If the acquirer's country makes foreign income exempt from further taxation once taxed in the foreign country, the correct tax rate would be the marginal tax rate in the foreign country because that is where taxes are paid. Otherwise, the correct tax rate should be the acquirer's country rate if it is higher than the target's country rate and taxes paid in a foreign country are deductible from the taxes owed by the acquirer in its home country. The acquirer must still pay taxes owed in the country in which it resides in excess of any credits received for foreign taxes paid.

Estimating the Cost of Capital in Cross-Border Transactions

While almost three-fourths of U.S. corporate chief financial officers surveyed use the capital asset pricing model to calculate the cost of equity, there is considerable disagreement in how to calculate the cost of equity in cross-border transactions.[32] To the extent a consensus exists, the basic capital asset pricing model or a multifactor model (e.g., CAPM plus a factor to adjust for the size of the firm, etc.) should be used in developed countries with liquid capital markets.

For emerging countries, the estimation of the cost of equity is more complex. There are at least 12 separate approaches to estimating the international cost of equity.[33] Each method endeavors to incorporate adjustments to the discount rate to account for potential capital market segmentation and specific country risks. Still other approaches attempt to incorporate the risk of investing in emerging countries, not by adjusting the discount rate but by adjusting projected cash flows. In either case, the adjustments often appear arbitrary.

Developed economies seem to exhibit little differences in the cost of equity, due to the relatively high integration of their capital markets with the global capital market. Thus, adjusting the cost of equity for specific country risk does not seem to make any significant difference.[34] However, for emerging market countries, the existence of segmented capital markets, political instability, limited liquidity, currency fluctuations, and currency inconvertibility seems to make adjusting the target firm's cost of equity for these factors (to the extent practical) desirable.[35]

The following discussion incorporates the basic elements of valuing cross-border transactions, distinguishing between the different adjustments made when investing in developed and emerging countries. Nonetheless, considerable debate continues in this area.

Estimating the Cost of Equity in Developed (Globally Integrated) Countries

What follows is a discussion of how to adjust the basic CAPM formulation for valuing cross-border transactions where the target is located in a developed country. The discussion is very similar to the capital asset pricing model formulation (CAPM) outlined in Chapter 7,

---

[32] Graham and Harvey, 2001

[33] Harvey, 2005

[34] Koedijk and Van Dijk, 2000; Koedijk et al., 2002; Mishra and O'Brien, 2001; Bodnar, Dumas, and Marston, 2003

[35] Bodnar et al. (2003) argue that in addition to the risk-free rate of return, the firm's cost of equity should be adjusted for such factors as the risk arising from variation in returns on a global stock market, country-specific stock market risk, and industry-specific risk. Other factors include exchange rate, political, and liquidity risk. Unfortunately, the substantial amount of information needed to estimate the adjustments required in such extensive multifactor models usually makes this approach impractical.

except for the use of either national or globally diversified stock market indices in estimating beta and calculating the equity market risk premium.

ESTIMATING THE RISK-FREE RATE OF RETURN (DEVELOPED COUNTRIES)

For developed countries, the risk-free rate generally is the local country's government (i.e., sovereign) bond rate whenever the projected cash flows for the target firm are expressed in local currency. However, the debt crises in a number of developed countries in 2010 and 2011 suggest that in such situations alternative measures of risk-free measures should be used.[36] The risk-free rate is the U.S. Treasury bond rate if projected cash flows are in terms of dollars.

ADJUSTING CAPM FOR RISK (DEVELOPED COUNTRIES)

The equity premium, reflecting the difference between the return on a well-diversified portfolio and the risk-free return, is the incremental return required to induce investors to buy stock. The use of a well-diversified portfolio eliminates risk specific to a business or so-called diversifiable risk. The firm's β is a measure of nondiversifiable risk. In a world in which capital markets are fully integrated, equity investors hold globally diversified portfolios. When measured in the same currency, the equity premium is the same for all investors because each security's β is estimated by regressing its historical financial returns, or those of a comparable firm, against the returns on a globally diversified equity index.

Alternatively, an analyst could use a well-diversified country index that is highly correlated with the global index. In the United States, an example of a well-diversified portfolio is the Standard & Poor's 500 stock index (S&P 500); in the global capital markets, the Morgan Stanley Capital International World Index (MSCI) is commonly used as a proxy for a well-diversified global equity portfolio. Thus, the equity premium may be estimated on a well-diversified portfolio of U.S. equities, on another developed country's equity portfolio, or on a global equity portfolio.

ADJUSTING CAPM FOR FIRM SIZE

As noted in Chapter 7, studies show that the capital asset pricing model should be adjusted for the size of the firm. The size factor serves as a proxy for factors such as smaller firms being subject to higher default risk and generally being less liquid than large capitalization firms.[37] See Table 7.1 in Chapter 7 for estimates of the amount of the adjustment to the cost of equity to correct for firm size, as measured by market value.

GLOBAL CAPM FORMULATION (DEVELOPED COUNTRIES)

In globally integrated markets, nondiversifiable or systematic market risk is defined relative to the rest of the world. Therefore, an asset has systematic risk only to the extent that the performance of the asset correlates with the overall world economy. When using a global

---

[36] Note that the debt crises in Greece and other developed countries in 2010 and 2011 suggest that in some instances the interest rate on the debt of a large corporation within the local country or the U.S. Treasury bond rate may be more appropriate to use as a risk-free rate. The Treasury bond rate should be adjusted (using the Fisher effect) for the difference in the anticipated inflation rates in the two countries. This converts the Treasury bond rate into a local country nominal interest rate.

[37] Berk, 1995

equity index, the resulting CAPM often is called the *global* or *international capital asset pricing model*. If the risk associated with the target firm is similar to that faced by the acquirer, the acquirer's cost of equity may be used to discount the target's cash flows.

The global capital asset pricing model for the target firm may be expressed as follows:

$$k_{e,\text{dev}} = R_f + \beta_{\text{devfirm, global}}(R_m - R_f) + \text{FSP} \tag{17.5}$$

where

$k_{e,\text{dev}}$ = required return on equity for a firm operating in a developed country.
R_f = local country's risk-free financial rate of return if cash flows are measured in the local country's currency or in the U.S. Treasury bond rate if in dollars.
$(R_m - R_f)$ = difference between the expected return on the global market portfolio (i.e., MSCI), U.S. equity index (S&P 500), or a broadly defined index in the target's local country and R_f. This difference is the equity premium, which should be approximately the same when expressed in the same currency for countries with globally integrated capital markets.
$\beta_{\text{devfirm, global}}$ = measure of nondiversifiable risk with respect to a globally diversified equity portfolio or a well-diversified country portfolio highly correlated with the global index. Alternatively, $\beta_{\text{devfirm, global}}$ may be estimated indirectly as illustrated in Eq. (17.7).
FSP = firm size premium reflecting the additional return smaller firms must earn relative to larger firms to attract investors.

An analyst may wish to value the target's future cash flows in both the local and home currencies. The Fisher effect allows the analyst to convert a nominal cost of equity from one currency to another. Assuming the expected inflation rates in the two countries are accurate, the real cost of equity should be the same in either country.

APPLYING THE FISHER EFFECT

The so-called Fisher effect states that nominal interest rates can be expressed as the sum of the real interest rate (i.e., interest rates excluding inflation) and the anticipated rate of inflation. The Fisher effect can be shown for the United States and Mexico as follows:

$$(1 + i_{\text{us}}) = (1 + r_{\text{us}})(1 + P_{\text{us}}) \quad \text{and} \quad (1 + r_{\text{us}}) = (1 + i_{\text{us}})/(1 + P_{\text{us}})$$
$$(1 + i_{\text{mex}}) = (1 + r_{\text{mex}})(1 + P_{\text{mex}}) \quad \text{and} \quad (1 + r_{\text{mex}}) = (1 + i_{\text{mex}})/(1 + P_{\text{mex}})$$

If real interest rates are constant among all countries, nominal interest rates among countries will vary only by the difference in the anticipated inflation rates. Therefore,

$$(1 + i_{\text{us}})/(1 + P_{\text{us}}) = (1 + i_{\text{mex}})/(1 + P_{\text{mex}}) \tag{17.6}$$

where

i_{us} and i_{mex} = nominal interest rates in the United States and Mexico, respectively
r_{us} and r_{mex} = real interest rates in the United States and Mexico, respectively
P_{us} and P_{mex} = anticipated inflation rates in the United States and Mexico, respectively

If the analyst knows the Mexican interest rate and the anticipated inflation rates in Mexico and the United States, solving Eq. (17.6) provides an estimate of the U.S. interest rate (i.e., $i_{us} = [(1 + i_{mex}) \times (1 + P_{us})/(1 + P_{mex})] - 1$). Exhibit 17.3 illustrates how the cost of equity estimated in one currency is converted easily to another using Eq. (17.6). Although the historical equity premium in the United States is used in calculating the cost of equity, the historical U.K. or MSCI premium also could have been employed.

EXHIBIT 17.3 CALCULATING THE TARGET FIRM'S COST OF EQUITY IN BOTH HOME AND LOCAL CURRENCY

Acquirer, a U.S. multinational firm, is interested in purchasing Target, a small U.K.-based competitor, with a market value of £550 million, or about $1 billion. The current risk-free rate of return for U.K. ten-year government bonds is 4.2%. The anticipated inflation rates in the United States and the United Kingdom are 3% and 4%, respectively. The expected size premium is estimated at 1.2%. The historical equity risk premium in the United States is 5.5%.[a] Acquirer estimates Target's β to be 0.8, by regressing Target's historical financial returns against the S&P 500. What is the cost of equity ($k_{e,uk}$) that should be used to discount Target's projected cash flows when they are expressed in terms of British pounds (i.e., local currency)? What is the cost of equity ($k_{e,us}$) that should be used to discount Target's projected cash flows when they are expressed in terms of U.S. dollars (i.e., home currency)?[b]

$$k_{e,uk}(\text{see Eq. } (17.5)) = 0.042 + 0.8 \times (0.055) + 0.012 = 0.098 = 9.80\%$$
$$k_{e,us}(\text{see Eq. } (17.6)) = [(1 + 0.098) \times (1. + 0.03)/(1 + 0.04)] - 1 = 0.0875 \times 100 = 8.75\%$$

[a]The U.S. equity premium or the U.K. equity premium could have been used, since equity markets in either country are highly correlated.
[b]The real rate of return is the same in the United Kingdom (r_{uk}) and the United States (r_{us}). $r_{uk} = 9.8\% - 4.0\% = 5.8\%$, and $r_{us} = 8.8\% - 3.0\% = 5.8\%$.

Estimating the Cost of Equity in Emerging (Segmented) Capital Market Countries

If the individual country's capital markets are segmented, the global capital asset pricing model must be adjusted to reflect the tendency of investors in individual countries to hold local country rather than globally diversified equity portfolios. Consequently, equity premiums differ among countries, reflecting the nondiversifiable risk associated with each country's equity market index. What follows is a discussion of how to adjust the basic CAPM formulation for valuing cross-border transactions where the target is located in an emerging country.

ESTIMATING THE RISK-FREE RATE OF RETURN (EMERGING COUNTRIES)

For emerging economies, data limitations often preclude using the local country's government bond rate as the risk-free rate. If the target firm's cash flows are in terms of local currency, the U.S. Treasury bond rate often is used to estimate the risk-free rate. To create a local nominal interest rate, the Treasury bond rate should be adjusted (using the Fisher effect) for the difference in the anticipated inflation rates in the two countries. See Eq. (17.6) to determine how to make this adjustment.

ADJUSTING CAPM FOR RISK (EMERGING COUNTRIES)

An analyst can determine if a country's equity market is likely to be segmented from the global equity market if the β derived by regressing returns in the foreign market with returns on the global equity market is significantly different from 1. This implies that the local country's equity premium differs from the global equity premium, reflecting the local country's nondiversifiable risk.

Nondiversifiable risk for a firm operating primarily in its emerging country's home market, whose capital market is segmented, is measured mainly with respect to the country's equity market index ($\beta_{emfirm,country}$) and to a lesser extent with respect to a globally diversified equity portfolio ($\beta_{country,global}$). The emerging country firm's global beta ($\beta_{emfirm,global}$) can be adjusted to reflect the relationship with the global capital market as follows:

$$\beta_{emfirm,global} = \beta_{emfirm,country} \times \beta_{country,global} \qquad (17.7)$$

The value of $\beta_{emfirm,country}$ is estimated by regressing historical returns for the local firm against returns for the country's equity index. In the absence of sufficient information, $\beta_{emfirm,country}$ may be estimated by using the beta for a similar local firm or a similar foreign firm. The value of $\beta_{country,global}$ can be estimated by regressing the financial returns for the local country index (or for the index in a similar country) against the historical financial returns for a global index. Alternatively, a more direct approach is to regress the local firm's historical returns against the financial returns for a globally diversified portfolio of stocks to estimate $\beta_{emfirm,global}$. Furthermore, the β between a similar local or foreign firm and the global index could be used for this purpose.

Due to the absence of historical data in many emerging economies, the equity risk premium often is estimated using the "prospective method" implied in the constant growth valuation model. As shown in Eq. (7.14) in Chapter 7, this formulation provides an estimate of the present value of dividends growing at a constant rate in perpetuity. This method requires that the dividends paid in the current period (d_0) are grown at a constant rate of growth (g) such that d_1 equals $d_0(1 + g)$.

Assuming the stock market values stocks correctly and we know the present value of a broadly defined index in the target firm's country ($P_{country}$) or in a similar country, dividends paid annually on this index in the next period (d_1), and the expected dividend growth (g), we can estimate the expected return ($R_{country}$) on the stock index as follows:

$$P_{country} = d_1/(R_{country} - g) \text{ and } R_{country} = (d_1/P_{country}) + g \qquad (17.8)$$

From Eq. (17.8), the equity risk premium for the local country's equity market is $R_{country} - R_f$, where R_f is the local country's risk-free rate of return. Exhibit 17.4 illustrates how to calculate the cost of equity for a firm in an emerging country in the absence of perceived significant country or political risk not captured in the beta or equity risk premium. Note that the local country's risk-free rate of return is estimated using the U.S. Treasury bond rate adjusted for the expected inflation in the local country relative to the United States. This converts the U.S. Treasury bond rate into a local country nominal interest rate.

EXHIBIT 17.4 CALCULATING THE TARGET FIRM'S COST OF EQUITY FOR FIRMS IN EMERGING COUNTRIES

Assume next year's dividend yield on an emerging country's stock market is 5% and that earnings for the companies in the stock market index are expected to grow by 6% annually in the foreseeable future. The country's global beta ($\beta_{country,global}$) is 1.1. The U.S Treasury bond rate is 4%, and the expected inflation rate in the emerging country is 4% compared to 3% in the United States. Estimate the country's risk-free rate (R_f), the return on a diversified portfolio of equities in the emerging country ($R_{country}$), and the country's equity risk premium ($R_{country} - R_f$). What is the cost of equity in the local currency for a local firm ($k_{e,em}$) whose country beta ($\beta_{emfirm,country}$) is 1.3?

Solution

$$R_f = [(1 + 0.04)((1 + 0.04)/(1 + 0.03)) - 1] = 0.0501 = 5.01\%$$
$$R_{country} \text{ (see Eq. (17.8))} = 5.00 + 6.00 = 11.00\%$$
$$(R_{country} - R_f) = 11.00 - 5.01 = 5.99\%$$
$$\beta_{emfirm,global} \text{ (see Eq. (17.7))} = 1.3 \times 1.1 = 1.43$$
$$k_{e,em} = 5.01 + 1.43 \ (5.99) = 13.58\%$$

ADJUSTING THE CAPM FOR COUNTRY OR POLITICAL RISK

Recall that a country's equity premium reflects systematic risk (i.e., factors affecting all firms). However, the country's equity premium may not capture all the events that could jeopardize a firm's ability to operate. For example, political instability could result in a government that assumes an antiforeigner business stance, resulting in potential nationalization, limits on repatriation of earnings, capital controls, the levying of confiscatory or discriminatory taxes, and the like. Such factors could increase significantly the firm's likelihood of default. Unless the analyst includes the risk of default by the firm in projecting a local firm's cash flows, the expected cash-flow stream will be overstated to the extent that it does not reflect the costs of financial distress (e.g., higher borrowing costs).

If the U.S. Treasury bond rate is used as the risk-free rate in calculating the CAPM, adding a country risk premium to the basic CAPM estimate is appropriate. The country risk premium (CRP) often is measured as the difference between the yield on the country's sovereign or government bonds and the U.S. Treasury bond rate of the same maturity.[38] The difference or "spread" is the additional risk premium that investors demand for holding the emerging country's debt rather than U.S. Treasury bonds.

A country risk premium should not be added to the cost of equity if the risk-free rate is the country's sovereign or government bond rate, since the effects of specific country or political risk have already been reflected. Standard & Poor's (*www.standardardandpoors.com*), Moody's

---

[38] Increasingly, country risk is measured by adding the country's credit default swap spread to the U.S. Treasury interest rate.

Investors Service (*www.moodys.com*), and Fitch IBCA (*www.fitchibca.com*) provide sovereign bond spreads. In practice, the sovereign bond spread is computed from a bond with the same maturity as the U.S. benchmark Treasury bond used to compute the risk-free rate for the calculation of the cost of equity. The U.S. benchmark rate usually is the ten-year Treasury bond rate.

GLOBAL CAPM FORMULATION (EMERGING COUNTRIES)

To estimate the cost of equity for a firm in an emerging economy ($k_{e,em}$), Eq. (17.5) can be modified for specific country risk as follows:

$$k_{e,em} = R_f + \beta_{emfirm,global} \, (R_{country} - R_f) + FSP + CRP \qquad (17.9)$$

where

R_f = local risk-free rate or the U.S. Treasury bond rate converted to a local nominal rate if cash flows are in the local currency (see Eq. (17.6)) or to the U.S. Treasury bond rate if cash flows are in dollars
$(R_{country} - R_f)$ = difference between expected return on a well-diversified equity index in the local country or a similar country and the risk-free rate
$\beta_{emfirm,global}$ = emerging country firm's global beta (see Eq. (17.7))
FSP = firm size premium reflecting the additional return that smaller firms must earn relative to larger firms to attract investors
CRP = specific country risk premium, expressed as the difference between the local country's (or a similar country's) government bond rate and the U.S. Treasury bond rate of the same maturity. Add to the CAPM estimate only if the U.S. Treasury bond rate is employed as a proxy for the local country's risk-free rate.

Estimating the Local Firm's Cost of Debt in Emerging Markets

The cost of debt for an emerging market firm (i_{emfirm}) should be adjusted for default risk due to events related to the country and those specific to the firm. When a local corporate bond rate is not available, the cost of debt for a specific local firm may be estimated by using an interest rate in the home country (i_{home}) that reflects a level of creditworthiness comparable to the firm in the emerging country. The country risk premium is added to the appropriate home country interest rate to reflect the impact of such factors as political instability on i_{emfirm}. Therefore, the cost of debt can be expressed as follows:

$$i_{emfirm} = i_{home} + CRP \qquad (17.10)$$

Most firms in emerging markets are not rated. Therefore, to determine which home country interest rate to select, it is necessary to assign a credit rating to the local firm. This "synthetic" credit rating may be obtained by comparing financial ratios for the target firm to those used by U.S. rating agencies. The estimate of the unrated firm's credit rating may be obtained by comparing interest coverage ratios used by Standard & Poor's to the firm's interest coverage ratio to determine how S&P would rate the firm. Exhibit 17.5 illustrates how to calculate the cost of emerging market debt.

EXHIBIT 17.5 ESTIMATING THE COST OF DEBT IN EMERGING MARKET COUNTRIES

Assume that a firm in an emerging market has annual operating income before interest and taxes of $550 million and annual interest expenses of $18 million. This implies an interest coverage ratio of 30.6 (i.e., $550 ÷ $18). For Standard & Poor's, this corresponds to an AAA rating. According to S&P, default spreads for AAA firms are 0.85 currently. The current interest rate on U.S. triple A–rated bonds is 6.0%. Assume further that the country's government bond rate is 10.3% and that the U.S. Treasury bond rate is 5%. Assume that the firm's marginal tax rate is 0.4. What is the firm's cost of debt before and after tax?

Solution

$$\text{Cost of debt before taxes (see Eq. (17.10))} = 6.0 + (10.3 - 5.0) = 11.3\%$$
$$\text{After-tax cost of debt} = 11.3 \times (1 - 0.4) = 6.78\%$$

Exhibit 17.6 illustrates the calculation of WACC in cross-border transactions. Note the adjustments made to the estimate of the cost of equity for firm size and country risk. Note also the adjustment made to the local borrowing cost for country risk. The risk-free rate of return is the U.S. Treasury bond rate converted to a local nominal rate of interest.

EXHIBIT 17.6 ESTIMATING THE WEIGHTED AVERAGE COST OF CAPITAL IN CROSS-BORDER TRANSACTIONS

Acquirer Inc., a U.S.-based corporation, wants to purchase Target Inc. Acquirer's management believes that the country in which Target is located is segmented from global capital markets because the beta estimated by regressing the financial returns on the country's stock market with those of a global index is significantly different from one.

Assumptions: The current U.S. Treasury bond rate (R_{us}) is 5%. The expected inflation rate in the target's country is 6% annually as compared to 3% in the United States. The country's risk premium (CRP) provided by Standard & Poor's is estimated to be 2%. Based on Target's interest coverage ratio, its credit rating is estimated to be AA. The current interest rate on AA-rated U.S. corporate bonds is 6.25%. Acquirer Inc. receives a tax credit for taxes paid in a foreign country. Since its marginal tax rate is higher than Target's, Acquirer's marginal tax rate of 0.4 is used in calculating WACC. Acquirer's pretax cost of debt is 6%. The firm's total capitalization consists only of common equity and debt. Acquirer's projected debt–to–total capital ratio is 0.3.

Target's beta and the country beta are estimated to be 1.3 and 0.7, respectively. The equity premium is estimated to be 6% based on the spread between the prospective return on the country's equity index and the estimated risk-free rate of return. Given Target Inc.'s current market capitalization of $3 billion, the firm's size premium (FSP) is estimated at 1.0 (see Table 7.1 in Chapter 7). What is the appropriate weighted average cost of capital Acquirer should use to discount target's projected annual cash flows expressed in its own local currency?

Solution:

$$k_{e,\text{em}}(\text{see Eq. (17.9)}) = \{[(1+0.05) \times (1+0.06)/(1+0.03)] - 1\} \times 100^{\text{a}}$$
$$+ 1.3 \times 0.7 (6.0) + 1.0 + 2.0 = 16.52\%$$
$$i_{\text{local}} (\text{see Eq. (17.10)}) = 6.25 + 2.0 = 8.25\%$$
$$\text{WACC}_{\text{em}}(\text{see Eq. (7.4)}) = 16.52 \times (1-0.3) + 8.25 \times (1-0.4) \times 0.3 = 13.05\%$$

[a]Note that the expression $\{[(1+0.05) \times (1+0.06)/(1+0.03)] - 1\} \times 100$ represents the conversion of the U.S. Treasury bond rate to a local nominal rate of interest using Eq. (17.6). Also note that 1.3×0.7 results in the estimation of the target's global beta, as indicated in Eq. (17.7).

Table 17.3 summarizes the methods commonly used for valuing cross-border transactions involving firms in developed and emerging countries. The WACC calculation assumes that the firm uses only common equity and debt financing. Note that the country risk premium is added to both the cost of equity and the after-tax cost of debt in calculating the WACC for a target firm in an emerging country if the U.S. Treasury bond rate is used as the risk-free rate of return. The analyst should avoid adding the country risk premium to the cost of equity if the risk-free rate used to estimate the cost of equity is the local country's government bond rate. References to home and local countries in Table 17.3 refer to the acquirer's and the target's countries, respectively.

Evaluating Risk Using Scenario Planning

Many emerging countries have few publicly traded firms and even fewer M&A transactions to serve as guides in valuing companies. Furthermore, with countries like China and India growing at or near double-digit rates, the future may be too dynamic to rely on discounted cash flows. Projecting cash flows beyond three years may be pure guesswork.

As an alternative to making seemingly arbitrary adjustments to the target firm's cost of capital, the acquirer may incorporate risk into the valuation by considering alternative economic scenarios for the emerging country. The variables that define these alternative scenarios could include GDP growth, inflation rates, interest rates, and foreign exchange rates. Each of these variables can be used to project cash flows using regression analysis (see the file entitled "Primer on Cash Flow Forecasting" on this book's companion site). The scenarios may also be built on alternative industry or political conditions. For example, a best-case scenario can be based on projected cash flows, assuming the emerging market's economy grows at a moderate real growth rate of 2% per annum for the next five years. Alternative scenarios could assume a one- to two-year recession. A third scenario could assume a dramatic devaluation of the country's currency. The NPVs are weighted by subjectively determined probabilities. The actual valuation of the target firm reflects the expected value of the three scenarios. Note that if a scenario approach is used to incorporate risk in the valuation, there is no need to modify the discount rate for perceived political and economic risk in the local country. See Chapter 8 for a more detailed discussion and illustration of scenario planning in the context of a decision tree framework.

While building risk into the projected cash flows is equivalent to adjusting the discount rate in applying the discounted-cash-flow method, it also appears to be subject to making arbitrary or highly subjective adjustments. What are the appropriate scenarios to be simulated?

TABLE 17.3   Common Methodologies for Valuing Cross-Border Transactions

Developed Countries (Integrated Capital Markets)	Emerging Countries (Segmented Capital Markets)
Step 1. Project and Convert Cash Flows	*Step 1. Project and Convert Cash Flows*
a. Project target's cash flows in the country's local currency.	a. Project target's cash flows in the country's local currency.
b. Convert local cash flows into acquirer's home currency, employing forward exchange rates that are projected using the interest rate parity theory.	b. Convert local cash flows into acquirer's home currency using forward exchange rates. Project exchange rates using purchasing power parity theory if there are few reliable data on interest rates available.
Step 2. Adjust Discount Rates	*Step 2. Adjust Discount Rates*
$k_{e,\mathrm{dev}} = R_f + \beta_{\mathrm{devfirm,global}}{}^a\,(R_m - R_f) + \mathrm{FSP}$	$k_{e,\mathrm{em}} = R_f + \beta_{\mathrm{emfirm,global}}{}^a\,(R_{\mathrm{country}} - R_f)^b + \mathrm{FSP} + \mathrm{CRP}$
$i = \text{cost of debt}^c$	$i_{\mathrm{local}} = i_{\mathrm{home}} + \mathrm{CRP}$
$\mathrm{WACC} = k_e\,W_e + i(1 - t) \times W_d$	$\mathrm{WACC} = k_e\,W_e + i_{\mathrm{local}}\,(1 - t) \times W_d$
a. R_f is the long-term government bond rate in the home country.	a. R_f is the long-term government bond rate in the local country or the U.S. Treasury bond rate converted to a local nominal rate if cash flows in local currency or if cash flows in dollars, the U.S. Treasury bond rate. Note that if local risk-free rate is used, do not add CRP.
b. $\beta_{\mathrm{devfirm,global}}$ is nondiversifiable risk associated with a well-diversified global, U.S., or local country equity index.	b. $\beta_{\mathrm{emfirm,global}}$ is nondiversifiable risk associated with target's local country β and local country's global β.
c. R_m is the return on a well-diversified U.S., local, or global equity index.	c. R_{country} is the return on a diversified local equity index or a similar country's index.
d. FSP is the firm size premium.	d. CRP is the country risk premium.
e. t is the appropriate marginal tax rate.	e. i_{home} is the home country cost of debt.
f. W_e is the acquirer's target equity–to–total capital ratio, and W_d is $1 - W_e$.	f. i_{local} is the local country cost of debt.

$^a\beta$ *may be estimated directly for firms whose business is heavily dependent on exports or operating in either developing or emerging countries by directly regressing the firm's historical financial returns against returns on a well-diversified global equity index. For firms operating primarily in their home markets, β may be estimated indirectly by using Eq. (17.7).*
$^b(R_{\mathrm{country}} - R_f)$ *also could be the equity premium for well-diversified U.S. or global indices if the degree of local segmentation is believed to be small.*
^{c}*For developed countries, either the home or local country cost of debt may be used. There is no need to add a country risk premium as would be the case in estimating a local emerging country's cost of debt.*

How many such scenarios are needed to adequately incorporate risk into the projections? What is the likelihood of each scenario occurring? The primary advantage of adopting a scenario approach is that it forces the analyst to evaluate a wider range of possible outcomes. The major disadvantages are the substantial additional effort required and the degree of subjectivity in estimating probabilities.

EMPIRICAL STUDIES OF FINANCIAL RETURNS TO INTERNATIONAL DIVERSIFICATION

Cross-border M&A transactions may contribute to higher average risk-adjusted financial returns for acquiring firms and improved corporate governance for target firms in emerging markets. These and other issues are addressed next.

International Diversification May Contribute to Higher Financial Returns

Empirical studies suggest that international diversification may increase financial returns by reducing risk if economies are relatively uncorrelated.[39] Higher financial returns from international diversification may also be due to economies of scale and scope, geographic location advantages associated with being nearer customers, increasing the size of the firm's served market, and learning new technologies.[40] Controversy continues as to whether returns are higher for multinational companies that diversify across countries[41] or across industries.[42] In either case, selecting an appropriate country remains very important. Buyers of targets in segmented markets realize larger abnormal returns than if they were to buy firms in globally integrated countries, since targets in segmented markets benefit from the acquirer's lower cost of capital.[43]

Foreign Buyers of U.S. Firms Tend to Pay Higher Premiums than U.S. Buyers

Foreign bidders have historically paid higher premiums to acquire U.S. firms than domestic acquirers of U.S. firms due to more favorable foreign currency exchange rates, which contributed to lower overall purchase prices when expressed in terms of foreign currency.[44] Between 1990 and 2007, the premium paid by foreign buyers of U.S. firms over those paid by U.S. acquirers averaged about 4 percentage points. The continued higher premiums paid by foreign buyers may reflect their efforts to preempt U.S. buyers, U.S. target firm shareholders' lack of familiarity with foreign acquirers, and concern that the transaction would not be consummated due to political (e.g., Unocal and CNOOC) and economic considerations (i.e., lack of financial resources).

Returns for Cross-Border Transactions Consistent with Domestic Results

Shareholders of target firms in cross-border transactions receive substantial abnormal returns. Such returns for shareholders of U.S. targets of foreign buyers range from about 23%[45] to about 40%.[46] Abnormal returns to shareholders of U.S. and non-U.S. buyers of foreign firms are about zero to slightly negative.[47]

[39] Delos and Beamish, 1999; Tang and Tikoo, 1999; Madura and Whyte, 1990

[40] Zahra, Ireland, and Hitt, 2000; Caves, 1982

[41] Isakov and Sonney, 2002

[42] Diermeier and Solnik, 2001

[43] Francis, Hasan, and Sun, 2008

[44] Harris and Ravenscraft, 1991

[45] Kuipers, Miller, and Patel, 2003

[46] Seth, Song, and Pettit, 2000; Eun, Kolodny, Scherage, 1996; Servaes and Zenner, 1994; Harris and Ravenscraft, 1991

[47] Kuipers et al., 2003; Seth et al., 2000; Eckbo and Thorburn, 2000; Markides and Oyon, 1998; Cakici and Tandon, 1996

In comparing returns in cross-border transactions to domestic deals, researchers have found that U.S. acquirers realize stock returns for cross-border transactions as much as 1% lower than for U.S. deals.[48] This may be attributable to increased competition for attractive foreign targets and reduced gains from diversification into formerly segmented markets due to increasingly global integration. Studies of U.K. and Canadian targets acquired by U.S. firms also found that bidders buying foreign targets underperform those acquiring domestic firms.[49] In contrast, acquirer returns increase on average by 1.65 to 3.1% when the targets are in emerging markets. This improvement is attributable to the achievement of control (e.g., enabling the protection of intellectual property), the elimination of minority shareholders, and the encouragement of investment in the target by the parent.[50]

Good Corporate Governance Supports Cross-Border M&A Activity

Higher firm valuations are often found in countries with better shareholder protections.[51] This is especially true in emerging countries, where firms have a single dominant investor.[52] Inflows of foreign investment are highest in countries that enforce laws requiring firms to disclose information and provide good shareholder protections. This finding underscores the importance of countries having in place legal systems that actively enforce contracts and prevailing securities laws.[53]

M&A activity is substantially larger in countries with better accounting standards and shareholder safeguards. Moreover, researchers have found that targets in cross-border deals are typically from countries with poorer investor protection than the acquirer's country. The transference of corporate governance practices through cross-border mergers may improve shareholder safeguards and, in turn, financial returns to target firm shareholders. Target firms in weaker corporate governance countries relative to the acquirer often adopt the better practices because of a change in the country of incorporation of the firm. When the bidder is from a country with stronger governance practices and gains full control of a target firm in a country with weaker governance practices, part of the total synergy value of the takeover may result from imposing the stricter practices of the bidder on the target firm.[54]

Foreign firms that invest less in corporate governance than a comparable U.S. firm have a lower market value than the U.S. firm.[55] This may be attributable to the characteristics of the country (e.g., legal system, extent of enforcement of exiting laws). The underinvestment is greatest in countries in which it is in the best interests of the controlling shareholders, who

[48] Moeller and Schlingemann, 2002

[49] Chatterjee and Aw (2004) for U.K. and Eckbo and Thorburn (2000) for Canadian targets.

[50] Chari, Ouimet, and Tesar, 2004

[51] La Porta, Lopez-De-Silanes, and Shleifer, 2002; Lemmons and Lins, 2003; Peng, Lee, and Lang, 2005

[52] Young et al., 2008

[53] Leuz, Lins, and Warnock, 2004

[54] Rossi and Volpin, 2004; Bris and Cabolis, 2004; Martynova and Renneboog, 2008b

[55] Aggarwal et al., 2007

often can obtain benefits at the expense of minority shareholders. Efforts to increase minority shareholder protection can increase the attractiveness of the firm's shares to a broader array of investors.

Foreign Institutional Ownership May Promote Cross-Border M&A Activity

Foreign institutional ownership in acquiring and target firms may promote cross-border transactions and increase corporate governance in developing countries. Cross-border transactions are more likely to be characterized by significant foreign institutional ownership intent on facilitating a change in corporate control in firms located in countries characterized by weak corporate governance or legal institutions and protections (see Ferreira et al., 2010). The foreign institutional investors facilitate change of control transactions by serving as brokers or intermediaries between bidding and target firms and by resolving information asymmetry problems by supplying information not publicly available. In doing so, the institutional investors hope to raise the value of their investments.

SOME THINGS TO REMEMBER

The motives for international corporate expansion include a desire to accelerate growth, achieve geographic diversification, consolidate industries, and exploit natural resources and lower labor costs available elsewhere. Other motives include applying a firm's brand name or intellectual property in new markets, minimizing tax liabilities, following customers into foreign markets, as well as avoiding such entry barriers as tariffs and import barriers. Alternative strategies for entering foreign markets include exporting, licensing, alliances or joint ventures, solo ventures or greenfield operations (i.e., establishing new wholly-owned subsidiaries), and mergers and acquisitions.

The methodology for valuing cross-border transactions is quite similar to that employed when both the acquiring and target firms are within the same country. The methodology involves projecting the target firm's cash flows and converting these future cash flows to current or present values using an appropriate discount rate. The basic differences between within-country and cross-border valuation methods is that the latter involves converting cash flows from one currency to another and adjusting the discount rate for risks not generally found when the acquirer and target firms are within the same country.

DISCUSSION QUESTIONS

17.1 Find a recent example of a cross-border merger or acquisition in the business section of a newspaper. Discuss the motives for the transaction. What challenges would the acquirer experience in managing and integrating the target firm? Be specific.

17.2 Classify the countries of the acquirer and target in a recent cross-border merger or acquisition as developed or emerging. Identify the criteria you use to classify the countries.

How might your classification of the target firm's country affect the way you analyze the target firm?

17.3 Describe the circumstances under which a firm may find a merger or acquisition a more favorable market entry strategy than a joint venture with a firm in the local country.

17.4 Discuss some of the options commonly used to finance international transactions. If you were the chief financial officer of the acquiring firm, what factors would you consider in determining how to finance a transaction?

17.5 Compare and contrast laws that might affect acquisitions by a foreign firm in the United States. In the European Union.

17.6 Discuss the circumstances under which a non-U.S. buyer may choose a U.S. corporate structure as its acquisition vehicle. A limited liability company. A partnership.

17.7 Which factors influence the selection of which tax rate to use (i.e., the target's or the acquirer's) in calculating the weighted-average cost of capital in cross-border transactions?

17.8 Discuss adjustments commonly made in estimating the cost of debt in emerging countries.

17.9 Find an example of a recent cross-border transaction in the business section of a newspaper. Discuss the challenges an analyst might face in valuing the target firm.

17.10 Discuss the various types of adjustments for risk that might be made to the global CAPM before valuing a target firm in an emerging country. Be specific.

17.11 Do you see the growth in sovereign wealth funds as important sources of capital to the M&A market or as a threat to the sovereignty of the countries in which they invest? Explain your answer.

17.12 What are the primary factors contributing to the increasing integration of the global capital markets? Be specific.

17.13 Give examples of economic and political risk that you could reasonably expect to encounter in acquiring a firm in an emerging economy. Be specific.

17.14 During the 1980s and 1990s, changes in the S&P 500 (a broadly diversified index of U.S. stocks) were about 50% correlated with the MSCI EAFE Index (a broadly diversified index of European and other major industrialized countries' stock markets). In recent years, the correlation has increased to more than 90%. Why? If an analyst wishes to calculate the cost of equity, which index should he or she use in estimating the equity risk premium?

17.15 Comment on the following statement: "The conditions for foreign buyers interested in U.S. targets could not be more auspicious. The dollar is weak, M&A financing is harder to come by for financial sponsors (private equity firms), and many strategic buyers in the United States are hard-pressed to make acquisitions at a time when earnings targets are being missed."

Answers to these Chapter Discussion Questions are found in the Online Instructor's Manual for instructors using this book.

CHAPTER BUSINESS CASES

CASE STUDY 17.2
Overcoming Political Risk in Cross-Border Transactions: China's CNOOC Invests in Chesapeake Energy

Cross-border transactions often are subject to considerable political risk. In emerging countries, this may reflect the potential for expropriation of property or disruption of commerce due to a breakdown in civil order. However, as Chinese efforts to secure energy supplies in recent years have shown, foreign firms have to be highly sensitive to political and cultural issues in any host country, developed or otherwise.

In addition to a desire to satisfy future energy needs, the Chinese government has been under pressure to tap its domestic shale gas deposits, due to the clean burning nature of such fuels, to reduce its dependence on coal, the nation's primary source of power. However, China does not currently have the technology for recovering gas and oil from shale. In an effort to gain access to the needed technology and to U.S. shale gas and oil reserves, China National Offshore Oil Corporation Ltd. in October 2010 agreed to invest up to $2.16 billion in selected reserves of U.S. oil and gas producer Chesapeake Energy Corp. Chesapeake is a leader in shale extraction technologies and an owner of substantial oil and gas shale reserves, principally in the southwestern United States.

The deal grants CNOOC the option of buying up to a third of any other fields Chesapeake acquires in the general proximity of the fields the firm currently owns. The terms of the deal call for CNOOC to pay Chesapeake $1.08 billion for a one-third stake in a South Texas oil and gas field. CNOOC could spend an additional $1.08 billion to cover 75%

of the costs of developing the 600,000 acres included in this field. Chesapeake will be the operator of the JV project in Texas, handling all leasing and drilling operations, as well as selling the oil and gas production. The project is expected to produce as much as 500,000 barrels of oil daily within the next decade, about 2.5% of the current U.S. daily oil consumption.

Having been forced in 2005 to withdraw what appeared to be a winning bid for U.S. oil company Unocal, CNOOC stayed out of the U.S. energy market until 2010. The firm's new strategy includes becoming a significant partner in joint ventures to develop largely untapped reserves. The investment had significant appeal to U.S. interests because it represented an opportunity to develop nontraditional sources of energy while creating thousands of domestic jobs and millions of dollars in tax revenue. This investment was particularly well timed, as it coincided with a nearly double-digit U.S. jobless rate; yawning federal, state, and local budget deficits; and an ongoing national desire for energy independence. The deal makes sense for debt-laden Chesapeake, since it lacked the financial resources to develop its shale reserves.

In contrast to the Chesapeake transaction, CNOOC tried to take control of Unocal, triggering what may be the most politicized takeover battle in U.S. history. Chevron, a large U.S. oil and gas firm, had made an all-stock $16 billion offer (subsequently raised to $16.5 billion) for Unocal, which was later trumped by an all-cash $18.5 billion bid by CNOOC. About three-fourths of CNOOC's

CASE STUDY 17.2 *(cont'd)*

all-cash offer was financed through below-market-rate loans provided by its primary shareholder: the Chinese government.

China National Offshore Oil Corporation's all-cash offer sparked instant opposition from members of Congress, who demanded a lengthy review and introduced legislation to place even more hurdles in CNOOC's way. Hoping to allay fears, CNOOC offered to sell Unocal's U.S. assets and promised to retain all of Unocal's workers, something Chevron was not prone to do. U.S. lawmakers expressed concern that Unocal's oil drilling technology might have military applications and that CNOOC's ownership structure (i.e., 70% owned by the Chinese government) would enable the firm to secure low-cost financing that was unavailable to Chevron.

The final blow to CNOOC's bid was an amendment to an energy bill passed in July requiring the Departments of Energy, Defense, and Homeland Security to spend four months studying the proposed takeover before granting federal approval.

Perhaps somewhat naively, the Chinese government viewed the low-cost loans as a way to "recycle" a portion of the huge accumulation of dollars it was experiencing. While the Chinese remained largely silent through the political maelstrom, CNOOC's management appeared to be greatly surprised and embarrassed by the public criticism in the United States about the proposed takeover of a major U.S. company. Up to that point, the only other major U.S. firm acquired by a Chinese firm was the 2004 acquisition of IBM's personal computer business by Lenovo, the largest PC manufacturer in China.

Many foreign firms desirous of learning how to tap shale deposits from U.S. firms like Chesapeake and to gain access to such reserves have invested in U.S. projects, providing a much-needed cash infusion. In mid-2010, Indian conglomerate Reliance Industries acquired a 45% stake in Pioneer Natural Resources Company's Texas natural gas assets and has negotiated deals totaling $2 billion for minority stakes in projects in the eastern United States. Norwegian oil producer Statoil announced in late 2010 that it would team up with Norwegian oil producer Talisman Energy to buy $1.3 billion worth of assets in the Eagle Ford fields, the same shale deposit being developed by Chesapeake and CNOOC.

Discussion Questions

1. Do you believe that countries should permit foreign ownership of vital scarce natural resources? Explain your answer.
2. What real options (see Chapter 8) might be implicit in CNOOC's investment in Chesapeake? Be specific.
3. To what extent does the Chesapeake transaction represent the benefits of free global trade and capital movements? In what way might it reflect the limitations of free trade?
4. Compare and contrast the Chesapeake and Unocal transactions. Be specific.
5. Describe some of the ways in which CNOOC could protect its rights as a minority investor in the joint venture project with Chesapeake. Be specific.

Answers to these questions are found in the Online Instructor's Manual available for instructors using this book.

CASE STUDY 17.3
Wal-Mart's International Strategy Illustrates the Challenges and the Potential of Global Expansion

With more than one-fifth of its nearly $450 billion fiscal 2010 revenue coming from its international operations, mega-retailer Wal-Mart would appear to be well on its way to diversifying its business from the more mature U.S. market to faster-growing emerging markets. With the announcement in late 2010 of its controlling interest in South African retailer Massmart Holdings, more than one-half of all Wal-Mart stores are now located outside of the United States (Table 17.4).

Massmart gives Wal-Mart entry into sub-Saharan Africa, a region that to date has been largely ignored by the firm's primary international competitors, France's Carrefour SA, Germany's Metro AG, and the United Kingdom's Tesco PLC. South Africa has embraced shopping malls for years, and an increasingly affluent middle class has emerged since the

TABLE 17.4 Global Distribution of Wal-Mart Stores

Country	Number of Stores
United States	4,400
Mexico	1,578
Brazil	452
Japan	414
United Kingdom	379
Canada	321
China	298
South Africa	288[a]
Chile	264
Costa Rica	172
Guatemala	170
El Salvador	77
Nicaragua	57
Honduras	55
Argentina	52
India	3
Total	**8,980**

Source: Wal-Mart.
[a] A small number of these stores are located elsewhere within the region.

CASE STUDY 17.3   (cont'd)

demise of apartheid. South Africa also has relatively little regulatory oversight. Furthermore, there is an established infrastructure of roads, ports, and warehouses, as well as an effective banking and telecommunications system. While the country has a relatively small population of 50 million, it provides access to the entire region. However, the country is not without challenges, including well-organized and sometimes violent labor unions, a high crime rate, and a 25% unemployment rate.

Wal-Mart's past missteps have taught it to make adequate allowances for significant cultural differences. With respect to Massmart Holdings, there appears to be no plans to rebrand the chain early on. The first sign of change customers will see will be the introduction of new products, including private label goods and the sale of more food in the stores. Wal-Mart also has publicly committed to honoring current union agreements and to working constructively with the unions in the future. Current Massmart management also will remain in place.

Its decision to buy less than 100% of Massmart's outstanding shares reflected a desire by institutional investors in Massmart to retain exposure to the region and by the South African government to continue to have Massmart listed on the South African stock exchange. As one of the nation's largest companies, it provides significant name recognition for investors and a sense of national pride. Wal-Mart has a history of structuring its international operations to meet the demands of each region. For example, Wal-Mart owns 100 percent of its Asda operations in the United Kingdom and 68 percent of Wal-Mart de Mexico.

The year 2006 marked the most significant retrenchment for Wal-Mart since it undertook its international expansion in the early 1990s in an effort to rejuvenate sales growth. Wal-Mart admitted defeat in its long-standing effort to penetrate successfully the German retail market. On July 30, 2006, the behemoth announced that it was selling its operations in Germany to German retailer Metro AG. Wal-Mart, which had been trying to make its German stores profitable for eight years, announced a pretax loss on the sale of $1 billion. Wal-Mart had previously announced in May 2006 that it would sell its 16 stores in South Korea.

Wal-Mart apparently underestimated the ferocity of German competitors, the frugality of German shoppers, and the extent to which regulations, cultural differences, and labor unions would impede its ability to apply in Germany what had worked so well in the United States. German discount retailers offer very low prices, and German shoppers have shown they can be very demanding. Germany's shoppers are accustomed to buying based primarily on price. They are willing to split their shopping activities among various retailers, which blunts the effectiveness of the "superstores" offering one location for all of a shopper's needs. Employees filed a lawsuit against the retailer's policy forbidding romantic relationships between employees and supervisors. Accustomed to putting their own groceries in shopping bags, German shoppers were alienated by clerks who bagged groceries. Moreover, German regulations limited Wal-Mart's ability to offer extended and weekend hours, as well as to sell merchandise below cost in an effort to lure consumers with so-called loss leaders.

CASE STUDY 17.3 *(cont'd)*

Strong unions also limited the firm's ability to contain operating costs.

Wal-Mart also experienced a loss of executives when it acquired several German retailers whose headquarters were located in different cities. When Wal-Mart consolidated the two headquarters in one city, many executives left rather than relocate. Perhaps reflecting this "brain drain," Wal-Mart's German operations had four presidents in eight years. Wal-Mart has not been alone in finding the German discount market challenging. Nestlé SA and Unilever are among the large multinational retailers that had to change the way they do business in Germany. France's Carrefour SA, Wal-Mart's largest competitor worldwide, diligently avoided Germany.

After opening its first store in mainland China in 1996, the firm had to face the daunting challenge of the country's bureaucracy and a distribution system largely closed to foreign firms. In India, Wal-Mart is still waiting for the government to ease restrictions on foreign firms wanting to enter the retail sector, which is currently populated with numerous small merchants.

Discussion Questions

1. Wal-Mart's missteps in Germany may represent an example of the limitations of introducing what works in one market (i.e., so-called best practices) into another. To what extent do you believe that Wal-Mart's failure represented a strategic error? To what extent did the firm's lack of success represent an implementation error?

2. In what ways does the Massmart acquisition reflect lessons learned by Wal-Mart from its previous international market entries? Be specific.

3. Given the challenges of international market entry and the probable substantial delay in experiencing a return on investment, do you believe that Wal-Mart should slow its pace of international expansion or even avoid it altogether? Explain your answer

4. In your judgment, what criteria should Wal-Mart employ in selecting other foreign markets to enter? Be specific.

Answers to these questions are found in the Online Instructor's Manual available to instructors using this book.

References

Aboutmediakit. (2006). *http://beanadvertiser.about.com/archive/news091606.html*.

Acharya, V. V., Franks, J., & Servaes, H. (2007). Private Equity: Boom or Bust? *Journal of Applied Corporate Finance, 19* (Fall), 44–53.

Adams, R., & Ferreira, D. (2007). A Theory of Friendly Boards. *Journal of Finance, 62*, 217–250.

Adegoke, Y. (2008). YouTube Rolls out Sponsored Videos in Revenue Drive. *Reuters*.

Adolph, G. (2006). Mergers: Back to Happily Ever After. In *Strategy and Business*. New York: Booz-Allen Hamilton.

Aggarwal, R., Erel, I., Stulz, R., & Williamson, R. (2007). *Differences in Governance Practices between U.S. and Foreign Firms: Measurement, Causes, and Consequences.* NBER. Working Paper No. 13288.

Aggarwal, R., & Rivoli, P. (1990). Fads in the Initial Public Offering Market. *Financial Management, 19*, 45–57.

Aggdata.com. (2008). *www.aggdata.com/business/fortune_500*.

Agrawal, A., & Jaffe, J. F. (1999). The Post-Merger Performance Puzzle. *Social Science Research Network.* Working Paper Series.

Agrawal, A., Jaffe, J. F., & Mandelker, G. N. (1992). The Post-Merger Performance of Acquiring Firms: A Reexamination of an Anomaly. *Journal of Finance, 47*, 1605–1621.

Akhigbe, A., Borde, S. F., & Whyte, A. M. (2000). The Source of Gains to Targets and Their Industry Rivals: Evidence Based on Terminated Merger Proposals. *Financial Management, 29* (Winter), 101–118.

Aktas, N., de Bodt, E., & Roll, R. (2010). Negotiations Under the Threat of an Auction. *Journal of Financial Economics, 98*, 241–255.

Alderson, M. J., & Betker, B. L. (1996). *Assessing Post-Bankruptcy Performance: An Analysis of Reorganized Firms' Cash Flows.* St. Louis University. Working Paper.

Alexander, G. J., Benson, G., & Kampmeyer, J. M. (1984). Investigating the Valuation Effects Announcements on Valuing Corporate Sell-Offs. *Journal of Finance, 39*, 503–517.

Allen, J. (2001). Private Information and Spin-Off Performance. *Journal of Business, 74*, 281–306.

Allen, J., & McConnell, J. J. (1998). Equity Carve Outs and Managerial Discretion. *Journal of Finance, 53*, 163–186.

Allen, P. (2000). Corporate Equity Ownership, Strategic Alliances, and Product Market Relationships. *Journal of Finance, 55*, 2791–2816.

Alli, K. L., & Thompson, D. J. (1991). The Value of the Resale Limitation on Restricted Stock: An Option Theory Approach. *Valuation, 36*, 22–34.

Almeida, H., & Philippon, T. (2007). The Risk Adjusted Cost of Financial Distress. *Journal of Finance, 62*, 2557–2586.

Altman, E. I. (1968). Financial Ratios, Discriminant Analysis and the Prediction of Corporate Bankruptcy. *Journal of Finance, 23*, 509–609.

Altman, E. I. (1993). *Corporate Financial Distress and Bankruptcy* (2nd ed.). New York: Wiley.

Altman, E. I. (2007). Global Debt Markets in 2007: A New Paradigm or Great Credit Bubble. *Journal of Applied Corporate Finance*, (Summer), 17–31.

Altman, E. I., Brady, B., Resti, A., & Sironi, A. (2005). The Link between Default and Recovery Rates: Theory, Empirical Evidence and Implications. *Journal of Business, 78*, 2203–2227.

Altman, E. I., & Kishore, V. (2001). *The Default Experience of U.S. Bonds.* New York: Salomon Center. Working Paper.

Altman, E. I., & Kishore, V. M. (1996). Almost Everything You Wanted to Know about Recoveries on Defaulted Bonds. *Financial Analysts Journal*, (November/December), 57–64.

American Bar Association. (2006). *Mergers and Acquisitions: Understanding Antitrust Issues* (2nd ed.).

Anand, J., & Delios, A. (2002). Absolute and Relative Resources as Determinants of International Acquisitions. *Journal of Strategic Management, 23*, 119–134.

Andersen Consulting. (1999). *Global Survey Acquisition and Alliance Integration.* Chicago.

Anderson, R. W., & Coverhill, A. (2007). *Liquidity and Capital Structure.* Center for Economic Policy Research. Working Paper No. 6044.

Anderson, U., Johanson, J., & Vahlne, J. E. (1997). Organic Acquisitions in the International Process of the Business Firm. *Management International Review, 37*, 67.

Andrade, G., & Kaplan, S. (1998). How Costly Is Financial (Not Economic) Distress? Evidence from Highly Leveraged Transactions That Become Distressed. *Journal of Finance, 53,* 1443–1493.

Ang, J., & Kohers, N. (2001). The Takeover Market for Privately Held Companies: The U.S. Experience. *Cambridge Journal of Economics, 25,* 723–748.

Ang, J. S., & Cheng, Y. (2006). Direct Evidence on the Market-Driven Acquisition Theory. *Journal of Financial Research, 29,* 199–216.

Angwin, J., & Drucker, J. (2006). How News Corp. and Liberty Media Can Save $4.5 Billion. *Wall Street Journal,* September 16, A3.

Annema, A., Fallon, W. C., & Goedhart, M. H. (2002). When Carve-Outs Make Sense. *McKinsey Quarterly, 2. https://www.mckinseyquarterly.com/home.aspx.*

Annema, A., & Goedhart, M. H. (2006). Betas: Back to Normal. *McKinsey Quarterly, https://www.mckinsey-quarterly.com/home.aspx.*

Arellano-Ostoa, A., & Brusco, S. (2002). *Understanding Reverse Mergers: A First Approach.* University of Madrid. Business Economics Series Working paper No. 11.

Armstrong, A., & Hagel, J. (1997). *Net Gain: Expanding Markets through Virtual Communities.* Boston: Harvard Business School Press.

Arzac, E. R. (2006). *Valuation for Mergers, Buyouts, and Restructuring.* New York: Wiley.

Aschwald, K. F. (2000). Restricted Stock Discounts Decline as Result of One-Year Holding Period. *Shannon Pratt's Business Valuation Update,* (May), 1–5.

Ascioglu, N. A., McInish, T. H., & Wook, R. A. (2002). Merger Announcements and Trading. *Journal of Financial Research, 25*(2), 263–278.

Aspatore Staff. (2006). *M&A Negotiations: Leading Lawyers on Negotiating Deals: Structuring Contracts and Resolving Merger and Acquisition Disputes.* Boston: Aspatore Books.

Asquith, P., Gerther, R., & Scharfstein, D. (1994). Anatomy of Financial Distress: An Examination of Junk Bond Issuers. *Quarterly Journal of Economics, 109,* 625–658.

Asquith, P., Mikhail, M., & Au, A. (2005). Information Content of Equity Analyst Reports. *Journal of Financial Economics, 340–355.*

Asquith, P., Mullins, D., & Wolff, E. (1989). Original Issue High Yield Bonds: Aging Analysis of Defaults, Exchanges and Calls. *Journal of Finance, 44,* 923–952.

Astrachan, J. H., & Shanker, M. C. (2003). Family Businesses Contributions to the U.S. Economy: A Closer Look. *Family Business Review, 15,* 211–219.

Atanasov, V., Boone, A., & Haushalter, D. (2005). *Minority Shareholder Expropriation in U.S. Publicly Traded Subsidiaries.* Babson College. Working Paper.

Auerbach, A. J., & Poterba, J. (1987). Tax Loss Carry Forwards and Corporate Tax Incentives. In F. Martin (Ed.), *The Effect of Taxation on Capital Accumulation.* Chicago: University of Chicago Press.

Auerbach, A. J., & Reishus, D. (1988). Taxes and the Merger Decision. In J. C. Coffee, Jr., L. Lowenstein, & S. R. Ackerman (Eds.), *Knights, Raiders, and Targets* (pp. 69–88). New York: Oxford University Press.

Avramov, D., Chordia, T., Jostova, G., & Philipov, A. (2006). *Credit Ratings and the Cross-Section of Stock Returns.* University of Maryland, Emory University, George Washington University, and American University. Working Paper.

Axelson, U., Jenkinson, T., Stromberg, P., & Weisbach, M. (2009). *Leverage and Pricing in Buyouts: An Empirical Analysis. http://ssrn.com/abstract=1344023.*

Ayers, B. C., Lefanowicz, C. E., & Robinson, J. R. (2003). Shareholder Taxes in Acquisition Premiums: The Effect of Capital Gains Taxation. *Journal of Finance, 58,* 2783–2801.

Aziz, M. A., & Dar, H. A. (2006). Predicting Corporate Bankruptcy: Where We Stand? *Corporate Governance, 6*(1), 18–33.

Bailey, W., Li, H., Mao, C., & Zhong, R. (2003). Regulation Fair Disclosure and Earnings Information: Market, Analyst, and Corporate Responses. *Journal of Finance, 58,* 2487–2514.

Baker, G., & Smith, G. (1998). *The New Financial Capitalists.* Cambridge, UK: Cambridge University Press.

Baker, G., & Wruck, K. (1989). Organizational Changes and Value Creation in Leveraged Buyouts: The Case of O. M. Scott and Sons Company. *Journal of Financial Economics, 25,* 163–190.

Ball, M. (1997). How a Spin-Off Could Lift Your Share Value. *Corporate Finance* (May), 23–29.

Bao, J., & Edmans, A. (2008). How Should Acquirers Select Advisors? Persistence in Investment Bank Performance. *Social Science Research Network.*

Barber, B. M., & Lyon, J. D. (1997). Detecting Long-Run Abnormal Stock Returns: The Empirical Power and Specification of Test Statistics. *Journal of Financial Economics, 43,* 341–372.

Barclay, M. J., & Holderness, C. G. (1989). Private Benefits from Control of Public Companies. *Journal of Financial Economics, 25,* 371–395.

Barkema, H. G., & Schijven, M. (2008). Towards Unlocking the Full Potential of Acquisitions: The Role of Organizational Restructuring. *Academy of Management Journal, 34,* 594–611.

Barkema, H. G., & Vermeulen, F. (1998). International Expansion through Start-Up or Acquisition: A Learning Perspective. *Journal of the Academy of Management,* 7–26.

Barker, R. G. (1999). The Role of Dividends in Valuation Models Used by Analysts and Fund Managers. *Accounting Review*, 195–204.

Barnett, T. R. (2008). Message from the AAG, U.S. Department of Justice. *Antitrust Division Update*, Spring.

Barzuza, M. (2009). The State of Antitakeover Law. *Virginia Law Review*, 95, 1973–2052.

Bates, T. W. (2005). Asset Sales, Investment Opportunities, and the Use of Proceeds. *Journal of Finance*, 60, 105–135.

Bebchuk, L., Coates, J., & Subramanian, G. (2002). The Powerful Anti-Takeover Force of Staggered Boards: Theory, Evidence, and Policy. *Stanford Law Review*, 54, 887–951.

Bebchuk, L., Cohen, A., & Ferrell, A. (2005). *What Matters in Corporate Governance*. Harvard University Law School. Discussion Paper No. 49.

Bebchuk, L., Cohen, A., & Wang, C. (2010). *Learning and the Disappearing Association between Governance and Returns*. Harvard Law and Economics Discussion Paper No. 667.

Bebchuk, L. J., Coates, J. C., IV, & Subramanian, G. (2003). *The Powerful Antitkeover Force of Staggered Boards*. Harvard Law School and NBER. Working Paper.

Bekaert, G., & Harvey, C. R. (2000). Foreign Speculators and Emerging Equity Markets. *Journal of Finance*, 55, 565–613.

Bekaert, G., Hodrick, R., & Zhang, X. (2009). International Stock Return Comovement. *Journal of Finance*, 64, 2591–2626.

Bekier, M. M., Bogardus, A. J., & Oldham, T. (2001). Why Mergers Fail. *McKinsey Quarterly*, 4, 3.

Bellovary, J. L., Giacomino, D. E., & Akers, M. D. (2007). A Review of Bankruptcy Prediction Studies: 1930 to the Present. *Journal of Financial Education* (Winter), 262–298.

Ben-Amar, W., & Andre, P. (2006). Separation of Ownership from Control and Acquiring Firm Performance: The Case of Family Ownership in Canada. *Journal of Business Finance and Accounting*, 33, 517–543.

Beneda, N. (2007). Performance and Distress Indicators of New Public Companies. *Journal of Asset Management*, 8, 24–33.

Bengoa, M., & Sanchez-Robles, B. (2003). Foreign Direct Investment, Economic Freedom and Growth. *European Journal of Political Economy*, 19, 529–545.

Benmelech, E., & Bergman, N. (2011). Bankruptcy and the Collateral Channel. *Journal of Finance* (April).

Bennedsen, M., Nielsen, K., Perez-Gonzalez, F., & Wolfenson, D. (2006). *Inside the Family Firm: The Role of Families in Succession Decisions and Performance*. New York University. Working Paper.

Berger, P. G., & Ofek, E. (1995). Diversification's Effect on Firm Value. *Journal of Financial Economics*, 37, 39–65.

Berggren, N., & Jordahl, H. (2005). Does Free Trade Reduce Growth? Further Testing Using the Economic Freedom Index. *Public Choice*, 22, 99–114.

Bergh, D., Johnson, R., & Dewitt, R. L. (2007). Restructuring through Spin-Off or Sell-Off: Transforming Information Asymmetries into Financial Gain. *Strategic Management Journal*, 29, 133–148.

Berk, J. B. (1995). A Critique of Size Related Anomalies. *The Review of Financial Studies*, 8, 275–286.

Berman, D. K., & Sender, H. (2006). Back-Story of Kinder LBO Underscores Web of Ethical Issues Such Deals Face. *Wall Street Journal*, A6.

Bernard, V., Healy, P., & Palepu, K. G. (2000). *Business Analysis and Valuation* (2nd ed.). Georgetown, TX: Southwestern College Publishing Company.

Best, R., & Hodges, C. W. (2004). Does Information Asymmetry Explain the Diversification Discount? *Journal of Financial Research*, 27(Summer), 235–249.

Betker, B. (1995). An Empirical Examination of Prepackaged Bankruptcy. *Financial Management*, (Spring), 3–18.

Betton, S., Eckbo, B., & Thorburn, K. (2008). Corporate Takeovers. In B. Eckbo (Ed.), *Handbook of Corporate Finance: Empirical Corporate Finance* (vol. 2, pp. 291–430). Amsterdam: NorthHolland/Elsevier.

Betton, S., Eckbo, B., & Thorburn, K. (2009). Merger Negotiations and the Toehold Puzzle. *Journal of Financial Economics*, 91, 158–178.

Bhagat, S., Dong, M., Hirshleifer, D., & Noah, R. (2005). Do Tender Offers Create Value? New Methods and Evidence. *Journal of Financial Economics*, 76, 3–60.

Bigelli, M., & Mengoli, S. (2004). Sub-Optimal Acquisition Decision under a Majority Shareholder System. *Journal of Management and Governance*, 8, 373–403.

Billett, M. T., Jiang, Z., & Lie, E. (2010). The Effect of Change in Control Covenants on Takeovers: Evidence from Leveraged Buyouts. *Journal of Corporate Finance*, 16, 1–15.

Billett, M. T., King, T. H. D., & Mauer, D. C. (2004). Bondholder Wealth Effects on Mergers and Acquisitions: New Evidence from the 1980s and 1990s. *Journal of Finance*, 59, 107–135.

Billett, M. T., & Qian, Y. (2008). Are Overconfident Managers Born or Made? Evidence of Self-Attribution Bias from Frequent Acquirers. *Management Science*, 1036–1055.

Billett, M. T., & Vijh, A. M. (2004). The Wealth Effects of Tracking Stock Restructurings. *Journal of Financial Research*, 27(Winter), 559–583.

Billett, M. T., & Xue, H. (2007). The Takeover Deterrent Effect of Open Market Share Repurchases. *Journal of Finance*, 62, 1827–1851.

Black, E. L., Carnes, T. A., & Jandik, T. (2000). *The Long-Term Success of Cross-Border Mergers and Acquisitions. Social Science Research Network Electronic Paper Collection.* Available at *http://papers.ssrn.com/5013/delivery.cfn/ssrn_id272782_010705100.pdf.*

Blackman, A. (2006). Your U.S. Fund May Be Scurrying Abroad. *Wall Street Journal,* C2.

Bloomberg.com. (2000). *Glaxo, SmithKline Agree to Merge.* January 18.

Blume, M. E., Lim, F., & MacKinlay, A. C. (1998). The Declining Credit Quality of U.S. Corporate Debt: Myth or Reality? *Journal of Finance, 53,* 1389–1413.

Bodnar, G., Dumas, B., & Marston, R. (2003). *Cross-Border Valuations: The International Cost of Capital.* Fontainebleau: France. INSEAD Working Paper.

Boehmer, E. (2000). Business Groups, Bank Control, and Large Shareholders: An Analysis of German Takeovers. *Journal of Financial Intermediation, 9,* 117–148.

Boer, P. E. (2002). *The Real Options Solution: Finding Total Value in a High Risk World.* New York: Wiley.

Bogler, D. (1996). Post-Takeover Stress Disorder, Summary of a PA Consulting Study. *Financial Times,* 11.

Boone, A. L., & Mulherin, J. H. (2009). Is There One Best Way to Sell a Firm? Auctions Versus Negotiations and Controlled Sales. *Journal of Applied Corporate Finance, 21,* 28–37.

Boot, A. W. A., Gopalan, R., & Thakor, A. V. (2008). Market Liquidity, Investor Participation, and Managerial Autonomy: Why Do Firms Go Private? *Journal of Finance, 63,* 2013–2059.

Booth, L. (2002). Finding Value Where None Exists: Pitfalls in Using Adjusted Present Value. *Journal of Applied Corporate Finance, 15* (Spring), 1–15.

Booz-Allen, L., & Hamilton, L. (1993). *A Practical Guide to Alliances: Leapfrogging the Learning Curve.* Los Angeles: Booz Allen Hamilton.

Borden, A. M. (1987). *Going Private.* New York: Law Journal Seminar Press.

Boston Consulting Group. (1985). *The Strategy Development Process.* Boston: The Boston Consulting Group.

Boston Consulting Group. (2003). *Weak Economy is Ideal Time for Mergers and Acquisitions.* Available at *www.srimedia.com/artman/ppublish/printer_657.shtml.*

Boyle, G. W., Carer, R. B., & Stover, R. D. (1998). Extraordinary Anti-Takeover Provisions and Insider Ownership Structure: The Case of Converting Savings and Loans. *Journal of Financial and Quantitative Analysis, 33,* 291–304.

Bradley, M., Desai, A., & Kim, E. H. (1988). Synergistic Gains from Corporate Acquisitions and Their Division between the Stockholders of Target and Acquiring Firms. *Journal of Financial Economics, 21,* 3.

Brakman, S., Garretsen, H., & Van Marrewijk, C. (2005). *Cross-Border Mergers and Acquisitions: On Revealed Comparative Advantage and Merger Waves.* CESifo Working Paper No. 1602, Category 10: Empirical and Theoretical Methods.

Branch, B. (2002). The Costs of Bankruptcy: A Review. *International Review of Financial Analysis, 11,* 39–57.

Brav, A., Jiang, W., Partnoy, F., & Thomas, R. (2006). *Hedge Fund Activism, Corporate Governance, and Firm Performance.* Duke University, ECGI-Finance Working Paper No. 13912006.

Brealey, R. A., & Myers, S. C. (1996). *Principles of Corporate Finance* (5th ed.). New York: McGraw-Hill.

Brealey, R. A., & Myers, S. C. (2003). *Principles of Corporate Finance* (7th ed.). New York: McGraw-Hill.

Briel, R. (2010). YouTube: Profitable in 2010. *Broadband TV News,* March, 3. *www.broadbanktvnew.com/2010/03/05/youtube-proffitable-in-2010/.*

Brigham, E. F., & Ehrhardt, M. C. (2005). *Financial Management: Theory and Practice.* Mason, OH: Thomson-Southwestern Publishing.

Bris, A., & Cabolis, C. (2004). *Adopting Better Corporate Governance: Evidence from Cross-Border Mergers.* Yale University Working Paper.

Bris, A., Welch, I., & Zhu, N. (2006). Chapter 7 Liquidation Versus Chapter 11 Reorganization. *Journal of Finance,* (June), 1253–1303.

Brookings Institution Press. (2000). *Antitrust Goes Global.* Alexander Lehmann, Benn Steil, and Simon J. Evenett, eds.

Brophy, D. J., Ouimet, P. P., & Sialm, C. (2009). Hedge Funds as Investors of Last Resort. *The Review of Financial Studies, 22,* 541–574.

Brouthers, K. D. (2002). Institutional, Cultural, and Transaction Cost Influences on Entry Mode Choice and Performance. *Journal of International Business Studies, 33,* 203–221.

Brouthers, K. D., & Brouthers, L. E. (2000). Acquisition, Greenfield Start-Up: Institutional, Cultural, and Transaction Cost Influences. *Strategic Management Journal, 21,* 89–97.

Brouthers, K. D., van Hastenburg, P., & van den Ven, J. (2000). If Most Mergers Fail Why Are They So Popular? *Long Range Planning, 31,* 347–353.

Brouthers, K. D., van Hastenburg, P., & Van de Ven, J. (1998). If Mergers Fail Why Are They So Popular? *Long-Range Planning, 31,* 347–353.

Brunnermeier, M. (2009). Deciphering the Liquidity and Credit Crunch of 2007–2008. *Journal of Economic Perspectives, 23,* 77–100.

Bryan-Low, C. (2005). European Telecoms Vie for Emerging Markets. *Wall Street Journal,* B2.

Buljevich, E. C. (2005). *Cross Border Debt Restructuring: Innovative Approaches for Creditors, Corporate and Sovereigns.* London: Euromoney Institutional Investor.

Burch, T. R. (2001). Locking Out Rival Bidders: The Use of Lockup Options in Corporate Mergers. *Journal of Financial Economics, 60,* 103–141.

Burch, T. R., & Nanda, V. (2001). Divisional Diversity and the Conglomerate Discount: Evidence from Spin-Offs. *Journal of Financial Economics, 70,* 233–257.

Burkhart, M., Gromb, D., & Panunzi, F. (1997). Larger Shareholders, Monitoring and the Value of the Firm. *Quarterly Journal of Economics,* 693–728.

Burrus, A., & McNamee, M. (2002). Evaluating the Rating Agencies. *Business Week, 8,* 39–40.

Business Week. (2000a). *Burying the Hatchet Buys a Lot of Drug Research,* p 43.

Business Week (2000b). *Jack's Risky Last Act,* pp. 40–45.

Business Week, (2001, February 5). *A Merger's Bitter Harvest,* p. 112.

Business Week (2008). *Easygoing Trustbusters,* p. 8.

Bygrave, W. D., & Timmons, J. A. (1992). *Venture Capital at the Crossroads.* Boston: Harvard Business School Press.

Byrd, J., & Hickman, K. (1992). Do Outside Directors Monitor Managers? Evidence from Tender Offer Bids. *Journal of Financial Economics, 32,* 195–207.

Cakici, N. G., & Tandon, K. (1996). Foreign Acquisitions in the U.S.: Effects on Shareholder Wealth of Foreign Acquiring Firms. *Journal of Banking and Finance, 20,* 307–329.

Campa, J., & Simi, K. (2002). Explaining the Diversification Discount. *Journal of Finance, 57,* 135–160.

Campbell, A., Sadler, D., & Koch, R. (1997). *Breakup! When Companies Are Worth More Dead than Alive.* Oxford, UK: Capstone.

Campbell, J. Y., Hilscher, J., & Szilagyi, J. (2008). In Search of Distress Risk. *Journal of Finance, 63,* 2899–2939.

Cao, J., & Lerner, J. (2009). The Success of Reverse Leveraged Buyouts. *Journal of Financial Economics, 91,* 139–157.

Cao, J. X. (2008). *An Empirical Study of LBOs and Takeover Premiums. SSRN.* Available at *http://ssrn.com/abstrat=1100059,* February 10 Available.

Capron, L., & Shen, J. C. (2007). Acquisitions of Private versus Public Firms: Private Information, Target Selection, and Acquirer Returns. *Strategic Management Journal, 28,* 891–911.

Carey, D. C., & Ogden, D. (2004). *The Human Side of M&A.* Oxford, UK: Oxford University Press.

Carleton, J. R., & Lineberry, C. S. (2004). *Achieving Post-Merger Success.* New York: Wiley.

Carline, F. N., Linn, S. C., & Yadav, P. K. (2009). Operating Performance Changes Associated with Corporate Mergers and the Role of Corporate Governance. *Journal of Banking and Finance, 33,* 1829–1841.

Carlton, D., & Perloff, J. (1999). *Modern Industrial Organization* (3rd ed.). New York: Addison Wesley Longman.

Carow, K. A., & Roden, D. M. (1998). Determinants of the Stock Price Reaction to Leveraged Buyouts. *Journal of Economics and Finance, 22*(Spring), 37–47.

Carrington, G. R. (2007). *Tax Accounting in Mergers and Acquisitions.* New York: CCH.

Caves, R. E. (1982). *Multinational Enterprise and Economic Analysis.* Cambridge, MA: Cambridge University Press.

CCH Tax Law Editors. (2005). *U.S. Master Tax Code.* New York: Commerce Clearinghouse.

Ceneboyan, A. S., Papaioannou, G. J., & Travlos, N. (1991). Foreign Takeover Activity in the U.S. and Wealth Effects for Target Firm Shareholders. *Financial Management, 31,* 58–68.

Chaffee, D. B. (1993). Option Pricing as a Proxy for Discount for Lack of Marketability in Private Company Valuation. *Business Valuation Review,* 182–188.

Chakrabarti, A. (1990). Organizational Factors in Post-Acquisition Performance. *IEEE Transactions in Engineering Management EM-37, 135,* 259–266.

Chakrabarti, R., Jayaraman, N., & Mukherjee, S. (2005). *Mars-Venus Marriages: Culture and Cross-Border M&A.* Georgia Institute of Technology Working Paper.

Chang, S. (1998). Takeovers of Privately Held Targets, Methods of Payment, and Bidder Returns. *Journal of Finance, 53.*

Chang, S. C. (2008). *How Do Strategic Alliances Affect Suppliers, Customers, and Rivals.* Social Science Research Network Working Paper.

Chan, K. C., Karolyi, G. A., & Stulz, R. M. (1992). Global Financial Markets and the Risk Premium of U.S. Equity. *Journal of Financial Economics, 32,* 137–167.

Chan, L. K. C., Lakonishok, J., & Sougiannis, T. (1999). Investing in High R&D Stocks. *Business Week, 28.*

Chan, S. H., Kensinger, J. W., Keown, A. J., & Martin, J. D. (1997). Do Strategic Alliances Create Value? *Journal of Financial Economics, 46,* 199–221.

Chaochharia, V., & Grinstein, Y. (2007). Corporate Governance and Firm Value: The Impact of the 2002 Governance Rules. *Journal of Finance, 62,* 1789–1825.

Chaplinsky, S., & Ramchand, L. (2000). The Impact of Global Equity Offers. *Journal of Finance,* 2767–2789.

Chapman, T. L., Dempsey, J. J., Ramsdell, G., & Bell, T. E. (1998). Purchasing's Big Moment—After a Merger. *McKinsey Quarterly, 1,* 56–65.

Chari, A., Ouiment, P., & Tesar, L. (2004). *Cross-Border Mergers and Acquisitions in Emerging Markets: The*

Stock Market Valuation of Corporate Control. University of Michigan Working Paper.

Charitou, A., & Trigeorgis, L. (2000). *Option-Based Bankruptcy Prediction.* University of Cyprus Working Paper.

Chatterjee, R. A., & Aw, M. S. B. (2004). The Performance of UK: Firms Acquiring Large Cross-Border and Domestic Takeover Targets. *Applied Financial Economics, 14,* 337–349.

Chatterjee, S., & Yan, A. (2008). Using Innovative Securities Under Asymmetric Information: Why Do Some Firms Pay with Contingent Value Rights? *Journal of Financial and Quantitative Analysis, 43*(4), 1001–1035.

Chemmanur, T., & Paeglis, I. (2000). *Why Issue Tracking Stock?* Working Paper. Available by email from *chemmanu@bc.edu.*

Chen, C., & Findlay, C. (2002). *A Review of Cross-Border Mergers and Acquisitions in APEC.* Canberra: Australian National University.

Cheng, C. S., Liu, C. S., & Schaefer, T. F. (1996). Earnings Permanence and the Incremental Information Content of Cash Flow from Operations. *Journal of Accounting Research,* (Spring), 173–181.

Chen, H. L., & Guo, R. J. (2005). On Corporate Divestitures. *Review of Quantitative Finance and Accounting, 25,* 399–421.

Child, J., & Faulkner, D. (1998). *Strategies of Cooperation: Managerial Alliances, Networks, and Joint Ventures.* Oxford: Oxford University Press.

Child, J., Faulkner, D., & Pitkethley, R. (2001). *The Management of International Acquisitions.* Oxford: Oxford University Press.

Cho, M. H., & Cohen, M. A. (1997). The Economic Causes and Consequences of Corporate Divestiture. *Managerial and Decision Economics, 18,* 367–374.

Christofferson, S. A., McNish, R. S., & Sias, D. L. (2004). Where Mergers Go Wrong. *McKinsey Quarterly.* *www.mckinseyquarterly.com/home.aspx.*

Claessens, S., Djankov, S., Fan, J., & Lang, H. P. I. (2002). Disentangling the Incentive and Entrenchment Effects of Large Shareholders. *Journal of Finance, 57,* 2741–2771.

Clark, K., & Ofek, E. (1994). Mergers as a Means of Restructuring Distressed Firms: An Empirical Investigation. *Journal of Financial and Quantitative Analysis, 29,* 541–565.

Claus, J., & Thomas, J. (2001). Equity Premia as Low as Three Percent? Empirical Evidence from Analysts' Earnings Forecasts for Domestic and International Stock Markets. *Journal of Finance, 56,* 1629–1666.

Clifford, C. (2007). *Value Creation or Destruction: Hedge Funds as Shareholder Activists.* Arizona State University. Working Paper.

Clubb, C., & Stouraitis, A. (2000). The Significance of Sell-Off Profitability in Explaining the Market Reaction to Divestiture Announcements. *Journal of Banking and Finance, 26,* 671–688.

Coates, J. C. (2000). Takeover Defenses in the Shadow of the Pill: A Critique of the Scientific Evidence. *Texas Law Review, 79,* 271–382.

Coates, J. C. (2001). Explaining Variation in Takeover Defenses: Blame the Lawyers. *California Law Review, 89,* 1376.

Coates, J. C. (2007). The Goals and Promise of the Sarbanes-Oxley Act. *The Journal of Economic Perspectives, 21*(Winter), 91–116.

Coffee, J., Seligman, J., & Sale, H. (2008). *Federal Securities Laws: Selected Statutes, Rules, and Forms.* New York: Foundation Press.

Colak, G., & Whited, T. (2007). Spin-Offs, Divestitures, and Conglomerate Investment. *The Review of Financial Studies, 20,* 557–595.

Coles, J. L., Daniel, N. D., & Naveen, L. (2008). Boards: Does One Size Fit All? *Journal of Financial Economics, 87,* 329–356.

Comment, R., & Schwert, G. W. (1995). Poison or Placebo: Evidence on the Deterrence and Wealth Effects of Modern Anti-Takeover Measures. *Journal of Financial Economics, 39,* 3–43.

Conn, R. L., Cost, A., Guest, P. M., & Hugues, A. (2005). *Why Must All Good Things Come to an End?* In *The Performance of Multiple Acquirers.* University of Cambridge Working Paper. Available at *http://ssrn.com/abstract=499310.*

Cooper Lybrand, S. (1996). Most Acquisitions Fail, C&L Study Says. *Mergers & Acquisitions, 47,* 2, Report 7.

Copeland, T., Koller, T., & Murrin, J. (2005). *Valuation: Measuring, and Managing the Value of Companies* (4th ed.). New York: Wiley.

Cossey, B. (1991). Systems Assessment in Acquired Subsidiaries. *Accountancy,* 98–99.

Cremers, M. K. J., Nair, V. B., & Wei, C. (2004). *The Impact of Shareholder Control on Bondholders.* Yale University and New York University. Working Paper.

Cremers, M., & Nair, V. (2005). Governance Mechanisms and Equity Prices. *Journal of Finance, 60,* 2859–2894.

Creswell, J. (2001). Would You Give This Man Your Company? *Fortune,* 127–129.

Croci, E., & Petmezas, D. (2009). Minority Shareholders' Wealth Effects and Stock Market Development: Evidence from Increase-in-Ownership M&As. *Journal of Banking and Finance, 34,* 681–694.

Cumming, D., Siegel, D., & Wright, M. (2007). Private Equity, Leveraged Buyouts and Governance. *Journal of Corporate Finance, 13,* 439–460.

Cusatis, P. J., Miles, J. A., & Woolridge, J. R. (1993). Restructuring through Spin-Offs. *Journal of Financial Economics*, *33*, 293–311.

Cyree, K. B., & Walker, M. M. (2008). The Determinants and Survival of Reverse Mergers Versus IPOs. *Journal of Economics and Finance, 32*, 176–194.

Daley, L., Mehrotra, V., & Sivakumar, R. (1997). Corporate Focus and Value Creation, Evidence from Spin-Offs. *Journal of Financial Economics, 45*, 257–281.

Dalton, D. R. (2006). CEO Tenure, Boards of Directors, and Acquisition Performance. *Journal of Business Research, 60*, 331–338.

Dalton, D. R., & Dalton, C. M. (2007). Sarbanes-Oxley and the Guideline of the Listing Exchanges: What Have We Wrought? *Business Horizons, 50*, 93–100.

Damodaran, A. (2002). *Investment Valuation: Tools and Techniques for Determining the Value of Any Asset* (2nd ed.). New York: Wiley.

Das, S., Sen, P. K., & Sengupta, S. (1998). Impact of Strategic Alliances on Firm Valuation. *Academy of Management Journal, 41*, 27–41.

Datta, S., Iskandar-Datta, M., & Raman, K. (2003). Value Creation in Corporate Asset Sales: The Role of Managerial Performance and Lender Monitoring. *Journal of Banking and Finance, 27*, 351–375.

Davis, A., & Leblond, M. (2002). *A Spin-Off Analysis: Evidence from New and Old Economies.* Queen's University Working Paper. Available by email from *adavis@business.queensu.ca*.

Davis, G., & Kim, H. (2007). Business Ties and Proxy Voting by Mutual Funds. *Journal of Financial Economics, 85*, 552–570.

Davis, P. S., Desai, A. B., & Francis, J. D. (2000). Mode of International Entry: An Isomorphian Perspective. *Journal of International Business Studies, 31*, 239–258.

Davis, S. J., Haltiwanger, J., Jarmin, R., Lerner, J., & Miranda, J. (2008). *Private Equity and Employment.* U.S. Census Bureau, Center for Economic Studies. Paper No. CES-WP-08-07.

DeAngelo, H., DeAngelo, L., & Rice, E. (1984). Going Private: Minority Freezeouts and Stockholder Wealth. *Journal of Law and Economics, 27*, 367–401.

DeAngelo, H., & Rice, E. (1983). Anti-Takeover Charter Amendments and Stockholder Wealth. *Journal of Financial Economics, 11*, 329–360.

Dechow, P. M. (1994). Accounting Earnings and Cash Flows as Measures of Firm Performance: The Role of Accounting Accruals. *Journal of Accounting and Economics*, 3–42.

Delios, A., & Beamish, P. S. (1999). Geographic Scope, Product Diversification, and the Corporate Performance of Japanese Firms. *Strategic Management Journal, 20*, 711–727.

DeLong, G. (2003). Does Long-Term Performance of Mergers Match Market Expectations? *Financial Management*, (Summer), 5–25.

De Mdedt, J., & Van Hoey, M. (2008). *Integrating Steel Giants: An Interview with the Arcelor-Mittal Post Merger Managers.* McKinsey and Company.

Demirakos, E. G., Strong, N. C., & Walker, M. (2004). What Valuation Models Do Analysts Use? *Accounting Horizons* (December), 229–235.

Demsetz, H., & Lehn, K. (1996). The Structure of Corporate Ownership: Causes and Consequences. *Journal of Political Economy, 93*, 1155–1177.

Deogun, N., & Lipin, S. (2000). "Big Mergers in '90s Prove Disappointing to Shareholders," Salomon Smith Barney study, quoted in *Wall Street Journal*, C12.

De Pamphilis, D. M. (2001). Managing Growth Through Acquisition: Time Tested Techniques for the Entrepreneur. *International Journal of Entrepreneurship and Innovation, 2*(3), 195–205.

DePamphilis, D. M. (2010a). *M&A Basics: All You Need to Know.* Boston: Elsevier.

DePamphilis, D. M. (2010b). *M&A Negotiations and Deal Structuring: All You Need to Know.* Boston: Elsevier.

Desai, H., & Jain, P. (1997). Firm Performance and Focus: Long-Run Stock Market Performance Following Spin-Offs. *Journal of Financial Economics, 54*, 75–101.

De Visscher, F. M., Arnoff, C. E., & Ward, J. L. (1995). *Financing Transitions: Managing Capital and Liquidity in the Family Business.* Marietta, GA: Business Owner Resources.

de Vroom, H. J., & van Frederikslust, R. (1999). *Shareholder Wealth Effects of Corporate Spinoffs: The Worldwide Experience 1990–1998.* SSRN Working Paper Series.

Dewenter, K. L. (1995). Does the Market React Differently to Domestic and Foreign Takeover Announcements? Evidence from the U.S. Chemical and Retail Industries. *Journal of Financial Economics, 37*, 421–441.

Dichev, I. (1998). Is the Risk of Bankruptcy a Systematic Risk? *Journal of Finance, 53*, 1141–1148.

Diermeier, J., & Solnik, B. (2001). Global Pricing of Equity. *Financial Analysts Journal, 57*, 17–47.

Dimson, E., March, P., & Staunton, M. (2002). *Triumph of the Optimists.* Princeton NJ: Princeton University Press.

Dimson, E., March, P., & Staunton, M. (2003). Global Evidence on the Equity Risk Premium. *Journal of Applied Corporate Finance, 15*(Fall), 27–38.

Dionne, G., La Haye, M., & Bergeres, A. (2010). *Does Asymmetric Information Affect the Premium in Mergers and Acquisitions?* Interuniversity Research Centre on Enterprise Networks, Logistics and Transportation, and Department of Finance, HEC Montreal.

Dittmar, A., & Shivdasani, A. (2002). Divestitures and Divisional Investment Policies. *Journal of Finance, 58*, 2711–2744.

Dong, M., Hirshleifer, D., Richardson, S., & Teoh, S. H. (2006). Does Investor Misvaluation Drive the Takeover Market? *Journal of Finance, 61*, 725–762.

Down, J. W. (1995). The M&A Game Is Often Won or Lost after the Deal. *Management Review Executive Forum*, 10.

Draper, P., & Paudyal, K. (2006). Acquisitions: Private versus Public. *European Financial Management, 12*, 57–80.

Drucker, J., & Silver, S. (2006). Alcatel Stands to Reap Tax Benefits on Merger. *Wall Street Journal*, April 26, C3.

D'Souza, J., & Jacob, J. (2000). Why Firms Issue Targeted Stock. *Journal of Financial Economics, 56*, 459–483.

Duffie, D., Saita, L., & Wang, K. (2007). Multi-Period Corporate Default Prediction with Stochastic Covariates. *Journal of Financial Economics, 83*, 635–665.

Dumontier, P., & Pecherot, B. (2001). *Determinants of Returns to Acquiring Firms around Tender Offer Announcement Dates: The French Evidence*. ESA Universite de Grenoble. Working Paper.

Dunning, J. (1993). *Multinational Enterprises and the Global Economy*. Reading, MA: Addison-Wesley Publishing.

Dunning, J. H. (1988). The Eclectic Paradigm of International Production: A Restatement and Some Possible Extensions. *Journal of International Business Studies*, 1–31.

Dutordoir, M., Roosenboom, P., & Vasconcelos, M. (2010). Synergies Disclosure in Mergers and Acquisitions. *Social Science Research Network*. Available at *http://ssrn.com/abstract=1571546*.

Dutta, S., Iskandar-Dutta, M., & Raman, K. (2001). Executive Compensation and Corporate Acquisition Decisions. *Journal of Finance, 56*, 2299–2396.

Dutta, S., & Jog, V. (2009). The Long-Term Performance of Acquiring Firms: A Re-Examination of an Anomaly. *Journal of Banking and Finance, 33*, 1400–1412.

Dyck, A., & Zingales, L. (2004). Control Premiums and the Effectiveness of Corporate Governance Systems. *Journal of Applied Finance, 16* (Spring/Summer), 51–72.

Easton, P., Taylor, G., Shroff, P., & Sougiannis, T. (2001). Using Forecasts of Earnings to Simultaneously Estimate Growth and the Rate of Return on Equity Investment. *Journal of Accounting Research, 40*, 657–676.

Eberhart, A. C., Altman, E. I., & Aggarwal, R. (1999). The Equity Performance of Firms Emerging from Bankruptcy. *Journal of Finance, 54*, 1855–1868.

Ebin, R. F. (1998). Legal Aspects of International Joint Ventures and Strategic Alliances. In D. J. BenDaniel & A. H. Rosenbloom (Eds.), *International M&A, Joint Ventures and Beyond: Doing the Deal* (pp. 315–360). New York: Wiley.

Eckbo, B. E., & Thorburn, K. S. (2008). Automatic Bankruptcy Auctions and Fire-Sales. *Journal of Financial Economics, 89*, 404–422.

Eckbo, B. E., & Thorburn, K. S. (2000). Gains to Bidder Firms Revisited: Domestic and Foreign Acquisitions in Canada. *Journal of Financial and Quantitative Analysis, 35*, 1–25.

Economic Report to the President. (2003). *Economic Report to the President*. Washington DC: U.S. Government Printing Office.

The Economist. (2006a). *Battling for Corporate America*, March 9.

The Economist. (2006b). *A Survey of the World Economy*, September 14.

Elango, B., & Rakeh, B. (2004). The Influence of Industry Structure on the Entry Mode Choice of Overseas Entrants in Manufacturing Industries. *Journal of International Management*, 107–124.

Elder, J., & Westra, P. (2000). The Reaction of Security Prices to Tracking Stock Announcements. *Journal of Economics and Finance, 24*, 36–55.

Ellis, C. (1996). Briefings from the Editors. *Harvard Business Review, 74*, 8.

Ellison, S. (2006). Clash of Cultures Exacerbates Woes for Tribune Co. *Wall Street Journal*, 1.

Emory, J. D. (2001). The Value of Marketability as Illustrated in Initial Public Offerings of Common Stock. *Business Valuation Review, 20*, 21–24.

Engel, E., Hayes, R., & Xang, X. (2004). *The Sarbanes–Oxley Act and Firms' Going Private Decisions*. University of Chicago. Working Paper.

Ertimur, Y., Ferri, F., & Stubben, S. (2008). *Board of Directors' Responsiveness to Shareholders: Evidence from Shareholder Proposals*. Harvard Business School. Working Paper.

Erwin, G. R., & McConnell, J. J. (1997). To Live or Die? An Empirical Analysis of Piecemeal Voluntary Liquidations. *Journal of Corporate Finance, 3*, 325–354.

Escherich, R. (1998). Selected Results from Our Survey of U.S. Valuation Techniques. In *Global Mergers & Acquisition Review*. New York and London: J. P. Morgan.

Eun, C. S., Huang, W., & Lai, S. (2007). International Diversification with Large and Small Cap Stocks. *Journal of Financial and Quantitative Analysis, 43*, 489–524.

Eun, C. S., Kolodny, R., & Scherage, C. (1996). Cross-Border Acquisition and Shareholder Wealth: Tests of the Synergy and Internationalization Hypotheses. *Journal of Banking and Finance, 20*, 1559–1582.

Faccio, M., & Lang, L. H. P. (2002). The Ultimate Ownership of Western European Corporations. *Journal of Financial Economics, 65*, 365–395.

Faccio, M., & Masulis, R. (2005). The Choice of Payment Method in European Mergers and Acquisitions. *Journal of Finance, 60*, 1345–1388.

Faccio, M., McConnell, J., & Stolin, D. (2006). Returns to Acquirers of Listed and Unlisted Companies. *Journal of Financial and Quantitative Analysis, 47*, 197–220.

Faleye, O. (2004). Cash and Corporate Control. *Journal of Finance, 59*, 2041–2060.

Fama, E. F. (1998). Market Efficiency, Long-Term Returns, and Behavioral Finance. *Journal of Financial Economics, 47*, 427–465.

Fama, E. F., & French, K. R. (1992). The Cross-Section of Expected Stock Returns. *Journal of Finance, 47*, 427–465.

Fama, E. F., & French, K. R. (1993). Common Risk Factors in the Returns on Stocks and Bonds. *Journal of Financial Economics, 33*, 3–56.

Fama, E. F., & French, K. R. (2006). The Value Premium and the CAPM. *Journal of Finance, 61*, 2163–2185.

Fama, E. F., & Jensen, M. C. (1983). Separation of Ownership and Control. *Journal of Law and Economics, 26*, 301–325.

Farzad, R. (2006). Fidelity's Divided Loyalties. *Business Week*, 12.

Fauver, L., Houston, J., & Narango, A. (2003). Capital Market Development, International Integration, and the Value of Corporate Diversification: A Cross-Country Analysis. *Journal of Financial and Quantitative Analysis, 38*, 138–155.

Federal Reserve Bulletin. (2003). *Board of Governors*. U.S. Federal Reserve System (December), 33.

Federal Trade Commission, Bureau of Competition. (1999b). *A Study of the Commission's Divestiture Process*.

Federal Trade Commission. (1999a). *Merger Guidelines*. Available at *www.ftc.com*.

Feliciano, Z., & Lipsey, R. E. (2002). *Foreign Entry Into U.S. Manufacturing by Takeovers and the Creation of New Firms*. Cambridge, MA: National Bureau of Economic Research. Working Paper No. 9122.

Fernandez, P. (2011). *Market Risk Premium in 2010 by Professors, Survey with 1500 Answers*. Available at *http://ssrn.com/abstract=1606563*.

Ferreira, M. A., Massa, M., & Matos, P. (2010). Shareholders at the Gate? Institutional Investors and Cross-Border Mergers and Acquisitions. *Review of Financial Studies, 23*, 601–644.

Ferreira, M. P., & Tallman, S. B. (2005). *Building and Leveraging Knowledge Capabilities through Cross-Border Acquisitions*. Presentation to the Academy of Management Meeting.

Field, L. C., & Karpoff, J. M. (2002). Takeover Defenses of IPO Firms. *Journal of Finance, 57*, 1629–1666.

Fields, L. P., & Mais, E. L. (1991). The Valuation Effects of Private Placements of Convertible Debt. *Journal of Finance, 46*, 1925–1932.

Financial Times (1996). *Bugged by Failures,* April 8.

Finnerty, J. D. (2002). *The Impact of Transfer Restrictions on Stock Prices*. Cambridge MA: Analysis Group/Economics. Working Paper.

Foley & Lardner LLP. (2007). *What Private Companies and Non-Profits Need to Know About SOX*. Report presented at Foley & Lardner's 2004 National Directors Institute Meeting, Chicago.

France, M. (2002). Bankruptcy Reform Won't Help Telecom. *Business Week*, 40.

Francis, B., Hasan, I., & Sun, X. (2008). Financial Market Integration and the Value of Global Diversification: Evidence for U.S. Acquirers in Cross-Border Mergers and Acquisitions. *Journal of Banking and Finance, 32*, 1522–1540.

Franks, J., & Mayer, C. (1996). Hostile Takeovers and the Correction of Managerial Failure. *Journal of Financial Economics, 40*, 163–181.

Freeman, L. S., & Stephens, T. M. (1994). Advantages, Key Issues, and Tax Strategies in the Use of Partnerships by Corporate Joint Ventures. In *Tax Strategies for Corporate Acquisitions, Dispositions, Spin-Offs, Joint Ventures and Other Strategic Alliances, Financings, Reorganizations, and Restructurings*. New York: Practicing Law Institute.

Frick, K. A., & Torres, A. (2002). Learning from High Tech Deals. *McKinsey Quarterly, 1*, 2.

Fuller, K., Netter, J., & Stegemoller, M. A. (2002). What Do Returns to Acquiring Firms Tell Us? Evidence from Firms That Make Many Acquisitions. *Journal of Finance, 57*, 1763–1793.

Fusaro, R. F. X. (1995). Issues to Consider in Drafting Joint Venture Agreements. In *Drafting Corporate Agreements*. New York: Practicing Law Institute.

Garlappi, L., & Yan, H. (2011). Financial Distress and the Cross Section of Equity Returns. *Journal of Finance*, forthcoming.

Gaspara, J. M., & Massa, P. (2005). Shareholder Investment Horizons and the Market for Corporate Control. *Journal of Financial Economics, 76*, 135–165.

Gell, J., Kengelbach, J., & Roos, A. (2008). *The Return of the Strategist: Creating Value with M&A in Downturns*. Boston: Boston Consulting Group.

Gelman, M. (1972). An Economist-Financial Analyst's Approach to Valuing Stock of a Closely Held Company. *Journal of Taxation*, 46–53.

Georgopoulos, G. (2008). Cross-Border Mergers and Acquisitions: Do Exchange Rates Matter? Some Evidence for Canada. *Canadian Journal of Economics, 41*, 450–474.

Gertner, R., Powers, E., & Scharfstein, D. (2002). Learning about Internal Capital Markets from Corporate Spin-Offs. *Journal of Finance, 57*, 2479–2506.

Ghosh, A. (2004). Increasing Market Share as a Rationale for Corporate Acquisitions. *Journal of Business, Finance, and Accounting, 31*, 78–91.

Ghosh, A., & Lee, C. W. J. (2000). Abnormal Returns and Expected Managerial Performance of Target Firms. *Financial Management, 29* (Spring), 40–52.

Gillan, S., & Starks, L. (2007). The Evolution of Shareholder Activism in the United States. *Journal of Applied Corporate Finance, 19*, 55–73.

Gilson, S. C. (1997). Transactions Costs and Capital Structure Choice: Evidence from Financially Distressed Firms. *Journal of Finance, 52*, 161–196.

Gilson, S. C., Healy, P. M., Noe, C. F., & Palepu, L. G. (2001). Analyst Specialization and Conglomerate Stock Breakups. *Journal of Accounting Research, 39*, 565–582.

Gilson, S., John, K., & Lang, L. H. (1990). Troubled Debt Restructuring: An Empirical Study of Private Reorganization of Firms in Default. *Journal of Financial Economics, 27*, 315–353.

Gitman, L. J. (2008). *Principles of Managerial Finance* (12th ed.). New York: Addison-Wesley.

Goldblatt, H. (1999). Merging at Internet Speed. *Fortune*, 164–165.

Gomes-Casseres, B., Hagedoorn, J., & Jaffe, A. (2006). Do Alliances Promote Knowledge Transfers? *Journal of Financial Economics, 80*, 5–33.

Gompers, P. A., Ishii, J., & Metrick, A. (2010). Extreme Governance: An Analysis of U.S. Dual Class Companies in the United States. *Review of Financial Studies, 23*, 1051–1088.

Gondhalekar, V., Sant, R., & Ferris, S. (2004). The Price of Corporate Acquisition: Determinants of Takeover Premia. *Applied Economics Letters, 11*, 735–739.

Gordon, J. N. (2007). The Rise of Independent Directors in the Unites States, 1950–2005: Of Shareholder Value and Stock Market Prices. *Stanford Law Review, 59*, 1465–1476.

Gorton, G., Kahl, M., & Rosen, R. J. (2009). Eat or Be Eaten: A Theory of Mergers and Firm Size. *Journal of Finance, 64*, 1291–1344.

Goyal, V. K., & Park, C. W. (2002). Board Leadership Structure and CEO Turnover. *Journal of Corporate Finance, 8*, 49–66.

Graham, J., Lemmon, M., & Wolf, J. (2002). Does Diversification Destroy Firm Value? *Journal of Finance, 57*, 695–720.

Graham, J. R. (2000). How Big Are the Tax Benefits of Debt? *Journal of Finance, 55*, 1901–1941.

Graham, J. R., & Harvey, C. R. (2001). The Theory and Practice of Corporate Finance: Evidence from the Field. *Journal of Financial Economics, 60*, 187–243.

Graham, M., Martey, E., & Yawson, A. (2008). Acquisitions from UK Firms into Emerging Markets. *Global Finance Journal, 19*, 56–71.

Grant, J. (2007). SEC Hopes Sarbox Fix Will Revive Foreign Listings in U.S. *Financial Times*, 2.

Greenaway, D., & Kneller, R. (2007). Firm Heterogeneity, Exporting, and Foreign Direct Investment. *Economic Journal, Deposition/Interrogatory Review, 117*, 134–161.

Greenwood, R., & Schor, M. (2007). *Hedge Fund Investor Activism and Takeovers.* Harvard Business School, *Working Knowledge Series* Working Paper.

Grice, S., & Dugan, M. (2001). The Limitations of Bankruptcy Prediction Models: Some Cautions for the Researcher. *Review of Quantitative Finance and Accounting, 17*.

Grice, S., & Ingram, R. (2001). Tests of the Generalizability of Altman's Bankruptcy Prediction Model. *Journal of Business Research, 54*, 53–61.

Grinblatt, M., & Titman, S. (2002). *Financial Markets and Corporate Strategy* (2nd ed.). New York: McGraw-Hill.

Groh, A., & Gottschaig, O. (2006). *The Risk-Adjusted Performance of U.S. Buyouts.* Paris: HEC. Working Paper.

Gugler, K., Mueller, D. C., Yurtoglu, B. B., & Zulehner, C. (2003). The Effects of Mergers: An International Comparison. *International Journal of Industrial Organization, 21*(5), 625–653.

Guo, R. J., Kruse, T. A., & Nohel, T. (2008). Undoing the Powerful Anti-Takeover Force of Staggered Boards. *Journal of Corporate Finance, 14*, 274–288.

Guo, S., Hotchkiss, E. S., & Song, W. (2011). Do Buyouts (Still) Create Value? *Journal of Finance*, forthcoming.

Gurung, A., & Lerner, J. (2008). *The Global Economic Impact of Private Equity.* World Economic Forum and Harvard Business School.

Habbershon, T. G., & Williams, M. L. (1999). A Resource-Based Framework for Assessing the Strategic Advantages of Family Firms. *Family Business Review, 12*, 1–26.

Hackbarth, D., & Morellec, E. (2008). Stock Returns in Mergers and Acquisitions. *Journal of Finance, 63*, 1213–1252.

Hall, B. (1992). *Investment and Research and Development at the Firm Level: Does the Source of Financing Matter?*

National Bureau of Economic Research. Working Paper No. 4096.

Hall, L. S., & Polacek, T. C. (1994). Strategies for Obtaining the Largest Valuation Discounts. *Estate Planning*, 38–44.

Hamel, G. C., & Prahalad, C. K. (1994). *Competing for the Future.* Cambridge, MA: Harvard Business School Press.

Hand, J. R., & Skantz, T. R. (1997). *Market Timing through Equity Carve-Outs.* University of North Carolina. Working Paper.

Hanouna, P., Sarin, A., & Shapiro, A. (2001). *The Value of Corporate Control: Some International Evidence.* Los Angeles: Marshall School of Business, University of Southern California. Working Paper.

Hanson, R. C., & Song, M. H. (2000). Managerial Ownership, Board Structure, and the Division of Gains. *Journal of Corporate Finance, 6*, 55–70.

Hao, K. Y., & Jaffe, A. B. (1993). The Impact of Corporate Restructuring on Industrial Research and Development. *Brookings Papers on Economic Activity, 1*, 275–282.

Harding, D., & Rovit, S. (2004). *Mastering the Merger: Four Critical Decisions That Make or Break the Deal.* Cambridge: Harvard Business School Press.

Harford, J. (1999). Corporate Cash Reserves and Acquisitions. *Journal of Finance, 54*, 1969–1997.

Harford, J. (2005). What Drives Merger Waves? *Journal of Financial Economics, 77*, 529–560.

Harper, N. W., & Schneider, A. (2004). Where Mergers Go Wrong. *McKinsey Quarterly*, No. 2.

Harris, O., & Glegg, C. (2007). The Wealth Effects of Cross-Border Spin-Offs. *Journal of Multinational Financial Management, 18*, 461–476.

Harrison, J. S., Oler, D., & Allen, M. R. (2005). *Event Studies and the Importance of Longer-Term Measures in Assessing the Performance of Outcomes of Complex Events.* Indiana University. Working Paper.

Harris, R. S., & Ravenscraft, D. (1991). The Role of Acquisitions in Foreign Direct Investment: Evidence from the U.S. Stock Market. *Journal of Finance, 46*, 825–844.

Hartman, T. E. (2005). The Costs of Being Public in the Era of Sarbanes-Oxley. *Foley & Lardner LLP Annual Survey.*

Harvey, C. R. (2005). *Twelve Ways to Calculate the International Cost of Capital.* Duke University and National Bureau of Economic Research. Working Paper.

Harzing, A. W. (2002). Acquisitions versus Greenfield Investments: International Strategy and Management of Entry Modes. *Strategic Management Journal, 23*, 211–227.

Haushalter, D., & Mikkelson, W. (2001). *An Investigation of the Gains from Specialized Equity: Tracking Stocks and Minority Carve-Outs.* University of Oregon. Working Paper.

Hayes, R. H. (1979). The Human Side of Acquisitions. *Management Review, 41*.

Hayward, M., & Hambrick, D. (1997). Explaining the Premiums Paid for Large Acquisitions: Evidence of CEO Hubris. *Administrative Science Quarterly, 35*, 621–633.

Heflin, F., Subramanyam, K., & Zhang, Y. (2001). Regulation FD and the Financial Information Environment: Early Evidence. *Accounting Review, 78*, 1–37.

Hennart, J. F., & Park, Y. R. (1993). Location, Governance, and Strategic Determinants of Japanese Manufacturing Investment in the United States. *Journal of Strategic Management, 15*, 419–436.

Hennart, J. F., & Reddy, S. (1997). The Choice between Mergers, Acquisitions, and Joint Ventures: The Case of Japanese Investors in the United States. *Strategic Management Journal, 18*, 1–12.

Hennessy, C. A., & Whited, T. M. (2007). How Costly Is External Financing? Evidence from a Structural Estimation. *Journal of Finance, 62*, 1705–1745.

Henry, D. (2001). The Numbers Game. *Business Week*, 100–103.

Henry, D. (2002). Mergers: Why Most Big Deals Don't Pay Off. *Business Week*, 60–64.

Henry, D. (2003). A Fair Deal—But for Whom? *Business Week*, 108–109.

Hermalin, B. E. (2006). Trends in Corporate Governance. *Journal of Finance, 60*, 2351–2384.

Heron, R., & Lie, E. (2002). Operating Performance and the Method of Payment in Takeovers. *Journal of Financial and Quantitative Analysis*, 137–155.

Hertzel, M. G., Li, Z., Officer, M. S., & Rodgers, K. J. (2008). Inter-Firm Linkages and the Wealth Effects of Financial distress along the Supply Chain. *Journal of Financial Economics, 87*, 374–387.

Hertzel, M., & Smith, R. L. (1993). Market Discounts and Shareholder Gains for Placing Equity Privately. *Journal of Finance, 48*, 459–485.

Hill, C. W. L., & Jones, G. R. (2001). *Strategic Management: An Integrated Approach* (5th ed.). Boston: Houghton Mifflin.

Hillyer, C., & Smolowitz, I. (1996). Why Do Mergers Fail to Achieve Synergy? *Director's Monthly*, 13.

Himmelberg, C. P., & Petersen, B. C. (1994). R&D and Internal Finance: A Panel Study of Small Firms in High Tech Industries. *Review of Economics and Statistics, 76*, 38–51.

Hitchner, J. R. (2006). *Financial Valuation: Applications and Models* (2nd ed.). New York: Wiley.

Hite, G. L., & Vetsuypens, M. R. (1989). Management Buyouts of Divisions and Shareholder Wealth. *Journal of Finance, 44*, 953–970.

Hite, G., & Owers, J. E. (1983). Security Price Reactions around Corporate Spin-Off Announcements. *Journal of Financial Economics, 12*, 409–436.

Hite, G., Owers, J., & Rogers, R. (1987). The Market for Inter-Firm Asset Sales: Partial Sell-Offs and Total Liquidations. *Journal of Financial Economics, 18*, 229–252.

Hitt, M. A., & Ireland, R. D. (2000). The Intersection of Entrepreneurship and Strategic Management Research. In D. Sexton & H. Landstrom (Eds.), *The Blackwell Handbook of Entrepreneurship*. Oxford, UK: Blackwell.

Hoffman, W. H., & Schaper-Rinkel, W. (2001). Acquire or Ally? A Strategic Framework for Deciding between Acquisition and Cooperation. *Management International Review, 41*, 131–159.

Hogan, K. M., & Olson, G. T. (2004). The Pricing of Equity Carve-Outs during the 1990s. *Journal of Financial Research, 27*(Winter), 521–537.

Holthausen, R. W., & Larker, D. F. (1996). The Financial Performance of Reverse Leveraged Buyouts. *Journal of Financial Economics, 42*, 293–332.

Hopkins, H. D. (2008). International Acquisitions: Strategic Considerations. *International Research Journal of Finance and Economics, 15*, 261–270.

Hotchkiss, E., Qian, J., & Song, W. (2005). *Holdup, Renegotiation, and Deal Protection in Mergers*. Boston College. Working Paper.

Hotchkiss, E. S. (1995). The Post-Emergence Performance of Firms Emerging from Chapter 11. *Journal of Finance, 50*, 3–21.

Houston, J., James, C., & Ryngaert, M. (2001). Where Do Merger Gains Come From? *Journal of Financial Economics*, 285–331.

Hsu, J. C., Saa-Requejo, J., & Santa-Clara, P. (2002). *Bond Pricing and Default Risk*. UCLA. Working Paper.

Hulburt, H. M., Miles, J. A., & Wollridge, J. R. (2002). Value Creation from Equity Carve-Outs. *Financial Management, 31*(Spring), 83–100.

Hunger, D., & Wheeler, T. L. (2007). *Concepts: Strategic Management and Business Policy* (11th ed.). Upper Saddle River, NJ: Prentice Hall.

Hunt, P. (2003). *Structuring Mergers and Acquisitions: A Guide to Creating Shareholder Value*. New York: Aspen.

Hurter, W. H., Petersen, J. R., & Thompson, K. E. (2005). *Mergers, Acquisitions, and 1031 Tax Exchanges*. New York: Lorman Education Services.

Huson, M. R., & MacKinnon, G. (2003). Corporate Spin-Offs and Information Asymmetry between Investors. *Journal of Economics and Management Strategy, 9*, 481–501.

Huson, M. R., Parrino, R., & Starks, L. T. (2001). Internal Monitoring Mechanism and CEO Turnover: A Long-Term Perspective. *Journal of Finance, 55*, 2265–2297.

Hyland, D. (2001). *Why Firms Diversify: An Empirical Examination*. Arlington: University of Texas. Working Paper.

Ibbotson Associates. (2002). *Stock, Bonds, Bills, and Inflation, Valuation Edition Yearbook*. Chicago: Ibbotson Associates Inc.

Inkpen, A. C., & Beamish, P. W. (1997). Knowledge, Bargaining Power, and the Instability of International Joint Ventures. *Academy of Management Review, 22*, 177–202.

Institutional Investor Study Report. (1971). *Securities and Exchange Commission*. Washington, DC: US Government Printing Office. Document No. 93-64.

Isakov, D., & Sonney, F. (2002). *Are Parishioners Right? On the Relative Importance of Industrial Factors in International Stock Returns*. HEC-University of Geneva. Working Paper.

Ismail, A. (2005). *Will Multiple Acquirers Ever Learn? The U.S. Evidence from Single versus Multiple Acquirers*. Available at *http://ssrn.com/abstract=765245*.

Jaffe, A. B., & Trajtenberg, M. (2002). *Patents, Citations, and Innovations: A Window on the Knowledge Economy*. Cambridge, MA: MIT Press.

Jain, P. C. (1985). The Effects of Voluntary Sell-Off Announcements on Shareholder Wealth. *Journal of Finance, 40*, 209–224.

Jarrow, R., & Turnbull, S. (1995). Pricing Derivative on Financial Securities Subject to Credit Risk. *Journal of Finance, 50*, 1449–1470.

Jensen, M. C. (1986). *Agency Costs of Free Cash Flow, Corporate Finance, and Takeovers*. American Economic Association Papers and Proceedings (May).

Jensen, M. C. (2005). Agency Costs of Overvalued Equity. *Financial Management, 34*(Spring), 5–19.

Jindra, J., & Walkling, R. (1999). *Arbitrage Spreads and the Market Pricing of Proposed Acquisitions*. Ohio State University. Working Paper.

John, K., & Ofek, E. (1995). Asset Sales and Increase in Focus. *Journal of Financial Economics, 37*, 105–126.

Johnson, B. (1999). Quantitative Support for Discounts for Lack of Marketability. *Business Valuation Review*, 132.

Johnson, S. A., & Houston, M. B. (2000). A Re-Examination of the Motives and Gains in Joint Ventures. *Journal of Financial and Quantitative Analysis, 35*, 67–85.

Jones, S., & Hensher, D. (2008). *Advances in Credit Risk Modeling and Corporate Bankruptcy Prediction*. Cambridge: Cambridge University Press.

Kahya, E., & Theodosiou, P. (1999). Predicting Corporate Financial Distress: a Time-Series CUSUM Methodology. *Review of Quantitative Finance and Accounting*, 13, 323–345.

Kaiser, K. M. J., & Stouraitis, A. (2001). Reversing Corporate Diversification and the Use of the Proceeds from Asset Sales: The Case of Thorn EMI. *Financial Management*, 30, 63–101.

Kale, P., Dyer, J. H., & Singh, H. (2002). Alliance Capability, Stock Market Response, and Long-Term Alliance Success: The Role of the Alliance Function. *Strategic Management Journal*, 23 (August), 747–767.

Kalmbach, C., Jr., & Roussel, C. (1999). *Dispelling the Myths of Alliances*. Andersen Consulting. Available at *www.accenture.com/xd/xd.asp?it=enWeb&xd=ideas/outlook/special99/over_special_intro.xml*.

Kamar, E., Karaca-Mandic, P., & Talley, E. (2006). *Going-Private Decisions and the Sarbanes-Oxley Act of 2002: A Cross-Country Analysis*. University of Southern California Law School. Working Paper.

Kang, J. K. (2008). *The Geography of Block Acquisitions*. SSRN. Available at *http://ssrn.com/abstract=891110*.

Kang, J. K., & Shivdasani, A. (1997). Corporate Restructuring during Performance Declines in Japan. *Journal of Financial Economics*, 46, 29–65.

Kang, N. H., & Johansson, S. (2001). *Cross-Border Mergers and Acquisitions: Their Role in Industrial Globalization*. Paris: OECD. STI Working Papers 2000/1.

Kantor, R. M. (2002). Collaborative Advantage: The Art of Alliances. In *Harvard Business Review of Strategic Alliances*. Cambridge: Harvard Business School Press.

Kaplan, S. (1988). *Management Buyouts: Efficiency Gains or Value Transfers*. University of Chicago. Working Paper No. 244.

Kaplan, S. (1989a). The Effects of Management Buyouts on Operating Performance and Value. *Journal of Financial Economics*, 24, 217–254.

Kaplan, S. (1989b). Management Buyouts: Efficiency Gains or Value Transfers. *Journal of Finance*, 3, 611–632.

Kaplan, S. (1991). The Staying Power of Leveraged Buyouts. *Journal of Financial Economics*, 29, 287–314.

Kaplan, S. N. (1991). The Staying Power of Leveraged Buyouts. *Journal of Financial Economics*, 29, 287–313.

Kaplan, S. N. (1997). The Evolution of U.S. Corporate Governance: We Are All Henry Kravis Now. *Journal of Private Equity*, (Fall), 7–14.

Kaplan, S. N., & Ruback, R. S. (1995). The Valuation of Cash Flow Forecasts. *Journal of Finance*, 50, 1059–1094.

Kaplan, S. N., & Schoar, A. (2005). Returns, Persistence, and Capital Flows. *Journal of Finance*, 60, 1791–1823.

Kaplan, S. N., & Weisbach, M. S. (1992). The Success of Acquisitions: Evidence from Divestitures. *Journal of Finance*, 47, 107–138.

Karpoff, J. M. (2001). *The Impact of Shareholder Activism on Target Companies: A Survey of Empirical Findings*. University of Washington. Working Paper.

Karpoff, J. M., & Malatesta, P. H. (1989). The Wealth Effects of Second Generation State Takeover Legislation. *Journal of Financial Economics*, 25, 291–322.

Karpoff, J. M., & Walkling, R. A. (1996). Corporate Governance and Shareholder Initiatives: Empirical Evidence. *Journal of Financial Economics*, 42, 365–395.

Katz, S. (2008). *Earnings Quality and Ownership Structure: The Role of Private Equity Sponsors*. NBER. Working Paper No. W14085.

Kennan, S. C., Shotgrin, I., & Sobehart, J. (1999). *Historical Default Rates of Corporate Bond Issuers: 1920–1988*. Moody's Investors Services. Working Paper.

Kennedy, K., & Moore, M. (2003). *Going the Distance: Why Some Companies Dominate and Others Fail*. Upper Saddle River, NJ: Prentice Hall.

Khanna, T., Palepu, K., & Sinha, J. (2005). Strategies That Fit Emerging Markets. *Harvard Business Review*, 83.

Kim, E. H., & Schatzberg, H. (1987). Voluntary Corporate Liquidations. *Journal of Financial Economics*, 19(2), 311–328.

Kim, I. J., Ramaswamy, K., & Sundaresan, S. (1993). Does Default Risk in Coupons Affect the Valuation of Corporate Bonds? A Contingent Claims Model. *Financial Management*, 22, 117–131.

Kim, M., & Ritter, J. R. (1999). Valuing IPOs. *Journal of Financial Economics*, 53, 409–437.

Kini, O., Kracaw, W., & Mian, S. (2004). The Nature of Discipline by Corporate Takeovers. *Journal of Finance*, 59(4), 1511–1552.

Kisgen, D. J., Qian, J., & Song, W. (2009). Are Fairness Opinions Fair? The Case of Mergers and Acquisitions. *Journal of Financial Economics*, 91, 178–207.

Klaus, M., Estrin, S., Bhaumik, S., & Peng, M. (2007). *Institutions, Resources, and Entry Strategies in Emerging Countries*. Bath, UK: University of Bath. Working Paper.

Klein, A. (1986). The Timing and Substance of Divestiture Announcements: Individual, Simultaneous and Cumulative Effects. *Journal of Finance*, 41, 685–697.

Klein, A., & Zur, E. (2009). Entrepreneurial Shareholder Activism: Hedge Funds and Other Private Investors. *Journal of Finance*, 64(1), 187–229.

Klein, K. E. (2004). Urge to Merge? Take Care to Beware. *Business Week*, 68, July 1.

Koedijk, K., Kool, C., Schotman, P., & Van Kijk, M. (2002). *The Cost of Capital in International Markets: Local or Global*. Centre for Economic Policy Research. Working Paper.

Koedijk, K., & Van Dijk, M. (2000). *The Cost of Capital of Cross-Listed Firms*. Rotterdam: Erasmus University. Working Paper.

Koeplin, J., Sarin, A., & Shapiro, A. C. (2000). The Private Equity Discount. *Journal of Applied Corporate Finance, 12,* 94–101.

Kogut, B., & Singh, H. (1988). The Effect of National Culture on the Choice of Entry Mode. *Journal of International Business Studies, 19,* 411–432.

Kohers, N., & Ang, J. (2000). Earnouts in Mergers: Agreeing to Disagree and Agreeing to Stay. *Journal of Finance, 73,* 445–476.

Koh, J., & Venkatraman, N. (1991). Joint Venture Formations and Stock Market Reactions: An Assessment in the Information Technology Sector. *Academy of Management Journal, 34,* 869–892.

Korteweg, A. (2010). The Net Benefits to Leverage. *Journal of Finance, 65,* 2137–2170.

KPMG. (2006). Mergers and Acquisitions. In *2006 M&A Outlook Survey*.

KPMG. (2006). When Hedge Funds Start to Look Like Private Equity Firms. *Global M&A Spotlight*, (Spring).

Kranhold, K. (2006). GE's Water Unit Remains Stagnant as It Struggles to Integrate Acquisitions. *Wall Street Journal*, C2.

Kuipers, D., Miller, D., & Patel, A. (2003). *The Legal Environment and Corporate Valuation: Evidence from Cross-Border Mergers*. Texas Tech. Working Paper.

Lajoux, A. R. (1998). *The Art of M&A Integration*. New York: McGraw-Hill.

Lang, L., Poulsen, A., & Stulz, R. (1995). Asset Sales, Firm Performance, and the Agency Costs of Managerial Discretion. *Journal of Financial Economics, 37,* 3–37.

Lang, L., & Stulz, R. M. (1992). Contagion and Competitive Intra-Industry Effects of Bankruptcy Announcements. *Journal of Financial Economics, 81,* 45–60.

La Porta, R., Lopez-de-Silanes, F., & Shleifer, A. (2002). Investor Protection and Corporate Valuation. *Journal of Finance, 57,* 147–170.

LasheCr, W. R. (2005). *Practical Financial Management* (4th ed.). Mason, OH: Southwestern College Publishing.

Lattman, P., Michael, J., & Dela, M. (2010). Old GM Being Sold in Parts. *The New York Times*, September 1, 23.

Leeth, J. D., & Borg, J. R. (2000). The Impact of Takeovers on Shareholders' Wealth during the 1920s' Merger Wave. *Journal of Financial and Quantitative Analysis, 35,* 29–38.

Lehn, K. M., & Zhao, M. (2006). CEO Turnover after Acquisitions: Are Bad Bidders Fired? *Journal of Finance, 61,* 1383–1412.

Lehn, K., & Poulsen, A. (1988). Leveraged Buyouts: Wealth Created or Wealth Redistributed? In M. Weidenbaum & K. Chilton (Eds.), *Public Policy towards Corporate Takeovers*. New Brunswick, NJ: Transaction Publishers.

Leland, H. E. (1994). Corporate Debt Value, Bond Covenants, and Optimal Capital Structure. *Journal of Finance, 49,* 1213–1252.

Lemmons, M. L., & Lins, K. V. (2003). Ownership Structure, Corporate Governance, and Firm Value: Evidence from the East Asian Financial Crisis. *Journal of Finance, 58,* 1147–1170.

Lerner, J., Shane, H., & Tsai, A. (2003). Do Equity Financing Cycles Matter? *Journal of Financial Economics, 67,* 411–446.

Lerner, J., Sorensen, M., & Strömberg, P. (2011). Private Equity and Long-Run Investment: The Case of Innovation. *Journal of Finance, 6*(2), 445–477.

Letto-Gilles, G., Meschi, M., & Simonetti, R. (2001). *Cross-Border Mergers and Acquisitions: Patterns in the EU and Effects*. London: South Bank University.

Leuz, C., Lins, K. V., & Warnock, F. E. (2004). *Do Foreigners Invest Less in Poorly Governed Firms?* University of Virginia. ECGI-Finance. Working Paper No. 43.

Leuz, C., Triantis, A., & Wang, T. Y. (2008). Why Do Firms Go Dark? Causes and Economic Consequences of Voluntary SEC Deregistrations. *Journal of Accounting and Economics, 45,* 181–208.

Levine, D. M., Berenson, M. L., & Stephan, D. (1999). *Statistics for Managers* (2nd ed.). New York: Prentice Hall.

Lichtenberg, F. R., & Siegel, D. (1990). The Effects of LBOs on Productivity and Related Aspects of Firm Behavior. *Journal of Financial Economics, 27,* 165–194.

Lim, S. C., Mann, S. C., & Mihov, V. T. (2004). *Market Evaluation of Off-Balance Sheet Financing: You Can Run But You Can't Hide*. EFMA Basel. Meetings Paper, December.

Linn, S. C., & Rozeff, M. S. (1984). The Corporate Sell-Off. *Midland Corporate Finance Journal, 2*(Summer), 17–26.

Linn, S. C., & Switzer, J. A. (2001). Are Cash Acquisitions Associated with Better Post Combination Operating Performance Than Stock Acquisitions? *Journal of Banking and Finance, 25,* 1113–1138.

Lins, K., & Servaes, H. (1999). International Evidence on the Value of Corporate Diversification. *Journal of Finance, 54,* 2215–2239.

Listokin, Y. (2009). Corporate Voting versus Market Price Setting. *American Law and Economics Review, 11,* 608–637.

Liu, J., Nissim, D., & Thomas, J. (2007). Is Cash Flow King in Valuations? *Financial Analysts Journal, 63,* 56–65.

Liu, J., Nissim, D., & Thomas, J. K. (2002). Equity Valuations Using Multiples. *Journal of Accounting Research, 40*(1), 135–172.

Logue, D. E., Seward, J. K., & Walsh, J. W. (1996). Rearranging Residual Claims: A Case for Targeted Stock. *Financial Management, 25,* 43–61.

Loh, C., Bezjak, J. R., & Toms, H. (1995). Voluntary Corporate Divestitures as an Anti-Takeover Mechanism. *Financial Review, 30,* 21–24.

Longin, F., & Solnik, B. (1995). Is the Correlation of International Equity Returns Constant 1960–1990? *Journal of International Money and Finance, 14*(1), 3–26.

Longstaff, F. A. (1995). How Can Marketability Affect Security Values? *Journal of Finance, 50,* 1767–1774.

Longstaff, F. A., & Schwartz, E. S. (1995). A Simple Approach to Valuing Risky Fixed and Floating Rate Debt. *Journal of Finance, 50,* 789–819.

Lopucki, L. M., & Doherty, J. W. (2007). *The Determinants of Professional Fees in Large Bankruptcy Reorganization Cases Revisited.* UCLA School of Law. Law-Econ Research Paper No. 06-16, Second Annual Conference on Empirical Legal Studies, July 1.

Lord, M. D., & Ranft, A. L. (2000). Acquiring New Knowledge: The Role of Retaining Human Capital in Acquisitions of High Tech Firms. *Journal of High Technology Management Research, 11,* 295–320.

Loughran, T., & Anand Vijh, M. (1997). Do Long-Term Shareholders Benefit from Corporate Acquisitions? *Journal of Finance, 22,* 321–340.

Loughran, T., & Ritter, J. (2002). Why Don't Issuers Get Upset about Leaving Money on the Table in IPOs? *Review of Financial Studies, 15,* 413–443.

Loughran, T., Ritter, J., & Rydqvist, K. (1994). Initial Public Offerings: International Insights. *Pacific Basin Finance Journal, 2,* 165–199.

Lovley, E. (2007). How Troubled Firms Skip Bankruptcy Court. *Wall Street Journal,* C2.

Lowenstein, L. (1985). Management Buyouts. *Columbia Law Review, 85,* 730–784.

Luo, Y. (2005). Do Insiders Learn from Outsiders? Evidence from Mergers and Acquisitions. *Journal of Finance, 60,* 195–198.

Lynch, R. P. (1990). *The Practical Guide to Joint Ventures and Corporate Alliances.* New York: Wiley.

Lynch, R. P. (1993). *Business Alliance Guide: The Hidden Competitive Weapon.* New York: Wiley.

Lyon, J. D., Barber, B. M., & Tsai, C. L. (1999). Improved Methods for Tests of Long-Run Abnormal Stock Returns. *Journal of Finance, 54,* 165–201.

Madura, J., & Whyte, A. (1990). Diversification Benefits of Direct Foreign Investment. *Management International Review, 30,* 73–85.

Maguire, S., & Phillips, N. (2008). Citibankers at Citigroup: A Study of the Loss of Institutional Trust after a Merger. *Journal of Management Studies, 45,* 372–401.

Maher, J. M. (1976). Discounts for Lack of Marketability for Closely Held Business Interests. *Taxes, 54,* 562–571.

Maksimovic, V., & Phillips, G. M. (2001). The Market for Corporate Assets: Who Engages in Mergers and Asset Sales and Are There Efficiency Gains? *Journal of Finance,* 332–355.

Malatesta, P. H., & Walkling, R. A. (1988). Poison Pills Securities: Stockholder Wealth, Profitability and Ownership Structure. *Journal of Financial Economics, 20,* 347–376.

Malekzadeh, A. R., McWilliams, V. B., & Sen, N. (1998). Implications of CEO Structural and Ownership Power, Ownership, and Board Composition on the Market's Reaction to Antitakeover Charter Amendments. *Journal of Applied Business Research, 14,* 53–62.

Malekzadeh, A. R., & Nahavandi, A. (1990). Making Mergers Work by Managing Cultures. *Journal of Business Strategy, 11,* 55–57.

Mallea, J. (2008). *A Review of Mergers of Equals.* Available at *FactSetmergermetrics.com.*

Malmendier, U., & Tate, G. (2008). Who Makes Acquisitions? CEO Overconfidence and the Market's Reaction. *Journal of Financial Economics, 89,* 20–43.

Manzon, K. G. K., Sharp, D. J., & Travlos, N. (1994). An Empirical Study of the Consequences of U.S. Tax Rules for International Acquisitions by U.S. Firms. *Journal of Finance, 49,* 1893–1904.

Maquierira, C. P., Megginson, W. L., & Nail, L. A. (1998). Wealth Creation versus Wealth Redistributions in Pure Stock-for-Stock Mergers. *Journal of Financial Economics, 48,* 3–33.

Marciukaityte, D., Roskelley, K., & Wang, H. (2009). Strategic Alliances by Financial Services Firms. *Journal of Business Research, 62,* 1193–1199.

Markides, C., & Oyon, D. (1998). International Acquisitions: Do They Create Value for Shareholders? *European Management Journal, 16,* 125–135.

Marks, M. L. (1996). *From Turmoil to Triumph: New Life after Mergers, Acquisitions, and Downsizing.* Lanham, MD: Lexington Books.

Martynova, M., & Renneboog, L. (2008a). A Century of Corporate Takeovers: What Have We Learned and Where Do We Stand? *Journal of Banking and Finance, 32,* 2148–2177.

Martynova, M., & Renneboog, L. (2008b). *Spillover of Corporate Governance Standards in Cross-Border Mergers and Acquisitions.* ECGI-Finance, SSRN. Working Paper No. 197/2008. SSRN. Available at *http://ssrn.com/abstract=1094661.*

Massari, M., Monge, V., & Zanetti, L. (2006). Control Premium in the Presence of Rules Imposing Mandatory Tender Offers: Can It Be Measured? *Journal of Management and Governance,* 101–110.

Masulis, R. W., Wang, C., & Xie, F. (2007). Corporate Governance and Acquirer Returns. *Journal of Finance*, *62*, 1851–1890.

Maxwell, W. F., & Rao, R. P. (2003). Do Spin-Offs Expropriate Wealth from Bondholders? *Journal of Finance*, *58*(5), 2087–2108.

McCarthy, P. (1998). Legal Aspects of Acquiring U.S. Enterprises. In D. J. BenDaniel & A. H. Rosenbloom (Eds.), *International M&A, Joint Ventures & Beyond: Doing the Deal* (pp. 27–57). New York: Wiley.

McConnell, J. J., & Nantell, T. J. (1985). Corporate Combinations and Common Stock Returns: The Case of Joint Ventures. *Journal of Finance*, *40*, 519–536.

McConnell, J. J., Ozbilgin, M., & Wahal, S. (2001). Spin-Offs: Ex Ante. *Journal of Business*, *74*, 245–280.

McNamara, G., Dykes, B. J., & Haleblian, J. (2008). The Performance Implications of Participating in an Acquisition Wave. *Academy of Management Journal*, *51*(1), 113–130.

McNeil, C. R., & Moore, W. T. (2005). Dismantling Internal Capital Markets via Spin-Off: Effects on Capital Allocation Efficiency and Firm Valuation. *Journal of Corporate Finance*, *11*, 253–275.

Megginson, W. L., Morgan, A., & Nail, L. (2003). The Determinants of Positive Long-Term Performance in Strategic Mergers: Corporate Focus and Cash. *Journal of Banking and Finance*, *28*, 523–552.

Mehran, H., & Peristiani, S. (2006). *Financial Visibility and the Decision to Go Private.* Federal Reserve Bank of New York. Working Paper.

Mercer Management Consulting 1995 and 1997 Surveys. (1998.) Cited in A. R. Lajoux (Ed.), *The Art of M&A Integration*. New York: McGraw-Hill.

Mercer, C. (1997). *The Management Planning Study: Quantifying Marketability Discounts*. New York: Peabody Publishing.

Metrick, A., & Yasuda, A. (2007). *The Economics of Private Equity Funds*. University of Pennsylvania, Wharton School of Finance. Working Paper.

Meuleman, M., & Wright, M. (2007). *Industry Concentration, Syndication Networks and Competition in the UK Private Equity Market*. CMBOR. Working Paper.

Meyer, K. E., Estrin, S., & Bhaumik, S. (2005). *Institutions and Business Strategies in Emerging Economies: A Study of Entry Mode Choice*. London Business School. Working Paper.

Mian, S., & Rosenfeld, J. (1993). Takeover Activity and the Long-Run Performance of Reverse Leveraged Buyouts. *Financial Management*, *22*, 46–57.

Michaely, R., & Shaw, W. H. (1995). The Choice of Going Public: Spin-Offs vs. Carve-Outs. *Financial Management*, *24*, 15–21.

Miles, J., & Rosenfeld, J. (1983). An Empirical Analysis of the Effects of Spin-Off Announcements on Shareholder Wealth. *Journal of Finance*, *38*, 15–28.

Mishra, D., & O'Brien, T. (2001). A Comparison of Cost of Equity Estimates of Local and Global CAPMs. *Financial Review*, *36*, 27–48.

Mitchell, D. (1998). Survey Conducted by Economist Intelligence Unit. In A. R. Lajoux (Ed.), *The Art of M&A Integration*. New York: McGraw-Hill.

Mitchell, M. L., & Mulherin, J. H. (1996). The Impact of Industry Shocks on Takeover and Restructuring Activity. *Journal of Financial Economics*, *41*, 193–229.

Mitchell, M. L., & Pulvino, T. C. (2001). Characteristics of Risk and Return in Arbitrage. *Journal of Finance*, *56*, 2135–2175.

Mitchell, M., Pulvino, T., & Stafford, E. (2004). Price Pressure around Mergers. *Journal of Finance*, *31*–63.

Moeller, S. B., & Schlingemann, F. P. (2002). *Are Cross-Border Acquisitions Different from Domestic Acquisitions? Evidence on Stock and Operating Performance for U.S. Acquirers*. University of Pittsburgh. Working Paper.

Moeller, S. B., Schlingemann, F. P., & Stulz, R. M. (2004). Firm Size and the Gains from Acquisitions. *Journal of Financial Economics*, *73*, 201–228.

Moeller, S. B., Schlingemann, F. P., & Stulz, R. M. (2005). Wealth Destruction on a Massive Scale? A Study of the Acquiring Firm Returns in the Recent Merger Wave. *Journal of Finance*, *60*, 757–782.

Moeller, S. B., Schlingemann, F. P., & Stulz, R. M. (2007). How Do Diversity of Opinion and Information Asymmetry Affect Acquirer Returns. *Review of Financial Studies*, *20*, 2047–2078.

Moeller, T. (2005). Let's Make a Deal! How Shareholder Control Impacts Merger Payoffs. *Journal of Financial Economics*, *76*, 167–190.

Molina, C. A. (2006). Are Firms Unleveraged? An Examination of the Effect of Leverage on Default Probabilities. *Journal of Finance*, *60*, 1427–1459.

Moonchul, K., & Ritter, J. R. (1999). Valuing IPOs. *Journal of Financial Economics*, *53*, 409–437.

Morck, R., Shleifer, A., & Vishny, R. W. (1990). Do Managerial Objectives Drive Bad Acquisitions? *Journal of Finance*, *45*, 31–48.

Morck, R., & Yeung, B. (1991). Why Investors Value Multinationality. *Journal of Business*, *64*, 165–188.

Morck, R., & Yeung, B. (2000). Inherited Wealth, Corporate Control, and Economic Growth: The Canadian Experience. In R. Morck (Ed.), *Concentrated Corporate Ownership* (pp. 319–369). Cambridge, MA: National Bureau of Economic Research.

Morellec, E., & Zhdanov, A. (2008). Financing and Takeovers. *Journal of Financial Economics*, *87*, 556–581.

Morgan, J. P. (1995). *Monitoring Spin-Off Performance.* New York: Morgan Markets.

Morgan, J. P. (1999). *Monitoring Spin-Off Performance.* New York: Morgan Markets.

Moroney, R. E. (1973). Most Courts Overvalue Closely Held Stocks. *Taxes*, 144–154.

Mulherin, J. H., & Boone, A. L. (2000). Comparing Acquisitions and Divestitures. Social Science Research Network. Working Paper No. 38.

Mulherin, J. H., & Poulsen, A. B. (1998). Proxy Contests and Corporate Change: Implications for Shareholder Wealth. *Journal of Financial Economics*, 47, 279–313.

Mun, J. (2006). *Modeling Risk: Applying Monte Carlo Simulation, Real Option Analysis, Forecasting, and Optimization.* New York: Wiley.

Murray, M. (2001). GE's Honeywell Deal Is More Than the Sum of Airplane Parts. *Wall Street Journal*, B6.

Muscarella, C. J., & Vetsuypens, M. R. (1990). Efficiency and Organizational Structure: A Study of Reverse LBOs. *Journal of Finance*, 45, 1389–1413.

Navarro, E. (2005). *Merger Control in the EU: Law, Economics, and Practice* (2nd ed.). Oxford: Oxford University Press.

Nenova, T. (2003). The Value of Corporate Voting Rights and Control: A Cross-Country Analysis. *Journal of Financial Economics*, 68, 325–351.

The New York Times. (2001). The Spread of Antitrust Authorities. April 22, C4.

Newbould, G. D., Chatfield, R. E., & Anderson, R. F. (1992). Leveraged Buyouts and Tax Incentives. *Financial Management*, 21, 1621–1637.

Nielsen, A. C. *Retailer Support Is Essential for New Product Success. Bases.* Available at *www.bases.com/news/news112002.html.*

Nixon, T. D., Roenfeldt, R. L., & Sicherman, N. W. (2000). The Choice between Spin-Offs and Sell-Offs. *Review of Quantitative Finance and Accounting*, 14, 277–288.

Ofek, E. (1993). Capital Structure and Firm Response to Poor Performance: An Empirical Analysis. *Journal of Financial Economics*, 34, 3–30.

Ofek, E. (1994). Efficiency Gains in Unsuccessful Management Buyouts. *Journal of Finance*, 49, 627–654.

Officer, M. S., (2003). Termination Fees in Mergers and Acquisitions. *Journal of Financial Economics*, 69, 431–467.

Officer, M. S., (2004). Collars and Renegotiation in Mergers and Acquisitions. *Journal of Finance*, 59, 2719–2743.

Officer, M. S., (2007). The Price of Corporate Liquidity: Acquisition Discounts for Unlisted Targets. *Journal of Financial Economics*, 83, 571–593.

Officer, M. S., Ozbas, O., & Sensoy, B. A. (2008). *Club Deals in Leveraged Buyouts.* SSRN. Available at *http://ssrn.com/abstract=1128404.*

Officer, M. S., Poulsen, A. B., & Stegemoller, M. (2009). Information Asymmetry and Acquirer Returns. *Review of Finance*, forthcoming.

Oliver, R. P., & Meyers, R. H. (2000). Discounts Seen in Private Placements of Restricted Stock. In R. F. Reilly & R. P. Schweihs (Eds.), *Handbook of Advanced Business Valuation* (chap. 5). New York: McGraw-Hill.

Opler, T., & Titman, S. (1993). The Determinants of Leveraged Buyout Activity: Free Cash Flow vs. Financial Distress Costs. *Journal of Finance*, 48, 1985–2000.

Oppenheimer & Company. (1981). *The Sum of the Parts.* New York: Oppenheimer & Company.

Otsubo, M. (2009). Gains from Equity Carve-Outs and Subsequent Events. *Journal of Business*, 62, 1207–1213.

Palepu, K. G., Healy, P. M., & Bernard, V. L. (2004). *Business Analysis and Valuation* (3rd ed.). Skokie, IL: Thomson.

Palter, R. N., & Srinivasan, D. (2006). Habits of the Busiest Acquirers. *McKinsey Quarterly, https://www.mckinseyquarterly.com/home.aspxy.*

Pan, Y., Li, S., & Tse, D. (1999). The Impact of Order and Mode of Entry on Profitability and Market Share. *Journal of International Business Studies*, 30, 81–104.

Pan, Y., & Tse, D. K. (2000). The Hierarchical Model of Market Entry Modes. *Journal of International Business Studies*, 31, 535–554.

Pehrsson, A. (2008). Strategy Antecedents of Mode of Entry into Foreign Markets. *Journal of Business Research*, 61, 132–140.

Peng, M. W. (2003). Institutional Transitions and Strategic Choices. *Academy of Management Review*, 28, 275–296.

Peng, M. W., Lee, S. H., & Lang, D. Y. L. (2005). What Determines the Scope of the Firm over Time? A Focus on Institutional Relatedness. *Academy of Management Review*, 30, 622–633.

Perez-Gonzalez, F. (2006). Inherited Control and Firm Performance. *American Economic Review* (December), 1559-1588.

Pergola, T. M. (2005). Management Entrenchment: Can It Negate the Effectiveness of Recently Legislated Governance Reforms? *Journal of American Academy of Business*, 6, 177–185.

Petmezas, D. (2009). What Drives Acquisitions? Market Valuations and Bidder Performance. *Journal of Multinational Financial Management*, 19, 54–74.

Petty, J. W., Keown, A. J., Scott, D. F., Jr., & Martin, J. D. (1993). *Basic Financial Management* (6th ed.). Englewood Cliffs, NJ: Prentice-Hall.

Phan, P. H. (1995). Organizational Restructuring and Economic Performance in Leveraged Buyouts: An Ex Post Study. *Academy of Management Journal, 38,* 704–739.

Pinkowitz, L. (2002). *The Market for Corporate Control and Corporate Cash Holdings.* Georgetown University. Working Paper.

Platt, D., Platt, B., & Yang, Z. (1999). Probabilistic Neural Networks in Bankruptcy Prediction. *Journal of Business Research, 44,* 67–74.

Porter, M. E. (1985). *Competitive Advantage.* New York: The Free Press.

Porter, R., & Wood, C. N. (1998). Post-Merger Integration. In D. J. BenDaniel & A. H. Rosenbloom (Eds.), *International M&A, Joint Ventures & Beyond: Doing the Deal* (pp. 459–477). New York: Wiley.

Poulsen, A., & Stegemoller, M. (2002). *Transitions from Private to Public Ownership.* University of Georgia. Working Paper.

Powers, E. A. (2001). Spinoffs, Selloffs, and Equity Carveouts: An Analysis of Divestiture Method Choice. *Social Science Research Network.* Working Paper Series, 2-4.

Powers, E. A. (2003). Deciphering the Motives for Equity Carve-Outs. *Journal of Financial Research, 26* (1), 31–50.

Pratt, S., & Niculita, A. (2008). *Valuing a Business: The Analysis and Appraisal of Closely Held Businesses.* New York: McGraw-Hill.

Prezas, A., Tarmicilar, M., & Vasudevan, G. (2000). The Pricing of Equity Carve-Outs. *Financial Review, 35,* 123–138.

PriceWaterhouseCoopers. (2006). Mergers and Acquisitions 2006. In *A Global Tax Guide.* New York: Wiley.

Raff, H., Ryan, M., & Stähler, F. (2006). *Asset Ownership and Foreign-Market Entry.* CESifo Working Paper No. 1676, Category 7: Trade Policy.

Raff, H., Ryan, M., & Stähler, F. (2008). *Firm Productivity and Foreign-Market Entry Decision.* Christian-Albrechts-Universitat Kiel, Department of Economics Working Paper No. 2008-02.

Rappaport, A. (1990). The Staying Power of the Public Corporation. *Harvard Business Review, 76,* 1–4.

Rau, P. R., & Vermaelen, T. (1998). Glamour, Value, and the Post-Acquisition Performance of Acquiring Firms. *Journal of Financial Economics, 49,* 223–253.

Ravenscraft, D. J., & Scherer, F. M. (1991). Divisional Sell-Off: A Hazard Function Analysis. *Managerial and Decision Economics, 12,* 429–438.

Ravenscraft, D., & Scherer, F. (1987). Life after Takeovers. *Journal of Industrial Economics, 36,* 147–156.

Ravenscraft, D., & Scherer, F. (1988). Mergers and Managerial Performance. In J. Coffee, L. Lowenstein, & S. R. Ackerman (Eds.), *Knights and Targets* (pp. 194–210). New York: Oxford University Press.

Renneboog, L., Simons, T., & Wright, M. (2007). Why Do Public Firms Go Private in the U.K.? *Journal of Corporate Finance, 13,* 591–628.

Renneboog, L., & Szilagyi, P. (2007). Corporate Restructuring and Bondholder Wealth. *European Financial Management, 14,* 792–819.

Rhodes-Kropf, M., & Viswanathan, S. (2004). Market Valuation and Merger Waves. *Journal of Finance, 59.*

Richtel, M. (2008). Hewlett-Packard Is Facing Skepticism on EDS. Deal. *The New York Times.* Available at *nytimes.com.*

Ritter, J. (1991). The Long-Run Performance of Initial Public Offerings. *Journal of Finance, 46,* 3–27.

Robinson, A. (2002a). Is Corporate Governance the Solution or the Problem? *Corporate Board, 23,* 12–16.

Robinson, D. T. (2002b). *Strategic Alliances and the Boundaries of the Firm.* Columbia University. Working Paper.

Roll, R. (1986). The Hubris Hypothesis of Corporate Takeovers. *Journal of Business, 59,* 197–216.

Romano, R. (1993). Competition for Corporate Charters and the Lesson of Takeover Statutes. *Fordham Law Review, 61,* 843–864.

Romano, R. (2001). Less Is More: Making Institutional Investor Activism a Valuable Mechanism of Corporate Governance. *Yale Journal of Regulation, 18,* 174–251.

Rossi, S., & Volpin, P. F. (2004). *Cross-Country Determinants of Mergers and Acquisitions.* ECGI-Finance Working Paper No. 25/2003, AFA 2004 San Diego Meetings, September.

Ross, S., Westerfield, R., & Jordan, B. (2009). *Fundamentals of Corporate Finance* (9th ed.). New York: McGraw-Hill.

Ruback, R. S. (2002). Capital Cash Flows: A Simple Approach to Valuing Risky Cash Flows. *Financial Management,* 85–103.

Ryngaert, M. (1988). The Effects of Poison Pill Securities on Stockholder Wealth. *Journal of Financial Economics, 20,* 377–417.

Sanderson, S., & Uzumeri, M. (1997). *The Innovative Imperative: Strategies for Managing Products, Models, and Families.* Burr Ridge, IL: Irwin Professional, Publishing.

Savor, P. G., & Lu, Q. (2009). Do Stock Mergers Create Value for Acquirers? *Journal of Finance, 64,* 1061–1097.

Scherreik, S. (2002). Gems among the Trash. *Business Week,* 112–113.

Schipper, K., & Smith, A. (1983). Effects of Re-Contracting on Shareholder Wealth. *Journal of Financial Economics, 12,* 437–467.

Schipper, K., & Smith, A. (1986). A Comparison of Equity Carve-Outs and Equity Offerings: Share Price Effects and Corporate Restructuring. *Journal of Financial Economics, 15*, 153–186.

Schmid, R. E. (2001). Post Office, FedEx Become Partners. *Orange County Register*, 2 (Business Section).

Schultes, R. AB InBev Shines in Tough Times. *Wall Street Journal*, November 12, C7.

Schweiger, D. M. (2002). *M&A Integration: Framework for Executives and Managers*. New York: McGraw-Hill.

Schwert, G. W. (2000). Hostility in Takeovers: In the Eyes of the Bidder? *Journal of Finance, 55*, 2599–2640.

Selim, G. (2003). *Mergers, Acquisitions and Divestitures: Control and Audit Best Practices*. New York: Institute of Internal Auditing Research Foundation.

Sender, H. (2006). High Risk Debt Still Has Allure for Buyout Deals. *Wall Street Journal*, C2.

Seoungpil, A., & Denis, D. J. (2004). Internal Capital Market and Investment Policy: Evidence of Corporate Spin-Offs. *Journal of Financial Economics, 71*, 489–516.

Servaes, H., & Zenner, M. (1994). Taxes and the Returns to Foreign Acquisitions in the U.S. *Financial Management, 23*, 42–56.

Seth, A., Song, K. P., & Petit, R. (2000). Synergy, Managerialism or Hubris: An Empirical Examination of Motives for Foreign Acquisitions of U.S. Firms. *Journal of International Business Studies, 31*, 387–405.

Seth, A., Song, K. P., & Petit, R. (2002). Value Creation and Destruction in Cross-Border Acquisitions: An Empirical Analysis of Foreign Acquisitions of U.S. Firms. *Strategic Management, 23*, 921–940.

Shahrur, H. (2005). Industry Structure and Horizontal Takeovers: Analysis of Wealth Effects on Rivals, Suppliers, and Corporate Customers. *Journal of Financial Economics, 76*, 61–98.

Shapiro, A. C. (2005). *Foundations of Multinational Financial Management* (5th ed.). New York: Wiley.

Sherman, A. (2006). *Mergers and Acquisitions from A to Z: Strategic and Practical Guidance for Small- and Middle-Market Buyers and Sellers* (2nd ed.). New York: AMACOM.

Sherman, D. H., & David Young, S. (2001). Tread Lightly Through These Accounting Minefields. *Harvard Business Review*, 129–137.

Shin, H. H., & Stulz, R. (1998). Are Internal Capital Markets Efficient? *Quarterly Journal of Economics, 113*, 531–552.

Shivdasani, A. (1993). Board Composition, Ownership Structure, and Hostile Takeovers. *Journal of Accounting and Economics, 16*, 167–198.

Shleifer, A., & Vishny, R. W. (2003). Stock Market Driven Acquisitions. *Journal of Financial Economics, 70*, 295–311.

Shumway, T. (2001). Forecasting Bankruptcy More Accurately: A Simple Hazard Model. *Journal of Business, 74*, 101–124.

Shuttleworth, R. (2004). *Twelve Keys to Venture Capital*. Tech Coast Angels. Available at *http://techcoastangels.com*.

Sicherman, N. W., & Pettway, R. H. (1992). Wealth Effects for Buyers and Sellers for the Same Divested Assets. *Financial Management, 21*, 119–128.

Silber, W. L. (1991). Discounts on Restricted Stocks: The Impact of Illiquidity on Stock Prices. *Financial Analysts Journal, 47*, 60–64.

Singh, H., & Montgomery, C. (2008). Corporate Acquisition Strategies and Economic Performance. *Strategic Management Journal, 8*, 377–386.

Sirower, M. (1997). *The Synergy Trap*. New York: The Free Press.

Skantz, T., & Marchesini, R. (1987). The Effect of Voluntary Corporate Liquidation on Shareholder Wealth. *Journal of Financial Research, 10*(Spring), 65–75.

Sloan, R. G. (1996). Do Stock Prices Fully Reflect Information in Accruals and Cash Flows about Future Earnings? *Accounting Review*, 289–315.

Slovin, M. B., Sushka, M. E., & Polonchek, J. A. (2005). Methods of Payment in Asset Sales: Contracting with Equity versus Cash. *Journal of Finance, 60*, 2385–2407.

Smith, A. (1990). Corporate Ownership Structure and Performance: The Case of Management Buy-Outs. *Journal of Financial Economics, 27*, 143–164.

Sojli, E., & Tham, W. (2010). *The Impact of Foreign Government Investments: Sovereign Wealth Fund Investments in the U.S.* Social Science Research Network. Available at *http://papers.ssrn.com/sol3/papers.cfm?abstract_id=1540555*.

Song, H. H., & Walking, R. A. (2000). Abnormal Returns to Rivals of Acquisitions Targets: A Test of the Acquisition Probability Hypothesis. *Journal of Financial Economics, 55*, 439–457.

Srikant, D., Frankel, R., & Wolfson, M. (2001). Earnouts: The Effects of Adverse Selection and Agency Costs on Acquisition Techniques. *Journal of Law, Economics, and Organization, 17*, 201–238.

Standard Research Consultants. (1983). Revenue Ruling 77-287 Revisited. *SRC Quarterly Reports, 1–3*(Spring).

Stefanini, F. (2006). *Investment Strategies of Hedge Funds*. New York: Wiley.

Stickney, C. P., Brown, P. R., & Wahlen, J. M. (2007). *Financial Reporting, Financial Statement Analysis, and Valuation* (6th ed.). Mason, OH: Thomson SouthWestern.

Stout, L. A. (2002). Do Antitakeover Defenses Decrease Shareholder Wealth? The Ex Post/Ex Ante Valuation Problem. *Stanford Law Review*, 845–861.

Stowe, J. D., Robinson, T. R., Pinto, J. E., & McLeavey, D. W. (2007). *Equity Asset Valuation*. Hoboken, NJ: Wiley.

Stromberg, P. (2008). The New Demography of Private Equity. In *Globalization of Alternative Investments: The Global Economic Impact of Private Equity Report*. World Economic Forum. 1, Working Paper, 3-26.

Stulz, R. M. (1995a). Globalization of the Capital Markets and the Cost of Capital: The Case of Nestle. *Journal of Applied Corporate Finance*, 8, 30–38.

Stulz, R. M. (1995b). The Cost of Capital in Internationally Integrated Markets: The Case of Nestle. *European Financial Management*, 1, 11–22.

Stulz, R. M., & Wasserfallen, W. (1995). Foreign Equity Invest Restrictions, Capital Flight, and Shareholder Wealth Maximization: Theory and Evidence. *Review of Financial Studies*, 8, 1019–1057.

Sullivan, M. J., Jensen, M. R. H., & Hudson, C. D. (1994). The Role of Medium of Exchange in Merger Offers: Examination of Terminated Merger Proposals. *Financial Management*, 23, 51–62.

Sweeney, P. (1999). Who Says It's a Fair Deal? *Journal of Accountancy*, 188, 6.

Sweeney, P. (2005). Gap. *Financial Executives Magazine*, 33–40.

Tang, C. Y., & Tikoo, S. (1999). Operational Flexibility and Market Valuation of Earnings. *Strategic Management Journal*, 20, 749–761.

Tashjian, E., Lease, R., & McConnell, J. J. (1996). Prepacks: An Empirical Analysis of Prepackaged Bankruptcies. *Journal of Financial Economics*, 40, 135–162.

Teslik, L. (2009, January 28). *Sovereign Wealth Funds*. Council on Foreign Relations.

The Deal LLC. (2006). February 6–10, online magazine.

Thompson Financial Securities Data Corporation. (2000). C. Tierney "The World's Urge to Merge." Press release, January 5.

Thompson, T. H., & Apilado, V. (2009). An Examination of the Impact of Equity Carve-Outs on Stockholder and Bondholder Wealth. *Journal of Economics and Business*, 61, 376–391.

Titman, S., & Martin, J. (2010). *Valuation: The Art and Science of Corporate Investment Decisions* (2nd ed.). Boston: Prentice Hall.

Travlos, N. G., & Cornett, M. N. (1993). Going Private: Buyouts and Determinants of Shareholders' Returns. *Journal of Accounting, Auditing and Finance*, 8, 1–25.

Trout, R. R. (1977). Estimation of the Discount Associated with the Transfer of Restricted Securities. *Taxes*, 55, 381–385.

Truitt, W. B. (2006). *The Corporation*. Westport, CT: Greenwood Press.

U.S. Attorney General. (2000). *Global Antitrust Regulation: Issues and Solutions*. Final Report of the International Competition Policy Advisory Committee.

U.S. Department of Justice. (1999). Antitrust Division. *www.usdoj.gov*.

U.S. General Accountability Office. (2008). *Private Equity: Recent Growth in Leveraged Buyouts Exposes Risk*. GAO-08-885.

U.S. Small Business Administration. (1999). *Financial Difficulties of Small Businesses and Reasons for Their Failure*. Office of Advocacy, RS 188.

U.S. Small Business Administration. (2003). *State Small Business Profile*. Office of Advocacy.

Uhlaner, R. T., & West, A. S. (2008). Running a Winning M&A Shop. *McKinsey Quarterly*, 17, 6–11.

United States v. Primestar, L. P., 58 Fed Register, 33944, June 22, 1993 (Proposed Final Judgment and Competitive Impact Study).

Uysal, V. (2006). *Deviation from the Target Capital Structure and Acquisition Choices*. University of Oklahoma. Working Paper.

Vachon, M. (1993). Venture Capital Reborn. *Venture Capital Journal*, 32.

Vasconcellos, G. M., & Kish, R. J. (1998). Cross-Border Mergers and Acquisitions: The European-U.S. Experience. *Journal of Multinational Financial Management*, 8, 173–189.

Vasconcellos, G. M., Madura, J., & Kish, R. J. (1990). An Empirical Investigation of Factors Affecting Cross-Border Acquisitions: U.S. versus Non-U.S. Experience. *Global Finance Journal*, 1, 173–189.

Veld, C., & Veld-Merkoulova, Y. (2004). Do Spin-Offs Really Create Value? *Journal of Banking and Finance*, 28, 1111–1135.

Vermeulen, F., & Barkema, H. G. (2001). Learning through Acquisitions. *Journal of the Academy of Management*, 44, 457–476.

Vijh, A. M. (1999). Long-Term Returns from Equity Carveouts. *Journal of Financial Economics*, 51, 273–308.

Vijh, A. M. (2002). The Positive Announcement Period Returns of Equity Carve-Outs: Asymmetric Information or Divestiture Gains. *Journal of Business*, 75, 153–190.

Villalonga, B. (2004). Diversification Discount or Premium? New Evidence from the Business Information Tracking Series. *Journal of Finance*, 59, 479–506.

Villalonga, B., & Amit, R. (2006). How Do Family Ownership, Control, and Management Affect Firm Value. *Journal of Financial Economics*, 80, 385–417.

Wagner, H. F. (2004). *The Equity Carve-Out Decision*. University of Munich. Working Paper.

Walsh, J. P., & Ellwood, J. W. (1991). Mergers, Acquisitions, and the Pruning of Managerial Deadwood. *Strategic Management Journal*, 12, 201–217.

Wasserstein, B. (1998). *Big Deal: The Battle for Control of America's Leading Corporations*. New York: Warner Books.

Weifeng, W., Zhaoguo, Z., & Shasa, Z. (2008). Ownership Structure and the Private Benefits of Control: An Analysis of Chinese Firms. *Corporate Governance*, 8, 286–298.

Weir, C., Jones, P., & Wright, M. (2007). *Public to Private Transactions, Private Equity and Performance in the UK: An Empirical Analysis of the Impact of Going Private*. Nottingham, UK: Nottingham University. Working Paper.

Weir, C., Liang, D., & Wright, M. (2005). Incentive Effects, Monitoring Mechanisms and the Threat from the Market for Corporate Control: An Analysis of the Factors Affecting Public to Private Transactions in the U.K. *Journal of Business Finance and Accounting*, 32, 909–944.

Welch, I. (2001). *The Equity Premium Consensus Forecast Revisited*. Yale University School of Management. Working Paper.

White, E., & Joann, S. L. (2007, January 13). Companies Trim Executive Perks to Avoid Glare. *Wall Street Journal*, A1.

White, M. (1989). The Corporate Bankruptcy Decision. *The Journal of Economic Perspectives*, 3, 129–152.

Wigmore, B. (1994). The Decline in Credit Quality of Junk Bond Issues, 1980–1988. In Gaughan, P.A. (Ed.), *Readings in Mergers and Acquisitions* (pp. 171–184). Cambridge, UK: Basil Blackwell.

Wilson, B. D. (1980). The Propensity of Multinational Companies to Expand through Acquisitions. *Journal of International Business Studies*, 11, 59–64.

Wiltbank, R., & Boeker, W. (2007). *Returns to Angel Investors in Groups*. SSRN. Available at *http://ssrn.com/abstracts-1028592*.

Woolridge, J. R., & Snow, C. C. (1990). Stock Decisions. *Strategic Management Journal*, 11, 353–363.

Wright, M., Burros, A., Ball, R., Scholes, L., Meuleman, M., & Amess, K. (2008). *The Implications of Alternative Investment Vehicles for Corporate Governance: A Survey of Empirical Research*. In Report of the Organisation for Economic Cooperation and Development, Paris. Available at *www.oecd.org/daf/corporate-affairs*.

Wright, M. N. W., & Robbie, K. (1996). The Longer-Term Effects of Management-Led Buyouts. *Journal of Entrepreneurial and Small Business Finance*, 5, 213–234.

Wruck, K. H. (1989). Equity Ownership Concentration and Firm Value: Evidence from Private Equity Financing. *Journal of Financial Economics*, 23, 3–28.

Wruck, K. H., & Yilin, W. (2009). Relationships, Corporate Governance, and Performance: Evidence from Private Placements of Common Stock. *Journal of Corporate Finance*, 15, 30–47.

Wulf, J. (2004). Do CEOs in Mergers Trade Power for Premium? Evidence from Mergers of Equals. *Journal of Law and Organization*, 20, 60.

Wulf, J., & Rajan, R. (2003). *The Flattening Firm: Evidence from Panel Data on the Changing Nature of Corporate Hierarchies*. University of Chicago. Working Paper.

Wu, Y. L. (2004). The Choice of Equity-Selling Mechanisms. *Journal of Financial Economics*, 74, 93–119.

Yago, G., & Bonds, J. (1991). *How High Yield Securities Restructured Corporate America*. New York: Oxford University Press.

Yermack, D. (1996). Higher Market Valuation of Companies with a Small Board Size. *Journal of Financial Economics*, 40, 185–211.

Young, M., Peng, M., Ahlston, D., Brinton, G., & Jiang, Y. (2008). Corporate Governance in Emerging Economies. *Journal of Management Studies*, 22, 44–59.

Zahra, S. A., Ireland, R. D., & Hitt, M. A. (2000). International Expansion by New Venture Firms: International, Mode of Market Entry, Technological Learning and Performance. *Academy of Management Journal*, 244–257.

Zahra, S., & Elhagrasey, G. (1994). Strategic Management of International Joint Ventures. *European Management Journal*, 12, 83–93.

Zellner, W. (2005). This Big Oil Deal Shouldn't Hurt a Bit. *Business Week*, 42.

Zingales, L. (1995). What Determines the Value of Corporate Control. *The Quarterly Journal of Economics*, 110, 1047–1073.

Zola, M., & Meier, D. (2008). What Is M&A Performance? *Academy of Management Perspectives*, 22, 55–77.

Zuckerman, G., Sender, H., & Patterson, S. (2007). Hedge Fund Crowd Sees More Green as Fortress Hits Jackpot with IPO. *Wall Street Journal*, A1.

Glossary

Abnormal return The return to shareholders due to nonrecurring events that differs from what would have been predicted by the market. It is the return due to an event such as a merger or an acquisition.

Acquirer A firm that attempts to acquire a controlling interest in another company.

Acquisition The purchase by one company of a controlling ownership interest in another firm, a legal subsidiary of another firm, or selected assets of another firm.

Acquisition vehicle The legal structure used to acquire another company.

Advance ruling An IRS ruling sought by acquirers and targets planning to enter into a tax-free transaction. A favorable ruling is often a condition of closing.

Affirmative covenant A portion of a loan agreement that specifies the actions the borrowing firm agrees to take during the term of the loan.

Antigreenmail provisions Amendments to corporate charters restricting the firm's ability to repurchase shares from specific shareholders at a premium.

Antitakeover amendments Amendments to corporate charters designed to slow or make more expensive efforts to take control of the firm.

Antitrust laws Federal laws prohibiting individual corporations from assuming too much market power.

Appraisal rights Rights to seek "fair value" for their shares in court given to target company shareholders who choose not to tender shares in the first or second tier of a tender offer.

Arbitrageurs ("arbs") In the context of M&As, arbs are speculators who attempt to profit from the difference between the bid price and the target firm's current share price.

Asset-based lending A type of lending in which the decision to grant a loan is based largely on the quality of the assets collateralizing the loan.

Asset impairment An asset is said to be impaired according to FASB Statement 142 if its fair value falls below its book or carrying value.

Asset purchases Transactions in which the acquirer buys all or a portion of the target company's assets and assumes all, some, or none of the target's liabilities.

Assignment The process through which a committee representing creditors grants the power to liquidate a firm's assets to a third party, called an *assignee* or *trustee*.

Asymmetric information Information about a firm that is not equally available to both managers and shareholders.

Automatic stay The requirement for a period of time following the submission of a petition for bankruptcy in which all judgments, collection activities, foreclosures, and repossessions of property are suspended and may not be pursued by the creditors on any debt or claim that arose before the filing of the bankruptcy petition.

Back-end merger The merger following either a single- or two-tier tender offer consisting of either a long-form or short-form merger, with the latter not requiring a target firm shareholder vote.

Bankruptcy A federal legal proceeding designed to protect the technically or legally insolvent firm from lawsuits by its creditors until a decision can be made to shut down or continue to operate the firm.

Bear hug A takeover tactic involving the mailing of a letter containing an acquisition proposal to the board of directors of a target company without prior warning and demanding a rapid decision.

Beta A measure of nondiversifiable risk or the extent to which a firm's (or asset's) return changes because of a change in the market's return.

Bidder See *acquirer*.

Boot The nonequity portion of the purchase price.

Breakup fee A fee that will be paid to the potential acquirer if the target firm decides to accept an alternative bid. Also called a *termination fee*.

Bridge financing Temporary unsecured short-term loans provided by investment banks to pay all or a portion of the purchase price and meet immediate working capital requirements until permanent or long-term financing is found.

Business alliance A generic term referring to all forms of business combinations other than mergers and acquisitions.

Business-level strategies Strategies pertaining to a specific operating unit or product line within a firm.

Business strategy or model That portion of a business plan detailing the way the firm intends to achieve its vision.

Buyout Change in controlling interest in a corporation.

Capital asset pricing model A framework for measuring the relationship between expected risk and return.

Capitalization multiple The multiple estimated by dividing 1 by the estimated discount or capitalization rate that can be used to estimate the value of a business by multiplying it by an indicator of value such as free cash flow.

Capitalization rate The discount rate used by practitioners if the cash flows of the firm are not expected to grow or are expected to grow at a constant rate indefinitely.

Cash-for-assets An acquisition in which the acquirer pays cash for the seller's assets and may choose to accept some or all of the seller's liabilities.

Cash-out statutory merger A merger in which the shareholders of the selling firm receive cash or some form on nonvoting investment (e.g., debt, or nonvoting preferred or common stock) for their shares.

Certificate of incorporation A document received from the state once the articles of incorporation have been approved.

Classified board election An antitakeover defense involving the separation of a firm's board into several classes, only one of which is up for election at any one point in time. Also called a *staggered board*.

Closing The phase of the acquisition process in which ownership is transferred from the target to the acquiring firm in exchange for some agreed-on consideration following the receipt of all necessary shareholder, regulatory, and third-party approvals.

Closing conditions Stipulations that must be satisfied before closing can take place.

Collar agreement An arrangement providing for certain changes in the share exchange ratio contingent on the level of the acquirer's share price around the effective date of the merger.

Common-size financial statements Financial statements calculated by taking each line item as a percentage of revenue.

Composition An agreement in which creditors consent to settling for less than the full amount they are owed.

Confidentiality agreement A mutually binding accord defining how information exchanged among the parties may be used and the circumstances under which the discussions may be made public. Also known as a *nondisclosure agreement*.

Conglomerate discount The share prices of conglomerates often trade at a discount from focused firms or their value if they were broken up and sold in pieces.

Conglomerate mergers Transactions in which the acquiring company purchases firms in largely unrelated industries.

Consent decree Requires the merging parties to divest overlapping businesses or restrict anticompetitive practices.

Consent solicitation A process enabling dissident shareholders in certain states to obtain shareholder support for their proposals by simply obtaining their written consent.

Consolidation A business combination involving two or more companies joining to form a new company, in which none of the combining firms survive.

Constant-growth model A valuation method that assumes that cash flow will grow at a constant rate.

Contingent value rights (CVR) Commitments by the issuing company to pay additional cash or securities to the holder of the CVR if the share price of the issuing company falls below a specified level at some future date.

Control premium The excess over the target's current share price the acquirer is willing to pay to gain a controlling interest. A pure control premium is one in which the anticipated synergies are small and the perceived value of the purchase is in gaining control to direct the activities of the target firm.

Corporate bylaws Rules governing the internal management of the corporation that are determined by the corporation's founders.

Corporate charters A state license defining the powers of the firm and the rights and responsibilities of its shareholders, board of directors, and managers. The charter consists of articles of incorporation and a certificate of incorporation.

Corporate governance The systems and controls in place to protect the rights of corporate stakeholders.

Corporate restructuring Actions taken to expand or contract a firm's basic operations or fundamentally change its asset or financial structure.

Cost leadership A strategy designed to make a firm the cost leader in its market by constructing efficient production facilities, tightly controlling overhead expense, and eliminating marginally profitable customer accounts.

Covenants Promises made by the borrower that certain acts will be performed and others will be avoided.

Cram down A legal reorganization occurring whenever one or more classes of creditors or shareholders approve, even though others may not.

Cumulative voting rights In an election for a board of directors, each shareholder is entitled to as many votes as equal the number of shares the shareholder owns multiplied by the number of directors to be elected. Furthermore, the shareholder may cast all of these votes for a single candidate or any two or more of them.

Deal-structuring process The process focused on satisfying as many of the primary objectives of the parties involved and determining how risk will be shared.

Debt-for-equity swap Creditors surrender a portion of their claims on the firm in exchange for an ownership position in the firm.

Debtor-in-possession On the filing of a reorganization petition, the firm's current management remains in place to conduct the ongoing affairs of the firm.

Debt restructuring Involves concessions by creditors that lower an insolvent firm's payments so that it may remain in business.

Definitive agreement of purchase and sale The legal document indicating all of the rights and obligations of the parties both before and after closing.

Destroyers of value Factors that can reduce the future cash flow of the combined companies.

Discounted cash flow The conversion of future to current cash flows by applying an appropriate discount rate.

Discount rate The opportunity cost associated with investment in the firm used to convert the projected cash flows to present values.

Dissident shareholders Those that disagree with a firm's incumbent management and attempt to change policies by initiating proxy contests to gain representation on the board of directors.

Diversifiable risk The risk specific to an individual firm, such as strikes and lawsuits.

Diversification A strategy of buying firms outside of the company's primary line of business.

Divestiture The sale of all or substantially all of a company or product line to another party for cash or securities.

Divisional organization An organizational structure in which groups of products are combined into independent divisions or "strategic business units."

Dual class recapitalization A takeover defense in which a firm issues multiple classes of stock in which one class has voting rights that are 10 to 100 times those of another class. Such stock is also called *supervoting stock*.

Due diligence The process by which the acquirer seeks to determine the accuracy of the target's financial statements, evaluate the firm's operations, validate valuation assumptions, determine fatal flaws, and identify sources and destroyers of value.

Earnouts Payments to the seller based on the acquired business achieving certain profit or revenue targets.

Economic value The present value of a firm's projected cash flows.

Economies of scale The spreading of fixed costs over increasing production levels.

Economies of scope The use of a specific set of skills or an asset currently used to produce a specific product to produce related products.

Effective control Control achieved when one firm has purchased another firm's voting stock; it is not likely to be temporary. There are no legal restrictions on control such as from a bankruptcy court, and there are no powerful minority shareholders.

Employee stock ownership plan (ESOP) A trust fund or plan that invests in the securities of the firm sponsoring the plan on behalf of the firm's employees. Such plans are generally defined contribution employee-retirement plans.

Enterprise cash flow Cash available to shareholders and lenders after all operating obligations of the firm have been satisfied.

Enterprise value Viewed from the liability side of the balance sheet, it is the sum of the market or present value of a firm's common equity plus preferred stock and long-term debt. For simplicity, other long-term liabilities are often excluded from the calculation. From the perspective of the asset side of the balance sheet, it is equal to cash plus the market value of current operating and nonoperating assets less current liabilities plus long-term assets.

Equity beta A measure of the risk of a stock's financial returns, as compared with the risk of the financial returns to the general stock market, which in turn is affected by the overall economy.

Equity carve-out A transaction in which the parent firm issues a portion of its stock or that of a subsidiary to the public.

Equity cash flow Cash available to common shareholders after all operating obligations of the firm have been satisfied.

Equity premium The rate of return in excess of the risk-free rate investors require to invest in equities.

Excess returns See *abnormal returns*.

Exchange offer A tender offer involving a share-for-share exchange.

Exit strategy A strategy enabling investors to realize their required returns by undertaking an initial public offering or selling to a strategic buyer.

Extension Creditor agreement to lengthen the period during which the debtor firm can repay its debt and, in some cases, to temporarily suspend both interest and principal repayments.

Fair market value The cash or cash-equivalent price a willing buyer would propose and a willing seller would accept for a business if both parties had access to all relevant information.

Fairness opinion letter A written and signed third-party assertion certifying the appropriateness of the price of a proposed deal involving a tender offer, merger, asset sale, or leveraged buyout.

Fair value An estimate of the value of an asset when no strong market exists for a business or it is not possible to identify the value of substantially similar firms.

Financial buyer Acquirers that focus on relatively short to intermediate financial returns and typically use large amounts of debt to finance their acquisitions.

Financial restructuring Actions by the firm to change its total debt and equity structure.

Financial sponsor An investor group providing equity financing in leveraged buyout transactions.

Financial synergy The reduction in the cost of capital as a result of more stable cash flows, financial economies of scale, or a better matching of investment opportunities with available funds.

Fixed or constant share-exchange agreement An exchange agreement in which the number of acquirer shares exchanged for each target share is unchanged between the signing of the agreement of purchase and sale and closing.

Fixed value agreement The value of the price per share is fixed by allowing the number of acquirer shares issued to vary to offset fluctuations in the buyer's share price.

Flip-in poison pill A shareholders' rights plan in which the shareholders of the target firm can acquire stock in the target firm at a substantial discount.

Flip-over poison pill A shareholders' rights plan in which target firm shareholders may convert such rights to acquire stock of the surviving company at a substantial discount.

Form of acquisition The determination of what is being acquired (i.e., stock or assets) and the way in which ownership is transferred.

Form of payment A means of payment: cash, common stock, debt, or some combination. Some portion of the payment may be deferred or dependent on the future performance of the acquired entity.

Forward triangular merger The acquisition subsidiary being merged with the target and the acquiring subsidiary surviving.

Fraudulent conveyance Laws governing the rights of shareholders if the new company created following an acquisition or LBO is inadequately capitalized to remain viable.

Free cash flow The difference between cash inflows and cash outflows, which may be positive, negative, or zero.

Friendly takeover Acquisition when the target's board and management are receptive to the idea and recommend shareholder approval.

Functional strategies Description in detail of how each major function (e.g., manufacturing, marketing, and human resources) within the firm will support the business strategy.

Generally accepted accounting principles (GAAP) Accounting guidelines established by the Financial Accounting Standards Board.

General partner An individual responsible for the daily operations of a limited partnership.

Global capital asset pricing model A version of the capital asset pricing model in which a global equity index is used in calculating the equity risk premium.

Globally integrated capital markets Capital markets providing foreigners with unfettered access to local capital markets and local residents to foreign capital markets.

Going concern value The value of a company defined as the firm's value in excess of the sum of the value of its parts.

Going private The purchase of the publicly traded shares of a firm by a group of investors.

Golden parachutes Employee severance arrangements that are triggered whenever a change in control takes place.

Goodwill The excess of the purchase price over the fair value of the acquired net assets on the acquisition date.

Go-shop provision A provision allowing a seller to continue to solicit other bidders for a specific time period after an agreement has been signed but before closing. However, the seller that accepts another bid must pay a breakup fee to the bidder with which it had a signed agreement.

Greenmail The practice of a firm buying back its shares at a premium from an investor threatening a takeover.

Hedge fund Private investment limited partnerships (for U.S. investors) or offshore investment corporations (for non-U.S. or tax-exempt investors) in which the general partner has made a substantial personal investment.

Herfindahl–Hirschman Index The measure of industry concentration used by the Federal Trade Commission as one criterion in determining when to approve mergers and acquisitions.

Highly leveraged transactions Those involving a substantial amount of debt relative to the amount of equity invested.

Holding company A legal entity often having a controlling interest in one or more companies.

Holdout problem The tendency for smaller creditors to hold up the agreement among creditors during reorganization unless they receive special treatment.

Horizontal merger A combination of two firms within the same industry.

Hostile takeover Acquisition when the initial bid was unsolicited, the target was not seeking a merger at the time of the approach, the approach was contested by the target's management, and control changed hands.

Hostile tender offer A tender offer that is unwanted by the target's board.

Hubris An explanation for takeovers that attributes a tendency to overpay to excessive optimism about the value of a deal's potential synergy or excessive confidence in management's ability to manage the acquisition.

Impaired asset As defined by FASB, a long-term asset whose fair value falls below its book or carrying value.

Implementation strategy The way in which the firm chooses to execute the business strategy.

Indemnification A common contractual clause requiring the seller to indemnify or absolve the buyer of liability in the event of misrepresentations or breaches of warranties or covenants. Similarly, the buyer usually agrees to indemnify the seller. In effect, it is the reimbursement to the other party for a loss for which it was not responsible.

Initial offer price A price that lies between the estimated minimum and maximum offer prices for a target firm.

Insider trading Individuals buying or selling securities based on knowledge not available to the general public.

Interest rate parity theory A theory that relates forward or future spot exchange rates to differences in interest rates between two countries adjusted by the spot rate.

Investment bankers Advisors who offer strategic and tactical advice and acquisition opportunities, screen potential buyers and sellers, make initial contact with a seller or buyer, and provide negotiation support, valuation, and deal-structuring advice.

Involuntary bankruptcy A situation in which creditors force a debtor firm into bankruptcy.

Joint venture A cooperative business relationship formed by two or more separate entities to achieve common strategic objectives.

Junk bonds High-yield bonds either rated by the credit-rating agencies as below investment grade or not rated at all.

Legal form of the selling entity Whether the seller is a C or Subchapter S corporation, a limited liability company, or a partnership.

Legal insolvency When a firm's liabilities exceed the fair market value of its assets.

Letter of intent Preliminary agreement between two companies intending to merge that stipulates major areas of agreement between the parties.

Leveraged buyout Purchase of a company financed primarily by debt.

Leveraged loans Unrated or noninvestment-grade bank loans whose interest rates are equal to or greater than the London Inter Bank Rate plus 150 basis points.

Liquidating dividend Proceeds left to shareholders after a company is liquidated and outstanding obligations to creditors are paid off.

Liquidation The value of a firm's assets sold separately less its liabilities and expenses incurred in breaking up the firm.

Liquidity discount The discount or reduction in the offer price for the target firm made by discounting the value of the target firm estimated by examining the market values of comparable publicly traded firms to reflect the potential loss in value when sold due to the illiquidity of the market for similar types of investments. The liquidity discount also is referred to as a *marketability discount*.

Liquidity risk See *marketability risk*.

Management buyout A leveraged buyout in which managers of the firm to be taken private are also equity investors in the transaction.

Management entrenchment theory A theory that managers use a variety of takeover defenses to ensure their longevity with the firm.

Management integration team Senior managers from the two merged organizations charged with delivering on sales and operating synergies identified during the preclosing due diligence.

Management preferences The boundaries or limits that senior managers of the acquiring firm place on the acquisition process.

Managerialism theory A theory espousing that managers acquire companies to increase the acquirer's size and their own remuneration.

Marketability discount See *liquidity discount*.

Marketability risk The risk associated with an illiquid market for the specific stock. Also called *liquidity risk*.

Market power A situation in which the merger of two firms enables the resulting combination to profitably maintain prices above competitive levels for a significant period.

Market power hypothesis A theory that firms merge to gain greater control over pricing.

Maximum offer price The sum of the minimum price plus the present value of net synergy.

Merger A combination of two or more firms in which all but one legally cease to exist.

Merger–acquisition plan A specific type of implementation strategy that describes in detail the motivation for the acquisition and how and when it will be achieved.

Merger arbitrage An investment strategy that attempts to profit from the spread between a target firm's current share price and a pending takeover bid.

Merger of equals A merger framework usually applied whenever the merger participants are comparable in size, competitive position, profitability, and market capitalization.

Mezzanine financing Capital that in liquidation has a repayment priority between senior debt and common stock.

Minimum offer price The target's stand-alone or present value or its current market value.

Minority discount The reduction in the value of their investment in a firm because the minority investors cannot direct the activities of the firm.

Minority investment A less than controlling interest in another firm.

Negative covenant A restriction found in loan agreements on the actions of the borrower.

Negotiating price range The difference between the minimum and maximum offer prices.

Net asset value The difference between the fair market value of total identifiable acquired assets and the value of acquired liabilities.

Net debt The market value of debt assumed by the acquirer less cash and marketable securities on the books of the target firm.

Net operating loss carryforward and carrybacks Provisions in the tax laws allowing firms to use accumulated net tax losses to offset income earned over a specified number of future years or recover taxes paid during a limited number of prior years.

Net purchase price The total purchase price plus other assumed liabilities less the proceeds from the sale of discretionary or redundant target assets.

Net synergy The difference between estimated sources of value and destroyers of value.

Nondiversifiable risk Risk generated by factors that affect all firms, such as inflation and war.

Nonrecourse financing Loans granted to a venture without partner guarantees.

No-shop agreement That which prohibits the takeover target from seeking other bids or making public information not currently readily available while in discussions with a potential acquirer.

One-tiered offer A bidder announces the same offer to all target shareholders.

Open market share repurchase The act of a corporation buying its shares in the open market at the prevailing price as any other investor, as opposed to a tender offer for shares or a repurchase resulting from negotiation such as with an unwanted investor.

Operating synergy Increased value resulting from a combination of businesses due to such factors as economies of scale and scope.

Operational restructuring The outright or partial sale of companies or product lines or downsizing by closing unprofitable or nonstrategic facilities.

Payment-in-kind (PIK) notes Equity or debt that pays dividends or interest in the form of additional equity or debt.

Permanent financing Financing usually consisting of long-term unsecured debt.

Poison pills A new class of securities issued as a dividend by a company to its shareholders, giving shareholders rights to acquire more shares at a discount.

Portfolio companies Companies in which the hedge or private equity fund has made investments.

Postclosing organization The organizational and legal framework used to manage the combined businesses following the completion of the transaction.

Prepackaged bankruptcies A situation in which the failing firm starts negotiating with its creditors well in advance of filing for a Chapter 11 bankruptcy in order to reach agreement on major issues before formally filing for bankruptcy.

Private corporation A firm whose securities are not registered with state or federal authorities.

Private equity fund A limited partnership in which the general partner has made a substantial personal investment.

Private placements The sale of securities to institutional investors, such as pension funds and insurance companies, for investment rather than for resale. Such securities do not have to be registered with the SEC.

Private solicitation A firm hires an investment banker or on its own undertakes to identify potential buyers to be contacted to buy the entire firm or a portion of the firm.

Pro forma financial statements A form of accounting that presents financial statements in a way that purports to more accurately describe a firm's current or projected performance.

Proxy contest An attempt by dissident shareholders to obtain representation on the board of directors or to change a firm's bylaws.

Public solicitation Public announcement by a firm that it is putting itself, a subsidiary, or a product line up for sale.

Purchase accounting A form of accounting for financial reporting purposes in which the acquired assets and assumed liabilities are revalued to their fair market value on the date of acquisition and recorded on the books of the acquiring company.

Purchase premium The excess of the offer price over the target's current share price, which reflects both the value of expected synergies and the amount necessary to obtain control.

Purchasing power parity theory The theory stating that one currency will appreciate (depreciate) with respect to another currency according to the expected relative rates of inflation between the two countries.

Purchase premium The excess of the offer price over the target's current share price, which reflects both the value of expected synergies and the amount necessary to obtain control.

Pure control premium The value the acquirer believes can be created by replacing incompetent management or changing the strategic direction of the firm.

Pure play A firm whose products or services focus on a single industry or market.

Real options Management's ability to adopt and later revise corporate investment decisions.

Receivership Court appointment of an individual to administer the assets and affairs of a business in accordance with its directives.

Retention bonuses Incentives granted key employees of the target firm if they remain with the combined companies for a specific period following completion of the transaction.

Revenue ruling An official interpretation by the IRS of the Internal Revenue Code, related statutes, tax treaties, and regulations.

Reverse breakup fee Fees paid to a target firm in the event the bidder wants to withdraw from a signed contract.

Reverse LBOs Public companies that are taken private and later are taken public again. The second effort to take the firm public is called a *secondary public offering*.

Reverse merger Process by which a private firm goes public by merging with a public firm, with the public firm surviving.

Reverse triangular merger The merger of the target with a subsidiary of the acquiring firm, with the target surviving.

Right of first refusal A contract clause requiring that a party wishing to leave a joint venture or partnership first offer its interests to other participants in the JV or partnership.

Risk-free rate of return The return on a security with an exceedingly low probability of default, such as U.S. Treasury securities, and minimal reinvestment risk.

Risk premium The additional rate of return in excess of the risk-free rate that investors require to purchase a firm's equity. Also called the *equity premium*.

Secondary public offering A stock offering by a private company that had previously been a public company.

Secured debt Debt backed by the borrower's assets.

Security agreement A legal document stipulating which of the borrower's assets are pledged to secure the loan.

Segmented capital markets Capital markets exhibiting different bond and equity prices in different geographic areas for identical assets in terms of risk and maturity.

Self-tender offer A tender offer used when a firm seeks to repurchase its stock from its shareholders.

Share-exchange ratio The number of shares of the acquirer's stock to be exchanged for each share of the target's stock.

Shareholders' interest theory The presumption that management resistance to proposed takeovers is a good bargaining strategy to increase the purchase price for the benefit of the target firm's shareholders.

Shark repellents Specific types of takeover defenses that can be adopted by amending either a corporate charter or its bylaws.

Shell corporation One that is incorporated but has no significant assets or operations.

Sources of value Factors increasing the cash flow of the combined companies.

Spin-off A transaction in which a parent creates a new legal subsidiary and distributes shares it owns in the subsidiary to its current shareholders as a stock dividend.

Split-off A variation of a spin-off in which some parent company shareholders receive shares in a subsidiary in return for relinquishing their parent company shares.

Split-up A transaction in which a parent firm splits its assets between two or more subsidiaries and the stock of each subsidiary is offered to its shareholders in exchange for their parent firm shares.

Staggered board election A takeover defense involving the division of the firm's directors into a number of different classes, with no two classes up for reelection at the same time. Also called a *classified board*.

Stakeholders Groups having interests in a firm, such as customers, shareholders, employees, suppliers, regulators, and communities.

Stand-alone business One whose financial statements reflect all the costs of running the business and all the revenues generated by the business.

Standstill agreement A contractual arrangement in which the acquirer agrees not to make any further investments in the target's stock for a stipulated period.

Statutory consolidation Involves two or more companies joining to form a new company.

Statutory merger The combination of the acquiring and target firms, in which one firm ceases to exist, in accordance with the statutes of the state in which the combined businesses will be incorporated.

Stock-for-stock statutory merger A merger in which the seller receives acquirer shares in exchange for its shares (with the seller shares subsequently canceled); also called a *stock swap merger*.

Stock purchases The exchange of the target's stock for cash, debt, or the stock of the acquiring company.

Strategic buyer An acquirer primarily interested in increasing shareholder value by realizing long-term synergies.

Subsidiary carve-out A transaction in which the parent creates a wholly-owned independent legal subsidiary, with stock and a management team different from the parent's, and issues a portion of the subsidiary's stock to the public.

Subsidiary merger A transaction in which the target becomes a subsidiary of the parent.

Supermajority rules A takeover defense requiring a higher level of approval for amending the charter or for certain types of transactions, such as a merger or acquisition.

Supervoting stock A class of voting stock having voting rights many times those of other classes of stock.

Syndicate An arrangement in which a group of investment banks agrees to purchase a new issue of securities from the acquiring company for sale to the investing public.

Synergy The notion that the value of the combined enterprises will exceed the sum of their individual values.

Takeover Generic term referring to a change in the controlling ownership interest of a corporation.

Takeover defenses Protective devices put in place by a firm to frustrate, slow down, or raise the cost of a takeover.

Target company The firm that is being solicited by the acquiring company.

Taxable transaction Transactions in which the form of payment is primarily something other than acquiring company stock.

Tax considerations Structures and strategies determining whether a transaction is taxable or nontaxable to the seller's shareholders.

Tax-free reorganization Nontaxable transactions usually involving mergers, with the form of payment primarily acquirer stock exchanged for the target's stock or assets.

Tax-free transactions Transactions in which the form of payment is primarily acquiring company stock. Also called *tax-free reorganizations*.

Tax shield The reduction in the firm's tax liability due to the tax deductibility of interest.

Technical insolvency A situation in which a firm is unable to pay its liabilities as they come due.

Tender offer The offer to buy shares in another firm, usually for cash, securities, or both.

Terminal growth value The discounted value of the cash flows generated during the stable growth period. Also called the *sustainable, horizon,* or *continuing growth value*.

Term loan A loan usually having a maturity of two to ten years and secured by the asset being financed, such as new capital equipment.

Term sheet A document outlining the primary areas of agreement between the buyer and the seller, which is often used as the basis for a more detailed letter of intent.

Total capitalization The sum of a firm's debt and all forms of equity.

Total consideration A commonly used term in legal documents to reflect the different types of remuneration received by target company shareholders.

Total purchase price The total consideration plus the market value of the target firm's debt assumed by the acquiring company. Also referred to as *enterprise value*.

Tracking stocks Separate classes of common stock of the parent corporation whose dividend payouts depend on the financial performance of a specific subsidiary. Also called *target* or *letter stocks*.

Transfer taxes State taxes paid whenever titles to assets are transferred, as in an asset purchase.

Two-tiered offer A tender offer in which target shareholders receive an offer for a specific number of shares. Immediately following this offer, the bidder announces its intentions to purchase the remaining shares at a lower price or using something other than cash.

Type A reorganization A tax-free merger or consolidation in which target shareholders receive cash, voting or nonvoting common or preferred stock, or debt for their shares. At least 50% of the purchase price must be in acquirer stock.

Type B stock-for-stock reorganization A tax-free transaction in which the acquirer uses its voting common stock to purchase at least 80% of the voting power of the target's outstanding voting stock and at least 80% of each class of nonvoting shares. Used as an alternative to a merger.

Type C stock-for-assets reorganization A tax-free transaction in which acquirer voting stock is used to purchase at least 80% of the fair market value of the target's net assets.

Valuation cash flows Restated GAAP cash flows used for valuing a firm or a firm's assets.

Variable growth valuation model A valuation method that assumes that a firm's cash flows will experience periods of high growth followed by a period of slower, more sustainable growth. Sometimes referred to as the supernormal valuation model.

Vertical merger One in which companies that do not own operations in each major segment of the value chain choose to backward integrate by acquiring a supplier or to forward integrate by acquiring a distributor.

Voluntary bankruptcy A situation in which the debtor firm files for bankruptcy.

Voluntary liquidation Sale by management that concludes that the sale of the firm in parts could realize greater value than the value created by a continuation of the combined corporation.

Weighted-average cost of capital A broader measure than the cost of equity that represents the return that a firm must earn to induce investors and lenders to buy its stock and bonds.

White knight A potential acquirer that is viewed more favorably by a target firm's management and board than the initial bidder.

Winner's curse The tendency of the auction winners to show remorse, believing that they may have paid too much.

Zero-growth valuation model A valuation model that assumes that free cash flow is constant in perpetuity.

Index

A

Abandon options, 312–313, 313b
Abbot Labs, 246t
ABN Amro, 416, 437
Abnormal returns, 565–566, 565t, 715g
Accountability, in business alliances, 546
Accountants, in M&A transactions, 28
Accounting
  in deal structuring, 180
  discrepancy red flags, 328b
  pro forma, 328–329
  purchase, 466, 469–474, 470t
  recapitalization, 474
  see also Generally accepted accounting principles
Accounting considerations, 450
  balance sheet, 469–473
  cash flow, 474
  divestitures, 586
  financial reporting, 466–469
  form, amount, and timing of payment and,
      414–415
  income statement, 474
  international standards, 474
  purchase impact on financial statements, 469–474
  recapitalization, 474
  spin-offs, 590
  tracking stocks, 596
Acquirers, 4, 715g
  acquisition plan for, 161b
  creeping takeover strategy, 104
  due diligence question list, 170
  experience, importance of, 42
  open market purchase, 23
  overpaying for targets, 10
  part of larger legal entity, 353–354
  returns, 39–42
Acquisition currency, 592
Acquisition plans, 137–138, 156
  for acquiring firm, 161b
  building, 156–161
  business plan linkages, 158t
  development of, 157
  financial objectives, 157
  management guidance, 160b
  management preferences, 160
  nonfinancial objectives, 157
  objectives of, 157
  resource/capability evaluation, 157–159
  timetable, 160–161
  see also Business plans; Planning
Acquisition vehicles, 180, 415, 715g
  choosing form of, 416–417
  corporate structure, 416–417
  cross-border transactions, 665–666
  form of acquisition and, 413
  form of payment and, 413
  joint ventures, 417
  see also Deal structuring
Acquisition/merger agreements
  allocation of price, 189
  assumption of liabilities, 189
  closing conditions, 190
  completing, 188–191
  covenants, 189–190
  deal provisions, 188
  indemnification, 190
  other closing documents, 190–191
  payment mechanism, 189
  price, 189
  representations and warranties, 189
Acquisitions, 22, 715g
  customer attrition related to, 206
  partial, 68–69
  process flow diagram, 139f
  two-step, 440–441
  see also Mergers and acquisitions
Activist investors, 32–35
Adjusted present value method
  advantage of, 517
  annual cash flow projection, 514
  applying, 513
  cost of capital method versus, 517
  in distressed businesses, 640–644
  justification for, 513
  in LBO valuation, 511–517
  present value of equity cash flow with, 516t
  present value of tax savings estimation, 514
  total value of firm calculation, 514

Note: Page numbers followed by *b* indicate boxes, by *f* indicate figures, by *t* indicate tables, and by *g* indicate glossary.

Adjustments, financial statements, 371–377
  accounting for inventory, 374–375
  auto expenses, 373
  benefits, 373
  commonly overstated areas, 375
  commonly understated areas, 375
  depreciation expense, 374
  owners and officers salaries, 373
  professional services fees, 374
  rent or lease payments, 374
  reserves, 374
  travel and entertainment, 373
Advance notice provisions, 116
Advance rulings, 715g
Affirmative protective covenant, 496–497, 715g
Alliances. *See* Business alliances
American depositary shares (ADS), 668
American depository receipt (ADR) market, 668
Angel investors, 32
Antigreenmail provisions, 113t, 116, 715g
Antitakeover defenses, 97
Antitakeover statutes, 75–76, 715g
Antitrust laws, 715g
  collaborative efforts guidelines, 69
  consent decrees, 65
  cross-border transactions, 81–82
  federal, 53t, 61–69
  horizontal merger guidelines, 66–69
  procedural rules, 64
  state, 76
  vertical merger guidelines, 69
Appraisal rights, 103, 715g
Approvals, gaining at closing, 188
Arbitrageurs (arbs), 34–35, 715g
Arbitration clause, 561–562
Articles of incorporation, 113
Asset purchases, 431, 433t, 434–437, 715g
  advantages/disadvantages from buyer's perspective, 435–436
  advantages/disadvantages from seller's perspective, 436–437
  advantages/disadvantages of, 433t
  cash-for-assets transaction, 434–435
  stock-for-assets transactions, 435
  taxable, 451–452
  see also Form of acquisition
Asset swaps, 150–151
Asset-based LBOs, 500
Asset-based lending, 495–497, 715g
Asset-oriented valuation methods, 297–300
  liquidation or breakup value, 298–300
  in privately held companies, 379–380
  tangible book value or equity per share, 297–298

Assets
  acquired, valuation guidelines, 472b
  deferred tax, 262
  fixed, 486
  impairment, 715g
  net acquired, 467–468
  net fixed, 363–364
  nonoperating, 266–270
  R&D, 468
  redundant, 492
  target, net, 343–344
  undervalued, buying, 11
  unutilized/undervalued, 268–270
Assignees, 621–622
Assignments, 621–622, 715g
Asymmetric information, 715g
Automatic stay, 715g

B

Back-end mergers, 440–441, 715g
Balance sheets
  adjustment mechanism, 363–364
  adjustments, 422, 422t
  considerations, 469–473
  impacts of purchase accounting, 473t
  pro forma, 526
  projections, 526
Bank Merger Act of 1966, 78
Banking industry regulation, 78–79
Bankruptcy
  Chapter 7 liquidation, 618–619, 627–629, 632, 715g
  Chapter 11 reorganization, 624–627, 632
  Chapter 15, 630–631
  cross-border, 630–631
  firms emerging from, returns and, 644
  involuntary, 719g
  motivations for filing, 631–632
  predicting, 637–640
  prepackaged, 632–633
  professional fees associated with, 632
  reorganization and liquidation in, 622–633
  U.S. laws/practices evolution, 622–624
  voluntary, 723g
  voluntary settlement outside of, 619–622
Bankruptcy Abuse Prevention and Consumer Protection Act (BAPCPA), 623–624
Bankruptcy Reform Act of 1978, 622
Bankruptcy Reform Act of 1994, 623
BCG. *See* Boston Consulting Group
Bear hug, 107, 715g
Bear Stearns, 26, 79
Benchmarking performance, 216

Best practices, 192
Best price rule, 59
Betas, 715*g*
   data for estimating, 243–244
   equity, 242–243, 246*t*
   estimating, 243, 243*b*
   estimating based on sample, 244
   estimating by regressing percent change, 246
   estimating example, 246*t*
   financial/operating leverage effects on,
      244–247
   leveraged, 244
   privately held companies, 380–381
   unleveraged, 244
Bidders, 715*g*
   auction environment with, 10
   casual pass, 107
   competition among, 10
   foreign, 684
   with low leverage, 37
   objectives summary, 108*f*
   returns, 36–37, 42
   toehold ownership position, 102
   see also Acquirers
Bidding strategies
   common objectives, 109*t*
   decision tree, 108*f*
   developing, 107–108
   toehold, 102–104
Black-Scholes model
   formula, 308
   option to abandon, 312–313, 313*b*
   option to delay, 311–312, 311*b*
   option to expand, 309–310, 310*b*
   real options valuation with, 308–313
   variance, 308–309
Block transaction premiums, 389
Blue sky laws, 76
Board of directors
   approvals, 441
   cause provisions for removing members, 116
   compensation, 97
   in corporate governance, 94–95
   defenses, strengthening, 113–116
   staggered or classified, 115
Bond ratings, 515*t*
Bondholders
   payoffs, 43
   takeover defenses and, 124
Borrowing capacity, determining, 520–521, 521*t*
Borrowing sources, 495–497
   asset-based lending, 495–497
   cash-flow lenders, 497

   secured lending, 495–497
   unsecured lenders, 497
Boston Consulting Group (BCG), 148–149
Breakup fees, 106, 715*g*
Breakup value, 298–300
   calculating, 300*b*
   when to use, 314*t*
Bridge financing, 497, 715*g*
Brokers, discretionary voting, 71*t*
Bullet loans, 503
Business alliances, 540, 715*g*
   abnormal returns, 565–566, 565*t*
   access to new markets, 544
   accountability, 546
   alternative legal forms of, 547–554, 548*t*
   buyout clauses, 563
   clarity of purpose, 546
   compatible time frames/financial expectations, 546
   consensus decision making, 226–227
   control, 555*t*, 560–561
   cooperation, 546
   coordination, 226
   corporate structures, 547
   cost reduction, 543–544
   critical success factors, 545–547
   C-type corporations, 547–550
   deal-structuring issues, 555–565, 555*t*
   dispute resolution, 555*t*, 561–562
   distribution issues, 555*t*, 561
   duration, 555*t*, 556
   empirical findings, 565–566
   equal division of power framework, 564
   equity and debt financing, 555*t*, 560
   equity partnership, 553–554
   financial modeling, 354
   financing ongoing capital requirements, 555*t*, 559–560
   franchise alliance, 553
   globalization, 544
   governance, 555*t*, 557–558
   growing role of, 566
   integration, 225–227
   key differences among, 541*t*
   leadership, 226
   legal form, 555*t*, 557, 557*t*
   limited liability company (LLC), 550–551
   logistic, 543
   majority rules framework, 564
   majority/minority framework, 564
   management and organizational issues, 555*t*, 564
   as mergers and acquisitions alternative, 25–26
   motivations for, 540–545
   multiple party framework, 564
   operational plans, 554

Business alliances (*Continued*)
    owner or partner financing, 555*t*, 560
    ownership and control methods, 564
    partnership structures, 551–553
    performance criteria, 555*t*, 561
    policies and values, 226
    prelude to acquisition/exit, 545
    regulatory restrictions and notifications, 555*t*, 565
    regulatory treatment, 545
    resource contributions and ownership determination, 555*t*, 558
    revision, 555*t*, 562
    risk sharing, 542
    scope, 555*t*, 556
    shared control, 227–228
    sharing capital outlays, 543
    sharing management skills/resources, 542–543
    sharing proprietary knowledge, 542–544
    steering committee, 564
    strategic plans, 554
    subchapter S corporations, 550
    supply sources, 543
    support from the top, 547
    synergy, 545
    taxes, 555*t*, 563
    teamwork and role clarification, 226
    termination, 555*t*, 562
    transfer of interest, 555*t*, 562–563
    win–win situation, 546
    written contract, 554
Business combination provisions, 75
Business failure, 618–619
Business objectives, 147
Business plans, 137
    acquisition plan linkages, 158*t*
    building, 139–154
    business strategy, 140, 147–150
    as communication documents, 154–156
    executive summary, 155–156
    external analysis, 139–140
    financials and valuation, 156
    format, 155*b*
    functional strategy, 140, 153–154
    implementation strategy, 140, 150–152
    internal analysis, 139–140, 144–146
    mission statement, 140, 146
    phase, 139–154
    risk assessment, 156
    strategic controls, 140, 154
    updating, 137, 715*g*
Business strategies, 136
    in business plan format, 155
    business-level, 137, 148

    corporate-level, 137, 147–148
    diversification, 147–148
    financial restructuring, 148
    focus/niche, 149
    growth, 147–148
    hybrid, 149–150, 150*t*
    implementation, 137–138
    operational restructuring, 148
    price or cost leadership, 148–149
    product differentiation, 149
    product life cycle and, 149
    selecting, 140, 147–150
Business-level strategies, 137, 148, 715*g*
Bust-ups, 596
Buyers
    due diligence, 182
    financial, 204, 487
    strategic, 204
Buyouts, 4, 716*g*
    firms, 487
    see also Leveraged buyouts (LBOs)

C

Capital asset pricing model (CAPM), 236–239, 380, 716*g*
    applying, 237
    country/political risk adjustment (emerging markets), 679–680
    in developed countries, 674–676
    firm size adjustment (developed countries), 675
    global formulation (developed countries), 675–676
    global formulation (emerging markets), 678–679
    limitations, 237–238
    risk adjustment (developed countries), 675
    risk adjustment (emerging markets), 678–679
    understatement, 380–381
Capital markets
    Dodd-Frank Wall Street Reform and Consumer Protection Act and, 71*t*
    globally integrated, 657–659
    segmented, 657–659
Capital outlays, sharing, 543
Capitalization multiples, 378, 716*g*
Capitalization process, 378
Capitalization rates, 378, 716*g*
    converted to multiples, 378
    discount, developing, 380–383
    in valuing small businesses, 378
    in zero-growth valuation model, 252
Carve-outs. *See* Equity carve-outs
Cash
    deals, shareholder returns, 41
    as payment form, 420

with stocks as payment form, 421
taxable purchase of target assets with, 451–452
taxable purchase of target stock with, 453
Cash-flow valuation, 235–279
DCF, 250–256
earnings versus, 290–291
equity value with enterprise method, 259–266
firms under special situations, 258–259
free cash flows calculation, 247–250
income or discounted-cash-flow methods, 250–256
nonoperating assets, 266–270
Operating and Nonoperating Assets case study, 235
required returns, 236–242
risk analysis, 242–247
subject to multiple growth periods, 256–258
Cash flows, 235–236, 250*b*
after tax, calculating, 582
annual, projecting, 509, 514
in combining firms, 8
determinants, 143–144
discounted value, 254
enterprise, 248–249
equity, 249–250
foreign, converting, 671–673
free, 247–250
normalized, 333–339
requirements, 192
Cash impact
deferred taxes, 262–265
employee options, 265
provisions and contingent liabilities, 266
unfunded pension liabilities, 265
Cash-flow lenders, 497
Cash-flow models, 250–256
constant-growth valuation, 253
enterprise discounted, 251
equity discounted, 251
variable-growth valuation, 254–256
zero-growth valuation, 252
Cash-flow multiples, 315
Cash-for-assets transaction, 716*g*
Cash-for-stock transactions, 438
Cash-out provisions, 75–76
Casual pass, 107
Celler-Kefauver Act, 53*t*
Centralized organizational structure, 213
Cerberus, 577
Certificate of incorporation, 113, 716*g*
Chapter 7 liquidation, 627–629
case study, 627, 628–629, 628*t*, 629*t*
effectiveness of, 632
see also Bankruptcy

Chapter 11 reorganization, 622
before BAPCPA, 623–624
corporate structure and, 624
effectiveness of, 632
filing for, 624–627
sales within protection of, 634–635
363 sales from, 630
see also Bankruptcy
Chapter 15, 630–631
Chief executive officers (CEOs)
board of directors and, 95
functions of, 94–95
pay disclosure, 98
see also Management
Choice of law provision, 561–562
Chrysler, 543, 630
Clawbacks, 71*t*, 96
Clayton Act, 14, 53*t*, 61–62
Cleveland Cliffs, 350, 357, 358*t*
Closing, 188–191, 716*g*
acquisition/merger agreement, 188–191
approvals, 188
conditions, 177, 190, 716*g*
customer and vendor contracts, 188
documents, 190–191
financing contingencies, 191
postmerger integration before, 209–210
see also Mergers and acquisitions process
Clubbing, 491
Collaborative efforts, 69
antitrust guidelines, 69
safety zones, 69
Collar arrangements, 427–431, 716*g*
fixed share exchange agreement, 429
fixed value (offer price) agreement, 429
Commercial banks, 29
Committee on Foreign Investment in the United States (CFIUS), 76
Common-size financial statements, 332, 716*g*
Communication plans, 191–192
postclosing integration, 191–192
postmerger integration, 211–212
Communications industry regulation, 79
Communities, in communications plan, 212–213
Comparable companies method, 287–289, 314*t*
Comparable transactions method, 289, 314*t*
Compensation, 214–215
board of directors, 97
merging, 214–215
recovery, 96
total, 214–215
Compensation committee independence, 71*t*

Competition
  dynamics, 142–143, 142*f*, 330–331
  intensity determinants, 143
Compositions, 620, 716*g*
Concentration, 67
Confidentiality agreements, 176, 716*g*
Conglomerate discount, 8–9, 716*g*
Conglomerate mergers, 21
Conglomerates, 8–9, 716*g*
Consensus decision making, 226–227
Consent decrees, 64, 716*g*, 65
  requirements, 65
Consent solicitation, 116, 716*g*
Conservatorship, 619
Consolidations, 716*g*
  industry, 661
  mergers versus, 20
  statutory, 20
Constant-growth valuation model, 253, 253*b*, 716*g*
Consumer Financial Protection Bureau, 71*t*
Contingency plans, 137–138
Contingent claim valuation, 305
Contingent considerations, 468
Contingent payouts, 425
Contingent value rights (CVRs), 426–427, 716*g*
  use example, 426–427
Continuity of business enterprise, 456
Continuity of ownership interests, 456
Contract-related issues, 186–187
Control, business alliances, 555*t*, 560–561
Control model, 368–369
Control premiums, 23, 388, 716*g*
  adjustments to, 392
  block transaction premiums, 389
  dual-class ownership, 389–390
  empirical studies, 389–390
  estimating, 391–395
  factors affecting, 392–393
  liquidity discounts relationship, 390–391
  in merger and acquisition transactions, 390
  in private business valuation, 394*b*
  pure, 388, 389–390
  size estimation table, 393*t*
Convertible bonds, 260–261, 498
Cooperation, in business alliances, 546
Coordinated effects, 68
Corporate bylaws, 105, 113, 716*g*
Corporate capital gains taxes, 464
Corporate charters, 75, 716*g*
  amending, 113
  business combination provisions, 75
  cash-out provisions, 75–76
  elements of, 113

  fair price provisions, 75
  share control provisions, 75–76
Corporate culture, 221
  building, 221–224
  as corporate governance factor, 97
  cultural differences, overcoming, 223–224
  cultural profiling, 221–222
  symbols of, 221
Corporate default prediction, 637–640
  alternative models, 637–638
  credit score models, 638
  CUSUM methods, 639
  models by methodology, 638–639
  models differing in choice of variables, 640
  structural models, 639
Corporate focus, exiting business for, 577
Corporate governance, 93, 716*g*
  alternative models of, 94, 94*t*
  antitakeover defenses, 97
  board of directors role in, 94–95
  control model, 368–369
  corporate culture and values, 97
  corporate takeover market, 98–99
  cross-border transactions, 685–686
  external factors, 97–99
  factors affecting, 93*f*, 94
  incentive systems, 95–97
  institutional activists, 98
  internal controls, 95–97
  internal factors, 94
  legislation and legal system, 97
  management role, 94–95
  market model, 368
  regulators, 98
  takeover market and, 92–93
Corporate minimum tax, 464
Corporate restructuring, 5, 716*g*
  alternative forms of, 19–22
  financial, 19–20
  mergers and acquisitions, 5
  operational, 19–20
  process illustration, 22*f*
  as takeover defense, 119*t*, 121
  see also Restructuring and exit strategies
Corporate shells, 396
Corporate structure, 417
  acquisition vehicle, 416–417
  C-type, 547–550
  LLC and, 550–551
  Subchapter S, 550
Corporate takeover market, 91–126, 92–94
  alternative takeover defenses in, 108–112
  alternative takeover tactics in, 99–105

corporate governance and, 92–93, 98–99
    friendly approach, 99
    hostile approach, 99
Corporate value chain, 21*f*
Corporate-level strategies, 137, 147–148
Cost leadership, 716*g*
Cost of borrowing, 8
Cost of capital (CC), 7, 241–242
    cross-border transactions, 674–682
    leveraged buyouts valuation, 509–511, 517
    present value of equity cash flow with, 511*t*
    privately held companies, 381–383
    reducing, 7, 8
    in variable-growth valuation model, 255
    weighted average (WACC), 241–242
Cost of debt, 239–241
    emerging markets, 680–682, 681*b*
    estimating, 239–240
    privately held companies, 381
Cost of equity, 236–239
    changing debt levels impact on, 247*b*
    estimating, 236–237
    market risk premiums and, 237–239
    as opportunity cost, 236–237
    privately held companies, 380–381
Cost of equity (developed countries), 674–677
    calculation in home and local currency, 677*b*
    CAPM adjustment for firm size, 675
    CAPM adjustment for risk, 675
    Fisher effect, 676–677
    global CAPM formulation, 675–676
    risk-free rate of return, 675
Cost of equity (emerging markets), 677–680
    calculating, 679*b*
    CAPM adjustment for country/political risk, 679–680
    CAPM adjustment for risk, 678–679
    estimating, 677–680
    global CAPM formulation, 680
    risk-free rate of return, 677
Costs
    deal, 468
    implementation, 341
    of preferred stock, 241
    reduction, in business alliances, 543–544
Country risk premium (CRP), 679
Covenants, 189–190, 716*g*
Cram down, 633, 716*g*
Credit bids, 630
Credit score models, 638
Creeping takeover strategy, 104
Cross-border bankruptcy, 630–631
Cross-border transactions, 81–82, 655–688, 656–657

acquisition vehicles, 665–666
corporate governance, 685–686
cost of capital and, 674–682
debt markets, 668
developed versus emerging economies, 656–657
in emerging countries, 669–670
empirical studies, 683–686
equity markets, 668
financing, 667–669
foreign cash-flow conversion, 671–673
foreign institutional ownership, 686
form of acquisition, 666–667
form of payment, 666
globally integrated capital markets and, 657–659
hybrid, 667
international expansion motives, 659–662
international market entry strategies, 662–665
marginal tax rate selection, 674
scenario planning, 682–683
shareholder returns, 684–685
sovereign wealth funds, 668–669
structuring, 665–667
tax strategies, 667
taxable, 667
valuation, 670–682
valuation methodologies, 683*t*
WACC, 681*b*
Cross-default provisions, 496
Cross-sectional comparisons, 332
C-type corporations, 547–550, 548*t*
Cultural compatibility criteria, 174
Cultural differences, overcoming, 223–224
Cultural profiling, 221–222
Cumulative sums (CUSUM) methods, 639
Cumulative voting, 115, 716*g*
Current ratio, 347–348
Customer contracts, assigning, 188
Customers
    avoiding conflict with, 581
    bargaining powers, 143–144
    collections of, 140–141
    communication with, 211
    exiting business for, 581
    following to international markets, 662
Cyclical firms, 259

D

Deadlock/impasse clause, 561–562
Deal costs, expensing, 468
Deal provisions, 188

Deal structuring, 179, 409–444, 410, 449–477, 717g
  accounting considerations, 180, 413
  acquisition vehicles, 180, 413, 415–419
  closing price gap, 421–427
  collar arrangements, 427–431
  common linkages, 413–415
  components, 181
  contingent payments, 423–426
  contingent value rights, 426–427
  Continued Consolidation in the Generic
    Pharmaceuticals Industry case
    study, 449
  cross-border transactions, 665–667
  decisions, 179–180
  distributed/staged payouts, 427
  form of acquisition, 180, 413, 431–442
  form of payment, 180, 413, 419–421
  key components of, 411–413
  legal form of selling entity, 180, 413, 419
  leveraged buyouts, 442, 500–504
  in negotiations, 179–180
  postclosing organization, 180, 413, 415–419
  postclosing price adjustments, 421–422
  primary objectives, 411
  process, 411–415
  process illustration, 412f
  rights, royalties, and fees, 427
  risk management, 421–427
  risk sharing, 411
  single firm recapitalization, 442
  special applications, 442
  tax considerations, 413
Debt
  book value, 260
  in cross-border transactions, 667–668
  long-term, 259–261
  mezzanine, 503–504
  net, 720g
  pretax cost of, 239–241
  reduction, 493
  restructuring, 717g
Debt markets, 668
Debt-for-equity swaps, 620, 717g
Debt-to-equity (D/E) ratio, 245–246
  on firm's creditworthiness, 347–348
  preacquisition, 247
  projecting, 510
Decentralized organizational structure, 213
Decision tree framework
  illustrated, 307f
  real option valuation with, 305–308
Default, 618
Defense industry regulation, 79

Deferred taxes
  assets, 262
  cash impact of, 262–265
  challenges, 263
  liabilities, 262
  reasons for, 262
Definitive agreement of purchase and sale, 717g
Delay options, 304
Department of Justice (DoJ), procedural rules, 64
Destroyers of value, 340, 717g
Developed economies, 656–657
  cost of equity estimation, 674–677
  emerging economies versus, 656–657
  examples of, 657t
  foreign cash flow conversion, 671–672
Direct mergers, 500
Discount rate, 717g
  adjusting, 510
  divestitures, 583
  in variable-growth valuation model, 255
  in zero-growth valuation model, 252
Discounted cash flow (DCF), 250–256, 717g
  applying, 250–256
  constant-growth model, 253
  discounted model, 251
  in distressed businesses, 640
  enterprise model, 251
  for leveraged buyouts, 509–517
  in privately held companies valuation, 378
  use of, 314t, 315
  variable-growth model, 254–256
  zero-growth model, 252
  see also Cash flow valuation
Dispute resolution, business alliances, 555t, 561–562
Dissident shareholders, 717g
Distressed business valuation, 640–644
  APV method, 640–644
  DCF methods, 640
  example, 640–644, 641t
Distributed payouts, 427
Distribution issues, business alliances, 555t, 561
Diversifiable risk, 242, 717g
Diversification, 8–9, 717g
  corporate, 9
  cross-border transactions, 659–662, 684
  discount, 8–9
  examples, 8
  as mergers and acquisitions theory, 8–9
  objectives, 147
  strategies, 147–148
  unrelated, 8–9
Divestitures, 22, 581–586, 717g
  accounting considerations, 586

after-tax market value estimation, 583
agency conflicts resolution, 603–604
assets transfer, 603
business value to parent estimation, 583
corporate portfolio reviews, 582
discount rate calculation, 583
financial distress mitigation, 604
focus increase, 602–603
key characteristics, 598*t*
motives for, 581–582
parent company operating units undergoing,
    598*t*
purchase price premiums factors, 587*t*
selecting, 600*t*
selling process, 584–585
selling process selection, 585–586
sell/not sell decision, 582–583
shareholder returns, 599–604
tax considerations, 586
timing of sale, 583–584
see also Restructuring and exit strategies
Dividends
    preferred stock, 499–500
    yields, 315
Divisional organization, 212–213, 717*g*
Dodd-Frank Wall Street Reform and Consumer
    Protection Act, 10, 29, 31–32, 52, 53*t*, 69–74, 78
    capital markets, 71*t*
    on compensation recovery, 96
    effects of, 78
    financial institutions, 71*t*
    governance and executive compensation, 71*t*
    government bailouts and, 73–74
    implementation of, 73
    implications, 70–73
    provisions, 71*t*
    scope, 69–70
    systematic regulation and emergency powers, 71*t*
    systemic risk and, 74
Dow Jones, 21
Drag-along provisions, 562–563
Dual-class ownership, 389–390
Dual-class recapitalization, 117, 717*g*
Due diligence, 180, 717*g*
    beginning of, 178
    buyer, 182
    components, 182
    conducting, 180–183
    data revalidation, 215
    demands of, 181
    information sources, 181*t*
    legal, 202
    lender, 183

LOI description, 177
    preclosing, 186
    reviews, 182
    seller, 182
    seller termination of, 181–182
    team, 186
Duration, business alliances, 555*t*, 556

E

Earnings after taxes (EAT), 378
Earnings before interest and taxes (EBIT)
    FCFF calculation with, 248
    operating leases and, 249
    tax rate selection and, 248
Earnings before interest, taxes, depreciation, and
    amortization (EBITDA)
    enterprise value to, 291–294
    for privately held companies, 372
    in same or comparable industry method, 290
Earnings before taxes (EBT), 378
Earnings per share (EPS)
    as financial objective, 326
    growth through acquisition, 14
    postacquisition, 350
Earn-outs, 423–426, 717*g*
    agreement, 423
    forms of, 423
    formula, 423
    IRS rules and, 426
    multiple targets and, 425
    requirement, 423
    on share of equity ownership, 424
    use of, 425
Ease of entry, 68
Economic value, 717*g*
Economies of scale, 5, 717*g*
    premerger/postmerger, 7*t*
    profit improvement from, 5
Economies of scope, 5–6, 717*g*
    premerger/postmerger, 7*t*
Effective control, 717*g*
Embedded options, 303
Emergency Planning and Community Right to Know
    Act (EPCRA), 80
Emerging economies, 656–657
    cost of debt, 680–682, 681*b*
    cross-border transactions in, 669–670
    developed economies versus, 657*t*
    examples of, 657*t*
    foreign cash flow conversion, 673
    political and economic risks, 669–670
    raw material/labor costs, 661
    risk assessment, 670

Emerging economies (*Continued*)
  risk management with insurance, 670
  risk management with options and contract language, 670
  unrated firms, 680–681
Empirical studies, 384–386
  corporate governance and cross-border activity, 685–686
  cross-border transaction returns, 684–685
  cross-border transactions, 683–686
  evidence from block transaction premiums, 389–390
  evidence from dual-class ownership, 389–390
  evidence from mergers and acquisition transactions, 390
  financial distress, 644–646
  foreign bidders, 684
  foreign institutional ownership, 686
  international diversification, 684
  IPO cost, 387
  liquidity discounts, 384–388, 385*t*
  option pricing, 387
  of parent subsidiaries, 387–388
  postbuyout returns, 507
  prebuyout returns, 504*t*
  pre-IPO, 386
  pure control premium, 389–390
  restricted stock (letter stock), 384–386
  restructuring and exit strategies, 599
  of shareholder returns, 398–399
Employee benefit plans, 80–81
Employee stock ownership plans (ESOPs), 717*g*
  as antitakeover defense, 25
  leveraged, buying private companies with, 397–398
  to restructure firms, 25
  role in M&As, 24–25
  stock acquired by, 24–25
  as takeover defense, 119*t*, 120
  valuations based on projections, 366
Employees
  availability, 214
  communication with, 211
  options, cash impact of, 265
  retention of, 192
  turnover of, 205–206
Enterprise cash flow, 248–249, 717*g*
  discounted model, 251
Enterprise value, 184–185, 251, 717*g*
Enterprise value to EBITDA method, 291–294
  example, 292*b*
  in LBO evaluations, 519
  shortcomings, 292–294
  total market value, 292
  uses, 292

Entry barriers, international markets, 662
Environmental laws, 53*t*, 80
Equal division of power framework, 564
Equity
  cost of, 236–239
  premium, 237
Equity beta, 242–243, 717*g*
Equity carve-outs, 22, 591–593, 717*g*
  agency issues resolution, 607
  financing sources, 607
  key characteristics, 598*t*
  motives for, 592
  parent company operating units undergoing, 598*t*
  selecting, 600*t*
  shareholder returns, 606–607, 608
  as staged transactions, 592–593
  subsidiary, 592
Equity cash flow, 249–250, 717*g*
  discounted model, 251
Equity markets, cross-border transaction financing, 668
Equity partnerships, 553–554
  advantages/disadvantages of, 548*t*
  key characteristics, 541*t*
Equity premium, 717*g*
Equity value
  deferred taxes, 262–265
  employee options, 265
  estimating, 259–266
  example, 270–274, 271*t*
  long-term debt, 259–261
  minority interests, 266
  nonequity claims, 259
  provisions and contingent liabilities, 266
  unfunded pension liabilities, 265
Equity-financed deals, shareholder returns, 41
Escrow accounts, 422
Exchange offers, 102–103, 717*g*
Exclusive agreements, 541*t*
Executive summary, 155–156
Exiting businesses. *See* Restructuring and exit strategies
Exon-Florio Amendment to the Defense Protection Act, 53*t*
Expand options, 309–310, 310*b*
Experience curve, 148
Exporting, as international market entrance strategy, 662, 663*f*, 664
Extensions, 620, 717*g*
External analysis, 139–140
  in business plan format, 155
  elements of, 140
  how to compete determination, 141–144
  where to compete determination, 140–141
  see also Business plans

F

Facilitation payments, 77
Failing firms
    alternative strategies for, 634t
    merging with another firm, 634–635
    out-of-court voluntary settlements, 635
    strategic options for, 633–635
    systemic risk and, 635–637
    voluntary/involuntary liquidations, 635
Failure, 44
    business, 618–619
    imminent, alternative to, 68
Fair disclosure (Regulation FD), 53t, 77–78
Fair market value, 377, 451–452, 717g
Fair price provisions, 75, 103
    as shark repellent, 113t, 117
Fair value, 377, 718g
    of reporting unit, 473
Fairness opinion letters, 27, 718g
Family-owned firms, 367–368
    governance issues, 368–369
    succession, 368
Federal antitrust laws, 53t, 61–69
Federal Communications Commission (FCC), 79
Federal Deposit Insurance Corporation (FDIC), 69–70,
    71t
    in firm seizure/liquidation, 636
    guarantees, 74
    OLA and, 74
    resolution authority, 636
Federal Insurance Office, 71t, 79–80
Federal security laws, 53t, 54–61
Federal Trade Commission Act of 1914, 53t, 62
Federal Trade Commission (FTC)
    actions at market share concentration levels, 67f
    procedural rules, 64
Financial buyers, 204, 487, 718g
    initial equity contribution estimation, 522
    LBOs and, 489
Financial data limitations, 327–329
Financial distress, 618
    contagious nature of, 645–646
    emerging from bankruptcy and, 644
    empirical studies of, 644–646
    IPOs, 645
    stock returns unexpectedly low, 645
Financial leverage, 244
    effects on beta, 244–247
    financial returns and, 245t
    Financial modeling, 326–327
    acquirer and target as stand-alone business, 329–339
    acquirer and target, including synergy, 339–341
    acquirer and target part of larger legal entity, 353–354

alternative applications of, 353–354
    balance sheet adjustment mechanism, 363–364
    business alliances, 354
    combined firms' ability to finance transaction,
        345–352, 348t
    competitive dynamics, 330–331
    destroyers of value, 340
    distribution of synergy, 344
    financing structure, 347, 348t
    four-step procedure, 354–357
    historical data normalization, 331–332
    implementation costs, 341
    joint ventures, 354
    magnitude and composition of offer price, 341–345,
        342t
    minimum/maximum offer price range, 342–343
    model building, 326
    normalized cash flows, 333–339
    offer price composition, 344–345
    process, 329–352
    in support of M&A negotiations, 349–352
    techniques, applying, 325–357
    uses, 326
    value sources, 339–340
Financial objectives, 326
Financial options, 302
Financial plans, 184
Financial ratio analysis, 332
Financial reporting
    of business combinations, 466–469
    GAAP, 466
    IFRS, 466
    SFAS 141R, 466, 467–468
    SFAS 157, 466–467, 469
Financial resources, 157–158
Financial restructuring, 19–20, 718g
    strategies, 148
Financial returns, analyzing, 523
Financial review, 182
Financial risk, 159
Financial Services Modernization Act, 10
Financial sponsors, 487, 718g
Financial Stability Oversight Council, 71t
Financial statements
    commonly overlooked areas, 375
    commonly understated areas, 375
    common-size, 332
    explaining adjustments to, 375–377
    informed adjustments, 372–375
    privately held companies, adjusting, 371–377
    purchase accounting impact on, 469–474
    target/acquirer, consolidated, 345
Financial synergy, 7–8, 718g

Financing
  bridge, 497
  business alliances, 555*t*, 559–560
  contingencies, 191
  equity/debt, 555*t*, 560
  junk bond, 486
  mezzanine, 497
  owner/partner, 555*t*, 560
  reverse mergers, 397
Financing transactions, 485–529
  asset-based lending, 486–487, 495–497
  borrowing options, 495–497
  cash-flow lenders for, 497
  common and preferred equity options, 499–500
  cross-border, 667–669
  leveraged loans, 499
  long-term, 497
  postbuyout returns, 507–508
  prebuyout returns, 504, 505–506
  revolving lines of credit, 495–496
  secured lending, 495–497
  seller financing, 500
  unsecured lenders for, 497
Firms
  buyout, 487
  change of control covenants and, 492
  competitive dynamics, 330–331
  creditworthiness, 347–348
  cyclical, 259
  failing, 633–637
  family-owned, 367–368
  going private, 495
  with longer-term problems, 258–259
  with temporary problems, 258
  valuing subject to multiple growth periods, 256–258
  valuing under special situations, 258–259
  see also Privately held companies
First contact
  approach for initiating, 174–175
  confidentiality agreement, 176
  intermediary for, 175
  legal documents, preliminary, 176–178
  LOI and, 177–178
  mergers and acquisitions phase, 174–178
  personal relationships, 175
  term sheet, 176
  value discussion, 176
Fisher effect, 676–677
Fixed share exchange agreement, 429, 718*g*
Fixed value (offer price) agreement, 429, 718*g*
Flexibility objectives, 147
Flip-in pills, 111–112, 113*t*, 718*g*
Flip-over pills, 111–112, 113*t*, 718*g*

Focus business strategies, 149
Foreign companies, tax-free reorganization, 667
Foreign Corrupt Practices Act, 77
Foreign institutional ownership, 686
Foreign investment, security-related restrictions, 76
Foreign laws, 53*t*
Foreign markets. *See* International markets
Form of acquisition, 180, 431–442, 718*g*
  acquisition vehicles and, 413
  advantages/disadvantages, 433*t*
  asset purchase, 431–432, 433*t*, 434–437
  cross-border transactions, 666–667
  form of payment and, 414
  postclosing organization and, 413
  staged transactions, 433*t*, 442
  statutory mergers, 433*t*, 439–441
  stock purchase, 431–432, 433*t*, 438–439
  stock-for-assets transactions, 432, 433*t*
  stock-for-stock transactions, 432, 433*t*
  tax considerations and, 414
  see also Deal structuring
Form of payment, 180, 419–421, 718*g*
  acquisition vehicles and, 413
  cash, 420
  cash and stock in combination, 421
  cross-border transactions, 666
  evaluating, 428*t*
  legal form of selling entity and, 414, 419*b*
  noncash, 420–421
  postclosing organization and, 413
Forward currency exchange rates, 671–672
Forward triangular cash mergers, 451
  illustrated, 451*f*
  international markets, 667
Forward triangular stock mergers, 718*g*
  advantages of, 459
  illustrated, 458*f*
  type A, 458
Franchise alliances, 553
  advantages/disadvantages of, 548*t*
  key characteristics, 541*t*
Franchises, 26
Fraudulent conveyance laws, 502, 718*g*
Free cash flows, 718*g*
  calculating, 247–250
  to equity investors (FCFE), 247, 249–250
  to the firm (FCFF), 247, 248–249
Friendly takeovers, 22–23, 718*g*
  control premium, 23
  corporate takeover market, 99
  purchase price, 23
  tender offers, 23
  see also Takeovers

Fully diluted shares outstanding, 345, 346*t*
Functional integration, 215–221
    benchmarking performance, 216
    finance, 219
    human resources, 220–221
    information technology, 217–218
    manufacturing operations, 216
    marketing, 219
    purchasing, 220
    research and development, 220
    revalidating due diligence data, 215
    sales, 219
Functional organization, 212
Functional strategies, 137–138, 153–154, 718*g*
    in business plan format, 156
    examples, 153
    focus, 153
    selecting, 140
    to support implementation strategy, 154
    see also Business plans

G

General partnerships, 548*t*, 552, 718*g*
Generally accepted accounting principles (GAAP), 28,
    718*g*
    application of, 328
    financial statements, 327
    financial statements under, 466
    IAS systems and, 327
Global capital asset pricing model, 675–676, 718*g*
Global CAPM formulation
    developed countries, 675–676
    emerging countries, 680
Global exposure, 144
Globally integrated capital markets, 657–659, 718*g*
    segmented capital markets versus, 658, 659
Going concern value, 718*g*
Going private, 495, 718*g*
Golden parachutes, 718*g*
    say on, 71*t*
    takeover defense, 113*t*, 118
Goodwill, 718*g*
    estimating, 471–472, 471*b*
    minimization of, 469
    negative, 470
Go-shop provisions, 178, 718*g*
Governance
    business alliances, 555*t*, 557–558
    control model, 368–369
    market model, 368
    privately held companies, 368–369
Greenmail, 718*g*
    payments, 464–465

    takeover defense, 118, 119*t*
Growing annuity model, 255–256
Growth
    in international markets, 659–660
    objectives, 147
    strategies, 147–148
Growth rates
    adjusting relative valuation methods for,
        294–296
    determining, 257–258
    diversification and, 8
    high-growth periods and, 257
    stable, 258

H

Hart-Scott-Rodino Antitrust Improvement Act, 53*t*,
    62–64
    regulatory prenotification filing requirements, 63*t*
    state antitrust regulators and, 64
    Title I, 62
    Title II, 62–64
Hedge funds, 30, 718*g*
    as activist investors, 34
    investment strategies, 30–31
    as investors of last resort, 490–491
    management fee, 31
    PIPES purchase, 491
    success of, 34
Herfindahl-Hirschman Index (HHI), 67, 718*g*
    ranges, 67
Highly leveraged transactions, 718*g*
Holding companies, 24, 718*g*
    postclosing organization, 418
    role in M&As, 24
    structure, 24
Holdout problem, 635, 719*g*
Hollinger Inc., 631
Home country, 656–657
Horizontal mergers, 21, 66, 719*g*
    alternative to imminent failure, 68
    antitrust guidelines, 66–69
    coordinated effects, 68
    ease of entry, 68
    efficiencies, 68
    market definition, 66–67
    market share and concentration, 67
    partial acquisitions, 68–69
    price discrimination potential, 66
    unilateral effects, 67–68
    see also Mergers
Hostile takeovers, 23, 719*g*
    advantages of, 104–105
    corporate takeover market, 99

Hostile takeovers (*Continued*)
  outcome dependencies, 105
  purchase price, 23
  successful, 105
  tender offers, 23
Hostile tender offers, 23, 101–102, 719*g*
  majority approval requirement, 101
Hubris, 719*g*
  as mergers and acquisitions causation theory, 10
Hughes Electronics Corporation, 416
Human resources, 220–221
Hybrid business strategies, 149–150, 150*t*
Hybrid securities, market valuation, 260–261
Hybrid transactions, 667

I

IASB. *See* International Accounting Standards Board
ICC. *See* Interstate Commerce Commission
If-converted method, 346*t*
IFRS. *See* International Financial Reporting
    Standards
Impaired assets, 719*g*
Implementation costs, 341
Implementation strategies, 136, 137–138,
    150–152, 719*g*
  assumptions analysis, 151–152
  in business plan format, 156
  comparison, 151*t*
  implications, 150
  intangible factors, 150–151
  selecting, 140
  see also Business plans
Incentive systems, 95–97, 154
Indemnification, 190, 435, 719*g*
Industries, 140–141
  attractive for LBO, 492
  competition, determining, 141, 143
  competitive dynamics, 142*f*, 330–331
  consolidation, international markets, 661
  information, 167
Industry-specific regulations, 53*t*
Information sources
  companies, 171*b*
  due diligence, 181*t*
  economic data, 167
  industry data, 167
  private firms, 372*t*
Information technology, 217–218
Initial equity contribution, 522
Initial public offerings (IPOs), 27, 592
  cash infusion, 592
  cost studies, 387
  public disclosures, 489

reverse mergers versus, 396–397
Insider trading, 56, 719*g*
  investigation of, 56
  regulations, 56
Insurance companies, 30
Insurance industry regulation, 79–80
Integration, 203–228, 204
  acquisition-related customer attrition and, 206
  activities, 206
  benchmarking performance and, 216
  business alliances, 225–227
  corporate culture, 221–224
  employee turnover and, 205–206
  finance, 219
  functional, 215–221
  human resources, 220–221
  information technology, 217–218
  manufacturing operations, 216
  marketing, 219
  mechanisms, 226–227
  in mergers and acquisitions, 204–206
  postmerger, putting in place, 209–210
  premerger planning, 207–208
  process, 206–224
  process illustration, 207*t*
  projected financial returns and, 205
  purchasing, 220
  rapid, 204–205, 206
  research and development, 220
  revalidating due diligence data and, 215
  sales, 219
  staffing plans, 213–215
  time constraints and, 224
Integration managers, 187, 208
Integration plans
  contract-related issues, 186–187
  decisions, 187
  developing, 186–187
  preclosing activities determination, 187
  preclosing due diligence, 186
  trust and, 187
Intercompany sales, 582
Interest rate parity theory, 671–672, 672*b*, 719*g*
Interest-coverage ratio, 347–348
Internal analysis, 139–140, 144–146
  in business plan format, 155
  output of, 144
  success factors, 144–145
  see also Business plans
Internal rate of return (IRR), 518, 523
International Accounting Standards Board (IASB),
    474
International accounting standards (IAS), 327

International Financial Reporting Standards (IFRS), 466, 474
International markets
 customers and, 662
 diversification, 659
 entry barrier avoidance, 662
 entry strategies, 662–665
 exchange rate fluctuations, 662
 exporting, 662, 663f, 664
 growth acceleration, 659–660
 industry consolidation, 661
 intangible assets, leveraging, 661–662
 joint ventures, 662, 663f, 664
 licensing, 662, 664–665
 lower costs, 661
 M&A, 662, 663f, 664
 motives for expansion, 659–662
 solo ventures, 662, 663f, 664
 tax liability minimization, 662
Internet bubble, 16
Interstate Commerce Commission (ICC), 79
Investment banks, 26–27, 719g
Investment credits, 12
Investment tax credits, 12
Investors
 activist, 32–35
 angel, 32
 commercial banks, 29
 communication with, 212
 hedge funds, 34
 hedge/private equity funds, 9–10
 mutual funds, 30, 33
 pension funds, 30, 33
 private equity funds, 34
 sovereign wealth funds, 32
 venture capital firms, 32
 vulture, 632

J

Joint ventures, 25–26, 719g
 as acquisition precursor, 150
 acquisition vehicle, 417
 financial modeling, 354
 as international market entrance strategy, 662, 663f, 664
 key characteristics, 541t
 managerial autonomy, 549
 ownership distribution case study, 559
 partners, 549
 postclosing organization, 418
 right of first refusal, 562–563
 services provided by, 563
 see also Business alliances

Junk bonds, 498, 719g
 as financing, 486
 in LBO capital structure, 503
 in long-term financing, 498–499

L

Labor and benefit laws, 53t, 80–81
Lawyers, in M&A transactions, 28
Leadership, 226
Leases. See Operating leases
Legal documents, preliminary, 176–178
Legal due diligence, 202
Legal filings
 proxy contests, 101
 tender offers, 104
Legal form of selling entity, 180, 419, 719g
 form of payment and, 414, 419b
 types of, 419
Legal forms, business alliances, 555t, 557, 557t
Legal insolvency, 618–619, 719g
Legal review, 182
Legislation, as corporate governance factor, 97
Lenders
 cash-flow, 497
 commercial banks, 29
 due diligence, 183
 unsecured, 497
Letter of intent (LOI), 106, 719g
 closing conditions, 177
 due diligence process, 177
 in first contact, 177–178
 go-shop provisions, 178
 legal liabilities, 178
 termination, 177
Letter stock, 595
Leverage
 financial, 244–247, 245t
 impact on shareholder returns, 487t
 intangible assets, international markets, 661–662
 limitations on, 71t
 operating, 244–247, 245t
 as screening process criteria, 174
Leveraged Buyout Model
 balance sheet projections, 526
 Equity Ownership section, 523
 Financial Projections and Analysis section, 523
 Internal Rates of Return section, 523
 output summary, 524t
 Pro Forma Capital Structure section, 523
 Sources and Use of Funds section, 523
 supporting statements, 523

Leveraged Buyout Valuation and Structuring Model, 487
Leveraged buyouts (LBOs), 14–15, 486, 719*g*
    acquisitions of private firms, 489
    analyses, 518
    asset-based, 500
    attractive industries, 492
    bankruptcies, 15
    borrowing capacity determination, 520–521, 521*t*
    capital structure illustration, 503*f*
    capital structures, 502–504
    challenging nature of, 488–489
    characterizing, 487–493
    deal structures, 500–504
    in deal structuring, 442
    debt reduction, 493
    direct merger, 500
    EBITDA in evaluating, 519
    effects on employment growth, 490
    effects on innovation, 489–490
    financial returns estimation, 523
    financial sponsors, 489
    firms without change of control covenants, 492
    formats in building models, 523–526
    growth explosion, 488
    improperly structured, 502
    initial equity contribution estimation, 522
    large company operating divisions, 492
    management competence/motivation, 492
    market competition, 491
    operating margin improvement, 493
    operating performance improvement, 493
    opportunities evaluation, 518–523
    overpaying for, 493
    postbuyout returns, 507–508
    prebuyout returns, 504, 505–506
    quick flips and, 489
    in retrenchment era, 15
    reverse (RLBOs), 504
    reverse stock split, 501
    subsidiary merger, 500–501
    success factors, 491–492
    target selection, 491–492
    targets, 486
    timing the sale of the firm, 493–495
    unused borrowing capacity, 492
    as valuation method, 236
    value creation, 493–495
    widespread transactions, 488
Leveraged buyouts valuation, 509–517, 518–526
    adjusted present value method, 511–517
    annual cash-flow projection, 509, 514
    basics, 518–526

    CC method, 509–511, 517
    DCF methods for, 509–517
    deal determination, 511, 514–517
    debt-to-equity ratio protection, 510
    discount rate adjustment, 510
    methods comparison, 517
    present value of tax savings estimation, 514
    target valuation, 514
    terminal value calculation, 510
    total value calculation, 514
Leveraged ESOPs, 397–398
Leveraged loans, 499, 719*g*
Leveraged recapitalization, 119*t*, 120
Liabilities
    acquired, valuation guidelines, 472*b*
    assumption of, 189
    deferred taxes, 262
    non-interest-bearing, 242
    in statutory mergers, 417
    unfunded pension, 265
Licenses, 26
Licensing
    as international market entrance strategy, 662, 664–665
    key characteristics, 541*t*
Limited liability companies (LLCs), 548*t*, 550–551
    drawbacks, 551
    management structure, 551
    outside United States, 666
Limited liability partnerships, 552–553
Liquidating dividends, 719*g*
Liquidation or breakup value method, 298–300
Liquidation value, 298
    calculating, 299*b*
    as valuation method, 298–300
    when to use, 314*t*
Liquidations, 719*g*
    Chapter 7, 627–629
    as failing firm option, 635
    voluntary, 596
    voluntary settlements resulting in, 621–622
Liquidity, 384, 619
    arbs and, 35
    market, 390–391
Liquidity discounts, 384–386, 719*g*
    adjustments to, 391
    control premiums relationship, 390–391
    empirical studies, 384–388, 385*t*
    estimating, 391–395
    factors affecting, 391
    IPO cost studies, 387
    option pricing studies, 387

parent subsidiaries studies, 387–388
pre-IPO studies, 386
in private business valuation, 394*b*
in privately held companies valuation, 384–388
restricted stock (letter stock) studies, 384–386
size estimation table, 392*t*
Litigation
    as takeover defense, 119*t*, 121
    as takeover tactic, 108
Local country, 656–657
Logistic (logit) regression models, 639
Logistic alliances, 543
LOI. *See* Letter of intent
Long-term debt
    attractiveness of, 497
    financially distressed firms, 260
    financially stable firms, 259–260
    hybrid securities, 260–261
    market value determination of, 259–261
Long-term financing
    convertible bonds, 498
    junk bonds, 498–499
    see also Financing transactions
Long-term performance, 44
Loss carryforwards, 12

M

Macro value drivers, 296
Majority rules framework, 564
Majority/minority framework, 564
Management
    acquisition plan guidance, 160*b*
    business alliance issues, 555*t*, 564
    competence/motivation, 492
    in corporate governance, 94–95
    entrenchment theory, 719*g*
    leadership versus, 226
    ownership and, 96
    preferences, 160, 719*g*
    in restructuring strategies, 599
    risk types confronting, 159–160
    risk-averse, 158
    skills and resources, sharing, 542–543
    structures, 213
    voting against, 33
Management attachment theory, 98–99
Management buyouts (MBOs), 486, 719*g*
    pure, 488
Management integration team, 210, 719*g*
    emphasis, 210
    responsibilities, 210*b*
Managerialism, 719*g*
    as M&A causation theory, 11

Manufacturing operations
    integrating, 216
    process effectiveness, 216
Marginal tax rate, 674
Market model, 368
Market power, 66
    hypothesis, 719*g*
    increases in, 69
    as M&A causation theory, 12
Market segmentation, 173
Market shares
    concentration and, 67
    concentration ratios, 66
    as screening process criteria, 174
Market structure, 66
Market value
    debt, 260
    long-term debt, 259–261
    minority interests, 266
    operating leases, 261
Marketability risk, 719*g*
Market-based approach, 379
Marketing
    alliances, 553–554
    integrating, 219
Markets, 66–67, 140–141
    collection of, 140–141
    competitive dynamics, 142*f*
    ease of entry into, 68
    profiling, 141
    target, identifying, 141
MBOs. *See* Management buyouts
Merger arbitrage, 35, 720*g*
Merger-acquisition plans, 720*g*
Mergers, 20, 720*g*
    back-end, 440–441
    conglomerate, 21
    consolidations versus, 20
    to consummate transactions, 439–441
    direct, 500
    economic perspective, 21
    of equals, 720*g*
    horizontal, 21, 66–69
    legal perspective, 20
    reverse, 395–397
    short-term, 441
    small-scale exception, 441
    squeeze-out, 440–441
    statutory, 20, 417, 439–440
    subsidiary, 20, 439–440, 500–501
    taxable, 451
    triangle, 441
    vertical, 21, 69

Mergers and acquisitions, 3–47
    accountants in, 28
    analyzing in terms of real options, 302b
    arbitrageurs (arbs), 34–35
    bondholders and, 43
    business alliances as alternative to, 25–26
    in business plan execution, 45
    buying undervalued assets theory, 11
    case studies, 47
    cash-flow valuation, 235–279
    as change agents, 4–5
    control premiums, 390
    cross-border, 655–688
    diversification theory, 8–9
    efficiencies resulting from, 68
    employee stock ownership plans, role of, 24–25
    failure to meet expectations, 44
    financial synergy, 4
    first contact phase, 174–178
    global transactions, 16
    holding companies, role in, 24
    hubris theory, 10
    integration role in, 204–206
    as international market entrance strategy, 662,
        663f, 664
    investment banks in, 26–27
    investors and lenders, 29–32
    laws affecting, 53t
    lawyers in, 28
    long-term performance, 44
    managerialism theory, 11
    market power theory, 12
    mismanagement theory, 11
    misvaluation theory, 12–13
    model-building process, 330t
    planning-based approach to, 137–138
    process, 138
    process participants, 26–29
    proxy solicitors in, 29
    public relations firms in, 29
    reasons for, 5
    shareholder returns, 35–43
    state regulations, 75–76
    strategic alignment theory, 9–10
    success rate, 45–47
    synergy theory, 5–8
    tax considerations, 12
    theories, 5, 6t
    trends in, 17t
    waves, 13–19
Mergers and acquisitions, the process, 138
    acquisition plan phase, 156–161
    business plan phase, 139–154
        closing, 188–191
        flow diagram, 139f
        integration plan, 186–187
        negotiation phase, 178–186
        phases, 138–139
        postclosing evaluation, 193–194
        postclosing integration, 191–193
        search phase, 170–173
Mergers of equals, 440
Merrill Lynch, 26, 169–170, 322–323
Metro-Goldwyn-Mayer, 633
Mezzanine financing, 497, 503–504, 720g
Micro value drivers, 296
Microsoft, 239–240, 240t, 283–284, 285f, 303,
    539–540, 542
Minority discounts, 388, 720g
    estimating, 391–395
    factors affecting, 394–395
    in private business valuation, 394b
Minority interests, 266
Minority investments, 25–26, 720g
Mismanagement, as M&A causation theory, 11
Mission statements, 140, 146
    business objectives, 147
    in business plan format, 155
    diversification objectives, 147
    flexibility objectives, 147
    technology objectives, 147
    see also Business plans
Misvaluation
    as M&A causation theory, 12–13
    as reason for M&A waves, 13
Morris Trust transactions, 466
Multifactor models, 238
Multiperiod comparison, 332
Multiple party framework, 564
Multitiered offers, 103–104
Mutual funds, 30
    as activist investors, 33

N

National trade associations directory, 167
Negative covenant, 496–497, 720g
Negotiations
    deal structuring, 179–180
    disagreement resolutions, 200
    due diligence, 180–183
    dynamics, 200
    financial models in support of, 349–352
    financial plan, 184
    iterative activities, 178
    as mergers and acquisitions phase, 178–186
    money, 200

one-on-one, 586
planning in, 200
price range, 720g
in problem solving, 178
as process, 179f
purchase price, 184–186
refining valuation, 178–179
win–lose approach, 200
Net asset value, 315, 720g
Net assets, 343–344
Net debt, 720g
Net fixed assets (NFA), 363–364
Net operating losses (NOLs), 463–464, 720g
valuation, 465t
as value for acquirers, 464
Net purchase price, 185–186, 720g
Net synergy, 339, 341, 720g
percentage of shared, 343
Network alliances, 541t
Niche business strategies, 149
Nondiversifiable risk, 242, 720g
Nonequity claims, 259
Nonoperating assets
cash and marketable securities, 266–268
investments in other firms, 237–239
overfunded pension plans, 270
patents, 269–270
trademarks and service marks, 270
unutilized/undervalued assets, 268–270
valuation of, 266–270
Nonrecourse financing, 720g
Normalized cash flows, 330
Normalizing, 331
historical data, 331–332
No-shop agreement, 720g

O

Offer price
composition of, 344–345
determination, 346t
fully diluted shares outstanding, 345
initial, 719g
magnitude and composition of, 341–345, 342t
minimum and maximum range, 342–343, 719g, 720g
purchase of stock, determining, 343b
share-exchange ratios, 344–345
simulation model, 350, 351t
variance of, 350
OLA. See Orderly Liquidation Authority
One-tiered offers, 720g
Open market purchases, 23, 720g
Operating budgets, 493

Operating leases
dealing with, 249
market value determination of, 261, 261b
Operating leverage, 244
effects on beta, 244–247
financial returns and, 245t
Operating risk, 159
Operating synergy, 5–6, 720g
Operation expenses, 370–371
Operational plans, 554
Operational restructuring, 19–20, 720g
strategies, 148
Option pricing studies, 387
Options, 302
to abandon, 312–313, 313b
to delay, 311–312, 311b
delay, 304
embedded, 303
to expand, 309–310, 310b
financial, 302
postclosing, 304–305
preclosing, 304
real, 302–313
Orderly Liquidation Authority (OLA), 73, 636
advantages of, 637
application of, 636
FDIC and, 74
initiation, 636–637
liquidation under, 636–637
regulation through deal making, 73–74
Organizational structure
centralized, 213
decentralized, 213
divisional organization, 212–213
establishing, 212–213
functional organization, 212
postmerger, 212–213
product or service organization, 212
Overfunded pension plans, 270
Overpayment risk, 159
Over-the-counter (OTC) derivatives, 71t
Ownership determination, business alliances, 555t, 558

P

Paid in kind (PIK), 499–500
Parent subsidiaries studies, 387–388
Parent-submerger exception, 441
Partial acquisitions, 68–69
Partnerships
equity, 541t, 548t, 553–554
franchise alliances, 548t, 553
general, 548t, 552

Partnerships (*Continued*)
   limited liability, 548*t*, 552–553
   postclosing organization, 418–419
   profits/losses and, 563
   structures, 551–553
   written contracts, 548*t*
Patents, 269–270
Payment-in-kind, 184, 720*g*
Payments
   facilitation, 77
   form. *See* form of payment
   greenmail, 464–465
   mechanism, 189
Payoffs
   bondholder, 43
   for society, 43
Payouts, 427
PCAOB. *See* Public Company Accounting
      Oversight Board
PEG ratio. *See* Price/earnings-to-growth ratio
Pension funds, 30
   as activist investors, 33
Pension Protection Act of 2006, 81
Performance
   benchmarks, 193, 216
   criteria, business alliances, 555*t*, 561
   long-term, 44
Permanent financing, 720*g*
Personnel requirements, 214
Pfizer Pharmaceuticals, 409–410, 497, 580
PIPES. *See* Private investment in public equities
Planning, 136–137
   key business concepts, 137–138
   in negotiations, 200
   premerger integration, 207–208
   prescriptive concepts, 137
   production, 216
   see also Acquisition plans; Business plans
Plant consolidation, 216
Poison pills, 110–112, 720*g*
   acquirer shareholder dilution due to, 112*t*
   flip-in, 111–112, 113*t*
   flip-over, 111–112, 113*t*
   use of, 112
   see also Takeover defenses
Porter Five Forces Model, 331*f*
Portfolio companies, 720*g*
Postbuyout returns
   empirical studies, 507
   factors determining, 507–508, 508*t*
   to LBO shareholders, 507
Postclosing evaluation, 193–194
   learning from mistakes, 194

performance benchmarks and, 193
   questions, 193
Postclosing integration, 191–193
   best practices, 192
   cash-flow requirements, 192
   communication plans, 191–192
   cultural issues, 193
   employee retention, 192
Postclosing options, 304–305
Postclosing organization, 180, 415, 417, 720*g*
   earn-out agreement, 418
   form of, 417–419
   form of payment and, 413
   holding companies, 418
   partnership or JV structure, 418
   see also Deal structuring
Postclosing price adjustments, 421–422
Postmerger
   share price, 44
   shareholder returns, 38–39
Postmerger integration
   communication plan development, 211–212
   management integration team, 210–211, 210*b*
   organization, 209, 210
   organization creation, 212–213
   in place before closing, 209–210
Postoffer defenses, 108–109, 118
   advantages/disadvantages of, 119*t*
   corporate restructuring, 119*t*, 121
   ESOPs and, 119*t*, 120
   greenmail, 118, 119*t*
   leveraged recapitalization, 119*t*, 120
   litigation, 119*t*, 121
   share repurchase/buyback plans, 119*t*, 120–121
   types of, 110*t*
   white knights, 119, 119*t*
   see also Takeover defenses
Prebuyout returns
   anticipated improvement in operating
         performance/tax benefits, 505
   efficient decision making, 505–506
   empirical studies, 504*t*
   factors contributing to, 505–506, 506*t*
   superior knowledge, 505
   to target shareholders, 504
   wealth transfer effects, 505
   see also Shareholder returns
Precedent transactions method, 289
Preclosing options, 304
Preferred stock
   dividends, 499–500
   market valuation, 260–261
   and PIK, 499–500

Pre-IPO studies, 386
Preliminary information request, 202
Premcor Inc., 11
Premerger
    integration planning, 207–208
    shareholder returns, 36–38
Preoffer defenses, 108–109, 110–112
    advantages/disadvantages of, 113*t*
    antigreenmail provisions, 116
    fair price provisions, 117
    golden parachutes, 118
    limiting shareholder actions, 116
    poison pills, 110–112, 112*t*
    reincorporation, 117–118
    shark repellents, 112–113, 116–118
    supervoting stock, 117
    types of, 110*t*
    see also Takeover defenses
Prepackaged bankruptcies, 632–633, 720*g*
Present value, 184
Pretender offer tactics
    legal filings, 104
    multitiered offers, 103–104
    tender offer implementation, 102–103
    see also Takeover tactics
Price
    in acquisition/merger agreement, 189
    allocation of, 189
Price or cost leadership strategy, 148–149
Price/earnings-to-growth (PEG) ratio
    applying, 295*b*
    calculating, 294–295
    in firm comparison, 295–296
    in market value determination, 295
Price-to-earnings (P/E) ratios
    in conglomerate era, 14
    relative valuation methods and, 294–295
    use of, 315
Price-to-free cash flow, 315
Private equity funds, 30, 720*g*
    as activist investors, 34
    investment strategies, 30–31
    management fee, 31
Private equity market, 488
Private investment in public equities (PIPES), 397, 490–491
    hedge funds and, 491
    with reverse mergers, 397
Private placements, 720*g*
Private sales, 584, 585
Private solicitations, 720*g*
Privately held companies, 365–401, 366, 394*b*, 720*g*
    acquisition returns, 399

buying with leveraged ESOPs, 397–398
cashing out of, 365–366
demographics of, 367–368
EBITDA for, 372
family-owned, 367–368
financial statements adjustment, 371–377
governance issues, 368–369
information sources, 372*t*
key characteristics, 367
ownership of, 398
Privately held companies valuation, 366
    accounting for inventory, 374–375
    asset-oriented approach, 379–380
    auto expenses, 373
    benefits, 373
    beta estimation, 380–381
    challenges, 369–371
    control premiums, 388–390, 391–395, 394*b*
    cost of capital, 381–383
    cost of debt, 381
    cost of equity, 380–381
    DCF approach, 378
    depreciation expense, 374
    discount (capitalization) rates, 380–383
    family members, 373–374
    firm-specific problems, 370
    inadequate reporting systems, 369–370
    lack of externally generated information, 369–370
    lack of internal controls, 369–370
    liquidity discounts, 384–388, 391–395, 394*b*
    market-based approach, 379
    methods, 377–380
    methods, selecting, 378–380
    minority discounts, 388–390, 391–395, 394*b*
    owners' and officers' salaries, 373
    personal life insurance, 373
    process, 372–375
    professional services fees, 374
    purchase price premiums, 388–390
    relative-value approach, 379
    rent or lease payments, 374
    replacement-cost approach, 379
    reported income manipulation, 370–371
    reserves, 374
    travel and entertainment, 392
    value definition and, 377
Pro forma accounting, 328–329
Pro forma financial statements, 526, 720*g*
Proactive sales, 584
Product differentiation, 149
Product life cycle, 148–149
    in business strategy selection, 149
    in valuing firm, 149

Product lines, 173
Product or service organization, 212
Production planning, 216
Product-market matrix, 8*t*
Profit determinants, 143–144
Profitability, 173
Projected financial returns, 205
Promissory notes, 496
Proprietary knowledge, sharing, 542–544
Proxy
    access, 71*t*
    contests, 99
Proxy contests, 720*g*
    forms of, 100
    impact on shareholder value, 101
    implementation of, 100–101
    legal filings, 101
    in support of takeover, 100–101
Proxy solicitations, 56
Proxy solicitors, in M&A transactions, 29
Public companies, capital structure, 348
Public Company Accounting Oversight Board
        (PCAOB), 60–61, 97
Public relations firms, 29
Public sales, 584, 585
Public solicitations, 720*g*
Public utilities regulation, 80
Public Utility Holding Company Act, 80
Purchase accounting, 469–474, 721*g*
    balance sheet impacts of, 473*t*
    example of, 470*t*
    guidelines for assets/liabilities valuation,
        472*b*
Purchase method of accounting, 466
Purchase premiums, 721*g*
Purchase price, 184–186
    negotiations on, 200
    net, 180
    total, 184–185
Purchase price premiums, 388–390
    adjusting valuation estimates for, 301–302
    factors affecting, 587*t*
    see also Control premiums
Purchasing, 220
Purchasing power parity theory, 673–674,
        673*b*, 721*g*
Pure control premiums, 388, 389–390, 721*g*
Pure plays, 595, 721*g*

Q

q-ratio, 11
Quality control, 216
Quick flips, 489

R

R&D. *See* Research and development
Railroad industry regulation, 79
Raising funds, for exiting businesses, 578–579
Reactive sales, 584
Real options, 302, 721*g*
    to abandon, 312–313, 313*b*
    analyzing M&As in terms of, 302–313
    to delay, 311–312, 311*b*
    embedded in M&A decisions, 303–305
    to expand, 309, 310*b*
    impact on mergers and acquisitions, 306*t*
    valuing target company using, 305–313
    valuing with Black-Scholes model, 308–313
    valuing with decision tree framework, 305–308
    when to use, 314*t*
Recapitalization
    accounting, 474
    leveraged, 119*t*, 120
    single firm, 442
Receivership, 619, 721*g*
Reduced form models, 639
Regulated industries, 78–80
    airline, 80
    banking, 78–79
    communications, 79
    defense, 79
    insurance, 79–80
    public utilities, 80
    railroads, 79
Regulation FD (fair disclosure), 52–53, 53*t*, 77
Regulatory change, 10
Regulatory considerations, 51–84
    antitrust laws, 53*t*
    collaborative efforts guidelines, 69
    consent decrees, 65
    cross-border transactions, 81–82
    Dodd-Frank Wall Street Reform and Consumer
        Protection Act, 69–74
    environmental laws, 80
    for exiting businesses, 577–578
    fair disclosure (Regulation FD), 77
    Foreign Corrupt Practices Act, 77
    foreign investment, 76
    horizontal merger guidelines, 66–69
    industries, 78–80
    labor and benefit laws, 80–81
    prenotification filing requirements, 63*t*
    procedural rules, 64
    securities laws, 53*t*
    state regulations, 53*t*, 75–76
    vertical merger guidelines, 69
Reincorporation takeover defense, 94, 113*t*

Relative valuation, 286
    adjusting for firm growth rates, 294–296
    applying, 286–294
    comparable companies method, 287–289
    comparable transactions method, 289
    enterprise value to EBITDA, 291–294
    in privately held companies, 379
    same or comparable industry method, 289
Replacement cost method, 300
    in privately held companies valuation, 379
    uses, 314t
Reported income manipulation, 370–371
Representations, 189
Repsol YPF, 288, 288t
Repurchase agreements (repos), 51–52
Required returns, 236–242
Research and development (R&D)
    integrating, 220
    in-process assets, 468
Resource contributions, business alliances, 555t, 558
Restricted stock (letter stock) studies, 384–386
Restructuring and exit strategies, 575–612, 576,
        617–648, 618
    Anatomy of a Spin-Off case study, 590–591
    Anatomy of a Split-Off case study, 593–594
    for avoiding customer conflicts, 581
    business failure, 618–619
    choosing, 597
    comparing, 597
    for corporate focus, 577
    decision process, 597–599
    for discarding unwanted businesses, 580
    divestitures, 581–586
    equity carve-outs, 591–593
    for increasing transparency, 581
    key characteristics, 598t
    for lack of fit, 578
    motives for, 576, 577–581
    preannouncement abnormal returns, 599–607
    for raising funds/worth more to others, 578–579
    for regulatory concerns, 577–578
    reorganization and liquidation in bankruptcy,
        622–633
    for risk reduction, 580
    shareholder returns, 599–607, 601t
    spin-offs, 587–589
    split-offs, 593
    tracking stocks, 595–596
    for underperforming businesses, 577
    voluntary liquidations (bust-ups), 596
    voluntary settlement outside of bankruptcy,
        619–622
Retention bonuses, 154, 721g

Retrenchment era, 14–15
Returns
    financial leverage and, 245t
    market, 243
    operating leverage and, 245t
    required, 236–242
    risk-free rate, 237, 675, 677
    stock, 243
    see also Shareholder returns
Revenue, manipulation of, 370
Revenue rulings, 379, 721g
Reverse breakup fees, 721g
Reverse LBOs (RLBOs), 504, 721g
Reverse mergers, 395–397, 721g
    corporate shells, value of, 396
    financing, 397
    IPOs and, 396–397
    PIPES with, 397
Reverse stock splits, 501
Reverse triangular cash mergers, 451, 452f
Reverse triangular stock mergers, 721g
    illustrated, 459f
    type A, 459
Revision, business alliances, 555t, 562
Revolving lines of credit, 495–496
Right of first refusal, 562–563, 721g
Rights, 427
Risk, 242
    assessment, in business plan format, 156
    CAPM adjustment (developed countries), 675
    CAPM adjustment (emerging markets), 678–679
    country premium, 679
    cross-border transactions in emerging countries,
        669–670
    diversifiable, 242
    equity beta, 242–243
    financial, 159
    market, 237–239
    nondiversifiable, 242
    operating, 159
    overpayment, 159
    reduction, exiting businesses for, 580
    shareholder view, 246
    types of, 159–160
Risk analysis
    cash flow valuation, 242–247
    financial/operating leverage effects, 244–247
Risk management
    cross-border transactions in emerging countries, 670
    deal structuring and, 421–427
Risk premiums, 721g
Risk sharing, 411
    in business alliances, 542

Risk-free rate of return, 237, 721*g*
  developed economies, 675
  emerging economies, 677
Royalties, 427

S

Sales
  integrating, 219
  private, 584, 585
  proactive, 584
  public, 584, 585
  reactive, 584
Sales-to-market capitalization, 315
Same or comparable industry method, 290–291
  earnings with stock returns, 290–291
  valuations based on projections, 290
  valuing target company using, 291*b*
  when to use, 314*t*
Sarbanes-Oxley Act, 52, 53*t*, 60–61
  implementation costs, 60
  PCAOB and, 60–61, 97
Say-on-pay, 96
Scenario analysis, 333
Scenario planning, 682–683
Scope, business alliances, 555*t*, 556
Screening process, 173–174
  cultural compatibility criteria, 174
  degree of leverage criteria, 174
  market segment criteria, 173
  market share criteria, 174
  product line criteria, 173
  profitability criteria, 173
Search process, 170–173
  criteria, 170
  information reliability, 172
  information sources, 171*b*
  Internet research, 171
  strategy, 171
Secondary public offerings, 504, 721*g*
Section 338 elections, 453–455
Secured debt, 721*g*
Secured lending, 495–497
Securities
  hybrid, 260–261
  OTC Market, 55
  valuation, 266–268
Securities Act of 1933, 53*t*, 54–55
Securities and Exchange Commission (SEC), 27
  enforcement powers, 55
  hedge funds registration with, 31–32
  insider trading investigation, 56
  PCAOB oversight, 97
  private equity advisors' registration with, 31–32

privately held companies, 369
  as regulator, 98
Securities Exchange Act of 1934, 53*t*, 55–56
  insider trading regulations, 56
  reporting requirements, 55
  Section 13: Periodic Reports, 55
  Section 14: Proxy Solicitations, 56
Securities Investor Protection Corporation (SIPC), 636
Securities laws
  federal, 53*t*, 54–61
  state, 76
Security agreements, 496, 721*g*
Security provisions, 496–497
Segmented capital markets, 658, 659, 721*g*
Self-tender offers, 23, 440, 721*g*
Sellers
  due diligence, 182
  financing, 500
SFAS 141R, 466, 467–468
  application of, 466
  expensing deal costs, 468
  in-process R&D assets, 468
  recognizing acquired net assets, 467
  recognizing contingent considerations, 468
  recognizing/measuring net acquired assets in
    step/stage transactions, 467–468
SFAS 157, 466–467, 469
Share acquisitions, 666
Share companies, 666
Share control provisions, 75–76
Share repurchase/buyback plans, 119*t*, 120–121
Share-exchange ratios, 344–345, 721*g*
Shareholder equity guarantee, 422
Shareholder interest theory, 98–99
Shareholder returns, 35, 41
  abnormal, around announcement dates, 37*t*
  acquirer, 39–42
  acquirer experience and, 42
  aggregate, 38
  cash deals, 41–42
  cross-border transactions, 684–685
  divestitures, 599–604
  empirical studies of, 398–399
  equity carve-outs, 606–607, 608
  equity-financed deals, 41
  large deals, 40–41
  leverage impact on, 487*t*
  minority, 104
  postbuyout, 507–508
  postmerger, 38–39
  prebuyout, 504, 505–506
  premerger, 36–38
  for private/subsidiary targets, 39

restructuring strategies, 599–607
small deals, 40–41
spin-offs, 604–605, 608
in successful/unsuccessful bids, 36
tracking stocks, 607
voluntary liquidations, 607
votes, 96
Shareholder value
aggregate, gains in, 43
collar arrangements to preserve, 427–431
proxy contest impact on, 101
takeover defense value on, 121–124
takeover impact on, 35
Shareholders
appraisal rights, 103
dissident, 717g
minority, 439
view of risk, 246
Shareholders' interest theory, 721g
Shark repellents, 112–113, 721g
antigreenmail provisions, 113t, 116
fair price provisions, 113t, 117
golden parachutes, 113t, 118
limiting shareholder actions, 113t, 116
reincorporation, 113t, 117–118
staggered or classified boards, 113t, 115
supervoting stock, 113t, 117
as supplements to poison pills, 113
see also Takeover defenses
Shell corporations, 25, 721g
merging with, 396
type of, 396
value of, 396
Sherman Act, 53t, 61
Shocks, 13, 14, 640
Short-form mergers, 441
Single firm recapitalization, 442
Size premium, 238–239, 238t
Small-scale merger exception, 441
Sources of value, 339–340, 721g
Sovereign wealth funds, 32, 668–669
cross-border transaction financing, 668–669
Spin-offs, 22, 587–589, 721g
accounting considerations, 590
case study, 590–591
examples of, 587–588
focus increase, 605
information asymmetries elimination, 605
key characteristics, 598t
motives for, 590
parent company operating units undergoing, 598t
selecting, 600t
shareholder returns, 604–605, 608

tax considerations, 590
wealth transfers, 605
see also Restructuring and exit strategies
Split-offs, 593, 721g
key characteristics, 598t
motives for, 594
as non–pro rata stock distributions, 593
Split-ups, 593, 598t, 721g
Spot exchange rates, 671
Squeeze-out mergers, 440–441
Stable growth rates, 258
Staffing plans, 213–215
compensation, 214–215
employee availability, 214
formulation, 213
personnel information systems, 215
personnel requirements, 214
strategy sequencing, 214f
timetable and, 214
Staged transactions, 442
advantages/disadvantages of, 433t
Staggered or classified board elections, 113t, 115, 721g
Stakeholders, 137, 721g
Stalking horse, 630
Stand-alone businesses, 329, 721g
value acquirer and target firms as, 330
Standstill agreements, 722g
State regulations, 75–76
antitakeover laws, 53t, 75–76
antitrust laws, 53t, 76
blue sky laws, 76
securities laws, 76
Statutory consolidations, 20, 440, 722g
Statutory mergers, 20, 432, 439–440, 722g
advantages/disadvantages of, 433t
cash-out, 716g
IRS regulations, 460
liabilities transfer, 417
type A, 457
see also Form of acquisition
Steering committees, 564
Step-transaction doctrine, 456
Stock lockup, 106–107
Stock purchases, 431, 438–439, 722g
advantages/disadvantages from buyer's perspective, 438–439
advantages/disadvantages from seller's perspective, 439
advantages/disadvantages of, 433t
cash-for-stock transactions, 438
stock-for-assets transactions, 438
taxable, 453
see also Form of acquisition

Stock-for-assets transactions, 435
  advantages/disadvantages of, 433*t*
Stock-for-stock transactions, 438, 722*g*
  advantages/disadvantages of, 433*t*
Stocks
  arbs accumulation of, 34
  with cash as payment form, 421
  in firm acquisition, 41
  issuance when overvalued, 41
  letter, 595
  as payment form, 420–421
  super voting, 722*g*
  target, 34–35
  tracking, 595–596
Strategic alignment, 9
  as mergers and acquisitions theory, 9–10
  regulatory change, 10
  technological change, 10
Strategic alliances, 25–26
  key characteristics, 541*t*
  see also Business alliances
Strategic and operational review, 182
Strategic buyers, 204, 722*g*
Strategic controls, 154
  establishing, 140
  monitoring systems, 154
Strategic mega-mergers, 15
Strategic plans, 554
Structural models, 639
Subchapter S corporations, 548*t*, 550
Subsidiary equity carve-outs, 592, 722*g*
Subsidiary mergers, 20, 439, 722*g*
  LBOs and, 500–501
  merger structure as, 439–440
Success factors, 144–145
Supervoting stock, 722*g*
Supermajority rules, 116, 722*g*
Supervoting shares, 94
Supervoting stock, 113*t*, 117
Suppliers
  communication with, 211
  cost of switching, 143
  leverage of, 144
  production schedules, 175–176
  securing in business alliances, 543
Surface Transportation Board (STB), 79
SWOT analysis, 139–140, 145–146
  example, 146*t*
Syndication, 722*g*
Synergy, 722*g*
  business alliances, 545
  distribution of, 344
  estimation of, 336*t*

financial, 7–8
as mergers and acquisitions theory, 5–8
net, 339, 341, 343
operating, 5–6
overestimation of, 45–47
as value source, 339

T

Tag-along provisions, 562–563
Takeover defenses, 108–109, 722*g*
  antigreenmail provisions, 116
  board strengthening, 113–116
  categories of, 108–109
  corporate restructuring, 121
  in corporate takeover market, 108–112
  destructive effect of, 123
  in early stages of firm development, 123–124
  ESOPs and, 120
  fair price provisions, 117
  golden parachutes, 118
  greenmail, 118
  impact on shareholder/bondholder value, 121–124
  leveraged recapitalization, 120
  limiting shareholder actions, 116
  litigation, 121
  poison pills, 110–112
  postoffer, 108–109, 118
  preoffer, 108–109
  public offerings and, 123–124
  reincorporation, 117–118
  share repurchase/buyback plans, 120–121
  shark repellents, 112–113
  supervoting stock, 117
  types of, 110*t*
  white knights, 119
Takeover tactics
  advantages/disadvantages of, 109*t*
  bear hug, 100, 107
  bidding strategy, 108*f*
  breakup fees, 106
  in corporate takeover market, 99–105
  friendly approach, 99
  hostile approach, 99
  hostile tender offer, 101–102
  letter of intent, 106
  litigation, 108
  pretender offer tactics, 102–104
  proxy contests, 100–101
  stock lockup, 106–107
  tender offer, 107–108
Takeovers, 4, 722*g*
  activity patterns, 17–18
  friendly, 22–23, 99

hostile, 23, 99
impact on shareholder value, 35
in retrenchment era, 15
strategy development, 107–108
unsuccessful, 36
Tangible book value or equity per share method,
297–298, 314*t*
Target, 470
Targets, 4, 722*g*
bylaws, 105
LBOs and, 486
net assets, 343–344
part of larger legal entity, 353–354
in play, 23
undervalued, 12
Tax considerations, 449–450, 722*g*
alternative corporate minimum tax, 464
amount, timing, and composition of purchase price
and, 414
in asset purchases, 436
business alliances, 555*t*, 563
corporate capital gains, 464
cross-border transactions, 667
as determining role, 12
divestitures, 586
for exiting businesses, 578
general, 450
greenmail payments, 464–465
international markets, 662
liability, 246
loss carryforwards, 12
as M&A causation theory, 12
Morris Trust transactions, 466
NOLs, 463–464, 465*t*
postclosing organization and, 414
spin-offs, 590
tax rate selection, 248–249
taxable transactions, 450–455
tax-free transactions, 456–463
tracking stocks, 596
Tax shields, 246, 722*g*
Taxable transactions, 450–455, 722*g*
alternative structures, 450*t*
key characteristics, 454*t*
mergers, 451
purchase of target assets with cash, 451–452
purchase of target stock with cash, 453
Section 338 elections, 453–455
see also Tax considerations
Tax-free reorganizations, 456–457, 722*g*
Tax-free transactions, 456, 722*g*
from 1031 like-kind exchanges, 462–463
advance rulings, 456

alternative, 457–460
alternative structures, 450*t*
continuity of business enterprise, 456
continuity of ownership interests, 456
expanding role of mergers in, 460–462
key characteristics, 461*t*
qualifying, 456–457
step-transaction doctrine, 456
target tax attributes, 462
as tax-free reorganizations, 456–457
type A, 457
type A forward triangular stock merger, 458, 459
type A reorganizations, 457–458
type A reverse triangular stock merger, 459
type A statutory merger, 457
type B stock-for-stock reorganization, 460
type C stock-for assets reorganization, 460
see also Tax considerations
Technical insolvency, 618–619, 722*g*
Technological change, 10
Technology objectives, 147
Telecommunications Act of 1996, 79
Telecommunications Reform Act, 10
1031 like-kind exchanges
taxes owed and, 462–463
tax-free transactions from, 462–463
Tender offer solicitation/recommendation statements, 59
Tender offer statements, 59
Tender offers, 23, 440–441, 722*g*
exchange, 102–103
hostile, 101–102
implementing, 102–103
legal filings, 104
multitiered, 103–104
process, governing, 59
revising, 103
self, 23, 440
as takeover strategy, 107–108
two-tiered, 59, 103
see also Hostile tender offers
Term loans, 722*g*
Term sheets, 176
Terminal value, 254, 254*t*, 722*g*
calculating, 510
Termination, business alliances, 555*t*, 562
Termination fees, 106
363 sales, 630
Times interest earned ratio, 347–348
Timetable, acquisition plan, 160–161
Toehold bidding strategies, 102–104
Topping fees, 630
Total consideration, 722*g*
Total purchase price, 184–185, 722*g*

Toxic Asset Recovery Program (TARP), 74
Tracking stocks, 595–596, 722*g*
   accounting considerations, 596
   examples of, 595
   key characteristics, 598*t*
   motives for, 595
   problems with, 596
   pure plays, 595
   shareholder returns, 607
   tax considerations, 596
   voting rights and, 595
Trademarks, 270
Transfer of interests, business alliances, 555*t*, 562–563
Transfer taxes, 722*g*
Transparency, increasing, 581
Trend extrapolation, 333
Trial-and-error method, 520
Triangle mergers, 441
Triangular cash mergers, 451
   forward, 451, 451*f*
   reverse, 451, 452*f*
Trigger points, 137–138
Trust, earning, 187
Two-step acquisitions, 440–441
Two-tiered tender offers, 59, 103, 722*g*
Type A reorganizations, 457, 722*g*
   forward triangular stock merger, 458
   reverse triangular stock merger, 459
   statutory merger, 457
   use of, 457–458
   see also Tax-free transactions
Type B stock-for-stock reorganization, 460, 722*g*
Type C stock-for assets reorganization, 460, 723*g*

U

Underperforming businesses, 577
Unfunded pension liabilities, 265
Unilateral effects, 67–68
United Nations Commission on International Trade Law
   (UNCITRAL), 624
Universal banks, 26
Unleveraged betas, 244
Unsecured lenders, 497
Unwanted businesses, discarding, 580
U.S. Department of Defense, 10
U.S. Federal Reserve System, 26
U.S. Foreign Corrupt Practices Act, 53*t*

V

Valuation, 285–286
   acquired assets/liabilities, 472*b*
   based on projections, 290
   with book value, 298*b*

   cash and marketable securities, 266–268
   cash flows, 235–279, 723*g*
   contingent claim, 305
   cross-border transactions, 670–682
   deferred taxes, 264–265
   distressed business, 640–644
   employee options, 265
   ESOPs and, 366
   estimates, adjusting for purchase price premiums,
      301–302
   firms, subject to multiple growth periods, 256–258
   firms, under special circumstances, 258–259
   investments in other firms, 268
   LBOs and, 509–517, 518–526
   minority interests, 266
   multiples, factors influencing, 289*t*
   NOLs and, 465*t*
   nonequity claims, 259
   nonoperating assets, 266–270
   overfunded pension plans, 270
   patents, 269–270
   real options, 305–313
   refining, 178–179
   trademarks and service marks, 270
   unfunded pension liabilities, 265
   unutilized/undervalued assets, 268–270
   value-driver-based, 296–297
Valuation and Structuring Model, 339
Valuation methods
   asset-oriented, 297–300
   cash-flow, 235–279
   comparable companies, 287–289
   comparable transactions, 289
   constant-growth, 253
   DCF and, 250–256
   enterprise value to EBITDA, 291–294
   LBO and, 236
   liquidation or breakup value, 298–300
   real options, 302–313
   relative, 286–294
   replacement cost, 300
   same or comparable industry, 290
   tangible book value or equity per share,
      297–298
   types of, 235–236
   used in practice, 315
   variable-growth, 254–256
   weighted-average, 300–302
   zero-growth, 252
Value, 377
   breakup, 298–300
   destroyers of, 340
   discussions, 176

enterprise, 184–185, 251, 291–294
equity, 259–266
fair market, 377
firm, 256–259
identifying potential sources of, 183*t*
LBO creation of, 493–495
liquidation, 298–300
NOLs and, 464
present, 184
sources of, 339–340
stand-alone, 343
synergy and, 339
terminal, 254, 254*t*, 510
Value chains, 21
Value-driver-based valuation, 296–297
Variable-growth valuation model, 254–256, 723*g*
    cost of capital, 255
    discount rate, 255
    practice example, 256*b*
Vendor contracts, assigning, 188
Venture capital firms, 32
Vertical mergers, 21, 723*g*
    antitrust guidelines, 69
Virtual data rooms (VDRs), 585
Volcker Rule, 71*t*
Voluntary liquidations, 596, 723*g*
    key characteristics, 598*t*
    shareholder returns, 607
Voluntary settlements
    as failing firm option, 635
    outside of bankruptcy, 619–622
    resulting in continued operation, 620–621
    resulting in liquidation, 621–622
Vulture investors, 632

W

Wallace Act of 1967, 122
Warranties, 189
Warrants, 423
Waves, in mergers and acquisitions, 13–19
    age of strategic mega-merger, 15
    anticipation, importance of, 19
    characteristics of, 18*t*
    conglomerate era, 14

    fifth (1992–2000), 15
    first (1897–1904), 14
    fourth (1981–1989), 14–15
    horizontal consolidation, 14
    increasing concentration, 14
    reasons for occurrence, 13–16
    rebirth of leverage, 15–16
    retrenchment era, 14–15
    second (1916–1929), 14
    similarities and differences, 17*t*
    sixth (2003–2007), 14–15
    third (1965–1969), 14
    U.S. historical, 18*t*
Weighted-average cost of capital (WACC), 241–242, 723*g*
    cross-border transactions, 681*b*
Weighted-average valuation, 300–302
    estimates, adjusting, 301–302
    example, 302*b*
    weights, 301
White knights takeover defense, 119, 119*t*, 723*g*
Wholly-owned subsidiaries, 353
Williams Act, 53*t*, 56–59
    disclosure requirements, 56, 57–58
    regulatory prenotification filing requirements, 63*t*
    Section 13(D), 57–58
    Section 13(G), 57–58
    Section 14(D), 59
    tender offer process, 59
Winner's curse, 10, 723*g*
Win–win situation, 546
Workouts, 620

Y

Yield to maturity (YTM), 239–240
    in cost of debt estimation, 240
    example, 240*t*
    weighted average, 239–240, 240*t*

Z

Z score model, 638
Zero-growth valuation model, 252, 252*b*, 723*g*

RKAKAR @ Visa.Com

Roopalikakar @gmail.Com